LEABHARLANNA CHONTAE FHINE GALL

FINGAL COUNTY LIBRARIES

Items should be returned on or before the last date shown below. Items may be renewed by personal application, by writing or by telephone. To renew give the date due and the number on the barcode label. Fines are charged on overdue items and will include postage incurred in recovery. Damage to, or loss of items will be charged to the borrower.

Date Due	Date Due	Date Due
14. JAN 04.		

D1422561

A TALE OF
FOUR HOUSES

A TALE OF
FOUR HOUSES

*Opera at Covent Garden,
La Scala, Vienna and the Met
since 1945*

SUSIE GILBERT and JAY SHIR

HarperCollins*Publishers*

HarperCollins*Publishers*
77–85 Fulham Palace Road,
Hammersmith, London w6 8jb

www.harpercollins.co.uk

Published by HarperCollins*Publishers* 2003
1 3 5 7 9 8 6 4 2

A catalogue record for this book
is available from the British Library

ISBN 0 00 255820 3

Set in PostScript Linotype Minion
with Janson display by
Rowland Phototypesetting Ltd, Bury St Edmunds, Suffolk

Printed and bound in Great Britain by
Clays Ltd, St Ives plc

TABLE OF CONTENTS

LIST OF ILLUSTRATIONS

PREFACE

The six decades since the Second World War have witnessed radical changes in almost every aspect of opera – in performance style, management, funding, training and in the greatly increased accessibility and popularity of opera for a far larger public than has ever been the case. These great developments are revealed through the stories of four of the world's leading opera houses: La Scala, the Vienna Staatsoper, New York's Metropolitan Opera and the Royal Opera House, Covent Garden. Concentration on the 'Big Four' has supplied a focus for an otherwise unwieldy subject and at the same time provides a representative sample of the larger story. Other opera houses in Europe and North America are discussed in the light of the Big Four.

A revolution in opera performance style and content began in the 1950s with the emergence of stage directors like Luchino Visconti, who established an integrated method of direction working in close collaboration with all his colleagues throughout rehearsals. He formed particularly creative partnerships with Carlo Maria Giulini and with the great Maria Callas who altered our conception of the singing actor in opera, perhaps for ever. While some opera lovers and opera 'buffs' may mourn the great singers of the first half of the century such as Conchita Supervia, Lauritz Melchior, Lotte Lehmann, Frida Leider and Kirsten Flagstad, the integrated productions of the new era gradually established standards of drama, design and music which provided singers with even greater opportunities for expression. Gone for ever were the pre-war painted flats and drop curtains, and directors who used to 'dress the stage' with pictorially placed choristers and supernumeraries, leaving the principals to their own histrionic devices. As part of this development the British contribution to bringing theatrical talent to opera began with the young Peter Brook in the 1950s and came into its own in the late 1960s and early 1970s with such figures as Peter Hall, Elijah Moshinsky, and John Dexter at the Met, all of whom helped to transform the art. In Europe the director Walter Felsenstein brought the audience into intimate contact with the drama and insisted that his singing actors work with emotional authenticity. His students and disciples, including Günther Rennert, Götz Friedrich, Joachim Herz and Harry Kupfer, have changed and influenced the direction of opera by moving it into a contemporary, and often controversial style.

While the role of the director has been the most striking development in post-war opera, the role of the conductor remains crucial. The greatest achievements in operatic performance are attained when there is a true collaboration between conductor and director, like that enjoyed by Visconti and Giulini, with La Scala's 1955 *La Traviata* and Covent Garden's 1958 *Don Carlos*. Other great collaborations were those of Giorgio Strehler and Claudio Abbado, Peter Hall and Bernard Haitink at Glyndebourne, Elijah Moshinsky and Georg Solti, and Haitink and Graham Vick for Covent Garden's 1993 *Die Meistersinger von Nürnberg*. These and other highly significant relationships and characters are all explored in depth, and their achievements analysed with constant reference to the words and thoughts of the artists themselves. The exciting legacy to opera of Herbert von Karajan – as maestro, administrator and even stage director – is also traced in these pages, along with the other great conductors of the period.

Together with talented directors came inventive designers with new and ever more sophisticated designs, construction materials and lighting techniques that have given directors enormous freedom to work in an abstract or realistic mode with equally powerful results. In Britain the young Zeffirelli's combined direction and design for *Lucia di Lammermoor* in 1958 launched Joan Sutherland's career with empathy and creativity. At Bayreuth Wieland Wagner renewed the understanding of his grandfather's operas by placing them in a stripped-down, symbolically charged visual setting. In the 1960s and 1970s great innovative designers like John Bury, Timothy O'Brien, Jocelyn Herbert and David Hockney, with sets ranging from the abstract to the naturalistic, freed the imaginations of both audience and directors alike.

Even if some opera 'buffs' nostalgically argue that the golden age of singing has passed, the general standard of performance and presentation at the millennium was extremely high, as was the standard of singing of both choruses and principals; there was no lack of exciting performers to challenge their great forebears. Training of young singers had become far more sophisticated and demanding. While it proved difficult in the late 1990s to cast dramatic Verdi roles, it had become easier to cast an ever widening repertoire, especially Mozart *opere serie*, Rossini, French works, baroque and twentieth-century operas. The youthful singers of today show not only a high level of competence, flexibility and intelligence, but an extremely high level of musical and dramatic understanding. Britain has developed from being a relative backwater to having its own solid infrastructure and training bases. What a distance has been travelled since Sir Thomas Beecham's ludicrous observation in 1956 that the British were a 'thin wiry race' who do not 'breed the throats'.

The operatic repertoire worldwide has also expanded in the course of the past sixty years. The works of Handel and other baroque opera composers have become common fare, as have Rossini's brilliant works and the magnificent music dramas of Janáček, Mozart's *opere serie*, and twentieth-century operas. Perhaps most significant among the last is Schoenberg's *Moses und Aron* which, after its first major production by Hall and Solti at Covent Garden in 1965 was performed throughout Europe and North America, and has taken its rightful place as one of the finest operas in the repertoire. The heightened level of opera training and of orchestral skill has enabled singers to meet the exacting demands of such a wide repertoire. Equally important in bringing these works before the public has been financial subsidy.

The role of the state in supporting cultural activities in different countries is a constant theme of our tale. The culture in which the art form thrives originates from 'civic pride' – a national or local cultural identity that enables the nurturing and development of talent and which entails a willingness to provide subsidy and a concern for the welfare and schooling of young artists, as well as a readiness to innovate and experiment. The narrative charts the different attitudes to support in the four opera capitals: Milan, Vienna, New York and London. In Milan and Vienna, subsidy has been a foregone conclusion, as a natural expression of civic responsibility and pride. Even in difficult economic climates national governments played their part, albeit at times on a reduced level. In Britain, although state subsidy for the arts was firmly established after the war, there has remained a certain amount of ambivalence to opera on the part of both governments and public. This ambivalence occasionally erupts into malevolence from the tabloid press and cynicism, occasionally even from the serious press, which spitefully colour the ongoing debate on the question of the value of the senior arts to society in general. Covent Garden has lurched from financial crisis to financial crisis, while constantly improving its standard of production and revivals, and continuing to maintain its tradition of keeping together well-rehearsed teams of artists for a series of performances. The Metropolitan Opera grew up in a country where private enterprise and private donations rather than state subsidy were always the main source of non-box-office income. It developed from being a semi-provincial institution with a strong society cachet to becoming a major private company, described in the Eighties as the General Motors of the arts world in its efficiency and power. During the nineties, following a lengthy and painful reduction in state support, La Scala underwent a far-reaching structural transformation from an institution that had once enjoyed generous government subsidies to that of a semi-privatised House receiving significant funding from large financial and industrial concerns. Even the Vienna Staatsoper, which benefited from the generosity of successive Austrian governments, has begun to operate with more limited state resources. However, like La Scala, the Staatsoper is still regarded as the flagship cultural institution of the nation. In continental Europe the state's ultimate responsibility for opera's existence is still firmly acknowledged, whereas elsewhere it is not.

While governments may ponder the role of the senior arts, the institutions themselves are dependent on financial support for freedom of expression and innovation. The story shows how opera, when freed from the restraints of private sponsorship and box office returns, can transform itself from merely being a particularly skilful form of entertainment to becoming a great art form, with all that implies in terms of emotional, intellectual and spiritual demands. It can also reflect political and social developments. This was particularly true in the 1970s when 'museum' opera was transformed to play its part in the political debates of the time. Italian stagings tended to reflect the leftist views current in intellectual circles. During Colin Davis's era Moshinsky's *Peter Grimes* in 1975 redefined artistic values at Covent Garden. Even Bayreuth dared to stage Patrice Chéreau's *Ring*, which infuriated Wagner traditionalists for its idiosyncratic socialist approach. Some of La Scala's brightest evenings since the war have been directed by Giorgio Strehler, whose Marxist views never pushed his stagings over the edge into ideological statements. When John Dexter was at the Met during the 1970s the House briefly touched on social realism, but by the early 1980s reverted to a comfortable, visually magnificent and recognisable form of entertainment with superb music, top singers and increasingly polished standards of performance. Franco Zeffirelli, who later in his career adopted an increasingly elaborate and decorative style, was entrusted with many new productions. The sumptuous productions of the 1980s were considered by the Met management to be an investment and found the enthusiastic support of major sponsors. They resulted in a style of opera very distinctively 'Met'.

The European and British Houses that do not depend solely on sponsorship and box office for survival can afford to make more demands on their audiences, and they have established relationships of imagination and emotional commitment with them. A substantial part of the story is that of the increasingly sophisticated education of the performers and of the audiences themselves. At his farewell performance on 13 July 2002 Bernard Haitink movingly thanked the Covent Garden audience, underlining the dialogue that had been established between performers and audience.

Sometimes the imagination of the directors is allowed too great a license, and seeking novelty for novelty's sake they disregard the text to such an extent that the composer's intentions are ignored and his work becomes unrecognisable. From the late 1970s there developed the tyranny of the postmodernist director whose approach all too often obfuscates or threatens the integrity of the works. The postmodernist approach was particularly evident in Germany. At Cassel in 1981 *Don Giovanni* was staged with Zerlina and her friends as punk rockers on skates who eventually stripped naked. In Berlin in 1984 Götz Friedrich set Wagner's *Ring* in a bombed-out Germany where Valkyries wore black leather motorcycle gear. Such obsessions as Nazi imagery, stylised choruses and expressionist gestures of the principals threaten the very humanity of the works and occasionally, as in the case of Covent Garden's 1990s post-political *Ring*, makes decoding an almost insurmountable challenge. Each House has faced the postmodern challenge in its own way – with the Met taking the most conservative stand. In recent years Vienna has slowly begun adding contemporary stagings to its vast repertoire of productions, while in Milan postmodernist readings have made occasional forays, often dependent upon the currents of the Italian intellectual climate. Covent Garden has sometimes strayed into postmodern waters while at the same time giving space to directors like Moshinsky, whose understanding of the historical imperative preserves the tradition of Verdian grand opera.

While placing the great changes in opera in their cultural and historical context, *A Tale of Four Houses* illuminates the process by which operatic performances reach the stage, and describes how good management and leadership provide the conditions which enable the greatest creative work. Susie Gilbert's work in the archives has uncovered new material on the workings of Boards and managements, and aims to give a balanced documented account for even the most controversial episodes such as the great crisis during the closure of the Royal Opera House when the company was nearly destroyed. Also explored are the roles of the important administrators like Bing and Volpe in New York, Tooley in London, Karajan in Vienna and Ghiringhelli, Grassi and Muti in Milan.

Jay Shir has written the chapters on La Scala and the Vienna Staatsoper, and the early Met chapters. He is also responsible for the critiques of music and singing throughout the book where critics attending actual performances are not quoted. Susie Gilbert wrote the chapters on Covent Garden, and the later Met chapters. Both authors maintain their distinctive styles as the European continental Houses require different treatment from the Met and Covent Garden. The Met archive, with its very helpful archivists, is a vast and generous resource, as is that of Covent Garden. The annual financial reports of Covent Garden and the Met provide an indispensable source to the researcher and in recent years British government inquiries have provided searchlight insights into the inner workings of the Royal Opera House. Susie Gilbert has therefore adopted a more historical approach, using sources wherever possible to provide a fair and accurate account. The culture of Vienna and La Scala is quite different, however, with an oligarchical administration drawing a veil of privacy over the workings of the institutions. Both the Viennese and Milanese regimes are ungenerous with their financial reports and other details of administration. Because of this lack of source material and because change has occurred in a less radical manner, and musical and vocal interest are more important in those Houses, Jay Shir has given greater emphasis to analyses of performances.

Opera has become one of the most popular art forms and, at the same time, is considered in a world where all the senior arts are viewed with 'politically correct' suspicion to be the most 'elitist' and exclusive. While its audiences have grown with the development of broadcasting, videos, recordings and cross-over work by singers, and its most famous artists such as Callas, Pavarotti and Domingo have become household names, ticket prices have gone up so much in recent years that opera is increasingly viewed as exclusive, snobbish and remote. As the millennium approached, the erosion in public funding in the subsidised world had caused sharp increases in ticket prices. The stalls were increasingly filled with corporate sponsors, which created a belief that exclusivity was a new phenomenon. In reality the opposite was true. In 1945 opera in England and America was an art form largely identified with the upper reaches of society and those whom the British musicologist Edward Dent referred to as 'all sorts of ridiculous people' who were trying to improve their social status. From viewing opera as an alien and 'exotic' art form the English-speaking countries had come to develop an infrastructure of training and developing talent to such an extent that by 2002 they had became equal partners in what had come to be described as 'international opera', and Covent Garden, with its inadequate but well-used subsidy, in some respects even emerging as a custodian of the great tradition of Italian grand opera.

The Houses have also become much more aware of their role as educators. Outreach, surtitles, promenade performances, outside broadcasts, children's performances and educational programmes are a must for the Houses fearful of losing the next generation and concerned that declining audiences would threaten their very right to subsidy. The great continental Houses have enjoyed the faithful support of their traditional audiences, which has meant that outreach has been less pressing. Even so, La Scala has felt the need to provide for students' and workers' performances, and has set up an education department.

All Big Four Houses faced great challenges during the economic difficulties of the 1970s when subsidies increasingly failed to meet spiralling costs – and, in the post-Reagan/Thatcher world, governments tried to quantify the value of the arts. In the Arts Council Annual Report of December 1970 Lord Goodman, its chairman, warned that 'in a society whose values are totally insecure' there was no economic protection for even the best cultural activity. 'We have contrived', he said, 'an economic world where it is a simple untruth that worthwhile activities must succeed.' Our tale is how these 'worthwhile activities' have survived and thrived, and shows the quite extraordinary ability of its talented practitioners to regenerate and re-create it.

ACKNOWLEDGEMENTS

One of the pleasures of writing this book has been the contact with the devoted archivists of the Royal Opera House Archive and the Metropolitan Opera archive. A deep debt of gratitude is owed to them for their kindness and generosity. At the Royal Opera House Francesca Franchi, Jane Jackson and Sue Whyte, under sometimes very difficult circumstances, gave warm and welcoming help and access. Francesca Franchi also read the Covent Garden chapters and made many helpful suggestions. At the Metropolitan Archive Bob Tuggle not only gave access but also read the Metropolitan chapters most carefully, and John Pennino helped with many queries. Jeff McMillan also helped. With their humour and enthusiasm they made it a delight to work in their archives. We would also like to thank Henry Hardy and the Berlin family for access to the Isaiah Berlin Archive at the Bodleian Library, Oxford and for permission to quote from many unpublished letters in the early Covent Garden chapters. Thanks are also due to the librarians at the Theatre Museum, Covent Garden, London, to Jon Tolansky and to Music Preserved (formally the Music Performance Research Centre) for giving access to their substantial and fine collection of recordings and broadcasts. We are also grateful to the trustees of the Britten Pears Foundation for permission to quote from letters from Benjamin Britten. A particular word of thanks is due to Frau Hackel of the Austrian State Archive, as well as Rosl Merdinger in Vienna and Martin Ruberger of the Austrian National Library.

We would also like to thank those who gave so generously of their time for interviews: Sir Thomas Allen, Sarah Billinghurst, John Copley, Bruce Crawford, Sir Colin Davis, Paul Findlay, Jonathan Friend, Peter Gellhorn, Sir Peter Hall, Lord Harewood, Ioan Holender, Joan Ingpen, Sir Jeremy Isaacs, Darryl Jaffray, Philip Jones, Michael Kaiser, Adele Leigh, James Levine, Elaine Padmore, Steuart Pearce, Marcel Prawy,

Lady Solti, Sir Colin Southgate, David Syrus, Frank Taplin (who also most kindly gave permission to quote from his unpublished diary), Sir John Tooley, Joseph Volpe and Francesca Zambello. Sir Claus Moser, as well as making time for two long interviews, gave many leads and introductions. Elijah Moshinsky not only generously gave time for interviews but was also illuminating, trenchant and inspiring at all stages of the work.

During the course of our six years of work many people have given support and help. Among them are Mel Cooper, Erica Hunningher and Naomi Shepherd, who also commented on the manuscript. Martin Gilbert read the manuscript and gave much good guidance, especially during the early and later stages of the work. Hella Pick and George Weidenfeld gave us important contacts in Austria. Arabella Pike at HarperCollins saw the book through with tremendous enthusiasm and patience over a rather longer time-span than had originally been envisioned. David and Joshua Gilbert helped Susie Gilbert with technical work, as well as giving strong moral support throughout. In Israel Tamar Har-Even and Dafna Vertesh gave Jay Shir technical assistance, as did Evan Cohen, Kirsten Cowan and Maya Gelcer. Professor Eliyahu Schleifer of the Hebrew Union College, Jerusalem, was a fount of helpful suggestions. In London Felix Aprahamian and E. H. Morgan gave Jay Shir of their time and advice.

Above all our heartfelt thanks go to Rodney Milnes who, as Editor of *Opera*, most kindly arranged for permission to quote extensively from the magazine, which is a trove of crucial and fascinating material. He also painstakingly read the manuscript and made a host of useful comments on questions of fact and content. With his fairness, humour, expertise and generosity, he has been a constant source of encouragement and inspiration.

PART ONE

THE 1940s
Building and Rebuilding

ONE

VIENNA 1940–55

'Some New Beauty Is Being Born'

IN WARTIME VIENNA music and death were joined in terrible partnership. On 30 June 1944 the last wartime performance was given at the Vienna State Opera House. The work, fittingly enough in view of the worsening situation in the Third Reich, was Wagner's *Götterdämmerung* (*The Twilight of the Gods*). The printed programme requested patrons to rise from their seats to honour wounded soldiers returning from the front. Opera goers were also begged to remain calm and follow instructions in the event of an air raid. That evening in Vienna Hans Knappertsbusch conducted a cast which featured guests from the Munich Staatsoper: Julius Poelzer as Siegfried, Helena Braun as Brünnhilde and Karl Kronenberg as Gunther. The role of Waltraute was sung by Elisabeth Höngen, a new star of the Vienna Opera ensemble who had recently arrived from Dresden. More than three decades later Höngen told an interviewer, 'If I had not been called to the Vienna Opera in 1943, I would most probably not be here in front of you. The bombardments in Dresden not only destroyed the most beautiful theatre ever built but killed a great percentage of the population. Most of the friends I had there were, in a matter of a few seconds, annihilated. One becomes fatalistic, but one can never quite be the same afterwards. Of course, the Vienna Staatsoper was turned to ashes too . . .'[1]

Upon the closing of the Staatsoper, singers were directed to war work. Gertrud Grob-Prandl, who had recently made her Vienna debut as Elsa, checked gas masks. Martha Mödl, who would become a great Leonore after the war ended, made hand grenades in a munitions factory.[2]

On the morning of 12 March 1945 Allied bombers penetrated the skies over Vienna, the seventh anniversary of the *Anschluss* – Hitler's annexation of Austria into the Third Reich. On the same day the Red Army was only a few dozen kilometres from the outskirts of the Austrian capital. At eleven that morning Dr Karl Böhm, the music director of the Vienna Opera, was making a recording in the Musikverein hall with some of the singers of the Opera. When they heard the sirens the artists and others present in the building took to the shelters beneath the Ringstrasse side of the Opernhaus, the only part of the edifice which did not take a direct hit in the bombardment. With few exceptions every portion of the House was wrecked. The auditorium, the stage and backstage areas were burnt to the ground. What remained was the foyer, the staircase, the loggia and the façade of the building that faced the Ringstrasse. The ruins went on burning for two days. Water was scarce. The Viennese were quick to blame the laziness of the 'foreign' Ukrainians manning the fire brigade and even hinted at sabotage. But the Ukrainians redoubled their efforts once the Opera's director, Ernst August Schneider, who had been conscripted as a soldier in the ranks, arrived on the scene. In a filmed interview some three decades later Böhm professed to have seen a 'mystical significance' in the date of the burning: 12.3.45.

How had opera in Vienna, and elsewhere in the Third Reich, fared – indeed, survived at all – until this late date in the war? The answer lies in the Nazi authorities' co-opting of music and musicians throughout the Reich into the service of their propaganda machines. The works of some composers were banned as 'decadent', while Wagner was enshrined as the leading prophet of Germanism. Art was manipulated to boost morale. Since the Germanic self-image – which at that time meant the Austrian self-image as well – was so intimately bound up with opera companies and houses, with opera stars and operatic works, it made good political sense to keep the art as healthy as conditions would permit. Conductors and singers who served the Nazi cause fared well, enjoying privileges denied the ordinary citizen. Indeed, the Nazis lavished funds and favours upon 'their' opera and bent it completely to their aims. The most pernicious result of this policy was the suggestion that the Nazis were the rightful inheritors of the spirit of Germanic culture. And that culture, they declared, was a thing the Jews and leftists had somehow perverted and nearly destroyed.

The Bayreuth Festival was taken over as a propaganda arm of the Reich. Richard Wagner's daughter-in-law Winifred effectively surrendered artistic and administrative control of the festival to Adolf Hitler. As Frederic Spotts writes in his history of Bayreuth, 'Winifred's letters to him make clear that she deferred to him for final decisions on every question – who was to sing, who was to conduct and what was to be performed. The main issue was the repertory, which was revised to suit the Führer's wishes and what he considered ideologically suitable for the audiences.'[3]

Bayreuth was not the only scene of 'politically correct' opera production under the Nazis. All over the Reich great works were twisted to serve nefarious political ends. In Aachen on 15 April 1938 Herbert von Karajan conducted a special new production of *Fidelio*, Beethoven's operatic hymn to human freedom. The occasion was engineered to celebrate the unification of Germany and Austria after the *Anschluss*. The administration of the Aachen Opera termed the *Fidelio* production a celebration of 'Adolf Hitler's great act of liberation and the reunification of Austria with the Reich'.[4]

Until 'total war' was declared by Hitler in mid–1944, every effort was made to pamper opera in Vienna and elsewhere in the Reich. Singers and conductors were given a variety of favours. This tradition of special treatment persisted, even under totally different political and economic conditions, after the end of the war, becoming a crucial factor in the recovery of opera in post-war Vienna.

In 1933 the Vienna Opera soprano Lotte Lehmann had been invited to Berlin to meet Hermann Göring, at the time the Reich's Education Minister. According to one account, Göring received her wearing a resplendent white uniform with a brace of lion cubs standing at his feet. He made her a lucrative offer to star at the Berlin Opera, demanding that she appear there exclusively and never sing outside Germany. She recalled him admonishing her, 'You should not go out into the world. The world should come to us, if it wants to hear you.'[5] Lehmann refused Göring's terms. The Minister reacted by forbidding her to sing in Germany. 'Göring himself dictated a reply to me,' she said. 'It was a terrible letter, full of insults and low abuse. A real volcano of hate and revenge poured over me.'[6]

In 1937 the great bass-baritone Hans Hotter had refused an offer from Bruno Walter, the exiled Viennese Jewish conductor, to leave Germany and put down roots in the United States. 'Hans said that he had a wife and small child, mother, and a brother who was a Catholic priest. Could he hope to take them all, and support them in America? No, said Bruno Walter, he could not undertake that. So Hans stayed.' Although Hotter refused to sing on tours organised by the Ministry of Propaganda, he confessed the temptation was great. 'If you were sent to other countries by Goebbels's organisation you could keep foreign currency. You could bring in food without being searched. . . . There were times when one wanted to say – to hell with politics, I will go and get some food for my children.'[7] But Hotter never sang at the intensely Nazified Bayreuth during the war.

Other singers in the Reich proved more tractable and obeyed the authorities' wishes. During a time of food rationing Viennese opera goers grumbled about the excess poundage carried by the Konetzni sisters, the sopranos Anny and Hilde. Hildegard Ranczak, whom Richard Strauss admired for her interpretations of Salome and the Dyer's Wife, in *Die Frau ohne Schatten*, admitted in an interview many years after the war that she married a German man 'in order to have a name that did not sound foreign, for one risked being thrown out of the country. Perhaps it would have been better, but every singer is haunted by the pension he is to receive after twenty-five years' uninterrupted work. We were expected to live in grand style, have expensive clothes, look like stars.'[8] Still other singers remained and worked in the Reich, but suffered according to the degree of their political opposition. Frida Leider had been an outstanding Wagnerian soprano in the last fifteen years before the war, performing throughout the German-speaking countries as well as at the Metropolitan and Covent Garden. At Bayreuth she had sung Brünnhilde, Isolde and Kundry to great acclaim. In 1935 her name had appeared on a Nazi blacklist of 'Musical Bolshevists' with the appellation 'Jewess'. After 1938 she had refused to appear at the festival after its 'rededication' as a temple to Wagner in his new guise as a prophet of Nazi views. During the war years she sang lieder recitals but no operatic roles.

Leider was married to a Viennese Jew, Rudolf Deman, who before the war had been concert master of the Berlin Staatsoper orchestra and had fled Germany for Switzerland in the year of his wife's last appearance at Bayreuth. In 1943 Leider was able to obtain permission to give concerts in Basle and Zurich, where she could visit the husband from whom Fascism had separated her.

Few singers – among those who survived the war – suffered more than Danica Ilitsch, a Yugoslav soprano who began her Viennese career during the 1930s. Ilitsch was thrown into a concentration camp for having sheltered a secret agent acting on behalf of the British. A few weeks after being liberated by the Red Army in April 1945 she returned to the Staatsoper as Cio-Cio-San. She was awarded the accolade – by some Viennese at least – of *'tapfere* [courageous] Madama Butterfly'. When asked to fill out a form for the Metropolitan Opera's publicity office before her debut there in 1947, she gave what must have been a unique reply to the banal question 'What are your antipathies?' 'Peas, beans, lentils,' she answered. 'Will never forget them for they consisted of my diet in the months of concentration camp in Austria.'[9]

Anti-Semitic measures were intended to blot out any indication of Jewish presence in the arts. Talented figures were declared non-persons simply because of their ancestry. After Hitler's rise to power all Jewish musical performers had been banned from working in their profession. In the summer of 1938, following Hitler's entry into Austria, the management of the Vienna Staatsoper drew up lists of its no longer welcome employees: Jews, half-Jews, three-quarter-Jews and even philo-Semites. All these people, from conductors to cloakroom attendants, were sent form letters of dismissal. Some Jewish performers managed to flee Germany and Austria, often finding refuge with great difficulty. The bass Alexander Kipnis was made to leave Germany in 1935; he eventually sheltered in America, where he became a Met stalwart during the war. William Steinberg, the conductor, was sacked as music director of the Frankfurt Opera in 1933. During the same year in that city he established the Jewish Cultural League, conducting its musical programmes until 1936, when he left for Palestine. Like Kipnis, Steinberg ended by establishing himself in the United States, where he had a highly respected career. The great Jewish conductor Bruno Walter had been named music director of the Staatsoper in

1936, but fled to France in the wake of the *Anschluss*. Eventually he made his way to America, where he was conductor of the New York Philharmonic from 1947 to 1949.

Many musicians perished in the Holocaust. Gustav Brecher, music director of the Leipzig Opera, was sacked by the Nazis in 1933. Trying in vain to escape the *Wehrmacht* advance in Belgium in 1940, he committed suicide on a beach near Ostend. Non-Jewish musicians who were opposed to the Reich suffered less gravely, particularly those with a measure of renown. Hans Knappertsbusch, the outstanding Wagner conductor, was a special case. After criticising the Nazi regime he lost his position as music director at the Munich Opera in 1935. However, he conducted at the Staatsoper from 1938 until its final wartime performance. Marcel Prawy recalls Knappertsbusch in Vienna pressing his luck by an outburst of temper: '[With] an unprintable oath he sent an ashtray flying against a loudspeaker from which one of Hitler's speeches was being broadcast. Hitler's speeches had to be listened to by the entire staff, and for big speeches that had been announced in advance, loudspeakers were installed in the auditorium. . . .' 'Kna', as he was generally known, was expressing his fury at Hitler's address having interrupted a rehearsal.[10] A few non-Jewish conductors fled out of political or moral conviction. Erich Kleiber, who had been music director of the Berlin State Opera, left for Argentina. In 1934 Fritz Busch became the first music director at Glyndebourne, afterwards spending time in Argentina and Sweden as well. He had been dismissed the previous year from his post as music director at the Dresden Staatsoper. Together with stage director fellow refugee Carl Ebert, Busch played an important part in developing opera in England before and after the war.

The great majority of non-Jewish German and Austrian musicians, however, remained at home and collaborated actively with the regime. In 1933 the composer and conductor Richard Strauss was named president of the Reich Music Chamber, at the time the chief musical organisation in Germany. Wilhelm Furtwängler, the musical director of the Berlin Philharmonic, was appointed vice-president. Strauss was at the centre of musical life during the Third Reich and he did his best to carry on operatic business as usual. His political perceptions were deeply impaired by his egocentricity. Hitler's rule and the war were to him not moral issues but a stroke of personal bad luck. For a superior creative spirit like himself these were times of difficult, even exasperating working conditions. During the years of the Third Reich he appeared at Bayreuth, Salzburg, Berlin, Munich and elsewhere, composing, rehearsing and conducting new works as well as old ones. During the Nazi era he completed three full-length operas and two one-act pieces. Although he did not particularly like Hitler, his self-absorption ensured that he would take no position against the regime that might jeopardise him. Stefan Zweig, the Jewish man of letters who had collaborated with Strauss on his opera *Die schweigsame Frau*, considered him an amoral pragmatist.

> He conducted wherever the new masters wanted him to, he set a hymn to music for the [1936 Berlin] Olympic games, at the same time writing me with little enthusiasm in his shockingly frank letters about his commission. In truth, in the *sacro egoismo* of the artist he cared only about one thing: to keep his work alive, and above all for a production of the new opera [*Die schweigsame Frau*] which lay particularly close to his heart.[11]

After the war's close, in October 1947, Lord Harewood was taken to meet Strauss at a concert of his music conducted in London by Sir Thomas Beecham. Harewood witnessed the composer's sensitivity to recollections of the Nazi era:

> I was taken up to him, presented, and stammered out in my best German how much I had enjoyed the music and the other programmes I had heard. '*Wo haben Sie ihr Deutsch gelernt*' ('Where did you learn your German?') he asked. Searching for an appropriate answer, I said, truthfully but irrelevantly, '*Ich war Kriegsgefangener*' ('I was a prisoner of war'), whereupon Strauss turned on his heel and walked away.[12]

Some found specious reasons to dislike the regime. Strauss's wife Pauline, who was her husband's model for the character of the Dyer's Wife, disapproved of the Nazis on the same grounds as she disapproved of Richard's social background (his father, Franz, was a horn player). For her they were simply too common. At a reception one evening in wartime Vienna, Pauline offered Baldur von Schirach, the Nazi Gauleiter who professed an interest in the arts, an ironic invitation to be her guest in the country. 'When the war is lost and over, I'll save a little place for you at Garmisch, when you're on the run. But as for that other trash . . .'[13] Nevertheless, neither Pauline nor Richard Strauss ever went on record as opposing the policies of 'that other trash'. Arturo Toscanini, an active anti-Fascist, put it succinctly: 'To Strauss the composer, I take off my hat. To Strauss the man, I put it on again.'[14]

Others followed in Strauss's wake, lending their talents to the service of the Fatherland. Unlike Hans Hotter, Wilhelm Furtwängler travelled willingly to Nazi-occupied countries to conduct operatic and symphonic performances in support of the German propaganda effort. In 1940, after the Germans had conquered Czechoslovakia, Furtwängler went to Prague to lead the Berlin Philharmonic in a gala musical event commemorating the occasion. He also conducted a concert in honour of Hitler's birthday and another at the Nuremberg Nazi party rally. These activities show an artist doing far more than the necessary minimum to preserve his position.

Although Furtwängler collaborated with the Nazi authorities, he also carried on a fitful, often quixotic struggle against Nazi control over musical life in Germany and Austria. When Paul Hindemith was denounced as having 'Jewish connections' and his operas banned, Furtwängler resigned his directorship of the Berlin State Opera and the Berlin Philharmonic. He also left his post as vice-president of the Reichsmusikkammer. Marcel Prawy remembered him after the *Anschluss* conducting an orchestral rehearsal at Vienna's Musikverein hall: 'He glared at the swastika hangings all over the hall and said in a loud voice, "I wonder whether it will sound all right with these decorations."'[15]

After the war the violinist Yehudi Menuhin – himself Jewish – took up Furtwängler's cause, arguing that the great conductor had tried on several occasions to help Jewish musicians. Indeed he had, but the majority of his efforts had the effect of supporting Nazism. Furtwängler's thinking was affected by an odd streak of misplaced poetic idealism. Even his champion Menuhin admitted that Furt-wängler's error, 'like my own perhaps, was to overestimate the power of music. If he did not expect it to absolve original sin, he did believe it proof against contamination.'[16]

Furtwängler gave too much credence to the moral force of music, believing that it could by itself draw people out of bondage into the light. 'Men are always free when Wagner and Beethoven can be played. And if they are not free, they will become so when they hear these works. Music will lead them into regions where the Gestapo will be powerless.'[17] Furtwängler's reason for protesting about the dismissal of Jewish musicians in an open letter to Goebbels in 1933 sounds odd to say the least: 'The contemporary world of music, already weakened by the world depression and the radio, can stand up to no more experiments.'[18] His secretary, Dr Berta Geissmar, herself Jewish, unwittingly underscores the naivety of his thinking when he made his objections to Goebbels. 'Furtwängler was relieved that he had been able to say what he wished; he had given expression to the opinion of the majority, and supported a principle that was of vital necessity both to himself and to the whole German nation. He hoped that things would gradually revert to normal and sound instincts prevail before too much had been destroyed.'[19] But Furtwängler's hopes for a saner Germany were to be fulfilled only after the Allies had totally defeated the Reich.

Other conductors had no compunctions about helping the Reich by making music. On 1 July 1933 Clemens Krauss stepped in to conduct the first performance of Strauss's *Arabella* in Dresden once Fritz Busch – who had been scheduled to lead the premiere – had been dismissed. Such major figures as Karl Böhm and Herbert von Karajan took active steps to demonstrate their allegiance and further the aims of the Reich through music. While music director at Vienna from 1943 to 1945 Böhm gave the Nazi salute on the podium, though to do so was not obligatory.

Robert Bachmann, one of Herbert von Karajan's biographers, has revealed, Karajan twice joined the Nazi party. In 1981 Bachmann asked him if he felt becoming a Nazi was a wrong thing to do. Karajan replied,

> No, quite certainly not. I would do exactly the same again. I was given a position as Generalmusikdirektor in Aachen, and after I'd held it a long time my secretary came and said, 'Listen, the district commanders . . .' That's what you can't explain to anyone. Nobody can understand it. For me that was as if you had said, 'We're going up the Eiger now, but listen, you have

to be a member of the Swiss Mountaineering Club.' Then I
would join. And that was then – then they used to say, 'That's
simply impossible, you are there, and you have to do it.' And
the important thing for me was that I could finally have – well,
in Aachen there was a big orchestra and a wonderful choir, a
medium-sized theatre. I was able to do whatever I liked.[20]

Bachmann points out the falsehood in Karajan's excuse that he was
already installed at Aachen and that Nazi party membership was a
necessity to continue the appointment. The conductor maintained in
several interviews that he became a member of the Nazi party in 1935.
In fact, as Bachmann showed, both Karajan's party cards date from
1933 and his audition for the Aachen appointment did not come until
8 June 1934.

At the war's end it seemed that nothing could stop the rebirth of
music in what had been the Third Reich. After the bombing of their
opera house the Viennese had to wait only a few short weeks before
they could attend another performance of their favourite art. Nazi
resistance in Vienna had ceased by mid-April 1945 and the Austrian
republic was restored on 27 April. The Soviet occupying authorities
ordered Alfred Jerger, a bass-baritone singer who was interim administrator of the Staatsoper, to resume activities at once. The speed with
which the order was carried out would have astonished anyone who
had not witnessed the Nazis' careful preservation and encouragement
of opera during the previous twelve years.

Opera in Vienna began to come alive again. As it did, a new
generation of brilliant singers arose, as one might expect in this cradle
of outstanding musical performance. On 1 May *The Marriage of Figaro*
was duly presented at the Volksoper theatre, whose frame and decor,
as well as its store of sets and costumes, had remained quite untouched
by the ravages of war. The conductor was Josef Krips, described by
the Staatsoper administration as a 'half-Jew',[21] who had spent the
wartime years in Belgrade as a refugee. Sena Jurinac, who went on to
establish a legendary name as a Mozart singer, made her Viennese
debut that evening in the mezzo role of Cherubino. As Jurinac recalls,
'The Vienna Opera simply did not have a mezzo for this part, and I

was given three days to learn it.'[22] One story has it that the Russian military, smitten by the opulent set for the *Figaro* performance they had demanded, decided to 'appropriate' a number of gilt chairs and curtains of gold cloth. The next production, a fortnight later, was *La Bohème*. Jurinac starred – this time in the lyric soprano role of Mimì. Her interpretation was acclaimed as 'tenderly poetic'.[23] The Rodolfo was Anton Dermota, who had been a leading lyric tenor in Vienna during the war and had won praise in Mozart roles. Irmgard Seefried, not yet twenty-six, sang Musetta. Like Sena Jurinac, Seefried soon became a first-rank lyric soprano with an international career as a Mozart specialist.

Jurinac was a leading light of the Vienna Mozart renaissance from the very day of her *Figaro* debut, aged twenty-four. In later life she recalled, 'My first year in Vienna I did over a hundred and fifty performances, which was of course totally irresponsible on the part of those in charge, but I was not yet in a position to argue with them.'[24] Her 1945 Cherubino was soon followed by a memorable Dorabella in *Così fan tutte*. As she shifted to soprano, she eventually added the part of Fiordiligi in the same work, but only at Glyndebourne and the Edinburgh Festival. In fact, she never performed Fiordiligi at the Vienna State Opera. Said Jurinac, 'They had Schwarzkopf, della Casa, and Seefried to do it and always found excuses not to assign it to me.'[25] In the course of Jurinac's long career she performed Wagner, Strauss, Puccini and Verdi, as well as Mozart. Her appearances at Salzburg, La Scala, Covent Garden, Glyndebourne, Chicago and San Francisco made her an international star of her day, although audiences at the Metropolitan never had the chance to hear her.

During the first few months after the war's end conditions in Vienna were appalling. Some half a million people died in the city during 1945. Singers were summoned to rehearsals by foot messengers, as the telephone network was down and the trams were not running. Alexander Witeschnik estimated that sets for 120 operatic productions had been destroyed in the course of the war. Stagehands were not paid. Food and electricity were scarce, but performances were given regularly and singers somehow did not become ill. The Volksoper House and the historic Theater an der Wien had to be pressed into service as twin replacement venues for the Staatsoper's productions.

In June Franz Salmhofer was named permanent head of the Vienna Opera, returning to the capital from a period in the provinces. Before the war Salmhofer had been a composer of theatre and ballet music, and, as a conductor had been active at the Burgtheater from 1929 until 1939. In his history of the Vienna Opera, Marcel Prawy recalls Salmhofer reappearing in town with no luggage and wearing a pair of leather shorts, 'in which attire he was officially confirmed in office by the State Secretary for Education'. Prawy continues,

> His first action [on 15 June] was to summon all the available singers and orchestral players to a meeting by the main stairway in the Opera House, which was the only part of the house that had survived the fire. After a short speech in which he instilled into all and sundry a feeling of pride at having a country to belong to once again, he set about assuring himself at first hand that to give any sort of performance in the ruins of the Opera House was quite out of the question. It was not until after this memorable little ceremony that he resolved to see about staging operas at the Theater an der Wien; because he was well aware that the Volksoper alone provided a far from adequate remedy.[26]

The Volksoper was inadequate because it seated only 1,473 people. Moreover, its plain interior was considered unsuitable for opera.

Salmhofer found the Theater an der Wien a decayed shell inhabited by an aged caretaker who had spent the war growing mushrooms on the stage. He demoted her to lavatory attendant. The theatre lacked windows and lighting equipment. The orchestra pit had rotted away and the cloakroom hosted a colony of rats. To refurbish the house he enlisted members of the Staatsoper chorus to work as carpenters and to sew costumes. The Vienna Philharmonic Orchestra – which then as now also played as the Staatsoper orchestra – had been preserved during the war for opera and concert performances. Salmhofer demonstrated his organisational ingenuity during a power failure by running an electricity cable from the Theater an der Wien to Soviet military headquarters, thus settling accounts after the incident of the *Figaro* gilt chairs and curtain. He is also said to have acquired food for his singers and fuel for his theatre by less than honest means. When challenged by an assistant, he announced, 'Please take note of this fact – the Vienna Opera does not steal!'[27] When Salmhofer's company reopened the Theater an der Wien on 6 October 1945 with *Fidelio*, funds were so scarce that part of the set was borrowed from a production of *Aida*. Moreover, the theatre's ravaged walls were made to serve as the walls of Florestan's prison. Krips conducted; Anny Konetzni sang Leonore, with Seefried as Marcelline and Dermota as Jacquino. So it was that the Theater an der Wien and the Volksoper amalgamated to constitute the joint venues of post-war Viennese opera. This temporary doubling went on until the Staatsoper building reopened nine years later.

Then as now, the Austrians felt the need to assert overall governmental control over the arts. Late in 1946 Egon Hilbert was named chief administrator of all the Viennese state theatres. Hilbert had been a police official before the war and more recently an inmate of Dachau concentration camp. His indefatigable efforts on behalf of opera led to his being nicknamed '*der Fanatiker hinter den Kulissen*', or 'the fanatic behind the scenes'. In short order, and largely as a result of Hilbert's and Salmhofer's efforts, the standard of opera in Vienna had been raised once again to a high level.

The resumption of opera in Vienna carries a double significance. On the one hand, the Viennese demonstrated bravery and dedication. They helped make it possible to resume performances at the point where they had been suspended at the closing of the theatres in 1944. And insofar as a particular artist had committed no offence, no one could bar him from performing. No reasonable person could wish to punish the Viennese – whether artists or audiences – by denying them their Mozart, Beethoven and Strauss.

On the other hand, the illusion of 'business as usual', fostered by the Nazis, lingered after the war's end. The Staatsoper building was no more, but the show went on as before. As Sir Georg Solti said sardonically in an interview on BBC international television, broadcast on 12 June 1997, three months before his death, 'In 1946 in Germany nobody was a Nazi.' The same was true of Austria. Eberhard Waechter was a schoolboy and frequent standee at the Vienna Opera just after the war. Later he would be one of its leading baritones and, eventually, its director. Recalling this period Waechter said, 'All these conductors in Vienna at that time – Böhm, Knappertsbusch, Clemens Krauss and the rest – they were all former Nazis. Or so it was alleged. I never checked it out. That was forbidden.'[28] It is unclear whether Waechter meant it was forbidden to be a Nazi – or to delve into the past. An Allied denazification order forbade Böhm to conduct for four years after 1945. However, lax enforcement of the order meant that Böhm took the podium at least twice during this period: in Graz in 1947 and in Salzburg the following year.[29]

After Karajan had been engaged to conduct the Vienna Philharmonic Orchestra in 1946 permission was withdrawn by the United States Army. He was brought before an Austrian denazification commission on 15 March 1946. Under cross-examination he admitted he had joined the Nazi party, an act which appeared to him mistaken in hindsight. He offered the excuse of the totally absorbed musician: 'I'm prepared to admit that was an error, but we artists live in another world, a self-contained one. Otherwise it would be impossible to play music properly, and music is the highest and only thing for me.' Karajan continued, 'One makes either music or politics.' Dr Horak, the interrogator, responded, 'I can't imagine today that even an artist can be completely unpolitical.'[30] The denazification commission approved Karajan's engagement in May of that year.[31] His final denazification did not come until August of the following year.

The contrast between the horrors the Nazi regime had perpetrated and the unbroken continuity of this great human art was almost too much for Marcel Prawy, a Viennese Jew and returning refugee, to grasp.

> During World War II, I was far from my native land. My very first evening as a refugee in the United States I spent in the standing-area at the 'Met'. I returned to Vienna in 1946, failed to find either my friends or my family, and gazed upon the ruins of the Opera House I had virtually grown up in.
>
> Moments of the deepest revulsion are very often followed by a reaction in the direction of self-delusion, a temptation to behave as if everything were just as it always had been. So I went to the opera. . . . I dropped in at the Volksoper to see *Tosca* with a cast including Maria Németh, Alfred Jerger and (if I remember rightly) Josef Kalenberg, who all seemed to be in good voice. Just like the 1930s . . . And then I realised it was no use trying to delude myself: the world I had known was no more.[32]

Although the Staatsoper did not then have a music director, Josef Krips soon became its guiding artistic spirit. Krips had been a staff conductor at the House from 1933 until the *Anschluss* year of 1938, when he was dismissed. After his return from Yugoslavia he became the prime mover in the Mozart 'renaissance' of the first post-war years. His devotion to this quintessentially Viennese composer ensured that infrequently performed operas like *Così fan tutte* would henceforth be considered good financial prospects rather than mere period curiosities. In fact, when Krips's *Don Giovanni* was announced at the Theater an der Wien, with a cast that included Ljuba Welitsch, Hilde Konetzni, Irmgard Seefried and Anton Dermota, the riot police were called to keep order in the ticket line. Krips often led the Vienna company in its post-war tours abroad. In 1947 the opera travelled to Nice and Paris in a French military train. Later that year it performed *Don Giovanni* at Covent Garden.

The Vienna musicians deserved these opportunities to show off their accomplishments abroad, for they were faithfully maintaining the local tradition of excellence even after the war's devastation. Krips's reputation is fully borne out in a 1950 Decca recording of *Die Entführung aus dem Serail* in which the Vienna Philharmonic gives of its very best. The conductor is in complete empathy with Mozart. The overture is brisk and jolly, almost Rossinian in humour were it not for the 'janissary' music with its severe precision and exciting dynamic contrasts. Krips never emphasizes the obvious – particularly not the accents and downbeats, and thumpiness is absent from this elegant, slightly understated *Entführung*. Krips accompanies the singers solicitously, while keeping the pace moving. These were the days when many singers did not blush to record less than perfect performances. They felt then – and some still feel today – that over-polished recordings fail to capture excitement and freshness. In this *Entführung* Wilma Lipp is a crystal-toned Constanze, fleet in the passage work but not quite in tune in the fiendishly difficult highest register. Endre Koréh's Osmin is refreshing for its elegance and lightness, portraying a merry, overgrown homicidal child. Koréh's technique, like Lipp's, is at once impressive and slightly problematic. Nevertheless, this 1950 recording shows that each singer had his or her own unique tone quality, a well-delineated conception of the role and the ability to express unambiguously, through the voice, the dramatic emotion of the moment.

Night after night in post-war Vienna there was magnificent singing to match the conducting. Hilde Konetzni's soprano displayed some of the best the Staatsoper had to offer. A 1937 recording of 'Abscheulicher!' conducted by Hans Schmidt-Isserstedt shows an exciting spinto, full of warm expression and nobility. Konetzni uses her voice for acting, precisely and with abundant Viennese good taste. Her Leonore is trans-figured by suffering, redeemed by hope. It contrasts with Martha Mödl's far more passionate interpretation recorded sixteen years later under Furtwängler. Konetzni's middle register is dependable and easy over the break. A recording of Agathe's aria, 'Wie nahte mir der Schlummer', from *Der Freischütz* demonstrates complete understanding between singer and conductor – again, Schmidt-Isserstedt. The tempo is abso-lutely right. Perfect pacing, easy but never over-broad, gives Konetzni room to observe every one of Weber's tenuti and accents.

Probably the most sensational star of the day was Ljuba Welitsch, whose stage presence grew out of her sexual allure. Born in a small Bulgarian town on 10 July 1913, Welitsch studied philosophy at Sofia University before making her singing debut in a minor role in *Louise* in the Bulgarian capital in 1934. After a Nedda at the Graz Opera in 1936, she went on to sing a variety of lyric and dramatic parts in German Houses during the war. In Vienna in 1944 her performance of the title role in Strauss's *Salome* created a sensation. The aged composer was fascinated by her interpretation and in later years Wel-itsch fondly recalled a letter she had had from Strauss. 'He wrote me once, "I never realised my Salome could be sung like that." It was so nice of him.' Welitsch went on, 'I've kept the letter, but I don't know for whom. My poodle Bobeline can't read.'[33] At the Metropolitan she also sang in English – as Adele in *Die Fledermaus* – besides Tosca, Musetta and, under Fritz Reiner, her incomparably acted Salome. She also made a great impression at Covent Garden.

However, Welitsch's free high register, her impetuousness on stage and her sharply focused stagecraft were not matched by her technique. A 1949 New York recording of the final scene from *Salome* shows her hoisting the voice up from beneath to attack top notes. Occasionally she even changes placement and focus after the initial attack. Register selection on the lower break is chaotic, and the break itself is an obstacle that interferes in rapid passages. In louder moments the weight of the voice is badly positioned, with a thinness in the upper-middle register. But the middle register is healthy and well-focused, with a good sense of line. Despite the lyric cast to Welitsch's voice, opera goers could generally hear her above Strauss's inimical orchestration.

Recorded selections from *Tosca* show Welitsch's voice in a more suitable role. Puccini's gently swooping line helps her stress the upper-middle register, which blooms as it fails to do in the Strauss. Nevertheless, here the top notes tend to go sour. Worst of all, she sings the role with little authentic feeling, as opposed to 'dramatic' accents and spat-out consonants. By the mid-1950s the voice had deteriorated. Welitsch began appearing in character roles, particularly at the Volksoper. She also sang in operetta and acted in films. Living in retirement with her Viennese policeman husband and, of course, Bobeline, she had a warm appreciation of her own past accomplishments. One critic tells of her listening to her recordings at home and 'gleefully crying *"Geschossen!"* [bull's-eye] as she hit the top notes spot on.'[34]

Several other opera houses in German-speaking lands have also played an important part in post-war opera history. In Berlin the Staatsoper, the Deutsche Oper and the Komische Oper, and in Hamburg the Staatsoper have been venues for fascinating and often innovative opera stagings. In Munich the Nationaltheater has presented consistently outstanding singers. And in Bayreuth Wieland Wagner created a production style close to modern abstract expressionist painting whereas previously productions had been in historical folkloric style. The Festspielhaus has taken imaginative steps to remove the Nazi taint from Wagner's music dramas. Opera has long enjoyed generous financial support in Germany and Austria. Civic pride, outstanding musical competence and a respect for performance traditions have helped create a relatively high standard. From the time of the Weimar Republic, and even before, non-musical German theatre has been marked by liveliness, intellectual seriousness and a penchant for innovation. Stage directors and dramatic values have been imported from the legitimate theatre to German opera houses, with interesting effect.

If the revival of opera in Vienna gave proof of the enduring value of the lyric stage to Austrians, the renewal of performances at Bayreuth sought to salvage the artistic legacy of Richard Wagner. The composer designed the Festspielhaus to suit his profoundly original operas, which took the form of integrated music-dramas, or *Gesamtkunstwerke* (complete art works). However, by the beginning of the Second World War operatic performance at Bayreuth had become stultified. Wagner's widow Cosima had enshrined the composer's every wish and indication as sacrosanct. Little room was left for musical and dramatic interpretation. Following the death of Siegfried Wagner, the composer's son, and under the stewardship of Siegfried's widow Winifred, Wagner's operas came to be identified with the national myth of Jewish conspiracy and German racial supremacy.

Bayreuth was not bombed by the Allies until late in the war. In April 1945, however, the town became the target of intensive air attacks because of the presence there of a railway marshalling yard. Damage was considerable. The Villa Wahnfried, the home of Wagner and afterwards of his descendants, was badly hit. Although the Festspielhaus – which Wagner himself had designed – was still intact, the town was in a state of chaos. The stores of costumes were pillaged, with bizarre results. Frederic Spotts, the historian of Bayreuth, writes, 'It is said that for miles around German refugees could be seen in the garb of characters from one or another opera.'[35] The American army confiscated the opera house, Villa Wahnfried and other family properties. The auditorium was used for dances, stage plays and other entertainments for the troops. After July 1946 control was handed by the American army to the city of Bayreuth. For a while the building sheltered Sudetendeutsch, ethnic Germans who were refugees from Czechoslovakia. Later the city ran it as a concert hall, incurring considerable losses. Mayor Oskar Meyer tried to transfer the Festspielhaus to politically untainted members of the Wagner family, who might be expected to find an honourable musical use for it. However, according to the will of the composer's son Siegfried, the building belonged to Winifred – whose unrepentant National Socialist beliefs made her an inappropriate guardian to the Bavarian government. They also made her liable under the Allied denazification laws to a prison sentence. After much temporising Winifred succeeded in avoiding all legal penalties – even probation – by promising 'to withdraw from all participation in the organisation, administration and leadership of the Bayreuth Festival'.[36]

In February 1949 the Bavarian government ended its temporary trusteeship arrangement over the festival. Winifred made Wieland Wagner and his brother Wolfgang leaseholders and sole managers, with control over the assets. The brothers agreed that Wieland would take responsibility for artistic matters and Wolfgang would work on the side of finance and management. Money was extremely scarce in Germany following the war. Wolfgang had difficulty raising funds. He was quoted as saying, 'In the year before the beginning of the Festival [1950], I travelled around for a total of six months; I chalked up nearly 40,000 kilometres on my motorcycle, going from pillar to post.'[37] But the Wagner family were not prepared to accept defeat. If worse came to worst, they announced their willingness to sell valuable Wagner autographs – even the score of *Tristan und Isolde* – in order to reopen the doors of the Festspielhaus. Funds were contributed by the state and municipal governments as well as by industrialists. Ticket sales – considerably better than expected – helped close the gap. Wolfgang's efforts had borne fruit and Bayreuth won back its primacy as a home for Richard Wagner's music dramas.

Determination and an insistency of vision bore fruit in Bayreuth as they had done in Vienna. After the war the festival underwent an artistic rebirth which was both profound and wide-ranging. Wieland Wagner, the composer's grandson, built on the festival's great musical tradition by introducing innovative stagings that were to have a far-reaching impact on the staging of opera generally all over Europe and indeed the whole world. And Wieland's stage practice arguably helped 'denazify' his grandfather's operas.

The reopening of the festival on 30 July 1951 showed how far Wieland's stagings amounted to an aesthetic, and conceptual revolution. In *Parsifal* scenic richness and quasi-realism had given way to a stage that was almost stripped bare. Frederic Spotts wrote:

> What amazed the audience was less what it saw than what it did not see. In place of the sumptuous, Constable-like woods and rippling lake of the conventional opening scene, there was

an all but empty stage. Even the background depicted no road ascending Monsalvat to the castle of the knights of the grail but merely hinted at a forest through which sifted the gentle morning light. The walk to the castle led not through rocks and woodland but across a barren desert. . . . When the scene shifted to the magic garden, rather than the 'tropical vegetation, luxuriant flowers . . . battlements of the ramparts, which are flanked by projecting portions of the castle (in rich Arabian style) with terraces', as prescribed in the composer's stage directions, there emerged a scene devoid of any object or decoration except a tenebrous, pastel backdrop, which in later years [of the production's life at the Festival] resembled a canvas by Jackson Pollock. The Flowermaidens had no flowers, just as the flowery meadow was neither flowery nor a meadow. There was no swan in the first act and no dove in the third. Klingsor had no spear. What else was missing was impossible to know in the dim lighting. When Hans Knappertsbusch, who had conducted, was asked by an outraged spectator how he could have had anything to do with such a production, he replied – only partly in jest – that he had assumed during the rehearsals that the settings were yet to arrive.[38]

David Harris in *Opera* magazine was impressed: 'All scenes are presented behind gauzes, stage properties reduced to the barest essentials and, for the singers, action and gesture kept to a minimum. This all serves to present the dramas more clearly and to distract one less from the music. The gain is tremendous.'[39] Bayreuth's first post-war season had opened to considerable critical acclaim. At its close only a small deficit had been registered.

A major influence for Wieland Wagner was the work of the early twentieth-century Swiss stage designer and theoretician Adolphe Appia, who had used expressionistically lit abstract volumes to suggest the dramatic content of settings rather than depicting them pictorially by the use of flats and drops. These volumes tended towards minimalism, in contrast to the maximalist representationalism of traditional Bayreuth settings, with each leaf painstakingly painted on each tree. Eventually the powerful influence of Wieland Wagner would help give birth to conceptualist operatic staging. A common link would be forged based on the clean simplicity of set pieces, suggesting ideas and notions, not merely dramatic situations or conflicts. But unlike many conceptualist stagings, which add a layer of subjective interpretation to the opera, Wieland's efforts were all in the service of the opera as the composer wrote it.

Rolf Liebermann, from 1959 to 1973 intendant at Hamburg and afterwards director of the Opéra de Paris, linked Wieland's work to the new spirit of the age in Germany, stripped of its wealth, power and illusions:

> The magnificent scenic deceptions put about by opera had vanished along with the vulgar theatrical palaces of the Hitler regime. It was no longer money or sets which determined the worth of a particular work. People just wanted to see human beings on the stage and hear music which would help them carry on. The hour for truth had come – that heightened sense of truth and reality in a performance which now became the aim of the singer as well.[40]

The brothers Wagner were intimately and passionately involved in almost every detail of the productions at the post-war Festspielhaus. Hugh Preston, a Briton, stood in the wings and watched a performance of *Lohengrin* during the Wieland–Wolfgang days. He noted the presence of a Wagner family quorum to make sure that all ran smoothly:

> ... It is not unusual for members of the chorus to faint, especially at a first performance. In the first act of *Lohengrin*, the chorus has to remain absolutely still for over an hour. Those who fail to last the course are quietly removed. All the time that the chorus is on the stage Wieland Wagner's wife Gertrude keeps a vigilant eye on them, continually seeking for improvements in grouping and gesture. Wieland and Wolfgang Wagner too spend most of their time in the wings, singing all the parts, beating time, and discussing points of gesture and production.[41]

Preston also recalled the horseplay backstage once the body of the slain Telramund was borne off by four knights:

> The scene is one of great visual and musical beauty, with the lights casting a soft chiaroscuro upon the departing Telramund and the chorus ranged in solemn tiers at the back of the stage. As Telramund reached the wings, Wieland Wagner poked him

playfully in the ribs and the knights emptied him unceremoni-
ously on to the floor. This caused loud and sustained laughter
and I was sure that the rumpus would be heard by the audience.
But I was later informed that the acoustics made it impossible
for such noises to be heard in the auditorium.[42]

The 1951 Bayreuth *Parsifal* was recorded in a live performance
conducted by Hans Knappertsbusch. His broad tempi suggest the old-
fashioned, reverential attitude to *Parsifal*, instead of a decision to
emphasise dramatic values. Even so, the music is paced better than
many more recent recordings. 'Kna' provides considerable dynamic
variation and a good sense of the moment. In the Prelude to Act Two
(Klingsor's castle) the low strings provide some truly grim gnashings
and the brass accents are beautifully balanced. The Grail Motif at
Parsifal's 'Es starrt der Blick dumpf auf das Heilsgefäss' shines out. The
orchestral playing is generally fine, but there are intonation problems
in the strings. As Parsifal, the young Wolfgang Windgassen relies
on spat-out consonants and vocal theatricality to make an impression.
In his 'traditional' Germanic singing, even 'Traute, teuerste Mutter!'
sounds as if he has been stabbed by his mother. But at 'Wes war ich
je noch eingedenk' Windgassen expresses confusion and uncertainty,
the lyric side of the knight-innocent that is Parsifal. Windgassen has
a good low register and is seamless and utterly reliable on the passaggio.
As Kundry, Martha Mödl's swoops also belong to an old-fashioned
style of German singing that has almost passed away; however, her
vitality, emotion and line are unforgettable. Wieland Wagner approved
of Knappertsbusch's conducting, especially his tireless drive and long
phrases. 'Kna' remained on the podium at Bayreuth for thirteen
seasons (1951–64). The combination of solid performances and, more
important, aesthetic innovation helped ensure a bright future for Bayreuth. By the early 1950s the finest performances of opera, found there
and in Vienna, were so outstanding that an uninitiated observer might
have found it hard to believe that the Second World War had disrupted
musical life in the German-speaking lands.

Once opera had become re-established after the war, the intricate
politics of the arts in Vienna often led to crisis situations. A long-

standing disagreement between Egon Hilbert and Dr Ernst Kolb, the Austrian Minister of Culture, resulted in Hilbert's suspension in October 1953. Hilbert had allegedly engaged guest singers at exorbitant fees. Kolb threatened to resign as minister if Hilbert did not go. On 4 October George London, singing the name role in *Don Giovanni* at the Staatsoper, made a speech before the curtain in which he attacked the 'disgraceful treatment of our chief'. The chancellor of Austria installed a finance ministry official to supervise Hilbert's expenses. Hilbert responded by resigning. On 30 October Ernst Marboe was named administrator of the Staatsoper and the Burgtheater.

The reconstruction of the Vienna State Opera building had been a central theme in the national consciousness since the very first days following the war's end. On 24 May 1945 the state secretary for public construction, Julius Raab, wrote an article in *Neues Österreich* calling for national and international funding to aid rebuilding:

> The Opera shall rise again on the same spot, in its former setting. Instead of burning ruins the noble, glorious structure of van der Null and Siccardsburg shall once more tower to heaven; once again its unmistakable silhouette shall be seen, recognised by the whole world as the crossroads of opera; from within it godly music and magical song shall once again resound. Obviously the reconstruction of the Opera will cost a large sum of money.... I am convinced that the city cannot bear the sole burden of this building, but rather that Austrians and lovers of art all over the world will find it a point of pride to enable this celebrated cultural institution to rise again.[43]

The reconstruction began with the laying of a cornerstone in May 1952. As Raab had urged seven years previously, the entire Austrian nation was taxed in a special levy to cover the huge costs – more than £4 million at the time. The parts of the House which had survived the bombing were incorporated into the new structure, itself a near-replica of the old one. Several public rooms, decorated in their original, charmingly tasteless *kaiserlich und königlich* kitsch, were left as relics of what had been. The grand staircase was, and remains, almost as bombastic as the one in the Salle Garnier in Paris. Modern hydraulic stage machinery was installed. The new playing area – comprising a forestage, a rear stage and two side stages – was fifty metres long, twice the length of the auditorium from the parterre standing-room area to the pit. The architects, Erich Boltenstern and Otto Prossinger, removed the balcony pillars and the box partitions in the third tier, but retained the rest of the auditorium's shape and layout. They also kept the keynote colours of gold, red and ivory. But in the opinion of some, a mistake was made when the rococo interior was radically muted to suit changing tastes. The walls and ceiling were sobered up, made Fifties-functional to the same degree that the Metropolitan's auditorium is Sixties-garish. Gold leaf was applied so sparingly it looked almost apologetic. The big chandelier, in particular, has a safe *Good Housekeeping* flavour.

By 1955 Julius Raab had risen to the position of chancellor of Austria. On 27 April in a speech to the Austrian parliament he publicly requested that the armies of occupation quit his country before the reopening of the Staatsoper and the first performance there, of *Fidelio*. 'It would be a splendid gift to the Austrian people if this immortal hymn to freedom and humanity by the greatest composer of all time, could resound in a free and independent Austria.'[44] On 15 May the treaty restoring Austria's status as a sovereign nation was signed. True to Raab's hope, the last troops left Austria on 28 October 1955.

Work having been completed, the gala reopening was held eight days later, on 5 November 1955, with a splendid and unprecedentedly expensive new production of *Fidelio*. Since Austria was about to regain its independence following the quadripartite military occupation, the musical event naturally assumed a national significance. Even the standees wore formal dress. The American Secretary of State himself, John Foster Dulles, attended the opening. Other honoured guests included Prince Pierre of Monaco, the Austrian president, and captains of industry including Henry Ford II, Dr Ferry Porsche, Signor Olivetti and the chief executive officer of Daimler-Benz, the composers Orff, Ibert and Shostakovich, the conductors Leopold Stokowski, Erich Kleiber and Bruno Walter, leading singers from Vienna and elsewhere in Europe – and even the painter Oskar Kokoschka and the photographer Henri Cartier-Bresson. The *Wiener Zeitung* went so far as to print a complete list of guests with precise seating arrangements. Another paper, *Die Presse*, ran a banner headline reading, THE GREAT FREEDOM FESTIVAL OF VIENNA, CITY OF MUSIC. Its sub-head spoke of *Fidelio* as symbolising the mission of uniting the nations.[45] A new fore-curtain, executed from a design by Professor Eisenmenger, showed Orpheus bearing his lute leading Eurydice out of Hades into a great aureole of light. The curtain hangs in the House to this day. A festive programme booklet was printed containing essays by the great and good of Viennese opera. It even included a swatch of the thick-ribbed and striped garnet-red wallpaper, supplied by a Swiss firm, which adorned the walls of the rebuilt House. The Viennese could imagine they held their opera house in their very hands.

Vienna had bequeathed to the world much of the tradition of classical music over the past two centuries. Clearly it deserved every festive moment of the musical revival it was bestowing upon itself – and which it had taxed itself so heavily to bring into being. No one would fault Vienna's almost superhuman efforts of opera folk to bring the art back into glorious – if underheated and underfunded – being as soon as possible after the defeat of the Reich. And few would grudge Austria its new-found independence and a rebuilt symbol of its national culture. But on that day there was a false suggestion of a noble cultural continuity which ignored the Nazi era. Ernst Marboe, the government official responsible for the state theatres, termed the reopening 'a page in the great Austrian legend'.[46] Karl Böhm had once again been named the Opera's musical director. As the press reported Böhm's speech at the opening, he made no mention of the Anschluss or the Nazis. He drew an equivalence between Austrian music, Austrian history and the noblest sentiments of the human soul.

> A higher power has chosen our country to be the Fatherland of great classical music. The musical mission which we have been permitted to celebrate is not something we have chosen through our own will. It has been bestowed upon us by Fate. We hold art and music in such lofty regard, beyond all other things, not so much because we are merely intoxicated by it externally, but rather because we wish to do justice to the task of fulfilling a great mission. The Genius of Austria has taken on the shape of music. And we have erected our noble opera house to be its homeland . . .[47]

Böhm's speech pandered to negative tendencies lingering from the pre-war Austrian national consciousness, including self-deception.

Those who could not afford seats stood outside in hushed silence to listen to *Fidelio* on loudspeaker relay. The Philharmonic under Böhm played exceptionally well, with British critic Peter Heyworth attesting to 'a nobility, inner fire, and outward loveliness of tone few members of the audience can ever have heard equalled'.[48] Marcel Prawy disliked some of the innovations of Heinz Tietjen's production, which featured a red wig and an odd reversal for Pizarro, who sang his 'Welch ein Augenblick' before receiving the letter announcing Don Fernando's visit. Prawy grumbled, 'I had a premonition that the age of the producer, with its innumerable horrors and its all too infrequent delights, had already dawned.' Prawy also found Martha Mödl, with faulty high notes, below her own best as Leonore. Heyworth raved, however: 'Since Frida Leider scarcely an interpreter of the role has gone so deep, creating a musical and histrionic totality of such broad scope and perfect integration of all the details.'[49] Mödl herself almost lost her grip on her emotions. It was 'a historic occasion', she recalled, 'one of the most memorable moments of my life. I have always managed to control myself on the stage – one must arrive at the end in one piece, if possible – but on that night I was overcome with tears. I knew how much this theatre meant, not only to the Viennese but to the entire civilised world.'[50]

Perhaps the most honestly moving moment arrived when Lotte Lehmann entered the hall. The audience rose to its feet, honouring the greatly beloved soprano who had 'come home' after resisting Nazi blandishments. 'Beauty had awakened in ruins,' Lehmann later wrote, and 'the heart of Austria was beating again'. She did not regret what was no longer present. 'I don't belong to those people who always sigh for the past. Nobody is irreplaceable. Wherever some beauty dies, some new beauty is being born.'[51]

Although much of opera in Austria had undergone a true rebirth since the war, old and negative patterns had not entirely died. The Staatsoper remained in thrall to the arts bureaucracy, which maintained its ultimate sovereignty. Opera continued to provide a field for political infighting and, worse still, for public-relations exercises which sought to blur Austrian guilt for ill-treatment of Jews and complicity in the wider crimes of the Third Reich. These patterns would continue to trouble the Staatsoper in years to come.

TWO

LA SCALA 1945–57

Reconstruction

IN CONTRAST TO the situation in Austria and Germany, La Scala of Milan carried out its task of post-war reconstruction under the guidance of an unflinching anti-Fascist who was also one of music's living immortals: Arturo Toscanini. As Harvey Sachs, Toscanini's biographer, put it, 'His existence was a terrible irritant to Mussolini.'[1] Before the outbreak of war the conductor had protested by word and deed against Hitler's racist policies. His boycott of the Bayreuth Festival, from 1933, was reported around the world and welcomed especially by Jewish musicians. The boycott did not, however, keep Richard Strauss from stepping in to conduct Toscanini's *Parsifal* performances at Bayreuth. Perhaps Toscanini, by way of compensation, had the satisfaction of hearing that Hitler used to 'see red whenever the maestro's name was mentioned'.[2] This was observed by Friedelind Wagner, the composer's granddaughter, who was privy to behind-the-scenes doings at Bayreuth. During the 1937–38 Salzburg Festivals Toscanini hired Georg Solti, then a young Hungarian Jewish musician, as his assistant. In April 1938 Mussolini issued a 'racial manifesto' on the lines of the anti-Jewish legislation by the Nazis. When Toscanini returned to Italy in the late summer of that year, after a series of concerts in Switzerland, his passport was cancelled. After it was returned he left Italy for the United States, where he spent the war years.

Many musicians suffered under the Italian Fascists. In 1938 Vittore Veneziani, La Scala's chorus-master, was removed from his position because he was Jewish. Veneziani had been first hired at the House by Toscanini in 1921. In 1940 the passports of a number of leading singers, including Ebe Stignani, Maria Caniglia and Mafalda Favero, were confiscated. In a letter of 9 November 1944 to his daughter Wally, who had stayed behind in Italy, Toscanini wrote of his agonised thoughts of home: 'I think of my poor, dear Italy, mishandled and torn asunder by enemies and friends alike, and I don't know why I'm not there to do something better than what I can do here. I assure you that I feel remorse because of it. . . .'[3]

At the same time Mussolini's regime did not exercise absolute control over Italian musical life. Art and architecture were turned into more obvious icons of the new order. The Venice Biennale became a forum for Fascist visual art.[4] No Italian opera composer had produced works which, like Wagner's in Germany, could be presented as a reflection of a grandiose and perverted mythic image of the nation. A few composers even used their talents in the service of humane values. Luigi Dallapiccola, who had flirted with Fascist ideology at the beginning of the 1930s, was appalled by the racist decrees promulgated at the end of the decade. Dallapiccola, whose wife was Jewish, wrote a strong musical protest against totalitarianism in his choral work, *Canti di prigionia* (*Songs of Imprisonment*), composed between 1938 and 1941.

At the time Toscanini was writing his letter in Riverdale, New York, La Scala was a wrecked shell. On the night of 16 August 1943 Allied bombers had scored a direct hit on the roof. Great beams crashed through to the auditorium, destroying boxes and burying red plush chairs in piles of plaster. Daylight poured in through the hole. As one historian of La Scala put it, the theatre was 'crushed, offended, ruined like the poorest houses of Milan beneath the destructive fire'.[5] But revolt rather than shame was uppermost in the hearts of some citizens. Soon after the bombing, notices appeared, in print and in scrawled characters, on the Scala's exterior walls: '*Evviva Toscanini.*' Although Mussolini had been overthrown, his successor Marshal Badoglio was leading Italy's war effort on the side of the Axis. What better place of protest than the damaged house from which the Risorgimento had been proclaimed in the previous century? Many citizens perceived a link between the spirit of free Italy, the personality of Toscanini and the opera house whose modern traditions the great conductor had fashioned more or less single-handed.

As in Vienna, opera performances in Milan could not wait for the theatre to be rebuilt. From December 1943 until mid-1945, opera was heard at three venues, two of them outside the city limits: Bergamo's Teatro Donizetti, Como's Teatro Sociale and, in Milan itself, the Teatro Lirico.

A year after the end of the Second World War, on 11 May 1946, Toscanini led La Scala's orchestra and singers in a concert of rededication. Answering an invitation from Hans Busch, the son of the conductor Fritz Busch, who was stationed with the Allied Military Government in Milan, Toscanini had flown on 22 April to Geneva. There he had discussions with the industrialist Antonio Ghiringhelli, whom Antonio Greppi, the mayor of Milan, had appointed to be La Scala's 'special commissioner'. Ghiringhelli was appointed its sovrintendente, or general manager in May 1945. Toscanini made it clear to Ghiringhelli that musicians and other opera workers who had been dismissed by the Fascist regime for their political views or on racial grounds – among them Vittore Veneziani – must be rehired. Italian newspapers ran large pictures of the conductor and traced his progress homewards day by day: 'He will be in Milan by April.' 'On the 24th he will arrive in Italy.' And, in the *Corriere d'informazione* of 23 April, '*Tra poche ore Toscanini*' ('In a few hours, Toscanini'). When his train crossed the Italian frontier he was welcomed with flowers, tears and applause.

As one Italian writer put it, Toscanini's concert programme was 'a homage to Italian music and thought'.[6] The composers represented were Verdi, Puccini, Rossini and Boito. Many of the singers had been long-standing associates of the conductor. Soprano Mafalda Favero, who sang the third act of *Manon Lescaut* that evening, had made her Scala debut under Toscanini in 1929 as Eva in *Die Meistersinger*. Mariano Stabile and Giuseppe Nessi had performed the title role and Bardolfo, respectively, in many a performance of *Falstaff*, one of the operas Toscanini loved best and took greatest care of in performance. Also singing that evening was the great bass Tancredi Pasero, remembered for his Verdi roles, including King Philip in *Don Carlo*, and for his portrayal of the title part in Rossini's *Mosè in Egitto*. A new discovery of Toscanini's was Renata Tebaldi, then only twenty-four. Her appearance in the concert brought her immediate international recognition and acclaim.

The concert was broadcast throughout Italy and, on shortwave, to foreign countries. Huge crowds filling the Scala square and the Piazza del Duomo heard the music over loudspeakers. The critic of the *Corriere della Sera* exploded into superlatives, lauding Toscanini's 'miraculous baton, which possesses a secret catalytic power'. According to one account, the baton the maestro used was painted in the colours of the Italian flag – which may explain its catalytic power.[7] Inevitably, the occasion was also associated with Italy's emergence from the war and the Fascist era. Toscanini made sure that the Slaves' Chorus from *Nabucco* and the overture to *I Vespri siciliani*, with their echoes of the Risorgimento, were performed, together with the Verdi *Te Deum*. The same critic in the *Corriere* understood that the programme selections were 'of the people and for the people'. La Scala, after all, was 'an authentic glory of the Nation'[8] and the Nation in this case equalled Italy minus Mussolini. A distressing note was sounded just before the concert. A basket of flowers appeared in Toscanini's dressing room with a message referring to 'the dead of Gorla', a village outside Milan where more than a hundred children had been killed in an American bombing raid on 20 October 1944. The inference was clear: Toscanini had been a traitor to Italy in supporting the Allies. The message was removed before the maestro saw it.[9]

A recording exists of the reopening concert. Although the recorded sound is extremely poor, the excitement of the occasion shines through. The overture to Rossini's *La Gazza ladra* is rich in contrasts of expression and dynamic, a remarkably crisp and objective reading, even by Toscanini's standards. In the 'Va, pensiero' chorus from Verdi's *Nabucco* the line soars, the tone is fervent and the breathing across the structural seams of the piece remarkable. The touching nobility – and again fervour – of the Act Three quartet from Rossini's *Mosè* is due above all to the singing of Tancredi Pasero as Moses. If Toscanini was ever criticised for being cold, the Intermezzo from *Manon Lescaut* provides convincing evidence of his human, even sentimental warmth.

Another crucial difference between the reopening of the Staatsoper and the festivities at La Scala had to do with the profound changes Italy was undergoing, changes which were conspicuously absent in Austria. Italians were making a serious attempt to purge Fascism from the national conscience. King Victor Emmanuel III had acquiesced in

Mussolini's dictatorship. Toscanini in hyperbolic mood had referred to him as 'that degenerate coward, the king of Italy, who has betrayed everything and everyone'.[10] On 2 June 1946, less than a month after the rededicatory concert at La Scala, the monarchy was swept away by referendum. In contrast, a great many Austrians had welcomed the invasion of their country by German armies in 1938. Not only that: Austria as a whole had never renounced Nazism, for many Austrians still believed the comfortable fiction that they had never accepted it. This is why the 1955 celebrations at the Staatsoper ring hollow and why La Scala's reopening was indeed part of an authentic national renewal.

Meanwhile the enormous devastation of the war was only slowly being repaired. Many Italians were going hungry, with the average caloric consumption falling from 2,795 calories during the period 1936–40 to 1,733 calories in 1945. Ten per cent of housing space had been ruined or gravely damaged. Sixty per cent of Italian roads were unusable.[11] Funds granted by the Allied Military Government and the United Nations Relief and Rehabilitation Administration, amounting altogether in the years 1945–47 to more than half a billion dollars, helped the country survive the immediate post-war crisis and take the first hesitant steps towards rebuilding its economy.

In this ambiance of devastation and suffering, opera shone brightly. La Scala's post-war return to superb performances, like the Staatsoper's, was astonishingly rapid. Although Toscanini held no official position at the House, he was often present in fact and in spirit. Claudio Sartori wrote:

> Sometimes, during a season of concerts at the Scala, one enters the darkened and almost empty auditorium during a rehearsal and senses his presence. There is sure to be someone who whispers: 'Toscanini's here.' . . .
>
> Once one gets accustomed to the dim lighting, his silhouette just becomes visible in a centre seat at the back of the stalls. One discerns the white hair, guesses at the details. But no movement betrays him. He seems insensitive to the sound that comes from the orchestra. One can just make out that his hands are tightly clasped, almost gripping one another, while his elbows are forcefully pressed into the arms of the seat. And

in the iron grip of the hands one perceives the tremendous tension of the man utterly absorbed in listening, but completely under control. Sometimes a finger, one finger only, will escape and wag in the air, beating a rhythm which may not be that of the orchestra. It is the only way in which he takes part in the rehearsal.[12]

It surprised many people that Toscanini did not accept the music directorship of La Scala. While he had held the post he had shaped the character of the modern House. At the end of the nineteenth century he had insisted that administrative control be removed from the hands of the wealthy box holders. In 1921 he had pushed through the notion that the theatre be made an '*Ente Autonomo*', or 'independent organism', in perpetuity. Under the Law on Musical Associations, or '*Enti Lirici*', state subsidies were granted to any 'autonomous musical association' set up by local or other authorities in order to put on a season of opera lasting one month or more. This ensured freedom for La Scala in both the artistic and the financial spheres. Toscanini's intense concern for every aspect of the production extended to stage design and direction. Mafalda Favero remembers him concerned with the least minutiae of detail. During one rehearsal he jumped on to the stage and demonstrated what should be done to a singer who was entering carrying a basket. Nicola Benois, one of the most prominent directors and designers at La Scala, was not too proud to take advice from the conductor.

> He gave me very valuable suggestions which I put into practice. One of the most interesting was that of dividing the third act of *Otello* into two scenes, in order to give the first part, which contains the handkerchief episode, a more intimate and dramatic setting. Toscanini suggested that I make the scene dark and small-scale, and advised me to use four large columns, which would serve to make the action, the play among the four characters, more interesting.
>
> Actually, Toscanini did not conceive the sets only in an aesthetic sense, but above all in relation to the action.[13]

It is a great pity that the production of *Otello* Benois refers to never took place. In fact, Toscanini never conducted a complete opera at La

Scala after World War Two. Nevertheless, the legacy he bequeathed the House was vast and profound. As Benois suggests, his interest in the stage was part of his concern for the whole work, the integrated performance. And as Lorenzo Arruga makes clear, opera under Toscanini was not 'a composite spectacle made up of concomitant events but ... a unitary and complex act of life, the ever-renewed creation of each and every performance'.[14] Toscanini could be tyrannical and demanding, sometimes flying into rages, but never capricious, never blind to the essential artistic purpose. An account of a National Broadcasting Corporation Orchestra rehearsal in New York in 1946 gives an indication of his tendency to temperamental behaviour. '*E passione, dolore* – sorrow, passion, *ENTUSIASMO* – *ma non* SLEEP when you play! Put *entusiasmo*, like me! I don't enjoy to conduct – no, no, I 'ate to conduct, I 'ATE! Because I suffer too much – *TROPPO!*'[15] Another great artist, Lotte Lehmann, was impressed by Toscanini's humility. The pianist Ivor Newton heard her tell the story in London: 'She told Toscanini how everybody at Salzburg worshipped him, to which he replied, "You must not use such extravagant language to me – you should reserve that for Mozart, Beethoven and Brahms. I am only a conductor, perhaps a good conductor, but that is all." '[16]

The tradition of performance, and of personal commitment, that Toscanini built before the war was sufficiently solid to be carried on afterwards. Wally Toscanini, by marriage the Countess Castelbarco, sat on the La Scala Board and advanced her father's views even when he was not present. A new generation of conductors appeared in Toscanini's wake. Older conductors like Tullio Serafin and Victor De Sabata also cared deeply for excellence of playing and singing. Like the maestro, they understood the importance of a co-ordinated performance based on an objective and sensitive understanding of the composer's intentions as indicated in the score. Perhaps most important of all, the custom continued to be observed that the conductor was the key figure in most Scala performances. Since the score had been entrusted to his hands, all parties concerned – singers, management, director and designer – agreed that he bore ultimate responsibility for the success of the production. Without deferring to him, they would not think of overruling him in the interest of their own particular contribution.

Serafin is remembered as Maria Callas's chief musical mentor and, in Italy, as the man who saved the Rome Opera from chaos in the mid-1950s. He has been variously described as 'wise, vigorous, impassioned', 'a retiring man, perfectly willing to leave the limelight to others', 'a combative figure and a connoisseur'. Serafin followed his Scala *Nabucco* of 26 December 1946 with a *Cenerentola* which opened two evenings later. The young mezzo Fedora Barbieri sang the title role in the Rossini opera. In January 1947 Serafin led a rarely staged performance of Berlioz's *Damnation of Faust*, as well as an *Andrea Chénier* starring Beniamino Gigli in his post-war return to the House. Even though Serafin continued to be active into his eighties, these operas, together with a *Traviata* which opened in March and a *Meistersinger* in May, constituted his last work at La Scala.

Serafin knew his scores intimately and conducted them with faithful attention to the composer's markings. He also had an extraordinarily empathetic understanding of singing and singers. His legacy of recordings demonstrates an impeccable cantabile, especially in the strings. Orchestral dynamics are consistently held 'under' the singer. He never rushed singers into shallow breaths when a relaxed, easy breath could be taken. At Serafin's death in 1968, in his ninetieth year, generous tributes came from many artists. The baritone Tito Gobbi wrote, 'Serafin's performances were like an arch, beautifully shaped in a curve from the first bar to the last; and we all took part, body and soul, with the same devotion and enthusiasm as he showed.'[17] And as that ultimate perfectionist, Elisabeth Schwarzkopf, declared in print for all the world to hear, 'Nobody else, apart from Toscanini, knew such an enormous amount about singing.'[18]

Victor De Sabata, artistic director at La Scala from 1953 to 1957, loved composition and women and, according to the London critic Felix Aprahamian, hated conducting. 'Sabata presented perhaps the most notable instance of what is, too often, almost an occupational disease of great conductors: the desire to compose, and the illusion that they are better composers than conductors.'[19] Certainly De Sabata was endowed with prodigious gifts of memory and mental organisation, rivalling Toscanini's. They earned him the respect of musicians wherever he worked, including London, Paris and Monte Carlo. One evening in Aprahamian's house in London the British critic decided to set the Italian conductor a memory quiz on Debussy's *Pelléas et Mélisande.*

> Every one of the dozen snippets I played on the gramophone he would continue at the piano, singing the voice part faultlessly. Then I tried to catch him out with a succession of just two chords. '*On a brisé la glace avec des fers rougis!*' he sang out immediately. 'And what is the scoring at that point?' I asked. 'Held E on second horn, violin harmonics and violas, with the four moving parts on *divisi celli*', came the prompt answer.[20]

Among other Scala conductors, Antonino Votto had been Toscanini's assistant before the outbreak of the war 'and conducted almost in his name'.[21] Votto led a number of Callas's great Scala performances at the height of her career, including the 1954 *La Vestale*. Critical opinion was divided over Votto's work. Harold Rosenthal dismissed him as 'a good routinier' devoid of taste or imagination.[22] But Claudio Sartori called Votto's Scala *La Forza del destino* a model of 'aristocratic restraint, which makes him an ideal interpreter of Verdi'.[23] And his opera recordings with Callas are frequently full of fire, although certainly not in excess. Nino Sanzogno made his Scala debut during the 1948–49 season at the relatively young age of thirty-seven. A champion of new repertoire, Sanzogno was initially assigned Italian operatic premieres by such composers as Ildebrando Pizzetti, Goffredo Petrassi, Luigi Ferrari Trecate and Gian Francesco Malipiero. Many of these works were justifiably forgotten. In 1951 Sanzogno conducted the Scala premiere of Menotti's *The Consul*, which was received by the conservative audience with completely undeserved catcalls. Sanzogno had an unusual gift for reading and understanding difficult new scores.

Guido Cantelli was Toscanini's particular protégé – and prodigy – during the early post-war years. Toscanini wrote to Cantelli's wife that her young husband's talents were truly exceptional. 'This is the first time in my long life that I have met a young man so gifted. He will go far, very far. Love him well, because Guido is also good, simple and modest.'[24] By 1955 Cantelli's career was well under way – but not yet at La Scala. He conducted at the Edinburgh Festival in 1950 and led London's Philharmonia Orchestra in live concerts and recordings from 1951. But his debut in Milan did not come until 27 January 1956, when he conducted – and, in the best Toscaninian tradition, stage-directed – a sparkling *Così* at the Piccola Scala. The singers included Schwarzkopf, Nan Merriman, Graziella Sciutti, Luigi Alva and Franco Calabrese. As if to make up for lost time, the same year he was named chief conductor at La Scala. But Cantelli was not spared to fulfil his talents. On 23 November 1956 he was killed in an aeroplane accident in Paris, ending one of the most promising conducting careers of the century. Toscanini, old and ailing, was never told of the death of the young man he had so admired and championed. At the funeral, the Scala orchestra, performing without a conductor, played Handel's 'Ombra mai fu', the last piece Cantelli had conducted.

Carlo Maria Giulini was appointed principal conductor at La Scala in 1953 at the age of thirty-nine. He had previously been music director for RAI, the Italian radio, and had first been engaged at La Scala in 1952 at Toscanini's instigation. In conducting opera Giulini's habit was to rehearse with great taste and care and, whenever possible, to extract from the score an element of profundity. Interestingly enough, the August 1954 La Scala recording of Rossini's *L'Italiana in Algeri* shows Giulini completely at home in *opera buffa*. The overture is elegant, joyous, without Toscanini's ferocity but with extremely careful attention to the composer's markings. As an indication of the Scala orchestra's supreme musicianship, the principal oboe phrases his solo lines with enchanting subtlety, managing to be noble and sly at the same time. Giulini brings out the long, sad line of the Act One male chorus 'Quà le femmine son nate solamente per soffrir' with sensitivity and taste. The rich, virile voices sob with a gentle, almost womanly charm. Tempi tend to the pensively slow, giving a sweet melancholy to moments such as the opening of Lindoro's cavatina, 'Languir per una bella'. Giulini handles the ensemble scoring with an almost infallible sense of balance and knack for placing climaxes. The stylish soloists are held together by Giulini in perfect comic timing. Cesare Valletti as Lindoro has a good leggiero, as well as the top of a true Rossinian tenorino. His tone, however, verges on the strident, and there is little evidence of feeling for the text or independent musical judgment. Graziella Sciutti as Elvira sings with admirable dramatic sense, if not with the richest of sound. Giulietta Simionato is delightful from her very first note. While reining in her powerful mezzo – even to the point of erasing the lower passaggio, soubrette fashion – she manages to invest Isabella's twirling lines with real joy, not merely stage sauciness. Though Mario Petri (Mustafà) is put at a disadvantage by the omission of his aria, 'Già d'insolito ardore', his bluff, almost ugly-voiced bass galumphs most characterfully. Altogether, the Scala forces, as revealed in this recording, showed that the devastation of war had done nothing to diminish the House's standards.

Although sovrintendente Ghiringhelli was not known as a judge of singing or music in general, he kept La Scala going at a time of transition and upheaval. He worked for continuity rather than change and strengthened the familiar Scala pattern of excellent performances of the traditional operatic repertoire. A leather manufacturer who had grown very wealthy during the war, Ghiringhelli had risen from extreme childhood poverty and turned himself into a 'tough, charming and gregarious' man of the world.[25] In order not to compromise his independence he declined to take a salary from La Scala or even the perk of a 'company' car. He adored the theatre and devoted himself to the House's best interests as he conceived them in his rather conservative outlook. Ghiringhelli had what was probably more an intuitive than a conscious sense of what was needed at the House. He knew when to play safe and when – very occasionally – to be innovative. Nor was he always pleasant or easy to get on with. However, his politician's make-up generally led him to make choices which the public and critics would approve. In setting his plans in motion he was greatly helped by his musical and administrative staff. He surrounded himself with people who could give competent advice.

At La Scala the vital tradition of Italian operatic performance also ensured the generous availability of fine conductors, instrumentalists and choristers. There, and in Germany and Austria, ample creative talent helped ease the task of post-war reconstruction. In New York, the Metropolitan Opera a policy decision to advance the careers of native-born American singers quickly bore fruit. At Covent Garden, however, the process was much slower. The tradition of operatic singing in Britain was still in its infancy.

Ghiringhelli's first challenge, the rebuilding of the House, had been successfully accomplished, restoring the auditorium to its pre-war excellence. As Arruga wrote,

> Technically, the work was unanimously judged to be perfect; the acoustics were not worsened and in any event proved almost miraculous, according to all the historians, despite the rather ticklish problems posed by the largeness of the building and its particular type of construction, designed at the beginning to provide good sound only for those who wanted it, that is, for those who sat in the boxes or got a good seat in the orchestra filled with unfastened chairs.[26]

During the immediate post-war period Ghiringhelli played to the conservative tastes of the Milanese as far as La Scala's sets, stage direction and repertoire were concerned. Direction usually consisted of what might be called movement management with an emphasis on utility. Singers must stand downstage and be heard, and the chorus and comprimarii must occupy space properly. The visual element took precedence over acting. The twin watchwords for designers were decorum and stylishness, in that order. Nicola Benois created for Scala productions literally dozens of sets of 'composed spectacular solemnity'.[27] Against these scenic backgrounds singers acted – more or less, and often less. Critics and audiences alike paid more attention to the set than to the stage direction. Arruga rhapsodises over Benois's suggestion of mood in his set for Ildebrando Pizzetti's *Fedra*:

> Rooted, one might say, in the bowels of the earth, from which emerged, confused with the rocks, almost formless cyclopean masses carved with mysterious reliefs, trunks of lopped-off columns nesting in the shadow and crushed by the barely squared forms of immense capitals; and from those shadows which seemed to contain the most distant origins of myth, between jagged and rusty stone dripping with the blood of sacrifices and crimes, red stairs rose from the darkness, ascending towards the distant glare of a Doric colonnade inundated with light. . . . [A] sense of implacable 'presence' which almost made one gasp.[28]

Such a 'theatrical' approach to opera is apt to occur when attention is paid mainly to the singing. It leads to the de-emphasis of intellectual values at the expense of emotional – and musical – ones. This unabashed theatricality was characteristic of many Scala stagings soon after the war.

One exception to run-of-the-mill Scala productions was the work of Margherita Wallmann, whose lavish sets tended more to the representational. Another even more exciting director was the young Giorgio Strehler, who staged his first opera at the theatre – a *Traviata* – in 1947. Strehler's was the first Italian production of Prokofiev's fantastical opera *The Love for Three Oranges*, which opened at La Scala on 30 December 1947. Strehler was praised by the L'Italia critic for his 'immense ability in scenic representation matched by his awareness of the text and his following step by step the lively inventiveness of the music'.[29]

At this period new repertoire at the Scala was undertaken at peril. Ghiringhelli knew and shared the conservative tastes of his Milanese public – certainly those who occupied the stalls, many of whom were businessmen and fellow industrialists. When Callas turned down the main soprano part in Gian Carlo Menotti's *Consul*, she may have shown a good sense of tactics. Although Callas's performances of Rossini, Bellini and Donizetti reintroduced fascinating bel canto works to the Scala repertoire, she did not sing contemporary opera. *The Consul* was received in 1951 with a rudeness which its quality – and its conservative musical style – scarcely deserved. The critic Guido Confalonieri protested by going up to the gallery. According to one account he booed throughout the performance. According to another he hissed. But *The Consul*, often considered Menotti's finest work, has since taken a firm hold in the international repertoire. Working from his own libretto, with a plot centred on underground political activity, the composer produced an opera of strong dramatic interest. Although its musical idiom owes much to Puccini, its tautness and its dissonant elements place it securely in the modern era. Lincoln Kirstein called it, when it was new, 'a work of distinction, of sincerity in sentiment and of a relentless theatrical efficiency'.[30]

In 1952 La Scala decided to mount Berg's *Wozzeck* for the first time. A serious production team was assembled: Dimitri Mitropoulos conducted, Herbert Graf directed and Tito Gobbi sang the name part. The Marie was Dorothy Dow, who had created the role of Susan B.

Anthony in Virgil Thomson's *The Mother of Us All* in America in 1947. Dow concentrated on unusual repertoire, from Cressida in William Walton's *Troilus and Cressida* to Agnese in Spontini's opera of the same name. From the very beginning disturbances were heard. Mitropoulos turned to the audience and begged for silence. The performance was completed, but some of the critics could not quite fathom the piece. The *Corriere della Sera* reviewer called Berg's score 'at times indecipherable',[31] while the critic writing in the *Corriere Lombardo* termed the work 'an interesting, important opera highly worthy of an attentive hearing'.[32]

Working in a traditional musical idiom, Ildebrando Pizzetti functioned more or less as House composer. From 1947 to 1959 no fewer than nine different Pizzetti operas were produced at La Scala, five of which were world premieres. Anglo-Saxon critics have frowned at Pizzetti's domination: 'One of those composers highly respected at home, virtually unknown abroad, and performed more often than one would really wish.'[33]

Italian opera would be the staple diet of Italy's premier House. However, Furtwängler and Herbert von Karajan brought German operas to La Scala in the early post-war years in idiomatic, authoritative performances which posed a challenge and set a standard for the future. Until their visits Wagner and Mozart had generally been performed in Italian. Even the great Wagnerian, De Sabata, had been accustomed to conduct at La Scala a work entitled *Tristano e Isotta*, rather than *Tristan und Isolde*. Furtwängler's unforgettable Scala *Ring* was mounted during March and April 1950, with Kirsten Flagstad singing Brünnhilde, Set Svanholm as Siegfried, Elisabeth Höngen as Fricka, Erda and Waltraute, and Hilde Konetzni as Sieglinde, Gutrune and the Third Norn.

Karajan, Furtwängler's young rival, opened his *Tannhäuser* on 27 December of that year. For some time previously Ghiringhelli had eagerly been seeking to engage him. Since artistic quality was supremely important at the House, and since the German repertoire needed strengthening, Karajan was a desirable catch. He had been born in Salzburg on 5 April 1908 to a family which had moved to Austria in the late eighteenth century from the town of Kozani, in what is now Greece but which at the time had been a part of the Ottoman Empire.

His antecedents had been successful doctors and academics. He studied conducting at the Vienna Academy of Music and occupied music directors' posts at provincial German-speaking opera houses from a very early age: his debut as an opera conductor came at Ulm a month before his twenty-first birthday. On 21 October 1938 Karajan had conducted *Tristan* at the Berlin Staatsoper to tumultuous acclaim. After his Nazi past proved a temporary barrier, he returned to full activity as a conductor after the end of the war.

In Milan, the Karajan *Tannhäuser*'s largely German and Austrian cast included Hans Beirer in the title role, Elisabeth Schwarzkopf and the imposing bass Gottlob Frick as Hermann. Karajan followed with a brilliant *Rosenkavalier* in January 1952, with Schwarzkopf as the Marschallin, Jurinac as Octavian, Lisa Della Casa as Sophie and Otto Edelmann as Ochs. Furtwängler returned the following month with a *Meistersinger* and, in March, with a *Parsifal*. Quite beyond the introduction of *la pura lingua tedesca* to performance of the German repertoire at La Scala, Karajan's visits in particular laid the precedent of exchanging productions between top international Houses. This would eventually result in Karajan's 'ensemble of stars', which he flew from one house to another, making opera truly an international art.

The opening of the Piccola Scala on 26 December 1955 marked an important new departure. By making available a venue of 500 seats, Italy's premier opera house could stage works that 'got lost' in the big auditorium. The *Ente Autonomo* owned an old building close by in the Via Filodrammatici which had suffered great bomb damage during the war. It was demolished so the 'Little Scala' could be constructed on the site. The first production was Cimarosa's *Il Matrimonio segreto*, conducted by Nino Sanzogno and staged by Giorgio Strehler. Writing in the *Corriere*, Orio Vergani praised Strehler for 'maintaining the comedy at the level of enchantment of the music'.[34] *Il Matrimonio segreto* was followed that season by *Così*, Alessandro Scarlatti's *Mitridate Eupatore*, and four other chamber operas, including Falla's *El Retablo de maese Pedro*. A permanent company was established, made up of carefully selected singers whose voices and styles of acting were suited to the works presented. Production and musical quality did not suffer by comparison with the Scala's larger-scale offerings, and fine singers whose voices were inappropriate to the big hall could have the hearing they deserved.

The Cimarosa opera was recorded in February 1956 in Milan as part of the celebrations of the Piccola Scala opening. Once again, quality and elegance are at the forefront. Sanzogno approaches the overture with humour, taste and style. Accents are nicely placed; the orchestra play with energy and a collective sense of timing. The young lovers are sung by Luigi Alva and Graziella Sciutti, both of whom went on to grace the Piccola Scala stage for years and achieved a special fame. In Alva's voice there always lurks a smile. Sciutti is the incarnation of charm and pertness. Her acting persona is rich in colour and nuance, with the voice always at her service to establish character and project emotion. Ebe Stignani as Fidalma – replacing Giulietta Simionato, who sang the part in the theatre – is well past her vocal prime. This great singer acquits herself honourably, even in the late autumn of her career. She assumed her last role at La Scala in 1956, at the age of fifty-three.

Franco Zeffirelli recalled the excitement of Scala performances during the early Fifties – especially the singers' contributions. He did not slight Ghiringhelli's part in facilitating this extraordinary era of singing.

> It was the most fantastic time for Italian singers. The list of great voices, all at their peak, seemed endless – Tebaldi, Callas, Di Stefano, Del Monaco, Corelli, Rossi-Lemeni, Barbieri, Simionato, Gobbi, Bechi, Christoff . . . it was unbelievable. The manager, Antonio Ghiringhelli, while no great artistic figure, was able nevertheless to hold all these thoroughbreds together.[35]

It was an extraordinary era for tenors. Giuseppe Di Stefano had supreme beauty of tone and a legato that he seemed to have been born with. Such natural, sensuous singing, rare in any era, is a moving thing in itself. At the same time Di Stefano was capable of lapses of taste and style, and had a tendency to push. Such lapses are revealed in the larghetto 'Fra poco a me ricovero' from the Karajan *Lucia*, recorded live in 1955. Di Stefano howls and bawls in the worst Italian-tenor style. There are blood-curdling aspirations, inexcusable portamenti, scoops, fustian accents, dynamic shifts, faulty rhythms. All this goes cheek by jowl with brief appearances of melting tone lasting for mere measures and half-measures. Karajan lets Di Stefano get away with it all, abetting his crimes with the slackest of slack tempi. The Scala audience applauds happily. In contrast, there is also an undated recording of 'La donna è mobile', conducted by Serafin, apparently during the mid-1950s. Serafin's genial slow tempo gives Di Stefano time to discover a wealth of cynicism and arrogance in the character. A 1956 live 'Nessun dorma' with Sanzogno is a model of restraint. Instead of bawling Di Stefano produces warmth, sweetness and passion. The climax is magnificent and the noisy fans manifest their approval well before the orchestra has finished playing. Listening to Di Stefano keeps the listener apprehensive.

Mario Del Monaco was arguably the leading tenore robusto of the immediate post-war generation. His Milan debut came at the age of twenty-five in 1940, with a Pinkerton at the Teatro Puccini. During the war years he sang a broad selection of the lyric and spinto repertoire throughout Italy. He quickly added the dramatic roles and became one of the two foremost Otellos of his day, a part in which he was challenged only by the Chilean tenor Ramón Vinay. Del Monaco's debut as Otello came in July 1950 in the Teatro Colón in Buenos Aires. He carefully worked towards singing the part in Milan, first performing it in Rio de Janeiro, then successively in Catania, Rome, Mexico City and the Met. Finally, on 7 January 1954, he was heard in the role at La Scala.

Del Monaco had an instrument of astonishing power and penetration. His stage presence was enhanced by his muscular good looks. He was not averse to appearing in tights, or even – as Pollione opposite Callas's Norma at La Scala – bare-legged. However, Del Monaco sometimes sang with scant regard for vocal subtlety or the deeper aspects of musicianship. A 1952 recording of *Aida* survives, conducted by Alberto Erede, with Tebaldi, Stignani and Fernando Corena as principals. Del Monaco's unique baritonal strength is apparent in 'Si quel guerrier io fossi'. However, the aggressive 'Celeste Aida' which follows has a primitive sound. As frequently happens with this tenor, the vowels are oddly distorted and swallowed, which prevents him from maintaining a consistent tone from word to word. In the death scene from a 1954 *Otello* Del Monaco's admirable instrument is misused. Though he is capable of pianissimo, he rarely chooses to use it. The last 'Un bacio' is a rudely trumpeted demand. The 'Pia creatura', which should be heartbreaking, is marred by sobs. The previous generation – not even Gigli at his most sentimental – never went as far in the direction of self-indulgence as both Del Monaco and Di Stefano could do. In spite of repeated lapses of taste, however, many loved the sheer force of Del Monaco's portrayal of Otello. Renata Scotto was one: 'I remember when I saw Del Monaco. He was a great Otello. He had this figure – and when he was on stage, he was Otello. Make-believe – Del Monaco had that, to make believe that he was the warrior and the conquerer and the big man that Otello was.'[36]

In contrast to Del Monaco, Siepi consistently displays musical taste. This intelligent bass was a young man of twenty-three when he made his Scala debut in December 1946 as Zaccaria in the Serafin *Nabucco*. Siepi's tone is consistently smooth, sweet and sensuous, with a wealth of lights and colours not often found in a bass. His Figaro in the great 1955 Vienna recording conducted by Erich Kleiber shows his understanding of the music and his sense of partnership with the conductor. In the 'Se vuol ballare' Siepi acts through the voice, delightfully delineating character and situation. His Figaro is warmly human, with a broad hint of fun rather than cynicism or perverseness. No matter how darkly he frowns at Cherubino in 'Non più andrai', Siepi maintains his smooth Italian legato. In the allegro patter of 'Aprite un po' quegl'occhi' he shifts with no problem to a baritone colour and even, almost, to baritone tessitura and range. Every word in the Figaro recitatives is given a dramatic and emotional character of its own. Giulietta Simionato remembered her colleague fondly: 'Cesare Siepi was for me the king of bassos, a *grand seigneur* on the stage, a rare thing these days. His voice was pure gold, so effortless and all-enveloping.'[37] Like Del Monaco, he elicited strongly favourable reactions from female opera admirers, although Siepi's appeal was rather more suave than tigerish.

Simionato herself is a leading example of what some would suggest has disappeared from opera singing since those glory days of La Scala: freedom, and individuality. Like Shirley Verrett and Marilyn Horne later on, Simionato had both a mezzo and a soprano in her. Unlike the judicious Horne, she tended to sing her Rossini parts with too heavy a sound. Even so, the very weight is exciting. A recording exists of Rosina's *Barbiere* aria 'Una voce poco fa', made with Alberto Erede conducting with special insensitivity. And where Callas's Rosina, recorded in 1957, has an edge of wildness, even savagery, Simionato's is grounded in determined optimism. In her 'Non più mesta' from *La Cenerentola*, Simionato takes the allegro at a mad gallop, a tempo she handles with aplomb. By the later stages of her career – again, to judge from recordings – Santuzza in *Cavalleria* is a more appropriate part for her. In Verdi, too, Simionato shone, with Preziosilla and Ulrica as two outstanding roles.

Antonino Votto, the Scala conductor, stopped Simionato going on as a soprano. She recalled him telling her that if she 'pushed up the voice, a hole would develop in the middle. "The voice is like a rubber band," he reminded me. "Pull it one way and it gives way elsewhere. You are a superb Azucena; be satisfied. A Leonora at this point of your career is not going to mean that much." He was right . . .'[38] Her friends and peers enjoyed her good nature and her superb imitations of her fellow singers. Gilda dalla Rizza vowed Simionato was greater than Callas: 'She became a luminous star not through publicity, but through exceptional merit.'[39]

Renata Tebaldi was making a splendid career in Italy, England and America. As the young primadonna at La Scala during the late Forties and early Fifties she sang a broad selection of the lyric and spinto repertoire. Her early parts there included Eva, Gounod's Marguérite, Boito's Margherita, Desdemona, opposite Vinay's Otello and Alice Ford. Beginning in the 1950s she began to take on heavier roles: Tosca, Wally, Tatyana, Leonora (*Forza*), Aida and Adriana Lecouvreur. In the last role, considered especially difficult, she triumphed at La Scala in May 1953. Tebaldi 'excelled herself both vocally and dramatically; in her death scene in the last act she entered into her part so realistically that the public began to cheer and clap before the curtain came down'.[40] The conducting of Giulini was also praised: 'His preparation of the work was in every detail perfect.'[41]

In the 1952 *Aida* recording opposite Del Monaco, with the Scala forces conducted by Alberto Erede, it is clear that the name part is not completely right for Tebaldi. (Nor is it for most sopranos: perhaps

Leontyne Price and Montserrat Caballé are the two stars of the post-war era who have come closest to singing it with ease.) Her rich, rounded, exquisitely smooth tone does not extend to the highest register. She abandons her top C in 'O patria mia' just as it is threatening to go squally. Nor has she Price's dark, creamy chest tones. Her vocal advantages lie in the wonderful weight carried in a long, generally seamless middle register and a tone that would be almost genteel were it not so caressingly lovely. The mezza voce is of unparalleled beauty. Tebaldi's rendering of this aria is rich in legato, which she puts to expressive use. Although her acting on stage may have sometimes lacked spontaneity, she brings such subtlety of tone and nuance to her acting through the voice that an Aida is created on the recording: noble and pathetic, pensive and declamatory.

The career of Maria Callas, arguably La Scala's greatest star during the 1950s, had a difficult birth. Callas was born in New York City to Greek-American parents in December 1923. Her early career unfolded in Athens, where she studied with Elvira de Hidalgo, a noted retired coloratura. Callas appeared from adolescence in a number of large and small roles. From the beginning there was a clear emphasis on the dramatic soprano *Fach*. After hearing favourable reports, Toscanini decided to audition her at his home in Milan. He was considering her for a one-off production of *Macbeth*, with Scala singers, to commemorate the half-century of Verdi's death. After listening to her sing on 27 November 1950 he told her, 'You are the woman for whom I have been looking for a long time. Your voice is perfect. I will do Macbeth with you.'[42] Callas for her part was overwhelmed by her meeting with the maestro. During the same period the possibility was raised at La Scala of Callas's singing the role of Magda Sorel in Menotti's *The Consul* – in Italian, *Il console*. Menotti wanted Callas for the part, but Ghiringhelli was extremely reluctant. Menotti recalled the story to Michael Scott, one of Callas's biographers:

> Ghiringhelli had assured me: 'Find a soprano who pleases you and I'll be glad to give her a contract.' It was Wally Toscanini who first mentioned Callas: 'She's fat, ugly and half-blind but with a remarkable voice and stage presence' and she urged Menotti to go and see Callas. He thereupon took the train to Rome, and 'heard her in *Turco* – instantly I realised she was

an extraordinary singer and went to speak to her ... I asked
her if she would be interested in doing the *Console* at La Scala.'
He telephoned Ghiringhelli and told him he had found a singer
– 'her name is Callas.' Ghiringhelli started to rant and rave:
'Oh! my God, never, never, never.' Menotti protested, 'You
promised me I could have whomever I wanted and De Sabata
was present at our meeting. You can't go back on your word.'
Ghiringhelli equivocated: 'Well, I promised any singer you
chose would be acceptable, but I will only have Callas in this
theatre as a guest artist.' Menotti went back to tell her, as
circumspectly as he could. He remembers how surprised and
indignant she became: 'Mr Menotti,' she said, 'unless I go back
as a regular artist I will never put my foot in that theatre again.'[43]

Callas's determination paid off. She had refused the part of Magda
Sorel, which was far from ideal for her. But Ghiringhelli was forced
to face facts. Callas was a star and he was running an institution that
traded in stars. Good business demanded that there be another House
diva besides Tebaldi.

In 1951 Callas sang a stunning Elena (*I Vespri siciliani*) at the Maggio
Musicale in Florence. Lord Harewood, present at one of the dress
rehearsals, was struck by her stage presence as well as her singing and
musicianship:

Act I of Vespri begins slowly; rival parties of occupying French
and downtrodden Sicilians take up their positions on either
side of the stage and glare at each other. The French have been
boasting for some time of the privileges which belong by rights
to an army of occupation, when a female figure – the Sicilian
Duchess Elena – is seen slowly crossing the square. Doubtless
the music and the production helped to spotlight Elena, but,
though she had not yet sung and was not even wearing her
costume, one was straight away impressed by the natural dignity
of her carriage, the air of quiet, innate authority which went
with her every movement. The French order her to sing for
their entertainment, and mezza voce she starts a song, a slow
cantabile melody; there is as complete control over the music
as there had been over the stage. The song is a ballad, but it
ends with the words *Il vostro fato è in vostro man*, delivered
with concentrated meaning. The phrase is repeated with even

more intensity, and suddenly the music becomes a cabaletta of electrifying force; the singer peals forth arpeggios and top notes and the French only wake up to the fact that they have permitted a patriotic demonstration under their very noses once it is under way. It was a completely convincing operatic moment, and the singer held the listeners in the palm of her hand to produce a tension that was almost unbearable until exhilaratingly released in the cabaletta.[44]

In his autobiography Harewood concisely summed up Callas's achievement in this great role: 'The technique and assurance seemed to have grown enormously, and what had formerly been an obvious aptitude for operatic tragedy had turned into nothing less than a sovereign dramatic authority.'[45]

On the opening night of this *Vespri*, on 7 December 1951, Callas received a telegram from the sovrintendente. Ghiringhelli offered congratulations and suggested a meeting to set up performance dates for the same opera at La Scala. Callas, however, did not rush to open her engagement book. Only in June 1952 did she agree to meet Ghiringhelli, who had to journey to Florence and meet the singer backstage. His offer was a handsome one: opening the 1951–52 Scala season in *I Vespri*, together with Norma, Elisabetta in *Don Carlo*, and Constanze in the Italian version of *Die Entführung aus dem Serail*. Callas accepted the offer, and Ghiringhelli confirmed the arrangements in writing. But Callas demanded in addition a Violetta, to which Ghiringhelli agreed reluctantly without committing himself in writing.

The reception of *I Vespri siciliani* was all Callas might have wished. She recalled, 'I had never faced so difficult a test in all my life. But the welcome given me by the Milan public was sufficient to remove my doubts.'[46] The director Luchino Visconti telegraphed congratulations as well. The *Corriere della Sera* critic waxed breathless over her miraculous throat – '*la miracolosa gola di Maria Meneghini Callas*': '[The] prodigious extension, as well as the tones in the low and middle registers, [have] a phosphorescent loveliness and an agility and technique rather more unique than rare.'[47] Like Harewood, himself a connoisseur of singing, the Italian critic emphasises Callas's peerless technique – which would become a point of contention years later when she encountered vocal difficulties.

At the end of that month, in Parma, Callas sang such a splendid Violetta that Schwarzkopf came backstage from the audience and vowed to her that she would never sing the part again. Fuelled with these latest triumphs, Callas insisted to her husband, the industrialist Giovanni Battista Meneghini, that he pin down the Scala management. 'Ghiringhelli thinks he can play me around with *La Traviata*, but he'll regret it. If he doesn't reassure me unequivocally, I shan't sing Norma in a couple of weeks. Write to him using precisely those words.'[48] Ghiringhelli responded by special delivery letter: 'Every problem with Madame Callas will always be solved with the utmost cordiality.'[49] His solution, which might have been deemed not entirely cordial, was to temporise and pay Callas off. At this point there would be no new production of *Traviata*, but Ghiringhelli wrote a cheque for 1,400,000 lire – the diva's fee for four unsung *Traviata* performances. In the long run Callas prevailed. The 1955 Scala *Traviata*, staged by Visconti and starring Callas, would be one of the high points in her career and a landmark in the history of twentieth-century opera production.

On 7 December 1952 De Sabata conducted Callas in *Macbeth* for the opening of the 1952–1953 Scala season. Macbeth was sung by Enzo Mascherini, Banquo by Italo Tajo and Macduff by Gino Penno. As critic Elvio Giudici shows, De Sabata's tempi in the recorded performance shift unevenly, possibly because the opera was at that time relatively unfamiliar to conductors as well as audiences. De Sabata gives Lady Macbeth's 'Vieni! t'affretto' a slack tempo and lack of drive exactly where this aria should thrust forward. Callas is not surprisingly put off balance as concerns breaths and initial attacks. Vocally, however, she is in excitingly top form. It is hard to recall another modern singer – with the exception, perhaps, of Gobbi at his best – who takes such care for each word of recitative. And the passion which ignites Callas's phrases, more moving by far than Gobbi, is matchless in our time.

Tebaldi was not satisfied by Ghiringhelli's efforts to keep her happy. She refused to share glory with Callas, just as at the Royal Opera House during the 1959–60 season Callas would be assured that Tebaldi would not be singing any of the parts with which Callas was associated. 'The atmosphere at La Scala had become stifling,' she recalled. 'Undoubtedly the administration at the opera house favoured Maria, but I decided that I did not want to endure it, so I accepted the offer from Rudolf Bing, who for years had been inviting me to sing at the Metropolitan.'[51] Like so many divas, Tebaldi needed to be adored, and New York was to become the place where she was most welcome and best loved. However superb Tebaldi's singing was, it was Callas who would set a new standard for acting on the post-war lyric stage. The rising careers of these new artists indicated how quickly the art of opera in Italy was reviving from the ruins of war.

THREE

———❦———

COVENT GARDEN 1945–55
'Making Bricks . . .'

WHILE LA SCALA AND THE STAATSOPER had been physically devastated by the Second World War, the foundation of the Royal Opera as a permanent international company was an unlikely but positive result of war's turmoil. Unlike the Staatsoper and La Scala, Covent Garden had never been home to a permanent company and had no great native operatic tradition to which to return after the war. Just how far the English public had to go to develop an operatic culture was revealed in an editorial in *The Times* on 6 July 1945: 'There has always been', it stated, 'something exotic about opera in England. Perhaps its inherent and occasionally ludicrous artificiality sets it apart from sophisticated rather than popular appreciation.'

In the three decades before 1939, opera had been presented only intermittently in London. Sir Thomas Beecham had organised seasons of international artists and visits of foreign companies, both at Covent Garden and other London venues, which in the early days had been produced largely at his own considerable expense. In 1910 alone the Beecham family had lost £40,000 on the summer season. Until the 1930s the main opera to be heard outside London was provided by the Carl Rosa Company, which had been founded in 1875 and had toured Britain since 1893, singing in English and keeping an awareness of opera alive in the provinces, and giving experience to young musicians and singers.*

From 1924 to 1931 a group of wealthy private patrons, the Grand

---

* Among those who performed with the Carl Rosa company were Joan Hammond, Heddle Nash and Otakar Kraus. Conductors included Peter Gellhorn and Vilem Tausky.

Opera Syndicate, with Colonel Eustace Blois as managing director, had put on summer seasons at Covent Garden, bringing such major artists as Bruno Walter. In response to criticism that he was choosing a repertoire that could be assured of filling the House, Blois issued a statement in 1925 after having made a careful scrutiny of the financial returns, in which he said, 'There seems to be no possibility of making such an undertaking self-supporting.' Blois was forced to include 'a certain number of popular favourites instead of considering nothing but pure artistic interest'.

In 1927 Beecham established the Imperial League of Opera to raise money from private subscription: he could no longer afford to finance his own opera company or seasons. The following year he issued a broadsheet in which he wrote, 'Owing to limited opportunity the bulk of the public has never heard opera' and he noted that there was 'no actual insufficiency of first-rate artists of British origin on the modern operatic stage. . . . The plain reason why they are not here is that there is no home to house them.'[1] Beecham's League collapsed in 1929 because subscriptions failed to materialise during the Depression. The chorus of his company was only kept together until 1932 at Covent Garden under Colonel Blois's auspices.

Maintaining high artistic standards could only become the major consideration when public funding became an accepted part of cultural life after the war. Public funding, however, was not yet a reality. Indeed, Beecham had been furious when he discovered that a joint season he was planning with the syndicate in 1931 was to be partially subsidised by the Exchequer, as a result of influence from Ethel Snowden, wife of Philip Snowden, the Chancellor of the Exchequer. The arrangement was tied to an agreement with the BBC whereby broadcasts would be assured for five years. The BBC would receive £17,000 a year from January 1931 and would pay the Grand Opera Syndicate an annual fee of £25,000. Beecham argued that no one would subscribe if they knew that some of the funding was coming out of taxation. This first attempt at public subsidy did indeed have a detrimental effect on his plans. As a result of the economic crisis and Depression in 1931 the government refused to renew the subsidy at the end of 1932 and subscriptions dropped, as did audiences.

In an attempt to combine the various operatic interests, Blois invited Beecham to conduct a short season of German opera at Covent Garden in May and June 1932. This entailed cancelling Bruno Walter's contract at the last moment, as well as replacing the London Symphony Orchestra with Beecham's new orchestra, the London Philharmonic. When Blois died in 1933 and the syndicate terminated its lease of the theatre, the opera house's very existence was threatened. Covent Garden Properties were planning to pull down the building and replace it with shops and offices. It was saved that December when Beecham, assisted by his good friend Lady Cunard, formed a new syndicate – the Royal Opera House, Covent Garden Ltd, with Philip Hill, the chairman of Covent Garden Properties Ltd, and some of the wealthiest men in England. Although the syndicate started with a nominal capital of £50,000, it included people of such affluence and social status that the short-term future was secured. Extensive modernisation was to be undertaken under the terms of the new lease. Beecham was made artistic director and Geoffrey Toye managing director.

Beecham appeared the next season with the London Philharmonic and remained in charge of Covent Garden until the war. He conducted *Götterdämmerung* with Flagstad in 1936 and brought Otto Erhardt to direct the *Ring* and, with the designs of Rex Whistler, *Fidelio*. The Dresden State Opera visited in November 1936, when Karl Böhm conducted *Rosenkavalier* and *Tristan*. The critics were impressed by the German company's well-rehearsed and dramatically integrated productions. During the international seasons from 1936 to 1939 the roster of great singers, later looked back to with nostalgia, included Conchita Supervia, Lauritz Melchior, Lotte Lehmann, Frida Leider, Kirsten Flagstad and Alexander Kipnis. English singers included Eva Turner and Maggie Teyte. Beecham also brought Felix Weingartner, Vittorio Gui and Erich Kleiber to conduct at Covent Garden. The last season, in May 1939, included Beniamino Gigli and Eva Turner in a performance of *Aida* and Vittorio Gui conducting Eva Turner and Giovanni Martinelli in *Turandot*.

When Toye left in 1938, Beecham appointed Walter Legge, the music administrator and critic, as assistant artistic director. There were further substantial financial losses, however, and in January 1939 Beecham wrote to the *Daily Telegraph* describing the insecure and disorganised state of opera in England. He derided the plan to close Covent Garden because of the international situation, pointing out that the thriving Vienna State Opera had a generous state subsidy, and was providing a wealth of opportunities for young singers to advance.

Not only had the Dresden opera company's performances introduced English audiences to a higher standard of opera production but also the productions at Glyndebourne had demonstrated the possibility of integrated music drama on the operatic stage. In beautiful rolling countryside in East Sussex, John Christie's opera house, originally seating 311 people, was built on his family estate. From 1934 Christie and his wife, the soprano Audrey Mildmay, endeavoured to put on privately subsidised opera productions of the highest quality, employing the experienced opera administrators, producers and musicians who had been driven out of Nazi Germany. Fritz Busch, who had been music director of the Dresden Staatsoper from 1922 to 1933, when he was dismissed because of his openly expressed dislike of the Nazis, was engaged as music director. Carl Ebert, with whom he had worked closely at Salzburg in the 1930s, was engaged as head of production. They were joined by another émigré, Rudolf Bing, who was engaged as manager. This triumvirate attracted top performers to Glyndebourne because of its unique rehearsal conditions – six to eight weeks in a community atmosphere, which helped create an unusual sense of ensemble.

Busch insisted that although the conductor's contribution was the major one, the producer was an equal partner in the preparation. Ebert worked with his singers using the music to define the movement of groups and individuals. The familiar 'but meaningless gymnastics of arm and foot' were no longer acceptable.[2] Peter Hall, who applied to be Ebert's assistant after the war but did not take the job, admired Ebert's 'command of the language of the theatre – the lights, the design, the grouping of the characters'. Hall was, however, critical of one aspect of Ebert's method: 'He had an irritating habit, common then in Europe, of illustrating the music; by which I mean drilling the singers for hours to walk and gesture precisely to the time and pulse of the score. This had a tendency to make everyone act like Mickey Mouse.'[3]

The Ebert–Busch belief in an equal collaboration between music and drama became a tradition at Glyndebourne that was maintained under Moran Caplat. Caplat, an ex-actor and arts administrator, took over from Bing in 1949 as general administrator, a post he filled until 1981. John Pritchard and John Cox, followed by Bernard Haitink and Peter Hall, also maintained the tradition. It was possible for director and conductor to refine productions over many years with the same or different casts. Hall later explained, 'You know that what you do is thought to be as important as what the conductor does. That's not so in any other opera house,' although it was, he added, 'spasmodically so at Bayreuth'.[4]

While not attempting to provide top-quality performances at high prices in the 'festival' conditions, Sadler's Wells had been the only other company in Britain that had put on regular performances of opera before the war. Socially it was the polar opposite of Glyndebourne, with its origins in Emma Cons's Royal Victoria Coffee Music Hall, opened on Boxing Day 1880 to provide an antidote to the 'gin and melodrama' of the Victorian music halls. As well as concerts, the hall had provided popular education.* By 1906, under Lilian Baylis's management, audiences for opera produced in tableau at the hall averaged between 1600 and 2000. Baylis was also one of the first managers to show films regularly at the hall. In the hall's 1912 season brochure it was called 'The People's Opera House'.

In 1925 Lilian Baylis decided to restore Sadler's Wells, which had been derelict since 1915, intending that performances of opera and drama should be shared with the Old Vic in south London. Opera was to be made available to audiences 'within the means of labourers and artisans'. She formed a committee and launched an appeal as a result of which Sadler's Wells reopened in 1931. Edward Dent, professor of music at Cambridge, in his book *A Theatre for Everybody* published in 1945, ascribed to Baylis the 'vision of a really national theatre' and

---

* Manufacturer Samuel Morley provided funding. Three years after his death in 1889 Morley College was founded in his memory to provide educational opportunities to working people. Music was represented on Emma Cons's committee by Arthur Sullivan, Carl Rosa and Julius Benedict.

the model from which a state-subsidised national theatre and opera company could evolve.*[5]

It soon became clear that drama should be housed at the old Vic and opera at Sadler's Wells. Baylis also offered a home to the ballet company which had been formed by Ninette de Valois. During the Thirties, Joan Cross, Edith Coates and Heddle Nash appeared regularly in productions of the popular operatic repertoire at Sadler's Wells. Dent acknowledged that in spite of Miss Baylis's belief that in the neighbourhoods of the Old Vic and Sadler's Wells there was 'a culture-starved proletariat hungering for Shakespeare and Mozart', in reality the audiences were predominantly middle-class, coming from central London and the suburbs.

The Second World War was a watershed in attitudes to the arts in Britain. The Council for the Encouragement of Music and the Arts (CEMA) was founded in January 1940 by the Pilgrim Trust and Lord De La Warr, President of the Board of Education, later the Ministry of Education. Its mandate was to bring music, drama and art to all corners of the country during the war, when ordinary sources of entertainment had collapsed and workers were concentrated in new factories. The conference that inaugurated the setting up of CEMA in December 1939 stated in its preparatory memorandum, 'This country is supposed to be fighting for civilisation and democracy and if these things mean anything they mean a way of life where people have liberty and opportunity to pursue the things of peace. It should be part of a national war policy to show that the Government is actively interested in these things.'[6]

CEMA's initial grant of £25,000 from the Pilgrim Trust, with a

---

* Dent recalled the lack of resources at Sadler's Wells at the time: 'Necessity', he wrote, 'was never very prolific of invention, and in many operas the wilful abstention from grandeur, the elevation of economy into a moral principle – "oh but it's so old-fashioned to be realistic! We leave all these things to imagination now" was depressing in the extreme. Lohengrin was not allowed to have a swan at all; the swan was "suggested" by a light which looked as if the operator had intended to "spot" the hero himself but always missed him' (Dent, *Theatre for Everybody*, p. 98). Strangely, a lighting effect for the swan was used by Robert Wilson in the controversial Met production of *Lohengrin* in 1998, although with no technical mishaps.

matching Treasury grant, was soon raised to £50,000 with the help of Dr Thomas Jones, former Assistant Secretary to the Cabinet and later secretary to the Pilgrim Trust. Jones had been involved in sending experts in music, drama and the visual arts to unemployed miners in the 1930s and his original concept for CEMA was the encouragement of community and folk arts and crafts, with local participation rather than professional performers providing cultural experiences for audiences.

Both Christie of Glyndebourne and the economist John Maynard Keynes had been critical of Jones's approach as being populist and tending to mediocrity. When Keynes was asked by R. A. Butler, De La Warr's successor as President of the Board of Education, to become chairman of CEMA he replied that he had been 'only limited in sympathy with the principles on which it has been carried on hitherto'.[7] At the end of 1941 CEMA was taken over by the Treasury and the Pilgrim Trust no longer contributed to its funding. Keynes became its chairman in April 1942, by which time it had established itself as a national institution, having organised 8,000 concerts and art exhibitions visited by 600,000 people.

Keynes, in keeping with his anti-Depression policies, believed that the state should assume responsibility for spending money on the arts. In 1933 he had written, 'For with what we have spent on the dole since the war we could have made our cities the greatest works of man in the world.' Keynes gave CEMA a forceful and clear-headed direction towards the provision of the fine arts for the great mass of the people but with the emphasis on supporting artistic excellence.* During his first broadcast as chairman he said, 'I would like to see the war memorials of this tragic struggle take the shape of an enrichment of the civic life of every great centre of population.'[8]

Sadler's Wells played a major role in CEMA's activities. When, in September 1940, the theatre became a refuge for people bombed out

---

* Keynes had been involved with supporting the arts before the war, in particular the ballet, after he married ballerina Lydia Lopokova in 1925. For Keynes 'the purpose of patronage was to make non-profit-making activities possible' not to provide 'a continual supply of something for which there was no demand' (Robert Skidelsky, *About the House*, no. 10, Christmas 1983). Keynes was a discriminating judge of theatre although, according to his biographer, his interests were narrow and he was not interested in either music or the visual arts.

of their homes, a grant from CEMA enabled the Sadler's Wells company to tour all over the country, at first with its leading singers, an orchestra of four, and conductor Lawrance Collingwood's piano accompaniment, and a chorus of two men and two women. By 1941 orchestra, chorus and principals had been augmented and audiences grew. When Joan Cross, Sadler's Wells's leading soprano since the 1930s, appealed to the general manager of the Met, Edward Johnson, on 8 November 1941 for a 'bundle' of costumes from the Met she told him that the big provincial theatres 'were packed from floor to ceiling' for their opera performances in English.[9] When the Old Vic itself was bombed, the company transferred its headquarters to Burnley in Lancashire, where it gave an eight-week season of opera, drama and ballet as well as continuing its touring activities. The company returned to London, to the New Theatre, in 1942 under the artistic directorship of Joan Cross.

The spreading of arts culture to a wider audience proved enormously popular. In Wales and the North, the public enjoyed the Old Vic's Shakespeare, and in the West End of London the general public was captivated by the Olivier–Richardson theatre seasons and ballet performances by Margot Fonteyn and Robert Helpmann. Equally successful were the re-creation of the Hallé Orchestra by Barbirolli in Manchester, and the film compositions of Walton and Vaughan Williams. By 1945 CEMA's Treasury grant was £235,000, with more than half going to music and increasingly to professional ensembles like the symphony orchestras.

After the war Keynes wanted to see both the Old Vic and Sadler's Wells brought under the Council's auspices, but Tyrone Guthrie, Sadler's Wells manager since 1933, was determined to maintain its independence. In November 1944 he and Edward Dent, who was on the Board of Sadler's Wells, had written a memorandum on opera policy. They suggested that English opera at Sadler's Wells should be subsidised for five years and should concentrate on acting, presentation and *opéra comique*, while Covent Garden should be used for visiting companies and occasional joint productions with the Old Vic.[10] In his book *Theatre for Everybody* Dent asked if it was time for Sadler's Wells to 'set to work to become the National Theatre and the National English opera'? He pointed out that although an 'idealist' theatre would not in peacetime boast the star casts it had enjoyed in wartime, it would gradually be able to build up a great tradition. A People's Opera, on the other hand, would always have a 'permanently subordinate status' and should aim to be the British Volksoper, humble but not humiliating, with a state-subsidised national House 'maintaining the artistic standards of the great continental opera houses'. If Covent Garden went back to its old international seasons it would bring back with it 'all sorts of ridiculous people' who were using it as a means of 'getting into Society'.*[11]

During the war there were no operatic performances at Covent Garden. The theatre was leased to the Mecca Company and used as a dance hall. When Mecca's lease was due to run out at the end of December 1944 Philip Hill, the chairman of the company which owned Covent Garden, approached Boosey and Hawkes, the music publishers, suggesting that they take on an opera season. Encouraged by CEMA, Boosey and Hawkes took out a lease for five years from 1 April 1945 and agreed that they would meet the rental, rates and running expenses if a non-profit-making company was set up to organise the running of opera at Covent Garden. They felt that the time had come for Covent Garden to become 'the home of the lyric arts in England'.[12]

On 12 June 1944 the Chancellor of the Exchequer, Sir John Anderson had announced that a new body was being created to take over from CEMA to continue in peacetime its work of encouraging and fostering the arts. Keynes, who had prepared the framework for this body, was to be its first chairman. The Arts Council of Great Britain would not be a ministry of culture but an autonomous institution, funded by and responsible to the Treasury but independent from political interference. At a press conference that day and later on the radio, Keynes enthused about the potential for stimulating artistic endeavour. 'I do not believe', he said, 'that it is yet recognised what an important thing has happened. State patronage for the arts has crept in. ... At last the public exchequer has recognised the support and encouragement of the civilising arts of life as part of their duty.'

---

* Dent wrote, 'My left-wing readers, if I have any, will say scornfully that after the present war there won't be any more "Society". People said that during the last war, too, and they will say it again during the next. *Plus ça change plus c'est la même chose'* (Dent, *Theatre for Everybody*, p. 136).

The Arts Council would 'create an environment' and 'cultivate an opinion' that would enable the artist and the public to create a union that would be mutually sustaining.*[13] The task of an official body, Keynes said, was not to 'teach or to censor, but to give courage, confidence and opportunity'.[14] Under Keynes's guidelines the Arts Council's objectives were to increase audiences, improve standards and aid professional training. It would make the fostering of opera and ballet a central objective. In its first year it made a grant of £25,000 to Covent Garden.

Covent Garden lay at the heart of Keynes's dream of making London the artistic capital of Europe. It was to be the base for a great national opera company, singing in English and encouraging the writing of English operas. Keynes set up a Covent Garden Committee including Boosey, Hawkes, Edward Dent, William Walton, Kenneth Clark and Steuart Wilson, the Arts Council's music director. As a result of their deliberations Sadler's Wells Ballet was asked to become resident at Covent Garden and it was decided that a resident opera company was to be built from scratch. It was also decided to form a charitable trust that would free the company from entertainment tax and enable it to receive gifts without tax. This Trust was formally set up on 5 February 1946, when the members of the committee became trustees.

The management of Covent Garden was not to include anyone with pre-war experience of running opera. One of the main contenders was Christie, but Keynes and Christie disliked each other from their schooldays at Eton, and Keynes resented Christie's accusation that Keynes at CEMA had copied his own ideas for a national council of music. Along with many others Dent, who was an excellent linguist and translator, passionately believed in the cause of opera in English and the development of an English 'style' of opera. This he successfully persuaded Keynes was the right course.

Keynes wanted a businessman to run Covent Garden. In April

---

* Arts managements would work with local government to build and adapt buildings for the arts. 'His proposals', wrote Andrew Sinclair, in his history of the Arts Council, 'were a curious amalgam of Bloomsbury elitism and state provision on the Soviet model' (*Arts and Cultures*, p. 46).

1944, therefore, the committee turned to David Webster, who had been chairman of the Bon Marché department store in Liverpool and had recently signed a contract to become chairman of the Metal Box Company. He had had some experience of music administration as chairman since 1940 of the Liverpool Philharmonic Orchestra, where Kenneth Clark had met him and been impressed by his knowledge of opera and his administrative skills. He also had some acting and directing experience as a student. Dent supported Webster's appointment, hoping to be 'one of the experts whose advice he takes'.[15] Webster signed his contract in August 1944 and was immediately given facilities by Boosey and Hawkes in their offices, from which he was to start forming the new company. His appointment was to begin formally on 31 December 1945 as the House was not to be vacated by the Mecca Cafés until October 1945. There was, in Webster's words, an 'appalling amount of work' to be done to restore the theatre.[16]

Neither Bing nor Beecham was considered for the position of general manager or artistic director of Covent Garden. Christie was furious, as he had been trying to buy the freehold of Covent Garden and since 1938 had expressed the hope that Glyndebourne and Covent Garden would be amalgamated with a twelve-week season involving thirty performances at each venue. Beecham and Legge were equally disgusted. They had been convinced that Legge's newly launched Philharmonia Orchestra would become the orchestra of Covent Garden and that they would resume the artistic direction they had controlled before the war. Dent was resolutely opposed to Beecham and, according to the Royal Opera House's official historian, Frances Donaldson, there is no evidence that Beecham was ever considered for the job. In his memoirs Beecham wrote that he was never consulted. Legge later wrote of Beecham, 'It seems that with this banishment from Covent Garden an iron entered his soul.' Legge recalled that Boosey had told him just before Covent Garden reopened that his 'standards were notoriously higher than those they aimed at ... and that I was too intransigent'.[17]

On 27 July 1945, the day on which the General Election brought Labour to power, *The Times* reported that negotiations were going on between the Arts Council and the management of Covent Garden to settle the 'division of function' between Covent Garden and Sadler's

Wells. Christie wanted a pooling of resources in a single management for all three companies. At this critical juncture, however, Webster and the trustees were determined to fight the idea of Sadler's Wells being incorporated into Covent Garden. Webster had no difficulty in persuading Keynes that the Sadler's Wells Charter meant that they had to charge lower prices and should serve the borough, whereas Covent Garden should serve the nation. Sadler's Wells was, he argued, 'a far more parochial affair'.[18] John Tooley, later Webster's assistant and then general director of the company, believed that Dent and Guthrie wanted no 'dilution or change of direction' of Sadler's Wells at its Rosebery Avenue home, where its tradition had developed and its audience been built up in the inter-war years. Another ally for Webster's autonomous Covent Garden was Ninette de Valois, whose successful Sadler's Wells ballet company was moving to Covent Garden. She was determined that her ballet company should not be used to subsidise the less successful Sadler's Wells opera. Sadler's Wells were also not too keen on closer co-operation. Steuart Wilson told Webster on 13 March 1947 that he had heard from those who had been involved in the negotiations that they had been a 'hopeless failure, owing to the fear of Sadler's Wells that they would be completely smothered'.[19] According to Tooley, those involved in setting up Covent Garden 'wanted to be totally different to Sadler's Wells'. They saw it, he explained, 'as the great national house, and it was to be the source of many new operas'.[20] The idea of singing in English was to encourage native talent and it was, in any case, still the norm in Europe to sing in the local language.

Covent Garden was to be the home of the major national and ultimately international company, but it was Sadler's Wells that reopened first, on 7 June 1945, with a landmark new opera, Benjamin Britten's *Peter Grimes*, conducted by Reginald Goodall and directed by Eric Crozier. Norman Tucker, director of Sadler's Wells from 1953 to 1966, later wrote that he would never forget that evening when 'before a capacity audience an accomplished company performed a work which seemed to herald the new birth of the native English repertory'.[21]

Britten's biographer, Michael Kennedy, ascribed Britten's success both at home and abroad to his brilliant technique and his 'discovery of a spiritual *Leitmotiv*'. *Grimes* was a parable of a man at odds with his nature and his social environment, in which Montagu Slater's libretto skilfully and speedily set the scene and outlined the personalities. *The Times* praised Britten's 'effortless originality' and its 'situations of great power ... intensified by orchestral music of diabolic cunning'.[22] Britten himself wrote to Imogen Holst on 26 June, 'I must confess I am very pleased with the way it seems to "come over the footlights", and also with the way the audience takes it. ... I feel it is perhaps an omen for English opera in the future.'[23]

The composer Michael Tippett heard *Peter Grimes* both at Sadler's Wells and in Budapest in 1948. He and William Walton were encouraged by the success of the opera, which soon worked its way into the standard repertoire. Within three years of its first performance it had been produced in seven cities including Budapest, Hamburg, Stockholm, Milan and New York, and had been conducted at Tanglewood by the young Leonard Bernstein. It was performed at Covent Garden in November 1947, conducted by the music director, Karl Rankl, directed by Tyrone Guthrie.

Sadler's Wells's general standard at this time was, however, far from remarkable. The music critic Hans Keller recalled how he was lying down in the gallery of Sadler's Wells during a performance of *Così fan tutte*, unwilling to look at the stage, because 'one production was as bad as another', when he heard a tenor 'who makes me, literally, sit up'. The tenor was Peter Pears. He was the first Peter Grimes and the central inspiration of Britten's work. Hans Keller wrote that the relationship between Pears and Britten – the 'creative genius who is basically a melodist and extremely susceptible to the human voice' – was to develop a hugely successful symbiosis 'between the composer's and the interpreter's work'. The seasoned performer Joan Cross was the first Ellen Orford, Britten having written the role with her in mind.

Britten was not happy with his relationship with Sadler's Wells. From the moment members of the company had seen copies of the first act four months before the opening night, there began a campaign against the work. The music itself was challenging for the company and there had been great tension during the rehearsals. The singer cast to sing Balstrode had refused to learn 'such outlandish stuff', and the orchestra and chorus struggled with the work. Edward Dent was reported to have likened the music of *Peter Grimes* to 'the noise of a motor bike starting up'.[24] John Lucas in Reginald Goodall's biography claims that Britten and Pears 'were sneered at as Joan's pansies'.[25] Leading singers also complained that the composer, leading tenor and producer had been conscientious objectors during the war – something that was intentionally reflected in the character of Grimes, the 'tortured idealist'.[26] In an interview with Alan Blyth in *Gramophone* in June 1970 Britten recalled that at the dress rehearsal he 'thought the whole thing would be a disaster'.[27]

In the event, even though orchestra and chorus struggled during the performances, the power of the opera was immediately recognised. Britten, however, realised that he would have to be an entrepreneur as well as a composer, and in March 1946 Crozier, Cross and Pears left Sadler's Wells to form a new company 'dedicated to the creation of new works', as Britten wrote. They approached Rudolf Bing at Glyndebourne and he agreed that Britten's newly formed Glyndebourne English Opera Company would produce one or two new English works every year alongside the regular company. The first was *The Rape of Lucretia*, which had its premiere at Glyndebourne on 12 July 1946, produced by Eric Crozier with sets designed by the artist John Piper. Pears and Joan Cross were the male and female choruses, Kathleen Ferrier was Lucretia, and Otakar Kraus was Tarquinius. Reginald Goodall conducted. Kraus, a Czech baritone domiciled in Britain since escaping from the Nazis, was from 1951 a stalwart of Covent Garden.

Ferrier had never sung in opera before and Britten and his librettist, Ronald Duncan, were 'relying completely on her natural simplicity and dignity'. Ferrier, however, later recalled her anxiety: 'Could I ever *walk* across the stage without falling over my rather large feet? ... I couldn't believe how difficult it was to do the simplest arm movements without feeling like a broken windmill.' Joan Cross advised her to stop worrying about her arms and feet, and said to her, 'Your voice expresses all you need.'[28] In her recordings of opera, lieder and folk songs, Ferrier's voice was indeed expressive, her emotion flowing naturally out of the tone: darkly shimmering, with a thrilling tight vibrato. She also had a fine sense of text, dramatic pacing and musical sophistication. The low register of her contralto was especially resplendent, although incomplete training meant she never developed her highest notes, and the slight 'English' covering of the tone and a 'refined' diction occasionally restricted full emotional expression.

The Times critic said that Britten was 'lifting opera out of the dead end in which it has been stuck by the death of Puccini'.[29] But the ending, in which the chorus answers the final ensemble of mourning with Christian promises of eternal life and redemption, on which Britten had insisted, was severely criticised both at the time and later.* Michael Fuller reassessed *Lucretia*'s theme of Christian forgiveness in an article in *Musical Times*, in the spring 2000 edition, tracing the piece to Britten's own 'definite religious sensibilities' as well as to its composition just after the composer had returned from a concert tour of Europe. That tour had included concerts at the recently liberated concentration camp at Bergen-Belsen. Fuller ascribed Britten's invocation of God to the need for a work of renewal and a 'contribution to the post-war healing process'.

Commercially the opera foundered, its provincial tour proving a box office disaster. Christie, who had disliked the opera, stood the financial loss of that season but refused to underwrite the next. Britten decided to found a non-profit-making company, the English Opera Group, with Peter Pears and Joan Cross his fellow trustees. Britten, Crozier and John Piper were the artistic directors. Britten's aim was to create a form of opera 'requiring small resources of singers and players'. They were responsible for the production of *Albert Herring*, which they staged on 24 June 1947 at Glyndebourne as a visiting company. Christie was heard to say at the opening, 'This isn't our kind of thing, you know.'[30] The arrangement was not a happy one and in 1948 the English Opera Group became the House company of Britten's Aldeburgh Festival, launched in June 1948 with Lord Harewood as its president.

The problems of starting a first-rate permanent English opera company at Covent Garden were formidable. On 19 January 1946 Desmond Shawe-Taylor expressed his concern in the *New Statesman* about the

---

* The revered critic Ernest Newman said it was 'rotten with insincerity and pretentiousness'.

'perpetual mediocrity and provincialism' of Covent Garden. He wrote, 'In Sadler's Wells we have a rough and unofficial, but promising, Volksoper; in Covent Garden the empty shell of a Staatsoper.' He urged that use should be made of 'what little first-rate material is available, *irrespective of nationality*', as Glyndebourne had with Ebert, Busch and Bing. These were, he emphasised, people 'who know the whole complex business of opera inside out'.

The decision to use English at Covent Garden was proving extremely hard to reconcile with the effort to create an opera company of international standing. Isaiah Berlin later described the English-language policy as 'an invention of the patriotic days after the war, when Keynes and Kenneth Clark developed a good deal of patriotism in the arts'. It had, he believed, 'in fact nearly proved our undoing'.[31] But for the time being the policy was sacrosanct. The Trust issued a statement on 5 June 1946 explaining its aim was 'to establish a resident opera company and a resident ballet company of the highest standard mainly of British artists'. This permanent national institution would give training and opportunity to British artists, as well as encouraging creative work in English. In other countries opera houses were often the 'centre of musical life', giving opportunities to local singers, composers, instrumentalists and conductors. It was hoped that this would become the case in England, where hitherto singers in particular had not had the opportunity to become 'finished products in the operatic sense'.[32] The Trust believed that the development of opera in England, and indeed the development of a style of performance, depended to a large extent on the use of the English language. The performances of the resident company would therefore be given in English. British artists would be engaged to prepare new scenery and costumes. It would be a permanent institution, learning from the 'great continental traditions' but developing its own tradition and style. Auditions were to be held for principals and they, together with known English singers, would form the basis of the company.* Peter Gellhorn, who later

---

* Adele Leigh, a company soprano from 1949, later recalled, 'You could never do *The Magic Flute* in German. It was just after the war and we were still rationed. By the time Solti came a lot of water had flowed under the bridge. We would sing very little in Italian – British people were still very wary about opera and wanted to know what it was all about – our diction was so good, one of the things Reggie Goodall and Norman Feasey taught us' (Interview, 23.4.98).

became assistant music director, defended the policy. It was not only the best way to build up a company of British singers, he said, but also the only way to build up the audience.[33]

The principle of the 'English-language' policy made the choice of music director especially challenging. Leon Goossens was the choice of the trustees and Hawkes approached him in April 1945. Goossens responded with interest to this approach and on 25 February 1946 Webster wrote to Goossens explaining why it had been decided that the company should sing in English: 'If we are going to organise a company that is going to last, and if we are going to attract audiences for a very large portion of the year, and if we are going to have a subsidy from the public purse, then it is clear that performances by the resident company must be given in English.' British singers had not developed as had ballet dancers, Webster explained and continued, 'Everything that we do by way of opera has more or less to start from scratch.' Covent Garden must 'give every encouragement to the British artist and consider him first'. Goossens would be the general director, there would be a principal producer and Webster would be in the chair. Together they would do 'a building job'.[34]

Goossens wrote to Hawkes on 7 March 1946 that he feared that 'there were not enough well-schooled English singers ready for the company' and that this would necessitate either the employment of foreign artists or the abandonment of the principle of opera in English. He also wrote about his alarm at the prospect 'of making bricks without straw' and questioned Webster's contention that 'opera has never really prospered anywhere unless given in the language of the audience attending the performance', citing the Met as his main example. Furthermore, he argued, the 'directorial set-up' of Webster presiding over the artistic and musical direction would mean responsibility without authority for the music director.[35] Goossens added, 'I can't suddenly reconcile myself to taking up the rather grim role of operatic pioneer with its chance of failure.'[36] He offered his services for the latter part of the year but declined the music directorship. On 12 March 1946 Keynes wrote to Hawkes to say that he was disappointed that Goossens had not understood the basic concept of building up 'an English opera that has its own traditions and standards'.[37]

Other conductors approached to be music director in 1945 were

George Szell and Bruno Walter. The latter said he was willing to come to Britain for four months a year, but must know all the artistic details before he committed himself. These details included 'singers, chorus, scenery, general organisations, casts, chorus-master, who will train the orchestra, and choice of repertoire'.[38] He also suggested that Covent Garden should take on Ebert. Webster explained to Goossens on 25 February 1946 why Ebert had not been invited to Covent Garden: 'We came reluctantly to the conclusion that the outlook was so Germanic, that we should not see it fitting with the state of affairs over here today.'[39]

Covent Garden reopened on 20 February 1946 with a ballet production of *The Sleeping Beauty* starring Margot Fonteyn and Robert Helpmann. Webster explained in the *Arts Council Bulletin* that the opera company was not yet ready for the opening: 'To prepare an opera company largely British in personnel, of a quality in any way worthy of the singing traditions of Covent Garden, takes time.'[40] Keynes, though ill, greeted the King and Queen at the opening, during which he suffered a minor heart attack. After the opening he wrote to his mother, 'Many people had come to fear in their hearts . . . that all the things from the old world had passed permanently away, and it caused an extraordinary feeling of uplift when it was suddenly appreciated that perhaps they had not entirely vanished.'[41]

Two weeks later, in April, Keynes died, which was a blow to Webster. A businessman, Sir Ernest Pooley, became chairman of the Arts Council and Sir John Anderson, who was to become Viscount Waverley in 1952, was suggested to take over the chairmanship of the Covent Garden Trust. Anderson had little previous involvement in opera or the arts but it was he who, as Chancellor of the Exchequer in 1945, had authorised the creation of the Arts Council. He was thus aware of the arrangements and difficulties of arts subsidy. Furthermore, his good relationship with the Labour Chancellor, Hugh Dalton, was to prove invaluable to the Opera House. Indeed, it started a tradition of direct links between successive Board chairmen and governments.

On 26 July 1946, before he accepted the chairmanship, Anderson sought an assurance from Dalton that the House's future had been 'placed on a sound financial basis'. He was particularly concerned because the 1946 budget had rescinded tax relief on charitable gifts made under seven-year covenants, making it impossible for charities to reclaim the amount paid in surtax and income tax. In his letter to Dalton, Anderson sought an assurance that the Chancellor would not 'rule out the possibility of a larger payment in certain contingencies' and asked for 'a definite obligation to see to it that, subject to others playing their part, opera is not let down'. In his letter Anderson foresaw difficulties that were only to come to a head in the late Nineties. He wrote, 'I am convinced that it would be disastrous if the Trustees were ultimately dependent on private benefactions for maintaining opera in this country on a worthy basis.' And he explained, 'Experience shows how easily undesirable influences can creep in under such conditions.'

In his reply Dalton recognised that the 'magnitude of the Covent Garden undertaking' placed it in a 'special position' and that, although the Arts Council would continue to be responsible for the allocation of funds, the government would assume 'a definite obligation to see to it that, subject to others playing their part, opera is not let down'. He accepted that there might be circumstances which made it necessary to increase the Treasury grant to the Arts Council – if the Trust could show the need for a grant exceeding £60,000. This concept of a Treasury with a sympathetic and watchful eye was also traditional until the redevelopment debacle in 1998.[42]

Anderson was satisfied with Dalton's assurance and accepted the position of chairman. His lack of a musical background was not unwelcome to Webster, for whom Anderson was to prove an uncritical, uninterfering and highly compatible chairman. His biographer, Sir John Wheeler-Bennett, wrote of Waverley, 'Having accepted his subordinates with confidence he never interfered with them; only expecting to be informed, expecting loyalty and giving it generously.' These were attributes that could have served as a valuable model for later chairmen. Webster was content. He could have been writing about himself when he wrote of Waverley, 'Procrastination, or if you would have another word, timing, plays a large part in good government of affairs and he was a good governor.' Webster said that Waverley 'never made a pretence to be an expert in opera and ballet, but he could listen to a discussion, sum it up, make the principles clear and bring his board to a decision'.[43] Later, Isaiah Berlin wrote to Wheeler-Bennett that the chairman used to 'let people patter on about artistic matters about which he knew nothing, with an air of amused contempt or indulgent indifference'. Berlin described Waverley as 'efficient, firm, just' and wrote that he could be 'rather cowing' and even 'severe' when he did not receive answers to his questions.[44]

The choice of music director finally fell on Karl Rankl, of whom Webster later wrote, 'He was a typical German Kapellmeister ... he knew the whole business of running an opera house, training choruses, orchestras and soloists.' It was for these skills that he was chosen, for he was not, in Webster's words, 'a virtuoso conductor'.[45] Rankl was highly experienced in opera organisation having been répétiteur and assistant conductor at the Vienna Volksoper and later music director at the German (Neues Deutsches) Theatre in Prague. He had also worked before the war at Königsberg and Wiesbaden, and with Klemperer at the Kroll Opera in Berlin. Rankl had been born into a peasant family near Vienna and, as with so many musicians of Germanic background, the opportunity for his earliest musical training had been as a chorister. He had also been a pupil and protégé of Schoenberg. Rankl had left Germany because of Nazi attacks on Klemperer – who was Jewish – and in August 1939 reached England where he spent the war. After being released from internment as an alien, he composed until in 1944 he was allowed to take on paid work.

When Rankl was asked by Webster to be music director of the new Covent Garden company he accepted with alacrity. The appointment was announced on 16 June 1946. In Rankl's statement to the press he said, 'Given support and confidence there is no reason why the Royal Opera House should not develop into an institution comparable with the Berlin, Dresden and Vienna State opera houses of the pre-war days, with a resident company playing a repertory of about fifty operas, nine months out of the twelve.' He was totally in harmony with the aims of the Trust, declaring that the ensemble had to be developed with local talent together with the occasional employment of 'eminent foreign singers' who would 'give home-bred talents an invaluable insight into the traditional approach which is so vital a factor in sound performance'.[46]

Douglas Robinson, a thirty-four-year-old organist and choirmaster from Harrogate, became chorus-master, a post he held until 1974. There was to be a total of seventy choristers, which became the standard number until Solti's time. In February 1946 Rankl and Webster began auditioning all over the country for the chorus, which had to be recruited from scratch. Very few of those auditioned had any professional experience at all. There was much excitement in the south Wales mining town of Amanford when two miners had to be given permission to leave the colliery to join the chorus. Wales, with its strong choral tradition and eisteddfods – local festivals for music competitions – provided a firm base for the development of operatic voices in the post-war period, both of choristers and soloists. Covent Garden's orchestra had to be formed from those who had worked with the Sadler's Wells Ballet, since demobilisation had not yet been completed. By 30 July 1946 the Trust was informed that auditions for nearly 200 singers and orchestral players were almost completed.

Rankl and Webster held auditions in England and America for principals. As Goossens had predicted, the problems were severe. An article in *Musical Opinion* in December 1946 criticised the state of vocal training in Britain. Training periods were too short, there were not nearly enough good teachers and many singers started performing far too early. The young soprano, Adele Leigh, who auditioned for Webster in New York and joined the company in 1949, recalled her good fortune in studying in New York, where some of the finest European teachers had sought refuge before the war. She was taught by Juilliard coach Paul Berl, who arranged for her to be auditioned. 'In England', Leigh recalled, singers were coming out of the colleges with this 'pure white and sexless sound; "my redeemer liveth" ... That wasn't for me.' Of the English singers the contralto Constance Shacklock had what Leigh described as a 'very, very British voice. A little hooty but beautifully controlled.'* Leigh added, 'It was different in Australia – you sing with your guts in Australia.'[47] In the early days of the company the Australian contingent included Sylvia Fisher, Elsie Morison and Joan Sutherland, as well as John Lanigan and Arnold Matters.

---

* Born in 1913, Shacklock studied at the Royal Academy under Frederick Austin. She sang at Covent Garden from 1946 to 1956, singing in 632 performances, including as Octavian, Cherubino and Brangäne for Kleiber both at Covent Garden and in Berlin, with Flagstad; and Magdalene in Beecham's 1951 *Meistersinger*. She sang oratorio and after her operatic career moved on to musicals, singing the Mother Prioress about 2,000 times in *The Sound of Music* from 1961.

Singers learnt stage and other skills on the job, under the direction of the music staff. Postgraduate training for singers only began in 1948 when Joan Cross and Ann Wood formed the National School of Opera in London as a non-profit-making public company controlled by a board of governors.* The music staff at Covent Garden consisted of a few people with pre-war experience as répétiteurs and some with no experience. Peter Gellhorn became head of the music staff and later assistant music director, preparing the rehearsal plans, as well as coaching and conducting. Reginald Goodall was also brought on to the music staff in 1946 and remained for many years; he was responsible, with Norman Feasey, John Gardner, Leonard Hancock and Eric Mitchell, for coaching.† Conditions were primitive. Adele Leigh remembered working with Goodall with a piano 'in the Bedford box, the Crush Bar and dressing room'.[48] Gellhorn recalled, 'We had to build a company from Adam. There were a number of people singing parts in operas they had never heard, never mind had the actual experience of singing! We were teaching and coaching. I was so tired at the end of the week that every Sunday I lay in bed till lunchtime. We just didn't stop.'[49] The company was at the time as much a training school as a performing company.

Rankl gave few opportunities to conductors other than Goodall and Gellhorn, and Goodall was mainly given French or Italian operas, which he was known to dislike. 'I hated the rum-te-tum. I was terrible,' he later said.[50] This was in keeping with the second-class status of Italian opera in the company's early years. After Rankl left in 1951 Webster told Goodall that he would no longer be required for conducting but could continue to coach if he wanted. Many years later Webster wrote to the Earl of Drogheda explaining that there had been 'many protests from artists of his conducting in terms of time and

---

* In 1963 it received a grant of £20,000 a year from the Arts Council in order to try to secure its shaky financial basis. It functioned with its grant for some years as the London Opera Centre.

† Peter Gellhorn, whose father, an architect, was Jewish, had come to Britain in 1935 from Berlin where he had received his musical education. He toured with the Carl Rosa Company after the war, before Webster asked him to conduct and work at Covent Garden. Hancock was described in his *Times* obituary as 'one of the most loved, most admired and most sought-after' répétiteurs in Britain. He later taught at the Royal Scottish Academy of Music and Drama, and the Royal Academy and the National Opera Studio in London.

accent and it was because of this that we tended to drop him'.[51] Adele
Leigh later recalled that Reginald Goodall was 'a pain in the neck . . .
and the *bête noire* of everyone. He walked around with his shoulders
hunched and his collar up and wouldn't even say good morning to
you. I teased him like mad. "Reggie have you had a hectic night? Why
aren't you smiling?" Grumpy is the word for Reginald Goodall. One
couldn't break him down.'[52]

Occasionally Goodall emerged to conduct performances of *Boris
Godunov*, *Fidelio*, or *Turandot*. It was to Wagner, however, that he
was most committed. Webster sent him to Bayreuth in 1951 to observe
Knappertsbusch. On his return Goodall retired to 'Valhalla', a small
room at the top of Covent Garden full of washbasins, where he became
one of the most sought-after Wagner coaches in Europe.* Goodall
gave legendary performances of *Walküre* in Croydon and Birmingham
during a company tour in 1954, but rarely conducted Wagner at Covent
Garden. Rankl, Kempe and then Solti dominated Covent Garden's
Wagner, although Solti gave him a *Parsifal* in 1971.

On 12 December 1946 Purcell's masque, *The Fairy Queen*, introduced
Webster's first opera season. Webster was nervous of making the first
performance too dependent on the singing and music, instead preferring to concentrate on the spectacle and staging of a masque. There
were splendid sets by Michael Ayrton, and Malcolm Baker-Smith was
brought from the theatre to direct. The solo singers included Audrey
Bowman, an English-born soprano who had been singing in the United
States, David Franklin, who had sung at Glyndebourne before the war,
and Constance Shacklock. The main attraction, however, was the ballet
company's stars, Robert Helpmann in the miming role of Oberon,
and Margot Fonteyn.

The Fairy Queen was not a success, Peter Brook in the *Observer*
praising Constant Lambert's musical direction and Margot Fonteyn's
dancing, but criticising the soloists as 'inadequate' and the chorus as
being 'good in tone but slipshod in articulation'.[53] The first pure opera

---

* Goodall coached Jon Vickers for his debut as Siegmund at Bayreuth in 1958. Others
whom he coached included Alberto Remedios, Rita Hunter, Margaret Curphey, Norman
Bailey, Gwynne Howell, Anne Evans and John Tomlinson.

performance was even less well received. It was *Carmen*, in January 1947, sung in English. There was general and severe criticism of the performance for being relentlessly English in style, as well as for Rankl's insensitive handling of the score. Martin Cooper in the *Spectator* wrote that 'all the inhabitants of Seville were aggressively English'. The voices were pleasant, he continued, 'but of the type associated with the musical play rather than with opera. Light and charming without any hint of dramatic let alone tragic power.' He asked of Edith Coates's Carmen, 'Would not anyone prefer unintelligible French to governess English?'[54]

Carmen showed clearly what problems the English-language policy was going to present Covent Garden with. In an article entitled 'Bricks without Straw' on 25 January 1947 the *New Statesman* pointed to the 'painfully simple problem' – the need for better singers. The subsequent productions of Massenet's *Manon* and *The Magic Flute* were also harshly criticised. Philip Hope-Wallace described the orchestra as 'like the town band in a hurry to get home to tea'.[55]

With the musical elements so weak, Webster turned to theatre directors and designers to improve standards. Malcolm Baker-Smith directed *The Magic Flute*. Oliver Messel, in keeping with the intention to employ English artists, designed both *The Magic Flute* and *The Queen of Spades*. Although Andrew Porter described *The Magic Flute* as 'generally execrable . . . the beginning of a long series of misconceived productions', he later had 'very happy memories of Oliver Messel's magic world, created in the spirit of Schikaneder's stage directions, with a lightness, elegance and decorative fancy'.[56] *The Times* critic on 21 March said that the stage spectacle and sumptuous effects actually detracted from the musical effect. Malcolm Baker-Smith had placed the singers high upstage and behind veils to create 'illusions of mystery' but audibility suffered as a result. Audrey Bowman's Queen of the Night and Victoria Sladen's Pamina were criticised, although Heddle Nash's Des Grieux in *Manon* found greater approval in February. 'One could wish for a bigger voice but Mr Nash spreads his tone stylishly,' wrote the *Observer* critic Eric Blom on 2 February 1947. Though no longer a young man, Nash's was a sweet, lyric tenor on the John McCormack model, with a well-produced even tone. However, as with many other voices in England in the pre-war and early post-war period, Nash's potential was not fully developed.

Joan Cross's production of *Der Rosenkavalier* in April 1947 was more successful, with musical considerations given due weight. It was kindly received by Shawe-Taylor, who described it as 'a thoroughly studied, professional, on the whole well-cast affair' and he praised the young English singer Victoria Sladen as Octavian.*[57] Philip Hope-Wallace said it was Covent Garden's 'first real success', although there was some poor singing in the lesser roles.[58] Cross's future career as producer was not in England, however, but on the Continent and at the opera school in London which she founded with Ann Wood. Her double disadvantage as a woman and someone with pre-war opera connections and experience was possibly too challenging for the Covent Garden administration.

On 27 April 1947 Ernest Newman asked in the *Sunday Times* if the management and Trust were not 'flying too high in their trial trip'. Newman's main criticism was levelled at the singing: 'It is no mitigation of the offence, in my eyes, to say that the performers were inexperienced but did their best.' Webster complained that the critics 'did not understand the problems'. He and Rankl had continued to hold auditions in England, the United States and even Vienna but it was very hard, as Goossens had warned, to find singers prepared to sing in English.

The Times repeated its refrain on 27 June at the end of the season: 'The history of operatic enterprise in this country is a long record of failure and persistence', but the newspaper took heart from the new-found interest in symphonic music, ballet and in opera which had resulted from the troops' exposure to opera 'as a normal art form' in Europe.

The weaknesses of the young company were highlighted during a short visit of the Vienna State Opera in September 1947, with singers of the calibre of Sena Jurinac, Elisabeth Schwarzkopf, Irmgard Seefried, Ljuba

---

* Sladen, dissatisfied with the Trinity School's determination to train her as a mezzo, had gone to Germany to study with Ernst Grenzenbach in the 1930s – 'a bold step for a young singer' at the time. She made her debut at Sadler's Wells as Butterfly in 1943, to Pears's Pinkerton; 1947–48 was her only season at Covent Garden (*The Times*, Obituary, 3.11.99).

Welitsch, Julius Patzak and Hans Hotter, and conductors Clemens Krauss and Josef Krips bringing the 1947 production of *Don Giovanni*.

Webster, in announcing the 1947–48 season, defended opera in English, but in March 1948 the Trust agreed that they 'might like to take advantage of offers from one or two foreign singers of reputation who would be willing to sing in English'. They also agreed that although the principle of opera in English should not be abandoned 'that did not mean that there should in no case be performances in other languages'. It was agreed by the Trust and Webster that if Kirsten Flagstad sang Brünnhilde in English she could sing Isolde in German.*[59] The season itself was improved by the appearances of other foreign guests including Paolo Silveri and Hans Hotter, the latter becoming a regular visitor to Covent Garden. Hotter's international career only began in 1947, although he had a very successful career in Germany before and during the war. The agent, Joan Ingpen, who was to play a great role in opera administration in England and America, arranged for him to give a live recital of Franz Schubert's song cycle *Winterreise* on the BBC early in 1947. Webster heard his broadcast in the studio and offered him a contract. Hotter later recalled that Webster got both himself and Flagstad to agree to sing in English by telling each that the other was keen to do so. They both found out the truth during the rehearsals for *Walküre* in March 1948 in a Friedrich Schramm production in pre-war sets.

Lord Harewood later wrote that for nearly twenty years Hotter was 'supreme' as Covent Garden's regular Wotan, writing that Hotter's was not 'conventional beautiful singing; he did not seem to mind forcing, he could sound harsh and out of sorts, he regularly went through the tone and recovered to sing magnificently a few phrases later. The whole performance was on a vast scale, but so grandiloquently expressive that criticism of detail evaporated in the face of such stature.'[60]

Hotter recalled the primitive conditions of these early days. For the final scene of *Walküre* he and Flagstad had to climb up a ladder at the back of the stage on to a narrow platform, where there was

---

* The Trust was informed on 2 April 1947 that Flagstad was indeed willing to sign for *Walküre* in English and Isolde in German at a fee of £300 per performance.

little room to move. 'We managed fairly well at the rehearsals,' Hotter recalled, 'but on the first night they changed the lighting plan without telling us, and there was one brilliant light immediately over our heads. . . . I could not see anything, and in those days Wotan had to wear a long cloak, armour and an enormous winged helmet which did not help.' After Brünnhilde lay down he was feeling with his feet for the edge to climb down, when he 'stepped into nothing and fell – armour, spear and all – about six feet'.[61]

On 14 August 1947 Shawe-Taylor in the *New Statesman* argued that the compromise of bringing over a few stars to sing in English was 'the worst of both worlds'. The visitors struggled with the English, failing to make it intelligible and giving the impression that they were 'capable of far better things in their own language'. When Hotter sang Hans Sachs, Shawe-Taylor said that he was 'plainly bothered by having to sing familiar notes to unfamiliar English words' and that he seemed to have caught from his English colleagues the 'trick of breaking up the longer lyrical phrases into a series of jerky, half *parlando* phrases'. Shawe-Taylor demanded a radical change in the management's attitude to the engagement of singers. 'There are', he complained, 'three or four singers in the company to whom the management obstinately clings although their inadequacy becomes more and more obvious with each new production.'[62] They included the American sopranos Audrey Bowman, and Doris Doree who sang Gilda, Queen of the Night, the Marschallin and Ellen Orford. Grahame Clifford, the baritone, was also regularly excoriated, as was the character tenor Hubert Norville. Steuart Wilson reported to Webster from Edinburgh on 16 March 1951 that Bowman in *Traviata* 'makes delightful noises occasionally but looks like a dump from the Middle West. She has no sense of licentious charm or of any style whatever in the arias.'[63] Gellhorn recalled Tyrone Guthrie telling Bowman during a rehearsal for *Traviata*, 'When you say this it has to mean something. It didn't mean a fucking thing!' but he added, 'Doree was a quite moving Marschallin. . . . I don't know who else we should have had – when we could get Schwarzkopf we had her.'[64] Sylvia Fisher, who joined the company in 1948, was to prove a more satisfactory Marschallin in 1950.

* * *

Anderson soon had to test his agreement with the Chancellor when, in July 1947, Webster told him that extra funds would be needed as the £30,000 he had hoped would be available for 'contingencies' had been eradicated in the current economic slump. Webster explained that the costs of the early working period were especially formidable, as even music had to be purchased and copied. Much rehearsal and preparation time was needed for the principals and chorus, as even for *Rosenkavalier* and *The Magic Flute* 'no one member of the cast has ever appeared in these operas before'.*[65] After Anderson received Webster's breakdown and explanation of expenses, he negotiated the first of many overdrafts for the House with its bankers, Coutts, and arranged with Dalton's successor as Chancellor of the Exchequer, Stafford Cripps, a special earmarked grant of £120,000 for Covent Garden as part of the £550,000 Arts Council grant. After a wage increase to the theatre employees which would cost £8,000, the Chancellor agreed to a further £25,000 to be retained by the Arts Council for Covent Garden's use 'only in the case of absolute necessity'.†[66]

The use of English, although bringing in the audiences that had been hoped for, was already proving a financial liability. In November 1947 members of the Trust were informed that although the cheaper seats were selling well, with attendance as high as 95 per cent in the gallery, the higher-priced tickets were not selling. Sales in the stalls were as low as 35 per cent and in the grand tier even lower, at 25 per cent. The standard of singing was just not high enough and could only be improved by the use of foreign singers, who were 'limited by the use of English'. Kenneth Clark pointed out that for those who had been used to the stars of the grand seasons there was a prejudice against English singers. The Trust realised that there was 'considerable ground for suggesting that the use of English was a deterrent for certain sections of the public'.

During the November 1947 meeting Rankl was criticised, but Webster defended him, as he had expended 'colossal energy' in training

---

* £98,322.0.2d had been put aside for the audition period alone.
† Anderson demanded a breakdown of expenses which Webster provided: £5,995 for lighting, electricity £75, stage staff £445, ballet management £275, music staff £340, wardrobe and dressers £170, chorus £615, ballet dancers £810, opera soloists £1100, orchestra £1,560. Repairs alone cost £3,000 (Royal Opera House Archives).

the orchestra and chorus. Rankl was also, in Webster's words, training the new English music staff – 'training the trainers'. There was talk in December of getting 'Karayan' to conduct at Covent Garden, as he was 'thought to be one of the best conductors in the world' and his political reputation had now been 'cleared'. Rankl, however, demurred, arguing that the lack of singers was the main problem. Guest conductors could be invited later. 'To do this now', he argued, 'would upset an organisation while it was still in its formative stage.'[67] On 22 December 1947 Rankl was defended by Webster's deputy, Steuart Wilson, who told Webster that 'no conductor can do more than make the best of his material'. Besides, a guest conductor would be 'a slap in the face without parallel for Rankl'. They had only heard about Karajan from Walter Legge who, as director of his recording company, had a 'direct interest' in publicising him on the English market.[68]

Finding adequate English-speaking singers was not easily resolved. In February 1948 Webster reported that during a trip to America he had heard 140 singers, but they were mainly young and inexperienced or past their prime. He had failed to find a Radames. In April he had spoken to the director of the Vienna State Opera, Franz Salmhofer, who did not want to lose his singers and even objected to Welitsch singing Aida at Covent Garden. Hotter had left the company because the Ministry of Labour, on the advice of the Incorporated Society of Musicians, objected to him giving lieder recitals.[69]

The early problems of the Covent Garden management left it open to criticism by those who had been left out. Both Beecham and Christie launched strong attacks in 1948 and 1949. Beecham wrote in the foreword to Stephen Williams's book *Come to the Opera*, 'We are in a pitiable plight. . . . We have touched rock bottom, and if we are to have opera again of any consequence we shall have to rebuild from a crude beginning.' At a Foyle's Literary Luncheon Beecham attacked English singers for their 'pleasant but woolly voices'.[70]

The dissatisfaction could not be ignored. In June 1948 Christie gained access to Cripps, to complain that 'the present Management organisation is not delivering the goods'. He claimed that Webster did not 'know anything about opera' and that Rankl was 'second rate'. During discussions between Treasury official P. D. Proctor and Sir Ernest Pooley of the Arts Council there were suggestions that Webster should be replaced. A meeting was held between the Chancellor, Webster, Pooley, Trust member James Smith and Anderson on 9 September 1948, when Anderson defended Webster's efforts to 'nurse the growth' of the company. The Trust were asked by Cripps to answer criticisms about standards of singing, production and conducting. On 16 November 1948 the Trust eschewed radical solutions in favour of the creation of a subcommittee which would look into the artistic criticisms.[71] Webster wrote a reply to Christie's criticisms in which he pointed out that Glyndebourne 'was an opera for the rich and the leisured in gala style of remarkable quality'. Christie, he argued, was 'totally out of touch with contemporary social views'. It would be, he stated, 'impossible to recreate the "Gala" scale of pre-war opera'.[72]

While the committee deliberated, the attacks continued. In January 1949 Beecham criticised the appointment of a foreigner as music director, demanding an enquiry into Rankl's appointment, which he called a 'disaster' – the work of 'ignoramuses and nitwits who . . . were under the impression that the functions of a musical director in an opera house were of such exotic, intricate and profound a nature that only a person of the sublime intelligence of a Teuton could grasp and manipulate them'. He bitterly denounced 'the keeping out of the running of Covent Garden of the leaders of the musical profession in England'. Peter Gellhorn later recalled, 'I suppose it wasn't very tactful to have two people with a German background for the national opera, five minutes after the war with Germany! The press certainly had their knives into us and we couldn't do anything right.'[73]

Anderson defended both the House and Rankl in a letter to *The Times*. 'The Trustees', he wrote, 'have the highest admiration for the manner in which he has addressed himself to his task.' By the time the subcommittee reported in April 1949 the management was able to point to some productions of a higher standard. The subcommittee also defended Webster's dubious contention that it was hard to find good singers, reporting a lack of 'good talent' all over Europe, even at a time when outstanding continental singers were heard touring in London. Webster's position was assured. His contract was renewed for five years.

The Trust's idea that there should be an artistic director was superseded in September 1950 when Webster took on Steuart Wilson as his deputy, with the title deputy general administrator. Wilson had been head of music at the BBC from 1948 to 1950 and music director of the Arts Council, as well as being a member of the Trust of the opera company. He was to have responsibility for the administration of the company, auditions and the well-being of the singers, supervision of répétiteurs and the co-ordination of stage and orchestra. On 2 March 1950 Webster assured Rankl that Wilson's name 'from the public relations angle' would be extremely useful for the House and that his 'direct standing with the musical world' was greater than that of Webster himself.[74] The appointment was not without potential friction, as Wilson was older than Webster and was by temperament not a natural number two.

Webster's position was now assured and the theatre itself was purchased by the Ministry of Works during 1949. Anderson played a major part in the negotiations that resulted in the lease being transferred from Boosey and Hawkes to the ministry, which undertook to maintain the building for forty-two years and ensure that it was used for opera and ballet. The Covent Garden Trust was replaced by the Royal Opera House, with its Board, which was incorporated on 1 April 1950.* The Board had two subcommittees, one for opera and one for ballet, which were attended by the general executive of each company and which enabled members to have a detailed knowledge of plans and to advise the Board on the conduct of affairs.

With the musical side so subject to criticism, Webster decided to improve the dramatic elements and bring in a radical and dynamic young theatre director, Peter Brook, as director of production. Brook had recently had great successes at Stratford with *Love's Labour's Lost* in 1946 and a less romantic, more controversial *Romeo and Juliet* in 1947. The Trust was informed on 2 July 1947 that the Stratford management felt that Brook 'had genius' and was adept at managing stage

---

* Trust members became members of the new Board, on to which Anderson had also brought the Hon. James Smith, the Hon. Edward Sackville-West, the Earl of Harewood, Eric Cundell, Sir Arthur Bliss, and Viscount Moore (later the Earl of Drogheda). The title 'Royal' was granted to all theatres that had been licensed for the first time by letters patent from the King, as Covent Garden had been in 1732.

staff. Trust members were concerned, however, that he had no experience with opera and needed reassurance from Webster that he had a 'first-class musical approach'.[75] Brook himself was undeterred by his lack of experience, later recalling that he 'did not feel at a loss' as the repertoire was 'unbelievably bad' and productions were 'still thrown together in a week each . . . five rehearsals each of three hours'. Brook also recalled his efforts to modernise the technical department, which was still wedded to painted scenery:

> The great days of painted scenery belonged to an era of dim lighting from gas-fed footlights or candles, which flattened the performer so that he and the picture became one. The day the first spotlight was hung on the side of the proscenium, everything changed: the actor now stood out, was substantial, and a contradiction suddenly appeared between his roundness and the two-dimensional *trompe l'oeil* behind his back.

Brook described the work of the German director, Dr Schramm, brought from Germany to prepare the *Ring*: 'He was called in because he and he alone knew all the moves that the great star singers were likely to make.' Dr Schramm coached the chorus and the secondary roles shouting, 'Flagstad, come down here and hold out left hand. So you must be ready give spear with right hand, so!' Brook laughed at this style of preparation, but later he came to appreciate Schramm's criticism that Brook made his singers move too much. He told the young director, 'That's ballet choreography. Opera choreography much different.' Brook also recalled his efforts to introduce acting skills to the singers:

> I made experiments with the principal singers, but soon saw that there was nothing I could do to improve their lamentable efforts to act. A tenor I worked with was an ex-policeman, and all he could do was move his arms about as though directing traffic. I even tried hanging on to them with both hands, only to discover that they were totally and inseparably locked in his brain to the pattern of the score.

The chorus was, Brook recalled, made up mainly of Welsh miners who 'stood in surly groups as though they were at a pit-head meeting'.*[76]

---

* Peter Gellhorn recalled Tyrone Guthrie during a rehearsal of *Traviata* telling the chorus: 'It's champagne glasses you're holding not cocoa mugs!!'

Brook's first production was Mussorgsky's *Boris Godunov* in April 1948 designed by the Russian stage, costume and film designer, Georges Wakhévitch, with Paolo Silveri as Boris. The singers wore platform shoes and large headdresses. Brook had chosen Wakhévitch to create a film-like realism, with the energy of *Battleship Potemkin* or *Alexander Nevsky*. They wanted to represent a harsh Russia, where 'ferocity, oppression and pain could be easily believable'. The critical reception was mixed. Ernest Newman in the *Sunday Times* said the production 'touched for the most part the lowest depths to which Covent Garden has yet fallen'.[77] Especially disliked was a long corridor of sliding doors closing one by one in the death scene, which Brook had intended to end with the last doors forming a 'gigantic icon, a head of Christ whose enormous eyes towered over the dying Boris'. The *Daily Telegraph* on 22 May 1948 said the doors looked 'like the lift gates at a tube station'. Shawe-Taylor, on the other hand, wrote that 'with its mobs and processions it is very much a producer's opera, and Peter Brook has seized his chance with both hands'. The last scene 'with its lurching wayside crucifix and crowds milling and scuffling against the cold sky, was unforgettable'.

Brook was also learning on the job. Gellhorn recalled that during a rehearsal of *La Bohème*, in October 1948, he had objected to a woman crossing the stage on stilts during Musetta's 'Waltz Song', explaining that it would detract from the music. Brook cut it out the next day. The production was in the old sets, which had been painted from Puccini's own photographs of Paris. The young Welsh baritone, Geraint Evans, appeared in this production. He said it was a thrill to sing in the sets that Caruso had sung in. Brook had originally 'fumed against the idea' of using them, but when he actually saw them, he found them 'magically beautiful' and they brought tears to his eyes.

The performances of *Bohème* were conducted by Rankl and Gellhorn, and starred Elisabeth Schwarzkopf as Mimì and Ljuba Welitsch as Musetta, with Welitsch apparently upstaging Schwarzkopf. Harewood wrote that Welitsch 'stormed onto the stage, singing fit to bust, but we were hardly prepared for the diamond brilliance of her singing of the Waltz Song; nor apparently was the audience, which went pleasurably mad. Joan Cross and I yelled with the rest of them.'[78]

Elisabeth Schwarzkopf was married to Walter Legge, who had

signed her up for EMI in 1946. Because Legge was based in London, Schwarzkopf agreed to sign a three-year contract with Covent Garden, as a guest member of the resident company at £60 a week. She had learnt English as a teenager when a League of Nations student in England before the war, and was willing to sing in English. Between 1948 and 1951 as well as Mimì she sang Pamina, Sophie, Violetta, Susanna, Marzelline, Eva, Manon and Butterfly, although Legge objected strongly to the last two roles. In almost every respect Schwarzkopf was the exact opposite of Ljuba Welitsch. Perfectly modulated. stylish and controlled in her vocal art, she was charming and cool on stage, with a gracious beauty that made her an ideal Marschallin. Her recording of the role with Karajan in 1956 shows her with meltingly beautiful, always appealingly feminine lyric tone, perfectly modulated. Gerald Moore, who often accompanied her in recital, adored her: 'It seems to me quite unfair for anyone to look so ravishing and sing so beautifully.' After hearing her Marschallin at Salzburg he wrote, 'I was too moved to visit her after the performance.'[79] Even Schwarzkopf, however, found singing in English troublesome. On 31 May 1950 her Manon was praised by Harewood but he commented that her singing was competent only when she did not 'put the coloratura on the back of the tongue and swallow it'.*

Brook's next production after his *Bohème* was *The Marriage of Figaro*, in 1949. It showed the beginnings of the ensemble which the management were endeavouring to create. Schwarzkopf was Susanna, Geraint Evans was Figaro and the Australian soprano Sylvia Fisher was the Countess. Brook worked sympathetically with Fisher, who became the first company prima donna. Adele Leigh was Barbarina in this production and became the next season's Cherubino. Leigh recalled that Brook was inexperienced and slightly in awe of opera singers, and that when Schwarzkopf 'swanned in with her great big Viennese thing, and said, "I have done the Countess in Vienna I know

---

* As much as any singer of the post-war period, Schwarzkopf's legacy is a question of taste. She was praised for her perfectionist attention to detail in matters vocal and musical, and her tone, which at its finest was ethereally pure, is still cherished among the admirers of her many recordings. Schwarzkopf's detractors, on the other hand, mention her frequently stiff operatic characterisations lacking in spontaneity and her mannered way with vocal colouring and expression.

all about this just leave it to me," he did, and it was a big success!'[80]
Geraint Evans was beginning to make his mark in the company with
a voice that Harewood at first found 'not especially beautiful' but
which also benefited from the opportunities afforded by the ensemble
system.[81]

Evans, like so many British singers of early post-war Britain, had
found great difficulty in carving out a musical career. There was as
yet no structure in which talent could be trained and developed, and
with so much poverty and so little prospect of a secure financial future,
most musicians and artists faced a near-impossible struggle. Evans had
been brought up in Wales, where his father was the conductor of the
Pontypridd Male Voice Choir. Like many servicemen at the end of
the war, Evans gained exposure to the European musical tradition in
the army and got his early experience performing in the Entertainment
Corps in the British Army of Occupation in Germany. After the war
he studied in Hamburg with the bass Theo Hermann. A rare achievement at that time, Evans managed to get a grant to study at the
Guildhall School of Music. In 1948, aged twenty-four, he was hired by
Covent Garden as the night watchman in *Meistersinger*. Webster
arranged for a scholarship so that the impecunious Evans could go to
Geneva to study with Fernando Carpi. Evans recalled that he and his
wife almost starved trying to keep financially afloat for the four months
of their stay in Switzerland.

Brook's production of *Salome* in November 1949 was his last at Covent
Garden. It caused great controversy. He later wrote, 'When I asked
Salvador Dali to design *Salome* for our 1949 season at Covent Garden,
it did not occur to me that it would be seen as a stunt. Quite simply
Dali seemed the best man in the world for the job,' for he was an
artist whose style had 'both what one would call the erotic degeneracy
of Strauss and the imagery of Wilde'.[82] Brook and Dali worked closely
together, studying the score and designing a stone slab which was
'perhaps an altar once' as a focal point for the action.

Relations between Brook and Rankl rapidly deteriorated during
rehearsals. Dali demanded a huge bed which Rankl did not like, as it
placed the singers too far backstage. When Jokanaan's head descended

on a tray during rehearsals Peter Brook was heard to say, perhaps apocryphally, 'I wish that was Rankl's head,' whereupon the latter was said to have left the rostrum and the opera house, swearing never to return.[83] Wilson reported to Webster on 19 October on his separate meetings with both men. The case was nearly 'quite hopeless' and he had suggested a ' "buffer" to whom they could both and continuously apply for remedies against each other'.[84] 'Webster then had to spend several hours mending injured feelings to get Rankl to agree to conduct the performances.'[85] Thereafter Rankl would only speak to Brook through an assistant and refused to take a bow after performances of *Salome*.[86]

The production was greeted by booing mixed with applause and most of the critics expressed hearty dislike. Philip Hope-Wallace on 19 November 1949 said the costumes 'touched a high watermark of absurdity'. Newman 'found it difficult to speak in the restrained language of a Sunday newspaper' and wrote that the decapitated head looked like 'a large steamed pudding'. The production 'beat even the present Covent Garden management's latest record for inanity'.[87] Eric Blom in the *Observer* said there was 'something rotten in the state of things' at Covent Garden. Harewood in February 1950's *Opera* found it the 'climax of a series of more or less unmusical productions', which had built up prejudice against Brook at Covent Garden. But for Frank Howes in *The Times*, 'the general effect was properly macabre and the special effects, pomegranates, peacocks and a pavilion' did not interfere with the drama. Furthermore, Welitsch's 'frontal assault on the emotion' was, he said 'a tour de force'.[88] William Mann wrote many years later that Brook's production was 'too powerful and idiosyncratic for opera goers of the time who howled their heads off in fury'.[89]

The Trust was perplexed – some members feeling that the production 'carried eccentricity to the point where it seriously distracted attention from the music'. Others felt that it had been 'an experiment worth making' and Webster pointed out that sales had improved with the controversy.[90] Brook himself later wrote, 'They all decided that Dali and I were out to annoy them. There at least, I might claim that they underestimated us; if that had been our intention, I think that between us we could have done far worse.' He left Covent Garden, telling the *Daily Mail* on 24 June 1950 that he had been ill for months after his 'fight against the reactionaries' which could only lead to a nervous breakdown. 'The decision to terminate his appointment', the *Daily Mail* reported, was mutual 'because the critics and performers seem bent on sending people like himself back to theatre'.

Christopher West became the resident producer after Brook. It was his task to rehearse revivals and to work with guest artists to try to integrate them with minimum rehearsal time into the productions. He was to have much success with his Tippett premiere of *The Midsummer Marriage* in 1955 and was to work with Rafael Kubelik when he became music director.

By the autumn of 1949 it was obvious that the insistence on English was creating insurmountable problems for casting as well as causing havoc with individual performances. *Aida* opened with Welitsch's Bulgarian English, Franco Beval's Italian English and Torsten Ralf's Nordic English. Later Marko Rothmüller was the Amonasro, a Yugoslav baritone and a member of the company from 1948 to 1952, who sang in English 'but here and there threw in a word of Italian to help the story along'.[91] In December Anderson suggested that there should be a more flexible policy and that the House 'need not be too slavish in adhering to the rule of presenting opera in English'. On the contrary, there should be a willingness to 'deviate a good deal more' from the policy, 'particularly when no satisfactory cast could be found'.[92]

Boris Christoff, the great Bulgarian bass, insisted on singing Boris in Russian in the revival on 26 February 1950. He also refused to accept some of Brook's – to him – outlandish inventions, such as the blood-dripping knives of the Hallucination scene, and had nearly left for Italy before Webster persuaded him to stay. Christoff was a master of characterisation with an uncanny gift for bringing life to a role. In a 1949–50 EMI recording with the Philharmonia Orchestra and the Royal Opera House chorus supervised by Walter Legge, Christoff displays his exemplary Italianate vocal production – the tone placed well forward in the mask, the upper register free and baritonal, as well as his ability to float pianissimi in any register. His vocal resources were combined with a remarkable ability to suggest feeling through melody, accent and diction. Harewood compared him with Callas in his 'exact and subtle realisation of Italian music'.

Another fine visitor was Victoria de los Angeles, who made her debut on 1 March 1950 in *La Bohème*. Harewood wrote that 'an expressiveness and at the same time an intimacy was obtained by the singer which amounted to perfection'.[93] De los Angeles also sang Manon, Elsa and Mimì in the 1950–51 seasons, each in the original language, and not in English. Philip Hope-Wallace wrote in *Time and Tide* on 24 June that her 'warmth' and 'natural legato' made 'nonsense of the English-language policy'.

Ivor Newton, who accompanied all the great operatic artists at that time, described de los Angeles as 'an aristocrat among singers, because of her musical intelligence, her ability to work and to work quickly, and emphasising that instinct for rhythm which is characteristic of most Spanish artists'. He continued, 'Her capacity to adapt her voice to all moods and styles of singing enables her to combine joy with pathos, delicacy with power, light with shade and yet never sacrifice tone, texture, accuracy, control or flexibility.'[94] As Mimì in the 1956 Beecham recording of *Bohème*, her sweetness of tone and nuances of phrasing help create a Puccini heroine full of pathos as well as erotic appeal.

While Covent Garden was receiving harsh criticism, except for its guest artists, Sadler's Wells was enjoying a period of consolidation and Glyndebourne reopened with help from the John Lewis Partnership, after financial difficulties had caused two seasons of total closure. Before the House reopened Bing had left for Edinburgh, where an International Festival was inaugurated in 1947, supported by a committee of Edinburgh dignitaries and the city's Lord Provost. Bing had suggested that such a venue would provide an international outlet for Glyndebourne until such time as the House could reopen. The Glyndebourne management put on performances of *Così* at Edinburgh in 1948 and 1949, conducted by Vittorio Gui, and *Don Giovanni* in 1949, with Ljuba Welitsch as Donna Anna and Richard Lewis as Don Ottavio.* Bing went on to the Metropolitan in New York in 1949.

* During the first Edinburgh International Festival, Bruno Walter accompanied Lotte Lehmann in a lieder recital and conducted Kathleen Ferrier and Peter Pears in Mahler's *Das Lied von der Erde*.

Moran Caplat took over as general manager at Glyndebourne and Ian Hunter at Edinburgh.

Philip Hope-Wallace was delighted with the reopened Glyndebourne production of *Così*, writing in the *New Statesman* on 27 November 1950, 'The orchestral playing under Fritz Busch is of a precision and vivacity which nowadays seems like a miracle and brings tears to the eyes before the end of the overture.' Sena Jurinac's Fiordiligi was greatly admired for its beauty and evenness of tone, and for its depth of feeling. Hope-Wallace was delighted that Glyndebourne's pre-war standards had so quickly been restored.

Sadler's Wells was, in its more modest way, developing 'a sincere and homogeneous style'. It was also developing young Commonwealth talent, according to Harold Rosenthal, writing in the new magazine *Opera*, founded that year by Lord Harewood.* In his review of *Faust* on 24 January 1950 Rosenthal was struck by the talent of the twenty-five-year-old soprano, Amy Shuard, who could become, if carefully nurtured, 'the finest dramatic soprano in this country since Eva Turner'. Shuard had studied at Trinity College of Music and with Eva Turner, and had sung in Johannesburg, before joining Sadler's Wells in 1949.

The Covent Garden Trust were increasingly concerned at the poor quality of the routine performances and singing. On 26 October 1950 they noted Webster's 'dilatoriness' in signing up singers and 'a general tendency to leave everything to the last minute, so we often end up with inferior singers'.†[95] But the most urgent problem in early 1950 was that of the music director and the inadequate level of conducting. Rankl was reluctant to allow foreign guests to appear, which meant that Fritz Reiner was not engaged to conduct either *Salome* or *Götterdämmerung* although he was willing to do both. The Trust began discussing the possibility of Erich Kleiber being invited to Covent

* *Opera* was founded by Lord Harewood in 1950. Harold Rosenthal became the editor in 1953, Rodney Milnes associate editor in 1976 and editor in 1986. John Allison became editor in 2000.

† In April 1952 Flagstad complained to Audrey Williamson that she had heard nothing from the Covent Garden management about signing her for Alceste for that June during her triumphant performances at the Met although she believed she had been promised the role (*Opera*, February 1966).

Garden. On 17 January Webster reported that Kleiber was demanding £100 tax free per performance as well as being in 'complete charge of what he was doing'. On 26 January the Trust agreed that Kleiber would be able to work with international singers and to improve the local talent as he had done in South America.[96]

Rankl's human relations were also problematic. The young Geraint Evans recalled that although Rankl conducted nearly everything, he never really 'got to know him'. Evans wrote, 'He had no favourites and he kept a distance from everybody. . . . He never forgave mistakes, and sometimes he made you even more nervous by shouting out in anticipation if he thought you were likely to make one.' Gellhorn remembered him as 'quite a sweet old thing', but agreed that he was a 'disciplinarian' who 'wanted to get it right'. Furthermore, although his English was good, his literal translation of German curses caused offence. Gellhorn recalled, 'When some section of the orchestra played some wrong notes he said, "Ach, these swine!" which is not a bad word in German!" '[97] Evans also remembered that 'there was little warmth or sympathy in him and no humour'.

Rankl was not only difficult to work with but his performances were all too frequently found lacking in accuracy and interest. In January 1948 the House put on a new production of *Mastersingers* – the first Wagner performance since the war. Shawe-Taylor found that Rankl's orchestra had 'dry, toneless strings and barking short-winded brass'. The *New Statesman* critic continued that he longed for 'beauty' as each fine moment was 'thrown away by roughness, poor balance and insensitive phrasing, sometimes even by downright howlers . . . there was one from the oboe in Act 2 which sent a gasp round the House'. Shawe-Taylor concluded, 'There is something cheap and shoddy about this *Mastersingers* which repels sympathy.' *The Times* on 22 January was more generous, saying that Rankl steadied the tempo after harrying the orchestra through the overture. According to *The Times*, although Hotter was uncomfortable with the English and although he could not 'put across to the full his conception of Sachs', he made his authority felt.* Shawe-Taylor commented that the

---

* *The Times* was glad that *Mastersingers* was back at Covent Garden as it 'expunges from the mind of those who hear it the evil associations that have lately overlaid the fair name of Nuremberg, city no longer of Hitler, but still of Hans Sachs' (22.1.48).

critics were 'showing extreme indulgence to the still struggling cause of native opera'.

A rare recording of Rankl conducting the company in Falstaff's drinking song from *The Merry Wives of Windsor* with New Zealand bass Oscar Natzka and the Covent Garden orchestra and chorus on 10 May 1947 reveals Rankl's heavy-handed approach. The conducting is literal and pedantic rather than accurate and it lacks line. Although the young chorus is unschooled, with accuracy and intonation left to chance and little sense of ensemble or unity of attack, it is bright and lively. Neither the orchestra, which is not together, nor the chorus, however, betray any sense of following a clear beat.[98] In June 1950 Rankl's *Ring* cycle was greeted with the familiar critical gloom, in spite of rapturous praise for Flagstad's Brünnhilde. Rosenthal complained of Rankl's 'lack of poetry' and his 'tension', which together with his fast tempi left both the brass and audience 'out of breath' by the end of the evening.[99] The *Gramophone* called the orchestral playing 'lamentable'.[100]

On 2 March 1950 Webster wrote to Rankl to tell him that his appointment would not be renewed after the 1950–51 season. He referred to the progress which had been made during Rankl's four years as music director and tried to be delicate. 'We have failed to find a conductor of sufficient ability to support you in any reasonable way ... you need freeing of some of the almost intolerable burden of work that has been placed on you.' But he also alluded to the dangers of continued failure and stressed how lucky they had been to have Cripps at the Treasury, supporting them in spite of so much criticism. In five years the subsidy had been increased from £25,000 to £145,000 a year. Webster informed Rankl that Erich Kleiber had been appointed for three months that autumn as guest conductor to do 'some works out of the repertoire and one new production'.[101]

On 1 November Rankl replied to Webster pointing out that he had been responsible for developing singers, orchestra, chorus, stage staff and repertoire from nothing. Among the singers he had brought into the company were Geraint Evans, Constance Shacklock, Sylvia Fisher and Adele Leigh. He had also brought in conductors Warwick Braithwaite and Reginald Goodall. Gellhorn later recalled the difficulties Rankl had encountered: 'We had to teach the orchestra all the repertoire. When Kleiber and Kubelik came they had an apparatus which we had built from nothing, everything was new. There was no one else with that experience who was available. There were fine musicians and fine singers all over England but they had not had the experience in opera.'[102]

However unsatisfactory Rankl was, his orchestra and chorus were both by then established instruments capable of development. On 14 November Webster told Rankl that Beecham wanted to conduct something at Covent Garden in spite of his virulent attacks on the House and on Rankl in particular. Beecham had expressed the view to Webster in October that the orchestra was now 'an instrument which he could use'.[103] It was decided that Beecham would conduct *Meistersinger* in June 1951 and *The Bohemian Girl* in August. Newman in the *Sunday Times* found 'ardour, passion, beauty, tenderness, thoughtfulness' in Beecham's performances.[104]

Other fine conductors were to work with Rankl's orchestra. Erich Kleiber's debut was on 6 December 1950, conducting *Der Rosenkavalier*. He was greeted with great enthusiasm, Shawe-Taylor commenting on 'the cheers which swept round the House'.[105] *The Times* on the following day noticed an extraordinary transformation in the company under Kleiber's direction: 'What caused the whole company to sing with their hearts as well as their voices was the orchestral playing, which provided a broad, flowing river, not a torrent of sound, on which the voices could float . . .' Eric Blom wrote in the *Observer* on 24 December 1950 that 'on the evidence of one's ears alone one would have sworn that he had brought some fine and assiduously drilled orchestra of his own with him, from goodness knows where'. Ruth Kleiber was delighted, writing to Rudolf Bing in New York, ' "Rosenkavalier" was very good here – and the orchestra received special praise in the notices, and had a big success.'[106] On 16 December 1950 Clark wrote to Webster to say that everything must be done to keep Kleiber, who was making an 'immeasurable difference' but, he added, 'When all is said and done, he couldn't have used the instrument unless Rankl had created it.'[107]

Richard Temple Savage, Covent Garden's librarian and bass clarinettist, wrote affectionately of Kleiber, 'His beat was small and clear and contained an uncanny power so that it was virtually impossible to take one's eye off it . . . his confidence in his own powers was quite obvious and he overcame all difficulties with almost schoolboy zest.'

He imbued the orchestra with new confidence. Temple Savage recalled a typical incident: 'I once had the misfortune to have a mechanical breakdown during a performance of Der Rosenkavalier, with the result that I stopped playing in the middle of a solo passage. Afterwards he sent for me and said, "Don't worry, only you and I and Strauss in heaven noticed!"' [108]

Kleiber also worked sympathetically with the singers. Sylvia Fisher was the Marschallin, and Constance Shacklock, Octavian. Harold Rosenthal observed that 'the singers themselves seem to feel a new confidence'. This was especially true of Sylvia Fisher who revealed 'her full possibilities at long last' and who recalled that Kleiber was wonderfully supportive. At the end of Act One of Der Rosenkavalier she remembered, 'he always gave me time to sigh. I complained to him that I couldn't sigh in a convincing natural manner as quickly as the music wanted me to. He said, "You just sigh and I'll be there." And he was.'[*][109] It was Kleiber who was responsible for Shacklock being engaged to sing Brangäne in Berlin in 1952.

Kleiber had earlier had a distinguished career at the Berlin Staatsoper, where he had worked for twelve years before the war with an extraordinary ensemble, and such musicians as Toscanini, Klemperer, Walter and Strauss. In January 1935 he had given up his post in Berlin because of his dislike of the Nazis. He spent the next four years as a travelling concert conductor until, in 1939, he went to Buenos Aires where he built up a new career. His experience in dealing with a less prestigious orchestra than he had been used to was to serve him well at Covent Garden. His biographer, John Russell, wrote that Kleiber had a reputation for being 'a super-disciplinarian, on occasion a monster of rudeness, stubborn at all times and subject in the face of others' shortcomings to a rage and contempt which he thought it pointless to conceal. Legend played a part in this: for, by nearly all those who had worked under him, he was loved as few men are loved.'

*   *   *

* Joan Ingpen recalled that Fisher was rather depressive. According to Ingpen, 'She would look in the mirror and say "I can't go on". Adele Leigh would say, "There we were getting Sylvia on to the stage – she would sing like an angel and we were all exhausted"' (Ingpen interview, 18.10.99; Leigh interview, 23.4.98).

In spite of Kleiber's great contribution at this time, the routine performances, especially of under-rehearsed Italian operas, continued to be sadly wanting in professionalism. On 6 November, during a seriously under-rehearsed *Rigoletto* 'there was a disastrous lighting mishap in Act 2 when Rigoletto and the abducting party spent some time commenting on their inability to recognise each other in spite of what was at the time a brilliantly illuminated stage'.[110] The use of English also continued to cause unease. The same unfortunate performance, in spite of Rothmüller's 'first-rate' Rigoletto, was castigated for its poor translation, which, Harold Rosenthal admitted, would 'cause even the most convinced supporter of opera in English to have second thoughts'. Joan Sutherland recalled in her memoirs that in general 'even the British contingent could not seem to disguise their local dialect'. Hans Hotter, in an interview in New York, complained that he had been required, as Hans Sachs, to begin the 'Wahnmonolog' in *Mastersingers* with 'Craze, craze everywhere craze'. Covent Garden, Rosenthal's conclusion was that Covent Garden was 'laying itself open to ridicule'.[111]

In early 1951 the Trust discussed the possible options for the musical direction of the House. Although Kleiber was then demanding the substantial sum of £200 per performance the directors felt he should be re-engaged. Kleiber did not, however, want a permanent position, suggesting instead two visiting periods of two months. On 3 April, Edward Sackville-West told the Trust that he felt it would be 'disastrous' to start another season under Rankl. Webster said that both players and singers were kept under Rankl's 'tight nervous control'.[112] There were also clashes between Rankl and Kleiber, Wilson reporting that during rehearsals for *Carmen* Rankl had refused to release trumpeters he was rehearsing for *Valkyrie* so they could sound the 'retreat' for Kleiber. Kleiber had told Wilson that he had been promised by Webster 'absolute priority in the House'. Wilson apologised for Rankl's behaviour, holding him responsible for the mix-up as he had refused to arrange Kleiber's rehearsals.[113]

The undermining of Rankl's authority was too much for him. After he learnt that Kleiber was going to conduct *Wozzeck*, which he had not been allowed to do, and having been greeted with shouts and hisses when he entered the pit on 30 January 1951, he announced his resignation on 7 May. The foreword to *Covent Garden Book Number 7* praised him for having performed 'an ungrateful task done with a will'. In general, however, Rankl got little credit for his achievements at Covent Garden and when, in 1953, he discovered that his name had not been mentioned in the coronation programme he wrote bitterly, 'Apparently Mr Webster has seen fit to omit any reference to the man who unaided by anybody and hampered by antagonism on all sides nevertheless succeeded in building up from scratch the opera company that still exists.'[114]

Edward Downes, who joined the company as a répétiteur and prompter in 1952, wrote that Rankl 'trained the orchestra, and indeed the whole company, in the routine that he had learnt in German opera houses before the war. Without the foundation of Rankl's training the company could never have grown. It did grow apace – it outgrew Rankl.'[115]

After Rankl's departure there was no full-time music director for three years. It was hoped that Barbirolli would take up the full appointment, but he was busy at the Hallé Orchestra. He agreed, however, as did Kleiber, to be a guest conductor in the 1951–52 season. Webster and the Board decided to wait for him, as he still hoped to be able to make a greater commitment after the 1951–52 season. In September 1952, however, Barbirolli finally declined the invitation, deciding he could not give up his commitment to the Hallé.[116] Between 1952 and 1954 Barbirolli conducted *Aida*, *La Bohème*, *Orphéo*, *Madama Butterfly* and *Tristan und Isolde*. John Pritchard and Vilem Tausky also appeared as guest conductors.

Edward Downes, recalling his early days as répétiteur, prompter, and coach, remembered Barbirolli, in 1953, sending him on stage to sing the whole of *Tristan* with the orchestra when the German tenor did not turn up in time for rehearsals. 'One was prepared for anything in those days,' Downes mused.[117] Downes was a great asset to the House's music staff. Adele Leigh recalled, 'He taught me Manon in four days. He has a wonderful way of teaching people parts. He said, "We are going to do this phrase six times and by the time we have done it six times you will know it" and I *did* know it!'[118]

Like many other British and Commonwealth artists, Downes had managed to get a musical education only with the utmost difficulty. His parents did not believe in education in general and in music in particular, but by taking organ lessons as a child and studying scores while working in the local gas department, he managed to win a music scholarship to Birmingham University in 1941. In 1946 he won a scholarship to study conducting with Hermann Scherchen in Zurich. He became a répétiteur with the Carl Rosa Company on his return and was soon taken on at Covent Garden, where his knowledge of Italian and German was indispensable as the company were doing more original-language performances. In 1957 a haemorrhage nearly cost him his sight.

In 1951 Lord Harewood, who had known Webster from his days in Liverpool, was invited to join the Board of Covent Garden. He was keen to improve the standard of singers, sending Webster a list of foreign and local singers who should fill more roles and some company singers whose roles were 'inadequately sung at present', including Michael Langdon's Angelotti.[119]

On 10 April that year Harewood saw what he described as the 'operatic highlight of the season'. It was not at Covent Garden but at Sadler's Wells – Leoš Janáček's *Kát'a Kabanová*, conducted by Charles Mackerras. In 1947 the twenty-two-year-old Mackerras, who had been principal oboist with the Sydney Symphony Orchestra in Australia, had won a scholarship to study with the Czech conductor Václav Talich in Prague. Mackerras became captivated by Janáček's music, which was at that time virtually unknown outside Czechoslovakia, and spent the year seeking out performances of Janáček's work and familiarising himself with the different styles of presentation. He was deeply struck by the 'dramatic impact and yearning lyrical beauty' of *Kát'a Kabanová* and in 1948 brought the vocal scores back to London to show Norman Tucker, joint director of Sadler's Wells. Mackerras became Janáček's leading champion and exponent, twenty years after the composer's death. He described Janáček's success in 'writing an opera in an entirely different idiom from anything I had ever known'; he 'used the human voice and the inflexions of his strange sounding language in an absolutely original way' and his 'instrumentation and harmony produced colours and sounds unlike anything I had heard before'.*[120]

After joining the music staff of Sadler's Wells, in 1948 Mackerras conducted the premiere of *Kát'a*, with Amy Shuard in the title role. Rosenthal felt that she lacked the experience, though not the intensity, for this taxing part. Some of the critics were uncomfortable with the unfamiliar work. Ernest Newman called Janáček 'rather a scrap by scrap composer, finding it difficult to think consecutively for more than two or three minutes at a time'. Shawe-Taylor, however, was struck by the work's 'undiluted strength and purity of human feeling'.[121]

The production of *Kát'a* revealed the limited experience and appetite of the English audience. Norman Tucker wrote that the 'toughest problem' of the post-war opera world was the education of the opera-going public. *Kát'a*, he wrote, was 'a work of extraordinary originality and beauty which proved the biggest box office failure since the war'.[122] Rodney Milnes later recalled this production, commenting that it underlined how crucial state subsidy was, as *Kát'a*, and later Kubelik's *Jenůfa* in 1957 at Covent Garden, 'continued to play to half-empty houses' until gradually the public became familiar with these great works.[123] In general, the post-war English opera-going public's range of experience was narrow, with Wagner and Strauss, Puccini and a limited range of Verdi, as well as *Carmen*, proving standard fare. In the 1954–55 *Opera Annual* Lord Harewood lamented the lack of a curious opera-going public after the critically well-received *Elektra* at Covent Garden failed to draw full houses. It was only gradually in the subsidised conditions of post-war opera that new and unfamiliar works were introduced to the public and slowly came into the mainstream repertoire.

Glyndebourne continued to flourish, and to widen the Mozart experience. In June 1951 Busch put on *Idomeneo* with Sena Jurinac as Ilia

---

* On his mother's side Mackerras was descended from Menahem Mona, the Jewish cantor of Canterbury who died in 1823 and was believed to be the natural son of the last king of Poland and his Jewish mistress.

and Birgit Nilsson as Elettra. Busch was a patron and supporter of Nilsson, whom he had met at the Stockholm Opera when she was finding it hard to get work and was ready to give up singing. During the *Idomeneo* performances, however, Busch was thought to be unusually inflexible. Later in the season he became ill in the middle of *Don Giovanni* and was unable to complete the performance. He died quite suddenly in London, that September, at the age of sixty-one.

In 1952, after a period of financial uncertainty, Glyndebourne was devising schemes to make a sound basis for the future. The management introduced the festival programme – a glossy brochure with full-page advertisements. That year the management also inaugurated the Glyndebourne Festival Society whose aim was to raise £25,000 a year – the shortfall between the cost of running Glyndebourne and the receipts.* By the opening of the 1952 season the Society already had 806 members and the experiment that year brought in receipts of £8,000. As this was not nearly enough, the idea of running Glyndebourne as a trust became increasingly attractive. The Covent Garden Opera Trust was formed before the 1954 season.

At Covent Garden there was increasing concern at Webster's dilatoriness. On 19 September 1951 Viscount Moore, who was to become Earl of Drogheda in 1957, attended his first Board meeting as its secretary, a position he maintained until he was elected to the Board in 1954. He later wrote of Webster, 'His chief virtue was his calmness and unflappability, and his ability to cope with crises, many of which it must be said arose from his own lethargy ... he was known as the arch procrastinator, or AP for short.'[124] At Moore's first meeting it was noted that there was as yet no Billy for Britten's new opera, *Billy Budd*, whose premiere was to be in December, Geraint Evans having decided the role lay too high for his voice. Webster told the Board that there was no point in delaying the premiere 'as the problem would grow no easier with time'. Three suitable singers had been found in America and Webster was sent to audition them.[125] By good luck

---

* The three kinds of membership would be corporate, individual and associated – each with its own privileges commensurate with the donation.

Theodor Uppman was suitable and available. But on 26 October two Board members, James Smith and Sackville-West, complained about Webster's procrastination, especially in signing up artists.[126]

Even Kenneth Clark, who was a staunch supporter of Webster, complained to Anderson that there were too many instances of delays.[127] By December the programme for the summer of 1952 had not been finalised and a less than ideal conductor had to be engaged for *Norma*.[128] On another occasion, the distinguished but elderly French conductor, Désiré Inghelbrecht, who had been engaged to conduct *Hoffmann* in the 1954–55 season was, Downes later recalled, 'virtually gaga at the time . . . I mean he would sort of fall asleep in the middle of it.'[129]

Harewood, however, admired Webster's qualities, describing him as 'totally loyal and unflappable'. Even in the 'darkest days' he 'kept a calm exterior . . . he hated explosions and defused trouble before it had a chance to blow up'. Harewood remembered Kleiber 'storming out of a rehearsal and marching up to Webster's room with an imposs- ible rehearsal ultimatum (his initial requests were usually phrased like declarations of war)', to be met by Webster offering him what he wanted as he got in the door.[130] Webster confided in Kleiber and his wife Ruth about his new colleague. Ruth Kleiber wrote to his secretary on 28 May 1953, 'It was charming to hear Mr Webster tell how he will curb his Earl, and make him fit into the Covent Garden family.'[131]

Kleiber had continued his relationship with Covent Garden after Rankl's resignation, even though he was not prepared to take on the role of music director. At the beginning of 1952 he conducted Alban Berg's *Wozzeck*, sung in English. Michael Ratcliffe later called this production, with Marko Rothmüller as Wozzeck and Christel Goltz as Marie, as a 'turning point', which showed how 'the company's sense of ensemble had grown'.[132] Sumner Austin, a baritone of pre-war Sadler's Wells, directed, but Kleiber kept a watchful eye over all aspects of the production. Hope-Wallace found it had 'none of the despair of the nineteen-twenties in Caspar Neher's "homely" set'. Mann, too, was critical of Neher, who had been among the leading designers of Weimar and Nazi Germany and had worked closely with Brecht. Mann called his sets 'pretty-pretty, wishy-washy'. Hope-Wallace also found that the '*Sprechstimme*' translated with great difficulty into 'a mixture of Old Surrey melodrama hamming and Burgtheater declamation'.[133] *Wozzeck* played to a capacity audience of 2,000 people and was revived eight times.

In 1953 Kleiber left, never to return, saying that Covent Garden could not afford him. His wife Ruth had written to Webster on 12 July 1953 to explain that at Covent Garden he received half the fee that he received elsewhere and only came out of 'love for you and the orchestra'. He had also pulled out of *Elektra* in February after many changes of cast. Ruth Kleiber told Webster on 28 February, 'He thinks the manoeuvres are nerve-racking and refuses to have any more to do with them in any way.'[134] Kleiber's financial demands were just too great for the hard-pressed institution and on 7 July 1953 the Board decided that his demand for £300–£350 per performance should be refused.[135]

Kleiber died in 1956. His biographer believed that he did not feel that at Covent Garden there was the 'determination to put art first, at whatever cost, and with no side-bets on friendship, or social position, or safety of one kind or another. Kleiber was by nature an absolutist.'[136]

On 15 June 1946 Webster had written to Britten asking him to compose a large opera for Covent Garden. He also offered Britten a home for his English Opera Group and wrote that he and Rankl 'would very much appreciate being taken into your councils and your discussions, completely unofficially', and would make their artists and staff available for him. On 15 May 1948 Britten had written an angry letter to Webster complaining of an under-rehearsed performance of *Grimes* that also failed to take due care with the work's 'dynamics and expression marks'.[137] These inadequacies did not deter Britten, however, from the new commission, and his *Billy Budd* was premiered at Covent Garden on 1 December 1951, subsidised by the Festival of Britain. It had been two years in gestation, Britten working in close collaboration with his two librettists, Eric Crozier and the novelist E. M. Forster. It was Forster who felt it should be a 'big' opera. Britten had wanted Sadler's Wells to put it on, but Norman Tucker felt it was beyond their resources. Basil Coleman directed and John Piper designed the sets.

Britten conducted reluctantly, Krips having decided to step down at the last moment. The young American, Theodor Uppman, recruited by Webster at short notice in the United States, sang Billy. According to Winton Dean he 'filled the part so exactly, both in voice and physique'. Peter Pears was Captain Vere and Frederick Dalberg was Claggart.

In the *Manchester Guardian* Philip Hope-Wallace described *Billy Budd* as 'stern and beautiful' with 'an originality, effectiveness and fineness of musical creation'.[138] The January 1952 edition of *Opera* devoted three long critical appreciations to it. Winton Dean thought it 'an even finer work than *Peter Grimes*'. Britten, he wrote, 'historically derives from Verdi, the true line of descent, from which Wagnerian music drama exiled opera for forty years hard labour in the wilderness'. Lacking Verdi's supreme melodic genius, Dean continued, Britten 'to some extent compensates by a pregnant and very English express-iveness in word-setting and a wonderful command of orchestral sonorities'.

The Crozier–Forster libretto is one of the most finely constructed in all modern opera: strong, spare and elegant, with sensitivity to its source, Herman Melville's novella. Britten follows natural speech rhythms to create a musical line interrupted organically by hesitation, regret and pain. Unlike Wagner, Britten and his librettists do not blur the distinction between good and evil. Billy is a good man, not a tormented spirit; evil is a force imposed upon him rather than emanat-ing from within his simple soul. Sexual attraction is presented as a positive force, with moral goodness as well as physical beauty as the sources of that attraction. Claggart, a man of moral darkness, not allowing his hellish world to be violated by Billy's decency, lightness and beauty, safeguards it by the cruel exercise of authority and sexual menace.

Britten often works in contrapuntal layers, giving the chorus and small roles simple melodic cells which often recall sea shanties without quoting them. The orchestra has independence and interest in its own right, but never takes centre stage as in Wagner. After the officers have sentenced Billy to hang, and after Vere has accepted the verdict, the confusion and horror of Vere's thoughts and feelings are expressed in a moving harp solo. Played in octaves, its strange pentatonic flavour

typifies Britten's imaginative, original and dramatically appropriate writing. This full-length opera is tightly written, with nothing discursive in the music, stage action or character development. Whereas Tippett's writing for the opera stage tends to be episodic, *Billy Budd* is a continuous narrative, engrossing and taut. Like its great literary original, it is a moving, thought-provoking, profound work, which was to prove a fine vehicle for great performers. It was warmly received and its first run was sold out, but it was some years before *Billy Budd*, with its all-male cast, in a revised, two-act version, became a regular part of the international repertoire, reaching the Met only in 1978.

Throughout the post-war period, and increasingly as the twentieth century drew to its close, Covent Garden rarely had sufficient funding to enable it to develop and then maintain the high standards to which it aspired. The year 1952 saw the first of Covent Garden's recurrent financial crises. On 14 February Ernest Pooley told Anderson that the Arts Council grant to Covent Garden had been cut back from the projected estimate to the previous year's figure of £150,000, in spite of what he called the strong representation of the House's needs to Anderson. The Board were told on 19 February that the chairman was to tell Pooley that there was a gap of £64,000 between the grant and the deficit of £214,695. He was to take up the 'Dalton promise' with R. A. Butler, the Chancellor of the Exchequer.[139] On 6 June the Arts Council told Webster that £90,000 was available as a 'rescue operation'.

This was the first of many 'rescue operations', the subsidy never being conceptualised as something that should sustain work at the highest level or allow for planned development. The subsidy provided to the Opéra in Paris by the French government at that time was the equivalent of £800,000 a year. Both the Stockholm and Buenos Aires operas received approximately double that of Covent Garden. In the next decades the Met's appeals to wealthy donors, in spite of various crises, enabled the House to be more ambitious in the scale, if not innovation, of its programming than was Covent Garden with its perennially inadequate subsidy. When Parliament approved the supplementary grant of £90,000 and the Chancellor called it a 'rescue operation', the Arts Council warned that the same amount would be needed again next year and added, 'We should like to see our national home of grand opera secured on a less sporting basis.'[140]

Italian opera, although still sadly neglected at Covent Garden, was given a much-needed boost in the original language in November 1952 when Callas made her electrifying British debut in *Norma*. The House could have been filled several times over. Cecil Smith wrote, 'One of her most stunning moments came at the end of the *stretto* to the trio "Oh non tremare" when she held for twelve beats a stupendous, free high D.... From this point on Miss Callas held her audience in abject slavery. She rewarded them by never letting them down.' With Vittorio Gui conducting, 'everything sounded completely lovely and unforced'. The lesson was not lost on Smith, who concluded, 'If Covent Garden is capable of attaining so satisfactory and unprovincial an international standard, I should think it might be expected to do so more frequently.'[141]

Callas returned the following year, each of her appearances causing even more excitement than her first. On 4 June her *Aida* 'was a gala event', wrote Andrew Porter in *Opera*, 'a return to the old days when the aim was to engage the best singer for each main part in an opera.... How beautifully she caressed the phrases in the final duet, touching gently the notes marked staccato, ravishing the ear with the downward portamento from the high B flat (a steady sweet one here).'

Webster and the Board were gradually being forced to recognise that Italian opera in the original language was more appealing to London audiences. In June 1953 a less than perfect Italian season at the Stoll Theatre sold out and Webster told the Board that although he thought it would be wrong to change the policy of opera in English 'there clearly was a great demand for opera in Italian'. He admitted that it was 'very difficult to persuade Italian artists to sing in English'. One member of the Board believed that 'great zest' was added to the performances when guest artists appeared and that this had 'strengthened' the company. Viscount Waverley (as Sir John Anderson had become) concluded that although the policy should not be reversed, the 'tendencies must be carefully watched'.[142]

One of Webster's strengths was the fostering of new talent within

the company. On 28 October 1952 a young Australian soprano, Joan
Sutherland, made her debut as the First Lady in *The Magic Flute* and
then as Callas's confidante Clotilde in *Norma*. Later in *The Magic Flute*
run, Sutherland was spotted by the critics and praised. 'Joan Sutherland
was one of the Queen of the Night's ladies, and helped form a trio
"quite above the average",' Andrew Porter wrote.[143]

Initially, Sutherland was considered to be a dramatic not a coloratura soprano. Her first, though unplanned, principal role was in
December in *A Masked Ball*, when she was asked to cover for Amelia
at the last moment, without knowing the part. She recalled in her
memoirs the hectic rush to run through the part and prepare the
costume. John Pritchard in the pit and Edward Downes in the prompt
box helped her get through the performance. She later recalled how
prior to that evening, at one of the regular weekly staff meetings,
Downes suggested that Sutherland should not be re-engaged the following season as he felt she was 'such a slow learner'. That performance, she added, 'changed his mind'. In May 1954 she had her first
planned principal role – Agathe in *Der Freischütz*. Both *The Times* and
Opera were impressed, *Opera* complaining that Covent Garden had
been keeping her talent 'hidden under a bushel'.[144]

A Masked Ball had been John Pritchard's Covent Garden debut.
Peter Gellhorn having resigned at the end of the 1952–53 season and
in the absence of a music director, Pritchard was given an increasingly
heavy workload in his first three seasons, so much so that he sometimes
sounded ill-prepared. He conducted more than eighty performances
of eleven different operas, many of them for the first time. He had
begun his career at Glyndebourne in 1949 as chorus-master and
the next year as an assistant to Busch. He remained associated with
Glyndebourne, becoming its music director in 1969, a post he held
until 1978.

The need to involve top conductors and, in Tooley's words, 'move
much more into the international scene' was clearly felt. In 1953 Harewood resigned both from the Board and *Opera*, and officially joined
the staff of Covent Garden as assistant manager in September. After
making what Tooley later described as a huge contribution to the
planning of repertoire and casting, he was given the official title of
'controller of opera planning' in 1959. One of his main contributions

was to establish links with many top European conductors, including Giulini and Kempe.*

Harewood admired Webster, later writing that he 'half-consciously contributed to an atmosphere within the House that most of us, myself unreservedly amongst them, found congenial'. The two men were in total agreement on the question of ensemble and the use of the English language, in spite of increasing criticism. In pursuing his objectives, Webster was a skilled and sympathetic manager of his developing company members. Adele Leigh remembered the company spirit that was being fostered under Webster's guidance: 'He was like a father to us all, he used to give parties after the first night in his house. We had an ensemble. It was like a big family. In those days we all helped each other.' They were, Leigh recalled, 'building something brick by brick'.[145] Geraint Evans later wrote that Webster had the 'gift of being able to see the potential in a singer' and to support them in the face of criticism while they were 'developing artistically'.†[146]

Webster was also exceedingly loyal. On 3 February 1953 Sir John Barbirolli conducted Kathleen Ferrier in *Orfeo ed Euridice*. Ferrier only managed to sing two of the four scheduled performances. She was dying of cancer and had been in great pain throughout the rehearsals, going to hospital twice a day for treatment. Her consultant had not felt able to guarantee that she would be able to complete the performances, but Barbirolli and Webster agreed that she had to be allowed to try.

The critic Winton Dean described the production as 'tasteful but languid and conducive to slumber'. But of Ferrier he wrote, 'The natural beauty of her voice is supported by so high a musical and dramatic intelligence that she expresses the very heart of the Orpheus legend, the poignancy of human loss on the one hand and the consoling

* Webster wrote about Harewood to Bing on 7 October 1966, explaining that he had hesitated to employ him earlier because he had been worried that his 'personal responsibilities' as a member of the Royal Family would interfere with his work. In the event 'his title was no impediment'. Harewood's knowledge was, in Webster's words 'very great indeed', he was also possessed of a 'phenomenal memory', had 'administrative ability', was 'a good mixer' and had a 'natural sympathy for the creative artist'. His only weakness was in the financial sphere (ROH Archives, Harewood, DW file).

† In 1960 Geraint Evans was the first British singer to sing at La Scala since the war, when he sang Figaro.

power of music on the other, in terms of the purest vocal and theatrical art.'[147] It was in the middle of the second performance that Ferrier's femur broke and she only managed to finish the performance in great agony, and with supreme courage.

Ferrier wrote to her American accompanist in her usual brave and cheerful way, 'The first night was a wow and the very elegant audience shouted their heads off at the end. The second night was going fine until I snipped a bit of bone on my hip and had to limp for the rest of the evening.' After this, only her second operatic role, she never sang again. She died that October.[148]

'Her successful career did little to ease her sadness,' Ronald Duncan wrote in his obituary of Ferrier, 'the cause of which was not only her unfortunate marriage but a need for love itself which life could not fulfil.' After an earlier *Orfeo* in Amsterdam she had told Duncan, 'Yes . . . that part suits me. Searching through hell for love is something I do all the time.'

On 8 June 1953 Britten's *Gloriana* had its premiere in honour of Queen Elizabeth II's coronation six days earlier. Britten had spent an intense year of effort composing it, at Harewood's suggestion. The novelist and poet, William Plomer, based his libretto on Lytton Strachey's book *Elizabeth and Essex*. Pritchard conducted, Joan Cross was Elizabeth, Peter Pears Essex, and Geraint Evans the Earl of Mountjoy. The occasion was a disaster. Lord Harewood later recalled, 'The audience, so far from being a gathering of artistic Britain to honour the Queen (as we had naively hoped) consisted of Cabinet, Diplomatic Corps, and official London first and foremost and the rest apparently nowhere. They applauded if at all with their kid gloves on, and the press, critics as well as journalists, gathered next day to castigate composer, performance and choice.'[149]

The *New York Herald Tribune* on 15 June reported that the 'critics set up a howl in their newspapers' because Britten had 'shattered the fairy tale mood which had been woven round the streets of London and in the nation's press' by writing about the 'down-to-earth tragedy of Elizabeth I, torn between her illicit love for a man who had betrayed the state and her duty as Queen to execute him'.[150] The main howl came from the Beaverbrook press, and in particular Beverley Baxter MP, who wrote articles in the *Evening Standard* and the *Sunday Express* deriding the 'clamorous ugly music', which he described as an 'insult to the young Queen'. The more serious critics, like Mann in *The Times*, recognised Britten's 'astonishingly fertile resource and invention' while criticising the work for a lack of vigour and dramatic coherence.[151]

Ralph Vaughan Williams pointed out the powerful if sombre fact, to those who had objected so strenuously to the cost of the venture, that it was 'the first time in history the Sovereign has commanded an opera by a composer from these islands for a great occasion'.[152] The episode did little for the concept of royal patronage of opera, nor did it encourage a general support for subsidy. The *Evening Standard* concluded that if *Gloriana* provoked such public dissatisfaction that there arose 'a determination to abolish all Arts Council activity' the cost would have been worthwhile.[153] Twenty years later, David Cairns reflected, 'In opposing state-subsidised opera, and Britten as the pampered symbol of it, traditional British philistinism was only acting according to its sad lights.'[154] Britten was philosophical, writing to Plomer on 20 July, after the last night, that the opera had been a box office success. He feared that Plomer was probably feeling more 'kicked around' than he did, as he was 'a bit more used to the jungle'. Nevertheless he was not untouched. 'The savageness of the wild beasts', he wrote, 'always is a shock.'[155]

When in 1966 *Gloriana* was brilliantly staged at Sadler's Wells, the critics reversed their view of Britten's work, although maintaining reservations about Plomer's libretto. In Phyllida Lloyd's austere production in a recognisably Elizabethan setting for Opera North in December 1993, the work's power and drama mesmerised the audience. Josephine Barstow's interpretation of Elizabeth, the Essex of Thomas Randle and Paul Daniel's conducting plainly revealed the opera to be what Michael Kennedy described as 'a great national opera worthy of its occasion'. He ended his review with the thought that if the Queen were to revisit the opera after her *annus horribilis* she might 'recognise what a long-sighted tribute Benjamin Britten laid before her in 1953'.[156]

*   *   *

In September 1953 there was a visit to Covent Garden by the Bavarian State Opera. Andrew Porter described the 'admirable wholeness and integration of performance' in Rudolf Hartmann's production of Strauss's *Arabella*. The singing was of an equally high standard: 'Nature seems to have made Lisa Della Casa for the role of Arabella,' Porter wrote. The professionalism, dedication and teamwork of the company impressed Porter, who observed that 'Covent Garden's famously inadequate lighting worked quite well in the right hands'.*[157]

Of great significance for the development of the Covent Garden company was the conducting of Rudolf Kempe, Munich's Generalmusikdirektor, who became the House's main guest conductor in the autumn of 1953. He wrote to Webster, 'I have to tell you how happy I am to conduct at Covent Garden and how much I like the orchestra. I am only sorry that my duties in Munich make it necessary for my visits to be so short.' By 1959 Kempe had conducted 125 performances with the company – more than any of his colleagues. In the words of *Opera*, he 'established himself as the most popular guest conductor', greeted with 'warmth and affection by both audience and orchestra'.[158] Adele Leigh recalled that Kempe 'had the most extraordinary effect on singers. He breathes with us, he sings the whole part with you, you feel you're not there alone.'[159] Kempe was of the generation of conductors who grew up in opera houses. Born near Dresden in 1910, he studied piano, oboe and violin, before joining the Dortmund Opera as an oboist and then répétiteur in 1928. In 1949 he became Generalmusikdirector in Dresden. He left East Germany when he succeeded Solti at Munich.

On 29 October Kempe conducted *Salome* at Covent Garden and, in April and July 1954, *Elektra* and *Rosenkavalier*. On 12 May 1954 he launched the new *Ring*, which was produced by Rudolf Hartmann and designed by Leslie Hurry, who replaced the travelling spotlights with some modern lighting techniques from Bayreuth.† Sung in German,

---

* It had been decided by the Board in May 1953 that the Vienna State Opera was too expensive for Covent Garden to bring over as, with their expenses, each performance would cost £4,000. Munich performances cost less, at £1,200 (Board meeting, Covent Garden Archives, 19.5.53).

† It was suggested that Henry Moore design the *Ring* but Kenneth Clark wrote to Webster on 4 June 1953 that Moore had 'never heard a note of the *Ring* and is not particularly in sympathy with Wagner' (Royal Opera House Archives, Kenneth Clark, 34/303).

it was very well received, Andrew Porter writing that the cast could be compared with that at Bayreuth, with Hans Hotter's Wotan, 'perhaps the noblest and most affecting performance in the theatre today'.[160] *Rheingold* was premiered on 10 May 1955. *The Times* saw a future Brünnhilde in Amy Shuard's Freia and wrote that Kempe's 'texture of sound was clear enough to permit all the inside of the score to be heard, rich but not opaque, sparing of climax and flowing'.* On 14 May *Walküre* was described by Hope-Wallace as 'lucidity itself ... the finest since the war', with some real acting.[161] During the 1954 season Kempe also conducted *Rosenkavalier*, *Fidelio* and *Tristan und Isolde*. On 9 December he conducted Sylvia Fisher in *Tristan*. His reading was described by Mann as 'authoritative and impassioned, notable for finely calculated nuances and for legato line'.[162]

In June 1954 Webster told Harewood that he had been impressed by Rafael Kubelik whom he had heard conducting Janáček's *Kát'a Kabanová* at Sadler's Wells. In July 1953 the opera subcommittee had noted that as Kubelik had decided to leave Chicago and live in England, his name 'should be borne in mind for music director'. In September 1954 the committee learnt that Kubelik was eager to come to Covent Garden. He was willing to work with Kempe and, as Kempe did not want a full-time job, there could be a satisfactory arrangement. Kubelik was also in total sympathy with Webster's and the Board's continuing policy of creating an ensemble company using the English language. On 7 October Kubelik's appointment as music director was announced. He was to receive £6,500 a year for not less than seven and a half months' presence.

Although Covent Garden's programming was still weighted heavily in favour of the German repertory, by the 1953–54 season there had been some acceptable performances of Italian opera. They were, however, not sung in English. On 13 November 1953 *Un Ballo in maschera* was sung in Italian. Gré Brouwenstijn's Amelia and Tito Gobbi's Renato were, in Andrew Porter's words, in 'the finest Scala tradition, with bearing and gesture geared to the grand scale, and big, confident, stylish singing'. Their performances caused Porter to ask, 'Can it be

* Webster told the opera subcommittee on 21 December 1951 that Shuard was to join Covent Garden as soon as possible as she was in danger of being overworked at Sadler's Wells (Opera Sub-Committee 1951–59, 6/1).

that one's ear is put out, during the London winter, by hearing too much opera in English?'[163] Tito Gobbi was to become a regular at Covent Garden. In February 1954 Webster admitted to the Board that it was difficult to find top singers willing to sing in English. Lisa Della Casa would not agree and even Schwarzkopf, who was changing her roles, was not willing to learn the new ones in English.

Language was not the only challenge. Fees were also a problem for the company, which was always facing deficits in its budget. Webster told the Board that Callas was asking for higher fees than Flagstad had received and that de los Angeles was asking for fees 'on the Callas scale'. Webster and his accountant Douglas Lund were constantly being asked to pare down the budget when, in early 1954, the Arts Council reduced a promised grant of £300,000 to £240,000.* On 30 March, Webster told the Board that the replacement of old productions was going too slowly. Only one standard work, *Carmen*, had been replaced since 1946, and the 1954 *Ring* was the first new production of Wagner. Arthur Bliss said that the grant was inadequate 'to enable Covent Garden to become a paramount influence in Europe'.[164]

Under these circumstances Covent Garden's efforts to widen the repertoire were appreciated. In reviewing a performance on 7 January 1954 of Rimsky-Korsakov's *The Golden Cockerel*, Porter pointed to a significant improvement in the House's general standards in spite of some specific criticisms of the production and the conducting. 'We have, now, a worthy company, and it is building up a varied and representative repertory.'[165]

The company, according to its brief, continued to put on new work by British composers. The 1949–50 season had opened with Arthur Bliss's *The Olympians* with a libretto by J. B. Priestley. In 1951 the company performed Ralph Vaughan Williams's *The Pilgrim's Progress*, which John Tooley described as a 'pageant with beautiful meditative music' but lacking theatrical appeal.[166] In December 1954 and January 1955 there were premieres of two more English works. One was Walton's *Troilus and Cressida*, which had a warm reception from the critics. On 4 December 1954 *The Times* went so far as to call

---

* Lund was the company's accountant and company secretary from 1946 to 1972. He died in 1974.

it a 'great tragic opera'. There was a general feeling that what Martin Cooper described as 'a strong traditional belief that opera is a fantastic irrational entertainment fit only for foreigners and cultural snobs' was at last being overcome by the development of a real British opera.[167] Harewood described *Troilus* as the operatic equivalent of a 'well-made play'. This was in contrast to Tippett's *The Midsummer Marriage*, premiered on 27 January 1955, which he called 'a long sprawling compendium of the many philosophical ideas and trends which he found appealing at the time'.[168]

Tippett, whose background in the provinces in Suffolk had lacked any musical content, had by sheer determination made it to the Royal College of Music in 1923. His early years of composing had been lonely and isolated until he had gone to work at Morley College in 1940 as music director. Like Britten he had been a conscientious objector. In 1943, in spite of William Walton's testimony in his defence, he had been sentenced to three months in prison for refusing to do approved work other than in the musical sphere. After the war, in 1952, he became artistic director of the St Ives Festival of the Arts and continued composing.

Tippett saluted the courage of Covent Garden for putting on his opera. Webster strongly supported the project, in the face of opposition from Steuart Wilson, who had said the work was too long, 'diffuse and exceedingly restless'. He warned Webster that it would require a 'vast amount of rehearsal to extricate the composer's meaning' and that in spite of a long article of explanation in the *Observer*, he confessed 'to being still in the dark' as to the work's meaning.[169]

The Midsummer Marriage was given serious coverage in the press. Andrew Porter in a long analysis explained that the opera 'does not proceed in terms of direct narrative. It has been described as a "quest" opera, like *Parsifal* and *The Magic Flute*, but its climate is quite different to these. It is a comedy of everyday life, set in the ordinary English countryside with ordinary English people – young men and women, a garage hand and a shorthand typist, an industrialist – as its characters.'[170]

Tippett described *The Midsummer Marriage* as 'the activation of the Great Memory, that immense reservoir of the human psyche where images age-old and new boil together in some demonic cauldron'. The storyline is a unique mixture of English folk themes, a mythic quest interpreted in a Jungian perspective, and a love story that begins with an elopement and ends in a happy marriage. Most striking is the musical writing. Tippett created extraordinarily dense contrapuntal lines and orchestral colours, which nevertheless retain clarity. He was an imaginative spirit and ingenious technician whose bonding of music to text works well in its own terms, even though the text itself, richer in thought than drama, may not be to every taste.

A recording was made of the first performance. The work proved difficult for the Covent Garden forces, the choral writing so demanding that it forced the voices out of tune and pushed the sopranos into shrieking the high notes. The orchestra played with more approximation than clarity, but the conductor, John Pritchard, balanced the sections and cleaned up as many lines as he could.

Joan Sutherland created the role of Jenifer. Although her character is conceived as cold, even harsh, Sutherland's tone was fresh, soft-grained, warm and limpid, with breathtaking floated pianissimi. Her trills and staccato coloratura presaged her 'stupendous' Lucia of 1959. Richard Lewis was an English tenor of the next generation, his voice richer and more developed than that of Heddle Nash, although in *The Midsummer Marriage* performance the lower register was lacking and the weight of Tippett's writing burdened him. Adele Leigh created Bella, with her pure and light sound, crystalline diction, an appealing personality and fine acting through the voice. In her first-act aria 'It is so strange' she managed Tippett's difficult leaps with aplomb and accurate intonation.

The Midsummer Marriage met with a mixed reception, although Barbara Hepworth's sets and John Cranko's inspired choreography were universally praised by the critics. Desmond Shawe-Taylor found it 'intellectually undisciplined and unselfcritical to a surprising degree' and wondered if it were not 'all conceived on the analyst's couch'.[171] Britten's more immediate and international appeal may well be due to the emphasis he places on dramatic conflict and deeply felt human themes. Tippett's characters often have a symbolic tinge, while Britten's are consistently individual. Only after a fine production in 1976 at Welsh National Opera, at San Francisco in 1983, in Tim Albery's 1985 production for Opera North and in David Alden's Munich production in 1998 did *The Midsummer Marriage* become recognised in the international as well as British repertoire.

In the immediate aftermath of the war, troops of the British and Allied occupation forces had been exposed to European opera for the first time. This exposure contributed to a greater awareness of opera which in turn enabled a general blossoming of British operatic life and creativity – from the amateur to the increasingly sophisticated. The creation and development of Welsh National Opera was part of this transformation. An ex-baritone, John Morgan, and Idloes Owen, a singing teacher and choral conductor, together with William Smith, a businessman, had managed to turn the dream of a semi-amateur grand opera company into the foundations for a new permanent ensemble.

Although opera was virtually unknown to the music-loving Welsh, choral singing and eisteddfods meant there was a powerful and popular vocal tradition. The opportunity to sing in the opera chorus brought a hugely enthusiastic response, even though the company could not offer fees in the early days and most chorus members were in full-time jobs, including mining. The only credential for joining the chorus was a good voice, of which there was no shortage in Wales. On the opening night, 15 April 1946, for *Cavalleria rusticana* and *Pagliacci*, coachloads of enthusiasts arrived in Cardiff from the valleys; and thereafter opera became as truly popular an art form in Wales as it was in Europe.

The Arts Council gave very modest support in the early years, but by 1951 it had recognised that Welsh National Opera could become a major force in Welsh cultural life and the company began to receive a proper grant (£6275 for 1952) to expand its activities. By then the ambitious William Smith had taken over the company and although knowing little about music had a nose for talent, inviting the young Sadler's Wells répétiteur, Charles Mackerras, down for the 1950 season. In November 1954 the company's productions of *Menna*, a Welsh opera, and Verdi's *Nabucco* attracted national visitors and critics. *Opera* reported that the company was 'developing into an institution of considerable regional, even national significance', with its 'admirable amateur chorus'.

A great deal had been achieved in British operatic life by the premiere of *The Midsummer Marriage* at Covent Garden in 1955. The formation of a national opera company coincided with a creative period in English opera. Cecil Smith in the 1955 *Opera Annual* wrote that the premieres of Walton's and Tippett's works had established Covent Garden 'in the eyes of the world as a truly national theatre'. Nevertheless, it was becoming increasingly clear that while English opera and operatic life were flourishing, opera in English was inhibiting the improvement of standards of singing at Covent Garden, however tenaciously the Board and administration attempted to maintain the policy. Webster's first ten years had been uneven. Cecil Smith said that foreigners still viewed Covent Garden as a place 'where operas are sung in appalling English translations by singers of unrivalled mediocrity'.[172] The many poor routine evenings were, however, interspersed with some fine performances and visits of distinguished guest artists and conductors, and there was a sure and gradual development of local talent and an ensemble. From nothing Rankl had laid solid foundations for the establishment of a permanent company, orchestra, chorus and principals, and a broad repertoire.

Webster, with his dilatoriness, allowed too much mediocrity, but his patience gave time for new talent and a company identity to develop. There was what Tooley later described as 'a natural momentum behind the company which needed guidance' and which Webster and Harewood provided. Webster's warm managerial skills had created a pleasant atmosphere and true company spirit remembered with affection by those who worked for him. Webster had also made a great contribution to the firm foundations of the company which was capable of developing into something of an international standard that would soon rival the great European Houses and the Met.

FOUR

THE MET 1941–50
Gentleman Johnson

DURING THE WAR YEARS the Metropolitan Opera, alone among
the Big Four opera houses, had remained open, with performances
proceeding uninterrupted. Many European stars who had been frequent guests at the Met before 1939 were prevented by wartime conditions from returning. Foremost among the absent singers were Jussi
Björling, Beniamino Gigli, Tito Schipa, Maria Caniglia and Kirsten
Flagstad. Nevertheless, other Europeans, including Licia Albanese
and Alexander Kipnis, came to help fill the gaps. Albanese herself
went on to sing 286 Met performances and after her retirement became
a regular member of the audience, eccentric, outspoken and much
loved.

Ever since Toscanini's retirement in 1915 as chief conductor and,
effectively, music director without the title, the Met had made its mark
as a singer's House. Now that foreigners were much harder to import,
American talent had to be actively encouraged if that reputation were
to be upheld. Even before the war Edward Johnson, the general manager, had instituted a policy encouraging 'the employment of artists,
preferably Americans, whose first consideration was their art, with
money of secondary importance'.[1]

During the first years after the war's end the Metropolitan Opera
remained a provincial institution. The crucial problem had not been
the drying-up of the supply of foreign singers; management had begun
to tap an ample fund of local talent. Rather, it was a chronic shortage
of money that kept the Met from realising its potential as one of the
supreme international venues for opera.

Money matters posed great difficulties for Johnson. Forced to rely largely on box office income, and with Johnson seeking as best he could to avoid large deficits, the Met's artistic level suffered. Johnson finished eight of his fifteen seasons with a budget surplus. During the year 1945–46 a net profit of $4,370 was recorded and the following year saw a surplus of $11,800. Meeting the budget resulted, however, in decrepit productions, underpaid orchestra and chorus members, and stinginess with the contracts of principals, who generally fared much better at other top Houses. Zinka Milanov, who first sang at the Met in 1937, actually left the company in 1947 out of dissatisfaction with the fees she was offered.

> Edward Johnson and I simply did not get on. When I first started I was paid $125 a week, and ten years later I received three hundred, which was totally ridiculous. I considered it insulting, but every time I talked to him about this untenable situation, he smiled – he was very good at that – and repeated that he could not afford more. So I packed up and went abroad . . .[2]

Milanov returned at the beginning of the Bing regime to make her mark as a great Verdian soprano. Until her retirement in 1966 she was loved by her many fanatical admirers at the Met for the tender beauty of her tone and excused by nearly all opera goers for her disinclination to act.

Today, when prominent Met donors regularly support lavish new productions with great generosity, it is hard to imagine the House's penuriousness during the Johnson era. The chairman of the Board, George Sloan, shared Johnson's conservative financial philosophy. He vetoed the idea of pensions for dismissed chorus members, declaring, 'The Met has no funds for pensions.'[3] Nonetheless, new productions initiated during the 1947–48 season did put the Met deeply into deficit – to the extent of some $220,000. Even Sloan, in a joint statement with Charles Spofford, the Board president, acknowledged the positive side of the red ink:

> While the financial results of the past season are obviously unsatisfactory, they do not of course constitute the measure of the results achieved. With the ambitious programme of new productions and revivals which was carried through during the

year, the extension of the spring tour to the Pacific Coast, and
the unparalleled public interest with which the Opera has been
greeted everywhere, we feel that the season has been one of the
most important in recent years.[4]

The following year's deficit was even larger: approximately $325,000.
Even so, Board chairman George Sloan in the Annual Report expressed
no interest in government support: 'The Metropolitan Opera Association [that is, the Board] is not asking for a federal subsidy, believing
that the cultural institutions of this country can be maintained by the
public which attends, and by the voluntary efforts of the increasingly
broad groups which are devoted to the support of fine music.' The
Met was following the traditional American path of private funding,
placing itself firmly outside the pattern of leading European opera
houses, including Covent Garden, all of which relied on government
funds for their very existence. The Met preserved its independence
but limited its artistic depth and range.

During the late 1940s the ladies and gentlemen of New York society
were still active in funding Met productions. The Metropolitan Opera
Guild, chaired by Mrs August Belmont, had a largely female membership. In 1947 the Guild raised tens of thousands of dollars for a new
Ring, towards which the Wagnerian tenor Lauritz Melchior himself
donated $5,000.[5] However, when Bing succeeded to Johnson's job he
found the Metropolitan Opera Club – in contrast to the Guild, a male
organisation – a band of cheapskates: '[It was] simply another social
club for businessmen and lawyers who in my early days sat around
in tails and top hats, paying the house a most inadequate rental for
their facilities.'[6] The Met stage director, Herbert Graf, recalled that the
money problem was the chief reason for the Met's mediocre stagings:

> The first thing to remember is that there was a terrible scarcity
> of money. New productions, in the sense of new costumes and
> scenery, were very rare indeed. And rehearsal time onstage was
> strictly limited. Most of the staging was done on the roof stage,
> where scheduling was no great problem, but the net result was
> that the singers didn't get to work in the set until the last
> moment; and given the general shabbiness of the physical pro-
> duction, the total effect was a good deal less than theatrical.[7]

Graf told an interviewer that there was so little money for staging that Lily Pons, the coloratura soprano, paid for the queen's pavilion in *Le Coq d'or* out of her own pocket.

Lack of resources also resulted in the failure to appoint an outstanding musical director. Two highly experienced conductors were available as exiles in America: Bruno Walter had worked extensively in Berlin and Vienna and at the Salzburg Festival, and Fritz Busch had been music director before the war at Dresden and at Glyndebourne. However, neither made more than the occasional guest appearance at the Met. Either one would have provided the competence, the artistic leadership, the familiarity with the European operatic tradition – and, most important, each in his own fashion the original vision of the work as a whole that a conductor like Toscanini insisted upon realising in performance. In a word, America needed European excellence to challenge local talent. But personalities like Erich Kleiber, who entered into fruitless negotiations with the Met, wanted a higher salary than the House was prepared to offer. Kleiber also demanded greatly increased rehearsal time with the orchestra, but Johnson felt he could not provide this: 'It is almost impossible to guarantee more than two stage rehearsals with the orchestra. As a matter of fact, the technical questions of operation cannot be formally incorporated in a contract.'[8] Nevertheless, Johnson's musical tastes often came to the fore. Although he named no permanent conductor, he did engage such outstanding guests as Walter, George Szell, Sir Thomas Beecham and Fritz Reiner.

Another problem at the Met was the personality of the man at the top. Edward Johnson was a former tenor who had been made general manager in 1935. His decision, as he put it, was to retire from the stage and 'to give away his purple tights'.[9] In 1940 he led a successful fund-raising drive to purchase the House from the box holders, thus loosening to some extent the grip of 'society' on opera in New York. Many recall him as a kind man, perhaps too kind. When Gilda dalla Rizza had made her Scala debut in 1916 as Madeleine de Coigny, her Chénier was none other than the Canadian Edward Johnson – 'or Eduardo di Giovanni, as he was called in Italy'. Dalla Rizza had high praise for her colleague on that difficult first night: 'The kindness and camaraderie of Johnson will never be forgotten, for if I came through it, much of the credit is his.'[10] Soprano Dorothy Kirsten recalled,

'Having been an excellent, sensitive singer himself . . . he knew voices and rarely made a mistake. He did, however, talk Lotte Lehmann into singing Tosca at the Met, which was accounted a mistake in view of her Teutonic seriousness on stage.[12]

As far as the promotion of musical standards was concerned, Johnson ran a loose ship. Helen Traubel and Lauritz Melchior, the reigning Wagnerian soprano and tenor respectively, were allowed a degree of liberty that amounted to indiscipline. Neither was accustomed to attend rehearsals at the House.

Stage direction was too often carried on by routiniers like Désiré Defrère, who tended to copy clichés remembered from German, French and Italian Houses of years earlier. Productions – especially in their physical aspect – were sometimes embarrassingly decrepit. A British opera critic visiting New York disparaged Met stagecraft: '. . . an Augean stable of bad lighting charts, unintelligent handling of crowds and individuals, and unduly permissive stage direction that lets the stars do just about as they like.'[14] When Rudolf Bing took up the post of general manager in 1950 he was shocked to find that the Johnson-era settings were, with few exceptions, 'simply collections of drop curtains and flats, leaving the singers standing on the bare stage with occasional prop pieces for variety'.[15] Some singers, especially foreign ones, were accustomed to bring their own costumes for their roles. Little thought was given to visual coherence. The notion of an integrated production was altogether unfamiliar. Quality suffered through the use of inexperienced artists. Vocal self-indulgence was all too frequent. The absence of a music director on the European model meant that on most evenings the Metropolitan would give the impression of being a routine, get-through-it-somehow House. 'The wisdom of allowing young singers with no more than a textbook knowledge of their subject the freedom of a stage traditionally the object of a lifetime's progress was dangerous. What should have been the tolerable exception became numbingly regular in a flighty, planless, artistically arbitrary shuffling about of personnel.'[16]

Irving Kolodin sums up Johnson's legacy: 'never other than a singer at heart; . . . the special talent for organization, detail, discipline, and creative thinking . . . which characterizes the able impresario was never in his make-up.'[17]

As a one-time performer, however, Johnson was a good judge of singers. Under his leadership the Metropolitan Opera actively promoted the discovery and nurturing of young American artists. The Met Auditions, a nationwide talent-scouting competition, were supported by the Sherwin-Williams Paint Company. A number of the American-born artists whom Johnson hired built outstanding careers in New York and abroad. Blanche Thebom was Covent Garden's first Dido in Berlioz's *Les Troyens*, and, at Glyndebourne in 1950, a lush and grainy-voiced Dorabella to Jurinac's Fiordiligi. At the Met, Thebom was an all-round mezzo whose repertoire extended from Orlovsky to Brangäne to Baba the Turk in Stravinsky's *The Rake's Progress*. The Met Auditions having turned up plentiful talent, Johnson's keen judgement of singing led him to engage the best Americans of the day: Dorothy Kirsten, Eleanor Steber, Risë Stevens, Regina Resnik, Jan Peerce, Richard Tucker, Robert Merrill and Leonard Warren. Besides forming the post-war generation of Met stalwarts, all these singers performed abroad. Each one, to a greater or lesser degree, helped create the awareness that American artists could hold their own with their European colleagues. In this respect the post-war Met performed a valuable artistic service for opera at large.

While some young singers were carefully tutored, others were rushed far too quickly into difficult roles. Blanche Thebom recalled the hectic, isolated atmosphere at the Met immediately after the Second World War:

> That period gave us young American singers unique opportunities. Today's young singers cannot imagine the meagreness of American operatic life in those days. Opera was not taught at any university. The Chicago and San Francisco seasons were extremely short. There was nothing in Boston and Washington DC. New York was it. And here we were, with minimal stage experience but virtually surrounded by refugee European coaches who came from the best schools, theatres and traditions. I had the benefit of studying with Paul Meyer, a very Germanically thorough and exacting teacher, and at the Met I learned a lot from stage director Lothar Wallerstein. We were rushed into big roles, making debuts that were more like auditions. At the same time, we had to compete at the top level.

You survived if you had guts and discipline. We learned to become individuals, not some generic singers cranked out by the system.[18]

Lothar Wallerstein's name had appeared on the Vienna Staatsoper's lists of employees to be sacked in 1938 under the notation 'full Jew'.[19] His work at the Met was funded by a grant from American philanthropist Kathryn Turney Long. His acting class at the Met gave young singers the basis in their craft they required, while inexperienced artists taking on new roles benefited from his dedicated individual coaching. Conductor Erich Leinsdorf praised Wallerstein's work: 'Without Wallerstein, I don't think some of these new and untried singers could have gone onstage at the Metropolitan to do these great parts.'[20]

The Johnson House was reluctant to engage African-American singers. In an era when racial segregation was often practised in the northern states as well as the Deep South, the Met did not see fit to give leadership in the struggle against racism. The archives contain several letters from black public figures protesting against the failure to hire such outstanding performers as Marian Anderson. In a response to the National Urban League, a group devoted to the advancement of black Americans, in April 1944, veteran assistant general manager Edward Ziegler went so far as to assert that non-white singers were on the whole incompetent to sing opera: 'While we have the greatest admiration for the voices and musical abilities of qualified Negro singers, we have not learned that they are qualified to fill important operatic roles.'[13] Given the unwillingness of American opera companies to give black singers stage experience, it is unclear how Ziegler imagined they might attain the desired 'qualification'.

In general, casting was fraught with difficulties. A serious problem was the dramatic soprano *Fach*. Kirsten Flagstad, the Met's paramount Wagnerian, had returned to Norway in April 1941 at the bidding of her husband, Henry Johansen. When her American manager, Marks Levine, asked her whether she would agree to sing 'in Germany or in Norway or elsewhere for the sake of propaganda', Flagstad made it clear she would not. 'You know me well enough, Marks, to realise that I can always lose my voice, get sick or in general make it impossible for myself to open my mouth.'[21] Flagstad remained in her homeland for the duration of the war except for two recitals in Sweden and appearances at the June festival in Zurich. She failed to respond to a number of invitations to sing in Germany. However, after the war was over Henry Johansen, a lumber dealer, was charged with being a Norwegian collaborator with the Nazis.

Under suspicion of collaboration because of her husband's complicity, Flagstad was not invited to perform after the war at the Met as long as Johnson was general manager. Many at the House lobbied for her reinstatement. In December 1948, wrote Met archivist Robert Tuggle, Mrs Belmont 'forwarded pro-Flagstad correspondence to George Sloan . . . and added, "Furthermore, it raises in my mind the question of whether the time has not come for the Association Board to consider the possibility of engaging Madame Flagstad for several performances next year. Surely she has, after two years of courageous struggle, won her way back to a first position in America as a great artist."'[22] Some of Flagstad's post-war appearances elsewhere in America had been greeted with opprobrium – a few had even been cancelled – and Met management were afraid of adverse reaction.

In Flagstad's absence Johnson had to cast the *Ring* somehow. Although he could parcel out her roles between Helen Traubel and Astrid Varnay, neither singer approached Flagstad's emotional range, ease, and tonal volume. Johnson had first engaged Traubel without much enthusiasm in 1937. During the next season, though, she became 'the year's new box office personality', as *Variety* put it.[23] In her speciality, the heaviest Wagner roles such as Isolde and Brünnhilde, Traubel was for years unexcelled at the Met. Her voice was big, ringing and warm. However, her minimal acting typified the era and the House. As one critic put it, 'Her principal effect was of majestic poise.'[24] Astrid Varnay made her Met debut on the day before Pearl Harbour, 6 December 1941, as Sieglinde, a part she was singing without rehearsal. A much more accomplished actress than Traubel, Varnay's repertoire eventually became much broader. Her lengthy international career displayed her talents as far more than a provincial dramatic soprano.

Eleanor Steber also helped fill the casting gap. Her debut at the Metropolitan had come on 7 December 1940, early in Johnson's tenure. A West Virginia girl of twenty-four who had studied singing privately, her first role – Sophie in *Der Rosenkavalier* – was warmly praised.

Somewhat heavier roles quickly followed. Unlike many singers, however, Steber was ready for the plunge. Her lyric soprano was both bright and deep in tone. She used that tone wisely to project phrase and text, rather than force accents or strive for a dramatic weight she did not possess. Her Marzelline in Toscanini's 1944 *Fidelio* broadcast recording (with the NBC Symphony and a number of other Met singers) shows real passion. Steber also exhibits her flair for colouring sounds, for exciting crescendi and decrescendi and messe di voce. In 'O wär' ich schon mit dir vereint' her relative inexperience is evident in a certain hesitancy after rests, in over-careful German diction and in some nervous breathing. But her contribution to the Act One quartet, 'Mir ist so wunderbar', is splendid.

On a good day the singers were generally more impressive than the conductors at the Johnson-era Met. A case in point is the live-performance recording of a *Rigoletto* of 29 December 1945 conducted by Cesare Sodero, who presided over 188 performances at the Met from 1942 until his death five years later. While Sodero's *Rigoletto* is competent and comfortably within the Italian idiom, his involvement is no more than routine. Although the orchestra plays crudely throughout, an effort is made to keep together, and Sodero observes Verdi's dynamic indications, if not his tempi. Jussi Björling sings the Duke of Mantua in his first post-war appearance at the Met. Although he is not giving his all, his technique is impeccable. The vocal production is clean and as easy as that of any outstanding post-war singer. In the title role, baritone Leonard Warren, aged thirty-four, is in the prime of his voice. The sound is completely mature, big and rich and flexible, with the weight in the middle and upper registers. The upper extension is excitingly free, giving this Rigoletto the happy impression of possessing a half-tone or even a tone beyond the final interpolated A flat. Warren acts through the voice with intensity and commitment, showing why he was considered – together with Tito Gobbi and Robert Merrill – among the leading Verdi baritones of his time. Bidú Sayão, the Gilda, is the image of the incandescent diva. At a number of points Sayão does all she can to drag the tempo and show off her gorgeous voice. In purely vocal terms, however, she was an exquisitely appealing singer.

Johnson had repeatedly threatened to resign during the Met's recurrent financial crises. On 30 January 1949 the House issued a statement recalling his past offers of resignation and stating that this time the resignation had been accepted. Johnson continued as general manager for one more year, with the Opera Guild undertaking to raise an additional $250,000 in order to give him a final, 'artistically outstanding season'.[25] But in the statement no successor to Johnson was named. A number of candidates were being bruited as replacements. Rudolf Bing, in America to prepare for a visit of the Glyndebourne company, decided to knock on the door of the Thirty-Ninth Street House. Kolodin wrote:

> While in New York, Bing looked up his old friend Fritz Stiedry, a colleague of Berlin days, and asked him to arrange a courtesy call on Johnson. Stiedry brought them together and presided over introductions. After some preliminaries, concerned mostly with the difficulties of producing opera in this era, Johnson looked in mock despair at Bing, saying, 'How would you like this job?' Somewhat startled, Bing replied, 'Mr Johnson, you must be joking.' Whether or not he was – and the chances are that he was – Johnson decided that this was an excellent idea, and arranged for Bing to meet Sloan. After much conversation in the next two days, Bing returned to England with a promise of serious consideration for the position.[26]

Some accounts portray Johnson as having second thoughts about a hasty decision about his resignation. He was seen to be unhappy during the 1949 Met tour. Staff conductor Max Rudolf detected signs of regret as early as Atlanta. Frank Daniels, a reporter for the *Atlanta Journal*, asked Johnson who his successor would be. His reply sounded despairing. 'Oh, anybody. Kullman, Brownlee.'[27] Rumour had several Met singers in the running to succeed him. Besides tenor Charles Kullman and baritone John Brownlee, the names of Lawrence Tibbett, Lauritz Melchior and Richard Bonelli were heard. Brownlee – who went on to head the Manhattan School of Music – was thought to have the backing of society. Bing's name was not mentioned. Another candidate was said to be László Halász, director of the New York City Opera. It was Frank St Leger who seemed to have Johnson's approval. St Leger, an Irishman born in India, had been a coach, accompanist and 'music administrator' at the Met. At the centre of things for years, his experience in musical matters – if not his genius as a musician – could not have been bettered. Johnson sent him on a scouting trip to Europe to bolster his reputation.

If Johnson had regrets, however, they did him no good. And if he preferred other candidates over Bing, his wishes had no impact. Once Board chairman Sloan had received Bing's expression of interest in the post, the die was cast. Mrs Belmont made a trip to Britain. According to Quaintance Eaton in her history of the Met, she spoke to two or more people prominent in society, who gave positive reports of Bing's tenure at Glyndebourne, where he had been general manager since 1936, as well as at the Edinburgh Festival, where he had been serving as artistic director since 1947.

Upon Bing's acceptance of the Board's firm offer of a three-year contract beginning 1 June 1950, he was asked to come to the Met as an 'observer' for the 1949–50 season. Bing recalled hearing the good news in the company of young British director Peter Brook. The pair were lunching in Soho. 'I swore Brook to secrecy, told him the contents of the telephone call that had summoned me from our table, and secured a promise from him that he would direct for me at the Metropolitan, which he did, twice, for *Faust* in 1953 and *Eugene Onegin* in 1957 . . .'[28] Bing gives his game away with the little phrase 'direct for me'. Once installed in power, he ran the Metropolitan Opera, for good and for ill, as his private fief.

PART TWO

THE 1950s
The Old and the New

FIVE

LA SCALA 1955–59

A Golden Age

ECONOMIC RECOVERY CONTINUED in Italy during the 1950s under the leadership of the Christian Democratic party. The lot of landless farmers and industrial workers was significantly improved, while the impoverished south began slowly to benefit from infrastructure investment by the central government. Although Italians as a whole were still far from well off, a pattern of gradual growth had been set. Another pattern was emerging: rapidly changing national governments which nevertheless were composed consistently of Christian Democratic members in coalition with other centrist parties. While Christian Democratic governments sought to help weaker elements in Italian society, Communists and other leftist parties were excluded from power. The Christian Democratic-run political establishment was supported by the Catholic Church and business interests. From the political and business establishment came La Scala's audience – or those audience members who occupied the *poltrone*, or stall seats, and set the social tone for the House.

During this period La Scala was not stinted. The House's government subsidy allowed it to spend wisely, if not lavishly, to fund new productions and pay singers' and conductors' fees. Like Vienna and in stark contrast to the Met and Covent Garden, Italy's cultural flagship did not release annual financial reports. Although figures are scarce indeed, in 1955 La Scala posted a deficit of $214,009. The following year this rose to $385,882, suggesting that deficit budgeting was at least tolerated by the government. Ghiringhelli used available funds to engage the finest artists, making Milan a venue for extraordinary productions and adding lustre to the name of the House.

With artistic excellence in mind, and with what might be called a policy of enlightened conservatism, Ghiringhelli had the luck to benefit from a happy conjunction of creative talent. In Italy the national consensus concerning the centrality of culture – including opera – was still intact. La Scala could get on with its business of what it did best. An unforgettable collection of singers was joined by outstanding conductors. A crucial development for this golden age was Ghiringhelli's decision to hire a brilliant, demanding and imaginative stage director-cum-designer who would be a pioneer of integrated opera production: Luchino Visconti. Visconti was eager to exploit the full measure of Maria Callas's talents.

Count Luchino Visconti di Modrone was born in Milan on 2 November 1906 in the ancestral palace of his father, Giuseppe Visconti, Duke of Modrone. The family of his mother, who was born Carla Erba, had made their fortune in pharmaceutical goods. Two of Luchino's relatives had held the post of sovrintendente at La Scala and Visconti himself studied the cello. The Visconti di Modrone family, like many other Milanese aristocrats and captains of industry, had owned a box in La Scala before the House was reorganised by Toscanini in 1921. In fact, Toscanini owed his first engagement as artistic director of the House to one of the Viscontis. When the commune of Milan cut off its financial support to La Scala in 1897, Visconti's grandfather, Guido Visconti, Duke of Modrone, organised a number of rich opera goers to fund the continuation of the House's activities. Guido Visconti then pushed through Toscanini's appointment. The young Visconti frequently attended performances at La Scala and even cast the eight-year-old Wanda Toscanini, the conductor's daughter, as Ophelia in his own childhood production of *Hamlet*.

Before the war Visconti was assistant to French film maker Jean Renoir. During the war he made a film, *Ossessione*, which fell foul of Mussolini's censors. Visconti was imprisoned by the Nazis for his underground activities. His post-war films, such as *La Terra trema*, display a deep sensitivity to visual and psychological values and to mood. His work for the Italian stage was also much acclaimed. Visconti's pupil and disciple Franco Zeffirelli recalled his formidable self-assurance:

He had an amazing amount of *grinta* – you know, grit – and he gave me a feeling of confidence in myself and my judgements, a feeling of arrogance almost, that the director is some kind of superior being. What you did was either great or nothing, there was no middle ground. And of course whatever anyone else did was junk. . . . He could be very charming and persuasive, but at times he was terribly cruel. Don't forget that it was then still fashionable to be the German-style 'mad director': you had to rant and rave and keep the rehearsals full of *Sturm und Drang*, and in your private life you were scandalous and sinful. (Nowadays you're expected to be very kind and calm and diplomatic with your colleagues.) Visconti was the superman-type director and he could be very demanding indeed.[1]

Zeffirelli also made the point that Visconti was steeped in the culture of pre-war Europe, which enabled him to bring 'an international flavour to the Italian stage. He'd . . . spent the last part of the thirties in Paris and knew everyone important in the world of the arts – Jean Renoir, Aragon, Chanel, for instance – and so he was able to import a wide-ranging mentality and taste into an otherwise provincial and moribund atmosphere.'[2]

When Visconti saw Callas in *Norma* at the Rome Opera in February 1950 he had been much impressed by her acting abilities. As William Weaver wrote, 'Callas is the first to give Visconti credit for his developing her as an actress.'[3] For her part, Callas confessed, 'I was thoroughly spoiled by him – a *grand seigneur* treating me as a prima donna.' She admired his work for what it was: 'The less I moved [on stage] without evident reason or profound reason the more it is my own personality. It did me enormous good, of course.'[4] In July 1953, Visconti turned down an invitation from Ghiringhelli to direct *Rigoletto*, with Callas as Gilda. Callas, he said, had 'the temperament of a great tragedienne'; he compared her with the immortal French actress Edwige Feuillière. He preferred to await a chance to work with her in an opera which would suit her unique talents.

In the end Ghiringhelli made a proposal which appealed to Visconti and brought Callas to work together with him in an appropriate vehicle. La Scala opened its 1954–55 season with Visconti's staging of Gaspare Spontini's *La Vestale*. The entire cast were the finest La Scala had to offer. Besides Callas in the role of Giulia, the singers included Franco Corelli (Licinio), Enzo Sordello (Cinna), Nicola Rossi-Lemeni (Il Sommo Sacerdote) and Ebe Stignani (La Gran Vestale). Antonino Votto conducted. For his Scala debut, management allowed Visconti to direct Spontini's seldom performed opera sparing no effort or expense. The production cost $140,000, at the time a record for the House. Votto recalled Visconti's having obtained a pair of silver candlesticks for a table used in the finale. 'On the table he placed authentic silver, not stage props. He wanted every detail perfect.'[5] Visconti could not have accomplished everything he wished, however, without Callas's inspired acting. He said, 'La Vestale is a difficult opera to stage because it needs great style. This Maria gave it. For me she was a wonderful instrument, which could be played as I wished and which responded in an inspired way. How different from contending with a singer from the old school!' The style Visconti chose was linked to the Napoleonic period. He recalled that he and Callas selected gestures 'from the French tragediennes, some from Greek drama, for this was the kind of actress she could be – classical'.[6] Visconti also studied the paintings of Jacques Louis David, who had brought classical themes to portrayals of the Napoleonic era. Toscanini attended at least one rehearsal, approving of Visconti's direction and Callas's singing. 'Very good,' said Toscanini, 'a beautiful voice and an interesting artist.'[7]

Although Visconti's work as an opera director was always identifiably his own, he had respect for the score and libretto. Eugenio Montale, reviewing La Vestale in Corriere d'informazione, praised Visconti's light touch. The direction 'has the great merit of not having imposed a heavy hand', he wrote.[8] Fedele d'Amico detected in the staging 'predominant notes of moderation [and] an absence of intrusiveness, with the music being given room to breathe'.[9]

Visconti's next collaboration with Callas followed quickly. The new Scala production of Bellini's opera La Sonnambula had its first performance on 3 March 1955, with Leonard Bernstein conducting and Piero Tosi responsible for the sets. Visconti concentrated on showing Callas how to walk as a ballerina might, which combined with her recent dramatic loss of weight gave her the appearance of a smaller, more fragile creature. Bernstein recalled the excitement he experienced while working closely with the great stage director and the immortal soprano:

> [It] was something marvellous, the closest to a perfect opera performance I've ever witnessed. The time expended on its preparation – the care, the choices that were made, the work Maria and I did together on cadenzas and embellishments and ornamentations – was enormous. I remember hours of sitting with Visconti in the costume warehouse of La Scala, picking feathers for the caps of the chorus! I had eighteen rehearsals for a score that is usually done in one rehearsal, because the orchestra doesn't have too much more to do than a series of arpeggios, but those arpeggios were something never to be forgotten. And Callas was just glorious.[10]

In emphasising the care and expense lavished on so many aspects of the production, Bernstein indirectly honoured the Ghiringhelli administration's willingness to do everything possible to facilitate this historic collaboration in order to achieve an evening of lyric art at the highest level.

Even more than he had done with *La Vestale*, Visconti set an idiosyncratic stylistic seal on his *Sonnambula*. The *Corriere della Sera* critic delighted in the ambience of early eighteenth-century French painting, which had been replicated in Bellini's Swiss location: '[One] may understand that Luchino Visconti had wished to see the female characters costumed and moving on stage in an atmosphere of *fête galante* or a ballet in the style of Taglioni as Théophile Gautier might have conceived it.'[11] Claudio Sartori in *La patria* noted Visconti's love for significant decorative details at work in the movement of the singers on stage: 'Out of this intelligent framing of the opera a vision and an interpretation of the work sprang up in Luchino Visconti's mind which, as it were, animated a most delicate narrative of transparent porcelain statuettes moving lightly with the unreal steps and gestures of the dance . . .'[12] Bernstein's contribution to the show was applauded for its energy and intelligence. Eugenio Montale called it 'the interpretation of a great artist', which for a thirty-six-year-old American conducting only his second opera at La Scala (the first had been *Médée*, also with Callas, in 1953) was high praise indeed. Montale called Callas's singing the greatest triumph of the evening, lauding 'this phenomenal leggero soprano-tragedienne with a tinge of expressionism – an unprecedented mixture'. For him Callas's portrayal of the sleepwalking girl was entirely 'her own creation, to the point of wiping out all memory of previous interpreters. And when in the final rondo her voice was unloosed in all the richness of its colours, trills and great arches of tone, the effect was such that the audience shouted enthusiastically for a quarter of an hour.'[13]

In the 1955 La Traviata a standard of integrated music drama was established for the post-war era. Carlo Maria Giulini's noble, tragic vision of the music was matched by Luchino Visconti's highly individual understanding of the characters. Visconti, who had for years been obsessed by Verdi's and Piave's tragic heroine, took stage direction into a new dimension of intelligence, creativity and sympathy for the score. Callas played Violetta with great vocal distinction and utterly involved and involving acting at a level unmatched by other opera stars. If any single Scala production after the war was the paragon of excellence, it was this one. Here the inspired collaboration – star singer, stage director and conductor – presents La Scala, and post-war opera altogether, at their finest. Visconti's direction integrated music and staging in a way that set new standards for opera production.

Once again Visconti made the decision to alter the time-frame of the opera, placing it in the 1880s. Many of those who saw the production felt that locating the story closer to our own time underscored its pathos and 'decadence'.[14] The 'intimate bourgeois romance' was never erased but expanded.[15]

There is an audio recording of the first performance on 7 December 1955. Giulini's conducting is shown to have been an essential part of this extraordinary group effort. The first emotional colour established in the orchestra is a restrained sadness. In the overture the divisi violins sob, but not heavily. In the first scene of Act One Giulini lays stress on Verdi's recurring forte diminishing to pranissimo. While Callas in her singing interprets this shift as darkly tragic, the conductor's feeling for the diminuendo is by contrast gently mournful. The combination of soprano and orchestra is magical: Violetta's wrenchingly unhappy tale is accompanied with a delicate, sympathetic warmth.

Visconti also staged Callas in Donizetti's Anna Bolena, a Scala production which opened on 14 April 1957. Sets and costumes were by

Scala veteran Nicola Benois; Gianandrea Gavazzeni conducted. Fedele d'Amico, writing in *Il contemporaneo* on 27 April 1957, found Visconti's interpretation exactly right, grounded neither in verismo nor 'melodramatic rhetoric'. 'There was no overt insistence, no overemphasis, no moments of indulgence ... and yet not a trace of clumsiness – everything was alive and functional ... And there was perfect attunement to the dialectic of the music: the placement of the characters in the ensemble scenes, and Callas's arms in the mad scene like the wings of some nocturnal bird.'[16] D'Amico also delighted in Giulietta Simionato's singing as Giovanna Seymour, calling her portrayal 'one of the greatest interpretations of her career'.

The last collaboration between Visconti and Callas at La Scala was Gluck's *Ifigenia in Tauride*, which opened on 1 June 1957. Nino Sanzogno conducted and Nicola Benois designed the production. On balance this *Ifigenia* succeeded visually where it failed to impress vocally. Visconti opened the show with Callas striking an iconic attitude of tragedy. As the director himself put it, Callas 'wore a majestic gown with many folds of rich silk brocade and an enormous train, over which was a large cloak of deep red. On her head was a crown of pearls, and loops of pearls hung from her neck.'[17] Pacing anxiously up and down stairs in the role, Callas created an unforgettable effect with the first words she sang. Visconti recalled, 'With the wind machine behind her she would run up the staircase and come back down again, trailing twenty-five feet of cloak, and with split-second timing and still enough breath to start fortissimo dead on cue. So extraordinarily co-ordinated for her was music and movement that at each performance she would hit her first note in exactly the same position.'[18]

These were the finest years of Maria Callas's career, with her recorded performances with the Scala company some of her most impressive and moving. Some operas were recorded in the studio, while others, frequently of poorer sound quality, were taken from live stage performances. Hearing several of Callas's Italian recordings over time traces the vicissitudes of the singer's vocal condition, as well as her peerless acting through the voice. They also provide an excellent picture of the Scala forces – conductors, orchestra, chorus – when spurred to give of their best.

In the 1953 studio recording of Bellini's *I Puritani*, conducted by Tullio Serafin, the results of the veteran conductor's inspired guidance of Callas's artistry are evident. Serafin had urged Callas to add the great bel canto heroines to her repertoire at a time when she was singing Aida and Turandot. In agreeing she set out on one of the great adventures of her career, one which was crowned with glory. Her technique enabled her to conquer the difficulties of the music and her creative actor's imagination brought the roles to vivid life. In so doing she helped restore several of Donizetti's and Bellini's operas to the modern opera stage after they had not been heard for decades. In this recording Serafin's imprint is evident in the delicate phrasing – Callas's Elvira is delineated with the lightest of vocal brushstrokes – and the perfect uniting of solo and orchestral line. Callas's mad scene is completely felt; in this music she uncovers the maximum of sincerity, for it is material from which a lesser artist would create vocal theatrics. The tone is as close to melting as Callas could make it. Her range of timbres is excitingly varied, always with a hint of darkness. Her technique is astounding. Diatonic and chromatic scales are articulated with an eager, almost tangible ease. The voice is not pushed; even the high notes are sweet and tender. There is an incredible diminuendo on a high B flat, and the solid high E flat at the close of the scene is held for what seems an age. Perhaps Sutherland's leggiero in bel canto was suaver and her tone more limpid, but Callas's interpretive capacities tip the balance in her favour.

In the same year Callas and Serafin collaborated in the studio on *Lucia*, with Di Stefano and Gobbi and the Maggio Musicale chorus and orchestra. In 'Regnava nel silenzio' the dramatic timing is breathtaking – and entirely at one with vocal and musical nuance. It is as though she and Serafin are one mind, conjuring up the rubati together at each moment. In 'Quanto rapita in estasi' Callas displays complete technical control, even to the extent of articulating her trills metrically. However, the tone lacks the beauty she found for Elvira.

By the time of the August 1955 studio *Aida*, conducted by Serafin, Callas's vibrato problems, as well as her squally high notes, are more evident. The pianissimi are particularly unsteady, suggesting problems with abdominal support. As she often does, Callas takes great vocal risks. One or two phrases towards the end of 'Ritorna vincitor!' are thrillingly stretched out and with her superb breathing the singer reaches her goal – only just. As Amonasro, Tito Gobbi joins a menacing tone and flexible vocal coloration with careful attention to text and musical nuance. In their scenes together, Callas and Gobbi push each other to greater and greater intensity. Callas's singing technique in this particular recording takes a big step forward at moments when Gobbi is partnering her.

In September 1957 Serafin conducted Callas in a studio recording of Cherubini's *Medea*, in the Italian version, again with the Scala orchestra and chorus. There are uneven attacks on upper-middle-register notes and frequent difficulty with the cruelly high tessitura. The intonation, uncertain at times, again indicates problems with support. However, musical expression and acting through the voice remain riveting. The range of emotion is paralleled in the striking variety of phrasing: interrupted lines are succeeded by strong, driving legato. At the age of twenty-three, Renata Scotto as Glauce sings with purity and delicacy of tone, as well as superb technical control.

The September 1959 recording of *La Gioconda* shows Callas at her greatest as a singing actress. It also gives the lie to the conventional wisdom that her voice was consistently failing by this time. In spite of difficulties – some top notes are forced to the point of unpleasantness – a great many vocal resources remain available to her. Again, without proper technique, those resources could never have been exploited. The 'Suicidio' and the subsequent scene with Enzo are hair-raising, with the unabashed full-out chest voice at 'Or piombo esausta fra le tenebre!' completely controlled, suggesting a maddening degree of pain. The sudden shifts from one emotion to the next are horrifyingly believable. Callas is a terrified little girl at 'Vergine Santa, allontana il demonio' – and a lunatic soubrette at 'Vo' farmi più gaia'. Votto conducts with empathy and imagination.

In the realm of singing Callas, to many opera lovers the greatest of post-war divas, held the Scala stage, even if her vocal problems grew more troubling and even if her leading men were not always a match for her. Extraordinary supporting casts, especially mezzos, shared the glory. The noble tradition of Italian opera conducting continued to be upheld, whether by inspired masters or competent journeymen.

The pantheon of Scala singers included Ettore Bastianini, who had made a very early debut as a bass in Ravenna in 1945, aged only twenty-three. By 1952 he had shifted to baritone and in the 1953–54 Scala season made his Milan debut as Eugene Onegin. In the part of Alfio in the Erede recording of *Cavalleria rusticana* in 1957, Bastianini has a virile, aggressive, growly sound, which he uses with considerable judiciousness.

Among leading Scala mezzos, Fedora Barbieri also made her debut in her extreme youth. Born in 1920, she first sang opera twenty years later at Florence as Fidalma in *Il Matrimonio segreto*. As Amneris in the 1955 Serafin *Aida* she allows a seductive womanliness free rein in her Act One duet with Radames, 'Quale insolita gioia'. While her instrument answers to almost any demand of emotion or dynamic, the tone is slightly inflexible. The rich mezzo lacks all bite; the civilised, rounded sound is in stark contrast to Callas's sharply cleaving tone. Where Callas drives through the vocal line, Barbieri's tendency is to light on a word to illuminate feeling.

Fiorenza Cossotto's Scala debut came in 1957 as Soeur Mathilde in Poulenc's *Les Dialogues des Carmélites*. Although she was only twenty-four in the 1959 *Gioconda* recording, and not yet a mature singing actress, her 'Voce di donna o d'angelo' was vocally outstanding. The sound was big, clear and rich in overtones. Cossotto would go on to become one of the star mezzos of the post-war era and a renowned interpreter of Verdi.

Composer Francesco Siciliani was named artistic director at La Scala from the 1957–58 season. He remained in the position until 1966 and returned to it from 1980 to 1983. Siciliani had previously been artistic director at the San Carlo in Naples (1940–48) and for the Maggio Musicale (1948–57). He was considered a knowledgeable musician who took care to uphold the musical standard. During this period, when a surfeit of fine voices and conductors was available in Italy, the standard was relatively easy to maintain.

At the same time that Ghiringhelli's administration was focusing on artistic excellence, Ghiringhelli was also eager to 'democratise' the theatre and make it more comfortable for opera goers. In 1955 foyers for the balconies were constructed. In the following year a new lobby and foyer were built for patrons sitting in the orchestra seats. A publicity release from the theatre congratulated itself for having added those public spaces. It spoke of 'carrying through work that has also an obvious social significance'.[22] At a time when Italy had a mixed economy and the government followed a fairly progressive social policy, La Scala's democratisation made the House more accessible to a wider public. Towards the end of the decade, however, the House began to suffer financially. In an interview on 22 February 1959 Ghiringhelli pointed out that the Scala season had been extended an extra month that year for economic reasons. The projected total admission for the season was half a million paid tickets. The House, he said, needed to be full each and every night to help reduce the deficit.

Ghiringhelli was also concerned over the administrative future of La Scala. In the same interview he spoke of his concerns about personal relations among staff and the social function of opera in the community. On the first point he stated, 'We have reached the point where we have to close our ranks tight or we lose everything we have won to date. The opera staff must have an esprit de corps, all for one, one for all. Times have changed. . . . The era of great names is gone. Our strength lies in group work, in good ensembles and competent technicians.' It must be noted that Ghiringhelli engaged star performers who would add lustre to the House, even when he sought to build up the ensemble. He also feared social friction unless the make-up of the audience was extended to include more working-class music lovers. 'We must be in contact with the factories. . . . We must get families of workers into [the boxes], people who are related through their jobs or their factory, who will meet in those boxes the way members of the same family used to meet there. Except that today Mother Factory should buy and distribute tickets.'[23]

The Scala management were also keen to channel funds towards developing new voices for the House. Ghiringhelli had established the Scala's school for young singers in 1946, the year the theatre was reopened. At that time the course was two years long, but was reorganised to three years as a 'School of Perfection' in 1951. It was also set up to channel graduates to careers as contracted Scala singers. From 1953 to 1956 the 'Cadetti della Scala' programme trained singers in repertoire drawn from eighteenth- and nineteenth-century works. The scale of these pieces suited a smaller stage and the roles fitted youthful, still-developing voices. When the Piccola Scala was founded it absorbed the best of the Cadetti, and the whole idea of the Cadetti began to be obsolete. Later the 'School of Perfection' was re-established and the graduate singers were again funnelled to the main Scala stage.

Ghiringhelli's concern to reach a wider public was shared by all leading Houses, and the exploitation of a new medium, television, was to play its part in the efforts to bring in new audiences. On 24 April 1954, a few months after television broadcasting began in Italy, the first opera was seen on the small screen. Giulini conducted *Il Barbiere di Siviglia*, with a cast including Rolando Panerai, Nicola Monti and Franco Calabrese. Direction was by Franco Enriquez. In these early days of the medium, the singers were pretending to sing to a previously recorded tape. Despite this severe technical limitation, William Weaver in *Opera* felt the dramatic effect was positive: 'In Enriquez's first [televised] productions the singers were all good actors and, thanks to careful training, were able to give the impression of spontaneity.'[24] Other television operas were crudely lip-synced, however, and remote cameras transmitted performances from inside La Scala only infrequently. Television broadcasting of opera still had far to go before it could be a bridge for those Italians who could not attend live performances.

At the same time La Scala sought to reach out to wider audiences, it found the time to mount several newly composed operas. In 1956 it officially commissioned an important work, one which has found its way into the standard repertoire: Francis Poulenc's *Dialogues des Carmélites*. The original dramatic text – a screenplay by Georges Bernanos – concerned the martyrdom of a group of Compiègne nuns during the French Revolution. Bernanos's mystical orientation was taken up by Poulenc, who began composing the work in 1953. Claudio Sartori in *Opera* found the score tasteful and refined but monotonous: 'The text, in fact, is too rich in its own sense of theatre and literary vitality to be fulfilled by this rather indifferent musical portrayal.'[25] Massimo Mila had faint praise for Poulenc's inventiveness: His 'music is generally melodious, but does not produce great melodies.'[26] The recitatives are indeed somewhat utilitarian and they owe rather too much to Mussorgsky – a debt which Poulenc acknowledged in the score. Later critics and audiences have been kinder to the *Carmélites*, appreciating the sincerity and effectiveness of the writing, if not its originality, and enjoying the dramatic power of the libretto. The work was quickly taken up by most other international Houses. Paris and San Francisco produced it later in 1957, Covent Garden opened its production in January 1958, and the Vienna State Opera gave it eleven performances in 1958 and fourteen in 1959–60. The Metropolitan Opera staged it only in 1977, after Rudolf Bing had retired.

In 1958 Ildebrando Pizzetti closed a series of works, today seldom performed, with his *Assassinio nella cattedrale*; the libretto was by the composer and Alberto Castelli after T. S. Eliot's verse drama. Sartori wrote, 'There is now a new maturity and mastery in musical speech which allows Pizzetti more sincere expression and lyrical expansion together with more natural writing. The public has appreciated the composer's abandonment of academicism and has welcomed the new score with true enthusiasm.'[27] While agreeing that the writing was unusually fine, Massimo Mila found the dramatic aspect of the opera rather static, just as Eliot's original text had been.

It was not, however, new repertoire that signalled a golden age for La Scala in the late 1950s, it was Luchino Visconti who brought to the staging of opera a new vision and a genius for collaboration. Together with Bayreuth, La Scala at this time constituted one of the few venues where opera could be seen, heard and appreciated for what it is, a unity of disparate arts and parts, all of which were brought individually to a high pitch of excellence and presented in their organic relation to each other.

SIX

VIENNA 1955–60
The Advent of Karajan

THE FESTIVE REOPENING of the Vienna State Opera continued through November and early December 1955 with a number of magnificent productions, most of them superbly sung. After the *Fidelio*, the Viennese were treated to a *Don Giovanni* with a dream cast: George London in the name part, Lisa Della Casa as Donna Anna, Sena Jurinac as Donna Elvira, Irmgard Seefried as Zerlina, Erich Kunz as Leporello, Walter Berry as Masetto and Anton Dermota as Don Ottavio. Karl Böhm conducted. The press was for the most part breathlessly enthusiastic, with *Die Presse* lauding Böhm for bringing out the opera's 'inner harmonies and providing the finest of stylistic polish'.[1] Then came Strauss, Böhm's great speciality after Mozart. Alexander Witeschnik recalled Böhm's *Die Frau ohne Schatten* as *unbeschreiblich* (indescribable) in mere words. The orchestra played with 'majestic luminous power'.[2]

The standard of the first few performances after the reopening could not be sustained. Subject to bouts of alternating enthusiasm and cynicism, the Viennese are often ready to turn into opera maniacs – *Opernnarren* – and then find the object of their mania has disappointed them. They eagerly savaged the very institution they had taxed themselves so heavily to rebuild. Marcel Prawy summed up the situation:

> The weeks after the gala was over were, therefore, a distinctly
> lean period. The gala performances had been planned well in
> advance, but now the Vienna Opera's 'own' admirable producer
> Josef Witt was saddled with the thankless task of transferring
> the repertoire productions from the Theater an der Wien. Most
> of them did not travel well. Furthermore, many of the stars

decamped after the gala performances, and at the repertoire performances some of the casts were distressingly poor. Some of these performances were advertised as 'new productions', which was an exaggeration, to say the least. Others were billed as 'special productions at increased prices of admission'.[3]

The young British critic Andrew Porter, visiting Vienna after the gala, was similarly glum: 'No performance that I saw could be deemed a living and total re-creation of a work of art.' Porter detected an 'almost complete poverty of ideas'.[4]

Clearly Viennese opera needed a strong leader with competence and vision. Although British record and television producer John Culshaw, among others, cites Vienna gossip as predicting a victory for Karajan, it nonetheless seemed natural that Böhm would be offered the position of Generalmusikdirektor and natural that he would accept it.[5] Böhm had filled the position from 1943 until 1945, and for nearly a decade before that time had been musical head at the Dresden Opera, where he had replaced Fritz Busch, who had left Germany and gone on to Glyndebourne before the war. Böhm's five-year contract in Vienna took effect from 1 September 1954. Not merely a consummate technician, Karl Böhm also had a penetrating musical understanding and the gift of communicating to the orchestra, simply and briefly, the essence of that understanding. Besides his Mozart, Böhm was well known for his premieres of Strauss operas and his devotion to new music in general. He believed in taking up the cause of 'any new work which is seriously and competently written'.[6] His idea of operatic performance for Vienna sounded appealing on paper.

> ... I take the view that, rather than on the basis of a one-time festival evening, the general level of a great opera house must be defined according to ongoing high quality. Only on this basis can we build up an ensemble and draw up a permanent plan of operatic presentation. With the closing of the opera festival on 5 December our task is far from complete. Now the real opera season begins, which, built on the same foundations as the festival, must make of everyday opera a festive experience.[7]

Even with his almost ideal credentials and experience, and with the best of intentions concerning solid quality in day-to-day performances,

Böhm quickly came to grief. His practice turned out to be the opposite of his theory. He was absent from Vienna during the running-in period, a crucial time for him as well as for the rebuilt House. Böhm was sorely missed and audiences agonised. Other conductors were unable to approach his standard. Productions were spoiled by dull routine. One interpretation placed the blame for his absences on the carping of the Viennese audiences. Even darker rumours were circulated about Böhm being a stalking horse for Karajan, who, it was said, was waiting to take over the job he had missed out on.

Böhm took sick leave beginning on 23 December 1955. The press had little difficulty tracking him down in Berlin, where, far from bedridden, he was conducting the Berlin Philharmonic. From that point on, wrote Joseph Wechsberg, in Vienna for *Opera* magazine, 'the artistic level of the performances dropped continuously and reached a deplorable low in January [1956], two months after the opening!'[8] Singers also took ill, leaving the House frequently starless and on the verge of embarrassment in the vocal field. This after Böhm had assured Wechsberg in a letter of May 1955, 'The ensemble will be so built up that first-class casts will be possible at all times.'[9] Most ominous of all, the incomparable Vienna Philharmonic, functioning as the House orchestra, began to play 'with less sensuous tone than usual'.[10] A call appeared in the Viennese press for Böhm's resignation.

On 28 February 1956 Böhm returned from America, where he had conducted the Chicago Symphony in a series of concerts. His press statement at the airport infuriated the Viennese opera lovers. He told the press: 'I have no intention of sacrificing my career to the Vienna Opera.' Böhm had been taking full advantage of his potential to achieve international fame, but he had not reckoned with the injured pride of the Staatsoper audiences. On 1 March, when he mounted the podium of the Staatsoper to conduct *Fidelio*, he was booed. He resigned the directorship the following day, charging that the booing had been staged by 'hooligans'.

Franz Endler, a Viennese music critic, an associate of Karajan's and one of his biographers, faulted Böhm for ignoring the warning signs. Endler suggests that Böhm's absences from Vienna displayed a certain naivety. And in a subtly sinister allusion to the struggles of Austrian cultural politics, Marcel Prawy suggests Karajan had been in the running for the job some time before Böhm resigned: 'I can recall many enjoyable conversations with Ernst Marboe, head of the State Theatres Administration, during the 1955–56 season. Many of them took place on the way out to Hinterbrühl, where Marboe used to enjoy kicking a football about with his children and his friend, the bass singer Ljubomir Pantscheff. The name Herbert von Karajan kept cropping up again and again.'[11] In conversations with Marboe and with the Ministers of Finance and Education Karajan set out his plans for the Staatsoper. They included collaborative productions with La Scala and performances of non-German operas in the original language. Endler states that the officials were convinced Karajan would provide excellent evenings for the Staatsoper, the nation's newly reconstructed artistic flagship, the beloved symbol of Austrian cultural hegemony. And they knew he would not come cheap: 'Billig wird's nicht,' they told themselves.[12]

After a brief interregnum Herbert von Karajan was named *künstlerischer Leiter* (artistic leader) of the Vienna State Opera. His title suggested he would not concern himself with administration. Indeed, Egon Seefehlner, a member of the Böhm regime, was named 'general secretary' to accomplish that task. Karajan was given a three-year contract.[13] At the outset he declined to commit himself to spend a certain amount of time each year in Vienna, since his presence could not be quantified in 'cold calendar terms of weeks and months'.[14] While heading the Vienna Opera, Karajan would simultaneously be acting as lifetime head conductor of the Berlin Philharmonic, permanent conductor of London's Philharmonia Orchestra, permanent 'concert director' of the Gesellschaft der Musikfreunde in Vienna, and head of the Salzburg Festival. He would also be maintaining a relationship with La Scala.

Having reintroduced German opera to Italy, bringing Italian opera to Austria, and conquering Berlin and Salzburg, Karajan would dominate European opera. Vienna, restored to the prominence it deserved, would be the greatest prize of all. But would Karajan be tempted to repeat Böhm's habit of absenting himself from the Staatsoper? He assured the citizens that he would conduct some forty to fifty performances annually and achieve a consistent standard of excellence. He also promised to bring in world-class guest conductors.

On 13 June 1956 Karajan began a brilliant series of performances of his *Lucia* imported from Milan. The box office queue began to form twenty-four hours in advance of the opening. Squally on her top notes, Callas nevertheless acted the title part superbly, with Di Stefano and Rolando Panerai as the male principals. The sextet was applauded for an encore. A reviewer suggested that Karajan's purpose may have been to 'show up lamentable shortcomings in home performances'.[15] Three days after the *Lucia* opening, the Staatsoper concluded an agreement with La Scala according to which singers, conductors and productions would be exchanged between the two Houses.

Karajan succeeded in obtaining a handsome addition to the Staatsoper's government subsidy, raising it to an annual total of $4 million. Although he maintained, 'Money does not interest me,'[16] he reportedly drew a monthly salary of 6,000 schillings as musical head. In addition, he was paid 18,000 schillings for every performance he conducted.[17] Even so, he would not agree to meet Callas's fee of $2,500 after her *Lucia* performances. Callas did not sing with him again, nor ever again in Austria.

For some time after the marvellous *Lucia* Karajan was not sighted in Vienna. The shortcomings that had been felt in the House when Böhm was absent were now even more glaring. Karajan had made no provision for a deputy 'artistic leader' while he was away. The redoubtable fans of the fourth gallery, who felt they constituted the House's artistic conscience, published a mimeographed sheet of opera criticism which monitored performances. Their work was cut out for them. The ship was rudderless. In a new production of *Tannhäuser* the tenor, Rudolf Lustig, gave what was by most accounts a dreadful performance, one 'which would not have even done credit to a small provincial theatre'.[18] The fourth gallery began booing. After the last curtain these self-appointed guardians of greatness chased poor Lustig round the opera building, from the stage door to the other side of the Ring, where he collapsed. Memories were raised of Nazi behaviour. By way of protest the other singers refused to take curtain calls for five days.

Standards remained low. No conductor of note arrived as a guest. The Vienna Philharmonic were on tour in the United States, leaving Staatsoper performances to be played by substitutes. Wechsberg, despairing, wrote, 'The last-ditch substitutes carry on with more courage than ability. Some nights one isn't sure which is worse: the notes that the musicians played or the ones they missed.'[19] He also noted mistaken entrances and exits, curtains coming down early, and commented on 'minor characters who 'steal scenes by cabaret methods'.[20] *Schlamperei* (sloppiness) had become the order of the day. Wechsberg observed a certain consistency: several opera goers fell asleep during each of several performances.

The problem of artistic quality that troubled the Staatsoper during the second half of the decade had a different origin than at the Metropolitan. Whereas Rudolf Bing sought to bring the House standard up from relative mediocrity, Karajan wanted maximum personal visibility and the conditions which would allow him to conduct breathtaking performances at a place where greatness could be coaxed from guest stars and existing personnel. Vienna provided him with a platform for further fame. He has been termed the sole owner and proprietor of 'Karajan's Worldwide Musical Activities, Inc.'. At the same time he brought lustre to the Staatsoper when he was present there. After the brief period of heavy international travel at the beginning of his tenure he curtailed his schedule abroad – for a time – and devoted his energies to the House. This move earned him critical approval for taking 'a gratifying interest in the Vienna branch of his empire'.[21]

Karajan's first new productions showed him in typical form. He insisted on staging his *Walküre* as well as conducting it. Before opening night he was said – in Viennese rumour, probably exaggerated – to have had twenty-five lighting rehearsals. The rebuilt Vienna auditorium had new lighting boards and instruments, which helped him realise his intentions. In fact, lighting came to be Karajan's stock in trade as a stage director. Relying on it to establish atmosphere, he relegated to second place helping actors to portray character and interact with each other. Prawy described his methods at this period:

> To Karajan, production means interpreting the music by technical media. He orders a seemingly endless sequence of rehearsals so as to work out a detailed lighting pattern for the entire work. Bar by bar, infinitely subtle nuances of lighting are devised, and to co-ordinate them with the music at rehearsals

Karajan usually has recourse to tape recordings of the work in question, conducted by himself of course, with extras acting as stand-ins. The singers are drilled at piano rehearsals and on the rehearsal stage; only relatively late do they attend rehearsals on the main stage, where the first thing they do is learn to co-ordinate their movements to 'their' light.[22]

Hearing *Walküre*, Wechsberg strongly approved of Karajan's 'flowing, soft approach' to Wagner. Karajan knew the score so well, Wechsberg wrote, that he dared 'to conduct by heart'. He added, 'he knows how to extract magnificent sound from the beautifully playing Philharmoniker. The score becomes transparent, the instrumental groups are clearly distinguished, the phrases sung out, and the transitions never abrupt.'[23] Karajan also dared conduct *Otello* in Italian and cast Mario Del Monaco as the Moor. This was a double heresy in conservative Vienna. At that time the supremacy of the German language was unquestioned, even in Verdi. Restraint and decorum were also held up as supreme virtues. 'K' was banishing sloppiness in favour of 'a welcome polish throughout and ruthless discipline'.[24] Even Del Monaco, who in other Houses generally declaimed his way through the part, was forced to adhere to the composer's indications. Tickets were three times the normal price. Even so, every seat was sold and the black market was feverishly active.

Karajan gave Vienna – and Salzburg as well – authoritative Italian opera performances, as he had given Milan authoritative German opera performances. This he did without neglecting Wagner. His first Vienna *Ring*, of 1957–60, has been deemed finer than his Verdi and Puccini. Whether or not Vienna had found her saviour in Karajan, she had an outstanding conductor.

Karajan's 1958 Salzburg *Don Carlos* was, fortunately, recorded for Austrian radio. He lets his generally excellent singers get on with the job, accompanying with sympathy, modesty and precision. Although Giulini's performance of the same opera in London has a dynamic pulse which this recording lacks, Karajan's performance can scarcely be called Teutonic. He is true to Verdi's style, if not to the score, which is much abbreviated. Ettore Bastianini, at his peak, is singing Posa. The voice is dark and gruff but without roughness, and with exciting idiomatic accents on the line – and at times, unpleasant aspirations as well. As King Philip, Cesare Siepi is arguably unmatchable, even by Christoff. 'Ella giammai m'amò' builds up in awful awareness from beginning to end, with the bass rather than the conductor taking the lead. Sena Jurinac's Elisabetta has a glorious upper-middle register that melts, glows and melts again. Her involved portrayal is suffused with sadness, especially in the last act, when she shows herself the consummate singing actress she could be.

During this period few young singers made their mark at the Staatsoper. However, an important debut came when Böhm engaged mezzo-soprano Christa Ludwig at the House in 1955. Born in Berlin in 1928 (according to one authority, in 1924), both her parents were professional singers. In 1946, while studying singing with her mother and with Felicie Hüni-Mihaček of the Munich Opera, she made her debut as Orlovsky in Frankfurt. At about the same time as her first performances in Vienna she was offered a contract at EMI by Walter Legge. Legge significantly advanced her career by persuading Karajan to accept her as Octavian in his recording of *Rosenkavalier*. He likewise convinced Klemperer to conduct her as Leonore in his *Fidelio* recording.

Even with a generous budget and the magnificent resources of the Staatsoper at his disposal, especially the orchestra and chorus, Karajan could not achieve his desire for perfection. The realities of operatic production and performance make for compromise and gradual improvement rather than consistent splendour. The scarcity of new singers meant that Karajan could not maintain uniformly high standards night after night. By this time established stars were no longer tightly linked with specific Houses, as they had been before and just after the war. As they flew from engagement to engagement, from continent to continent, their fees were inevitably increasing. These mundane realities lay behind Karajan's reluctance to remain faithful to the Staatsoper podium. In 1988, a year or so before his death, he confessed, concerning this period:

> When I finally left Vienna, it was not at all clear yet what had really happened. Today I know that the standards of artistic practice which I held up before myself at that time could not possibly be realised in an opera house staging works in repertoire. When one is focusing above all upon an ideal situation

in which every evening of opera must be a sensation, then one is raising a demand which is incapable of fulfilment. There are not enough sensational singers in the world for even a unique opera house to perform night after night at the highest level. Already in the search for a third sensational tenor one must come to grief.[25]

Karajan's attention began to turn to Salzburg as a venue for the sort of excellence he sought to create. In the framework of an annual festival, without the obligations of performing a repertoire, he could programme the operas he wished and lure stars to perform them. The cachet of the Salzburg Festival, with its high ticket prices, wealthy audiences and media attention, also appealed to his instincts for self-promotion.

After considerable controversy over the advisability of constructing a new festival theatre in Salzburg, the proponents of art prevailed over those who felt Austria's social needs took precedence. The new Grosses Festspielhaus, built at great expense, was opened for the 1960 season. It reflected the plans and expectations of Karajan, the festival's artistic director. Technical specifications were, and remain, impressive. The stage was at the time the world's largest, its seventy-foot depth having been achieved by blasting out a portion of the rocky hill behind it. The width was no less than 120 feet. The architect, Clemens Holzmeister, made certain the lighting and stage machinery were as up to date and flexible as possible. The orchestra pit can be raised and lowered, and the proscenium arch varied in size and shape. The auditorium can be quickly and easily reshaped into a concert hall. The acousticians who worked at the rebuilt Staatsoper took responsibility for Salzburg's new theatre as well. Karajan liked the results: 'perfect for Mozart, an intimate sound in spite of the size of the auditorium'.[26] Many other musicians and critics, however, faulted the acoustics and the chilly, impersonal feeling of the Salzburg hall. The opening production, conducted by Karajan, was *Rosenkavalier*, an opera which made relatively few demands on the technical aspects of the new House during its running-in period. The Salzburg summer festival lasts scarcely a month, from late July until late August of each year. To provide it with a grand new venue, in addition to the already existing halls known as the Kleines Festspielhaus and the Felsenreitschule, meant that Austrian music was intended to be at the forefront of the world. And at the forefront of Austrian music stood Karajan.

While Bing remoulded the Met to his specifications and Karajan strode from peak to peak of acclaim, Walter Felsenstein was quietly laying the groundwork for the stage directors of the future in the operatic backwater of the Komische Oper, East Berlin. His revolutionary 1959 production of *Otello* at the Komische Oper was quite different from anything being mounted at the time in New York, London, Milan or Vienna. Felsenstein completely rewrote the German translation of the text, by Boito after Shakespeare. He also had the forestage extended at the price of half covering the orchestra pit, thus enabling intimate scenes to be played in close proximity to the audience. The orchestral sound was reported by Horst Koegler, the *Opera* critic, to be, at times 'rather thin, indeed'.[27] Felsenstein's direction of Verdi's masterwork had the effect of revealing character, motivation, conflict and feeling to an unparalleled degree; the intensity of the theatrical experience was at times even painful. Rudolf Heinrich's designs radiated 'a spaciousness and magnitude which is extremely powerful and completely in harmony with the strong Venetian flavour of the whole production. The Venetian character is further emphasised through the wonderful costumes, make-up and hairstyle, which seem to come straight out of Botticelli.'[28] Koegler was transfixed by the show, which he called 'the greatest ... experience I have ever had during twenty years of opera going'.[29] Felsenstein's work at the Komische Oper provided opera staging with one of its most exciting and influential directions in the post-war years. It also helped give birth to a new generation of stage directors who – contrary to Karajan's way of working – began to displace the conductor's dominance in the process of production.

If Felsenstein was one of the few revolutionaries in a conservative artistic genre, Karajan made opera fascinating. His personal glamour and artistic achievements brought him to the level of an international cultural icon. Closer to home, he gave the Viennese the satisfaction that their city could once again be the venue for extraordinary musical performances.

SEVEN

THE MET 1951–59
Bing Rampant

RUDOLF BING, a no less obsessive and prickly individual than Karajan, was determined to remedy the weaknesses of the Johnson regime and reclaim the House's international position. On 8 December 1949, during his 'observation year', he told the Board that he intended to widen the basis of the House's public support and bring in more young people by changing the system of subscription. Instead of one subscription offering eighteen performances, there would be two of nine in which some of the operas would be repeated. He hoped that the reduced cost and greater availability of the subscriptions would bring in between five or six thousand more people each season. The new system was announced to the press by Bing who explained that it would also enable a 'fairly drastic reduction' in the number of operas performed each season and thus radically improve the artistic quality of the stagings. Fewer operas performed would mean an increase in the amount of rehearsal time for each production. Top artists such as Bjoerling and Warren would be available for longer periods. Boris Christoff would be appearing for the first time at the Met, and Flagstad would be returning to sing Isolde. There would also be 'more contemporary ideas with regard to scenery and staging'.[1]

Bing reflected the conditions he had to deal with once his observation year was over.

> The more I learned about the technical resources of the Metropolitan, the more alarmed I became. The auditorium was of course one of the glories of the world – that deep Diamond Horseshoe that gave the box holders, who had once owned the house, an opportunity to look at each other unrivaled in any other opera

house anywhere. But the depth of the Horseshoe meant an immense number of side seats that had limited views of the stage, and the public areas were seriously inadequate for those who were not members of the Metropolitan Opera Guild or the Metropolitan Opera Club, which had their own exclusive spaces. . . .

Behind the proscenium and its golden curtain, however, the theater had nothing at all to recommend it. Everything backstage was cramped and dirty and poor. There were neither side stages nor a rear stage: every change of scene had to be done from scratch on the main stage itself, which meant that if an act had two scenes, the audience had just to sit and wait, wondering what the banging noises behind the curtain might mean . . .

Dressing rooms were inadequate – and had to be used during the day for coaching sessions, because of the lack of rehearsal space. (The chorus rehearsed in the public bar!) A single roof stage had to be used for both orchestral rehearsals and dramatic rehearsals, alternately. Not that there was any overwhelming demand for rehearsal facilities. New productions were scarce (there were only two of them during my observation year, and that was more than the house had seen in most recent seasons), and repeats from last year received few ensemble rehearsals. When casts were changed, which happened very frequently, the newcomers might do their individual scenes with a coach and with such of the holdovers as deigned to attend.[2]

Bing set to work with laudable energy. He determined to make a real impact in the area of staging, seriously neglected under Johnson. He found new donors for the much needed new productions. He retired the worn-out, old-fashioned sets and replaced them with solid structures with multiple elevations. As announced, he cut the number of operas presented in the first season by about one-third, thus giving more time for musical rehearsals for each one. He succeeded in persuading international stars to give more time to the Met. Björling increased the number of his annual performances almost tenfold – to twenty, from a previous average of two or three. Bing's attention to everyday detail was similarly constructive. He fired memos at each and every miscreant. The orchestra manager was informed that the players must rise upon the conductor's entering the pit. The assistant stage manager was berated over the ragged condition of the caged canary in *Pagliacci*.

Most important, professional discipline was raised to a level more appropriate to a great opera house. Star singers could no longer decide where – and even whether – they might rehearse, as Traubel and Melchior had done in Johnson's day. House rules were declared sacred for all. Star baritone Robert Merrill was suspended for a season when he accepted a Hollywood contract, thereby reneging on his commitment to participate in the Met tour. Adherence to schedules made for tighter performances. Bing hired men who would run the House in his own more efficient style. Horace Armistead was given the task of trying to 'tame the wild dragons of the technical staff, the stage crews, and the physical productions they manipulated (or manhandled)'.[3] John Gutman, a musicologist and before 1933 a music critic in Berlin, had been an old friend of Bing from the days before the war in Europe. In 1950 Bing named him assistant manager. Gutman translated libretti into English, interpreted the Italian of Signor Meneghini (Callas's husband) for Rudolf Bing, negotiated with music publishers, radio and television networks, and auditioned singers. He eventually came to head the Metropolitan Opera Studio for young performers. Bing paid tribute to Gutman: 'For almost twenty-three years he was available for help in any emergency; and in the early years, when there were plenty of emergencies, he was invaluable.'[4] Given Bing's authoritarian personality, it was inevitable that there would be few if any hold-overs from the Johnson era in high administrative positions. St Leger had to move on and staff conductor Max Rudolf was brought in as his replacement as 'music administrator'. Bing recalled, 'St Leger was the symbol of the old regime. To a much greater extent than I would want from an artistic administrator, he rather than the general manager was really running the Metropolitan. He was an older man than I and would expect to tell me what could and could not be done. Under the circumstances, I decided not to retain him.'[5] However, Bing did not name a chief conductor or music director for the Met.

Bing's tenure had an average of three new productions each year. His first season, 1950–51, had four. He opened with a new *Don Carlos*, conducted by Fritz Stiedry. Tyrone Guthrie, approached in London to direct, was unavailable, and Margaret Webster was chosen instead. Rolf Gérard designed the sets. Bing was proud of his tightfistedness with fees for directors and principals, writing:

> What we had to offer [Webster], unfortunately, was nothing but an exciting opportunity: her total fee for directing *Don Carlo*, including expenses, was $2,500. Rolf Gérard agreed to design the sets and costumes, months of work for so lavish an opera, for $4000. Including these fees, and extra payments for rehearsals, I budgeted *Don Carlo* at $65,000, which Mrs Nin Ryan raised, as I have recounted, by selling one of the family Rembrandts. This production, which several members of the board considered desperately extravagant (it did run over budget), must now be counted one of the bargains of operatic history: counting the performances in my final season, the Metropolitan has done this *Don Carlo* more than eighty times. . . .[6]

The cast was superb, even though Boris Christoff could not come to sing King Philip II because, as a citizen of a Soviet-bloc country, Bulgaria, the provisions of the anti-Communist McCarran Act kept him from being admitted to the United States. Cesare Siepi, making his Met debut, was his replacement. Also taking part in what Kolodin described as an 'excellently integrated vocal ensemble'[7] were Björling as Carlo, Merrill as Rodrigo, Jerome Hines as the Grand Inquisitor, the Argentine soprano Delia Rigal as Elisabetta di Valois and Fedora Barbieri as Eboli. A British critic described Barbieri's Eboli as 'rather coarse-grained and punchy'. He warmly praised Siepi, however. 'In his first appearances his voice was a bit muffled – though "Ella giammai m'amò" won an opening-night ovation – but as time went on his delivery came to seem quite natural, as he learned to cope with the special acoustical problems of the house.'[8] Stiedry, Bing's friend and ally in obtaining the Met post, had had considerable experience in New York and in Europe, and was recognised as extremely competent, but was not quite the top-class artist one would have expected Bing to choose to lead such an important production. In Bing's own words, Stiedry 'was an outstanding personality and musician, though not a great conductor'.[9] Press reviews stressed Bing's taste, experience and good judgement in putting the show together. Most of all, the Bing *Don Carlos* stood the test of time. Another reviewer, James Hinton, seeing the production late in 1954, praised it as 'the most impressive at the Metropolitan'. It was, he wrote, 'Planned and executed with the greatest care, it served both as a kind of down-payment on promises and a statement of future policy. It also set an artistic standard – or, at least, achieved a unanimity of praise – that has not quite been equalled by any production since.'[10]

A recorded performance of *Don Carlos* on 6 November 1950 largely bears out Bing's assessment of Stiedry. The orchestra and chorus are well rehearsed and carefully controlled. But Stiedry's pacing is uncertain, his tempi are sometimes inflexible, and he lacks an imaginative understanding of this great music. Björling and Merrill in particular surpass their maestro, singing the grand third scene of Act One with passion, conviction and glorious, ringing, virile tone. Siepi's King Philip is another memorable vocal interpretation of a tragic figure. For Siepi's 'Ella giammai m'amò' Stiedry rises to the occasion, eliciting a nearly human expressiveness from the strings. But Fedora Barbieri's Eboli has problems with strained high notes, and lines in 'O don fatale' are spat out with a vehemence foreign to the character and to Verdi. Rigal, an Argentinian lirico-spinto, sings Elisabetta's big moments with frequently pushed tone – a bad habit that would curtail her career. But her scene with Björling at the close of the opera is vocally admirable and dramatically sublime.

Besides the *Don Carlos*, Bing brought three other new productions to the Met in his first year: *Der fliegende Holländer*, *Fledermaus* and *Cavalleria rusticana/Pagliacci*. *Holländer* was beset by cancellations. Robert Edmond Jones, hired to do the sets, left the production. Ljuba Welitsch bowed out of the role of Senta. Mihály Szekely, scheduled to sing Daland, was not allowed to leave his native Hungary by the Communist authorities. However, Hans Hotter's debut as the Dutchman was warmly acclaimed, with the German bass-baritone praised for his acting abilities as well as his voice.

A 'centrepiece', as Bing himself termed it, of his first season was a new *Die Fledermaus*. Bing's idea was to select an opera that would have popular appeal and stage it to enhance its popular aspect. In a daringly original decision, he asked Broadway lyricist Howard Dietz to provide an English translation of Strauss's operetta. He wanted Rouben Mamoulian to direct, but Mamoulian had undertaken a new Broadway project. Then, Bing recalled, 'Someone proposed Garson Kanin, who came to my office with his splendid wife Ruth Gordon to tell me that the whole idea was nonsense, he knew nothing of operas and opera houses, but ultimately agreed to take on the job.'[11] Kolodin considered that some of Bing's hiring decisions were made in order to gain press coverage. For example, during the controversy over the new *Fledermaus* it was reported that the comedian Danny Kaye had been approached to play the speaking part of the jailer Frosch. Kolodin was horrified: 'Was this the kind of front-page play which could regularly be expected from Bing's Metropolitan?'[12] But nothing could stifle Bing's pride in his new show. Years later Garson Kanin recalled, '. . . I remember that Bing used to come to almost every rehearsal. One day I came and sat beside him, and he was just simply kvelling [Yiddish for drooling with pride] over it – and he was sort of conducting.'[13] Cast member Patrice Munsel remembered, 'Oh, he would conduct in every performance. With a banana, always with a banana.'[14] Ljuba Welitsch did show up at last as Rosalinde, and Patrice Munsel was delightful as Adele giving a 'fresh and pert characterisation, splendidly under control in every aspect of acting technique.'[15] Eugene Ormandy conducted the opening night, in a rare departure from his work with symphony orchestras. 'Eugene Ormandy, called in as guest conductor for the *Fledermaus* first night, whipped the orchestra into a state of brilliance, but some listeners complained that his interpretation was not *echt* Viennese.'[16]

Bing approached Italian film director Vittorio de Sica to stage *Cavalleria rusticana* and *Pagliacci*. De Sica, who worked in a gritty realist style, was then famous worldwide for films such as *Bicycle Thieves*, which depicted the sordidness of post-war Italian life. De Sica turned down the offer, thus depriving Met audiences of a meeting between cinematic neo-realism and operatic verismo. In the end Horace Armistead's designs for the double bill were savaged by the critics: Olin Downes called it 'the most atrociously inappropriate scenic setting' he had ever seen.[17] The tenor, Richard Tucker, sang 'in green shirt, red tie, fawn-coloured suit, and buckskin shoes'.[18] The season as a whole was criticised for its emphasis on the German repertoire, two highlights of which were a Stiedry *Rheingold* and a Walter *Fidelio*.

Bing's second season, like the first, was on the whole a success. Cecil Smith, writing in *Opera* magazine, gave credit to the conductors, especially Fritz Reiner:

> Musically, every opera profited from the renaissance of the Metropolitan orchestra. I am not sure that I really remember how the orchestra sounded when I first became acquainted with the Metropolitan back in the mid-twenties; but since that time, it is safe to say, such gleaming sounds have never consistently emerged from the pit as those we have heard in the past six months. Largely at the demand of Fritz Reiner, one of the company's staff conductors (the others are Fritz Stiedry, Fausto Cleva and Alberto Erede), many replacements have been made. There is a good deal of young blood in the orchestra, and the men play with precision, balance, singing tone and, on occasion, real virtuosity. The chorus, too, under the stern discipline of Kurt Adler, has become first-class. As the consequences of these improvements in the basic ensembles, every opera this season, whether well or ill cast, has had firm musical outlines and a general air of complete professionalism.[19]

One of the great stage successes of the second season was *Così fan tutte*, directed by the distinguished American actor Alfred Lunt and translated into English. Lunt devised a complex mixture of pictorial tableaux and balletic stage movement in the eighteenth-century manner, as well as finding 'a happy balance among the elements of farce, aristocratic comedy and sentiment'.[20]

Apart from these successful productions in the early Bing era, a number of others were misconceived or aborted. Eager to make changes on the directorial front, the new general manager approached famous directors and designers from Broadway and London's West End. Some, like Margaret Webster, accepted, creating three successful productions of Verdi operas. Others declined, pleading prior commitments. Still others did not understand the special needs of the opera stage. Oliver Smith, also brought in from Broadway, provided the first act of a new *Traviata* with such a colossal staircase that it was hard to imagine that Flora was a mere courtesan, not a railway tycoon. In 1953 the Hollywood director Joseph Mankiewicz staged *Bohème* to broad acclaim. The *Opera* critic found it 'in general comfortingly lively and effective while hewing to traditional lines'.[21] However, one very non-traditional directorial touch which seems to have escaped that critic's notice was Rodolfo's and Mimi's tarrying in the studio at the close of Act One, 'with the obvious intent of consummating their relationship before joining the Christmas Eve merriment at the Café Momus'.[22] For this production Howard Dietz translated the *Bohème* libretto into what many considered an off-brand of English, allowing every other consideration than singability 'to go by the board, including dramatic sense and good taste.'[23]

Continuing money problems at the Met were partly responsible for the absence of a music director. Although fine conductors were available, and were hired for many productions, the vacancy at the top meant fluctuating standards. From time to time Bing made serious attempts to secure the services of outstanding permanent conductors – though not in the role of music director. In late 1950 Bing offered Erich Kleiber $1,000 per week as an absolute maximum for two or three performances per week, but it was clear that Kleiber was not to be engaged as a music director. At the most, wrote Bing, Kleiber 'would be consulted in case of new engagements for orchestra, chorus and solo singers. Though again in these respects I must reserve the right of final decision. . . .'[24] Kleiber wanted $1,000 per performance and a briefer, eight- or ten-week guest engagement. At the same time Bing asked the agent Alfred Diez to sound out Knappertsbusch for the permanent conductor's job, but begged Diez to try to acquire his services more cheaply: 'Also, please do not offer him $1,000 a week. I think I would hope to get him for a little less – say $750–$800.'[25] As staff conductor, Fritz Reiner led 143 performances in his five seasons at the Met (1949–53). He had considerable success in improving the orchestra's playing, but he never appeared there after 1953, when he was named music director of the Chicago Symphony.[26] In that year George Szell returned to the Met, where he had conducted for four years during the Johnson era (1942–46). Szell had been engaged for *Tannhäuser*, but he fell out with Bing and left after only four performances. Press reports suggested he was unhappy over lack of influence in casting decisions. 'Without the authority he considered due him, he was having no more of the Bing monarchy.'[27] The Italian repertoire was covered adequately by Cleva and the Italian-Swiss conductor Alberto Erede. The brilliant Romanian conductor Jonel Perlea had remained for only one season at the Met – the last of Johnson's tenure. Perlea and Bing could not agree on repertoire. Bing held artistic policy decisions very much in his own hands.

Efforts in 1953 to engage Wilhelm Furtwängler for a twelve- to fifteen-week stint failed; the German conductor, old and ill, died in November of the following year. From 1953 to 1955 Rudolf Kempe was also courted as a 'leading conductor' for the House, but proved a difficult catch. Eventually he came to the Met for some two dozen performances, including the *Ring*, but without providing the permanence Bing sought. In 1954 and 1955 Bing worked out an agreement with the Greek-American conductor Dimitri Mitropoulos to conduct regularly at the Met in a wide repertoire of operas, although with the title neither of music director nor of permanent conductor. Mitropoulos is remembered as an intensely dramatic conductor whose readings were sometimes eccentric but seldom boring. Erich Leinsdorf was an authoritative and experienced conductor of opera whom Bing engaged as 'music consultant' from 1957 until 1962. Born in Vienna in 1912, he had been assistant to Toscanini and Bruno Walter at Salzburg from 1934 to 1937 and had conducted a number of German-language operas at the Met from 1938 until 1943. During the year before his consultancy appointment he had been music director at the New York City Opera. His successor there was another Austrian-born musician, Julius Rudel.

Bing's staging successes were reflected in the box office receipts: subscriptions purchased in advance of the season's opening rose from $900,000 in 1949 to $1.4 million the following year. However, his investments in improved standards resulted in an overall deficit for 1950–51 of some $430,000 and, for 1952, of $473,000. The board were increasingly concerned about the House's financial situation. Such was the pressure on Bing that on 27 May 1954 he warned them that although he was 'mindful of the necessity for due economy', he was also responsible for 'the maintenance of artistic standards commensurate with the position of the Metropolitan Opera'. If the Board felt the need for a further drastic economy of operation, 'he was not sure he was the right man to carry out the Board's intentions'.[28]

Mrs August Belmont remained Bing's greatest ally on the Board. Although her 'friends' organisation, the Met Opera Guild, had grown in membership from about 1,300 in the Thirties to some 50,000 in the mid-Fifties, the contributions the Guild amassed were insufficient to cover the deficit. Rising taxes were biting into American private fortunes. New methods of fund-raising were needed. In 1952 Mrs Belmont helped start a new organisation called the National Council of the Metropolitan. Membership cost a great deal more than the Guild: the minimum contribution was $1,000. From the ranks of the National Council individuals and foundations were approached to underwrite new productions. The National Council also supported the Met Auditions scheme to help further the careers of young singers throughout America. This organisation marked a new departure in funding opera in America, and one which would prove crucial in later years for the Met. It set a precedent for wealthy people to contribute to opera rather more generously than they had done previously. Besides Mrs Ryan, Mrs John D. Rockefeller was an outstanding benefactress.

To supplement the work of the Guild and Council, a public appeal in 1952–53 raised $1.5 million, of which $400,000 was earmarked for improvements backstage and in the auditorium. The front-of-house changes were in the nature of an infrastructure investment. Kolodin noted the replacement of 315 orchestra circle fauteuils by 479 orchestra 'seats', meaning leaner-width accommodation for presumably thicker pockets. Another quarter-million of the appeal funds went towards drawing up preliminary plans for a new House, underscoring yet again the decrepitude of the lovely old leviathan with its forests of columns restricting sight lines. It was Bing's idea to raise money for the new House and for a permanent endowment fund by broadcasting Saturday matinée performances over live radio. In a memorandum of 19 December 1952 to Mrs Belmont and key members of the Board he proclaimed that it was

> the time to show the world that the whole American nation rallies to the support of its most important cultural assets: there are an estimated 14,000,000 radio listeners and every one of them should contribute a dollar or more. It should be emphasized that [the present financial needs of the House are] only a trifling part of the stream of money that could come in that

way and if this appeal to the nation succeeds and every radio listener contributes a minimum of one dollar for eighteen enjoyable Saturday afternoons then an enormous endowment fund would be set up which would secure the future of the Metropolitan for decades to come and, indeed, would supply the funds for the new national opera house.[29]

Bing's suggested appeal – which was never aired – reflected the Met's financial plight, which was so serious that in June 1956 it was necessary to borrow $1 million from the Bank of New York in order to assure curtain up in the 1956–7 season.[30] In a 1955 speech to the National Press Club in Washington DC, Bing pointed out that opera houses in West Berlin and Milan received an annual government subsidy of some $1 million, while the American federal government gave not a penny to the Met.

At this singers' Met, the 'Italian wing' was safe in the hands of the American artists Johnson had hired. The Wagnerian singers were the problem. In the spring of 1953 Bing approached Kirsten Flagstad, ignoring the taint of collaboration with the Nazis that had attached to her husband. He argued that 'Miss Flagstad was obviously a non-political person, and the time for punishing her for her husband's misdeeds had ended. . . . Asked by the press to justify my actions, I said simply that the world's greatest soprano should sing in the world's greatest opera house.'[31] Upon being invited by Bing to perform in the 1950–51 *Ring*, Flagstad generously requested that Traubel be kept on. 'She is a very great singer,' Flagstad is quoted as having said, 'and kept Wagner going during my absence. I could not possibly consider being the cause of her being pushed aside.'[32] But a scandal had arisen. Objections were raised in the press to engaging Flagstad on grounds of guilt by association. Bing swore, when listening to her sing, 'I am listening to God.'[33] Even though Flagstad sang a *Ring* and a *Tristan und Isolde* during the 1950–51 season, it was too late to use her to secure the *Fach* of the Wagnerian dramatic soprano. Not until Birgit Nilsson reached the Met stage late in 1959 would Bing have a star to sing Isolde and Brünnhilde whose qualities approached those of Flagstad.

Flagstad in her prime came very close to the then current ideal of the Wagnerian soprano. In an age when singers took stances rather than created roles on the stage, her personal sincerity won over the audience. Lanfranco Rasponi writes, 'With few gestures and the stateliness of a regal figure of ancient times, she dominated the stage and made everyone else around her disappear. As she said to me in [our] interview, "I don't think of acting; I only remember to express the words of the text." '[34] The famous recording of live performances from the Furtwängler Scala *Ring* of March and April 1950 shows Flagstad in her still-luminous twilight. As she told Rasponi, 'I was born with a voice already placed.'[35] Flagstad – with the crucial exception of some high notes – continued from strength to strength. She sang until the age of sixty. Her innate vocal power allowed her to dominate any orchestra ever assembled.

Elisabeth Höngen, who sang opposite Flagstad in the Furtwängler Scala *Ring*, paid tribute to her powers of empathy. 'She had ... the most astonishing vocal force, and at the same time a profound tenderness. There were moments when the instrument gave the impression of almost breaking because of the emotion she felt – do not let anyone ever tell you that she was not a tremendously sensitive human being, for she was, even if she did eat sausages for breakfast!'[36] Rasponi summed up Flagstad:'In my opinion, she was way over and above any other singer I have ever heard. Her voice was unique in its grandeur and flexibility. After a heroic phrase she could utter one of shattering delicacy, almost as if the thread to which it was attached might break off at any second. It never did.'[37]

In the lyric soprano wing, Eleanor Steber was acclaimed in Vienna in 1957 as Tosca. And when the Met finally staged Berg's *Wozzeck* in 1959 she undertook the role of Marie. Her daring paid off. Her 'well-fleshed outlines hardly suggested a Marie mired in poverty, but she made a searing vocal effect in some high-lying passages and humanized the character she performed, especially in the scenes with the child'.[38] Steber's speciality at the Met, however, was Mozart. She sang both Donna Anna and Donna Elvira as no other American soprano of her day could. When Bing took over the House he treated Steber inconsiderately. In 1962 she sang Donna Anna in a dress rehearsal, declining to sing the part in half voice even though she had a cold. In the following two performances she had an attack of nerves which resulted, during the second evening, in her being unable to sing a difficult passage. Bing's punishment was a refusal to speak to Steber until the end of the season. At that point, she recalled that Bing

> said that as long as I couldn't do *Don Giovanni*, he had nothing for me. I was out two seasons. Then he had to call me to replace [Dorothy] Kirsten [in *La Fanciulla del West*] in January 1966. I suppose I was a fool to do it. But he would have had to cancel.

Steber sang Minnie, the name part in the opera, on forty-eight hours' notice. She was given what she remembered as a 'shouting, screaming, stomping' standing ovation.[39]

While fine singing remained the Met's hallmark, a general improvement in musical standards since Bing had led the House is apparent in two recordings of the late 1950s. A fascinating recorded performance of *Otello*, conducted by Cleva on 8 March 1958, with Del Monaco and Victoria de los Angeles, shows the orchestra playing at its very best.

Cleva holds the players tightly to Verdi's subtle indications, while moving briskly through the score at a pace verging at times on breathlessness. The chorus sound positively Italian in their depth of tone, accuracy and fervour. Del Monaco roars his way through the title role, while de los Angeles is the acme of sweetness and light, bringing a wealth of gentle sadness to the 'Willow Song'. Her amalgam of tasteful restraint and emotional freedom is uniquely appealing, and the delicacy of the voice is only enhanced by its golden richness.

Relatively few commercial recordings of Met productions were made during the first decade or so of the Bing era. The *Macbeth* of the 1958–59 season, recorded by RCA under Erich Leinsdorf, is an interesting exception. It too demonstrates the increased musical accomplishments of the Met forces since the 1951 *Pagliacci*. Orchestral attacks are clearer and the balance more coherent. Leinsdorf demonstrates musical intelligence and an understanding of the overall structure of the work. It is hard to imagine him tolerating the musical laxities and vocal excesses of the Johnson House. Bing recalled that the new staging was 'our most expensive production to that date . . . the first to break the $100,000 barrier'.[40]

The Met principals were impressive. As Macbeth, Leonard Warren's tone has gone slightly ragged round the edges since the 1945 *Rigoletto*, but his technique is still dependable, the voice itself ample and far from dry, and expression projected more subtly and intelligently than fourteen years earlier. Leonie Rysanek had made her Met debut as Lady Macbeth in this production when Callas cancelled. Still young at thirty-two, Rysanek's dramatic soprano is solid and free. Carlo Bergonzi sings Macduff with dedication. In his aria, 'O figli miei . . . Ah, la paterna mano', he conjures the maximum of drama from his light voice. Style and understanding are impeccable. The tone is pure, manly and consummately Italian.

Bergonzi sang frequently at the Met, helping to fill a growing gap of first-class tenors. Björling was singing less often, and Bing faced fierce competition from the European houses in fees for singers. In March 1953 he had reported to the Board that it was proving difficult to secure contracts for the 1953–4 season as La Scala was not only offering equal fees but also tax exemption. La Scala also had greater flexibility over scheduling as it did not have to contend with a subscription system.[41] In October 1952 there was a contretemps with Bing over Di Stefano's unwillingness to arrive as agreed to rehearse a new production of *Bohème*. While Johnson's correspondence with singers was consistently cordial and businesslike, Bing took the opportunity to patronise Di Stefano:

> The fact that you have done *Bohème* so often makes the situation much worse because if this production is to be a good one I do not believe that anything of what you have done so far in the way of acting will be acceptable. Of course, this does not apply to you only but to practically the whole cast. Therefore, you will have to unlearn what you have done and to learn new ways of moving and acting on the stage. I had hoped that you would be interested in such possibilities which could lift you from being a very good singer to becoming a very good artist, but apparently you are only thinking of making a few extra dollars at the Scala and trying to cut rehearsals.[42]

Di Stefano sang in Milan a *Bohème* and a *La Gioconda* at the same time that he had been contracted for the Met production. Bing terminated the House's contract with him. He did not return there until 1955–56, and then for only a few performances.

In May 1957, to insure that the Met could compete with the European Houses as well as some of the American Houses, the Board agreed to Bing's request to end the system where the top fee was $1,000 dollars. He persuaded the Board to make the change by arguing that the interest and excitement generated by outstanding singers had contributed to the successful selling out of 94 out of the 148 performances that season.[43]

The tale of Maria Callas's career at the Metropolitan illuminates her artistry and personality, as well as illuminating Bing's approach to managing the House. In the course of 'l'affaire Callas' his proprietary attitude sometimes verged on tyranny, while Callas's pride, perfectionism and hypersensitivity made her exceedingly difficult to deal with.

Callas's first encounter with the Met came in 1945 during Johnson's tenure, when she was twenty-two years old. Despite two auditions she received no firm offer of a part. During the late 1940s, however, her artistry and career flourished outside the United States and her Scala debut made her, with Tebaldi, the brightest international star soprano of the early 1950s. On 20 November 1950 Bing wrote to Erich Engel, a colleague at the Vienna Staatsoper, enquiring about Callas's suitability for the Met: 'I gather she does not look well and is an uninteresting actress. Does the beauty of her voice make up for all these defects?'[44] Engel replied on 12 December that Callas was extremely flexible as far as her roles were concerned, having sung Turandot, Norma and Aida at the Teatro Colón in Buenos Aires. He added, 'As far as I remember, she is by no means ugly, [has] a good appearance, and [is] a thoroughly skilled actress.'[45] In spring 1951, after receiving Engel's favourable assessment, Bing auditioned Callas in Florence. He later wrote: 'The lady I saw in Florence in spring 1951 bore only a slight relationship to the Maria Callas who later became world-famous. She was monstrously fat, and awkward. I wrote to her agent: "I heard her and had a long talk with her. She has no doubt remarkable material but still has a lot to learn before she can be a star at the Met."'[46] As a matter of fact, Callas was an already known quantity. Audiences already considered her an impressive singing actress. Bing does not mention Callas's supremacy – acknowledged by Harewood and Ghiringhelli, among many others – in projecting emotion and character through music and movement. Nor does he refer to her beauty, evident in contemporary photographs despite her weight.

Bing's change of heart came in the summer of 1954, when Callas lost weight: 'Now it became urgent for the Met to have her.'[47] At this point Bing suggested roles better suited to her voice and personality: Violetta, Santuzza, Tosca. He also wanted her to begin rehearsals that November. Fees were once again uppermost in Bing's mind: 'I would not like to have to pay her more than $750 per performance,' he wrote. In 1954 the lack of funds to pay singers was still causing Bing great problems, and Callas opted to make her American debut at the Chicago Lyric Theater, a respected venue which offered her the fee she deserved.

In 1955, after further successes at La Scala, Florence, Mexico City, London, Rome and elsewhere, Callas was offered by Bing a contract to sing the Queen of the Night – in English. The choice of role, although paired with an offer of a Lucia, represented an error of judgement. As Callas herself admitted, the part was quite unsuited to her voice. And as Ernest Newman put it, the Queen of the Night is 'a vulture with the throat of a nightingale'. The second-act aria in particular, 'Der Hölle Rache', has florid arpeggiated passages up to a high F which are appropriate to a lighter voice – a coloratura 'nightin-gale' that can negotiate the transition from head to pharyngeal tones or, better still, execute the arpeggios all in the head voice. However, Callas's tendency was to carry a mixed voice, including a suggestion of chest voice, to dangerous heights. This would be a stunning 'vulture' effect in another context. It might, for example, suggest Lucia's mad-ness. But it would be a recipe for top-note instability in Mozart, and consequently a potential fiasco in a crucial debut. Sensibly Callas refused Bing's offer. She awaited something more appropriate from the Met.

Callas finally appeared in New York to open the 1956–57 Met season as Norma. She also performed the title roles in productions of *Tosca* and *Lucia di Lammermoor*. The logistics of opening night were carefully planned to keep the adoring crowd at bay. Herman Krawitz, Bing's point man backstage, received a memo from his boss asking him to discuss with her 'when and how she wants to leave after the performance. It may be difficult to get her out the 40th Street stage door, unless she enjoys that sort of scramble. It may even be advisable to have her car pick her up at the scene dock door entrance on Seventh Avenue.'[48]

By the end of her engagement Callas was having difficulty reaching high notes and, even more worrying, a debilitating fear of not reaching them. Callas's partisan Irving Kolodin admitted a top E flat in Lucia showed 'vocal weariness'.[49] Robert Sabin frowned: 'Notes above the staff in climaxes frequently approximated screams.' At the same time she was giving evidence of a matchless acting ability grounded in empathy with the character. Those who spoke of her stagecraft agreed that as a singing actress she was unsurpassed. Kolodin, attending the *Norma* opening, was deeply impressed by her musicianship: 'Rounded musical phrases, a musician's way of curving a melodic line, a superior vocalist's sense of dynamics and colour.'[50] Kolodin also summed up the critics' ambivalence: 'That she moved in a realm of dramatic artistry inaccessible to those whose voices were not "puzzling" and all of whose top tones were "well placed" apparently registered not at all. The uncommon talent sought in vain for the uncommon appraisal.'[51]

The sensational atmosphere that can accompany an important Met debut was in evidence. *Time* magazine ran a tell-all cover story on Callas's troubled relations with her mother. Much of her achievement was lost in a wash of yellow journalism. Callas did not help matters with her own tendency to petty bad behaviour. There was an imbroglio over a sustained high note with Enzo Sordello, the baritone who sang Enrico to her Lucia. On Callas's return to Italy it was revealed in the press that the diva had flown first class while her spouse, the Italian industrialist Giovanni Battista Meneghini, sat in the tourist-class cabin. The Callas–Tebaldi feud grew to monstrous proportions. Callas was reviled by the papers as the dark witch who spurned her penniless mother. Tebaldi was enshrined as the good girl, sweet and virginal, who cherished her mother and scarcely left her side.[52] In the face of such flummery it was hard for the critics to maintain equilibrium.

In 1951, hearing Callas as Elena (*I Vespri siciliani*), Lord Harewood was convinced of her technical accomplishment: 'She has . . . the technique to deal with music of apparently any date, and is the only soprano I know who could cope with the technical demands made by Meyerbeer's operas and in much of Verdi's earlier output too.'[53] But a number of writers agree that Callas's fear of attacking high notes, and even of performing at all, affected her singing. Accounts from as early as 1952 depict the singer as an emotionally vulnerable perfectionist who often sought reassurance from those around her.[54] Objectively grounded self-confidence is essential to a singer. When it is absent tension may build up in the throat, chest and shoulders. Simultaneously, the abdominal muscles can lose tone and fail to provide sufficient support. This combination can make for a shrill top. It is likely that emotional problems underlay the tragic fraying of her voice. This hypothesis is strengthened by Bing's account of a late Callas performance as Norma. He heard Callas crack on an exposed high note, then watched her signal for the conductor to repeat the passage and, once she had her second chance, succeed in sustaining the note. If technique were fundamentally lacking, no amount of courage could have helped her. This anecdote suggests sudden and extreme variations in the singer's self-confidence. Callas's emotional problems included narcissistic belligerence and a tendency to act manipulatively and vindictively to achieve her goals. Unfortunately, Bing's personality also reflected many of the same traits.

Before Callas began her second season at the Met, Bing made an effort to control her American media appearances, as well as her engagements at other opera houses. When he heard that she was to sing Medea in Dallas, he tried to discourage her: 'I don't know whether in your wildest imagination you can realise what sort of performances you would be letting yourself in for. They will be pickup orchestras, most likely amateur choruses and the scenery, I suppose, will be picked from last Christmas's pantomimes.'[55] Bing also disapproved of Callas's friend Miss Elsa Maxwell, who achieved notoriety during the 1950s as a hostess of celebrities and a gossip in the daily press. He entreated Callas 'to instruct Miss Maxwell to keep absolutely quiet. She is neither your business manager nor your publicity agent. Anything she says or writes is immediately suspect by anybody in this country who matters.' Bing added: '. . . Please keep her out of everything. Her interference may really be dangerous.' Bing also begged Callas to present a gentler image to the media: 'Please – no more arguments, no more accusations, no more fighting spirit. Please do not attack Rome or the Italians or the press or AGMA [the singers' union, the American Guild of Musical

Artists] or San Francisco or any of your colleagues. Believe me, I am your friend and I have learned a little how to handle the American press and public. Calm, quiet and sweetness are required – now and then, as I said, a few brilliant performances.'[56] Bing was not pleased about Callas's decision to be a guest on the Eddie Fisher television programme: 'The last thing I would want would be for you to appear on a third-rate variety show two days before you appear at the Metropolitan.' He urged Callas to cancel the Fisher show in order 'to preserve the dignity of this House and that of its leading artists'. Notwithstanding Bing's aversion to undignified television variety programmes, he had asked Callas a year and a half earlier to sing on the *Ed Sullivan Show*, telling her that Sullivan, 'an immensely popular commentator', had 'the most popular Sunday television show in the United States'. The reason behind Bing's admiration of Ed Sullivan – no commentator at all, and certainly no highbrow host – was apparently Sullivan's agreement with Bing to showcase the Met in 'Six or eight "Great Scenes from the Metropolitan"'.[57] Bing was seeking safe publicity and a positive public image for his House rather than nasty media barbs from Callas. In 1958, Bing also disapproved of her plans to be a guest on Ed Murrow's TV programme, even though he considered it 'of a very different calibre [from the Fisher show] and it is entirely in keeping for a distinguished artist to appear on that programme'. But once again, Bing feared Callas's sharp tongue: 'Naturally he will ask you about all sorts of controversial subjects and your answers are not always the most even-tempered, angel-tongued replies!'[58]

Callas's last-minute second thoughts about her contract for the 1958–59 Met season provide an insight into her erratic behaviour, and also reveal her terror of high notes. She had contracted to sing two *Traviatas* on 13 and 17 February 1959, sandwiched between two performances of *Macbeth* on the 5th and 21st. She wrote to Bing to express her doubts about singing such a heavy role as Lady Macbeth so soon after performing Violetta. At a face-to-face meeting of 19 February 1958 she also complained about the prospect of participating in the Met's upcoming tour. But Callas had signed a contract covering the tour, the repertoire and the performance dates. What was the general manager to do?

Bing's strategy was to fire a barrage of letters during the months of

September and October 1958 in which he demanded clear, immediate answers to three distinct questions. First, he asked whether Callas was willing to sing in the Met's next season – that is, 1959–60. Bing's suggestions for roles for that season did not reflect awareness of, or sympathy with, Callas's vocal difficulties. He proposed some which would be extremely difficult for her, including Norma, Violetta and Lucia, and others such as Rosina and even Kundry, which would be well-nigh impossible. Second, Bing wanted to know whether Callas was willing to sing Lady Macbeth in the upcoming February 1959 production. Third, he wondered whether she might be about to renege on her agreement to participate in the Met's tour that spring. One of Bing's letters, dated 23 October, was sent to Callas's Milan address, while he was aware she was singing in Dallas; a letter of 21 October had been sent to the Adolphus Hotel in that city. The final letter in Bing's salvo, dated 29 October 1958, included a cutting reference to the tone of one of Callas's replies. Bing said the letter sounded more like 'the Maria Callas of whom I have been warned rather than the Maria Callas I know, like and respect. It seems that you are determined to make life difficult for both of us just for the sheer pleasure of being difficult.'[59]

Speaking in Italian, Callas's husband stated in a telephone call to John Gutman at the Met on 1 November that Callas would be willing to perform the contracted *Traviatas* once Tebaldi had sung one performance of the same opera in the same Met production. Gutman asked Meneghini whether Callas would agree to sing *Lucia* instead of *Traviata*. According to the English-language précis of the phone conversation, 'Meneghini retorted that she no longer wanted to be bothered with any of those "broken-down, mouldy, old productions" such as *Lucia*. He also mentioned *Norma* as a "ten-year-old" production which was unworthy of Maria Callas.'[60] Bing himself knew there was justice in Meneghini's complaint. He wrote in his autobiography that 'The *Lucia* in which Miss Callas had been appearing was one of our oldest and poorest productions still on the boards', and that Lily Pons had also expressed her intense dislike of it.[61] As for the tour, Meneghini was afraid 'that he just had to give us fair warning about the strain and stress to which the tour subjects a singer. He suggested that at least in those tour cities where Maria Callas was scheduled to appear twice, one of those appearances would have to be cancelled.' Gutman said that this was impossible.[62]

On 2 November Callas replied in fury to Bing's letter of 29 October: 'There arises a question and that is do you make your judgements with the brain of some little fool or rather with your own brain, basing yourself on facts and not on gossip?' She declared, 'I am not interested in what the Metropolitan offers' – for the 1959–60 season – and 'I cannot put myself at the disposal of the Metropolitan for the old standard routine'. The *Traviata* production in which she had sung was 'obnoxious', and she could not appear once more in such a lame, unchallenging vehicle. Tebaldi, she said, had after all been given right of refusal for her performances of *Traviata* – an allegation which Bing never refuted; she, Callas, felt she was merely demanding equal treatment.[63] Meanwhile, on 31 October, Callas had sung what turned out to be the last Violetta of her career. At least one Dallas music critic had been worried on her behalf as she sang the treacherous 'Sempre libera'. 'The ear was ready with a tense concern,' he wrote.[64]

On 3 November Bing issued an ultimatum in the form of a telegram to Callas in Dallas:

> If you are definitely unwilling perform three Traviatas as con-tractually agreed request immediate confirmation that you agree replace these performances with three Lucias. Planning necessities force me request telegraphic confirmation not later than tomorrow Tuesday afternoon.[65]

Two days later Bing's ultimatum was extended:

> Your letter November 2 not clear reply my proposal contained my letter October 29 or request for confirmation for replace-ment of Traviatas by Lucias proposed my telegram of November 3. My proposal in letter October 29 did not contemplate reduc-ing total number of agreed performances but was predicated upon your acceptance of substitute operas in your contract repertory list if our schedule permitted. In accordance with my letter October 29 and telegram November 3 I have proposed three Lucias which is only opera we can substitute within requirements of our schedule. Renew my request contained in telegram November 3. Unless such confirmation received by

telegraphic reply tomorrow Thursday morning ten oclock New York time we have no alternative but consider you in breach of agreement and contract terminated.[66]

Callas's cabled reply, translated here from the original Italian, failed to relate to Bing's demand to replace the *Traviatas*. She focused instead on *Macbeth* as a work difficult to combine in sequence with *La Traviata*, which she termed a 'light opera'. By this she apparently mean that the part of Violetta called for a more lyric weight of voice than Lady Macbeth.

> Most astonishing and irksome your manner and unacceptable as usual. I repeat and shall insist that it is absolutely impossible to mingle. Macbeth a heavy opera with any light opera whatever. I thought I was making your task easier eliminating straightaway clearly incompatible and contrasting operas but in view your incomprehensible insistence I propose now reasonable substitution with opera of appropriate repertoire.[67]

Callas's cable was sent at 4.26 p.m., Central time, on 6 November. New York's local time was two hours later. Apparently Bing had not received it when he sent his reply, which has no indication of the hour: 'Since you have not seen fit to reply my telegrams November three and November five or furnish confirmation as requested please consider your contract for Metropolitan 58–59 season cancelled.'[68] Perhaps it is a matter of legal opinion whether Callas was still negotiating with management and was not standing in breach when Bing seized the opportunity to rid himself of her.

The American press made much of Callas's dismissal, with she and Bing carrying on a slanging match in the newspapers. Viewing the situation from outside the House, B. H. Haggin, the music critic and biographer of Toscanini, concluded that Bing was running the Met 'by public martinet-like assertion of power'.[69] Kolodin maintained that, in Bing's relationship with Callas, the star 'in this instance was Bing himself, who wanted things his own way regardless of the consequences.'[70]

Francis Robinson, at the time the Met's assistant manager, was in a good position to assess Bing's motives. Robinson writes, 'He got her on a technicality. It was a little like getting Al Capone for income tax. Those dates [for *Traviata* and *Macbeth*] could have been patched up.

Bing's real reason was her non-delivery of the tour, which he couldn't prove – but he was quite right.'[71]

Few would maintain Callas was easy to deal with. But her singing, until her last performing years, repaid huge investments of administrative frustration. In spite of flaws of voice and character, Maria Callas was a great artist. But Rudolf Bing never offered her a chance to realise her full talents in New York. The Met seldom proposed a superior conductor or outstanding singers as partners in creating an organic interpretation. On the contrary, Callas showed up the weaknesses of Bing's House. These were impatience, favouritism, short-sightedness and an attitude to art as something that had to be subordinated to managerial authority. In a number of respects Bing was seriously wanting. He lacked tact, consistent aesthetic judgement and, at times, common humanity. Since the Met had no artistic director, music director or even chief conductor, no countervailing force was present to heal wounds and give alternative creative leadership.

At the same time, Bing gave his much-beloved institution the full measure of his devotion and persistence. Under difficult financial conditions he and his staff led it to a much higher standard of performance, one that could take a proud place among leading opera houses worldwide. In addition, it was during his tenure that heroic attempts were made to resolve the financial dilemmas of putting on worthy opera without a subsidy. It is impossible to imagine the present-day Met, with its efficiently and intelligently presented productions, without the contribution of Rudolf Bing.

EIGHT

COVENT GARDEN 1955–60
Kubelik and Beyond

WHILE BING WAS IMPOSING substantial changes at the Met, Covent Garden's new music director from September 1955, Rafael Kubelik, was to continue the process of gradual yet solid improvement and to provide the day-to-day leadership that was needed to build a more rigorous artistic control within the institution. There was, however, a growing disagreement between the management and those members of the Board who felt that the only way to improve the general standard was to bring in leading foreign guests to sing and conduct, particularly after Viscount Waverley's death in 1958. More international visitors would inevitably mean compromise over the use of English and the development of the local company. Ironically, it was at the same moment that the 'international' lobby gained sway that the policy of developing British and Commonwealth talent began to bear fruit.

Kubelik's background put him firmly in the camp of the local talent supporters. Born in Bohemia in 1914, he had started conducting the Czech Philharmonic at the age of twenty. In 1939 he was appointed music director of the Brno Opera House until it was closed by the Nazis in 1941. From Brno, Kubelik went to Prague, where he stayed until 1948, when he went to Edinburgh to conduct the Glyndebourne company at the Festival. This visit gave him the opportunity to leave Communist Czechoslovakia and later to become domiciled in Switzerland. It was as a result of his experience at Brno, where the use of the Czech language had contributed to the development of local talent and a native tradition in opera, that Kubelik was so in harmony with Webster's and Harewood's determination to maintain the English-language policy. On 30 September 1955 he told the BBC that he 'disliked the international star system intensely and believed in years of hard work on ensemble between artists'.[1]

Kubelik's musical direction was greeted with enthusiasm. On 4 May 1955 he conducted his first opera after being appointed music director, Smetana's *The Bartered Bride*, which was produced by Christopher West and was to be the first of many such collaborations. Cecil Smith wrote that Kubelik's interpretation came as a shock to an audience used to the Sadler's Wells *Bartered Bride* and its 'clodhopping folk rhythms'. Smith enthused, 'How slow, how gentle, Mr Kubelik made some of the sentimental melodies! How spontaneously he let the dance rhythms move.' Cecil Smith added that 'the orchestra and chorus responded eagerly to the new conductor'.[*2]

As planned, Kempe continued his relationship with Covent Garden as a guest conductor after Kubelik's appointment. From 10 to 27 May 1955 he conducted two cycles of the *Ring*, which was produced by Rudolf Hartmann with costumes and scenery by Leslie Hurry. Andrew Porter wrote, 'A Wagnerite surveying the international scene will now have to reckon with the Covent Garden *Ring* as something he will not be able to find elsewhere.' He went on to praise Kempe's 'great tenderness in the lyrical passages, with pianissimi much softer than most conductors dare, climaxes built up by an increase of emotional intensity rather than swelling of the orchestral volume, and a remarkable feeling for the shape of the acts and the operas in relation to the whole drama'. Although he spoke of the orchestra's playing as of 'rare subtlety and beauty of tone', he also mentioned the lack of warmth and rounded tone in the strings and the faulty playing in the horns and Wagner tubas.[3] Porter admired the 'superb' Wotan of Hans Hotter, among a fine cast that included Birgit Nilsson, Wolfgang Windgassen, Una Hale, Hermann Uhde, Otakar Kraus, Kurt Böhme and Joan Sutherland.

In October 1955 Kubelik's first new production as music director was *Otello*. This was one of the few productions to be sung in Italian as Kubelik agreed it was an opera whose 'colour' could only be captured

---

* Sadler's Wells had expressed regret in December 1954 that Covent Garden was going to produce *The Bartered Bride*. Webster told the opera subcommittee that there was bound to be some duplication with 'certain basic operas' though efforts would be made to avoid them. *Bartered Bride*, he believed, was an 'excellent debut for Kubelik' (Opera Sub-Committee, 1951–59, 6/1).

in the original language. It was a carefully rehearsed production and when Tito Gobbi said he was going to arrive late for the piano and stage rehearsals Kubelik, determined to show discipline, replaced him with Otakar Kraus. In Rosenthal's words, Kraus had 'one of the greatest triumphs of his career', his Iago 'evil incarnate, subtle, reptilian, repulsive'.[4] The two guests were Ramón Vinay as Otello and Gré Brouwenstijn as a moving Desdemona.*

The critics were divided in their responses to Kubelik's reading. Peter Heyworth in the *Observer* praised Kubelik for his 'grasp of this music's pulse, its melodic contours, and immense range of mood'.[5] Rosenthal, on the other hand, felt that Kubelik sometimes lost the 'natural momentum' and that the 'tempo sagged'. There was universal recognition, however, of the careful preparation and what Heyworth described as the 'unity of conception that extended from Wakhévitch's highly romantic sets and costumes to Kubelik's impassioned conducting'.

As at the Met, where Bing's stricter rehearsal discipline led to greater artistic quality, Kubelik's *Otello* marked the beginning of Covent Garden's policy of putting well-rehearsed shows on the stage. This tradition was to be further developed under Solti, and adhered to with greater or less success thereafter. Tooley later described this as Covent Garden's version of a *stagione* system, although the concept had different meanings in different Houses. For Tooley this was to mean: 'A good rehearsal period and half a dozen performances, maybe seven or eight if you could keep the cast, well spaced, with the same cast there throughout – everybody had to be there from day one'. According to Tooley, Kubelik's sacking of Gobbi was 'a bit of an exaggeration on Rafael's part but nevertheless he wanted to make a point. That echoed round the world in twenty-four hours.'[6]

Kubelik was also chasing Webster over casting and scheduling, writing to him on 13 December that if they were to avoid the 'bigger and smaller mistakes' of the current season they must finalise plans

---

* Brouwenstijn had been so depressed by her reception from the critics at the time of her debut in 1951 in *Aida* that she had considered not returning to Covent Garden, but she established a warm working relationship with Kubelik and gave some outstanding performances. She later went on to sing at Bayreuth and in 1956 sang, for the first time, Fidelio, a role that was to become one of her favourites. She was a warm, good-natured performer much liked by her colleagues.

for the 1956–57 season that month.[7] Critics Rosenthal and Porter recognised Kubelik's contribution and hoped that *Otello* would bode well for the Italian repertoire and the 'more professional and realistic, less dilettante, approach which has obtained at Covent Garden recently'.[8] Kubelik's *Bohème* in December was similarly welcomed by Mann as showing a serious approach to the 'bread and butter' performances.[9] The new production of *The Magic Flute* in January 1956 was very much a company achievement with Elsie Morison, Jess Walters, Richard Lewis and Adele Leigh. Kubelik had worked closely with designer John Piper and producer Christopher West over many months. Once again the preparation was universally recognised, while Kubelik's conducting inspired differing responses. It was described variously as 'doughy' by Porter and 'truly Mozartian' by Mann.[10]

In the early summer of 1955 Webster's deputy, Steuart Wilson, whose relationship with his director was increasingly strained, resigned shortly before his contract came to an end. Wilson had resented Harewood's appointment in 1953, writing to him, 'Your arrival causes many misgivings. . . . David has told nobody about it, not even his deputy. That is the kind of trust that he puts in us all.' Harewood recalled that Wilson's 'constant sniping at David Webster was barely concealed and it came as a relief to know he had reached official retirement age in summer 1955'.[11] In April 1955, the Board approved the appointment of John Tooley as assistant general administrator.

At the time of Harewood's appointment Wilson had discussed his complaints about the administration with Waverley. In May 1955 Wilson circulated a memorandum extremely critical of Webster to which Waverley had replied that it was 'not proper for an employee to appear before members of the Board in order to criticise the administration'.[12] Wilson left Covent Garden abruptly the next month.

On 24 July Wilson was quoted in the *People* as saying that there was at Covent Garden 'a kind of agreement among homosexuals which results in their keeping jobs for the boys'. The quote appeared in an article that declared that Wilson was launching a campaign against 'homosexuality in British music' in an effort to curb the 'influence of perverts in the world of music'. Wilson wrote to the Board in August to apologise, saying that he had not authorised the statement. The following year, however, he circulated a memorandum on the same subject to the Board, who decided to ignore him, at which he wrote to the *Daily Telegraph* calling for an investigation into the running of Covent Garden. It was at this time that the police and press were leading a campaign to expose and bring homosexuals to trial with newspapers like the *People* and the *News of the World* giving maximum coverage to the cases. Among those arrested and imprisoned were Lord Montagu of Beaulieu in 1953, the *Daily Mail* diplomatic correspondent Peter Wildeblood and author Rupert Croft-Cooke. John Gielgud was also arrested, but not imprisoned, in 1953.*

Wilson's attack did not, however, destroy Webster and was not picked up by other newspapers. It is probable that Moore's position as proprietor of the *Financial Times* enabled him to protect Webster from further press coverage. Nevertheless, Wilson's dissatisfaction with the standards of the House was shared by Moore who soon had a staunch ally in his desire to see more international artists employed at the House, when Isaiah Berlin, Professor of Social and Political Theory at Oxford, joined the Board in 1955 and the opera subcommittee in June 1956.† Berlin quickly made himself, as Drogheda recalled, 'indispensable'. He was to prove an active member of the Board and Opera Board, involving himself in details of opera planning and casting. Drogheda described Berlin as 'mercurial, hypersensitive, with antennae stretching out far in every direction, omniscient, prejudiced, funny, human and lovable'.[13] Drogheda later told Berlin he was a 'heaven-sent colleague, so wise and penetrating' in his judgements.[14] For his part Berlin recalled Drogheda as a 'most effective director, a civilised and well-travelled man of cosmopolitan taste and very masterful'.[15] On 14 June 1956 the opera subcommittee discussed the need to win over the Ministry of Labour, who constantly made difficulties over long-term work permits, to the fact that more foreign singers were needed in the company.

* The drama critic Kenneth Hurren wrote an article in the *Spectator* in which he accused the theatre impresario Hugh 'Binkie' Beaumont of only giving jobs to homosexual actors and directors (Sheridan Morley, *John G: The Authorised Biography*, London: Hodder, 2001, p. 240).
† Berlin served on the Board from 1955–65 and from 1974–87. He was the founding President of Wolfson College, Oxford, 1966–75.

Webster, although hampered by his tendency to procrastinate, was determined to persevere with his efforts to improve the stock of English-speaking artists and had held auditions in Canada the previous November. One of those auditioned was tenor Jon Vickers, who had what Harewood later described as 'a strong, youthful, all-purpose kind of voice'. Once again Webster's procrastination nearly lost a potential star for the company. After the audition Vickers had gone to New York to work with Leo Taubman, the distinguished coach and accompanist, intending to 'have a bash if anything happened in London'. Taubman had invited people to hear Vickers and offers were coming in when Webster finally invited him to London in May 1956 after so many months of silence that Vickers had almost forgotten. When the invitation did come Vickers was disconcerted to find out that it gave him only five days' notice and offered only one week's work. He nevertheless took it up and, after two further auditions, was offered a three-year contract. He accepted a contract for eighteen months, not wanting to become a resident in the UK and be subject to its taxes.*

In 1956 Waverley faced the House's first major crisis. Financial pressures had been growing the previous year as the Arts Council had again failed to extract enough from the Treasury to provide Covent Garden with the grant they themselves had recommended. Moore had written to the chairman of the Arts Council, Kenneth Clark, on 10 January to warn that the House could not continue through 1958–59 with such a low grant and that if it was forced to close it would be a 'national disaster'. Webster told the Board on 18 January that he could find no more room for cuts, both orchestra and chorus were in any case smaller than those of Houses abroad. Indeed, Kubelik was asking for an extra reserve of players. On 22 March Waverley told the Board that he had told the Chancellor, R. A. Butler, that the 1946 undertaking was not being honoured. 'While the Treasury had a right to kill opera,' Waverley had told the Chancellor, 'they could not be allowed to starve it.'[16]

---

* Vickers had always sung as a child as an amateur and in 1949, aged twenty-two, he won a $400 scholarship to the Royal Conservatory of Music, Toronto. After working with voice teacher George Lambert he decided not to go back into business, in spite of great financial struggles at the beginning of his career.

This theme was to echo down the decades. Starvation remained the diet during the international tensions of the Suez crisis, during the summer and autumn of 1956. Waverley told the Board on 15 May that the Chancellor had to reduce public expenditure and the House had, for the third year running, not received the recommended £300,000 grant. In November 1956 Waverley told the Board that the discussions with the Treasury had been postponed because of 'the international situation'.[17]

On 5 June 1956 Covent Garden published the first of its Annual Reports of the House's activities with a review of the first ten years. It was Professor Lionel Robbins – who had been Professor of Economics at the London School of Economics and had been on both the Board and the finance committee since January 1956 – who had persuaded Lord Waverley to publish the report. Such an open and public account was in contrast to Vienna and La Scala, where management did not publish a breakdown of their income and expenditure.

The Annual Report underlined how far the peripheral position of the arts in the nation's attitudes was affecting Covent Garden. Waverley wrote, 'No opera house has paid its way . . . but any European country deems it essential to its dignity to have a national opera house in its capital, and sometimes municipal opera houses in its largest cities.' Waverley called a press conference during which he said that if the overdraft of £150,000 was not covered and the government found it impossible 'to provide what we think necessary', Covent Garden would have to close down.[18]

Responding to Waverley's angry statement, Martin Cooper launched a strong attack on the administration in the *Daily Telegraph* on 9 June. He agreed that the Arts Council grant was small compared with other countries, but argued that the public was not getting what it wanted and that the House was too big for singers with a 'characteristically small, drawing-room type of voice'.* Beecham supported Cooper on 16 May in the same newspaper and said that the subsidy

* There were also criticisms of Kubelik's conducting and constant references to his slow tempi and dispiriting performances in 1957–58. In June 1959 his *Tristan* led Rosenthal to write, 'Kubelik is not by nature a Wagnerian . . . the music stopped and started.' When Kubelik was not in charge, Edward Downes was sometimes conducting six times a week and the routine evenings caused the administration to come under heavy criticism.

should be radically reduced. Kubelik defended himself and English singers in a letter to *The Times* without consulting the Board. The difference between the Briton and the continental, he argued, was not the size of their voices but the fact that the continental had 'no inferiority complex and almost no inhibitions', and was thus able to project his voice. The critics did not help because they had the same complexes. He urged support for a British national opera, built on an ensemble of confident soloists, not what he called a *stagione* system with 'a few singers gathered together with almost no rehearsal for ad hoc performances'. Martin Cooper responded on 25 June with a sarcastic letter to *The Times*, expressing the hope that Kubelik was not thinking of employing a resident psychiatrist at Covent Garden.

Beecham again weighed in, writing in the *News Chronicle* on 5 July 1956 that the British were a 'thin wiry race' who do not 'breed the throats' and with a letter to *The Times* on 27 June, again lashing out at British voices in his familiar refrain, and suggesting that Covent Garden go back to its short seasons. Beecham attacked the administration for both Rankl's and Kubelik's appointments: 'In defiance of all common sense they engaged as Musical Director a foreigner. . . . Now we have another foreigner in charge. But does he possess any of the qualifications essential for the creation of a truly national organisation?' Such personal attacks from critics and the press, which failed to address the root issue of inadequate subsidy, were to become a pattern at Covent Garden.

Kubelik was wounded by the attack, particularly as he had 'very great respect for Sir Thomas Beecham'. He had also had a similarly bad experience in Chicago, where he had suffered 'hostile criticism because he was a foreigner'.[19] He immediately offered his resignation to the chairman, proposing to write a letter to *The Times*: 'Through the recent attacks on the policy of the administration of Covent Garden, I learned that my status as foreigner might be regarded as a handicap to creating a British national opera.'[20] Isaiah Berlin was angered, writing to Webster on 28 June to say that Beecham's attack was 'absolutely monstrous' and 'dictated by perversity and a desire to assume charge himself'. Berlin urged that Kubelik should be assured he had the 'solid confidence and admiration' of the Board and that he would be defended 'against sordid xenophobia'.[21]

Moore was despatched to stop Kubelik sending his letter of resignation and to encourage him to stay. The Board drafted a letter to *The Times* rejecting his resignation and Moore told Kubelik that 'he and his colleagues would be greatly distressed if Mr Kubelik was to leave the opera house'. Frances Donaldson wrote, 'It is said that when Kubelik heard the terms of this letter he cried "It is finished" and embraced Lord Waverley.'[22]

Moore assured Kubelik that critics would be approached in order to rally support and on 17 July Oliver Franks told the Board that Beecham's attack had 'been substantially neutralised by generally favourable articles in the press'.[23] One such article was written by Desmond Shawe-Taylor, who analysed the improvements in the company in its first decade. He wrote in the *New Statesman* on 7 July, 'In its early post-war days I made no secret in these columns of my conviction that the operatic side of its work was in the wrong hands: the singers ill-chosen, the orchestra rough, the stage designs outlandish, the productions absurd. But since those days there has been an immeasurable improvement.' Great conductors like Kleiber and Kempe had 'transformed the musical scene out of recognition' and he urged that Kubelik be given time. Mann in *The Times* wrote, 'To say that all is not well at Covent Garden on a mere ten years' working is to show a lamentable ignorance of operatic history.' And he reiterated the basis on which Covent Garden was founded: 'Without singers you will have no opera, but it is equally true that without opera you will have no singers.'[24]

Kubelik, in spite of this support and that of the Board, had, according to Drogheda, been 'deeply wounded'.[25] When Webster offered to renew his contract in January 1957 he told him he felt that his most important function was that of performer and that the music director role did not give him enough time. On 14 May 1957 he told the Board that he was honoured by the offer to extend his contract and would like to continue his 'close association' with the House but not as music director.[26]

Webster defended the opera house from its detractors in *Opera* in October 1956, arguing that the money 'at present being spent on opera is completely inadequate'. Inflation and the lack of rehearsal space were causing the House serious problems.[27] Webster also continued staunchly to defend the English-language policy both within and outside the House. 'For opera to develop it must be a popular art,' he argued. In November the opera subcommittee decided not to recommend 'a radical change of accepted policy', while 'the pronunciation of foreign languages by English opera singers left so much to be desired'. It was noted, however, that Italian opera in Italian would improve the box office and persuade foreign singers to come.[28] The Board agreed in December that the policy must be 'fluid', and that works should be given in their original tongue 'where this appeared to be more satisfactory'.[29]

Kubelik stood firmly behind the English-language policy, Isaiah Berlin characterising his attitude as 'Prague mustn't be subservient to Vienna'.[30] On 28 January 1957 Kubelik conducted *Mastersingers* in English. There had been pressure from the Board and from the Wagner Society for it to be sung in German with guest singers like Hotter. But Webster was adamant, arguing that he was trying to train singers for the future and that in any case, '*Mastersingers* is not a star opera but an ensemble work which requires the kind of rehearsal that can in fact only come from the conditions that surround resident artists.'[31] Although *Meistersinger* is unquestionably an opera that demands ensemble work and ample rehearsal time, it is also a work that contains extremely demanding principal roles and is difficult to cast even from an international pool. Nonetheless, Rosenthal applauded Kubelik's meticulous preparations and pointed out that the conductor got better as the run went on. He needed, Rosenthal believed, to find 'the feeling of shape for the whole'. The last scene provided 'a glorious blaze of sound from stage and pit' when the orchestra redeemed itself from some uneven playing earlier in the performance.[32] The *Manchester Guardian* also commented on the orchestra's erratic standards, feeling that it lacked 'depth and splendour of sound which the ear so longs for and is not beyond the players' powers'.[33] The ensemble included James Pease as Sachs and Geraint Evans as Beckmesser, a role for which he had prepared every move and which he was to sing for many years. Joan Sutherland sang Eva with opulent tone but with a slight lack of personality.

The language debate was being conducted inside and outside Covent Garden. Andrew Porter, who was to become one of the major translators of Wagner, believed in sensible flexibility. By allowing Sylvia

Fisher, Constance Shacklock and Adele Leigh to repeat their roles in *Rosenkavalier* they had had a chance to improve and develop, even though it would have been exciting to have had Jurinac as Octavian. A local cast, he argued, was far preferable to the 'constantly shifting unrehearsed casts that they have in Vienna'. Italian opera, on the other hand, could not be cast at home and so it made more sense to sing it in Italian.[34] One company member who was gaining experience in both English and original-language performances was Geraint Evans, who made his debut at Glyndebourne in the summer of 1957 as Falstaff. He remembered the preparations with Ebert and Gui and the company as one of the 'greatest times in his life', rehearsing certain scenes with Ebert again and again. Evans could feel Gui 'breathing the part with me and phrasing accordingly'.[35]

Another company member who was about to make his talent known was Jon Vickers, who made his debut at Covent Garden on 27 April 1957 in *A Masked Ball*, having sung Gustavus in Cardiff on 4 March during the spring tour. Vickers was instantly recognised by Rosenthal as having 'a true dramatic tenor voice, not inherently beautiful but of exciting timbre'. He hoped Vickers would stay at Covent Garden, not be overworked, and would one day sing Siegmund and Otello. Shuard was 'obviously inspired' by her partner. Edward Downes's conducting was also enthusiastically received. Downes, who later recalled Kubelik's warmth and humanity, was playing an increasingly important role at Covent Garden, conducting 115 performances during the three Kubelik seasons. Downes's *Trovatore* in June 1957 showed his 'determination to treat Verdi's orchestral score as a work of art and imagination, an attitude to which the orchestra gladly responded'.[36]

Kubelik's musical direction continued to widen the Covent Garden audience's experience, introducing some interesting repertoire. In December 1956 the House presented Janáček's *Jenůfa* in English with Shuard, Edgar Evans, John Lanigan, and Sylvia Fisher as the Kostelnička. Desmond Shawe-Taylor welcomed Kubelik's close rapport with the stage and the expressiveness of the musicians, as 'when the woodwind pick up some vocal phrase and give it all the tenderness or sorrow of the human utterance from which it is derived'. Christopher West's production was 'scrupulously prepared under a conductor ideally suited for the task'.[37] Peter Heyworth, however, found the opera 'too diffuse'[38] and *The Times* felt the English translation lay 'uneasily on the vocal line'.[39] David Webster later told Rosenthal that attendance for the eight performances of *Jenůfa* were 'the worst in the history of post-war Covent Garden'.[40] The gradual development of a knowledge-able and responsive public could not have taken place without the subsidy which enabled Covent Garden to persevere with such inno-vations. The House's growing band of passionate opera lovers, no matter how impecunious, were able to afford seats in the stalls. In 1955 rows P–W cost 17s 6d in the evenings and 13s 6d for matinées. Rodney Milnes later recalled how, as a student, he had seen the ill-attended *Jenůfa*, *The Midsummer Marriage* and Gerda Lammers in *Elektra* several times, sitting in the stalls.

On 4 June 1957 the English-language production of *The Trojans* was recognised as a landmark for the company. It was cast largely from Covent Garden's resident company, except for the American mezzo, Blanche Thebom, who sang Dido. Amy Shuard was Cassandra and Jon Vickers Aeneas. Vocally and dramatically the performance was dominated by Thebom and Vickers. *The Times* declared that *Les Troy-ens* was 'no longer a problem opera'. The French critic, Jacques Bour-geois, reviewing *The Trojans* in the September edition of *Opera*, claimed that the production 'puts French music heavily in England's debt' as Berlioz at that time was little performed in France.

The critics were unanimous in their praise, recognising it as a 'red letter day in the history of British operatic effort'.[41] As director, John Gielgud was applauded by *The Times* on 7 June for coming from the theatre and putting music first, and for encouraging the singers to 'employ the economic gestures of the ordinary actor'. Building further on this achievement, Covent Garden gave its first performance of Poulenc's *Dialogues of the Carmelites* on 18 January 1958. William Mann thought that Kubelik 'shaped and balanced the phrases and colours of the orchestral parts to admiration'. Joan Sutherland, who was Madame Lidoine, the new prioress, had a 'dignified bearing and vocal authority'.[42]

In November 1958 Boris Christoff refused to sing *Boris Godunov* in English and Kubelik, determined to do away with mixed-language performances, agreed that it should be sung in Russian. A live recording of a performance shows clearly the standard of company work at this time, with moments of great dramatic excitement juxtaposed with ragged orchestral playing, uncertain entrances and pallid choral singing. Secondary roles were less than adequate, Edith Coates as the Hostess singing with a curious and unattractive coyness and David Kelly's Varlaam often pushed to coarseness. Christoff in the title role, however, sang with even greater liveliness and vitality than is sometimes evident on his recordings. The dark voice, shot through with lights, was flexible in timbre and range. In fine partnership with Kubelik, Christoff moved effortlessly from lyric to intensely dramatic singing, with impeccable phrasing and consistent care in putting the character across.[43]

On 4 January 1958 the death of Lord Waverley was a blow to Webster and was to alter the balance of power between the Board and the management. Waverley had not interfered with Webster's plans. His favourite saying, if there was criticism during Board meetings, was 'this is a matter that we can safely leave to Mr Webster'.[44] Lord Moore, who had inherited the title Earl of Drogheda on 22 November 1957 and had deputised for Waverley during his illness, took over officially as chairman of the Board and was to prove a very different kind of chairman. He intended to make his views clearly felt, constantly sending out memos on topics great and small. Relations between the chairman and his director soon became strained. The new chairman proved to be a 'shock' to Webster, demanding to know 'every detail and have a hand in everything'. An undated letter from Drogheda to Webster betrayed the former's irritation at Webster's response to his suggestions about repertory and singers. 'I find it most depressing', he wrote, 'that I have only to support an idea for you to oppose it.'[45] Tooley later recalled the poor communications between the two men: 'Webster never wanted to tell the Board anything and Drogheda used to ring me; it was a nightmare at times.'[46]

Drogheda was active in improving the working conditions of company members, initiating the benevolent fund to assist operatic artists, musicians, technical and other staff at Covent Garden in times of illness, hardship, or misfortune. The inaugural annual gala was in June 1961 with de los Angeles singing in *Cavalleria rusticana* and *Pagliacci*. Drogheda also worked steadily from 1954 to introduce a pension scheme for company members.

The new chairman was constantly to face financial problems. Arts funding was not at the top of the list of priorities for the new Harold Macmillan government in January 1957. That month the chairman of the Arts Council, William Emrys Williams, wrote an introduction to the Council's Annual Report entitled 'Art in the Red', in which he high-lighted the fact that the Council's budget of less than a million pounds a year had to assist 125 bodies professionally engaged in opera, ballet, music and drama. The Arts Council and its music panel spent a great deal of time discussing the deficits of the opera companies and in particu-lar the failing Carl Rosa Company, which was finally disbanded that year, its touring role being taken on by Sadler's Wells. There was no capital expenditure on the arts and the only new building provided by public funding since the war was the Royal Festival Hall. Austria, Italy, Hol-land and Germany – countries that were in a worse economic situation than Britain – had between them built fifteen opera houses and concert halls in bombed cities. Peter Hall recalled how shocked he had been when he had visited Germany in 1949. He found the country 'still poor, still ruined, yet to my amazement spending money on the arts. No houses, yet building new opera houses . . . It was a revelation to me, as I had left a country where art was not in the centre of a town's life.'*[47]

The financial problems of the House and its estimated £406,000 deficit remained so great a concern in 1958 that, in January, Clark and Drogheda were again faced with the prospect of closing down Covent Garden.[48] Worries had been compounded by another Arts Council initiative in July 1957 to amalgamate Sadler's Wells and Covent Garden, in order 'to eliminate both Houses' deficits'.[49] When the grant of £362,000 was announced in February, the Arts Council again agreed that it was 'substantially below' its own estimate of the House's needs.

---

* The director of decor at the Berlin State Opera, Hainer Hill, who came to Covent Garden in 1961, urged British technicians to visit Germany to study the numerous theatres built since the war as well as scientific treatments of costumes and sets (*The Times*, 1.3.61).

Drogheda wrote to the Arts Council in March warning that the estimates had already been cut to the point where seat prices had had to
be raised and maintenance work, including 'urgent repairs to stage
machinery', deferred.[50] Both the size of the grant and the annual uncertainty were detrimental to long-term planning, he warned.*[51]

In May, recognising the 'accurate and alarming picture' that Drogheda had painted of the House's predicament, William Emrys Williams
at the Arts Council suggested that Covent Garden and Sadler's Wells
management visit the Chancellor.[52] As a result the Treasury proposed
a new arrangement whereby Covent Garden would receive a grant at
43 per cent of the House's approved expenditure. This would mean a
grant of £453,000. The Treasury would also pay off the overdraft.
Williams told Webster that although this 'created dilemmas over the
other arts', he recognised that Covent Garden deserved more than it
was receiving. The arrangement was concluded in January 1959.[53]

In 1957 Harewood, who was playing a substantial role in planning,†
persuaded the Board to accept *Don Carlos* as one of the House's
centenary productions for May 1958, and succeeded in bringing Giulini
to Covent Garden with Visconti to design and direct. It was a landmark
production for, unlike *The Trojans*, it had an international cast, including Gré Brouwenstijn, Boris Christoff, Tito Gobbi and Fedora Barbieri,
as well as Vickers, and was to be sung in Italian. There was intense
co-operation between Visconti and Giulini during the four-and-a-half-
weeks of rehearsal. Edward Downes later recalled that there were no
rehearsals unless both director and conductor were present.

Visconti's sixth opera production and his first outside Italy had its
premiere on 9 May. A live recording of the 12 May performance clearly
shows that it was an exciting turning point in the history of Covent
Garden, with a truly integrated musical theatrical production and
exciting performances from the assembled artists. Vickers as Don

---

* *The Times* reported on 19 November 1958 that Covent Garden's subsidy of £362,000
compared with Vienna's £1 million subsidy.
† Harewood was eventually given the official title of controller of opera planning in
October 1959, after Webster explained to the Board that he occupied a 'key position'
(Board, June 1959).

Carlos had an almost animal vitality with which he expressed a complete range of emotions and created an authentic involvement in the
character. Gré Brouwenstijn's Elisabetta conveyed nobility, gentleness
and tragic dignity, while Gobbi's vocal dryness was more than out-
weighed by his virile, forward tone and by his forceful acting.

The star of the performance, however, was Giulini. His tempi
were invariably just and the climaxes exquisitely positioned. Giulini
captured the dark *tinta* of the work, its anguish and melancholy,
especially by careful attention to note values, line and accents. In the
ensembles his understanding of the weight and colour that Verdi
accords each character was on a level with the wisdom of Tullio Serafin.
The chorus, responding to the conductor, sounded fresh, youthful
and almost Italian. The orchestra outdid themselves throughout,
responding to Giulini's nuances and playing as one.[54] Downes later
said that Giulini taught the orchestra 'how to play with nobility'.[55]

The critics were unanimous in their approval, recognising that this
was a landmark in British operatic history. Harold Rosenthal called
this *Don Carlos* a 'highly integrated musical production such as none
of us can ever remember having experienced'. To those who said that
it reminded them of the good old pre-war performances he retorted,
'We never had such a finished and rehearsed production as this.'[56] On
11 May, Peter Heyworth in the *Observer* called the production 'one of
the outstanding operatic productions to be seen in Europe today'.
Shawe-Taylor called it a 'manifestation of musical theatre at its
grandest and most complete'.[57] Peter Hall later remembered it as 'the
greatest operatic experience of my life'.[58]

The success of *Don Carlos* had a decisive effect on future policy
at Covent Garden. Lord Harewood wrote in his memoirs, 'Ironically,
the success of that international cast presaged the end of our ensemble
policy, as the Board was quick to twig that this brought success much
more certainly and easily than did our efforts to develop native talent.
From then on the cry was for more and more international singers.'[59]
Callas's Violetta, in June 1958, also encouraged the 'international'
lobby, Porter calling it 'a revelation, thrilling in its intensity'. Although
Callas was ill and below her best vocal form, and the production was
not a new one, Porter was overwhelmed by her 'wonderful fluency and
delicacy, ravishing tone in the soft passages and intense and exciting

emotional colour' and the 'artistry and imagination' she expressed in every phrase.

While great foreign singers were coming to London, successful company singers were keen to go abroad and, like the top international conductors, no longer wished to be tied to one place. Vickers's performances had been going from strength to strength, his singing marked by consistent ease and exuberance. In 1957 and 1958, as well as Gustavus, Aeneas in *The Trojans* and Don Carlos, he had also sung Radames under Kempe's baton and a triumphant Handel Samson in November 1958. He decided in early 1958 not to renew his contract with Covent Garden until after his Bayreuth debut as Siegmund, with which he had a huge success. This was the first time a singer had gone to Bayreuth from the company. He was followed by David Ward, Otakar Kraus and Amy Shuard. In July, Vickers asked Webster for a contract for £175 for each performance, as he could get £200 per performance in Canada and America, and for his Vienna debut he would be getting double what he had received for his London debut just eighteen months earlier. He also insisted on spending no longer than 180 days in England for tax reasons. Webster replied to Vickers's London agent, John Coast, 'You know as well as I do that I have to give in to his demands.'[60] Vickers later wrote a warm letter to Webster, thanking him for his help and guidance: 'You have done far more for me than can really be appreciated – you have given me opportunities, experience, guidance, moral support, artistic and business advice, to such an extent that you have so to speak taught me the profession.'[61] Vickers had seven important debuts within three and a half years of *The Trojans*, including the Met, La Scala, Bayreuth and Vienna.

The Covent Garden management were now being forced to recognise that the use of English could not much longer be adhered to. It was increasingly difficult to get international singers to learn their roles in English, and air travel, which facilitated the exchange of top artists, was making vernacular performances less attractive all over Europe. The many dreary and routine performances of the mainstays in English were not filling the House, and when the head accountant Douglas Lund's figures of attendance and costs during the previous season had been scrutinised in April, it became clear that losses on special nights were in fact no greater than on routine nights. A Board member, Jack Donaldson, had suggested that the repertory in English, with its 'less satisfactory attendance records should be reduced'.

Webster endeavoured to stand behind his English repertory operas which, he argued, provided 'invaluable and in many cases irreplaceable opportunities for British artists to develop'. He cited Evans and Sutherland as examples.[62] On 8 May, however, the opera subcommittee decided to recommend that in order to maintain an average audience of no less than 72½ per cent of capacity, the well-known operas should be put aside until they could be revivified in new productions or with star singers or conductors.

The Trojans had been both a company show and a 'special' night, and audiences had numbered 2,086 out of a possible 2,199 in June.[63] *Don Carlos* had been performed to capacity audiences of up to 2,195. The future, however, lay in the *Don Carlos* international style of casting rather than with *The Trojans*.

As part of the move towards a more international tone for the House, some members of the Board had been considering inviting Walter Legge to join them. Legge had much influence with musicians in his capacity as head of the EMI classical section and was publicly highly critical of the management. He had written a letter to *The Times* on 27 December 1957 in which he accused the Board of being 'innocent amateurs on musical matters'. On 21 April 1958 Drogheda wrote to Berlin to suggest that it would be sensible to prepare a statement of policy before issuing any invitations. There was, he wrote, 'a great fear of the consequences of Legge'.[64]

In the summer of 1958 Webster strongly opposed Legge's appointment to the Board and to the opera subcommittee, an appointment which was to prove very troublesome for him. Berlin was in favour of Legge, believing that he 'knew more about opera than anyone else in England'.[65] So too was Drogheda, who hoped he would be less critical if he saw the problems at first hand.* Berlin later described

---

* Drogheda did not appoint Legge in order to persuade him to encourage Schwarzkopf to appear at Covent Garden, as Legge alleged on 27 December 1975 in *The Times*. Frances Donaldson described Legge as 'arrogant, unreliable and with a contempt for other people easily aroused', but nonetheless 'a power in the music world'.

Legge as 'a force of nature – a kind of managerial Beecham'.[66] Some members of the Board had even considered him as artistic director, but Drogheda was afraid of the 'shock effects' Legge might have on the organisation, which he felt was 'improving all the time'.

It was decided on 20 May that Legge should join the Board. That same day, the Board approved the opera subcommittee's recommendation of 8 May that 'Where there is a conflict between quality of performance and performance in English the latter may be sacrificed'. The main concern was to fill the House to between 70 and 75 per cent capacity, except in the case of 'prestige operas' such as *The Midsummer Marriage* and *Jenůfa*.[67]

There were criticisms about the change in the language policy from the music panel of the Arts Council, and from critics including *The Times*, as well as from the Society of British Composers and the Incorporated Society of Musicians. The opera subcommittee decided on 14 October 1959 that the policy should be confirmed and defended in the Annual Report. Kenneth Clark at the Arts Council expressed his 'sympathy to the original-language decision' but 'regretted that the change had not been made more gradually'. The Arts Council, however, would not challenge the decision as it wanted Covent Garden to be 'as independent as possible'.[68] By the 1960–61 season only *Carmen*, *Wozzeck* and *Orpheus* were sung in English.

The move towards abandoning the English-language policy was strengthened by Kubelik's decision not to renew his contract. Webster, however, fought a rearguard action for his English ensemble and, keen to maintain his position, was not unhappy to be without a music director. Both he and Harewood felt they could get by with guest conductors until they found the right person. In May 1957 Webster had told the Board that a music director was not necessary except in a small House. According to both Kempe and Kubelik post-war conditions were so different from the 'heyday of the musical director' between 1880 and 1939 that 'no conductor good enough to be considered as a music director in a metropolitan centre could afford to accept the job'.[69] Members of the Board, however, disagreed, believing that 'responsibility for the day-to-day supervision and musical standards should be assumed by one person'.[70] In June, Legge told the Board 'that the search must go on for a music director'.

Harewood suggested that his friend Benjamin Britten become music director, in order to 'turn the promising ensemble into something far more important'. On 11 July 1958 the opera subcommittee discussed the question of the music director, Thomas Armstrong pressing for Britten and Berlin opposing, although Berlin agreed that Britten's would be a 'prestige' appointment that would satisfy the critics. There were, however, underlying attitudes that precluded Britten as far as Berlin was concerned. He believed, as he wrote to fellow Board member Jack Donaldson,* that Britten was 'part of the same gang as Webster and not to put too fine a point on it, opera is an essentially heterosexual art, and those who do not feel affinity with this tend to employ feeble voices, effeminate producers etc., which is a very large factor in our present misfortunes'. The minutes stated that the appointment should be 'seriously considered' by the Board.[71]

Kubelik's last appearance as music director was a performance of *The Trojans* with Shuard and Vickers on 19 July 1958. Harewood wrote of Kubelik, 'It was sad that there was some bitterness in his leaving, as he was much loved inside the building.'[72] Tooley later called him 'a man of extraordinary humanity and understanding'.[73]

With the question of replacing Kubelik unresolved the balance of power between Board and management was unsettled and centred on the question of the next music director. On 16 September 1958, when the Board again discussed the appointment of Britten as music director, Berlin continued to express his opposition to the composer who, he felt, 'would either devote himself to Covent Garden and thus frustrate his own genius' or would be unable to give enough time to the House. Webster argued that if Britten were to be made music director he would be an ally in the effort to develop the 'national character of Covent Garden' and that his appointment would give prestige to the House. Britten

* Jack Donaldson, whose wife Frances wrote the official history of the Royal Opera House, which was published in 1988, was a director of both Covent Garden 1958–74 and Sadler's Wells. A member of the Labour party until 1981 when he became a member of the Social Democrats, he was Minister of State at the Department of Education with responsibility for the arts in Callaghan's Cabinet, from 1974 to 1976. In 1967 he was made a peer.

would not be asked to deal with administration. The Board, however, was too divided for an official approach to be made.[74] On 21 October it was decided to delay the decision as there were a number of guest conductors who had agreed to appear during the next season.

The Board was increasingly uncertain about the 'national character' emphasis. In particular, Legge and Berlin were sceptical of Webster's and Harewood's conviction that home-grown talent could reach the heights of foreign stars and were hesitant when they proposed that Joan Sutherland sing Lucia. Sutherland, like Vickers, had been singing many roles in recent seasons with great success. Her Gilda in May 1957 was praised for its vocal qualities and had received a wildly enthusiastic response from the audience. She had also been a fine Desdemona in the revival of *Otello* with Vinay in December 1957 and an Israelite Woman in the October 1958 Handel *Samson* with Vickers on tour in Leeds. During this performance, Rosenthal enthused, her 'Let the bright seraphim' 'aroused the House to a frenzy of enthusiasm'.[75]

Lord Harewood wrote, 'David Webster and I were convinced from the start that even though she always looked a big girl on stage, she possessed so rare a vocal talent that we should set about putting her forward in something special.' Her husband Richard Bonynge 'favoured Lucia, maintaining that she was going in that direction rather than towards Wagner and the dramatic Italians. He had been working on the role with her.' Sutherland still, however, seemed self-conscious and uncomfortable on stage, and she later recalled that at one point during the autumn she had been told that Lucia was being cancelled.[76] In June 1958 the Board was still hesitant about her singing Lucia and on 11 June Harewood defended the choice, arguing that her voice was 'one of the best in the company'. Legge suggested that Sutherland study with an Italian conductor for the role.[77] The Board finally agreed she should sing Lucia if Tullio Serafin would conduct and coach her. Harewood recalled, 'She sang for him, he professed himself delighted, and said he would conduct the new production – but only in Italian.'[78] Harewood was relieved, telling Webster that with Serafin the risk would be 'justified and calculated'.[79]

Legge, however, was still not convinced about Sutherland, writing to Berlin on 11 December to suggest 'a plan of campaign' to improve what he considered to be Covent Garden's inadequate and amateur standards. 'The pious hope of individuals', he wrote, 'that it is possible to give first-class opera with local talent has no foundation.' Berlin invited Legge to Oxford to discuss 'a joint policy of attack', but felt that they should wait until after *Lucia* in order to prove that 'the proposition that first-class opera with local talent is a utopian term at present'. He urged Legge to try to enlighten Harewood, who was 'the main defender of local talent'.[80]

With Webster maintaining his usual dilatory style of management and in the absence of a music director, the Board assumed a more activist role than management would have liked and tensions grew between them and within the Board itself. Legge was causing Drogheda distress. After eight months his hopes of lessening Legge's hostility were in no way fulfilled and Legge continued to show, in Drogheda's words, 'the most thorough contempt for the whole organisation'.[81] In December Drogheda wrote to Berlin to say that he, like Berlin, was considering resigning, because he could not 'stand the atmosphere of mutual distrust and dislike'. Although Drogheda admired Legge, he could not but be aware that he took 'the dimmest possible view of all his colleagues', other than Berlin and Donaldson. Drogheda complained about Legge's disdainful attitude to the Board and its deliberations: 'He either doesn't come to meetings at all or else drops in late and leaves early, having caused the maximum of embarrassment and ill-feeling all round.'[82]

Legge was indeed disdainful. He had written to Drogheda on 5 November, 'Five years on the Covent Garden Board have convinced me that I have almost every possible disqualification.' Among those he listed were his passionate love of music, his hatred of inefficiency and 'the imprudent spending of public money', his knowledge of singing and music, and his maintenance of a great orchestra and chorus. He concluded 'that in your gallery of distinguished dilettantes I have no place'.*[83]

Webster's own relationship with the Board was increasingly strained.

---

* An example of a clash between Legge and other Board members was the meeting of 16 December 1958, when Legge responded to the suggestion that Kempe wanted to conduct *Forza* with the comment, '*Forza* conducted by a German conductor would be a cosmopolitan venture of doubtful artistic merit.' After Legge left the meeting, the Board agreed that a conductor's desire to conduct something should be 'of considerable account' if their presence was of value to the House (Royal Opera House Archives, Board meeting, 5/1).

Early in 1958 Drogheda had been enraged when he heard of plans to mount Handel's *Samson* with Vickers at the 1958 Leeds Festival without consultation with the Board. In September Drogheda sent Webster a letter in which he wrote, 'I do hope you understand my desire and indeed right to be consulted and realise that I am unwilling to be a rubber stamp for decisions where I have been allowed no opportunity of expressing a view.'[84] That autumn Webster told Harewood that 'he was doubtful that he should continue under pressure of this kind'. He saw the appointment of Walter Legge to the Board as a deliberate threat to his authority. Harewood later explained to Berlin how 'awkward and sometimes downright hampering' the Board's interference had been for him and Webster, in particular the many detailed suggestions about casting. Harewood quoted such remarks by members of the Board as 'We shamefully neglected someone else who ought to be a regular appearer (because a friend of the Chairman's liked him in Verona) . . .'

In reply to Harewood, Berlin later defended the role of the Board. He pointed out that in the absence of what he termed a 'single Napoleonic intendant or impresario', the role of a responsible body 'of half-or quarter-time dilettantes' was bound to assume more weight, however tiresome. He admitted that the Board sometimes made mistakes – his own opposition to *The Trojans* and Sutherland's Lucia had been proved 'howlers' – but he nonetheless felt that the 'advantages of the system outweigh its vices'.[85] According to Berlin, one of the Board's main contributions had been the 'whole Giulini connection'.

So long as there was no 'Napoleonic intendant', Berlin continued to press Webster to activity. On 9 January 1959 he wrote to him, detailing problems that had to be worked out for the following season. He was angered to discover that Gobbi had declined to sing in the revival of *Don Carlos* as he had 'not been engaged early enough' and that Schwarzkopf had not been approached about anything. Berlin continued to hope that Legge would 'keep Webster in check' and 'get the chariot moving on all its wheels'.[86]

Relations between Legge and Webster, however, were so bad that he and Donaldson were forced to try to work out 'some kind of modus vivendi'. Their efforts worked and on 17 January Berlin was able to report to Drogheda that they had made good progress at their meeting and that ambitious plans for the 1959–60 season were developing, including keeping Callas 'at all costs'.* It was even agreed that if Callas insisted, she should be promised that Tebaldi would not be invited to sing any of 'her' roles. Berlin reported that the meeting was so harmonious that Legge promised Schwarzkopf for the next year, possibly in *Rosenkavalier*. Webster's usual tactic of avoiding difficult subjects had been overcome and the committee learnt that Sutherland was indeed being coached by Serafin for her forthcoming *Lucia*.

At this meeting, Webster denied that Gobbi had been approached late and stressed that he had, in fact, agreed to sing in three performances of *Don Carlos*. In general, however, Webster was no less dilatory than usual and, on 24 February, Legge informed Berlin that Webster, 'the AD' Artful Dodger was 'living down to his title'. Webster had failed to discuss any role with Legge's wife, Schwarzkopf, although he had talked to her before and during a rehearsal of *Lucia*. Legge warned that both she and Nilsson might accept other engagements if Webster did not make a move. In spite of more confrontations in the committee, however, Berlin believed that Webster should not be sacked but that he should be subjected to 'constant pinpricks'.[87]

The combination of Berlin's and Legge's 'pinpricks' and Harewood's planning were beginning to make a noticeable contribution to the performances. The 1958–59 season included a Jurinac *Butterfly* in January 1959, and a revival of *Don Carlos* with Giulini in the pit in April and May 1959 when Evans successfully took over from Gobbi. Also in May was a finely sung *Aida* with Vickers, Regina Resnik and Leontyne Price, and in June *Medea* with Callas and Vickers. In May 1959 Vickers sang a thrilling *Parsifal* in a new production under Kempe. But it was Harewood's and Webster's support for Joan Sutherland that resulted in the most exciting achievement at this time.

While Sutherland worked with Serafin in Venice in the new year, the maestro decided that Franco Zeffirelli would be the person to help Sutherland realise her dramatic potential. He told Zeffirelli over the

---

* Callas's engagement, Berlin believed, might not be too difficult as she had broken with most of the leading Houses except Paris. Both Webster and Harewood agreed that Callas should sing in *Medea* and *Traviata*, even though the role of Violetta was proving vocally difficult for her.

telephone that it was not Callas who would be singing but someone with probably as great a talent but who had some problems. He said, 'Don't worry, I know you can work miracles.' Zeffirelli recalled his first impression of Sutherland: 'Before us was a stout, awkward, badly dressed woman with a cold. My heart sank.' Serafin quickly urged her to sing and Zeffirelli saw 'the awkward person and the divine singing'. It reminded him of the young Callas.

Zeffirelli realised that 'the main problem was her own fears and frustrations: she knew she lacked grace, and was withdrawn and diffi-cult to reach'. He continued, 'I moved close and put my arm round her shoulder, and to my surprise she pulled away, frightened, almost angry with me.'[88] Geraint Evans also recalled her sensitivity. During a rehearsal of *Figaro* when he had put his arm round her and accidentally touched 'the bare skin' between her jumper and skirt, she had swung round and slapped him across the face 'with all her strength'. Everyone was amazed because it was so out of character and they were old friends and colleagues.[89]

Zeffirelli, however, managed to make a virtue of his own impro-priety, telling her how difficult it was for him as he was 'a tactile animal'. At that, he remembered, 'she took a deep breath and gave me a real hug'.[90] Sutherland herself recalled her first costume fitting. At the beginning she was very embarrassed, but then 'much feeling, pushing, pummelling went on until he achieved the effect he desired and I became his most adoring fan'.[91]

Lucia was premiered on 17 February 1959. The tenor, João Gibin, had a cold and the Australian Kenneth Neate stepped in at the last moment. Porter in the *Financial Times* on 18 February 1959 wrote, 'Franco Zeffirelli's production of *Lucia di Lammermoor* for Covent Garden takes its place beside the great Scala revivals of *ottocento* opera which have been so striking a feature of post-war musical life: and with her performance of the title role the young Australian soprano Joan Sutherland becomes one of the world's leading prima donnas.' He was struck by her 'new dramatic power. The traces of self-consciousness and awkwardness on the stage had disappeared; and at the same time she sang more freely, more powerfully, more intensely – also more bewitchingly – than ever before.'

Sutherland received a standing ovation at the end of the first act. Porter continued, 'Particularly notable were the sustained notes followed by an octave drop. Her decorations were tastefully and justly conceived and beautifully executed. Arpeggios were delicate and lovely. Trills were confident. But beyond this there was *meaning* in everything she did.'[92] Serafin told Noël Goodwin of the *Daily Express*, 'When I started audiences were only interested in voices. And singers were only interested in applause. Now we expect singers to put the music above all. But it is not enough to sing. They must create life as well. That is what your Miss Sutherland did.'[93]

In the live recording of the performance Sutherland's tone quality is indeed unmistakable and uniquely appealing. Fresh, crystalline and chaste, there was a hint of dramatic weight behind the free, untrammelled lyric sound. In 'Quando rapita in estasi' she seemed capable of doing anything she liked in the way of trills and roulades. She was aided in this great performance by Serafin, whose sense of rubato and instinctive empathy with the singer was miraculous. He 'breathed' Sutherland's phrases as she sang them. As an actress Sutherland was far less fiery than Callas. Rather, she was a well-schooled, willing, dedicated performer. Musically, however, she was consistently intelligent – her rhythms correct, the sustained top notes politely cut off at the right moment. And in the mad scene the white satin tonal texture and the repetitions of the name Edgardo gave a powerful impression of insanity: this was no gentle Romantic illusion.[94] In future years the absence of such strong and sensitive direction might sometimes result in less convincing dramatic realisations, but vocally Sutherland was by then recognised as unique.

Donaldson wrote to Berlin on 18 February, '*Lucia* was a riot, with the longest applause in mid-stream that I've ever heard at CG' and continued, 'Last night was so good, that it is in fact as well as in fancy some vindication of David's whole policy. I have written him a very fulsome letter saying how delighted I am to have been absolutely wrong in opposing Sutherland in the first place.'*[95]

*   *   *

* According to Peter Diamand, who wrote to Harewood on 15 January 1959, Callas was 'bitter' that not only had Webster not given her Lucia – a role she had always told him she wanted to sing at Covent Garden, with 'her' Serafin' and 'her' Zeffirelli – but that 'no one had thought of writing her a line of explanation or regret'. (Royal Opera House Archives, Harewood papers).

The debate about a new music director continued, Legge pushing for Leinsdorf with Berlin, as he told Smith, giving 'qualified support' in order to get the 'subject on the map again'. On 17 July 1959 Drogheda, Harewood, Webster, Berlin, Smith and Donaldson discussed the issue and it was agreed that 'any man who is to make a success at the job must first make a success with the public in the opera house'. Georg Solti was the first conductor to be invited, the Board hoping that he might meet the House's needs 'at the top level'. Others could be considered later, including Erich Leinsdorf, Lovro von Matačić, Heinz Wallberg and at a 'slightly lower level, Nello Santi'.

After the meeting Berlin wrote to Webster on 20 July to support his argument that anyone other than a top conductor like Giulini would do more harm than good.[96] Legge was pushing the idea of an official position for Klemperer, as well as raising the spectre of the Philharmonia being the Covent Garden opera orchestra. Both suggestions were firmly rejected by Drogheda.[97] Harewood wrote to Berlin on 30 September to say that inviting Klemperer to be music director was 'a ludicrous suggestion'. He was, Harewood wrote, 'to put it mildly, an extremely unfit man'.* He could conduct his performances without being music director. He and Webster were discussing plans with Giulini including *Barber* and *Falstaff* in the hope that he would like to conduct three works over the next two years.[98]

By 1960, when the search for the new music director was reaching its conclusion, it was clear that Covent Garden had come closer to its goal of being an opera house with an international standard of production and singing. With foreign singers no longer prepared to sing in English or stay in any one place for long, this would mean the end of an English-language repertory system based on the company singers. An 'international' policy would fill the House and ease the financial situation.

Lord Harewood, who was about to accept the artistic directorship of the Edinburgh Festival,† was quoted in *Opera* as saying that one of

---

* Apart from suffering from recurrent bouts of manic depression, and having been operated on for brain tumours in 1939, Klemperer had only the previous September suffered second- and third-degree burns after setting fire to his bed. He endured complications from the accident for a long time afterwards.
† A position he held 1961–65. He was also artistic director of the Leeds Festival 1958–74.

the House's greatest problems was that the subsidy was insufficient to provide enough new productions. This meant that the few excellent new productions were 'shown in too fierce a light' and that the general repertoire was not refreshed often enough.[99] *Tosca* and *La Bohème* both had ancient scenery, and the newer *Aida* and *Carmen* had been through so many performances that they also soon showed wear and tear. New productions could not be mounted for company stars like Amy Shuard or visitors like Björling, as would have been the case in Europe. It was Covent Garden's good fortune that Georg Solti was in sympathy with the House's new orientation and aspirations, as well as being experienced and brave enough to take it on with all its financial and technical problems.

PART THREE

THE 1960s
Changing Stages

NINE

COVENT GARDEN 1960–65

The Solti Revolution

BY THE TIME Georg Solti's appointment as music director of Covent Garden in 1960 was being considered by the Covent Garden Board, his artistic reputation was well known, as was his long and thorough experience of European opera and music organisation. At the Liszt Academy in Budapest between the wars, under Ernó Dohnányi, Zoltán Kodály and Leó Weiner, Solti had received what he called 'a wonderful musical education', having obtained a diploma in piano, conducting and composition.[1] At the age of nineteen he had become répétiteur at the Budapest Opera, where he learnt not only all the skills of coaching but also of running an opera house and conducting the main operatic repertoire. He worked with many of Hungary's leading singers, helping them to learn their roles and himself learning 'an enormous amount about good singing and good music-making'.[2] Knowing that as a Jew who had not been baptised he would not be allowed to conduct at the opera, Solti left Budapest in 1932 to work with Josef Krips in Karlsruhe, but Hitler's coming to power the following year forced both these musicians of Jewish origin to leave Germany. Solti was re-engaged at the Budapest Opera as assistant conductor and coach. Many of the great Jewish and anti-Nazi conductors worked in Budapest until the war, including Erich Kleiber, whom Solti greatly admired and from whom he learnt much, especially his 'great feelings for the singer'.[3]

Solti was working with Toscanini at the Salzburg Festival in 1937 when an influenza epidemic gave him the opportunity to take over as rehearsal pianist for *Die Zauberflöte*. Solti later said that he learnt from Toscanini that 'music is an eternal fight – you cannot study enough.

I never saw him without a score.' During rehearsals of *Zauberflöte* Solti later recalled that Toscanini exclaimed '*Bene!*' and forthwith engaged him to work the following summer at Salzburg.

Bryan Magee later described Solti's conducting as having 'unparalleled drive and excitement without loss of control, technically or expressively, and without loss of sight of the whole or the part'. These qualities he believed derived from Solti's experiences with Toscanini: 'They are quite simply Toscanini's characteristics – though Solti is an altogether more "nervous" or febrile conductor.'[4] Later Solti also came to admire Furtwängler, although at first he 'hated him . . . first of all as a musician and second as a human being'. Later, at Munich, Furtwängler opened Solti's eyes to a less strict keeping of tempo than that which he had learnt from Toscanini: 'When I was too stiff he liberated me, so that I am a kind of mixture.'[5]

Toscanini's recognition, and the Hungarian press's reporting of it, gave Solti the confidence to persuade the opera's administration to let him conduct. The night of his Budapest debut in *Le nozze di Figaro* was the night when Hitler marched into Austria, 11 March 1938. It was his first and last performance in Budapest. In 1939, as a result of the Hungarian anti-Semitic laws, Solti lost his job at the opera and had to earn his living by privately coaching singers. He left his family that summer. His mother told him not to return and he was never to see his father again. When war broke out he was visiting Toscanini in Lucerne, trying to get help to reach America. He was 'grudgingly' allowed to stay by the Swiss authorities, although he was not allowed to conduct during the war. Instead, he played and taught the piano, winning a competition in 1942, which brought with it the opportunity of some concerts and a limited work permit. It was a lonely and unhappy time. As Solti recalled many years later, 'A stranger, friendless and a Jew, in Switzerland!'[6] He married Hedwig Oechsli in 1942.

At the end of the war, the message the 'homesick Solti' heard from his homeland was, 'Thank you, we don't need you, we have already conductors here in Hungary.'[7] This rejection left what his second wife Valerie called 'a tremendous scar' and a love–hate relationship with his native land. He became music director at the Bavarian State Opera in Munich, an appointment that he believed he had achieved in spite of his lack of conducting experience because of the temporary banning of senior German musicians in post-war de-Nazified Germany.

Munich and its opera house were shattered, the auditorium was a hole in the ground. Solti stayed for six years, learning the repertoire as each opera was rebuilt from scratch. He was, he recalled, 'rushing to make up for the missing years in my career, and this required a terrific struggle'. Although he conducted at Strauss's funeral in September 1949, he was never fully accepted by the Munich music establishment. In 1951 Solti's new contract in Munich so curtailed his powers that he happily accepted an offer from Harry Buckwitz, the new general manager at Frankfurt, to become its music director. Solti spent ten happy years at Frankfurt, building his international reputation, particularly after guest appearances in America in 1953.

Lord Harewood went to Frankfurt in 1959 to hear Solti conduct *La Forza del destino*. As a result of his enthusiastic response, Solti was invited to conduct *Der Rosenkavalier* at Covent Garden on 4 December that year with Elisabeth Schwarzkopf as the Marschallin, Sena Jurinac as Octavian, Kurt Böhme as Ochs and Hanny Steffek as Sophie. Solti recalled demanding from Webster 'more and more rehearsals than he wanted to give', as well as an international cast, as the 'reputation of English singers was so bad'. Solti won praise from Shawe-Taylor, who described his conducting as 'exemplary in tempo and balance, in Viennese rhythm and consideration for the singers'.[8] *The Times* critic was reminded of the 'pre-war summer performances' and wrote of Solti's 'fluent, transparent, refined and rhythmically strong' direction.[9]

Drogheda, not wanting to risk Webster's delaying tactics, decided to talk to Solti directly. Solti recalled Drogheda saying to him 'in his typical manner, "I want you to become music director of the Royal Opera House. There are just two points about this offer; firstly you cannot refuse and secondly we cannot afford to pay you but you must accept."' At first Solti declined Drogheda's offer and the salary of £7,000 a year, as he had just accepted the musical directorship of the Los Angeles Philharmonic and did not feel he could do justice to both positions. He had also become 'disheartened' at Frankfurt, which maintained a repertory system, by the difficulties of keeping casts together and creating anything resembling ensemble theatre.[10] Drogheda, however, was deeply impressed by Solti: 'I was instantly attracted,' he wrote. 'His mind worked with astonishing rapidity, and he saw very clearly what he wanted.'[11] He asked Solti not to make a final decision, telling him, 'We can wait, we haven't got anyone else!'[12]

In Los Angeles Solti discussed the offer with Bruno Walter, who urged him to accept, telling him, 'We, the older generation of conductors, no longer conduct opera. You of the younger generation must carry on our tradition and pass it on to the next generation. . . . Nobody will know what German operatic tradition meant at the beginning of the century.'[13]

On 21 December Drogheda informed Berlin that he was hopeful that when Solti's contract with Frankfurt expired in the summer of 1961, 'he would like to settle in London'. Solti was 'bored with Frankfurt, & he wants to establish a home here for he has roots nowhere else'. Hedwig Solti, Drogheda added, was 'London-mad'. Drogheda believed that Solti could do more for Covent Garden than anyone else and could 'place CG in the premier operatic position in the world'. He urged Isaiah Berlin to send Webster a note to encourage him.[14] In response, Berlin wrote to Webster encouraging him to 'keep after Solti' so that Bing would not offer him a post at the Met. 'Do send him blandishing letters, flowers, anything,' Berlin urged.[15]

On 21 February 1960 Drogheda wrote to Solti to persuade him to take up the invitation, 'I do hope', he wrote, 'you are already aware that if you do come to London you will have my fullest support and encouragement and assistance and I will do everything in my power to assure your contentment here.' He added, 'Under your Mus Direction I believe that the ROH can attain a position second to none in the world.'[16] Hedwig Solti wrote to Drogheda on 25 February to thank him for his encouragement, which made 'all the difference' at a time when her husband was inclined to take on the Covent Garden post, in spite of a highly successful tour in the United States.[17]

On 2 April Hedi Solti wrote to Drogheda to say that he had offered Covent Garden five months so that he could give Los Angeles twelve weeks. David Webster, she wrote, had expressed himself 'delighted', but she nonetheless asked Drogheda if Solti could have a confidential meeting with him in Germany before he finalised the arrangements with Webster.[18] Drogheda went to see Solti in Frankfurt on 19 May. 'He was suffering agonies of doubt,' Drogheda later wrote, 'because he felt that David did not seriously wish him to come to London.'

Webster was indeed reluctant to see Solti take the job. His relations with Drogheda remained strained and at the time of the Solti negotiations Drogheda wrote to Webster, 'Your unwillingness to consult or inform one is chronic. Beyond a certain point it can become insupportable.'[19] Drogheda himself admitted to Berlin that he was 'an officious busybody with an itch to interfere' and that he was 'terribly unsure' of his judgement.[20]

Before Solti came to London in May, Drogheda wrote a memorandum for the Board in which he stated, 'Solti has one main doubt, namely that DW does not really want him.' Drogheda hoped 'that he had persuaded him that this was not the case'. He urged Solti to list his needs and try to resolve them with Webster on 23 May, so that the Board could reach a final decision the following day. Solti was considering a three-year contract, with five months a year in England. He supported the engagement of Giulini and was anxious to employ English conductors like Colin Davis. He recognised the need for international singers while at the same time wanting to develop English talent.

Although Berlin had doubts as to whether Solti was 'the best procurable', he realised that strong new leadership was needed and agreed that Solti was the best cosmopolitan conductor that Webster and Harewood 'would swallow'. He had been angered in January when Webster allowed Sutherland to perform her first Violetta when she had been under-prepared, describing the performance as a 'real fiasco'.[21] Webster admitted that Sutherland's lack of preparation had not been discovered until it was too late to postpone the opening night.[22] Porter had found Sutherland 'ill at ease, nervous, uncertain of her effects'.[23]

Berlin reported to fellow Board member Burnet Pavitt* that Harewood had shown a 'stiff upper lip' and taken the blame for the much criticised conductor, Nello Santi.[24] Fortunately, it was agreed to treat Sutherland gently and give her another chance, for on a return visit on 30 January, Porter found that Sutherland, recovered from tracheitis, was 'brilliantly successful' even without the help of a first-rate producer or conductor. Porter wrote that he could not have hoped for a more 'exquisitely sung Violetta ... equipped for every part of the role'.[25] Sutherland later admitted that she had not had enough time to prepare

* Pavitt was a member of the Board from 1957 to 1980.

the role, with much travelling, and many concerts and performances in December in Vienna. She later wrote that she and her husband Richard Bonynge 'vowed never to accept a new role unless we were sure of sufficient time not only to learn the part but also to sing it well into the voice'.[26]

Berlin, in a letter to Drogheda, contrasted Covent Garden's management to that of the Met: 'The administration slipped up badly in a way which could never have happened at the Metropolitan, where Bing lives in the Opera.' Even though Berlin described Bing as a 'dictator' with far from 'impeccable' taste, he was, according to Berlin, a 'genuine intendant'. In November, however, Berlin was reconciled to Sutherland when he found her performance in *Sonnambula*, under Serafin's direction, 'absolutely marvellous', and he even wrote her a fan letter. He also admitted that he had been pleasantly surprised by the fact that the production was composed of company members.[27]

In February 1960 Sutherland made her debut in Italy, at Venice's La Fenice, singing in a new Zeffirelli production of *Alcina*. By the end of the second act she had been given the title 'La Stupenda', and by the end of the third act the floral decorations on the boxes and galleries had been torn loose and showered down on to the stage. Franco Abbiati in *Corriere della Sera* called her a 'faultless artist' and even compared her with their own Callas. In April she made her debut in Paris with a similarly ecstatic reception.

Solti's advent was clearly going to shake up Covent Garden's administration. When he came to London in late May to finalise the details of his contract, Berlin met him and wrote on 29 May to tell Legge of his impressions. 'I do not think', he wrote, 'we shall have an exactly easy time with him. He knows what he wants a great deal better than poor old Kubelik and although his ideas are more enlightened than those of the administration, they have a very strong central European flavour about them.'

Berlin was especially concerned that Solti would upset the relationship that was developing with Giulini, who had been invited to conduct a Mozart cycle, starting with *Don Giovanni*, a work Solti seemed determined to tackle. Berlin had told Solti that the Giulini connection was 'a priceless jewel' in Covent Garden's crown, but Solti insisted that if he was to be music director he 'must be allowed to do at least one opera that he had set his heart on, namely *Don Giovanni*'. Solti told Drogheda, Berlin and Webster that he admired and loved Giulini and 'realised that he was now acclaimed as the greatest conductor of Italian opera since Toscanini'. But he argued, 'Mozart was a universal possession and he could not be pushed out.'* Webster discussed the problem with Giulini, who agreed that the music director should have first choice and agreed to do *Figaro* instead of *Don Giovanni*. Giulini also agreed to do one new production a year.†

The decision to give Solti the opera Giulini had been promised enraged Legge, who accused Covent Garden of double-crossing Giulini 'over the Mozart cycle'. Berlin urged Legge to stay on the Board and told Legge that he was 'the only person that keeps the AD at bay.' He added, 'The general rise in standards during the last three years is in large part attributable to you.' There had, he said, not been 'the slightest resistance' from Giulini about *Don Giovanni*, no doubt because of his 'saintly character'. There was, he argued, no alternative to Solti's appointment if a further drift into 'amateurishness' were to be avoided, especially with Harewood's imminent departure to Edinburgh.[28] Giulini seemed unperturbed: when Drogheda spoke to him, the maestro 'expressed general contentment' with the situation.[29]

To Webster, Berlin wrote on 28 May, 'I liked Solti but I doubt if it will be plain sailing, from time to time I think we shall have to "fasten our seat belts".'[30] The impending arrival of Solti and Drogheda, and Berlin's active involvement in the running of the House were depressing to Webster who, in spite of his knighthood in the New Year's Honours List, was considering taking a job as managing director of Southern Television. Solti recalled a three-hour car journey to Aldeburgh in late June to hear the premiere of Britten's *A Midsummer Night's Dream* during which Webster did not address one word to

---

* Berlin was urging Webster to pin Giulini down to a Verdi cycle: *Rigoletto* in 1962, *Traviata* in 1963 and *Boccanegra* in 1964. The latter date seemed far off with planning still so last minute, but Berlin stressed, 'The more he ties us up with Giulini the better for us and our relations ultimately with Solti.'

† Giulini was at Covent Garden for performances of a new production of *Barbiere* with Teresa Berganza and Luigi Alva. Solti also wanted to conduct *Fidelio* which had been promised to Klemperer.

him. Webster's assistant, John Tooley, met Solti and his wife in Vienna later that summer and recalled 'an air of suspicion'.[31] On 24 October Drogheda wrote to Berlin to thank him for making substantial revisions to the Annual Report. 'Sometimes I wonder', he wrote, 'whether the AD realises what he owes to you (and in some measure also to myself).'

While he was in England, Solti learnt that Mrs Dorothy Chandler, the chairman of the Los Angeles Orchestra Board had, without consulting him, invited Zubin Mehta to conduct the concerts which Fritz Reiner had cancelled after a heart attack. Solti had been warned of her propensity to interfere and cabled that her proposal was unacceptable and that under such conditions he could not honour his contract. Mrs Chandler did not reply and later made Mehta the music director, leaving Solti sad but free to concentrate on Covent Garden.

The weaknesses of the Webster regime had left the Board with executive powers and involvement in details of planning that would be revised in the Solti era. Drogheda told Berlin that Solti was asking for it 'to be laid down in black and white that all final decisions rest with him'. Solti wanted powers over casting, arrangements with singers, players and other conductors, but the Board would retain the 'final word on issues of policy', in effect the right of veto. Drogheda was reluctant to 'concede him a position of virtual dictatorship'. Berlin, however, realised that the Board and opera subcommittee would 'have to contract themselves somewhat to make it possible for him to make decisions without us and indeed bully us to the degree needed by any Generalmusikdirektor'. Berlin concluded, 'If he is a success we shall not want to interfere too much; if not we shall, and he will have to go.* Although Berlin found Solti 'ambitious' and 'thrusting', he immediately recognised his 'large views, energy and temperament' and hoped all would 'go well'. He felt that Solti's preference for German work might well create a 'just balance' with the Board's love of 'Bellini and bel canto'. After recently seeing an 'appalling' *Traviata*, Berlin wrote, 'Anything for a new hand at the helm, even if it leads us into some rapids.'[32]

*   *   *

---

* Webster told the opera subcommittee on 23 June 1960 that the Board and subcommittee's 'active intervention in the execution and even to some extent in the framing of artistic policy would be likely to diminish if Solti was appointed music director by the very nature of the appointment' (Royal Opera House Archives, Opera Subcommittee).

Solti was not due to take up his appointment until September 1961. On 26 July 1960 he attended his first Board meeting, where he outlined his plans for his first season. 'Everyone was attracted by his friendly manner and impressed by his determined and astonishingly practical approach.'[33] Solti felt that in the absence of a music director the repertoire had become unbalanced, with no Mozart in the last season and little Wagner. Solti told the Board of his plans to do more Mozart and a new *Ring*, as well as *Arabella, Salome, Lohengrin, Forza* and *Simon Boccanegra, Pelléas* and *Lulu*.[34] He also hoped to do *Moses and Aaron* in English, but warned that it would need six weeks' rehearsal.

Webster had soon to face the realities of the new relationship. In December Solti angrily complained that he was not being kept informed of planning. 'When I signed my contract', he wrote, 'it was on the premise that I would be consulted on all matters of artistic policy' and he refused to give a press conference 'until the entire repertory was settled'. Webster, in his reply on 23 December, revealed his discomfort, writing, 'You reiterate what you have already said before, namely that I have been successful for a number of years and therefore must hate giving up what you feel must have been almost a one-man show.' He also reminded Solti that the employment of British singers was 'an important political problem' – more so than that of the employment of English producers of whom he did not think highly in any case. Solti was conciliatory in his reply, although he had been disappointed by Webster's response. He explained that he would do everything in his power to see that 'gifted English singers' were 'utilised and introduced' and would be going through the role of Sieglinde with Amy Shuard.[35]

Solti was determined to improve performances by replacing the repertory system with what was loosely described as a *stagione* system, putting two or three operas in repertoire for a four-to six-week period, each thoroughly rehearsed, with the same cast and conductor through-out the run. At German opera houses, and at the Met before Bing's reforms, an opera could appear at any time during the season, with many different casts, and as many as forty operas performed in a season. What Solti was aiming at, he explained in his memoirs, was 'a far smaller number, but with greater care'. Solti's objection to the repertory system was that the inevitable changes of cast, with too few rehearsals, inevitably resulted in lower artistic standards. Even before his appointment, and under Kubelik's direction, the Board had recognised that revivals needed more rehearsal time. Covent Garden already had three or four orchestral rehearsals a week compared with Vienna's one hundred a year.*[36]

In spite of criticism, particularly from *Opera*, which was to wage a determined campaign in favour of a repertory system with the resident company, and more English-language performances, Drogheda firmly supported Solti's plans, sharing Solti's belief that his version of the *stagione* system was essential to ensure sufficient rehearsal time and the higher standards required by an international House. At his press conference on 20 June 1961 Solti also sought to answer the concerns expressed in *Opera* about the use of English. Comedies and *Singspiel* operas, and operas which require the audience to understand every word of the text like *Erwartung* or *Wozzeck*, would, he explained, be given in English, as would Slavic-language operas. Solti planned to work with local musicians and bring in guests from time to time. He warned that quick results should not be expected and that it needed four to five years to achieve his aim of making Covent Garden the best in the world.[37] The House would be, he told the press conference, 'a wonderful instrument' with which to realise his plans.[38]

In February 1961 the seventy-five-year-old Otto Klemperer made his Covent Garden debut, conducting and producing *Fidelio*. He had conducted relatively little opera since the pre-Hitler days and it was due to his friendship with Walter Legge and Isaiah Berlin, as well as the encouragement of Webster, Kubelik and Harewood, that he chose Covent Garden to make his first appearance for eleven years in an opera house. Klemperer insisted on directing himself and chose a

* On 11 March 1959 Webster had told the opera subcommittee that revivals could not have as much rehearsal time as new productions and quoted 'Rennert's law': that the first few performances were 'really good', those of the second season 'not so good' and those of the third 'unrecognisable' (Opera Subcommittee minutes, 1951–59). In December 1963 Solti told Webster that Covent Garden did not actually play a *stagione* system as they had an eleven-month season and put on twenty to twenty-five operas, and a true *stagione* system meant a maximum of a six-month season with a more limited number of operas. Covent Garden's system was a combination of repertory and *stagione*.

designer with a naturalistic approach, Hainer Hill. It was a happy time for him, his daughter Lotte writing that he was 'so happy to be doing it again' that he 'really blossomed', leaping on to the stage without his stick to show what he wanted.[39]

Klemperer's *Fidelio* was, as Webster told Solti, a 'conventional' production. It was also, according to Webster, 'in many respects dramatically inept' as when Fidelio was off stage to hear the words which provoke her to cry 'Abscheulicher Leonore'.[40] It was nonetheless historic in its inspiration. Critics were unanimous in their admiration, *The Times* on 25 February referring to the 'supreme power' of the performances resulting from Klemperer's letting 'everything grow from the music'. It was Sena Jurinac's first Leonore and she was 'vocally and interpretatively the embodiment of ideal womanhood'. The cast also included Vickers, Gottlob Frick and Hotter.

The following year Klemperer recorded *Fidelio* with Walter Legge who, against Klemperer's desire to use the Covent Garden cast, insisted on a different cast except for Vickers. This great recording has been called majestic, tragic, splendidly architectonic. It is all these things and much more, glowing moment by moment with human warmth and tenderness. Klemperer was profoundly sympathetic not only to the drama of the music but to its sheer beauty. The unusually slow tempi actually aided the singers to bring out emotion to the full. Jon Vickers as Florestan sang with a fire at once spiritual and completely human.

While great conductors were coming to Covent Garden, efforts to improve the stock of new productions were inconsistent. Zeffirelli's work was generally appreciated and before Solti took up his post he helped replenish the Italian stock. In December 1959 he directed *Cavalleria rusticana* and *Pagliacci*. Hope-Wallace wrote of the production's 'richness, realism and dramatic power'. Vickers, although somewhat upstaged by the horses and goats, was a formidable Canio.[41] Evans, who was Tonio in *Pagliacci*, was struck by the powerful stage effects of *Cavalleria*: 'The dawn of Easter day broke over shadowy figures in the village street beside the church, the scene gradually becoming brilliantly sunlit in the hard, Mediterranean contrasts of light and shade.' Santuzza did not lie ideally for Shuard's voice, but the production played to packed houses in March and was made up wholly of the 'home team', including the conductor, Edward Downes.

On the whole, however, Berlin felt that the problem of finding good directors still hung over the company, 'like a black cloud'.[42] In September 1959 Webster had told the opera subcommittee that Hall, Brook and Olivier had been approached to prepare Covent Garden's first-ever production of *Macbeth*, premiered on 31 March 1960.* In the event, theatre director Michael Benthall's production and lighting, together with Georges Wakhévitch's sets, provided what Rosenthal described as 'some fine stage pictures', but not an integrated production of the calibre of *Don Carlos* or *Lucia*.[43] A live recording of the performance of 8 April 1960 shows Francesco Molinari-Pradelli conducting with understanding of the score, albeit with occasionally slack pacing and insufficient attention to detail for an orchestra which still required a firm hand to produce good results. When singing loudly the chorus had a good open sound, but turned pallid in quiet passages. Entrances and cut-offs were ragged, and expression was lacking. In fine vocal form, Tito Gobbi was perhaps too forceful a Macbeth, even though the hint of roughness in the voice was appealing. Amy Shuard, who had been working with Eva Turner, made good use of her wide range and penetrating, gleaming tone. Moments of a slightly genteel, head-voice-filled sound were followed by a more Italianate vocal production, with tonal weight carried up from the rich lower register.[44]

In May 1961 Zeffirelli directed Geraint Evans as Falstaff, in Italian, conducted by Giulini. Many critics were hostile, *The Times* suggesting that the 'ultra sophisticated production', with its unusual effects like Herne's oak disappearing at Nannetta's entrance, weakened Falstaff's 'Tutto nel mondo è burla'.[45] Rosenthal, however, was impressed, stressing that normally only under festival conditions would such a high quality of performance and preparation be encountered. The whole show, he wrote, 'bubbles over with invention'. Geraint Evans had made Falstaff 'his own, warmer and more human' than at Glyndebourne. Regina Resnik was Mistress Quickly, and Mirella Freni, Nannetta. Giulini created a 'wonderful musical ensemble', revealing a 'myriad of orchestral detail'.[46] The decision to perform *Falstaff* in Italian marked

---

* It was only the second English production in the twentieth century, following a Glyndebourne production in 1938. It was the eighth Verdi opera to be staged at Covent Garden since the war.

another stage in the acceptance of original-language productions being the norm rather than the exception.

Drogheda was delighted, telling Berlin that Zeffirelli's success in getting the singers to act made for an 'enchanted evening'. He was, however, disgusted by the 'carping critics, who are utterly without the power to discriminate and who make our job of getting distinguished foreigners back here most dreadfully difficult'. Drogheda felt that Zeffirelli's association with Covent Garden was 'almost as important as anything else' and that he must 'be wooed like mad'.[47]

Berlin continued to be devoted to Giulini, writing on 22 May 1961, 'My heart is lost to the austere and saintly Giulini ... a conductor freer of intrigues, ambitions and normal weaknesses (this is sometimes very daunting and makes him remote and over-intense) than any musician I have ever met. He conducts Italian opera marvellously, better than anyone now living.' He added that the orchestra loved Giulini and continued, 'He has kept himself pure of all the intrigues that surround him at La Scala (which does not realise what a wonderful man they have).' Solti, according to Berlin, was a very different individual, 'extroverted, vain, brilliant, dynamic, not anxious to conceal his gifts or bow down to the gifts of others'. On the whole, Berlin was proud that the House could now boast a roster that included Solti, Giulini, Kempe and Klemperer.[48] Covent Garden was indeed developing a tradition as the 'conductors' House'.

On 2 February 1961, before taking up his position, Solti conducted *A Midsummer Night's Dream*, directed by John Gielgud with designs by John Piper. Solti had told Drogheda that he thought it 'the most beautiful contemporary work'[49] and his fondness for the piece was apparent to the critics, who praised his interpretation. Andrew Porter found 'magic in the sound from those first warm sighs that portray the midsummer forest'. Solti had 'understood the different kinds of lyricism – fairy, mortal and rustic'.[50] He was enthusiastically received by the audience.

Even before Solti took over at the start of the 1961–62 season, he set about improving what he considered to be the weak elements in the company. He later recalled, 'At Covent Garden I found a very good orchestra but not very firm leading. A sort of nice English atmosphere. So I tried to change it.' The co-principal flautist remembered, 'He was often correcting what we would regard today as basic mistakes.' When asked by Bryan Magee in 1971 how he raised the standard of the orchestra, Solti said, 'It is the same as with the singers – you set a standard, you know what you want and you try to achieve it, working very hard for it and never giving up – this is probably my best quality that I *never* give up – I am very tiresome in the rehearsal because I want always more and more.'[51] Harold Nash, the principal trombonist, remembered, 'When he arrived he was just like a storm hurtling through the door. He had very good ears – he could balance a thing properly, make a thing transparent.' Although Nash remembered that the rehearsals were 'entertaining and amusing' they were extremely demanding and exacting. 'If you said something was impossible he simply would not believe you. He would say, "Yes, yes, I know it is possible – you must practise, my dear." It was not a threat. It was encouragement. He really meant to encourage you to go away and practise, and most people did.'[52]

Years later, Solti admitted that at first he thought that 'there was no one there who knew anything at all about how to run an opera house'. During rehearsals for A Midsummer Night's Dream he tried to introduce some continental work practices, such as morning rehearsals followed by a long lunch break and reassembling at six. As soon as it was explained to him that most of the musicians had a long way to travel home, he reinstated the old system, but not before he had, as he recalled, 'inadvertently stirred up some ill will'. He was not so flexible about what he considered the slack discipline, planning and production practices that he encountered. 'I was used in Germany to be a dictator. The German general music director is a dictator and has to be because the people need a different kind of discipline than I learnt in England. If you put upon people very hard here they don't react. Only if you have a sense of humour. . . . It's no good shouting – here you don't get anything. Joking yes.' And he added, 'I tried too hard – I wanted to show how good I am.'[53]

At the beginning, Solti remembered of the company members, 'They hated me like anything. But I wasn't used to that way of working in Germany. When I came here they called me a Prussian bastard, or

something like that, a "Hungarian disaster", all sorts of nice things.'
Private Eye, the satirical magazine, called him 'The Screaming Skull'.
In particular, Solti recalled the hostility of William Bundy, who was
the opera's technical director. As Bundy wrote to him when Solti left
Covent Garden, 'I hated you at first, I called you a Prussian Field
Marshal, because you enforced discipline.' Webster was so concerned
that he wrote to Drogheda to express his fear that the orchestra who
worked out of interest and decent working conditions, as their pay
was not 'over generous', was in danger of dissolution under Solti.[54]

But Solti's efforts were also appreciated. John Tooley later recalled,
'His arrival here was very timely. What the House needed was energis-
ing ... On his arrival he said, "I am going to make this into the
greatest opera company in the world." That was what everybody in
this House wanted to hear.'[55] His future wife, Valerie, later recalled
that behind her husband's drive there was 'always this *joie de vivre*
and a desire to share' and his fundamental ambition to do 'the best
for his masters', the composers. When he arrived at Covent Garden
'they did not understand what this "extraordinary creature" was'.[56]

The Board were also wary of Solti. On 1 June 1961 Berlin wrote to
Drogheda, 'I think you will find that once he is in the saddle our
powers will be seriously diminished and he will not be at all easy to
deal with and his tastes will not really coincide with ours.' Berlin
added, 'Still, I think we were right to have him.' Berlin was worried,
mainly on financial grounds, about the 1960–61 season's proposed
repertoire, which included Gluck's *Iphigénie en Tauride*, a Stravinsky
triple bill, Tippett's *King Priam* and Weber's *Freischütz*. Although he
agreed that commercial considerations should be balanced with artistic
ones, he shared Legge's view that what was needed was 'a solid base
of classical works as against one-time wonders'.

Berlin's financial concerns were based on what the 1960–61 Annual
Report referred to as the 'precarious position' of Covent Garden, which
resulted from increased costs as well as increased activity. The existing
subsidy arrangement of 43 per cent of costs with a £500,000 ceiling
was obsolete. Drogheda pointed out that 'an increase in subsidy is
urgently needed if the enterprise is to go on at all' and he warned, in

an oft-repeated refrain, 'If the Nation wishes to continue to have and to develop a national opera and ballet, then it invariably follows that the needs must be met.'

Solti was going to develop the Royal Opera no matter how adverse were the conditions he encountered. He was fully aware that planning was haphazard with some artists being engaged only weeks in advance and some at just a few days' notice. Berlin had encouraged Drogheda to warn Solti in October 1960 that he should plan 'a very long way in advance if he really wants to cast the operas he conducts successfully' – hinting that 'unless he makes the administration do it, they will move without energy'.[57] In reply, Drogheda told Berlin that Solti needed no prodding on the matter but 'finds it hard to persuade DW of the necessity'. As to forward planning, Solti had, according to Hedi Solti, 'been preaching it ever since he had negotiations with Covent Garden'.[58]

Drogheda also told Berlin that he had changed Webster's title from that of 'AD' – Artful Dodger – to the 'AP' – Arch Procrastinator. Solti recalled the horror with which Webster greeted his demand for planning three years in advance.[59] On 30 November Hedi Solti wrote to Drogheda to tell him that were it not for Drogheda himself and Ingpen, her husband 'would never know what is going on in London at the opera house'. In December he wrote to Bernard Keefe to say he could not believe that he had received no communication other than a telegram for four weeks and that he could not work in such a way. Drogheda sought to reassure him on 21 December that in future there would be 'less cause for annoyance'.[60] Thereafter communications were improved by Webster and Keefe.

Solti's first production as music director was Gluck's *Iphigénie en Tauride* on 14 September 1961, presented at the Edinburgh Festival. Solti had wanted Peter Hall to direct but Hall was too busy at Stratford. Hall's mentor, Michel Saint-Denis, the radical French theatre director who influenced a generation of British theatre directors, also declined. In the event, Göran Gentele's production of *Iphigénie* was judged to be a musical rather than a dramatic success, William Mann writing, 'The evening's triumph was Georg Solti's – his and Gluck's. Triumphantly acclaimed as he took his place in the pit, he treated us to an evening of dedicated music making, which augurs well for the future. His Gluck is by turns grand, noble, passionate and moving.' Mann also praised the improvements in the choral singing and expressed the hope that the administration would expand the seventy-one-member chorus to the size of that in Munich (eighty) or Berlin (eighty-eight). 'Vienna's 105 or Milan's 106 would', he realised, 'be too much to ask for.'* Rita Gorr, while magnificent vocally, was dramatically 'somewhat placid', with no evidence of the producer having worked with her on such basic details as entrances and exits.[61]

On 29 September Solti introduced *Die Walküre* – the first instalment of the *Ring* cycle he was to conduct every autumn for the next nine years. It was a new production directed by Hans Hotter, with whom Solti had worked in Munich. Hotter and Solti had been exercised by the problem of how to stage Wagner after the abstract productions of Bayreuth. Solti wanted to find a 'more naturalistic style of presentation'.[62] Hotter's solution, Harold Rosenthal concluded, was to produce it 'in direct human terms', letting the music provide 'primary dramatic impulses'. Rosenthal was impressed, finding 'much to admire in Hotter's simple but intelligent production', in which the 'characters all moved naturally and with point'.

Hotter worked closely with the designer, Herbert Kern, to ensure the sets were subservient to the action, while aiming for warmth and harmony of colours. Hotter felt Kern's spacious and simple sets supported his own production style, but they were not well received by an audience that was to remain conservative in its visual tastes for many years. Rosenthal expressed disappointment that the scenery was not more naturalistic, noting the lack of shields, helmets, pine forests and mountains. One critic complained there was no door to Hunding's hut. Andrew Porter in the *Financial Times* missed the 'bearskin rugs, grassy knolls'. Solti later said that one of the problems had been the lighting, which was later solved.[63]

Looking back, Rodney Milnes had fond memories of the original set which he found 'clean and traditional' with its Walküre's rock up which he remembered Marie Collier running to deliver the 'Walkürenruf'.[64] The next year, however, Kern was replaced by Günther Schneider-Siemssen, who created his great 'adjustable circular disc nicknamed the pineapple ring'.[65]

---

* The size of the Covent Garden chorus was sixty-seven in 1962.

Hotter's direction functioned closely and harmoniously with Solti's intense conducting. Rosenthal was excited by Solti's interpretation: 'Although his approach was very different to Kempe the orchestral playing was superb.' The supreme climax before Wotan's farewell was such 'that even Mr Hotter was momentarily inaudible' but despite the occasionally overwhelming sound, Rosenthal could not but admire Solti's 'wonderful musicianship, his ear for sonorities and balance . . . and the intensity and drive'. Porter called it an 'immensely distinguished performance'. Solti 'by a rightness of judgement, an absence of exaggeration and a combination of bounding vigour with refinement of phrasing', had succeeded in sustaining 'fidelity to the score and vividness of execution'. Berlin, not a fan of Wagner, found *Walküre*, as he told Drogheda, 'wonderful'.[66]

The first performances starred Birgit Nilsson, Jon Vickers and Hotter himself as a moving and compelling Wotan. Later Solti brought in members of the company, including Amy Shuard as Brünnhilde, Josephine Veasey as Fricka and David Ward – who, coached by Solti, took over from Hotter. It was after this production that Vickers refused to work with Solti, claiming that he had felt bullied. Tooley recalled that the two men were 'determined, self-willed, highly opinionated musicians' and continued, 'It always seemed to me that Vickers was saying "Don't you tell me how to do it!" and that Solti was saying "I don't want to know how you do it. I want you to do it my way!"'[67] Solti had written to Vickers after the production that he had felt that Vickers's 'co-operation was somewhat lacking'. Solti explained that he did not want to enforce his ideas, but rather 'to have the opportunity of exploring the singers' potentialities and to understand the conception'. Although they had not had much time together, Solti felt that when they had met he had encountered 'rejection of almost every suggestion'.[68] Solti insisted that there must be sufficient time for them to work together on *Otello*, and he withdrew from conducting *Un Ballo in maschera* because Vickers did not have enough time for rehearsals.

Edward Downes took over the rehearsals for *Ballo*, which were reduced to less than a week. Vickers was distraught. When Drogheda went backstage after the first night he found him in tears in Amy Shuard's arms. Berlin hoped that Webster could heal the breach, but on 13 October Drogheda, after talking to Vickers, told Berlin that he feared it was irreparable. Vickers told Drogheda that rehearsals had been reduced to one week after Solti withdrew and this had added to the pressures he was feeling. He also told Drogheda that he would never forgive Solti for having made him rehearse one evening in September from 7.30 p.m. to 9.30 p.m. and again the next morning, demanding he sing at full voice in rehearsal when he knew Vickers was singing three *Walküres*, rehearsing and performing four *Fidelios* and recording *Walküre* between 8 September and 9 October.[69] Tooley told Vickers's biographer that the tenor was convinced that 'his voice was God-given' and believed that 'any conductor who caused him in his view to strain his voice was in fact acting against his Maker'.[70]

The blame, Drogheda felt, was 'about equally divided' between the two artists.[71] Vickers could not be persuaded to sing the planned *Otello* and was replaced by Del Monaco. In 1963 Solti wrote a conciliatory letter to Vickers saying he hoped that Vickers would sing Siegmund in the autumn's *Walküre*, and *Tristan* in 1961–62, but Vickers did not relent. He told Drogheda that in future he would treat Covent Garden as though it were like any other House in the world, 'demanding exact dates and details before he signed contracts'.[72] Joan Ingpen recalled that although Vickers said his non-appearance was due to Solti, in fact, he had to have a 'certain absence for tax problems'.[73] In April 1962 his agent had told Webster that the inland revenue considered him subject to United Kingdom taxes and were looking into his past earnings, and that until he had established that he was not a resident he could not sing in England at all.[74] According to Tooley, Vickers's insistence that the orchestra had been too loud became part of a budding anti-Solti mood.[75]

From 1958 to 1967 Solti made history by recording the entire *Ring* for the first time since the new stereo and long-playing record technology made such an enterprise possible. The project was put together by the producer John Culshaw of Decca, who recognised Solti's recording talents before anyone else. Solti was quick to adapt to the problems of the recording studio, easily grasping the differences between recording and live performances. For the *Ring* recording Solti won the

Académie du Disque and Grammy awards.* The *Walküre* recording of October 1965 reveals Solti as a sensitive and supportive accompanist to Nilsson and Hotter. There were moments of great lyricism as in the 'Winterstürme' and the Act One duet when there was a compelling ebb and flow, a murmuring in the strings, and then a clear vision of the tenor line – a conscious simplifying and clarifying. Solti focused on a clarinet line or a dotted figure in the strings, which is heard subliminally but which creates the lyric spring atmosphere.

Solti's Mozart was to prove more controversial and added to the growing anti-Solti hostility. At its premiere on 9 February 1962 Franco Zeffirelli's new *Don Giovanni* had a mixed reception. It was the first of four Mozart operas to be staged under the music director. Porter later wrote that the cycle did not attempt any consistency of style and already, in December 1961, Webster had expressed concern at how heavy and cumbersome were the sets for *Don Giovanni*.[76] Tooley later recalled, 'It was a monster of a set.... This was Zeffirelli indulging, as is his wont, in spectaculars.' It should, he added, 'never have been allowed to happen'.[77]

Don Giovanni was indeed designed in Zeffirelli's most grandiose manner, with sumptuous costumes in sombre colours encrusted with gold.† Andrew Porter wrote, 'Arches soar in the flies; Zerlina's wedding picnic is held in a Watteau park; the Commendatore's monument is many times larger than life, and looms through a swirl of night vapours' and continued, 'This is romantic Mozart for a grand opera house.' Porter also found, however, the long waits between scene changes 'fatal to the dramatic tension', as was Solti's 'broad, non-incisive handling of many numbers'. Cesare Siepi's voice he described as 'too bass and backward for a Don' though his general portrayal was 'excellent'.[78] *The Times* critic was obscurely negative: 'The orchestra played as well as they always do for Mr Solti, yet the result was strangely inhuman, alternating between extremes of tension and languor. The performance as a whole certainly had grandeur, yet Mozart's infinitely diverse humanity remained only partly realised; a film of romanticism blurred the conception.' Perhaps he was blaming Solti for a flaw he

---

* Solti won thirty-three awards throughout his career; the last was posthumous.
† *The Times* critic found the protagonists so overdressed as to be 'impregnably fortified by their dresses against Don Giovanni's advances' (16.2.62).

had found in Zeffirelli's work: 'It is clearly his intention to create an atmosphere thick with passion, heavy with sensuality but what he has achieved as a designer, he has missed as a producer.'[79]

Peter Heyworth in the *Observer* agreed that the 'ravishingly beautiful' visual element was stronger than the characterisation: 'Siepi fails to convince . . . a worried gentleman a little harassed by his commitments.' But he felt that Solti responded 'intensely . . . to each nuance of the drama' and conducted 'superbly'. On 16 February *The Times* critic wrote that his heart had sunk when he had read that Solti planned to put Mozart's last five comic operas on the Covent Garden stage, after his efforts with *Don Giovanni* 'to strike sparks in the air resulted in an un-Mozartian hard gloss that coarsened the emotional richness of the music'.

Harold Rosenthal defended *Don Giovanni*, arguing in *Opera* that there was no reason why it should not be produced as 'a sensuous romantic opera in a large theatre'. Many of the delays were eliminated by the second performance, when 'Mi tradì' and 'Non mi dir' were sung in front of the act-drop. Rosenthal wrote, 'Musically Mr Solti's reading was at one with the producer. His was a frankly romantic and dramatic approach – and yet the exquisite details and charm were there too.'[80] Desmond Shawe-Taylor, in his review of the Solti years at Covent Garden – in *About the House* in the summer of 1971 – also felt that Solti's Mozart had been 'undervalued' and recalled a 'sensuous beauty' in the 1962 *Don Giovanni* as well as his 1968 *Così*, which he called a 'balanced and rounded whole'. He had enjoyed the way Solti had 'revelled in the voluptuous bloom of the score, encouraging his excellent woodwind in particular to spin the finest and most delicate of lines'.

As Shawe-Taylor suggested, the London critics' view of Solti's Mozart performances was less than balanced. In the recordings made at the time, both live and in the studio, Solti's tempi were not consistently fast, while his vital, muscular rhythms anticipated a later generation of Mozart conductors, particularly Abbado. As Rosenthal indicated, his alertness to the drama in the music meant that his readings were generally better paced and less episodic than the carping critics were prepared to admit. Solti was in no way superficial – even if he did not always bring out the nuances that Krips found in Mozart, or Böhm's nobility, he touched other depths. His Mozart was full of emotional tension and warmth, bringing out the erotic glow which so often suffuses the music.

Solti cast *Don Giovanni* with Richard Lewis as Ottavio and Geraint Evans as Leporello. In an archive recording these British singers were generally shown to advantage: Evans's legato is as Italianate as it needed to be and he responded to Solti's energy, drive and sense of line. Lewis's smallish sound was not inappropriate to the part, while his beautiful timbre positively added to the characterisation in spite of pitch problems and less than idiomatic Italian. Solti kept the Covent Garden orchestra under tight control, using a thrusting line with considerable expressive effect. The attacks were still messy, however, and articulation in the strings had room for improvement. Sena Jurinac's Donna Elvira, after a somewhat too careful start, reached a high level of purity, expressiveness and emotional focus.

In the title part Siepi was convincing, although his voice was placed quite far back. He was, however, so upset by the critics, according to Berlin, that he decided not to return to London. Schwarzkopf and Nilsson had also expressed such sentiments. There was, in Berlin's words, 'nothing to be done about this: the critics are proud, independent and uncorrupt, that they are very bad is simply a misfortune'. He did not feel that Drogheda's 'angry letters to the proprietors of newspapers' helped, as the proprietors 'quite rightly defend their critics'. In general, Berlin was satisfied with developments, writing, 'Without undue boasting it can be said that the standard of performances really has gone up, and the preoccupation with British singers singing British works is waning, in spite of the anguished yowls of protest of our more chauvinistic critics.' He did, however, feel that the critics were 'nastier in London than elsewhere', telling Webster, 'They know perfectly well that our difficulties are greater than those of other opera houses, and that what we achieve we achieve in the face of far greater odds, both financial and cultural.' He added, 'We have to make our own tradition ourselves – heroic, noble, but difficult.'*[81]

---

* The critics and booing groups always caused intermittent distress to singers, conductors, composers and directors at Covent Garden and the Met, while at the same time providing a necessary stimulus to the constant improvement of the companies' work.

Solti was deeply upset by what he called 'the terrible experience' of *Don Giovanni*, writing to Webster on 12 February to say that it was due not only to illnesses in the cast but also to 'bad planning, organisation and lack of a rehearsal stage'. If Webster did not provide 'urgent assistance' he would have to ask to be released from his contract. Solti demanded the new rehearsal stage be ready by September and asked that Joan Ingpen, the music agent, be made director of opera planning.*

Ingpen had negotiated Solti's first contract in 1959 and Solti had immediately recognised her organisational talents. Ingpen herself recalled how one weekend Solti rang up and said to her, 'I can't go on like this. I think you should sell your business and come to Covent Garden.' Ingpen had been running a successful artists' management company for sixteen years, but in September 1962 she left to spend nine years planning opera at Covent Garden. 'He was known to us as "Soltissimo",' she recalled, 'he always wanted everything yesterday.'[82]

Solti wrote that Ingpen carried the planning charts around with her and could immediately answer any scheduling query. Ingpen recalled the relationship between music director and opera planner: 'Since you have more time than they do it's up to you to make a plan and make suggestions. He'd say, "I want to do a new production of this" and I'd say "It would be better to do that because so and so is available" . . . We clicked.'[83] Solti also brought in Enid Blech, wife of the conductor Harry Blech, as his personal assistant. They were a formidable organisational team.

Some critics, such as Ernest Newman and Andrew Porter, were extremely well informed and based their reviews on a deep knowledge of music history and textual scholarship. Even they, however, could sometimes be slow to recognise the value of some new work or directorial approaches. Drogheda continued to be distressed by the critics, writing to Noël Goodwin in response to his review of *Aida* in October 1968, when there had had to be a last-minute change of cast, 'It would really do you good having a spell trying to run an opera house.' An undated letter in the Royal Opera archive from Drogheda to Sheila Porter, sister of Andrew Porter, and a member of the Covent Garden staff, complained that the critics 'appear collectively to take delight in holding up Covent Garden to ridicule, without any thought for the consequences, or the pain they cause' (Drogheda papers, 4/48/1/7).

* Ingpen had worked for Walter Legge at the music department of ENSA during the war and after the war organised visits of such groups as the Hallé Orchestra and Sadler's Wells Opera to Europe to entertain the occupation forces. It was at this time that she met Solti and in 1958 she organised his engagement with the London Philharmonic.

Solti's relationship with Webster improved as Webster came to appreciate the results of the music director's leadership. Solti also continued to enjoy a good working relationship with Drogheda, who believed in him: 'He protected me and helped me to resolve difficulties,' Solti recalled.[84] This relationship was crucial, for whatever charges were levelled against Solti or the Board, at this period Board and management were working together with the joint objective of bringing the best quality of performance before the public. Even Legge was reconciled to the new music director, writing to Berlin on 15 March 1962, 'Although as you know I was not in favour of Solti's appointment I have to admit that in the weeks Solti has been in London I have had more co-operation from Covent Garden than in the years I have been on the Board.'[85]

A critical area of planning over which Solti maintained a watchful eye was the auditioning and engagement of singers, keeping himself 'well informed' about the international situation from both live performances and recordings. After a few unfortunate experiences, he tried not to engage a singer he had not personally heard. As a pianist, he was also able to take on the responsibility for coaching singers, working closely with them on matters of interpretation, phrasing, breathing and text – 'Having lots of English singers one has to work on the German and Italian,' he explained. He preferred to demonstrate at the keyboard rather than give verbal explanations or try to sing. He had perfect pitch but 'an ugly voice', Valerie Solti later recalled. The director Elijah Moshinsky, who worked with Solti many years later, said of him, 'His sense of authority is never malicious and never without a sense of helping the artist. The artists absolutely love being worked over and coached this way, and they don't get it anywhere else. He has this amazing charm by which he can bully the artists and pester them, with this kind of Hungarian glamour and charm, it's absolutely brilliant.'[86]

On 16 June 1962 Solti conducted his triple bill directed by Peter Ustinov, whom he believed to be an 'extraordinarily gifted musician . . . and linguist'. Solti liked the idea of pieces composed in the first quarter of the century – but from very different musical traditions – being presented together: Ravel's *L'Heure espagnole*, Schoenberg's *Erwartung* and Puccini's *Gianni Schicchi*, which he saw as the 'immediate descendant of *Falstaff*'. Solti explained that they were to be given in English because they were comic pieces, except for *Erwartung*, and that he had 'worked very hard to obtain an English parlando style of singing'. He was most anxious to show that English could be sung 'musically and spontaneously and in a lively fashion'. The response was mixed, Hope-Wallace finding *L'Heure espagnole* like 'comic vaudeville', Peter Heyworth not liking the mix of repertoire.

On 30 June, in spite of Vickers's withdrawal, *Otello* ended Solti's first season on a more positive note. Andrew Porter reported in *Opera* 'eloquent playing from the Covent Garden strings', as well as 'precise colouring from the winds'. Solti's conducting was 'full of vigour and excitement, of pathos and passion'. Raina Kabaivanska, the young Bulgarian graduate of the Scala school, had a 'beautifully clear and pure' voice, and Del Monaco, although he had lost the 'bright, savage ring', had gained some pathos. Apart from *Otello* and *Don Carlos* Solti did not conduct much of the Verdi repertoire, with Downes on the staff and Giulini as visitor. His June and July 1965 recording of *Don Carlos*, however, reveals the excitement and drama he brought to his Verdi interpretations, which were described by Porter. Produced by John Culshaw for Decca at the London Opera Centre, the recording was made with the Royal Opera House orchestra and chorus, and a top international cast. Evident throughout was Solti's usual vitality and involvement, as well as his consistently careful attention to detail: upbeats, accents, precisely articulated lines, clear tempo changes, and expressive tone in the brass and woodwinds. The recording also charts the progress of the orchestra and chorus, with the wind players functioning at a much higher level than in the 1958 *Don Carlos* performances. The chorus sing well together to Solti's beat and dynamic indications, and in terms of overall musicianship they may be favourably compared with the Met chorus of the time. This was, however, the only recording that Solti made with the Royal Opera House forces.

Solti's efforts to make Covent Garden a major international House continued almost as if without reference to the vicissitudes of subsidy changes and financial pressures. The 1958–59 arrangements with the

Treasury and Arts Council whereby payments of £20,000 a year for five years would be made to cover the House's overdraft of £183,000 and to pay 43 per cent of 'allowable' costs had alleviated the situation. But a new formula based on the percentage of receipts during the preceding year (17s 6d for every pound of 'reckonable receipts') proved to be unreliable. Although the 1961–62 Annual Report showed that 'the attractive power of the performances' had increased receipts and contributed to a surplus of £61,000, the following year receipts were again down owing to a closure for rewiring. Receipts went down, but costs, which were based on the year-round employment of staff, could not be reduced. The chairman warned that if the rate were too tightly drawn there would be pressure to plan the programmes with an eye to the box office only.

Efforts would also have to be increased to raise money from private sources. The 1961–62 report therefore announced the establishment of the 'Friends of Covent Garden' in January 1962, to organise lectures and rehearsals, quizzes and parties, and publish a House magazine called *About the House*, in order to raise money. The Board had decided in January 1962 to found both a Friends and a Society of the Royal Opera House, which would exist to raise funds from wealthy individuals and corporate bodies.* Berlin had expressed his doubts to Drogheda in June 1961 about the Friends' priority booking scheme, as he felt it made the House vulnerable to criticisms of being 'socially discriminatory'. Berlin had also warned Leon Bagrit, who was to be in charge of both organisations, to handle the scheme 'with the utmost care' so as to avoid charges of 'favour shown towards the rich' on the part of a state-supported institution.[87] Berlin's concern was to prove to be well-founded.

At the beginning of the new season in September, the second instalment of Solti's *Ring*, *Siegfried*, again saw a half-hearted response, Shawe-Taylor complaining that it 'had not coalesced into greatness' and that it showed 'some want of poetry and tenderness in the forest scene', although it was not lacking in 'bounding vitality'.[88] Heyworth in the

---

* The Society was wound up in 1973, when the Royal Opera House Trust was set up in its place.

Observer said Solti failed to 'reveal the work's full stature'. He admitted, however, that there was more lyricism than would have been expected from Solti's much-criticised *Tristan* recording, and that there was 'exceptional subtlety in its rhythms and textures, its melodic flow and colour', and that 'the themes were brilliantly characterised', with the climaxes showing 'weight and power'. But, also according to Heyworth, there was a 'lack of a strong sense of musical continuity', and Solti 'failed to seize the symphonic lifeline'. Wolfgang Windgassen as Siegfried did not help with his 'curiously lackadaisical gestures and phrasing'. Nilsson, however, was a 'great glistening spear of sound, she sang with uncanny sureness and power . . . riding every note and phrase with complete mastery'. Rosenthal described the design by Schneider-Siemssen as 'massive and gigantic in conception'. He still found Hans Hotter's production unobtrusive, with some nice individual touches.[89]

There had been no resolution yet of the problem of lack of rehearsal time and space. The ballet and opera companies shared the stage, which was the only large space available. In October 1961 Solti had told the Board that 'most of the difficulties of the opera side stemmed from the lack of a rehearsal stage' and that he did 'not feel able to continue as music director' without the assurance that a special rehearsal stage would be provided 'in the not too distant future'.[90] At the annual press conference in July 1962 Solti had defended Ande Anderson, the resident producer, who was responsible for revivals when the original producer was not available, explaining that the lack of rehearsal space and the late arrival of some international singers meant that sometimes there was less than ten days for rehearsals.* The Troxy Cinema in London's East End was acquired in early 1962 and was soon ready for rehearsals.

John Copley became a resident producer in 1962, working with Anderson on the revivals of the 1960s. Copley later recalled some of the problems at the time. He had asked Webster to do *Bohème*† with Jurinac, but Webster instructed him to work on the *Lohengrin* revival

---

* Anderson had started working as Peter Brook's assistant in 1948. He had been Christopher West's assistant responsible for stage managing revivals. He was resident producer at Covent Garden from 1959 to 1971, when he became manager of the opera company, responsible for revivals.
† Copley's 1974 *Bohème* was still going strong in 2001.

in 1964 – a work he told Webster he was unsuited to. Webster told Copley, 'I know *that*, but there isn't anybody else.' Copley remembered it had been a 'frightful' production and that Webster had told him the next day, 'It was no good, but it was a considerable improvement.'[91]

The problem of creating a consistently distinguished standard of design had exercised the Board before Solti's arrival and was to continue to trouble Solti himself, who later felt it was one area where he had failed, in spite of some individual successes.[92] Solti's first production, *Iphigénie en Tauride*, had been criticised for its poor design, and Klemperer's *Zauberflöte* in January 1962 had been criticised as ugly and the production old-fashioned and static.*

Solti tried to improve the situation by bringing in powerful theatre directors such as Michel Saint-Denis and Peter Hall – then at the Royal Shakespeare Company – who worked with the extraordinarily gifted designer John Bury. Bury was perhaps the most influential designer at this time, leading British theatrical design away from 'realistic box sets and decoratively painted scenery' towards 'striking architectural images' made out of authentic materials such as metal, wood, bricks, tarpaulins and glass.[93]

Solti understood that Hall was a theatre director who had a deep understanding of the operatic medium, which he loved because it is 'passionate and sensual', not 'didactic and dry', although he believed it should never be 'escapist or reassuring'.[94] But although Hall himself had approached Webster in 1954, describing himself as 'a reasonably accomplished musician' and stressing that his 'chief ambition' was to produce opera,[95] both he and Bury were immersed in their work at the Royal Shakespeare Company at this time.† Hall later recalled,

> In 1961, I had a very long talk with Solti in the Musical Director's office at Covent Garden. He screamed at me in his beautiful –

---

* There had been discussions at the Board in 1960 about Kokoschka designing the *Ring*. Pavitt had written to Berlin, 'Do you think that the vivid colours of Kokoschka, closely juxtaposed, would be the right setting for the sinister Nibelungen saga?' Henry Moore had already refused the task. Pavitt continued, 'Unless somebody can think of an alternative, we may be left with Wieland Wagner's Crumpet or some dreary Teutonic realism.' Italians like Visconti or Zeffirelli appealed most to Pavitt (Berlin papers, 26.10.60).

† Webster had offered him *Macbeth* in 1959, Britten's *Dream* in 1960 – when he was busy launching the London and Stratford seasons – and *Forza* in 1961, none of which he felt he had time to do (Fay, *Power Play*, p. 235).

because I love him dearly – Hungarian way because I would not come to work with him at the Opera House. I would not because I could not. I was at Stratford. And he said, 'It's all very well, I come here to this House, and I'm going to try to help opera in England and all you producers are so busy with your bloody theatre that you won't come and help me.'

Solti pleaded, 'How am I to do it?' Hall believed that had Solti been able, as he had wished, to assemble a group of producers in 1960, 'he would have made not only a musical style but an operatic style during his musical directorship'.[96]

With Hall too busy, Solti and Webster turned to stage director Sam Wanamaker, whose production of Tippett's new *King Priam*, in 1962, designed by Sean Kenny, was much praised and had held the audience 'spellbound' in spite of its unfamiliar music.[97] But on 28 September 1962 Wanamaker faced the full wrath of the critics and public for his production of *Forza*.

Wanamaker had not got on with Webster's original designer, the Italian painter Renato Guttuso. After dispensing with him he decided to prepare the designs for the production himself, without informing the Board. Webster, Drogheda and Solti were each unhappy with the set, which projected Goya paintings on to a picture frame above the stage. Drogheda also had doubts during the rehearsals about the soprano, Floriana Cavalli, who was standing in for Leontyne Price after many other sopranos had been approached.* Solti had reassured Drogheda that the soprano would be all right on the night, but she sang flat throughout the performance and scarcely made it to the last notes. Porter found her 'often out of tune, sometimes acid in tone and generally dull in interpretation'.[98]

There was also a mishap in the last act when Carlo Bergonzi's hat came off 'and his wig with it'. Solti ruefully recalled that the audience burst out in 'uncontrollable laughter that later turned to booing' when he and Wanamaker took their curtain. In a letter to *The Times* Rosenthal called the response 'sadistic to a degree' and said that he had 'never experienced such a display of boorish manners'. Solti never conducted

---

* Joan Ingpen later recalled that Giulini had recommended her and she discoursed on the problem of the recommendation of singers who then turned out to be going through a bad patch.

Forza again in the theatre and considered it was one of his few real disasters.

Wanamaker defended his production from what he believed to be unfair criticism. He had intentionally concentrated on characterisation, he explained, and had avoided long scene changes in order to facilitate the music drama. He singled out Andrew Porter's criticism in the *Financial Times* for concentrating on the background rather than the central drama, and in particular for his portrayal of Preziosilla as a 'sordid, sinister gypsy' camp prostitute rather than a 'high-spirited and attractive vivandière'. Wanamaker replied that prostitutes were indeed used for recruitment and as camp followers, and that he had deliberately tried to convey the misery resulting from the war, with suffering people that bore no resemblance to the 'conventional choruses of happy peasants in pretty colourful costumes' that were so familiar on the operatic stage.[99] Wanamaker argued that *Forza* was 'a drama of man caught in the grip of his time in which the values of honour, revenge, prejudice, the church, God, all impinge to destroy two innocent people and their simple desire for peace and happiness'. He added, 'That is *why* I emphasised the background.'[100]

Some critics recognised Wanamaker's attempt at dramatic realism. *The Times* on 29 September found his simple and manoeuvrable sets – 'low lying movable platforms, a few significant architectural façades and the free, bland sky of a cyclorama' to be an 'enlightening' method of conveying the drama. Philip Hope-Wallace in the *Guardian* found it a 'highly original, interesting, intelligent and largely successful new production of a notoriously intractable opera' and could not understand why Wanamaker had been 'vilely and violently booed for his pains'. Hope-Wallace pointed out that 'nothing in Mr Wanamaker's production would have struck a German provincial audience as bizarre'.[101] Indeed, when Wanamaker's *Forza* was revived in May 1975, Elizabeth Forbes in *Opera* wondered 'what on earth all the fuss could have been about'. The production then seemed 'one of the most reasonable, practical and workable in the Royal Opera's repertory'.*[102]

* Wanamaker later complained that Bergonzi had behaved in the 'worst opera tradition', only attending one full rehearsal and rejecting 'the entire, carefully worked out production to come smack down to the footlights, face the audience squarely – with no pretence of character or situation – and belt it out' (*Opera News*, 18.1.64).

Solti's reading was praised for having 'immense drive and vitality', but in a later performance on 15 October, when Floriana Cavalli was replaced by the robust Marcella De Osma, according to Rosenthal his spirits seemed to have been 'somewhat dampened by all that had gone before'.[103] Although *Forza* was Solti's only disaster as music director, he had not yet had an outstanding critical success. The continuous carping of the critics, in particular about his Mozart, together with the practical problems he was encountering, caused Drogheda to be concerned that he might not want to renew his contract. Drogheda wrote to Berlin on 19 October that after the first performances of *Forza*, 'Solti nearly threw his hand in altogether and David (who, I fear, did wrong to allow Wanamaker's sets to be put in hand without consulting anyone) did a very good job in restoring his morale.'[104] Webster also told the Board on 23 October that he was making efforts to identify the hooligans who had started the *Forza* booing.[105]

Drogheda was determined not to let Solti go, writing to Webster on 29 September,

> I am personally clear that we should be heavily condemned if we do not secure an extension of Solti's contract for at least a year or preferably two. . . . What really matters is that he is outstandingly good and if he is allowed to be lost to us we shall stand to be heavily criticised. Indeed a position of real crisis would arise, with widespread repercussions on the Board and throughout the organization. . . . Watching him at rehearsal as I did last night, observing his fantastic grasp of detail without losing command of the broad sweep, his power to stimulate – his tremendous versatility, his practical and resourceful nature, one realizes that to lose him would be a tragedy.[106]

On 29 November Isaiah Berlin, who was teaching at Harvard, warned Drogheda that Bing 'admires Solti extravagantly, thinks he is a conductor of genius'. Covent Garden, Berlin wrote, 'certainly must not lose him to America. I think the Board must somehow be injected with the idea that he is much wanted elsewhere, and that it is a piece of good fortune on our part to be able to have him at all, despite the occasional failures as must occasionally happen to us.'[107]

On 13 December Solti told Webster and Drogheda that he did not want to stay. He was unhappy with the conflicting claims on the orchestra of the opera and the ballet, and the lack of rehearsal time. At a ballet performance recently he had been 'distressed by the poor quality of playing, and the poverty of the music they were required to play. How could the orchestra play *Walküre* one night and the next day *La Fille mal gardée*?' Orchestral playing at one of the performances of *Walküre* had 'dismayed him'. He urged that the orchestra be increased by twenty so that there could be a rota system whereby the players could have more free time. The orchestra director had said extra players could not be found but Solti said this was due to his reluctance to employ women. He felt, too, that the orchestra should appear on the concert platform. If such measures were implemented the problems could be overcome in twelve months. Solti also felt that though the raw material of the chorus was excellent, it would never be developed under Robinson, the chorus-master, and urged that an assistant be found and trained up, and that the Bayreuth chorus-master, Wilhelm Pitz, should help with Wagner. In addition, Solti was worried about a lack of imagination in the lighting department. Webster said that the system was to be replaced in 1964.

Solti's main concern was that he felt Covent Garden was not building up his name and that he was working 'almost anonymously'. He believed he was 'expending much energy for very little return' and that 'his presence at Covent Garden was adding little to his stature'. The press focused more on the scenery and production than on the standards of performance. He was particularly upset that Porter, in his *Walküre* review, had compared him unfavourably with Goodall. During the course of their meeting Webster 'became avuncular' and agreed to meet Solti's demands, including the employment of an additional press officer to deal specifically with the music director.[108]

Berlin wrote to Drogheda to support the increase in the orchestra. Of Solti's feelings he commented, 'Virtuosi need constant spoonfuls of jam, honey etc., and I have no objection to feeding him as much as he feels he needs.'[109] Urged by Drogheda and Berlin, Solti agreed to sign on for another three years. Downes later recalled that for Webster the situation had became more acceptable – Drogheda provided the money, Ingpen planned the rehearsals and casting, and he and Solti worked out the musical problems. Downes recalled that Webster 'presided over the whole thing like a great amiable spider'.[110]

It was Covent Garden's good fortune that Drogheda and the Board stood behind Solti at the difficult start of his regime, having faith in his abilities, the foresight to give him time and the certainty that he would be snapped up elsewhere if he was lost to the House.

Having decided to stay on at Covent Garden, Solti's critical reception remained disheartening. On 18 January 1963 he conducted *Falstaff* with Geraint Evans and later Tito Gobbi. Philip Hope-Wallace was ambivalent: 'The instrumental sound seemed at moments to quiver in the air with delicate vivacity, yet I could rarely perceive any strong sense of overall musical shape. . . .'[111] Evans, however, received 'paeans of praise' for his 'countless small subtleties – of irascibility, vanity, breeding, decay, ardour, wounded pride – his voice is equally varied in colour without ever losing its basic richness and smoothness of quality'.[112]

The response to Solti's Mozart, however, remained the most depressing for him. The new *Figaro* had the same mixed reception as his *Don Giovanni*. On 5 June 1963 *The Times* headline read MR SOLTI SKATES OVER THE SCORE. He was accused of giving a 'super-charged chromium-plated account' of the score, which 'did not help the singers'. Felix Aprahamian wrote in the *Sunday Times* of a 'tendency to brashness, where the music cries out for expressive warmth'. In the *Financial Times* David Cairns wrote, 'I must say that I prefer Mozart both more rhythmically articulated and more expansive', although he praised Solti for the 'superb pitch of ensemble into which he has worked and shaped the whole cast'.

A recording of a performance of this *Figaro* on 11 June 1963 belies the hostility of the critics. Solti's was a humane reading of the work, stressing character delineation and bringing out the score's blend of eccentricity, sensuousness and human wisdom. The orchestral playing was crisp and controlled, with brilliant articulation in the strings, near-perfect balance between the sections and Solti's trademark high-lighting of an inner voice or a fetching woodwind motif – a clarinet here, a bassoon there. Although his pace was brisk, especially in the recitatives, his tempos were slow compared with later conductors such as Abbado.[113]

Figaro was directed by Oscar Fritz Schuh, and designed by Teo Otto and Erni Kippert. It starred Evans, Freni, Ilva Ligabue, Gobbi and Teresa Berganza. There had been some light-hearted moments during the rehearsals. Evans recalled in his memoirs how Berganza had had to wear a very tight pair of breeches as Cherubino, 'a snug fit on a trim figure'. She soon realised that everyone's eyes, including Solti's, were following her around the stage. 'After some whispered plotting with colleagues,' Evans continued, 'Teresa made her next entry with apples strategically placed in the breeches, causing Solti to collapse helplessly and the rehearsal to disintegrate. . . .'[114]

William Mann thought the production 'carefully prepared and brilliantly polished', and the orchestral playing 'superb'. But like his colleagues, he was 'acutely disturbed by its lack of depth', calling Teo Otto's decor 'at worst, an affront to the eye'.[115] Solti himself wryly recalled that there had been a better reception for his *Figaro* than there had been for *Forza*: 'There was no booing this time.' John Tooley remembered Solti's disappointment:

> Mozart was Solti's first love and it was consequently particularly harmful to him that the critical response to his performances was generally negative. My own belief is that Solti in this regard, as was to be the case with his approach to some of his productions, was ahead of his time. Here it was a matter of his choice of brisk tempos, now the hallmark of period style.[116]

It was a difficult time. As Solti later recalled, 'They didn't believe in my way of doing Mozart. The new production of *Figaro* – they hated it. . . . It was depressing.'[117] In his memoirs Solti wrote that, apart from William Mann in *The Times*, the critics 'maintained a basically negative attitude' causing him to adopt a 'voluntary censorship'.[118] Equally distressing was the intermittent booing and hostility he faced throughout the early part of his directorship. Tooley recalled that some of the hostility focused on the loudness of the orchestra. At one point Webster received an anonymous letter urging Solti's dismissal: 'Who wants to hear the *Ring* or *Otello* under Solti's selfish baton,' wrote one of the House's 'faithful galleryites'.[119] Tooley was eventually able to bring an end to the campaign, by meeting the booers who had been identified by a friend. He told them, 'The House cannot afford to lose Solti. You clearly do not understand the kind of destruction you bring to a human being by shouting and booing.' He urged them to show their disapproval by refraining from applauding.[120]

Drogheda was worried that the standard of the repertory performances was not good enough and wrote to Solti in March to urge him to spend more time at Covent Garden. He begged him not to take on other commitments when he was at the House. There was, he wrote, no one to supervise the production, decor, costumes and stage business and 'in many cases some terribly silly things are allowed to happen'.* Solti replied that it was 'absolutely impossible' to find someone of sufficient stature both to supervise revivals and repertory performances – it was a problem in all repertory Houses.[121]

Design also continued to be erratic, particularly in the less than integrated productions such as the *Lohengrin* Klemperer conducted on 8 April 1963. It was unanimously considered to be musically superb, but Josef Gielen's production was depressing to look at, with really 'grotesque costumes', and what Shawe-Taylor described as 'plastic legal wigs'.[122] The sparse Bayreuth-like first and last scenes, and the realistic and more conventional middle act, prompted Rosenthal and other critics to ask, 'Are we to return to naturalism or are we to go the whole Bayreuth hog?' Porter referred to Covent Garden's scenically 'muddled' and 'misconceived' course.[123]

Innovation in design fared no better with the Covent Garden audiences. Designer Sean Kenny and director Clifford Williams of the Royal Shakespeare Company prepared *The Flying Dutchman* in January 1966. They were criticised and even booed by the audience for bringing a symbolic approach to a romantic subject. Some years later Andrew Porter put the innovative and controversial designs of the early Sixties into some perspective, seeing a link with both Wieland Wagner's work

---

* On 22 March Drogheda wrote to Hedi Solti, 'I hear that in order to satisfy Georg's commitment of going to Berlin at the time of the *Figaro* we are having to give performances of the same opera on two consecutive nights. This is really a bit rough on everyone. I must refrain from commenting however because no doubt I shall only make you rather angry and Georg as well. I would only say that I do not think it is setting a terribly good example'. (Drogheda papers, Royal Opera House Archives).

and the oriental theatre. The means for presenting the stage picture could be extremely spare, using the newly invented powerful lighting projectors and materials such as polystyrene: 'One rope on an otherwise bare stage can tell us we are on board ship, and two fir branches conjure up a forest.'[124] But the conservative opera audiences had yet to familiarise themselves with the use of illusion rather than 'imitation'. Despondently, Solti wrote at the time of his retirement from Covent Garden, 'In Germany everything now is surrealism ... cubes and strong, hard lines. The Italians partly accept this and partly do their very old-fashioned way. But here the visual outlook is very conservative.'[125]

Peter Hall who, like Kenny and Williams, came from the subsidised theatre, recalled in his memoirs the excitement of the early experiments which were facilitated by the new technology. 'A gauze was no longer painted to look like an old, sun-drenched wall,' he explained. 'Instead, there would be an actual wall of old bricks on the stage, splashed with strong sunlight. We revelled in the power and brilliance of our new lights and the beauty of texture that they could reveal.'[126]

Drogheda was wary of innovation, writing, 'I myself was always convinced that in the main with basic repertoire works it was quite wrong for Covent Garden to engage in experiments.' Nonetheless he believed in a 'diversity of approach' rather than the elusive concept of a House style. He continued to blame Webster, however, for the failures in design, as he saw them: 'At heart I think that the ideal would have been to have as general administrator a man of infallible judgement and taste, with the personality to impose his will.'[127]

Götterdämmerung on 11 September 1963 was at last a triumph for Solti. As he had insisted, the male chorus had been coached by the Bayreuth chorus-master Wilhelm Pitz. At last the critics were unanimous in their praise. Porter in the *Financial Times* wrote, 'It was the Solti we have been longing to hear, confident, not assertive' and he noted that Nilsson, Windgassen and Frick – the finest of interpreters – had all benefited from Solti's guidance. Nilsson was singing with 'new light and shade ... a new depth of musical characterisation'. *The Times* described Frick's portrayal of Hagen as 'terrifying not by any baleful glee, but by its fanaticism'.[128] Shawe-Taylor was also impressed: Solti was 'unhurried in pace, extremely taut and scrupulous in rhythmic pointing, clear in contrapuntal delineation, and often sumptuous in sound' and, he continued, 'Mr Solti's energy and attack were again in evidence; but they did not lead him on this occasion to any neglect of the finer points of the larger structures. I doubt if a better *Götterdämmerung* could be heard anywhere in the world.'[129]

After *Götterdämmerung* Solti went to New York to conduct some performances at the Met, and Drogheda again urged him to consider staying longer at the beginning of the next season as the current one was proving disappointing both from the artistic and box office perspectives.[130] While Solti was still away, at the end of the year there were two interesting, though not popular, productions. On 4 December 1963 Shostakovich's *Katerina Ismailova* – the revised version known as *Lady Macbeth of Mtsensk* – marked the first staging in Britain of a Soviet opera. Edward Downes, an authority on this music, conducted and translated. When Christoff refused to sing Boris in English, Downes had been sent by Kubelik to learn Russian so that he could coach the chorus in the original language.[131] The cast included Otakar Kraus and Marie Collier. Frances Donaldson described the production as a '*succès d'estime*' but a 'failure at the box office'.[132] According to Drogheda, Shostakovich himself was impressed by Covent Garden's efforts. In spite of the artistic success, Solti was as disappointed as Drogheda by the box office returns but reminded the chairman, 'Even if the public like only *Bohème* and *Rigoletto* we get the subsidy and we might present other operas than these two.'[133]

Downes had developed a close working relationship with Solti. He would play for the rehearsals, coach the singers, then conduct the first scene while Solti listened from the back of the stalls to ascertain that the balance was right and note corrections on the score. They would then reverse roles and Downes would check if the changes had 'come right'. They worked this way for ten years. 'We had', Downes recalled, 'a sort of rapport – lots of things Solti did I hated, but it was my job to try to do them as he did – but much of what he did I liked very much.'[134] Berlin believed Downes to be more appreciative of Solti's qualities, in spite of his 'fiery self-assertiveness', than other members of the staff.[135]

Not only artistically but also financially the 1962–63 season had been more successful. According to the Annual Report this was due to 'the attractive power of the performances'. The takings were £47,032 ahead of budget and there was a surplus of £70,117, so that the overdraft could be paid off. The chairman warned, however, that rising costs and the need for improvements to the building meant the next year might entail a deficit.

Webster was determined that Callas should sing *Tosca* at Covent Garden in spite of her erratic form at that time. Peter Diamand, the Dutch arts administrator and artistic director of the Holland Festival, wrote to Webster on 22 January 1964 acknowledging the act of faith that Webster had shown in arranging for Callas's London return. It 'would not only provide her audience with a unique experience but will also undoubtedly help her to resume her task which she, temporarily, seemed to have neglected'.*[136]

Callas agreed to perform at a fairly late moment. Luckily Zeffirelli was in the House rehearsing *Rigoletto* with Solti, and took on the production of *Tosca*. Carlo Felice Cillario was called in to conduct. Beginning on 21 January 1964, Callas's performances, together with Tito Gobbi's Scarpia, became legendary. Callas's portrayal of Tosca, while full of passion, was that of a vulnerable woman rather than a tigress. Her most poignant rendering of 'Vissi d'arte' was quiet and introspective rather than declamatory, as Puccini intended. Harewood wrote that they were among her supreme portrayals: 'She had complete confidence in Zeffirelli, who had created a well-observed production around her. Within this framework she was uniquely expressive.'[137]

The season continued to provide excitement. On 1 April 1964 Solti again conducted *Otello* with James McCracken. There was a rave review in *The Times*: 'Every element in the performance was ideally calculated, every voice and every actor, the playing of a superb orchestra, the

---

* During the war Peter Diamand had been in a concentration camp and later in hiding. After the war he organised tours for young Dutch singers including Brouwenstijn. He had been director of the Holland Festival from 1948 to 1965, where he mounted avant-garde works including Berio and Boulez, and succeeded in getting top artists such as Giulini to appear.

direction of an inspired and understanding conductor, and a production which almost by accident proved worthy of the great play.'[138] Harold Rosenthal wrote that it was the 'finest thing Georg Solti has so far done at Covent Garden'. He ventured to say that it was '*his* opera beyond any doubt . . . he combines the nervousness of a Beecham with the burning incandescence of a De Sabata, to which he adds his own special gifts of virility and the ability to judge and calculate orchestral sonorities'. It was James McCracken's debut, standing in for Del Monaco, who had had an accident. According to Rosenthal he sang 'beautifully and pointedly'. Gobbi was a potent Iago.

Solti was thought to be much more relaxed in the revival of *Figaro* on 16 May 1964, and was given a warm welcome as he entered the pit, in recognition of the recent exceedingly high standards. *The Times* called it a 'tour de force, exhilarating, indeed stunning'. The critical and public storms did indeed seem to be abating as the 1963–64 season drew to its close. Drogheda wrote to Solti to tell him how happy he was that his 'impact on the whole operatic position was being felt with increasing force'. It was, he added, 'a splendid thing that you are here'.[139] Solti himself was content, telling the opera subcommittee after a visit to the Met that he had been made 'keenly aware of two priceless assets at Covent Garden; the happy atmosphere and *esprit de corps* in the House, which extended to all concerned, and the interested, attentive and fundamentally friendly support of the opera-going public'.[140]

During the summer of 1964 Covent Garden was closed for rewiring and improvements. In thirteen weeks the builders demolished the old gallery and amphitheatre, and constructed a new large amphitheatre with 600 seats instead of benches. New stage lighting, as Webster had promised Solti, was installed, spotlights were placed in the dome with the ceiling replicated afterwards, and the whole electrical system on stage was replaced. Covent Garden now had the largest control system in the country situated in a 'central apparatus room' behind the grand tier.

Solti's marriage to Hedi Solti was dissolved in 1966. He met and fell in love with Valerie Pitts, a young journalist and television personality, who had come to interview him. She and Solti were married in November 1967. The same month that they met Solti was busy

preparing the final instalments of the *Ring* cycle. He later wrote that
his first ever complete *Ring* cycle was greatly helped by his completion
of the recording and his consequent intimate knowledge of the score.[14]
On hearing Solti's *Rheingold* on 3 September, Porter in the *Financial
Times* referred to the music director as 'a reformed character' who
'never drowned the singers, never forced the pace, never wrenched
attention away from the stage. But positively he brought the music to
life again and again with a curiously athletic phrasing and tangy tone
... strong and definite character, hard to describe, fascinating to hear.
The Times called Solti's conducting 'increasingly glorious with each
opera in this cycle'. In *Siegfried*, the critic continued, 'he gives us
dramatic excitement, sensuous beauty, a rhythmically vital articulation
of phrase and paragraphs that make the music almost physically visible
and a grand appreciation of structure'.[142] Aprahamian reported that
some Wagnerites enjoyed the *Ring* at Covent Garden that year 'rather
more than at the shrine'.

It was in the annual *Ring* cycles that Solti's work with the British
and Commonwealth members of the company was most strikingly
apparent. Amy Shuard, Marie Collier, Josephine Veasey, Joan Carlyle
Gwyneth Jones, Monica Sinclair, Elizabeth Bainbridge, David Ward
and Michael Langdon were all involved in the development of the
cycle. Edmund Tracy in the *Observer* was moved to write, 'The music
director really means it when he claims that he is quite as interested
in developing a strong team of British artists as in putting on glittering
assemblies of international stars.' He singled out Veasey for praise
with her beautiful tone and the 'extra edge to her stage personality'.[14]
'It was wonderful to see the growth of our own singers,' Joan Ingpen
recalled. 'Even Solti was surprised.'[144]

Porter, however, could not help looking back nostalgically to
Hotter and Flagstad, feeling that vocally only Veasey as Waltraute was
really up to standard, singing with 'ringing tones, firmly projected'
Ward lacked 'projection', his voice too 'soft grained to give the necessary authority' to Wotan/Wanderer. David Ward was one of the young
British singers whose careers Solti was helping to develop, and whom
Hotter had coached and inspired. Porter found him more impressive
in *Walküre* than in *Rheingold*, 'but perhaps lacking godliness'.[145] There
was also criticism of the inconsistencies of casting: Anita Välkki went

to sleep in *Walküre* and Shuard woke up in *Siegfried*. Shuard was, however, warmly praised for her vocal skill, *The Times* finding her in 'purer, more radiant voice than her heavy dramatic roles had suggested possible' with 'smoothly eloquent phrasing and clean easy top Cs and with undiminished strength and attack'. It was her 'spiritual progress' that was found somewhat lacking.[146]

Marie Collier was another of the Commonwealth artists brought on by Covent Garden. She had a keen dramatic instinct and a vibrant, powerful soprano, which because of its versatility tended to be much in demand, and sometimes overworked. Milnes remembered her as 'a beautiful woman, extremely temperamental'.[147] Like Edward Downes, she had received no encouragement from her parents and had struggled to pursue her career. Born and brought up in Melbourne, she had managed to find her own way to the Conservatory and then in 1952 to the Melbourne Opera Company, and from there to Milan. In Milan she was interviewed by Harewood and Ingpen, and was offered a contract. In London she studied with Joan Cross, singing at Sadler's Wells and completing 293 performances in fifteen seasons at Covent Garden. The critics often commented that she showed signs of vocal strain with both wobbles and problems with high notes. Tito Gobbi, who had worked with her and helped her, described her as 'highly strung, restless, impulsive, she was always searching for something she could not find, feeling tormented, tired and uncertain'. Marie Collier fell out of a window to her death in December 1971.[148]

In September *Das Rheingold* and *Die Walküre* also featured a largely company cast: David Ward and Amy Shuard as Wotan and Brünnhilde, Peter Glossop as Donner, John Lanigan as Mime, Marie Collier as Freia, and Michael Langdon as Hunding. The American soprano Claire Watson was Sieglinde. Solti was praised for bringing on the company artists, John Warrack in *Opera* commenting, 'More native singers are appearing in the four operas than ever before in the history of the company . . . to Georg Solti much of the credit for this often thrilling, rarely less than absorbing new *Ring* must go.'[149] After his initial reluctance Solti was, as Ingpen recalled, 'very good about the English singers'.[150]

*   *   *

The United Kingdom was at last developing an opera culture that was not only becoming more deeply established, more sophisticated and critical, but was also producing fine practitioners and expanding into the provinces. Welsh National Opera, which had developed steadily since its inception in 1946, was well established when Scottish Opera came into being in 1962 with a £40,000 grant from the Arts Council and £4500 from the Gulbenkian Foundation. It was a small organisation headed by Peter Hemmings and its founding conductor, Alexander Gibson. The company began with week-long seasons in Glasgow, renting the King's Theatre, and an amateur chorus of sixty-five members, who in May 1963 showed its mettle in a 'blazing' opening to *Otello*.

Hemmings was determined to bring the best to Scotland and not to allow its regional status to result in provincialism. Audiences, he warned, would no longer accept the old Carl Rosa touring efforts and he was careful not to expand beyond the ability of the young company. The amateur chorus was gradually given some professional 'stiffening' and, in 1966, the company mounted its first *Ring* cycle. Critic John Warrack reported that there was an 'infectious sense of excitement that has suddenly gripped Scottish opera. . . . All the arguments about regional opera are simply swept to one side by the enthusiasm with which the Scots are taking to opera now they have a chance to do so.'*[151]

Glyndebourne continued to be active with its new head of production Günther Rennert, who took over in 1960, after a very successful production of *Fidelio* in 1969 which starred Gré Brouwenstijn. Rennert was responsible for eight productions in a wide range of repertoire from that year until 1967. His work included Monteverdi's *L'Incoronazione di Poppea*, Cavalli's *L'Ormindo*, Handel's *Jephtha*, Rossini's *La Pietra del paragone*, Strauss's *Capriccio* and Henze's *Elegy for Young Lovers*. Rennert was another director whose German origins were evident in the heavy-handed preparation of his stagings. George Christie wrote of him in 1978, 'He was very methodical and precise in the way he

---

* Hemmings had worked at Sadler's Wells for Stephen Arlen and later as repertory and planning manager at the New Opera Company. In 1984 he joined the Los Angeles Music Center Opera and was responsible for establishing a permanent company for the first time in the city's history. He brought in Plácido Domingo as the company's first artistic adviser and after Hemmings's retirement in 2000 Domingo succeeded Hemmings, who died in 2002.

realized his concept of a production, each detail being worked out in advance of his starting work on the stage. His orders – and there was something almost military in the way in which he marshalled his forces – were issued to each department in a somewhat autocratic fashion during the first few days after his arrival at Glyndebourne each year.'[152] John Jolliffe later wrote that 'all Glyndebourne trembled before Ebert and Rennert, like Rome before Scarpia in *Tosca*'. Some members of his casts went so far as to make 'irreverent jokes about life at "Glynditz"'.[153]

With Vittorio Gui as music director, Glyndebourne continued to expand its repertoire. Gui added early nineteenth-century operas by Donizetti, Bellini and Rossini, and 'discovered' Rossini's *Le Comte Ory*. Bellini's *I Puritani* was added during the 1960 season, with Sutherland stunning audience and critics with her brilliance, purity and style. Glyndebourne played its part in the revival of bel canto works, which was facilitated internationally by the availability of such singers as Callas, Sutherland, Berganza and Simionato, who were technically capable of negotiating the runs and trills, and able to bring the music excitingly to life. Gui's conducting of *I Puritani* convinced audience and critics of the value of the work. There was also an exuberant *Falstaff* with Evans and a revival of Ebert's moving *Rosenkavalier*.

In 1962 the London Philharmonic, whose principal conductor was John Pritchard, replaced the Royal Philharmonic as Glyndebourne's resident orchestra. On its thirty-fifth anniversary John Allison wrote that the orchestra's association with Glyndebourne gave it an 'individual voice' and great versatility.[154] The orchestra's first season saw performances of Raymond Leppard's edition of *L'Incoronazione di Poppea* in the first modern professional staging of a Monteverdi opera in England. It was conducted by Pritchard, but later Leppard himself usually conducted. Leppard arranged the original texts in a free manner, with transpositions, cuts and enhanced sonorities. His work, however, inspired the 'early music' movement. Kent Opera produced Monteverdi works with its own 'baroque' orchestra, and John Eliot Gardiner conducting Rameau in a more authentic manner.*

With all the great strides that opera was making in the United

---

* Singers who had sung in the Glyndebourne chorus included Janet Baker, Anne Howells, Ryland Davies, Thomas Allen, Philip Langridge and Richard Van Allan, who had earlier been a policeman and a coal miner.

Kingdom there remained the problem of operatic training. The main institution for practical instruction had been the National School of Opera founded by Joan Cross in 1948. Compared with schools abroad, however, it was limited in its range of activities, particularly language teaching. Heather Harper later recalled that practical teaching was limited everywhere. When she was studying, 'no stagecraft was taught at Trinity College or much elsewhere' and she added, 'I've just had to pick it up as I go along.' The opera school also suffered from a shortage of rehearsal and performance space. In 1963 the Arts Council provided a grant for the setting up of the London Opera Centre, which was to give musical and dramatic training. When Solti insisted on more rehearsal space for the Royal Opera, a rehearsal studio was fitted out in the Troxy Cinema, which was shared with the Opera Centre.

Humphrey Procter-Gregg – not Joan Cross or Ann Wood – was made director by the new centre's Board, which included Webster. In April 1964 Joan Cross and Ann Wood and members of the Board, including Lord Harewood, resigned as directors, believing that the connection to the Royal Opera was not beneficial to the opera school. The Troxy Cinema's rent and upkeep alone took up half of the school's Arts Council grant of £29,500, so that only 27 per cent was used for actual teaching, and the opera house's rehearsal time got priority over the school's need for public performances. The centre only got access to the stage in December because Solti refused to rehearse in an unheated hall. By 1976 the centre had outlived its usefulness 'given the improvement offered by the colleges'.[155] It continued until 1978, when it was replaced by the smaller National Opera Studio, first under Michael Langdon and, from 1986, under Richard Van Allan.*

On 29 January 1965 Solti conducted his first new Strauss production, *Arabella*, an opera for which he felt much affection and the first Strauss

---

* On 19 February 1976 Tooley had written a memorandum on the London Opera Centre, in which he stated that the Troxy Cinema, which was costing £40,000 a year, was too 'great a burden for Covent Garden because of its location'. Its training was outmoded and it would be better to have a studio at the House, giving small roles to young singers. Tooley recommended abandoning the lease when it came up for renewal in July 1977 (Board, 19.2.76).

that he had conducted since his 1959 *Rosenkavalier*. He enjoyed collaborating with his friend, Rudolf Hartmann. He was, said Solti, 'a wonderful director, the sort of director I would like to be myself. He had a natural, no-nonsense approach to the staging, he knew the score, he knew the music, and he understood the singer's point of view.' Hope-Wallace referred to the 'energy and voluptuous glee of Mr Solti's conducting'.[156]

Harold Rosenthal found Solti's 'fine ear and loving hand were on the score', drawing 'some of the most ravishing sounds from his orchestra heard in recent years at Covent Garden' and faithfully capturing 'the tender, nostalgic moods of the piece'. Rosenthal also found Solti especially 'solicitous' of his singers, Della Casa and Fischer-Dieskau. Della Casa was as 'beautiful and ravishing' as in 1953, when she first sang Arabella in England with the Munich company. Her extraordinarily soft, bright, sweet lyric voice and purity of tone were ideally suited for portraying the intrinsic decency of Arabella. She also combined an astonishing breath control with the power over infinite gradations of pianissimo to create a remarkable sense of intimacy and dramatic response. Fischer-Dieskau sang with 'skill and subtlety', although Solti himself found him 'more suited to Schubert recitals'.[157] Joan Carlyle, another British singer ready for the international scene, was praised for her portrayal of Zdenka.*

The *Times Educational Supplement* raved about the Covent Garden production which, like the recording, it described as 'something quite exceptional, a glimpse of paradise in a world which is usually proof of man's fallen condition'.[158] Drogheda commented on the problems inherent in the production's very success, writing to Solti, 'Everything we put on is going to be compared with this great triumph.' He advised against a revival the next year, which would degrade it.

It was still not the case that as much care was consistently put into revivals as into new productions or the productions of the music director, who enjoyed longer rehearsal periods than the ordinary repertory pieces. *Arabella* nonetheless underlined the improvements, and Drogheda wrote to Solti on 11 March, 'There is no doubt that your tremendous drive, energy, high musicianship and all the other great

---

* The full glory of the Solti–della Casa partnership is revealed in Solti's 1958 recording of *Arabella* with the Vienna Philharmonic, also starring George London and Hilde Gueden.

qualities which you have brought to bear have been the prime cause of the turn in our fortunes.' Solti replied that Drogheda's help and support and 'needling' were crucial to the achievements.[159]

Having only just failed to hound Solti out in the early and difficult days of his regime, the critics now came to recognise the generally high quality of his work. Musical standards went hand in hand with a competent Board and management. In January 1965 Claus Moser, who was Professor of Social Statistics at the London School of Economics, was appointed to the Board.* In his letter seeking approval for his appointment from the Arts Council, Drogheda described him as 'a man of great personal charm as well as high intellectual ability' and 'an extremely good amateur musician'.[160] Moser immediately became a member of Lionel Robbins's finance committee and soon after joined the opera subcommittee. Drogheda asked him to prepare a professional analysis of attendance figures and seat prices, which soon helped the pricing policy of the House.[161] Two years after he joined the Board, Moser became head of the government's Central Statistical Office.

Although the recognition of high musical standards and 84 per cent capacity houses did not insure financial stability, they did insure that the music director was willing to renew his contract. The Opera House's Annual Report for 1963–64, published in February 1965, welcomed Solti's renewed contract and 'the achievement of its opera company under Mr Solti'. But, as the chairman had warned the year before, there was a deficit of £82,516 compared with the surpluses of 1961–62 and 1962–63. The Annual Report put the loss in the context of maintaining high standards, at a time of rising costs, increased wages and salaries as well as rents, rates and insurance, which alone accounted for £104,000. As Solti had insisted, there had been seven new productions in 1963–64, which 'enhanced the standing of Covent Garden'. During 1964–65 discussions were held with the Ministry of Education about the 'grave deterioration' in Covent Garden's financial

---

* Born in Berlin in 1922, educated at the LSE. Professor of Social Statistics at London School of Economics, 1961–70. Director of Central Statistical Office and head of Government Statistical Service, 1967–78. Chairman of N.M. Rothschild & Sons, 1978–84. Chairman of the Royal Opera House, 1974–87. Warden of Wadham College, Oxford, 1984–93.

position. The chairman urged that the grant should not be so rigid and should take changed circumstances into account. The bankers were pressing and the company was finding it hard to plan ahead.

For once, government responded to the crisis, and Covent Garden was saved by the bell. Shortly after the General Election in October 1964 the new Labour Prime Minister, Harold Wilson, had appointed Jennie Lee the first Under-Secretary of State at the Department of Education and Science with responsibility for the arts. In 1967 the position was elevated to that of Minister of State, just below Cabinet rank. In offering Lee the job Wilson promised her that if she produced a coherent policy for the arts in the form of a White Paper, and the Cabinet accepted it, he would support her.

On 7 February 1965 Jennie Lee's White Paper, 'A Policy for the Arts', announced that responsibility for the arts was to be moved from the Treasury to the Department of Education and Science. There would be an extra £2 million for the arts, and an increase in local and regional activity 'while maintaining the development of the national institutions'. Artistic enterprises in Scotland and Wales were to be properly funded, as were the orchestras and provincial repertory theatres. The policy statement stressed that 'the Government appreciate the need to sustain and strengthen all that is best in the arts, and the best must be made more widely available'. It also stated that there must be more co-ordinated planning.[162]

Lord Drogheda was worried that for Jennie Lee, who was a doyenne of the radical left, he stood for everything of which she disapproved. Quite soon after her appointment, however, he invited her to Covent Garden and 'instantly warmed to her'.[163] Lee's early irritation with Drogheda soon gave way to a highly constructive partnership. On 16 June 1965 Lee wrote to Drogheda, 'You have my sympathy in trying to do the impossible.'[164]

In April Jennie Lee asked Arnold Goodman – known in political circles as 'Mr Fixit' – to be chairman of the Arts Council. He agreed, taking up the position on 1 May. They immediately sought to clarify the priorities. All the 'flagship' companies, theatrical and operatic, were in trouble financially and all, apart from Covent Garden, needed homes as well as money. Goodman wrote in his memoirs that a tranquil five years followed thanks to Lee with whom his relationship was 'idyllic'.

He had a great influence over her in artistic matters – they would meet regularly and go through departmental memoranda in his flat. Goodman saw in her a true champion of high artistic standards, someone with 'none of the confused thinking of later administrations'. According to Goodman, Lee had spent much time with artists of all kinds and 'knew that the genuine artist was an uncompromising creature who would not relax his standards'. Even more significant was Lee's determination to make 'the unalloyed product' more available. 'What she wanted fervently and what we worked with her to achieve', Goodman wrote, 'was that the artistic product should be made intelligible, acceptable and available to more and more people; and during her period of office she achieved this to an extent that will, I think, only be formally recognized many years hence.'

Goodman considered that the independence which the Arts Council system of funding gave to artistic enterprise was essential. He abhorred the concept of a 'Ministry of Culture' that would mean 'political control of artistic matters'. Government departments, he believed, 'were calculated to interfere, in the ultimate analogy, with real freedom of thought'. The Arts Council's task was to ensure proper financial controls but never to influence the repertoire or artistic decisions of its grantees.*[165]

The Arts Council was, however, only as effective as its members and the prevailing attitude of government to subsidy for the arts. Even when government policy was in favour of subsidy, as it was during Wilson's Labour administration, civil servants showed a lack of goodwill. There was an ominous incident when Treasury officials met to look into costs of the Royal Opera House with Tony Field, the finance director of the Arts Council. Field discovered that none of the civil servants had visited a theatre or an opera or ballet. He wrote,

> They were appalled at the need to have so many sopranos and contraltos, tenors and baritones all singing at the same time.

* Joan Ingpen, when she went to Paris, quickly became disenchanted with the French bureaucracy: 'The opera was completely government subsidised and entangled in political problems.' Even a 500 franc piece of material had to be signed for by someone in the Ministry of Finance: 'It could take weeks.' She later said categorically, 'One cannot run a successful opera house with bureaucrats who don't know what they're talking about telling one what to do' (Ingpen Interview, 8.10.99).

Why could economies not be made in the numbers of the chorus? In desperation I flayed around for a counter argument and pointed out that if the chorus was cut they could not be heard above the orchestra. 'Ah,' said the three wise men in triumph, turning back a page, 'but not if you cut the orchestra accordingly!'[166]

Jennie Lee herself was not keen on opera, thought Wagner 'immoral', rarely went to Covent Garden and only enjoyed her visits to the first nights at Sadler's Wells and, when the company moved, at the Coliseum.[167] But as Goodman wrote of both Lee and Harold Wilson, 'Neither of them claimed any great knowledge of the arts, but both held the firm political view that the promotion of the arts was a simple necessity to procure a more civilized world and – a view about which there is now much disagreement – that the cost of its adequate promotion should fall on public funds.'[168]

While Jennie Lee was the Minister and Arnold Goodman the chairman of the Arts Council, the budget of the Arts Council rose from £3 million annually to over £7 million. Covent Garden's grant rose by 70 per cent between 1964 and 1970–71, with inflation reaching 40 per cent. Among the achievements resulting from this rare period of committed government support for the arts were the burgeoning of the subsidised theatre and the consolidation of a national operatic infrastructure. Goodman's determination to give every artistic enterprise a hearing also helped to 'foment an atmosphere of artistic freedom'.[169]

Tooley later criticised Lee and Goodman for showing a lack of discrimination and encouraging 'new companies and organisations without any awareness of how they fitted into a plan'. He believed this resulted in 'thin spending' in the inflation of the Seventies, and that the Arts Council was too reactive and should have been asking, 'What do we need and what can we afford?'[170] Goodman's policy, however, was not to direct from the centre but to respond to the needs of local bodies, and there is little doubt that during this period there was an explosion of creativity, which consolidated and strengthened public arts institutions and influenced their development for the rest of the century. In the words of the Arts Council's report of 1966, they had set out to make a 'revolutionary change ... namely a transition from the Poor Law technique of limiting our assistance to a bare subsistence level, with stringent means test, towards a system of planned subsidies for improvement and growth'.[171]

Most important of all, it was as much the audience as the creators whom Goodman and Lee wanted to develop. Goodman said shortly after his appointment, 'The major purpose for which we must use our money is to cultivate new audiences for the arts.' It was a tough battle, he told an audience at the Guildhall. 'It must be made quite clear . . . that one can appreciate simple things without effort and complicated things only by effort.'*[172]

The Opera House's Annual Report for 1965–66 announced agreement between the Education Ministry and the Arts Council that the old rigid formula of subsidising Covent Garden was to be abandoned. In its place was to be an annual estimate based on the financial situation as it developed. It was also agreed that a series of yearly instalments would pay off Covent Garden's debt. The Opera House specifically thanked Jennie Lee and Arnold Goodman. The happy juxtaposition of a minister responsible for the arts who believed in excellence, and a music director supported by a chairman of the Board who was determined to provide it, was a unique moment in British operatic life. It gave rise to the hope that opera would become an indispensable part of British cultural life.

---

* Subsidised by local authorities and helped by the Arts Council, new theatres sprang up in the regions, including at Coventry, Nottingham, Guildford, Leicester, Chichester, Edinburgh and Leatherhead, with major improvements and rescue for other local theatres. A splendid array of talents from theatre, literature, drama, art and music was added to the various panels of the Arts Council. The National Theatre was built, the National Film School established, and increased funding made available to art galleries in London and the provinces. The Maltings at Snape was converted into a concert hall for Britten's festival.

TEN

COVENT GARDEN 1965–70
'The Greatest Opera Company in the World'

JUNE 1965 BROUGHT a triumphant production of Arnold Schoenberg's *Moses and Aaron* to Covent Garden in spite of the great difficulties of preparing such a piece. The Board had been discussing the venture since 1959 and trying to overcome the problem of the time needed for rehearsal. On 30 May 1960 Isaiah Berlin had written to fellow Board member Edward Sackville-West that everyone but Legge wanted to do it and that there had been a plan to do a joint production with the Edinburgh Festival in 1961 in order to save between £10,000 and £15,000.[1] Solti recalled that at the time he had felt too ashamed to say no, although he had never before conducted 'twelve-tone music of such complexity', and by the winter of 1964 he had begun to have grave misgivings. He contrasted the 'predominantly spoken and contrapuntal *Moses*' to *Lulu* which, he said, had 'a bel canto, legato quality'. Solti continued, 'I remember feeling depressed as I grappled with the score during my 1964 Christmas holiday. I simply did not know how to learn the piece, how to get it into my bloodstream.' In fact, he nearly gave up: 'Many times I was on the verge – I can't do it.'[2]

In February Solti informed Drogheda he did not wish to conduct the work, telling him that he did not believe it was a great masterpiece. Berlin was deputed to persuade Solti not to drop the project and on 16 February he wrote urging Solti to convince himself of the value of the piece, which was 'genuinely revolutionary and original'. Covent Garden would create the 'right mood' by organising articles, lectures and getting the Schoenbergians involved. Solti would 'surely and deservedly become a great opener of gates'. Covent Garden would be breaking new ground as no first-class performance of this work had yet been performed in a great opera house.[3] Solti was persuaded by Berlin's impressive array of argument and incentive, and later told *The Times*, 'This is the most difficult and the most rewarding task of my life ... it must be accounted a landmark in the history of the Royal Opera House to present what I consider the greatest opera of the century.' *Moses and Aaron* was, he believed, exactly 'the sort of work that an opera house supported by public funds should undertake'.

Peter Hall, who directed *Moses and Aaron* in a new translation by playwright David Rudkin, also believed it to be 'one of the key works of the twentieth century', with its 'debate between the inspired, dogmatic prophet and the pragmatic politician who does what is possible rather than what is right'. The debate on the nature of monotheism and an indivisible and invisible God reflected Schoenberg's return to Judaism in the Twenties after many years of estrangement. William Mann in *The Times* gave substantial space in preparation for the production, writing,

> Maybe I exaggerate out of love and admiration. It is perfectly possible to be bowled over by the warm, translucent sonority of the vocal harmonies in which God speaks from the burning bush at the beginning; to recognise the crucial contrasts between the austere speech-sung [*Sprechgesang*] utterances of Moses and the honeyed fluency of Aaron's cantabile in the duet where Aaron accepts the role of God's public mouthpiece to the Hebrews; and then the vigorous, diversified choruses of the suppressed Chosen Race ... the brilliance and rhythmic vivacity of the dance-destined music that portrays the rites around the Golden Calf; and afterwards the solemn spectacle of the people walking behind the Pillar of Fire by night and the Pillar of Cloud by Day.

The 'conflict of Idea and Image', wrote Mann, lies at the heart of the work: 'Every elucidation of the nature of an invisible, unimaginable God, weakens and vulgarises the vulnerability of that ideal.'*[4]

Belief in the profundity of the work, however, did not lessen the

---

* *Moses und Aron* had first been produced in the Zurich Stadttheater in 1957 and then in West Berlin in October 1959.

challenge of preparing it for the stage. It was, Hall wrote, 'fearsomely difficult and had to be allocated seven weeks for rehearsals', which was 'a vastly long time for an opera house'.*[5] Solti remembered that everyone involved was afraid of the rehearsals. Things were made even more difficult by the journey to the Opera Centre rehearsal studio in London's East End. He later regretted not having closed the theatre completely for three weeks for rehearsals when there was criticism of the very poor standard of revivals during the *Moses* preparation period.†[6]

Solti's task during the rehearsals was to make 'the textures clear and to ensure that the solo voices were always audible'. This was difficult because, he explained, 'the orchestration is so heavy and the individual orchestra parts are so demanding that the players are hard put to think about anything except playing the right notes at the right time'. But as time progressed Solti 'discovered the solution to such atonal music was to approach it expressively, to play it like a Brahms symphony, so that it sounds simple rather than harsh'. The chorus, on the other hand, which had been studying the opera for a year with chorus-master Douglas Robinson, had to 'cultivate a short, sharp, even ugly mode of delivery'.[7] Robinson was impressed by Hall's working method, writing to him on 1 February that he had an ability to 'inspire' the choristers and 'make something very special in our theatre's history, even in the history of opera'.[8]

Hall had to manoeuvre more than 300 people: dancers, singers, a double chorus, acrobats, actors and a 'menagerie of animals'. At the dress rehearsal, he recalled, 'a camel teetered down the precipitously raked stage, causing the whole opera house orchestra to flee the pit in consternation. The creature then shat copiously. He had to be cut.' Hall was concerned about 'overdoing it', but as he believed one of the

---

* Such long rehearsals were far from the norm. In March 1965, Webster had discouraged talk of inviting Felsenstein to direct *Gloriana* as his presence would lead to 'trouble in the future' as other directors might seek to copy his technique and demand longer rehearsal time (Royal Opera House Archives, Drogheda papers, Drogheda to Solti, 11.3.65).

† After a particularly poor revival of *Bohème*, Drogheda wrote to Solti on 9 June to say he did not know who should be supervising revivals when the music director was busy and that Ingpen should reconsider the 'routine Puccini revivals as fillers' (Royal Opera House Archives, Drogheda papers).

themes of the opera was the danger of excess, he felt that it was essential to present this element on stage. For the orgy he also insisted on using 'large ornamental penises, painted garishly and decked out with muffs of goat hair', which were designed to be strapped to the performers' middles but which disappeared into the desk of David Webster. With great reluctance Webster was persuaded to allow them out. Hall believed that 'nakedness in the theatre is a basic truth', and should be used responsibly and for a purpose. The 'lust of orgy round the golden calf' could only, Hall felt, be expressed by 'some degree of nudity'. Since the Lord Chamberlain, responsible for censorship, was still the arbiter of obscenity, Hall had to be careful with the half-dozen strippers hired from Soho. They had to wear pads of false pubic hair and 'Elastoplast patches over their nipples'. Hall called them the 'most noticeable breasts in Old Testament history'.[9] Isaiah Berlin recalled that because of the Lord Chamberlain's censorship policy the extras were 'not allowed to wriggle'. Solti did not feel the orgy was overdone. 'The quiet close after so much excitement is effective and the final coming to rest on F sharp with Moses's last, despairing words is overwhelmingly moving.'[10]

News of the orgy was leaked before the opening night and caused an uproar in the popular press, thus unintentionally helping to ensure a good box office. The less popular press was also excited. On 29 June *The Times* was delighted, calling *Moses and Aaron* a 'triumph for Mr Georg Solti', and for Peter Hall 'whose production of the crowd scenes alone sets new standards in the staging of opera'. Andrew Porter in the *Financial Times* wrote that the performance was 'so assured, so powerful that it is surely the greatest achievement in Covent Garden's history'. Rosenthal in *Opera* seconded Porter's assessment: 'The achievement of Covent Garden cannot be overrated.' Hall called it 'the only great tragedy this century has produced' and added that 'only Covent Garden could have staged it'.

The public reactions were extraordinary. The booing claque, which had warned Hall that they would be on duty, never materialised. *The Times* reported that the 'roar of applause at the end was of a volume and enthusiasm that one expects for a concourse of great prima donnas but not for a dodecaphonic opera about the nature of God'. John Warrack in the *Sunday Times* called it 'nothing short of a triumph. . . .

'ouglas Robinson's chorus have absorbed the music so deeply that it ounds their natural utterance.' By mixing singers and actors, Hall as created a picture both frightening and oddly touching of the any-headed monster, capricious yet idealistic touching degradation nd groping out of it to salvation'.[11]

Solti and Peter Hall enjoyed this first of several successful collabor-ions, each appreciating the other's intelligence, sense of humour and rofessionalism. In particular Hall valued Solti's precision and ability work with directors. 'In a sloppy world, which frankly, opera both usically and dramatically usually is – a sort of sentimentality and pproximation – his precision was a wonderful corrective.' Solti's etermination to get the best out of the people he worked with could reate, Hall observed, 'an electricity, a tension which can have the ost extraordinary results'.[12] Solti, for his part, was pleased that Hall inlike many German directors, realised that his production must ork with, not against, the music'. And he added, 'Any idea of his or iine has been thrashed out, accepted or rejected after experimenta-on.' Solti said it had been 'a rewarding collaboration' for both men nd was to ask Hall to do the *Ring* with him in Bayreuth in 1980.[13]

Jennie Lee brought the Soviet Minister of Culture, Ekaterina Furt-eva, to see *Moses and Aaron*. Hall recalled her reaction: 'At the end, y courtesy of an embarrassed interpreter, she harangued me soundly. he said that she thought that it was completely wrong for the country grant me public money so that I could create such an erotic and eprehensible spectacle; it was pandering to decadent tastes ... the lought of staging him (Schoenberg) as a crowd pleaser was something treasure.'[14]

'he 1965–66 Covent Garden season opened once more with *Ring* cycles om 22 September to 8 October. The orchestral playing was of a high tandard and the cast was by then, and as a result of Solti's nurturing, early entirely British. The new Sieglinde was Gwyneth Jones, one of olti's protégées, who made a great impression. Rosenthal reported lat it was 'generally agreed that Miss Jones was the most moving, 'omanly, and ardent Sieglinde seen or heard since Lotte Lehmann'.

Jones's Welsh background had provided her with experience

singing in choirs and winning song competitions, but the poverty of the Welsh industrial valleys meant that she had started out her working life as a secretary. Having managed to gain admission to the Royal College of Music, she had gone to study in Siena and from there to Zurich on a scholarship, helped by Edward Downes and Joan Ingpen who had heard her in a singing competition when Ingpen was still an agent. When Solti told Ingpen he needed two new mezzos, Ingpen immediately thought of Jones, who came back to audition for Solti. Although she auditioned as a mezzo, by the time she joined the company she had decided that she was a soprano. She was taken up by Covent Garden in 1963 but made her debut at Welsh National Opera as Lady Macbeth, where her dramatic and vocal talents were instantly recognised. Solti told her she could take on Santuzza in her second season but that she could also cover for Régine Crespin in *Fidelio* and sing in the last performance on 21 October 1964, if Solti felt she was ready. She later recalled of her Covent Garden debut, 'The House just went wild and they tore up their programmes up in the gods and threw it all down like confetti.' She also stood in for Leontyne Price in the new Giulini–Visconti *Trovatore*. According to Joan Ingpen, Jones, who was studying in Rome, had contacted Giulini on her own initiative and, after hearing her, he had agreed to her taking part in the performances. Ingpen felt that it was too soon for her, that her voice was still raw, but, she explained, 'You couldn't hold Gwyneth back.'[15] Offers soon started pouring in and her career, Jones recalled 'took off like a rocket'.[16]

From the earliest days of Gwyneth Jones's career there were anxieties about pressure and premature exposure. When she first tackled Leonore in *Fidelio*, in October 1965, Arthur Jacobs found her voice 'insufficiently varied, not always pleasant and not always on pitch'. At the time of her debut at La Scala in 1970 the critic thought she was singing too much and that such a natural talent should be more carefully guarded. Members of the Board also expressed concern that, with her 'great talent', she might be tempted to 'do too much too quickly'.[17] But Jones did not take kindly to the criticism. She had, she explained, to work 'extremely hard in the first years' in order to establish herself and build a soprano repertory. She was singing seventy-five performances a season but at the same time she turned down offers from Solti to sing Isolde and from Kempe to sing Elektra.

Solti's period as music director saw no diminution in the visits of first-class conductors. These conductors, working with some fine casts, ensured a consistently high standard of performance. Klemperer continued to be a regular visitor, returning for more *Fidelios*. In a performance of the opera in March 1969 Arthur Jacobs found that some 'slow tempos and a beat sometimes ill-defined' led to some untidy orchestral playing.[19] Nevertheless, London musicians of this era responded to Klemperer's profound understanding of Beethoven. A film of a 1964 performance of the Ninth Symphony at the Royal Albert Hall shows the New Philharmonia following the muddled beat perfectly, executing every nuance. Klemperer was a great intuitive conductor. As Yehudi Menuhin put it, he lacked 'technique or method or manner. He stood there with music coming out of him with great authority – without talking or doing. . . . He was a kind of magician.'[20]

Giulini also continued his relationship with Covent Garden. He found the House's professionalism and organisation under Solti more satisfactory than that of other opera houses, with which he was becoming increasingly disenchanted. Drogheda wrote to Webster from Rome, where he had gone to see the Visconti–Giulini *Figaro*, to say that Giulini 'finds the *spirito de corpo* something unique'.[21] Giulini's appearances at Covent Garden were much appreciated. On 25 October 1965 Rosenthal found Giulini's *Trovatore* series the 'greatest single performances of Italian opera we have heard at Covent Garden in recent years'. Giulini 'with his burning sincerity, musical integrity, complete belief in Verdi's music, is without a doubt the greatest conductor of Italian opera, and Verdi in particular, since Toscanini'. Giulini's conducting of Visconti's controversial black-and-white *Traviata* in 1967 had his usual 'intensity, feeling, firm rhythms, a fierce belief in the music itself', to which the orchestra heartily responded.

Kempe conducted *Parsifal* in February 1966 and in 1968 Abbado came to conduct *Don Carlos*. Kubelik received a great response on 16 February 1968 when he conducted *Jenůfa*. In December 1969 Pierre Boulez conducted *Pelléas et Mélisande*. Charles Mackerras, who was familiar to Sadler's Wells audiences, made his debut at Covent Garden with *Katerina Ismailova* in 1963. Thereafter he conducted Mozart, Puccini and Verdi at the House.*

The House's music staff also continued to make its contribution. Edward Downes was entrusted by Solti with many performances, both new productions and revivals. He was appreciated for his Verdi interpretations and the Italian repertoire in general. Solti in his memoirs called him 'a talented man and a wonderful support to me'. In October 1965 Downes conducted the *Ring* for the first time, the first Englishman to do so at Covent Garden since Beecham in 1939. In spite of difficulties stemming from Hotter's late withdrawal, Downes was warmly praised by William Mann. In November and December 1966 Downes had conducted a revival of *Simon Boccanegra*, in which he showed great understanding as well as a great feel for the 'ebb and flow of Verdi'. Rosenthal said of Downes, after a performance of *Rigoletto*, that he 'gets the last ounce of excitement from the score'. Reginald Goodall had over the years become one of the great Wagner coaches. James King learnt Parsifal, Vickers specially came to learn Tristan, and Shuard, Veasey, Ward, Gwyneth Jones, Donald McIntyre, Gwynne Howell and John Tomlinson all studied with him. Solti, however, did not entrust him with actual performances. He felt that Goodall did not have 'the technical skills to transmit his love of the score'. Webster was later uncomfortable when Goodall went to English National Opera and prepared his highly successful *Ring*, but there was no question of Solti relinquishing his *Ring* to Goodall.†

*   *   *

---

* Mackerras was interested in period style. On 30 December 1965 he prepared his famous *Figaro* for Sadler's Wells, fulfilling the roles of 'music editor, conductor and harpsichordist'. Grove notes that 'his appoggiaturas and added ornamentation had a lasting influence'.

† It was said that Goodall's career had been impeded by his pacifism and 'spouting of blackshirt and anti-Semitic slogans'. His friends defended him as 'naive, inconsistent, illogical, quite potty and perfectly harmless', and biographer John Lucas said that his hero was Klemperer (Lucas, Obituary, *Opera*, July 1990). Tomlinson later recalled that Goodall was a 'totally dedicated and patient' coach who had suggested coaching him for the role of Hagen many years before he actually sang a Wagner role and for no payment. 'It was his philosophy,' Tomlinson explained, 'almost like a pilgrimage' (*Guardian*, 8.10.93).

Solti was appalled in July 1966 when one of his detractors defaced his car with the words 'Solti go home'. Tooley recalled receiving a telephone call from Solti to say that he 'could not remain in London'. It was, Tooley remembered, 'a horrible, horrible experience'. In his memoirs Solti says that it reminded him of what Fritz Busch had suffered at the hands of the Nazis in the 1930s. Drogheda wrote to him, 'How absolutely damnable for you. I can imagine nothing more unpleasant. . . . Everything possible will be done to discern the identity of the particular idiot who is plaguing you.' A private detective employed by management failed to find anything more sinister than some stickers with the words 'Solti must stay' placed in various parts of the theatre.

In spite of this unpleasantness, Solti's contribution was now recognised even by the early doubters, Berlin writing to Drogheda on 5 July, 'With all his faults the musical director has proved of terrific value to us; he really has transformed the reality and the image of Covent Garden.' He added, 'But do not tell David this – even though it is true and he knows it.'[22]

The happy collaboration of Hall and Solti continued that summer with the fourth production of *Magic Flute* since the war. 'Mozart', Hall said, 'is Shakespearean in his love of human ambiguity,' comparing *The Magic Flute* with *The Tempest*.[23] The basis of Hall's successful collaboration with Solti was his respect for the other people in the team. Hall wrote, 'The relationship with the conductor is very important to me. . . . It is a partnership, no one element is subservient to the other.' Geraint Evans, who sang Papageno, recalled that Hall was never 'dogmatic about opera staging; he was always ready to talk over ideas with the artists, and to reach a balance between what he had in mind and what was best for them. I'm sure that his concern for the artist is a major part of his success in the theatre.'[24] Peter Hall later recalled of Solti:

> He was a wonderful collaborator, but you had to stand up for yourself, because if you knew what you wanted to do with strength and conviction, he wouldn't obstruct you. But with weaker directors I have seen him be terribly overbearing – simply in the sense that what he loved most of all was to have everybody in the cast looking at him and watching his baton

and not doing anything about acting ... But he was excited
by creation and talent and drama when it worked. ... Georg
challenged you – it was a bit of a fight with Georg, I loved it.[25]

Solti's and Hall's partnership again proved to be an inspired one.
When *The Magic Flute* was premiered on 5 July Solti's Mozart talents
were at last given full recognition. He showed, wrote Shawe-Taylor in
the *Sunday Times*, 'perfect tact and understanding'. *The Times* on
6 July said Solti made 'natural, affectionate but never forced or reverential music'. Rosenthal in *Opera* magazine felt it was one of the best
Magic Flutes he had ever seen anywhere. Hall, having dispensed with
Oscar Kokoschka's designs, had worked inspirationally with his Royal
Shakespeare colleague, John Bury, confounding Webster's fears that
Bury, with his 'stern, masculine qualities' would not find 'enough
magic for the job'.[26] Their teamwork, together with Solti, not only
'struck a blow for ensemble opera but it also showed that the British
straight theatre can contribute something to the world of opera'. It
was sung in English, in a new translation by poet and novelist Adrian
Mitchell, with 'most, if not all the tricks of the stage. The pace was
smart, the staging a constant delight.' Hall and Bury had 'faithfully
imitated the mechanical devices of the original production of 1791'.
Of special delight were 'the appearances and disappearances through
various trap doors, the three (real) boys in their flying chariot, Sarastro's lions and a very convincing serpent'. It was, concluded Rosenthal, 'one of the best things that Solti has done since he came to
Covent Garden'. Shawe-Taylor wrote that the three boys were a 'smash
hit', and that, 'serene benevolent and unpretentiously wise, they sit
aloft in their stout chariot and embody the spirit of Mozart'.[27]

Drogheda felt that Solti's marriage to Valerie Pitts in July made
Solti 'altogether more relaxed and at ease with himself than he had
previously been'.[28] At the annual press conference it was announced
that Solti's contract had been renewed to the end of the 1969–70
season, when he would have completed nine years. Solti said that he
felt it was fair to say that the level of performances at Covent Garden
was 'as high as anywhere in the world'. He later signed a contract for
another year to enable him to complete ten years.

*   *   *

Solti had another Strauss success with *Die Frau ohne Schatten* on 14 June 1967. The opera was one of his great loves in spite of the heavy orchestration and problems of balance.[29] It was once again produced in a traditional way by Hartmann, with 'magic and other-worldly' designs by Josef Svoboda. William Mann later wrote that he believed it was during revivals of *Die Frau* that Solti 'matured as a conductor'. Mann added that with this maturity, Solti 'had not ceased to lead his audiences in working up a healthy sweat, nor in looming over his orchestra, shoulder blades never idle, poised for the panther's spring in case any of his players should for an instance relax the highly sprung tension which makes the complete musical ensemble'.[30]

In 1967 Solti was invited to become music director of the Chicago Symphony Orchestra and agreed to assume the position in 1969. He decided, however, that he could only manage the double workload with Covent Garden for two years, and told the Board that he would stay on until the summer of 1971. The Board deliberated on the question of a successor throughout 1967. There was general agreement that a British musician should be chosen. After three successive foreign music directors it was felt that to appoint a fourth would be 'tantamount to saying that despite all the years of operatic experience gained in London since the war, there was still no native-born conductor worthy of the job'.[31] Kempe and Giulini would have been considered, both because of their close relationship with the House and their popularity with the public, but neither was prepared to tie himself down and both were conducting less opera.

Of the British candidates, Drogheda felt that Charles Mackerras's 'qualities and attributes made him a powerful possibility'. He had become a staff conductor at Sadler's Wells in 1948 and main conductor from 1956 with the English Opera Group. He had been connected with the development of operatic life in Britain since 1947, including conducting premieres of many of Britten's works at Aldeburgh and bringing Janáček's work out of Czechoslovakia. At the time of the deliberations he was first conductor at Hamburg (1966–69) but it was announced in March 1969 that he would become music director of Sadler's Wells from January 1970.* Drogheda

---

* He was a guest conductor with Welsh National Opera, and in Australia, Canada and East Berlin 1961–62.

also wrote that John Pritchard was considered very gifted and had given some 'impressive performances', but it was thought that he might find 'the intricacies of Covent Garden' too daunting. Edward Downes, as well as being an excellent musician, was deeply experienced in the running of the musical side of the House.

Colin Davis, however, was the preferred candidate of Webster, Drogheda and Solti himself, ideally with Downes staying on in a position of 'appropriate status' – with the title of principal conductor.[32] Davis seemed to Drogheda to have 'a passionate intensity in all that he did, and one felt that there was a fire raging inside him'.[33] The decision became urgent because Davis had been offered the Boston Symphony Orchestra. Drogheda wrote to Webster on 28 November that although he was very keen not to lose Downes, he felt Davis's stature would grow to a greater extent than that of Downes and that they would be 'very criticised, and rightly, if we allowed Colin to be lost to the USA'.[34] Solti had entrusted Davis with many performances since his debut, conducting *Figaro*, on 10 November 1965. Perhaps because of nervousness he had rushed the first act and 'seemed ill at ease with his soloists, often differing with them over questions of tempo'. It was felt that at that time he had not quite made the transition from the Sadler's Wells ensemble to Covent Garden's international line-up. His *Wozzeck* with Collier and Evans on 23 March 1970, however, was more successful, *The Times* praising his 'admirably lucid account of this marvellous score'.*[35] In April 1967 he conducted *Der fliegende Holländer* and in July, at the end of the season, a very successful *Don Giovanni* with 'strong dramatic lines'.[36] He also conducted a *Midsummer Marriage*.

Davis came from a non-musical background, but after hearing Beethoven's Eighth Symphony at the age of fourteen, music became his consuming interest and he studied clarinet at the Royal College of Music. His difficult early struggles to become a conductor had been alleviated in 1959, when Walter Legge had arranged for him to take over from an indisposed Klemperer at the Festival Hall in a performance of *Don Giovanni*. Davis later ascribed this opportunity to 'Legge's sense of humour and malicious delight in shocking the international Estab-

---

* Evans was knighted on 23 March 1970.

lishment' by putting in 'an insignificant squit of an Englishman'.[37] But his performance had made a fine impression and he had become Sadler's Wells's music director in 1961. He had also worked at Glyndebourne and had gained popularity in appearances at the Proms.

In December 1967 the Board formally asked Colin Davis to be music director after Solti's retirement in 1971. His first contract would run from September 1971 to August 1976 and the appointment would be announced in December 1968. The Board, Solti and Webster agreed that Downes should be retained with the title of 'associate music director', but in October 1968 he resigned, not wanting, Solti recalled, 'a lesser title'. Downes went to Sydney as music director of Australian Opera in 1972 and came back, according to Solti, 'disillusioned' in 1976.*

There was to be not only a new music director but also a new executive director. Webster was getting old and difficult, and his slow retirement was worrying Drogheda. It was finally agreed, however, that he should go at the end of the 1969–70 season, on his sixty-seventh birthday, even though he ought to have retired two years earlier. In January 1967 Berlin made the strange suggestion that Drogheda himself take on the job, doubling it with his chairmanship of the Board, as 'enlightened noblemen have always done it – and very brilliantly too – in Petersburg, Munich, Vienna etc.'. He was worried about the programming of Janáček, Britten and 'various Swedes' that would result if Harewood were to take over. The idea of a Board chairman assuming the role of the executive was at this juncture – though this was not to be the case thirty years later – laid quickly to rest by Drogheda himself. Although he was flattered, he told Berlin that the suggestion was 'totally unpractical'.†[38]

There was also a move to bring in an artistic director, inspired by Drogheda's growing friendship with Peter Hall. There were

---

* Downes conducted Prokofiev's *War and Peace* as the official opening production of the new Sydney Opera House on 28 September 1973. The new House had taken sixteen years to build at a cost of $100 million. There were many technical problems with the 1,500-seat opera auditorium at the beginning, even though the 2,700-seat concert hall and 550-seat drama theatre proved more workable initially, and the building became one of Sydney's most striking landmarks.

† At the Met, Anthony Bliss and Bruce Crawford had during their careers the position of both president of the Board of Directors and general manager.

conversations about Hall producing a *Ring* with Solti, and by 1968 actual dates had been specified, to begin with *Rheingold* and *Walküre* in 1970, the cycle to be completed in 1971. Hall had refused to cast Brünnhilde from the company of British singers and insisted on the same singer for Wotan throughout the cycle.[39] Drogheda decided to introduce Hall to the music director elect to discuss the possibility of doing a *Ring* and in early 1969 Davis met Peter Hall at Drogheda's house. Hall recalled that he and Davis found an immediate rapport:

> We were of the same generation – both young lions of the new artistic establishment, both impatient of formality and what we saw as the old, stuffy British way of doing things. We found an identical enthusiasm about what opera should be, how it should be created and how the audience for it should be broadened. We both wanted to bring the theatre back into the opera. . . . Our wives and the Droghedas stared at us dumbfounded. We talked on and on. It was a magical evening.[40]

Hall later recalled, 'Within a week Colin Davis had done an extraordinary thing: he had offered me half his crown. He wanted me to share his directorship of the Royal Opera. This was an act of immense generosity. It was absolute proof of his feeling that music and drama should be equal partners. I accepted with alacrity.' The two men met again soon after to examine, in Davis's words, their 'intuitive enthusiasm under the cold light of reason'. Davis told Drogheda that he wanted Peter Hall to be associated with him in the artistic direction of the House on 'equal terms'. This was important, he argued, because 'musicians on the whole are ill educated visually and are, besides, far too concerned with their own problems'. There was, he said, a possibility of the two men 'approaching the whole problem of opera from a shared attitude'. Davis suggested that they both be given the title of artistic director.[41] Hall told the Board, 'We will be directors together. Otherwise I will not do it because there will be no point.'[42]

By March 1969 it was agreed that Hall would become artistic director, devoting twenty-six weeks a year to Covent Garden, and that he would direct a number of productions while Solti was still music director. Plans were already in hand for the proposed *Ring* cycle, which was to be completed in 1971. John Higgins in the *Spectator* felt that

Hall would be the English answer to Felsenstein. Hall recalled, 'It was very simple – they asked me to go in and provide some RSC thinking for the cause of opera and modernise it.'[43]

The future was looking exciting but costs were starting to increase. The 1967–78 Annual Report showed an increase in both expenses and income of about £400,000. The increase in expenditure was due to a general increase in wages and materials on a level with the general inflation, but nearly £200,000 of the income increase was from the Royal Ballet tour in the United States, which was a one-off source. The remaining income was £130,000 from increased seat prices of about 10 per cent, and the Arts Council grant of £100,000. Salaries and wages had increased by £30,000 and new ballet and opera productions accounted for increases of over £50,000.

The management staunchly defended its policy of at least eight new opera and ballet productions a year, as 'the lifeblood of a repertory company'. Their role was to 'maintain the vitality and variety of the repertory; if the repertory gets stale, not only the morale of the company but also the interests of the public – and thus receipts at the box office – are diminished. . . .'* The report explained that an outside firm of business consultants had been called in to find room for greater economies and efficiency, but that they had reported there were few ways to reduce costs. The report concluded, 'We are not here to produce opera and ballet on the cheap.'

In July 1968 Solti, in an interview with *Opera*, gave a rounded view of Covent Garden's achievements and status. He felt justified in saying that Covent Garden was the best opera house in the world: 'We have on average more performances that maintain a consistently high standard musically, dramatically and visually, than Milan, Vienna, Munich or New York.' He believed that the system he had introduced and developed at Covent Garden was a good compromise between repertory and *stagione*, facilitating 'really integrated performances'.

Charles Mackerras reinforced Solti's confidence in the system in

---

* Donaldson points out that European Houses did from eight to ten new productions of opera alone.

operation at Covent Garden. At that time he was first conductor in Hamburg and spoke of the difficulties inherent in the repertory system. There was no chance to integrate the singers in a revival in Hamburg as there 'were never orchestral rehearsals for operas already in the repertory'. A production was never 'rethought' as it was at Covent Garden where every season, 'although it's not a new production, the cast (old or new) is rehearsed by the resident producer, who can make certain changes to suit a new artist coming in'. With a few differences of detail, the same difficulties were felt in Vienna, where a similar repertory system held sway. In answer to the question as to why Hamburg's standards seemed so high to the outside critics, Mackerras pointed out that visiting critics were only invited to the best and best-rehearsed performances.[44]

Solti was also proud that British singers had been encouraged: 'The public and the press have both advanced in recent years in accepting native singers on equal terms with the artists from abroad.' Two exciting young talents whom he was nurturing were Yvonne Minton and Margaret Price. Minton had performed in Solti's revival of *Rosenkavalier* in March and Margaret Price made her debut in a revival of *The Magic Flute* on 21 October as Pamina. Solti was pleased that there was a young and 'well-informed' audience who would come to a *Ring* without stars.

Together with the increasingly lustrous ensemble of local artists, the international stars had continued to come to Covent Garden. Nilsson sang a magnificent *Turandot* in January 1967 – her icy hard tones, according to Rosenthal, melting into 'something beautiful and warm'.[45] She had been encouraged to come back after some problems with British income tax had been resolved. Sutherland visited regularly. One of her roles was Marie in a new Sandro Sequi production of *La Fille du régiment* with Luciano Pavarotti in May 1966, a production which the Met borrowed in the 1970–71 season. Jon Vickers began once again to be a regular visitor, returning for Radames in January 1968, Grimes in May 1969 and for Florestan in January 1970, with conductors Downes and Davis, 'sounding like the Vickers of several years ago'.[46]

One of Solti's disappointments at Covent Garden was the low box office for modern works. In July 1968 he conducted a visually and musically exciting *Billy Budd* to small audiences and Colin Davis's fine revival of *The Midsummer Marriage* in 1970 was also not a box office success. Solti was nevertheless optimistic about Covent Garden's future. London, he felt, had become the 'musical and operatic centre of the world', as Berlin had been 'in the days before Hitler' and, he concluded, 'There are also musicians to take over when I go.'[47]

The whole operatic scene in Britain was indeed unrecognisable from twenty years earlier. As well as the by now established companies, the festivals had continued to develop. In 1965 Peter Diamand, the experienced arts administrator who had been director of the Holland Festival from 1948 to 1965, had taken over from Lord Harewood as director of the Edinburgh Festival. His aim at Edinburgh was to develop the sort of conditions, including long rehearsal periods, that had originally encouraged top artists to come to Glyndebourne, as well as to create a place for Scottish opera. Scottish Opera produced a triumphant *Trojans* in May 1969. The Aldeburgh Festival continued to present new works by Britten and other composers such as Harrison Birtwistle's *Punch and Judy*, which had its premiere in June 1967. Alan Blyth called it a 'real firework'.

In the last heady days of arts expansion in 1969, Arnold Goodman and Lord Harewood prepared an Arts Council report that provided a blueprint for establishing opera and ballet on a solid footing throughout the country, and not to the detriment of London, as was the case with William Rees-Mogg's plan in 1984 when he was chairman of the Arts Council. While touring theatre was on the decline, local theatre with Arts Council support was flourishing. The committee believed 'there was a moral to be drawn from this' – that local opera could thrive similarly with sufficient subsidy. They urged the construction of new opera theatres for Scotland and Wales, and suggested Manchester as a suitable location for a regional opera house, as the city showed 'strong feeling' for it. The funding could be divided equally between local funds and government subsidy, as was the case with the Greater London Council and the new National Theatre.

The report also emphasised the need for increased subsidy for Covent Garden: 'Full value from the Royal Opera House and other institutions will only be extracted by substantial increases in their grants, which is at present restricted or prevented.' A portion of the hoped-for additional grant should be used for 'contemporary or experimental works particularly of British composers'. Benjamin Britten in his evidence believed that opera houses in the regions would help composers to obtain performances of their works. The report also urged the redevelopment of the House, including a second smaller theatre, when the fruit and vegetable market moved out of Covent Garden.

In December 1969 Kent Opera gave its first performances in Tunbridge Wells, and later in Canterbury, presenting *The Coronation of Poppea* produced by Norman Platt and sung by an ad hoc professional company to full houses. It was the first step in the establishment of the regional company described in the Goodman–Harewood report, the plan being to have a permanent company of twelve to fifteen singers to play regularly in the provinces. Roger Norrington conducted what Andrew Porter called an 'intelligent, well-executed performance'. Young singers like Sarah Walker and Benjamin Luxon were deemed worthy of belonging to a 'city company if, say, Canterbury were Cassel'. In addition to the growth of professional companies, amateur groups such as Morley College and Hammersmith Municipal Opera, performing in February 1967 at the Camden Festival, found critical favour and encouragement.

Sadler's Wells was about to make a decisive step. The decision as to whether a new opera house should be built on the South Bank had been dependent on the outcome of the Goodman–Harewood report. In May 1967 Stephen Arlen, Sadler's Wells's new director, was distressed at a press conference when Jennie Lee announced that the first of many South Bank schemes was to be abandoned. In its stead there was to be a new opera house in Edinburgh, as well as an arts centre for Manchester at a cost of £2.3 million. Arnold Goodman, as chairman of the Arts Council, had opposed the South Bank scheme as being 'absurdly extravagant'. The Arts Council decision had also been taken in the light of the soaring costs of the National Theatre, which was being built.* Goodman, however, strongly supported Sadler's Wells's

---

* Costs had risen from the estimated £2 million in 1961 to £7.5 million in 1968.

move to the Coliseum Theatre and spent many hours negotiating with the owner of the theatre and other individuals to make the move financially feasible.[48] Sadler's Wells moved to the Coliseum in August 1968.

Although the Sadler's Wells company was freed from the restraints and remoteness of the Rosebery Avenue theatre, moving to the Coliseum brought its own problems. With a 2,354-seat theatre, Sadler's Wells Opera now occupied the larger and less intimate of the two London opera houses, and it was feared that the acoustics would be a strain for young and inexperienced singers. Tooley later said that it 'deprived British opera of a wonderful breeding ground for singers', which was only partially solved by the regional companies.[49] The orchestra would sound better, but a larger chorus as well as a larger audience would be needed, and the size of the threatre would make the relationship with Covent Garden even less clearly defined. Sadler's Wells also had to work out its identity since the demise of the Carl Rosa Company, and to decide if it still had a role as a touring company or whether its London base would dominate.

In January 1968 Goodall had conducted the first of his highly successful Sadler's Wells Wagner productions. It was a 'memorable' Mastersingers. In it appeared the young British-born baritone Norman Bailey, who had been working at the Deutsche Oper am Rhein. In January 1969, while Bailey was rehearsing The Flying Dutchman for Sadler's Wells, he stepped into the first night of the Covent Garden Die Meistersinger when Hubert Hoffman was taken ill. Goodman recalled that this incident underlined the rivalry which was building up between the two London Houses. Drogheda was by chance at a meeting with Goodman when Hoffman's withdrawal had become known. He and Webster were finding it impossible to find a replacement, according to Drogheda, in spite of 'phoning all over Europe', until Goodman pointed out that Norman Bailey was available down the road. In spite of Drogheda's antipathy to using a Sadler's Wells singer they had no choice but to ask him. Goodman recalled, 'They returned with their faces as black as thunder: Norman Bailey had been delighted to accept.' Bailey's Covent Garden debut as Hans Sachs was rewarded with an enormous ovation for what Goodman described as 'one of the most beautifully acted and sung Hans Sachses in my experience'. It was achieved without a rehearsal.[50] A few days later, on 29 January, Bailey's *Flying Dutchman* opened at the Coliseum to critical acclaim. In his May 1976 recording of the Dutchman with Solti for Decca, Bailey's distinctive tone quality is apparent as he forges through the consonants, clearing the way for a beautiful legato line and displaying great feeling with his masky Italianate focus and clear, dark and virile timbre.

In January 1970 Charles Mackerras became music director of Sadler's Wells Opera at the Coliseum. He was to stay at the Coliseum for seven years, seeing the company through financial crises during one of its most creative and formative periods. In the early years of his regime, lack of money and poor attendance dogged the company until threats of resignation galvanised the Board of Directors and administration. On 29 January 1970 Goodall introduced his *Valkyrie* at the Coliseum. It was the beginning of the cycle which was to be a milestone in the company's development. Rosenthal was delighted with Andrew Porter's translation, which he believed provided the basis for 'a complete musical-dramatic experience'. The production was by Glen Byam Shaw and John Blatchley, with 'modern, daring and generally convincing' sets designed by Ralph Koltai. The cast was mainly from the company. Rita Hunter was Brünnhilde, her voice attractive and voluminous, though her dramatic skills were limited. Norman Bailey's Wotan was, however, 'world class'.

Glyndebourne's fortunes had been mixed during the late Sixties. The Pritchard–Rennert team* was not as dynamic as that of Ebert and Busch, or Gui. John Christie had died in 1962, leaving his son George in control. Great singers like Jurinac, Sciutti and Evans were now unwilling to come and spend summers rehearsing and working at Glyndebourne. In general, the differences in rehearsal and preparation standards between what were considered festival conditions and the regular conditions at Covent Garden were no longer of any significance. Indeed, Covent Garden was more like a continuous festival

---

* Pritchard had taken over from Gui in 1964 (until 1977) and Rennert from Ebert in 1959 (until 1968).

with expertise developing in all areas because of the constant work and use of all its departments, and thoroughly rehearsed casts. Covent Garden had also created a better-educated and more enthusiastic opera-going public.

In May 1966 George Christie, after a difficult 1965 season, announced changes. Glyndebourne would have a shorter season with four instead of six operas, a greater proportion of which would be new productions rather than revivals. In 1966 Janet Baker sang Dido in Purcell's *Dido and Aeneas*, and Michael Redgrave directed *Werther*. Rennert resigned his position as artistic counsellor in 1967. Pritchard was promoted to the title of music director in 1969 and continued to give unstinting service until his retirement in 1977.

During the May–August 1970 season, Glyndebourne gave Francesco Cavalli's *La Calisto*, which had been composed in 1651. It had been unearthed by Raymond Leppard, who had been Hall's musical adviser at Stratford and was an early-music missionary. It was the first of many splendid Glyndebourne productions by Peter Hall with designer John Bury. It marked the beginning of Hall's close relationship with Glyndebourne, which continued for twenty years and was to have a substantial effect on the institution. He enjoyed the rural surroundings and working conditions, and received support and encouragement from Moran Caplat, the general manager. Caplat insisted that sets and props once ordered were used, but was otherwise relaxed in his attitude to budgeting, a system which Hall and his great designer colleague John Bury found congenial.[51]

Both with *Calisto* and two years later with Monteverdi's *Il Ritorno d'Ulisse in patria*, Hall and Bury sought to re-create the baroque stage using modern materials and machinery. In *Ulisse* cues were given which 'enabled Jupiter to fly towards the audience on his eagle and Neptune to rise from the deep while the seas parted and clouds filled the sky, covering the setting sun'. Hall's intention was to give the spectacle 'the metaphorical weight of the baroque world – where the Gods live above in the flies; men walk on a stage which is the earth; and underneath, with access by trapdoor, are darkness and devils and the supernatural'.[52] Robert Donington felt Hall had succeeded with *Calisto*: 'The production was spectacular in exactly the baroque sense.' Noel Annan, the Provost of King's College Cambridge, wrote to Hall in appreciation of the production,

'Pastoral is the hardest thing to do', he noted, but the 'routs of satyrs and bevies of nymphs' had been 'dazzling'.[53]

Hall's work with his principals was also remarkable. He asked Janet Baker to double as Diana and as Jove disguised as Diana in *Calisto*. Diana was a lyrical role, the other comic. The result was an 'extraordinarily clever and amusing travesty' of Jove which Hall found both 'funny and heartbreaking'. Baker wrote to Hall, 'I emerged from *Calisto* a different person and a better performer ... You give us such a wonderful sense of freedom; your sense of creating moment by moment, is the most exciting way of working I have ever seen.'[54]

Although opera was reaching out to an ever-widening audience all over the country, and British singers were making their mark at home and abroad, Lord Goodman felt compelled to defend the company from the first charges of elitism, writing in the 1969 Annual Report of the Arts Council, 'We are not a luxury: we do not cater for a small elite out of the pockets of a protesting multitude; we supply a commodity which a great many people require and which can make a better life for a great many more, once their interest and appetite have been awakened.'* Covent Garden's grant that year was £1,280,000, including £30,000 towards the reduction of the annual deficit.

As Goodman had warned, the Board and administration were forced to seek ways both to fill the House and insure income. Drogheda further developed his 'premium stalls' scheme, which had been introduced in 1959. According to this scheme the Bank of England and businesses like Marks and Spencer bought seats for a whole season for about £1,000 a stall. Sometimes they were not occupied, but the advantage of the scheme was that even with the less popular shows the seats had been paid for. The disadvantage was that the scheme laid the basis for the growing perception of Covent Garden as an exclusive institution. Colin Davis later said that there were often empty seats because the corporate sponsors did not take them up. 'If it is a national opera house then everybody should have access.'[55]

---

* Of Arts Council grants totalling £3,212,886, £2,344,520 went to opera and ballet, and £1,280,000 to Covent Garden. The total sum spent on all seventy theatre companies amounted to £1,700,000.

The flagship company continued to be worthy of pride and to generate excitement. On 9 May 1969 Solti conducted a John Copley revival of Elektra and as usual his effect on the well-rehearsed revival was impressive. In Alan Blyth's opinion there was 'complete involvement and emotional response to those purple patches, such as the pounding Agamemnon theme and the recognition', as well as 'precise attention to detail, such as the sensuous oboe solo when Elektra sets the bait for her mother.... Solti's response was unfailingly right.' Elektra was 'among his major achievements in Bow Street'. Also praised was 'the undiminished opulence' of Birgit Nilsson's voice, which left Blyth 'quite limp by the end of the evening'. He found Regina Resnik's Clytemnestra 'unsurpassed as a study in nightmarish decadence', while Marie Collier's 'dithering Chrysothemis was keenly sung and projected; she and Solti between them caught the passionate yearning of her big solo'. The audience recognised the splendour of the occasion by bestowing upon it more than thirty curtain calls.[56]

The new regime in waiting was caught up in the exhilarating atmosphere engendered by the outgoing music director as well as its own enthusiasm for future plans. On 21 May 1969 the music director elect, Colin Davis, injected 'a sense of excitement in the House and tension on the stage' in a company performance of Peter Grimes.[57] The chairman of the opera subcommittee on 16 September 1969 was pleased when Hall and Davis said they intended to demonstrate 'catholicity of taste' in their plans for new works and new productions, and to encourage the composition of 'contemporary operas of contemporary relevance'. Drogheda sounded a note of caution in October, however, when he warned Davis of the 'financial difficulties of being too adventurous'. The budget demanded 82½ per cent capacity in the House and even Peter Grimes usually played to less than 50 per cent houses. Davis said he attached a great deal of importance to his objective of including four operas, preferably modern, from outside the existing repertory each year.[58] In November, Davis urged Drogheda that management should 'first decide what we want and then think of trimming our desires to the financial need'. His aim was to get young people into the House as well as to keep up standards. He also apologised to Drogheda for being 'too ferocious at meetings' and assured the chairman that although he was a performer he knew 'about money'.[59]

The Annual Report for 1968–69 stressed the difficulties of forward planning as well as presenting operas 'outside the standard repertoire', in spite of an average of 90 per cent box office. On 17 April 1970 Jennie Lee underlined her support for the company when she published a statement of policy towards the arts. She stressed that the government's aim was to maintain and improve standards, and make 'the best in the arts more generally available – not less'.[60] When Solti's long dreamt-of foreign tour finally came to reality that month, Lee sent a telegram of congratulations to Munich: 'We are all proud of you.' During the tour, Solti conducted *Don Carlos* and *Falstaff.* The company, according to Rosenthal, 'covered itself with glory'. As Solti entered the pit 'there was an ovation which meant he had to bring the orchestra to its feet three times'. *Falstaff* was a particular triumph. Geraint Evans and Solti were the heroes of the evening, receiving further overwhelming ovations.

In the summer of 1970 Joan Sutherland, who had continued to appear regularly at the House, sang Norma with Marilyn Horne, conducted by Richard Bonynge. When she had sung the role in 1968, Rosenthal had praised the 'great beauty of tone, the mood of other-worldliness' of Sutherland's 'Casta diva' but had criticised the 'over-decorated cabaletta, which gave the impression of being completely externalised'. For Marilyn Horne, however, he had found nothing but praise. She phrased musically and dramatically and 'coloured her singing according to the relevance of the text'. Horne's and Sutherland's inspired partnership was to become legendary. In March 1970 they had performed a triumphant series of *Normas* at the Met, which had helped Sutherland to overcome the difficulties of the role. Irving Kolodin wrote of her 'vocal splendour undiminished, with her all but inhuman accuracy wholly at her bidding, and the fastidious kind of musicianship . . . more subtly employed than before'.[61] At Covent Garden, on 25 June 1970, Arthur Jacobs found that Sutherland had added 'to her habitual radiance of tone, vocal agility, and fine timing . . . a new meaningfulness of words, with well articulated consonants and differentiated vowels'. Jacobs thought Horne was Sutherland's 'ideal partner . . . The chain of thirds in the duet cadenza of Act 1 scene 2, when Norma reaches high C and

Adalgisa A, was irresistibly delivered. The beauty of Miss Horne's soft singing is, I think, unmatched among today's mezzo sopranos, and her full voice is powerfully exciting.'

It was at the end of the 1969–70 season that Webster finally retired. His health had been declining for some time, as had his decision-making powers. When Drogheda discussed the question of his successor with him his unequivocal choice was John Tooley, who had a keen knowledge of and support for the ballet as well as skill in labour negotiations and touring arrangements, and had also been virtually running the place during the last two years. Drogheda wrote that Tooley was supported by the whole Board and that he had 'the confidence and trust of the staff'. He added that the consequences of appointing anyone else 'could have been dire'.[62]

Jennie Lee and Arnold Goodman held up the appointment, however. Goodman did not object to Tooley himself, thinking him 'a most able man and probably the most suitable candidate', but they both felt that such an important office should be advertised. Of the other potential candidates, Lord Harewood in particular felt that he was at least as familiar with the workings of Covent Garden as Tooley. Later Solti himself wrote that his choice to replace Webster would have been Lord Harewood.[63]

When Harewood asked Webster if there was any point in applying, 'Webster was evasive and it was not hard to deduce that the succession was already promised – presumably to John Tooley'.[64] Arnold Goodman described Harewood's indignation: 'He felt that the Arts Council should know what was being discussed and insisted that the post must be advertised. He was told this was not to be.'* Drogheda wrote to Harewood to say he envisioned him taking over the chairmanship of the Board when he, Drogheda, retired. On 19 April Harewood replied that he would like to join the Board.[65]

Goodman wrote to Drogheda, explaining that the Arts Council did not accept the 'proposition that a deputy can in a public institution

---

* Drogheda had written to Harewood in November 1966 to say he did believe that after Webster's retirement someone more sympathetic to the ballet should take the position in order to provide a 'balancing act'. If the ballet moved out of the House that would be the opportune moment for Harewood to take over (Royal Opera House Archives, Drogheda papers, Drogheda to Harewood, 16.11.66).

be "groomed" for a senior appointment'. Such a proposition, he argued was 'a nepotistic view which might have validity in a private or family firm but is totally incompatible with the principles of public engagement'. The compromise agreed upon did not please Goodman. They concluded that 'a trawling operation' would be carried out and a few select names put forward for consideration, including that of Lord Harewood. Goodman later wrote that the trawling operation was 'conducted in a strangely anaemic fashion', the prospective candidates given 'discouraging intimations that if they wanted to apply they could but their prospects were minimal'.*

The Queen made Webster a KCVO and on 30 June 1970 there was a farewell gala in his honour. On 28 July Webster attended his last Board meeting. Tooley took over formally in September. On 18 September Webster wrote to Drogheda his letter of thanks for the gala, in which he acknowledged that Drogheda's enthusiasm had 'been a fund of strength'. Drogheda recalled, 'At times he simply maddened me ... But I was genuinely fond of him.' Webster died less than a year later, on 9 May 1971. Geraint Evans had been asked to make an address on the presentation of a portrait to Webster that February. During it he called Webster 'a great administrator, an eloquent speaker, a shy man with a sense of humour, and above all a person with a deep concern for his fellow men'. For Evans and his colleagues he was '"DW": adviser and friend'.

The early Seventies still saw politicians in power who were in sympathy with the needs of the arts, but support nevertheless began to erode as the effects of inflation became more damaging. Already by the end of 1973 inflation was 3 per cent higher than the grant-in-aid increase of 15 per cent. In June 1970 the Conservatives won the General Election, and Edward Heath became Prime Minister, with Lord Eccles responsible for the arts. Both men were committed to the arts and in December 1970 Lord Eccles granted a £2.6 million increase to the Arts Council. In the Arts Council Annual Report of December 1970

---

* Among those approached were John Denison of the Festival Hall, Moran Caplat of Glyndebourne and Peter Diamand.

Goodman warned, 'In a society whose values are totally insecure' there was no economic protection for even the best cultural activity. 'We have contrived an economic world where it is a simple untruth that worthwhile activities must succeed,' he wrote and suggested that other forms of support would have to be sought. A return to the bad old days of 'Poor Law' subsistence-style assistance was not far away. Goodman only stayed on at the Arts Council for another two years, being replaced by a businessman, Patrick Gibson, who shared Eccles's concern for the regions.

The Board would be increasingly responsible in the next decade for finding 'other forms of support' but it still felt its greater role was in maintaining standards within a restricted budget. Shortly before Webster's retirement, Drogheda had asked Isaiah Berlin what he hoped for in the new era. Berlin had written to him candidly on 13 January 1970. He believed that the Board's role was 'to goad the enterprise on to greater and greater heights'. He believed that the danger of complacency was far greater than that 'of excessive self-criticism'. The Board should 'go on nagging and nibbling', and not accept the accusation of 'carping and destructive criticism if they do'. Drogheda had rescued the old Covent Garden of David Webster from that kind of relationship. Berlin wrote that there were now very few bad performances and that sometimes the heights were achieved. Covent Garden's reputation had shot up 'since those difficult and ill-attended, rightly attacked, early patriotic days'. Management and Webster in particular had been unwilling to accept any criticism. There was, Berlin wrote, a 'feeling that it is caddish or unjust to harass a sorely tried and very worthy body of workers who are doing their best'. Although this attitude was in the 'best British tradition' it was not 'good for art'.[66]

'Covent Garden is now as traditional and national as the BBC,' Berlin pointed out. But although the battle for creating a tradition had indeed been won by 1970, a deep sense of pride in its artistic institutions never really established itself in Britain. Geraint Evans's personal experience highlighted this weakness. Evans recalled that there were never British embassy visits or parties when he and other singers were singing abroad, which they did with increasing frequency. In particular he recalled being in Vienna in March 1961 for a gala performance of *Figaro* with Karajan. The other singers had been visited by their ambassadors – not so Evans. He said this was true time and time again in spite of invitations to many other embassies for receptions. When asked, the Foreign Office would say they were concerned only with trade and commerce. During Evans's first Salzburg *Figaro* in 1962 the BBC made a film about the festival in which he was not invited to appear, even though Graziella Sciutti had reminded them there was a British Figaro. Cultural achievements remained a source of indifference rather than pride in British public life.

In his letter to Drogheda, Berlin expressed a worry that the new team was too concerned about 'contemporary relevance' in an art form which has not proved very amenable to this form of treatment'. He admitted, however, his own preference for 'the human voice at the expense of acting, decor, the personality of singers.' and reflected, 'Still we are all aged men and it may be that Peter Hall and Colin are right. They must be given a free run without chivvying from us I suppose.'

The 'aged men' were about to have an interesting time. It soon became very clear that the new directors were indeed determined to make opera more socially relevant, dangerous and dramatic while bringing new audiences to Covent Garden. In February 1970 Davis gave an interview to the Oxford University magazine *Isis* in which he made some remarks about Solti for which he later had to apologise. New operas under Solti, he was quoted as saying, had played a 'peripheral' role – he and Hall intended to 'make the new pieces central'. He also said that although Solti had given the impression of having a lot of young singers, in fact the 'company had never been smaller'. He and Peter Hall were gradually going to 'turn the whole place upside down'. They were agreed that 'a higher standard of acting' was required in order to 'make some kind of statement about the condition of being a human being'.[67]

Drogheda reprimanded Davis for his criticisms of the man he was to succeed and said he hoped that Davis was not contemplating a 'repertory company à la Sadler's Wells', which would deny the public the opportunity to hear the leading international singers. In reply Davis wrote that the article had misrepresented him. He went on to explain that he was 'indiscreet, somewhat ferocious, fairly honest, affectionate, insolent, but not wittingly treacherous'. He and Hall were, he added, 'terrified at our responsibility'.[68] Davis also sent a note of explanation to Solti.

Berlin's preference for the 'human voice' also seemed threatened by the new team's plans for 'a permanent ensemble of young singers, under thirty-fives'. With these younger singers they hoped to do all the new productions, then, 'when the productions were revived, the canaries could come with their own costumes'. There were many extraordinarily talented young singers who, Hall hoped, might be persuaded to spend longer periods in Britain. These future stars included Frederica von Stade, Ileana Cotrubas, Kiri Te Kanawa, Janet Baker and Thomas Allen. Davis and Hall hoped to persuade them to give three or four months a year so that they could 'build up a company . . . to create new productions with them and revive productions when the stars turned up. A two-tier system.'[69] The 'two-tier' price system would enable a new, younger and possibly smaller audience for the more adventurous repertoire and ensemble cast to pay less than would the 'canary fanciers' who would continue to favour 'international' opera.[70] The 'canary' fancying or voice-loving preferences of some Board members were not, however, an insoluble source for conflict with the Board. Davis and Hall were both fully aware that the team they envisioned would always be augmented and inspired by the 'stars' who had to be employed, Hall explained, 'otherwise, you can't do a lot of the works'.[71]

Despite this understanding, relations between the artistic directors and the Board were becoming increasingly strained. Davis attended Board meetings when future plans were discussed and, in Drogheda's words, his representations before the Board tended to be 'rather intemperate'. In January 1970 Lady Drogheda had written to Berlin to say that she thought the Davis–Hall partnership was 'a risky experiment'. Davis, she felt, with his 'left-wing "chippy" attitude' lacked humility and always thought he knew best 'in a tiresomely aggressive way'.[72] Both Hall and Davis were keenly aware of their social origins, Davis telling Tooley, 'Peter and I have no great background, he's the son of a station master and I'm the son of an extraordinarily penurious bank clerk with too many children.' He sensed, he said, 'slight opposition in some quarters to the fact that we are these kind of people'. Hall felt it too, but suggested that 'it provokes an over-defensive attitude in us sometimes'. It had also, he admitted, created 'a good deal of misunderstanding before we have even begun'.[73]

Hall's and Davis's plans were developing fast. Among them was that of bringing Harold Pinter together with Harrison Birtwistle for a new opera for 1972, which Hall himself would help to edit and shape. Davis and Hall were also keen to bring in musical men of the cinema, such as John Schlesinger and Satyajit Ray, and the controversial film director, Ken Russell.* Russell was suggesting Debussy's *Martyrdom of St Sebastian* or Martinů's *Julietta*. Hall also wanted to bring in his RSC colleagues, Trevor Nunn, Peter Brook, John Barton and Terry Hands because, he explained, 'there are shared assumptions'. Hall and Davis would prepare the *Ring* and all the main Mozart operas. The solutions for these diverse challenges would, Hall explained, 'come from the doing'.[74] On 19 January 1970 he wrote to Tooley that he would shortly be introducing his 'hair-raising ideas' to the opera sub-committee. 'Let battle commence,' he wrote.[75]

Battle did soon commence. On 18 February Drogheda expressed strong opposition to Russell, who was, he argued, 'entirely without experience as an operatic producer'.[76] Drogheda, Claus Moser and William Glock had been appalled by Russell's film about Richard Strauss.[77] Furthermore, the plot and libretto of Martinů's *Julietta* would give 'every opportunity for psychologically distorted and sensational interpretations to be imported into the production'.[78] Martinů was not, in his and Solti's opinion, a 'first-rate composer' and it was felt that it would be better to try to get a 'new English opera'.[79]

Such was the growing tension that Burnet Pavitt sought to bring Drogheda together with his new directors to smooth the relationship. The two men were, he believed, 'flexible' and sufficiently aware that 'canaries' could 'bring success all around'. Pavitt also believed that Hall and Davis did not want to disappoint the existing Covent Garden audience. It was clear from their choice of the *Ring* and all the Mozart

---

* Ken Russell emerged from the world of television documentaries where he made respected programmes about composers. His film career began with *Women in Love* about D. H. Lawrence but soon encompassed composers like Strauss, Mahler and Tchaikovsky in increasingly surreal and wildly imaginative film biography not famous for factual reliability. His later work was deemed increasingly self-indulgent by both critics and public with a completely a-stylistic production of Gilbert and Sullivan's *Princess Ida* for English National Opera in the 1990s being the high point of camp excess.

operas, and also of *Figaro* as their opening work, that they realised 'the real point of it all' was 'beauty of sound and sight'.[80]

Hall was increasingly worried that the Board might not support their directors in the 'new directions' they were seeking. On 18 March he told the opera subcommittee that he and Davis believed profoundly 'in the need to extend the range and language of opera, to bring on not just new works but works of new kinds, combining music and theatre'. Risks would have to be taken with such potential new works as those of Birtwistle, Peter Maxwell Davies and John Taverner. Hall agreed that Russell's film about Strauss had been deplorable but he believed him to be a man of genius who would never seek merely to shock. Although Harewood, Glock and Berlin 'wholeheartedly endorsed' Hall's and Davis's aims, they did not feel that *Julietta* was 'a very good case on which to make a stand'.[81]

The first major breach between the Board and their new directors was in September 1970, when Hall and Davis planned to do *Don Pasquale* in English. Drogheda again warned them that he did not wish Covent Garden to become 'a glorified Sadler's Wells'.[82] *Don Pasquale* would, he argued, sound 'rather silly in English'.*[83] Davis reacted strongly, telling Drogheda on 22 September that he and Hall were 'not to be denied freedom of thought, which is the only creative freedom! Restriction', he added, 'is Death!'

There were further disputes in October and November about whether *The Trojans* should be sung in English or not. Drogheda warned that the language question involved fundamental issues, including the relationship with Sadler's Wells, the employment of foreign artists and the training of company members. Davis, on the other hand, tried to persuade his chairman that it was not language that differentiated Covent Garden from Sadler's Wells but rather 'better singers, a better orchestra and international goodwill'.

Drogheda was not assuaged, telling Moser on 8 October, 'Our

---

* Solti, however, in his July 1968 *Opera* interview, had expressed the view that the language issue was in fact in the process of resolution, both because of the audience's greater familiarity with the works through records and radio, and also because Sadler's Wells's move to the Coliseum would enable bigger audiences to hear opera in English. He and Hall had agreed, however, that 'conversational operas' should be in the vernacular so they could be understood.

young friends take themselves very seriously.' And he added, 'Covent Garden under the new regime is in danger of becoming extremely earnest.' He was considering resigning after Solti's departure, telling Tooley, 'The outlook under the new regime is indeed rather frightening.' The dispute reached a climax over *Figaro* in December 1970, when Davis told the opera subcommittee that his reasons for wanting an English-language production were 'partly dramatic and partly social'. He was anxious, he explained, 'that the audience should not be left out of the drama'. English would bring 'a great gain in communication with the audience', who would be able to understand the large amount of factual information conveyed in the recitatives. *Figaro*, he stressed, was a social opera, not a myth like *Don Giovanni* or *The Magic Flute*.

Drogheda was totally opposed, arguing that singers had already been engaged to sing in Italian. '*Figaro* in English at Covent Garden', he wrote to Tooley, 'goes against all we have been attempting to achieve.' He found in Hall and Davis's statements 'overtones of antagonism' and their mood to be 'prickly and defiant'.[84] He also found their public statements, suggesting that the affairs of the House had been hitherto conducted by 'fuddy-duddy reactionaries', to betray a 'very mistaken and rather adolescent attitude'. In the opera subcommittee it was argued, in opposition to Davis and Hall, that the work had a universal rather than contemporary relevance and that the audience should study the libretto. Translation, it was argued, would harm the box office. The only reason it had been agreed to sing *The Magic Flute* in English was 'to avoid the embarrassment of extended spoken dialogue in faulty German'.[85] Drogheda told Tooley that *Figaro* as a 'sort of "down with social privileges" social tract' was 'insupportable'.[86]

Behind the language debate there also lurked the perennial British question of class consciousness and snobbery. Drogheda was worried about losing the House's 'present loyal supporters',[87] while Hall, Davis and Tooley were all keen to widen the audience, believing that 'a lot of people are worried that they don't have a place in the Opera House – worried about the plush and the supposed snobbery'. Tooley wanted to make it easier to buy tickets, and both he and Davis were determined to do promenade concert performances in Covent Garden, taking out the seats in the stalls.[88]

Harewood prepared a paper for the Board in which he expressed the unspoken argument for translation, writing that companies that did not sing in translation, like Covent Garden and the Met, tended to 'breed an audience with social, perhaps snobbish, certainly canary-fancying tendencies'. The employment of international stars contributed to a greater 'emphasis on the singer and performer rather than what is performed', which in turn led to a 'superficial approach' as well as higher ticket prices. He described Covent Garden's happy position of being able to choose between original language and translation but 'came down firmly in favour of translation for this particular opera in this particular case'.

Drogheda felt that the issue was part of 'a power struggle' and told Tooley that he would not stay on as chairman if the decision were to be for *Figaro* in English. Other members of the Board were less anxious. Moser urged, in a paper prepared for the meeting, that although there should be no general departure from the original-language policy, an exception could be made in the case of *Figaro* in order to give the 'new directorate every chance and support to develop the work of the House in the ways they feel to be right'.[89] Board member and later chairman, John Sainsbury, wrote that while the directors could seek to persuade and they could replace their artistic directors, they should not veto their decisions.[90]

Hall wrote to Drogheda on 12 January 1971 to say that he was relieved that after a meeting their differences with Drogheda had been cleared up. He and Davis, he wrote, had felt that they were 'not wanted as policy makers – men, that is, whose convictions about such work are what the Board wants and supports'. He explained to Drogheda that *Figaro* had been an exception and that it was understood and accepted that 'basic policy must be opera in the original language' in order to maintain the international standing of the House. They needed, he wrote, Drogheda's 'support and backing' for the 'difficult task ahead'.

Tooley supported Hall and Davis, telling Drogheda that neither he nor they were trying to reverse basic policy, even though he was not convinced that 'the whole of Covent Garden's subsidy and purpose' was 'connected with the presentation of international artists'. He also warned that the continual pushing up of prices might leave the company with 'no audience at all in 10 or 15 years' time', which would be a 'disaster'. Tooley added, 'The children of the refugees from Hitler may not be as persuaded of opera's value as their parents, and they may not even understand German so well!'[91] The conflict was only reconciled by Tooley having the entire Board to dinner, where a compromise was reached whereby the *Figaro* decision would not constitute a precedent.[92] In the end, Reri Grist refused to sing in English, and, as her contract specified Italian there was no way out apart from the whole cast following suit. Although the *Figaro* debate was resolved it had revealed the same differences that the Met was about to face, between the artistic team's will to adopt a more radical approach and the Board's need to maintain a 'safer' approach, which would not endanger the box office by attempting to reach a new audience.

Before Solti's retirement, Hall worked closely with him on *Eugene Onegin* and *Tristan*, and with Colin Davis and designer Timothy O'Brien on Tippett's *The Knot Garden*. Davis was very excited about working with Peter Hall: 'The possibility we have here is of two men approaching the *whole* problem of opera from a shared attitude.'[93] The excitement was mutual. Hall recalled, 'Colin and I thrived in a frenzy of discovery, and found we had a real rapport in the rehearsal room.'

The efforts of the new management to define the role of the Royal Opera House in the new era were recorded in an undated transcript of a meeting between Davis, Hall, Tooley, John Bury and Timothy O'Brien at the time of the *Knot Garden* rehearsals. Hall recognised the anxiety of the doubters. 'The devil's advocates think', Hall said to Davis, 'that we will end up doing 50 per cent modern works and 50 per cent grey, Brechtian versions of Mozart. They fear that in five years' time their nice candy box of entertainment will have been destroyed.' This would not be the case, Davis explained: 'We shall go on playing the best pieces in the repertory because we'd be damn fools if we didn't,' but he added that there was a one-sixth margin for choosing the new repertory that they were interested in.

Hall said that another central aim was to work together as a team with designers Bury and O'Brien. They were going to do what only Ebert and Busch had achieved at Glyndebourne 'because of the freedom', said Davis, 'with which designer, musician and producer could trespass on one another's ground'. Both Davis and Hall had worked with Michel Saint-Denis and Glen Byam Shaw at Sadler's Wells and the Royal Shakespeare Theatre. These 'theatrical masters' had taught both men to ask, 'It is nice, but is it necessary? . . . What is it for and what does it mean?' Only Felsenstein had achieved consistent dramatic standards but he had not managed 'a musical standard at the same level'.[94]

On 2 December 1970 Hall described working with Tippett on *The Knot Garden* to Rosenthal. Tippett was, said Hall, a 'humanist, mystic and humorist'. Of the work itself, Hall explained, 'It's a contemporary piece – it deals with marriage, sex, the colour problem – but it uses the architectural form of opera.' In Act Three the psychoanalyst asks the characters to take part in a charade with characters from *The Tempest* – as Hall explained, 'to see the inner motives of their characters and to help them in understanding themselves'. Hall sought to make the whole thing real and convincing. 'We must', he said, 'avoid it becoming pretentious. People on the stage must look at each other and react to one another.'

On 21 February 1971 Solti conducted Peter Hall's production of *Eugene Onegin*, in English, designed by Julia Trevelyan Oman. There had been doubts in the Board as to whether Hall and Solti were the right people to prepare the work. Berlin had even feared that they might be 'antagonistic' to it, given that he felt the piece to be 'a meltingly lyrical, irresistibly charming work to do with country houses in the nineteenth century in backward but terribly attractive countries like Russia and Ireland, very remote from the neuroses of Central Europe'. There had been casting problems, with Solti considering Joan Carlyle and the Board wanting Elisabeth Söderström for Tatyana. Pavitt wrote to Berlin, 'Truth to tell, conductors are unsound about singers and they just do not see that an inadequate leading soprano drags everything down.' In the event, Hall refused to work with Carlyle and Söderström decided not to sing the part.[95] Ileana Cotrubas, after some doubts on the part of Solti and Hall as to whether she could get 'the measure of the House',[96] was given the role. It was to be her Covent Garden debut.

Confounding the doubters, *Onegin*, sung in English, was a sensitive and moving interpretation. John Warrack was excited by the implications for the new regime as an era of 'drama in music'. Hall's attention was 'concentrated on the characters', he wrote, and Oman's settings placed them in 'the emptiness stretching away'. Solti was 'unexpectedly delicate; he can let the dances go with a swing . . . accompanies the singers watchfully and affectionately'.[97] Desmond Shawe-Taylor, writing in the *Sunday Times* on 21 February, admired Hall's presentation of *Onegin* as a 'lyrical masterpiece that is . . . nearer Turgenev than Pushkin'. Shawe-Taylor found Cotrubas's 'small-scale' Tatyana 'so touching, so sensitive, so deeply human' and that her voice had a 'forward even quality and limpid utterance of the notes'. Arthur Jacobs wrote that 'this Romanian sang the English text with clarity and meaning'. Victor Braun was a 'caddish and heartless' Onegin. Robert Tear's Lensky was 'withdrawn, tender, even distorted in its anguish – but marvellous in its expression'.

Solti and Hall's last collaboration during Solti's directorship was *Tristan und Isolde* on 14 June. Solti was present at all production rehearsals and had even joined in discussions with Hall and Bury on the design – how to make it look like a ship and somehow dissolving until 'there is no more ship'.[98]

Once again Hall's skills enabled the artists to move naturally and logically, and stand still with economical gestures both as individuals and groups. The result was another integrated dramatic experience. According to Rosenthal, Ludmila Dvořáková was 'the very embodiment of a Celtic princess', Jess Thomas a 'very fine Tristan'. When the pair sang the love duet lying down, Hall was actually following Wagner's stage directions. Veasey's Brangäne was 'consistently lovely'.[99]

Controversy was aroused, however, by Hall's Royal Shakespeare style, realistic blood-letting, when Tristan's guts gushed out as he tore the bandages from his wounds. Drogheda was said to have hated this moment. On 19 May Pavitt wrote to Berlin to say that 'Garrett is beginning to wonder, and to suffer from a Frankenstein complex'. Pavitt himself had confronted Hall, saying that nothing could be more bourgeois than 'trying to *épater les bourgeois*' and that he could not understand 'why in all directions art has to go through this seemingly endless phase of violence'. He was worried about the 'John Bury – *Midsummer Marriage* school of design' with its potential for 'oodles of gore and fire'. Pavitt added, 'As Peter Hall keeps saying, we knew what he was like when we appointed him.' He went on, 'He is a clever fellow.'[100]

Nilsson sang the last performance of *Tristan* at Solti's request, but refused to agree to Hall's decision that at the end Tristan should rise up and clasp Isolde's body in an embrace. Without telling Hall during their four-hour rehearsal, at the actual performance she stood up, arms outstretched as usual. Drogheda asked Nilsson why Tristan had not been resurrected and she replied, 'As it was the last performance, I told him that he could stay asleep.' Amusing though her response was, there were those who saw a more serious implication in the diva ignoring the director's instructions. Peter Hall later recalled that he had found it 'rather out of order, actually, bloody rude!'[101] After the performance there was a farewell party for Solti, where he was presented with the KBE by the Prime Minister, Edward Heath.

Solti's ten years had transformed Covent Garden into what he could indeed argue was 'the greatest opera company in the world'. Although La Scala could always boast great singers on its roster, the House's repertoire was still limited. At the Met, Bing continued to be daunted by financial restrictions, and Vienna, as was so often its wont, was slipping into the second-rate – an attitude of getting the job done. At Covent Garden, Solti, building on the basis that had been prepared by Rankl, Kubelik and Kempe, supported by a devoted Board, and from 1965 with a realistic subsidy, had been able to achieve his main objective of consistently high artistic standards.

John Tolanski later described Solti as 'a real music director in the style of the great European music directors of the first half of the century. . . . He was really in charge of nearly everything at the Garden and although he was a very tough cookie his aspirations, integrity and charismatic personality won those people over.'[102] One of Solti's greatest contributions was the creation of a system that facilitated the thorough rehearsal of both new and revived productions. It allowed top international singers to participate and, in increasing the number of original-language performances, also enabled British singers to make increasing inroads into the international scene. By 1970 London had a truly international House and a local British ensemble.

At the time of his retirement Solti told Bryan Magee, 'I needed a certain security as a musician to be able to be more generous or mellow. This, of course, reflects in my music. I'm not as tense as I was.' Magee reflected that ten years earlier some of Solti's performances were so tense as to be 'frenetic' and that sometimes the voices of the singers 'would be consumed and they would become exhausted'. But Solti's supreme gift was 'to generate excitement. . . . His musical gift is essentially dramatic, and it makes him a better opera conductor than others of equal talent.' Solti could sweep his audience along 'in a single blaze of excitement through a whole evening'.

Solti's determination to provide enough rehearsal time helped improve the orchestral standards beyond expectations, and the orchestra was ready to make distinguished recordings with Davis.* Edward Downes wrote, 'The brilliance and rhythmic incision which are the hallmarks of Georg Solti's conducting have marked the latest stage in the orchestra's rise to distinction.'[103] Downes afterwards added the thought that, in his later years, Solti had achieved this with his special charm: 'insofar as someone who can be as authoritarian, as strict, as precise, as rhythmically demanding in his music, can be such an amiable man'.

Magee felt that Solti had made more of a contribution to London's musical life than any other individual since the Second World War. For his part Solti admitted that England had also given much to him: 'I am a much better human being, more tolerant – I was a very intolerant man.' He said he felt at home for the first time since he had left Hungary in 1939. Bruno Walter had told him that he would love England but hate the weather. He had thought this was nonsense but never got used to the climate. Valerie Solti recalled that her husband 'would look out on rainy days and say how right he was', but she added, 'He loved the people – the fairness and integrity.'[104] When he retired from Covent Garden, Solti was sad to leave his 'child' but he added, 'In the meantime that child has grown up and got married and Papa has to retire.'[105]

On Solti's departure William Bundy, the technical director who

---

* There was criticism that Solti only made one recording with the Covent Garden forces during his directorship, Don Carlos, and that this was at a time when his own recording career was flourishing with Decca who preferred the Vienna Philharmonic (Tooley, In House, p. 33).

had so disliked him during the early years, told him, 'You taught me how to make the theatre work properly – how to create a proper production ... And I just want to tell you that I am grateful to you.' Stella Chitty, the cherished stage manager, went even further: 'Gradually we came to like him – always respected him – and eventually came to – shall I say – love him?'[106]

ELEVEN

THE MET 1960–72

The Met Moves to Lincoln Center

WHILE COVENT GARDEN and the European Houses were striving to create and maintain a higher standard of day-to-day performance, Rudolf Bing, at the Metropolitan Opera continued to build on the House's strengths, while leaving many of its weaknesses unremedied. Many fine young Americans based their careers at the Met – although many others, equally capable, were ignored. Beverly Sills was America's leading diva in bel canto roles, singing at the New York City Opera, but she did not make her debut at the Met until 1975, at the age of forty-six. European singers like Elisabeth Grümmer and Elisabeth Schwarzkopf were also brought to the Met, in the autumn of their careers. Gradually – very gradually – the orchestra was strengthened. A reviewer in 1963 wrote that it 'can be a hack one night and a thoroughbred the next'.[1] Under Kurt Adler, chorus-master from 1945 until 1973, the chorus also improved. The Met's repertoire was gradually extended to include works which had long been standard in Europe, especially in the German repertoire. Above all, Bing knew what made the Met the Met: he carried on feeding the House with top singers.

Two sopranos made their Met debuts with enormous and justified éclat. Birgit Nilsson's Isolde was greeted with great enthusiasm on 18 December 1959. The *New York Times* reviewer felt her superior to Flagstad in the part. A British critic wrote, 'Whatever one's opinion, the ringing high Bs of the first act, the sumptuous, cello-like tones of her lower register, and the poise and assurance of her portrayal in the dramatic moments won the singer an immediate following.'[2] Kolodin considered Nilsson's voice ideal for the large Met auditorium. Nilsson 'proved herself . . . to be the greatest of rarities, a performer – like Flagstad before her and Caruso before her – to whom the size of the Metropolitan was not a hazard, but an advantage'.[3]

Nilsson was born in 1918 in Skane, a small community in southern Sweden. Her father, a sixth-generation farmer, objected to Nilsson studying singing. He was 'terribly upset,' Nilsson later recalled in an interview. 'He did not want his only child going out into the great world.'[4] Before her first appearance at the Met she had assumed major Wagnerian roles at Stockholm, Munich, Bayreuth and Covent Garden, among other venues. At the Met she sang more than 200 performances from her debut until 1982. Opinion is divided about her acting. Some considered her stiff, while others found her passionate and involved. Harold Rosenthal called Nilsson's recording of the *Salome* name part 'the most staggering recording of an opera I have ever heard'. He continued, 'Her characterization is complete, so much so that the closing pages become quite repulsive, and one cannot but agree with Herod's final instructions to the soldiers: *"Man töte dieses Weib!"* ("Kill this woman!")'[5] Many remember Nilsson as a finer actress through the voice than through stage movement.

Ten days after Nilsson's debut, illness struck the Met's *Tristan* production. Disaster was narrowly averted and a measure of farce was injected. Ramón Vinay, the Tristan scheduled to sing that evening, told Bing he was too tired to get through the role, having sung this most taxing of tenor parts only four days previously. Karl Liebl, who had been Nilsson's partner on opening night, had a cold. Albert da Costa, a youthful singer who was also on call, was ill as well. Bing's curtain announcement was one of a kind. 'I began by saying, "Ladies and gentlemen, Miss Nilsson is very well," which brought a sigh of relief from almost 4,000 people. Then I went on, "However, we are less fortunate with our Tristan. The Metropolitan has three distinguished Tristans available, but all three are sick. In order not to disappoint you, these gallant gentlemen, against their doctors' orders, have agreed to do one act each." . . . Never has *Tristan und Isolde* started so hilariously.'[6]

Nilsson's instrument was very dependable and she rarely cancelled. In a 1963 Met *Aida* she sang with such aplomb as to give no evidence of her indisposition. Even a non-musician like Clive James, attending a Covent Garden performance in the 1960s, could sense Nilsson's indomitable professionalism: '. . . Birgit Nilsson kept drilling Brünn-hilde's climactic notes right through the middle while Valhalla, which was supposed to fall, got caught in the scrim up which the Rhine, in the form of projected green light, was supposed to rise. She sang like a train coming while the set malfunctioned all around her.'[7]

Bing brought to the Met the first black singers in an age when discrimination was the norm in America. In this respect his policy stood in direct contrast to that of Johnson's House. He was responsible for Marian Anderson's debut in 1955 as Ulrica in *Ballo*. Anderson was fifty-six years old at the time, and though her artistry was still at its peak the voice had lost a certain amount of lustre and power. However, no matter how tardy, it was to Bing's credit that he used his authority to take such a step. Great excitement accompanied Leontyne Price's Met bow as Leonora in *Il Trovatore* on 27 January 1961. She had more than half an hour of sustained applause at the final curtain, much to the discomfiture of her Manrico, Franco Corelli.

Corelli was also making his debut at the Met. Years later Price recalled, 'I believe that Corelli had words with Mr Bing the next day.'[8] Harold Schonberg wrote in the *New York Times*, Price's voice, 'warm and luscious, has enough volume to fill the house with ease, and she has a good technique to back up the voice itself. . . . In the convent scene she took some fine-spun phrases in a ravishing pianissimo. And her top is exceptionally secure. She does not lunge for notes, attacking them from underneath and sliding into them.' Schonberg was not so positive about Corelli, whose voice, he felt, was 'a large-sized but not an especially suave instrument, and it tends to be produced explosively. It has something of an exciting animal drive about it, and when Mr Corelli lets loose, he can dominate the ensemble.'[9]

Price was not only the first black American opera star; she was also one of the finest interpreters of Verdi. Born in 1927 in the small town of Tupelo, Mississippi, her first singing lessons were funded by a sympathetic white family, but she emphasised in interviews that her parents' encouragement was an even stronger factor in her becoming a singer. A milestone was reached at the age of nine, when she heard Marian Anderson in recital. Another crucial event in her young adult-hood was hearing Ljuba Welitsch as Salome. Before her Met debut

Price had already been an outstanding Bess (debut in the part 1953), Aida in Vienna, Milan, London and Verona, and Tosca, among other roles. Leontyne Price had a positive appreciation of her own vocal talents. She is quoted as having told an interviewer, 'I think I've one of the most beautiful lyric soprano voices I've ever heard. I'm mad about my voice. It was gorgeous.'[10] More to the point, she knew her *Fach* and liked it. 'I'm a lyric soprano – a juicy lyric, yes – but I've never said I was a dramatic soprano. We lyric sopranos have special problems. We can't just get away with trilling; we don't have the power to stamp out an orchestra like "Big B", as I affectionately call Birgit Nilsson.'[11]

At least two casting choices for Leontyne Price show the Met management at their most insensitive to singers and singing. The part of Minnie in *La Fanciulla del West* demands extraordinary flexibility and strength in the top register. In 1961 Price was forced to cancel after a performance and a half. Although a 1965 *Così* was not disastrous, the principals did not acquit themselves well. Martin Bernheimer thundered in *Opera*:

> Whoever advised Leontyne Price to undertake Fiordiligi should never be asked for counsel again. Ease in coloratura and Mozartian elegance were never Miss Price's forte, not even in her best days. And February 4, when I heard her, was anything but one of her best days. The two arias ['Come scoglio' and 'Per pietà'] were negotiated with the same desperate awkwardness that marked her attempts at stylized high comedy.[12]

When Price was well cast and functioning at her best she was a legend, well-nigh unsurpassable in her finest roles. In the 1964 RCA recording of *Forza*, conducted by Thomas Schippers, her portrayal of Leonora is a masterpiece of singing, acting and, above all, emotional commitment. The dark lustrous tone, 'masky', sensuous, perfectly clean, is ultimate diva material. Price's sound is to the post-war era what Rosa Ponselle's was before the war: beauty revealed, with suggestions of reserved mystery. The phrasing is exquisite, the pathos sincere, and the lush, deep high and upper-middle notes, approached without hurry, electrifying. Comparing her recorded 'La vergine degli angeli' with Tebaldi's, Elvio Giudici is at a loss for words. He finds in Price 'a blend of the maximum of passion and religious exaltation, moulded in a thrilling something which Verdi's female characters had never before known – a something quite unknown in Tebaldi's regal vocal tranquillity'.[13] Schippers, only thirty-four at the time the recording was issued, had conducted extensively at the New York City Opera and at the Met. This is one of his most memorable opera recordings; Giudici praises his 'innate sense of the fantastic and the picturesque', which 'allows him to bring the great choral scenes to life in a magnificent manner'.[14]

As the old Met's days began to be numbered, new legends arose in the House. On the evening of 4 March 1960 Leonard Warren went on stage in *Forza* opposite Tebaldi and Richard Tucker. That night Tebaldi was making her return to the Met, wearing as a British critic wrote, 'a gorgeous henna coiffure and singing for the most part like an angel'.

> Then disaster struck: after the recitative 'Morir, tremenda cosa!' and the aria 'Urna fatale del mio destino' Warren turned to reply to the Surgeon's '*Lieta novella, è salvo*' but no words came; he took a step or two towards the wings, collapsed, and the music stopped. Forty-five minutes later he was pronounced dead of a cerebral haemorrhage.[15]

Under Bing, labour relations seriously deteriorated. Facing a deficit of $840,000 for the 1960–61 season, Bing felt he could not meet the orchestra players' demand for a pay rise – from $170 per week to $268. The American Federation of Musicians twice reduced the demand, at first to $248 and then to $220. The orchestra members also sought to play six performances a week instead of seven. Bing travelled to Europe, entrusting the continuing negotiations to his assistant manager. After a strike was threatened the dispute was finally settled when Secretary of Labour Arthur J. Goldberg conducted arbitration binding on both sides. The Met musicians felt the agreement was unfair to them. Resentment remained that would fuel future contract disputes.

Bing complained to Board president Anthony Bliss in June 1962 that the Vienna Staatsoper was subsidised by $5 or $6 million a year, and Berlin nearly $4 million. The Met, he added, had to get along on

The façade of the Vienna Staatsoper undergoing reconstruction, 1949.

Below Herbert von Karajan, music director of the Staatsoper from 1957 to 1964, and the artistic director of the Salzburg festival from 1956 to 1988, rehearsing in the Staatsoper auditorium.

Right below Kirsten Flagstad as Brünnhilde, and Hans Hotter as Wotan, in *The Valkyrie*, Covent Garden, 1948.

Right La Scala in ruins, after being bombed in August 1943.

Below The collaboration of Carlo Maria Giulini and Luchino Visconti set new standards for integrated music drama, notably in their 1955 La Scala *Traviata* and their 1958 Covent Garden *Don Carlos*. This photograph shows them during rehearsals for *La Traviata* at Covent Garden in 1967.

Maria Callas in *La Traviata*, Covent Garden, June 1958. Her collaboration with Visconti at La Scala in the 1950s transformed the concept of the singing actor, as well as restoring many *bel canto* works to the repertoire.

Below The 1958 Visconti-Giulini *Don Carlos* at Covent Garden: Act II Scene 2.

Above Edward Johnson, Met general manager from 1935 to 1950, Eleanor Belmont, Met benefactor, and Rudolf Bing, Met general manager from 1950 to 1972.

Left The golden horseshoe – the old Met auditorium.

Below The new Met auditorium.

Opposite
Above John Gielgud and Rafael Kubelik rehearsing *The Trojans*, Covent Garden, June 1957.

Below Joan Sutherland's Lucia, in Zeffirelli's Covent Garden production in February 1959, turned her into an international star.

Above Georg Solti, Covent Garden's music director from 1960 to 1971, January 1964.

Below The Peter Hall, John Bury, Georg Solti production of Schoenberg's *Moses and Aaron* at Covent Garden, June 1965.

I Vespri Siciliani directed by John Dexter, designed by Josef Svoboda, and conducted by James Levine. A controversial production for the Met, January 1974.

James Levine, the Met's music director from 1976, with John Dexter, director of productions from 1974 to 1981, seen here during the creative period of their collaboration during rehearsals for *Aida*, 1976.

Right Louis Quilico with Luciano Pavarotti in the Met's *Ballo in Maschera*, February 1980.

Above The radical and socially committed director Giorgio Strehler rehearsing *Die Zauberflöte* at Salzburg in 1974.

Right Claudio Abbado, as music director, artistic director and later chief conductor, gave La Scala great leadership, restoring quality and variety to its repertoire.

Below The Abbado-Strehler collaboration inspired such productions as the 1971 La Scala *Simon Boccanegra*.

private sponsorship amounting to only $1 million – and no government subsidy at all. Money difficulties had brought him, he wrote, 'to the end of rope'.[16]

In spite of financial difficulties Bing persisted in his efforts to raise the standard of Met stagings. Director Nathaniel Merrill and designer Robert O'Hearn were brought in as resident artists in 1960 and given a degree of creative autonomy. They gave Met stagings a boost in favour of stronger characterisation and dramatic impact. The team were responsible for more than a dozen Met productions. The first of their collaborative efforts was the *L'Elisir d'amore* of 1960–61. At the age of thirty-six O'Hearn had designed many productions in the American theatre and opera, including Shakespeare at the New York City Center and other words at the Brattle Theater in Cambridge, Massachusetts. Disliking stylised settings, he defined his style as 'decorative' or 'imaginative'. O'Hearn sought to lighten the approach to *Elisir* by setting the work in northern Italy – 'but really northern Italy. I'm not using the usual heavy southern Italian scenery with the long stucco walls. This is wrong for the opera – heavy scenery for light music. I've made up my own village – grape arbors, vertical buildings broken up by balconies, windows and lattices, hills in the distance.'[17] O'Hearn placed the *Elisir* chorus on elevations to enable them to have a view of the conductor.

Given the size of the stage and a certain Met philosophy of grandeur, it was natural that Merrill and O'Hearn would create imposing spectacles. This was epitomised by the October 1963 Merrill – O'Hearn *Aida*. As other designers would do later in the Lincoln Center House, O'Hearn put the depth of the old Met stage to good effect by angling the set, allowing the chorus plenty of room to move about among the monumental set pieces. He costumed the dancers with extravagance. 'Tall African warriors shake their arm and leg bands of plumes; a bevy of belly-dancers gyrate their gilded navels; and a group of female witch-doctors (presumably) are fascinating in blue paint and veils. At the climax of the ballet in the Triumphal Scene, a seven-foot Watusi runs in and spreads an ostrich-plume cape that looks about twenty feet broad. (The production cost about $150,000, and for that sum you can afford a lot of ostrich plumes.)'[18] Merrill's direction was deemed acceptable: 'The characters are consistent in their actions and the large masses of stage figures are moved smoothly.' The ballets, by Katherine Dunham, were 'a potpourri of everything from African tribal to the twist'.[19] The standees hissed and booed them. Nilsson sang the name part with great success despite suffering pain from an attack of gallstones. Bing dismissed the critics' carping. He wrote in a letter to William Fisher, the president of the Fisher Governor Company in Marshalltown, Iowa, who had given funds for a production of *Salome*, telling him that while the music critics' level 'was fairly low when I came, it has now deteriorated to unbelievable depth. Neither their praise nor their condemnation means a thing. The vast majority of them are totally ignorant and tasteless, and nothing they can say makes the slightest impression on me one way or the other. . . .'[20]

At the same time that they presented big, splashy shows, Merrill and O'Hearn also did thoughtful, balanced work at the Met. A number of their productions gave opportunity for serious acting. During the 1964–65 season their *Samson et Dalila* was far more positively reviewed. The chorus's gestures and movements were restrained by comparison with typical old-fashioned productions. In a move that showed the impact of Wieland Wagner at Bayreuth, lighting was employed to create dramatic effect. 'The result', said *Opera* magazine's reviewer, made Samson 'an exciting theatrical experience instead of the usual semi-dramatic oratorio. It is good by any operatic standard – extraordinary by the Met's.'[21]

In addition to his permanent staff, Bing eagerly sought the services of the very finest international opera conductors and stage directors. The conductor of the Merrill–O'Hearn *Aida* was Georg Solti, who visited the Met for three seasons in the 1960s. Kolodin appreciated the originality of Solti's reading. 'Musically, the distinctions of this *Aida* stemmed from the ability of Solti to treat the score as an expert restores a painting – by erasing accumulated grime from the sound of the orchestra, bringing "up" and making fresh the whole.'[22] Solti's financial demands at the Met were largely satisfied. Bing went so far as to promise him payment for unconducted performances, a nefarious practice encountered at some European Houses:

> Our top fee for conductors is $1,000 per performance. This is what Mitropoulos had and what Böhm and Stokowski have. Nobody else so far has had more.

However, I want you to feel as happy as possible and I suggest that we guarantee you in the period twenty-five performances at $1,000 per performance, although you won't conduct anywhere near that number.[23]

Solti's difficulties at the Met largely concerned casting questions. Bing could not always deliver the outstanding artists Solti wished to work with. For the name part of Boris in 1963 Solti would have preferred either Cesare Siepi or George London. Bing replied, 'I cannot promise you that it can only be Siepi and/or London. . . . Also we cannot completely ignore other first-rate singers like [Jerome] Hines and [Giorgio] Tozzi.'[24] Siepi accepted a part in a Broadway show. Hines, according to Bing, refused to sing Pimen and insisted on having Boris; and 'The same applies to Tozzi (who used to do our Pimen) unless he also gets a Boris'.[25]

In 1964, when Bing began planning a new production of *Peter Grimes* to be conducted by Solti, he insisted that Lucine Amara sing Ellen Orford. His reasoning reflected a characteristic Met attitude: 'Her lack of a strong personality may not be a disadvantage in that particular part, while her exceptionally beautiful voice would give it all the warmth it requires.'[26] Solti replied, 'I cannot accept Lucine Amara in this role, as in my view it is just bad casting. I understand only too well that you (as indeed I at Covent Garden) sometimes have to cast a member of your company, for policy reasons, into a role for which they are not pre-eminently suitable, and if this is the case with Miss Amara I see your point, and am quite willing to withdraw from conducting the opera. . . .'[27] Calling the Amara question a matter of 'artistic conscience', Solti abandoned the planned *Grimes*.

In May 1962 Bing offered Carlo Maria Giulini a chance to conduct the Verdi *Requiem* at the Met on Good Friday in 1964. His suggestions for the soloists included Price, Rosalind Elias, Bergonzi and Siepi – artists who had performed, or would soon perform, the solo parts with such conductors as Toscanini, Reiner and Karajan. Giulini did not take up the offer.[28]

Early in the same year Bing approached Franco Zeffirelli with an offer to stage *Falstaff*. The idea appealed to him: '. . . I retain my keen interest for producing and designing *Falstaff* particularly since I have learned that it is to be conducted by Mr Leonard Bernstein.'[29] Zeffirelli also mentioned his wish to stage *Carmen* at the Met, suggesting that Bernstein conduct and that Callas sing the name part. Bing demurred, pointing out that he had already asked Callas to star as Carmen at the Met and that she had not accepted his offer. Bing added that Callas was by then in questionable vocal condition. Casting Don José would also prove difficult: '. . . I know that at the present moment there are no more than one or two tenors and one or two baritones in the world whose vocal equipment would qualify them to sing Don José and Escamillo at the Metropolitan Opera; I consider it totally unrealistic to assume that those tenors or baritones could deliver French dialogue to an audience of close to four thousand from the stage of the Metropolitan.'[30] Zeffirelli angered Bing when his designs did not arrive on time. Bing wrote to Zeffirelli:

> I cannot tell you how upset I am about your discourteous and unreliable attitude. We had a firm agreement with you which you confirmed in writing that certain models and designs for drops were to be delivered to us by the end of July. . . .
>
> You have chosen completely to ignore repeated [letters], cables and telephone calls and have not even had the courtesy to acknowledge my personal cable from Siusi . . .
>
> It is a most unhappy experience.[31]

In spite of Zeffirelli's tardiness and Bing's wrath, the *Falstaff*, presented in 1964, was a triumph, a truly integrated production. Zeffirelli had done *Falstaff* in many countries, including Israel, when he was engaged to design and direct it for the Met. In fact, he wanted to sue one major opera house whose settings showed his influence, he felt, a little too obviously.[32] The London production was called 'arty', while the Rome staging was termed 'a kind of village practical joke', set in 'a rural, simple world'.[33] The New York version steered a middle course, with a tilt in the direction of broad humour. That broadness was summed up in the slogan embedded in the final fugue, 'Tutto nel mondo è burla' ('The whole world is a jest'). In the spirit of 'burla' Zeffirelli had the notion – which he rejected eventually – to fly the scenery away at the end of the opera and have the singers remove their costumes to show street clothing. The new lighting effects were greeted with the same enthusiasm as they were at Covent Garden.

Francis Robinson of the Met wrote, 'For the first time we saw real sunlight on a stage, several sunlights in fact, for they were different, as they are in nature. The pale sun through the cobwebs of the Garter Inn was as different from midday in the garden as that was from the slanted glow of late afternoon when Falstaff comes dripping from the Thames.'[34] Alan Rich in the *New York Herald Tribune* was fulsome in his praise of the director: 'In Zeffirelli's enchanted hands everything becomes a means toward a single end.'[35] Bernstein's conducting stressed the work's vigour. 'Bernstein was as meticulous in detail, as rich and unflagging in imagination, as Zeffirelli, and the result was a revelation to Metropolitan audiences. Almost never, at that house, is a production so unified, so carefully worked out, so obviously conscious that opera is a blending of all the arts and not a musical performance with appendages.'[36]

Although Bing had disparaged Callas's vocal state to Zeffirelli in 1962, after her triumphant Covent Garden Toscas he was considering her for the role of Carmen. In October 1964, he approached Luchino Visconti with the idea of him producing *Carmen* 'sometime in November 1966' and he presented the project to Visconti in terms which suggested that he and Callas were still actively considering the possibility of her singing the lead role. 'The project, of course, depends on the solution of innumerable problems; one of them is that at this stage I have no Carmen. I have been in communication with Maria Callas, and Maria has expressed interest but has not yet made up her mind. The trouble is I simply must come very soon to a decision on the whole matter. If Maria agrees, I will be delighted to offer it to her.'[37] Callas's vocal state was still erratic. In his reply, however, Visconti sounded ready to explore Bing's suggestion: 'In reply to your letter, yes, I would be very interested in staging a new production of *Carmen* for the Metropolitan Opera. I would also be willing to commit myself for a definite period in October, November, 1966, depending on the terms of the offer which you extend to me. . . . If you are still considering Maria Callas, perhaps I might speak to her myself.'[38] On 9 November Bing was pessimistic: 'I am afraid Maria Callas simply cannot make up her mind right now about our *Carmen* project two years from now.' He suggested that Visconti might wish to stage Callas in Cherubini's *Medea* – if Maria might by chance be willing – or, 'failing all that, would a new production of *Gioconda* with Renata Tebaldi and Franco Corelli conceivably be of any interest to you?'[39] These vague suggestions met with no response from Visconti. On 19 December Bing adopted a tone at once wounded and hectoring: 'I confess that I am a little upset not to have had even the courtesy of an acknowledgement from you of my various letters.' He also confessed that the *Gioconda* project would prove impossible – 'For various reasons, I think this, too, may be doubtful.'[40] Bing offered the *Gioconda* to Margherita Wallmann, who accepted. In later correspondence the two men could not agree on an opera for Visconti to direct.

During this period Bing's negotiations with world-class artists were seldom easy, with frequent power skirmishes on both sides. After a lengthy correspondence with Bing, Karajan agreed to stage and conduct Wagner's *Ring* at the Met over a four-year time period beginning in the 1967–68 season. Karajan's fee was high for the Met: a total of $33,500 for the two and a half months he would be spending in New York during the first two years of his engagement. The contract also stipulated that no artist engaged by the House during that time would be paid more than Karajan. For *Die Walküre*, the first instalment of Wagner's tetralogy of operas, Bing agreed to up to seven rehearsals with orchestra alone, as well as five six-hour days of lighting rehearsals. Karajan also convinced Bing to pay up to $20,000 for new lighting instruments which would duplicate the effects of his Salzburg *Ring*. 'You will doubtless agree with me', he wrote to Bing, 'when I tell you that when and wherever I conduct, my approach to my work is based on a standard of a festival *en permanence*.'[41]

However, if Bing thought that by signing a contract he had finally agreed terms with Karajan, he was mistaken. By February 1967 Karajan was demanding two casts for his *Ring*, a proviso which if accepted would have proved very expensive. He sought to alternate Birgit Nilsson as Brünnhilde with Régine Crespin, casting deplored by Bing, who felt Crespin's high notes were failing. Karajan also claimed, over Bing's objections, that Leonie Rysanek was unsuitable for Sieglinde, being 'too old . . . and not virginal enough'.[42] He also sought to convince the Met to reschedule the *Ring* performances in a way which Bing maintained would wreak havoc with the House's prearranged programming. When Bing received a cable from Michel Glotz, Karajan's representative in Paris, announcing that Karajan expected Bing to telephone him in Italy at five in the morning, New York time, to discuss outstanding issues, Bing was more than indignant. He told Karajan and Glotz that the Met was prepared to cancel the *Ring* project unless he, Bing, did the casting.

> I hope you will agree that this is the moment of truth, if we go forward with the scheme, you must face up to the fact that you are not and cannot be, by nature of the circumstances, in complete control as you are everywhere else. . . . I cannot abdicate my responsibilities as General Manager, and in the event that in one or the other case we cannot agree, the decision of the General Manager of the Metropolitan Opera must be the final one. If that is unacceptable to you – and it really is as simple as that – then please say so and let us abandon the plan.[43]

In March 1966, seeking to contract Claudio Abbado to a twelve- or fifteen-week stand at the Met, Bing offered him a *Tosca* with Nilsson starring. A lengthy correspondence ensued, spread out over eleven months. In the end Abbado, who was accustomed to conduct from memory, declined on the ground of lack of time to memorise the score. Abbado also felt, according to the Met's Italian scout Roberto Bauer, that 'he would not dare to conduct such a well-known and popular work as *Tosca* for the first time in his life just at the Met. He thinks he should try that opera out in another theatre before and then present it to the public of the Met.'[44] Abbado likewise declined what was for him the questionable plum of *Cavalleria* or *Pagliacci*, to be staged by Michael Cacoyannis, as well as an offer to take *Boris Godunov* on the gruelling spring tour of 1971. On 27 December 1967 Bing wrote to Abbado, 'I am terribly disappointed with your letter of December the eighteenth. We are talking of the tour of 1971, which is approximately three and a half years from now and it is inconceivable that with a little goodwill and desire this could not be arranged for you.'[45] Further negotiations with Abbado to conduct at the Met, carried on by Robert Herman and Bing himself, led to a single series of performances of *Don Carlos* in 1968.

*   *   *

Booing is heard, at least from time to time, in most opera houses round the world. At La Scala it rises at different periods to the level of an institution. Since opera is a visible and cherished emblem in Italy, politics, both national and musical, are frequently expressed noisily in the galleries of the venerable House. In Vienna the *Opernnarren*, or 'opera fools', who have occupied the fourth gallery, have occasionally issued manifestos for or against this or that singer or conductor – and could be aggressive, as when they chased tenor Rudolf Lustig round the corner of the Staatsoper in 1956. At Covent Garden booing was sometimes heard in the amphitheatre, where strong opinions on musical issues were held and expressed, and where management very much discouraged booing as detrimental to the performers. More often, booing was the conservative audience's reaction to more radical stagings or designs, as with Peter Brook's *Salome* in November 1949 or Wanamaker's *Forza* in September 1962.

The Met standees were the approximate equivalent of La Scala's noisy, catcalling *loggionisti* and the *Opernnarren* of Vienna. But in America the standees' behaviour was generally milder and their protests were confined to singing of which they disapproved. By 1962, however, they were drawing Bing's ire. In that year, management issued an ultimatum that referred in arctic tones to 'ill-mannered, noisy and annoying shouting demonstrations', most of which 'emanate from the standing-room areas'. If this behaviour was not controlled, the ultimatum continued, the Met 'either will have to curtail drastically admittance to standing room or, if worse comes to worst, cut out standing room entirely'.[46] By early 1964 a line had clearly been crossed, independent of management's threats. A faction opposed to Leonie Rysanek had deluged the soprano's hotel room with telephone calls only an hour after she had arrived there in advance of singing Desdemona. Some of the callers had threatened to kill her, which in those gentler days was interpreted as 'a threat to "kill" the performance'. Clearly inside information had been obtained from the hotel and an artist had been criminally harassed. On Valentine's Day Bing declared the sale of standing-room tickets suspended. 'I will not abdicate to mob rule,' he stated. The next day the theatre was picketed at a Saturday matinée. One sign read, 'Mr Bing – do you want to get rid of the claque? Then fire your third-rate singers who pay them.' Maria Jeritza was enlisted by the standees to intercede. She was seen walking into Bing's office. By the end of the performance Bing relented and withdrew the ban on standee ticket sales. No further threats to artists were recorded.

Bing had called the annual spring tour 'the albatross hung around the neck of the manager of the Metropolitan Opera'.[47] Even in those long-gone days when the tour cities came up with $50,000 per performance, Bing wrote, a loss was incurred. 'A sold-out house in New York also yields about $50,000, and can be gained without the expense of carting about costumes and scenery and paying transportation plus a $25-a-day per diem to 300-odd members of the company.'[48] Foreign singers hated the tour. Nilsson flatly refused to participate in a seven-week tour of *Tristans* and *Turandots*, writing to Bing in no-nonsense terms, 'A fee of 1,500 dollars does not at all cover what I can get for that time from other companies.'[49] At this period the tour proceeded from city to city in special trains. During the 1959 tour the sets travelled in twenty-seven goods waggons. Bing, ever mindful of caste distinctions, recalled with a certain frisson that star singers, administrative staff and wig-combers 'all ate in the same dining cars'. Bing also recalled: 'I never knew what went on all night, the comings and goings between the compartments.'[50] Those on the train included an orchestra of ninety or more, a chorus of about seventy-five and a ballet of more than twenty dancers. In addition, there were principal singers, conductors, technical and administrative staff. After 1968 the tour abandoned the rails and travelled in chartered planes. A fleet of some thirty trucks carried the sets.

Venues for tour performances were sometimes not up to standard. The Public Auditorium in Cleveland, seating some 9,000, is shown in one photograph full nearly to capacity. The orchestra are placed on the same level as the front-row patrons, separated from them with velvet ropes in bank-queue fashion. Intervals in Cleveland, Bing confessed, are 'endless'. 'The stagehands have to hand things through holes in the wall, to and from the truck.'[51] The social cachet of the occasion is unmistakable. Women in floor-length gowns and men in black tie wait for the curtain to rise. Fashions are far from provincial. But when the Met company returned home the Cleveland Public

Auditorium was once again booked by trade fairs and circuses, much more suited to the hall.

Atlanta, one of the Met's annual tour destinations, was one of its heartiest supporter cities. Atlantans gave the Met company more delightful parties than any other town. Southern ladies would buy their tickets months ahead of time, prepare their mink stoles and line up their Southern gentlemen to accompany them. Performances took place in the post-Moorish movie palace known to Atlantans as 'The Fabulous Fox'. Bing recalled conductor Pierre Monteux striking a blow for racial equality in the then-segregated Georgia Piedmont. 'I took him for a drive into the countryside around Atlanta, and we stopped for tea at a simple place by the road. A fat old black lady came out and said she couldn't serve us: "We only serve coloured." Monteux said with that wonderful smile under the wonderful white moustache, "But we are coloured; we are pink." '[52]

Met productions were seldom toured abroad. One exception was the summer of 1966, when Jean-Louis Barrault invited the company to Paris to perform in the little Théâtre de l'Odéon. Since the Met's reputation had been built for years on 'big' opera, the choice of *Il Barbiere di Siviglia* and *Le Nozze di Figaro* was curious. French critical and popular reception was so negative that Bing felt compelled to apologise afterwards in print – although not in Paris itself. In a letter to the *Vienna Express* he wrote, 'Probably it was a mistake, my mistake, to come to Paris after more than fifty years with works like *The Barber of Seville* and *The Marriage of Figaro*.' Perhaps the better idea, Bing concluded on reflection, would have been to 'wait until we could come with *Aida* and *Turandot* – most likely another fifty years'.[53] Lucine Amara as Mozart's Countess was booed at the end of 'Porgi, amor', but Teresa Stratas's Cherubino was eagerly applauded. With Maria Callas in the audience, Roberta Peters in *Barbiere* was much insulted, as Eaton wrote, 'after Roberta Peters had concluded her second-act aria with a note less than perfect, a coarse shout came from high in a balcony: "Brava, Callas!" '[54] Some said the Parisians' sense of inferiority lay behind their savaging of the Met performances.

The note of Paris' artistic inadequacy had been sounded in Harold Schonberg's first dispatch [to the *New York Times*] after

Barbiere: 'Of the world's major opera houses, the two in Paris
. . . occupy a low position in the international world. The French
know this as well as anybody else.' Bing later echoed this more
pungently in an interview: 'So Peters had a bad night. Paris has
had a bad century.'[55]

At a time when opera was reaching relatively small audiences in
America, the Met decided in 1965 to establish a permanent touring
company called the National Company. Initial funding was provided
by the Met and the John F. Kennedy Center for the Performing Arts
in Washington DC. Anthony Bliss, then president of the Met Board
and later the House's general manager, wrote that the new company
would be 'made up almost exclusively of American singers'. It was
intended to 'present opera in sixty-odd communities throughout the
nation. For many in its audiences, this will be their first experience
of operatic theatre.'

The idea was also to provide young American singers with experience.[56] Mezzo Risë Stevens was co-general manager, together with
Michael Manuel. The curious idea was instituted of performing 'standard' operas (*Carmen* and *Butterfly*) in both the original language
and in English in order to 'discover whether operatic truth lies in
understanding the language of the drama as well as the charm and
beauty of the music'.[57] At a time when there were no surtitles, this
was an unusual admission by the Met that an operatic text – and its
language – might be hard for an audience to understand. The National
Company was also set up to produce a comedy and a contemporary
opera – in the first year, *Cinderella* (Rossini's *Cenerentola* sung in
English) and Carlisle Floyd's *Susannah*. By the middle of its second
season the company's accumulated loss amounted to $1 million. Board
president Bliss was in favour of the troupe, but Bing and Board treasurer George Moore felt it was a drain on Met resources. Even so,
Bing approached Walter Felsenstein – whose work he had much
appreciated in East Berlin and Hamburg – to help out with the National
Company's stagings. The offer was not taken up.

The insufficiencies of the old Metropolitan Opera House had been
obvious as early as 1908. In that year, when Giulio Gatti-Casazza took

up his post as general manager, he complained to Board chairman Otto Kahn about the lack of rehearsal space and storage for sets. There was nowhere in the old building to park sets for a day or two when they were not needed. Stagehands had to shift them into a back alley, leaving them at the mercy of the weather. When they were not required for a longer period they were trucked back and forth to a warehouse far uptown on St Nicholas Avenue. The storage facility and transportation cost the Met sums it could ill spare. Kahn is reported to have replied to Gatti-Casazza, 'We have noticed these things before you. But don't worry about it, and have patience. In two or three years a new Metropolitan Opera House will be built, answering all needs.'[58] But fifty-eight years were to pass before the new House would be dedicated. In the meanwhile, as Irving Kolodin remarked, it was good to reflect that no opera goer had been killed in the decaying building.

Besides considerations of civic and national prestige, and a typically American wish to renew and improve on the old, the problems Gatti-Casazza had perceived at the beginning of the century were more than enough reason to build a new opera house in New York. An earlier idea had been to move the Met to a new building in Rockefeller Center. However, the Depression weakened the House's finances to the point that the idea had to be shelved. Turning seedy tenements in the West Sixties into an arts centre was a joint plan of Mayor Fiorello La Guardia and Met Board member Charles Spofford, which began to evolve during the late 1930s. The centre would also include a permanent home for the New York Philharmonic, which was performing at that time in Carnegie Hall.

In 1955 Spofford and Arthur Houghton of the Philharmonic Board enlisted the aid of John D. Rockefeller III to sponsor an 'Exploratory Committee for a Musical Arts Center'. Bing strongly objected to including a 'Philharmonic Auditorium' in the same space as the new Met opera building. He wrote in a memo, 'I think it may be wise to reflect upon the fact that, to my knowledge, in no city in the world are the opera house ... and the large concert hall ... on the same block.'[59] Bing was also concerned about the traffic problem. But his objections were overruled, and planning for Lincoln Center – as it was then being called – went ahead. The architectural supervisor was the firm of Wallace K. Harrison. The prestige value of a unitary arts centre for New York City overruled custom, tradition and even parking problems. It also overruled the convenience of the residents of the slum that was to be demolished: 188 buildings were torn down and 1,647 families were moved elsewhere.[60]

In 1963, at an extraordinary meeting of the Met Board, it was revealed that the Ford Foundation had granted the House the sum of $600,000 for helping it over the move to Lincoln Center. An additional $2.5 million from the same source, contingent on the Met's raising matching funds, would help the company expand and allow it to give more performances.[61]

In spite of the Met's money troubles a new era seemed to be dawning for the arts in America. Lincoln Center, and the Met with it, was to be the flagship of a 'cultural explosion' in which the federal government began to take an interest. In 1965 President Lyndon Johnson signed legislation setting up the National Endowment for the Arts, with the purpose of funding selected cultural projects with a potential country-wide impact. While Met Board chairman George Sloan had politely renounced any desire for federal money in 1949, by the mid-Sixties the idea was beginning to look more attractive. Big business was also enlisted in the hope that America's self-interest, and self-image, might be bound up more with the arts. Although corporate sponsorship continued to be an important element in the financing of the arts in America, the National Endowment was shortlived, and curtailed its support after the 1970s.

Board treasurer George Moore and his colleagues had much success at raising funds to help with the Met's share of building Lincoln Center. With the total cost of the complex at $184 million, $40 million was provided by governments – national, state and local. The Ford Foundation and the Rockefellers gave $25 million each. Business and individual contributions made up the rest. Moore drew up a list of potential corporate sponsors for the attention of the Met Opera Association. Clarence Francis, Board chairman of General Foods, headed a committee of corporate contributors. He was quoted as saying, 'The thing that fascinated me was that New York now could be made the cultural centre of the world.'[62] Corporate sponsorship took on importance at the Met rather earlier than in the United Kingdom and at La Scala. It suited the companies' need for image promotion.

Bing had early insisted on an extraordinary building that would make the appropriate impression on the public. In a meeting with the architects in 1959 he declared 'that to build only an adequate and not the best opera house possible today in New York City would make the country "the laughing stock" of the world and the opera a subject of Russian propaganda'.[63] Business sponsorship would help the Met renew itself on a large and luxurious scale. Some Board members wanted an even bigger auditorium than the Thirty-Ninth Street build-ing, with up to 5,000 seats. The need for size was clear in view of the House's dependence on box office income. But Bing demurred: singers' 'lung power' would be insufficient and he feared empty seats as well.[64] This time his view was accepted. The new House would have 3,778 seats, 163 more than the old one. Of these only 170 would have partial or obstructed view. Bing also objected at first to the New York City Opera sharing the same plaza as the Met. But in the end he changed his mind, concluding that the City Opera gave the Met 'no particular difficulties'. After all, its shows were 'simply not in the same league as Metropolitan productions'.[65]

Leaving the old Met was a long, agonised process. Montserrat Caballé advanced her New York debut in order to have had the honour of singing in the old House. Fund drives and court cases were launched. Demonstration after demonstration was held to 'Save the Met'. To no avail, alas. Wrote Harold Schonberg in the New York Times, 'It so happens that there is nothing the Metropolitan Opera would rather see than have the old building interred with all decent speed.'[66] Moreover, Louis Sismondo, manager of Sherry's, the Met restaur-ant, was happy about the move. 'The kitchen here, she is lousy. Very, very lousy. Most of the time to get the dinners out we did some miracles.'[67]

On the evening of 16 April 1966 a 'Gala Farewell' was held, with dozens of Met artists present on stage. In the audience were social, political and artistic luminaries, including Prince Michael of Kent and his mother Princess Marina, Cornelius Vanderbilt Whitney (grandson of two co-founders of the Met in 1883), Mrs Cornelius Vanderbilt III, Mrs W. Vincent Astor, Abby Aldrich Rockefeller, Nin Ryan, Mrs Joseph Kennedy, Arthur Goldberg (then American delegate to the United Nations), Walter J. Kohler Jr (former governor of Wisconsin and a plumbing millionaire), Lotte Lehmann, Blanche Thebom and the retired boxer Gene Tunney. Risë Stevens wore a necklace of eleven big emeralds set with diamonds. But the diamonds in Mrs C. Buxton Love's parure, according to Charlotte Curtis in the *New York Times*, were even more impressive – 'as large as pop-bottle caps'.[68] Irving Kolodin wrote, 'The couture was not merely haute, but, in some instances, excessively so.'[69] The gate was $292,000, some nine times the average evening's takings.

Leopold Stokowski was among the conductors who took the podium. He made a plea to 'save this beautiful House'. The operatic selections put Kolodin in mind of 'a gaudy sound montage of all the operas ever written, pieced together from the choicest morsels of Verdi, Wagner, Mozart, Rossini, Puccini, even Giordano and Ponchielli'.[70] He found it too long, too contrived, but full of fine moments. As first alphabetically, Marian Anderson was the first to take the stage. Nilsson, singing the Immolation scene from *Götterdämmerung*, and Price, singing 'D'amor sull'ali rosee', received much praise. At five minutes past one in the morning everyone joined in 'Auld Lang Syne' and the curtain came down. Kolodin had noticed in it an unrepaired rip.

At three in the afternoon of 17 January 1967 the demolition of the old Met began. 'The sound of wreckers' hammers echoed from the roof, crowbars began to pry at the secrets of dimmed footlights, marble water fountains were dragged from their moorings and the interior of the dusty old auditorium, struck with mortal chill, disintegrated.'[71] After the building had been turned to dust, Licia Albanese put on her *Butterfly* costume and sang 'Un bel dì' in the ruins. The great gold curtain was sold off bit by bit in little squares.

The land, worth $10 million, would be used to construct a new office building; an annual income of almost half a million dollars would accrue to the House. Together with increased ticket prices and savings on operating costs, this would be of some help. But the crucial factor in overcoming the financial crisis would have to be outside contributions. By this time the emergency fund drive had already raised $2.1 million and thought was being given to build an endowment fund which would take many years to achieve.

* * *

The new Met was a conceived on a massive scale. The publicity department gave out formidable statistics: a length of 451 feet, a front width of 175 feet and a rear width of 234 feet. 'At the front it is seven stories high, six above ground level and one below, at the back thirteen. Below the stage level we go three floors right into the solid rock of Manhattan.'[72] When excavation began, an underground body of water was uncovered, much to the builders' surprise. It became known as Lake Bing. The stage machinery and scene-building facilities were unsurpassed anywhere. Harrison, the architect, made 7,000 drawings for the House; 4,000 rolls of gold leaf were used for decoration, largely on the exterior shells of the boxes. The façade was made of 156 glass panels; 42,000 cubic feet of travertine marble were used in the outside plaza. As the Met was happy to point out, that marble was taken 'from the same quarry at Bagni di Tivoli that provided the marble for the Colosseum in Rome, much of which later found its way to St Peter's Basilica'.[73]

The cost of the entire construction amounted to $50 million. In a situation where 'the new Met is deficient in visual elegance' – to quote such a Met partisan as Martin Mayer[74] – the accent was placed on the magnificence. The increased width of the auditorium meant a loss of intimacy, especially in the stalls: in the old House there had been a greater feeling of closeness to on-stage action. The Met seemed proudest of its 'starburst' chandeliers, a gift of the Austrian government. When the House lights are dimmed, many of these chandeliers rise out of sight to the ceiling. When installed they were so fascinating to some New York society women that they demanded they be duplicated for them in miniature as brooches. The Met has described them as 'magic chandeliers' whose beauty 'hits you in the throat as well as the eye'.[75] They were donated as a thank offering for American aid to Austria after the war. But any Viennese who was irked by the wartime destruction of his opera house, then taxed to the hilt and dunned for 5,000 Austrian schillings for a ticket to *Fidelio* at the 1955 reopening, might have thought twice about thanking America.

The new Met's acoustic designers consulted extensively with music personnel. After examining the acoustics of other top opera houses round the world, they took as their model the sound of the old Met. Although it is generally agreed that the acoustics are excellent in the new House, its sheer size makes it very difficult for many singers to project that personalities and subtleties of interpretation. When Cyril Harris, the head acoustician, stood in the Family Circle listening to a student matinée of *Fanciulla*, he knew things would be all right. 'I could hear every card go down,' Harris recalled of the poker game when Minnie plays the sheriff for the life of Dick Johnson. 'I knew we really had a winner.'[76] Lord Harewood, on a visit for the opening, was also happy. He spoke of 'an acoustic that – praise be to the gods of opera! – seemed excellent from wherever I sat'.[77] But the matinée left a sour taste in Rudolf Bing's mouth. 'The triumphant nature of the occasion was somewhat marred when the audience left and we found how many of our student guests had slashed the plush seats with their little knives; but that's New York.'[78] In the end, rather like the new Grosses Festspielhaus at Salzburg, dedicated in 1960, the Met auditorium was a technically efficient playing space which nevertheless lacked warmth.

During the time of moving to the new House, Bing was trying hard to keep salary increases to a minimum, which did not sit well with employees who considered themselves underpaid. In 1966 the unions threatened to stop negotiations in the middle of the season, thus jeopardising the opening of the new House.

The dedicatory production was *Antony and Cleopatra*, a commissioned work by Samuel Barber to a libretto by Zeffirelli, who also directed and designed the production. He came up with a visually rich show conceived on a very grand scale, which played havoc with the Met's budget. Thomas Schippers conducted. The first night, 19 September 1966, was another grand social occasion. Some of the sophisticated new stage machinery failed to work. During the interval Bing announced that the threat of a strike had lifted and that the full season would continue following successful contract negotiations.

The production – with Zeffirelli responsible also for direction and designs – cost more than $400,000, a grand sum at the time. A decade and a half later Met general manager Joseph Volpe remarked that such a production would now cost more than $1 million. '"Anthony Bliss would never stand for that," said Volpe.'[79] The Dean of the Yale School of Drama was scathing: 'Lincoln Center is what America produces instead of art.'[80] Zeffirelli later announced, 'I didn't really believe in it from the beginning ... When I tried to tell Sam that he must reinforce the score, he was adamant. I kept sensing a precipice facing us and did all I could to compensate with a lavish spectacle.'[81] At the time, most critics agreed that the production was overblown and inappropriate. Writing after the event, Bing pleaded with Zeffirelli not to repeat his extravagance: 'May I also say right here and now that in the serious financial situation which we find ourselves, I must ask you and, indeed, every other designer and director, not to plan again too elaborate a production.' Bing objected to 'the immense expense of the production itself' as well as the enlarged stage crew whose extra salaries had to be paid.[82]

After Barber rescored the work, to a revised libretto by Gian Carlo Menotti, opinion began to turn. The present consensus is that the revised work is better than its premiere production. Did Leontyne Price feel *Antony and Cleopatra* was a disaster? 'Not as far as I was concerned. Cleopatra was written specifically for me, much of it in my own sitting-room, with Sam at my piano. I count it a success. But I'm not talking about the sets and staging. Franco Zeffirelli is usually a theatrical genius, but not that night. Sam never got over the hurt.'[83]

Even before the move to the new House the deficit had increased alarmingly. At the Board meeting of 9 November 1966 chairman Spofford indicated that the Met Association was no longer capable of filling the gap. He praised Bing's efforts for quality, saying that while the executive committee of the Board had reached 'the consensus that artistically the company had achieved its goals, . . . financially it placed a definite burden on the resources of the Association'. In a significant departure for the House, outside financial support would have to be sought. Corporate patrons would be approached; a credit line of $5 million would have to be negotiated; and Bing would have to do his part by finding a way to save $200,000 in the annual operating budget and increase audience capacity.[84]

On 12 December the Board reported an anticipated operating loss for 1966–67 of almost $5.5 million, and a forecast of contributions for the season of approximately $3.7 million.[85] By April 1967 it was apparent that the new Met was a very expensive institution to run. Operating the building, including heating and air conditioning, cost three times as much as at the old Met. Unexpected building problems cost $307,000; operating costs in excess of budget were $796,000. Management and Board members mentioned that the new House placed 'almost unmanageable technical and administrative burdens on the staff', with control over costs being lost altogether for a time. Bing told the Board that the season had been the most 'difficult and harrowing in the Metropolitan's history'. There had been too many productions and many technical difficulties.[86]

Robert Craft, Stravinsky's friend and chronicler, attended a performance of the Met's new production of *Carmen* on 15 December 1967. Craft's reaction indicated that the production style and musical standards of the new Met, soon after its opening, were not appreciably different from those of the old one.

> To the Met's new *Carmen*, as the opera is billed, though both musically and visually it is unrelated to the traditional character of the piece. The set for the entire opera is a bullring of Colosseum proportions. In the first act it is an esplanade for strolling couples, fashion models apparently dressed in lavish Goya and Manet costumes. In opposition to this preposterously rich apparel, the children are gotten up like Cruikshank chimney-sweeps or the waifs in photographs advertising the plight of starving earthquake survivors.
>
> The principal shortcomings of the musical reading are simply that the tempi are too fast, the orchestra is too loud, and the performance is innocent of all nuances, shadings, inflections. Singers and orchestra are seldom synchronized, moreover, despite Maestro Mehta's heroic strivings – between prize-fighterly cues to cymbals and brass – to bring them together.[87]

Craft noted the enthusiastic and indiscriminate applause that remains a characteristic of many Met audiences.

In 1968–69, in an overall budget of $17.4 million, the deficit came to $3.5 million. The opening of the 1969 season was delayed until 29 December because of contract disputes with orchestra, chorus, dancers and stagehands. Employees did not walk out, but Bing decided not to begin the season until agreements were reached. He feared financial ruin: if the season went ahead and there were an eventual strike, there would be no box office income to refund subscriptions. Union leaders, as well as the rank and file, felt animosity towards Bing, considering his moves tantamount to a lockout. Anthony Bliss wrote to George Moore, 'He is the principal target at the moment, and I am sure is reluctant to face hostile negotiating committees.'[88]

This time the unions declared they were ready to work during the negotiations, but Bing refused the offer. In a letter to Met subscribers he maintained that he sensed a 'trap', worried that the unions would pull out as they nearly had done in 1966:

> After years of 'negotiating', on the eve of the opening of the new House when enormous amounts of money had been laid out for rehearsals and productions, the orchestra threatened to strike and thereby forced us to accept their terms. The continued refusal of the unions to accept our very substantial offers confirms our belief that they seek to repeat the 1966 experience – to strike when the Metropolitan is most vulnerable – when the season is on.[89]

Many union members termed this management-initiated shutdown a lockout. '"Normally, a lockout only happens when an employer decides to break a union," one labour representative said. "Here it was a device to pressure employees into a quick settlement and an attempt to shift the blame for closing the House from management to the unions."'[90] On 4 August 1969, while negotiations were continuing, management affixed an announcement on the stage door which read, 'Rehearsals and related activities are suspended until further notice.'[91] Bing thus effectively refused to start the 1969–70 season while still negotiating with chorus, ballet and orchestra. In his letter to subscribers he had expressed the hope that something of the season could be salvaged, but meanwhile his salary offers were declined by the artists. Not surprisingly, perhaps, since members of the corps de ballet were offered the sum of $10,000 annually – as opposed to the previous season's even more meagre $6,500. Nor was it surprising that the offer was so small: the Met was still struggling to keep the expensive new House going and the financial crisis was far from over. The season finally opened on 29 December 1969. Donal Henahan recorded the bad feeling that permeated the bargaining.[92] Herman Gray, a lawyer for the musicians, stated after one meeting that the toughest barrier to an agreement was 'the wave of hate blowing across that table'. Sitting across from him was, of course, Bing.

Not only was Bing the object of hatred, but so too was the establishment from which the membership of the Met Board was chosen. Journalist Jane Boutwell viewed the Board as alien and alienated from rank-and-file members of the company.

> Professionally speaking, the board consists of law, banking and a little business; economically it is people who have money or access to money; socially it forms part of the interlocking cultural establishment that finances music, dance and art in New York. Since most board members are busy and successful executives, few of them have the time or the inclination to wander backstage and get acquainted with the company. There has not been a professional musician on the board since Lucrezia Bori died in 1960, and there is no one in the present group with any direct experience in collective bargaining.[93]

After the initial rush to support the building of Lincoln Center it turned out that big-time opera financing in America was still in its infancy. By the early 1970s foundation and corporate donations were increasingly being channelled to social needs, especially education and housing for slum dwellers. Other leading Houses around the world benefited from government subsidy, but not the Met. George Moore stated, 'Box office income can never pay our bills. We have to develop new sources of income from broad-based corporate and individual giving, electronics, a substantial endowment fund, and government support on all levels.'[94]

The urgent need for broader funding helped spur the Met to take steps for education. The Met was awakening to the need for developing a wider audience and informing the public at large about opera. If the art were not merely the preserve of a favoured few, the case for public support could be made that much stronger. In a memorandum by the Met's committee on government support dated 21 May 1970 it was stated that the National Endowment for the Arts would 'probably . . . only support proposals that will make opera available to a greater number of the citizenry'. These included performances in parks and studio workshop evenings. Otherwise, pessimism was expressed about the National Endowment's readiness to give: It would be 'virtually impossible to gain general support for the main programme of the opera since the audience is so limited.'[95] The committee's recommendations included opening rehearsals and performances to students, and making television broadcasts from the House.

Despite financial stringencies, Bing's administration had done splendid work in audience-building. By 1965 Met audiences had reached 97.2 per cent of capacity. Even so, a major problem remained insufficient funds to put on opera properly. After the 1969 contract settlement was finally reached, the *New York Times* printed an editorial calling for a 'broad appraisal of the financial problems': 'The present agreement will almost double the $3.5 million annual deficit that already besets the opera. Further sharp increases in ticket prices next season would tend to restrict patronage even more rigorously to the richest of New Yorkers. The Met ought to be a community institution enriching the cultural endowment of all citizens, not an elitist sanctuary.' Simultaneously the *New York Times* reprimanded Bing for his tough stance: 'Coercive tactics boomerang, to the detriment of both sides.'[96]

Bing was being well and truly assailed on all sides. After George Moore told him in the autumn of 1970 that there was no money for new productions in the 1972–73 season, Bing turned to the executive committee of the Board for guidance. How was he to put on the scheduled *Götterdämmerung* under such stringent conditions? In the end money was found for this new production alone; others would have to wait. And in the minutes of a meeting of the executive committee on 3 December 1970 it was noted that Bing's artistic policies – dictated partly by financial considerations – were causing difficult relations between artists and the Met management.

Bing's attitude to singers remained a sore issue. He made some damaging revelations in a television interview transcribed and published in *New York* magazine and in London's *Opera* magazine. *New York* turned to singer Beverly Sills for a rebuttal.

BING Opera singers are poor, pitiful creatures; they tremble before they go on stage. Their success is only due to some abnormality of the vocal cords, a kind of throat disease. Most of them come from humble backgrounds, and fame is not easily digested by someone who can barely read or write.

SILLS It's distressing to hear him refer to what he has to sell in such scornful terms. If you don't feel that what you're selling is the greatest thing in the world, you're in the wrong profession. I really wish he'd produce one singer who can't read or write; it's just ludicrous to make a statement like that.

BING In 20 years I have never once set foot in a singer's home. I haven't been to the movies in years.

SILLS Yet, there he was at Roz Elias's house in a bathing suit. My husband and I sat in back of him at *Midnight Cowboy*. He went to sleep.[97]

Bing's determination and administrative ability had helped him preside over the successful running-in of the new House. By December 1970, when Göran Gentele was announced as Bing's successor, the stage machinery was functioning as it was supposed to. The dysfunctional revolve, which had caused so much grief, had been replaced at a cost of nearly a quarter of a million dollars. The press announcement was predictably size-oriented: the new machine measured 57 feet in diameter, and was capable of turning at any speed between 15 and 150 feet per minute.

Music and singing took precedence in December 1970, when Karl Böhm came to New York to conduct *Elektra* and *Fidelio*. The Beethoven opera was given a new production by Austrian director Otto Schenk. Böhm's tempi were slow, but his sympathy for the score was warmly approved. Critic Herbert Weinstock found Leonie Rysanek as Leonore 'generally cherishable' despite vocal problems in 'Abscheulicher', her difficult first-act aria. Weinstock's hero of the evening was Jon Vickers as Florestan: 'Vickers was altogether superb. Indeed, this was an entry into legend, for both his extremely affecting singing and his sympathetic visible existence ... were, quite simply, great.'[98]

Bing's last season as general manager opened on 15 September 1971 with *Don Carlos*, the opera which had marked the beginning of his tenure. It was characteristic of the difficult financial climate that the work was mounted in the same production which had been new in November 1950. One observer found it suffering from 'very visible tiredness'. But on balance the singing was exceptionally fine. Plácido Domingo, who made his Met debut in September 1968, sang the title role. Despite singing with a cold, he was favourably compared with Björling. It was a source of pleasure to Bing that three singers were repeating the roles they had sung in the 1950 production: Cesare Siepi as King Philip ('a triumph of style and insight'), Robert Merrill as Rodrigo ('astonishingly bouncy and in the best condition of his current voice') and Lucine Amara as the Heavenly Voice (who 'did little to justify the adjective').[99]

Two months later, on 18 November, August Everding staged a landmark production of *Tristan und Isolde* for the new Met. Günther Schneider-Siemssen designed, and Erich Leinsdorf returned to conduct after a lengthy period away from the House. Birgit Nilsson as Isolde was praised for adding nuances to her already electrifying interpretation. Jess Thomas as Tristan was excused for not being able to fill the huge auditorium with his voice. 'That is more a criticism of the new House than of the singer,' wrote the *Opera* critic. Harold Schonberg of the *New York Times* found the Met, for the first time since the opening of the new House, had made intelligent use of its ample stage facilities. He termed the Everding – Schneider-Siemssen production 'a very interesting attempt to combine neo-Bayreuth symbolism with realism'. The intention seemed to be to isolate Tristan from Isolde in order to underline the transfigured nature of the couple's love. Visual values were emphasised over acting: The direction kept Nilsson 'relatively static; in this production the singers are adjusted to the stage mechanisms, not the reverse.' In the first act, after the drinking of the love potion, 'everything on stage disappears but the lovers. In the background are changing patterns that can be interpreted at will. Is it a cosmos, Stanley Kubrick style? Psychedelic swirls of libido? The electrical charges of love? No matter. The intent is clear; the lovers are on another plane of existence.'[100]

On 17 February 1972 Met audiences heard Sutherland and Pavarotti in a merry *La Fille du régiment* conducted by Richard Bonynge. Sutherland put aside her noble mien and array of careful graces to succeed in light comedy. 'She romped, she made funny faces . . . she had a thoroughly agreeable time, yet the singing was as pure and as honeyed as anything she has ever done here.' Schonberg praised her for producing 'arch after arch of pure tone. What is more, it was expressive tone. There has not been more beautiful or expressive singing in any opera house than in Miss Sutherland's second-act romance, "Il faut partir". This was bel canto at its best – secure in technique, melting in tone, delicately shaded, long-breathed.'[101] Pavarotti's high notes were fast becoming legendary: 'During "Quel destin" he shot off those nine ballistic high Cs. The cheers must have been audible in New Jersey.'[102] The tenor's reputation was much enhanced by the opening performance and he was called back to the curtain twelve times. Even Bonynge, whom one faction of the Met standees was accustomed at that time to dismiss as 'Boing-Boing', was roundly applauded. And beloved Ljuba Welitsch was welcomed back to New York in the speaking role of the Duchess of Crakentorp. Schonberg also liked the unpretentious production: 'Nobody was out to aggrandize the basic simplicity of the opera, and the sets were no more sumptuous than were necessary.' The *New York Times* headline summed up the evening: SHOW-STOPPING AT MET.[103]

In June, Bing held a Verdi festival at the House. Productions, singing and conducting were generally panned by the critics. Changes of cast occurred with embarrassing frequency between the time the publicity material was issued and opening night, and even in mid-performance. Martina Arroyo fainted in the wings after singing the first scene of *Aida*. She was replaced by Elinor Ross, who the *New York Times* felt 'performed like the fine, experienced artist that she is'. But beyond powerful singing by Fiorenza Cossotto as Amneris, the paper's critic called the performance 'routine'.[104] In *Don Carlos* Ruggero Raimondi filled in for the 'indisposed' Nicolai Ghiaurov as King Philip. According to Donal Henahan, Raimondi merely 'read over the surface of the part'. The prime miscreant was Francesco Molinari-Pradelli, the conductor. 'He let the singers set their own pace throughout, and that meant abandoning any overall dramatic or musical line.' After more than two decades of Bing's hard work, it seemed that consistent quality still eluded the Met.

The Bing farewell gala combined spectacle, top-singer power and nostalgia. It was also a very long evening, with the curtain falling at half past one. Proceeds went to benefit the House pension fund. Critic George Movshom wrote, 'Since the musicians started out playing for the matinée *Don Carlos* at 2 p.m. on Saturday and were not dismissed until twelve hours later, each of them must have made a packet.'[105] According to Mrs Kenyon Boocock, who chaired benefit performances for the Metropolitan Opera Guild, the 'packet' amounted to a net of $125,000 for the opera company's retirement and benevolent funds. Numbers were also at the fore of the Met's public relations material:

> The demand for tickets for the gala honoring Sir Rudolf on his retirement was the greatest in the history of the company up to that time. Forty leading artists, some of them the greatest singers in the world, and the chorus, orchestra and ballet went through 29 numbers. It was one of those nights only the Metropolitan Opera can produce.[106]

Musical high points included Caballé and Domingo's performance of the Act Two duet from *Manon Lescaut* and Leontyne Price's 'Dove sono' from the Mozart *Figaro*. The proceedings closed with two particularly moving moments: Nilsson's 'stunning, impassioned singing'[107] of the last scene of *Salome*, and Marian Anderson's 'lovely and haunting'[108] 'Auld Lang Syne'. Bing spoke only briefly, thanking everyone and introducing Göran Gentele, the new general manager.

Born in 1917, Gentele was a Swedish stage director who had worked as producer (1952–63) and later managing director (1963–71) of the Swedish Royal Opera. His productions in Stockholm had been acclaimed for their originality; he had also invited world-renowned artists such as Felsenstein and Ingmar Bergman to do opera stagings. One critic termed Gentele's goal 'to make living drama out of opera'.[109] The Royal Opera in Stockholm had an annual subsidy of some $2 million, allowing for ten new productions in the 1964–65 season alone and forty-eight opera performances at provincial Swedish theatres. Funds were also available for the commissioning of new works. Gentele was quoted as saying, 'We have various subscription series of five or six operas, one of which is inevitably what you might call modern. We simply don't allow people to hear the "good old" things if they won't hear the new ones. Oh no, we don't force them ... We just expose them.'[110]

Gentele's fresh ideas about education and popular exposure to opera were exactly what the Met Board sought. He had been recommended to the Board by Schuyler Chapin, vice-president for programming at Lincoln Center. Chapin, whose background was in concert management and recording, had also organised a number of projects on Leonard Bernstein's behalf. Board chairman George Moore 'checked out the Swede's credentials and reputation, and made the choice'.[111] The selection of a creative artist who also had experience in opera administration was significant for the future of the House. Even more important for the Met, in a time of upheaval, was Gentele's background as head of a government-subsidised arts institution. The House spelled out its thinking in a 'White Paper' published in June 1971:

> Coming from a country with a strong tradition of government support of the arts, Gentele believes the American government should provide support for the Metropolitan as a national opera company. To strengthen the Metropolitan's position in that respect, Gentele has said that he plans to make even greater use of American singers and other talent 'because we can't ask the American people to support a company that doesn't provide opportunities for its own citizens'. He also indicated that he plans close co-operation with other American opera companies.[112]

Gentele's approach to staging was decidedly untraditional for a House which felt most comfortable with gradual artistic change. The *New York Times* commented: 'It was obvious that Mr Bing meant it more than jokingly when he said ..., "The poor dear doesn't know what he's in for."'[113]

Gentele had been used to the free rein – and the lack of worry over the box office gate – which government subsidy permitted. He expressed the wish to present innovative stagings at the Met based on a de-emphasis of spectacle. He also conceived the notion of a 'mini-Met' or 'Piccolo Met', a smaller auditorium where operas unsuited to the huge stage could be mounted. This theatre was to have only 299 seats and be located in Lincoln Center's Vivian Beaumont Theater.

Funds were raised for construction; in order to appeal to a younger audience ticket prices were to be only $5. Gentele intended to 'change the image of the Met by adding a contemporary aspect. We must do our best to attract a young public that do not come to the Met now, and we must do so by offering this public opera of its own time at a price it can pay.'[114] Gentele's innovative approach also included plans for a series of opera performances for children to be called 'Look-ins'. An interviewer asked him what an opera house ought to be. 'Alive,' he replied.[115]

The new general manager made a number of personnel choices that would prove important for the future. He broke a Met precedent of long standing by insisting on the naming of a music director.[116] His choice was Rafael Kubelik, who had been music director of the Bavarian Radio Symphony Orchestra since leaving Covent Garden in 1958. At first it appeared that Kubelik's contractual obligations in Germany would prevent him from taking up the New York position at once. He could not even be free to conduct at the Met until the 1973–74 season, when he and Gentele planned a production of Berlioz's *Les Troyens*. Gentele again discussed the problem with Kubelik at the Plaza Hotel in February 1971, when he was in New York as guest conductor of the Cleveland Orchestra. According to Gentele, speaking at a Met press event in June of that year, they reached on that occasion 'a good mutual agreement'. 'I feel so relieved,' Gentele declared. 'A House such as this one is so enormous, no one should try to handle it all himself.' Gentele went on to state that 'he and Mr Kubelik would "share artistic responsibility" in planning repertory and new productions, supervising the orchestra, chorus and musical staff, and choosing casts and conductors'. Kubelik later changed his mind about availability, announcing he would be present at the Met for five months of the year, devoting three months to the Bavarian Radio Symphony.[117]

Gentele had been pleased by James Levine's conducting of *Luisa Miller*. The Executive Committee offered the young American the post of principal conductor. Levine was born in Cincinnati on 23 June 1943; his father had been a band director. A child prodigy, he made his piano debut with the Cincinnati Symphony at the age of ten, playing the Mendelssohn Second Concerto. He assisted George Szell at the Cleveland Orchestra from 1964 to 1970. The following year, at his first performance at the Met, he led *Tosca*. Wrote Allen Hughes, '. . . Mr Levine, who is 28, may be one of the Metropolitan's best podium acquisitions in some time. He conducted a performance that was vital, precise and splendidly paced. The balances between orchestra and voices were excellent, and those within the orchestra were adjusted to achieve a nice interplay of textures and colours.'[118]

In a climate of financial problems, with empty seats in the House, rising production costs and an economic recession in America, and with as yet unfulfilled hopes for broad-scale funding from the federal government, Gentele nevertheless managed to negotiate contracts with the unions. 'Greatly assisted by the strong feelings of "Never Again" on both sides of the bargaining table, Gentele got agreements with nearly all the unions in the first week of his incumbency . . .'[119] Gentele named his ally Chapin as his assistant general manager. Chapin signed a four-year contract at a salary of $50,000. All this activity had taken place before Gentele's first season opened. Gentele also enjoyed considerably greater support from the Board than Bing had in the last years of his tenure. On 18 February 1971 Bing complained to the Board that Gentele was allowed a number of new productions after his, Bing's, new plans had been cancelled.

The first production scheduled under the new administration was *Carmen*. Marilyn Horne, James McCracken and Sherrill Milnes were to sing the principal roles; Leonard Bernstein would conduct. Josef Svoboda, the Czech artist, would be designer and Gentele himself would direct the opera. But Gentele's debut at the Met was forestalled by tragedy, as were all his innovative plans for the House. On 18 July 1972, vacationing in Sardinia, he was driving his family in a hired car down a narrow, curving road. The car collided head-on with a lorry laden with cement. Gentele was killed in the crash, as were two of his children. Marit, his wife, survived, along with a daughter from a previous marriage.[120] The House would have to come to terms with an appalling and unforeseen event at a time when it needed courageous, effective leadership.

TWELVE

VIENNA 1961–68
Karajan Resigns

THE STAATSOPER OF THE EARLY 1960s, enjoying government support and buoyed up by the activities of a highly visible artist, shared
few of the Met's problems. Its record was nonetheless inconsistent.
Outstanding operatic performances were threatened by entrenched
bureaucracy and Viennese disaffection. Just as it had seemed fated that
Böhm would be named as music director and then resign, so Karajan's
arrival and departure appeared inevitable. While both Bing's tenure
at the Met and Solti's at Covent Garden were far from serene, both
men provided strong leadership, a quality appreciated in New York
and London. In contrast the Viennese tendency to cynicism, and a
certain distaste for highly visible excellence, contributed to undermine
Karajan's leadership. He nonetheless endeavoured to rise above the
periodic upheavals and realise his vision of an 'ensemble of stars'
performing in optimal conditions under his complete and unquestioned control.

One of the first things that comes to people's minds when they
speak of the Karajan they knew was his star quality. Born in 1908 in
Salzburg to an aristocratic family whose origins were in what is now
the Macedonian province of north-western Greece, his father was a
leading surgeon in the city. Karajan's ambitiousness and competi-
tiveness were evident from his early youth, as was his hauteur. As a
student at the Vienna Hochschule für Musik from 1926 to 1928 he
declined to address his peers with the familiar *du*, preferring the formal
Sie for everyone he spoke to. Richard Osborne, his biographer, states,
'Herbert was generally well liked by his fellow students despite a *de
haut en bas* manner that bordered on the autocratic.'[1] In adulthood

Karajan was perhaps the first conductor to assume the mantle of glitter usually associated with a singing star. The American soprano Grace Bumbry recalled: 'The maestro had this gorgeous Ferrari, and I had my gorgeous Lamborghini. That was why we were always quarrelling a bit.'[2] The glamour offended a number of Viennese. Prawy defined the anti-Karajan mood as a peculiar mixture of envy, ignorance, mindless conservatism and chip-on-the-shoulder nationalism:

> Although Karajan frequently deserved the criticism he got, a great deal of it was due to pure jealousy: 'Just look what he earns!' Mingled with relatively good-humoured banter like 'world champion in conducting', 'the Greta Garbo of the rostrum', or 'the twenty-second-century conductor' were genuine anger at *Carmen* sung in French and sarcasm about his villa at Saint-Tropez. There was no harm, of course, in his skiing in the Engadine if he wanted to, but why on earth must he choose to fly to the skiing grounds in a helicopter? (Franz Schalk [the Viennese conductor and director of the Staatsoper, 1924–29] would never have done a thing like that!') People who regularly lent their own villas for exorbitant rents boiled with moral indignation if Karajan leased somebody his private aeroplane. 'Did Gustav Mahler need yoga for concentration and relaxation?' And when Karajan was voted Vienna's best-dressed man, it was just 'cheap publicity'. And worst of all, 'He squanders our precious Schillings' abroad by having his Salzburg costume made by a Milan tailor!
>
> Even his tax problems were all at once the concern of every good Austrian music lover. Karajan was careful never to spend more than 180 days a year in Austria, otherwise he would have been deemed to be domiciled in Austria and would have had to pay Austrian tax on all his earnings from whatever source. A lot of people would have been only too glad if the tax authorities had made things difficult for him over his Buchenhof property at Mauerbach near Vienna. The most diehard reactionaries became convinced Republicans overnight and indulged in caustic comments of Karajan's aristocratic 'von'. People with none too edifying records themselves started delving back into his activities during the Third Reich . . .[3]

Karajan's generous royalties from his recording contracts, together with his salary from the Staatsoper and other musical activities, allowed him to enjoy himself away from the podium. He was passionately fond of a range of non-musical sports: skiing, yoga, sailing, piloting his own aircraft. At different times he owned a variety of fast automobiles, including a Mercedes 300 sports car and – in America – a Thunderbird, a marque also favoured by Zeffirelli. His obsession with clothes was profound. Winthrop Sargeant, writing in the *New Yorker*, was fascinated by his collection of pullovers:

> The sweaters change with every rehearsal; he has scores of them, turtle-neck and open-neck, in all sorts of designs and colours. For dress rehearsals, he puts on a lily-white turtleneck, which, in its informal way, is the last word in sartorial splendour. The sweaters strike a note of violent contrast in a scene where every man is wearing an ordinary suit, and with them he usually wears loud plaid sport socks and moccasins, which along with his deeply tanned face and hands, enhance the out-of-doors, man-of-action effect. This effect is somewhat theatrical, but then von Karajan is as much a man of the theatre as any actor . . .[4]

Karajan used his acting talents to craft a public image of a modified Byronic hero: a brilliant, demanding, energetic, sexually electric star who held within a hint of menace. At the same time, his stunning musical successes, his cultivated demeanour and his frequenting of haunts of the *beau monde* – Ischia, Portofino, St Moritz – made him appear a safe social catch rather than 'mad, bad and dangerous to know'. The terms of his contract at the Staatsoper were a secret at the time and remain a secret to this day.

The Vienna Festival of 1961 featured Karajan's second *Ring* cycle. The festival, held annually in the late spring, presented among a variety of musical performances new opera productions as well as repertory works. The first Karajan *Ring*, premiered work by work from 1957 to 1960, had had designs by Emil Preetorius, one of the leading German stage designers of the pre- and post-war periods and a close friend of Thomas Mann. Prawy had considered Karajan's first *Ring* overly restrained. Musically, Pravy wrote, the performance of *Die Walküre* in April 1957 'already presaged the unemotional, almost chamber-music quality of Karajan's later performances of Wagner that have aroused so much controversy.'[5] The second *Ring* of 1961, by contrast, was praised by Joseph Wechsberg for its human warmth and nobility: 'Musically, Karajan's reading was even more powerful, more lyric, more exciting' than in his first Vienna *Ring*.[6] Just as Karajan insisted on doing his own staging, he also insisted on making his signature lighting style – moody and dim – a major feature of the show. Wechsberg criticised what he saw as Karajan's ill-lit stage and chaotic blocking: 'Large stretches of important action are still camouflaged by Karajan's lack of decision and deep darkness; the mass scenes in *Götterdämmerung* are confused, haphazard, everybody wandering all over the stage, though the powerful crescendos in the score obviously point the way for a powerful, co-ordinated movement on the stage.'[7] Even if acting and movement were not fully realised, the cast was superb. Birgit Nilsson was an 'incredible' Brünnhilde and Hans Hotter a 'magnificent' Wotan and Wanderer.[8] Jon Vickers sang Siegmund, Wolfgang Windgassen Siegfried, and Gottlob Frick Hunding and Hagen. Even the Rhinemaidens were the brightest of stars: Wilma Lipp, Sena Jurinac and Hilde Rössl-Majdan.

Many Viennese critics and opera lovers chose Karajan's 1962 *Pelléas et Mélisande* for special praise. His designer for the production was Günther Schneider-Siemssen, who was named chief of design at the Staatsoper in the same year and went on to collaborate with Karajan in many opera stagings. The work, sung in French, won over the audience completely. People were moved to the point of remaining seated after the applause had finished and the House lights had come up. But Wechsberg again criticized the lighting: 'Long stretches and even climactic scenes – Golaud killing Pelléas – are obscured by dimness; the colours are mostly dark, and rarely are there moments in Günther Schneider-Siemssen's sets when the lights remind you of Monet or Cézanne or Corot.'[9] Nevertheless, Wechsberg waxed ecstatic over the music:

> This is a lyrical and dramatic interpretation and, when the inexorable climax comes towards the end, one sits spellbound. And at the same time Karajan opens the delicate texture of the score, lovingly displaying its beauty, making everything clear and always transparent, changing the rhythms imperceptibly so that one feels they may be rubati, and always painting, painting with music.[10]

Karajan's dramatic sense was fitful. While he could also create a satisfying new interpretation of score and libretto, he might on the other hand include elements of staging that appeared at odds with the composer's intentions. The 1962 Vienna Festival featured Karajan's new *Fidelio*. This production replaced Heinz Tietjen's and Franz Holzmeister's version, which had opened the rebuilt Staatsoper in 1955. Prawy had even at that time spoken of a tendency to conceptualism. Seven years later, in the Karajan version, Wechsberg reported, 'There is a conception from beginning to end. The visual impressions are of grey, sombre blocks of stone, of grey lights, of men in grey concentration-camp suits, with bare skulls. The guards have the ominous black uniforms of you know whom.'[11] It seemed a crass move by Karajan, who had twice joined the Nazi party and staged a pro-Nazi *Fidelio* in Aachen in 1938, to endeavour to arouse anti-Nazi sympathies in this new production of Beethoven's hymn to liberty. Musically speaking, Wechsberg detected a chill. Karajan's was 'a symphonic presentation of the score, with the singing voices treated as instruments . . .'[12]

The Theater an der Wien was reopened in time to stage this Karajan *Fidelio*. It had been closed since the reopening of the Staatsoper seven years earlier, and restoration and modernisation meant that its long and honourable history as an opera venue could continue. The intention was primarily to stage smaller-scale operas, particularly eighteenth-century works, which were unsuitable for the larger stage of the Staatsoper. The Volksoper continued as it had since 1955 performing operetta and musical comedy.

Karajan's first resignation from the position of *musikalischer Leiter* anticipated his second resignation from the post in February 1962. Although the immediate circumstances were different, the basic reason was the same. He wanted complete control of the Staatsoper and was prepared to brook no bureaucratic interference. For its part, the Austrian federal government had for decades kept close watch over all cultural institutions. Theatres and operas came under the purview of the Bundestheaterverwaltung (State Theatre Administration). And Ernst Marboe, Karajan's erstwhile ally in the bureaucracy, had died unexpectedly, at the age of forty-eight, in September 1957.

Karajan made enemies by his high-handed tactics. He erred politically in making public his wish in 1962 to 'take the State Opera out of the Administration'.[13] His high profile was antithetical to the way things were done in Vienna: quietly and behind the scenes. Soon Karajan was trapped in a situation where no matter what he did he would lose face. For months the technical staff of the opera had been carrying out industrial action over the problem of overtime. Productions could not go ahead as planned without the stagehands' extra hours. Karajan had to stage his January 1962 *Pelléas et Mélisande* with fewer rehearsals than planned. Heinrich Drimmel, the Education Minister, at first asked Karajan to head the negotiations with the technical staff. But soon afterwards, when Karajan happened to be briefly absent from Vienna, a wage agreement was suddenly signed between the technicians and the government. The 'musical leader' was not informed. Prawy explained:

> Karajan felt that he had been bypassed and claimed that the terms of the agreement were impracticable because the stagehands, instead of accepting a fixed and specified amount of overtime, merely bound themselves 'to volunteer to work unlimited overtime as occasion demanded', a formula that became known as the 'on request' clause. The real reason why an agreement was reached so suddenly was to save the Opera Ball, which, for all State functionaries, is a social occasion of the first magnitude but for Karajan was a matter of no importance.[14]

In February 1962, a month after the *Pelléas* opening, Karajan submitted his resignation and left Vienna. Despite past carping, the majority of Viennese opera lovers were on his side. At least one performance during that month – conducted by Tullio Serafin – was interrupted by shouts of support for Karajan. The opera personnel also showed their appreciation of their boss. Following the technicians' wage settlement, they as well as the artists decided to go out on strike. Such expressions of warmth, as well as Karajan's charisma and musicianship, strengthened his position considerably.

Karajan was seeking financial independence from the Austrian government. In March he made demands to which Minister Drimmel had to accede if he, Karajan, were to return to his post. He extracted a promise that the Staatsoper's budget be separated from the supervision of the State Theatre Administration, and that Walter Erich

Schäfer, intendant of the Stuttgart Opera, be brought to Vienna as co-director. Authority over money was the key: if Karajan did not have to go to the ministry for budget approval, he could hire the desired artists, particularly guests, thereby further enhancing his 'ensemble of stars'. He also sought autonomy in money matters in order to initiate further new productions. During the first seven years of his tenure there had been two new productions each of *Tannhäuser, Fidelio* and *Don Giovanni*. Karajan duly resumed his position and once more received the effusive support of the public. On his return to the podium for a performance of *Aida* in March 1962 he was presented with a bouquet of roses – and, after the second act, with a standing ovation.

Besides the question of financial independence, Karajan's grand scheme for international opera production was another, even more potent, cause of friction with the Austrian government. In July 1960 Drimmel had spared no words in telling the audience at the dedication of the Salzburg Festival's new auditorium that he strongly objected to any plan to ally the Staatsoper with another musical institution – or let it be ruled by a musical empire builder:

> I say today what I have always said: full freedom of artistic creation for the artistic director of the State Opera. . . . But the liberation of the State Opera for a completely new existence, perhaps in some worldwide conglomerate – No! No minister and new government can take it upon themselves to make the Vienna State Opera a worldwide combine.[15]

The notion of pooling resources for international opera production was an imaginative one, which, if realised, would have placed Karajan at the peak of the opera world. But in an interview a year and a half later, while he sardonically denied that he had sought anything resembling sovereignty, he admitted his plans had been impractical:

> My solution was a proposal to pool the first-rate talent in every field of opera production so that the same singers, conductors, and scenery for a given opera could first be properly integrated and then shifted from one great opera house to the next, ensuring audiences the best possible performances. My God, the cry that was raised over this in some quarters! I wanted to be the Generalmusikdirektor of the World. I wanted to control a

worldwide cartel on opera production. Finally, I had to give up this idea. It cannot be done.[16]

During 1962 Karajan worked on his new *Tannhäuser* production. Wolfgang Windgassen had originally been cast in the title role, but late into the rehearsal period it was announced in the Viennese papers that he was ill and would not be singing. The *Tannhäuser* opening was postponed from 12 December until after the new year. After the second night of the production Karajan left Vienna. Busy elsewhere, especially at La Scala, he did not conduct at the Staatsoper for two months. Standards plunged in his absence, as they had in the mid-Fifties as soon as Böhm left town. Without its 'artistic leader' the great House sank almost overnight into mediocrity. But meanwhile in Milan the landmark Karajan–Zeffirelli *Bohème* of 31 January 1963 opened to rapturous acclaim as a leading instance of an integrated operatic production.

On his return to Vienna, Karajan began rehearsing a ground-breaking production of Monteverdi's *L'Incoronazione di Poppea*, at the time almost completely absent from the international repertoire. Günther Rennert was lavishly praised for his unconventional direction – a particular exception for the Staatsoper, which at that time had few daring stagings. 'He has courage – he is unafraid of asymmetry and simplicity, of a slackening of the pace, even of inactivity.'[17] Born in 1911, Rennert had been Felsenstein's assistant when the older man was directing opera in Frankfurt before the war. His appointment as head of the Hamburg Staatsoper in 1946 gave him scope to stage twentieth-century operas and explore some of Rossini's *opere buffe*, which were relatively neglected in German-speaking theatres at that time. Rennert's work generally delved into the characters' motivations and interactions while presenting visual elements in abstract or expressionistic terms. Concerning the Vienna *Poppea*, he later recalled his collaborator Stefan Hlawa's designs: 'Together with designer Stefan Hlawa, a classical architectonic semicircle was worked out whose form was derived from the Colosseum in Rome. . . . In all, ten round arches could be seen stretching to the horizon, indicating with baleful splendour the jewelled focal points of the drama in a number of variations from bright glittering gold to purplish black.'[18] Karajan's own contribution to

Monteverdi's opera was deemed no less impressive: 'Karajan conducted with devotion and authority. There was never any hint of the museum, but always the beautiful, transparent texture of great music and great drama; it was all very much alive, and the tension never relaxed.'[19]

Meanwhile a new government had been installed in Austria after a lengthy period of transition. A new director of the Bundestheaterverwaltung was named: Dr Alfred Weikert, a lover of the arts. The authorities moved quickly to alter a central provision of the previous agreement with Karajan. On 10 June Herr Schäfer was replaced as co-director of the Staatsoper by Egon Hilbert, who had been director when it was revived immediately after the war in the Theater an der Wien. Prawy felt Hilbert had hated Karajan from the start.' 'According to a rumour Prawy wrote, 'Hilbert had sworn that only over his dead body should Karajan be admitted to the Vienna Opera.'[20] The stated reason for the replacement was Schäfer's having had a heart attack, but the real reason was unclear. Hilbert was quoted as saying, '*Ich freue mich wahnsinnig*' ('I am madly happy').[21] Wechsberg, guardedly optimistic, saw Hilbert as a key to a potential grand reconciliation – even though on the face of it the two men did not get along. 'If Hilbert and Karajan can reconcile their temperaments for the sake of the Vienna State Opera, there should be a new, fruitful and perhaps great era for the great house – provided the outsiders, clique members and interested intriguers keep away.'[22]

One effect of Hilbert's presence was a truce between Karajan and Böhm, at least for musical purposes. An announcement was made of Böhm's return to the Staatsoper podium. Josef Krips, too, was announced for Mozart, Verdi and Strauss. A Krips *Don Giovanni* was a memorable delight, Wechberg reported: 'Everything was just as it should be with Mozart: it sounded like Mozart. It was "*dramma*" and it was "*giocoso*" at the same time', and added that Krips 'obviously worked with the singers and gave help to those who needed it, and made them sound much better than they usually do.' Krips's triumphant return led to 'hope that the crisis of conductors would at last come to an end'.[23]

Prawy concluded that Karajan's acquiescence to Hilbert's replacing Schäfer was 'a quite unaccountable sign of weakness on Karajan's part'. Hilbert's personality was ebullient and verbose, in contrast to Karajan's lofty silences. The two men's professional goals and styles were also diametrically opposed. 'What Karajan wanted at this juncture was someone to take the administrative chores off his hands; whereas what Hilbert wanted was to be a full-blown Director of the Vienna Opera with full authority in artistic matters. What Karajan wanted was an ad hoc assembly of stars for limited periods; what Hilbert wanted was the ensemble of the good old days.'[24]

During the brief Karajan–Hilbert duumvirate the next fracas to turn the Staatsoper upside down was the 'prompter war' of November 1963. When Karajan imported to Vienna the Scala *Bohème* on which he had collaborated with Zeffirelli he also imported from Milan a prompter – or, in Italian, a *maestro suggeritore*. Austrian trade unions protested and the man, Armando Romano, was denied a work permit. Nevertheless, Hilbert insisted on employing him. The unions went out on strike. The opening was ceremonially cancelled when Karajan and Hilbert came on stage before the curtain. Prawy recalled: 'Hilbert read out a résumé of the facts of the case, stressed his loyalty to Karajan, and sealed it with a kiss (no one who saw the episode will ever forget Karajan's face). The audience, asked to go home, protested vigorously. There was some disorder and a first-class sensation all over Europe.'[25]

Scandal overwhelmed Vienna. Prawy recalled

> The episode split little Austria into two irreconcilably hostile factions. My grocer, who had never been to the Opera in her life, regarded it as uncivilised to deny Karajan his '*mastro zutsch-erritohre*'. My boot-maker on the other hand, who had also never been to the Opera in his life, regarded it as an impertinence that this Karajan should squander the taxpayers' money on a '*mestro dschuzerridoore*'.[26]

Karajan made the magnanimous decision to open the show *senza maestro suggeritore*, even though a roster of top international singers had joined the protest on the prompter's side. The opera itself was a sensation. 'I went home after the fifth curtain,' reported Wechsberg, 'but over the radio I heard that I had missed thirty-three more.'[27] In the annals of post-war opera it is hard to recall a more effervescent time or place than Vienna under Karajan.

*   *   *

By the spring of 1964 Hilbert and Karajan were gravely at odds. Hilbert objected to the inclusion of Karajan's secretary André von Mattoni in the Staatsoper management. Mattoni was the one who had hired the luckless *maestro suggeritore*. In a move reflecting the Viennese obsession with titles and his own wish for sole control, Karajan objected to Hilbert's styling himself Staatsoperndirektor. More appropriate, he felt, would be Direktor der Staatsoper. Wechsberg reported:

> Karajan does not talk to Hilbert. Hilbert does not talk to anybody. Everybody talks about Karajan and Hilbert. Top secret intelligence claims that the entire personnel will strike if Karajan attempts to have an Italian prompter for his next *La Bohème*. Also: the members of the Vienna Philharmonic (who provide the orchestra of the State Opera) are said to be hurt because Karajan has signed up to record exclusively for Deutsche Grammophon. Karajan's urging the orchestra to move to DG was described by a Viennese journalist as 'Balkan behaviour'. [Karajan took the journalist to court and won the case.] And no one knows how the new Austrian Minister of Education, Dr Piffl-Perčević, feels about the mess. End of report from the battlefield.[28]

In spite of the tension, Karajan went on conducting performances which were frequently outstanding – that is, when he was present in Vienna, which was not often. His heavy recording schedule and highly visible concerts with the Berlin Philharmonic were bringing his name before the public even more prominently than before. His work outside the House was lucrative. During the first quarter of 1964 his royalty statement at EMI showed earnings from recordings of £10,903 7s 8d, making him the most successful classical artist under contract to the company. At the Staatsoper, Karajan's *Rheingold* in the spring of 1964 'seemed to penetrate more deeply into the psychological content of the score than ever before'.[29] Even so, Karajan's choice as Wotan of the fine baritone Eberhard Waechter, who would in 1991 become joint head of the Staatsoper, was not well received. At a time when the House could call on at least three other Wotans/Wanderers, the invidious comparison to Waechter seemed to be with Hans Hotter, then in his mid-fifties. Waechter was 'never godlike, never in command of the stage and its action, and he seemed to strain vocally. Karajan is a great Wagner interpreter but less great as a judge of Wagnerian voices.'[30]

Hilbert scheduled a performance of *Tannhäuser* for 17 May 1964 in the knowledge that Karajan had committed himself previously to conduct in the Musikverein hall that evening. Hilbert refused Karajan's request to delay the *Tannhäuser* performance and, on 7 May, engaged another conductor in Karajan's stead. That evening the audience chanted, 'Hilbert must go!' On 8 May Karajan resigned with effect from the end of the season. He left open the possibility of continuing as guest conductor and guest stage director, depending 'on what artistic assurances "the new Director or Directors" would guarantee'.[31] According to the *Frankfurter Allgemeine Zeitung*, 'All Vienna is agreed that a complete break with the charismatic maestro must be avoided. Yet only a miracle could prevent this from being the ultimate consequence. That would be the miracle of a freely chosen act of self-sacrifice on the part of Dr Hilbert, which no one considers within the realm of possibility, or else a miracle in the mould of imperial Austrian diplomacy, which over the centuries consistently brought about the reconciliation of opposites in this multi-ethnic realm.'[32] Several names of potential replacements for Karajan were already being mentioned in the Viennese press: Egon Seefehlner, Rudolf Gamsjäger, Oscar Fritz Schuh, Rolf Liebermann. But the *Opernnarren* feared Hilbert already had the upper hand. On 21 May, when Karajan was conducting *Fidelio*, the gallery gave forth with a pessimistic prediction. Florestan sang, 'Who is the governor of this prison?' and the shout came back, 'Hilbert!'

The Vienna Festwochen were opened on 24 May with Karajan's *Parsifal*. For Wechsberg it was 'perhaps the greatest *Parsifal* I have ever heard'.[33] Karajan's *Die Frau ohne Schatten* of 11 June marked what would be his last appearance at the Staatsoper for thirteen years. His partisans granted it a delirious reception, in spite of his reordering of scenes in the second act. Throughout, Karajan demonstrated his 'ability to create the mysticism of sound, when music becomes absolute beauty, and one stops analysing'.[34] A mingled atmosphere of ecstasy and impending doom was felt – or was being confected by the press and the *Opernnarren*. On 21 June 1964 Karajan's resignation took effect. He announced, 'After eighteen years in the concert halls of Austria, and eight years as artistic director of the State Opera, I am ending my activities in Austria.' Minister Piffl-Perčević announced that, as of 31 August, Egon Hilbert would be the one and only director of the Staatsoper.

Karajan himself stated that he left Vienna because he was not allowed artistic and financial control:

> When I saw that everything I had laboriously built up over eight years was not to be continued according to my wishes, when I was not to be granted the working conditions I demanded, I came to the obvious conclusion. . . . I was probably the last individualistic operatic director with full responsibility. . . .
>
> I will certainly never take over the running of an opera house again, because the existing system of the so-called repertory opera is growing increasingly dubious from the quality point of view. . . . I see no reason why something should be kept alive when you've been convinced for ages that it can't survive much longer, for the simple reason that the relationship between costs and the quality on offer is no longer correct.[35]

Although Karajan had taken frequent leave to further his career, he had made the House a place where opera could truly thrive. Walter Legge felt Karajan's tenure at the Staatsoper would be esteemed 'even higher than Mahler's'. He wrote:

> He transformed a complacent national institution into the world's most prestigious opera house. His activities as a regisseur often caused heated dispute, but his conducting (40 or more performances a year) won almost unstinted praise and admiration. . . . Most probably he was bored by the job and saw no stimulating future in it.[36]

The next season's offerings caused the Karajan camp to despair. They felt government bureaucracy had vanquished the muses. Prawy and Wechsberg agreed that Staatsoper performances were sorely wanting. Die Zauberflöte, the opera that opened the season in September 1965, 'should put the management into an apologetic mood', Wechsberg reported. Contrary to custom at the season's opening, the work was not given a new production. The Rudolf Hartmann–Günther Schneider-Siemssen staging of 1962, according to Wechsberg, 'was never an inspiration, now appears less attractive than ever. There is more light now but what it reveals is certainly not a fairy-tale, just make-believe.'[37] Nevertheless Fritz Wunderlich as Tamino and Wilma Lipp as Pamina received lavish praise. In October, during a performance of *Die Entführung aus dem Serail*, cries were heard of 'poor Mozart'. However, a December 1965 *Elektra* featured memorable singing by Resnik, Nilsson and Rysanek, and authoritative conducting from Böhm.

Amid the tribulations of its opera, Austria's past did not fail to catch up with it. During the autumn of 1965 Dr Alexander Witeschnik, the author of a book about the Staatsoper and its press spokesman, was revealed as an anti-Semite when he was about to be promoted to the position of press officer for all the Austrian state theatres. The *Vienna Express* reprinted facsimiles of some extremely distasteful articles Witeschnik had written in 1938, the year of the *Anschluss*. Worst of all, the Minister of Education, Dr Piffl-Perčević, acknowledged he had known about Witeschnik's anti-Semitic beliefs when he made the appointment, as had Austria's Vice-Chancellor, Herr Pittermann. The affair was crowned by the Austrian government's astonishing offer to Witeschnik of a medal and the honorary title of professor.

The following year Hilbert programmed Rossini's *Il Barbiere di Siviglia* in German. The audience had been well trained by Karajan. This time the shouts were 'Rossini in German? A disgrace!' Otto Schenk's 1967 *Don Giovanni* was booed. It was not only Karajan's musical genius that was missed. Revivals of Karajan's stagings were gradually being changed and at times debased. The weird, dark-and-floodlit *Trovatore* degenerated into parody. *Opera* reported in November 1965 that the best aspect of revival director Bruno Prevedi's "Di quella pira" 'were the extra searchlights – just like in front of Grauman's Chinese Theater in Hollywood, *circa* 1940. That is the way the whole production looks now. Even the wonderful *Bohème* is only a pale facsimile of the original.'[38]

While Karajan's presence was missed, Hilbert made some much-praised changes at the Staatsoper. He named the highly competent stage director Otto Schenk resident chief producer. He hired outstanding guest stage directors, including Luchino Visconti, Wieland Wagner and August Everding. Wieland's *Salome*, premiered on 25 November

1965, stripped Strauss's opera of much of its setting and colour to concentrate on horror. Wechsberg described it as 'No exotic moon, no courtiers, no fancy footwork to brighten up the mood of unrestricted brutality and bestiality'. The following month Wieland's new production of *Elektra* was similarly reduced to the essentials: 'No backstage activities, no slaves, no playing with torches. Just black tragedy between black walls from which bones dangle down.'[39]

Hilbert brought welcome fresh air to the House. Although Karajan's partisans were reluctant to admit it, the overall level of routine performances was raised somewhat under Hilbert. In so doing he alleviated, albeit temporarily, one of the severest chronic problems of the House. He returned Böhm and Krips to the podium and brought Leonard Bernstein to the Staatsoper. During the late 1960s Bernstein began an important, though informal, presence as guest conductor of opera and orchestral works in Vienna. Although he was welcomed by much of the Viennese musical public as a potential successor to Karajan, his conducting and composing commitments in America only made it possible for him to come to Vienna occasionally. There he led a 1966 *Falstaff* and a 1968 *Rosenkavalier*.

The *Falstaff* was directed by Visconti with great respect for Verdi's intentions. Wechsberg wrote: 'There were no gags, no jokes, no "interpretations". Everything was so normal that it was abnormal, considering the present-day standards of producing.' Visconti collaborated with Ferdinando Scarfiotti on the sets and costumes, which were deemed 'just right, in the style of Vermeer or Frans Hals'. Visconti Wechsberg continued: 'handled the singers with great skill and a light hand, and sometimes the singers seemed to have as much fun as the audience.' The director also took care to create a true acting ensemble and the conductor followed suit, polishing the orchestra to something near perfection and helping create untrammelled joy on stage:

> Bernstein did not miss a single subtle nuance in the great score yet he never lost himself in detail; there was a continuous excitement, a sort of super-brio, clearly expressed by the way he conducted, lifting both arms high in the air, lifting the music from earth into Olympian space. During three hours the laws of musical gravity were cancelled, and everybody was in a cloud of happiness.

Regina Resnik, playing Mistress Quickly, was 'terribly funny and never overplayed'. Rolando Panerai as Ford was 'witty and elegant, singing with great feeling and great refinement'. Dietrich Fischer-Dieskau's Falstaff was generally admired, but nonetheless failed to please Wechsberg, who found his portrayal 'boisterous and clumsy'. He went on, 'I missed the subtlety and self-irony, the intrinsic humour and light wit, the transfigured melancholy and the sense of optimism.'[40] The same critic termed the Bernstein–Otto Schenk *Rosenkavalier* a mixed bag, acquiescing in director Schenk's slapstick touches but objecting to the conductor's slow pacing.

The last new production of the Hilbert administration which Hilbert himself lived to see was a *Tristan* which opened on 17 December 1967. It was a mixed success. Böhm conducted and August Everding, in his debut production at the Staatsoper, staged the work, which was designed by Schneider-Siemssen. The stage team had the odd notion of 'showing the principals' emotions way back on the cyclorama, in operatic Twenty-First-Century Fox style'.[41] But Böhm's 'transparent, classical' conducting, Nilsson's 'perfect' Isolde and Jess Thomas's Tristan were warmly received.

Although the anti-Karajan camp had disparaged his spending habits as director, Hilbert was hardly frugal. During the 1966–67 season his administration was reported in the Vienna press to have paid 'twelve million Austrian schillings for performance fees that were contractually signed but never sung by the artists'.[42] Prawy confirms that Hilbert had the habit of paying singers for performances they never gave. Hilbert was reluctant to leave the Staatsoper. Following the successful Bernstein–Visconti *Falstaff* it was announced that his contract would be renewed through 1969. But in 1967 he fell gravely ill. Following a long struggle Erwin Thalhammer, Alfred Weikert's successor as head of the Bundestheaterverwaltung, convinced Hilbert to resign not long after the opening of the December 1967 *Tristan*. In January of the following year Hilbert signed a document confirming his resignation 'with effect from the first of February'. Having done so, 'he got into his government chauffeur-driven car outside his house in Penzing, and fell back dead.'[43]

Although Hilbert's reputation suffered by comparison with Karajan's, it is wrong to portray him merely as an enthusiast or a philistine.

He had clear opinions on singers and music, some of which were better grounded than others. He was obsessed with carrying his point, and had the habit, not limited to the Viennese, of uttering pleasant words to disguise unpleasant deeds. 'Hilbert was the first legal official to be Director of the Vienna Opera, yet he was the most anti-juridical Director in the Opera's history. He was a past master in the art of not honouring contracts if it was in the Opera's interest (as he conceived it) to break them.'[44]

Karajan had ostensibly resigned from all music making in Austria. But given his preference for the finest possible casts and performances with ample finances and rehearsal time, Salzburg tempted him to reconsider. In a telegram of 24 July the president of the festival Board, Hans Lechner, wrote, 'Salzburg will give you every assurance that in future you will find all the preconditions here that you require for your work, and which will perhaps enable you to consider your decision about Salzburg as other than final.'[45] Karajan quickly took up Lechner's suggestion. On 5 August, Bernhard Paumgartner, the festival's president, wrote to Lechner advising that 'K' be appointed a director of the festival.

The fascination that accompanied Karajan's efforts on behalf of opera in Vienna now shifted to Salzburg. His shows were granted more rehearsal time than those of other conductors, including Böhm. His work at Salzburg during the 1960s tended to the idiosyncratic. A 1965 *Boris Godunov* suffered from extensive cuts and rearranging of scenes by the conductor. Some also felt that the production was excessively sumptuous. Nevertheless, there were many moments of great dramatic impact and 'triumphal instrumental bel canto playing from the Vienna Philharmonic'. The Bulgarian Nicolai Ghiaurov, thirty-five at the time and not yet a polished actor, displayed an 'adaptable bass-baritone voice, capable of majestic fortissimo and mezza voce gentleness'. He was considered a great find and dubbed Kurt Honolka 'the ideal Boris of the future'.[46]

An even more adventurous Karajan *Carmen*, however, was not well received the following year. Harold Rosenthal disapproved both of Karajan's cuts and the high notes interpolated by Grace Bumbry in the title role. Worse still, Karajan altered the score with a crudeness seldom heard of in a modern opera house.[47] According to Rosenthal, Karajan provided 'some even more startling additions to the orchestral score in the final scene, when Carmen's stabbing of José was accompanied by some very Hollywood-like fortissimo chords; we had a seemingly endless nightclub entertainment by Mariemma's Ballet de España in the second act with long extracts from *L'Arlésienne* and *La Jolie fille de Perth*'.[48] Karajan also shifted the location of Act Three from the mountains to the seashore. Peter Conrad wrote: 'The set was a mile-long stretch of beach, strewn with hulks.' The explanation was given that the sense of liberty suggested by the original mountain setting would not 'read' in Salzburg, surrounded as the town is by mountains.[49] When the production was seen at Salzburg again the following year the same abuses were perpetrated on Bizet's music. Peter Katona wrote: 'Karajan treats the score like chamber music, with a lightness which might be suitable anywhere except in the Grosses Festspielhaus, where it was completely lost. He plans a production fit for an arena and then provides music for the first three rows of seats.'[50]

Since the summer festival gave him an ideal forum for his productions, which could be repeated the following year or recorded – it was inevitable that Karajan should seek to extend his work at Salzburg. In 1967 he founded the Easter festival, whose emphasis lay at first upon Wagner's operas. Karajan's *Walküre* of that year was judged superior even to the second Vienna *Walküre*, with critics remarking on the intimacy and tenderness of the orchestral playing. With almost exactly the same personnel, Karajan recorded this *Walküre* for DG as one instalment of his new *Ring*, thus consolidating his work at the festival as a springboard for other activities.

The 1967–70 recording of the Karajan *Ring* has been called one of the conductor's finest achievements. In *Die Walküre* Karajan brings out the chamber-music quality of the score – as he had been doing with Wagner ever since his first Vienna *Ring* – while never neglecting its declamatory aspect. Honest dramatic emotion is realised moment by moment, with the Berlin Philharmonic Orchestra, particularly the principal players, moved to give of their very considerable best. Energy, flexibility and warmth unify Karajan's musical conception, with no hint of the fierceness and occasional insensitivity to the score's dramatic values that mar a number of his operatic performances. This overriding gentleness, so rare for Karajan, stands in contrast to Georg Solti's brilliant, pagan, Nilsson-ignited *Walküre* of the same era. The singing on the Karajan recording is for the most part breathtaking. As Elvio Giudici remarks, Gundula Janowitz as Sieglinde is simply stupendous. Using the utmost economy of means, avoiding all suspicion of histrionics, Janowitz creates a Sieglinde born only to love, somehow magically innocent of the crime of incest. Jon Vickers's Siegmund is likewise humane, and very movingly sung. Vicker's vocal resources include a mezzo voce whose deep resonance gives little hint of the crooning head tones which he can sometimes emit when seeking to sound gentle. Martti Talvela's Hunding is phenomenal. This Finnish bass, only thirty-two at the time of the Easter festival performances, seems to harbour endless reserves of sound, endless gradations of colour and nuance. Josephine Veasey as Fricka sings richly and incisively, with an appealing tone, if somewhat cautiously on a few entrances. Régine Crespin is a surprising choice as Brünnhilde. Her 'Ho-jo-to-ho' comes over as pallid, even with the addition of a studio echo. In the end, though, it is her delicacy and musical intelligence which are convincing. Karajan's *Walküre* was one memorable imagination, humanity and taste.

Although few newly composed operas were staged at Salzburg during the 1960s, Hans Werner Henze was an important presence. His *Die Bassariden* (*The Bassarids*) was premiered at the Grosses Festspielhaus on 6 August 1966. The libretto, by W. H. Auden and Chester Kallman, had originally been written in English.[51] Henze had written music prolifically from an early age. He felt culturally and politically alienated from post-war Germany, his homeland, and adopted a leftist political position. Some time after abandoning the exclusive use of serialism for a generally more traditional and eclectic compositional approach, he asked Auden and Kallman to produce a libretto for his opera *Elegy for Young Lovers* (1961) that would leave room for 'tender, beautiful noises'.[52] Henze's opera written just before *The Bassarids* was a comic piece, *Der junge Lord*, cast in a Rossinian mould.

In one sense *The Bassarids* may be considered a strong, dense libretto set to music. In another it is a four-movement symphonic work with text running through. Basing themselves loosely on Euripides' 'The Bacchae, Auden and Kallman created a dramatic-cum-symbolic tale of the overthrow of old gods and the installation of new ones. Although the libretto is intellectual and allusive, it is a good basis for a stage show. Emotion and dramatic interest are real, not stylised or synthetic. Theatrical elements carry the ideas along, somewhat in contrast to Tippett's operas, particularly The Knot Garden. Perhaps the unusual musical structure chosen by Henze was a way of coping with the imposing text. Rather than acts there are four 'movements', each of which recalls an element of symphonic form. The first movement is even structured as a sonata, with Pentheus's stern music as the main theme and the Bassarids given a more lyric secondary theme. Immediate interest is derived from the emotionally charged vocal lines and the flexible, highly suggestive orchestral colours.

Besides Salzburg, Karajan was seen in his other habitual haunts. At the Deutsche Oper Berlin he staged and conducted an extraordinary *Trovatore* starring Leontyne Price. With ticket prices doubled, every seat was sold for all four performances. He handed his critics ammunition by making the action take place on an almost completely dark stage while satisfing his admirers with this 'apotheosis of non-realism'. Principal singers stood in tableau downstage centre to deliver their arias in the old-fashioned static manner, while behind them stood weird, phantasmagorical set pieces. The effect was one of expressive mood painting integrated with the work of the singers. The *Opera* critic H. H. Stuckenschmidt wrote:

> Spotlights carve out fragments of the inhabited world from Night – the face of a singer, a chorus group, parts of a wooded landscape or a Romanesque castle, a half-curtain tall as a tower, two or three column capitals, and all the other things which replace the customary stage settings. . . . This is great singing theatre, completely ruled by the score, in which even the orchestra constitutes only a background. Karajan directs all this musical entertainment as a passionate, omnipresent arranger and organizer. . . . And yet his whole achievement is put behind the singers: Karajan's rich adaptation, his fluctuating beat, softening of the strong beats and accents, are all theirs.[53]

* * *

At Bayreuth, Wieland Wagner built upon the work he had done during the 1950s. He continued to shun the traditional Wagner stagings in favour of a symbolist-inspired, visually centred presentation in which gesture was minimised, as were physical and emotional interactions between characters on stage. As Frederic Spotts put it, Wieland's 'abstract style demonstrated that as silence is an essential element of music, so emptiness can be a vital part of staging'.[54] In his work during the 1960s, he brought out certain ideas – and ideals – which he found latent in his grandfather's 'musical dramas'. Wieland's Bayreuth production of the *Ring* in 1965 was received with intense and contradictory feelings. Harold Rosenthal wrote in *Opera*, 'Whatever else Wieland Wagner has done, he has certainly made it as difficult to get seats at Bayreuth as it is for a Callas performance, and has made opera houses all over the world reconsider their approach to Wagner operas.' Wieland's reinterpretation of the content of the cycle was influenced by reflection on 'archaic fields, an art of archetypes' extending even to prehistoric icons. Wieland's model for Fafner's and Fasolt's idol was the plump, erotic votive figurine known as the Venus of Willendorf.

Walter Felsenstein also created influential and fascinating integrated productions in Germany during the post-war years and made a great contribution to post-war operatic production. At the Komische Oper in East Berlin from 1947, Felsenstein built upon the early twentieth-century theatrical traditions of Stanislavsky and Brecht, and banished routine performing; each musical-dramatic moment was to be created as if for the first time. Banished also was pictorial staging as a visual substitute for authentically involved acting. Forbidden was any concentration on vocal virtuosity to the detriment of teamwork and the emotional truth of the score. Instead came a focus on stagecraft that enlisted each singer's unique emotional make-up. Felsenstein placed the singer in the composer's service: together with the stage director and the conductor, the singing actor became personally responsible for the realisation of all the composer's intentions as expressed in the markings of the score.

Felsenstein emphasised the primal emotional experience as that which inevitably issues into song. This to him was the reason that opera is opera, and not a moment on the legitimate stage. He wrote that in opera 'everyday sobriety is pushed aside' in favour of vivid, unstudied passion, 'heightened experience'. A leading instance for Felsenstein was Verdi's reworking of Shakespeare's *Othello* in order to allow the music to bring primal emotional experience into being on stage:

> Verdi and the librettist Boito omitted the first act of the Shake-spearean drama, thereby making room for music. A new exposition was created: unchained powers of nature, thunder and lightning, storm, the roaring sea, chaos. Out there the battle is raging. Everybody knows what depends on its outcome. The crowd trembles for the fleet, trembles for Cyprus, trembles for Venice. Boito and Verdi have heightened the situation until it touches elemental nature itself. The cosmic power of this new beginning must release the furioso of the singing and out of this tempestuousness the human being Otello is hurled into the action. After the victorious battle he finds at last, and per-haps for the first time, fulfillment of his dreams of happiness and peace. Otello's sorrow-filled life and Desdemona's love and understanding are fused into a situation in which two people must sing, 'driven by love'. This is the origin of singing on the stage.[55]

In a great many instances singers were cast at the Komische Oper by Felsenstein himself, rather than the opera house administration. Sometimes he would use a particular musical 'exercise' in an attempt to get the singing actor into the 'right state' for a scene or character. If the singer failed to give satisfaction, he would be sacked. 'We rehearse with him together, the assistant conductor and I, until we feel that he has reached the necessary state. If for any reason he does not live up to expectations, we can still put someone else in his place.'[56] Given this declaration of the paramountcy of directorial values, it was fortu-nate that Felsenstein was intensely musical. 'As soon as you take a Verdi score literally, which unfortunately many interpreters are not prepared to do, it becomes a stage director's workbook', Felsentein wrote, 'Every eighth note, every change of tempo, every dynamic indi-cation is a scenic direction in itself.'[57] After the stage director has brought the singing actor into the score, the latter re-creates within himself the composer's original creative process. The singer-actor 'feels, sings, and "plays" the notes as if he had written them himself. At the peak of necessity the musician in him becomes liberated. In that moment, in a rehearsal or during a performance, he discovers within himself the capacity to compose the opera in the way intended by Mozart or Verdi. What happens then between him and the conductor – if the conductor is ready to go along – is a miracle, one of the most beautiful experiences imaginable. It is perfect music theatre.'[58]

The singer Ella Lee told the astonishing tale of her work with Felsenstein, who engaged her for Tytania at the Komische Oper. She recalled that Kurt Masur, then music director, was present at all the stage rehearsals except when they conflicted with a scheduled perform-ance. Lee's rehearsal period with Felsenstein lasted an extraordinary seven months, whereas a typical new opera production is rehearsed in six weeks or so. In praising Felsenstein's enthusiasm and 'naive honesty,'[59] she felt that 'He brought out in me feelings I did not know I possessed'.[60] His work as a director, in contrast to Wieland Wagner's externalised, visually orientated style, was concerned not with symbols but with social motives and sought to prod the actor into finding the character inside himself. 'I had to soul-search and find within my own experience a way to get across to the public what I was trying to say', Ella Lee recalled, and she added that Felsenstein 'only told me where I was to make my exits and entrances; the rest was up to me. If I did not dig into myself and find the real Ella I was going to be insane and without a job.'[61]

Felsenstein's approach differed from Wieland Wagner's stripped-down, symbolist orientation. 'If one wishes to be abstract', he told Rolf Liebermann in 1962, 'it is best not to use human beings for it. A human being is a reality. If I try to use this reality abstractly, I am simply guilty of wrongly utilizing my basic material.'[62] Felsenstein was likewise opposed to the kind of conceptualism that characterised much opera staging after 1970: 'Anyone who thinks he can reshape or modernize a valuable work would do better to have a new work written for him, rather than to misuse the existing one for his own purposes.'[63] Nevertheless, his pupils and assistants, including Götz Friedrich, Joachim Herz and Günther Rennert, formed a new generation of conceptual opera directors who sometimes departed from their men-tor's faithfulness to the composer's intentions. Besides East Berlin, Felsenstein staged opera extensively in the German Federal Republic.

His Hamburg *Rigoletto* of 1962 was granted ten weeks' rehearsal time and had a resounding success.

Together with Callas, Bernstein, Giulini, Visconti and notable British stage directors, among them Peter Hall and Elijah Moshinsky, Felsenstein paved the way for an even fuller integration of acting, staging and music. His example has made it more difficult for any contemporary opera director to be ignorant of the score. He has also helped ensure that singers can no longer trust their vocal glory alone to carry them through a performance. Felsenstein also gave an answer to the 'elitist' argument against opera. Since his vision of the genre is one of passion – the 'passion of the soul' rather than a rhetorical or assumed emotion – it points to the deepest sources of creativity. 'Modern man has lost his connection with his creative core. But a certain longing for this creative core has remained with him. It can find its fulfilment in art.'[64] This creative core is, of course, universal. It is as democratic as primal emotion itself.

THIRTEEN

LA SCALA 1960–69

New Divas and Divos

THE SCALA OF THE 1960s lacked some of the excitement of the previous decade. With Visconti no longer creating stagings for the House, Ghiringhelli was sometimes at a loss to build on the triumphs of the recent past. Giulini, also absent, was beginning to tire of conducting opera altogether. He longed for better conditions, especially a longer rehearsal period. And Callas, though still singing, was continuing to decline vocally. The rare and wondrous collegial artistry of the middle and late 1950s was no more. Nonetheless, respectable and sometimes imaginative work could be seen on the stage in Milan.

Scala stagings, even those by veteran stalwarts, were beginning to head in new directions. A *Parsifal* at the end of the 1960 season was given new decor by Nicola Benois and a production by Frank de Quell. Claudio Sartori wrote that the pair 'renovated the traditional Scala spectacle, getting rid of the old floral realism, using coloured projection and psychological illumination, stylising the action and reducing it to a minimum – sometimes omitting necessary details. The spectacle gained in dignity and suggestive power, and amply corresponded to the intentions of the conductor André Cluytens, who always obtained, in this performance in German, a fine balance between massed forces and soloists, and between stage and orchestra . . .'[1]

Franco Zeffirelli was able partly to fill the breach opened by Visconti's departure from La Scala, using his sharply honed visual sense to excellent effect. While Zeffirelli often expressed the wish to do more work at the House and longed to direct Callas there, he was engaged for relatively few productions. La Scala awaited a stage director both creative and reliable who could be counted on to goad fine singers into becoming fine actors as well.

Callas's last Scala appearances were as Paolina in Donizetti's *Poliuto* (four performances in December 1960) and as Medea in Cherubini's opera of the same name (two performances in December 1961; one in May and one in June of the following year). Visconti had been scheduled to stage *Poliuto*, but abandoned the production during an emotional crisis: he was reportedly angry at the censoring of his film *Rocco and His Brothers*. In the end Herbert Graf directed the opera and Nicola Benois designed it in 'grandiose and splendid' style.[2] The audience was equally grandiose and splendid. Eugenio Montale, writing for the *Corriere d'informazione*, witnessed the 'complete mobilisation of the Milan and Monaco "high life"'.[3] Michael Scott recalled the presence of Prince Rainier and Princess Grace, the Begum Aga Khan, Erich Maria Remarque and his wife Paulette Goddard, and Callas's lover Onassis. Paolina was to be the last new role Callas took on stage. Even at a time of diminishing vocal achievement, it was far from a failure for her. Massimo Mila in *L'Espresso* found relatively little to disparage: 'Her voice is no longer what it was ten years ago, but it is scarcely extinct. There is a bit of strident, metallic tone in the high notes and in the pointless virtuosity of the "Perchè di stolto giubilo" in Act I.' But, Mila wrote, 'the musical intelligence and innate nobility of her tragic manner are unchanged.'[4] Michael Scott also praised her musicianship and technique:

> Like a tight-rope walker her vocal cords wobble under the slightest pressure; but her technical, as well as musical, skill remains on a virtuoso level. Even at this stage of her career we can still hear precisely what Donizetti writes. Even in 1960 she could execute the most intricate and demanding music with her familiar accuracy. It is customary to talk of singers losing their voices; but it would be more precise to discriminate between losing their voices and losing the ability to sing. For most it is the latter but, even with only a whisper of tone, which was all Callas had left by this time, she could still sing.[5]

Opinion was rather more negative concerning the Medea. Elvio Giudici found Callas's performance on the live recording to be poor: 'Callas has ceased being a great singer and become that most uncomfortable thing, a legend, a living myth.' She was 'struggling with a recalcitrant instrument', a voice in decline which produces an 'obviously cracked' high B flat in 'Dei tuoi figli la madre'. Nonetheless, Giudici concludes that Callas's acting was more refined, more tragically intense than ever after her experience gained in singing this role around the world.

Tebaldi's career was also in decline. During the 1960s her top notes, never her strongest point, grew even more unreliable. She tended to take verismo parts such as Fedora and Adriana Lecouvreur. Some critics maintained her role choices emphasised her vocal shortcomings, but others felt they gave her added scope for acting. At Naples in December 1968 she sang an appealing Gioconda. Enrico Tellini wrote: 'In the old days Tebaldi had one of the most beautiful sweet voices, with splendid filati and great accuracy. Very little of that remains. Now she has a more powerful voice, with almost mezzo-like notes, and she is troubled only at the very top of her still very remarkable voice.' Her acting of the part was considered 'quite vehement and alive'.[6] During the 1960s she pursued her career in several Italian provincial Houses and especially in America, where her fans stayed loyal. Tebaldi remained convinced that La Scala was still interested in her. When Scala singers performed the Verdi *Requiem* in Carnegie Hall during the autumn of 1967 she was in the audience. At the end Ghiringhelli bestowed upon her 'the famous kiss on the forehead'. 'They're waiting for me at La Scala!' wrote Tebaldi in a letter. 'But, at present I have no plans to accept.'[7] It seemed that La Scala was 'waiting' for her in her imagination.

Casting problems began to beset the House. As the careers of Callas and Tebaldi faded, a serious diva gap opened up. But the haste to fill their place resulted in more than one young soprano being advanced too quickly, and others were assigned too heavy roles. Baritones were similarly at a premium, although for a briefer period. New tenors came up, among them Plácido Domingo and Luciano Pavarotti, who have become enshrined in the pantheon of twentieth-century singers. If one sought fine singing one could often find it in Milan, though not at the level of the previous decade.

For brilliant vocal performances La Scala could rely on Joan Sutherland's occasional appearances. Even though she was not a fixture at the House, she could fill a portion of the vacuum left by Callas, singing the Donizetti and Bellini heroines. And though she did not have Callas's fire, Sutherland provided an abundance of elegance and purity, as well as predictable quality.

On 28 May 1962 Sutherland starred at La Scala in a splendidly cast *Les Huguenots*, Meyerbeer's ambitious grand opera. Franco Corelli sang Raoul, Fiorenza Cossotto Urbain, Nicolai Ghiaurov Marcel, Giorgio Tozzi Saint-Bris, and the youthful bass-baritone Wladimiro Ganzarolli the Comte de Nevers. Giulietta Simionato as Valentine was 'at the top of her form in an impassioned interpretation'. It should be noted that Simionato, a mezzo, was singing a soprano part at the age of fifty-two, four years before her retirement. Although Sutherland too was acclaimed, Massimo Mila was not happy about the bass-baritone. To him Ganzarolli's voice 'had a grim, gloomy complexion inappropriate for this character, who ought to be portrayed as a kind of baritonal Duke of Mantua'.[8] Gianandrea Gavazzeni conducted competently and with a measure of involvement. Nicola Benois's set was opulent and, typically, traditional.[9]

The pair of Sutherland and Ganzarolli opened the 1962–63 season with Rossini's *Semiramide*, a work little heard at the time: the Rossini 'revival' was not to begin for nearly another decade. Harold Rosenthal found the evening boring, writing that neither 'neither Margherita Wallmann whose strong point is the massing of the chorus and bringing on processions who march and counter-march, nor Gabriele Santini, who conducted the piece at funereal pace with noise a plenty, seemed particularly equipped to deal with this particular opera.'[10] Sutherland as Semiramide was technically superb, but left the character 'a one-dimensional figure most of the evening'. As Assur, Ganzarolli was praised for his voice and stage presence.

Franco Abbiati, writing in the *Corriere della Sera*, called Sutherland's 12 June 1964 performance of Lucia 'miraculous' and, in the Mad Scene, 'perhaps unsurpassable'.[11] Nevertheless bel canto, whether sung by Callas, Sutherland or Scotto, was still not at the core of the Scala repertoire. What the House urgently needed was a top Verdi soprano. Montserrat Caballé was not yet known in Milan. She had sung the First Flower Maiden in a 1960 *Parsifal*, but did not appear in the limelight of the opera world until 1965, when she sang a stupendous Lucrezia Borgia in New York's Carnegie Hall.

As management searched for a diva to sing the bread-and-butter Italian repertoire, Renata Scotto emerged as a candidate. Born in Savona in 1934, Scotto's career began remarkably early, with a Violetta in the town of her birth in 1952. Her first role at La Scala – Walter in *La Wally* – came in 1954 and an early starring role in the House was Adina in *L'Elisir d'amore* in 1958. By the early 1960s Scotto had developed into a real bel canto find. Her pure, fresh, accurate soprano leggero made her a natural choice at La Scala as Elvira in Bellini's *I Puritani*, Giulietta in *I Capuleti e i Montecchi* and, from 1967, as Lucia. Massimo Mila considered her 'predestined' for this role, which she portrayed in the 'great Italian tradition' of Toti dal Monte and Lina Pagliughi. Mila also delighted in her vocal timbre, identified with the 'innocence and unhappiness of such romantic heroines as Lucia and Giulietta'.[12] According to Eugenio Gara, Scotto's acting as Lucia was particularly admirable: 'Take the celebrated Mad Scene: her heart-rending answers to the flute's questions are not simply a device on the part of the composer to allow his leading ladies to indulge in a vocal free-for-all. They are the cries of a soul in despair responding to the mysterious voice in the air announcing her imminent death.'[13] Claudio Sartori was less impressed. Renata Scotto as Lucia, he wrote, 'sang with great ability and polish, but she is a little short of the dramatic power so essential to bring the character to life'.[14]

Critical opinion was sharply divided over Scotto's shift to the heavier soprano repertoire, which began during the 1960s. She sang Violetta at Vercelli's Teatro Civico on 6 June 1965, earning praise for her beautiful timbre and line as well as her sense of drama. Although she managed a successful high E flat at the close of 'Sempre libera', and was compared not unfavourably with Callas, mention was also made of stridency in the tone. In the 1966 Barbirolli *Butterfly* with the forces of the Rome Opera there are difficult moments, as in 'Un bel dì' where wide register seams open up, and where Scotto pushes fortes beyond Puccini's markings. In uncomplicated lyric moments, she can be effective. Other listeners have enjoyed Scotto's Butterfly, however. Elvio Giudici delights in this selfsame 'Un bel dì', in which he hears 'a magnificent purity and homogeneity of line placed in the service of an enchanted lyricism'.[16]

Like her almost exact contemporary Renata Scotto, Mirella Freni's career began very early. She was only twenty when she sang Micaëla, her first operatic role, in her home town of Modena in 1955. After a number of appearances at Glyndebourne from 1960 to 1962 she made her Scala debut as Mimì in 1962.

With her creamy lyric soprano and her warm simplicity of demeanour Freni was the natural choice for Mimì in the *Bohème* premiered at the end of January 1963. The production was staged by Zeffirelli and conducted by Karajan, at a time when Zeffirelli's interest in getting singers to act was apparently lessening and he was beginning to concentrate upon spectacle. He felt it made his reputation at last in his native land: 'That first night, on 31 January 1963, was precious to me as it represented a recognition I had been accorded in London and New York, but had so far been denied in my own country. To many people in the Italian theatre and opera I was just one of Visconti's boys, someone with no identity of his own. Elsewhere I could be Franco Zeffirelli but not, until that *Bohème*, on my home ground.'[17]

In this *Bohème*, certainly one of his visual masterpieces, the director-designer solved a long-standing problem in Act Two: how to differentiate the main characters from the Christmastide throngs at the Café Momus? Zeffirelli placed the action on two separate levels, with the crowd milling about on the upper level and the principals in the foreground below. Particularly in Act One there is considerable visual interest but relatively little movement on stage, even though the quicksilver shifts in the music clearly suggest movement. The visuals are nevertheless cleanly effective in portraying moods and states of mind. All was done with taste and sensitivity, albeit with a lack of dramatic tension.

Since Karajan did not want Di Stefano as Rodolfo, Gianni Raimondi sang this part. In addition to Freni as Mimì, Eugenia Ratti sang Musetta (replaced on the film-for-television by Adriana Martino). Rolando Panerai was cast as Marcello, Gianni Maffeo as Schaunard, and Ivo Vinco as Colline. The cine-film of the production, one of the earliest of its kind, gives a good impression of the conducting. Karajan takes pains to understate dynamic contrasts in Act One. In contrast Act Two is extremely loud in some places and extremely soft in others – as if Karajan had consciously sought to underscore the intimacy of the garret and the contrasting public whirl of the Café Momus. While bringing out the richness and brilliance of Puccini's orchestration, he seems insensitive to the pacing, to the line, to the pathos and the gentle feminine element in the music. The Scala orchestra play cleanly and responsively, with beautifully achieved balance and legati. The chorus are nothing short of marvellous.

As Mimì, perfect for her at this stage of her career, Freni's voice is delectable. Softly produced, beautifully focused, tasteful and graceful, hers is consistently honest singing, even when, still in her youth, she has not found all the feeling in the music. A warning is sounded, however, in the top notes, which, although open, verge on the harsh. Gianni Raimondi is a more than serviceable Rodolfo, in the swing dramatically and vocally, and displaying an easy high C. Indeed, the *Corriere della Sera* critic found that Raimondi's acting surpassed Di Stefano's in the same part, at least 'from the psychological viewpoint'.[18]

Two years later Freni fell victim to Karajan's misguided decision to cast her, then a light lyric soprano, in the far more taxing part of Violetta in *La Traviata* in December of 1964. Ominously, she had once before announced for Violetta – in Bari – and cancelled. Tebaldi had also come to grief at La Scala her first time there in the role, even though she had sung it previously at half a dozen Italian Houses, as well as in Lisbon. The Scala audience were hostile, booing both Freni and Karajan. According to Zeffirelli the conductor was 'shattered'. 'I could see that he was debating whether or not to walk out, but in the end professional pride drove him on.'[19] Zeffirelli, responsible for the production, had sensed oncoming disaster from Freni's nervousness late in the rehearsal period. Besides Freni's vocal unsuitability for the part he felt the still fresh memory of Callas's great Violetta inhibited her work. Zeffirelli urged Karajan to transpose down for Freni's benefit 'Sempre libera', the difficult Act One aria, but the conductor refused. Zeffirelli recalled that when he took Freni to one side:

> I discovered that she was the victim of the most horrendous hate mail sent by the supporters of other divas who had sung the role or wanted to. Inevitably there were poison-pen letters from Callas fanatics – that I expected – but even the Tebaldi claque had joined in and, most surprising of all, the crudest threats came from admirers of Scotto and [Antonietta] Stella – what a bunch! I begged Freni's husband to intercept all this

hate mail and to keep it from his wife, who was clearly being destroyed by it, but he chose to ignore my advice.[20]

Zeffirelli recalled Freni cracking twice during 'Sempre libera', to the accompaniment of boos from the gallery. He thought her decision to take a solo bow at the first-act curtain an even greater mistake. When Freni heard renewed booing over the unenthusiastic applause, the 'poor woman, who must have been on the verge of a nervous break-down, raised her fist like a fishwife and shook it at her tormentors. The entire audience was stunned and the booing became more general. We dropped the curtain and got her off.'[21] When Karajan took the podium after the interval, he too was booed, apparently for having chosen Freni to sing the part. But soprano and conductor persevered until the final curtain. Freni cancelled her remaining performances, even though critical opinion was not unanimously negative. The *Corriere della Sera* critic, for one, admired her emotional expressiveness and tended to be forgiving of her vocal shortcomings.[22]

By the time Anna Moffo stepped in to sing the remaining Violettas, the galleries were overcharged with emotion. Zeffirelli recalled that, at one point, 'a cat attached to a parachute was launched from the gods and floated, screeching all the way, down on to the stage . . .'[23] How-ever, the *Corriere* reporter noted a gradual easing of tension during the performance, and the hissing of Karajan was less pronounced than on the first night. The production was scrapped, much to Zeffirelli's chagrin. Sharing Tebaldi's superstitions about numbers, he had argued that 17 December, the date of the opening night, was unlucky for him. But the Scala management had refused to listen. When he next met Visconti he was given some sage advice. ' "My dear," he said, "as an old friend, may I suggest you keep away from the Lady of the Camellias, she doesn't seem to be doing you much good." '[24]

Karajan never forgave the Milanese for questioning his choice. It is interesting that Eugenio Montale also found a good deal to like in Freni's single performance as Violetta that December. Besides her voice – '*bellissima, ferma, sicura*' – Montale approved of the pathos and honesty she brought to the part: 'Freni is doubtless no tigress, no high-rent *demi-mondaine*, rather a good girl marked by a cruel fate, and not only by sin.'[25] It is also true that Freni recovered from the

incident at La Scala and went on to sing, and record, Violetta successfully.

The conductors Toscanini had brought to the House – among them
Votto and Gavazzeni – were ageing, although together with Nino
Sanzogno they still constituted arguably the finest permanent conducting staff of any opera house anywhere. Giulini was no longer
active at La Scala, and Vittorio Gui had shifted much of his activity
to Rome after leaving Glyndebourne.

The brilliant, scholarly and exceedingly taciturn Claudio Abbado
came on the scene as a youthful successor to the older generation.
Abbado had been born to a musical family in Milan in 1933. Some
commentators linked the political awareness of his adulthood to his
wartime memories of his mother being sent to jail by the Nazis for
sheltering a Jewish child in Milan. As a young man he had witnessed
Toscanini and Furtwängler conducting rehearsals. Years later he told
an interviewer, 'They taught me that nothing should ever sound routine.'[26] He graduated from the Milan Conservatory in 1955, studied
conducting in Vienna with Hans Swarowsky, and made his debut in
a concert at La Scala in 1960. The following year he began conducting
there regularly. He conducted *Atomtod* by Giacomo Manzoni at the
Piccola Scala, which opened on 27 March 1965. This fantastical opera
took place in nuclear bomb shelters occupied by a decadent and des-
picable bourgeoisie. Its political slant was not at all foreign to Abbado's
leftist views. His first major assignment in the main House was a more
familiar work: the *I Capuleti e i Montecchi* (opening 26 March 1966)
that was also Pavarotti's debut vehicle. He made a new version of
Donizetti's score, which assigned the part of Romeo to a tenor, sung
at La Scala by Giacomo Aragall, rather than a high mezzo. An Abbado
Lucia, with the title part performed by Scotto, opened the 1967–68
season. Reactions to the conductor's contribution were lukewarm:
'Though perfectly adequate, it did nothing to erase the memory of
other productions of the same opera already seen at La Scala. Claudio
Abbado's conducting, while extremely skilful, somehow suggested a
slight lack of conviction and a failure to surrender completely to the
rather wonderful old piece.'[27] Franco Abbiati in *Corriere della Sera*

gently suggested that Abbado's deletion of traditional 'rhetorical' interpolations in Donizetti's score was an act of youthful rebellion: '*nonconformisti . . . anticonvenzionali*'.[28]

Abbado often conducted from a polemical or cerebral standpoint, and while he was always sparing with words – 'You can't talk during a concert,' he once told an interviewer, 'so why should you talk much during a rehearsal?'[29] He was also capable of fiery emotion from the podium. He created an 'incandescent' *Don Carlos*, which was first presented at La Scala on 7 December 1968. Massimo Mila praised his 'vibrant enthusiasm' and called him a 'great artist'. Abbado proved a sensitive, intelligent collaborator with stage directors. Jean-Pierre Ponnelle's scenic work for this *Don Carlos* was 'an elegant stylisation in black and silver which was more successful in the interiors, inspired by the gloomy ambience of the Escurial'. Ponnelle, who also directed, staged the finale of Act Two 'in the most grandiose possible manner . . . monks, notables, guards, uproarious crowds, condemned men, dwarves, pyres, gallows and crucifixions – the entire armamentarium of the grand spectacle'.[30]

The Scala administration was doing everything it could to maintain the ancient tradition of singing at the House. At the same time, changes were becoming manifest in the Italian body politic which eventually were felt in the cultural sphere, including opera. While the establishment had not loosened its grip on political and economic life, the ruling coalitions had come to realise that further improvement in the standard of living was an absolute necessity. Even though a consumer society had arisen, with automobile production trebling between 1960 and 1967, there was still much poverty in Italy. The electorate were angry at a variety of breakdowns in national life. With the judiciary strangled by 2 million pending cases, the social security system failing to live up to demands and the Mafia threatening the fabric of society in Sicily and the south, voters were beginning to demand more of the Christian Democrats. A tendency to strengthen the Left was beginning to be evident in elections.

La Scala itself became a stage for some of the political arrest. Abbado's debut in *Atomtod* presaged a more unruly political event that same year. On the first evening of the 1965–66 season a new Scala tradition was begun: political demonstrations using the House as a spotlit venue. The first act of *La Forza del destino* witnessed three noisy interruptions. Piero Cappuccilli cracked and left the stage to boos. Soon afterwards leaflets were thrown from the balcony to the seat of Felice Riva, an industrialist whose cotton factory had gone bankrupt, putting several thousand workers out of their jobs. The leaflets were launched by Riva's former employees. They read, 'Riva, your place is not at La Scala but at San Vittore' – the Milan jail. And finally a demonstration by the singers near the close of the first act included a shower of leaflets as well objecting to what they termed 'the Mafia of opera houses'. The demonstrators appeared to be seeking a place to air their political views rather than the democratisation of the House.

During the turbulent period there was an evident willingness on the part of the Scala management to programme new operas. Such an extension of the standard repertoire stood in strong distinction to the conservative programming of the 1950s. Works already known to audiences abroad – especially in Germany – were introduced, and new works were commissioned for the House. These were daring acts for an established Italian artistic institution. As he had been for more than a decade, Nino Sanzogno continued to be a linchpin in these efforts. His quick musical intelligence allowed him to enjoy reading and assimilating new scores, and his sense of the dramatic seldom failed him. Sanzogno led Berg's *Lulu* in a borrowed Hamburg Opera production which opened on 11 February 1963. The audience greeted it with yawns rather than boos. However, the Italian critics were waking up at last to the realities of the modern repertoire. 'Berg has composed the true music of our century,' wrote *Il Giorno*.[31] The same reviewer stressed the conductor's competence and sensitivity: 'Sanzogno conducted Berg's extraordinary, highly intricate and difficult score with careful attention to the theatrical values of the singing and *Sprechgesang*.'

The first staged version of Manuel de Falla's posthumous opera *Atlántida*, which depicted Columbus's discovery of the New World, was welcomed by Scala audiences in June 1962. However, reviewers focused on its un-operatic nature. Its three-hour playing time and absence of dramatic interest made it boring. Eugenio Montale termed it a '*cantata scenica*' and concluded that the work probably ought to have remained unstaged. Massimo Mila agreed and added an original thought for the next time round: 'Would it be possible to try another staging? A popular show perhaps, with a minimum of scenic trappings: an open-air spectacle in the square, little more than an oratorio modestly and honestly presented.' The score, completed after Falla's death by his pupil Ernesto Halffter, was summed up in *Opera* as uneven: 'Alongside magnificent pages there are others which are weaker, less inspired, less able.'[32]

In June 1964, in a double bill with Schoenberg's *Erwartung*, La Scala staged *Volo di notte*, an early opera by the highly regarded Italian composer Luigi Dallapiccola which had first been performed in 1940 in Florence and afterwards in a number of Houses round the world. The work had a libretto by the composer after Antoine de Saint-Exupéry's novel *Vol de nuit*. The relatively simple scoring seems scarcely daring, a quarter-century after its premiere. The *Corriere lombardo* wrote, 'This opera contains unusually expressive passages which ought to have been given a fitting staging. Its text and gestures – whether seen or understood – should have found a perfectly exact correlative, altogether lacking in fluff, just as [the composer has] demanded of the orchestra.'[33] Sanzogno's conducting, unusually, was faulted: 'Nino Sanzogno conducts the two works without going much beyond a functional beating of time.'[34]

Not all unfamiliar repertoire had a success at La Scala in the 1960s. From time to time a new production seemed on the verge of disaster in rehearsals. Management generally had something dependable on hand to serve up in a difficult hour. When a January 1966 production of *Olimpie*, by the Italian-born early nineteenth-century composer Gaspare Spontini, never got beyond its dress rehearsal, it was replaced on the *cartellone* by the trusty Zeffirelli *Bohème*, with Sanzogno conducting and starring the team of Freni and Pavarotti.

At the same time that La Scala was experimenting with new works and long-forgotten older operas, Mozart, Strauss and Wagner were heard less often than in other houses. The problem was many-sided: the conducting staff did not make a speciality of these works, the Scala singers were not familiar with them and the audiences did not demand them. Even so, German operas were staged, if not in abundance, and an occasional Mozart performance could reach a high standard.

Rosenthal found Lorin Maazel's and Luigi Squarzina's April 1966 *Don Giovanni* 'fast moving and convincing', and 'by and large the best performance and production of the opera I have ever seen in a large house'.[35]

During the latter half of the decade the procession of new singers continued. The young Elena Suliotis's star rose and declined rapidly. Her dramatic soprano seemed the sort of raw material that might fill the diva gap, particularly in the Verdi repertoire. In Naples in February 1966 her Leonora (*Forza*) sounded to Enrico Tellini 'exceptionally powerful' but lacking in control.[36] Lord Harewood delighted in her Scala Abigaille (*Nabucco*) two years later: 'Excitement goes with her and she is plainly a star, who fills the box office by her presence in the cast and the theatre with her voice.'[37] However, Harewood deplored her amateurish, frequently uninvolved acting, a fault also noted by Harold Rosenthal late in 1967 during a BBC programme devoted to the Greek singer. Problems soon overcame Suliotis's youthful voice, as she took on very heavy parts. In December she cancelled two appearances in Florence as Norma in the opera of the same name, while in the two she sang, according to Giorgio Gualerzi, 'her vocal estate was precarious'.[38] In the same role in Chicago in October 1968 Roger Dettmer panned her performance outright: 'Her technique is imperfect: she cannot trill; she cannot sing an even scale; swell or diminish volume once a phrase has begun; or act; or dress suitably for the occasion. All this promises shortly to be the ruin of a potentially viable instrument.'[39]

Simionato closed her career with a farewell both sad and modest. She had begun singing in the Italian provinces in 1928, at the age of eighteen. She told no one she was going to retire until one winter evening in 1966 in Milan. After nearly forty years on the opera stage she had the intention of marrying an older man and wished to make the most of his company. She asked to be allowed to sing a single performance of *La Clemenza di Tito* in the Piccola Scala on 1 February. She told the make-up man that this would be 'the last time I shall appear on this or any other stage'.[40] Italy being Italy, the audience got wind and reacted emotionally. Rasponi wrote: 'No one could believe it, and the performance ended with the audience stomping and in tears.'[41]

Just before the advent of Domingo and Pavarotti, the House was experiencing a fairly severe tenor gap. Franco Corelli had made his Scala debut in 1954 and had since learned to open up his top register. He was capable of tackling roles requiring the utmost vocal stamina, but he was also apt to sing and act bombastically. Rosenthal had written of this tenor, when he had sung Poliuto opposite Callas in December 1960, 'He looks magnificent and is obviously the darling of the young Milanese opera fans. He possesses a magnificent, virile tenor voice, with exciting top notes in which he and the audience clearly revel. As yet, however, his singing lacks much refinement, and his phrasing, or rather lack of it, makes for an inartistic and sometimes vulgar performance. If only a really strong conductor could get hold of him he might well become a great singer as opposed to being just a handsome young man with a magnificent voice.'[42]

Di Stefano was in vocal trouble, with numerous pre-performance 'indispositions' dating back to the late 1950s. Pavarotti, his disciple, describes him as a victim of nerves. He went on committing egregious errors of taste and vocal production, but with his characteristic inconsistency he would sing at times with great sweetness of tone and a sense of style. In the early 1960s Di Stefano added new roles, some of which were appropriate for him and others which seemed not to be. His Nemorino in an *Elisir* which opened at La Scala on 11 March 1964 was well received. In June, however, he sang the heavy name part in Wagner's *Rienzi*, in a liberally cut version conducted by Hermann Scherchen. Even though it seemed to many a strange choice of role, notices were also generally positive. *L'Unità* called Di Stefano's performance a courageous act with 'profound musical involvement: yet again he gave of his rich talents of voice and stagecraft'.[43] On 27 January 1965, at the Met, Di Stefano sang a single performance of *Les Contes d'Hoffmann* that verged on disaster: *Opera* wrote that Di Stefano 'was not averse from rewriting when the required notes lay too high for comfort.'[44] Di Stefano sang no further performances after the first night. In Rome he was announced for a Lohengrin in the Terme di Caracalla in July 1966, but the young tenor Nicola Tagger sang instead. Di Stefano was announced for the tenor role of Lucano in La Scala's 17 January 1967 *L'Incoronazione di Poppea* and cancelled.

The 'tenor gap' was short lived. Carlo Bergonzi was a breath of fresh air. He shaped his exceedingly beautiful tone with a highly sophisticated musical intelligence. Phrases were completely organic, with music, text and emotion presented as a single unit. Not only that: in the recorded performances – of Verdi, Puccini, Ponchielli, Giordano and other composers – Bergonzi scarcely seems to take a breath between his flexible, endlessly spun lines. Rhythms and accents are clear, satisfying, revealing character and feeling. His unusually express-ive and tasteful singing made up for a lack of acting commitment and vocal force. He was never a heroic tenor in the mould of Corelli and Del Monaco, which meant that listening to his spinto parts took some readjusting of expectations concerning tonal weight. Given that readjustment, Bergonzi's Verdi was a special delight: the Met used him again and again as Radames, and his partnership with Solti in record-ings of *Un Ballo in maschera* (1959) and *Don Carlos* (1965) shows two outstanding musicians sensitively making music.

Although he sang at Covent Garden, as well as in 249 performances at the Met, Bergonzi's work at La Scala was limited. His debut in 1953 was in the name part of Jacopo Napoli's newly commissioned opera *Masaniello*; he did not sing afterwards in the House until 4 March 1964, in Gounod's *Faust*. In the following year he sang Radames and, to open the 1965–66 season, Alvaro in *Forza*. Bergonzi had replaced a tragically alcoholic Jussi Björling in the Solti *Ballo* recording. With Björling dead (in any case, he had sung very rarely indeed at La Scala after the war), and Bergonzi himself frequently occupied in New York, Italy needed new tenor blood.

Luciano Pavarotti was twenty-five when he made his professional debut on 29 April 1961 as Rodolfo in the Teatro Municipale of Reggio Emilia. He went on to perform half a dozen other lyric tenor leading roles in the standard Italian repertoire before his Scala debut four years later. His father, a Modena baker who had also sung tenor in the local opera chorus, passed on his love for singing to his son and encouraged his vocal studies with a well-known local tenor, Arrigo Pola. Another young singer in Modena at the time was Mirella Freni. She and Pavarotti were childhood friends. Said Pavarotti, 'I have done everything with her except make love.'[45]

Pavarotti studied further with the renowned Ettore Campogalliani in Mantua, who also taught Bergonzi, Scotto, Freni and Tebaldi, among many others. He fervently admired Di Stefano's singing. Pavarotti worked as an insurance salesman and a primary-school teacher, as well as taking his athletic talents seriously. 'When I was young,' he declared, 'I played a lot of sport. At 18 my weight on form was 172 pounds, and in football I played "striker" centre forward for a little team on the outskirts of Modena . . .'[46] But weight became a problem for Pavarotti, and one which would eventually inhibit his work as an actor, which was never his strongest point. Pavarotti's vocal idol was Di Stefano. He admired the older tenor's lyricism and, above all, his diction. Pavarotti's own Italian diction would become a standard for opera singers in his own time. In his youth – and later on – his stage persona was that of a vital, sunny, embraceable bear of a man. His voice was equally bright and liquid in tone, with an appealing glint that matched his projected self. As a musician he was not outstanding, lacking a certain depth of understanding and finding difficulty in learning new roles. As a warm human being and astonishingly talented singer, however, he was loved by his admirers in a way few twentieth-century tenors ever have been.

Although Pavarotti had previously substituted at La Scala for two performances as Rodolfo, his official debut in the House came on 9 December 1965 as the Duke in *Rigoletto*. Montale was ready to love him, as 'the chief surprise of the evening'. 'The young and still unknown Luciano Pavarotti' had, he wrote, proved to be 'endowed with notable quality. . . . He acts with ease and possesses a quite agreeable voice which blooms in the high register.'[47]

On 26 March of the following year Pavarotti sang his first Tebaldo in Bellini's *I Capuleti*. Montale found him 'especially noteworthy'.[48] That summer, as Alfredo in the Terme di Caracalla in Rome, the *Opera* critic treated him as a known quantity: 'Pavarotti sang Alfredo with his customary mixture of ardour and technique, and, perhaps because he felt unrestricted on the gigantic platform, acted without some of the self-consciousness he shows indoors.'[49] Pavarotti was becoming a reliable star: his soaring high register, translucent timbre and obvious love of singing made his audiences adore him.

Though it would be far from the truth to say that La Scala 'discovered' Plácido Domingo, it was in Milan that he made his most important debut. Born in Spain in 1941, he had been brought to Mexico as a child by his parents, who were singers in the Spanish-language zarzuela music dramas. Domingo's first professional role came in 1957, when he performed in Mexico as a baritone in a zarzuela. He studied piano, conducting and singing at the National Conservatory in Mexico City and, while singing there and in the United States, gradually made the transition to tenor roles.

Domingo spent a formative period of two and a half years from 1962 to 1965 at the Israel National Opera in Tel Aviv, during which he sang tenor parts in ten operas, repeating performances again and again in that city and elsewhere in Israel on tour. He felt he learned his craft the hard way. Domingo recalled the Tel Aviv summers. They were, he wrote: 'terribly hot, especially in the dressing room – a single, large area with a curtain down the middle to separate the ladies from the gentlemen. The room would become so stuffy that we could hardly breathe; then we would walk on to the stage and get hit in the face by the air-conditioning of the auditorium. Having sung under those circumstances, I knew that I could sing anywhere.'[50]

Soon after leaving Israel, Domingo sang Don José at the New York City Opera. By the following year, 1966, he had become a star at New York's second opera company. Following his Vienna Staatsoper and Met debuts, both in 1968, he accepted the title role in Verdi's early opera *Ernani* to open the 1969–70 Scala season. Mila was aware that the House had in Domingo an unusual performer: 'an excellent Verdi tenor, with a ringing voice, outstanding in high notes and intonation but with intelligence and taste as well: in short, a cherished addition to the Verdi repertoire'.[51] Abbiati in the *Corriere* called him 'a lead tenor with rare ringing sound, pure intonation [and] fine phrasing'.[52] In due course Domingo would make his mark as one of the finest singing actors of this or any other era, and even as a conductor of opera. During this period, however, it was his heroic timbre and sensitive musicianship that gained him admiration. Underlying these singer's qualities was a generous and magnetic personality, which would also grow and deepen in time.

For excellent musical reasons Domingo loved performing at La Scala. In his own words:

> The orchestra is incredibly flexible – those players can follow
> the most incompetent singer to hell and back. And the chorus

... When the *Ernani* ensemble rehearsals began and I heard those tenors singing B flats and B naturals like real tenors, I was truly impressed. . . .

Singing under the baton of Antonino Votto was a great opportunity for me. He had been hired as a coach and staff conductor at La Scala by Toscanini nearly 50 years earlier, and that was one of his last seasons at the house. What was wonderful about Votto was the life, the pulsation, he gave to a work when he rehearsed singers at the piano. I remember the vigour and subtlety of his playing of my cabaletta, 'O tu che l'alma adora'. When he went before the orchestra, the fire and feeling of command waned a bit, but that may have been due to his age.[53]

By the time of his maturity Domingo had turned himself into a complete musician who had sufficient wisdom and humility to understand his art at depth. His friend and mentor Franco Iglesias once pointed out the honest dedication in Domingo's work: '[From] the beginning to the end of a performance, he doesn't let anything bother him. He's as if in a temple for a few hours, with only the music and the role and what he has to do for that time. He sings everything the way the composer wrote it, and he cares about this, while others think it doesn't matter and sing it whatever way. He studies well and uses his technique in a perfectly clear way. . . . He was always strong, prepared, ready.'[54]

Another new tenor, Alfredo Kraus, first sang at La Scala in 1960 as Elvino to Scotto's Amina in *La Sonnambula*. Born to an Austrian father and a Spanish mother in the Canary Islands in 1927, his career as a *tenore di grazia* flourished in the Italian provinces during the late 1950s. His polished sense of style – in the French as well as the Italian repertoire – and his intelligent acting and musicianship made him a connoisseur's singer. His voice, while perhaps lacking in opulence, was beautifully produced and blessed with an unusually open high register. His highly successful career continued well into the 1990s.

Wladimiro Ganzarolli, once hailed as a successor to the great Mariano Stabile, was a bass-baritone whom the House used frequently during the early 1960s. He was assigned the most difficult roles early on, including Falstaff. These first parts at La Scala coincided with the period just before a wealth of young baritones and basses began their distinguished careers at the house. Claudio Sartori, perhaps over-enthusiastically, found the young man full of potential as Falstaff. After overcoming first-night hesitancy under the careful leadership of veteran conductor Antonino Votto, Sartori wrote that 'a new Falstaff has been born and is assured of a long and successful career.'[55] But Ganzarolli failed to last the course in a profession which can be cruelly demanding. Following the *Semiramide* of December 1962 with Sutherland, critics began to disparage his voice and artistry. Elvio Giudici could not abide Ganzarolli's Jorg in the first recording of Verdi's *Stiffelio* (1979), writing that his participation as Jorg 'is terrible. By now he is incapable of sustaining and modulating even a single phrase. . . .'[56] Ganzarolli's career was far too short and one wonders why the House pushed him so quickly into these taxing parts.

Later in the 1960s an exciting new crop of Italian basses and baritones began appearing at La Scala, together constituting the start of a golden age for male low voices. Ruggero Raimondi, born in Bologna in 1941, sang his first opera role at Spoleto in 1964. Raimondi's Timur, his Scala debut part in 1968, was considered by Lord Harewood 'remarkably fine', perhaps the best' Timur that he had ever heard.[57] In London's Royal Festival Hall in 1968 Raimondi sang Alfonso in a concert performance of *Lucrezia Borgia* with Montserrat Caballé. Harold Rosenthal wrote, 'Signor Raimondi is without doubt the finest Italian-born bass since Ezio Pinza. The voice is rich, full and noble.'[58] Raimondi's impeccable technique and ability to make his presence strongly felt on stage have helped him become one of the outstanding singer-actors of the late twentieth century.

Although Verdi baritone Renato Bruson first appeared somewhat belatedly at La Scala in 1972, he began his long and distinguished career at a number of Italian Houses during the 1960s. Born in 1936 at Este near Padua, Bruson grew up as an orphan. He was once described as an inwardly turned man. 'Bruson . . . displays traces of his painfully difficult childhood and adolescence in his almost unsociable shyness and cautious reserve, and in the composed nobility of the actor-singer and the stiff, even uniform severity of the interpreter.'[59] He studied with only one teacher, Elena Fava Ceriati, and made his debut at Spoleto in 1961 in *Il Trovatore*.

Another Italian baritone who became a world star was Piero Cappuccilli. Born in Trieste in 1929, his first moment of fame came in 1959 when he sang Barnaba in Callas's recording of *La Gioconda*. In his Scala debut, on 12 June 1964, he appeared as Enrico opposite Sutherland's Lucia.

Baritone Ettore Bastianini, who had sung opposite Callas and had a highly respected career as a Verdi specialist, died tragically in 1967 at the age of forty-four. He had been ill for the previous two years with cancer of the vocal cords and the epiglottis, but had gone on singing, without telling his fellow singers or the press of his condition.

On 14 August 1967 the Italian parliament approved a bill to regularise government funding of opera. This had the effect of reducing the Scala subsidy. Called the Corona law after its promulgator, the culture minister, it allocated 12 billion lire among thirteen nationally supported opera houses, including La Scala, the Teatro dell'Opera in Rome, the Teatro Comunale of Florence and La Fenice in Venice. Opera lovers criticised the sum as insufficient.

In 1968 Gianandrea Gavazzeni announced his resignation from the artistic directorship of La Scala. Cited in *Opera* as the reason for his departure was 'the imminence of the operation of the Administrative Council provided by the new laws regulating Italian operatic and symphonic organizations'.[60] Gavazzeni, who had worked at La Scala since 1948 and had been artistic director since 1965, had established a reputation as a considerable musical intellect. When emotionally committed to the score on a given night he was a force to be reckoned with, but at other times he remained a careful, scholarly conductor. He was succeeded as artistic director by composer Luciano Chailly, who had been music consultant to RAI, the Italian broadcasting organisation.

In a 1968 report from La Scala, Lord Harewood was generally enthusiastic but anxious about a number of lapses of taste and quality, finding casting occasionally problematic. He heaped blame on the acting of Rita Orlandi Malaspina, who replaced Leontyne Price as Amelia in *Ballo*. Orlandi Malaspina's 'involvement in the proceedings reached a peak of a sort in Act II, when she promenaded round the gibbet and its surroundings with all the emotion of a hostess showing off her roses after rain when the slugs are out'.[61] However, Nicolai Ghiaurov's 'truly wonderful voice and spacious singing' made him an ideal Zaccaria in *Nabucco*. Harewood found the chorus 'at the peak of its form, which means I suppose singing better than any other ... chorus in the world'.[62] About the same period Harold Rosenthal found much to respect in Karajan's – and La Scala orchestra's – account of *Cavalleria rusticana*: 'Karajan possesses the ability to make music like *Cavalleria* sound much better than it actually is. There was nothing tawdry about this performance, and the playing of the Scala orchestra was superb. It was the kind of performance that left the listener with the impression that La Scala's orchestra is the best opera orchestra in the world – and the same remarks apply to the chorus.'[63] Rosenthal also enjoyed Giorgio Strehler's direction for *Cavalleria*, which used stylised movement of the characters to suggest the doomed, ritualistic aspect of the Sicilian plot.

If La Scala was beginning to suffer from a financial squeeze and not quite living up to its creative potential, the House was far from moribund at the end of the 1960s. Claudio Abbado would soon come into his maturity as a musician and artist, and bring the House new vigour.

By 1962 quality, fitfully present in Milan, was quite lacking in Rome. The Italian capital's Teatro dell'Opera had been suffering for some time from slack artistic standards and poor box office figures. There was no sovrintendente, and Rome's mayor sacked the deputy head who had been in charge in the absence of an intendant. The eighty-four-year-old Tullio Serafin was brought in as 'artistic consultant', which meant excellent conducting.

Massimo Bogianckino was appointed Rome's artistic director as from the 1963–64 season, with Serafin continuing as the 'consultant'. Bogianckino had studied piano with Alfred Cortot in Paris and composition at the Santa Cecilia Academy in Rome. He was a professor of musicology at the University of Perugia and eventually served, from 1986 to 1989 as the mayor of Florence. He possessed a keen aesthetic sense, and had written a book on stagecraft in opera, *L'interpretazione scenografica nel teatro musicale*, Perugia, 1979.

The first production organised by Bogianckino was an acclaimed *Falstaff*, which Giulini conducted and which Zeffirelli staged and designed. The star was Tito Gobbi. Although William Weaver for *Opera* heartily approved, he stopped short of ecstasy:

> Zeffirelli's production was apparently much less arty than his London *Falstaff* (of which I know only the newspaper reports); this was a rural, simple world. The opera's plot became a kind of village practical joke, and the sadistic sting was taken out of the last act by having Falstaff pummelled by elf-like children. Giulini made the orchestra play as it has seldom played in years, and the chorus in the last act was faultless. Gobbi's Falstaff is well known. Personally, I find it somewhat heavy and humourless; but this artist's authority is such that even in a mistaken interpretation he carries the evening.[64]

Lord Harewood welcomed Giulini's strong presence in Rome and hoped it might continue. 'So much can be learnt from Giulini's thoroughness of work, and so much does he give to all artists who come in contact with him, that it would be to the general gain of opera if he had a permanent musical home where he could work steadily and regularly under conditions congenial to him.'[65] But Giulini insisted on stable casts and lengthy rehearsal periods for his new productions, and no Big Four House was prepared to offer him such 'congenial conditions' on a regular basis. Zeffirelli, however, shone in the Rome setting at a time when he might have preferred to work at La Scala.

Bogianckino brought Rome very close to Big Four standard for the four brief years of his tenure. His first season closed with a Giulini–Visconti collaboration: a 'revolutionary' *Nozze di Figaro* with sets designed by the director and Filippo Sanjust. The production, which reflected the leftist ideology of the time, indicated a growing politicis-ation of opera in Italy. In keeping with Visconti's habit, however, the political 'tilt' could be justified by suggestions inherent in da Ponte's libretto. Working from an 'assertive' directorial personality, Visconti pitted the oppressive Count against an angry, proletarian Figaro – 'a role symbolized by the riding-boot that Figaro polishes ominously on the stage, while in the music he vows much less bitterly to play the guitar and make the Count dance to his tune'.[66]

Another Giulini–Visconti collaboration, which opened in Rome on 20 November 1965, was the Paris version of *Don Carlos* in Italian. William Weaver wrote, 'Giulini's conducting was beyond praise; I have never heard him give a more penetrating, well-paced reading of an opera.'[67] Bogianckino, in a filmed BBC interview, called Visconti a demanding director. He pointed out that Visconti seldom changed his ideas during the rehearsal period. Bogianckino said: 'He works hand in hand with the conductor, and when the conductor is good, the result is good.'

Once again the team of Visconti and Giulini had consciously created an integrated production. In a significant assessment, Visconti stated in the same interview that the overall purpose of staging is to 'serve the music'. He continued, 'I try to listen when Maestro Giulini is working with the singers in the beginning – I try to see what he is asking of the singers . . . I try to serve his conception.' Giulini himself felt that a production should not go against the music, but that it would be wrong to say that the music was the most important element. 'The difficulty is to find a producer with great talent, personality and sensibility.' Giulini sought 'a collaboration where the chorus, the singing – everything – is one thing'.

The 1966–67 Rome season opened with a notable *Rigoletto* directed by Eduardo De Filippo with sets by Sanjust. Giulini again conducted. Although Renata Scotto as Gilda seemed involved, Weaver did not entirely approve, writing of how she 'keeps "acting" as if her life depended on it, and the amount of waste motion (and emotion) is immense.' Pavarotti as the Duke was by contrast indulging in a rather easygoing performance. In Weaver's words, he 'obviously does not ponder problems of interpreting the Duke; he simply opens his mouth and sings. His Duke is traditional, all exterior, but likeable. And he was in very good voice.'[68] In spite of his general approval of Giulini's conducting in this production, Weaver deplored his wholesale cuts. The next generation of conductors, chief among them Abbado and Riccardo Muti, made it a common practice to restore traditional cuts in an effort literally to fulfil the composer's intention.

Bogianckino's tenure at Rome came to an end a few weeks before the opening of the 1967–68 season. Critics felt the production of *Trovatore*, which opened the season, typified Bogianckino's fondness for venturesome stagings with a polemical twist. An unusual creative spirit, allied with administrative ability, had enabled Bogianckino to bring the House lustre for a few years. But for the time being Rome's glory days were over.

PART FOUR

THE 1970s
A Radical Era

FOURTEEN

LA SCALA 1970–80

There'll Always Be an Italy

THE STUDENT UNREST of the 1960s, which grew out of protests in America against the Vietnam war, extended to Europe late in that decade and during much of the following one. In the early 1970s high unemployment and inflation throughout the continent led to social, political and cultural unrest. Awareness of the gravity of these issues inspired practitioners of the senior arts to make social commentary through their work. The operatic world was drawn into the arena of political comment and debate, reflecting social upheavals.

Italy witnessed its own specific manifestations of these phenomena. Throughout the country, popular disaffection with the establishment was increasing dramatically from the level of the previous decade. Political and economic questions coloured the work of many Italian Houses. Student and leftist demonstrations in protest against economic conditions were held throughout Italy, with La Scala not exempted. Many opening nights at the theatre were turned into highly visible focal points for rallies against government policy. Political ideology also became a crux in a number of important opera stagings.

In an atmosphere of crisis, battle was joined over scandals within Italian opera houses. At one point a singer's denunciation led the police to seize La Scala's accounts. Chief administrator Antonio Ghiringhelli was put on trial for embezzlement. The staff of the Rome Opera rebelled, alleging management incompetence and favouritism in the distribution of free tickets. The Rome staff also claimed that certain singers received larger fees than the maximum agreed scale. But despite public outcry, many Italians of this time tended to react fatalistically to revelations of disorder and corruption within their national institutions, which meant that grass-roots pressure for change was lacking.

Inflation was a worldwide problem during this period, and badly affected opera houses. The Met and Covent Garden suffered severely, but La Scala also felt the effects. Since corporate sponsorship was not yet part of the life of Italian artistic institutions, the government had to pick up the slack. As opera house deficits increased, the government found it more and more difficult to cover them. Although the insufficient subsidy allocated under the Corona law of 1967 was raised in 1971 by another 3 billion lire, the total sum remained less than generous. In 1972 the *New York Times* underscored the secrecy surrounding financial matters at the House. It termed La Scala's total budget 'something of a mystery, believed to be somewhere near $10 million a year. The city of Milan and the central government in Rome cover the deficit, which is said to have amounted to an average of $3 million in each of the last few years.'[1]

Inefficiency, wastage and misplaced priorities characterised Italian society at large. Guido Carli, the governor of the Bank of Italy, said, 'The efforts of the State have provided Italians with excellent sweet cakes distributed in plenty along a magnificent network of motorways, but not schools nor hospitals nor law courts.'[2] Similar problems troubled La Scala, where there were a great many mouths to feed: by the 1970s staff totalled 1,200. They were organised into elected 'commissions', which had a say in artistic decisions as well as working conditions. The latter had been significantly improved by the early 1970s. Workers at the House enjoyed pension and sickness benefits, as well as overtime payments and abbreviated working hours. At the same time, these additional expenses proved a burden for a financially overstretched House, whose management made few moves to increase its efficiency. In 1972 Roger Brunyate, a British observer at the House, found a disorganised and inefficient body of creative individuals.

> The orchestra, for example, takes a vote at the end of each season for or against the return of each conductor, and it is difficult for the management to resist its wishes. . . .
> Chorus rehearsals with piano generally last two hours, but as they rarely start on time and are interrupted by a fifteen-minute

coffee break this works out as two periods of about 45 minutes each. Not only are discipline problems more acute in the absence of a professional force of stage managers, but the time taken up in organizing such large numbers is enormous. Imagine that the scene to be rehearsed involves sections of the chorus entering from two or three different places. The chorus members have to be assembled in their respective wings, and maestri have to be given their cues to send each group onstage, another maestro has to go around with a large mouth-organ giving the chorus their note, and still more maestri have to be stationed at the point of arrival to reinforce the conductor's beat. If something goes wrong there is no easy mechanism for making adjustments. . . . Two or three false starts . . . and half a rehearsal will have been expended on a mere 30 seconds of music.

It is not surprising that nearly half the remaining time should be wasted in argument. This is most amusing to watch from the sidelines as the person will typically explain at great length exactly why it is impossible for him to do what is asked, only to end with a long-suffering '*però*' ('however') and then go off and do it after all! . . . Yet there is a wealth of talent and enthusiasm there: occasionally, when it is drawn together by a powerful conductor or producer, or gets kindled in a moment of spontaneous combustion, it can result in a performance that virtually defines the nature of opera in at least one of its aspects.[3]

Tradition and professional competence, as well as collegial pride, helped this quintessentially Italian institution to function under chaotic conditions, however erratically. At times the swing was towards disaster, at others towards genius. But La Scala did not need to strive hard to achieve world-class quality, as Covent Garden had had to do under Solti in the 1960s. If the right principals were present, there was latent quality in the House, ready to be drawn upon. La Scala personnel shared a respect for the operas of the standard repertoire and an understanding of what makes for a great performance.

Composer Luciano Chailly resigned as artistic director at the end of the 1970–71 season. He was replaced by Massimo Bogianckino, who had held the same post in Rome. At the end of 1971 Ghiringhelli was acquitted on all counts of embezzlement. The following year, after his name had been cleared, his retirement was announced. He had been sovrintendente at the House for twenty-seven years and recently had been in poor health.[4]

During this period, politicisation began to be a factor in the management of Italian opera houses. The Italian establishment was opening up to new blood as leftist candidates were more and more successful in elections. Ghiringhelli's successor was Paolo Grassi, a man of the theatre and an avowed Socialist. Shortly after the end of the war Grassi had been theatre critic for the leftist journal *Avanti!* and a strong advocate of a politically involved theatre. With his friend Giorgio Strehler he had founded and directed Milan's outstanding Piccolo Teatro in 1947. The two founders' manifesto linked social awareness to a policy of pluralism:

> After the rhetoric of theatre for the masses and the restrictions of fascist propaganda we believe it is time to begin to work in depth so that later we can gain a wider audience. We hope that the theatregoers who come to us will become the nucleus who will help to fill bigger theatres; unless we deceive ourselves, every civilisation works by bringing different groups of people together and integrating them into a richer and more varied unit.[5]

Grassi brought his views of a popular theatre to La Scala. His task was exceedingly difficult. The House had many constituencies to please. Besides a desire to improve the level of performances, Grassi warmly agreed with those who wanted to make La Scala more open to middle and working-class audiences. Beginning a 'dialogue with the public', he planned performances especially for factory workers and regional tours to towns in Lombardy. He issued invitations to dress rehearsals. Lists of recipients were well balanced: they included students and soldiers, as well as 'people of some social, intellectual and political importance'.[6] Audiences for workers' and students' concerts grew from 15,958 in the 1972 season to 102,555 in 1977.

Grassi found an additional role for the Piccola Scala as a venue for experimental repertoire, including operas by Luciano Berio, Luigi Cortese and Salvatore Sciarrino. The Piccola Scala's productions were also toured in the Lombardy area. Nor did Grassi neglect the physical aspect of the House: a new lighting system was installed, as well as electronically operated stage machinery, and even a new curtain, as the old one had seen eighty years' service.

In 1973, caught in an inflation squeeze, the Italian government decided to stop covering La Scala's overdraft. It began for the first time to allow the state-subsidised opera houses to accumulate debt to banks. In a fit of misguided generosity, permission was extended retroactively as of 1969. This meant that already by 1974 bank interest alone for La Scala's overdraft totalled 1.4 billion lire annually. Aliki Andris-Michalaros wrote at that time in *Opera News* that true reform of state opera funding 'remains an illusion: not only has it not yet appeared on the parliamentary agenda, it is now the centre of one of the government's most torrid political debates'.[7]

Premieres commissioned by La Scala during Grassi's tenure included Luigi Nono's, *Al Gran sole carico d'amore*, which had its first performance not in the opera house itself but in the Teatro Lirico of Milan in April 1975. Nono's strongly ideological opera broadly reflected Grassi's own political stance. The work – whose title may be translated as *In the Great Sunlight Charged with Love* – featured militant women characters in the days of the Paris Commune and the Russian Revolution, and eschewed stage directions in favour of improvised movement. Nono used a wide range of musical resources, including live and recorded sound, two choruses, and even the singing of political texts by a quartet of sopranos. Witnessing a 1978 concert performance at the Edinburgh Festival, William Mann called it 'eventful, excitable, beautiful and ultimately moving', despite its pastiche structure and its programmatic ideological content.[8] The conductor of the premiere, Claudio Abbado, was also sympathetic to leftist politics. The stage director, Yuri Lyubimov, was allowed to travel from Moscow to work in Milan after Enrico Berlinguer, the chief of the Italian Communist party, pleaded Lyubimov's case with the Soviet authorities. La Scala was taking on some of the political colour of its time and place. The Milanese audience began once more to be fascinated by the goings-on at their local temple of high musical art, as they had been in the days of Callas and Tebaldi.

Although the standard fairly remained high, during the early 1970s new Scala productions did not quite attain the level of the previous decade. Borrowed productions appeared more frequently, as they did elsewhere around the world of opera. However, by this time it was normal in Milan – and elsewhere in Italy – for a home-made new production to be assigned a serious stage director. Harold Rosenthal wrote in *Opera* that provincial Italian Houses like the Fenice in Venice, the Massimo at Palermo 'and of course the Comunale in Florence, are as much concerned with the visual and dramatic side of opera as the musical.'[9]

The opening production of the Scala season, on 7 December each year, generally showed the House at its finest. But other new productions often presented less well-known works, many of which were of inferior quality. Besides, some productions of standard works were as much as two decades old. Routine performances suffered from cast changes. Brunyate reported that major roles in a repertory work were often sung by 'three or four different singers over the course of the season, so that the same group of singers seldom perform together more than once, let alone find time for rehearsal. Tradition in such circumstances, without the constant expenditure of time and talent, quickly becomes mere routine.'[10] Even worse, planning sometimes went wildly astray: in the 1974–75 season, nineteen previously announced opera evenings and seventeen concerts were erased from the *cartellone*.

In 1971 La Scala experienced multiple calamities in a single production. *I Puritani*, due to open on 19 February, was postponed for three days because the baritone, Dan Jordanescu, fell ill. Then Freni and Pavarotti, the stars, became indisposed, causing another postponement. On 27 February conductor Riccardo Muti left the production. On 1 March the stage director, Franco Enriquez, 'said he found it impossible to guarantee a performance with the new cast in so short a time'.[11]

The 1972–73 season, Grassi's first as sovrintendente, was marked by extremes of splendour and mediocrity. In a *Ballo* staged by Zeffirelli, Abbado fell ill at the last moment and was replaced by Gianandrea Gavazzeni, whose work was summed up as 'dull' by the *Opera* critic. An American soprano rather lacking in experience, Lou Ann Wyckoff, sang Amelia, while Domingo's Riccardo was resounding. 'The second act was bel canto at its best ... while his death scene was dramatic enough to satisfy everyone.'[12] The great team of Caballé and Cossotto played in an unforgettable *Norma* which opened on 22 December. 'Rarely have the duets sounded more beautiful or been sung with greater care and love. The voices seemed to melt into one another, the incredibly difficult cadenzas seemed as light as butterfly wings, no shouting, no distortion, no squeezing. These were moments which will be cherished for a long time.'[13] However, Peter Hoffer wrote that the *Don Pasquale* which opened on 15 January 1973 'must surely rank as one of the worst productions put on by this theatre for many years. . . . Donizetti himself would have left during the first act.'[14] Wladimiro Ganzarolli was a well-known singer who abandoned the cast of this show. The production was replete with gags and slapstick turns which the *Corriere della Sera* critic found inappropriate: they did not have 'too many stylistic scruples, but simply the intention to get a laugh'. The entire production was 'a game which Donizetti would perhaps not have liked very much'.[15]

Worse still was the January 1974 *La Favorita*. Designer Tito Varisco 'decided the old sets [by Nicola Benois] could not be used, and proceeded to design his own, in the Benois style, but just not quite making it beyond ponderous dullness'.[16] The conductor, Bruno Bartoletti, became indisposed. Pavarotti, singing the tenor lead, fell ill, but decided to appear nonetheless. The chronic booers went into action. The American critic, Susan Gould wrote:

From the first sagging phrases of the overture, the infamous '*loggione*' [the gallery] began to express its more or less justified disapproval, which of course did not help put the performers at ease. As the curtain rose on the dreary scenery, Ivo Vinco, as Baldassare, set the pace for the evening by emitting a series of dry, wildly off pitch sounds, followed immediately by an unrecognizable (except visually) Pavarotti: husky voice with uncertain high notes. It must be said that Pavarotti, while sounding obviously ill, did have a few good moments, whereas Vinco had none whatsoever. Grumblings from the audience were not quieted by the arrival onstage, nude midriff atremble, of Luisa Machinizzi as Inès, who in the terror of her Scala debut succeeded in singing a quarter-tone sharp for the entire evening. Piero Cappuccilli did not sound any better than his two gentlemen colleagues, and what was worse, he kept hesitating, singing out of rhythm, or stopping altogether; during rehearsals he had been flying back and forth from Bari, at the other end of the country.[17]

Mezzo Fiorenza Cossotto attempted in vain to salvage the situation:

Cossotto came forth with some reassuring rich tone and relatively refined style. She tried desperately to keep Cappuccilli in line during their duet, but even a rapid turn of her head and a fulminating dart of her eyes could do nothing to stop him from singing several bars in front of her. By now the public, even that of the boxes and stalls, was in constant turmoil, and it remained for Cossotto to calm it with a respectable rendition of 'O mio Fernando'. But 'ahimé!' in an excess of self-assurance and a paucity of taste, La Cossotto shot forth at the end an unwritten high note and missed. Result, a theatre-wide groan, then defensive applause, then comments, as she stood apparently unmoved, and little by little the applause won out, so much so that the poor Inès, who had begun to make her next entrance, backed hastily offstage. Laughter, more applause, more protests, and the opera dragged on its excruciating, embarrassing way through oceans of hoarse sounds, lopsided rhythms, broken high notes, orchestral imbalance, and the one saving grace, magnificent choral singing thanks to chorus master Romano Gandolfi.[18]

While some productions floundered, Claudio Abbado's conducting restored a generous measure of quality to the House. He had been named resident conductor in 1969 and music director in 1971. In contrast to Karajan, Abbado spent a good deal of time in Milan and took care to give opera performances at La Scala a recognisable character. He also adopted an original and highly influential view of opera performance. Taking his cue from the movement towards 'authentic' performance of pre-twentieth-century works that arose in the 1960s, Abbado reconstructed the original score by restoring traditionally cut passages, forbidding singers' bravura interpolations and insisting on a general tightening of musical decorum. An early instance of a 'reconstructionist' performance was Abbado's Salzburg *Barbiere* of 1968 and 1969, later transferred to La Scala. The conductor revised the working score against a copy which had belonged to the composer. Harold Rosenthal felt Abbado had purged it 'of 150 years of bad operatic traditions'.[19] A 1972 video recording with the Scala forces, presents Abbado's clearly delineated approach to the work. The orchestra gives him an astonishing variety of tone and indeed every single detail he asks for. What he seeks is sometimes more thoughtful than humorous – or 'fun'. Many – though not all – of the singers' interpolations in the big arias have been removed, something which deprives the work of some of its beloved wit and playfulness. But Abbado is a magician at blending voices. The 'Zitti, zitti' trio (Count, Rosina and Figaro) seems to have been so thoroughly rehearsed as to allow for a nonchalant and very funny performance.

Abbado was not the first Italian conductor to rid Italian operas of their excess baggage. In 1969 Vittorio Gui recalled that Rossini's autograph score of *Barbiere* had been published by Ricordi thirty years previously, and that he, Gui, had conducted from it at La Scala. Abbado, however, was the conductor who made reconstruction 'official' for performances of Rossini operas. In 1969 the Italian conductor and musicologist Alberto Zedda published his own critical edition of *Barbiere*, removing the latterly added parts for trombone and timpani, restoring the original pair of piccolos and replacing the triangle with bells as Rossini had intended. Zedda also corrected dynamic and phrase markings to reflect the composer's manuscript indications. Crucial arias were stripped of their traditional embellishments, which had crept into editions previously held to be standard. In 1972, at Florence, Riccardo Muti continued the Rossini reconstructionist movement by leading what was probably the first uncut performance of *Guillaume Tell* in the twentieth century.

In one sense the reconstructionist conductors were following in the path of Toscanini, who, insisted that the marks in the composer's score were meant for conductors to understand and interpret faithfully. Excising florid embellishments from bel canto arias was felt by many opera lovers, however, to be puritanical censorship, a foul subtraction of beloved – and harmless – vocal fireworks. Likewise, moving the spotlight away from the singers to the conductor's vision of the score, no matter how loyal, implied a deep shift in the perception of opera. It shed a different light upon the central focus of the performance.

The 1973–74 season was opened not with Verdi but with Rossini's *L'Italiana in Algeri*, with Abbado conducting with great restraint. The *Opera* critic thought the effort puritanical. Under Abbado's direction, Susan Gould wrote:

> the cleaning process tends almost to be overdone: rigorously strict rhythms, dynamics meticulously held to a level rarely above or below mezzo forte, voices treated as additional members of the orchestra, all contribute to a sleek atmosphere of academic correctness which, while undoubtedly refined and safe from all risk of vulgarity, is also self-conscious, constrained, and lacking in spirit.[20]

Massimo Mila was also unhappy with Abbado's 'austere' approach, writing, 'This new, more reserved orchestral sound suits the interpretative criteria of the conductor Claudio Abbado, who in his orchestral direction is the most authoritative representative of the Calvinistic tendency to precision, equilibrium, and objectivity, in reaction to the nineteenth-century imbalances and excesses.'[21] However, the *Corriere*'s headline called the show 'irresistible'. Abbado's conducting, wrote the critic, fittingly underscored the Mozartean elements of the score. Jean-Pierre Ponnelle's staging went hand in hand with Abbado's light and elegant touch. The delicacy of scenic elements and expressive lighting helped bring about what the writer called 'the maximum of directorial felicity'. Teresa Berganza as Isabella joined vocal virtuosity with 'a musical nature of the rarest, most joyous simplicity'.[22]

Grassi brought his friend and collaborator Giorgio Strehler to do stagings at La Scala. Strehler's ideological convictions were woven into his work. His 1971 Scala production of *Simon Boccanegra*, which reached the stage even before Grassi was made sovrintendente, was a memorable example of politically involved direction which had full objective justification in the score and libretto. Sets were by Ezio Frigerio. Abbado conducted the premiere. The fruitful Abbado–Strehler collaboration, which would be repeated in the future, reflected the two men's shared political and social vision. Peter Hoffer wrote:

> Strehler's political and social commitments found their expression in a story which, shed of its silly patina of family entanglements, is of great topicality: Establishment versus

People. The aristocratic Fiesco's dislike of Simon, Paolo's ple-
beian dealing and scheming mixed with political opportunism,
and Simon's losing fight against both, defended only by his
honesty, are repeated on today's political scene ad infinitum;
and Strehler therefore concentrates on this aspect of the opera,
making it as dramatically taut and contemporary as possible.
Claudio Abbado ably seconds him in this, as his fiery temperament, brilliant attack and spanking pace amply bear witness . . .

It is said that *Simon Boccanegra* has a special place in
Abbado's heart. After hearing his reading, this is easy to believe.
Tender and violent in turns, he makes every bar count.[23]

A local Italian critic emphasised the unity of the Abbado–Strehler
collaboration. The action of the opera, he wrote, 'issues from the
details of Abbado's and Strehler's artistic work – clearly, flowingly,
and derived out of the richness of the emotions. Music, staging and
singing are united in a single concept: Verdi's artistic vision.'[24] Abbado
had done spring cleaning on Verdi's score as well. This time Massimo
Mila, writing in *La Stampa*, enjoyed the result: 'Claudio Abbado's
conducting purges the score of all those hellish *sforzati* accents which
cheap conductors strew over Verdi's music, treating the notes as if
they were meant to be forced out with cudgels. Nor does it work to
the detriment of the virile energy which, in this drama of iron men,
is the supreme strength of Verdi's art.'[25]

Another Abbado – Strehler collaboration at La Scala was the 1975
Macbeth, one of the finest of all post-war opera stagings. It was reported
that the production had been granted ninety hours of stage rehearsals,
whereas most new productions have a fraction of that figure: lengthy
on-stage rehearsals are costly and tend to interfere with other operas
being presented during the same time period. Strehler read Shakespeare's text as 'the drama of two lonely people who never meet on
the same ground, who sink into the void of madness – an "infantile"
madness, a reversion to childhood in the case of Lady Macbeth, progressive self-destruction for him'. Not surprisingly, Strehler emphasised in his production 'the "political part", and the great theme of
liberty for the "oppressed"' – a theme he found in the chorus that
opens Act Four. He dressed the pair in voluminous costumes, 'meaning
that the Macbeths are overwhelmed by roles too big for them to fill.

Both principals were almost engulfed in colossal robes, with virtually unmanageable trains.' Shirley Verrett as Lady Macbeth 'gave a tigress interpretation altogether at odds with this conception of the work, though in every other way magnificent'.[26] Piero Cappuccilli as Macbeth fitted Strehler's vision. From the start, wrote Brian Magee, 'the performance took off. It swept through the evening with huge, self-confident ease, in a single span. Claudio Abbado's conducting was electrifying, the voltage at climaxes just about as high as this music can carry.'[27]

Abbado's musical maturity enabled him to conceive and elicit from his Scala forces a degree of emotional intensity that Karajan arguably never attained. In a 1976 recording of Verdi's *Macbeth*, made in Milan with the original cast, Abbado was at the peak of his career as an opera conductor. The orchestra plays with extraordinary emotional range and an almost singer-like cantabile. The chorus under Romano Gandolfi is more mixed in quality. In the Act One chorus, the witches generate excitement, even if the sound is a bit too covered for some tastes. The Act Four choral opening could not have been bettered. The Scala forces seem infinitely flexible, as intense and dolorous in a *ppp* as in a *fff* roar.

Nicolai Ghiaurov is a rich-toned Banquo. Light glints dance on top of a deep timbre. A majestic performer, he uses his great reserves of power wisely, stylishly and tastefully; and acts through the voice most effectively at times. In 'Studia il passo . . . Come dal ciel precipità', Abbado guides Ghiaurov into what is again a black intensity. The conductor emphasises the lines in the horns and low strings to bring out the fear in the scene. Plácido Domingo makes a most impressive Macduff, with his impassioned delivery and his baritonal low register suiting the *tinta* of the opera.

Piero Cappuccilli's Macbeth is more conventional. A consummately Italian performer, he brings the role to life through the voice, controlling the breath brilliantly but not displaying emotional involvement at every moment. His low register is very good for a Verdi baritone, his top is sound and he has an appealing range of tonal colours. Verrett's 'Vieni! t'affretta!' which is moving indeed, has an imposing low register remaining from her days as a mezzo. The top here is sound, with the C and even the D flat successfully produced.

The treacherous aria makes for exciting listening and Verrett sings full out, with intelligence and musicianship. In the great duet that closes Act Three, 'Ora di morte e di vendetta', Cappuccilli acts convincingly and Verrett, at the height of her passionate singing, recalls Callas. By the time Cappuccilli's Macbeth approaches his death ('Sol la bestemmia, ahi lasso! la nenia tua sarà!') he is as emotionally mighty as the rest of the cast: a bitter man lying in the wreckage of his own barbaric power.

Together with memorable achievements, controversies also loomed over the Scala stage. Luchino Visconti, who had agreed to return to the House in a new staging of the *Ring*, fell ill and abandoned the project. Two years later, on 17 March 1976, he died. In a much-criticised move, the House's artistic director, Bogianckino, handed over *Walküre* and *Siegfried* to Luca Ronconi, with the assistance of Pier Luigi Pizzi on sets and costumes. Ronconi, who had started in the theatre as an actor, was making his mark in Italy as a director of opera and stage plays, particularly at the Scala and Florence's Teatro Comunale. With a flair for irony, Ronconi often sent up the work he was staging rather than treating it on its own terms. He also considered opera in general a rather laughable art, a balloon deserving to be pricked. Ronconi's Wagner signalled the beginnings of a shift at La Scala to ironic, highly personal stagings by directors who did not consistently keep the composer's intentions in mind.

Bogianckino resigned from the Scala at the end of the 1974 season and went on to become artistic director of Florence's Teatro Comunale. In an interview evidently alluding to the controversial Ronconi *Ring* over which he had presided, he stated that 'it was the very lack of possibility to create, caused by the hierarchical system at La Scala, that had led him to leave, even though his rapport with his colleagues was of the best'.[28] When Bogianckino left La Scala for Florence, he had the *Ring* moved to the Teatro Comunale.

Financial difficulties were an even more serious problem for La Scala than artistic controversy. Inflation and rising salaries were a worldwide bane of opera houses at this time, particularly at Covent Garden, where costs were rising at a rate well beyond the annual increase in the government grant. Even though La Scala's difficulties did not threaten the House's very existence, they were scarcely petty. In 1974 the Scala's Moscow tour was threatened with cancellation and went ahead at the last moment only after the Istituto San Paolo, a major Italian bank, granted the House a loan of 400 million lire. Another problem occurred when the annual state subsidy was delayed in reaching the House's account, which frequently happened. This meant the administration had to cover immediate expenses by more borrowing at a high bank rate. Debts mounted and government intransigence grew. On 20 March 1976 the Italian press reported the cancellation of another Scala tour, this one in celebration of the bicentenary year of American independence. The government had refused to allocate the needed extra funds for the tour. Even worse, Rome imposed an ultimatum upon all the thirteen Italian opera theatres which it funded: budgets must be balanced before the federal subsidy (60 billion lire altogether) would be deposited into the Houses' accounts. La Scala's share was to be 9.5 billion lire, a sum widely deemed insufficient to ensure continued functioning at a high artistic level.[29]

With the Italian government less and less willing to underwrite the activities of opera, Paolo Grassi concluded that the House's financial straits made his position untenable. He called a press conference on 25 March to protest against the cancellation of the American tour and to present an appeal, signed by himself and the mayor of Milan. Referring to La Scala's distinctive position in the culture of Italy and the entire world, Grassi pleaded that 'special legislative measures be taken to insure the maintenance of the artistic level and international dimensions which are the characteristics of this great theatre'.[30] Even though he was a man of the left, Grassi also found it necessary to demand that 'archaic' union rules be abrogated, mentioning music rehearsals that had to be cut short because of work schedules. He threatened to resign, taking Abbado with him, if his demands were not met. Several other Italian sovrintendenti blasted Grassi for 'cultural Gaullism' at the expense of the other national opera houses. Scala staff initiated strikes, which affected a number of performances and brought about the postponement of a new work by Sylvano Bussotti, the composer who was artistic director of La Fenice Opera in Venice. At this point, on 9 April, Grassi resigned, with immediate and supposedly irrevocable effect. But all the Italian political parties, together with leading cultural figures, united to beg him to rescind his resignation. On 10 May he agreed.

In July a new work agreement was drawn up. It stipulated a measure of worker participation in the management of the theatre – including questions of costs, work schedule and even programming – but left veto power in the hands of the administration. This enabled Grassi to continue the administrative running of La Scala. As for the House's heavy expenses, Grassi agreed to cut salaries to guest singers, conductors and directors. New productions were to be cut back and additional performances of each production were added. These changes were agreeable to the federal government, which reinstated its support for the American tour.

The Kleiber–Zeffirelli *Otello*, with Domingo in the title role, opened the 1976–77 season. Youthful leftists took advantage of the musical event to stage a big, noisy demonstration in front of the theatre. An extra 1,000 police were placed on duty and the whole spectacle, both opera and demonstration, was broadcast live on Italian television. The viewing audience was almost as large as a typical televised football game. Susan Gould wrote in *Opera*, that the 'TV reporters at the end of each act all-but-gleefully announced the stages of protest, destruction, and injury as the youthful mob was dispersed and in part arrested'. Grassi, when interviewed, 'felt called upon to defend his theatre from Sylvano Bussotti's accusations of "triumphalism"'.[31] Domingo later expressed surprise that the young people chose to attack the Scala, which under Grassi had recast its image as an elitist institution:

> I thought it strange that this protest came precisely when the then general director of La Scala, Paolo Grassi, a brilliant man with forty years' theatrical experience, was doing everything in his power to open the theatre to everyone, when La Scala was registering a hundred thousand special attendances annually, at very low prices, of young people, students, and trade union members, and when television was finally beginning to bring some important productions into millions of homes throughout the country.[32]

While the political furies raged outside the House, an outstanding performance was being witnessed within. Gould found that Freni's Desdemona encompassed the whole of the character, including 'warmth, tenderness, femininity, yet also pride and anger'. Domingo had sung his first Otello the previous year at Hamburg, despite the admonitions of critics who feared the demanding part would do him vocal damage. Gould praised his 'passion, lyricism, virility, and touching portrayal of a noble being capable of violence as well as of compassion, destroyed by conflicting feelings too strong for him to conquer'. Nor did she long for a more declamatory performance: 'If there are those who miss the more powerful high notes of other tenors, I for one would not sacrifice the musicianship, intelligence, and beautiful singing of Domingo for a few bars of music.'[33]

A videotape of the opening performance displays great singing, playing and conducting. While Kleiber's musical direction is knowledgeable and competent, there is nothing safe about it. The rhythms, attacks, cut-offs and crescendi flash with pagan fire. The phrase 'elemental force' might have been invented to describe the opening scene. In Domingo's own words, Kleiber 'made the orchestra play feelings, not notes'.[34] Domingo sings with absolute assurance and spontaneity, as well as forceful dramatic impact. His low register is so strong that one might mistake him for a baritone, lending even more weight to the character.

Zeffirelli's production, however, was less than triumphant, reflecting his recent bias in favour of spectacle and grandeur. Domingo enjoyed working with Zeffirelli, who had learned much from Laurence Olivier's portrayal of Othello. But Zeffirelli seems not to have reached Piero Cappuccilli as Iago, who strikes attitudes instead of acting, and casts rhetorical gestures into the air. The director, relying on props and stage business, overemphasises the obvious: Iago fiddling with an hourglass at 'la morta è il nulla', patting the handkerchief and even placing it on his head before folding it and inserting it in his doublet. Worse, Zeffirelli distorts emotion by sometimes physically distancing Otello and Desdemona in their duets.

While La Scala was mounting traditional productions like Zeffirelli's Otello, the House went on experimenting. Moses und Aron opened on 6 February 1977, twelve years after the brilliant Covent Garden production; the Met would not present Schoenberg's great work until 1999. Two days earlier a fire had broken out in the House. The velvet curtain had been ruined and stage machinery damaged, but the stage crew banked the flames before the fire brigade could reach the theatre. 'The Scala workers threw themselves into the task of repair with the same energy that had rebuilt the theatre in 1946 (Christoph von Dohnányi said he had never seen any human feat so impressive as the stage swarming with almost violently laborious men), and the first night of *Moses und Aron* went ahead as scheduled. . . .'[35] At the end of the performance the audience applauded the stagehands.

The 200th anniversary year of the theatre was celebrated with a feast of Verdi operas, including some rarely heard ones. On 7 December 1977 was seen the first Scala performance of the 1867 *Don Carlos*, in a re-edited version with new material discovered by Andrew Porter at the Paris Opéra. Peter Conrad recalled Luca Ronconi's staging:

> Ronconi's *Don Carlos* treated Schiller's pageant as a Brechtian epic. It directed the traffic of history in obedience to political imperatives. Throughout the opera, in a protracted funeral march, a crowd of three hundred plodded across the stage from right to left, disappearing to re-enter and begin their unprogressive toil anew. This mob of troops, monks and grandees trundled trolleys of corpses, dragged crosses or wheeled floats with statues of the Grim Reaper: life unrolled endlessly toward annihilation. History was thus dramatized as a Triumph of Death.[36]

Ronconi's revisionist *Don Carlos* underscored the anti-establishment views prevailing at the House. At the same time, conceptualist stagings started to emerge there, the earliest of such efforts among the Big Four. In works where no political subtext could be discerned, a director might take a highly personal, even idiosyncratic view of the score and bend it to his vision. Jorge Lavelli directed a *Butterfly*, which opened 5 March 1978. Amazingly, the whole sequence of events in Giacosa's and Illica's libretto turned out to be the heroine's neurotic dream. According to the Milanese critic, Sergio Castagnino 'She rejects reality and creates for herself the people in her life, Sharpless, Goro, Yamadori, as puppets with whom she plays. In the end the fiction can no longer be supported. . . . The puppets become real people, and her suicide is the logical conclusion for a girl fully unprepared for life.'[37]

In 1977 Abbado was named artistic director, a position he held concurrently with the music directorship. His dedication to the musical well-being of the House, which recalled Solti's, paid considerable dividends. In a November 1978 news conference he addressed the issue of revivals and routine performances. He stated that the crucial thing was not how many revivals were done at La Scala – certainly financial stringencies ensured that there would be many – but 'how they were performed, the seriousness of the preparation and the casting'.[38] Towards the end of the 1970s, critics agreed in general that the level of routine performances had risen. Harold Rosenthal wrote that Abbado enjoyed his work and conducted many non-subscription performances, 'including those given for workers and students'.[39] Yuri Lyubimov had high praise for Abbado's artistry and dedication. After collaborating with him on the December 1979 Scala *Boris Godunov*, Lyubimov decided his early worries over Abbado's youth and lack of knowledge of Russian had been unfounded: 'Mussorgsky demands great maturity from a conductor. I later found out that Abbado has a veritable passion for his music, and I was surprised by the profoundness and meticulousness with which he approached the score, and by the power and subtlety of the orchestral sound he produced.'[40]

During this decade La Scala audiences continued to be given excellent singing. The period witnessed achievements by artists who, though perhaps not of Callas's calibre, were impressive. Opinion was divided over Shirley Verrett's shift upwards from mezzo. Peter Hoffer wrote of her Scala performance in *Samson et Dalila*, 'Verrett's voice has a rich, honey-like texture and a range nearer to a soprano's without loss of volume or quality within its range. To this is added her strong personality, temperament, physique, acting ability and musicianship – a combination ideal for Delilah.'[41] However, Walter Legge disagreed: 'I wish Verrett would listen to plain common sense. She is by achievement the best mezzo in the world. She should be forbidden to sing Norma.'[42]

Norma was a difficult part, which found few successful interpreters at this time. As Verrett had come to grief so too did Scotto in Turin: 'Scotto lacks the density of vocal colour, the heroic, metallic timbre and the breadth of sound needed to portray the extraordinarily complex psychology of the character.'[43] But she was commended for depicting the character through technique and musicianship. Montserrat Caballé was one of the few singers who were succeeding as Norma. Caballé was Scotto's polar opposite as a singing actress. Although she was less than successful in her efforts to open up on stage, her mezza voce, impressive breath control, legato line and pure, caressing tone, made her possibly the most revered diva of her day. In her Scala debut on 24 February 1970 she sang the name part of Donizetti's *Lucrezia Borgia*. A 14 May 1970 Rome performance of *Maria Stuarda*, by the same composer, typified her enthralling way with bel canto. 'To some spectators she recalled Tebaldi in her halcyon days. Above all in the third act, Caballé's singing was magical, enchanting, spell-binding. In the finale her interpretation was incomparably human and warm, her phrasing supple and her mezza voce ravishing.'[44]

In the audience at Rome during one of Caballé's *Maria Stuarda* performances was Luchino Visconti, in the company of Queen Frederika of Greece. In the dressing room, when Caballé began to disparage her own acting skills, Visconti demurred, telling her that her greatest assets were her remarkably expressive face and hands: so long as she used those to best effect, it was wholly unnecessary for her to engage in histrionics, for with a voice like hers, a look, a gesture were all she needed.'[45] In her youth Caballé had attended ballet school, where she was first introduced to music. She admitted in an early interview that her full figure had precluded a career in dance, but she sought afterwards to make movement an important part of her stage work. 'My favourite role,' she said, 'my very favourite role – is Salome. There is a little of everything in that role. . . .' Caballé smilingly recalled her dance training when she mentioned the part, with its celebrated Dance of the Seven Veils.[46] Singing the *Trovatore* Leonora, a relatively heavy role, in Naples in 1971, her attempts to engage in 'histrionics' were criticised: 'Caballé has one of the most beautiful voices of this century and her singing is always a lesson in style. However, she should not try to be dramatic and vehement because the effect sounds unnatural and forced.'[47] Performing the role of Leonora (*La Forza del destino*) for the very first time, Caballé entranced La Scala in June 1978. Her aria 'Madre, pietosa Vergine' was cheered so lustily that the performance was halted for several minutes.

Katia Ricciarelli was also notable among new singers. Born in 1946, she studied with Iris Adami-Corradetti, a leading Italian soprano of the 1930s and 1940s. At La Scala her Suor Angelica in 1973 met with a mixed reaction from the *Opera* critic: 'Ricciarelli has an attractive voice, well schooled and even, smooth and round. But it still lacks real personality and expression. That spells death in Puccini.'[49] Her debut as Violetta in Trieste, on 12 February 1976, was vocally commended, while her acting was not. 'Ricciarelli is, however, on the right road, and the triumphant success she achieved here should be the most encouraging stimulus.'[49] The following year Gualerzi was enthusiastic over an Anna Bolena Ricciarelli sang in Modena, calling it, perhaps 'the most convincing performance I have heard from her. The long melodic line and plangent cantilena so peculiar to Donizetti suit to perfection the timbre and emotive colour of "angelical" sopranos, especially when, in Ricciarelli's case, they are enhanced by polished beauty of sounds, mastery of legato, elegance of phrasing, more persuasive diction than usual...'[50] All too often, however, Ricciarelli showed vocal insecurity on stage. Her Alice Ford at Covent Garden in 1982 under Giulini was still deficient in character and in time she began to lose control over her voice. She tended to take on roles too heavy for her in a time when Verdi sopranos were scarce, and gradually her career declined.

Renata Tebaldi's many fans welcomed her back in two final Scala recitals in 1974. They closed the career of a unique singer. Her inimitable tone – as beautiful, at its best, as any sounds made by a human throat – her profound devotion to opera and her unique stage persona, all made her a diva among divas. Young mezzo Lucia Valentini (later Valentini-Terrani) replaced Teresa Berganza with great success in a 1973 Scala *Cenerentola*. In the 1982 *Falstaff* under Giulini she was a memorable Mistress Quickly, with the veiled tone working wonders.

Among tenors, Alfredo Kraus continued to draw enthusiastic admiration. In a 12 February 1976 performance of *Werther* at La Scala he had the audience in tears with his 'Pourquoi me réveiller'. Critics agreed that, despite a dry and not very big tone, Kraus's taste, style and 'nobility of vocal line' made him one of the memorable tenors of this century.[51] Kraus maintained that keeping physically fit helped him stay the course in his unusually long career. Reserved and intelligent, concentrated on his art, he gave much attention to singing technique and characterisation on stage. He confessed that the death of his teacher, Mercedes Llopart, magnified his tendency to introversion. 'After that, since I didn't have anyone to talk to, I had to think more.'[52]

José Carreras began his rise to stardom during the early 1970s. Born in Barcelona in 1946, his family toiled to survive in a Spain which was still suffering from the aftermath of its civil war (1936–39). His father had difficulty finding work after having fought on the Republican side. When his mother opened a hairdresser's establishment, young José would sing to her customers. 'With the tips they gave me,' he wrote later, 'I bought Coca-Cola, ice cream, and other wonderful children's nonsense.'[53] His parents urged him to develop his vocal potential. After graduating from the Barcelona Conservatory he began a rapid professional ascent; his youthful charm on and off stage, no less than his appealing lyric voice, helped him carve out a niche among tenors. From 1971 to 1973 he accepted engagements throughout Europe and North America in more than a dozen operas, including several lesser-known works. Working towards his first role at La Scala, he delighted audiences in provincial Italian theatres. In Parma in 1974 he was warmly praised as Arvino in *I Lombardi*: he 'conquered the audience with sheer beauty of timbre, sensitively judged phrasing and warmth of temperament'.[54] Harold Rosenthal also enjoyed his Alfredo (*La Traviata*) at Covent Garden in the same year: 'His fresh and often beautiful voice promises well.'[55]

Carreras's 1975 Scala debut, as Riccardo in Verdi's *Un Ballo in maschera*, was a triumph. Before the opening night the young tenor's morale was lifted by a moving gift from Giuseppe (Pippo) Di Stefano. Carreras tells the story in his autobiography:

> Pippo showed up unexpectedly at the opera house to watch our dress rehearsal. With his professional eye, he quietly observed the first act. Then, during the break, he burst into my dressing room and objected excitedly: 'Listen here, José! You can't make your debut at La Scala in that costume! It doesn't fit you, and besides it's dreadful! That won't do!' . . . When the

rehearsal was over, Di Stefano whisked me off to his apartment. When we got there he showed me his private costume collection. It was unbelievable. Pippo had absolutely hundreds of costumes stored inside wardrobe crates. He rummaged through all kinds of outfits for some time, finally pulling out triumphantly what he'd been looking for. He announced with satisfaction, 'This is the costume I wore when I sang my first Riccardo at La Scala.' The debut he was referring to was the now legendary production in which he had appeared [on 7 December 1959] with Maria Callas, Giulietta Simionato, and Ettore Bastianini. Then he added, 'Now you will sing in it.'[56]

In a 1976 studio recording of *Lucia*, Carreras is paired with Caballé: the New Philharmonia Orchestra is conducted by Jesús López-Cobos, who besieges Donizetti's score with thumpiness and rigidity. The protagonists' duets are delectable. The tonal blend – Carreras's bright gold with Caballé's canary-diamond sound – is exquisite. During the same summer in London, and once again opposite Caballé, Carreras recorded the part of Cavaradossi in *Tosca*, this time with the Covent Garden orchestra under Colin Davis. Except for a few over-effulgent blasts, Carreras uses his glorious tone judiciously to portray Cavaradossi as a vital, believable lover of life, art and women. Indeed, as Elvio Giudici has pointed out, with this tenor the sound becomes the persona:

> [The] timbre – sunny and very vibrant in the middle range, and moreover, homogeneous and soft – is a marvel, superior even to Di Stefano's; the accent is always spontaneous and incisive, sometimes with roaring outbursts; certain high notes, as usual, leave something to be desired, but this is a mere quibble in a character who in the end is defined through the medium of the voice.[57]

During the following decade Carreras would worry many critics and colleagues by his choice of roles, which tended to the vocally taxing. At this time, however, freshness was his stock in trade, and he exploited it to the full.

Among the baritones, Piero Cappuccilli had been 'established securely as a considerable artist by the early 1970s', with increased vocal and dramatic security, and singing better in tune. But Ruggero

Raimondi was to many the finer singer and musician. He sang an acclaimed Silva in *Ernani* at Verona in 1972: 'Leaving aside the natural advantages of his great stature and a voice perfectly defined from bottom E to the high A flat he gave us to end his first-act cabaletta, there is an extraordinary musical and histrionic intelligence. In this work it was evident in the use of an almost exaggerated legato, achieving thus a convincing ageing effect, and an astonishing assumption of restless vindictiveness.'[58] The name of Leo Nucci had also begun to appear among the roster of leading Italian baritones. His Scala debut, as Figaro, was in 1976. A Nucci *Rigoletto* in Trieste on 26 October 1979 was notable for 'clear, incisive vocalization', a 'mature sense of style' and 'obvious vocal distinction'.[59]

On 1 January 1979 Paolo Grassi was replaced as sovrintendente by Carlo Maria Badini, ending a difficult, productive and frustrating term of office. Although Grassi was by no means fortunate enough to pursue his anti-elitist, aesthetically sound plans in a climate of financial security and administrative calm, he had been able nonetheless to remind Italians that they had a splendid national artistic institution which preserves, even enhances quality, while accepting a degree of social responsibility. Badini came with the socialist credentials deemed requisite in the Italian political climate of the time. He also sought to calm passions and resolve disputes. He said, 'I seize the need for mediation as an instrument for progress.'[60]

Provincial Italian opera houses served a number of functions during the last quarter of the twentieth century. They catered to the Italian love of the art by presenting works from the standard repertoire. They functioned as a clearing house for rising singers and conductors. The finest of them, including Florence's Teatro Comunale and its international festival, the Maggio Musicale, have often taken a leading role in the tale of Italian opera.

In the early 1970s Florentine opera flourished, due largely to the brilliant, patient and persistent efforts of the youthful conductor Riccardo Muti. Born in Naples in 1941 and reared in the little southern Italian town of Molfetta, Muti had a father who encouraged his musical studies. During his adolescent years Muti developed a passion for

opera and was allowed backstage at the Teatro San Carlo. Muti later
stressed the importance of these early experiences. 'I was very much
loved by the staff and musicians at the San Carlo. Watching backstage
out of curiosity, I started to see how an opera takes place. You know,
when some symphonic conductors start to conduct opera, they have
never seen and therefore do not know what the real life of the theatre
is. It is another world.'[61] Although Muti studied piano at the Naples
Conservatory, he enjoyed his experience conducting a student orchestra. He went on to study composition and conducting at the Verdi
Conservatory in Milan, where his conducting teacher was Antonino
Votto, who had been Toscanini's assistant. Votto bequeathed to the
young man the essence of the tradition of Italian opera conducting.
Equally important, he confirmed Muti in his passionate, devoted and
methodical approach to his task. Muti recalled in an interview,

> In Milan I followed the rehearsals when maestro Votto was
> preparing *Falstaff* in 1964 at La Scala. These rehearsals are some-
> thing I will remember for ever. . . . Votto learned *Falstaff* staying
> for months near Toscanini, playing the piano for ten hours
> every day. His rehearsals with the orchestra were unbelievable
> – the facility that man had! Votto had *Falstaff* in his blood.
> One of the most important things I learned from Votto was
> that he never asked for a pianist when he prepared the singers
> – he always played the piano himself. He played everything and
> I follow this concept. It is very important, because when the
> conductor plays the accompaniment, a singer understands from
> his playing exactly what he wants. When you have another
> person in the middle, it is not the same thing.[62]

After winning the Guido Cantelli international conductors' competition in 1967, Muti's future seemed assured. Indeed, he would go on
in 1986 to succeed Abbado as music director of La Scala.

Muti first conducted Florence's Maggio Musicale orchestra in 1968,
in a performance by pianist Sviatoslav Richter. The following year he
was made principal conductor of the festival. He was deemed by
William Weaver, to be 'sound' at the opening of the Comunale's
season on 21 December 1970. 'Though his operatic experience is obviously limited (Muti is still in his twenties, I believe), he clearly has
sound ideas about opera and how it should be conducted. This *Puritani*

performance was notable for its musical coherence, its nobility of line, and its drama. . . . Though this was a well-paced reading, it did not make sudden dashes or spurts. It flowed.'[63] In the same year at Florence he was faulted by Weaver for a *Cavalleria rusticana* and a *Pagliacci* lacking in passion. 'There was nothing careless or superficial about his interpretation; in fact, I felt that each note, each phrase had been carefully studied, pondered, and long rehearsed (the orchestra played with wonderful precision and beautiful tone). But there was, in the end, a "studied" air about the performances, too. . . . The operas needed more blood, more surge, perhaps even a bit of vulgarity.'[64] Four years afterwards a critic found opposite qualities in his *Forza* at Florence: a 'customary misplaced energy . . . unwarranted harshness, excessive volume, and periodic bursts of exaggerated speed'. Muti gained further orchestral experience as a guest conductor of the Philadelphia Orchestra – his debut there was in 1971 – and, at Karajan's invitation, at Salzburg the same year.

In 1974 Muti resigned as music director of the Teatro Comunale and the Maggio Musicale; he expressed anger at the naming of 'a non-theatrical and non-musical personality as artistic director of these two organisations'.[65] This personality was Massimo Bogianckino, whose appointment as sovrintendente of the Comunale took effect on 1 January 1975. By November his job had become the shuttlecock in a power game between the Italian Socialists and Communists. Muti's slur was at least half incorrect: Bogianckino had studied composition and performed publicly as a pianist. The Socialists supported Bogianckino, while the Communists favoured Paolo Barile, who had administrative experience but none in the theatre. For some months paralysis reigned and future planning at the theatre could not be carried out.

Muti insisted that opera performance should be a faithful representation of the composer's intentions. Not only was he keen to purify musical elements of the score; he also took an interest in what was happening on stage.

> As a conductor, it is my responsibility to perform the score
> as the composer left it, without cuts and without interpola-
> tions. But I must also take responsibility for the production,
> to make sure that the production and design reflect my musical

viewpoint. In most theatres, the singers are the stars. In my theatre in Florence and everywhere else I conduct, the composer is the star.[66]

In time sceptics would claim that Muti was in fact the star of his shows. He freely admitted to having a 'polemical' personality; his aggressiveness and authoritarian approach helped him achieve what he wanted. His goal was exciting, faithful – and passionately Italianate – opera performances, and he was sure he knew how to achieve them. Certain other well-known Houses, he maintained, did not:

> The Vienna State Opera kills Italian opera more than any other theatre in the world. It is unbelievable what you hear there. They have no respect for our composers. In Vienna, in Covent Garden too, you have these routine evenings. We don't speak about the Metropolitan. That is another *scandalo*. I saw a *Traviata* there that is something I will never forget. I couldn't believe what I saw and heard. If you like, you can write this: I will not conduct at the Metropolitan.[67]

During the same period the Rome Opera was in stalemate. Luigi Bellingardi wrote that the 'crisis is total, because the political parties will not reach agreement on the appointment of a new board of directors; and as long as the governmental crisis ... lasts, it is not even possible to have a state-appointed provisional administrator. Moreover, the municipality of Rome is in a state of crisis, and the mayor, who is chairman of the opera house, has resigned.' Even worse was the administrative squalor: 'Balance sheets gone mad, an incredible amassing of interest paid, indiscriminate clashes between factions, miserable incompetents elevated to leading roles ...'[68] Régine Crespin had been announced as Tosca, but another soprano, Ilva Ligabue, had in fact been contracted by management. After the affair blew up in the press, Ligabue maintained she was suffering from appendicitis. Tito Gobbi withdrew from the part of Scarpia. It proved difficult to find a conductor willing to take over. In the end Pier Luigi Urbini assumed the task and the veteran Antonietta Stella sang the name part to considerable acclaim. Gradually the vacuum at the top was filled.

On 6 April 1976 Gioacchino Lanza Tomasi was named artistic

director; he had held the same position at Palermo. Lanza Tomasi worked to expand the theatre's repertoire. Rome's 1977–78 season was opened with Rossini's *Tancredi*, a rarity which formed part of the great Rossini Foundation (Pesaro) edition of the composer's complete works. Marilyn Horne as Tancredi 'was capable of decorating the part with fairy-tale beauty in the coloratura arabesques, and expressing the most noble pathos in the recitatives. The latter were such a model of poetic feeling that the stark finale was even more moving than the amazing virtuoso acrobatics.'[69]

Then trouble arrived. At the end of May 1978 a group of Italian opera administrators were arrested and charged with violating the 1967 law forbidding agents to operate in Italian opera. *Opera* reported:

> According to which newspaper one read, either 39, 34 or 26 leading figures in the Italian opera scene were arrested at the end of May and were held by the police for questioning about alleged corruption as well as the infringement of the 1967 law. . . . The arrested men included Lanza Tomasi, artistic director of the Rome Opera, Francesco Siciliani, former artistic director of the Florence Festival, La Scala Milan and Radio Italiana, Sylvano Bussotti, the composer and until recently artistic director of the Teatro La Fenice, Venice, and Lucio Parisi, who is former secretary general of the San Carlo, Naples. Tomasi, in a statement to *Il Messaggero*, said of the 8 or 9 million dollars paid to performers in Italy each year, an estimated 2 million went to agents.[70]

The following month the opera administrators were released. Lanza Tomasi resigned. However, in Italy politics often holds the keys to fate. *Opera* reported '[It] is not impossible that Lanza Tomasi may reoccupy the artistic leadership of the opera with the final removal of Senator Todini, a right-wing Christian Democrat whom many hold to be responsible for the theatre's decline.'[71]

ATER, the association linking provincial Italian opera houses, sponsored an exchange scheme which allowed productions to travel from city to city. In a time of financial squeeze the scheme proved helpful. But politicisation of Italian opera was an even greater common denominator. In Bologna, the Teatro Comunale opened its 1977–78 season with *Fledermaus* and went on to *Fedora*. This choice of works met with the disapproval of 'official Marxist and affiliated criticism', expressed 'with a ferocity akin to the utmost contempt'.[72] The currents of the Italian 'discourse' concerning intellectual and artistic issues were turning strongly against works which lacked social relevance.

As a new generation of musicians took over at La Scala, the older ones began to fade. After a conducting career spanning sixty-eight years, Vittorio Gui died on 16 October 1975 in Florence, as did Antonio Ghiringhelli on 11 July 1979 at the age of seventy-seven.

On 16 September of that year Maria Callas died of a heart attack, following a disastrous world tour with Di Stefano and several semi-reclusive years in her beautiful and sumptuous Paris flat in the avenue Georges Mandel. The transcription of her master classes for singers at the Juilliard School of Music in New York was published in book form and provided inspiration for a Broadway play. It was not simply that Callas's acting was considered unparalleled on the operatic stage in the twentieth century, recalling Adelina Patti's in the nineteenth. Verdi had written of Patti, in words that could have been applied to Callas, 'She is perfectly organised. Perfect balance between singer and actress, a born artist in every sense of the word.'

Callas did pioneering work as a singer. She revived operas from the bel canto era which, since her time, have become staples of the repertoire. In doing so she 'reinvented' the technique necessary to execute the difficult passage work and paved the way for later bel canto singers such as Sutherland, Sills, Horne and Caballé. The critic Giorgio Gualerzi recalled her splendidly Rossinian Armida in Florence in 1952: 'Callas stood apart from her five well-intentioned tenor colleagues by the simple fact of her command of the correct technique, and by extension, correct style.'[73]

Most of all, in her work with producers like Visconti, who had himself died on 17 March 1976, and conductors like Giulini, Callas redefined the artist's function on the opera stage. In collaboration with their talents, and ever sensitive to the composer's intentions, she created a conceptual, verbal, vocal and musical unity of performance. Giulini wrote in appreciation of her life:

There are three fundamentals necessary for the realization of the melodrama: words, music and acting. Many artists possess one or two of these, but how rare it is to find the three embodied in one person! They were in Callas. She was melodrama. She realized the value of the text; she possessed a natural musical instinct, and an immense knowledge; and on the stage she had a radiance which reflected every mood and movement. There was a unity and logic in everything she did.[74]

FIFTEEN

VIENNA 1970–80

Manifold Pleasures of Routine, Rarer Joys of Excellence

WHILE RAGING POLITICAL QUESTIONS invaded the Italian cultural world, the Vienna State Opera, like Austria at large, continued to stand aloof from outside issues and problems. If energy and controversy were present at the House in the early 1970s, they were most evident in the rapid turnover in the top administrative post. Intrigue among arts bureaucrats was the sad staple, while the creative forces at the Staatsoper did their best to present a huge repertoire night after night with little rehearsal time and without the challenging novelty of fresh ideas and approaches.

Dr Heinrich Reif-Gintl, Egon Hilbert's successor at the Staatsoper, had a brief and unremarkable tenure. The sixty-eight-year-old Reif-Gintl, formerly one of Ernst Marboe's colleagues in Austrian arts administration, had been employed at the House for decades in a variety of posts, most recently as vice-director. Little remembered and less cherished by colleagues and artists, he had something of a bureaucrat's vision of opera. Even before the war, as a Staatsoper functionary, he had forbidden star tenor Jan Kiepura to perform popular songs: 'One simply cannot sing Schlager with piano accompaniment before a performance on the Vienna Staatsoper stage!' Kiepura announced with a grin that he would therefore perform them without piano accompaniment.[1]

Although no artistic director was named along with Reif-Gintl, Horst Stein was brought from Mannheim in Germany as 'first conductor' with the proviso that he be in residence for seven months of the year. Stein, born in 1928, had been a staff conductor at Hamburg and the Berlin Staatsoper during the 1950s before taking up the music directorship at Mannheim in 1963. He had previously conducted a variety of operas at the Vienna Staatsoper, ranging from Mozart through Wagner and Strauss. As for Reif-Gintl himself, he was known as a Viennese gentleman of the old and circumspect school, although not as an artist nor even an outstanding leader. Wechsberg wrote, 'He studied law and music; he played the horn and violin. Above all he loved the theatre and the opera. He knew everybody, saw everything, but he won't tell. A Hofrat [court privy councillor] does not gossip; he keeps his secrets to himself.'[2]

In 1970, with Reif-Gintl in charge fifteen years after the reopening of the Staatsoper, critical opinion was dissatisfied with the overall level of performances. After all the work that Karajan and Egon Hilbert after him had done, consistent quality eluded the House. Wechsberg summed up the situation: 'There is too much mediocrity and too little excitement; too much improvisation and too little planning. [The Staatsoper] is still run along the lines of the turn of the century but times have changed.'[3] It was generally agreed that the singing was competent or even better than competent. The orchestra could play gloriously when encouraged to do so, and the chorus was consistently fine. There was, however, an enervating atmosphere of routine and *Schlamperei*. Erich Leinsdorf recalled that the Staatsoper in the 1930s, 'when I went there three to four times a week, alternated between great evenings and wretched routine.'[4] In the early 1970s rehearsing a repertory production was a rare event in Vienna, in contrast to Covent Garden.

Excellent evenings could still happen. In the 1969–70 season Stein's conducting of Gluck's *Iphigénie* was praised by Wechsberg. Sena Jurinac 'sang the title role with great warmth and a thorough understanding of Gluck's vocal line; not many singers are able to do that today'.[5] Karl Böhm came to conduct a *Macbeth* starring Christa Ludwig and Sherrill Milnes, which was acclaimed as 'a great and glorious evening for the Vienna Opera. . . . Milnes as Macbeth did the almost impossible by living up to Miss Ludwig's great portrayal. He became a star almost immediately: a beautiful, well-timbred dark voice, a typically healthy American voice of power and conviction, an intelligent singer who does not "act".'[6]

In 1970, the bicentenary year of Beethoven's birth, Leonard Bernstein conducted a commemorative *Fidelio* at the Theater an der Wien. Otto Schenk directed. Writing in *Die Presse*, Franz Endler approved the unified quality and taut pacing of the entire production. He found in Bernstein's conducting a remarkable emotional validity: 'When Florestan falls to the ground at the close of his aria in the dungeon there is no time to pay homage to the singer's performance. Rather one hears in the orchestra how the prisoner's ecstatic outcry breaks down and dissolves into profound hopelessness.' To Endler's ears Gwyneth Jones's Leonore was 'glorious' and Theo Adam's Pizzaro 'vocally grandiose'. He considered Lucia Popp's Marzelline the most beautiful he had ever heard.[7] Wechsberg wrote in *Opera*, 'It was not, thank goodness, a perfect production; like Beethoven's dearly beloved child, it was full of human weakness. Bernstein's devotional reading of the score had unorthodox tempos and exaggerated accents, to say the least; and Schenk's actors were often "overreacting", hamming it up.' Günther Schneider-Siemssen's sets 'were absolutely right. Direct and dramatic, without phoney symbolism and contrived modernism. When the prisoners said goodbye to the "*Sonnenlicht*", there was sunshine.'[8]

It was a tribute to his extraordinary personality and musicianship that Bernstein, an American Jew, should have established such a warm rapport with the Staatsoper singers and orchestra only a quarter-century after the fall of the Third Reich. Bernstein also reminded the Viennese of the works of their neglected symphonic master Gustav Mahler.[9] In a film produced by Humphrey Burton about the making of the Vienna *Fidelio* it is clear that Bernstein is taking almost complete control of the production. Ebullient and light-hearted, in conversations with the singers he encourages them to portray three-dimensional characters rather than types of good and evil. In Schuyler Chapin's account of the making of the film, Bernstein is seen working closely with Schenk, suggesting ideas for stage business and props:

> Next we see a stage rehearsal with piano: Bernstein and Otto Schenk, the director, are talking about the Pizarro problem. Bernstein is explaining his theories and Schenk listens, nodding in agreement. 'Let's have him wear spectacles to read the message about Don Ferando's arrival,' says Bernstein. '*Wunderbar!*' exclaims Schenk and, going up onstage, he takes off his own glasses and hands them to [bass-baritone Theo] Adam. 'And be paranoid!' exclaims Bernstein. 'Otto, he should tug at his

collar; he should sweat with fear and look around to see if his weaknesses are observed.' 'Right, right!' says Schenk, and in German and pantomime he shows Adam what he wants. Adam shakes his head and in German says that he's played this role all over the world and never before has he been asked to do things like this. 'He's afraid he'll mar his good looks!' exclaims Bernstein, and laughs.[10]

The next season the unexpected happened: another stunning Lady Macbeth was sung on the Vienna stage, this time by Birgit Nilsson. 'While some of the fleeter passages were little more than sketched in, the rest of [Nilsson's] portrayal was on a level which even she rarely reaches. . . . While rarely raising her voice above piano throughout the sleepwalking scene, no two consecutive phrases used the same colour, nor did she shy off downright unpleasant sounds when she felt them appropriate, thereby substantiating the composer's oft-quoted wish for an actress who did not just sing beautifully – which is not to say that there was any lack of beautiful and brilliant singing when this was in place.'[11] At this moment in the history of operatic performance there were no fewer than four sopranos capable of giving outstanding accounts of Lady Macbeth – one of the most difficult of all Verdi roles. They were Nilsson, Ludwig, Rysanek and Shirley Verrett. Verrett's Vienna debut as Eboli in late 1970 was rapturously received, in advance of her great Scala successes.

Earlier in the same season Horst Stein's *Don Carlos* was booed by a faction of the Staatsoper standees. Before the opening Stein had received poison-pen letters written on lavatory paper. Stein's opinion of the *gemütlich* Austrian capital was adversely affected. He speculated to reporters that he might not wish to renew his contract when it expired the following year.[13]

On 23 May 1971 a worthy new opera had its world premiere at the Staatsoper – a rare event for the conservative House. The work was Gottfried von Einem's *Der Besuch der alten Dame*, with a libretto adapted by Friedrich Dürrenmatt from his play of the same title (known to English-speaking audiences as *The Visit*). The cast – starring Christa Ludwig and Eberhard Waechter – was strong, Horst Stein's conducting sympathetic and the score generally praised for its expressiveness. But Endler in *Die Presse* expressed an unfavourable minority view, remarking on the repetitive quality of the music and its 'insipid' dramatic impact.[14] In time *Der Besuch der alten Dame* proved to have been a happy choice for the Staatsoper: the opera has stood the test of time and been performed frequently.

Reif-Gintl's final season, in 1971–72, was notable for Ileana Cotrubas's Violetta on 25 December. The Romanian soprano was singing the role for the first time, following on her great Covent Garden success as Tatyana earlier the same year. Even though she came to grief at 'Sempre libera', Wechsberg found her Violetta the finest since Callas's. 'Miss Cotrubas coped with the most improbable details of her taxing part. When she died a part of the audience died with her; those who still "live" opera.' Krips's conducting treated Verdi's orchestration lightly, to Cotrubas's advantage, and director Otto Schenk 'managed to turn stock operatic characters into human beings, and created a wholly convincing "Love Story", anno 1853'.[14] Endler was no less enthusiastic: 'This was a performance so great as to cause rejoicing – so beautiful that it actually succeeded in Vienna.'[15]

A few months after Reif-Gintl had taken over his post his successor was announced. Rudolf Gamsjäger would take up the position of 'administrator' of the Staatsoper beginning in the 1972–73 season. Rolf Liebermann, who had worked wonders as intendant at the Hamburg State Opera since 1959, had been approached for the position, but declined. Instead he went on to the Opéra de Paris, where he used his imagination – and a generous government subsidy – to revive a somnolent institution. Reif-Gintl told journalists that he was happy that his 'old friend Rudolf Gamsjäger' was to be his replacement in 'this not entirely simple job'.[16]

When he succeeded Reif-Gintl in 1972, Rudolf Gamsjäger's past career seemed to encourage hope for improvement at the House. Born in Vienna on 23 March 1909, he studied mathematics, then chemistry and eventually singing. In 1945 he was hired as general secretary of the Gesellschaft der Musikfreunde. This organisation, better known as the Musikverein, ran the leading Viennese concert series; Karajan was later named its director for life. Gamsjäger ran it until his appointment at the Staatsoper. Wechsberg wrote, 'Gamsjäger is that refreshing personality in Vienna – a fellow who is not afraid. Some say he can be a tough guy. . . . He has taste and erudition, he knows the big business aspects of today's musical industry, he has shown sound executive ability and a sense of old-fashioned diplomatic skill in his present job.'[17] Albert Moser, the administrator of the Volksoper, was named to replace Gamsjäger at the Musikverein, while Gamsjäger was simultaneously named manager *pro tempore* of the Volksoper. In due course the Volksoper position was assumed by a singer, Karl Dönch. Many Viennese opera goers hoped that Gamsjäger's connection with Karajan would carry enough weight to persuade him to conduct again at the Staatsoper. It was also hoped, perhaps over-optimistically, that if Karajan returned he could somehow share the podium with Böhm, Krips, Bernstein and talented younger conductors.

As Gamsjäger took up his appointment, Horst Stein left Vienna to become music director at the Hamburg Opera. Stein continued to guest-conduct performances at the Staatsoper. The first Staatsoper evening under Gamsjäger's directorship was a revival of *Fidelio* on 1 September 1972. It was not a happy occasion. The orchestra, conducted by Krips, sounded tired following the Salzburg Festival. Helga Dernesch, making her debut as Leonore, forced her sound, drawing catcalls from the gallery. Gamsjäger's first new production was a *Don Giovanni* which opened on 31 October. Krips's conducting was deemed faultless and stage director-designer Zeffirelli's visual contributions, including footmen with candlesticks illuminating the principals, worked well. However, the title role, according to Wechsberg, was badly sung by Theo Adam, 'who seems much more at ease as Wotan or Hans Sachs. Adam had neither charm nor glamour, elegance nor humour, nor sex appeal. Instead he carried on with a certain low-class brutality that is neither in the character nor the music.'[18] The next new production of the Gamsjäger regime was a *Fliegende Holländer*, which opened on 1 December. Wechsberg excoriated it as 'dull' and 'mediocre'. Otmar Suitner conducted 'in a rough way, without subtlety'. The direction of Wolfgang Zörner, who had replaced Herbert Graf at a late date, 'got lost in the labyrinth between abstract and realistic moments. Often there were effects instead of emotions, and gimmicks instead of feelings.'[19]

An art nouveau *Salome* turned out beautifully on 22 December 1972, with extraordinary ensemble singing. Rysanek as the heroine 'gave an astonishing performance which was never a tour de force.

She presented Salome as a capricious, badly spoiled girl, underplaying the more shocking aspects . . . and she fully used the sensuous beauty of her warm soprano, especially when she went up and on and on.' Wechsberg added that Rysanek 'gave the visual illusion of Salome, even bringing off the devilish dance without visible strain.'[20] Böhm's approach to Strauss was admirable: 'He kept the large orchestra down so that it sounded with chamber-music clarity. One could almost always understand the words – exactly as Strauss wanted – and Böhm rose magnificently to the emotional climaxes.'[21] However, as he grew older the veteran conductor was faulted for lack of accuracy and a vague beat. Franz Endler admitted that the Vienna Philharmonic under Böhm's direction in *Salome* 'glowed in every colour of the palette, but it can scarcely be reported that it played with precision as well'.[22]

Internationally acclaimed singers helped raise the level of Staatsoper performances. Teresa Berganza, who performed the mezzo roles of Rossini, Mozart, Cherubini and other composers throughout the world during the 1960s and 1970s, had a triumph in May 1973 in Vienna as Cenerentola. Endler called her 'a singer of the highest accomplishment, an artist so magisterial and intelligent that appropriate adjectives for her have long since been lacking. Happy is the opera house that could engage her as a guest star in this role.'[23]

Nicolai Gedda, an intelligent singer who was a master of a wide variety of roles, found his high-lying lyric tenor in wide demand across Europe during the 1960s, 1970s and 1980s. A 1973 Vienna Festival *Elisir* showed him in top form. According to Charles Osborne, 'As Nemorino, Nicolai Gedda was incomparably fine. It is usually difficult to fault him musically; but, in this production, he not only sang beautifully but also acted the role of the diffident country bumpkin to perfection.'[24]

Schoenberg's *Moses und Aron* was a brave choice for the 1973 Vienna Festival. The Viennese public could not be expected to welcome such a daring work; in fact, it was the first Viennese performance of the opera ever. Endler found it 'dissonant from the first bar to the last'.[25] This was hardly surprising, since it is composed in the twelve-tone style, in which consonant harmony is irrelevant. Endler observed that Götz Friedrich 'staged the work solely according to his own ideas' – in other words, he located it in a concentration camp.

The infamous Vienna standees were again getting out of hand. At that year's festival they jeered their enemies and shouted approval of their favourites. The standees had been partly responsible for the failure of a new production earlier that year when Nathaniel Merrill's splashy staging of *Aida* was offensively booed. 'Confusion was compounded by Nathaniel Merrill's production, with ridiculous crowd assemblies, and few ideas during the important private scenes of the opera, with the singers gesticulating in grand-opera style *circa* 1900.'[26] Arias were jeered while the singers were still singing. The Staatsoper brought in police to eject 'a small minority of the listeners'.[27] Also at fault, Wechsberg wrote, were Günther Schneider-Siemssen's sets, which recalled Hollywood rather than the Egyptian Middle Kingdom: '[Schneider-Siemssen] created laughter with his incredibly "kitschy" sets for Amneris' boudoir (with private swimming pool) and the scene of Radames' victorious return. It was not only "kitsch", but bad taste and ridiculous, the action cramped in a very narrow space at the front of the stage, and there were ugly colours and pseudo-Egyptian "symbols", an orgy of phoniness.'[28]

Such grandiose stagings of *Aida* were a staple item in the Met's programming, where they were well-received. In Vienna, the conducting was what gained approval. Riccardo Muti, making his Staatsoper debut, conducted the show excitingly. Wechsberg wrote: 'Muti has youth and brio and temperament (which sometimes gets away from him) and he obviously knows and loves Verdi. He has a fine ear for detail, and the music sounded lucid and transparent and the orchestra played beautifully.'[29] It is characteristic of Muti that he would give generously of his talents to lead a successful performance in an opera house whose professional habits did not entirely please him. Plácido Domingo also received plaudits as Radames.

Gamsjäger was not successful in enticing Karajan back to the Staatsoper. Occupied with the Berlin Philharmonic, the Salzburg Festivals and recording commitments, the maestro had reduced his opera conducting and was even making time for rest and meditation in a schedule that had been hectic for years on end. Karajan's acclaimed performances of Verdi and Wagner at Salzburg during the first half of the decade, kept his name shining brightly in the opera firmament. He turned down an offer from Vienna of the October 1973 *Tristan und Isolde,* which Carlos Kleiber eventually conducted. If Karajan returned to Vienna, it would be on his own terms – as what his biographer Richard Osborne called 'a kind of laureate superstar'.[30]

Kleiber, who was allowed no fewer than fourteen orchestra rehearsals, went so far as to cancel the second *Tristan* performance when Hans Hopf, cast in the name part, fell ill: Kleiber would not substitute a singer he had not rehearsed. Again, it was Wechsberg who commented: 'Carlos Kleiber has done the almost impossible: with a single performance he has firmly established himself as one of the few great conductors at the House since the days of Mahler. He did this without magic, by sheer hard work and dedication to the music. . . . He produced miracles of dynamic shading, articulation of chamber-music care, and clear phrasing, and abundant excitement and climax. The orchestra played happily for him as it has not played for months.'[31]

Intending to bring about change, Gamsjäger instituted forward planning of performances and rehearsals for the first time at the Vienna State Opera. And even though a number of worthwhile productions were being mounted, the occasional debacle recalled the failures that were also rife at La Scala. Late in 1973 Gamsjäger tried and failed to organise a Russian-language production of *Onegin.* Mstislav Rostropovich was announced as conductor, and Vladimir Atlantov and Galina Vishnevskaya for the main roles. Before rehearsals began, all three artists had become 'unavailable'. An alternative German-language production ran into difficulty because of dissension between Jürgen Rose, the set designer, and Rudolf Noelte, the director. Cotrubas, who was to replace Vishnevskaya as Tatyana, fell ill and was in turn replaced by Eva Marton. In the end the singing was applauded. Wechsberg wrote of the standees, 'The Tupamaros . . . behaved quite well, for a change.'[32] Such veterans as Anton Dermota, Hilde Konetzni and Hilde Rössl-Majdan took small parts, in the good Viennese tradition of allowing ageing singers to work as long as possible, even as comprimarii. Hilde Konetzni once told an interviewer, 'I simply could not afford to retire, and when I did, it was because of a heart attack . . . So I went on to mezzo roles, then smaller, cameo parts at the Volksoper, where Ljuba Welitsch is still doing pretty much what I did. It is no shame there in Vienna to go on making a living, you know.'[33]

In contrast to the overdone Merrill *Aida*, Joachim Herz's staging of Janáček's *Kát'a Kabanová* was much applauded. Herz, another Felsenstein protégé, had also staged the work at the Komische Oper. Harold Rosenthal wrote, 'He had the same designer, Rudolf Heinrich, and between them they built a stark, unromantic and very working-class looking small town Kalinov, on the swamps of the Volga. All the outdoor scenes were played on a series of duckboards or catwalks, and the feeling of water and sky, and of virtual isolation was intensified by the use of blacks and whites and brilliantly cold lighting.'[34] But this was before Janáček's works had found their way into the Staatsoper repertoire and conservative Viennese audiences stayed away. Another Herz effort, a serious-minded *Zauberflöte* of 30 November 1974, was a highly unusual event for the Staatsoper. Wechsberg could not abide it. 'The Herz–Heinrich production had dialectic materialism, *Tiefenpsychologie*, pseudo-analysis, bright ideas and a generally disenchanting story line. . . . Here Sarastro is a dictator, and the Queen of the Night a sex symbol, and Pamina *das süsse Wiener Mädel*, very late Schnitzler, and Tamino is just another nice guy. And so on. . . . A couple of West German intellectuals thought it was splendid. It was, they said, clever and new and profound. As the late Wieland Wagner told me, "When we Germans try to be profound, we are merely obscure." '[35] Nevertheless Herz returned to Vienna with his *Lohengrin* of 20 February 1975. At the curtain, the chorus director, Norbert Balatsch, was booed by mistake for Herz, who did not come out for a bow.

By contrast, the new production of *Forza* which opened on 29 September 1974 seemed lacking not only in controversy but in originality and creative energy as well. There were, wrote Wechsberg, 'some nondescript dark sets, and a conventional approach to all problems of staging. The work was also given uncut, and seemed too long.'[36] Wechsberg did, however, like Muti's energy, while deploring his big bangs. 'Riccardo Muti is full of youthful enthusiasm and loves a great fortissimo climax, which is fine but eventually he will realize that Verdi's fine, emotional music does not need such tremendous power.'[37] Wechsberg wondered why Gamsjäger's administration went to the bother of initiating a new production while coming up with so little. 'The question is rhetorical, because unpleasant questions, of which there are many now, are never answered around Vienna's Staatsoper.'

A fracas erupted in early 1974 when Böhm objected to Zubin Mehta's conducting at the Staatsoper. The matter was carried as far as the office of the Chancellor, Bruno Kreisky. It was only resolved when Mehta was paid not to conduct. The amount was 300,000 Austrian schillings. Wrote Wechsberg, 'Maybe some people in America are right when they say that subsidised opera is a dangerous business. The general manager of the Metropolitan would certainly have grave problems with his board of directors if he spent $15,000 on non-performances.'[38]

By 1976 accusations of spendthrift management were filling the papers. Exact figures were impossible to come by, since the Staatsoper's budget was added together with those of the other state theatres and published as an approximate lump sum. The Austrian government controller called the Staatsoper 'the most wasteful, inefficient and scandalously expensive opera house in the world'.[39]

Marcel Prawy, by this time head dramaturg at the Staatsoper and the Volksoper as well, later pointed out Gamsjäger's shortcomings: 'Gamsjäger had considerable strengths as head of the Musikverein, but in opera he was rather out of his depth (*etwas fachfremd*).'[40] Prawy recalled him searching for the addresses of tenors and basses in his desk drawers, trying to recall the names of the 'best ones', namely Domingo and Ghiaurov. Speaking in parliament, the Austrian Education Minister said he expected to announce a successor to Gamsjäger in the summer, even though Gamsjäger was still at his post. That successor turned out to be Egon Seefehlner. Seefehlner had been deputy director of the Staatsoper from 1954 to 1961. When the Deutsche Oper of West Berlin was opened in 1961 he was named its deputy general manager, moving up to the post of intendant in 1972.

On taking office Seefehlner gathered the entire staff in the auditorium and made a speech from the stage. He said, 'I have no need for power. But whatever may happen, I shall only do what I wish.'[41] His ambition to be a benevolent dictator was furthered by the first new production undertaken during his tenure, the ambitious Vienna premiere of Berlioz's *Les Troyens*. The American director Tom O'Horgan staged the mammoth opera, with his countryman Robin Wagner responsible for the sets. There were gimmicks and spectacle galore, which were liked by some and disliked by others.[42] On balance, the unusual (for Vienna) choice of work and director represented a laudable attempt to breathe a new spirit into the House.

Seefehlner's House continued to prosper as Böhm conducted a popular *Ariadne auf Naxos*, which opened in November 1976. Filippo Sanjust directed and designed the production.

In a coup for the Seefehlner, Böhm's great rival 'K' agreed at last to a three-year stint as occasional guest conductor, returning to the Staatsoper on 8 May 1977 with *Trovatore*. The production was Karajan's landmark Salzburg version. The television crews appeared and special floodlighting had been installed. Karajan's march to the podium was wildly applauded by the entire audience and not merely the *K-Narren*: late in 1974 he had suffered a life-threatening spinal ailment and had been spared permanent paralysis by a hair's breadth. The *Frankfurter Allgemeine* reported that a mere 300 or so tickets, out of a total of 1642, were available for free sale; all the rest had been commandeered in one way or another.[43] José Carreras was present, provided with a complimentary ticket from Pavarotti, who was singing Manrico.

Carreras recalled, 'When the maestro stepped into the orchestra pit, the theatre reverberated with shrieks and commotion the likes of which I'd never heard before. The ovations lasted so long that I wondered if the performance was ever going to begin. Suddenly, almost brusquely, Karajan turned to face the orchestra. He directed one of the orchestra servants to remove a huge bouquet of red roses from the conductor's dais and then, amidst the roar, raised his arms. Instantly, a hush fell. The performance began.'[44] Five days later in Vienna, Carreras sang Rodolfo with Karajan conducting the Zeffirelli production of *Bohème*. The Austrian Chancellor, Bruno Kreisky, attended the final performance of the Puccini work on 20 May. During his Staatsoper engagement Karajan also conducted performances of the Ponnelle *Figaro* from Salzburg.

Although little new artistic ground was broken in these *Trovatore* performances, Endler found that Karajan 'inspired the singers, improvised with the orchestra, stirred up passion, and corrected the errors of all his colleagues'.[45] The singers whom Karajan inspired – Price, Ludwig, Pavarotti and Cappuccilli as Luna – were judged capable but not outstanding. Wechsberg found Cappuccilli 'good but never exciting in a part that can be very exciting; and Miss Ludwig needed some

time before she grew into the part that is not strictly hers'.[46] Pavarotti
was acclaimed, and Leontyne Price, though considered by some to be
no longer in her vocal prime, was commended for her intelligent and
emotionally committed singing. For Wechsberg, the 'most memorable
moment was Karajan's cautious and loving conducting while Leontyne
Price, with true bel canto training, sang "D'amor sull'ali rosee"'.[47]

More than one singer has praised Karajan's moments of empathetic
conducting, while he was actually getting the singer to do what he,
Karajan, wanted. Carreras wrote,

> It was fascinating how Karajan made you feel that he was like
> your father, conducting for you alone. There you were on the
> stage, under the impression that you were calling all the shots
> and that he would always follow you with the orchestra. It was
> all an illusion because in reality everything was turned around.
> He did it in such a way that you wouldn't notice it. Here
> was one of the great professional secrets of Karajan's art of
> conducting. You thought you were singing as freely as you
> pleased and your confidence soared; yet all the time he was
> leading you from the beginning through to the end of the work.
> Mirella Freni once put it this way: 'Singing with Karajan was
> like going to sleep in a comfortable bed.'[48]

Wechsberg had great appreciation for the Karajan phenomenon.
Witnessing Price's Leonora at the 1977 Salzburg Easter Festival, he
wrote, 'She has often remarked on Karajan's ability to get the best out
of her, and it was fascinating to watch him do it; here we saw him in
the role of the ideal accompanist, the servant, not the master, of his
singer on stage, nursing her and giving her maximum support, while
allowing her the essential freedom to interpret the role with most
subtle phrasing and accentuation of words within the phrase.'[49]

Elisabeth Schwarzkopf described Karajan's precision and economy
of effort when working with an orchestra:

> Karajan knows the psychology of an orchestra I think probably
> better than anybody else. He is a man who does everything
> with the greatest economy of his time. He spends a great deal
> of thought preparing everything, trying out the effect of differ-
> ent sorts of beat on an orchestra – to make everything clear to
> the orchestra with the minimum of effort. . . .

And I have never heard him raise his voice at a rehearsal. Hardly a word spoken: the whole thing done visually. He knows exactly what he wants and has this strange quiet authority. As he has said to me many times, 'If I don't raise my voice, they'll listen to what I say, and the less I speak, the more important each word is.'[50]

Seefehlner, fond of bel canto, introduced Bellini's *I Capuleti e i Montecchi* to the Vienna repertoire. On 23 March 1978 *Lucia* was heard once again after a lapse of many years. Gruberova, cast in the title role, had been helped in her career by Seefehlner. Wechsberg approved of his choice: 'The fact is that she gave a vocally faultless performance, and that she also gave a modern one. She not only sang Lucy, she was Lucy. . . . Her suffering did not affect her coloratura technique. It was truly amazing.'[51] Seefehlner also extended the repertoire to include Henze's *Der junge Lord*, which opened on 9 June 1978. The audience were not amused. There were many empty seats on the first night. 'Vienna's traditionally conservative audiences have accepted *Wozzeck* and, reluctantly, *Lulu* and *Moses und Aron*, but the rest is silence.'[52] Herr Pallavicini, who once had owned Demel's coffee shop, designed the sets. 'There was applause at the end but I heard a woman say she should have spent the money at Demel's.'[53]

During the 1978–79 season Erich Leinsdorf made a brief and much welcomed return to his native Vienna to conduct Pfitzner's *Palestrina*. A big Zeffirelli *Carmen* was filmed by Austrian state television and distributed worldwide, with Carlos Kleiber's magical conducting.

Seefehlner's tenure during the latter half of the decade did much to revive the Staatsoper's flagging fortunes. His understanding that excellent conductors and imaginative stage directors must be lured to the House meant the occasional glorious evening. But not even Seefehlner could overcome the brutal demands of the schedule, which meant a performance almost every night and consequently a good deal of routine work.

Karajan had escaped the conundrum of routine by moving his opera work to the Salzburg Festival. He had also devoted much of his time since leaving the Staatsoper to the exploration of mass media. He sought to make his music available to all, not merely to concert goers. Beginning with filmed and televised symphonic performances, he went on to consider the possibilities of presenting opera as well to the wider public. He decided to use Salzburg as a laboratory for developing his own productions, which would eventually be seen and heard around the world:

> I imagine the future of big musical productions for the theatre as follows: first a gramophone record, so that the music is already there down to the smallest detail when we are doing the subsequent staging. After that comes the film and television recording. . . . Everything I have in my head will be made possible in Salzburg in an ideal way. I feel committed to the house as to no other: here I was born, and here I should like to work.[54]

Sales of Karajan's opera recordings were enhanced by the film and television exposure. But Karajan's film of *Otello* (1973) fails almost completely in the visual and dramatic senses. The interiors are ugly and the exteriors generally look artificial. Often the main characters are ignored in favour of the set. The camera has a curious way of scouting round walls and ceilings in search of a detail of decoration whose higher significance in the drama is less than obvious. Theme and directorial viewpoint are similarly obscured. The sublimity of the love relationship and the tragic anguish of its wrecking are not brought out. It must be said in defence of Karajan that by the early Seventies, when he made *Otello*, the medium of film had not been developed for opera to any degree of sophistication. In the 1960s and 1970s the Munich-based firm of Unitel made rather indiscriminately three sorts of opera films: operatic productions more or less in the form they were staged; a few original projects especially for film, like Karajan's *Otello*; and some staged productions radically altered to accommodate the cinema lens, such as the Karajan–Zeffirelli *Bohème*. It took time for directors to understand the special needs of opera for film.

Salzburg productions were by and large recognised by critics and audiences as very fine indeed. Karajan and Böhm conducted; Strehler and Günther Rennert directed. As William Mann put it, management engaged 'casts of the most distinguished singers who will give Salzburg first call on their services, so great is the réclame involved'.[55]

However, Joseph Wechsberg was disenchanted with the Salzburg ambience. 'Salzburg at festival time is a super carnival with too many tourists, too many buses, too many ticket scalpers, too many rumours, too many gossips. There is often good opera but the people rarely talk about the music. They gossip about the stars, the intrigues, the feuds, and who-did-what-to-whom. The stories are often amusing but rarely nice. The Salzburg Festival has become cool and distant, and the atmosphere at the Grosses Festspielhaus pompous and expensive. The last person to be remembered is a certain Mozart.'[56] Wechsberg once saw Karajan making a telephone call during a rehearsal while the musicians carried on playing.

Karajan's staged *Otello*, premiered in 1970, was a much appreciated staple at the festival. But during its first year in the repertoire it became the occasion for a revival of the Karajan–Böhm feud. Karajan had appropriated the Grosses Festspielhaus for his *Otello* rehearsals, which meant that Böhm's *Fidelio* had to be mounted in the not entirely suitable Felsenreitschule. This auditorium, seating 1,568, had recently been redesigned, with a roof that echoed with pounding rain during Böhm's show. In the 1974 Easter festival Harold Rosenthal did not approve of K's *Meistersinger*. It 'lacked heart and compassion, and I never felt caught up and involved in this most human and universal of operas'.[57]

Following his controversial practice in Vienna and New York, Karajan stage-directed his own 1975 Salzburg *Don Carlos*, with sets by Günther Schneider-Siemssen. Plácido Domingo was part of a splendid cast, which included Christa Ludwig – who, however, left the role of Eboli after the first performance. Wrote William Mann, 'Domingo . . . sounded happier in duets and other ensembles . . . than in his opening solo "Io la vidi": his portrayal was, perhaps deliberately, not heroic, but his singing was not helped by Karajan's zestful conducting.'[58] Domingo had mixed feelings about Karajan's unique rehearsal methods:

> He insists on having all rehearsals, from the very first one, on stage rather than in a rehearsal room, and in full costume. These are tremendously helpful techniques. The stage rehearsals make us singers think right from the beginning about projecting our characters, and the costumes make us all feel completely comfortable and natural with what we have to wear by the time we go before the public. . . .

The one Karajan technique that I am not so enthusiastic about is that of rehearsing from a pre-recorded tape of the work in preparation, instead of having the singers sing along, half-voice or otherwise, to piano accompaniment. He claims that the purpose is to rest the voice during staging rehearsals, but I feel that it creates bad habits because we hear the same timing, the same phrasing, the same breathing, every time. . . . As a result, our concept of the role is kept from growing during that all-important rehearsal period. At the Don Carlo rehearsals I was not even following my own recording, but an earlier one made by a different tenor. And even when your own records are being used, it is distracting to hear yourself singing all the time – the same good moments and the same discouraging bad ones.[59]

Karajan's Don Carlos opened the summer festival in 1976, with one of the finest casts that could be assembled: Freni, Cossotto, Carreras, Cappuccilli, Ghiaurov. Carreras had stepped in for Domingo after the latter could not undertake to sing all six Salzburg performances. While Domingo maintained he had to honour previous Japanese commitments, the press reported disagreements with Karajan concerning rehearsal schedules.[60] Wechsberg delighted in Karajan's 'coaxing by turns the grandest and most tender tones from the Vienna Philharmonic'.

As the Salzburg Festival flourished under the Karajan cachet, the Bayreuth Festival took another new turn. After Wieland Wagner's death of lung cancer in October 1966 his brother Wolfgang assumed sole control and dismissed most of the staff who had worked with Wieland. Wolfgang also attacked Wieland's memory, publicly criticising his stagings and announcing that he had been a Nazi. In fact, however, Wieland had never taken steps to join the Party; he had been declared a member by Hitler at the 1938 festival. Wolfgang even destroyed models of Wieland's sets. Ever since the 1950s many of Wolfgang's own Bayreuth stage productions had come in for adverse criticism on the grounds of lack of imagination and taste. Now staging was opened to outside producers. Frederic Spotts writes, 'Keeping Wagner's works alive, Wolfgang insisted again and again, meant constantly reinterpreting them to make them relevant to contemporary audiences. "The continuous, active contact with what is topical, with our present day, that is what we encapsulate in the idea of Werkstatt Bayreuth" is the sort of comment he made over and over. By the same token the Festival was no longer to be the end point but the launching platform of a career for singers, conductors and producers.'[61] But in the 1970s the productions of 'Werkstatt Bayreuth' (Workshop Bayreuth) deeply disturbed many traditional Wagnerians, as Wieland's productions had done twenty years earlier.

While Viennese opera production at this time remained apolitical, political issues began to invade stagings in Germany as they had in Italy. Wolfgang Wagner made the daring decision to have Götz Friedrich stage an innovative *Tannhäuser* after Giorgio Strehler turned down the project. Harold Rosenthal recalled that Friedrich's production 'did not prove less shocking than Wieland's in his early, daring days'. It was booed in 1972 – 'and rapturously received the following year!'[62] Friedrich viewed Tannhäuser not as a man engaged in a spiritual quest but as 'a rebel, striving in Faust's way. His personal drama is not a struggle between heavenly and earthly love – Venus and Elisabeth are identical, mere variations of Eros. Transcendency is simply left out.'

Friedrich depicted Wagner's hero as an artist struggling against social norms – a situation which Friedrich felt corresponded to Wagner's own. The abstract sets were bare and grim: the confining society they sketched was a thinly veiled allusion to Nazi Germany, while the redemptive force in the opera was not religion but 'leftist' social tolerance. Erich Leinsdorf 'accused Friedrich of having compromised his artistic integrity for the sake of politics. In his preparations the producer "must have reread the whole opus of Marx, Engels, Trotsky, Liebknecht, and the lot. What he did not read up on was Wagner." '[63] On opening night the principals gave a clenched-fist salute, a gesture which was not repeated in later performances. Members of the audience yelled 'Revenge!' at Friedrich, and Wolfgang Wagner became the target of bomb threats. There were violent scenes when Friedrich took his bow. Gottfried Wagner, Wolfgang's son, later recalled shouts of 'Go back to your dirty communists in the GDR, we don't need you here.' Gottfried added: 'The fronts between right, liberal and left, blurred since 1951 by Wieland's apolitical, psychoanalytical stagings, became clear again'.[64]

Wolfgang's invited producers brought their political concerns to Bayreuth, where they created scandals. On the opening night of the new 1976 centenary production of the *Ring*, conducted by Pierre Boulez and staged by Patrice Chéreau, opera goers objected to the innovative staging created havoc. 'Wolfgang Wagner's new wife had her dress ripped and another woman had her earring torn off – and the earlobe with it.'[65] Ultraconservatives formed an Aktionskreis für das Werk Richard Wagners (Action Group for the Oeuvre of Richard Wagner), handing out leaflets condemning the Chéreau–Boulez *Ring* to audience members as they entered the House. The following year Bryan Magee still reported dissension: 'A theatregoer would scarcely raise an eyebrow at it, yet at Bayreuth a good part of the audience once more divided after each performance into two mobs, one mindlessly outraged by the production's newness as such, the other equally mindlessly thrilled by it.'[66] Magee's main objection was that the music was subordinated to the stage goings-on. 'The result is to reduce long stretches of the orchestral score to little more than soundtrack music, and to void the whole of it of autonomous expressive content.'[67] Rosenthal reported that Boulez had made sure Chéreau would direct the new *Ring*, after failing to convince Bayreuth to hire Ingmar Bergman or Peter Stein. The latter, active on the German legitimate stage, had only once before directed opera, that same year in Paris, collaborating with Solti on an experimental staging of *Rheingold*.[68]

The Chéreau Wagner Ring cycle turned out to be a seminal operatic staging for the late twentieth century. Chéreau focussed on the seeds of political meaning that lie latent in the *Ring*. Andrew Porter considered Chéreau's work 'an allegory of economic history in the last century; untrue to the music and untrue to the text, it was enlivened by keen family scenes and some amusing anachronisms'.[69] Indeed, Chéreau scatters allusions to the industrial revolution and the power politics of the nineteenth and twentieth centuries. Siegfried's forge resembles an early Bessemer converter. The characters of Wotan, Alberich and Mime are tweaked, although not distorted beyond recognition. In contrast to traditional Wagner productions, the characters are frequently in motion on the stage and actually seem to enjoy touching each other. Ensemble acting encourages the audience's emotional – and not merely intellectual – involvement. Chéreau seems to be working forward from Wieland Wagner's dictum, 'The Ring appears to me nowadays to be a giant dialogue . . . about the incompatible contradiction between the concepts of power and love.'[70] In another estimate, written after witnessing performances in the 1979 festival, Robert Hartford found this *Ring* particularly human: 'The greatest strength of Chéreau's direction lies in the treatment of the characters – not as puppets, but as real people. I have never seen a *Ring* with so much human feeling and emotion displayed; I have rarely seen singers act so well.'[71] Wrote Rosenthal, '*Siegfried* was full of provocative touches – Mime was portrayed as if he embodied all the composer's anti-Semitic tendencies; when Siegfried was being perfectly beastly to him he produced an attaché-case ready-packed for his journey. . . .'[72] If Chéreau's aim was to put people off, observed Rosenthal, he achieved it: 'That he must have succeeded to some extent was shown by the hostility of large sections of the audience, especially the German portion of it, who clearly saw some of their rather nastier characteristics mirrored in Chéreau's treatment of certain of the personages on stage . . .' *The Times* critic neatly summed up the production: 'The fury would have been less intense if Mr Chéreau had simply bungled his job; the real aggravation is that his production makes so many illuminating, often unkindly truthful, points about the *Ring*.'[73]

Boulez is so passive that he almost deconstructs his own role in the proceedings. He gives no clear 'read' of the music beyond a pedestrian account of the composer's markings. Rosenthal found that the orchestra 'played for Boulez in a lacklustre manner, hardly sounding as if it was made up of leading front-desk players from all over Germany. Boulez, in his attempt to purge Wagner of bombast and grandiosity, merely succeeded in making him sound dull, small-scale and quite lacking in magic. The great moments passed by almost unnoticed. . . .'[74] By and large, the singers are likewise less than memorable. Peter Hofmann (Siegmund), a sometime rock singer, has not got a large voice, but acts well, has a youthful appeal and uses his vocal resources wisely, if not in a classically Wagnerian manner. Gwyneth Jones (Brünnhilde) encounters far too many vocal difficulties to justify her tackling this demanding part at this stage of her career. Although Donald McIntyre (Wotan) is perhaps the best, he tends to use his fine instrument in a graceless and inflexible way, while his acting is often static.

During the 1970s the Wagner family relinquished part of their control over the festival. A national foundation was established called the Richard-Wagner-Stiftung Bayreuth. The Board of this independent institution was made up of representatives from the federal government, the Bavarian government, the Wagner family, the Society of the Friends of Bayreuth and other interested parties. The Board leased the Festspielhaus to the festival's director, who by preference would be a member of the Wagner family. The advantage to the Wagners was the assurance of fiscal subsidy from government sources.

Opera also came vividly to life during the 1970s in many of the leading Houses of the German provinces. Controversial productions stood in sharp contrast to the safe goings-on at the Vienna Staatsoper. When Rolf Liebermann left Hamburg for Paris in 1973 he was succeeded as intendant by the well-known German stage director August Everding. At the same time Götz Friedrich was appointed principal stage director, while Horst Stein had already been in place for a year as general music director. Emphasis was thus clearly placed on staging as the business of the House. Years of generous government subsidy, a tradition of creativity and innovation and a succession of enlightened, talented managers, helped Hamburg achieve excellence. But disaster struck late in 1975 when props and scenery went up in flames. The fire had been started by a temporary employee angered at being sacked. Fifty-five of the fifty-nine repertory productions were destroyed. Somehow, the season went on almost as planned.

During 1973 Friedrich staged new productions of *Così fan tutte* and *Freischütz*. In the Mozart opera he hung a banner across the curtain with the *e* in *tutte* crossed out and an *i* substituted. This changed the meaning of the title from 'The way of all women' to 'The way of all men'. By this device Friedrich twisted da Ponte's libretto right round to place the blame on Guglielmo and Ferrando for making the wager to test their girlfriends' fidelity. According to *Opera*, the action itself 'did not begin in a café, but backstage in a ragged travelling theatre company, where the two gallants were amusing themselves with the actresses – and in a way which would not have been possible with their ladies. Thus the meaning of *"tutti"* was exposed . . .'[75]

A Götz Friedrich *Zauberflöte*, which opened in Hamburg on 17 April 1977, failed, in Jürgen Kesting's words to bring together 'the disparities inherent in the opera'. Ernst Fuchs was the designer. It was nonetheless of great interest:

> Friedrich sees the opera as a drama of enlightenment and puri-
> fication, as a journey through inner worlds towards the goal of
> self-knowledge in the form of a Love in which 'Eros and
> Humanitas have become as one'. He sees the visual and dra-
> matic riches of the work as a 'multi-faceted montage of the
> stimuli and influences of the Viennese popular theatre'. The
> decor by the Viennese painter, Ernst Fuchs, started out from
> this premise: far from being stylistically unified, his sets were
> rich in contrast and variety. . . .
>
> In the second act the stage was in two split levels, rep-
> resenting the upper and lower worlds. On the bare upper stage
> the priestly scenes were played, and underneath the fantasy-
> Disneyland Papageno episodes took place. In short, all this
> suggested a revue-type succession of scenes, if in a rather tor-
> tured arrangement. At the end of the opera the lovers emerged
> from their ordeals and stood alone on the upper stage bathed in
> a blue light, while the boys presented them with pink betrothal
> garlands.[76]

Horst Stein took over as conductor at the dress rehearsal from Hans Werner Henze, who had been intimidated by members of the orchestra. Stein's direction was considered 'too smooth and lacking in tension'.[77]

Everding resigned from Hamburg in 1977 to become intendant in Munich, and Stein left the House in the same year. Christoph von Dohnányi, engaged as Hamburg's music director from 1977, was greeted with invective from some sections of the press. But he won over the critics in his first season with *Ballo* and *Die Frau ohne Schatten*. The Verdi was marked, wrote Kesting, by 'analytical clarity of tone from the violins and cellos . . . Dohnányi captured the hearts of most of the unprejudiced.' In *Die Frau* he imposed on the score 'a shape and form as strong and forcible as Strauss himself might have conceived . . . He juxtaposed the almost chamber-music-like scenes and the over-whelming sounds at the end of the second and third acts, and managed to achieve, in addition to the contrast value, a dovetailing of the two moods. One should mention the fact that the singers, in spite of this, remained entirely audible throughout.'[78] Dohnányi began to offer new commissions, which he wanted to share with four other Houses in northern Germany. An Everding – Horst Stein *Rosenkavalier*, Everding's farewell production, was considered by Kesting to be too literal, 'full of gimmicks and scenic frivolities and lacking any clear concept'. Stein 'squeezed the last drop of schmalz out of the famous waltz. The orchestral playing was so loud that the sense of the parlando passages was almost lost.'[79]

Günther Rennert was intendant at the Bavarian State Opera in Munich from 1967 until 1977. He had been intendant at Hamburg when the opera was reopened in temporary premises in 1946. Rennert's Munich production of Janáček's *Jenůfa*, which opened on 17 March 1970, was warmly acclaimed as 'one of the most important and successful new productions of recent years'. It formed part of the growing trend towards greater appreciation of Janáček's operas. The work was sung in German in a translation by Kafka's great friend Max Brod. In an exception to the Munich House's habit of failing to keep first-rate conductors, Kubelik was hired for *Jenůfa*. Wrote Greville Rothon, 'Janáček could scarcely have had a more persuasive ambassador than Rafael Kubelik. He drew ravishing playing from his orchestra, relishing the folk-music-inspired lyricism of the score and its nervous vitality.'[80] Kubelik and Rennert received no fewer than forty-eight curtain calls. Even so, Rennert was the target of criticism in the Munich press. As in Vienna, Munich critics tended to the waspish and they were partly blamed for the departure of fine conductors from the House, including Solti, Kempe and Eugen Jochum. Rothon continued, 'As the Kostelnička, Astrid Varnay towered above all other members of the cast. In the same way that Kubelik dominated the whole performance, her presence dominated the stage throughout the evening. Totally immersed in her role, she caused the blood to run cold with the frightening impact of her dramatic portrayal, sung with steely intensity. The memory of it will haunt me for the rest of my opera-going days.'[81]

Rennert left his position at the end of the 1976–77 season and died a year later. Wolfgang Sawallisch, who had been Munich's music director from 1971 to 1982, administered the House for an interim year until Everding took over. Under Sawallisch's guidance the Bavarian State Opera retained its honoured place among German Houses. Sawallisch had a special affinity for Strauss. Charles Pitt wrote: 'His Strauss, like that of his predecessor, Rudolf Kempe, is at the other end of the spectrum from Solti's. It is intellectually refined, finely controlled, never over-exuberant, just clearly laid out.'[82] Conceptual stagings were not absent, however, from the Munich seasons. A new production of *Fidelio* by Götz Friedrich in early 1978 was an uneasy blend of naturalistic and symbolic elements. 'The shaft in Florestan's dungeon,' wrote Karl Heinz Ruppel, 'through which a beam of heavenly light fell after his liberation by Leonore, was a not entirely convincing symbol; but this was mainly the fault of the staging, which failed to suggest the frightening atmosphere of a Spanish gaol of around 1800, with its subterranean dungeons; it resembled rather a somewhat neglected atomic power station. (It appears that today's stage designers are able only to conceive a work of terror and tyranny in terms of life-destroying technology.)'[83] The audience booed Erich Wonder's designs for the production.

Everding's House was the venue for the premiere of Aribert Reimann's *Lear*, with a libretto by Claus Henneberg, first performed on 9 July 1978 to open that year's Munich Festival. The critic for *Opera*, Horst Koegler, wrote, 'Characters are drawn precisely, situations are evoked in strong atmospheric density. There are songs bordering on arias, duets and ensembles. The male choruses even suggest *Götterdämmerung* leanings, and there are beautifully spun out intermezzos. It is an opera deeply rooted in the Schoenberg–Berg traditions without following their twelve-note doctrine.' Jean-Pierre Ponnelle was praised for his craftsmanlike, dramatically effective staging.[84] James Helme Sutcliffe was no less moved the following year at repeat performances at the Munich Festival: 'Reimann's opera still impresses me, on third viewing, as one of the finest new stage works this century has yet brought forth. . . . What is so refreshing about *Lear* in the theatre is that you are little by little compelled to take opera seriously again, to believe in it, as Reimann so evidently does himself.'[85] Each of the nine performances at this year's festival was sold out, down to the last standing-room place.

In a live performance recording of 9 July 1978 the seriousness and dramatic intensity of *Lear* is apparent. Henneberg's German adaptation of Shakespeare is concise and faithful, eschewing all metaphor and literariness. Reimann's having abandoned dodecaphonic composition several years earlier makes for a more expressive vocal line. His richly nuanced *Sprechgesang* likewise is turned into a supple medium for emotional expression. Indeed, the element of feeling is so marked that this work stands in contrast to a good deal of late-twentieth-century music. Contemporary opera composers such as Berio and Glass often deal in ironic or mock-naive postmodernist 'send-ups' of the genre by composers. Occasionally, however, Reimann's excess of expressive power, often associated with thick orchestration, means that text and characterisation, vocal and instrumental lines, may be lost in a welter of sound and emotion.

After more than forty years of richly creative labours Walter Felsenstein died on 8 October 1975 in East Berlin. Perhaps his most lasting legacy to opera staging was his view of the centrality of acting in the genre. The work of his disciples has been highly influential as well. Friedrich, Herz and other directors grafted on to Felsenstein's views of the theatre an ideological commitment which owed a great deal to Brecht as well. In a few brief years ideologically oriented stagings would lead to the conceptual productions which for the past two decades have become common in major opera houses around the world.

In West Berlin, conductor Lorin Maazel was an activist music director from 1965 to 1971. Maazel's work demonstrated the benefits of a conductor's consistent presence in the House and his faithful attention to detail, a combination which had worked so well at Covent Garden. Bryan Magee was enthusiastic: 'By all accounts Lorin Maazel has done with the orchestra what Solti has done with Covent Garden's, namely developed it to symphony-orchestra calibre.'[86] However, Magee criticised the House's costumes and sets as typically 'cheap looking, reminiscent in style of the 1940s, and action is too often mimetic when realism is cried out for. As for the way sex and violence are presented, that is strictly for Aunt Edna.'[87]

Jean-Pierre Ponnelle was active throughout Germany during this period. His new *Salome*, which opened in Cologne on 17 October 1976, was conducted unemotionally by Leif Segerstam. In a geographical miracle, Ponnelle transferred *Salome* to India. *Opera* decided that it 'must rank as the top example of sexual outspokenness. Strauss's "chaste virgin . . . with the most simple and noble gestures" seemed to have been abandoned to the orchestra pit, while on Jean-Pierre Ponnelle's stage an erotic pandemonium raged. It was as if Ponnelle had, for the first time, released the elementary forces of the music and translated them into stage terms.' The musicologist, H. H. Stuckenschmidt continued:

> What went on between this Salome and this Jochanaan had to be seen to be believed! Without actually touching his body, Salome started by voluptuously bathing her sinuous curves in his hair. Then she crouched between his legs, and closely inspected his body. After being interrupted in her inspection by his retreat, she still had the ropes with which he had been tied up; these she fondled and amorously wrapped around her body. Later, in her topless striptease act, she again used the ropes, knotting them so that they resembled the head of the desired Jochanaan, and achieving a sort of ersatz orgasm. After which her actual act of necrophilia, with the severed head, came as a poor letdown.
>
> Can you imagine Gwyneth Jones as this type of Salome . . . ?[88]

Although the gracefully spoken arts administrators in Vienna might not have appreciated the implications of this erotic staging in a German provincial opera house, they would have to contend with much more revolutionary and sometimes brutalist stagings in the years to come.

SIXTEEN

COVENT GARDEN 1971–80

Colin Davis 1: 'A Drama and Not a Birthday Cake'

IN BRITAIN, political developments were reflected in the performing arts by gritty social realism as much as by overt ideological statements. Hall and Davis's impact on what Hall had referred to as Covent Garden's 'nice candy box of entertainment' was soon felt. A tough interpretation of *Peter Grimes* presented a stern realism, very much in keeping with an era of political and social awareness in the performing arts in Britain, Italy and Germany, and even briefly at the Met. Andrew Porter found Davis's reading 'intense and powerful . . . vivid, passionately expressed, keenly projected'. He and Vickers were, he said, almost 'too violent, too vehement, almost brash'.[1] On 1 July 1971 Alan Blyth also recognised the potential for the 'indigenous style and ensemble', which Hall and Davis were so anxious to develop. Davis helped the singers, Blyth wrote, to surpass themselves. Heather Harper's 'voice seems to have taken on new strength' and Norman Bailey was 'the best Balstrode' in Blyth's experience, 'bluff sea captain to the life with a nutty, full voice to match'.

The new era was, however, over before it began. Hall's anxiety and irritation at the disagreements with the Board had grown. 'I remember', he recalled, 'one Board member talking about a singer and saying "I think her top is questionable" and I thought you don't know anything about singing and voices, shut up! – it was like me talking about investments.' Hall added, 'I thought it was intolerable, in spite of all the efforts of John Tooley and Colin, whom I loved and admired, to keep it together.' Drogheda had been the 'marriage broker but then he didn't dare do it'. Hall concluded, 'They wanted their visiting stars and their crush-bar culture.'[2] Davis shared Hall's attitude to the 'crush-bar culture' – the culture of a wealthy, conservative audience interested in star singers, traditional productions and glamorous events. He, like Hall, also recalled how members of the Board 'liked to have their opinions' about singers: 'They didn't like Miss so-and-so and why have we got her again.'[3]

On 4 July 1971 Hall told Lord Drogheda that he was resigning, explaining that 'temperamentally', he was not suited 'to the needs of a repertory opera house'. He would have to do the job full time if he were to succeed, and it had been a mistake to think that a twenty-six-week commitment would be sufficient to control and improve revivals of his productions. While musical standards sometimes benefited from revival, if there was a new cast, there was not sufficient time to work 'through the individuality' of the artists and improve on the dramatic standards. Hall felt guilty about letting Davis down: 'He gave me half of his kingdom gladly and it is a poor way to answer his generosity.'[4] Drogheda replied on 7 July, describing how 'distressed' he was, particularly as he felt a 'considerable sense of personal responsibility' for originally bringing Davis and Hall together.[5]

Hall later wrote that both Davis and Tooley were 'wonderfully magnanimous' in the face of his change of heart, and that he later came to feel that a great chance had been missed. 'I realised as time went by that I had made a terrible mistake,' he said, and added, 'I dreamt to do for opera what I had done for Shakespeare at Stratford and in Colin Davis I had found the ideal partner.' Hall believed that progress and great work in the theatre and opera 'always comes out of companies' and what he called 'a settled group, working together with a common aesthetic' such as that of Felsenstein and Wieland Wagner. Such an achievement was not beyond Covent Garden's aspirations, Hall later ruminating, 'We could have done that.'*[6]

*   *   *

* Hall's biographer believed that Hall was also unhappy that his contract did not give him total artistic control. It specifically stated that final decision rested with the opera subcommittee of the Board, and that any disagreements with Davis should be submitted to Tooley for binding arbitration (Stephen Fay, *Power Play*, p. 266). Tooley did not believe that this was a cause of strain, later recalling, 'It was all very friendly and constructive, with Peter saying, "If at the end of the day there is any dispute – you, John, tell us what we do"' (Tooley Interview 4.12.00).

Davis was bitterly disappointed at Hall's departure. In an interview in the *Evening Standard* he said, 'So much store was set by his coming ... and I actually think he is giving up the thing he is really best at. He is a genius with opera. I am desperate about it.'[7] Davis was at a loss to know where to look for someone who would develop the dramatic and visual aspects, telling the *Observer*, 'When you have offered a man loyalty, friendship and half your kingdom, small though it may be, you don't do it again lightly.'

Kenneth Pearson in the *Sunday Times* of 11 July 1971 laid the blame for Hall's resignation squarely on the Board, and especially on Drogheda, who, he argued, 'in bringing Davis and Hall together has created a monster he could not manage'. Pearson alleged that the 'monster' was a threat to Drogheda whose task as chairman of the Board was to maintain high box office returns by employing top international singers in the principal roles. Drogheda was enraged by the *Sunday Times* article, but Hall again apologised abjectly for the 'terrible mess' he had landed everyone in, and said that he had had nothing to do with the article.[8]

Neither Tooley nor Ingpen was surprised at Hall's resignation. Even during the rehearsals for *Tristan* it had become clear to Tooley that Hall's other commitments conflicted with his own preference for long periods of rehearsal.[9] Tooley also realised that Hall had been unhappy with the technical standards at Covent Garden upon which he had attempted to impose a rigorous discipline during his recent productions, and upon which Tooley believed he would have had a highly beneficial influence.[10] Hall later told Tooley that the *Tristan* opening had been 'the worst first night I have experienced in twenty years'. The stage, he wrote, had failed him 'on every occasion'.[11] As Tooley recalled, 'It wasn't always the technicians' fault – it was sometimes just sheer lack of time, cumbersome arrangements for focusing lights etc., which in fact caused approximation at the end of the day. Peter saw that being permanently attached to a year-round opera house was going to result in too much compromise.'[12]

Tooley was nonetheless saddened, writing to Colin Anderson on 6 July 1971, 'It is a tragedy that the triumvirate of Colin Davis, Peter Hall and myself should have come to an end before it started.'[13] Hall was a complicated individual who needed total backing from those around him and although disagreement with Drogheda and the Board was not the sole reason behind his withdrawal, it was certainly an important influence on his decision. Although Hall denied it, Tooley also believed that he was waiting for Laurence Olivier to step down at the National Theatre. In April 1972 it was announced that Hall would indeed succeed Olivier at the National Theatre. Hall denied that the National appointment had affected his decision, Lord Goodman having sounded him out about it ten days after he had withdrawn from Covent Garden.[14] On 3 August Goodman wrote to Drogheda to say that he knew 'nothing about Peter Hall and Covent Garden'.[15] A letter from Goodman to Drogheda on 14 July 1972 shows clearly that whatever Hall's own motives, there was relief on the part of the establishment that Hall was to return to full-time theatrical work and that Covent Garden had escaped a dangerous leap into the dramatic unknown. 'You and I both know', Goodman wrote, 'that opera is only in a very small degree theatre.'

Without Hall's active presence, this was to be a self-fulfilling prophecy. Faced by ever-growing financial stringencies, Davis was to find it hard to give the artistic direction that the two men had jointly envisioned. Davis had spoken to Tooley in the heady days of December 1970 of his work with Hall, Bury and O'Brien: 'I don't want to be everywhere. I want to be with these men, because when I am with these men, I'm twice the man I might be.'[16]

The young singing talent with which Hall and Davis had intended to create an ensemble was abundant and extraordinary in 1971. Of the English-based singers alone, Thomas Allen, Benjamin Luxon, Valerie Masterson and Margaret Price were at the start of fine careers, as was John Tomlinson, who made his debut at English National Opera in 1974 and went on to a great international career in the 1980s and 1990s. Kiri Te Kanawa was also about to make her debut at Covent Garden. This was a generation of singers brought up in a new cultural world in Britain. John Tomlinson, one of five children whose early experience was singing in the Accrington Male Voice Choir, recalled the sudden possibilities that had emerged in the 1960s: 'There was a new feeling of daring and optimism. When I finally made the decision to sing, I was on the crest of that wave.'[17] David Syrus, who was later head of music at Covent Garden, had a similar experience of the openness of the 1960s, recalling, 'I came from a working-class background. My father worked in the same shoe shop all his life. I went to grammar school, luck of good teachers – off you go to Oxford.' He continued, 'That seemed to be absolutely what was assumed in that period – nothing was closed to you, there was such idealism.'[18]

Janet Baker was another artist who had benefited from the developments in cultural life in Britain since the war. Coming from York, she had not even seen an opera until she first appeared in the Glyndebourne chorus in 1956. Like Heather Harper she had been a member of the Ambrosian Choir, which she described as a 'university' for so many singers in Britain. Anthony Lewis helped her to lift her voice into the dramatic mezzo range from contralto.* Her ability to communicate with her audience and her solid training were recognised from her earliest appearances. On 27 September 1969 she had sung Lucretia at the Coliseum, when she was recognised as a great artist with a strikingly beautiful and individual voice. She was singing opposite Benjamin Luxon, the talented baritone whose career was to be cruelly cut short by deafness.

Another impressive young artist, Thomas Allen was described by John Steane as 'the best lyric baritone singing in opera since the war'.[19] Born in 1944 in County Durham, the grandson of a miner, Allen's extraordinary talent emerged from an unpromising environment. 'Where I come from there is no theatre,' he recalled, 'at school you were knocked down, physically knocked down, if you showed any aspirations to the arts, and speaking "proper".' He also recalled, however, that his father and some of his schoolteachers encouraged him and instilled in him a love of music and singing, at a time when choral societies were very much part of the English way of life. In 1964 he was offered a place at the Royal College of Music. Arriving there, Allen recalled, 'was a mystery, and finding out about composers called Mahler and Bruckner was a mystery. I had no proper education of music . . . I think the transition from a Northern pit village to London

---

* Janet Baker joined the English Opera Group, singing many roles at Aldeburgh until in 1967 Scottish Opera cast her as Dorabella for Anthony Besch.

was a hell of a shock.' Allen also remembered the kind of teaching he encountered at college: 'I wasn't aware of many voice teachers at the time who seemed to really know what the physical process of singing was about. . . . The teachers I have come across in the last few years have an understanding such as I never came across as a student. As luck would have it I had someone who did me no harm and left nature to take its course.'[20]

At the Royal College, Allen was coached by James Lockhart who, when he was made music director of Welsh National Opera, took Allen with him. Lockhart, Michael Geliot and John Moody gave Allen three years of invaluable experience as a contract artist with Welsh National Opera, where he learnt stagecraft by observing and 'jumping in at the deep end'. As Allen put it, 'You observe and then something instinctive and organic comes from inside.' Geliot pushed Allen, who recalled, 'The lessons I learnt then about pitching your voice into a theatre for dialogue have stood me in good stead ever since.'[21] Geliot's May 1971 *Magic Flute*, which was set in a South American forest with Tamino a conquistador and Papageno an Indian, provoked a lively response. At first Allen found the producer's vision hard to take, and 'there were some awful rows'. But in the end, wrote Max Loppert in *Opera*, Allen's 'lithe impersonation, decked with feathers and paint, cracking the jokes in a broad Wearside accent, was one of the show's undoubted triumphs'.[22] Loppert also found Allen 'infinitely pathetic and touching' in scenes with Margaret Price's 'poignant Pamina'. Price herself was yet another impressive young artist, admired by *Opera* critic Elizabeth Forbes for her 'fearless attack, firmness of line and the way she pours her voice into the music so that every note and phrase is completely filled'.[23]

Allen's talent was immediately recognised in London when he started giving recitals in 1973 and appearing at Covent Garden. Loppert wrote of Allen's 'high, firm, precisely placed lyric baritone, easy of emission and wide of compass, particularly bright of tone in its top octave. The voice was apparently master of a wide range of tone colours; there was a combination of thrust, warmth, and emotional openness about its employment that lent everything he sang a strongly dramatic focus.'

Margaret Price was making a greater career in Germany and Vienna than at home. On 22 September 1971, in a Ponnelle production of *Don Giovanni*, she 'swept an elegant Cologne audience off its feet as Donna Anna. . . . Her vocal delivery was steady as a rock and marvellously projected.' The local press called her '*Die perfekte Sensation*'. Covent Garden, wrote Alan Blyth, was slow 'to see they had a star in their midst'.[24] Tooley later recalled that Price's relatively few performances in England were not because she was not offered roles, but that she could not bear to be parted from her dogs who were subject to the English quarantine laws.[25] In a 1972 Glyndebourne recording of *Entführung*, conducted by John Pritchard, Price's vocal accuracy is impressive and the sound is most attractive. The trills are clean, as are the attacks, with no suggestion of scooping from below. The top notes are free; the middle and upper registers appealingly creamy toned.

Hall's departure from Covent Garden left plans in disarray, Drogheda telling the opera subcommittee on 21 July 1971 that all their 'high hopes had been dashed by Hall's withdrawal'. The opera committee were told that Tooley and Davis would share the responsibility for choosing repertoire and singers, and major decisions had to be taken about the work Hall was to have prepared, including *Figaro, Nabucco, Don Giovanni* and the *Ring*. Hall, supported by Moser, was still extremely keen to direct the *Ring* with Bury and O'Brien as joint designers. Harewood also favoured Hall, believing that Davis needed 'a very strong collaborator with whom he can discuss any dramatic possibility which occurs to him'. Only Hall, he believed, could translate such thoughts 'into exciting stage fact'. Tooley, however, was sceptical that Hall would have enough time for such a major undertaking. In October he told Harewood that his main doubt 'centred around Peter's personal reliability in keeping his commitment to us over an extended period'. Hall's personal situation made it difficult for him to withstand outside pressures.[26] He told Isaiah Berlin on 11 November 1971 that the 'suspicion and tension' that would exist between Hall and Davis would result in a production that would not reflect their talent.[27] In December Hall told Davis and Tooley that he no longer wished to direct the *Ring*.[28]

The most urgent decision concerned the imminent *Figaro*, about which there had already been so much dissension. It was decided that John Copley, the associate resident director from 1966 to 1972, would take over the new production with Stefanos Lazaridis as designer.* Premiered on 5 December 1971, this *Figaro* was sung in Italian. Many of the critics would have preferred it in English, as Hall and Davis had originally wanted, but they nevertheless sensed a new spirit in the House. Seat prices were reasonable, there seemed to be a less glittering audience and it was not a star cast, although Kiri Te Kanawa, singing her first major role as the Countess, was about to be launched on a great career. William Mann wrote of Te Kanawa, 'How lovingly Mr Davis is nursing the miracle in his charge.'[29] Peter Heyworth liked Davis's first *Figaro* as music director, finding it a 'most lively, warm, humane and blissfully unaffected performance of the opera'.[30]

The production was Beaumarchais-inspired, with a young-looking Almaviva household and realistic scenery, the blinds keeping out the hot Spanish sun. 'Sexual passions', wrote Rosenthal, 'were never far below the surface.'[31] The cast included Geraint Evans and Reri Grist, as well as Te Kanawa, who made a great impact, William Mann going so far as to say she 'looked like a teenage Goddess'.[32] Shawe-Taylor wrote of Te Kanawa's 'stream of pure radiant ample tone, which remained ringing and assured'.[33]

Colin Davis later remembered how he and Hall had auditioned Te Kanawa in 1969, fresh from the Opera Centre, where Joan Ingpen had heard her. Davis recalled, 'I couldn't believe my ears. I've taken thousands of auditions but it was such a fantastically beautiful voice that I said, "Let's hear her again and see if we're not dreaming."'[34] Copley had originally been reluctant for Te Kanawa to sing the Countess. He had been her teacher at the Opera Studio and she had been, according to Copley, 'a terrible student, she never knew her stuff and

---

* Copley was central to British opera production from the late 1960s until the 1990s, since when he worked mainly abroad. He was originally trained in ballet; later Joan Cross and Tyrone Guthrie were his mentors. He worked on design at Stratford with Leslie Hurry and Tanya Moiseivich. In 1960 he joined the stage management at Covent Garden and was present at rehearsals, including Kleiber's *Elektra*. He played the piano for Sylvia Fisher while she learnt her roles. He had been given a chance by Solti to prepare the 1968 *Così* and had worked as resident revival producer with Ande Anderson, and was resident director from 1972 to 75. His musicality, and ability to make singers feel comfortable on stage, contributed to his extraordinarily long and fruitful career.

we had to send her home for being lazy'. Copley later recalled that Te Kanawa 'always talks about it and she's quite right, she really didn't have a very good time there at all – we weren't very nice to her'. He felt she was not ready for the role, but Tooley and Davis insisted and Copley started working with her months before: 'I really did groom her, in every way, how to use fans, how to move and she was absolutely receptive and she was fantastic.[35] We had a marvellous time. Colin Davis was very involved in that.' Ingpen recalled that in order to secure Te Kanawa's future was not rushed, as she felt Gwyneth Jones's had been, she had urged Covent Garden to give Kiri a five-year contract to protect her from taking on too much too soon. In December the Board congratulated Te Kanawa on her 'outstanding debut' and offered her a contract to 1975.[36]

In spite of the auspicious *Figaro* and *Grimes*, Davis soon came to feel the same hostility that Solti had faced in his early years, particularly in the Italian repertory, with which he seemed to be less in sympathy. Davis told Tooley that he was criticised for having no knowledge of the Italian repertory, but that he was unrepentant about having no interest in Bellini. It was his task, he believed, to find someone who did have such an interest.[37] Davis's first Verdi was the new *Nabucco* that Hall was to have directed. It was the first time it had been presented at Covent Garden since 1850. It opened on 27 March 1972, when both he and soprano Elena Suliotis were greeted with a barrage of booing, which Porter thought undeserved. Rosenthal, however, found Davis 'un-Verdian, unidiomatic' and felt that the work 'did not flow, did not throb with that primitive emotion'. Peter Heyworth thought Davis to be in 'one of those fretful moods in which he hurls himself at the music'.[38] The producer who had taken over from Hall, Václav Kašlík, and his designer Josef Svoboda – with his black, white and grey sets – had not decided whether to make it realistic and traditional or modern and stylised. According to Porter the original idea of Jewish prisoners in a Czech ghetto, which had been rejected by the Board, had not altogether been dispensed with and there were moments of amateurishness such as 'the village hall swordplay of Nabucco's army' in the first scene.[39]

After the performance a woman booed Davis in the street. According to the *Evening Standard*, Davis said to her, 'Don't do that. That's no way to behave' and held on to her coat collar. Her husband came up and said, 'Take your hands off my wife.' Davis continued, 'She said I hadn't conducted Verdi with enough Italian blood. I wouldn't have minded except that my shirt came to pieces in three places during the performance. . . . In the end she asked for my autograph.'[40]

The booing claque performed intermittently during most of Davis's regime, and in February 1973 Tooley told Drogheda that he was attempting to find the source and stop it, as he had with Solti.[41] Tooley later recalled that Davis generally tended to brush aside these attacks, only occasionally responding with moments of defiance that 'did him no good with the public but which eased the tension for him'. The going was, in Tooley's words, 'rough and hard for him', with particular criticism of his Puccini, Verdi and Wagner in his early years when he lacked experience.[42] The Italian repertoire was particularly vulnerable and a recording of Bohème in 1979 indeed revealed a lack of the caressing line so essential to Puccini. Nevertheless, the Covent Garden orchestra played very well for Davis, with clean attacks, good intonation, and good expression within the limits set by his hard-nosed interpretation of this very warm music. The Covent Garden orchestra, very much at Davis's instigation and in contrast to Solti, made in all twelve recordings, with Davis, for Philips.

The standard of revivals was to prove a major problem during the Davis era after Hall's resignation. There was a major row in the summer of 1972 when Hall was enraged to discover that his Tristan production had been substantially altered and the lighting projectors removed without his permission for reasons of economy. Davis sought to soothe relations between them, telling Hall that if he had been in the House they could 'have hammered out these problems'. But Hall was not there to convince Tooley or improve his work and felt that he had reached the 'end of a journey' begun when he left the House the previous year. Hall wrote to Tooley on 9 August 1972 that although they should not behave like enemies in public, their partnership was ended. Tooley replied that they did not need to be enemies 'in public or in private' and good relations were eventually restored.[43] On 22 January 1973 Rosenthal mourned the dismantling of Peter Hall's Tristan and deplored 'its concert-like stances for the love duet'. He recognised that the alterations to the lighting plot severely affected the production.

In Rosenthal's words, Davis gave a 'committed and impassioned reading' but once again he was booed.*[44]

Hall's absence and the presence of 'canaries' in what was labelled 'international' opera did not tend to the well-rehearsed, taut, integrated performances that Davis and Hall had envisioned. On 23 June 1972 Copley failed to get Caballé to fit into a production of Traviata, which disappointed in spite of her fine singing. On 1 April 1973 Carlo Bergonzi and Grace Bumbry gave magnificent vocal performances in Tosca, but also with no attempt to integrate themselves into their surroundings. Milnes found 'Bergonzi's genuine, instinctively felt Mediterranean gut reaction . . . completely compelling'. But his acting was rudimentary: 'At the end of the duet where he sails up to a B flat, he stepped back from Tosca, got into a comfortable legs apart position, set the arm in motion and really gave the phrase the works. C'est magnifique, mais ce n'est pas l'opéra, and the laughter it generates, while tinged with admiration, is still laughter.'[45]

'International opera' entailed the appearance of other great 'canaries' throughout the decade, including Alfredo Kraus, Lucia Popp, Brigitte Fassbaender, Freni, Pavarotti, Domingo and Carreras. Vickers again became a regular visitor. In June 1972 he sang his first Otello at Covent Garden. Porter wrote that his 'sudden movements of swift savagery recalled Olivier – a fury so intense as to border on madness'. He also pointed out perceptively that Davis needed 'great music to get the best from him'. Otello, Porter noted, 'engaged him on all levels – the orchestral playing was keen and colourful'.[46]

On 8 December 1971 Plácido Domingo had made his Covent Garden debut in Tosca. John Higgins found 'virility and metal in the voice' and 'sweetness too'. Downes, a master of the Italian repertory, gave a 'dramatic, fast-moving' account.[47] In July 1973 Domingo appeared with Solti in an unexceptional new production of Carmen by Michael Geliot, who had taken over from Zeffirelli at six months' notice. Solti was happy to be back at Covent Garden and produced what Stanley Sadie described as a 'rhythmic vitality which set the nerves tingling'. The critics did not immediately respond to Domingo's

---

* On 21 May 1975 the opera subcommittee noted that a revival of Onegin had fallen to 'an unacceptable level' (OSC, 19/3/6).

talents, Heyworth finding him to be 'too soft and lachrymose', although master of 'a rich and ardent voice'.[48] Thomas Allen was Morales, and Te Kanawa's warm, creamy tone was praised, while her characterisation of Micaëla was thought a shade too homely. Ingpen later recalled that from the time of *Carmen*, Kiri was 'Solti's pet'.[49]

In January 1974 Domingo's talents were given full acknowledgement when he sang Radames in what was otherwise a poor *Aida* revival. Domingo 'in excellent voice and looking considerably more heroic than as Don José last summer, is probably the best all-round Radames that there is today, and that is not to forget Jon Vickers or Carlo Bergonzi'.[50] Domingo became Tooley's favourite tenor, usually singing twice at Covent Garden every season. For his part, Domingo testified to the pleasant atmosphere at Covent Garden at that time. 'There is no doubt that London's Royal Opera is one of the friendliest in the world,' he wrote in his memoirs. 'Everyone there from the maintenance staff and telephone operators to the top of the administration does everything to make life as easy as possible for the performers. Their courtesy and friendliness is amazing.' Of John Tooley, Domingo wrote that he was 'a man who cares not only about the welfare of his theatre but also about that of his artists'.[51]

Some of the Davis–Hall plans survived Hall's departure. On 12 July 1972 Michael Geliot's production of Maxwell Davies's *Taverner* was premiered, causing such excitement that on its third and fourth performances people were turned away from the box office. Set during Henry VIII's Reformation, the story traces the composer John Taverner's conversion from Roman Catholicism to Protestantism, his involvement in the persecution of the Catholic priesthood and his subsequent loss of musical creativity. William Mann found the work loaded with symbolism and the music abundant in 'passion and sensuous colour'. He felt that the harmonic writing, however, sounded 'like thick fog under an audible tune'.[52] Rosenthal concluded that Geliot's excellent production made the work 'more enjoyable for theatrical than musical reasons'.[53]

Martin Cooper considered the libretto of *Taverner* 'too intellectual for opera'. Historical events, he believed, were better presented in terms of personalities, as in Verdi's *Don Carlos*. He felt that the 'imbalance between words and music' was a 'fundamental weakness' and was caused by the 'wide disparity between the composer's intellectual and his emotional grasp'. The musical language also worked against the drama: 'the multiplicity of micro-rhythms seriously weakens any overall sense of movement in the music'.[54] The orchestra and Edward Downes, however, were praised for mastering the extraordinarily difficult music and for the successful realisation of the enterprise.

Unfortunately, the revival of *Taverner* only resulted in modest box office returns of 49 per cent. There were even lower returns for Richard Rodney Bennett's *Victory*, at 30 per cent, and Tippett's *The Knot Garden*. Based on Conrad's novel, *Victory* had been premiered in April 1970, sponsored by the Friends of Covent Garden and directed by Colin Graham. It showed, in Rosenthal's words, 'a real feeling for the theatre' and its music 'evoked atmosphere' for its varied dramatic situations.[55] Set in the Dutch East Indies in 1895, the work included thirteen sung roles, three spoken roles, two choruses and an 'on-stage Ladies' orchestra, with the young Anne Howells as the Chanteuse. Masterfully conducted by Edward Downes, *Victory* was a demanding piece. New work, recalled Davis, entailed a 'huge investment for very little return of interest from the public'.*[56]

Although Davis was recognised as a Berlioz specialist, he again had a mixed reception, including some boos, for *The Trojans*, sung in French on 21 September 1972. The cast included Vickers, Elizabeth Bainbridge and Josephine Veasey, who became ill during the run. Janet Baker took on Dido at short notice and sang in English, the language in which she had performed the role at Scottish Opera. Baker, who had not performed with the company before, made an enormous impact during her performances in October. On 3 October, Baker sang with a 'spellbinding restraint and complete involvement in the role' which, in Rosenthal's words, 'cast a spell over the house'.[57]

Davis had recorded *Les Troyens* with the Covent Garden orchestra for Philips in 1969. In the recording, his love of the French repertoire

---

* Richard Rodney Bennett's other operas were *The Ledge* (1961), *The Mines of Sulphur* (1965), *A Penny for a Song* (1967) and *All the King's Men* (1969).

was clearly apparent. He showed complete understanding of Berlioz's unusual and highly expressive orchestration, with crisp rhythms and sharp contrasts of tempo and dynamics building great excitement and, when necessary, accenting the primitive, atavistic elements in the score. Vickers sang Aeneas with epic breadth and ecstatic involvement. Although he was gruff and often tonally invariate, his larger-than-life stage persona suited the role perfectly and his scarcely restrained roar created a wonderful mix with Veasey's dark, plangent tones.*

Davis's new *Don Giovanni* on 18 April 1973 was poorly received. Copley had unwillingly taken over the production from Hall at the last moment. He had warned Drogheda in December 1971 that Geraint Evans and Peter Glossop were 'temperamentally completely incompatible'.[58] His and Lazaridis's concept of hell as a filmed 'horde of beautiful women who gradually become lewd and distorted' was abandoned at the last moment by the management as too expensive and was replaced by the dreaded 'flames and smoke', which were accompanied by strenuous booing.[59] Davis reacted defiantly, in a manner that Board member John Pope-Hennessy described to Drogheda as 'undignified and reprehensible'. He also found it 'one of the coarsest performances' of the opera that he had ever heard and wrote that Davis had the 'brain of a sparrow, little operatic experience and a minus quantity of taste'. Public taste, he wrote, was 'fundamentally conventional' and required 'visually orthodox, musically excellent performances'.

Drogheda defended Davis, but the Board as a whole were disturbed by the 'juxtaposition of a realistic production and costumes set incongruously against unrepresentational scenery'.[60] Readers of *Opera* wrote complaining that Lazaridis's mirrors and steel rods sets were 'tatty' and impractical, and that the ladies' seventeenth-century dresses got ensnared in them.[61] As a result of the mainly hostile reception Copley had his *Magic Flute* taken away and felt 'lacerated' by the experience.†[62]

---

* Davis's love of Berlioz also brought *Benvenuto Cellini* into the Covent Garden repertoire on 29 January 1976. Davis had recorded the complete works of Berlioz by the late Eighties and conducted a complete cycle of Berlioz operas with the London Symphony Orchestra in 2000–01.

† Copley had another difficult experience at Covent Garden in 1987, when Margaret Price fell ill during rehearsals of *Norma* and the show was consequently seriously under-rehearsed. The management never explained what had happened, and he had two years' estrangement, from the company.

Davis explained to Drogheda that he had been endeavouring to 'make a drama and not a birthday cake'.[63] Harold Rosenthal was one of the few to recognise the production's merits, both for its interpretation of 'the dissolute punished' – the sub-title of the opera – and the absence of elaborate and naturalistic scenery. He also praised its 'unified sense of purpose', superb lighting and beautiful costumes, and feared that the 'forces of reaction and conservatism' had taken over Covent Garden.[64] Later revivals managed to correct most of the problems, and it proved a flexible basis for reworking for many years.

Much of the booing Davis was to encounter during his time as music director had as much to do with steel rods as with his musical contribution. According to Stanley Sadie, he made the score sound 'so varied, so intense, so full of character, so big . . . a thrilling realisation'.*[65] The singing was, however, disappointing. Felix Aprahamian thought that Gwyneth Jones had lost the 'bloom' in her voice and that Glossop's Giovanni 'failed to establish his seductiveness'.[66] In the November revival with Siepi, Alan Blyth, who had known Davis's *Don Giovanni* since the 1950 Chelsea Opera Group performances at the Holywell music room in Oxford, felt he was looking for something new and hurrying things along too much, and that as a consequence he had lost 'the fiery, lean interpretation, full of dynamic contrasts', as well as 'that direct, dramatic vision of the score that we all so much admire'.[67]

Perhaps Davis was anxious, for his recording of May 1975 for Philips Classics indeed reveals the qualities Blyth so admired. The Covent Garden orchestra responded warmly to Davis's direction, giving a cleanly delineated performance with striking contrasts of colour and emotion. Where Solti was vital, transparent and energetic, Davis was insistent, virile and menacing. A sensitive accompanist who appreciated Mozart's nuances, Davis highlighted sour horns and clarinets and nasty, chuckling, low strings, and succeeded in matching the orchestral sounds to those of the singers. However, there were occasional indications of a lack of empathy with the singers – in 'Mi tradì' his fast tempo did not give Te Kanawa time to melt with anguish and

---

* Davis would have been pleasantly surprised by Sadie's review, as he had warned Drogheda that he would probably say that he drove the music too hard and that he had not developed since his Cambridge days (Davis to Drogheda, Royal Opera House Archives, Drogheda papers 15.4.73)

in spite of some lovely sounds the singing was generally characterless.

Te Kanawa's expanding repertoire continued, however, to give delight. On 16 October 1973 she sang her first Amelia in *Simon Boccanegra*. Rosenthal was bowled over by her 'ravishing sounds'. Verdi showed to great advantage her 'amazing breath control and technique', and she looked as ravishing as she sounded. In the middle of the lyric soprano *Fach*, the role was a perfect match for Te Kanawa's warm and slightly vulnerable stage persona. In her early prime she was peerless, with her soft-grained sound, marvellously well-knit registers and free top. The voice lacked Italian pungency, that hint of edge: instead, the timbre was mellow and elegiac, with a delicate and most appealing touch of sadness. The effortless tonal production was matched by her easy and appealing stage demeanour.

When it was finally decided that Hall would not direct the *Ring*, Tooley felt that Davis needed another strong collaborator and suggested, in January 1972, that Götz Friedrich, the East German director, might be a suitable substitute. He was, Tooley told the opera subcommittee on 19 January, 'particularly imaginative and stimulating'. In early 1972 Davis went to Berlin to talk to Friedrich. He recalled, 'I took to the man at once, he was my sort of person.' Friedrich then came to London and the two men spent two weeks going through the *Ring* 'word by word and note by note'. Davis continued, 'Those were some of the most marvellous days of my life.'[68]

In September 1972 the subcommittee decided to recommend Friedrich's engagement to the Board. Davis was sure that Friedrich was the right man to direct the *Ring*, even though Board members were concerned, in the light of reports of his *Tannhäuser* from Bayreuth, that he was 'a dedicated Marxist'. Friedrich's Bayreuth *Tannhäuser* had raised a storm of booing and controversy with its vision of the knights of the Wartburg as medieval Nazis. Davis defended him, explaining that he was 'a man of real intellectual and artistic stature, great integrity, a fertile mind and a stimulating and exciting personality'. Davis assured the Board that the attacks on him at Bayreuth had been politically motivated and his approach to the *Ring* was 'wholly undogmatic'. Tooley was equally convinced of Friedrich's suitability as 'a German-speaking producer steeped in Wagner who had not yet produced it'.[69]

Drogheda recalled that when he and Moser met Friedrich in December 1972 they too were 'impressed if slightly apprehensive'. Friedrich's *Ring* plans, Drogheda felt, revealed 'a highly original and creative mind at work'. Tooley recalled that in spite of his asking for an overall plan for the *Ring*, Friedrich was unconcerned about 'visual unity' and never provided one. Friedrich's concept of the stage representing the world and the action taking place on a hydraulic platform, with Wotan, Loge and Alberich addressing the audience from outside it, was felt to be 'imaginative and original'.[70]

Davis was getting a hostile reception from some members of the audience and a mixed one from the critics, and his relationship with the Board continued to be strained. On 28 June 1973 Drogheda told Tooley, 'I think he went a bit too far in his dismissal of the Board as being of no use or value at all unless they devote themselves to raising funds from private sources.'[71] Moser recalled that in his early years, Davis felt the need 'slightly to put the Board in its place'. He came, Moser continued, 'with a suspicion that the Board would interfere too much and in a way he was right, as Drogheda had not hesitated to give his opinion on musical matters'.[72]

Davis himself later admitted, 'I created most of the problems simply by being the kind of person that I was.' He realised that he had not been 'very good at handling the Board – they loved opera but they were not professionals . . .' and he regretted having been 'irascible'.[73] Davis told Tooley that his 'sharp' responses at Board meetings 'reflected a situation that has existed since I was a child in which I appear to be pitting my own pitiful self against a world with values other than mine'.[74] Tooley, who greatly admired Davis as a 'remarkable' and 'intuitive' musician, believed he lacked confidence, and later recalled, 'I used to say to Colin, "For God's sake stop humbling yourself!"'[75] On the whole, however, he found Davis 'a splendid person with whom to work'.*[76]

---

* On 7 December 1972 Davis suggested to Drogheda that if Michael Tippett were appointed a Board member he would help to break down the 'club' atmosphere. He was 'our greatest composer, successful manager of the Bath Festival & a highly responsible person' (Royal Opera House Archives, Drogheda papers).

Although Drogheda was seen as the main adversary, in fact, he defended Davis from Pope-Hennessy, who had gone so far as to suggest taking artistic responsibility away from the music director after *Don Giovanni*. Davis was, Drogheda wrote, 'a man of great fondness of heart and depth of feeling, a fine musician needing above all to be upheld and reassured'. He explained to Pope-Hennessy that the Covent Garden Board's powers, even if only those of 'persuasion and advice', were far greater than those of any European opera house, where the intendant 'is a virtual dictator subject only to occasional ministerial whim' and greater even than those of the Met Board.

Davis indeed required reassurance. He wrote to Drogheda on 4 April, 'Just at the moment we cannot win . . . because we cannot expand efficiently because we have not enough money.' Davis felt the House needed a bigger chorus, bigger orchestra, fewer performances and more new productions to attract better conductors. Drogheda urged him not to be despondent, as Covent Garden was putting on first-rate performances and playing to nearly full houses.

At a press conference on 5 July 1973 Davis was attacked for the erratic standard of orchestral playing and admitted that in the previous season some of the performances had made him blush.* On 13 July, during an interview for the *Evening Standard*, Sydney Edwards found Davis 'hurt and upset' although he said that his conscience was clear as he spent more time in the House than had previous directors. Davis asked, 'Are they out to destroy me?' To Max Loppert he said, 'They'll get over it, or I will or they will get rid of me . . . I have no intention of being too solemn about it.' Drogheda tried to reassure Davis, writing to him on 26 August, 'Please do not say "we cannot win" . . . It is tantamount to saying that performances of inspirational quality have no place in London and this I find it terribly hard to accept.'[77]

*   *   *

* In June 1972, Davis had told the Board that resources were urgently needed to improve the morale of the orchestra; £10,000 to improve the salaries of outstanding players and £25,000 for more string players. It was twenty-five years since the orchestra had been established and the older members were staying, whereas the talented younger ones were leaving (Board meeting, 27.6.72).

Davis had complained to Drogheda in April 1973, 'In their eyes Sadler's Wells can do no wrong, and we no right.'[78] It was true that Sadler's Wells was reaping the rewards of a steady development of its ensemble company. The music director from January 1970 to December 1977 was Charles Mackerras, who had a sure grasp of the company's musical standards and had successfully brought them through the difficult first seasons after the move to the Coliseum. Milnes wrote of Mackerras: 'The versatility of the man is truly bewildering' with his repertory of 110 operas. During his directorship Mackerras shaped a repertory 'balanced between bread-and-butter and caviar', building up the orchestra and nurturing the singers.[79] In 1972 Sadler's Wells's director, Stephen Arlen, died tragically young, just as things were beginning to settle down after the move. Lord Harewood took over his position, resigning from the Covent Garden Board.

Mackerras created his own 'stars', as well as inviting British guests to appear. In August 1972 he conducted a highly successful John Copley – Stefanos Lazaridis *Trovatore* with a company cast including Rita Hunter and Norman Bailey. Copley was to produce many classic productions for Sadler's Wells during the 1970s. In October of that year the company mounted an ambitious project, which played to packed houses. It was Prokofiev's *War and Peace*, a little performed opera with an episodic libretto, whose strengths Colin Graham managed to emphasise.* Norman Bailey dominated as Kutuzov, and the cast also included Josephine Barstow, another increasingly well-known member of the company, who had sung a much praised Violetta in March 1973.

Sadler's Wells Opera was progressing with its English-language *Ring* cycle, which reflected the coherence of the company. Its principals were all company members: Norman Bailey's Wotan was world class,

---

* Colin Graham was a central figure in English operatic life in the 1960s and 1970s, directing nearly all the English Opera Group's premieres of Britten's works. He then oversaw EOG's transformation into English Music Theatre, which was axed by the Arts Council four years later. He also worked at Sadler's Wells Opera and ENO as director of productions (1978–83). He directed premieres in Britain of *The Cunning Little Vixen* and *From the House of the Dead* for Sadler's Wells. As director of Opera Theatre of St Louis from 1978 to 1984 Graham became a central figure in United States opera also teaching at Yale University opera department. He has since rarely worked in Britain with the exception of the 1992 *Death in Venice* for Covent Garden.

Alberto Remedios's Siegfried was lyrically sung with good strong tone, and Rita Hunter was a sturdy Brünnhilde. The joint producers, Glen Byam Shaw and John Blatchley, together with the designer, Ralph Koltai, received much praise for what Rosenthal described as a 'musically and visually . . . completely integrated' production, although some of the critics were once again disturbed by Koltai's 'space age' and monotone sets, which included more 'cubes, tubes and spherical objects'. Early in 1972 Siegfried completed the Sadler's Wells Ring so that two complete cycles could be given in the summer. Andrew Porter's translation was praised by Rosenthal for its singability and naturalness, and for enabling a new and wider public to enjoy the Ring. Although some of Goodall's tempi were so slow as to create difficulties for the singers, and often caused the tension to flag, his reading won high acclaim from most critics.

On 3 August 1974 Sadler's Wells Opera changed its name to English National Opera, in order to end the confusion between Sadler's Wells at the Coliseum and Rosebery Avenue. The company continued to present new and adventurous repertory, sometimes in co-operation with the Opera Factory and the New Opera Company. On 10 October 1974 they produced The Bassarids by Hans Werner Henze.

Not only were Sadler's Wells at the Coliseum and its music director 'doing no wrong' at this time, but Peter Hall was finding great artistic satisfaction directing the Mozart – da Ponte operas at Glyndebourne, where the conditions of a summer festival and the constant support of general manager Moran Caplat released Hall's full creative energies. Glyndebourne was, for Hall, a harmonious environment where the stage held equal status with the pit.[80] Hall's fascination for Mozart was also given full scope at Glyndebourne, where the scale of the theatre was, he believed, 'absolutely right for releasing the complex riches of his operas'.[81]

Hall continued to work with designer John Bury, with whom such a close understanding had grown up that 'the briefest exchange could result in a remarkable conception'.[82] Bury was a designer of genius, even though the Covent Garden Board had been slow to recognise his talent and had been nervous of what Pavitt had called the 'John Bury

– *Midsummer Marriage* school of design'. Hall's and Bury's first production at Glyndebourne was *Figaro* in 1973, for which Bury's sets and costumes firmly set the drama in its social context, rendering both the palazzo and its inhabitants strikingly and delightfully recognisable.

In contrast to many of the German producers, Hall's working method was undogmatic and flexible. 'Almost dangerously but always constructively,' John Higgins wrote, 'he avoids reaching the opera house with a pat, blocked-out idea of what he wants to achieve.' Rather, Hall worked 'with and through his singers, asking them to create their characterisations, their relationships in partnership with him. Sometimes there is a clash of wills; more often the result is a happy amalgam of suggestions from players and director.'[83]

Hall used the uncut text of *Figaro* – working closely on the recitatives with the singers so that they would deliver them with expression and emphasis. He also collaborated closely with the conductor, John Pritchard, throughout the rehearsals. A video recording of the production was made the following winter, sensitively and effectively directed by Dave Heather.[84] Hall's staging was revealed as both imaginative and respectful of the work, using nuances of acting to draw out the implied conflicts stemming from class and social stratification. As Spike Hughes commented, the whole production conveyed 'the shadows of human sadness cast by the sunlight of comedy'.[85]

In the recording the cast was exemplary. Frederica von Stade's Cherubino was a gentle, sunny, life-loving zany. Her silvery mezzo with its big free top was combined with sensitive, intelligent phrasing, consummately easy breath technique and considerable acting skills. Benjamin Luxon's beautiful baritone was also full of nuance and expression – from frustrated bully to childish charmer. Te Kanawa's warm and creamy-toned Countess, though sometimes distracted in mien, was vocally well paired with Cotrubas's thinner, spinnier, floated sound as Susanna.

Pritchard's conducting was snappy and nicely articulated – after a routine and rather dull beginning and in spite of not giving it quite enough line and lilt. His conducting, however, did little to support the singers in the video recording. He is often ahead of von Stade who, completely in control of the role, quite rightly sings at her own pace. During his last seasons at Glyndebourne, Pritchard's work came sometimes to lack concentration and his insensitivity was a problem in this production as well as in other Mozart operas he recorded at Glyndebourne. Peter Heyworth found a conflict between Hall's and Bury's 'austerely rustic, modest country household' and Pritchard's 'fresh and sunny' musical direction.[86]

Glyndebourne was also introducing a more varied repertoire, with Jonathan Miller's moving production of Janáček's *The Cunning Little Vixen* in 1975 and a fine *Rake's Progress* directed by John Cox, with David Hockney sets, conducted by Bernard Haitink. It was this production that showed Haitink how fruitful operatic work could be when the conductor could collaborate as an 'equal partner with the director and designer in a production team'.[87]

Haitink, who was to become Glyndebourne's music director in 1978, had conducted very little opera, and no Mozart, until he came to Glyndebourne to conduct *Entführung* in 1972. His early experiences with the Netherlands Opera in the 1960s had not been encouraging, but by 1972 he had decided that he no more wished for a reputation as a 'concert conductor' than as an 'opera specialist'. He had become artistic director of the London Philharmonic, which had been the resident orchestra at Glyndebourne since 1964, and his relationship with the orchestra, together with Glyndebourne's long rehearsal times and pleasant company atmosphere, convinced him to accept Moran Caplat's invitation. *The Times* called him a 'Mozartian to his baton tip' and one who was sensitive in his support of the singers.[88] The collaboration between Hall and Haitink at Glyndebourne was to prove as creative and mutually satisfying as that of Strehler and Abbado at La Scala in the mid and late Seventies.

Opera in Britain, although always underfunded and constantly beset by financial problems, was at last firmly established. By November 1970 the Welsh National Opera, although still without its own theatre, was a substantial company, performing from September to January in Cardiff and on tour with permanent chorus and staff.* Most of the company's productions were traditional but Michael Geliot

---

* The Prince of Wales Theatre where Welsh National Opera had begun had become a cinema showing sex films, and in 1977 Cardiff City Council gave Rank the go-ahead to turn the Capitol Theatre into a multi-cinema and bingo complex.

was responsible for low-budget more daring productions. One of Geliot's outstanding successes was *Billy Budd* with Thomas Allen in September 1972.

Billy was to become one of Allen's great roles. In March 1979 he sang it at Covent Garden and in 1988 Tim Albery's production at ENO was captured on video.[89] Allen, a passionately involved actor, whose work stems from an essential honesty, had an instinctive feel for the dramatic moment. His talent, skill and dedication were unusual even in an age of better acting on the opera stage. His voice was no less appealing: a richly resonant and 'wet' baritone, even throughout the range and, in his youth, an almost tenor-like top. Allen's versatility made him a most useful star in the major opera houses, with roles ranging from Orff's *Carmina Burana* to Mozart's *Figaro* and including Janáček's Forester (Covent Garden 1990) and Monteverdi's *Ulysses* (Salzburg 1985).

In June 1973 Claus Moser was elected to take over from Drogheda as chairman of the Board during the next season. Shortly after, Drogheda wrote to him, 'I am so terribly aware of the legacy of debt and artistic problems I have bequeathed to you.' The House's finances were indeed about to enter an even more challenging era. The economic depression resulting from the October 1973 Middle East war and the subsequent increase in fuel prices resulted in a cut of £1.2 billion in public spending and, indirectly in February 1974, to Edward Heath losing the General Election to Harold Wilson. Moser wrote to Drogheda that the general economic situation terrified him. On 22 January Robbins told the Board that the prospective deficit for the 1974–75 season – £178,000 – was so serious that a special meeting would have to be convened to decide what part of the programme would have to be cut, and to consider the prospect of reducing 'long-term commitments' which were the basis of the House's international reputation.* Davis was adamant that a new production of *Freischütz* should not be cancelled:

* Although La Scala's deficit was greater at this time, reaching $3 million, Covent Garden, with its much smaller subsidy of £2 million and no firm commitment on the part of government to bail it out in time of trouble, was much more vulnerable than its European counterparts.

'I am passionately addicted to *Freischütz*,' he pleaded, and he and Friedrich were already deeply involved.[90]

In February the Board decided to reduce costs by spreading the production of the *Ring* over a longer period, and Moser was negotiating with the Treasury to refund the £150,000 that had been lost in VAT. The finance committee met frequently between February and April, with the proposed total abandonment of the *Ring* a constant theme.* Tooley contemplated the prospect of becoming a 'relatively moderate home-brewed House, occasionally doing something good: eschewing expensive singers, elaborate productions, high-quality orchestra and chorus ... continually dismissed with contempt by the big musical names'.[91] Faced by the gradual erosion in its subsidy, the Board decided that more money should be raised from commerce and private individuals, and in January 1975 set up the Royal Opera House Trust with Lord Kissin its first chairman. Kissin selected an influential body of trustees and invited industrial firms to become sponsors. The Trust's sole function was to raise money and was highly successful, producing more than Kissin's promised £50,000 a year. George Christie, who had also been feeling the results of inflation, in 1975 set up his own finance subcommittee of the Glyndebourne Arts Trust under Sir Alex Alexander, to encourage sponsorship from industry. By January 1976 the Trust had succeeded in raising more than its £70,000 target.

At a time when it was becoming increasingly difficult to meet running costs, the closure of the Covent Garden fruit and vegetable market meant that at last there could be a serious redevelopment of the House's antiquated and inadequate facilities. It was during January 1974 that the government told the Opera House it could buy the site next to the theatre. The House also bought the land on which the theatre sits. The Treasury, however, announced that this was the only contribution it was going to make towards the House's redevelopment, although it quietly gave two further separate donations of £1 million. The Greater London Council offered £1 million, leaving the House to

---

* The designs for Friedrich's *Ring* were already £50,000 over budget and in April Robbins urged that the production should be cancelled (23.4.74). There were further problems for the House when ENO gave a substantial increase in salary to their musicians. The Royal Opera House orchestra were demanding £65 for an eight-session week and Tooley warned that they had a strong case.

find £4 million; Moser and Lord Sieff began the appeal for the first stage of the development. A documentary about the shocking backstage conditions was made with Prince Charles's participation and shown in cinemas all over the country. By 1982 the Appeal had raised just over £9.5 million, allowing the first stage of the modernisation plan, phase 1, to be completed that year. The extension, consisting of an opera rehearsal studio and a chorus rehearsal room, offices and modern dressing rooms, was opened by Prince Charles on 19 July. Money had run out before double-glazing could be installed.

In October 1973 the Board decided not to 'get rid' of Davis, Drogheda having recommended that he be offered a fresh contract. Davis was, Drogheda had argued, only just recovering from the great blow of Hall's withdrawal and was finally settling into his job. Drogheda also recommended that as Davis, supported by Tooley, wanted to share artistic direction with Friedrich, the German director should be invited to work at Covent Garden for three months a year until 1977, when he would be free to come full time. Davis's contract could then be renewed to 1980. Friedrich's engagement to direct the *Ring* from 1974 to 1976 was confirmed in November.[92]

There was unreserved praise at last for Colin Davis, when he conducted *La Clemenza di Tito* on 22 April 1974. William Mann in *The Times* wrote that Davis 'will have justified his post as music director with the reinstatement of a great and half-neglected Mozart opera, even if he never does another hand's turn in Floral Street'.[93] In his book, *The Operas of Mozart*, Mann praised the Covent Garden production for helping to contribute to the acceptance 'into the Mozartian operatic canon' of *Clemenza*. Anthony Besch's production, he wrote, by combining 'opera seria style with human, realistic behaviour, may be regarded as exemplary'. Mann added the proviso, however, that 'a successful production of *La Clemenza di Tito* will depend on scrupulous casting of each part, physically and vocally', with Sextus and Annius convincingly male, Titus 'heroic as well as clement' and Vitellia a 'riveting stage personality, with a voice of unusual range'.[94]

These necessary ingredients were present in the Covent Garden production. Andrew Porter wrote, 'Colin Davis touches greatness in works that he passionately believes in. . . . The orchestral playing – the balancing, the timbre, the shaping of phrases – was very beautiful.' In short, he concluded, 'this is the *Clemenza di Tito* we have been waiting for, warm, romantic, dramatic and gripping from first to last'. Of Janet Baker he wrote, 'Great music becomes incandescent when she sings it. She is so bold, so passionate, so delicate. Weight, timbre, line, words are all expressive.'[95] The success was all the more welcome because it came after what Rosenthal called an 'over-long depressing period'. There was 'exquisite orchestral playing . . . almost virtuoso clarinet and basset horn obbligatos from Ian Herbert and Frederick Lowe'. The result was 'a wonderfully integrated operatic production in which all elements, musical and visual, were beautifully fused into one'.

Davis was more relaxed than before. 'What was so welcome was that Colin Davis neither hectored nor worried the music (except briefly in the overture), but let it speak for itself,' Rosenthal wrote.[96] The July 1976 Philips recording with the Royal Opera House forces underscores Davis's authoritative and truly Mozartean account – the overture full of momentum and spirit, the tempi and phrasing consistently intelligent, with gentle, 'feminine' lines. Janet Baker spins marvels of beautifully breathed phrases, with clean passage work, a broad palette of vocal colour and feeling, and fascinating ornamentation.

Covent Garden was also replenishing its old stock. On 6 February 1974 John Copley's new production of *La Bohème* replaced the original 1897 one, with sets and designs by Julia Trevelyan Oman. It was a sensitive framework and a sound investment, and was still performed in 2002. According to Rosenthal, Domingo gave the 'best-sung Rodolfo since Björling' but he was 'far more convincing dramatically and more emotionally involved than the great Swedish tenor ever was'.[97]

Claus Moser took over the chairmanship of the Board in July 1974. Relations between the executive and the Board were to be less tense under Moser, who later recalled that although other members of the Board might have 'felt awkward about Davis's forthrightness' he never did. There was always, Moser said, 'a smile hovering'.[98] Moser was also to prove a totally committed chairman, going to more than 2,000 performances and becoming part of the international opera scene. He remained director of the Government Statistical Office and head of the Government Statistical Service (1967–78) directly responsible to the Prime Minister – Edward Heath – one of whose main loves in life was music. Heath was Prime Minister when Moser was asked to be chairman and agreed to his appointment. Drogheda was also evidently satisfied with the appointment, telling Pope-Hennessy that Moser's financial acumen and links to Whitehall would be invaluable, with 'finance such an eternal problem' and with the forthcoming redevelopment being of 'such paramount importance'.

In July, there was a last frisson of tension with the outgoing chairman over Friedrich's working methods. Drogheda and the Board expressed concern about Friedrich's *Ring* rehearsals and at reports of his Holland Festival *Figaro*. Drogheda wrote to Davis in July to say that he had heard that Friedrich was 'very good at reducing the artists who work for him to a state of tears'. Davis responded by telling Drogheda that he had a 'small, but sharp suspicion that the Board still wants to administrate, produce and conduct!' After reading this letter, Drogheda wrote to Moser on 26 August 1974 of Davis, 'He is a strange chap!' and added, 'All I can say to you is jolly good luck.'[99]

Friedrich was indeed a hard taskmaster. Hall later described him as 'authoritarian, very, very German, of the German school, the school of Ebert and Reinhardt'. He was 'very much concerned with working it out beforehand' and telling the singers 'what to do'.*[100] Davis himself later recalled Friedrich's authoritarian style, which was the antithesis of his own. Although he greatly admired much of his *Ring* and his *Freischütz*, he did not like much of his later work. At the time Davis, in David Syrus's words, 'deferred very willingly to him on the *Ring*'. Syrus added, 'On the *Ring* he had so many insights one was glad to do so.'[101] Davis himself later said, 'I think the production we did of the *Ring* was really quite revolutionary.'[102]

Tooley recalled some of the difficulties of working with Friedrich,

---

* Thomas Allen later described working with the generic 'Teutonic overlord', whose background is 'of the highest academic qualification', but with whom the process of working is 'stupefyingly boring and permits no space whatsoever for the inventiveness and special skills of his cast' (Allen, *Foreign Parts*, p. 229). Allen was referring particularly to Herz and Kupfer at the Coliseum, and doing a 'deeply studied style of performance'. His own worst experience was a *Barber of Seville* with Michael Hampe (Interview 21.12.99).

who seemed unconcerned about the technical details and was unimpressed when warned that Valhalla could not be seen from the amphitheatre. He seemed, said Tooley, 'to be content as long as the critics
saw it'. He also insisted on continuing with what Tooley described as
a 'catapult to transport the bodies of the heroes to Valhalla' in spite
of Tooley's accurate warning that it would 'appeal to the British sense
of the ridiculous and provoke laughter'.[103]

On 30 September 1974 Friedrich's *Ring* was launched with *Rheingold*. The action took place on Svoboda's movable platform that could
rise, fall and tilt, and provided a 'succession of spectacular and appropriate acting areas', according to David Cairns: 'Beneath the platform
the Nibelungs work, illuminated by magic-lantern techniques and
supervised by Alberich on a glass dome. More mirrors convey the
depths of the Rhine with the twirling, tumbling nixies.'[104] The stage
for *Walküre* was broken up by boulders representing a 'terminal epoch
personified in Wotan'. *Siegfried* would have elements of the comic strip
and *Götterdämmerung* 'the glittering glamour of the last civilisation'.
Throughout, Friedrich used the stage characters to address the
audience.[105]

Andrew Porter disliked the production, which he called a 'disaster
scenically, dramatically and therefore, as the elements cannot be separated, musically'. For Porter, the crucial element, nature, was lacking.
'A designer', he argued, 'needs to have made a Rhine journey.'[106]
But Rosenthal praised Friedrich for observing the details of Wagner's
instructions and for having enabled the characters to act and react to
one another 'naturally and intelligently', as well as for some powerful
visual moments such as the slow 'pavane of the Gods entering into
Valhalla ... with Loge nonchalantly leaning against the proscenium
arch'. It was the first time Colin Davis had conducted the *Ring* and
there was some criticism of his slow tempi after his work with Goodall.
Rosenthal missed 'the overall span and pulse that are the hallmark of
more experienced (or dare I suggest) natural Wagner conductors'.
Matti Salminen was a fine Fasolt, McIntyre a 'somewhat soft-grained
Wotan'.[107]

On 3 October 1974 *Walküre* 'looked like an anthology of Expressionist film and theatre'. Costumes were silver, black and shiny,
'make-up was brutally formalised often into primitive painted masks

with huge white lips, which compound the producer's depersonalising process'. Crichton felt there were other cinematic references in Friedrich's work, such as the vassals in *Götterdämmerung* looking like the Teutonic Knights of Sergei Eisenstein's *Alexander Nevsky*.[108] The work was greeted by 'a cacophony of boos and cheering', wrote Peter Heyworth, who recognised the political subtext of the gods representing the *ancien régime*, although he had not quite managed to work out the more obscure references.[109] Once again Davis was criticised for his pacing. Mann wrote that the 'symphonic perspective sagged again and again. In addition, the singers found it difficult to sustain tone steadily at a snail's pace.'[110] Casting, however, was strong, with Norman Bailey's Wotan both dramatically powerful and musically sung.

In August 1974 Moser warned Gibson at the Arts Council that because of inflation the financial situation was 'desperate' and he was not sure the House would 'survive at all'. Salaries were so low that two senior staff members had left. The raising of seat prices was 'hazardous' and was making the House less accessible'. On 17 December 1974 the Royal Opera House announced the postponement of *Siegfried* from the end of the year to September 1975, which would make a saving of £115,000 for 1975–76, for which the deficit was estimated at £1 million.*

Moser's first Annual Report (1974–75) was concerned with inflation that had resulted in the year closing with a deficit of £209,000. Support from public funds was down to 50 per cent of expenditure, a situation that had been described by a German opera house intendant to Moser as 'sensational'. European Houses were only expected to get about one third of their receipts from the box office. Moser explained in his report that no more could be obtained from receipts in spite of high attendance – at this time the opera was playing to 90 per cent and ballet to 93 per cent capacity. The House was particularly vulnerable

---

* On February 1973 Davis wrote to Drogheda to report a conversation with Board member Jack Donaldson. Donaldson had cited a 'gentleman who had paid £30.00 for a bottle of wine at Sothebys; however, this gentleman probably does not like wine at all but what he does enjoy is spending money'. Davis added, 'We certainly don't want the expensive seats in this House to be filled by people who like spending money and who do not really love opera' (Royal Opera House Archives, Drogheda papers, 2.2.73).

to cost inflation, because 75 per cent of its expenditure consisted of wages. He appealed for an increase in the subsidy to make it closer to the European level of 60–70 per cent of expenditure and to English National Opera's 61 per cent.

All opera house managements were faced by increasing financial pressures in the inflation of the 1970s. In June 1976 the International Association of Opera Directors met to discuss artists' fees and the economic problems facing Houses all over the world. In October 1975 the Board heard that a meeting of the association had recognised the need to co-ordinate artists' fees, some of which had reached 'wholly disproportionate levels'.[111] In July 1976 *Opera* reported that the International Association of Opera Directors had decided not to raise the fees of producers, conductors and leading singers for the next three seasons.*

In the 1978–79 Annual Report Moser was able to announce that fees for guest artists had been reduced. Tooley recalled the association as a 'useful forum for the exchange of views, exchange of information'. Ultimately it failed to control fees, however, as the Americans could not participate wholeheartedly because of their anti-trust laws and there was always what Tooley described as 'some rogue intendant who would step out of bounds'. In particular, Tooley had many discussions with Rolf Liebermann in Paris but failed to convince him of the need to curb fees.†

As costs, and therefore ticket prices, mounted, Tooley, Davis and Moser became sensitive to the need for outreach. Like the Met, Covent Garden was aware of the need to build audiences for the future. In the summer of 1977 Moser announced that there would be further schools' matinées, which had proved very popular since their

---

* Intendants of West Berlin, Brussels, Chicago, Florence, Hamburg, London (Convent Garden and English National Opera) Milan, Munich, New York, Paris, San Francisco, Stockholm, Vienna and Zurich.

† Tooley recalled that 'Liebermann would say, "Come on, John, it doesn't make any difference to you if I pay a bit over the odds" and I would say, "It makes a hell of a difference." And he would say, "I've got to have so and so – I've got to get Paris on the map again – don't argue with me." And of course the whole basis of the enterprise was severely compromised by this kind of attitude' (Interview, 4.12.00). The Board learnt in September 1975 that Hans Sotin had broken his contract with Covent Garden because Paris would pay more (Royal Opera House Archives, Opera Sub Committee, 1974–75, 19/3/6).

introduction at his instigation the previous year. On 13 December 1976 Rosenthal had attended the first school matinée of *Bohème* – in which seventy schools participated, each child paying £1. 'The opera house was bubbling with excitement,' Rosenthal reported, the audience 'emitted gasps of pleasure as the curtain rose, laughed at the horseplay of the Bohemians, could hardly believe their eyes when they saw the live model nude in the last scene, and audibly sobbed when Mimì died'. The cast were 'obviously stimulated by this audience'. Carreras sang 'with honeyed tone and much warmth'. It was one of the best Rodolfos heard at Covent Garden in the post-war period.

The hugely successful Promenade weeks, which were sponsored by the Midland Bank, had been inaugurated in 1971 – the inspiration of both Davis and Tooley. The seats in the stalls were removed and members of the audience sat on the floor at greatly reduced prices. Tooley later wrote, 'Fear of not feeling at home and being welcome in a grand opera house has been as much the cause of some people not coming to Covent Garden as price. Hence the importance of the Promenade performances in creating an atmosphere of informality as well as providing one of the best bargains in London.'[112] Davis also believed that the Proms did much 'to reduce the snobbish image' of the House.

The first Prom was *Boris Godunov* with Boris Christoff, revived by Ande Anderson in July 1972. Milnes, on Tooley's retirement in 1988, remembered the occasion: 'I shall never forget the look of saucer-eyed amazement on Boris Christoff's face when he took his call after the coronation scene to a roar like that of a football crowd from the tightly packed stalls area. He realised that something special was happening and it was: as the performance under Edward Downes grew steadily in intensity and theatrical tingle, it was as if a century of cobwebs had been blown away.'[113]

The Proms flourished until 1997. Davis recalled getting into trouble for making a little speech at the end of a Prom *Ring* performance when he said, 'We are very grateful to the Midland Bank but what a pity it's the Midland Bank and not the government.' And he added, 'It was politically provocative.'[114]

Television relays, which had been the victim of industrial disputes, were resumed in the 1973–74 season when there were televised performances of La Bohème and Ballo. On New Year's Eve 1977 Die Fledermaus with Kiri Te Kanawa and Hermann Prey was sung and spoken in different languages, and was relayed around the world to 20 million viewers. Tooley's deputy, Paul Findlay, was instrumental in developing another area of access with Covent Garden Video Productions Ltd, announced on 2 January 1981. Findlay recalled, 'We did about fifteen television videos in the first five or six years.' The videos did not make money, however, and as at the Met, proved to be of more value for access and audience building.*

In the mid-Seventies Tooley suggested to Colin Davis that a talented twenty-nine-year-old director, Elijah Moshinsky, join the production staff after seeing his production of As You Like It at the Oxford Playhouse. Moshinsky was an Australian who had come to Oxford to do a doctorate in history before going on to work with Peter Wood at the Royal Shakespeare Company. He was assistant director in February 1975 on a revival of Svoboda's and Kašlík's 1974 Tannhäuser, and later in the year he revived the Ballo of Jürgen Rose and Otto Schenk, which had been premiered on 30 January with Domingo.

Moshinsky's first virtually new production was Peter Grimes, on 9 July 1975. The old Moiseivich production had fallen to pieces and, when Covent Garden decided to take it on tour, Moshinsky was asked to replace it for the price of refurbishing it, although according to Peter Heyworth Covent Garden 'bashfully called it a restaging'.[115] In the event, the only things that were recycled were the costumes which the designer, Tazeena Firth, used as undergarments 'as they wore a lot of clothes on the Suffolk coast'.[116]

The Brecht-inspired production was ground-breaking in the seriousness of its intent and achievement, creating real people in a recognisable social environment. A video recording of 1980 reveals the production to have been a triumph both in musical and dramatic terms. Timothy O'Brien's sets, Tazeena Firth's costumes and Moshinsky's staging worked powerfully in close harmony with the musical

---

* Findlay began working at Covent Garden as assistant press officer in 1968 and was personal assistant to the general director 1976–87, assistant director 1987–93.

elements to give Britten's work an intellectual and philosophical frame. The audience was transported to a grim, lowering sea coast where the salt air and fish could almost be smelled. Grime's descent into madness and the destruction of the society around him were traced within this powerfully suggestive setting.

A member of the chorus who worked with Moshinsky on a revival of *Grimes* in 1989–90 described the production's 'almost empty stage' and its 'steeply raked floor that draws the audience in and makes them use their imagination but is not patronising'. During the storm, the chorister continued, 'the door opens and closes and it is possible to see right round it'. He had doubted during rehearsals that such a device could ever work, but concluded that Moshinsky's 'intrinsic musicality' meant that he allowed Britten's music 'to paint all those pictures'. Colin Graham, who had worked closely with Britten on many of his operas, recalled in his obituary that Britten had a very keen eye and built visual ideas into his work in conjunction with the designer and director at an early stage of creation.[117]

Colin Davis conducted with sympathy, modesty and commitment, with clarity and balance, and with careful attention to detail. Jon Vickers was less ferocious than usual in this particular performance and very moving. Moshinsky's sharp pursuit of truth and commitment, and his method of getting the singers to *do* very little on stage at critical moments – such as Vickers's stillness in the courtroom before the magistrate announces his verdict – created great dramatic tension. Vickers's use of sotto voce in 'Now the Great Bear' suggested a public confession and powerfully underscored Grimes's vulnerability and the inevitability of his tragic situation.* Heather Harper as Ellen Orford made moving use of her long cantilena lines to suggest great sadness. Norman Bailey's Balstrode was faultlessly sung. Each chorus member, as well as the principals, was presented as a clearly delineated character in the action. The same member of the chorus recalled, 'The chorus

---

* Britten never liked Vickers's interpretation of Grimes, finding it too manic. Tooley recalled that when he saw the second act of the new production, he said 'Jon sentimentalises the ballad ["in dreams I've built myself some kindlier home"] and it's not to be sentimentalised.' He also told Colin Graham angrily that Vickers was 'cavalier with the score, changing words and notes as it suited him'. Moshinsky, however, argued 'at times a composer may not realise what he has wrought: it takes the interpretation of others to spread fully the wings of his creation' (Jeannie Williams, *Jon Vickers*, pp. 148, 142).

are a character in Elijah's show.' The production showed how far the Covent Garden company had come over the years and how it reached a point at which the vocal, musical and theatrical resources available in London had been carefully brought together, sharply honed and brilliantly integrated.

The cost of Moshinsky's *Grimes* was about half that of a normal new production. William Mann wrote, 'Economy draws attention not only to the shingle and planks but to the drab black clothes of the locals' and that it 'sharpened characterisation everywhere'.[118] Rosenthal felt that Moshinsky's team had revolutionised Covent Garden's production methods, making 'many of the existing heavy, cumbersome and expensively lavish settings look old-fashioned and unnecessary'.

Moshinsky's success with *Grimes* led to a good working relationship with Davis and Tooley who, Moshinsky believed, 'kept the thing together at the time and made it a lovely place to work in and the best in the world at the time'.[119] His next low-budget production was *Lohengrin* in 1977. This production inspired Tooley to write of Moshinsky's 'ability to distil the essence of the work and make a production which was faithful to the music and at the same time illuminating in its statements'.*[120] In February 1975 Tooley had told the opera subcommittee that unless great singers and conductors continued to come to Covent Garden it would be impossible to maintain its reputation, but that there was also a need for 'greater austerity on the stage'. And on 22 July the Board noted, 'It might be possible to redefine artistic standards without lowering them.' *Peter Grimes*, it was suggested, 'could be a portent of the future'.[121]

Benjamin Britten died shortly after the Covent Garden production of *Peter Grimes* on 4 December 1976. The February 1977 edition of *Opera* devoted five articles to his 'magnificent operatic legacy'. Lord Harewood said his contribution in the twentieth century was rivalled only by Strauss, Berg and Janáček, and continued, 'No other composer has recently gone so far to restore confidence in opera as a medium.' Harewood added, 'Benjamin Britten made a unique world of music theatre in which many of us have found solace and joy over the span

---

* Moshinsky was spending seven months at the National Theatre but Covent Garden was to have first call on him during the remaining five months (Royal Opera House Archives, Opera Sub Committee, 1974–75, 19/3/6).

of nearly a generation's length, and his loss at the tragically early age of sixty-three leaves us all irreparably the poorer.'[122]

Clemenza and *Grimes* were turning points in Davis's directorship, their success giving him confidence. In an interview with John Higgins in *The Times*, Davis said he felt that with the production of *Peter Grimes* Covent Garden was 'moving down the right path'. He continued, 'The real satisfaction of last season came from beginning to see on stage some of the images I have always wanted to see.'[123] Similarly encouraging was the company's exchange visit to Milan in March 1976. The exchange with La Scala was subsidised by a £250,000 grant from a British Council fund. Davis conducted *Benvenuto Cellini* and *Grimes*, and John Pritchard *Clemenza*. Milan was thrilled and the critics were impressed, not only by the level of ensemble but also by the fact that the announced casts actually appeared. The orchestra sounded splendid in the Scala acoustic, especially the strings, which were dampened by the shelf at Covent Garden, and the chorus, which had been strengthened in numbers for the tour.

Davis's ongoing partnership with Friedrich, whose delayed *Siegfried* was first performed in September 1975, also helped bolster his self-esteem. In March 1976 the Board decided to confirm Friedrich's appointment as principal producer. He would be working with Davis on a number of productions from 1976 to 1980, and Davis was keen for him to be given recognition. Although Moser acknowledged that the appointment was controversial, he was in favour of it and it would not entail a contract, extra fee or position in the managerial hierarchy.[124] Friedrich's *Ring* cycle was completed in September 1976 with *Götterdämmerung*. Peter Heyworth found it 'a dazzling piece of theatre', full of excitement both visual and intellectual. Unlike some conceptual directors, he felt that Friedrich 'makes his points obliquely and leaves us to take them if we will'.[125]

The complete cycle was performed in October. Alan Blyth felt that it would not be remembered for its 'rectangular turntable, the arresting mirrors, the expensive dragon or the tagliatelle forest, but for the producer's ability to rethink each role from the start and for persuading his singers, who seem to revere him as much as does their conductor, to follow him and thus turn themselves into more accomplished singing actors than they had been heretofore'.[126] Davis was, according to Cairns, emerging as 'a full-scale Wagnerian talent', sensitive to his singers and with a 'sense of the purely musical flow'.[127] Shawe-Taylor called it a 'sensuously beautiful account'.*

Gwyneth Jones had become the leading Brünnhilde of the late Seventies and early Eighties. 'Many aspects of her Brünnhilde are overwhelming,' wrote Milnes, 'vocally in her swordlike top . . . and her sumptuously coloured lower register, where many phrases are most sensitively turned; and dramatically in her innate nobility, heroic stature . . . and eager involvement. But he added, 'What can happen between the extremes of her range remains wholly unpredictable.'† In October 1975 the Board had congratulated Davis and Friedrich on the *Ring*, and Davis thanked the Board for supporting the project at a time when the decision had been 'an act of faith'.[128]

Tooley and Davis were still committed to contemporary work. After Webster had decided not to put on Henze's *The Bassarids* and it was produced by ENO in 1974, Tooley commissioned a highly complex work from Henze which was premiered on 12 July 1976. *We Come to the River*, with libretto by British playwright Edward Bond, had as its original conception eight singing parts, with action taking place in different areas of the stage and auditorium, each accompanied by a separate orchestra. In the event the action was confined to the stage and pit, which lessened the work's impact.[129] Hans Keller, while acknowledging the interest the work had generated, criticised it as 'dramatised reiterations of the common-or-garden rationale of communism' with the 'occasional poetic line'. Henze, he argued, totally evaded the problem of individual liberty as well as 'making political statements which could be far more clearly formulated without music'.[130]

---

* The opera subcommittee congratulated Davis on the *Ring* on 2 October 1976, and in particular on the improvement of the orchestra. Davis said that the quality of those applying to join the orchestra was improving (Opera Sub Committee, 2.10.76).
† Tooley recalled of Jones, 'She had this huge Welsh emotional force which she seemed unable to control, unlike Jon Vickers, who possessed the same kind of emotional force but used it sparingly to maximum effect.' (Interview, 4.12.00)

On 7 July 1977 Tippett's *The Ice Break* was described by John Warrack as a 'worthy successor to *Midsummer Marriage* and *The Knot Garden*'. This opera, more than his others, expressed the need for the breaking down of stereotypes in order to achieve human reconciliation. Sam Wanamaker returned successfully to Covent Garden for the first time since the *Forza* debacle. Colin Davis, 'the worthy dedicatee, gave the music all the dynamic charge it contains in the violent early music, and clearly took much pleasure in the subtleties of a score that still has much to reveal'.[131] Peter Heyworth felt that although it was imperfect it was worth a dozen of the 'meretricious novelties by Ginastera and Henze'. The opera asked the question: 'How far can liberal humanism survive in a world that increasingly seeks violent solutions to its problems?'[132]

Covent Garden, following La Scala, was also introducing early and less familiar Verdi operas. It was the pioneering team of José Carreras and Lamberto Gardelli which brought *I Lombardi* to Covent Garden in June 1976. Gardelli, Osborne wrote, conducted with 'well-judged tempi'. In spite of András Mikó's highly regimented and consequently 'inhumane' production, the audience showed an enthusiastic response and Osborne urged more experiments with early Verdi. In July 1978 Blyth found that Maazel's 'coarse and unsubtle' conducting of *Luisa Miller* 'did not make out a very good case for the piece' but that the singers were 'ardent in their advocacy'. Carreras sang Rodolfo 'with a winningly plaintive timbre and tremendous panache'. Rosenthal admired Katia Ricciarelli as Luisa for her 'amazing agility, dramatic power' as well as a 'wonderful feeling for the text'.[133]

It was not until the Nineties, when Covent Garden boldly initiated the Verdi festival, that most of the less known works of the Verdi canon were aired at Covent Garden, some, like *Stiffelio*, in very fine productions.

In an interview which Davis gave in July 1986, reviewing his time as music director, he described his first five years as 'pretty awful'. He felt he had not been accepted: 'There were singers who did not like me,' he recalled and 'there were members of the orchestra who did not like me'. He felt that he had been 'criticised for not doing things the Solti way'. He had not given up the struggle, however. 'You have to stay and fight,' he said, 'or just chuck the whole thing in.'[134] As Findlay recalled, 'Colin did not come in with international experience. After years of Solti, this was levelled against him at the time. Colin had a very tough time in overcoming this hostility, that he was just the English conductor.'[135]

During Davis's next five years, fine conductors appeared with great regularity at Covent Garden; as Davis was willing to relinquish even new productions to guests. Between 1981 and 1984 he did not conduct any new productions, being content to supervise revivals.[136] Tooley was delighted to secure the appearances of Carlos Kleiber, whom he described as a member of 'a small band of conductors who are head and shoulders above their peers and who possess a special, yet indefinable, quality which enables them to make music of a standard and of a luminosity unattainable by most others'.[137] Kleiber conducted *Rosenkavalier* in 1974 and, in May 1977, an illuminating and shattering *Elektra*. In 1979 Böhm conducted *Figaro* and in March 1981 Muti conducted *Macbeth* in a new production by Moshinsky.

Bernard Haitink made his debut at Covent Garden in March 1977, conducting Copley's 1973 *Don Giovanni*, re-rehearsed by Ande Anderson. It was not a happy experience. Haitink's recently acquired confidence in opera was undermined by the size of the House, the rushed rehearsals and the audience, which the *Financial Times* referred to as a fine example of multinational philistinism 'with much whispering, rustling and cases of terminal whooping-cough on all sides'.[138]

This experience was, however, in striking contrast to his next operatic experience at Glyndebourne, working on Peter Hall's new production of the same work. Pritchard conducted the first performance on 31 May 1977, which 'opened the season with a dramatic force that had the critics and pre-dinner-interval audience reeling by the end of Act I'.[139] Hall's was a dark interpretation, he and Bury setting the scene in the Seville of Goya in 'oppressive black'. Milnes wrote that Benjamin Luxon submerged his own personality 'selflessly into Hall's cold-blooded, baleful, pasty-faced murderer'. Although Luxon's was a calculating, dour Giovanni, he 'fielded just enough charm for his purposes and the smiles when they came (with the mouth only) were all the more disturbing'. Milnes found Giovanni's 'extremely creepy house-hold staff, who looked half drugged and prone to nameless vices' contributed to an evening that 'made one think afresh about every aspect of this bewildering masterpiece'. He added, 'I shall remember and treasure it, rather nervously, as long as I live.'[140]

Bernard Haitink took over the production from John Pritchard in July 1977. His approach was much more in keeping with Hall's interpretation than Pritchard's gracious version. The second cast in Haitink's 'measured, wonderfully paced reading', was if anything more powerful than the first. Thomas Allen took over from Luxon, and Milnes was overwhelmed by his performance: 'Something happened on stage and in the audience . . . a Giovanni who holds the stage by right, not by accident in the title role.' Allen recalled looking at the production before he took over and 'feeling I knew exactly what I would be doing when I put myself on that stage . . . knowing exactly what your body is telling you. I don't think I have experienced that with any other role. I knew there was something inside me waiting to express itself.' Allen says of the role, 'The start of Don Giovanni is as violent as it gets. The kind of electricity that flashes between two artists on stage, and what can happen is primeval really – it is an enormous force.'[141]

Allen's Don, Van Allan's Leporello, John Rawnsley's Masetto and Philip Langridge's 'unusually masculine' Ottavio lent a passion and sense of inherent violence to the production which became 'an instant yardstick against which others were judged'.[142] Haitink later spoke of these performances as the best he ever collaborated in: 'That was a very special, electrical event and I loved it.'[143]

The Glyndebourne anniversary recording of 1984 with the London Philharmonic, on EMI, maintained the darkness of Hall's 1977 pro-duction, although it did not fully capture the power of the original performances.* The overture opened slowly with a sense of impending tragedy and the jocose quality, leading into 'Notte e giorno faticar', was downplayed. Haitink proved himself a master of timing and pac-

* The recording featured Thomas Allen, Richard Van Allan, Maria Ewing, Carol Vaness and Keith Lewis. Vaness later recognised Hall's contribution, 'I have been forced to draw on productions like the Peter Hall one at Glyndebourne as Anna, as all they do is give you a hanky and tell you to weep.' (Opera, 1989, p. 422)

ing. The broad tempo of 'Là ci darem' suggested love gone wrong, with Thomas Allen in most seductive mode. Even though Haitink underscored the tragic, a ray of light and humour shone out in 'Batti, batti'. He did not crush the humour out of the show but nevertheless brought out the tragic bleakness of the denouement, eliciting a maximal weight of tone from the orchestra. In a performance marked by sensitive timing this was a fitting climax.

Hall later said, 'Bernard Haitink is pre-eminent because he leaves his ego outside the rehearsal room. . . . Collaboration only works if the conductor is secure enough to allow himself to be challenged, which Haitink is.'[144] Hall explained:

> Unless the conductor modifies his musical views because of what the director is doing and unless the director modifies his views because of what the conductor is doing, there's no hope of getting anywhere. In most opera productions the director stages it and then towards the end the conductor comes in and waves his baton and makes his music and the two don't coalesce . . . the general public don't notice but they know when it's wrong.

Hall added, 'Bernard collaborated with you, Georg challenged you.'[145]

Hall worked happily and extremely successfully again with Haitink on Così in 1978, just after Haitink became music director, and on Fidelio in 1979. Hall's conviction, repeatedly proven, that equal collaboration is the most creative working method in the theatre, which the small space of Glyndebourne made particularly powerful, lies at the heart of the debate about the primacy of roles between musicians and directors. The critic Tom Sutcliffe, in defence of conceptualist directors argues, 'The hierarchy governing operatic performances must have the producer or stage director at its head, while the conductor is in charge of the tactical execution of the performance where the singers do the most vulnerable hard work, taking the main responsibility for focus and impact themselves.'[146] This theory belies a misunderstanding of the way effective theatre performances work in reality. As Hall said,

> True work in the theatre or opera is organic and collaborative and you don't stage an opera in the abstract. You stage in a particular way because you have a particular cast. . . . You

walking across the stage means something quite different to someone else walking across the stage. But if you're a conceptual director you're riding a motorbike anyway. The conceptual director often takes less time to rehearse because he's not finding the piece – he's already decided what the piece is. Also in a very small repertory of some fifty pieces of regularly done opera he draws attention to himself. He stops the critics being bored who have seen the pieces too many times. I don't believe that's theatre, myself – I believe that's imposition. In music and in theatre collaboration is the important thing.[147]

At Covent Garden the combined dramatic, visual and musical elements were less consistent than during Glyndebourne's summer seasons, although attendance was high at 91 per cent in 1977–78. After another happy Friedrich–Davis collaboration with *Der Freischütz* in February 1977, the March 1978 *Idomeneo*, with designer Stefanos Lazaridis, was less successful. Relations between Davis and Friedrich were deteriorating and after this production they had what Davis later called a 'messy divorce'. There was, he believed, 'a straightforward clash of temperaments and cultures', about which Davis was 'terribly upset'.[148] Janet Baker, the production's Idamante, recalled Friedrich as 'difficult, cruel even', though 'enormously challenging'.[149] Davis believed that Friedrich, after he left East Germany, was 'tremendously ambitious' and wanted to 'take on everything and make a lot of money'. He added, 'He did much too much. . . . It made him very tense and abusive, and I got very distressed about it and very, very angry once or twice.'[150] Tooley later recalled, 'Colin became more and more impatient – terrible scenes – fisticuffs, very dramatic stuff. Some were quite hilarious. Götz's glasses broke I remember one night.'[151]

Idomeneo was visually unattractive, with what Rosenthal described as its 'ugly black military-like block houses'. He continued, 'I wonder whether Mr Friedrich has learned the dangers of over-rehearsing. I enjoyed the malicious rumour going around that the first night might well have been given at Drury Lane, so that the Covent Garden stage could be free for further technical rehearsals.' The *Observer* critic, Peter Heyworth, observed once again Friedrich's reference to film, with what he called 'heightened cinema realism'. The final act stage was 'littered with mangled corpses, which are ostentatiously removed by the Red

Cross during the quartet'. Some members of the audience booed John Bacon, the chorus-master, thinking he was Friedrich. This was the production which provoked Clive James to remark 'that producing opera was what Germans do nowadays instead of invading Poland'.[152] William Mann, however, praised the production for giving the 'strongest demonstration of the opera's dramatic coherence, its extraordinary vitality and a totally human compassion that bursts the conventions of Italian *opera seria* which Mozart had been trained to master'. Janet Baker was a 'truly great' Idamante.[153]

After *Idomeneo*, Friedrich's role as principal producer became little more than a title, according to Tooley, and in February 1980 the Board decided his connection with the House was 'so tenuous' that he should no longer maintain the title of 'principal producer'.[154] His revivals suffered as a result of his lack of involvement. By 1981 his *Ring* was looking rather shabby. With the passage of time and without the director to supervise, Milnes found the 'element of farce' and 'one-dimensional characterisation' to be tedious. At the same time he found that Davis's mastery of the work had become of 'towering stature'. Max Loppert wrote in 1986, 'As the seasons passed, the command of the long paragraphs grew easier, the movement more buoyant (and the shadow of Goodall receded).'[155]

Davis believed that after Friedrich settled down in Berlin as superintendant in 1981 he mellowed considerably. As Friedrich mellowed, so did his differences with Davis. But at the time Davis sadly came to realise that he was 'outdated' in his hope for a collaboration such as Busch and Ebert had enjoyed at Glyndebourne or he himself had experienced with Glen Byam Shaw at Sadler's Wells. He believed that such relationships could not 'feature on the international circuit',[156] although Glyndebourne could still provide a more settled and creative environment for Hall and Haitink.

With no such partnership, musical standards were often more impressive than that of the staging. On 28 June 1978 Davis gave a 'spirited quite passionate reading' of *Pelléas* – in its old and somewhat shabby Svoboda set.[157] Davis's love for the score of *Simon Boccanegra* gave him a chance to gain a striking success in the Italian repertoire in June 1980. Te Kanawa was Amelia and Sherrill Milnes Boccanegra, in glorious voice. But the director, Filippo Sanjust, according to Rosenthal, lined up his singers 'in a rather old-fashioned kind of way' in a 'yellow greyish, poorly lit setting'.[158] On 6 July 1978 Caballé appeared in *Norma* looking, in Ronald Crichton's words, 'for the most part merely lethargic' and 'in poor voice'.[159] Peter Heyworth called attention to a lack of 'artistic commitment' at Covent Garden in the *Observer* on 15 July 1979.

The main problem then, as always, was, above all else, the lack of resources. In November 1975 Davis had told the opera subcommittee, after a poor *Rosenkavalier* revival, that preparing good performances was impossible without 'sufficient time for rehearsal' and that even attempting to do so 'damaged orchestral morale'. Tooley added that he had long been urging that 'too much was being attempted with too few resources'. Claus Moser agreed 'entirely with the administration in what was a not entirely successful struggle' and the committee suggested that 'intricate scores like *Rosenkavalier*' might have to be 'deleted from the repertory' if the grant were not increased. In his 1977–78 Annual Report, Moser warned that 'to maintain an international company would require a grant 35 per cent above the present level'. The grant had gone up by 11 per cent, whereas the Retail Price Index had risen by 14 per cent, and the House's costs by 18 per cent. Not only was an inadequate grant causing artistic compromises, there were already signs that seat prices were changing 'habits in seat purchasing'. Raising seat prices by the necessary 15 per cent was not compatible with the grant being made to enable Covent Garden 'to serve the community and not a rich minority'.[160]

In spite of these pressures, Tooley and Davis were determined to expand the repertoire with such works as *Luisa Miller* (1977–78), *The Rake's Progress* (1978–79) and Taverner's *Thérèse* (1979–80). Martin Cooper described *L'Africaine* in November 1978 as 'a kind of "exhibition-opera" of more interest to historians than to music lovers'. It was, however, a splendid vehicle for Domingo, whose Vasco set the House alight with his 'strong, youthful exhibition of a superbly handsome voice'. The May 1979 production of *The Rake's Progress* was its first at Covent Garden. Rosenthal found it a 'good production' at the end of 'one of the most dispiriting seasons in recent memory'. The Davis–Moshinsky, O'Brien and Firth team, which had prepared *Grimes*, again showed, according to Rosenthal, that 'an integrated, carefully rehearsed production, resulting in a true ensemble, is what opera should be'.[161]

In his 1978–79 Annual Report, Moser gave the first of many unheeded warnings that increased costs were threatening Covent Garden's achievements and urged that the grant be increased in line with inflation. 'Few things', he said, 'have added so much to this country's reputation in recent decades as the unprecedented advance in the arts supported with quite modest means by successive governments through the Arts Council.' But the new era about to be entered into was to prove even more disheartening for those who worked in the arts, and even more threatening to the achievements of the previous decade.

SEVENTEEN

THE MET 1972–80

'Faces, Not Windmills'

GÖRAN GENTELE'S TRAGIC death left the Met facing the same increasingly grave financial problems as Covent Garden and, as he would inevitably have found, neither hopes for meaningful government support nor plans for a more challenging approach to production and repertoire at the Met were to be realised.

Board member Frank E. Taplin Jr wrote in his diary on 18 July 1972 that Gentele's death was 'a tragic loss', as he had 'healed a divided company' and had 'concluded labor negotiations with the Musicians' Union in a new and constructive spirit of mutual cooperation'. Schuyler Chapin was appointed acting general manager on 19 July 1972, accepting his responsibilities, as he told the Board, 'with a heavy heart'. Gentele's plans were 'well advanced', he said, and he would carry them out in 'spirit and letter'. The extraordinary response of the staff to the tragic event was testimony to the 'great impact Mr Gentele had in improving staff morale'.[1] Chapin's most immediate decision was that of choosing a director for Gentele's *Carmen*. Svoboda's sets were already coming out of the workshops, and in August, Bodo Igesz, who had been Gentele's assistant and had worked with Bernstein, was chosen.

Like Gentele, Chapin brought a new warmth and democracy after the Bing era, as well as courtesy and honesty, which was recognised by artists, employees and journalists alike.[2] His style of management was genial. One unnamed Met star told the *New York Times* on 9 May 1973, 'In all the time I was with Mr Bing, I always called him Mr Bing or Sir Rudolf, and I already call him Schuyler. Mr Bing had, I think, a certain – well, I wouldn't say dislike – but I don't think he held many singers in very high esteem. This man seems to think we are real persons.'

Like all opera companies, the Met was suffering from the effects of inflation and the increased costs of the new House continued to prove formidable. In June 1973, Chapin pointed out that the cost of maintaining the building alone was $2 million. Expenses, James J. Jaffray, treasurer and chairman of the Finance and Budget Committee, told the Board in September 1972, were now rising three times as fast as income and although contributions were up by $1 million, the box office remained disappointing at 87 per cent.[3]

Chapin's first hurdle – that of getting *Carmen* successfully on to the stage – was overcome on opening night, 19 September 1972. The show was well received in spite of the many pre-opening hazards. These had included conflict between Svoboda and the Met's chief electrician, Rudolph Kutner, and Marilyn Horne's threats to leave the production because she took exception to a rug that Svoboda said was needed for the special lighting effects.[4] The Guiraud recitatives were replaced by spoken dialogue, as in the 1875 premiere production, and traditional musical cuts restored. George Movshom in *Opera* commented, 'In particular the choral activity was considerably enriched and many of the new-found juxtapositions were startlingly effective, even though some of the tension was lost in the expansion of the first act to a duration of about one hour. (The performance ran from eight till midnight.)'[5]

Svoboda's set was suggestive rather than realistic, with projections giving an atmosphere of Seville. The stage was flooded with 'vertical downward blasts of Spanish sunlight'. Departing from her usual bel canto repertoire, Marilyn Horne sang a 'bold and bawdy' Carmen without excessive chest tone. Lacking the physique for the role, she nevertheless realised her own interpretation of the character, in part through her personality. Peter Conrad called Horne's Carmen a 'brash and bouncy American farm girl, her ebullience tightly restrained by her stays'.[6] McCracken's Don José was vital and energetic, if unsubtle. Movshom wrote that Bernstein's conducting of *Carmen* was of such 'architectural nobility and wise restraint as to reveal unimagined miracles in a score most opera goers think they know'.[7]

*   *   *

Chapin's relationship with Board president George S. Moore was strained, in spite of his immediate and strenuous efforts in October to get a grip on the expenses by tightening rehearsal schedules and reducing the number of operas in the repertoire. The Board continued to delay making Chapin general manager, instead undermining him in his efforts to gain control of a difficult situation. In his memoirs Chapin recalled efforts by Moore to appoint as artistic director Maria Callas and then Massimo Bogianckino, artistic director of La Scala, in both cases without consulting him.[8] There was a clash between Moore and Chapin when Chapin insisted on instituting Gentele's planned 'Mini-Met', where repertoire more suitable for a smaller stage and auditorium would be performed. Chapin hoped it would bring a new audience to the Met and had found three-year independent funding for the project. In spite of Moore's strong opposition to the plan on financial grounds, the donor refused to give his donation to the general funds and the plan was accepted by the Board on 19 October.

The first season's productions were Purcell's *Dido and Aeneas* and Virgil Thomson's *Four Saints in Three Acts*. The Mini-Met did not make a loss, and was well received by the critics and the public. Another of Gentele's plans to introduce a new audience to the Met was that of the children's 'Look-Ins'. Unlike Covent Garden's schools matinées, which were given straight, the 'Look-Ins' involved a celebrity talking about operatic presentation and giving highlights from several operas. On 26 October Chapin approached Danny Kaye, who agreed to prepare and present the shows for no fee.[9]

On 5 January 1973 Chapin presented his plans for the next season, explaining that the twenty-two operas proposed for the 1974–75 season were five less than during the current season. There would be seven new production, but of those, scenery for *Hoffmann* was to be borrowed from another production and *Götterdämmerung* was 'a hold-over' from previous seasons. Careful scheduling was intended to reduce overtime.[10] As Chapin was receiving little support from the Board, he himself found sponsors for *Hoffmann* and *L'Italiana*.[11]

In December, Moore praised management for its efforts to cut expenses but still argued that Chapin was planning more new pro-ductions than the House could afford. He questioned the need to do *Les Troyens* with its large chorus and eleven scenes.[12] Chapin's relationship with Moore continued to be tense and explosive. Moore was often absent and was not well pleased when Chapin turned to the Board's Chairman, Lowell Wadmond, for advice.[13]

On 8 May 1973 the Board, after much hesitation and with great reluctance, made Chapin general manager, and that same month accepted his plans. He immediately faced a major financial crisis. On 28 June, Jaffray told the Board that the financial situation had 'taken a turn for the worse' and that the Met faced a net loss of $2.1 million, which had risen to $2.8 million by September. This loss would increase the working capital deficit to $5.6 million.* Chapin later recalled the tensions:

> The scope of the Met's financial plight became increasingly horrifying. With the dollar slipping and European theatres having a direct edge relative to our fees, pressures from artists and their agents pyramided as we tried to plan the next two or three seasons. Everybody wanted decisions. Moore, as he raced in and out of the country, told me to balance the books or out I'd go.[14]

Chapin immediately initiated savings – each opera being examined with a view to cutting down labour expenses. The tops of the giant towers in *Otello* were to be removed, and for *Carmen* the steps leading into the square would be replaced with a flat area that would free three stage elevators and reduce the amount of labour required for the construction. A set of designs for *Les Troyens* was rejected as too lavish. There was to be stricter scheduling of orchestral personnel at rehearsals, and in *Tristan* thirty choristers would be employed instead of forty-five – and they would sing through megaphones. The company realised, Chapin told the Board in June, 'that the crunch is on'.[15]

While Chapin was aware of the need for economies, he also appealed to the Board to 're-examine our total fund-raising resources'. The Met, after forty-one years of broadcasting and seventy-six years of touring was a national institution, he argued, and should exploit its position more effectively. Chapin also urged a more effective co-ordination between the Guild, the National Council and the Patrons

---

* Income was $141,000 under budget and expenses $678,000 over budget (Board, Met, 28.6.73). The finance director had overlooked recent changes in the social security laws, which meant that 'the Met would owe the federal government an additional $300,000 in withholding taxes by the end of the fiscal year' (Chapin, Musical Chairs, A Life in the Arts, pp. 335–6).

programme. He had discovered during the tour that Met representatives in the tour cities were unaware of the company's plight and had never been asked to participate in any co-ordinated fund drives. Management, Chapin exhorted, could not rethink the general approach to the Met's problems without the Board's help and support.*[16]

The Board's immediate reaction to the crisis, however, was to concentrate on cutting expenses rather than try to increase revenue. In September 1973 the new treasurer, James Smith, told the Board that there had been a net loss for the 1972–73 season of $2.8 million. It was decided that every phase of operations would be examined in by-weekly discussions between management and Board members, with Anthony Bliss responsible for backstage operations.† There would also have to be staff cuts, increased seat prices and the programme of concerts in the New York parks would be cut. The new Rennert–Jo Mielziner production of *Don Giovanni* was cancelled. The *Don Giovanni* sets had not yet reached the carpentry shops, but Karl Böhm, whose eightieth birthday it was to mark, was deeply angered. Only under pressure did he agree to conduct the contracted *Der Rosenkavalier* during the season. James Levine took over the old *Don Giovanni*. At the same time the Mini-Met was also suspended.

Kubelik expressed to the Board his 'grave concern' about the cancellation of rehearsals. He warned that the House was jeopardising its commitments to artists 'who had been contracted with the promise of certain minimums of rehearsal time'. There was a limit, he stressed, to how many economies could be effected if artistic standards were to be maintained. The Met's very survival was at stake, however, Moore warning that the House now had a $5.6 million working capital deficit and that in order to borrow from the banks it was crucial to show a break-even budget.[17]

Chapin recalled telling Danny Kaye, while discussing the children's

---

* On 6 September Chapin wrote to Nilsson to tell her that there was no way the Met, 'in its worst financial crisis that it has faced since 1932', could afford to compensate artists for the dollar devaluation, even though he believed that she was 'entitled to all the money minted by the several treasuries of the several countries of the world' (Nilsson contracts 3, Met Archives).

† Other Board members given specific responsibilities were Francis Goelet, new productions; Irving Mitchell Felt, the House; Lawrence Lovett, artistic matters; and Paul Hallingby, financial matters.

'Look-Ins', that rather than argue with Moore about the new productions he was 'out raising the money' himself.[18] In spite of Moore's continued opposition and the loss of one of its sponsors, Chapin was determined to press on with the new Merrill–Peter Wexler production of *Les Troyens*. He wanted the Met 'to take a major, bold step to inaugurate its real first season under a new management'.[19] The production opened on 22 October 1973 and was described by George Movshom as 'very big stuff indeed'. In the end the production was sponsored by two private patrons at a cost, according to management, of $400,000. *Les Troyens* was warmly received and sold out, but the Executive Committee was not won over. Their scepticism was shared by Movshom, who was censorious: 'Visual concept', he wrote, 'has been degraded by the application of irrelevant spectacle, needless and costly detail, fussy decoration.' He was less critical of Kubelik's conducting which, he thought, entailed 'careful, well-articulated and logical ensemble work, at the cost of the passion and impetus that Colin Davis might have given us'. *Les Troyens* starred Vickers and Shirley Verrett who sang both Dido and Cassandra when Christa Ludwig became ill before opening night.

The box office continued to improve, maintaining 92.5 per cent in the autumn. In September, James Levine conducted *Trovatore* with Domingo, and in January 1974 *Salome*, for the first and last time. Marilyn Horne's *L'Italiana*, in a new Ponnelle production, also enjoyed a box office success. *Hoffmann* in November 1973 starred Domingo and Sutherland, in a dark Bliss Hebert production with Bonynge conducting. Domingo stole the show with 'melody sung surely and with melting tone'. The composer might have been thinking of him, enthused Movshom.[20]

The financial crisis, however, was worsening. In 1965, the last season in the old House, losses before contributions had been $1.9 million. By the 1974–75 season they were $9.3 million. Wages, which accounted for 81 per cent of expenses, were soaring, as they were in Europe.*

---

* In 1975–76 it cost $2,800,000 to maintain the House with no grant from state or city government. Costs included: singers $5.4 million, orchestra $2.8 million, chorus and ballet $2.3 million, stage directors $900,000, stagehands $4 million, shops $1.4 million, administration and staff $1.6 million, scenery and costumes $700,000, transport $1.7 million, building operations $1.5 million.

The Met employed 1,500 people, 700 of them full time – their wages accounted for 78.8 per cent of the total budget.[21] In 1974–75, box office income was $13.3 million but wages alone were $20 million. The percentage of expenses covered by contributions had gone up from 19 per cent in 1965 to 31 per cent in 1974. To make matters worse a blaze in the Met's warehouse on 7 November 1973 destroyed costumes for forty-one productions, including all the 'general use' props, at an estimated loss of $3,443,037. The insurance received, $2,626,500, was 76.28 per cvent of the estimated loss.

On 15 November 1973 Chapin was obliged to read to the assembled company members a financial review in which the stark realities of the situation were made abundantly clear. He urged everyone at the Met to work together to solve the House's problems, but he later recalled:

> In my heart of hearts I felt that we were sinking steadily under the crushingly dead hands of our board leadership, who were, at that moment, casting around for the knight in shining armour rather than realistically rolling up their collective sleeves and admitting that the problems had to be worked out in a joint management–board mutual trust manner.[22]

Chapin's efforts to make the Met more adventurous did little to reassure the Board. Premiered on 31 January 1974, the John Dexter–Josef Svoboda *I Vespri siciliani*, conducted by Levine, proved highly controversial. Chapin had seen Dexter's production in Hamburg and decided to use it to replace the *Ballo* which Gentele was to have directed. Levine was recording the work in London with much the same cast that had been engaged for *Ballo*. The production had earlier been given a warm reception in Hamburg in 1969 and was to be well received in Paris in April 1974. *Village Voice* critic Leighton Kerner later reflected that it was the first of Dexter's productions to employ 'lean and suggestive rather than realistically and fully detailed scenery'. Dexter would, said Kerner, 'rather give the audience the merest, most essential elements of a scene and make the audience concentrate on what matters most, the music and the drama'. Kerner was well aware, however, that some members of the audience still lived in a nineteenth-century world when everything was 'thrown to the spectators'.[23]

Wary Met audiences were indeed less convinced than Kerner by Dexter's approach, greeting Dexter's curtain call with a 'chorus of boos' which, according to Chapin, greatly upset him. Chapin recalled that when he came off the stage Dexter looked 'absolutely seasick green'.[24] Most critics were similarly unhappy. George Movshom was not won over by what he called an 'angular and harsh' as well as unfamiliar work, finding that the production 'did not sweeten the pill'.[25] Smith found Svoboda's brilliantly and harshly lit black-and-white set on an enormous staircase, and Jan Skalicky's grey-and-black costumes, 'insufficiently evocative of Palermo'. Harold Schonberg thought Dexter's and Svoboda's Palermo looked like 'Exxon storage tanks ... everything is trimmed down to essentials ... the set unadorned is a rocky beach. Drop some bars stage front and it is a prison.'[26] According to Movshom one member of the audience on the first night called it a 'neo-Fascist production'. Another wondered whether the 'Bayreuth style' should be applied to Verdi. Movshom himself thought that the interiors asked 'for quite a lot in the way of suspension of disbelief' – an activity that Met audiences have not always proved willing to try to engage in.[27]

Some Met critics and audience members were, however, excited by the singing as well as the production's dramatic pace and the removal of operatic convention: 'Arm thrusts and body lunges were suppressed, and strong postures and expressive repose substituted for them,' wrote Irving Kolodin.[28] On the whole, Dexter had succeeded in keeping the flow of the action so intense that there had been no opportunities for outbursts of applause. On the opening night, however, Caballé kept tradition alive with her rendition of 'Ah, parli a un core' which raised a great cheer. Thrilling though her vocal acting was, her physical acting was as usual rudimentary, with 'arms outstretched and pointing outward for moderate tension, arms outstretched upwards for moments of high drama'. Levine's conducting was praised, Movshom finding 'solid pleasure' and emphasis on 'every long-lined phrase'.[29] In the revival, Rosenthal found that Levine conducted with 'an unrelenting drive, a strong rhythmic sense, and often exciting results – very much like Solti'.[30]

During the season, a series of mishaps with the run of *Tristan* performances also did little to boost confidence in Chapin. The Isolde,

Catarina Ligendza, had cancelled, and Chapin's choice of Klara Barlow as her replacement caused a crisis with Vickers and Leinsdorf when Leinsdorf threatened to withdraw, publicly stating that the Met was being run by 'amateurs and commissars of optimism'.[31] Chapin was determined to get the show on the stage so that he could ensure that the only two performances scheduled with Nilsson and Vickers would not be lost. In the end there was just one performance by the two stars, on 30 January, which was described as a 'summit *Tristan* of our age'. Nilsson had, according to Movshom, 'at last found a fully worthy partner, a tenor with the metal, the manliness, the dramatic insight and the musicality to do justice to this music'. In February, Vickers had also sung a 'memorable' Otello to Te Kanawa's much praised and unexpected Met debut as Desdemona.[32] Te Kanawa had taken on the part at short notice to replace an ailing Stratas. The performance was broadcast and the Met switchboards were instantly jammed by enthusiastic callers.

In February 1974, as a result of the economising decisions, and following Leinsdorf's attacks on the administration in the press, Kubelik resigned. It was less than a year since he had taken up his post, and his resignation was accompanied by front-page attention in the *New York Times*. According to Chapin, their relations had become strained, because Kubelik was 'impatient with the reorganisation of the artistic administrative personnel' demanding changes in the orchestra, chorus and comprimarii. They had also had differences over the handling of the *Tristan* crisis, Kubelik having urged Tristan's replacement with *Tosca*.[33] On his resignation, Kubelik cited the 'changing financial conditions of the Metropolitan', which had made it impossible for him 'to carry out the artistic ideals' to which he had committed himself when he had signed his contract as music director. After Kubelik's departure James Levine continued as principal conductor, officially becoming music director in 1976.

Determined to make the Met's work 'the most compelling and provocative of any in the country', Chapin was concerned to find someone to be in charge of productions.[34] In February 1974 he chose the British theatre director John Dexter as director of productions, to start in the

1974–75 season. Dexter had worked at the Royal Court Theatre in London from 1957, during its most radical era under George Devine. He had, he later recalled, worked 'for and with a minimum of everything except acting talent'. Economic problems and the consequent lack of materials resulted in the English theatre's success in 'putting less on stage and suggesting more'.[35] At the Royal Court, Brecht had provided, in Richard Eyre's words, a 'philosophical basis and a cue for visual style'. 'The Brechtian tactic', Eyre wrote, 'of "doing new plays as though they were classics and classics as though they were new plays" gave working-class characters the fully dimensional quality that the West End had denied them, while at the same time restoring a long-forgotten realism to Shakespeare, Middleton and Otway.' Its aim was 'to reveal social realities of character, story or situation'.[36]

Dexter had brought this approach to the National Theatre in London, where he had been an associate director from 1963, and it was to influence his work at the Met. His previous operatic experience had been acquired directing *Benvenuto Cellini* for Covent Garden in 1966 and with Rolf Liebermann in Hamburg from 1969 to 1972. Chapin had known him since 1967 and it was he who had introduced him to Liebermann. Dexter was to be responsible at the Met for all production aspects of the repertoire for three years, the second two of which were to be optional. He and Levine were to report to Chapin. Dexter enthused, 'Every opera house should be run by a triumvirate: a music director, a theatre director and a general manager or intendant.'[37]

The completion of Dexter's contract was, however, delayed[38] and he, like Kubelik, was concerned that artistic standards would be sacrificed amid the financial turmoil. On 16 March 1974 he wrote to Chapin about plans for the 1974–75 season, criticising the lack of time for rehearsals for *Death in Venice* and *Forza*. The planning represented, Dexter wrote, 'a triumph of optimism over common sense and the need for standards'. He insisted on the 1975–76 season being reconsidered, and told Chapin that improvement could only be achieved by spending a far greater proportion of the money hitherto 'lavished on physical production' on rehearsal time – an approach that flew in the face of Met tradition since 1883. Dexter also intended to reorganise the workshops so that there would be room to experiment and develop 'an aesthetic slightly more practical in terms of twentieth-century economy, and post-war developments in European operatic production'.[39]

Moore resigned as President of the Board in June 1974 when it was learnt that the accumulated debt would reach $6.3 million by the end of the year. His place was taken by William Rockefeller. The endowment would soon be used up, as would the only remaining assets – the old opera house and insurance money from the warehouse fire.[40] During the summer of 1974 the Executive Committee of the Board met outside New York to try to ensure the Met's survival and to control the growing deficit. Chapin later recalled how a 'we versus they' situation developed between the Board and management at the meetings, and it became clear that whereas Chapin was pressing for a 'major capital campaign', the Board felt that new leadership would solve the Met's problems more easily.[41] In September the Executive Committee decided to reduce the 1974–75 season to twenty-nine weeks and to curtail the House's activities, but merely chewed over once again the need for a major capital campaign. They would also try to ensure 'greater government support for the arts'.[42]

The early part of the season saw Domingo's Roméo, to Judith Blegen's Juliette. *Death in Venice* in October 1974 was adapted from the production created in Benjamin Britten's theatre at Snape in Aldeburgh, Suffolk, and planned with Kubelik before he left. After Kubelik's departure Chapin engaged Steuart Bedford, who had conducted the premiere at Snape the previous year. Peter Pears and John Shirley-Quirk assumed the roles they had created for Britten. Chapin wrote to director Colin Graham on 14 November 1974, 'It seems that *Death in Venice* is still very much talked about and the performances are sold out.'[43] The production was praised although some of the 'talk' was whether the opera was suitable for the Met at all, and Chapin received a heavy mailbag of disapproval. Peter Davis in his *New York Times* piece welcomed *Death in Venice* to the Met in the light of the Met management's 'need to cater for the most conservative patrons in the world', who want to be 'comforted with standard works and star personalities'. Nevertheless he felt that the work and the production were 'swallowed up in the vast spaces of the Met auditorium'.[44] 'Conservative Met patrons' were to be challenged by other unusual and stimulating twentieth-century works during this period. In November

Günther Rennert's *Jenůfa*, in English, was conducted by John Nelson after Kubelik's withdrawal, with a winning Teresa Kubiak as Jenůfa and Jon Vickers heroically moving as Laca. According to Schonberg it was 'handsomely done'.[45] Levine conducted *Wozzeck* in October and November for the first time, with what Movshom called 'a rather detached view of the score'. Peter Glossop was a similarly restrained *Wozzeck*.[46] Box office returns reflected the 'challenge': *Death in Venice* doing 86.9 per cent, *Vespri* 83.6 per cent, and *Wozzeck* 77.5 per cent, as opposed to *Bohème* at 100 per cent.

In spite of box office resistance and Board anxiety, Chapin and Dexter were in harmony in their desire to bring more challenging work to the Met, both in terms of repertoire and production style. Chapin wrote to Solti on 8 October 1974 with plans to bring him and Dexter together for *Moses und Aron* in the 1977–78 season.* When he wrote to Solti to suggest a delay to the 1978–79 season for *Moses*, Chapin was still hopeful: 'Despite our current financial problems, I'm optimistic that we will keep this great institution moving ahead and that financing will be found from various governmental sources.'†[47]

Chapin's optimism was misplaced, and his own position continued to be undermined. He had long been receiving from Board members what he later described as gleeful reports of gossip about his lack of follow-through and consequent loss of artists. In October 1974 he had been questioned with animosity by the Board as to why he had not finalised his management appointments – neither Dexter nor Levine having been finally confirmed and Helga Schmidt having decided to go to Covent Garden instead of the Met.

On 21 November 1974 the Met's Board of Directors decided to create the position of executive director above the general manager, and to establish an administration committee of the Board, consisting of five members under the chairmanship of the executive director.

---

* Solti replied saying he was hoping to sort out his tax problems and preferred Götz Friedrich to Dexter as director for 'such a purely choral work' (Solti contracts 14.10.74,).
† On 2 May 1975 Chapin informed Bliss and Levine that Solti was no longer interested in *Moses und Aron* and wanted to do a new *Meistersinger*. Chapin had told him that that they had a 'beautiful' if fifteen-year-old production. Solti was also considering *Dutchman* (Solti contracts).

Anthony Bliss as executive director was to assume 'responsibility and authority for all non-artistic decisions'. Artistic decisions were delegated to Levine and Dexter, with the executive director providing 'ultimate decision in the event of disagreement'.[48] Bliss would be paid a salary so he could take leave from his law office for up to three years.

Just as in Europe, the severe economic depression was causing an acute financial situation. At the Met the falling off of box office receipts was such that Moore told the Board that by 24 August 1975 the Met's total assets would be reduced to $2.8 million, which would not be enough to continue operations.[49] Bliss's appointment was described by Board member Frank Taplin as 'a last-ditch move to strengthen the financial affairs of the Met'. He was welcomed to the Board meeting with applause but told members that he had 'no magic wand' and that everyone 'would have to work harder'.[50]

Notwithstanding his long and committed connection to the Met, Bliss was not given the job of restoring the House's solvency because of his potential skills in dealing with artists. Bliss, unlike Chapin, 'considered it improper to spend social time with artists'. He was described by Leonard Silk in the New York Times as 'Roman-visaged and patrician-voiced'.[51] Mayer commented, 'There were no social graces at the Met in his tenure.'[52] Bliss suffered from a heart condition and was by nature a reserved man. 'Bliss was not a warm guy,' Levine later recalled, 'but even that was skin deep.'[53] He was, however, determined to maintain the Met's artistic progress.

Taplin hoped that Chapin would regard Bliss's appointment as 'the best thing that could have happened to him'.[54] But, not surprisingly, when Rockefeller, who had replaced Moore as President of the Board in May, told Chapin of Bliss's appointment, Chapin responded by offering his resignation. He was only persuaded to stay by Bliss stressing that he did not want to be general manager and that they should endeavour to work together. Chapin decided to stay to complete the plans for the next two seasons, as well as to finalise Levine's appointment. According to Chapin there was no communication with Bliss in the next few weeks, and he later learnt that Bliss was secretly negotiating with Levine's agent for the conductor to have control of all artistic decisions at the same time as Chapin was negotiating a 'troika' arrangement with himself, Dexter and Levine to be equally responsible for artistic decisions.[55] By November Dexter was complaining of 'leaderless chaos' at the Met.[56]

The artistic team was, however, managing to create a fruitful collaboration, and one that was to challenge the Met audience. At the beginning of their partnership, Levine and Dexter worked in harmony and with enthusiasm. 'We've got such an extraordinary way of working together,' Levine said, 'and we're finding the company so responsive.' Dexter shared Levine's determination to 'put into the repertoire some of the missing masterpieces'. Both men wanted to include twentieth-century works such as Lulu, and also important eighteenth- and nineteenth-century works not yet included, like Meyerbeer's Le Prophète, as well as preparing new productions of the standard repertoire. Dexter said, 'Sometimes we will refurbish an old production with new costumes or lights from economic necessity.'[57] Levine explained their vision to the Production Committee of the Board on 19 November 1974: 'The Metropolitan needed a production style with great imagination, great artistic presence' but which took into account 'the necessity for playing productions in repertory, playing on tour and spending money where it is artistically important but not for window-dressing'. Levine and Chapin urged the Board to accept plans for the 1977–78 season so that major artists could be engaged.[58]

In December 1974 the new Everding production of Mussorgsky's Boris was the first performance of the authentic score, in a combination of the 1869 and 1872 versions, to be heard at the Met. It was conducted by Thomas Schippers with Martti Talvela, Paul Plishka, Donald Gramm and Mignon Dunn, and was received with great enthusiasm. The production, wrote Schonberg, evoked the 'power of the great score' and the cast 'plunged itself into the music'. Schippers, fully exploiting the fluid staging and scenery, kept things 'moving steadily and logically along'.[59] Kerner praised Everding for moulding the Met chorus into an 'explosive slice of humanity'.[60] After the opening Chapin wrote to Joe Volpe in the technical department on 18 December, 'I know the enormous amount of work that you and every one of the people in your area put into our beautiful production of Boris Godunov. The exceptional talents and skills of the individuals who make up the Metropolitan Opera are extraordinary and I firmly believe that there is no theatre in the world that can carry out the high standards that we have in our shops and on our stage.'[61]

On 17 January 1975 Dexter, with Levine, skilfully revamped an old Eugene Berman production of *Forza* with the same amount of rehearsal time as would have been accorded a new production. There were new costumes by Peter J. Hall, the old ones having been destroyed in the fire. Vickers sang Don Alvaro. In the spring there was the first *Ring* cycle for twelve years, with Nilsson singing Sieglinde to Vickers's Siegmund instead of an indisposed Rysanek. Nilsson then sang Brünnhilde as scheduled. At the end of the season Sills made her debut at the Met in *L'Assedio di Corinto*, with Shirley Verrett as Neocle.

Bliss soon came to realise that there was no hope of being bailed out by public funds, and that 'substantial improvement' would have to be in the area of contributions from the private sector. When he met representatives from the National Endowment for the Arts in February he failed to prevent the grant being reduced from the requested $1 million to $550,000, and even that was tied to specific projects.[62] Bliss wrote in his White Paper that the company would have to 'raise its artistic activities to higher and more exciting levels than ever before', and develop long-range plans to increase financial support.

In the new year 1975, fears of insolvency within the next two years led to a proposal by Bliss and the financial Board in February to make a 10 per cent pay cut.[63] Dexter noted in March, 'Whoever decided to build the biggest opera house in the world owes us all 10 per cent of his money for the 10 per cent wage cuts that had been agreed.'[64]

In May 1975 the Executive Committee decided that they and Bliss would run the company, and that the position of general manager should be eliminated. Bliss would not be seeking to take artistic control from Chapin's team, but he would review their plans 'from a budgetary point of view'.[65] Rockefeller was deputed to ask Chapin to become president of the newly created Metropolitan Opera Foundation, in charge of fund-raising. After some hesitation Chapin declined the position – he did not believe in the arrangement and could not face being in the House with no control over policy.

Chapin never had the time to prove whether he had the ability to run the House. Mayer later wrote that Gentele's death had elevated the forty-eight-year-old Chapin beyond his skills and temperament: 'The leadership of the company passed into hands that would never in other circumstances have been given such responsibilities.'[66] Chapin, a man of culture and a good diplomat, lacked the ruthlessness and toughness required for the job at this time of crisis. The financial problems had totally overshadowed him and the Board's lack of support had undermined him in everything that he tried to do. Chapin himself ascribed his eclipse to Board members J. William Fisher and treasurer James J. Smith who, he later wrote, were 'determined on a reorganisation that decentralized all authority and set up the Met along the lines of a new multinational company'.[67] Frank Taplin, when he read Chapin's memoirs, reflected that Chapin had 'suffered from lack of leadership at the Board level' but nonetheless concluded that Chapin's gifts had been for 'people, for artistic questions' and not for administration.[68] Movshom complained that in the new arrangement there was no one with 'outstanding taste and close knowledge of the character and quality of the world's operatic singers'.[69] Eleanor Belmont wrote to Bliss on 22 August that she thought Chapin would 'be a genuine loss to the Met', especially with 'the many friends professional and non-professional he and Betty Chapin have all over the world'.[70] Dexter was also not pleased, writing, 'Schuyler had wit, grace, knowledge, style and all one expects of a great intendant. His successor did not.'[71]

Bliss immediately set about stabilising the Met's finances. On 9 June 1975 he wrote to Levine and Dexter to say that the company faced bankruptcy by July 1976 unless 'urgent short-term measures' were taken. He wrote to John Tooley at Covent Garden, on 2 July, 'At present we are engaged in what is almost a death struggle.'[72] On 21 August 1975 Bliss announced the sale of the Met's last 'tangible asset' – the land on which the old Met had stood. The $5 million sum obtained was needed to repay bank loans and salaries.

Strenuous efforts were made to improve the subscription situation. On 16 October 1975 Bliss was able to report to the Board that subscriptions were up to 61 per cent from 55 per cent in the last season. He also reported the best box office gate since 1968, with 27 performances sold out. By December 600 volunteers were working in the subscriber departments and Al Hubay was able to report that new subscriber packages, such as the 'Met Samplers', were helping to improve the box office. On 26 August 1975 Bliss could inform Tooley that the proposed pay cut had been dropped, as the anticipated loss of $2 million had been reduced to $1 million due to a 'substantial increase in contributions' – $880,000 more than budgeted. This improvement was exactly the amount they had hoped to save by the 10 per cent cut.[73]

Although the 10 per cent pay cut was dropped, Bliss explained to Tooley the shortened forty-two-week season, which had been agreed to two years earlier by Chapin and the Board, would still cause 'considerable economic hardship'.[74] Bliss wrote to Eleanor Belmont on 12 September that the shorter season had been 'a bad decision made without thorough exploration' and that, if combined with the pay cut, it would have meant a real loss in earnings of 30 per cent. Even so, some Board members still wanted to impose both. 'Unhappily,' he wrote, 'some of our colleagues seem totally unaware of the human elements involved in the House.'[75]

Once the pay cut was dropped it was possible to reach agreement with the unions on 5 September 1975. Bliss was able to write to Chapin that agreement with the Guild was reached at 3 a.m. that day 'on terms with which I am very pleased'. These included forty-three weeks plus three weeks of guaranteed concert performances in the parks, no increase in rates, and some work rule changes including authority to start rehearsals at 10.30 a.m. whenever there is a twelve-hour gap between the time they leave the stage and report the next morning. On 16 September Bliss wrote to Tooley that company members were to receive partial pay during the weeks of unemployment resulting from the shortening of the season and an increase in rates of pay of 5 per cent for the 1975–76 and 1976–77 seasons. 'The settlement', Bliss wrote, 'will cost the company more than we can afford but less than our employees need in times of inflation.'[76]

In February 1976 Bliss reorganised the subscriptions department, putting all income-generating activities under the Department of Planning and Public Affairs. Patrick Veitch was appointed head of subscriptions and mail orders, and Al Hubay in charge of VIP ticket allocations. They, together with Marilyn Shapiro, were to liaise more closely with the press department on all public-affairs activities. Shapiro, who had worked in city and federal government, invited member of the Congress and New York State government and was to make useful contacts for the House.* In March, Veitch was able to report that the erosion in subscribers had been halted and that by 27 February 25,000 subscription bills had been mailed and one-fiftieth was already in the bank. Their goal was to raise the sub-scription base to 70 per cent.[77] Bliss also worked on budgeting, as budget controls were not giving a clear enough picture of what the deficits were going to be. Richard Clavell who had become finance director in 1974 – a post he held for the next eleven years – set about reorganising budgeting procedures and tightening up the Met's financial controls.

Bliss's central concern remained that of increased fund-raising, without which the 1977–78 season was still at risk. The shortened season had reduced income and the reduction of assets had further eroded income. $10 million would have to be raised.[78] In March, Taplin noted in his diary that at last there were plans to reduce the size and increase the effectiveness of the Board with the managing directors reduced to fifteen or twenty actively directing the overall operation.[79] Taplin was voted to be one of the managing directors. In May it was announced that there would be twenty-five managing directors who would control the company with forty other advisory directors who would meet twice a year.

In 1976 James Levine officially became music director. Responsible to the executive director, his duties included planning and scheduling, the choice of new productions and casts, the selection of musical assistants and orchestra members, as well as determining the size of the orchestra. He would be a full-time music director and was required

* Marilyn Shapiro was development and public affairs administrator, 1977–78; develop-ment and public affairs director, 1978–79, 1980–81; assistant manager, 1981–82, 1989–90. She was executive director, external affairs 1990–91, and 1999–2000. In 2000 she moved to Washington Opera.

to be physically present for seven months a year at an annual salary of $50,000, with his travel costs also paid for.[80] One of his main priorities was to improve the performance of the orchestra, by rehearsing consistently in a broader repertoire and in great depth. The orchestra was, he later recalled, 'clearly not functioning at what its capacity ought to be'. Likewise, he added, 'the chorus and the ensemble'. Another was to continue to redress the results of Bing's policy which had 'put the Met behind in active international repertory'.[81]

Initially, Bliss expressed the belief that Bing's conservative artistic policy would no longer be necessary, if there were to be good marketing and if costs of new works were kept down and performances balanced with the regular repertoire.[82] Dexter was the ideal man to keep down costs. On 25 November 1975 he explained to the Board, with the use of models of proposed sets for *Aida* and *Carmelites*, how sets would involve simplified and interchangeable parts and how much would depend 'on the effective use of lighting'. Action would be set far forward on the stage. In general, Dexter was aiming at 'achieving manageability of productions within the House'.[83]

Although Dexter was fully aware that the size of the House meant it was more suited to large-scale works than 'small' opera, and that Verdi 'must predominate at the Met',[84] he was not as passionately committed to the nineteenth-century works as he was to those of the twentieth century. Elijah Moshinsky later went as far as to describe Dexter as a modernist who 'hated grand opera'.[85] Unfortunately for Dexter, the Met needed a new production of *Aida* because the old one had been destroyed in the warehouse fire, and it was always a central piece of the Met repertoire. In 1975 Dexter wrote, 'No way was I going to do *Aida*. It wasn't part of the bargain at all. I picked it up because there was no one else around to do it and get it on for under half a million.'[86] *Aida*, designed by David Reppa, was the first collaboration between Levine and Dexter since their respective appointments, and in spite of Dexter's reluctance, both men found the preparation period exciting. 'The rehearsal atmosphere', said Dexter, 'was magical, a bit like an opera workshop.' Levine continued, 'We had everybody there all day long, every day, restudying an opera they knew. It was the best set of rehearsals I'd ever had here. . . .'

Dexter hoped that the atmosphere they were creating would encourage singers to work at the Met even though they could not 'match Paris or Milan in paying astronomical fees'.*[87]

The *Aida* production was received with boos and shouts of 'Dexter go home'. Dexter did not take a bow and most of the critics were harsh. Byron Belt called it 'misguided, vulgar, dangerously racist', and started his review, 'Come back, Rudolf Bing, all is forgiven!'[88] Andrew Porter suggested that if Dexter 'cannot bring himself to produce the opera that Verdi wrote he should let *Aida* alone' and try his hand at *Die Soldaten*.[89] Harold Schonberg, however, found it 'quite handsome' with its stylised set and tilted turntable. The production was, he wrote, 'an interesting amalgam of the new and traditional with the traditional predominating'.[90] Kerner was also less hostile, and felt that Dexter, in eschewing 'scenic spectacle', had been more successful than his predecessors – Margaret Webster in 1951, and Nathaniel Merrill in 1963 – in making 'the drama dominate the spectacle'. Kerner recognised the influence of Wieland Wagner in the triumph scene being held at night with imitation torches reminiscent of Nazi rallies. He also found that the drama was well served by the 'suffocatingly elaborate costumes' and stylised gestures of the principals that other critics, including Porter, found disturbing.[91]

Levine was excited by the innovations, telling *Opera* magazine in 1977, 'It's driven me crazy over the years that all people are interested in is seeing a Cecil B. de Mille spectacle.'[92] Dexter was less enthusiastic, later writing that it was 'an *Aida* whose main virtue was its economy and adaptability to its singers'.[93] He later admitted that the movement of the crowds was improved in revivals, but he was unrepentant about the triumph scene, explaining that at night 'ritual in Egypt is more dangerous, more mysterious, more significant. . . .'[94] He also said that it was 'the best sung *Aida*' he had ever heard.[95] The *Aida* singers' roster was indeed not out of keeping with Met tradition. Leontyne Price, according to Kerner, after a shaky start, soon found her old 'tones of floating, unearthly ravishing beauty'. McCracken, loved at the Met for his heroic roles, 'took the end of "Celeste Aida" on true, pianissimo

* Alan Rich in the *New York Times* in August 1980 quoted $6,000 as top fee at the Met compared with $10,000 at Dallas or San Francisco. Liebermann's fees in Paris were so high that disclosure of them caused a shock among French taxpayers.

head tones' and with input from Dexter, brought 'intense credibility' to his acting. Kerner praised Levine for obtaining an improved response from the orchestra although the chorus sounded 'downright scrawny in the triumph'.[96]

That same season, in February 1976, the Met was on more familiar directorial ground with Sandro Sequi's traditional new production of *I Puritani* which had not been seen at the Met for fifty-eight years. It starred Sutherland, Pavarotti and Milnes. A month into the run, Sutherland, after recovering from a cold, and Pavarotti from his apprehension, provided a 'night of vocal glory': 'Their legato line, their uniquely luminous timbres, and their obvious joy in dealing with Bellini's magnificent arcs of melody were treasures for history.'[97] The production was underwritten by the 'Met family': the National Council, Met Opera Guild and Patrons. But the cost of new productions showed just how challenging the new economic climate was. Bliss wrote to Mrs Edgar Tobin on 5 August 1976 that inflation meant that the 1975 *Aida* had cost $365,000, whereas the far more elaborate 1962 one had cost $135,000. Because of the steep rise in production costs it was increasingly difficult to get individuals to underwrite the cost of whole productions. Bliss therefore organised a new production fund whereby gifts would be accepted on the basis of a three-year pledge, with amounts intended to average $50,000 to $70,000. All donors would be credited in the programme and any donor contributing the cost of a whole production would be listed in the programme on the title page of the production.*[98]

The quintessential New Yorker, Tatiana Troyanos, finally made her Met debut in 1976, when she sang Octavian in *Rosenkavalier* and the Composer in *Ariadne* in March. The daughter of Greek and German immigrants, Troyanos was brought up in a New York tenement. In the words of her obituary in *Opera News* in 1993, 'Just as Lincoln Center rose from the rubble of that same West Side neighbourhood, so Troyanos conquered the challenges of a trying youth to become a

---

* In the 1975–76 season *Il Tabarro* and *Suor Angelica* were the joint gift of the William Penn Foundation and Mr and Mrs Alan J. Broder.

world-class artist.' She grew up in Queens, singing in choirs, then trained at Juilliard in lieder and oratorio. In 1965 she went to Hamburg, where she spent ten years working her way up under Rolf Liebermann's guidance. Joan Ingpen brought her to Covent Garden in 1969 to sing Octavian, which launched her international career, and a year later Carmen, after which Solti chose her for his *Carmen* recording. She was a highly strung artist, recognised for the intensity she brought to her roles. Troyanos's Composer in *Ariadne auf Naxos*, as seen in the Met video, showed both passion and freedom with her well-schooled, near-soprano top, open and vibrant. By the time of her early death on 21 August 1993, she had sung more than 270 performances at the Met. She was 'larger than life yet intensely human, brilliant yet warm, lyric yet dramatic . . . a great trouser role performer she was every bit as formidable in a dress, a poignant Charlotte . . . majestic Dido, enigmatic Carmen, white-hot Eboli'.[99] Troyanos was also an exciting singer-actress in the classic roles, especially Mozart.

Troyanos's Met debut focused attention on the growing number of fine singers coming out of the United States in the late Seventies and early Eighties. There were more Americans being trained as opera singers and there were more opportunities for them to develop. By 1976 there were forty-six opera companies with budgets of $100,000 or more, as opposed to twenty-seven in 1965. Frederica von Stade and Carol Neblett were appearing in top Houses in Europe. Von Stade, whom Ingpen had launched in Paris as Cherubino, was singing in the United States, along with fellow mezzos Horne, Dunn, Bumbry and Verrett. So too were baritone Cornell MacNeil and bass-baritone James Morris.

More familiar favourite singers also appeared regularly. Sherrill Milnes's baritone in its glory days was an astonishing instrument. With a broad tonal palette, a rich timbre, superb breathing and legato, great penetration and a high register that ascended to tenor B flat, he was ideal for Verdi. He also had considerable success as Don Giovanni, Jack Rance and Scarpia among his many roles. Milnes's acting varied from involved to melodramatic, but was always memorable, and both on stage and in recordings he could be relied upon to deliver a finely sung account of the role. In a 1976 recording of *Macbeth*, with Riccardo Muti conducting at the peak of his form, Milnes finds in Macbeth a belligerent, terror-ridden bully with little hint of neurosis, the tone appealingly warm, with a tendency to darkness appropriate to the role. That same year Milnes and Domingo recorded *Forza* and sang it at the Met under Levine. In *Forza* Milnes was even more exciting than in *Macbeth*, sparking off his colleague Domingo and thrillingly accompanied by Levine. In peak form, as he is on this recording, Levine shows an uncanny sense of how much to demand at a given moment from orchestra and singers. In a revival of *Forza* in March 1977 Domingo was again outstanding as Alvaro, setting, in Smith's words, a 'standard for that role which has not been matched at the Met in a long time for power, enunciation and sheer lyric beauty. Old Met goers', Smith added, 'rummaged in their minds for comparisons back to Martinelli.'[100] The 1976 performances were praised in the *New York Times* by John Rockwell as an example of 'the full-throated singing of Italian Opera' that had been missing at the Met 'under its new directorial triumvirate'.[101]

It was not just the scarcity of such singing that was being called into question. There were other criticisms of the management, and of Levine in particular. Erich Leinsdorf, who in 1978 was to celebrate his fortieth anniversary with the Met, wrote angrily to Bliss on 27 April 1976 to complain that 'a third echelon executive', Richard Rodzinski, had delayed finalising plans for *Rosenkavalier* for the 1976–77 season while 'four months were spent on a fishing trip for Carlos Kleiber'. By the time he came back, Leinsdorf had made other plans and was insulted to be offered what he called 'warm-ups', and no new productions in 1978–79. He warned of a system where 'the "Generalmusikdirektor" picks his own menu and assigns the rest in the most practical manner'.[102]

Bliss told Leinsdorf that the effort to bring 'outstanding' conductors to the Met meant that 'proven friends' were not offered so many options. Bliss replied that it was he who had insisted on Levine conducting more operas in his first two years 'than he would have wanted later'. It was, he believed, 'essential through continual supervision that the orchestra should be revitalised and raised to the highest possible standard'. He added, 'I am sure that Jimmy has the capacity to do the very difficult job that lies ahead in restoring the Metropolitan's artistic thrust.' After the first two or three seasons Bliss did not believe Levine would conduct more than two or three operas a season.[103] In February 1977 Leinsdorf returned to conduct *Salome* and *Walküre*.

There was criticism that Levine was not only monopolising the repertoire but that he was also learning many of the scores on the job. Some of his early presentations, such as *Lohengrin* in November 1976, his first Wagner with the company, and *Tristan* in January 1981, were not yet seen as definitive accounts. In June 1980 Kolodin criticised Levine for using the Met as a testing ground for *Parsifal*, which he was preparing for Bayreuth and was to conduct there at the centennial production in 1982.*[104] Levine's *Traviata* in March 1981 was described by Mayer as his 'first crack' and was seen as the 'formative stages of the interpretation of a great opera by a great conductor'.[105] Plácido Domingo, who sang Alfredo in this production, defended Levine: 'Those who sometimes accuse him of not going extremely deeply into the music do not realise that he is growing at an amazing pace ... that he is not now trying to give his definitive accounts of the works he conducts.'[106] In May 1980 the Board expressed its appreciation for Levine's devotion to the House but they also felt that the House should have the opportunity to hear other great conductors.[107]

Solti, in December 1976, mourned the passing of opera conductors who had grown up in opera houses and who had learnt the repertoire and skills of an opera house 'as an apprentice, as a coach'. With Böhm over eighty and Giulini no longer conducting opera, Solti felt that only he and Karajan represented the old school, which had included a generation from Toscanini and Kleiber, to Furtwängler, Mahler, Strauss and Walter.[108] The Met historian Irving Kolodin felt that Levine's musical intellect, fine pianistic musicianship and 'unflagging vigour' were not enough to counterbalance his lack of experience. Levine, however, had had a fair amount of practical experience in opera for his years. In 1956, at the age of thirteen, he had been a chorus-master at Serkin's Marlborough Festival and summer school on a production of *Così fan tutte*. In 1957 he attended the first of fourteen summers at the Aspen Festival and school of music, first as

* According to John Rockwell, Levine had told Wolfgang Wagner that he would not conduct the *Ring* at Bayreuth until he had the Met *Ring* 'under his belt' (*New York Times*, 21.9.86). Kolodin felt that Levine also used the Met as a testing ground for *Elektra*, *Dutchman*, *Otello* and *Onegin* (*Saturday Review*, June 1960).

a student, but from 1960 as a performer. There he also conducted *Così*, as well as twentieth-century works including Strauss's *Ariadne auf Naxos*, Stravinsky's *Mavra* and Britten's *Albert Herring*. In 1970 Levine conducted an exciting *Ballo* at Welsh National Opera and San Francisco, and *La Traviata* in 1971 at the Hollywood Bowl, with Sills, Domingo and Milnes, and began a long connection with the Salzburg Festival in 1976. Kolodin felt that Levine had gained 'a sure command of a sizeable symphonic repertory' at Cleveland, though not, he believed, the kind of operatic experience to which Solti was referring.[109] Kolodin also accused Levine of confusing 'physical energy with creative vitality' and a tendency to conduct at 'a ceaseless mezzoforte', as in his 1980 *Manon*.

Kolodin, however, underestimated the excitement generated by the youthful zest and enthusiasm evident in this same *Manon*. In the early days Levine was full of delight in the music making; there was no hint of routine in his performances. His colleagues responded to his enthusiasm and warmth. Domingo loved working with Levine. 'It is always fun to make music with Jimmy', he wrote, 'because he is so enthusiastic. I feel I have a friend and collaborator in the pit when he is there . . . if there is a difficult moment, he looks up with a smile, he is encouraging and reliable rather than panic-stricken and angry.'[110] Raymond Gniewek, concert master since 1957, wrote later that Levine 'radiates a feeling of warmth, integrity, and purpose that inspires our team to play more gloriously and eloquently than we ever believed possible'. Levine 'never raises his voice or yells at anybody. If he wants to make a correction he steps down from the podium and goes over and talks to the musician privately.'*[111]

Levine was also a supporter of young singers. One of his protégées was Maria Ewing, to whom he had given advice and encouragement since they had met in Cleveland in 1971. She recalled ten years later, 'He gets a hell of a lot of pleasure out of seeing his babies, as he calls us, develop properly. He's delighted about that and he's terribly concerned.'[112] Another protégée was Kathleen Battle, a former school-teacher who began singing late in life, and who was introduced to

* Levine, concert master Gniewek and Jascha Silberstein, the company's principal cellist, regularly played chamber music together.

Levine by Thomas Schippers in Cincinnati. Levine became what *Opera News* described as her 'friend, mentor, counsellor'.[113] Battle made her debut at the Met in 1978. With her high lyric voice in the tradition of Lily Pons and Roberta Peters, she sang many roles at the Met, including Despina and Rosina and Sophie in *Rosenkavalier* – usually to sold-out houses. Barbara Hendricks was another of Levine's protégées.

As a pianist Levine had the great advantage of being able to work closely with his singers 'one-on-one in his studio' at the keyboard going through the roles phrase by phrase as did such conductors as Abbado, Muti and Solti.* Samuel Ramey later said that Levine's true genius lay in his ability to explore the 'secrets behind the printed note on the page' in this way.[114] In June 1980 Sherrill Milnes said of Levine that he 'has an amazingly profound knowledge of vocal matters that belies his age. He can make specific suggestions regarding the voice that other conductors simply don't know.'[115]

The chorus was also improving under chorus-master David Stivender, who had taken over in January 1973 and remained until 1985. Henahan later said that within a year Stivender had given the chorus a sense of professional pride, and that they were 'functioning at a level that would have been thought Utopian ten years ago'.†[116] Comprimarii were also to have increased security and professional support under Levine's direction. Betsy Norden, a company soprano since 1972, married with two small children, was happy to stay at the Met all year round. She felt that 'the current management – and Levine, because of his infectious enthusiasm – boosts morale in the House'. Although learning while already in the exalted position of music director, Levine was given time and space to refine and develop his interpretations, and become steeped in the repertoire, as well as to become immersed in the running of the House.

The artistic team brought several unfamiliar works as well as non-naturalistic productions to the Met during the 1976–77 season, including Massenet's *Esclarmonde* and Poulenc's *Dialogues of the Carmelites*,

---

* Levine had by 1978 recorded Beethoven's sonatas for cello and piano with Lynn Harrell.
† Stivender died in 1990.

in February 1977, produced by Dexter in English. *Lohengrin* directed by August Everding, Generalintendant of the Hamburg Opera, opened in November 1976, with René Kollo making his Met debut as Lohengrin. Patrick J. Smith, had he not seen the programme, would have thought that Dexter and not Everding was responsible for the austere and dark production. He missed dawn and dusk, and found Ming Cho Lee's sets 'continued evidence of the new brutalism' as were the mostly 'monochromatic costumes' of Peter J. Hall.[117]

Esclarmonde, also in November, was borrowed from San Francisco in a grand-scale production starring Joan Sutherland.[118] It was an example of the growing practice of borrowing productions, as opera companies grew in number and costs spiralled. *Esclarmonde* was a vehicle for Sutherland and a rarity, which would probably not stay in the repertory.[119] Of Sutherland, Smith wrote, 'Strong as it is, the voice no longer has the effulgence and freedom it used to possess, so that her singing is everywhere more careful.' Giacomo Aragall's voice, however, had 'grown in size and filled the House' in spite of 'moments of strain'.[120] Meyerbeer's *Le Prophète*, which followed in February 1977, had not been produced for nearly fifty years, and starred Horne, Scotto and McCracken. It had a unit set which Dexter believed to be more fluid as well as more economical, at $300,000. Shortly after *Le Prophète*, Dexter recalled a conversation at one of the few cocktail parties he attended, when a 'grand lady with a loud voice' came up to him and said, 'Mr Dexter, I trust you will not make *Carmelites* as austere as *Le Prophète*.' To which Dexter had replied, 'Madame, the production of *Carmelites* will make Bert Brecht look like a Renaissance voluptuary.'[121]

Dexter, together with set designer David Reppa and costume designer Jane Greenwood, was determined to put on *Carmelites* as a preparation for other modern works and to show that productions could be both cheap and dramatically effective. 'The nuns' costumes', wrote Dexter, 'came from *Suor Angelica*, the peasants' costumes from *Andrea Chénier*, the raised floor was taken from *Boris Godunov*, the copper tubing was donated by a patron.' The entire production cost $65,000, which was $3,000 under budget.[122]

Spareness was part of Dexter's philosophy: 'Even with all the money in the world we still wouldn't be putting more clutter on the stage. We would be buying more rehearsal time. We'd be buying more choristers, more orchestral players.' In an interview with the *New York Times* on 28 January 1977 he explained why he favoured the use of a unit set:

> It's not just economics that dictates the use of a unit set. .... A realistic set locks you in. You have to line up your chorus in a tableau, three or four rows in front or in a semicircle or in straight lines. I don't think that's acceptable to today's audiences. A unit set is more fluid, and allows us to use different patterns.

Levine was in total agreement with Dexter's priorities. Working closely with him on planning repertoire, casts and rehearsal schedules, he hoped that all the House's work would soon be of a uniformly high standard, 'long on conceptual strength and on drama and on the integration of the musical and dramatic elements and very short on clutter'.[123]

Dexter's *Carmelites* was indeed both convincing and well received. He had insisted on an international cast, at one point approaching Maria Callas for the Mother Superior. In the event Régine Crespin took it, moving on from the role written for her, the New Prioress, to the Old Prioress. Michel Plasson conducted. It opened on 5 February 1977. Action took place on a huge white cross on the floor, a construction at the back of the stage suggesting Gothic arches under stark lighting. According to Schonberg, Dexter 'successfully threw the focus where it belongs', emphasising the psychological elements of the drama.[124] Byron Belt said of the revival, later in the season, 'From the opening tableau of prostrate nuns through the hideous impact of the scene at the guillotine, the Met's *Dialogues* is a shattering emotional and artistic experience.' Crespin was 'outstanding'. Maria Ewing as Blanche 'projected the youth and pathos of this difficult role'.

Schonberg complained that the excellent English translation could not be heard, but on the whole Dexter was delighted by the reception of *Carmelites* and was convinced that the public wanted to see 'some difficult works'. When a member of the Board had said to him in a critical tone, 'You're not really attracting a Met audience,' he had been happy to agree and suggested that he was bringing in a new audience rather than losing the old one.[125] Ten years later, when *Carmelites* was revived, Leighton Kerner in the *Village Voice* pointed out that in a season that included five major extravaganzas, including three Zeffirelli Puccinis, Dexter's *Carmelites* had been 'an oasis of theatrical sanity and poetry in a desert of antidramatic indulgence'. Dexter and Levine had another success in a modern work with *Lulu* in March 1977.

On 21 October 1976 Bliss called a special meeting of the directors and members of the Association and told them that without finding $4 million the next season could not be undertaken. Dexter told the meeting 'survival is the question', but that nonetheless new productions were essential to keep the place exciting and attract top artists as well as the public. Bliss told the meeting that contributions had to be increased and the Met recognised as the 'vital artistic centre of the United States'. In January 1977 the Board urged that there be a 37.4 per cent ticket price increase, but Bliss objected on the grounds that such a rise would reduce the box office, which was currently 94 per cent. Instead, he urged that an intensive, highly visible fund-raising campaign was to be initiated and committees formed to solicit various members of the Met 'family'.[126]

In April the Board voted for Taplin to become president of the Board to tackle all the fund-raising activities on a full-time, unpaid basis. Bliss argued that the most important job was fund-raising and that that role now needed a 'full-time president'. The task was, he felt, incompatible with being a working partner in a major law firm, as Rockefeller had been.* Bliss told Taplin that he had 'the right combination of experience in administration and the arts'.[127] Taplin, a lawyer by training, had been on the Met Board for many years as well as the Boards of cultural and educational institutions such as Sarah Lawrence College and the Marlboro Music Festival. He was also an amateur musician, who had grown up with the Cleveland Symphony Orchestra and enjoyed the company of musicians and artists.

Both Taplin and Bliss were convinced that the financial crisis had resulted from the Board not being active enough in raising the money

---

* Taplin had been a Board member since 1960 and had been president of the Cleveland Institute of Music 1952–56.

needed to cover the operating deficit, and they set about a complete overhaul of all the Met's income-generating activities. On 20 July 1980 John Rockwell of the *New York Times* was able to report that Taplin and Bliss had reordered an 'old-fashioned, rather stuffy private club into a modern operation based on the principles of efficient business practice and drawing from the fund-raising techniques of the business world'.

Taplin and Bliss vigorously set about organising a development office to take charge of all the Met's fund-raising activities. On 30 June the Board were informed that Marilyn Shapiro was to become director of development and would co-ordinate all fund-raising efforts in one programme. All fund-raising would be seen as a 'totality': membership, annual giving, project giving, capital giving and deferred giving. Representatives from each department would meet and agree on a schedule of activities. The goal for the next season's fund-raising was set at $13 million.[128]

'We spent money', Taplin recalled, 'creating the structure of a development office and tied it into the marketing of tickets.' The cornerstone of the annual giving was the patrons' programme where donors gave at higher levels – $1,000 and above. Taplin continued, 'We built a hierarchy of giving levels and matched those with levels of recognition': plaques with donor names, dinners, parties and rehearsals, and tickets were held back, to be ordered through a special hotline.[129] By 1980, Taplin explained, the 'backbone of the annual fund-raising' consisted of about 1,400 patrons who accounted for most of the $4 million annual revenue. On 6 October the Met marathon raised $250,000, with Taplin himself along with volunteers taking pledges on one hundred telephones. The confidence that Taplin and Bliss engendered brought back old sponsorship like Frank Greenwall of National Starch and Chemical, as well as bringing in new donors. Taplin also visited tour cities, including Houston, San Antonio and Dallas, stressing the 'national character' of the Met.*[130]

Solvency also depended on realistic wage settlements. During the union negotiations in July, treasurer Smith again pointed to the danger

---

* After touring for many years for the National Council as president, Taplin was able to build on his familiarity with supporters around the country.

of bankruptcy, and some members of the Board actually felt that bankruptcy would be beneficial, securing a 'clean start' for the Met. After three months of tense negotiations, with closure always a possibility, on 9 September the unions agreed to a three-year contract, with a 7 per cent increase compounded over three years. Bliss reported high morale after the settlement and a high box office at 93 per cent.[131]

Television was to prove another vehicle for widening the Met's support nationally. On 28 June Bliss applied to the National Endowment for the Arts for funding for the Met's live telecasts, explaining that one of their 'mutual primary concerns is exploring ways to expand the accessibility of performances of the highest quality to as many people as possible' and thus build up audiences. On the basis of the success of the telecast of *La Bohème* on 15 March 1977, Texaco agreed to underwrite two telecasts for the next season at $225,000 and promised that if the Met could find a 'non-corporate sponsor' the series could be expanded.[132]

As a result of Bliss, Shapiro and Taplin's efforts over the next four years, the Met increasingly became the national company, its donor base increasing from 75,000 in the mid-Seventies to 200,000 by 1981, two-thirds of whom lived outside New York City. By 1983 Shapiro was using 200 volunteers as well as a paid staff of thirty-two. On 23 May 1978 Bliss reported to Gordon Getty that they had 'come close enough to our $13.2 million goal to assure the unbelievers of the importance of the Met and our ability to sustain it'.[133]

The final element in Taplin and Bliss's long-range strategy for the Met was the decision to embark on an endowment campaign on 16 February 1978, after many years of discussion about such a campaign. Taplin, having learnt from the fund-raising activities of educational institutions like Princeton University, knew how to organise a major capital campaign, and because of the Met's advantage as a national institution he was confident that 'the money was there'. In the 1977–78 Annual Report, Bliss announced the initiation of a 'centennial fund' campaign. The major effort was directed to the larger givers: corporate, foundations and major individuals giving $10,000 and up. The Golden Horseshoe club was for donors of $100,000.

In the 1977–78 Annual Report, Bliss was able to state that the 'Association had met operating expenses for the second successive year with a modest surplus which helped it to replenish its severely depleted working capital'. The operating deficit for 1977–78 was $12.2 million. Taplin and his team succeeded in raising $12.4 in contributions. Taplin noted in his diary on 29 August 1978, 'The greatest "plus" is the confidence felt on all sides that we have turned around and are operating on firm financial and artistic foundations.'

Bliss also reported in his 1977–78 Annual Report that the Dexter–Levine team were raising artistic standards by widening the repertoire, expanding rehearsals, improving lighting and scenery, and strengthening the ensemble work of the orchestra and chorus. The box office had increased from 95.8 per cent capacity to 96.3 per cent in 1977–78. Bliss referred to *Rigoletto* and *Tannhäuser* as 'daring new interpretations of standard repertory works'. The critics were less sanguine than Bliss about *Rigoletto* on 31 October 1977, finding that Dexter's lack of empathy for the nineteenth-century repertoire had resulted in a coldness and lack of drama. Mayer wrote, 'Time and again dramatic moments were glossed over – Monterone's entrance, his curse, Gilda's entrance and her exit after "Caro nome" – time and again one could not pick out the central action because of the aimless and huddled crowds.' MacNeil was 'throaty and insecure', his acting 'little more than good routine'. Levine's conducting also lacked drama, and even Domingo's Duke and Cotrubas's Gilda did not enliven the proceedings.[134] In December 1977 a traditional production of *Tannhäuser* by Otto Schenk, with the naturalistic designs of Günther Schneider-Siemssen, met with a warmer response from critics, audience and Levine himself. He conducted with vigour and conviction, with a cast that included Rysanek, Grace Bumbry, McCracken and Bernd Weikl.

Levine was consolidating his power at the Met and was anxious to answer criticism that it was no longer up to standard as the singers' House. Unhappy with the state of planning and casting, he started to look for a new casting assistant. Domingo told him there was a woman in Paris who 'somehow manages to get one to rehearse more than one meant to'. This was Joan Ingpen. Other respected singers also spoke well of her. When offered the job of artistic administration director at the Met, she hesitated at first – it was far from home, in her words two decades later – but when she met 'Jim' she found that they 'really hit it off'. She came to New York in January 1978 and stayed until the 1983–84 season, by which time the plans for 1986–87 were well advanced. When she arrived there were still holes in the current season and there was a preliminary plan in Levine's desk for the following season. Ingpen recalled, 'It took two or three years to get it right.' As she explained, 'Jim was busy. Unless you bullied Jim and said, "I've got a list like this now, you've got to give me an hour." He could take a quick decision and that was it.'[135]

Ingpen was responsible for casting 3,000 singing roles a season, plus 3,000 covers. Covers remained a challenge – even with the development of local singers and companies – the time zones being in the wrong direction and making last-minute changes impossible. Ingpen planned rehearsal schedules three to five years in advance. 'Basically all opera houses are after the same thirty people,' she later explained, and added, 'One simply has to get there first.'[136] Ingpen later recalled her working relationship with Levine. They would, she remembered in 1999:

> make up a repertoire for the season and then we would go and talk to Tony Bliss, and he would immediately say, 'You're emptying my House . . . we can't have *Wozzeck* and this and that.' Al Hubay was there and he could tell you what the takings would be. He would reel off half a dozen that he knew would sell out and Jim and I would say 'we can't exist on that!' So it had to be a very careful mixture and that should not be more than two, and if we got our way two or three interesting things.[137]

Management had begun to take a firm stand on fees. Ingpen recalled, 'We had a top fee and never to be paid to more than ten – at a great stretch twelve – top artists at a time. Munich said no, La Scala had something extra on the back page . . .' On 25 July 1978 Bliss wrote to James McCracken that he had put an end to the system of 'side agreements'. The top fee which applied 'to a very limited handful of artists in the grandfather category' was $6,000 plus Guild rehearsal compensation and economy transportation. 'There are', he added, '*no* exceptions I will make with you or anyone else. If you doubt my word on this after all the years we have known each other, you should not be member of this company.'[138]

Even great stars like Sutherland were subject to management strictures. In 1978 she and Bonynge said she only wanted to sing *The Merry Widow*. Levine and the Board agreed as long as she would do *Semiramide* and *Seraglio* as well. She could not fit in *Semiramide* and turned down Constanze because it had become now 'uncomfortable' for her.[139] The Bonynges had also proposed a version of *The Merry Widow* that Dexter felt unsuitable for New York audiences. Bliss suggested to her the Christopher Hassell version on 5 July 1978, but she replied on 28 July, 'Either we do the version we have prepared and performed with love (and not a little success) or we do not perform at all.' When the Mozart *Seraglio* fell through, Levine dropped *The Merry Widow* and rumours flew around that Sutherland had been 'fired'. Bliss wrote to Dexter and Levine on 23 June 1978, 'I want to go on record that I think that regardless of how wonderful the artists involved may be, there is a limit to how far the Metropolitan Opera should go in giving into individual demands that affect our artistic policy.... I think the fewer special terms we make, the happier we shall be in the long run.'[140] Alan Rich in *New York* magazine supported management, arguing that stars had no right to dictate policy and that the Met was 'artistically better run now than at any time in its history'.[141]

On 21 September Levine told Taplin that 'progress on the artistic side had gone much faster than he had dared hope'. He added that he wanted to spend many years at the Met 'putting his stamp on the House, and perhaps in his fifties taking on guest appearances with symphony orchestras'. Taplin felt that Levine, 'confident, enthusiastic, thirty-five years old', would give continuity of artistic leadership to the Met.[142] Bliss told the Board on 8 January 1979 that regular performances had been 'drastically improved'.

Although few top international conductors appeared at the Met at this time, one who did was Karl Böhm, in October 1978, when he conducted *Fidelio* with Hildegard Behrens. Andrew Porter, who had settled in New York and was writing for the *New Yorker*, found the 'Met orchestra rough and raucous: the brasses brayed, the drums were banged, the ensembles see-sawed, and chords that call for a unanimous attack spattered into life'. He added, 'The eminent conductor got a great reception; people must have been hearing through to the carefully paced, classical *Fidelio* which underlay the rude execution.'[143] On 25 March 1978 Böhm's appearances conducting *Die Frau ohne Schatten* had become 'the hottest ticket in New York', but Böhm himself was nearing his eighty-fourth birthday and was at the end of his career.

The 1978–79 season continued to be innovative with *Luisa Miller* and the Svoboda–Skalicky–Dexter–Levine *Bartered Bride*. Early the next season Dexter directed an intimate *Die Entführung aus dem Serail*, which was surprisingly well received by audience and critics, and in September 1978 *Billy Budd* had its Met premiere. The British designer, William Dudley, worked closely with Dexter. Making full use of the Met's elevators, he created an ingenious single scenic machine which could smoothly adapt itself into four deck levels, from the gun decks to deep in the hold. The ship was harshly lit against 'a sea of unchanging black'.[144] James Morris gave a fine performance as Claggart, Richard Stilwell was Billy and Peter Pears was Vere, in what was described as 'a memory of a performance'. It was conducted by Raymond Leppard. The scenery, according to Schonberg, 'brought down the House' and was one of the few well-received new productions of the season, even though its box office averaged only 83 per cent.[145] 'From that point it was downhill,' Schonberg added.[146]

The first step 'downhill' for some critics was Dexter's *Don Pasquale* in December 1978, which was further evidence for Smith that British theatre directors were not suitable for American audiences. Smith felt that Dexter had turned *Don Pasquale* into an Oscar Wilde type comedy – moving up the time of the piece to 1900s Rome and replacing his more familiar Brechtian approach with what he called traditional English 'middle-brow boulevard or drawing-room comedic writing'.[147] Andrew Porter felt that although Dexter eschewed broad clowning, he was 'fussily focused upon stage properties' – cigarettes, wineglasses and notebooks and the like.[148] Sills sang Norina in her last role at the Met with what Manuela Hoelterhoff described as 'difficulty in popping out the notes'.[149] Harold Schonberg called it 'a triumph of experience and professionalism'. Nicolai Gedda was stylish if lacking sensuosness and warmth as Ernesto.[150]

Kolodin was less critical. He felt Dexter had put his 'knowledge aptly, effectively and – to his enduring credit – elegantly to work' on Donizetti's behalf.[151] Dexter, however, had not been in sympathy with the piece. 'Much against my better judgement,' he later wrote, 'I was persuaded to do *Rigoletto* and *Don Pasquale* by James. Whilst I hope they never went over their budget and achieved a little dramatic coherency, they are not works I enjoyed dramatically and that lack of enjoyment and energy shows on the stage.'[152]

The size of the Met stage was a constant problem. 'The audience', Dexter had written in January 1977, 'should be looking for faces, not windmills. The size of the Met creates a fight between the volume of the auditorium and the volume of the human figure, which has got to be made dominant to 4,000 people.'[153] For *Don Pasquale* Dexter had attempted to scale down the Met stage by framing it with a 'marvellously gaudy golden border decorated with huge flowers and butterflies'.[154] The problem of scale in the 4,000-seat theatre remained, however, in Dexter's words, 'very, very difficult'[155] and also became the source of increasing friction, which added to Dexter's isolation. When he directed *Don Carlos* in February 1979, with Scotto, Milnes, Horne and Ghiaurov, many of the critics, including Harold Schonberg, preferred Bing's grand opera 1950 production to what Schonberg called Dexter's 'mini-opera philosophy', which he felt was better suited to 'some little provincial House than the great Metropolitan'.[156]

During rehearsals Dexter's wrath had been aroused by Mrs Donald D. Harrington, the opera's sponsor, when she had insisted, against his judgement, that Elisabetta's white stallion and Irish wolfhounds remain in the first act. Despite this ominous clash, and his original reluctance to tackle *Don Carlos*, Dexter later felt it was the one grand opera with which he had had some success. The Dexter–David Reppa production incorporated the forest of Fontainebleau act, heard for the first time at the Met and welcomed by Leighton Kerner for its music which 'once heard is hard to do without'.[157]

On 8 March 1979 Jean-Pierre Ponnelle's *Flying Dutchman*, which had caused a sensation in San Francisco, came to the Met. Levine had worked with Ponnelle at Salzburg in 1978 on *The Magic Flute* and greatly admired him. Kurt Herbert Adler had brought Ponnelle to San Francisco in 1958 to design *Carmina Burana*, and he had subsequently designed eleven productions for that House, eight of which he had directed as well. Sometimes critics complained that Ponnelle's concepts paid scant regard to the librettos, and Domingo described Ponnelle's lack of reservation in his work. When Ponnelle was convinced he was right, Domingo explained, he went 'all the way'.[158] Levine did eleven productions of eight different works with Ponnelle, and believed that Ponnelle got the closest to what he thought 'a stage director should do'. Ponnelle had, he said 'many new images but was in such touch with the music and with the style and the implications'.[159] Ponnelle's early death at the age of fifty-six in 1988 saddened Levine greatly. He admired Ponnelle, recalling at the time of his death:

> He was the only director I worked with who directed from the full orchestral score. He knew the music, knew the text, and he understood the technical as well as the subliminal relationship between the two. . . . He had an innate feeling for the colours of the score.[160]

Ponnelle's *Dutchman* was conceived as the Steersman's dream, Steersman and Eric being sung by the same person. Levine believed it to have been 'a vivid theatrical result that came from an organic point of departure'.[161] At the Met it was greeted by extraordinary booing, cheers and a few scuffles. Robert Jacobson said it was 'so perverse, so arbitrary and so anti-musical . . . that one suspects a search for novelty at any cost'. The Dutchman, according to Jacobson, looked like Count Dracula, and Daland 'suddenly becomes some half-dozen Mad Hatter figures'. He continued, 'The sleeping steersman all along has been doubled by a writhing mute. . . . What is left is more the Steersman's obsession with Senta than Senta's obsession for the Dutchman – with no suicide or redemption.'[162] Harold Schonberg wrote, 'To ignore completely everything that a creator has indicated for a work is an ego trip.'[163] Leighton Kerner added that the music 'came from Wagner's opera of the same title', which was even more confusing as Levine conducted 'an uncommonly idiomatic performance of Wagner's romantic opera'.[164] José van Dam was a commanding Dutchman but Carol Neblett as Senta had 'pressing vocal problems'. Porter commented, 'Angry booing is an ugly sound, yet it must be welcomed if managements accept it as a sign that the public wants no more of such jejune rubbish.' He continued by referring to Dexter's 'deplorable' record as a House director and his two and a half successes in the twentieth-century repertoire against his 'string of nineteenth-century messes'.[165] On 19 April Board member Bruce Crawford warned the Board that the 'less than upbeat press', especially about *The Flying Dutchman*, and the Sutherland dispute, had affected subscriptions.*[166]

There was talk of Dexter resigning in April 1979, when he admitted to feeling over-pressured by administrative responsibilities. Bliss told the *New York Times* that he would 'never stand in the way' if Dexter 'were offered a better opportunity elsewhere'. He added that he was not sure that Dexter would be replaced if he left.[167] The director of productions was, however, on much happier territory with the Weill–Brecht *Aufstieg und Fall der Stadt Mahagonny* in November 1979. Collaboration between Dexter and Levine generated great excitement, Levine telling the Board that 'an unusual amount of time had been devoted to the production in order to reach a balance in terms of the musical and dramatic values of the work'. Levine defended their record, explaining that there was inevitably unevenness in performance when there were twenty-four works in the repertoire, but that the aim continued to be to raise levels 'so that the quality of performance on a regular night is higher than it ever has been'.[168]

Smith said that *Mahagonny* 'went a long way to vindicating' Levine's and Dexter's 'faith in the opera and the company's abilities'. The careful preparation was evident in the 'sure-hand ensembles, the clean and clear articulation of the English translation (by David Drew and Michael Geliot) and the professional sureness of the entire production'. Brecht's directions were followed closely and Jocelyn Herbert's sets and costumes powerfully evoked the 1930s. Teresa Stratas's Jenny and Richard Cassilly's Jimmy were both highly praised.[169] In spite of some letters of disapproval, *Mahagonny* became the 'hottest ticket in town'.†[170]

*   *   *

---

* Bruce Crawford was a Board member 1976–77, on the Executive Committee 1977–81, president of the Metropolitan Opera Association 1981–89 and general manager from 31 December 1985 to 1 April 1989. He returned to the Executive Committee as chairman from May 1990 to May 1991, when he returned to the Board as president until May 1999.
† The show also managed 98.6 per cent houses.

In December 1979 Bliss was able to announce that the Met had met
its expenses for the third consecutive year, with a small surplus of
$138,000.* It was due to Taplin and Bliss that the company survived
this perilous period. Shapiro later said of Bliss. 'He embodied the faith
that we would survive, even though we had run out of money.'[171]
Taplin also made a point of meeting the orchestra after the negotiations
to thank them for their support. He told them that he hoped to
improve pensions and ensured them that scheduling would in future
avoid four-hour operas back to back, as had occurred during the
previous season. He wanted to let the company know that they have
'a president who understands and will listen'. He believed that his
position 'as an amateur musician makes them feel that I understand'.[172]
Taplin and Bliss had succeeded in restoring the Met's solvency, but
the adventurousness of the artistic team was to prove short-lived and
there was a steady return to the main tasks of the Met – entertainment
combined with high musical standards.

Ingpen also continued to endeavour to redeem the Met's reputation
as the singers' House. In the January 1980 *Fidelio* Hildegard Behrens
sang her 'currently peerless Leonore'. Smith described her voice as
'a shining sword, gleaming and effulgent'. He found her intensity
'overwhelming' and wrote that 'her dungeon scene with Jon Vickers
and Paul Plishka was gripping to the point of emotional exhaustion'.
Domingo was also in peak form during the 1970s and 1980s, and made
a major contribution to the Met, often bringing keen dramatic tension
as well as vocal splendour to his roles. He acknowledged Ingpen's skill
in the early Eighties: 'Joan is so good at arm-twisting', he wrote, 'that
she manages to convince many of us to give more time to the Met
than we in fact wish to give.'[173]

Ingpen's advent, however, resulted in Dexter's increasing isolation.
In January 1980 Bliss told the Executive Committee that Dexter was
proving 'such a troublesome colleague' that he could no longer want
him to remain 'as director of production and a member of the
"troika"'. Bliss continued, 'His temper tantrums and abuse of colleagues have proved intolerable.' He was trying to arrange a peaceful

---

* The expenses had been $39.6 million, revenues $26 million and contributions
$13.3 million. Patron gifts had been raised by $3.5 million.

'divorce' by having him retained as a consultant. Although Taplin admired Dexter he recognised that 'under pressure he becomes imposs- ible to work with'.[174]

Dexter's behaviour underlined his frustrations, which caused him to interpret developments in terms of politics and intrigue as well as those of artistic policy. He had been suffering from a severe bout of shingles and was feeling isolated from his colleagues. On 4 February 1980 he wrote, 'Divisiveness is built into the system as long as the Rule of Three lacks a philosophic core as well as a productive one.'[175] The 'philosophic core', whereby thought-provoking drama had equal status with the music and the visual aspects, which had been at the centre of the early collaboration between Dexter and Levine, was indeed being undermined, as early 1980 again saw a downturn in the economic situation and a change in artistic priorities. Specific project donations had become an increasingly difficult method of funding new pro- ductions. In the late Seventies, however, Mrs Donald D. Harrington, described in her *New York Times* obituary as 'a fierce defender of private philanthropy', became a major sponsor.[176] She underwrote whole productions, like the 1979 *Don Carlos*, Elijah Moshinsky's *Ballo* in February 1980, and *Manon Lescaut* in March 1980. In February 1980 she also promised $20 million for the Centennial Fund, in response to which Bliss recommended renaming the auditorium in her name. It is hard to conceive, Taplin wrote in his diary, 'of what this woman's generosity and concern mean to the future of the Met'.*[177]

The Met became Sybil Harrington's 'family', according to Joan Ingpen, who recalled saying to her, ' "I don't know whether to envy you or be sorry for you, that you have nothing else in your life." And she said, "I worked very hard entertaining when my husband was alive. He made all this money and I have to do things in Texas but there is a limit to what you can do in Texas." So she made a life for herself. I'm not criticising that she did not like some of the things we wanted to do,' said Ingpen, but her money and attitude were 'very

---

* Tooley recalled of Harrington, 'It gives these very wealthy people the kind of elevation and status that they long for. Sybil Harrington I got to know and she told me, "I have no standing in New York, none, I'm interested in opera. I am going to give them money and I think it will have results" and it did. You can buy your way very rapidly in certain areas' (Tooley, Interview 4.12.00).

important factors' in the choices that were made.[178] In Levine's words, 'She loved opera on a lavish scale and that's what she wanted to pay for – anything that came under the heading of grand opera in representational terms.'[179]

In February 1980 Elijah Moshinsky's *Ballo in maschera* failed to fit Harrington's definition and was another blow to Dexter's hopes for a 'philosophic core'. It was only the second opera Moshinsky had directed. Dexter, impressed by his first production, *Peter Grimes* at Covent Garden, had invited him to prepare *Ballo* in the Boston–Riccardo version. Moshinsky updated the story to 'Tea Party' Boston, in order, as he explained, to 'select a recognisable turning point in history upon which to base the assassination of Riccardo'. Porter found it 'a brilliantly right solution' with the opera's distinctively Northern 'colour'.

The set by Peter Wexler, inspired by the paintings of John Singleton Copley, attempted to create, in Moshinsky's words, 'a stage space in which the feeling of Boston woodwork and the texture of colonial life will come across through suggestions of light and shade as well as through the people that inhabit that space'.[180] Moshinsky was endeavouring to render the working area more intimate, by means of wooden slats on three sides of the steeply raked and raised stage. He later recalled that Wexler 'didn't really get what I was on about – this European Brechtian thing – instead what I got was a fruit crate. At the time I thought it was fine. I don't blame him, he did what I asked. It came out wrong, because it's the wrong sort of thing to do on the Met stage, too big – you can't put a box on the Met stage, it's too big a stage.'[181] The effort, however, was not entirely unsuccessful. Act Three's simple, earth-coloured colonial surround, with a large portrait of an unhappy couple as a backcloth, was particularly evocative and Moshinsky's characteristically minimal use of props gave pointers to a setting rather than distraction from the proceedings. In Moshinsky's own words, 'It wasn't small, it was just uncluttered.'

Moshinsky was in any case less concerned with the scenery than with getting the singers to register the proper emotions. 'For me,' he explained, 'Verdi is a humanist who surrounded his characters with a social reality, not a scenic reality.' He encouraged Pavarotti to make simple gestures, for instance, to convey Riccardo's heartbreak by simply placing a pen down on a table. The tenor agreed doubtfully and instructed Moshinsky, 'You must tell the press that I am acting.'[182] Moshinsky recalled of Pavarotti:

> He was a very simple man and I thought he was terrific. He loved the music and he understood the irony and he could do it. It was just before he became a superstar and he knew the Met wanted this big Met approach and he was very happy with what we were doing in the rehearsal room, and then he got frightened.[183]

From the video recording it is clear that Moshinsky was successful in restraining the sometimes over-ebullient Pavarotti, with his familiar gesticulations. Pavarotti gave an unusually moving and involved performance, concentrated, acting from within, with animated eyes.[184] Reviewers were impressed by Pavarotti's realisation of the role, although they failed to recognise Moshinsky's contribution to the phenomenon. Schonberg spoke not only of Pavarotti's 'lovely focus of tone and generous outpourings of sound' but also of his 'dramatic intensity'. Byron Belt wrote, 'For the very first time at the Met the singer did not depend on his charm and singing to carry him to triumph . . . The result was a strangely touching and noble creation.'[185] Moshinsky later said of Gustavus and the work itself:

> The character himself is ironic, like the Duke in *Rigoletto* – he loved this woman and he half loved her and he didn't know if he should love her and he destroyed her marriage. He is a very painful sort of character. It plays a lot with prophecies and there are wonderful twists in the libretto all the time, but the setting is really weird – it has no reality around it. And so in terms of visual style there was no choice – it was the only way I could do things at that time, that Brechtian time – it was the second opera I'd done.

Manuella Hoelterhoff was one of the few critics to share Moshinsky's view that *Ballo* 'exists in opera time not historical time' and she praised his 'bold new production'.[186] Porter was also impressed by Moshinsky's work, and wrote that he had never seen *Ballo* treated 'quite so seriously as a drama of real and recognisable human behaviour'.[187] In general, however, it became a shibboleth at the Met that Moshinsky's production was a dismal failure. Many critics were outraged, Mayer referring to his 'strikingly unfortunate ... entirely infelicitous and frequently very stupid' debut.[188] Schonberg described the production as a 'directional nightmare, so frequently encountered today in which the intent of the composer and the basic quality of the opera are loftily ignored'.[189] Some of the hostility evoked was more of a nationalistic than artistic nature, as Moshinsky, by updating *Ballo* from the Boston of the seventeenth century to the eve of the revolution, inevitably made the colonial governor the hero and the 'fathers of the revolution (one of them was costumed as Sam Adams) the reactionary assassins'. Smith was indignant: 'This is not only a distortion of history but a calumny.'[190]

As so often when Levine was not conducting, the orchestral performance was not up to standard. In the video recording, conductor Giuseppe Patanè shows remarkable insensitivity to Verdi's markings and intentions, seldom, if ever, allowing the principals space to breathe freely, float a line, suggest a rubato, or sustain a beautiful tone. The orchestra plays with an unvaried mezzo forte that had become its way on below-average evenings.

Peter G. Davis in the *New York Times* recognised Moshinsky's talent for 'creating a maximum of dramatic tension against a minimum of scenic trappings'. This was not a talent, however, that was to be in demand at the Met. By October the whole of Act Two had been restaged and Moshinsky had asked for his name to be removed from the programme. Furthermore, because his production had not found favour with its sponsor, Sybil Harrington, the Executive Committee of the Board insisted according to Dexter that there were to be no such experiments in future.[191] Bruce Crawford later recalled that Harrington 'thought it was ghastly and hoped that she would not be underwriting anything like that again'.[192] Moshinsky was not asked to direct Verdi at the Met until *Otello* in 1994, when he took over from John Schlesinger at the last moment. 'The strange thing s,' Moshinsky later recalled, 'I didn't realise that different audiences look at the stage in the perspective of their own history and they didn't get it.'[193]

The next production that Harrington sponsored was *Manon Lescaut*, on 17 March 1980. Produced by Gian Carlo Menotti, it was a clear indication of the future. It was, in Schonberg's words, 'a traditional production through and through'. It was also far from spare, the designer, Desmond Heeley, Schonberg added, 'had studied his French baroque'.[194] Dexter later recalled that, only after a 'parade' of potential directors, Ingpen chose Menotti, who had not worked at the House before. Dexter therefore insisted on Heeley who had already worked there. Restricted by its realistic orientation and by the Met's big stage, Menotti's literal-minded staging was carried out in an unfocused manner, in a set both grand and cluttered. It proved popular with critics and audiences, Harold Schonberg expressing relief that there were 'no symbolism' and no 'ego trips'. Dexter, however, later described Menotti's direction as bringing to bear 'the acting techniques of the silent movie, allowing the principals to indulge in every acting cliché that has been used since Thespis'.[195] Plácido Domingo was responsible for whatever drama worked its way into the show.

Levine, whose power was increasing as that of Dexter was waning, was also a force for liveliness in this production. Unlike Patanè's Ballo, Levine's conducting was remarkable for its clarity and pacing. In the second act, supporting the singers without overwhelming them, he built ever increasing suspense. Levine also succeeded in bringing out the dramatic values of the music, and supporting Scotto and Domingo in their stagecraft. Levine expressed a great deal through the hands and arms, rather than through the body, which functions more as an appendage to his warm musical personality. In an interview with Howard Kissel he said, 'What's so ridiculous about emoting is that you encourage the audience to listen with its eyes. You make them comfortable – you let them know what they are supposed to feel . . . I am a conductor who does an awful lot by eye contact.'[196]

Levine's musical range and experience were fast growing. One of his great loves was Strauss's Ariadne, which he had conducted in February 1979 with 'gleaming sensitivity and warmth', as well as 'a thorough view of this treacherous score'. Levine was particularly sensitive to Strauss and Berg, whose rich harmony and orchestration were increasingly well served by the precision of the Met orchestra. Schonberg thought Elektra in February 1980 'simply superb . . . well proportioned, not rushed, with a very strong lyric feeling'.[197] Smith, however, felt that though it was 'broad and lyrical', it tended to slackness.[198] Nilsson's singing was overwhelming when she warmed up, and her fans went mad with enthusiasm.

Levine was full of energy, finding the diversity challenging. He told *Opera News* in March 1980 that he was working on four different operas – *Elektra, Otello, Don Carlos* and *Wozzeck*. 'These diverse styles are incredibly stimulating and give you a better perspective on viewing each of them, but you have to make sure you have enough sleep to keep up your energy.' He felt that his interpretations improved from year to year, citing in 1980 *Otello, Don Carlos* and *Tannhäuser* as operas that had grown with each revival.*

In spite of Levine's achievements, as his power grew there was growing criticism of the artistic direction of the House. The criticisms were aimed, however, not at the change of direction and philosophy but at his personality and musical direction. Kolodin's article in the *Saturday Review* in April 1980 was headlined IS JAMES LEVINE WRECK-ING THE MET? Kolodin felt that Levine had 'stepped into shoes several sizes too large for him', choosing not only singers, conductors and all matters connected to the music but, as Dexter's involvement declined, also repertory, directors and designers. Kolodin questioned Bliss's acceptance of 'Levine's demand for greater authority'; he wondered if he had sufficient 'breadth of experience, background and vision', contrasting his background with that of Liebermann and Bing. He also accused Levine of allowing his 'ambitions as a conductor to cloud his judgement' and was critical, too, of the conductor's summer absences at the Ravinia Festival and Salzburg.[199]

When Levine was not conducting the casting was indeed erratic, even provincial. Bernheimer cited the second cast of *Aida* or *Carmen* for conductor James Conlon in the 1979–80 season when the cast included Gwendolyn Killebrew, Patricia Craig and Richard Kness.[200] Furthermore, Levine was criticised for overusing singers such as Cornell MacNeil, Richard Cassilly and Renata Scotto. Scotto was Levine's

---

* One of Levine's achievements at this time was the inauguration of the Met's apprentice programme in 1979, which gave young singers a living wage for two years and intensive coaching by the opera staff, on condition that they took on no roles that Levine did not agree to. Risë Stevens joined the staff in 1980 to advise Levine on the programme. Neil Shicoff and Kathleen Kuhlmann graduated from the young artists programme in the early Eighties.

favourite dramatic soprano, since he first conducted her in *Vespri* in 1974. They were, he recalled, 'amongst the most memorable perform-ances I have ever participated in . . . since then she has asked for me and I have asked for her.' In 1976–77 Scotto was contracted to do forty performances for the Met, including Musetta in the forthcoming new production of *La Bohème*. She appeared in seven Met broadcasts between 1977 and 1982. Heavier roles, such as Lady Macbeth, however, were taking their toll on her voice, and her increasingly divaesque behaviour – including appearing in the Blackglama's mink coat adver-tisement – created passionate partisanship among the opera-going public. In 1979 a documentary was made in San Francisco of rehearsals for *Gioconda* during which her feuding with Pavarotti, her late arrival for rehearsals and her alienation from general manager Kurt Herbert Adler were revealed. Her refusal to take a solo curtain call and her storming into the dressing room 'calling down imprecations on Pavar-otti' were all recorded for television. 'People said she was doing her "Suicidio!" on camera.'[201] In his critical article Kolodin questioned casting Scotto as a 'teenaged maiden' in *Manon Lescaut*, not least because of her declining vocal powers.

Levine defended his casting record, telling Bernheimer that there were not enough fine singers to go round, particularly for *Aidas* and *Carmens*. Indeed, Levine decided in January 1980 to take *Aida* out of the repertoire for a while. Even when first casts were on a high level it was hard to maintain such standards for all 200 performances in any one year. Nevertheless, he argued, average standards in the House were improving all the time.[202]

There was also continued criticism that none of the world's great conductors was to be heard at the Met, and that when Levine was not conducting himself there were second-class conductors, like Patanè and Nello Santi. Where, asked Richard Dyer of the *Boston Globe*, were Abbado, Solti, Davis, Karajan and Mehta?[203] Kolodin added Bernstein, Maazel and Ozawa, Kleiber, Boulez and Haitink to the list of absen-tees.[204] American audiences had to hear them in the occasional concert performance such as Muti's *Macbeth* with the Philadelphia Orchestra, Solti's *Moses und Aron* with Chicago, and Abbado's three *Wozzecks*, also with Chicago. It was at this time that Claus Moser, John Tooley and Colin Davis felt that one of their greatest achievements was in luring great conductors to Covent Garden under difficult economic conditions.

Top international conductors had, however, been invited to the Met. Solti, Levine went on to explain, had been invited many times, and for repertoire that Levine would normally conduct, such as *Tristan* or *Don Carlos*. Levine explained to Dyer that Solti had put his children in British schools, which kept him in Europe. Colin Davis was similarly tied, and when he did offer to bring Tippett's *The Midsummer Marriage* for two months in 1984 he was turned down on the grounds that the Met had commissioned operas from three American composers and 'Tony Bliss does not think that the box office will stand another new production of a contemporary opera in that time-span'. Other top conductors were also reluctant. Abbado was busy at La Scala and with the London Symphony Orchestra, and when offered *Ballo* declined when it was decided that Moshinsky would do the Boston version instead of Peter Hall the Swedish one. Discussions with Muti, who was not interested in conducting *Turandot* in 1980–81 and insisted on coming in with a new production, similarly came to nothing.[205]

Bernard Haitink was one of the few top-ranking conductors to work at the Met. His debut had a mixed reception in March 1982 when he conducted *Fidelio*, with Shirley Verrett as Leonore. Henahan found him 'possibly hampered by tentativeness and mediocrity on the stage' and that his was a 'symphonic approach' that resulted in the singers having to force their voices. He did, however, find that the orchestra played with more than their 'usual degree of finesse and polish'.[206] Smith was more impressed, writing of Haitink's 'nobility of utterance and an unaffected beauty that are in contrast to Levine's work while bringing out the variety of orchestral timbre, especially in the strings'. He had 'never heard the brass more mellifluously controlled and expressive'. He felt it was a pity that 'the Met does not attract more top-level conductors, for its orchestra is now so accomplished that it would be a pleasure to hear a variety of musical approaches'.[207]

But Haitink did not come back. He was also unwilling to come for a revival in 1983–84, and Levine was to take all the new productions. Haitink's agent explained, 'It must be something very important since he will have to give up at least two months of his European commitments.'[208] Negotiations with Karajan failed too. On 25 January 1979 Bliss wrote to Karajan about alterations to his *Ring* saying, 'We need your presence here, and Jimmy and I would move mountains to make it possible.'[209] 'Everywhere', Levine told Dyer, 'you find people who are busy, who are dug in, who cannot leave for economic or domestic reasons.'

Levine was not, however, unduly concerned about the failure to bring distinguished conductors from outside, telling Dyer that only in the hands of a full-time music director could standards be maintained as they had by Fritz Reiner at the Chicago Symphony. 'I conduct a third of the repertoire,' he explained, 'eight operas out of twenty-four. What should the music director do? Less?' He continued, 'When you are working with the same chorus and orchestra day in and day out and you add new repertoire, in certain respects you can get better results than a guest conductor right away, because of the rapport you build up.' The more he worked with the Met orchestra 'the more you can look for ways to show the exceptional things'. He believed that what had been achieved by 1980 was 'a higher night-to-night standard than has been seen in modern times'.

In his Dyer interview Levine made a last-ditch defence of Dexter's role, pointing out that his work always has 'a point of view', that it was 'work that is always strong and dedicated', and that 'the mistakes, if you feel they are mistakes, come out of a great conviction'. Levine argued that there was no danger of superficiality or anonymity with such directors as Dexter, Ponnelle, Strehler and Schenk. The improvements in the visual standards at the Met were, he stressed, the result of Dexter's work in the technical department. 'The general dramatic credibility at the Metropolitan today is clearly John's work.'[210]

Dexter's work in the technical department was indeed one of the few areas where he himself felt he had had unqualified success, although he was generally disenchanted and was still suffering from shingles. He pulled out of *Traviata* in April 1980, to be replaced by Colin Graham. He later recalled that he had been too ill to argue the case with the Executive Committee against 'expensive cosmetics', which he believed had been decided on in panic when, according to rumour, his own visual taste and sense of drama had been called into question. In a letter of 3 March 1980, however, he told his friend, the British playwright John Osborne, about his one success, which was 'to organise the technical aspects of the place so that my job would become redundant'. Technical operations backstage were firmly in the hands of assistant manager Joseph Volpe, together with his assistant, Joseph Clark and Gil Wechsler, the first fully qualified lighting director, whom Dexter had brought on to the Met's staff in 1977. Dexter had said in 1978, 'The backstage crew of about 275 are to me what the orchestra is to Jimmy.'*[211]

Volpe, although with a reputation for toughness, was one of the few in management who did not have an upper-class image. His ability to communicate with the unions was to prove invaluable. He and Dexter had established good working relations, and it had been Dexter who had suggested Volpe as technical director, so he could 'come up with ideas and quick sketches and I could tell him whether or not it would work and what it might cost'.[212] Volpe later recalled, 'John would have ideas and there was no one in the management he could talk to. . . . I was head of the shop – because of him I moved into the management.'[213] Volpe had begun at the Met as an apprentice, moving on to the office to make drawings, and from there to the shop and stage. His job was to break down set designs and visual effects into the costs of man hours and materials. He collaborated closely with Dexter on many productions and the revitalising of existing productions.

By the 1980s Volpe had found various economising methods, including using more screen projections or adapting components from one production to another. Volpe was also responsible for keeping an eye on stage management. On 28 October 1976 he had reported to Dexter Everding's 'shock and bewilderment 'at the serious confusion and time wasting during rehearsals of the 1976 *Lohengrin*. He urged that stage management should be made responsible.[214] Volpe later said of Dexter, 'He taught everybody the way you work and you operate

---

* Wechsler was a graduate of Yale Drama School. Described by Johanna Fiedler as a 'charming and handsome man', he became a friend of Sybil Harrington, who paid for a computerised lighting system.

... he was a crazy man but there isn't anybody I can think of that would be completely successful if he was sane.'*[215]

Volpe later said that the conflict in management was 'about power'.[216] But Dexter's demise was also about finances and 'philosophy'. The 1979–80 season's budget was \$44.4 million, of which \$29 million was earned income and \$14 million was contributed by individuals. The 1979–80 season had, according to Bliss, seen declining box office returns: *Don Pasquale, Prophète* (78.7 per cent) *Onegin* (81.8 per cent) and *Werther* (69 per cent) had failed to fill the House. The performances of *Wozzeck* in February 1980, reworked by David Alden in his debut and with Anja Silja and José van Dam, and finely conducted by Levine, although 'done brilliantly', were also 'not accepted by the public'. There were empty seats and some members of the audience walked out.[217] The 1979–80 season box office averaged 90 per cent, in contrast to 1978–79 at 94 per cent. Dexter was the first and last director of productions at the Met and according to Levine his role came at a good time, when 'newer, simpler production styles had to be seen' and newer works introduced. It had, however, as Levine later said, 'run its course'.[218]

With his 'power' diminishing, Dexter contemplated how far his efforts had succeeded. The first job of improving technical operations was, he wrote to John Osborne, 'almost complete' and the second, which was 'to take that great dinosaur, wild and screaming, into the twentieth century' was finished 'at least in the sense that it will not be possible to say that there is no audience for modern opera at the Met'.[219] Dexter's main battle, however, of bringing demanding drama on to the Met stage and somehow revealing 'faces not windmills', was not only being lost but was to remain the Met's greatest challenge.

Dexter reflected, 'Only at the Met has time stood still. The curtain can still rise on a performance and the audience can be transported back to the nineteenth century and sit and wallow in an imaginary world ... Imagination costs more in the mind but less in the purse.

---

* The British playwright Arnold Wesker, who worked with Dexter on his play *Shylock* in New York in 1976, recalled, in 2001, Dexter's 'ferocity'. 'Some of it', he wrote, 'was just malicious, unpleasant; some of it was what he felt, perhaps knew, was what was needed to keep prima donnas in control, and lackadaisical backstage crew on their toes'. (E-mail to the author, 11.2.02).

But the imagination must swing out from the stage to embrace the audience and the audience must be trained to join in the act of imagination.'[220] By 1980 it was the obvious and comfortable visual world and not the world of the imagination that was set to dominate the Met stage. Indeed, the efforts of all the Big Four Houses to bring more of what Patrice Chéreau later described as 'the description of social reality'[221] to its audiences, were being challenged both by great financial difficulties as well as by the growth of deconstructionist vagaries and diversions.

PART FIVE

THE 1980s

Conceptuals versus Museums

EIGHTEEN

LA SCALA 1980–90

Italian Tossed Salad

LA SCALA'S PROBLEMS at the beginning of the 1980s reflected to some extent the general malaise affecting the country. A lack of national purpose and consensus was joined with politicians' cynical tendency to pursue private interests. Historian John Earle pointed out the fragmented, leaderless nature of Italian politics. It seemed that decency and honour had abandoned a country in which noble political institutions had once, long ago, arisen:

> Governments do not govern, but struggle to survive. The politicians, if we are to judge by their achievements, seldom rise above mediocrity and inefficiency. Men of stature are rare. The largest party, the Christian Democrats, is composed of cliques which do not give the country a lead but fritter away time on internal squabbles and manoeuvres to extend their sectarian influences over activities outside politics. The main opposition, the Communists, though less disorganised, appears strangely reluctant to come to power and intellectually indolent in searching for ideas beyond comfortable faith in the Soviet Union; it, too, is not immune from the general air of mediocrity.[1]

Although the financial lot of Italians at large continued to improve, the plight of Italian opera houses was worse than ever. Since it was not in the central government's parochial interest to support the work of La Scala, funding grew even scarcer. No strong opera administrator emerged to plead opera's case to the central government and lead the House out of its doldrums. Nor did new creative leadership arise until well into the decade; mediocrity frequently filled the vacuum.

The level of artistic quality began to suffer at La Scala soon after

Claudio Abbado relinquished the position of artistic director in 1980. Although he announced his intention to stop conducting in Milan altogether, he changed his mind and continued as chief conductor until 1986. At various points during this decade Abbado, as well as Lorin Maazel, shuttled between Vienna and Milan, helping create some of the best operatic performances of the time. International star singers also graced the Scala stage. However, on many evenings when La Scala did not have an outstanding musician on the podium or an excellent soprano downstage centre, an unwelcome touch of slackness could be felt.

When working at La Scala, Abbado still led performances marked by profound involvement, musical understanding and concern for detail. His new *Boris*, which opened the 1979–80 season, was called 'masterful'.[2] Even so, some critics felt producer Yuri Lyubimov made a muddle of the show. 'In the event it was practically impossible for anyone not closely familiar with the work to follow the action. Lyubimov's production was very stylized; the drama unfolded in a series of static pictures. Pimen was ever present on stage from the beginning, taking note of all that happened, and what we saw was what he had recorded.' Lyubimov's work, which like Chéreau's had as its inspiration Brecht's theatre of alienation, tended rather to be programmatic than strictly conceptual. It was also felt that Nicolai Ghiaurov 'still manages the part with great authority' – not surprisingly, as Ghiaurov was only fifty at the time and was still singing Boris at the Met ten years later.[3]

Lorin Maazel's Scala performances were energetic and intelligent but occasionally lacking in nuance and delicacy. His *Falstaff* of 7 December 1980, staged by Giorgio Strehler, was acclaimed for its polished orchestral playing. The *Opera News* critic wrote that the opera was 'vibrant throughout, and obviously inspiring the singers to give their best. Not a single word was lost; not once was a voice covered, despite some brilliant dynamics.'[4] By this time Strehler was acknowledged as Italy's leading director, both in opera and the theatre. 'Strehler's staging was paced at almost breakneck speed, requiring quite a bit of acrobatic agility from everybody, not least of all Falstaff, who almost caused a tidal wave when thrown into the stream in Act II, the enormous splash soaking all those onstage.'[5] In spite of slapstick touches, Strehler's view of the hero anticipated Giulini's muted *Falstaff*. 'Strehler had talked a lot in the weeks of rehearsal of removing the customary comic, even clown-like aspects from the character of Falstaff, and displaying him instead as a rather tragic figure.'[6] Juan Pons in the name part was warmly praised: 'Pons proved a captivating Falstaff, his voice full and expressive, his musical instinct serving him well in overcoming the role's many hurdles.'[7]

As Abbado, with his leftist views, was no longer music director, Scala productions tended less to take on a political coloration. Very gradually Riccardo Muti, who was not known for his political involvement, began to fill the conductor gap. Muti's *Ernani*, the opening production of 1982–83, brought out the best in this early work. Although Verdi's orchestral music, at times recalls, military-band tunes, Muti provided a welcome measure of good taste. In contrast, when Giuseppe Sinopoli encountered early Verdi, he tended to emphasise the pleasing coarseness of the music. For his part Abbado, the selective stylist, tended to avoid Verdi's operas altogether until the middle period, beginning with *Macbeth*. The video recording reveals the orchestra and chorus to be well rehearsed. Brass and woodwinds performed at their peak. Muti led with authority and a patrician mien. His beat was simple and clear, with far fewer complex movements than, say, Solti's. Muti's passion for the music gave the Scala forces the boost they needed to perform at their best.

Ronconi apparently left the principals to their own devices, leaving them with stock expressions in the harmless old Italian mode. David Hirst in his book about directors, pointed out that Ronconi's static direction was entirely appropriate for star singers who flit, scarcely rehearsed, into parts in La Scala, the Met or the Staatsoper and flit out again: moving about in stylised fashion is easily and quickly learned.[8]

The 1982–83 Scala season as a whole proved less interesting than the previous one, with fair-to-middling shows in the big House and higher-quality performances at the Piccola Scala. Fewer and fewer performances were scheduled, with the House frequently dark. Even star singers often came to grief. Unrest was rife among the *loggionisti*, or demons of the gallery, who blamed management for allowing aesthetic standards to slip. They expressed open disapproval at the 15 March opening of *Lucia*, a show which had been much hyped prior to its first night. Other sections of the audience applauded Pavarotti, who was singing the role of Edgardo. The *Opera* critic felt that soprano Luciana Serra, making her Scala debut in the name part, was 'the only singer to emerge with credit . . . Her interpretation is not dramatically intense: its merits lie in her sense of style and perfect vocal technique, in her lovely though not especially large voice.' However, it seemed that Milan had not found a dependable soprano for this difficult role. Singing opposite Alfredo Kraus on 3 July 1983, 'Serra's Lucia was, compared with her performance last year, ill-focused and shaky in intonation'.[9] During the same season Pavarotti 'was not at his best, with apparent vocal problems'.[10] A Chénier from Carreras in December 1982 proved that he could, at a stretch, succeed in a heavy-ish verismo role. Sergio Castgnino wrote that his 'memorable performance silenced the voices that have over recent months been questioning his present vocal state and suitability to the part. He had everything: fine voice and stage presence, exceptionally musical phrasing, and passionate delivery.'[11]

Two chapters in the recent history of the House were closed in 1983. Romano Gandolfi, the outstanding chorus-master, left La Scala to accept a conductor's position at Barcelona's Teatro Liceu. Gandolfi had been widely recognised as the leading figure in his profession worldwide. To the disappointment of those who loved chamber opera, the Piccola Scala was shut down in 1983. During a time of continued financial retrenchment, its limited seating made it much more expensive to operate. Many opera lovers particularly regretted the Piccola Scala's closure, as its performances in recent years had been judged superior to those at the main House. During the final season the Piccola decided on some daring programming: Alexandre Sergeyevich Dargomyzhsky's opera *The Stone Guest*, based on the Don Juan legend as dramatised by Pushkin and translated for this production under the title *Il Convitato di pietra*. The composer avoided the usual aria-recitative construction in favour of what César Cui, who completed it for its posthumous first performance in 1872, termed 'melodic recitative'. Although Stanley Sadie has declared that the opera can only succeed in Russia – 'Export is out of the question,' proclaimed Richard Taruskin[12] – critical opinion of the Piccola Scala production was favourable and the composer's memory extolled: 'Vladimir Delman's conducting, as ever fervent and instinctive, paid due attention to the music's astonishing modernity of idiom.'[13] In 1988, following the closure, the House announced tentative plans to acquire the far larger 1,800-seat Teatro Puccini within the next two years 'as an additional base for the company's productions'. The additional seats were meant to help generate needed box office income. The intention was also announced to acquire a turntable for the Scala stage 'as part of a programme of theatrical modernization'.[14]

The opening performance of the 1983–84 season was a *Turandot* presided over by Maazel and Zeffirelli. Tickets cost as much as 350,000 lire. Zeffirelli's work by this time had lost much of its delicacy and imagination. Wrote Castagnino in *Opera*, 'Grandiose, colossal, kitschy or extravagant (and very expensive) are the adjectives that spring to mind that describe Franco Zeffirelli's fairy-tale staging . . . [Masses] of people and masses of movement . . . [The] ceaseless movement eventually became tiresome: it was all a bit too much like Hollywood.' Even this *Turandot* was no match, however, for the excesses of Zeffirelli's production of the same opera at the Met in 1987. At the Scala, Maazel, conducting, 'opted for a solemn, slow overall pace and for massive sonorities', wrote Massimo Mila, who added that Maazel 'was attentive to detail and very colourful, and he brought out strongly the elegance and modernity of Puccini's scoring'. Mila also approved the 'splendid musical execution' of the Scala forces under Maazel. Everything 'worked exceedingly well: the orchestra resounded splendidly, and the chorus – now entrusted to the care of Giulio Bertola – no less so.'[15] Plácido Domingo was replaced at the last moment by Nicola Martinucci. Katia Ricciarelli as Liù was well received, and Ghena Dimitrova's Turandot was considered steely, powerful and unrefined. Martinucci 'managed to hold his own with so powerful a partner and matched up to the high standards expected of a leading tenor at an opening night at La Scala'.[16]

Newly commissioned work contributed much to the liveliness of the House. By and large, new European operas oscillated between seriousness and irony. Some works suggested an underlying ambivalence concerning the operatic medium: should the composer accept it as it is, renew it, or take the mickey out of it? Should one strive to be musical, or perhaps insistently anti-musical? Should one's work be clever, passionate? And in the less politically supercharged 1980s, was there still room for social content?

Luciano Berio's *Un Re in ascolto* fused autobiographical content with a self-referential use of the operatic form: mirrors mirroring mirrors. The work, with a libretto by the noted Italian author Italo Calvino, was first performed at La Scala on 14 January 1986, after a premiere at Salzburg a year and a half earlier. Max Loppert wrote after seeing the Salzburg production, 'In the immediate background of *Un Re in ascolto* lie the Fellini of *8½* and the Pirandello of *Six Characters*, not to mention Berio's own *Opera*. . . ; the self-consciousness, denseness and allusiveness of the structure make all the Strauss–Hofmannsthal collaborations seem like "Baa Baa Black Sheep" by comparison.' Loppert – who neglected to mention echoes of the ballet impresario Serge Diaghilev in the protagonist's personality – also enjoyed the energy of the work. 'The score finds Berio (who in some recent works has given the impression of compositional "coasting") working at full stretch; in it, the poetic possibilities of the libretto are realized with exuberant flair and love of theatrical device from the simplest to the most complex.'[17] Berio himself stated that the piece was an '*azione musicale*' rather than an opera: 'There is neither prologue nor plot nor plan of events, nor sentiment expressed by characters who set up moral conflict in song. But there is the analysis of a musical-dramatic situation and the representation of a farewell.' The farewell is that of Prospero, whom Berio portrays as a theatre administrator planning a new production of Shakespeare's *The Tempest*. The director of the show is a temperamental character who was said by Italian critics to be a stand-in for Giorgio Strehler. Nothing goes smoothly in the production; crisis follows crisis; Prospero dies and the piece is over. Marco Vallora wrote, 'As may be seen, there is no opera, only its shadow, its reflection as in a dream, and this may be a little old hat as a formula of theatre-within-theatre which creates an opera at the same time as repeating again that it is no longer possible to compose an opera.'[18]

The work manifests a sophisticated creative imagination. Mood, colour and feeling are established with a huge variety of rhythmic and melodic language. The orchestra's resources are stretched to the maximum. Singer-actors are likewise taken to the outer edge of technical possibility and the whole continuum of vocalism from mundane speech to aria is employed.

During the 1980s three instalments of Karlheinz Stockhausen's monumental multi-partite work *Licht* were performed by La Scala. Growing out of the composer's preoccupation with myth, symbol, ritual, spirituality and formal innovation, these three 'days of the week' met with mixed receptions. In 1981 Dominic Gill enjoyed the music in Act Two of *Donnerstag aus Licht*, terming it 'a marvellous journey of sound' full of 'extraordinary and visionary energy' with snatches of music from all over the world. Nevertheless he disliked the 'kitschy stagecraft' and muddled symbolism.[19] The same act was also praised by Andrew Clements, who found it 'as richly coloured and imaginative as anything he has written to date'.[20] The huge production of *Samstag aus Licht* was mounted in 1984 in the Palazzo dello Sport in Milan. *Montag aus Licht*, which opened on 7 May 1988, was called an 'expensive folly' by the *Opera* magazine reviewer:

> What a disappointment is the third part of this endless week on the origins of the universe set to music by Stockhausen! Set to music? . . . There is really none in Act I, entirely devoted to the presentation of mythical and grotesque characters to whom a giant figure of Eve gives birth one by one, and who mumble snatches of words and noises. And that is not all. A geometric ballet of women with perambulators full of animal-babies to whom they give bananas; women wrapped in rags polishing Eve on the stairs; a small train with eyes projected on the back-cloth; a pianoforte attacking Eve and impregnating her; the voice of Hitler followed by the noise of a water closet flushing. Enough said.[21]

Evidently Stockhausen did not feel enough had been said. Writing in the year 2000, after having completed six days of *Licht*, he reflected on the contents of his huge work:

> I have seen and heard . . .
> . . . Markus trumpeting through seven windows of a tele-command 27-foot polyester globe rotating above a south pole with a penguin orchestra;
> . . . Julian the tenor as Michael flying like an angel through space, singing beautifully; . . . Suzee the reborn harlequin, now

Mondeva playing basset-horn and landing with trumpeter Michael like a master acrobat . . .

. . . the public driven in buses to an airfield to listen to and watch a dancing quartet of helicopter grasshoppers in the air. What else? What else?

I could continue touching on the highlights of my scenic music *Licht* of the past 23 years: look at the scores, listen to the hundreds of compact discs, study thousands of pictures and films, talk to people who were there!

And you ask me 'Why?' Creation has no time limits. Spiritual art will live forever; if it is revealing, beautiful, perfect and universal.

Stockhausen also disparaged opera administrators who 'don't like electronic or acoustic installations of the kind needed for *Mittwoch*, for example, where four helicopters with four string players fly for about 40 minutes above the opera house, to be transmitted directly by screens and twelve-channel radio transmission to the public in the hall'.[22]

In March 1984 the Scala management announced that Muti would take over as music director beginning with the 1986–87 season. This was none too soon for a great opera house which had been floundering for several years. Abbado's contract as chief conductor ran out at the end of June 1986. Although he had been accused of avoiding taxes, the major reason for his leaving the Scala seemed to be his wish for fresh challenges. In any case, he kept silent in public. The following month he was announced as Maazel's successor at the Staatsoper. Cesare Mazzonis, the Scala's artistic director, stayed on at the House.

In December 1984, before the change-over, Abbado opened the House on the feast of Sant'Ambrogio. The work chosen was *Carmen*. Once again Abbado used a more authentic edition of the score and the audience received him warmly. The *Corriere della Sera* critic also delighted in Domingo's 'reserved but tormented' Don José.[23] However, the *Opera* critic was not as fulsome. 'The main reason for disappointment was the poor vocal condition of Shirley Verrett's Carmen, which influenced the entire evening, with Abbado's concern for the singer adding to an already dry and over-analytical reading of the work. Help was at hand in the person of Plácido Domingo, whose stage performance was 'totally convincing' Ruggero Raimondi 'made a towering Escamillo, and Alida Ferrarini a tender, fresh-voiced Micaëla.'[24] After Domingo and Verrett left the production, Agnes Baltsa and Carreras took over the leading roles.

Even when Abbado was off form, his work on the podium was considerably superior to that of other Scala conductors. A videotaped performance of Verdi's *I Lombardi alla prima crociata* in 1984 finds conductor Gianandrea Gavazzeni piloting a leaky ship at age seventy-three. Rhythms are slack, tempi puzzling, choral entrances ragged and the orchestral playing lacklustre. The evening is saved, more or less, by dedicated performances from Dimitrova (Giselda) and Carreras (Arvino). Carreras refrains from outsinging his instrument, giving Verdi's lines nuance and emotional interest. He also demonstrates star quality on an evening when he is sometimes the only hardworking artist on stage. Dimitrova plunges bravely into the vocal difficulties of the part, which recalls Abigaille (*Nabucco*) in its rapid register shifts, high tessitura and dramatic fire. Apart from intonation difficulties and a hint of unsteadiness in the middle range, Dimitrova's spinto is both attractive and exciting, with a surprisingly rounded tone.

Il Viaggio a Reims, a 'scenic cantata' by Rossini, which had been rediscovered in 1984, had an exciting rebirth on 9 September 1985. Abbado conducted and Luca Ronconi staged this amusing parody of the opera genre, which at the same time is a vocal tour de force. Marco Vallora wrote that the *viaggio* 'which, ironically, is a static "journey" that never was, turns into a sort of theatre concert with all the virtuoso artists featuring their special "party pieces" to honour an absent King who is in the audience.'[25] Ronconi's staging drew the city 'into the theatre by means of television, showing the arrival of a procession passing through the galleria and the square outside, and erupting into the auditorium in a *coup de théâtre* worthy of René Clair. It was not only an amusing diversion but the disturbing sign of something cracking, the crumbling of theatrical certainty, like marionettes on stage suddenly finding themselves dancing in empty space. The glowing intensity shining through Claudio Abbado's conducting was incomparable. . . .'[26]

When the stars were singing and conducting elsewhere, however,

Scala shows were all too frequently patchy. The *loggionisti* continued to howl their disapproval. A revival performance of *I Lombardi* on 28 January 1986 'had an air of being thrown on haphazardly and caused a near-riot'. The American conductor Thomas Fulton replaced Gavazzeni on short notice. Vallora wrote: 'The conductor's chief problem was a poor cast, consistent only in their generally erratic performances. Passages of clean, almost refined ensemble in some trios and quartets were followed by moments of sudden disintegration, and the same applied to the solo voices. Elizabeth Connell (Giselda) showed grave signs of vocal wear and rashly took too many risks with intonation, producing some melting tones but unpleasant shrieks and ugly top notes as well. The cavernous Russian [actually Georgian] bass of Paata Burchuladze (Pagano) lacked the technique of making words a means of communication; he simply emitted sounds, proceeding by trial and error.'[27] On 14 March of the following year, in a performance of *Ballo*, Gavazzeni was hounded from the gods. Pavarotti, singing Riccardo, forced his voice in an apparent attempt to divert attention from the conductor's failings.

As his farewell opera at the end of the 1986 season, Abbado led a brilliant *Pelléas* using an edition newly edited by David Grayson and based on Debussy's own score. Wrote Harold Rosenthal: 'I am afraid that I am not well enough acquainted with the score of *Pelléas* to know just what the alterations made by Grayson are. All I know is that never before have I heard Debussy's music so beautifully played as it was under Abbado. The strings shimmered, the woodwind detail was wonderfully clear, and there was a sense of other-worldliness, almost magic, in the web of sound that Abbado spun.'[28] François Le Roux sang the title role. As Mélisande, Frederica von Stade displayed a 'fey-like, even cool personality and keen musical intelligence'. And Nicolai Ghiaurov's 'very human and gentle Arkel was most moving, and sung with great beauty of voice'.[29]

The new music director, Riccardo Muti, was committed to becoming the prime force for quality at La Scala. He specifically sought to bring the House to a level above that of New York and Vienna. 'I will not conduct at the Metropolitan,' he once declared – and to date, he has kept his word.[30] In his first appearance on the Scala podium as music director, Muti opened the 1986–87 season with a rapturously applauded *Nabucco*. The press treated it as a great event. Muti's taut pacing was emphasised by his not waiting for applause but forging ahead to create a dramatic flow. The *Opera* critic praised his 'magnificent, monumental conducting . . . which fired the colours of the opera, sometimes with too intensely passionate waves of sonority. But his quite special reading of "Va, pensiero", not as a victory hymn but as a lament for the defeat of a people, was most convincing, so much so that he was forced by the audience's wild enthusiasm to grant an encore.' The singers were outstanding. Renato Bruson's 'supremely noble, betrayed sovereign seemed to embody the dream never realized by Verdi of writing *King Lear*. . . . Paata Burchuladze made a satisfactory Zaccaria on the whole, though his unconventional diction calls for attention. As the four acts develop the psychology of the character, so Ghena Dimitrova portrayed a tormented, defeated Abigaille, capable of adapting her steely voice to singing of exceptional sweetness.'[31] Robert de Simone's staging, with sets by Mauro Carosi, was more harshly received, as he 'seemed to wallow in a welter of styles: he . . . put Saint Ambrose among the Hebrews, brought in tourists to hot springs, labyrinths and catacombs, reflecting a basic lack of understanding'.[32]

One of the best-remembered productions of the 1980s was the *Don Giovanni* which opened the 1987–88 season under Muti's baton. In the stalls the great and the good were even more in evidence than usual on opening night, with politicians and captains of industry rather more numerous than nobility and leaders of society, even given the notable presence of the Prince of Wales. The powerful among the Milanese were once again taking an interest in the local opera house, an interest which would grow under Muti in the years to come. The show, like the previous year's *Nabucco* much hyped in the papers, starred Thomas Allen, with direction by Strehler, sets by Ezio Frigerio, and costumes by Franca Squarciapino. The *Corriere della Sera* assessed the evening as a triumph all round in a work which had not been performed at La Scala for two decades.

Milanese critic Laura Dubini praised Strehler's 'magisterial' handling of stage movement and his managing to elicit solid acting from each member of the chorus.[33] Massimo Mila approved the integrated production: 'A production replete with harmony and stylistic coherence. . . . A spectacle of the highest class.'[34]

In a video recording of the production, Muti's stick technique is once again marvellously clear, expressive and economical. Until the very end his sense of the music's fierce excitement is usually conveyed through nuances of expression and phrasing rather than excessive dynamics or fast tempi. Strehler gets each and every principal singer to act with honesty and originality. Frigerio's painterly designs are delectable: the grace and grandeur of a baroque-period Italian staircase framed with columns and cypress suggest the heights of civilisation from which Don Giovanni has fallen. Squarciapino's luscious costumes are elegant and evocative. The close collaboration between conductor and stage director is apparent, revealing the working out of a shared personal vision.

Even though daring stagings were sometimes seen – and great ones occasionally as well – Italian productions, even at this late date, were by and large unprepossessing. Writing in 1989, Rodney Milnes found direction existing chiefly to give the music and the singer a platform for expression:

> For all the stress laid on communication, the Italians have very different ideas about staging. In a word, they don't 'do' production as we know it. In general, singers have a limited stock of simple gestures of the sort that Bergonzi in his time has used at Covent Garden; singers know what they mean, and so do audiences – they are a kind of dramatic shorthand (some tenors, I should add, don't even bother with the gestures). In a curious sort of way this method of performance is rather refreshing: certainly nothing comes between the music and the listener, and basic feelings are clearly, if a touch abstractly, conveyed.[35]

Singing may have been the *raison d'être* of Italian opera productions, but the opening work of the 1989–90 Scala season, *I Vespri siciliani*, was roundly booed. Voices suitable to Verdi's music were becoming rarer in the opera world; Cheryl Studer and Chris Merritt in the main parts had lighter instruments, which could not easily stand the weight. Hearing a later performance, Marco Vallora wrote, 'Chris Merritt as Arrigo showed himself to be nothing like a Verdi singer, and the worrying lapses in intonation which he has displayed since the beginning of his career now seem apparent to even his most devoted fans.' His voice sounded 'forced and the high notes painful.'[36]

At a time when there was a serious lack of young native Italian singers, June Anderson continued to make her mark in bel canto roles. In *La Sonnambula* on 19 March 1986, she faced problems with both the conductor and the audience. The seventy-seven-year-old Gianandrea Gavazzeni received 'shamelessly disrespectful' catcalls for his 'inward, dream-like Bellini, consistently lyrical and sad', wrote Vallora. 'The very tense atmosphere reflected on June Anderson, whose excellent performance in the title role challenged memories of Callas 30 years ago.' Vallora also referred to Anderson's 'elegant, impeccable, razor-edged poise, maybe just a little too cold.'[37] In another production of *Sonnambula*, at Rome's Teatro dell'Opera on 2 February 1988, Anderson was praised for her technique, which 'enables her to cope with Amina's elegiac and sentimental music and the abstract perfection of bel canto'.[38] And, at the Fenice in Venice in October 1987, she scored a triumph in the title role of Beatrice di Tenda being described as 'perhaps the best singer of Bellini at the moment.'[39]

Veteran singers like Pavarotti were as deeply loved in their native land as they were worldwide, even if the Scala *loggionisti* overstated their disapproval of his occasional vocal lapses. During this period Pavarotti's, then 50 years old, voice usually sounded relaxed and free. In the new production of *Aida* that opened the 1985–86 Scala season 'Pavarotti, thought by some to be unsuited to Radames, proved unusually elegant with his voice miraculously rested, and brought out in his phrasing all the pain of the conquering hero who loses his right to live'.[40]

Since La Scala was enshrined in law as the premier opera house in Italy and consequently received what was relatively speaking the most generous state funding, provincial Italian Houses were affected even more severely by the ongoing financial squeeze. By the spring of 1983 Rome's Tgeatro dell'Opera was suffering from financial woes and was even closed by a magistrate on behalf of the fire safety authorities. Cited were structural decay, faulty electrical wiring, and a general 'absence of solidity and safety'.[41] With the benefit of a 4-billion-lire loan guaranteed by the city, work was duly carried out and the theatre soon reopened. By June a new intendant was installed: Alberto Antignani, who had the appropriate socialist credentials, succeeded Giorgio Mosconi, who himself had received only a year's tenure in the position.

New repertoire was still not easy for some Italian audiences to assimilate, even when it was not so very new. In Rome, on 26 February 1983, a performance of a new work by Aldo Clementi entitled *Es* was not allowed to proceed in silence. Luigi Bellingardi wrote: 'As often happens at the Rome Opera with contemporary works, the audience showed their considerable disapproval . . . from the moment the curtain rose.'[42] The chaos continued. The chorus went out on strike before the opening of a new production of *Carmen*; the show went on without the choristers. Obraztsova gamely sang the opening, but Carreras as Don José cancelled, returning for later performances. On 12 March 1986 the Teatro dell'Opera, which at that time was without an artistic director, was forced to stage *Iphigénie en Tauride* in concert form: the chorus had struck the show the day before the dress rehearsal, alleging that the main actors had been given more interesting stage business than they, the chorus, had.

In Florence the 1984–85 season was restricted to two operas because of limited funding. The artistic director, Luciano Alberti, was dismissed with no announcement of a replacement. The programme of the 1984 Maggio Musicale – which did not consist of opera alone – was planned by the composer Luciano Berio. The festival as a whole was positively received by the *Opera* critic, who noted that the 'success of the subscriptions, more numerous than usual, seemed to vindicate Berio. . . . The success was due to a judicious choice of repertoire, mixing the novel with the familiar. An especially interesting bit of programming was the selection of three works based on the Orpheus legend: Monteverdi's *Orfeo* in Roger Norrington's edition; a ballet called *Sul filo di Orfeo* with music by a young composer from Turin, Ludovico Einaudi; and an *Orfeo* based on Monteverdi's score, which engaged a workshop of young musicians in a collective task of transcription under the guidance of Berio who devised the entire enterprise, and brought it to life in the courtyard of Palazzo Pitti with Pier Luigi Pizzi as producer.'[43]

The *Rigoletto* directed by Yuri Lyubimov was however pounced on by the public, who protested about the director's impositions upon the work. Lyubimov decided to remove Rigoletto's hump – and thereby 'the deformity of his character' – and to place in the middle of the set a swing on which Gilda was to rock as she sang 'Caro nome'. 'In the last act the same swing became a sort of fork lift in the hands of Sparafucile who rested upon it the sack containing Gilda's body.' But Peter Conrad understood the swing as the cloud of an 'untainted angel', hanging as she does 'above the mean muddle of a world which kills her but which she blesses all the same'.[44] Clearly not appreciating this subtle point, Piero Cappuccilli abandoned the name part before the dress rehearsal. The story was heard in Florence that Edita Gruberova as Gilda had reservations about the staging, which led her to protest by arriving late for the dress. This led Bruno Bartoletti to resign as conductor. Berio took Lyubimov's side in the quarrels. In a typically Italian compromise Gruberova 'allowed herself to be persuaded to mount the swing as long as the rocking was kept to a minimum'. '[The] first night performance was received with noisy expressions of disapproval, sparking off another round of protests when Lyubimov responded to the whistling from a box where he sat with Berio by making a gesture of scorn which is readily comprehensible in every part of the world.'[45]

While Rome and Florence suffered financially, Muti's wish to put his personal stamp of tradition and quality upon La Scala was brought a step closer to accomplishment when Carlo Maria Badini left the post of sovrintendente at the end of the 1989–90 season. As Giuseppe Barigazzi wrote, Badini had 'inherited a thing of prestige and handed it on again'.[46] While in possession of his inheritance Badini had hardly enhanced its quality, not to say its prestige. His successor, Carlo Fontana, had been politically weakened during the collapse of the Italian Socialist party, of which he remained a member. For the opening of the following season Fontana made a positive impression on many of those concerned about La Scala's future by programming Mozart's *Idomeneo* – a worthy and at the time seldom heard work – under Muti's capable and imaginative direction. Fontana pointedly invited writers and other intellectuals to the opening night, thus widening the focus beyond the social and political establishment. Fontana's leftwards political leanings did not appear to set a strong ideological tone for the House. Perhaps symbolically, on that evening La Scala was hung with 13,000 carnations – not red ones, but a moderate pink.

NINETEEN

VIENNA 1980–90

Efforts to Revive the Gleam

UNLIKE LA SCALA, the Staatsoper of the 1980s found itself little affected by political events and social trends. As a neutral country with strong links to the West, Austria was pursuing an idiosyncratic course in the international arena. It served as a meeting ground for opposing sides during the Cold War. Kurt Waldheim, elected president in 1986, was exposed in the international media as having lied about his activities during the Second World War.

With the country was more visible on the world stage, questions were raised, more pointedly than ever before, about Austrian complicity during the Nazi era. In 1985 the *New York Times* correspondent in Vienna referred to the country's 'half-buried Nazi past'. He detected 'widespread and compromising links' to the Third Reich in the political establishment which thrived in a culture of denial.[1]

None of this controversy touched the Staatsoper. The House was not made the target of protests – except by booers who disapproved of one or another singer or stage director. Politically 'aware' opera productions were scarcely to be found within the borders of Austria. In a city where tradition was sacred, it was traditional that the business of opera be carried on within its own enclosed realm. During this decade the Staatsoper's bosses were occupied not with politics but with their difficult struggle to bring fresh ideas to an opera house that had grown rather stale and hidebound.

Intendant Egon Seefehlner continued to be an activist on the artistic front. He took pains to lure as many good conductors to the House as possible, telling an interviewer late in 1979, 'We now have Bernstein, Böhm, Dohnányi, Hollreiser, Carlos Kleiber, Leinsdorf, Mehta, Patanè,

Horst Stein as conductors, a list to be augmented soon with López-Cobos, Ozawa, Santi and Solti . . .'[2]

Solti's belated Vienna debut was a *Falstaff* which opened on 24 February 1980 in a new production by Filippo Sanjust replacing Visconti's. Sanjust's simple staging was deemed appropriate and effective. Solti was allotted unusually generous rehearsal time and conducted five performances. Wechsberg called the orchestra's playing subtle and transparent: 'No details were lost, and details often do get lost in this complex score. Solti was a real "conductor" between orchestra and stage; he made a cohesive unit of both. Perhaps it was just as well that he waited such a long time to conduct here, and that it was *Falstaff* in which he could show the astonishing range of his virtuosity.'[3]

Seefehlner was an imaginative man in a city where creative imagination was lying dormant. He had the interesting idea of putting on experimental and chamber opera in the little Schlosstheater in the Schönbrunn Park, which had been opened in 1747, but this was not realised. Instead, the Schlosstheater provided a venue for the productions of the Wiener Kammeroper, or Vienna Chamber Opera, as well as serving as a rehearsal stage for the Music Academy – the Hochschule für Musik und Darstellende Kunst.

The Seefehlner administration also succeeded in delicately expanding the horizons of opera consciousness in Vienna. Repertoire new to Viennese audiences opened on 15 November 1980: a double bill of Menotti operas, which the conservative public welcomed, possibly because of their post-Puccinian musical idiom. Johannes Strassel, a singer from the Vienna Boys' Choir, performed the title role in Menotti's *Amahl and the Night Visitors*, which like *Help, Help, the Globolinks!* was sung in German. The composer himself staged the works, enlisting the young pupils of the Staatsoper's ballet school to play the Globolinks (aliens who transform music into electronic sounds). The Staatsoper's 1980 Christmas production was Verdi's *Attila*, another new departure. This time Seefehlner chose to perform an unfamiliar work by a great composer and join the burgeoning Verdi 'renaissance' around the world. Ghiaurov sang Attila and Cappuccilli the part of Ezio, the Roman general defending Italy against the invaders. Wrote Wechsberg, 'Under the Italian composer-conductor Giuseppe Sinopoli, *Attila* became a popular success – people cheered and Cappuccilli even had to repeat an aria – but perhaps not an artistic one. The best Verdi could say about his music was when he wrote to Contessa Maffei: "It is not inferior to the others." (He also later admitted that *Alzira* was "really terrible", but sooner or later we are going to have to hear *Alzira* too.)[4] To date *Alzira* has not been performed at the Staatsoper, but the Verdi renaissance has changed the thinking of audiences worldwide about the works of the composer's early years.

In an even more daring move for the Staatsoper, Bernstein's *Mass* was given its Vienna premiere on 16 February 1981. Its first performances had been in Washington. The composer did not term it an opera, but rather 'a piece for singers, instrumentalists and dancers'. Wechsberg wondered with some trepidation if it ought to be called a 'show', commenting: 'Unlike in the Anglo-Saxon countries, there is something derogatory about a "show" in Vienna. This being the age of threats, especially telephonic threats, there were ominous calls to Marcel Prawy, who had translated *Mass* into German and was the producer, and some extremists said there would be demonstrations. It was remembered that Bernstein was an outspoken leftist, and that he is a Jew. The whole issue was dynamite, and Vienna was delighted.'[5] Prawy, himself Jewish, reported acclaim mixed with boos, which did not faze Bernstein as he took bows. 'I was happy', Prawy wrote in his memoirs, 'that I could help Bernstein to be heard as one of the great artists of the Seefehlner era. Every opera director has enemies. I believe that Egon Seefehlner had none.'[6]

The final new productions of what turned out to be Seefehlner's first reign, in the spring of 1981, were *Rheingold* and *Walküre*, the first two operas of the *Ring*. These productions were meant to replace the Karajan *Ring* of two decades earlier. Zubin Mehta was engaged to conduct, and Filippo Sanjust to stage the two works. Wechsberg's reaction was carefully phrased: 'Whether or not Mehta will one day be a great *Ring* conductor will only emerge later. The orchestra sounded marvellous, but the rejuvenated Vienna Philharmonic always does on a good evening.' Mehta 'was not as translucent as Boulez can be, and the sound was not as beautiful (some would say "glossy") as Karajan's.'[7]

On 7 February 1982 *Macbeth* was brilliantly conducted by Giuseppe Sinopoli, whom Wechsberg called admirable, 'especially when he inspires with thrillingly hectic life the less frequently performed operas of Verdi. His speciality is rubato within each phrase; he changes the tempo within each melodic arch, holds the performers' attention by his extravagance, and less sophisticated listeners experience an "entirely new" Verdi.[8] Born in Venice in 1946, Sinopoli had made his debut as an opera conductor there with *Aida* in 1978. He was also trained as a physician and composer; his opera *Lou Salome* had its first performance at the Munich Staatsoper in 1981. Some critics disparaged Sinopoli's conducting for its exaggeratedly rhetorical approach, while many others admired him for his energy, especially in early and middle Verdi works. Responsible for the staging of the Staatsoper *Macbeth* was Peter Wood, the English director. Wechsberg concluded that Wood 'provided one of the most conventional productions imaginable – the Vienna audience went into raptures over it and that in itself is all that needs to be said'.[9] Mara Zampieri as Lady Macbeth acted movingly but was less than effective vocally.

Lorin Maazel took over as director of the Staatsoper from See-fehlner from the 1982–83 season. For the first time since Karajan a leading musician was in the chair. As Solti had done at Covent Garden, Maazel came with the firm intention of finding ways to improve quality. Also like Solti, he had the notion of converting the Staatsoper to the *stagione* scheme, in which several performances of the same opera are repeated over the span of a few days. *Stagione* performances help reduce cast and conductor changes to a minimum. They also enable added rehearsal time: a luxury generally lacking at the Staatsoper. For Vienna, a House accustomed to performing almost every evening of the year with frequent changes of cast and show, this would have been a revolutionary step. The new director announced his intention to conduct a single new production each year, with a total of only thirty performances annually under his baton. Maazel's schedule reflected the phenomenon of the overstretched musical star: he held simultaneous appointments as music director of the Cleveland Orchestra and head conductor of the Orchestre Nationale de Paris.

Maazel launched his tenure with an ambitious programme of productions. The first opening night was *Otello*, with Domingo in the title role. Adam Fischer conducted, Margaret Price sang Desdemona and Siegmund Nimsgern Iago. Shortly afterwards, on 16 October, followed *Tannhäuser*, which came to grief when Reiner Goldberg as the protagonist had to quit the stage in the middle of the first performance because of what Christopher Norton-Welsh described as 'vocal difficulties'. The same critic felt that Maazel, conducting, 'stressed the Italian over the German aspects of the score, but generally opted for fast and unyielding tempi'.[10]

A *Falstaff* starring Walter Berry opened on 2 February 1983. Norton-Welsh wrote, 'Lorin Maazel let the music flow naturally without losing wit or pace, and kept the orchestra down for the singers.'[11] Berry's portayal was 'not an Italianate Falstaff in the rumbustious, extrovert mould but a more thoughtful character, slightly pompous and a bit of a bully to his subordinates. . . .'[12] The Mistress Quickly was Christa Ludwig, who had been married to Berry from 1957 to 1971.

Maazel was not averse to engaging brilliant guest conductors. Riccardo Muti sufficiently overcame his distaste for the House to conduct *Rigoletto*, but ran into considerable trouble using a new critical edition of the score. Tenor Veriano Luchetti was let go, then replaced by Franco Bonisolli. Afterwards Bonisolli was sacked, but eventually brought back to replace his substitute, Peter Dvorsky. The audience disapproved of the missing high notes, these traditional opera-house interpolations having been deleted, as was Muti's wont, from the cleaned-up score. The Vienna audience reacted lustily: 'The result was a bear-garden of boos, counter-bravos, stentorian comments, laughs for Bonisolli's brave attempt at a trill to end "Parmi veder", and any other excuse for a row. Bonisolli and Muti fought each other for control, with Muti inflexibly resisting the tenor's liberties. [Once] both had established the point, Muti allowed more latitude and the tenor went his merry way, degenerating into buffoonery in the tavern scene and hurling out "La donna è mobile" like a challenge to a duel.'[13]

Muti had previously expressed his strong objections to the House's traditional approach to Verdi, particularly the refusal to adopt the original score. In 1980 he declared, 'The Vienna State Opera kills Italian opera more than any other theatre in the world. It is unbelievable what you hear there. They have no respect for our composers. . . . A musicologist spends months of his life, even years, to be sure that Verdi put an accent in the second oboe part. He goes to the villa of Verdi at Sant'Agata and looks at the autograph score, compares this and that and takes a lot of trouble, just because we need to know what Verdi wrote. Then conductors and singers completely destroy the work of these gentlemen. They not only don't care about the accent of the second oboe, they change everything.'[14]

For a qualified success, the Maazel era had to wait until 12 June of the same year with a new *Turandot*. Although an effort had been made to create a serious, unconventional production, the audience booed the director Hal Prince, the stage designer Timothy O'Brien and the costume designer Tazeena Firth. However, Norton-Welsh found the quasi-expressionist staging and the use of masks appropriate. The idea of 'an alienated society fossilized through Turandot's *idée fixe* was well expressed in the masks for the whole populace bar the old Emperor, who could only save his humanity by total renunciation down to a Gandhi-like robe and a small box instead of a throne to sit on. This made sense and brought the work back from the realms of mere fairy-tale.'[15] Norton-Welsh went on,

> Musically, matters were more sumptuous and the audience roared its approval for ages at the close. Maazel had the orchestra in top form and produced a very hard-contoured, aggressive reading, often at maximum decibelage but rarely too much for the singers and always flexible and transparent. The Turandot was Eva Marton, who scored a huge success in this new assumption. She coped magnificently with the fearsome climaxes but was always able to give the lyrical passages due measure. Here and there I thought she had not fully mastered the musical phrasing but no doubt that will come. José Carreras (Calaf) disappointed the prophets of doom, which does not mean that his voice really has the weight for the role, simply that he did fair justice to the figure and to the music within his means and without apparent fatigue. The same cannot be said of Katia Ricciarelli, whose Liù was too resolute and lacked the vulnerability of the character. In compensation, she sang some exquisite soft high notes.[16]

Abbado's Staatsoper debut was delayed. It finally came on 22 March 1984, with the well-known *Boccanegra* staged by Strehler. Abbado's reading was described as 'luminous with a tenderness and warmth that is all too rare in modern Verdi conducting but so essential to this work.' The timing of the Abbado debut was significant. It emerged that director Maazel was on his way out. Three days earlier the first in a series of complex personnel shifts in the Staatsoper administration had been announced. Helmut Zilk, the Minister responsible for the Bundestheaterverwaltung, the organisation comprising the four Austrian national theatres – in order of seniority: the Staatsoper, the Burgtheater, the Volksoper and the Academy Theatre – informed the press that Maazel would be leaving the Staatsoper once his contract ran out at the end of the 1985–86 season. His replacement was to be Claus Helmut Drese, at that time intendant at Zurich. Drese would not take office until the 1986–87 season. The following month Abbado's appointment as music director was made public. He would be joining the new intendant, Drese, when his term began. Egon Seefehlner was named to return to the Staatsoper and run it *ad interim.*

Prawy was relieved at Maazel's fall from grace, which he attributed to 'a series of unlovely intrigues' surrounding the conductor-intendant. He also claimed Maazel was responsible for some of the intrigues. Although Prawy vowed that he esteemed him 'as a truly great conductor', he added, 'I ask myself whether he truly felt comfortable in the role of director of the Opera.'[17] Prawy also claimed Maazel 'had no experience as an opera director, was very frequently absent, personally not very accessible and could (or would) not delegate authority'.[18] According to Prawy's recollection, when Robert Jungbluth, the general secretary of the Bundestheaterverwaltung, informed Minister Zilk of Maazel's resignation, Zilk exclaimed, '*Gleich her mit dem Seefehlner!*' – in other words, 'Let's get in Seefelhner right away!' Maazel was furious at the way his appointment had been truncated. He blamed the establishment, concluding that 'The city is deadly. It opens its heart to no one. Anti-Semitism is more prevalent than ever.' Vienna 'trusts no politician'.[19] Maazel had a particular dislike for the political learnings of Minister Zilk, the then Austrian Minister of Education.

Maazel's final new production as opera director was a less than sublime *Aida*, opening on 30 April 1984. The staging was by Nicolas Joël, 'who was more concerned with the pictorial aspect than personal conflicts; and while there was plenty of pomp, there was also plenty of unnecessary or even ludicrous movement'. Maazel's conducting was placed in the same category of insensitivity: '[Joël's] generally superficial view seems to have been shared by Lorin Maazel. Though his tempos were mostly well judged and he gave the singers sufficient but not excessive freedom, he often drowned them and there was little subtlety, and transitions were often blunt.'[20]

Even though Seefehlner was a *locum tenens*, occupying the director's seat until Drese and Abbado took office, he brought fascinating guests to the House with the same creative energy that had marked his first term. Ken Russell's infamous staging of *Faust* opened on 16 March 1985. He took a manic, provocative stance, having Méphisto-phélès urinate into the cathedral font. He assured the Staatsoper management that the House would have 'the most glorious scandal in its history'.[21] Among other radical reconceptions, Russell chose to treat Marguérite as a tutor for the deaf and dumb. The *Opera* reviewer's reaction was mixed:

> Act I of Russell's two-dimensional, kitschy production was the most successful and the church scene the most striking, with Marguérite arraigned before Méphistophélès who was a black-clad bishop standing on the altar. The troupe of scantily dressed dancing girls who constantly appeared to keep things moving at all costs merely emphasized the superficiality and, ultimately, tedium of the proceedings. The production was generally well served by Carl Toms's scenery and costumes, though, with the exception of the Golden Calf fruit-machine, the floats introduced into the Kermesse were more gaudy than apposite.[22]

The final new production of Seefelhner's second regime, in the summer of 1985, was *La Gioconda*, starring Domingo and Eva Marton. A rash of cancellations before the opening marred the show. Stage director Piero Faggioni was fired following an incident in which he slapped the face of Herr Sertl, a top administrator of the Salzburg Festival. Two conductors left: Gianandrea Gavazzeni for reasons of health, and Giuseppe Patanè because the Vienna orchestra refused to have him. At last Adam Fischer was engaged to conduct. Although, judging from the videotape, Fischer's beat is at times unclear, communication was nonetheless established with the orchestra, who play satisfyingly if not excitingly. Filippo Sanjust was engaged to direct and design sets and costumes, and his work was called by the *Opera* critic 'a sorry effort'.

Sanjust tried to resurrect stage pictures from the period of composition but without any stylistic consistency or splendour. The opening scene was picture-book cut-out; Enzo's ship a most unseaworthy affair, Alvise's room bare with *trompe l'oeil* effects on the walls, and the final ruined palace was in the opera's currently favoured super-detailed realism. The costumes were Renaissance for the men and late nineteenth-century for the women. This might not have mattered if Sanjust had had any bright ideas for the action but he plunged us back into banal, old-fashioned postures and groupings.[23]

Although Domingo had taken a temporary rest from opera, because of his concern for the victims of the Mexican earthquake, he agreed to sing these *Gioconda* performances. To the *Opera* critic it was clear that Domingo was 'indisposed' on the evening of 27 May, as he had been on opening night.

Seefehlner quit the Staatsoper in 1986 when Drese's contract took effect. At the same time, Abbado took up the post of music director at Drese's side. Born in Aachen, Germany, in 1922, Drese had been active since 1950 as a stage director in German opera houses. His equally broad experience in opera administration included the directorship of Houses in Heidelberg (1959–63), Wiesbaden (1962–66) and Cologne (1968–75). At Zurich, which he had headed from 1975 to 1986, Drese had put together Monteverdi and Mozart cycles staged by Jean-Pierre Ponnelle and conducted by early-music specialist Nikolaus Harnoncourt. Drese understood musical values and respected Abbado's work. 'As a conductor he was not only a sovereign stylist in Italian opera. His artistic interest extended to the stage as well, witnessed by his ongoing collaboration with directors like Giorgio Strehler and Luca Ronconi, and with scenic designers such as Luciano Damiani and Ezio Frigerio.'[24] Drese also was happy to discover that Abbado shared his 'progressive' political outlook, even though, unlike Strehler, he had not consistently brought it to bear on his opera stagings. When Drese travelled to Milan to meet Abbado he found that the conductor was pessimistic about their future in Vienna: 'What was difficult for me', wrote Drese afterwards, 'was his scepticism about overcoming the Viennese mentality. From the start he had the gravest doubts about the repertoire system. But all in all, he seemed interested to make a new beginning.'[25]

Drese also approved of Abbado's lack of personal ambition. He felt that, unlike Karajan, Abbado was no 'egomaniacal star of the podium full of charisma and prejudice'. Instead he was a consummate professional: 'Abbado – or rather Claudio, as everyone quickly began to call him – was an approachable man with a variety of interests. When working, though, he was absolutely unshakeable. In a staging he sought to understand everything perfectly; he coached the singers from the first rehearsal onwards and learned the work down to the least nuance in order to conduct it later by heart.'[26] Although Staatsoper orchestra members sometimes complained about Abbado's unclear beat, they appreciated his control over performances. Singers liked his light touch in accompaniment.

Abbado was welcomed in Vienna, even by some sections of the press. Norton-Welsh wrote in 1986 that he had 'shown with a series of performances of *Simon Boccanegra* that the repertory system can provide glowing evenings to justify the House's reputation. He further consolidated this return to older standards of excellence with his conducting of the new production of *Un Ballo in maschera*, which opened on 19 October. With the orchestra on their best behaviour on 26 October, he gave a reading that left one marvelling at beauties hardly noticed before, revealed by subtle pointing and tempos that always felt perfect. If I have one cavil, it is that he emphasized the passion of the score at the expense of the elegance which is such an essential ingredient in this opera.'[27] Given Abbado's occasional tendency to over-intelligent conducting, this adds weight to the critical consensus that he can also be over-emotional at times.

The new team heading the Staatsoper concentrated on new productions, some of them perilously expensive. They deemed the gamble necessary: new productions, more than anything else, give vitality to an opera house. Drese and Abbado also favoured works unfamiliar to the Viennese public, either because they belonged to 'foreign' operatic traditions or because they had rarely been performed anywhere. Notable Vienna premieres included Dvořák's *Rusalka*, the first performance of which, on 10 April 1987, was conducted not by Abbado but by the Czech conductor Václav Neumann, who 'kept his orchestra subdued most of the time and caressed the phrases to bring out all the Slav lyricism. However, his forces were in sloppy form and frequently failed to respond to his demands.'[28] Director Schenk and designer Schneider-Siemssen were in their familiar realistic mode, 'with no attempt at over-subtle psychological point-scoring'.[29]

Staatsoper audiences also continued to be given more conventional fare, some of it at a higher pitch of quality. Many in Vienna 'preferred to follow series of performances by their favourite singers – the celebrated trio of tenors, Carreras, Domingo and Pavarotti, and also Agnes Baltsa, Edita Gruberova and Jessye Norman'.[30] With a personality both fiery and intelligent, Baltsa continued to build a career as a superb interpreter of roles. In her first performance of Charlotte on 3 December 1986, opposite José Carreras as Werther, she displayed 'fine singing and sensitive acting'.[31]

Born on the Greek island of Levkas, Baltsa drew sustenance from occasional visits to her native land. 'People ask what I do with my leftover time,' she told a journalist. 'I have no real time left over, because I always must find time to return to Greece for a rest. I like to swim and talk to the farmers.'[32]

Abbado's *L'Italiana in Algeri* of September 1987 was marked by brisk tempi. Norton-Welsh underscored the show's energy and force: 'The State Opera orchestra plays little of this kind of music and they were a little dry in the overture,' but they could not help but respond to Abbado's 'infectious rhythms.'[33] Concerning the singers, he concluded that 'Agnes Baltsa avoided many of Isabella's highest passages and the break between her upper and lower voices has become more pronounced; however, she put over the role in the grand manner and with a lesser artist than Raimondi [as Mustafà] she would have over-dominated the show'.[34] Norton-Welsh liked Frank Lopardo as Lindoro: 'He has it all: even coloratura; a pleasing quality all the way to a secure top, if a little throaty; finely spun pianissimo; good looks and a great sense of rhythm . . .' An *Il Viaggio a Reims*, also conducted brilliantly by Abbado, opened 20 January 1988. Caballé as Madame Cortese proved herself a successful comedienne, as well as a dab hand at the Spanish castanets in Don Alvaro's dance. Samuel Ramey as Lord Sidney received 'such an ovation for his cadenza to "God Save the Queen" that even his colleagues begged Maestro Abbado for an encore, which was not granted'.[35]

Drese himself staged Gluck's *Iphigénie en Aulide*, which had not been performed in Vienna since the end of the war. Drese 'made no attempt to force the essentially static action with unnecessary business, letting the music speak for itself and contenting himself with scenic changes that pointed up the events without interrupting them, and movement only where needed'. Gundula Janowitz as Clytemnestra gave 'a grandly passionate rendering of her great Act II aria'. Charles Mackerras conducted intelligently but the orchestra 'stubbornly refused to catch fire'.[36]

In May 1988, for the Vienna Festival, Abbado undertook the challenge of conducting Schubert's little-known romantic opera *Fierrabras*. Although the work is long and suffers from a loosely woven plot, Schubert's music was felt to be worth the effort of staging. Abbado consulted the autograph in revising the printed score. The critic for *Opera* was positive:

> Granted Josef Kupelwieser's text for *Fierrabras* is not a model of literary achievement either verbally or dramatically, but the basic premise of love crossing the front between warring factions is hardly new and the impossible nobility of Fierrabras – accepting dishonour in place of the man loved by the woman he loves – is not so far from that of Wolfram and others. The question remains of Schubert's music. Everyone who bothers to look at the score can see that it is as lovely as one would expect, but is it dramatic? The answer ... is an unqualified affirmative. The work is long but it never feels so, even though some numbers are dangerously protracted.[37]

Audiences were likewise appreciative. *Fierrabras* was given repeat performances at the Staatsoper from 1990 and Abbado recorded it to considerable acclaim.

Abbado and Drese were succeeding, by and large, in broadening the tastes of the Staatsoper's audiences. Their work had not come cheap. 'The Vienna Opera', wrote Drese, 'requires the world's best singers, cost what they may.'[38] By late 1987 *Opera* magazine was reporting that 'financial thunderclouds [were] gathering fast over the House. Sponsorship is now the name of the game, even for the State Opera.'[39]

In 1988 there was an unpleasant flap over Drese's tenure which, even more than Seefehlner's, had been marked by memorable artistic successes. Drese disliked the city and its byzantine politics. He admitted he felt a foreigner in the Viennese ambience of 'false compliments and the delicate manners of antechambers'.[40] He also indicated his displeasure with the financial juggling acts the Staatsoper's intendant was forced to perform. Nothing could be done straightforwardly: 'In the budget one must list receipts as minimally as possible in order to have reserves for expenditure.... To justify extra expenses one can always come up with a rationale after the fact.'[41]

It emerged that Drese's liberal attitude towards expensive new productions raised hackles in the ministry. In the middle of that year an announcement was made that Drese's term as Generaldirektor would not be extended when his contract expired in 1991. His replacement would be the well-known former baritone Eberhard Waechter, who meanwhile would continue running the Volksoper. Ioan Holender, an artists' agent, was named simultaneously to fill the newly created post of general secretary.[42]

In spite of his impending dismissal, at a subsequent press conference Drese announced his wish to continue as director, stating that he would rather go on contending with the 'Viennese tigers' than battle a different set of enemies. The Minister of Education and the head of the Bundestheaterverwaltung refused to let Drese go on. However, the government made a gesture in Drese's direction by issuing a 'letter of intent' outlining revised terms concerning the Staatsoper's over-the-top budget. These terms proved acceptable to Drese, but his contract nonetheless was allowed to run out in mid-1991.[43] The House's next *Ring*, to be conducted by Bernard Haitink, was to be postponed until Waechter took over.

Claudio Abbado planned his departure from the Staatsoper to coincide with Drese's, citing ill health. He went on to take over the music directorship of the Berlin Philharmonic Orchestra, giving emphasis in this new phase of his career to the orchestral repertoire rather more than to opera.

One of Abbado's last new scores for Vienna, the *Khovanshchina* of January 1989, demonstrated his understanding of one of Mussorgsky's most difficult works and brought out the best in the Staatsoper orchestra. Max Loppert believed that Abbado's conducting of Mussorgsky 'must count as one of the great performances of our day, an unforgettable display of skill and sympathy combined. The House's great orchestra flooded his spare lines with warmth – not cosy warmth, but colourful, vibrant, charged with dramatic electricity. . . . The desire to communicate the burning intensity of vision that underlies the awkward surface was paramount, and swept all before it.'[44] But after 1991 Abbado would return to the Staatsoper only as a guest: his brilliant mind, care for the score and generous emotional involvement would be sorely missed in an artistically and financially impoverished House.

While the Staatsoper was seeking to evolve beyond its past, the Volksoper had consolidated its position as Vienna's respected second House for opera, operetta and musical theatre productions. By 1984 it was putting on 300 performances a year of a repertoire that extended to 40 highly assorted musical works, many of them of unusual interest and quality, including rarely performed operettas. It still adhered to its policy of putting on works in German translation. The Volksoper employed an ensemble of 60 singers, with another 150 or so on board as choristers, dancers, orchestral players, technicians and administrators. General Director Karl Dönch, still active as a bass-baritone specialising in comic roles, extended the House's activities in the direction of chamber opera, newly composed works and the musicals that Vienna had grown so fond of ever since Marcel Prawy put on *Kiss Me, Kate* in 1958.

The accent at the Salzburg Festival remained on star singers and excellent music, with dashes of innovative repertoire. Agnes Baltsa's *Carmen* was rapturously received at the 1985 Easter festival. Karajan was conducting. The *Opera* critic was fulsome: 'I cannot overpraise Miss Baltsa's Carmen. Vocally supreme, by her acting she gave a fascinating portrayal of the sensuous, irresistible and dangerous wildcat that the heroine should be. . . . José Carreras was in excellent voice and totally involved dramatically in his role.'[45] The pair's first *Carmen*, at Zurich in 1982, had been called 'sensational'. The summer festival of the same year saw an audacious re-creation of Monteverdi's *Il Ritorno d'Ulisse in patria*. Hans Werner Henze, working from Giacomo Badoaro's libretto and an incomplete and problematic score, had pub-

lished his eccentric realisation three years previously. He heavily orna-
mented vocal lines and gave the sketchy orchestral parts a radically
contemporary flavour. The *Financial Times* critic, David Murray wrote:
'Brass is mostly reserved for the gods, but there are plangent woodwinds in panoply (even a heckelphone), and banjo and electric guitars,
a prominent accordion as chief continuo, and a still more prominent
concert piano.'[46] Henze omitted violins from the score, however.

Salzburg continued to mount lavish shows with outstanding casts
and conductors, including, of course, Karajan. Top ticket prices at this
period reached £130. In 1987, nearly forty years after the *Anschluss*,
Salzburg audiences were treated to a new production of Schoenberg's
Moses und Aron. The work was composed by a Jew born and bred in
Vienna who had fled Germany after Hitler's access to power. It was
conducted, as reviewer Horst Koegler did not fail to point out, by
James Levine, a Jewish musician. Jean-Pierre Ponnelle did the provocative staging. Horst Koegler wrote:

> The production emerges out of complete silence. The huge
> stage and the galleries of the Felsenreitschule resemble a giant
> museum of Jewish history, with books stacked in the recesses
> of the galleries, an enormous seven-flamed chandelier placed
> in the centre, Jewish cult vessels and instruments, with Torah
> scrolls scattered around and tombstones everywhere. We watch
> a silent crowd of Jews viewing these objects, studying the books,
> reading the Torah or deeply absorbed in prayer, until a piercing
> cry is heard, a mob of uniformed men storms on the stage,
> demolishing everything ... When the members of the chorus
> enter again, they all wear the yellow star on their robes, and
> the memory of the [*Kristallnacht*] ... is painfully evoked and
> omnipresent through the whole evening.[47]

Levine brought out, 'rather like Solti ... the espressivo quality of the
music, looking not so much forward to the distant horizons of Webern
as glancing backward to its roots in Brahms and even Wagner'. Philip
Langridge as Aaron was dressed to resemble a cabaret compère: 'He
used his light and malleable tenor like a sword and impressed through
his pointed declamation of the text.' As Moses, Theo Adam 'spoke
Schoenberg's texts so musically and so music-consciously, actually
balancing on the tightrope between speaking and singing, that one

sensed the abstract melody behind his utterances – the very idea of a vocal music which never materializes as real sound'.[48]

In the 1988 festival Riccardo Chailly conducted Ann Murray in the title part of *Cenerentola*. Koegler wrote of how Chailly drew from the Vienna Philharmonic, and Walter Hagen-Groll's chorus and the soloists, 'utterly refined, tiptoe sounds. The finesse of the ensembles could hardly have been more sophisticated, and the crescendos escalated irresistibly. Just occasionally Chailly seemed so enraptured by the sounds emanating from the orchestra that he drowned his singers, but generally he approached this score as filigree Brussels lace. Maybe Abbado's reading has more fizz and dash, but Chailly's seems the more philosophically minded – he stresses the melodramma giocoso classification of the work rather than its buffo antecedents.'[49]

Chailly was the son of the former artistic director of La Scala, Luciano Chailly. He had made his first appearance as a conductor in Padua at the age of fourteen, when he led the Solisti Veneti. He was named assistant conductor at La Scala in 1972, when he was only nineteen. He recalled, 'The first rehearsal was always the worst. Imagine me as a nineteen-year-old taking on the La Scala orchestra. It can be very tough and aggressive when the musicians want to be in a Latin kind of way. But things settled down after we got used to each other.'[50]

For the 1989 Salzburg Festival only one new production had been scheduled – *Un Ballo in maschera*, to be conducted by Karajan. Before the opening, however, Karajan died, on 16 July 1989, at his home at Anif near Salzburg. Prawy called him 'a charismatic, hypnotic personality', adding, 'Karajan's magic word was beauty: the beauty of sound, the beauty of women, the beauty of stage direction.'[51]

Soprano Gundula Janowitz praised Karajan's musical understanding: 'I shall always be grateful to this man. First, for being able to sing under him, and more than anything else, because what I learned and experienced through him in music truly cannot be expressed.'[52] Michael Haas, a producer of recordings, underscored Karajan's contribution to making serious music known to a wider audience through his audio and video recordings: 'Karajan's death was more than just the loss of an important artist, he changed the entire perception of classical music on the part of the public.'[53] Creative, determined, controversial, Karajan led the Staatsoper out of the wilderness and helped focus popular attention upon opera all over the world.

Important developments in the staging of opera were taking place in German Houses. There the conviction was growing that the 'museum pieces' of the standard repertoire needed a shake-up. New developments in the spoken theatre, especially here in Germany, also helped encourage conceptual productions. The German stage was becoming an arena for confrontational plays and productions heavily weighted with ideology, as well as nihilistic, even violent portrayals of contemporary life. In addition, French thinkers and critics such as Jacques Derrida and Roland Barthes helped foster an international trend to post-structuralist and deconstructionist textual criticism. Deconstructionist readings of literary texts were generally fragmented, revisionistic, ideological and highly personalised. They paralleled a shift in the aesthetic 'spirit of the age' from modernism to postmodernism. This shift entailed a neutralisation of ethical values, severe alienation, and a fracturing of perception and vision. Deconstructionism encouraged an attitude among some stage producers that there was no such thing as an objective reading of a play or a libretto. If that was the case, anyone's subjective approach, no matter how extreme, was a fair basis for an opera staging. In conceptual productions the director assumed the freedom to remould an opera in his or her personal aesthetic and intellectual terms which were often quite different from those the composer intended. Such a 'deconstruction' might make the work appear new, but it often failed to shed new light on its beauty or its meaning.

Conceptual producers also tended to put themselves at the centre of interest in opera, displacing the conductor and even the singers. Herbert Graf, a traditionally oriented director who staged operas at the Met, Salzburg, Zurich and Geneva, pointed out a growing tendency to the use of performers as producers' tools. Graf was also concerned that visual elements not become the main focus of a production:

> The greatest opera performers have had this in common –
> Lehmann, Flagstad, Melchior, Callas – the ability to sing mean-

ingfully, even if they were not all wholly convincing as actors in the conventional sense.

That's why, in training opera singers today, superficial technique must not be allowed to dampen or replace the expressiveness that is opera's only *raison d'être*. In the days when the conductor dominated the production, there was less danger of undervaluing this factor; the point of departure then could be summed up with the phrase 'In the beginning was the Word'. These days, the business of realising opera's dramatic content is in the hands of the director and designer. So the singer, with everything around him 'looking good', is called on less and less to use his own resources in the interests of expression.

Initially the conservative Staatsoper was immune to innovative stagings, with the very occasional exception such as the Joachim Herz *Zauberflöte* and *Tannhäuser* in the 1970s. However, a number of other important German-speaking Houses were beginning to adopt, not merely lively new direction, but radically conceptualist stagings as standard fare. At Frankfurt in October 1980 a particularly scandalous *Aida* was premiered, 'accompanied by fortissimo storms of booing and applause in equal proportion, both during and after the performance'. The writer for *Opera* decided that Hans Neuenfels, the producer, must have welcomed the boos, 'as he is obviously keen to shock the public at all costs, and has become the *enfant terrible* among the German producers'. Amneris was presented as an animal tamer and Aida as a cleaning woman. There were also 'lively goings-on in Amneris's bed'. In the final scene the underground chamber was filled with gas: Aida goes to Auschwitz. Gratuitous references to the Holocaust were becoming a cliché of conceptualist opera stagings. In the end, for this *Aida*, the *Opera* critic wrote, 'Verdi's music played a minor role'. José Carreras declared of the production, 'This is not true theatre.'[54] Generous state support lay behind such productions. The annual state subsidy at Frankfurt during the 1984–85 season was £12 million. (The Deutsche Oper Berlin received £17 million and the Paris Opéra £26 million.)

The premiere of *Don Giovanni* on 28 February 1981 at Cassel was conceived in a similarly shock-the-bourgeois vein. The *Opera* critic wrote: 'Zerlina . . . and her peasants were punk rockers on roller skates, she drawing her chewing gum up and out at Elvira's ascending coloratura and indicating masochistic tastes at "Batti, batti", her later scream being evidently one of disappointment at Giovanni's performance.' When the punk rockers removed all their clothing at the Don's 'Viva la libertà' pandemonium broke loose in the auditorium. Although some elderly opera goers quit their seats, others stood up to get a better view, with several approaching the stage.[55]

Not all avant-garde stagings in Germany at the time were conceptualist in orientation. At the Komische Oper of East Berlin, Felsenstein's protégé Joachim Herz had succeeded the master as intendant in 1977. Born in Dresden in 1924, Herz studied musicology before beginning to work with Felsenstein in 1953. Herz's activities outside East Germany had been limited until the 1970s. His stagings tended to emphasise ideological elements and took a polemical, anti-capitalist stance. At the same time his work with actors was careful, dedicated and often highly successful, as one might expect of a leading disciple of Felsenstein. In his Komische Oper production of Britten's *Peter Grimes* in January 1980, wrote the *Opera* critic, the chorus-collective emerged 'as the most impressive feature. Herz worked unbelievably intensively with the fishing people, modelled separate identities for them, and brought them to life. There are none of those exaggerations of music-theatre that merely announce the action; here we have simple people rising to the story and expressing themselves by singing.'[56]

After Herz left the Komische Oper in 1981, Werner Rackwitz succeeded as intendant, with Harry Kupfer as chief producer. One of Kupfer's most notable East Berlin productions was Reimann's *Lear* in 1983. Kupfer, wrote the *Opera* critic, 'has taken the appalling accumulation of atrocities – brute force, treachery, torture, murder – quite literally. He mercilessly opens up the tragedy, employing visual images, actions, gestures and psychological attitudes to create a suggestive stage language that disregards everything that is attractive in operatic terms. The work is presented in a new, emphatically menacing light.'[57]

Late in 1984, at the Deutsche Oper, West Berlin, Götz Friedrich staged a conceptual *Ring*, which was acclaimed for its imaginative basic premise: that the gods have taken refuge in a great tunnel from their errors and, indeed, from the end of the world. 'They then re-enact the events that led to their downfall as a means of achieving understanding.' At the same time Friedrich and designer Peter Sykora filled the stage with what James Helme Sutcliffe felt were irrelevant icons of destruction and decadence:

> ... models of bombed-out Berlin (Reichstag, Gendarmenmarkt and all, plus an abandoned doll's pram) ... the Valkyries, seemingly all black-leather motorcycle girls ... The towering wreckage of a mechanical horse, on which Wotan no longer forayed forth to delight in human self-destruction.[58]

It seemed that many conceptualist directors, including Friedrich, could take an approach that illuminated the work at hand while simultaneously obscuring it with arbitrary gestures, notions and, most of all, visual elements. It also was the case that ideas rather than emotions constituted a particular temptation for directors to commit irrelevancies.

After Patrice Chéreau's *Ring*, the management of Bayreuth turned to Peter Hall for a new staging of Wagner's masterpiece. Georg Solti conducted. Hall had expressed a lack of fascination with what he called 'the political side' of Wagner's work, which had been fully treated in the Chéreau staging. He favoured a return to 'the sensual side' of Wagner's tetralogy – 'not only the sexuality of Siegmund and Sieglinde, but the pure love of Brünnhilde'. Hall continued that for him the *Ring* expressed the concept that 'life goes on, seasoned by some forgiveness, some humanity, and some love; Fortinbras gives us the same message at the end of *Hamlet*.'[59] Hall insisted that the settings follow Wagner's stage directions explicitly. When Wagner asks for giants, a dragon, a huge worm, or a frog 'we have tried to provide them.' Andrew Porter enjoyed the faithfulness: 'For the first time in over thirty years of *Ring*-going, I saw Fricka arrive in a ram-drawn chariot and saw Brünnhilde leap on to a horse and ride into a blazing pyre.'[60] But Porter complained about inadequate visuals, misconceived costumes and 'a puzzling mixture of literalness – the real water ... and bleak ineffective abstraction'.[61] He also faulted Hall's imperfect understanding of German and Solti's 'engagement of several singers who were clearly not up to Bayreuth standard'.[62] Harold Rosenthal also demurred: 'Even had the Hall–Solti collaboration worked perfectly, I wonder whether we can ever return to a fairy-tale approach?' Moreover, wrote Rosenthal, 'I was rarely involved with the characters that Peter Hall had created, with the exception of Brünnhilde – and that was thanks to Hildegard Behrens's magnificent performance, and the Siegmund and Sieglinde of Siegfried Jerusalem and Jeannine Altmeyer.'[63]

In a press conference, Hall blamed the brevity of the rehearsal period for not allowing him to work out his vision of the *Ring*. In a 1988 interview with Michael Billington he recalled that he had had no more than thirteen rehearsal days before the technical rehearsal for *Götterdämmerung*. Hall summed up his Bayreuth *Ring* by confessing, 'Well, it had an inevitability about it, an excitement, and a horror. I wouldn't have missed it for the world, and it was a terrible experience. All those contradictory things are true.'

Several years later, Solti spoke of his own mistakes in the Bayreuth *Ring*. He regretted his choice of Reiner Goldberg as Siegfried. In rehearsal for the *Ring* his voice 'was a miracle – the best, I think, since Melchior in the forties. There are tapes to prove it. But he got frightened, he had no memory for more than 16 bars, so he was finished. The *Ring* I now think of as my own special disaster.'[64] On the evening that Rosenthal saw *Siegfried*, Manfred Jung had replaced Reiner Goldberg after an unsuccessful dress rehearsal. Jung was greeted at the first-act curtain, Rosenthal recalled, by 'a noise that I can only describe as sounding like hundreds of savage wolves baying for blood!' Wolfgang Wagner appeared before the curtain and threatened to stop the performance, and indeed the performance of all subsequent *Rings* at Bayreuth, and demanded understanding for Jung's predicament. Rosenthal went on, 'Then, like obedient children or good Germans they did exactly what they had been told, applauded and even cheered Mr Jung at the end of the evening.'[65]

Solti, who had not had the benefit of Wolfgang Wagner's plea for indulgence, was also booed at every curtain call. Solti had had some of the orchestra shell removed, which to Rosenthal's ears 'thus destroyed the wonderful Bayreuth magic sound which we have come to know so well. So the orchestra this year sounded just like any opera-house orchestra playing under Solti.'[66]

Porter was devastating concerning Solti's shortcomings:

> He sentimentalizes tender episodes, and he trivializes excited passages by charging through them. The great Wagner conduc-

tors inspire their singers and then seem to accompany them. With Solti, nothing sounds natural for long. He often begins an act well and then starts worrying at the music – pushing, nudging, jabbing, driving, or else dragging. Instead of glorying in the warm, broad, blended Bayreuth sound, he tried to turn it into Solti sound – hard-edged, forcible, clear, strident at climaxes – and to this end he removed a large section of the 'blending screen' Wagner installed over the orchestra.[67]

Porter was also aware, he wrote, of 'individual instrumentalists bowing, blowing, or banging away'. This minority view of Solti's conducting did not, however, mention the vigour, dramatic immediacy and transparent voicing which he elicited from opera orchestras worldwide.

Hall made changes the following year. The stage was better illuminated, but as Rodney Milnes wrote, in general the lighting 'was often flat and unimaginative, and this together with the clumsiness of those few scenic effects that still play "in view", especially the arrival of spring in *Walküre*, suggested that the technical staff's hearts were not in their jobs'.[68] Milnes suggested, as a panacea for all the ills in the Bayreuth Hall *Ring*, 'If] I were chairman of Covent Garden . . . I would commission a new *Ring* from Hall the moment he retired from the National Theatre, lock him in the opera house for a year, and give him a design budget of precisely 75p. Then we would see something. It is plain . . . that most of the Bayreuth rehearsal period was spent ironing out – or rather not ironing out – insuperable technical problems instead of directing singers.'[69] Solti did not return to conduct in 1984. His replacement was Peter Schneider from Bremen: 'Musical and consistently felt,' as Milnes judged him, but 'not quite of the quality one expects from Bayreuth – but then nor was any of the conducting I heard there this year'. Milnes also praised Behrens, returning in her last year's role: 'For dramatic intensity and force of intellect, I have not seen a Brünnhilde to touch her.' He was appropriately grateful that the Rhinemaidens 'were presumably cast with skinny-dipping in mind'. Manfred Jung was once again Siegfried: 'This year he had the advantage of being rehearsed and obviously profited; I cannot think of anyone today who could perform the role better.'[70] Nevertheless, Jung was booed once again; apparently the Germans had forgotten Wolfgang Wagner's finger-wagging.

In 1985 Wolfgang staged a *Tannhäuser* called by *Opera* 'an old-style Wagner family production'. The main set was 'a series of concentric circles in the centre of the stage' and the blocking consisted of 'dumping the principals down on the stage and leaving them there until it was time to move them off again. In the end there simply was not sufficient dramatic impulse generated on stage to convince us that this opera deals with issues of any import.' Wolfgang appeared before the curtain, 'smiling appreciatively at the audience as they boo in his face'.[71]

In 1988 Harry Kupfer's *Ring* was unveiled at Bayreuth. Its orientation was postmodernist and its provocative design elements were central. Even so, the visual aspect was superimposed upon, rather than integrated with, the energetic ensemble acting and imaginative stage movement organised by Kupfer. John Tomlinson's Wotan, thrillingly sung and acted, was given coldly phallic visuals: a long, thick spear, a floor-length black leather coat. But his leonine striding on stage and the majestic warmth of his singing humanised the character in contrast – to tell the truth, in opposition – to the way he is presented visually. Critical reaction was mixed. Milnes felt the 'grey section of motorway' which stretched into infinity 'looked hideous and was doubtless meant to'. The employment of lasers lent Wagner's tetralogy 'all the grandeur and mystery of a pub disco'. Milnes also objected to Kupfer's use of stage action 'to undermine the power of the music'.[72] However, John Allison, attending the last series of performances of this staging in 1992, appreciated 'the directness and intimacy of Kupfer's interpretation. Gods, giants and dwarfs are all demystified, given very human characteristics, their emotions laid bare. This is often achieved by dispensing with visual distractions: the image of a few characters, or of the solitary Wotan, alone on the vast Bayreuth stage was powerful indeed.' Allison felt that the motorway was 'an apt symbol for a modern setting', even though 'other visual aspects of the production seemed uncomfortably at odds with the poetry and romance of Wagner's score'.[73] Daniel Barenboim drove the Bayreuth orchestra to an arguably excessive degree of volume and dramatic tension, well beyond Solti's fieriest efforts in Wagner performance.

The dichotomy between true creative imagination and gratuitous provocation in opera staging reflected a long-standing problem for the genre. How can renewal be brought about in an art whose traditions are so strongly entrenched, and sometimes so cherished? If opera were to find new vitality towards the end of the century, this difficult question would have to be addressed.

COVENT GARDEN 1980–87

Colin Davis 2: Prima la Musica

FOR LA SCALA AND VIENNA the determining factor in the insti-tutions' performance was the quality of their leadership rather than severe financial shortage. At Covent Garden, however, the 1980s were to see a further financial erosion in the Royal Opera's development while the company was also faced by the need to maintain its identity during an era of conceptual and postmodern productions. On 4 May 1979 Margaret Thatcher became Prime Minister and the arts were soon to face a very different attitude to public funding from that which had been the consensus since the war. In November 1979, against a continuing background of international recession, Norman St John-Stevas, Minister for the Arts (1978–81) warned that it was going to be a very hard time for the arts in general. The government's policy was to bring down inflation, running at 10 per cent at the time, and to 'establish a healthy economy by reducing public expenditure'.*

Claus Moser wrote in his 1979–80 Annual Report, 'These are rough times for everyone, and the Arts cannot escape some pressure, but we are grossly underfunded in relation to comparable houses abroad and this year the increase in our grant has been substantially less than the rate of inflation.' The 1980–81 Annual Report showed that with careful management and at the expense of the cancellation of two operas, £704,000 could be carried forward. But the increase in the grant had been 15 per cent whereas the increase in the Retail Price Index had

---

* The government's first budget, announced on 12 June 1979, cut the basic rate of income tax from 33 to 30 per cent and the highest rate from 83 to 60 per cent. Value Added Tax (VAT) was raised to a unified rate of 15 per cent. There were to be savings of £3.5 billion in public spending. Cuts of £6.5 billion were proposed for the following year.

been 16 per cent, causing even greater anxiety for the following year, in spite of attracting audiences at an average of 94 per cent of capacity. 'No opera house of international standing', Moser reiterated, 'can operate on so fragile a basis.' He set out argument in favour of subsidy that was to be viewed with increasing scepticism: 'Opera and ballet bring unique experiences of joy and happiness and enrich the life of the community. They are not a luxury but a necessity, and a country which does not subscribe to this would be a poor place.'

In an effort to stave off the growing 'elitist' accusation caused by increased ticket prices, Moser reported the continuation of touring, promenade concerts and children's matinées, as well as television and radio broadcasts. Paul Findlay later recalled that amid all the cuts, Moser insisted that the schools matinées 'were sacrosanct'.[1] In the last quarter of the 1981–82 season there was according to the Annual Report, an 'alarming falling off in receipts', experienced by all theatres and due to recession, which reduced the average audience to 86 per cent.

Moser later recalled that during the 1970s and early 1980s there had nearly always been a deficit – but that it had been 'under control' and had always been covered by the Arts Council. In those days it was 'a true buffer between the government and us. You were dealing with friends, you could not go endlessly asking for money but they were sympathetic.'[2] The Arts Council was, in Moser's words, a very different kind of body from that which it became later in the Thatcher era. In 1982 Sir William Rees-Mogg became chairman of the Arts Council, a post he held until 1989, and Lord Gowrie became Minister for the Arts in 1983 until 1985. Both men were staunch supporters of Mrs Thatcher's monetarist financial policies, placing great emphasis on private funding. Rees-Mogg was, in David Pountney's words, to prove 'commitedly unhelpful'.[3] Tooley recalled him slamming the phone down on him.[4] Lord Gowrie doubled the roles of Minister for the Arts with that of Treasury spokesman in the House of Lords. The deputy chairman of the Covent Garden Board, Denis Forman, pointed out that because of this arrangement the arts had no independent spokesman in debate.* Tooley, who met the

---

* Denis Forman was deputy chairman of the Board from 1983 to 1991. He was chairman of Granada Television from 1974 to 1987 and a member of the Council of the Royal Northern College of Music from 1975 to 1984. Forman had some trenchant thoughts on

Prime Minister on a few occasions, was convinced that she 'distrusted arts managers and believed them to be profligate, incapable of controlling expenditure and ignorant of good business practice'. He continued:

> The theory of market forces so dominated her thinking and that of her government that the true purpose and significance of public arts funding was lost on them. Financially, they were immensely difficult years for the arts, and ministers seemed reluctant to come to terms with the real issues. The amount of money at stake was trivial, and a willingness to listen and join in a dialogue in quest of solutions would have made a big difference to all of us in our attitude to the government.[5]

In Thatcher's 900-page memoirs, four pages are devoted to the arts. Her attitude was simple and set the stage for the gradual erosion of public support for cultural activity in the next decade: 'I wanted to see the private sector raising more money and bringing business acumen and efficiency to bear on the administration of cultural institutions. I wanted to encourage private individuals to give by covenant, not the State to take through taxes.'[6]

Government policy, combined with inflation, was very rapidly forcing arts institutions into looking for other sources of income. Nicholas Payne, financial controller at Welsh National Opera, in an article in 1981 recognised the need for vastly increased private sponsorship. The company had suffered a deficit of £75,000 for the 1980–81 season, in spite of the cancellation of a new production. Amoco's promised £500,000 over five years had become a crucial part of the company's planning. Payne warned, however, that sponsorship was an unreliable resource, for it was dependent on a good economic climate. Furthermore, the sponsorship would, as Thatcher intended, weaken, perhaps fatally, the concept of State support. Roy Shaw, secretary-general of the Arts Council, pointed out that sponsors

---

musicians. Of Levine he said: 'Very versatile, bull-like determination, strength, very sound on Wagner, not as exciting as Georg or as profound as Bernard. Big Verdi is his heyday – a band conductor. Great precision. Georg more exciting, more dramatic power. Bernard piles on the agony' (Interview with the author, 29.6.99). Philip Jones, later finance director, described Denis Forman as 'one of the great non-executives I have had the privilege to work with'.

advertised their contribution in such a way that the role of public funding was becoming increasingly obscured in the public mind. The Midland Bank sponsorship of the *Ring* cycle, with big advertising banners outside the Royal Opera House, was such an instance. Milnes, on Radio 3's *Music Matters*, warned with remarkable prescience that if fund-raising were to prove successful it might enable a future government 'to back out of its obligations to prevent the companies from going bankrupt'.[7]

These problems were to prove more damaging to the House than the effect of sponsors on artistic policy. Tooley later recalled the difference between Covent Garden and the Met:

> The social circumstances here are so different – people are not going to make the same kind of progress socially that a Sybil Harrington could make in New York. We always had an absolutely clear, fundamental rule that we would regard sponsorship as funding but the sponsors would have no artistic influence at all. Once or twice people tried but we said in effect 'if you want to stay with us, we must be free to exercise artistic discretion'.[8]

As at the Met, however, even if sponsors favoured the more popular repertoire, they released other sources of income to pay for the less popular works. Colin Davis was less sanguine than Tooley, later recalling that at one point he had asked the Board why they expected the administration to make plans at all and that he had told them, 'Go and ask the sponsors what they want.' The management, he recalled, 'began to realise that the product was going to pass out of control of the opera house'. According to Tooley, 'this was a word of warning expressing his own doubts and fears' with which Tooley was 'totally in sympathy'. Both men were agreed on the general attitude to artists from both government and private paymasters. Davis felt that artists were not given enough respect: 'Musicians were not particularly welcomed. In this country serious artists, actors, composers, are not treated as entirely responsible people.'*[9] Isaiah Berlin was also concerned at the changing make-up of the Board, writing to Moser on 14 January 1982 to express concern that there was an over-

---

* Davis had been knighted in the 1979 New Year's Honours list.

preponderance of people with financial skills rather than great musical or artistic knowledge. 'I honestly think', he wrote, 'that *prima la musica* should rule in this case.'[10]

In January 1980 it was announced that Colin Davis had renewed his contract to 1983–84. By the mid-eighties, Davis admitted that while he had had no time for stars in his early days, he had come to accept their value, even though they were spread too thinly.[11] Findlay recalled that Davis 'certainly welcomed the opportunity to work with the greatest singers in the world, when you introduce that extra element of the very greatest voices you realise what a Covent Garden stands for'.[12] The House also continued to welcome the greatest conductors. One such moment was on 5 February 1980, when Plácido Domingo sang *Otello* with Carlos Kleiber conducting. As with their joint appearances elsewhere in Europe and the States, the partnership was greeted with rapture. 'The House was ablaze,' Peter Heyworth wrote. 'The Covent Garden chorus sang as if terrified out of its wits by the conductor.'[13] Bernard Haitink later said of Kleiber's *Otello*, 'Carlos Kleiber has spoilt it for me entirely. I admire that man so much and he did an *Otello* here which was so fantastic that I just can't do it any more.'*[14]

On 15 December 1980 Domingo made another exciting appearance, in John Schlesinger's inventive production of *The Tales of Hoffmann*. Kleiber had pulled out of the production because of uncertainty about the edition of the work being used, as well as about Schlesinger. Having heard Domingo sing *Hoffmann* and *Otello* in one year, Rosenthal was convinced that he was 'the finest singing actor, at least in the tenor repertory, of the present day'. There were other fine productions. On 16 February 1981 Friedrich prepared *Lulu*, working more relaxedly with Colin Davis. In March 1981 Muti conducted a new Moshinsky production of *Macbeth*.

While Covent Garden was fighting for its artistic standards under Moser and Tooley's stewardship, the English National Opera under

---

* Black market tickets for *Otello* were being sold for £1,000.

Lord Harewood continued to develop a strong ensemble with such company stars as Valerie Masterson, John Tomlinson and Ava June. Lord Harewood, with 'catholic tastes', continued to be adventurous in the company's programming, bringing German director Joachim Herz to direct *Salome* in December 1975, as well as including new operas in the repertoire. Iain Hamilton's *Royal Hunt of the Sun*, based on Peter Shaffer's play, was staged in February 1977 and, in November, Alberto Ginastera's *Bomarzo*, from the New York City Opera. That same year David Blake's *Toussaint* told the story of a house slave in Haiti who rose to be ruler of the island. The quality of the structures and librettos of these new works was not entirely successful, but *Toussaint* was brilliantly staged by David Pountney in one of his earliest productions for ENO, and conducted and prepared by Mark Elder. Mackerras's powerful last production as music director at ENO was Janáček's *From the House of the Dead* on 30 December 1977. He was succeeded in January 1978 by Sir Charles Groves, who decided not to renew his contract after a year, following a serious illness.

In 1978 Lord Harewood announced the formation of English National Opera North, to be based in Leeds, in order to obviate the ENO's need to tour. Opera North opened in November 1978 with a production of *Samson and Delilah* for a two-week season, which was later lengthened in order to take in visits to other centres in Northern England. David Lloyd-Jones was their director.

Mark Elder became the ENO's new music director in January 1980. Born in 1947, he had studied music as a choirboy at Canterbury Cathedral and won a scholarship to Cambridge. He had been on the music staff at Covent Garden and Glyndebourne, and had served his apprenticeship with Edward Downes at Australian Opera (1972–74). Elder was to prove an active hands-on music director, with a substantial say in the choice of producers and designers as well as casts. He believed that satisfactory performances could only be achieved by 'building an audience from within a company, from within a group of people who are used to working together; by working towards a finished product backed up by a management who understand style, values and priorities'.[15]

Even before Elder took up the reins at ENO there had been interesting intimations of what was to come. Daring and controversial productions, frequently involving juggling of period, were to be the flavour of the era, starting with *Gianni Schicchi* in February 1978. It was set in late nineteenth-century Florence. Colin Graham and Mark Elder argued in the programme notes that the change of period allowed 'an actor greater freedom of movement and expression without any need for period stylisation. More important, he is able to project a character and situation with which a contemporary audience is more easily able to identify – the clothes, the manners and behaviour patterns are much nearer home than the fancy dress of 1400.' This belief is a recurring theme in Tom Sutcliffe's defence of postmodern and conceptual productions in his book *Believing in Opera*:

> Their common factor was a rejection of naturalism, a belief in an expressive and emotional visual discursiveness, and a conviction that the purpose of the theatrical representation was not to define the nature of the work, to limit it to a particular narrative context, but to stimulate the audience's response to the material generally and to its subtextual associations.[16]

'The less natural the action on the stage,' Sutcliffe argued, 'the more audiences wonder why and what it portends.' The argument that modern dress makes emotional involvement easier for the audience shows little faith in the intelligence and sensitivity of either audience or composer, or in the ability of composer and director to illuminate the universal from the specific. It was, however, to be a recurring theme in the advocacy of conceptual production.

As well as expanding the modern repertoire and giving modern interpretations of the classic repertoire, the ENO under Harewood and Mackerras, and later Elder, played a major role in the Handel revival. Several of Handel's oratorios had been known and loved in Britain for decades in modernised orchestrations, but his operas had been almost completely neglected. In the revival of the operas the Handel Opera Society had been the torch bearer since it was founded by Anthony Lewis and Charles Farncombe in 1955.* On 3 June 1955 it

---

* The Handel Opera Society was constituted as an amateur choral society whose chorus sang with professional soloists and orchestra. By the time of its closure in 1985 it had

had given a performance of *Deidamia* at St Pancras Town Hall in London, and by 1990 nearly all sixty of Handel's operas had been staged in Britain. The professional companies took time to find a modern equivalent of the baroque love of elaborate spectacle, or to solve the dramatic problems of the several-part arias, but by the mid-1970s, singers emerged who could skilfully cope with the music, including Marilyn Horne in the United States and Janet Baker in Britain.

Charles Mackerras played a major role in the British revival. He was responsible for the musical and dramatic preparation of the December 1979 *Julius Caesar* at ENO. It was one of the first successful professional Handel performances, in John Copley's lively and skilfully considered production. Copley later spoke of Mackerras's 'enormous knowledge' and said that he was 'the best Handel conductor without any doubt because he will find the tempo'.[17] Mackerras and Copley preferred working with mezzos of strong character rather than counter-tenors, as great interpretative singers like Baker and Horne could solve the dramatic problems posed by Handel's writing. In the 1990s, however, the emergence of counter-tenors with powerful voices and a strong stage presence helped to tilt the balance in favour of using male voices, as eighteenth-century composers had frequently intended. David Daniels became an international star in the Nineties.

In Mackerras's 1979 *Julius Caesar* ornamentation sounded 'tailored' for the singers, who responded joyously to the challenge. Janet Baker was triumphant. In the 1984 video recording her Caesar is beautifully sung, with great artistic purpose in her understanding of the phrasing and the articulation on the line. Her breathing is miraculous, making the fiendishly difficult arias look effortless. Alan Blyth wrote of 'the total conviction she brought to Caesar's moods of anger, love and determination'. Valerie Masterson was a 'delightfully kittenish Cleopatra'.[18]

In November 1982 the Royal Opera had a noted success with John Copley's delightful production of Handel's *Semele*, 'the greatest comic opera to an English text', as Milnes was quoted in the Covent Garden

---

staged eighteen Handel operas. The Unicorn Theatre Group at Abingdon 1959–75 and the Barber Institute at Birmingham University 1959–68 also played their part in the revival. It was the Society that had pressed for original vocal registers, the emergence of counter-tenors and the use of period instruments.

publicity. Rosenthal was worried lest Handelians were upset with what might be considered 'wilder extravagances' – such as Juno looking at Semele in Act Two through a telescope or Somnus lying on an 'enormous *Rosenkavalier*-like bed'. But these touches, along with the ochres, sepias and cobalt blues of Henry Bardon's luminescently glowing eighteenth-century setting, ensured that *Semele* was lively, humorous and enchanting. Robert Tear 'looked good and sounded even better' as Jupiter and 'never became ridiculous'. Rosenthal was full of admiration and wonder at Handel's genius, leaving the theatre 'with a happy smile'.*[19]

Covent Garden's staging of *Samson* in February 1984, for Handel's 300th anniversary, was much less successful, due to Vickers's refusal to use an up-to-date edition of the work and his insistence on bringing Julius Rudel with him to conduct.† Stanley Sadie wrote that Rudel was not a Handel specialist and, in using 'continuo organ, new viola parts, violins in octaves', had shown 'an ostrich-like unawareness of all that has been going on in Handel performance over the last decades'. Nor, Sadie added was Vickers's voice suited to Handel.[20] Tooley recalled that Vickers 'remained adamant that decoration was out of order . . . that it was merely an invention of Mackerras and the like'. At its revival the following year, Tooley insisted on 'authentic performing practice' and Roger Norrington to conduct,[21] even though this involved breaking the contract with Vickers who was 'bitterly disappointed'.[22]

In February 1985 Nicholas Hytner, the young associate director of the Royal Exchange Theatre, Manchester, produced a stimulating *Xerxes* for the ENO.‡ Max Loppert found under Mackerras's direction once again, 'how well and stylishly a Handel opera can be played on

---

* At this time, Copley encouraged and guided as his assistants at ENO three highly successful directors of the Nineties: Graham Vick, Steven Pimlott and Nicholas Hytner, whose work with Copley on *Julius Caesar* encouraged him to ask to prepare *Xerxes* for ENO.

† Tooley believed that Vickers might be 'unidiomatic' but that he would have 'other virtues'. Board member Professor Alexander Goehr warned that 'when performing pre-classical opera, it was of the highest importance that the performance should be authentic' (Opera Sub Committee, 19/3/9).

‡ Nicholas Hytner began his career at Kent Opera and had mounted twenty new opera productions by 1990, when he was in his early thirties, as well as straight theatre productions for the Royal Shakespeare Company and the National Theatre where he became an associate director in 1989 and director designate in 2002.

modern instruments in a big theatre'. Hytner placed the action in Vauxhall's eighteenth-century garden, treating the staging as 'a kind of illustrated, enacted mini-lecture about the curiosity of the age for exotica, for feats of natural wonder, for fantasy and highly wrought engineering in intricate partnership'. The strong cast included Ann Murray and Valerie Masterson. Loppert was amused by the cleverness and bright humour in Hytner's 'elegant visual conceits' but he was troubled by the cleverness 'as the work progressed to its more serious moods'.[23] Much later, in 1991, Hytner himself admitted that there had been something of himself saying 'Hi folks, aren't I clever?' in this production.[24]

In May 1984 the Arts Council announced a cut in the Handel Society's modest grant. Rodney Milnes, although mourning what would prove to be the death knell of the Society, acknowledged that it had in effect done itself out of a job, as Handel was by then standard repertory in Britain and internationally. In 1982 Peter Sellars's *Orlando* for the American Repertory Theatre, Cambridge, Massachusetts made the central character an astronaut at Cape Canaveral. Sellars's *Giulio Cesare*, set in a bombed-out Cairo hotel under terrorist siege in 1985, also created a stir. The counter-tenor Jeffrey Gall as Caesar had both great virtuoso skills and dramatic presence. In January 1984 the Met itself staged its first ever production of Handel, *Rinaldo*, in a somewhat tampered-with edition. By the 1998–99 season the Met's own production of *Giulio Cesare* achieved 98.5 per cent at the box office.

The ENO was fast developing the company identity. Mark Elder was creating what David Pountney called a 'truly exciting theatre with a European reputation'.[25] In May 1980 Joachim Herz came to direct *Fidelio* with Elder conducting. In December 1981 Harry Kupfer's *Pelléas et Mélisande* again dispensed with a period setting. On 10 February 1982 the English National Opera's new *Dutchman* with Norman Bailey was the first Pountney–Elder collaboration since the announcement of the latter's appointment as director of productions. Pountney and Elder had worked closely together at Cambridge and at the ENO were to create the mutually supportive partnership which had eluded Colin Davis at Covent Garden. The two men remained in their posts until 1993.

Pountney's *Dutchman* was a traditional staging, using modern lighting techniques, a revolving stage and projections, given in one act. In both Pountney's production and Elder's lively conducting 'youth and raw energy' were evident. There was also an early warning of some of the more striking features of the Pountney–Elder era – in the shape of what Rosenthal ascribed as 'embarrassingly awful blood-stained corpses that descended from the flies'.[26]

On 22 October 1981 Jonathan Miller's *Rigoletto* at ENO, excitingly conducted by Mark Elder, was one of the most successful of the time-and-place transpositions of the Eighties. The opera was set in Mafia-controlled Little Italy in New York of the 1950s, with the 'Duke' as a Mafia boss and Rigoletto as barman and joker. It worked well, in Rosenthal's words, because 'passion, revenge and killing were as much part of the 1950s Mafia scene as of sixteenth-century Mantua'.[27] The production also showed what a high level of ensemble the company had reached with John Rawnsley's Rigoletto, Marie McLaughlin's Gilda, Arthur Davies's Duke and John Tomlinson's Sparafucile. Pountney and Elder ensured that the best English singers would work as 'friendly artists' at ENO. These included Ann Murray, Benjamin Luxon, Thomas Allen, Gwynne Howell, Anthony Rolfe Johnson and Philip Langridge.

Pountney and Elder soon began to ride the crest of the new wave more seriously. On 26 January 1983 Pountney's production of Tchaikovsky's *Queen of Spades* cast Hermann not with a romantic tenor but with a character tenor, Graham Clark, and it gradually became apparent that the action took place in his mind. The use of a stern, stylised chorus in static lines, here used for the first time in 'quasi-military uniforms of field-grey', was also to play an increasingly familiar role in conceptual productions. According to Arthur Jacobs, Elder's conducting of *The Queen of Spades* secured 'bold choral tone' and well-articulated solo performances.[28] Throughout the Elder era, however much controversy the productions raised, there was consistent praise for ENO's musical values.

Pountney's *Rusalka* in March 1983, though powerful, also dictated its message. Pountney explained that fairy stories and myths provide 'a means of discussing things which are difficult because of social taboos', and that Rusalka's story is about 'a typical initiation into social and sexual experience'. He worked with designer Stefanos Lazaridis to transform Dvořák's lakeside glade into a Victorian nursery with white walls and ceiling enclosing a 'dreamlike world of repression and surreal fantasy'. There was 'a case history of archetypal symbolism, of rocking horses, moving furniture and rag dolls that take on a menacing life of their own'. The Witch was a 'governess brandishing scissors and with plenty of other castration symbolism'.*[29] Within the concept Lazaridis's beautifully lit set, with its water reflections, beguilingly transformed the nursery's bare walls into Dvořák's enchanted world.

As in many German postmodern productions, Nazi and Fascist imagery soon became an overworked cliché at ENO. It made its first appearance in Nicholas Hytner's *Rienzi* on 29 September 1983. With money at a premium, David Fielding designed an all-purpose set, menacingly marble-like with steel-panelled doors. The chorus was placed above it, seated in Mao caps with their scores on stands before them and, in Alan Blyth's words, 'many blow-ups of Kenneth Woollam as the dictator'. As well as old film clips from the days of Hitler and Mussolini youth camps, there was an 'incursion of tanks, armoured cars, and lights on the audience at the moment of truth when Rienzi is shot rather than dying in a conflagration'.[30] Later Hytner admitted that some of what they had done had been 'jokes – maybe brilliant, maybe horrible –' which by 1991 had become 'simply appalling clichés'.[31]

At the beginning of the 1985–86 season Peter Jonas took over from Lord Harewood, who had been managing director since 1972. Rodney Milnes, summing up the Harewood years, praised above all the 'communication between artists and audience' that had grown up at ENO. The 'lively two-way conversation' was, he said, the 'lifeblood of the theatre'.[32] The two-way conversation continued and when a journalist on the *Evening Standard* called the ENO triumvirate of Pountney, Jonas and Elder 'the power house that drives the opera machine forward' the phrase 'Power House' rapidly became attached to the company.†[33]

---

* After this production *Rusalka* became a more frequently produced work, reaching the Met in 1993 and receiving a fine recording by Sir Charles Mackerras in 1998.
† Keith Cooper was director of public relations at ENO when the company gained its unofficial title. Previously from 1981 to 1988 and later from 1995 to 2000 Maggie Sedwards did a fine job of modernising the marketing image of ENO and improving relations with the press and critics.

Just before Harewood's departure in December 1984 the production of Tchaikovsky's *Mazeppa*, by American director David Alden together with designer David Fielding, caused members of the audience to walk out. Harewood later recalled the excitement of the piece but admitted that Alden 'wouldn't tell us what he was going to do.'[34] Milnes found the production's 'by now famous trimmings – the chainsaw massacre, torture by power drill, generous blood-letting, extremely peculiar treatment of the Hopak' to be 'gratuitously disgusting' and 'ultimately silly'.*[35] Sutcliffe, however, saw it as 'a symbol of ENO's brave new production world', in contrast to what he called Miller's 'deodorised Mafia *Rigoletto*'. Sutcliffe, again underestimating his audience's intelligence, believed that *Mazeppa*, updated to the time of the twentieth-century Great Dictators:

> provided a framework of reference in which design and choreo-graphed movement could be combined to authenticate ritualised thoughtless political violence. Alden anyway seems to need to draw on the audience's memory of the Nazi holocaust, to establish a continuum of political violence and systemic cruelty. Such associations challenge the audience to identify morally because the more recent experience of evil is always taken more seriously than cruelty softened by history.[36]

Alden and Fielding now turned their attention to Verdi. Milnes found their *Simon Boccanegra* 'deliberately ugly', with its 'crudely outlined sets in primary poster colours – livid red, shrieky blue, black, and decidedly off white ... deliberately tattily built'. It contained 'a ragbag of references taken from the cinema, pop video and comic books', and employed 'alienation, the use of stage business to distract one's attention from the music and a deliberate refusal to match musical and visual images'. It also contained Alden's familiar props: 'kitchen chairs and strip lights (two of Mr Fielding's calling cards that could now be given a rest) a fire bucket, sledgehammers, a huge hand that descended amidst much clattering of ropes for the Council Chamber scene'. The Doge ending 'Plebe! Patrizi!' in his braces was 'certainly an unconventional image'.[37] Sutcliffe accused Milnes of failing to notice 'how scrupulously Alden had managed the energy flowing

---

* The dancers slashed their own wrists as they danced.

in relationships on stage'. According to Sutcliffe both *Boccanegra* and the 1992 *Masked Ball* showed that 'operas were not simple costume dramas where characters happen to sing rather than speak, but psycho-historical mysteries whose resonances and implications (submerged in music) invited daringly imaginative amplification and experimental synthesis – so that they merged with the imagery and philosophy of life and art today'.[38]

Behind these controversial stagings lay a practical consideration – a lack of great voices. According to Elijah Moshinsky, ENO was creating 'an ideological shell' whereby 'the singing didn't matter and the style and presentation did'. It was, he explained, 'simply style over content'.[39] Sutcliffe himself was not unaware of this aspect, explaining in his essay about *A Masked Ball*, 'Neither Arthur Davies as Gustavus nor Cairns's Amelia could quite match the climactic thrill of their great duet, but the staging expressed a lot of what the voices could not.' The staging provided distraction, such as a 'great blood-red square stage-flat teetering above her, and a pock-marked moon that 'turned into a clock-face, its hands performing a lunatic dance around the eleventh hour'.[40]

While appreciating the function of their style, Moshinsky wrote a powerful article in *Opera* in October 1992 questioning its validity for Verdi. He believed that symbolism and postmodernism were 'antipathetic to the very core of Verdi's work' which reveals 'the power of opera to express our own feelings and experience'. Verdi was not just 'a composer concerned with the expression of passion in its dramatic form' but also 'a moral philosopher and realist of great perception' who used 'the rather crude forms at his disposal to dramatize ethical and social questions'. As part of the Romantic movement in Italian opera, Verdi addressed issues of politics, adultery, religion, family life and women. 'The mixture of long narrative, multi-plot structures, easily achieved verisimilitude of character, the epic and humanistic point of view relate to and mirror the novels of George Eliot and Victor Hugo and especially Tolstoy.'

Verdi's operas, Moshinsky explained, 'far transcend the operatic conventions which they use to express their ideas'. The director is also often confronted with problems of location that had to be changed for reasons of censorship and also that of heightened dramatic conflict with 'unbelievable consequences ("you mean you burnt the wrong baby?")'. The postmodern or conceptual director, in order to solve the problems, resorts to 'the use of expressionism' and treats the past as 'something to be looked at ironically'. They do not involve themselves or the audience 'in their great emotions' but rather treat the classics as 'familiar cultural icons which can be taken apart and reassembled in new forms. . . .' They seek out the neurotic implications and alienate audiences from 'the direct experience of the opera'. Moshinsky felt this to be an inappropriate method for Verdi, sharing Isaiah Berlin's belief that 'there is a bedrock of positiveness and wholeness in Verdi which gives his operas a sense of sanity and nobility'. In his own productions, therefore, Moshinsky seeks to 'embrace Verdi's humanism directly' giving 'life to his great themes and characters without a protective layer of irony'. A work like *Trovatore* does not have to be treated in a realistic way, but he stressed that whatever the director does has 'to take the characters' aspirations and passions seriously'.[41]

In the December 1992 *Opera*, Pountney defended David Alden's *Boccanegra* and *Ballo*, arguing that they had nothing to do with irony. The point of Alden's work, he believed, was 'the raw emotional intensity he releases in his performers, which drives them towards a miraculous reinvention of the high melodramatic style'. He and Sutcliffe attacked Moshinsky, with Sutcliffe calling him the 'poor man's Visconti'. But Moshinsky, resolutely undeterred by fashion, remained true to the spiritual centre of the works he tackled and his productions of Verdi at Covent Garden in the late Eighties and Nineties were among the most penetrating and integrated that the House has presented.*

Like ENO, Welsh National Opera was developing a distinctive style in the late seventies and early eighties. In 1976, after repeated financial problems, the Arts Council insisted that Lord Davies become the new chairman with a new executive in return for bailing out the company.

---

* Nicholas Hytner had also become increasingly disenchanted with what he described as 'style-obsessed' work and in particular the resulting dehumanisation of the chorus – something he admitted himself to have been guilty of in his productions of *Rienzi* and *Xerxes* (*Opera*, July 1991, p. 761).

In 1976 Brian McMaster took over as general administrator. Nicholas Payne became financial controller.

There was excitement and interest in the ensuing seasons, as with Göran Järvefelt's *Magic Flute* in 1978 and Goodall's *Tristan* in 1979, which resulted in growing audiences and increased performances. Box office revenues doubled by 1978 to £500,000. Increased activity, however, did not win an increased grant and financial problems continued to impede the company's ambitions.

McMaster's second season included Harry Kupfer's *Elektra*, first seen in Amsterdam the previous year. The production opened in an abattoir with maids scrubbing away the blood of carcasses, and it included the sacrifice of a naked slave girl, to emphasise the violence and cruelty of the piece, which might otherwise have escaped the notice of the audience. Pauline Tinsley, who was Elektra, spent much time dangling from a rope on a huge statue of Agamemnon and suffered injuries that included a dislocated shoulder. Tom Sutcliffe wrote that this production showed that WNO's new production team had 'come into their own'.[42] Kupfer's *Fidelio* in the 1980–81 season was, in the overworked cliché style, set in a modern prison camp with an SS-type commandant and a backdrop of freedom fighters from Christ to the Palestine Liberation Organisation.*

In May 1983 the Romanian director Lucian Pintilie's *Carmen* was staged as a 'post-revolutionary, improvised, unofficial performance during a carnival',[43] with a chorus dressed as guerrillas, and Micaëla on points singing in a little-girl voice, El Remendado in drag, and El Dancairo as Long John Silver. Sutcliffe sought to explain: 'The audience was invited to see *Carmen* as both an historic cultural artefact and meaningful contemporary tale.' For those less committed to postmodernism, however, too often the boundary between humour and ridicule seems blurred and scepticism appears to have been replaced by cynicism, diminishing all those involved – singers, composer and audience.

* In April 1985 Scottish Opera, in financial straits and sorely needing public support and sponsorship, presented Graham Vick's *Don Giovanni*, which, according to Raymond Monelle in *Opera*, was an 'out and out exercise in alienation, working against the drama and against the music and against the text' and took place in a huge public lavatory. Masetto was sick into a 'a ghoulishly grotty loo'. Kirov principal Sergei Leiferkus in his British debut somehow managed to reveal his qualities as 'a singer of great intelligence and restraint' as Don Giovanni (June 1985).

Less controversial work was also going on that revealed the deepening opera culture in Britain. In 1984 WNO presented its own *Ring*, introducing a new star, Anne Evans, to the Wagner firmament and, in October, bringing the production to Covent Garden – something that would have been unthinkable a few years earlier. The company also put on a series of remarkable productions by the German director Peter Stein, the first of which was *Otello* in February 1986 followed by *Falstaff* in September 1988.[44] At Tunbridge Wells, Norman Platt and Roger Norrington had successfully been developing Kent Opera. Houses were often filled to capacity, with a large subscribing membership and local business and councils making substantial contributions. Jonathan Miller, Elijah Moshinsky and Nicholas Hytner, the future director of the National Theatre, gained their early experience and successes at Kent. The concept of replacing touring opera with regional companies based on local involvement was meeting a great response.

The ENO and provincial companies had decided to produce their innovative and sometimes provocative work on increasingly limited budgets, but Covent Garden had somehow to find another path, balancing innovation with the highest musical standards. In his 1985–86 Annual Report, Moser stressed that '*prima la musica* should never be forgotten by all those involved in opera production'. He later felt that there had been too much 'producers' opera', even at Covent Garden, and said that he had 'little patience with the self-indulgence of some modern producers and designers'.[45] Isaiah Berlin called Peter Wood's November 1981 *Don Giovanni* 'anti-Mozartean'. He accused it of doing 'violence to both the music and libretto', and was particularly troubled by 'the portrayal of Elvira as a frustrated nymphomaniac'.[46] Tom Sutcliffe scathingly dismisses the concept of *prima la musica*, labelling it 'the wounded *amour propre* of conductors, too: sticking to the primacy of music, and in some cases leading the pack of reactionaries against the "usurpation of 'producers' opera"'.[47] But its maintenance under very challenging circumstances was the chosen task of Covent Garden's management in the Eighties.

In his 1981–82 report Moser again stressed that European Houses spent at least double per performance, and announced that it was only possible to do two new productions next season. This situation, he urged, was not 'compatible with a front-ranking House'. The problems of accessibility and artistic standards were beginning to prove insurmountable. Tooley in the same report stressed that ticket prices were 'causing regulars to come less regularly and causing some not to come at all'. The Board had held endless discussions about which new productions should be abandoned, and the 1980 *Hoffmann* had only been saved because the Board felt they had already asked Domingo to forgo a new production of *Chénier* the previous season and were worried that they might antagonise him.[48]

Moser, unlike the new political masters, understood the fundamental incompatibility between artistic excellence and rigidly balanced budgets. He later recalled, 'Hardly any opera house I know has found a good way of combining artistic freedom with financial efficiency.' Time and again, he said, 'we have failed to control the finances for a simple reason – we wanted to achieve the best performances'. The most unpredictable area to control was that of design: 'By the time the designer and director had agreed on the project it was getting quite near the deadline and then the designers came in and it was too late. We tried endlessly to stick to strict budgets – we tried like hell and a lot of things we got more efficient like catering and ordering cloth or wigs. It was never solved.'[49]

One designer who had a striking success, in spite of producing his set designs at the last moment and with no costume designs at all, was the Australian artist Sidney Nolan. Tooley had long wanted Nolan to work at Covent Garden and he invited him to design the sets for Saint-Saëns's *Samson et Dalila*, in close collaboration with Elijah Moshinsky, with whom Davis had been keen to work again after *Grimes*. Nolan was, however, wandering around in the Gobi desert just a few weeks before opening night. Tooley recalled, 'We got a model-maker and put the whole thing together in three weeks.'*[50]

---

* Tooley remembered, 'Sidney was late and I still have this image which arises from Sidney ringing Elijah in May and saying, "I am still in the Gobi desert and I will be back at the beginning of June. Tell John not to worry, I know exactly what I am going to do and I've got some samples of Dalila's dresses." Eventually Sidney came back but I still have an image of a red telephone box in the middle of the Gobi desert with Sidney in it.'

Nolan's love of landscape and the primitive were reflected in his sensuous Aboriginal-inspired designs and his powerful series of paintings on the drop curtains, including 'Samson Eyeless in Gaza' and a 'Ram Caught in a Thicket'. Equally effective was his 'evocation of the desert oasis, mysterious fronds, and floating moons and suns'.[51]

The production was premiered on 28 September 1981. Davis, Moshinsky and Nolan proved to be forceful and committed advocates of a work not previously highly valued. Critics were surprised by its power, both Mann and Cairns admitting to a strong prejudice against it before this production, which gave them 'heightened respect for the music and the drama'.[52] Moshinsky was praised by Cairns for his ability to convey his 'belief in and keen response to its truthfulness, sense of place and dramatic atmosphere'. Max Loppert found Davis 'in one of his most ardent and communicative acts of interpretative sympathy'.[53] Mann wrote that Davis performed 'Beechamesque magic in transforming what some thought was dross into manifest treasure'.[54]

That same season, in June 1982, Giulini's *Falstaff* came to Covent Garden – with *prima la musica* unquestionably at the forefront of all minds. For ten years Tooley had been urging Giulini, who had given up opera conducting fourteen years before, to come back to Covent Garden. He had written to him on 10 May 1977 to tell him that his and Moser's affection for him as a person and musician was 'unbounded', and to suggest that if three Houses shared a production the maestro would be able to avoid the compromise he so disliked.[55] Giulini agreed to do a joint Los Angeles–Covent Garden–Florence *Falstaff*, insisting on strict conditions. He told Martin Bernheimer that he wished to avoid 'a haphazard repertory system'. He also did not wish 'to argue with eccentric stage directors, cope with inadequate rehearsals, or juggle his schedule with those of jet-propelled singers'.[56] Zeffirelli, who had been Giulini's choice of director, failed to turn up, but Tooley's subsequent choice, Ronald Eyre, worked in harmony with the maestro. Giulini told Bernheimer that he was responsible for every aspect of the production; it represented 'my thoughts, my visions, my conceptions, my decisions'. Giulini insisted on a five-week rehearsal period with all the principals present, casting singers who had not appeared in the opera before and consequently had 'no preconceptions'. The cast included Renato Bruson as Falstaff, Katia

Ricciarelli as Alice Ford, Leo Nucci as Ford and Barbara Hendricks as Nannetta.

Tooley recalled that Giulini rigorously refused to allow any element of humour into the show.[57] Indeed, he had told Bernheimer, 'For my taste Falstaff cannot be too serious.' It was a sensible and straight-forward production, with serviceable and pleasant costumes. Ronald Eyre, however, was held responsible for what Rosenthal called a 'sombre staging' which, though filled with many telling details, lacked 'the sparkle and spirit of the Zeffirelli staging'.

By the time the show reached London, expectations had been raised so high that there were inevitable disappointments, expressed by Tooley who felt that even with its marvellous musical interpretation it lacked humour and poetry.[58] Loppert called it a 'dull Falstaff'[59] and Peter Heyworth did not find it the 'great operatic experience we had been led to hope for'.[60] Rosenthal found Ricciarelli, in spite of Giulini's strictures, tired after performances of Traviata in Geneva. She appeared nervous, singing carefully and achieving little character or projection.[61]

In spite of these reservations, there were those who appreciated the honesty and seriousness of Giulini's reading, Conrad writing, 'He never parodies the sentiments of his characters, but validates them.'[62] Indeed, both Bruson and Giulini made the show life-enhancing even within the constraints of a muted interpretation, with the accent on Falstaff's accumulated wisdom. Bruson gave clarity to every move-ment, gesture, facial expression, syllable and note. His voice shifted with no apparent effort from a soft-grained, floated head tone to a fully open roar. The tone colours varied from ironic smarminess to insulted virility. The only problem, as often with Bruson, was the weak low register. As actor he moved gracefully from physical tomfoolery to elegance, from self-pity to wise self-knowledge.

Giulini, pouring in his accumulated experience and devotion, eschewed rhetoric, ready both to accompany and take charge, depending on the dramatic and musical needs of the moment. He was equally precise about legato, leggiero, accents and the building of climaxes. The orchestra responded to his lead with the utmost flexi-bility. Peter Heyworth found the 'music bathed in a pellucid autumnal light'.[63] This production paved the way for a Falstaff of mellowness and a tinge of sadness rather than the traditional buffo light-hearted Falstaff. It did not, however, altogether reconcile Giulini to the demands of working in an opera house. Tooley later recalled, 'Giulini sat down with me one day and said, "John, if we were true to ourselves we wouldn't be doing this. The amount that we have to give away, in order to achieve the end result, is actually too great a compromise." '[64]

The compromises continued. The 1982–83 season was, as predicted, reduced to two new productions: the Copley *Semele* and a borrowed Friedrich production of Puccini's *Manon Lescaut* from Hamburg with Domingo and Te Kanawa and conducted by Giuseppe Sinopoli and directed by Piero Faggioni. In early 1983 August Everding did not spend enough time rehearsing his *Magic Flute* as he had gone to Munich to revive *Tristan* in the middle of rehearsals. He had told Tooley 'his fee at Covent Garden was only 50 per cent of his fee at Munich' for the revival.[65]

During the 1982–83 season, according to the Annual Report, opera audiences averaged 89 per cent, which was better than theatres and classical concerts were achieving during this period of recession. Expenditure, however, had risen by 10 per cent and box office receipts by 6 per cent. As predicted, sponsorship was not keeping up its previous levels and the Arts Council grant for the next year was a reduction of 2.3 per cent on the previous year. The company was faced by a deficit of more than £1 million.

In order to reduce the deficit, the Arts Council brought forward its guarantees of £380,000 and the Treasury made a supplementary grant of £450,000 in December 1982. When the Minister for the Arts, Paul Channon (1981–83), made the announcement of this supplementary grant he announced a government scrutiny into the financial affairs of the Royal Opera House and the Royal Shakespeare Company, to be undertaken by Clive Priestley, head of the government's Management and Efficiency Group.

Lord Goodman was horrified when, as a member of the Board, he found Priestley sitting in on Board meetings. He later wrote, 'No one present raised the slightest objection until I announced that he had no business to be doing what he was doing, that this was the most outrageous breach of the time-honoured principle that artistic subsidy was not related to government control.' Goodman was sorry that the Arts Council was not able to maintain 'the determined, indeed warlike, attitude that we had previously maintained, whereby in no circumstances would we have allowed government to interfere with the conduct of artistic affairs in this country'.[66] Moser later recalled that the system had been the envy of European Houses: 'What the Austrian and German Houses were envious of was that although our money came from the state we were totally uninterfered with and it was a family House.'[67] This was the beginning of a process that led directly to the appointment of a Board chairman by a government minister in 1998.

In spite of Goodman's rightful indignation at government intrusion, Priestley's report, published in September 1983, was surprisingly sympathetic to the House's plight. His findings were not what the government wanted to hear nor, after an initial response, did it pursue his recommendations. Findlay recalled, 'Priestley gave us five years, because he wouldn't accept that increasing the box office was the answer – that was the one omission in the report that Thatcher was looking for.'[68]

Priestley confirmed that by the end of 1984–85 the accumulated deficit after funding was expected to be £3 million and the annual deficit £1.8 million. He recommended that the government cover the deficit and raise the basic level of grant to the budgeted funding requirement of £12.35 million, an increase of £1.8 million on the existing projections. He explained that the Royal Opera House's expenditure was rising faster than the general level of price and wage inflation, because it was a very labour-intensive organisation and there was much overtime working. Although the Arts Council grant had almost kept pace with the Retail Price Index it had not kept pace with the more appropriate Average Earnings Index. The report emphasised that there was nothing the company could do to reduce its estimated deficit unless it was 'required to lower substantially its artistic sights, to try and withdraw from commitments necessarily entered into in planning ahead and to change its nature'.

Priestley recommended that the grant should in the future be based on what he called 'targeted funding', which broke the business down into a number of key areas such as the orchestra, chorus, and stage, and worked out the grant, which should be indexed each year, depending on the use of each resource and its cost.* The government should make a three-year commitment, so that management could plan ahead with greater security. The House should try to make savings of £600,000 per annum in two years. Priestley also recommended the establishment of separate cost centres for the three performing companies.

In order to implement Priestley's 'cost centre' concept each company was to have its own chief executive. Anthony Dowell was to be the new director of the Royal Ballet and Eva Wagner-Pasquier was appointed opera director in 1985. She had worked at Unitel, the classical music production company that made films for television and video, and with her father Wolfgang Wagner for nine years at Bayreuth. From April 1986 the directors would be responsible to the general director for the financial and administrative control of the performing companies. Eva Wagner's role was not, however, very long-lived, as Haitink took against her and, according to Jeremy Isaacs, Tooley did not want his authority undermined.[69] She departed in May 1987. There would also be a director of finance to work with the general director to resolve the claims of the three performing companies. Accountant Philip Jones was engaged as finance director.†

* The 'cost centre' suggestion was not thought helpful by Moser, who later explained that apart from the problems of extricating the joint costs, it added to the rivalry and disagreements between the two companies. The ballet might have argued, for instance, that as they were cheaper they should pay less of the running costs (Interview, 1.6.01). Findlay on the other hand thought it would have greatly benefited the efficiency of the two companies. 'Priestley wanted to say to the companies, "Now this is your money now you spend it" – dividing the opera and ballet subsidies up. Each should have its own planning and run its own affairs, then you can really determine how much it costs to run an opera and a ballet company.'

† Adrian Doran resigned in June 1984. Philip Jones was finance director of the House from 1985 to September 1993. He recalled how the cost centre system worked: 'We worked out as closely and accurately as we could the cost and incomes of running each of those companies. We then ended up with a hard core of costs which we tried to keep to a minimum, which was really your central administration. This we then farmed out in a predetermined percentage. Opera tended to get more because we spent more time on it, but the final allocation was as small as we could keep it. So each company knew exactly what its budget was, what its box office was going to be, its other income, its private funding and what the costs of putting on its productions were.' Jones continued, 'It focused attention much more – the opera and ballet Boards could more easily identify where there was a soft spot, and be responsible for dealing with any such problems' (Philip Jones, Interview 6.1.00). The first Annual Report reporting the cost centres was that of 1988–89.

In his Annual Report Moser, praised Priestley for the care with which he and his specialist advisers, Peter Diamand (with the Orchestre de Paris) and Hugues Gall (director of the Geneva Opera) had carried out their scrutiny. 'We welcome', he wrote, 'the report's support for our activities and its firm conclusion that the House is underfunded by some 17 per cent.' Nevertheless Moser was justifiably anxious. He warned that there were 'nagging doubts as to whether this country, and many people in key positions in government, central and local, in business and elsewhere, are really committed to a policy of sustaining what has been achieved'.

Moser was able to report the next year that the Treasury and Arts Council had eliminated the deficit and balanced the books for 1983–84 with a supplementary grant of £1,025,000 and a special grant of £219,000. The total raised from private funds was £1,531,000. But the future did not look promising, and by December 1984 the Board was once again discussing which prospective new productions should be dropped.[70] Moser told the Board on 31 January 1985 that the government had no intention of implementing Priestley's recommendations for three-year funding commitments. This was confirmed by the Arts Council in February. Gowrie told Moser on 11 February that the government would not institute 'targeted funding' as it could not be reconciled with the government's rejection of automatic index-linking in the field of public expenditure as a whole. Moser, in response, argued that the arts should indeed be a special case in government spending policy and have a special priority in a civilised country, as they did in Europe, reminding Gowrie that Vienna had rebuilt its opera house after the war.[71] There were those who had long been connected to the Royal Opera who described Gowrie's behaviour over the Priestley report as less than courageous. There was a belief that having promised that he would ensure that he would push Priestley through, Gowrie had come under pressure from the Treasury and announced that, as between monetarism and the arts, he was for monetarism. This was not a suitable position for a Minister for the Arts.

The government's declining role in 'paying' for culture had been enshrined in the 1984 strategy document for the Arts Council. Entitled 'The Glory of the Garden', the policy proposed 'to decentralise the dramatic and musical life of this country'. In fact, it meant spreading the increasingly inadequate resources yet more thinly, as there were no extra funds available for such a policy change. The Arts Council acknowledged that carrying out their new strategy would cause 'hardship for respected clients'. As a result, sixty-two companies lost funding altogether, and the major companies were increasingly underfunded. The report was concerned at the high levels of expenditure on opera – the subsidy per ticket sold averaged £19 whereas that for drama was £2.80. It would be impossible for the regional companies' funding to be brought up to the level of ENO and therefore very hard for them to maintain standards.*

Opera analysed what government policy meant in March 1985 in an editorial entitled 'The Axe Falls', which stated, 'With the most philistine government since the end of World War Two in office, it is hardly surprising that the grant to the Arts Council has effectively been savagely cut.' Reflecting the government's 'lack of commitment', about which Moser had warned, was a public response that had begun to find crude articulation in the press. The *Daily Telegraph* published an article on 2 April 1984 headlined WHY NOT LET THE CULTURE LOVERS PAY? WHAT YOU CAN'T AFFORD YOU CAN'T HAVE.

In 1983–84, during its all too brief Priestley interlude, the House managed to present eight productions of opera and ballet new to Covent Garden. These included Dexter's Met *Nightingale* and *L'Enfant et les sortilèges, Andrea Chénier*, Tarkovsky's *Boris Godunov* conducted by Abbado, and *I Capuleti e i Montecchi* conducted by Muti. A bold new production was Andrei Serban's *Turandot*. It was first seen in July 1984 at the Olympic Games in Los Angeles, where Davis and the company received a euphoric response for what Martin Bernheimer described as its 'old-fashioned ensemble values and teamwork' with its 'great conductor, a great chorus and a great orchestra'. Davis elicited

* In the light of this trend towards regionalism, Moser had explained in his 1982–83 report that, even in the context of increased regional funding, the Royal Opera had a strong claim to funds. In 1981 a survey had shown that 48 per cent of its audience came from outside London, three out of four per cent from the United Kingdom and the rest from abroad. Furthermore, 25 per cent of the grant was spent on touring.

a 'fervent response from orchestra and chorus with no hint of bathos'. Jones and Domingo, who was 'inadvertently made up to look a bit like Boy George', led the action which 'unfolded unfussily and fascinatingly in a colourful series of narrative devices borrowed from primitive Kabuki and Baguku'.[72]

Designer Sally Jacobs created a small-scale, almost claustrophobic and threatening, tiered amphitheatre which loomed over the stage and from which a masked Chinese chorus observed and commented on the action. A bank of stark modern spotlights above the pagodas added a further ominous element.* In striking contrast to the Met production, which Zeffirelli was to prepare three years later, Serban and Jacobs, according to Milnes, treated the piece as a 'serious work of art, one that visually places it firmly in its time – between two world wars, which makes its unfinished state even more disturbing'. Milnes felt that they showed that Puccini had succeeded in elevating his 'fascination with cruelty from a personal to a universal level; as a study in unreasoned mass violence it is a work of chilling power'.[73]

During the 1984–85 season John Schlesinger produced a new *Der Rosenkavalier* for Solti's twenty-fifth anniversary, and Moshinsky staged *Tannhäuser*. Domingo sang Chénier and Samson. In the 1984–85 Annual Report Moser was able to report that the season's box office takings were a record £9 million with 92 per cent attendance. These, combined with higher than budgeted private funding, meant that there was no deficit that year, but the next year (1985–86) the Arts Council grant was to be increased by only 1.9 per cent, which was a cut in real terms. Private funding, which even at its peak had only made up 3 to 5 per cent of the annual income, was by now affected by the recession. Fund-raising, Moser believed, could make little further progress without changes in tax arrangements.†

In June the Minister told Tooley and Moser that he recognised there was no 'substantial room for further economies', but he was not optimistic that he could help. Philip Jones told the Board on 29 July

---

* Jacobs had been responsible for the set of Peter Brook's landmark *A Midsummer Night's Dream* for the Royal Shakespeare Company in 1970.
† Forman told the Board on 14 January 1985, there would soon have to be staff reductions in various parts of the House, perhaps even in the orchestra as the cancellation of productions did not produce large enough savings (Royal Opera House Archives, 18/2/3).

1986 that neither a reduction in performances nor longer runs would help because of the 'heavy incidence of fixed costs'. The company was like 'an under-capitalised business which operated with only limited scope for improving profitability'. The decline in the grant in real terms was 'causing the House's position to grow progressively weaker'. Both the conducting and singing of *Donna del lago* in September 1985 left Moser, as he told the opera subcommittee, 'in despair'. Tooley replied that there were not enough new productions to encourage outstanding conductors to come to Covent Garden.[74]

Moser mourned the failure to implement Priestley: 'Alas the recommendations have now been effectively abandoned.' He was worried that the new Minister for the Arts 'appeared to dismiss the arguments' that 'public investment in the arts brings good returns in terms of employment, taxes and tourism'. He warned: 'If for the sake of "candle ends" (to use the phrase the Prime Minister once used in this context) the Royal Opera House and other arts institutions are forced to cut activities and standards built up over decades, both country and Government will lose much more than our masters in the Treasury may realise.'

Ironically, at the exact time when the decline in public funding was to make the House vulnerable to charges of inaccessibility, a technical development that could make opera performances comprehensible to a wider public than ever before, came into general use. In 1984, at Paul Findlay's urging, Covent Garden used surtitles for the first time in schools performances of *La Bohème* and *Falstaff*, and by 1988 the company introduced titles to all performances of foreign-language operas. Titles were a major development in operatic life, which some abhorred, and some welcomed as the conclusive answer to the vernacular versus foreign-language performance debate – the debate, as Isaiah Berlin put it, between 'accessibility of meaning' and 'fidelity to the composer's intended fusion of word and sound'.[75]

The debate was heated. Rodney Milnes in *Opera* waged a veritable war against surtitles, writing in October 1984, 'As stealthily as the cholera that creeps across the world on low brass in Britten's *Death in Venice*, a plague is threatening the world of opera.' Surtitles would, he believed, result in singers giving up trying to enunciate clearly and people would stop looking at the stage. In the early days the standard of many titling efforts was poor, 'scaling heights of illiteracy'. Berlin, however, believed that titles were the 'least imperfect solution'. He ascribed the unexpected success of the televised Bayreuth Chéreau–Boulez *Ring* to the captions as well as to its artistic merit. He believed that those who 'underestimate the beauty and depth of operas because they cannot follow the words ... can be converted and illuminated and made enthusiastic by becoming able to understand the meaning musically and emotionally, of what is going on, instead of being made to listen to mumbo-jumbo'.*[76]

David Pountney argued that surtitles upset 'the intricate synthesis of music, text, action and image'. Charles Mackerras, on the other hand, was a 'fanatical admirer of surtitles', arguing that 'the vocal line is matched to the original language'. In any case, he wrote, most singers pronounce 'even their own languages so poorly that you end up needing titles anyway'.[77] Haitink was also strongly in favour, telling the opera Board that 'surtitles enormously increased audience response'. This was, he argued, 'immediately heartening for the singers and the orchestra in the pit'. To Tooley's argument that surtitles made singers lazy, Haitink responded that they inspired singers, 'to give of their best in every way'. The argument was sealed when, in January 1988, Board member John Sainsbury said that it was 'clear that surtitles helped to sell performances'.[78] In May 1988 Covent Garden decided to use surtitles in all performances after a survey showed that 90 per cent of the audience favoured their use.

James Levine said that the Met would introduce surtitles over his dead body, and held out until the technology enabled the House to install the titles in little computer screens on the back of each seat rather than above the proscenium, which was far too high to be visible to most of the audience. He was immensely proud of the system finally developed because of his insistence. Terry Teachout in *Commentary* hoped that the advent of titles would help to transform

---

* Early surtitles were of variable quality. During Eva Marton's first United States tour a Houston Grand Opera performance of *Tosca* degenerated into hysterical laughter when Tosca's '*ma falle gli occhi neri*' was translated as 'give her black eyes' (*Opera News*, September 1985).

the Met from being chiefly the singers' House into a setting 'for unified dramatic presentations' which depended on an understanding of the text. The Met introduced titles in the 1995–96 season at a cost of $2.7 million.[79]

Another attempt to maintain accessibility at Covent Garden was the Paul Hamlyn weeks, due to begin in January 1986. They would enable 'thousands of newcomers to experience ballet for the first time at nominal prices'.* The Hamlyn weeks, together with the Midland Bank Proms and the schools matinées, attempted to stem the tide of audience erosion. In 1983 in another initiative taken by Findlay to increase audiences, a ballet education officer, Kate Castle, was appointed and started a programme of workshops in schools. The following year an opera education officer, Pauline Tambling, was appointed. The first opera project was a participatory project for young people based on *The Bartered Bride*. Two schools mounted productions of *Carmen* with members of the Royal Opera. One-off workshops in schools involving the participants' own creativity formed the basis for the company's educational activities, but there was also work with adults. In 1985 the Metropolitan Opera Guild team ran a 'Write an Opera' course which the Royal Opera's education department redeveloped for use in British schools, using Royal Opera artists and professionals. By 1999 the course had four levels and had gained accreditation at higher degree level through the University of Leeds. Darryl Jaffray joined the education department in 1987 and was involved in the development of its programmes, which increased in ambition and variety over the years. The House was among the first major performing arts organisations to institute a substantial educational programme.

Live relays to the Covent Garden piazza began in July 1987, with a splendid *Bohème* with Ilona Tokody and Domingo 'in amazingly fresh and youthful voice'.[80] Two thousand people watched the big screen in the piazza under the usual drizzle, and responded, as did the Prom audience inside, with abandoned enthusiasm. In later years

---

* Paul Hamlyn, whose family had moved to Britain from Berlin in the 1930s, made his fortune in publishing. He published populist good-value series which were sold in huge numbers at cheap prices. The Paul Hamlyn Foundation was set up in 1987 with an endowment of £50 million.

Domingo also sang Don José and Samson for Prom and relay audiences. Such relays cost £50,000 per performance.

These gallant efforts could not, however, fully compensate for the further increases in seat prices and the perceived and real narrowing of the social range of audiences. Tooley later revealed his anger: 'While I am not remotely opposed to mixed patronage and think that there are certain advantages in it, what eats me is the way the balance between public and private went wrong.' He continued:

> It got out of gear, and we were plunged into the need to find private money far too quickly. The Priestley Report was set up by the Government because they thought it would be adverse, and that that would enable them to wash their hands. It came out the reverse way.[81]

It was Tooley's influence that kept the House stable during such difficult times. The Priestley report praised him for his 'immense personal contribution to the preservation and development of the House'. It gave him credit for the House's 'high world standing and reputation', as well as its reputation for being a 'House free of intrigues', and for being 'welcoming, friendly and supportive to visiting performers and others'. It was this atmosphere, they wrote, that meant some performers were willing to come to Covent Garden 'at fees somewhat lower than they might command elsewhere'.*

Moser endorsed this view of Tooley: 'He knew everybody in the House – a thousand people – if I walked across Floral Street with John and he saw a stagehand he would say "George, is your wife's back better?" and that wasn't for show, that was real. . . . The ROH in my days, and I spent a lot of time in foreign opera houses, was a happier more family-type House until not all that long ago than any House I have visited.'[82] David Syrus, then a senior répétiteur and from 1981 head of the music staff, remembered both men as able to relate 'to people across the entire spectrum of the House'. They 'knew who everybody was', Syrus said, 'and always had time for them'. It had

---

* Tooley received a knighthood in the June 1979 Honours list. The Board congratulated him on 18 June, saying, 'Both at home and abroad he was held in the greatest admiration and affection' (Royal Opera House Archives, Board, 18/2/1).

been a 'wonderful' system that had preserved an old-fashioned man-agement-type status – you wouldn't argue with them'.*[83]

Tooley believed that the 'family atmosphere' that he had inherited from Webster made Covent Garden unique:

> Not to understand this, or to ignore it could only change the environment and lead to a situation where performers and staff would see Covent Garden merely as a place to work . . . more than professionalism is needed to make great performing companies and opera houses.†

Crucial in maintaining the House's international standing and yet increasingly challenging in the prevailing financial climate, was the continued introduction of contemporary works into the repertoire. Stockhausen's *Donnerstag aus Licht* (*Thursday from Light*), premiered on 16 September 1985, had survived the discussions about which new productions to abandon. It was an extremely complex and costly work to produce, involving electronic music, forty microphones and a large cast, as well as reduced seat prices. It had also cost Tooley salt tears trying to fit the rehearsals into the pre-season period of the 1985 season, as well as keeping Stockhausen happy.[84] In a spectacular production, directed by Michael Bogdanov and designed by Maria Björnson, it won over critics, who found it increasingly impressive and engaging as its four-and-a-half hours wore on, in spite of what Milnes described as its 'massive egotism'.‡[85]

In April 1987 Nicholas Hytner produced Aulis Sallinen's *The King Goes Forth to France*, a joint commission of the Royal Opera, the Savonlinna Festival and the BBC. It was based on a play by Finnish poet Paavo Haavikko. With Bob Crowley's decor it was a 'spicy brew of farce and horror'. Hytner, who appreciated the new work, said of the opera, 'It chucks experience around and hurls it back at you in order to dislocate you and then relocate you.' He saw it as a

---

* David Syrus was made head of music at Covent Garden in 1993. He was also in the 1970s and 1980s on the music staff at Bayreuth, and at Salzburg from 1991. In 1999 he was assistant conductor on the San Francisco *Ring*.

† Tooley wrote that in 1971, when silver medals were introduced for those with twenty-five years' service, 10 per cent of the company were eligible (Tooley, op. cit., p. 236).

‡ In his *Isis* interview in February 1970 Davis had expressed the opinion that Stockhausen was 'beyond' him, that he felt that 'music is not just a series of noises, of assault and battery . . .' He added that it was too abstract, 'there is nothing tangible to grasp'.

contemporary fable with all the 'cruel sardonic wit that all sorts of modern writers are rediscovering in the idea of fable'. Opera, he believed, is the best medium for myth, and he compared the libretto to Tippett's *Midsummer Marriage*. Some time in the near future in a new Ice Age subservient people wait for a political master who turns into a tyrant. The king seizes power and takes his four fiancées, his population and his cannon, and invades France in a time warp Hundred Years War.[86]

Peter Heyworth found the music second-hand, with traces of Puccini, Janáček and Mussorgsky or Shostakovich and although lacking in personal identity not without dramatic timing.[87] David Cairns, however, found that it made a 'distinctly dim impression' with neither libretto nor music revealing a sense of direction.[88] The search for new work had been disappointing. Tooley, reflecting in his memoirs, wrote that there was not the flourishing of English composers that had been hoped for, nor sufficient funding for young composers: 'Too often money set aside for a contemporary work has been swallowed up in the mêlée of budget balancing.' There was no place in Thatcher's economic world for the arts to 'find new and stimulating ways of communication'.*[89]

Davis wanted to renew his contract, but the Board and Tooley had decided in 1982 that it was time for a change. Moser, who would have been content to let him continue, later recalled that Davis was 'upset when it came to an end'.[90] Davis reflected, 'I don't think I stayed too long – I enjoyed the last five years very much . . . things were getting worse but we had a wonderful group of people working there – it became almost a family.'[91] In his last Annual Report (1985–86) Moser wrote of Davis's 'engaging informality coupled with the power and enthusiasm of his music making'.

Tooley, Moser and Berlin had met Muti in 1982, and had found him not only 'most impressive', but also 'keenly interested in the idea of becoming music director'. His main concern centred on the amount of time he could give to the House.[92] He therefore decided against the

---

* Even at reduced seat prices *The King Goes Forth* had only played to 70 per cent houses.

position, taking on the direction of La Scala in 1986. Discussions with Zubin Mehta had been initiated, but according to Tooley he had declined because of his 'poor standing with the London critics'. Abbado declined because he did not want the administrative chores after his experience at La Scala.[93] Moser recalled the deliberations about the new music director. 'We did flirt with Barenboim,' he recalled, 'but he turned it down.' Haitink had doubted his own suitability, saying a decade earlier that he felt a music director should 'start very young, work through the whole thing from the bottom to the top . . . I don't think I have the temperament for running an opera house – as you know you need about five extra skins.'[94] But as the discussions continued it seemed to Moser and Tooley that Haitink would be the right man, with Jeffrey Tate as principal conductor to deal with planning.

Bernard Haitink's appointment as principal conductor from 1986 to 1988 and as music director from 1988 was announced in December 1983 when he was still music director at Glyndebourne. In 1985 Hall became Glyndebourne's artistic director, taking over from John Cox. Hall wrote of Haitink's Covent Garden appointment, 'I think he knew it could turn out to be a poison chalice, but felt that it was a risk he had to take: it gave him the opportunity to conduct Wagner.'[95]

Together with John Bury, the Hall–Haitink team at Glyndebourne had continued to work creatively with an enchanting *Midsummer Night's Dream* in May 1981. It was one of Glyndebourne's greatest successes 'evoking an atmosphere that made the opera house and the gardens as much a part of Shakespeare's enchanted Athens as the set'. Bury created 'a ravishing picture of moonshine with black trees and bushes against a milky background'.[96] There was also a flesh-and-blood *Carmen* with Maria Ewing and a brilliant staging of *Albert Herring*. There was only one less than successful production – *Simon Boccanegra* in 1986. Charles Osborne was moved to write in the light of Hall's achievements, 'Surely the Royal Opera's worst moment in its modern, post-war period was when it failed to retain Sir Peter as its artistic director.'

Hall's Glyndebourne life, however, became gradually less contented and fruitful after Moran Caplat's retirement in 1981. His relationship with the new general administrator, Brian Dickie, failed to provide him with the support he needed to flourish and his many commitments elsewhere sometimes prevented him from overseeing productions other than his own.[97] In the late Eighties, Hall embarked on a second Mozart–da Ponte series with Simon Rattle and the Orchestra of the Age of Enlightenment, and without John Bury, who had retired after an extraordinarily creative and inspired collaboration of thirty-five years. The new, *Figaro*, designed by John Gunter, failed to recapture the excitement of Hall's earlier work. Hall resigned in 1991 when he was not consulted about Peter Sellars's decision to remove the dialogue from *The Magic Flute*.

Colin Davis's last new production as music director on 2 July 1986 was Serban's and Jacobs's *Fidelio*, after their great success with *Turandot*. At Davis's request the first night was a Midland Bank Prom performance with Davis in shirtsleeves. He received a storm of booing, however, when he took his curtain – as so often, the music director had shouldered the abuse aimed at the stage director or designer, who did not accompany him. Loppert found the production 'so roundly unworthy of the piece that Wednesday's performance came as near collapsing in ignominy as the sublime work ever could'.[98] Critics and audience particularly objected to the death mask of Beethoven in front of which children pranced during Leonore Number 3, as well as the finale, with assorted angels and devils and a big bat of death. Even the Board found 'the chill Blakean vision completely at odds with the warmth and idealism of the work', in spite of a 'very beautiful musical performance'.[99] Serban later revised it, throwing out the good with the bad according to Tooley. Max Loppert in the *Financial Times* made a general criticism of Davis, sometimes also made of Levine at the Met. As a good team member Davis sometimes seemed to be conducting the production 'and go dull in apparent sympathy with the loose, dull happenings on the stage'.[100] Also like Levine, and although Covent Garden had far fewer opera nights than did the Met, Davis sometimes felt the demands made of an international opera house were too great, telling John Higgins in 1986 that he was 'expected to run what is tantamount to a year-long festival and it is just not possible'.[101]

That season, in July 1986, the new *Der fliegende Holländer*, directed by Mike Ashman and designed by David Fielding, was also severely criticised. Taking place in a nuclear-powered submarine and a clinical, rope-making factory, with Fielding's familiar props including fluorescent light bulbs and mob-caps, the production betrayed, in Cairns's words, 'little engagement with the characters'.[102] In spite of his own reservations, Moser defended the impulse to experiment in the 1985–86 Annual Report: 'Innovation at Covent Garden inevitably causes more extreme reaction than elsewhere if it fails to please. But we must take care not to retreat into the safe and conventional.' Tooley admitted that although the House placed 'stricter constraints' than most Houses on producers, there were limits as to how far this could be pursued. After another 'disappointing' new production – Rudolf Noelte's *Manon* in June 1987 – Tooley told the opera subcommittee that it had been 'the worst production period he could recall'.*[103]

There had, however, also been fine achievements during the season. On 17 November 1986 Haitink had conducted his first new production as music director designate. It was Yuri Lyubimov's *Jenůfa*, Max Loppert writing that it was 'an evening to make one grateful to be at Covent Garden'. He referred to the production's 'surging theatricality' and its 'psychological and social honesty of vision' as well as its 'poetic lyricism of sound'. Loppert described the scene: 'A bare stage is bounded by revolving panels, a blank backcloth, and a small grave with cross placed permanently over the prompt box.' During the run, he added, Haitink's interpretation 'became magical'.[104]

In January 1987 the company had a great triumph: Elijah Moshinsky's new production of *Otello*, conducted by Kleiber and sung by Domingo, when staging, conducting, acting and singing came together in what Milnes called a 'shining example of the art that

---

* David Syrus wrote a paper on 22 July 1987: 'Thoughts on the music staff'. In it he wrote that he believed that production values had slipped lately because of what he referred to as 'a Germanic attitude' among guest and staff producers whereby the music and language staff were not involved in the creative process nor encouraged to make comments. A succession of producers, like Schlesinger, Serban, Noelte and Terry Hands had a 'sketchy knowledge of the language they're working in'. He was deliberately keeping the music staff numbers down for reasons of economy and also so that there would be space in the schedule to try out 'good young reps' who were freelance (Royal Opera House Archives, Opera Subcommittee, 19/4/2).

conceals art adding up to one of the Royal Opera's great evenings'. It vindicated Moshinsky's belief in an honest and direct approach. Tooley appreciated Moshinsky's work, writing that he 'understood the need to create productions which were the product of sound research and of examination with fresh eyes and ears'. A plan for a *Ring* produced by Moshinsky and designed by Nolan was, however, vetoed by the incoming music director, Haitink, who had not got on well with Moshinsky during the *Lohengrin* rehearsals.*

Before his retirement in 1986, Claus Moser revealed plans for phase two of the extension to the theatre. Stage machinery had to be replaced and the ballet company and opera house staff housed under the Covent Garden roof. Moser was determined that the new House should integrate the ballet company, which was increasingly frustrated with its second-class status. Two wealthy Board members, John Sainsbury and Vivien Duffield, would supervise the redevelopment appeal.†

In 1984 architect Jeremy Dixon had won an open competition to design the redevelopment, together with engineers Building Design Partnership. In 1986 Dixon presented the plans for modernising the stage, building and ballet rehearsal rooms, for providing a second small auditorium, and for completing Inigo Jones's Market Square. On 30 June 1987 Westminster City Council gave permission for phase two of the development. At that time the Council was insisting on underground parking and on commercial buildings, which would be constructed to help to pay for the development. The architects disliked the office blocks, which would create a monolithic unity in an area they saw as individual buildings in harmony and conjunction with Barry's auditorium. Furthermore, there was not enough space both to

* The Opera Subcommittee congratulated Tooley on mounting such a 'superb' *Otello* just a year after a planned Peter Hall production collapsed because Domingo cancelled following the Mexican earthquake (Royal Opera House Archives, Opera Subcommittee, 19/4/20, 12.2.87). Tooley later recalled that it was one of Nolan's 'last ambitions to design the *Ring*' and that it was a 'huge pity that the project had been lost' (Interview, 15.4.02).
† Vivien Duffield was the daughter of property developer Sir Charles Clore, whose empire at the time of his death in 1979 included Selfridges and high street shoe shops. Clore had entrusted her with the running of his charitable foundation. In 2000 she gave £7 million to help the education departments of major galleries.

provide the office areas and to meet the House's technical needs. There was also much opposition to the development of office blocks in an area which contravened the Greater London Council planning guidelines.

At the beginning of 1987 the Board decided not to renew Tooley's contract, although Haitink wrote, strongly urging the Board to keep him on.[105] Tooley pressed Moser to find a successor as soon as possible. Among the potential candidates were Hugues Gall, director of the Grand Théâtre in Geneva, Brian McMaster of Welsh National Opera, Michael Hampe, the Cologne intendant, Paul Findlay and Anthony Russell-Roberts, the administrative director of the Royal Ballet. Although he was a very strong candidate, Gall declined even to come over for an interview, judging the difference in culture in France and England, both in levels of subsidy and management, to be too great.*

Moser and Forman had decided on Jeremy Isaacs, who was a highly successful television producer and had been chief executive of Channel 4 from 1981 to 1987. According to Moser, he had suggested Isaacs as a Board member with the possibility of him taking on the role of general director in mind. Moser found him 'incredibly knowledgeable and a genuine impresario – a wonderful showman in the best sense'. He was also, according to Moser, in tune with modern communication methods like television.[106] There was a general feeling that someone with a background in television, rather than an arts administrator, would be 'more attuned to financial imperatives', with 'the ability to market and the ability to control costs'.[107] Moser recalled, 'John Tooley's relative weakness was financial control' and he added, 'To focus his mind on the financial crisis that was looming up clearly for me, because I am more financial, was quite difficult.'[108] The Board agreed to Isaacs's appointment with the proviso that he would be compatible with the incoming chairman of the Board, Sir John Sainsbury.

The Covent Garden position was not Isaacs's first choice. He asked

* The selection panel included Moser, Lord Gibson, Denis Forman, Colette Clark and Brian Nicholson. Gall had worked at the French Ministry of Culture before becoming Liebermann's assistant at the Paris Opéra.

if he could wait until the decision about the new director general of the BBC was made, and only when he did not get that position did he agree to take on Covent Garden. Isaacs left Channel 4 earlier than expected, in December 1987, and shadowed Tooley until 1 September 1988, when he officially became general director.

Moser himself retired at the end of the 1986–87 season and was replaced by Sainsbury for a five-year period. Married to ballerina Anya Linden, Sainsbury's main interest was the ballet. He was later described by Jeremy Isaacs as 'one of Britain's most successful businessmen, who, with his two brothers had given the nation the new Sainsbury wing at the National Gallery'.[109]

On his retirement, Moser, in an interview in *The Times*, begged the government 'to think again, and as positively as possible, about arts funding'. People working in the arts, contrary to Ministers' beliefs, were 'responsible, cost-conscious, for the most part lowly paid and dedicated to serving the community'. Moser once again vainly repeated his view that governments should be proud of Britain's success in the arts since the war.

The new chairman, John Sainsbury, had a very different approach to the government. He was determined, in Isaacs's words, to 'demonstrate to Margaret Thatcher and to her government that the arts were capable of helping themselves, by increasing steeply, self-generated income'.[110] Sainsbury immediately decided on a 40 per cent increase in seat prices in the 1987–88 season, as a result of which the company made a surplus of £101,000. The year's expected deficit had been reduced from £1.2 million to £522,000, in spite of the Royal Ballet's losses on tour. The 1987–88 Annual Report showed that Arts Council funding then accounted for 46 per cent of total revenue as opposed to 54 per cent in 1983–84. In this Annual Report, Tooley's last, he deplored this 'very substantial increase in seat prices', as it had put them 'in some parts of the House, beyond the reach of many people'. This in turn 'put even greater pressure on the less expensive seats and is causing greater disappointment as more people fail to obtain tickets in the balcony stalls and amphitheatre'.

In his report, the outgoing director described the 'hand-to-mouth existence' the House led not knowing what its funding was to be from year to year. He spoke of the 'irony' of the Arts Council now proposing a three-year grant at a time when inflation ensured that it would decline in real terms.

As well as hiking up seat prices, Sainsbury also sought to increase sponsorship, bringing in Alex Alexander, chairman of Allied Lyons, to be chairman of the Royal Opera House Trust to head fund-raising, a role in which he had been outstandingly successful at Glyndebourne. In October 1987 Alexander reported £360,000 funding for *Entführung*, *L'Italiana* and *Parsifal*. Isaacs told the Board on 29 March 1988 that the aim was to raise £5 million by the 1990–91 season. Some members of the Board were concerned that Arts Council funding as a total proportion of revenue would fall even further to 41 per cent in 1990–91.[111]

The new chairman was determined to institute stronger financial controls. In September 1987 Sainsbury amalgamated the former finance, opera and public affairs committees in order to integrate artistic and financial planning.* He also sought to maintain Priestley's 'cost centre' concept. In his 1987–88 review Sainsbury described the progress of the 'cost centre' arrangement and the working of the subsidiary Boards covering opera and ballet, which had been set up the previous year and were to underscore the separate accounting of the three companies.

By demonstrating the House's new self-reliance, Sainsbury hoped for a deal with the government. 'In view', he wrote in the 1987–88 report, 'of the initiative we are putting into raising greater income not only from private sponsorship but also through new retail and catering activities, we believe we have every reason to expect a significant addition under this new Arts Council policy of greater reward for those who most help themselves.'

This was to prove a costly miscalculation. Once management had proved that Covent Garden could help itself, extra funding became an even more remote possibility, while the sharp increase in seat prices was to cause irreparable damage to the House's public image during the next decade. In March 1987 *The Times* began what was to be an increasingly virulent press attack on Covent Garden. It published an

---

* When *Andrea Chénier* was cancelled because of Carreras's illness in January 1988, Sainsbury asked the administration to make sure that when changes were made to the repertory for any reason, an estimate of the budgetary effects should be made immediately and explained to the Board (Royal Opera House Archives, Opera Board, 19/4/3, 12.1.88).

article by Alan Peacock, chairman of the Scottish Arts Council, which warned that Covent Garden would have its subsidy cut if it did not become more accessible. Rodney Milnes, with foresight, pointed out that 'since there is no rational argument for subsidising the rich at their pleasure' the company would 'seem increasingly unworthy of receiving support of any kind'. He concluded, 'One hates to ponder the logical outcome of this particular vicious circle.'*

The future looked bleak. 'Quite frankly,' Tooley wrote, 'I don't envy the new management, but at least they will have the joy of working with the thousand men and women who go to make up a great institution, people whose energies are directed towards the success of this House and who care passionately about it.' Maintaining the standards of an international House would be a huge, perhaps impossible, challenge in the next decade. Hugues Gall had said in the Priestley report, 'In the pyramid of British lyrical life, the ROH must be the summit and not the base.' As the Jeremy Isaacs–Bernard Haitink era approached, the financial clouds were already threatening this apparently incontrovertible truth, as well as threatening the devoted workforce who gave it substance.

---

* Rodney Milnes had become editor of *Opera* in 1986.

TWENTY-ONE

THE MET 1980–90
'That Plush and Crystal Whorehouse'

THE MET was also faced by major financial problems in the 1980s and was looking for radical solutions. On 15 May 1980 the first drive of the Met's Endowment Fund campaign was launched by Frank Taplin in the grand tier. The appeal was to continue until the centennial in 1984, when the target of $100 million would be reached. The endowment was to be permanently invested to generate annual income, but it would not obviate the need for annual fund-raising at increased levels.* The goal was $100 million, of which $33 million had already been raised. John McKinley, the chairman of Texaco, who was to be national chairman, announced Texaco's $5 million leadership gift. He built a strong team to drive the campaign forward.

Anthony Bliss later said that the announcement of the Centennial Endowment Fund might have helped to give the unions the false impression that the company was 'rolling in wealth' and thus caused a 'real confrontation as a result'.[1] Volpe had already warned Taplin in December that trust between management and unions needed to be built up and that the negotiations would be 'very tough indeed'. He was right and the confrontation was not long in coming. That autumn the Board failed to reach agreement after nine months of negotiations with the orchestra and other unions. Philip Sipser, the arts-labour lawyer representing the Musicians' Union (Local 802), said, 'Just as the Met is seeking an endowment for its future, so we are seeking a decent wage and work week for our future.'[2] The orchestra's main – and to the

---

* Taplin later explained that $80 million was for the endowment of which only the income could be used, and $20 million was for certain works in the building.

management unacceptable – demand, was for four performances a week instead of five.* It was, Sipser said, a question of 'the quality of work life' and not just of wages as it had been ten years before.

The Met management argued that the demand for a four-performance week would cost an additional $750,000 annually because of the need to hire a pool of 'steady regulars' and management were worried that if the other unions made similar demands the cost could reach $5 million. Management's final offer was 9.5 per cent that year and 9 per cent the next, in a two-year contract, as well as improvements such as an additional week of holidays in the second year and increases in the touring allowance. Unable to reach agreement, Bliss announced the closure of the House on 29 September, explaining that acceptance of the unions' demands would return the Met 'to the dark ages, season after season, burdened with overwhelming deficits'. He was adamant that nothing should threaten his Endowment Fund drive, which would be the case if the administration 'knowingly entered into a contract that would then produce a substantial deficit beyond our potential fund-raising capacity'. Management's final offer was not put to a secret ballot and Taplin was saddened that the moderates in the orchestra had not made their voices heard.[3]

President Carter appealed to both sides to resume talks on 2 October. Levine later said that when he saw plans for *Turandot, Samson, Pique Dame* and *Così* unravelling, he thought of resigning.[4] The 1980–81 season would have been 'one of the best periods in the history of the House' he told the Board on 18 September.[5]

There was bitterness on both sides after the autumn breakdown of negotiations. One cause was the rumour that the Board were considering closing down the House altogether in order to cancel all existing contracts and start a new company under more favourable financial conditions. Bernard Holland later reported Bliss as having pounded his fist on the table and threatening to close down the House for the whole season. Bliss reported that a management lawyer had

* Other demands were an increase of 12.5 per cent each year in a two-year contract, first-class hotel accommodation on tour and two more weeks of paid holiday. Met orchestral players earned a basic pay of $525 weekly for a forty-four-week season. With extra services such as telecasts, the average annual wage was $30,000 a year according to the unions and $37,000 according to the Met.

been threatened with violence. The unions called for Bliss's resignation.[6] There was a background of class bitterness, the Board representing the new American establishment – partners of banks, legal firms and top corporations – and the musicians being men and women of working- or middle-class families with many ethnic groups represented. Taplin, although he felt that the issue of class was overstressed, was nonetheless aware that the orchestra perceived itself to be 'the oppressed dregs of the Metropolitan Opera family'.

Final agreement was reached with the unions on 13 October, and on 14 November Bliss announced that there would, after all, be a 1980–81 season. Management accepted the principle of the four-performance week, but on the basis that members of the orchestra would give five 'services' a week instead of five performances, i.e. four performances and one rehearsal. In order to obtain the four-performance week, the orchestra compromised by agreeing to reduce the first year's pay rise from the demanded 9.5 per cent to 9 per cent and to eliminate paid vacations. Taplin and Bliss were relieved that the contract was for four years and would go beyond the centennial.* It was Taplin who contacted the chairman of the orchestra negotiating committee after the strike in order to restore good relations, as there was 'too much bitterness on both sides' for Bliss to have made the call. Taplin gave a gift of a new cafeteria near the stage, writing in his diary that there was a need to build a 'sense of community within the Met organisation'.[7]

In order to restore relations with the unions, Bliss made Volpe management's labour relations chief. Volpe insisted that he would be the sole negotiator, with no lawyer involved, and succeeded in establishing multi-year contracts negotiated six to nine months ahead of schedule. Instead of saying that management could not afford certain demands, Volpe would say, 'I could never agree to that. 1. It wouldn't be a prudent business decision and 2. if we could afford it I wouldn't agree to it anyway. The answer is "No".'[8] In October 1981 Bliss reported high morale and thanked Volpe for the 'better working relationships in the House'. The company committee, made up of forty representatives of the unions, was also meeting regularly.[9]

---

* Wage increases would be of 9, 9, 8.5, 8.5 per cent over the next four years, with a possible increase to a maximum of 10.5 per cent in years three and four.

After the strike, Ingpen somehow managed 'to fit the jigsaw back together again'.[10] On 10 December 1980 the Met finally opened its season with a concert performance of Mahler's *Resurrection* Symphony, followed by John Dexter's highly praised *Lulu* on 12 December, starring Teresa Stratas, followed by performances of *Carmelites*. Alan Rich in *New York* contrasted the 'embarrassing' orchestral evening of Mahler with the powerful Dexter shows at a time when management was increasingly tending to speak of him as 'superfluous'.[11] Porter called *Lulu* 'the most faithful presentation of Berg's opera I have seen'. He referred to Levine's 'long broad line, a vivid feeling for passing dramatic incident, and the ability to find and express the sense of each particular sound'.[12] The strike had destroyed the proposed *Ring* cycle, as well as the opening *Turandot* with Pavarotti and Caballé. As a result of the strike the loss for the season was 4.5 million dollars.

After the strike it became clear that the House's new orientation would not include Dexter's participation. Dexter had set out his concern at his growing isolation in a memorandum to Bliss, written during the strike, on 24 September 1980. Since *Mahagonny* in 1979, and after Ingpen's arrival, he had become aware of 'a rift' and lack of contact between Levine and himself, and that his 'authority has been undermined within the House'. Management muddles, he wrote, were resulting from his being left out of planning discussions. He had been shocked to discover that Levine had engaged Zeffirelli for *Bohème* without consulting him, before they could afford him and without 'budgetary controls in his contract'. As a result, Zeffirelli was producing a *Bohème* which 'not only cannot tour in its present state but is costing half a million'. Dexter thought this was 'iniquitous in view of the gargantuan efforts of other directors and designers who were aiming at economy, style and lightness'. It was a 'monument to bad planning' which he found 'particularly galling' as *Bohème* had been 'one of the first things I mentioned to you as something I would like to do . . .'*

Dexter had received no reply to letters he had written suggesting the repertoire he would like to do. Nor had there been any clarification of the Executive Committee's dictum 'that experiments (à la *Ballo*)

---

* Dexter wondered if he had said something which Levine thought inappropriate when he had said that *Bohème* was 'really all about keeping warm in the cold if you have someone to cuddle up to'.

with major works are forbidden'. No one, he argued, had yet described to him 'the difference between an experiment, a success and a failure. *Abduction* was an experiment, a success, so was *Don Carlos; Mahagonny* was traditionalist.' Dexter would like to 'discuss their reasoning with them as it is clear they do not understand mine'.

Dexter's days at the Met were numbered. People who worked there remembered him as an acerbic and difficult individual, and he had received from Bliss frequent complaints about his behaviour. Bliss suggested a new relationship whereby Dexter would concentrate on planning the future staging of new works and touring, as well as giving Bliss advice on artistic matters. Dexter was still not clear, however, what the 'lines of authority' were to be, and did not want to continue with 'responsibility and no power'. He proposed forming a close technical committee of Joe Volpe, Gil Wechsler and Joe Clark, who could comment on plans early.

Dexter's suggestion was not taken up. Instead, in January 1981 Bliss was officially given the title of general manager, with three assistant managers, Ingpen in artistic administration, Volpe as operations director and Marilyn Shapiro in development and public affairs. Under them was Joseph Clark, as head of the technical department, and Phoebe Berkowitz, who became executive stage director. Dexter was 'relieved of his administrative responsibilities'. Bliss praised Dexter for identifying Volpe and others 'for leadership roles because of their extraordinary expertise', but explained in an *Opera News* interview that 'since this is a musical house, the primary selection of repertory and casting lies with Jimmy Levine assisted by Joan Ingpen and her staff'.[13]

Deeply frustrated, Dexter resigned as director of productions early in 1981, taking the title 'production adviser' and having decided to work only on the operas he had staged himself. He was contracted to do one new production a season until 1984. Bliss, when asked if he was 'sounding more and more like an old-fashioned general manager', responded, 'I don't feel that all the creativity and all the programming and planning must *start* in this office, but I feel it should *end* here.'[14]

Although Dexter was no longer involved in planning, his three short French pieces, Eric Satie's ballet *Parade*, Francis Poulenc's farce *Les Mamelles de Tirésias* and Ravel's *L'Enfant et les sortilèges* survived the strike and were premiered in March 1981. Dexter had intended to use the triple bill to keep the flame alive for twentieth-century works as well as 'so-called intimate works', which could be toured with ease and could even be taken to foreign festivals.[15] He also wanted to use the new ballet company and the children's chorus, and after working with children on opera in schools he hoped to bring more children into the audience.

Dexter, whose father had been wounded in the First World War and had died in 1965, was drawn to the works because they were all written in 1917–18. In a long letter to Manuel Rosenthal, the conductor, on 29 April 1980, he set out his thoughts on the pieces and the way in which he was working with David Hockney on the sets. For Dexter *Parade* was, in Richard Buckle's words, 'the doorway to the twentieth century, and that it opened out of that First World War'. He felt the evening was taking on a life of its own 'for the first time in a long while'.[16] He believed that children – created in *Mamelles*, as he explained to Rosenthal, to replace those lost in the 1914–18 war – could redeem the world, but that they must be redeemed by art. His aim was to present 'a full-scale display of the kind of totally illusionist theatre to which I believe opera belongs'.[17]

Dexter collaborated closely and happily with David Hockney and Manuel Rosenthal the conductor, although Rudolf Nureyev walked out of *Parade*, disagreeing with Dexter's ideas.[18] Nureyev had been demanding trucks on stage but, Dexter wrote to Bliss, 'it is desperately urgent for us to keep the stage clear of impedimenta, leaving the space clear for action'.[19]

Hockney's sets made a great impact. In his stage work he was determined to break up 'the anti-pictorial movement' which had dominated the theatre for twenty-five years. He harked back to the 'wonderful *trompe-l'oeil* scenery of the nineteenth century, which psychology and photography had made unacceptable'.[20] He convinced Gil Wechsler, the Met's lighting director, to use coloured lights on painted sets of the same colour. 'When you put blue light on blue paint, it comes *alive*, as something *physical*.' In order not to swamp the works in the Met's vastness, Dexter explained, 'You put everything as far downstage as you can and make sure you have a backdrop for the voices to bounce off.'[21]

Critics were struck by the decor and production. Satie's *Parade* had First World War barbed wire and searchlights behind Hockney's beige-pink fleurs-de-lis on a powder-blue background, which looked like an 'arrangement of crosses on a military graveyard'. Ravel's *L'Enfant* was also full of invention and 'effervescence', matched by Manuel Rosenthal's music making. Poulenc's surrealist *Mamelles*, whose cast included Catherine Malfitano, was 'very amusing'.[22] The triple bill showed some critics, too late, that the 'Met need not restrict itself to the vocal or pageant blockbusters'.[23] *Wall Street Journal* critic Manuela Hoelterhoff had wondered if the works were more suited to the City Opera, but she had found her doubts vanishing.[24] Illusion and invention, economy and imagination were not, however, to be the basis of solvency, as Dexter had hoped. Instead the Met's stability was to be based on visual splendour, unashamed expenditure and a parade of reliable 'repertory fillers' of varying standard.

On 21 September 1981 the season opened with Scotto's Norma and a lavish party for 700 members of what Marilyn Shapiro called 'the Met family' from all over the country. Ticket sales reached $350,000, a record only surpassed on the opening of the new House. Domingo was a 'splendidly heroic' first-time Pollione, but Scotto had great trouble with the role and – in Rockwell's words – 'in the upper regions, intonation and vocal technique deserted her'.[25] Increasingly Scotto's detractors and supporters made themselves felt, a certain section of the standees referring to her as Renata Screecho, and on opening night she was greeted with boos and laughter. Groans could be heard even before she attempted a high note. Porter was convinced that Scotto's early 'delightful lyric soprano' had suffered from the move to the heavier repertory, and in spite of the power and earnestness of her delivery she often pushed her voice. '"Casta Diva" was a disaster', the repeated 'A's at the climax lapsing into what Porter termed 'curdled screams'.[26] She determinedly sang the remaining performances and took on *Il Trittico* later in the same season with greater success.

The public were not deterred by the critically poor start to the season. What Smith called an almost shameful 'repertory filler' performance of the 1958 *Butterfly* on 28 September sold 3,000 seats. Gilda

Cruz-Romo's Cio-Cio-San, wrote Smith, 'strains credibility to the limit when she appears looking like a sumo wrestler'. The staging and scenery showed signs of much wear. Levine was quoted as saying, after a performance had to be cancelled at the last moment, 'I have accepted artistic compromises this year that I would not ordinarily accept – just to keep the House open.'[27]

Zeffirelli's production of *La Bohème* on 14 December was the 'blockbuster' that Dexter had feared would totally undermine his efforts at economy, and finally laid to rest his plans for a leaner and more imaginative production style. Its $750,000 cost was, however, totally underwritten by Sybil Harrington, who adored Zeffirelli and shared his fondness for animals on stage. Joan Ingpen later recalled, 'After the strike, she really came to our rescue – she gave so much money.' She did not interfere, Bruce Crawford later explained, but she did 'want to do standard work that suited management, which needed to replace the existing productions, and she loved Zeffirelli's because she thought that they were beautiful'.[28] Zeffirelli's *Bohème*, although it did indeed go over budget, was viewed as a long-term investment. It was performed hundreds of times over many seasons and was to have a consistent box office average of well over 97 per cent. As Jonathan Friend, who was director of the rehearsal department, and was to take over from Joan Ingpen in 1983, later explained, 'The curtain goes up, the audience says, "Oh Yes, got it – I'm in there with them." '[29]

Zeffirelli, who had been staging *Bohème* for twenty years all over the world, said he had been inspired by the Met's revolving stage to formulate an idea that had been in his mind for some time. He wanted to show 'the fragility of the Bohemian group as against the large, grey French capital. While the garret is small and intimate, the public is treated to Parisian skies, roofs, chimneys and balconies. . . . I want to underline the helplessness and humanity of these nice young people lost in the large city.'

Moshinsky thought Zeffirelli had successfully resolved the perennial question: 'How do you do a garret with a stage that's like a football pitch? They had an inset house and in order to inset it you have to put it that far back.'[30] Porter, however, felt that Zeffirelli's theme had been so well realised that the resulting 'oddly distanced effect of the drama' was 'hardly Puccinian'. On the first night, applause drowned the music four times according to Porter.[31] Rockwell wrote that in Act Two there were 280 people on stage and added, 'The sheer lavishness of detail – and demonstrable expense to realise it – brought appreciative, nostalgic comments from the first night audience.' He said it was 'a production for people who come *wanting* to applaud the scenery'.[32]

Zeffirelli was more concerned with the visually grand gesture than psychological insight. In the video recording there is no indication of Zeffirelli having directed Teresa Stratas as Mimì. Although she sustained an appealing, resonant lyric sound that suits the big House, her stagecraft seems shallow and external. Scotto indulges in excess and overacting, which sends her Musetta beyond narcissism into the realms of melodrama, with very little evidence of vocal control.

Zeffirelli was as adamant that his approach was right as Dexter was about his. 'People who think that they can do better than previously, interpreting works of art in a new key, are very foolish,' Zeffirelli argued and he continued, 'The reason I am box office everywhere is because I am an enlightened conservative continuing the discourse of our grandfathers and fathers, renovating the texts but never betraying them.'[33] Zeffirelli and the management had gauged the Met audience correctly. Dexter had not.

Levine later spoke of himself as a fan of Zeffirelli's *Bohème*, describing the garret as a small space with a 'great acoustic' and believing that the Café Momus act had never been better produced.[34] But Ingpen was not certain that the new direction was 'altogether by Jim's wish. . . . If you've got two people fighting the finance general manager perhaps you can get something through but you can't if you're one person.'[35] Naturalistic and occasionally extravagant scenery, combined with occasional magnificent individual performances, were to compensate for less than integrated dramatic productions and resulted in a successful box office. Many years later Moshinsky reflected, 'The naturalistic wasn't naturalistic, it was just pretty – Disneyfied tourism: you're in Nuremberg, you're in Egypt, you're in China – it was dioramas – they didn't actually act as real people.'[36]

On 8 March 1982 the designer Günther Schneider-Siemssen and the director Otto Schenk, a team that was to produce many shows, particularly Wagner, in the late Eighties and Nineties, prepared *The*

Tales of Hoffmann. The audience went 'dizzy with applause' at 'Spalan-
zani's infinitely crammed laboratory of inventions, all in motion'.
Domingo ensured that there were queues waiting for tickets. He was,
in Henahan's words, 'the Hoffmann of Everywoman's dreams'.[37] Smith
agreed: 'This is of course Domingo's show and the effortless flow of
his voice at every point – it sounds in better condition than ever –
disguises the real craft he brings to the role . . . one of his finest roles
and he knows it.' Troyanos's Giulietta was 'seductively sung' and the
opera was excitingly conducted by Riccardo Chailly.[38] *Hoffmann*'s average attendance was 98.2 per cent, the average for the season 92 per
cent. In spite of the high box office, there was an estimated $1.8 million
variance due to 'serious overruns on new productions', especially
Bohème.[39]

During the 1981–82 season Levine conducted three of the five new
productions, the opening night, all gala events and all four televised
operas. But he could not conduct every night and the roster of conductors for the 1983–84 season, apart from Klaus Tennstedt conducting
Fidelio, did not include any of the conductors whose absence had
already been commented on. Donal Henahan felt that the repeated
cheering at Tennstedt's performance was 'perhaps an expression of
gratitude at finding one of the world's foremost conductors in the
Metropolitan pit, even as a passing guest'. His performance was one
of 'heart-stopping melodrama and a musical line that never fell slack
for a moment'.[40]

Levine's work with the orchestra continued to develop its strengths.
In the early Eighties, he told Patrick J. Smith, he was reasonably content
with the orchestra's Verdi and Wagner, but that it was 'just in the ball
park' when it came to Mozart, a shortcoming he was determined to
remedy.[41] 'By working on one Mozart opera and then another and
another, then repeating the first one and adding a new one,' Levine
later explained, 'this gradual way of making the knowledge of the
repertoire go deeper and deeper into the company not only trained it
to a much higher capacity but also gave us a much better consistency.'[42]
For Levine, Mozart and Verdi constituted 'the pillars of the operatic
repertoire'. He saw it as 'a moral thing in the sense that there is a

wholeness in the approach of these people to the human soul'.[43] In January 1982 he expressed the wish that Così, for example, could be heard in more intimate surroundings than the Met provided. He called the work an essential part of the repertoire and regretted that it had to be performed in the large auditorium so long as the 'Piccolo Met' remained unbuilt.

The new production of Così in January 1982 was graceful and highlighted 'ensemble singing and fluidity of pacing'. Colin Graham at last repaired the English directors' reputation for perversity or gentility. His was a realistic approach, taking into account 'the work's innate humanity and ambivalence rather than its buffo artificiality'. Te Kanawa's Fiordiligi was 'supremely moving and gorgeously sung'. Henahan put her 'in the great tradition of Mozart women'. James Morris's Guglielmo was vocally a bit gruff and brassy but 'able to cannon forth to give of his emotions'. Kathleen Battle was Despina.[44] Henahan found Maria Ewing as Dorabella to be 'an irresistible comedian' who reminded him alternately of Leslie Caron and Olive Oyl. Her partnership with Te Kanawa brought back memories of Christa Ludwig and Elisabeth Schwarzkopf in the same roles.[45]

Levine's affection for Mozart and his attention to orchestral balance, dynamic levels and emotional nuance were revealed in a recording of Così, which was made with the Vienna Philharmonic for Deutsche Grammophon in 1989. In contrast to Krips and Erich Kleiber's Mozart, however, Levine tended to emphasise downbeats to the detriment of the subtle phrase structure. Pacing in this recording was often questionable, the charm and line of Mozart's music too often blunted. In 'Come scoglio', a tricky aria for Te Kanawa as Fiordiligi, Levine abetted the soprano's too-careful steps by slowing the tempo down. In contrast, Despina's 'Una donna a quindici anni' moved at an insensitively rapid pace, passing over melodic subtleties and textual irony.

Levine was, however, dedicated to Mozart and his devotion was shared by Jean-Pierre Ponnelle, with whom he collaborated in October 1982 for the Met premiere of Idomeneo. Works new to the Met were to prove more acceptable if they hosted an all-star cast. Idomeneo fitted the bill with Pavarotti as Idomeneo, Behrens as Elektra, Ileana Cotrubas as Ilia and Frederica von Stade as Idamante. Robert Jackson called it a 'brilliant musico-theatrical experience', successfully blending classic and baroque, and clearly delineating character with costume, acting and interaction. Ponnelle set the work in decaying classical ruins with the head of Neptune lowering behind, controlling events, and he used a stylised chorus to powerful effect. Levine's conducting was, according to Jackson, of 'Beethovenesque tragic intensity while maintaining suppleness of texture and chamber music delicacy for accompaniments with his finely attuned elegant orchestra'.[46] Henahan, however, found Levine's a 'large-scaled kind of Mozart'.* Ponnelle returned to direct *Clemenza* in 1984.

On 18 November 1982 Peter Hall's *Macbeth* was even worse received than Moshinsky's *Ballo* had been. According to Mayer, it was 'rubbished' by the critics and caused havoc in the audience. Donal Henahan in the *New York Times* said that it 'may just be the worst production to struggle on to the Metropolitan opera stage in modern history'.[47] 'I did it', Hall later reflected, 'as an all-out naive early romantic show.'[48] He explained: 'I attempted to take it back to nineteenth-century melodrama, which, rather more than Shakespeare, is at its heart.' It was, he said, 'close to the world of the Gothic novel and *Freischütz* romantic melodrama – that's why it has all those ballets and all those witches'. Hall continued:

> Met audiences had become used to a very heavily cut and Shakespeareanised version of the opera, deliberately short on fantasy. So what we presented, which included warlocks, sprites, goblins, flying witches and a full ballet – all the romantic vocabulary – affronted them. They thought we were mocking Verdi.
>
> At the first night there were not only catcalls; fights broke out in the audience between those who approved and those who did not. Peter Shaffer got thumped on the head with someone's programme when he loudly voiced his enthusiasm.[49]

Andrew Porter defended Hall in one of his learned *New Yorker* articles, explaining that Verdi had intended the opera to be 'in the *genere fantastico*'. Hall was, he wrote, 'perhaps the first modern director to attempt the witches of Verdi's description'. Even Hecate, wearing noth-

---

* *Idomeneo* was performed in the 1781 Munich version with cuts, including Idamante's 'Nò, la morte'.

ing but an illuminated tiara, seemed to Porter 'an authentic and beautiful nineteenth-century vision'. Even he had to admit, however, that the latex dummy three Oracles, which caused much mirth when they emerged from the cauldron, were 'ill-designed . . . and did look rather comic'.*[50] Sherrill Milnes 'sang beautifully', wrote Martin Mayer.

By the time of its revival in January 1984, as with Moshinsky's *Ballo*, Hall's *Macbeth* had become almost unrecognisable. Paul Mills, a House director, made crucial changes, including eliminating the flying witches and the cardboard apparitions from the cauldron. Gone too, wrote Smith, were Bury's 'beetling expressionist sets' – some of the most individual designs ever done for the Met. The result was that the revival had 'the air of a quasi-normal production'.[51] Jonathan Friend later said, 'By removing the things that the audience had found offensive it became very bland – there was then no point of view.'[52] It was not unusual for idiosyncratic or unusual shows to be transformed into 'Met' shows. A close observer considered that *Carmelites* was one of the few shows they 'didn't manage to water down'. In 1987, after substantial changes to his production of *Carmen* insisted upon by Baltsa, Hall asked Crawford to remove his name from both the *Carmen* and *Macbeth* programmes, writing that the *Carmen* changes represented 'the most awful rat-bag of old opera clichés' and that management had 'eloquently demonstrated its contempt' for his work.[53] Hall was bitter, later recalling of the Met, 'It's a factory – if you can deliver a large enough gesture on time, fine. If you are trying something difficult or dangerous . . . I wouldn't work there again.'[54]

Levine's control over what went on the stage was now nearly complete. Dexter revealed his bitterness about Levine in his diary on 25 March 1983: 'I do not enjoy the political atmosphere he creates and the relentless pursuit of popularity in which he drowns himself.'†[55]

---

* Porter first wrote for the *New Yorker* in 1972. While living in New York in the 1970s and 1980s he undertook some university teaching and was editor of the American Institute for Verdi Studies newsletter. Porter returned to England to write for the *Observer* in 1992.

† Johanna Fiedler in describing Levine's 'benevolent detachment' quotes Richard Dyer, a writer on the *Boston Globe*, on his friend Levine: 'Total friendliness as a way of guarding yourself is a Midwestern trait.' Fiedler adds, 'Everyone speaks of him with affection – the press, the public, his orchestra, the singers, the Met staff – and refers to him as Jimmy. But no one knows him' (*Molto Agitato*, p. 270).

Levine – a man who, in the words of his biographer 'hates confrontations' and works surrounded by 'individuals who are prepared to keep things moving smoothly and with the minimum friction' – was indeed the polar opposite of Dexter.[56] Later Levine said that Dexter's early enthusiasm for getting things right at the Met had diminished and that he had changed. He became, in Levine's words, 'one of the most irascible, difficult, unconstructive, overreactive, negative people to work with I ever met'. He gave credit, however, to Dexter's contribution, describing his work as 'always knowledgeable, always stimulating, always with a kernel of genius and brilliance'. Dexter also provided the Met with some of the House's classic productions, especially in the more modern repertoire. Levine concluded, 'I loved the guy and I adored working with him, and for quite a while it was very stimulating. Little by little it became increasingly impossible to work with him successfully.'*[57]

In September 1983 the forty-year-old Levine was negotiating a contract for a further five years beyond 1986, telling Taplin that life at the Met was 'tough and demanding' and that his 'ultimate goal was to direct a symphony orchestra'.[58] As a result of these negotiations Levine was given the title artistic director beginning in 1986–87. He was to be responsible for 'all musical and artistic aspects of the Metropolitan Opera'. He would choose all repertory, casting directors and designers, and decide day-to-day artistic policy, with the power to make oral commitments to artists and directors. Financial and contractual authority would remain with the general manager. Met officials described the new position as a normalisation of a de facto situation.[59] Mayer in *Fortune* magazine reported that in order to get him to sign the five-year contract covering 1986–91, the Met had to give Levine control over everything that was to appear on the Met stage. Levine explained

---

* Arnold Wesker, the British playwright, who worked with Dexter, described how Dexter could 'switch his abrasive warmth on and off with alarming, confusing and unpredictable rapidity'. He also described his 'bullying', how he would find a whipping boy or girl in the cast upon whom to 'exercise his scorn, vaunt his reductive wit, vent his ill-temper for what had gone wrong the night before with his love life . . .' On the other hand, Wesker wrote, 'when he was high on his cleverness, his skill, his imagination, when he buzzed with elation from an inspired day's work, he was electrifying in a way that few other directors I know have been, and it communicated itself to the cast who would then give him their all' (Wesker, *As Much as I Dare*, p. 505).

that 'the separation of musical and dramatic' had become intolerable to him.[60] He would no longer have to conduct productions with which he was 'not in sympathy'.[61] There had not been a director of productions before Dexter, Levine later recalled, and there was not one after his demise.[62] Jane Boutwell writing in *Opera News*, had asked Taplin if the Met had not become 'a sort of cultural General Motors'. Taplin had replied that he was confident Levine's artistic vision would ensure high standards.[63]

With power went responsibility and much administrative work. Sometimes Levine admitted to the pressures, telling Mayer in 1983, 'People don't digest what it means to do seven performances every bloody week. . . . This is not like Covent Garden, where they do only two operas for six weeks, or Vienna where the only thing that gets rehearsed at all is the new production. We don't have the relief of ballet evenings, or the relief of a small House.'[64]

Levine's dominant position at the Met emphasised the exciting fact that here was a successor to Bernstein, a native-born conductor who was taking his role seriously and full-time: 'I look at the press and sometimes they criticise. But mostly they approve and encourage, and when you consider that I don't have the stamp of coming from a foreign country, I am not old and not a grey-haired man with a beard, I feel appreciated for what I do.'[65] Far from suffering from the stigma of not being foreign, Levine was sometimes idolised for being American. Robert C. Marsh wrote, 'James Levine is the international symbol of the stature of American talent, American musical education and American musical institutions, enthusiastically welcomed in the citadels of European musical culture because their guardians are fully aware that, in his generation, Europe has not produced his equal.'[66]

Since Ingpen had taken over and instituted longer-term planning, the roster of singers had improved. The 1982–83 season included Te Kanawa and Kurt Moll in *Rosenkavalier*, Eva Marton and Domingo in *Gioconda*, Cotrubas, von Stade, Behrens and Pavarotti in *Idomeneo*, Te Kanawa and Weikl in *Arabella*. Freni returned after many years for *Don Carlos*, Sutherland came back for *Lucia*, with Kraus. The 1983–84 centennial season presented an extraordinary assembly of stars at the birthday gala in October and included the debuts of Samuel Ramey in *Rinaldo* and Jessye Norman.*

Jessye Norman had been singing in Europe for quite a while before she appeared at the Met in the production of *Les Troyens* which opened the centennial season on 26 September 1983. It was a grand opening, bringing in $601,000. The production was revamped by Fabrizio Melano from Nathaniel Merrill's 1972 production with sets by Peter Wexler. It was staged in a semi-oratorio manner with serried ranks of chorus and lines of solo singers to the front. In the video recording Levine found no way of patching together the grand, fascinating, but episodic musical moments. The musical aspect of the opera came across as rhetorical, spectacular and full of pleasant sounds. 'The Met production depends upon its principals,' Porter wrote, and the principals were splendid. Although Domingo, worried by the high tessitura, retired after the televised performance, he nonetheless provided 'poetry and caressing of the music'. Troyanos, overflowing with passion, was a consummate actress. Her tone was rich, warm, powerful and flexible, with a great feminine appeal. The instrument was also big enough to compete with the dense Berlioz orchestration and the huge Met auditorium. Jessye Norman as Cassandra switched with Troyanos's Dido in the second cast. Porter described Norman's Dido as 'warm, regal of manner, opulent of voice. Her instrument . . . often torrential in its lava-like outpourings, seductive in Berlioz's long, sensual phrases, matched the prodigiousness of her majestic presence.'[67] With never a suspicion of effort, Norman, like Vickers, was a phenomenon of nature. But unlike Vickers's frequently tormented stage persona Norman gave an impression of inner serenity.

At the time of her Met debut Norman said that the previous successes of black singers like Marian Anderson and Leontyne Price had made possible the varied career she enjoyed, performing in French and German operas and not just *Porgy and Bess*.[68] She had won a scholarship to study at Howard University, and after winning the

---

* The gala's roster included Behrens, Caballé, Cotrubas, Freni, Marton, Price, Rysanek, Söderström, Sutherland, Te Kanawa, Horne, Verrett, Troyanos, von Stade, Carreras, Domingo, Gedda, Kraus, Pavarotti, Vickers, Capecchi, MacNeil, Milnes, Ghiaurov, Plishka, Salminen and Talvela. The two-part afternoon and evening gala for the Hundredth birthday on 21 October made $1.5 million.

female division at the International Munich Music Competition in 1969, was given a contract to work at the Deutsche Oper Berlin, before she settled in London. She had great success with her Cassandra at Covent Garden in 1972 and later at Salzburg. In the 1988 videotaped Met *Ariadne auf Naxos*, gorgeously and elegantly costumed in dark sapphire and wide sleeves of old lace, her stage presence and opulent voice were mesmerising. The registers of her voice were extraordinarily imposing, from almost tenor-like low notes to a free top. Her pianissimi were floated, the tone 'spinny', nobly breathed and excitingly deep. She 'underacted' – yet a single pose or gesture commanded complete attention. In the same production, Kathleen Battle's Zerbinetta was pert, charming and fresh but with some weakness of tone quality when she approached a high note.

Another black soprano appearing on the Met stage was Leona Mitchell, who sang with Pavarotti and Milnes in *Ernani* in October 1983.* Mitchell, one of fifteen children of a black minister in Oklahoma, was born in 1949. She patterned her singing after Price, 'who', said Mitchell, 'acted so much with the voice, but also gave you the smoothness of the line and the high D flat, emotionally powerful but always the singing'.[69] In January 1982 Simon Estes had his debut in *Tannhäuser*. His voice was pleasing although 'reedy and light' at the bottom, more like a basso cantante than a deep bass.[70] Even though black singers felt little of the prejudice that Marian Anderson had encountered, Estes felt that he had been ready for the Met long before he was called, and Norman had been singing in Europe for a long time before her Met debut. There were, by the early Eighties, fifteen black artists on the Met roster, including Mitchell, Norman, Price, Battle, Verrett and Bumbry.

Another important and somewhat delayed debut had been that of Samuel Ramey in *Rinaldo*. Ramey, like Norman, had established his career elsewhere, having appeared at the City Opera for many years and having had both his Vienna and La Scala debuts in 1981, and his Covent Garden debut in 1982. It had taken a while for the Met management to recognise his talent and offer him a suitable vehicle for his

---

* Martin Mayer wrote that this *Ernani* was 'satisfactory even by Golden Age standards', although Mitchell was not yet quite in the league of Leontyne Price who had been the Met's last Elvira (*Opera*, March 1984, p. 272).

debut. Ramey pointed out that many City Opera stars had not been invited to sing at the Met, including both Norman Treigle and Beverly Sills.[71] Ingpen later recalled that Ramey used to say she was against him and that the Met was prejudiced against City stars. Ingpen sought to explain that because Met audiences found it difficult to accept someone from the City Opera, she had had to think of a role that would be both suited to his voice and not be comparable to his City Opera performances.[72]

Ramey, like so many American singers, had benefited from the American education system, which provided opportunities for developing talent under difficult circumstances. Born in Colorado, his father died at the time Ramey went to Kansas State University to study music. After an apprenticeship at Santa Fe Opera in 1970 he went to New York, where he studied with Armen Bovajian, the bass specialist. In 1972 he made his City Opera debut. His Don Giovanni there was seen by Zubin Mehta, who took him to Covent Garden and thence to Salzburg, where he worked with Karajan on the role in 1987. Ramey sang much Rossini, being the Pesaro Festival bass from 1981 to 1989. Bovajian said of the retiring, 'low-key' Ramey, 'He just walked on stage and he was a live wire. . . . From the very first, back in Central City, he observed other artists and simply absorbed that energy, that presence.'[73]

At the Met in 1990, Ramey alternated the Don and Leporello with Ferruccio Furlanetto. He was equally at home in Mozart, Italian bel canto roles, Handel, and 'devil roles' such as Boito's Mefistofele. Ramey's debut was in the first ever Handel to be given by the Met, *Rinaldo*, in January 1984, with Marilyn Horne. Borrowed from the National Arts Center Ottawa, with costumes by Mark Negin and production by Frank Corsaro, it was not a polished production as had been Ponnelle's *Idomeneo* in October 1982. Nor was the orchestra familiar with the work, and failed, according to *Opera News*, to respond to Mario Bernardi's direction.[74] Ramey's late debut at the Met was, however, 'triumphant'. He handled every moment of Argante's music 'with breathtaking command and quality'. Ramey's delivery of the bravura *aria di entrata* 'Sibilar', which is very florid and full of high F sharps, 'rightly brought the house down'. According to Mayer, Ramey instantly established himself as the Met's premier basso cantante.[75]

Henahan concurred that 'he made a tremendous impression with his powerful, pliable bass voice, particularly at his dazzling first entry in a wonderfully baroque chariot'.[76] Horne also sang with 'awesome breath control, a gorgeous array of colours . . . bravura and panache'.[77]

In 1984, Levine's 'artistic vision' brought a work unfamiliar to the Met. It was Riccardo Zandonai's *Francesca da Rimini*, a post-verismo, heroic work of the new romanticism with Gabriele d'Annunzio's libretto, full of 'decadent atmosphere laden with love, melodrama and cruelty'. Porter pointed out that d'Annunzio had learnt all the wrong things from Wagner: 'The over-amplification of detail, the insistence on so many things besides the essential things.' Levine, however, believed the work to be a 'masterpiece', and Porter wrote that Levine conducted it on 9 March 1984 'as if he admired and loved the score'.[78] Piero Faggioni's first production for the Met was lavish, intending to enhance the work's lushness but in fact overwhelming it. 'Ezio Frigerio's huge sets', wrote Smith, 'showed the influence of the pre-Raphaelites for the domestic scenes and out-and-out spectacle for the battle scene.' Its effort to 'duplicate the kind of stagy acting of the time when the opera was written' had, for Smith, 'a certain camp attraction'.[79]

Dexter was disgusted that the Board had seen fit to support *Francesca* when a new production of *Boccanegra* was abandoned in favour of a borrowed one. Peter Hall was to have directed *Boccanegra* but was told in October 1983 that it had been cancelled, although he and Bury had already been working on it.[80] Dexter still hoped to take *Boccanegra* over himself, and in May 1984 made one last and futile attempt to prove that it was possible to prepare a major Verdi work with 'economy and style'.[81] He felt that it was his last chance to forestall the visual style of the 'design clones' such as *The Trojans* and *Francesca*. But it was not to be, and it was Volpe who was deputed to tell Dexter that his *Boccanegra* was unacceptable. Dexter never forgave Volpe for apparently going over 'to the other side', telling Volpe that he was the person he had taken 'out of the trenches'. Volpe recalled, 'I said, "John, that's my responsibility, it's not personal." '[82] In his notebook, Dexter wrote bitterly:

(1) SH [Sybil Harrington] offered a huge endowment to the Met centenary fund.

(2) She likes 19th century opera

(3) AB [Anthony Bliss] chooses the money over policy.

(4) JL [James Levine] also chose the money over art.

(5) (This hurt) My own discovery, someone I took from the floor and trained and promoted to an office position betrayed me. JV [Volpe] chose the money over loyalty . . .

Dexter wrote to Phoebe Berkowitz on 21 November, 'To be completely honest with you I am relieved to bring my association with that plush and crystal whorehouse to an end.' He had, he told her, been waiting in vain for some sign from Levine that what had been achieved in their few productive years together 'had not been done entirely on his own'. He wrote to Bliss on 7 December 1984 to say that he had had no communication from Levine, 'neither good wishes nor regrets that ten years of work was coming to an inconclusive end'.[83] Dexter, despite his irascible personality, had made a great contribution to the Met in improving backstage practices and in assembling the staff who would continue to maintain those standards. He also opened up Met audiences to the possibility of a more radical approach to operatic direction and drama on the stage. These were not negligible achievements but the latter was constantly faced by ambivalence or indifference at the Met, and Dexter's demise coincided with a decided backtracking away from this dangerous departure.

The Met had managed to stabilise its precarious economic position of the mid-1970s, playing to 1 million people in its thirty-week season, in seven performances a week, and on tour. Its budget for 1983–84 was $74 million, larger than the total of its ten main competitors and double what it had been ten years earlier. Net contributions had tripled and ticket sales were up two and a half times. The New York Times said on 25 September 1983 that the Met had decided to 'throw its energy and resources into becoming known as a solid grey institution in which a contributor's money could be soundly invested'.

A successful area of long-term investment was the widening of public consciousness through the media. In 1980 Taplin had pointed out that the 'long-range future of the Met will depend on our ability to enlarge our audience through the media'.[84] By the 1980s the Texaco–Metropolitan Opera radio network, which had begun broadcasting in 1931 (it celebrated its 1,000th performance on 9 February 1991), reached more than 300 radio stations in the United States alone. Television was also to prove a crucial development in this widening process. Dexter had initially been against televising opera for artistic reasons and the technical difficulties were enormous, but satellite technology revolutionised the development of televised opera. From 1980 listeners could hear a broadcast note of music with a 'quarter of a second difference'.[85]

Between 15 March 1977, when *La Bohème* was broadcast, and 2 November 1979, there were eleven televised productions which achieved high ratings. Telecasts of *La Bohème* and *Rigoletto* in 1977 reached 10 million people, and the Met received 100,000 enthusiastic letters. Texaco agreed to fund three broadcasts a year with matching funding from the National Endowment for the Arts and public television. In 1978–79 there were four productions at a cost of $1.2 million. The first producer, Christopher Sarson, explained that an audience of 15 million people could be reached by television, which, as he pointed out, was probably more people than had seen each work in the theatre since it had been written. In 1990 sixteen countries signed on for access to the Met broadcasts, including the BBC, which found it cheaper to broadcast from the Met than from Covent Garden.[86]

Televising techniques improved during the late Seventies. Early colour was poor, but with time, designers and scene painters became more aware of the needs of the camera. The British television director Brian Large became the great television producer of the Eighties and Nineties. Trained as a musician, and then by the BBC as a film director, Large became the BBC's chief opera producer in 1974. Encouraged by John Culshaw, he filmed Patrice Chéreau's *Ring* cycle at Bayreuth in 1979 and 1980. This work was recognised as breaking ground, as had Culshaw's own work with Solti recording the *Ring*. Large worked in all the main opera houses and in 1979 *Mahagonny* brought him to the Met. He was admired for his 'phenomenal mastery of detail, the ability to select the shots with complete fidelity to the score and to the production'.[87]

In 1984 the first Met laserdiscs and video cassettes were issued but the sales proved less rewarding than was hoped, and in 1995 *Opera News* reported that sales were 'doing horribly'. The president of the retail company Opera World said that Francesco Rosi's *Carmen* had sold well, 1 million copies by 1995, because 'in the public mind it was a movie'. It was in the widening of its audience rather than in any financial benefits that videos were to prove their value. Disappointing as video sales were, television unquestionably underscored the Met's role as the national company and helped to build up future audiences.*

The 'national company' was part of an ever growing interest in opera in America. In November 1977 *Opera News* carried out a survey, which concluded that opera was flourishing in the United States and that the 'more opera is heard the more popular it gets'. Attendance was high throughout the country and by 1977 there were sixty major companies, including twelve organisations with budgets over $1 million. Municipal support was negligible but state aid had been between 18 and 26 per cent in Utah, Texas, Minnesota and upstate New York. Grants from private sources accounted for the largest percentage of support and repertoire remained mainstream.

All over the United States regional companies were developing and expanding. The Rescigno–Lawrence Kelly regime at Dallas, approaching the company's fiftieth anniversary in 1980, continued to expand its activities, and fine singers continued to appear there regularly. Smaller and newer companies such as Jackson's Opera South continued to widen the audience for locally staged opera. Norfolk, Virginia's company was launched in January 1975, under music director Peter Mark, professor of music at Santa Barbara and husband of the Scottish composer Thea Musgrave. In 1979 Musgrave's *Christmas Carol* was mounted to sold-out houses in Norfolk. Her *Mary Queen of Scots* was put on in San Francisco in 1979 and displayed a rare example of a

---

* In August 1982 came the conclusion of twenty-nine years of negotiations with unions for television broadcasts and cable television, videos etc. on a 50–50 split of all revenues between the association and its workforces. Conclusion of the contracts made possible a long-term contract with Beta Film Co. in Germany for live-by-satellite performances of the Met on Saturday afternoons.

warm lyric line and a keen sense of music drama. In March 1985 Musgrave's opera *Harriet: the Woman Called 'Moses'*, commissioned by the Virginia Opera Association and the Royal Opera House, told the story of Harriet Tubman, the escaped slave who helped free 300 fellow slaves along the Underground Railroad to freedom. Musgrave wove Negro spirituals into the rest of the musical texture with passion and intensity. Cynthia Haymon as Harriet gave a most moving leading performance. Covent Garden, however, despite having commissioned it, decided in April 1985 that in the difficult financial circumstances it could not put it on.[88]

In the early 1980s the small regional companies such as Fort Worth, Texas, sturdily maintained their effort to survive and reach reasonable standards of performance. In 1980, Tulsa, Oklahoma presented the first local Wagner, *Die Walküre*, to the Wagner-starved South-West, in a respectable if patchy production. Even little Anchorage in Alaska, with its population of 220,000 and a hearty state oil-rich subsidy, established itself in its first two seasons as the Western hemisphere's most westerly and northerly outpost of opera. Audiences thronged to the productions, which included *Tosca*.

As well as the new companies, bolder repertoire was steadily expanding the American operatic experience. *Jenůfa* was produced by David Pountney at Houston Grand Opera in an area more used to standard fare. That season, in November 1977, Houston brought Te Kanawa's much praised *Arabella* under Charles Mackerras's baton. In Boston, Sarah Caldwell, who had been influenced by Felsenstein, continued to stage and conduct lively and dramatic readings of classic repertoire and also unfamiliar and new repertoire. Her *Fanciulla* and *Macbeth* in the 1976 season were dramatic triumphs – the former being one of its earliest productions. She was responsible for a production of Verdi's *Stiffelio*, which was only to become part of the standard repertoire in the early Nineties. She also gave the first professional performance of a Tippett opera in the United States, *The Ice Break*.

In Washington, the Kennedy Arts Center, helped by a $43 million gift from Japan, was establishing itself as a major cultural centre while sticking to safe repertoire. Chicago's Lyric Opera celebrated its twenty-fifth season in 1979. Carol Fox, Chicago's director for twenty-six seasons, had been following the Met recipe for success, relying more heavily on spectacle and stage effects, as well as presenting star singers to maintain the audience at increased seat prices. Ezio Frigiero and Virginio Puecher's $200,000 *Tales of Hoffman* included lifts, a smoking locomotive, a carousel horse and buggy, and a fleet of gliding gondoliers, as well as Plácido Domingo – all of which caused the audience to gasp. In an anniversary article in October 1979 Fox complained that fiscal restraints and modern-day logistics meant high seat prices, which greatly encouraged the smaller and newer companies like Chicago Opera Theater and Opera Midwest. In 1978 Lyric Opera commissioned Krzysztof Penderecki's *Paradise Lost* which incurred such high production costs that the company did not recover financially under the existing management. The Board realised that it had to keep a closer curb on the company's finances and in January 1981 Carol Fox's twenty-six-year era ended with her forced resignation.[89] She died in July 1981. Ardis Krainik took over to try to eliminate the budget deficit of $4.2 million. By the end of the following season Krainik had succeeded in raising $4,352,134.

In 1982, in San Francisco, Terry McEwen took over from Kurt Herbert Adler, with whom he had been working for two years. The 1981 summer festival had left a debt of several million dollars with its adventurous programme and its holiday timing. McEwen's rigorous promotion succeeded in a 100 per cent improvement in subscriptions. Top singers continued to come, and forays into conceptual productions, with Jean-Pierre Ponnelle's controversial *Cavalleria rusticana* and productions by Christopher Alden and his brother David, reached San Francisco in the late Seventies and Eighties.

In 1982–83, in spite of plummeting public funding and against a background of economic recession, American opera companies managed to increase performances and audience attendance, by increasing subscriptions. City Opera's adventurous programming (*Alceste, Hamlet* and *Candide*), at a time of economic recession, resulted in loss, and from July to September the theatre was closed by a strike. Beverly Sills had become director in 1978 (a position she held until 1989) and she successfully improved the box office with a less adventurous repertoire, while at the same time vastly increasing fund-raising. Just as stars such as Domingo, Carreras, Troyanos, Milnes and Ramey had gained experience at City Opera in a previous era, so did a new generation of fine singers that included Carol Vaness, Jerry Hadley and Renée Fleming.

There were many new operas being given in America's provincial opera houses during the period 1975 to 1985. In 1976–77 alone, 179 American operas were performed, including thirty-three world premieres. America was unique in the world in the readiness of its opera houses to commission new works – often at minimal fees. One of America's most prolific composers was Thomas Pasatieri, whose *Ines de Castro* was premiered at Baltimore Opera in April 1976, and his *Seagull* at Seattle. Robert Ward's *The Crucible*, skilfully reduced from Arthur Miller's play, was presented at Milwaukee. Sarah Caldwell at Boston presented Roger Sessions's *Montezuma*. Another premiere in this season was Dominick Argento's *The Voyage of Edgar Allan Poe*, which was one of the few new works to be performed more than once. Carlisle Floyd's *Willie Stark*, described as a musical drama, was put on in Houston to mark the company's twenty-fifth anniversary. Many of the new works lacked dramatic coherence and most were not repeated; but they revealed a great vitality in operatic life.

A new work that received many airings was Leonard Bernstein's *A Quiet Place*, commissioned jointly by Houston Grand Opera, the Kennedy Center and La Scala, and premiered in Houston in June 1983. Porter called it a 'bold, ambitious and very interesting opera, containing some of Bernstein's most richly wrought music'. Since its theme is alienation and the difficulty of authentic communication, much of the strongly theatrical text is stammered, or conversely a fluent skein of clichés. The tragic, sound-bite-ridden characters are driven to find out what love may exist beyond their automatic responses to the death of Dinah – their wife, mother, best friend.

The expressive quality of the music, bringing the cleverly banal text to life, is remarkable in view of the multiple difficulties of the collaboration. As the librettist Stephen Wadsworth has recounted, Bernstein began their work together in a state of profound pessimism. Although his musicals *West Side Story* and *Candide* had been recognised as landmarks of the twentieth-century lyric stage in America, he had grown dissatisfied with his efforts to create, in Wadsworth's words, a 'national musical theatre'. Bernstein had lost his estranged wife, the actress Felicia Montealegre, to cancer in 1978. Traumatised by her death, he found work on *A Quiet Place* from 1980 to 1983 to be difficult but rewarding. The twenty-seven-year-old Wadsworth had just lost his sister in a car crash. With a keen sense that there was 'not much time' and in need of reassurance, the insomniac Bernstein, who died in 1990, insisted on working side by side with Wadsworth, frequently asking him for his opinion of the music he drafted.

After negative reviews following the opera's premiere performance in Houston, Bernstein and Wadsworth cut and radically revised the work for further performances at La Scala and Washington in 1984, and the Staatsoper in 1986. The result is a work of great melodic, rhythmic and harmonic inventiveness, as well as verbal flexibility and expressiveness.

Another significant contributor to the American lyric theatre was Stephen Sondheim – whose *Sweeney Todd, The Demon Barber of Fleet Street* (1979) straddles the fence more ambivalently between musical and opera. It has been produced at the New York City Opera, the New Israel Opera and Opera North, among other traditional opera venues. Christopher Bond's brilliant narrative exposition contains sympathetic and even humorous characters like Mrs Lovett, at the same time as chilling horror. The balance between lyrics and music is very much in the Broadway idiom with reference to music hall and ballad forms. This approach helps define *Sweeney Todd* as a musical. The orchestral element, while mainly serving as an accompaniment, is written in an extremely sophisticated and flexible idiom.

Rodney Milnes wrote of Sondheim's *Into the Woods* that 'words and music are an indissoluble entity as they are in Janáček'. He also found 'more music in any two bars of it than in the collected works of Philip Glass'.[90] In spite of Milnes's unfavourable comparison, however, by far the most successful of new stage composers was Philip Glass. His 'operas' played to packed houses in Europe and America, and his six-movement *Glassworks* composed for the recording studio, sold 100,000 copies. *Einstein on the Beach* was performed at the Met, which was rented for two performances in November 1976.* Patrick J. Smith wrote, 'Glass's music is well known in avant-garde circles: it

* The opera was presented by the Byrd Hoffman Foundation in co-operation with the Metropolitan Opera and with grants from New York State Council and the National Endowment for the Arts.

consists in short motifs – often only three or four notes reiterated thousands of times and ever so slowly changing . . . In musical terms it has reference to Indian ragas and African tribal music.' The unfolding of each scene, Smith explained, is extremely slow: 'for perhaps five minutes the stage is static, except for one person moving backwards and forwards with angular gestures and someone writing on an invisible blackboard, while a chorus transmutes syllables and solfège notes into patterns of sound. Everything is amplified via an immense sound mixer, to which is added an electric organ, suddenly a paper aeroplane darts across the stage . . .'[91]

Glass was a tirelessly enthusiastic advocate of his own work. His published writings concerning *Einstein on the Beach* show his enjoyment of the processes of composition, rehearsal and performance. His main collaborator was Robert Wilson with whom he discussed potential subjects. The collaboration was a happy one, Glass wrote:

> There were a number of presumptions Bob and I made about the work which, though they might be common ideas in the emerging New York counterculture, would appear quite startling in a larger cultural context. Interestingly enough these were things that Bob and I never needed to discuss . . . For example it never occurred to us that *Einstein on the Beach* would have a story or contain anything like an ordinary plot . . . It seemed to me that in Bob's previous work the title merely provided an occasion for which a theatrical/visual work could be constructed. . . . The point about Einstein was clearly not what it 'meant' but that it was *meaningful* as generally experienced by the people who saw it.[92]

Glass was equally enthusiastic about his minimalist music, which he found revolutionary. Certain techniques used by Glass in his minimalist idiom, such as developing motifs by adding or taking away notes, is standard compositional practice. The snappy, casual approach to cultural icons, which are such a strong feature of *Einstein* – Marilyn Monroe, Jackie Kennedy Onassis, Campbell's Soup – had emerged in the 1960s in the hands of pop artists led by Andy Warhol.

During *Einstein*'s performances at the Met there was a whiff of excitement as well as marijuana smoke in the air. The audience was generally young and excited to see a new and unusual work staged in

such a bastion of tradition. Patrick Smith was verging on pretentiousness when he wrote that it was like 'watching clouds or surf on a
beach ... In a sense monotonous; in another sense, not. Perhaps it
helps to be a little brain-hazy.'[93]

Milnes could not understand why Sondheim was on Broadway
and Glass in opera houses, asking why 'the problem of writing opera
in the closing decades of the 20th century should be resorting to
non-music'.[94] Andrew Clements pointed out that Glass's *Satyagraha*
and *Akhnaten* also avoided narrative, explaining: 'Each glosses and
amends a historically grounded theme to yield a complex bundle of
allusions and cross-cultural references which does not require any kind
of musical narrative to hold it together.'[95] William Mann posed the
question directly: 'How can an opera exist without a narrative, with
no more than a few known facts and with little reliance on language
to convey its meaning?'[95] But the whole question of where text and
drama lay in opera in the United States was unanswered even at the
Met. Dexter had written in his diary in November 1974: 'Only when
the operatic stage can share the freedom of the dramatic stage can the
medium exist in the twentieth century and maybe help us understand
the world and ourselves, instead of remaining the morphine of the
over-privileged.'[96]*

The Met's finances were again giving cause for concern. By the 1983–
84 season responsibility for a $7 million deficit was laid at Bliss's door
for his failure during the previous two years 'to run the House with
a tight hand'.[97] According to Bruce Crawford, who was president of
the Metropolitan Opera Association, the box office had fallen off
sharply, the capital campaign had 'cannibalised the regular annual
giving', and the House had used up all its working capital. In October
1984 Crawford, who came from the world of business promotion
and marketing, and had been president and chief executive of the
sixth-largest advertising agency in the world – BBDO International –
was chosen to succeed Bliss as general manager, starting in 1986. Some
of the 'sins' of management, Crawford later explained, had been

---

* Dexter died in March 1990 during heart surgery.

covered up by Sybil Harrington's largesse. The $8 million deficit translated into 2001 terms would be more like $20 million – almost the equivalent of the total government subsidy to Covent Garden that year. When the deficit emerged, Crawford recalled, 'some panic had set in', many Board directors were 'deeply upset'. He added, 'Things go wrong very fast in an opera house.'*[98]

Crawford was to prove a more 'hands-on' manager than Bliss, involved in the artistic planning and ensuring that certain singers and directors were engaged.[99] While Bliss's background was the legal profession, Crawford, coming from the world of business promotion and marketing, wanted 'to be involved in everything'. He wanted to know about the schedule before it was 'put to bed', and was determined to make sure that all the departments were making plans in coordination with each other.[100] He had taken a strong hold of the Met's leadership before he officially became general manager, writing to Bliss in February 1984 that there should be 'no contracted commitments with producers, artists, conductors etc.' for the next ninety days. On 24 September 1984 Crawford told the Board that as well as much improved housekeeping and fund-raising, there must be a policy 'that will bring in attractions that will bring in revenue'.[101] The repertory had included things that were not good box office and not tied to marketing through subscriptions. Crawford later recalled that the *Parade* triple bill had once done 29 per cent on a non-subscription evening and *Francesca da Rimini* 40 per cent.[102] The Met, he stressed, must 'move away from a policy of expansion to one of tighter management and increased working capital'.[103] Although Levine would initiate programming, final decisions would be taken in consultation with Crawford.

Crawford focused on repertory and stars to revive the box office, combining box office certainties with the less popular works, which would receive even fewer performances and would be included in the subscriptions with appearances by Domingo and Pavarotti. Pavarotti had become 'upset' with the House, Crawford later explained, and

* Crawford was a Board member 1976–77; vice-president of the Metropolitan Opera Archives 1981–84; president of the MOA 1984–85; general manager 1985 to 1989; chairman of the Executive Committee 1990, president and chief executive officer 1991–99 and honorary chairman 1999.

had not been performing at the Met Domingo was not giving enough performances on his own to sell sufficient subscriptions. Crawford made sure that both singers would guarantee at least fifteen performances each at the Met. Their appearances would immediately ensure thirty 'sell-outs' and help the subscriptions, because at that time the only way to see Domingo and Pavarotti was to buy a subscription.[104] The new general manager was keen to get rid of performers who had been 'around too long', particularly what he described to Peter G. Davis of *New York* as the archetypal 'dreadful Italian tenor'.*[105]

Levine professed to be content with the new relationship, as he wished to take on more international conducting.[106] As Crawford put it, 'The last thing in the world he wanted was a half-empty House' and he added, 'Properly approached, he was not intransigent.'[107]

According to Taplin, Levine had been feeling the absence of a 'strong general manager'. Under Crawford this was certainly not the case. In May 1984 Levine was told by Crawford, 'If you had deliberately set out to sabotage the tour, you couldn't have done a better job' – *Peter Grimes*, *Francesca da Rimini* and *Rinaldo*, he told Levine, were all ill-suited for tour audiences.[108] At the end of the 1984–85 season the decision was taken to end the Met tour after 103 years. According to the 1984–85 Annual Report the tour had become a 'financial drain on the company', and it had become 'increasingly hard to maintain artistic standards'. The stars no longer wished to travel with the company and some of the more modern repertoire had been playing to empty houses. The productions of the standard repertoire had become so elaborate and costly that they could not be taken on tour. Technical director Joseph Clark pointed out in September 1991 that the old Met *Turandot* set of painted flats could be packed away in four trucks and that the new production would have needed eighteen. The tours of the future were mainly abroad – to Japan in 1998 and Europe in 1999.

In January 1985 Crawford thanked Volpe for making a substantial cut in expenses and establishing a 'solid foundation for better management'. The box office still remained a problem, however, and 'serious attention' should be directed towards 'repertory and artists'.[109]

* Levine told Crawford, 'If the artist is famous and doesn't work out it is her fault, if we cast somebody who isn't particularly well known and she doesn't work out it's our fault.' (Crawford, Interview 31.5.01.)

Although Crawford was aware that there was criticism of the House's 'conservative profile', directors like Zeffirelli and Schenk would remain Met choices as they received, in Crawsford's words, 'extremely favourable customer approval'.[110]

'Serious attention' soon manifested itself in another of what Dexter had termed the 'design clones'. It was Zeffirelli's 'lavish' *Tosca* on 11 March 1985. Never was the church of Sant' Andrea della Valle 'so sunny or so pretty or so big', nor were costumes so 'gorgeous'.[111]

The new productions caused Andrew Porter to 'dismiss the House as a place of serious artistic endeavour' and to argue that the season was only redeemed by a fine revival of Dexter's *Lulu*, which had played to empty houses. Porter contrasted Zeffirelli's London *Tosca* for Callas, which had served 'as an enhancing frame for more ordinary interpreters'. His *Tosca* for the Met, like his *Bohème*, was a 'spectacle that must steal the show from all but very strong performers'.[112] Very strong performers were, however, what the Met was now determined to provide. In the 1985 *Tosca* recording Plácido Domingo was heard in a spate of long-breathed tone, his Cavaradossi ringing and virile, shining with joy. Domingo's vitality swept Hildegard Behrens as Tosca along. Giuseppe Sinopoli made his Met debut in this production. His passion and enthusiasm gave this familiar music a fresh glow – he and Domingo together rendered 'E lucevan le stelle' heartbreaking. Singing to the very end of his immensely long breath, Domingo seemed to find in himself the last ounce of feeling.

Crawford thanked Harrington for the production, whose opening had grossed $460,000, with top prices reaching $250 for the first time. The financial situation was improving, with the box office reaching 90 per cent and the deficit being reduced from the previous year's $8 million to $2.3 million.[113]

The autumn revival of *Tosca*, with Caballé and Pavarotti, followed Crawford's decision to bring in the stars, but in no way reversed Porter's critical assessment. There was, of course, fine singing, but conductor Cillario let both stars 'get away with murder'. Peter Hall described their performances. The two singers were, he recalled, 'lolloping about the stage like two dinosaurs' and he continued:

Pavarotti judged the mural in the church in the first scene to be too far upstage, so he had a little easel and a picture downstage and he stood there merrily painting with a palette in his hand. Caballé refused to throw herself off the battlements and walked off into the wings in triumph and I thought: Opera has a capacity for stupidity which is greater than any other art form – providing the music is there and is in tune, it's accepted. What is the point? You don't have to see Pavarotti and Caballé.[114]

Levine's artistic vision now focused on musical and singing standards, combined with attractive and immediately recognisable visual effect, rather than dramatic and musical integration. The size of the House remained a problem. Levine always stressed the fine acoustics of the Met and explained that well-designed sets with reflecting surfaces gave singers the same acoustical advantage as in any House.[115] He admitted, however, that the Met was too large for expressing nuance. Operas like *Werther*, he told Robert Marsh, which were designed for smaller European Houses, could not be successfully given at the Met as the audience has to see 'every nuance, every eye blink'.[116]

Even for the stars who came to the Met and often provided many extraordinary performances, the scale was sometimes overwhelming. Thomas Allen recalled performances of Almaviva, with Ruggero Raimondi as Figaro, in November and December 1985 when the two men were

> . . . blasting off at one another in the second act and we stared at one another and had the same thought at the same time: 'Why are we screaming like this?' and we suddenly realised that we were making more noise than we had ever felt the need to in our entire lives. For some reason the whole thing had become overblown, which it can tend to be at the Met. The sound coming from the pit with Jimmy encouraging that richness of sound.[117]

Allen added, 'The Met playing is thick and luscious, and sometimes hard to get through, when you combine that with the size of the House too, which tho' it has a wonderful acoustic, is physically very daunting because all you see is a vast space going out, out, out and thousands of faces in the orchestra stalls and you think, "My God you see more people down there than you see in an entire theatre elsewhere."'

Levine's orchestra and chorus had indeed achieved a 'richness of sound' and improved beyond measure during his first ten years. *Parsifal*, always a favourite opera of his and one he regularly conducted at Bayreuth, showed off his, and the orchestra's skills in April 1985. Porter described the opening bars: 'The five and a half bars of unison line ascending through an octave, then falling back, gave assurance of a lovingly rehearsed, pondered, serious performance . . . James Levine's conducting, and his players made it marvellously eloquent – a unison of blended, living, subtly shifting colours.'[118]

By 1986 the Met felt ready to produce a new *Ring* cycle. The orchestra and chorus provided the basis for success. 'Not outside Bayreuth', Rodney Milnes wrote after a visit to the United States in December 1986, 'have I heard choral singing of such precision, fullness and steadiness of tone . . .'[119] In keeping with the Met's conservative mood, the *Ring* was a faithful realisation of Wagner's intentions. Otto Schenk, the fifty-six year-old Viennese director who had prepared the Met's successful *Tannhäuser* in December 1977 and *Hoffmann* in 1982, was chosen to direct both the *Ring* and many other productions in the next decade. Working with his regular designer, Günther Schneider-Siemssen, he would hopefully continue to find 'customer approval'. Jonathan Friend, who had taken over from Joan Ingpen after the 1983–84 season, explained that Schenk and his designer fully responded to the Met's needs, as in *Siegfried*: 'When the curtain goes up on the second scene of the first act the audience immediately thinks, "Oh Yes . . . I can go for a walk in that forest." It engages people, they don't have to work out in advance what the director has inflicted on the piece.' Friend added, 'The audience immediately warmed to it.'*[120] As Leighton Kerner put it, 'Wagner's myth is to take place in a recognisable world.'[121]

Schenk had declined to do a *Ring* in Europe as he wanted a 'Romantic *Ring* for today, a fairy tale . . .' not quite what was standard European fare at the time.[122] Mayer wrote that it 'looked and felt like the *Rings* produced at Bayreuth in the decade after the composer's

---

* Friend's first position had been that of director of the rehearsal department in March 1982 with the title of company manager.

death'. The *Walküre*, premiered in September 1986, was 'rough-hewn, suitably outsize and all grey, brown and (for the *Lenz* and the *Wald*) green, with suitable and evocative projections on cyclorama and scrim'.[123] Headgear was refined medieval rustic with spears, shields and winged caps; bearskins and antlers on the walls. On 15 October 1987 *Das Rheingold* was 'very nineteenth-century with water in the Rhine and a rainbow bridge to Valhalla, everything out of the master's stage book'.[124] *Siegfried* and *Götterdämmerung* followed in 1988.

James Morris, the Wotan of later cycles, loved the naturalistic setting, explaining that it allowed 'the singers to portray the characters without fighting the production'. It was, he pointed out to Levine – when the Met was thinking of replacing it in the mid-Nineties – 'the only traditional production in the world'. Morris added, 'I'm so sick of *Ring* cycles in outer space and in tunnels and gas stations and concentration camps.'[125] Andrew Porter, however, called it a 'big, meaningless show, stolidly representational in design, with no dramatic life in it beyond what individual singers might bring'.[126]

It took a few years before the cast was uniformly strong and appropriate for the Met's scale. In *Walküre*, Hildegard Behrens was throughout equal to the demands of the House, as was the giant Texan Gary Lakes who took over Siegmund in 1987. Jeannine Altmeyer's Sieglinde, however, was somewhat overwhelmed, Henahan wrote, and the Wotan of Simon Estes ranged from 'compelling ardour' to 'stolid blandness'.[127]

In April 1989 the Met presented the complete cycle *Ring* for the first time in fifty years. The cast had been strengthened and included James Morris, Hildegard Behrens, Siegfried Jerusalem and Franz Mazura as Alberich. Voices survived the four-day challenge in the large auditorium with distinction.*

Levine's first *Ring* was well received. In an interview with John Rockwell he said that his aim was to 'achieve a maximum impression', eschewing the post-Toscanini–Furtwängler generation's inclination to bring the *Ring* 'down to human dimensions, to lighten the textures and speed things up'.[128] *Walküre* was praised by Kerner in October 1986 for its warm expansive love duet and the 'Toscaninian power' of

---

* Other members of the cast included John Macurdy (Fasolt), Helga Dernesch (Fricka, Waltraute), Matti Salminen (Fafner, Hunding and Hagen), and Mari Anne Häggander (Freia). The augmented eighty-voice chorus almost raised the roof in *Götterdämmerung*.

its 'Ride of the Valkyries'.[129] By 1988, it is clear from the video recording that Levine's intense conducting was demonstrating a mature mastery of the score. Wagner's music was played with style and sensitivity – the string sound warm and lyrical, the lines long-breathed, the singing generally impressive – and Jessye Norman's Sieglinde tonally magnificent. Hildegard Behrens's 'Ho-jo-to-ho' was sung judiciously, Levine holding the orchestra under her rather small voice, allowing her to act the part and draw emotion movingly from the text. At *'Hier bin ich, Vater'*, her colourless, vibrato-less tone movingly expressed her shame, humanising the divine daughter of the furious Wotan. Levine was quoted by Mayer as saying that Behrens lacked 'the tower of sound you got from Nilsson' and 'that warm bath from the stage that Flagstad gave', but, he asked, 'Have you ever been so moved by a Brünnhilde when she stands there in Act 2?'[130]

James Morris's Wotan was convincing without being stentorian. His legato phrasing reflected the time spent studying with Hans Hotter, who convinced and helped him to sing Wagner with a sensitive line. His bass-baritone gave him sufficient depth in the low and middle registers to give the part its due weight, while he managed the high tessitura with ease. His ability to lighten his tone in the upper-middle register eloquently expressed Wotan's pain at betraying those he loves. Nevertheless, Morris's acting was far from intense – a point not lost on the critics. When he sang Wotan in the September 1989 Covent Garden *Ring*, Milnes wrote that no one sang Wotan more beautifully than Morris, but he added, 'It is still hard to comprehend how an artist of such boundless musical insight can remain so blank dramatically – at neither a divine nor human level did Wotan's anguish project across the footlights.'[131]

Together with John Tomlinson, Morris established himself as one of the two Wotans of the generation. Tomlinson's Wagner portrayals, while sometimes rough-voiced and gruff, even occasionally forced, are intensely acted, and sung with a passion for textual expression, every syllable made meaningful. Morris, in contrast, and in keeping with Met tradition, deals more in mood and attractive homogeneous sound and the smoother tone that he found suitable for such Verdi roles as Banquo and, in later years, Iago. After turning down Bayreuth for the Kupfer *Ring* in 1988, Morris never appeared there, Tomlinson becoming the resident Wotan for ten years, even when Levine was conducting.

Many fine young singers were coming out of the United States in the late Eighties and early Nineties. Carol Vaness made her debut at the Met in February 1984 in a revival of *Rinaldo*, when she showed that she had 'evolved into a splendid, dynamic artist musically and theatrically' with 'clean, penetrating tone, flashing technique, security and dazzling ease in this fiendish music'.[132] Donna Anna, which she sang at Glyndebourne that same year, was a role she was to sing more than 150 times by 1996. Early in her career she was thought of as potentially the leading Mozart soprano of her generation. In the Nineties she diversified into Bellini, Donizetti, Verdi and Puccini.

Another young soprano who caused particular excitement when she sang *Aida* in October 1986 was Aprile Millo. Her thrilling sound and intense stage presence made it seem that at last there was a Verdi soprano of real quality on the scene. But Henahan in the *New York Times* warned against overusing her: 'Promise such as Miss Millo offers should be guarded zealously, not dissipated to the convenience of a vocally needy opera company.'[133] Some felt that her vocal technique was not steady enough to allow her to sing a heavy diet of Verdi roles, but the lack of such voices meant she was much in demand. Other emerging talents at this time were Neil Shicoff, Catherine Malfitano and Barbara Daniels, as well as Cheryl Studer, who was encouraged by Hans Hotter to study in Vienna and worked mainly in Europe.

On 27 May 1987 Crawford told the *New York Times* that plans to do *Moses und Aron* had been dropped. By the time the chorus was ready to face the challenge, the City Opera had scheduled the work and Crawford told Levine it would have to be postponed.[134] A commission by Jacob Druckman was also cancelled. The Met, Crawford told the *New York Times*, was 'financially and artistically ill-suited for anything but popular, large-scale spectacles', and he continued, 'The people who contribute to opera are not too excited about contemporary work. . . . You encounter extreme resistance among the public.' Company policy was henceforth to concentrate on popular operas that could fill the theatre. New work and experimental productions would be accommodated in the promised Mini-Met.[135] The Met auditorium was renamed the Sybil Harrington Auditorium 'in honour' wrote Porter, of 'the woman who paid for the Zeffirelli supershows there – *La Bohème, Tosca* and now *Turandot*'.[136]

Zeffirelli's *Turandot*, in March 1987, was the quintessential supershow. It caused what was becoming known as the 'Metropolitan gasp' which entailed 'the sudden, communal drawing-in of breath, followed by fervent hand clapping'.[137] The Sunday *New York Times* slammed the Met with its review article entitled 'Exit, Humming the sets'. The Met was not the director's House, wrote John Rockwell, it could more accurately be called the designer's House. 'If the Gods eat dim sum,' wrote Bernard Holland, 'they certainly do it in a place like this.'[138]

Zeffirelli phrased it differently, echoing the Met's new focus. 'A spectacle is a good investment,' he said.[139] He was right. His *Bohème* and *Turandot* would consistently sell out no matter who was singing.

For his sets Zeffirelli used a new type of clear fibreglass, which had been shipped from Italy and painted in the Met workshops. Technical director Joe Clark said that actually *Turandot* was not as big as *Bohème* – only needing two as opposed to three of the movable stages behind the curtain.

Zeffirelli filled the stage with a host of fairground extravaganzas, including an executioner with magnificent bare torso and a Chinese New Year's dragon. 'Virtually the whole city of Peking and its population on stage,' as Milnes wrote.[140] The Deutsche Grammophon video captured the spectacle. The ballet-cum-dumbshow in Act Two, revealing Altoum, was half Cecil B. de Mille and half Disney World, with a huge stage population engaged in seemingly random movements. In keeping with the goings-on on stage, Levine laid down great washes of sound, emphasising the lush and pretty rather than the sinister elements in Puccini's dense, magical score. Music was altogether sacrificed to grandeur at times such as 'Signore, ascolta', when Levine slowed the tempo down well beyond Puccini's markings, expunging all sense of line. Dynamic subtleties were also ignored; Leona Mitchell's Liù kept a steady mezzo forte, with rubati misplaced or exaggerated. The notes of the poor little aria, which is a humble plea to the prince, fell like boulders out of the sky.[141]

Acting and drama altogether became victim to excess. Porter observed that in Act Three, Eva Marton's Turandot had difficulty 'negotiating the small circular platforms stilted high above a fish pond, approached by narrow bridges and steep steps . . . in long voluminous robes, topped by a towering headdress like a chandelier'. Such an environment, he wrote, left 'little scope for acting'.[142] As Calaf guessed each riddle, huge carnival streamers – green, red, then white – were pulled from Turandot's shoulder blades. This raised a laugh as did the frenetic kiss of Act Three. At the close, glitter dust showered down on the lovers. Marton got through the cruel tessitura but not without strain, while Domingo was full of passion and fire in his role of bringing excitement and dignity to the spectacle.

The Met was proud of its achievement, Jonathan Friend later saying of the production, 'I think it is a wonderful *Turandot* in this theatre.'[143] Indeed, the spectacle has a powerful allure. During a revival in December 1987 Rodney Milnes 'secretly' enjoyed 'the visceral excitement of ear-splitting and unison top Cs', as well as the visual elements. Moshinsky, too, expressed admiration for the sheer bravura. 'It was', he later said, 'an amazing statement of design in the second act – breathtaking, and in many ways absolutely suits the music, which is high camp.' He added, 'Design done properly has an emotional and intellectual impact which is astonishing.'[144] On the other hand there were those like Porter who felt that *Turandot* was 'the Met's answer to *Star Wars* and *Starlight Express*'.[145] Paul Goldberger agreed, adding that he found *Turandot* and *Starlight Express* 'evidence of visual overkill in our culture'. Along with what he called a 'rise in visual literacy' had come 'an almost desperate desire to be stimulated, a belief that our eyes will not see properly unless they are bombarded'.[146]

Zeffirelli was the perfect director to realise this impulse. Moshinsky said of him, 'You can't write him off, but I do think he became over-decorative. I think it's like the whole history of Italian art in the biography of one person. He went from the Renaissance to the Rococo in one lifetime.' Moshinsky also identified a serious problem in *Turandot*'s very success: 'It has taught the New York public, because it is so overwhelmingly exciting, to think that that *is* opera.'[147]

Although Levine professed to being contented with the management structure, there was evidence of friction with Crawford, particularly over casting. Maria Ewing withdrew from all Met engagements when Agnes Baltsa was given a telecast of *Carmen* which she believed Levine had promised her. Crawford was later reported as saying that he had recommended dropping *Carmen* from the 1985–86 television schedule for budgetary reasons, and because there was an existing video of Ewing in the role at Glyndebourne. But when Baltsa was released from a contract to televise *Carmen* at Salzburg, it was decided to add one of her performances with Carreras to the Met television schedule in 1986–87. Levine, in an interview, said that he did not always get what he wanted in planning, but that he was sincere when he said he would try.[148]

Levine seemed discouraged, hinting that he felt overwhelmed by some of the problems. He told Peter Davis, in an interview in *New York* on 20 April 1987, 'Maybe some day they will think I was crazy putting all this work and energy into an art form in decline. Frankly, I'm not at all sure it isn't a losing battle.' It was not clear how much he welcomed the visual excesses. He told Davis that he admired Wieland Wagner above all other directors and, echoing Moshinsky's concern, said that he regretted the Met audience's ' "isn't-it-pretty" reaction', whereby the 'scenery and costumes *are* the production'.

It was the problem of finding big voices that Levine found most daunting. 'This is a bloody war,' he said and went on to ask, 'Where are the great Verdi tenors . . . There is virtually no choice any longer. But we still have to perform Verdi and Puccini.' Verdi sopranos were also rare, as were Wagner voices. 'But this is an international House and we've got to play the *Ring*. . . . If we don't keep these things in front of the public they will die.' He was concerned at the state of vocal training and felt that even the potentially great voices were not properly trained and developed. 'They don't go slowly enough,' he lamented, 'they have no one to teach them tradition and style, they have nowhere to go to learn interpretation, they have no place to turn to when they get into vocal trouble.' But Levine's determination and innate optimism caused him to seek answers to the pressing problems, including trying to develop voices in his young artists programme, as well as coaching young singers himself.[149]

Some of the programme's graduates were Dawn Upshaw, Heidi Grant Murphy, Dwayne Croft, Stanford Olsen, Stephanie Blythe and

Gregory Turay.* Other Houses were also developing programmes, like the Houston Opera Studio's, which was to bear fruit a decade later when it was able to boast Denyce Graves, Bruce Ford and Susanne Mentzer among its graduates, along with San Francisco's Merola programme which produced Deborah Voigt and Susan Graham. But it was early days and dramatic Verdi voices remained a rare commodity. Levine told Davis, 'This is a terrible time for opera.'

By building such a large House, the Met had reduced its chances of finding singers to fill it in both vocal and dramatic terms, and by staging such spectaculars as *Turandot* they all but submerged the talent they did have. To solve these and other problems, Levine hoped to be able to create his long desired Mini-Met. 'We can stage new operas of all kinds and in all sorts of experimental ways.' He even hinted in his *New York* interview that he might not renew his contract when it expired in 1991 if there was no progress on the Mini-Met. By 1991, he forecast, 'I will have done everything that I could – at least in terms of my own development.' He would only want to continue with major projects and guest conducting. His new project in the Mini-Met would be devoted to new music, together with Peter Sellars, reinventing the Kroll Opera.† 'Imagine not needing production values that must fill up a yawning space for 4,000 spectators,' Levine said with enthusiasm.[150] By the year 2002, however, Levine was still in harness, and there were no concrete plans for a Mini-Met.

During the late Eighties, Levine's absences often resulted in slackness. In February 1987 Kerner was highly critical of the conductors who were in the pit when Levine was absent – Christof Perick conducting *Fidelio*, Thomas Fulton *Rigoletto* and *Madama Butterfly*, Nello Santi *Aida* and *Butterfly*. In March 1987 Jean Fournet conducted a dull *Werther*. When Levine conducted *Clemenza* in January, orchestra, chorus and cast, which included Vaness, Troyanos and Upshaw, were in splendid form, but the performance only caused Kerner to reflect that he wished there were 'more arms in the bullpen'.[151] He also described the occasional visits of top international conductors such as Carlos Kleiber, and Giuseppe Sinopoli for *Macbeth* in 1988, as 'famous-

---

* Others were Paul Groves, Anthony Dean Griffey, Michelle de Young, Christine Goerke and Sondra Radvanovsky.
† The Kroll Opera flourished in Berlin from 1927 to 1931, under Klemperer.

guest tokenism'. Kleiber was warmly welcomed when he made his debut on 28 January 1988, conducting *Bohème*. In Mayer's words, 'People who work at the Met found ways to sneak into all five performances, and they say it was even more wonderful on each rehearing.'[152] In March 1990 the Kleiber–Domingo *Otello* made the same indelible impression that it had in Europe. In the 1990–91 season Levine gave up *Rosenkavalier* for Kleiber.

The general fare was, however, less exciting. Mayer nominated the 21 November 1987 performance of the new production of *Trovatore* 'the worst single performance of anything I have ever heard this company give'.[153] Sutherland was 'unpleasant to hear' and Richard Bonynge 'conducted with a kind of bored if gentlemanly malice against Verdi, forbidding his singers to make Italianate phrases'. Fabrizio Melano's staging, together with Ezio Frigerio's set, was cold, static and almost cynical in its refusal to allow any room for the opera's dramatic values. If Verdi's *Trovatore* is rich, warm and melodramatic, the Met's production was dry and grandiloquent. Massive black pillars were shunted about in front of static clouds on a painted backcloth, with a pop-up castle and hundreds of shiny stairs. The chorus shifted about in ranks like robots and the principal singers scarcely moved at all. In any case, as Milnes noted, Pavarotti and Sutherland were no longer 'very nippy on their pins'. He reported that *Trovatore* 'has locals waving wreaths of garlic and wielding crosses. . . . The duel at the end of Act 1 made *A Night at the Opera* look like Aeschylus. . . .'[154]

Even Levine's presence at this time did not always ensure inspiration. When he took over the revival of *Trovatore* for a television recording in 1989, for Deutsche Grammophon, the chorus sang well and the orchestra played brilliantly, but Levine's pacing often dragged, letting the dramatic tug of the recitatives go slack and only awakening interest in the great arias. Pavarotti's Manrico was chilly and at times harsh, and Eva Marton's steely-voiced performance underscored the difficulty of casting Leonora at this time, even though she could, and did, easily overwhelm Pavarotti in their duets. Instead of channelling her huge voice and dramatic sense into what could have been a moving performance, all sense of emotion and line were quite lost – as was even intonation.

Similarly disheartening, in October 1989, was a performance of the new Sonja Frisell – Gianni Quaranta *Aida* with Domingo, Millo, Zajick and Milnes, which had been premiered the previous December. In spite of its powerful line-up, like *Trovatore* it lacked intention and commitment. Bruce Crawford had rejected the original Zeffirelli designs for the new *Aida* as too heavy and expensive, much to Zeffirelli's amazement, as he believed that Sybil Harrington would successfully back him up. 'I just decided that I had had enough,' Crawford later said.*[155] Crawford employed designer Gianni Quaranta to work with director Sonja Frisell. The substitute sets, which Harrington paid for as planned, reminded Peter Davis of 'Hollywood in a Fifties land-of-the-Pharaohs mood'.[156] Although not on such a grand scale as *Turandot*, there was once again much distraction from the intimate drama supposedly being enacted on stage. The triumph scene was dangerously close to kitsch, with Domingo's Radames borne in on a golden horse-drawn chariot, holding aloft a turquoise-coloured sickle reminiscent of the Grim Reaper against a campy background of male flesh.† Meanwhile the orchestra was busy banging on the beat. Martin Mayer wrote, 'The show sold out (*Aida* always does) and the Met does not have to think too much about *Aida* for a while.'[157] It did not have to think – just perform it – in order to ensure up to 99 per cent box office, at any time, almost regardless of who was singing and for many years to come.

In November 1988 Crawford had announced that he would be resigning in April 1989 to head the Omnicom group – the world's third-largest advertising agency. Crawford stated that he had achieved what he had set out to do, reducing the bureaucracy and building the box office up from an average 89 per cent to 90 per cent. He had succeeded in eliminating the deficit altogether by 1988, mainly by cutting expenses in the administration. He had also managed to increase fund-raising and to complete the Centennial Endowment Fund campaign. Volpe believed that the job was too 'hands-on' for

---

* Crawford explained that if a production went too far over budget even Harrington would not be willing to pay for the whole production, which left the House with a shortfall. Of Zeffirelli he said, 'I don't think he brought anything in on budget.'
† 'The Metropolitan's famous stage machinery moved scenes up and down in spectacular fashion, to great applause from elevator connoisseurs' (Henahan, *New York Times*, 10.12.88).

Crawford, who was by inclination and experience 'a high-level corporate businessman who delegates a lot and makes decisions'. At the Met, said Volpe, 'if you delegate too much, nothing gets done'.[158] Crawford himself later wrote that his reasons for leaving stemmed from 'a combination of some boredom and impatience' together with 'the lure of a package of stock options'.[159] When Crawford left in April 1989 the Met, having come firmly down on the side of the 'museum', was financially sound but artistically in the doldrums.

PART SIX

THE 1990s
'A Measure of Our Civilisation'

TWENTY-TWO

LA SCALA 1990–2002

The Primacy of Muti

THE TALE OF OPERA IN MILAN during the 1990s centres firmly upon Riccardo Muti. By the end of the century his musical intelligence had raised La Scala once again to its rightful place in the constellation of the Big Four. It is true that political upheavals seldom ceased, even if they were milder than before. Political affiliation continued to be a factor in the choice of high opera administrators and the selection of new works for the repertoire. Carlo Fontana's Socialist party credentials helped him be chosen as La Scala's sovrintendente. On the other hand it was Muti's devoted, non-partisan artistic leadership that gradually raised the level of quality at the House. He was consistently present to conduct major productions, supervise casting and coach singers in their roles. He also extended his interests as a conductor, embracing Wagner, Gluck and Spontini, among other composers, with generally positive results. Among the music directors of leading opera houses since the war, Muti wins high marks for keeping his attention focused upon quality.

It was not an easy task for Muti. Casting Verdi voices posed a problem for a number of years. The opening evening of the 1989–90 season, a production of *I Vespri siciliani*, was roundly booed by the *loggionisti*. American singers Cheryl Studer and Chris Merritt, in the main parts, had relatively light instruments, for voices suitable to Verdi's music were becoming rarer in the opera world. Hearing a later performance, Marco Vallora wrote, 'Chris Merritt as Arrigo showed himself to be nothing like a Verdi singer, and the worrying lapses in intonation which he has displayed since the beginning of his career now seem apparent to even his most devoted fans.' His voice, Vallora continued, sounded 'forced and the high notes painful.'[1] Merritt had been experimenting with heavier repertoire after a successful career as a Rossinian tenor with a wide range. He had also been having throat problems for about a year, and a course of steroids prescribed by a specialist had been a factor in his becoming seriously ill. Telling his side of the story, Merritt believed the Scala booing had been unfair:

> By the time Cheryl got to the Bolero everyone's nerves were on edge: her C sharps didn't quite work the way she wanted them to, and they booed her mercilessly. . . . Then Muti's nerves were getting frayed and he was giving the *loggionisti* dirty looks over his shoulder, and of course the next thing was my Melodia. Riccardo started the music and I couldn't hear it because of the booing. It died down just before I had to sing, and I barely got the note. But they didn't want to hear it anyway. We planned to present this strange, almost Offenbachian little love song gently and tenderly, but they wanted me to bellow it. Riccardo gave me a sign of 'Give more, they don't like this', so I started singing full out, but all along he and I didn't want the high D in the coda to be sung loud. We wanted it to be soft and ethereal. Well, that threw them into a tizzy. They didn't want that.[2]

Shortly afterwards Merritt resigned from a planned *Ernani* in Parma, which opened on 8 March 1990. His replacement, Lando Bartolini, sang too loudly – possibly to please the audience – but was booed nevertheless.

When Pavarotti essayed the role of Don Carlos on opening night in 1992, he was greeted with boos. According to Rodney Milnes, the raucous *loggionisti* were settling grievances: 'The *loggionisti* were out to get Pavarotti; he had achieved superstardom outside Italy, had turned the Scala down in earlier years, and more recently had cancelled an *Elisir d'amore* run at a late stage. So he needed a lesson, and a couple of cracked notes – one in the auto-da-fé, one in the final duet – gave them the excuse.'[3] But the question of booing is far from simple. Many booers, especially at Covent Garden and the Scala, care passionately about the quality of singing on stage. Sir John Tooley, while stressing the destructive effect that booing has on artists, realised that it was sometimes inevitable: 'In my experience booers are serious opera goers, who find it impossible to contain their anger at what they perceive to be poor vocal or musical performances, or in contradiction of composers' intentions. Sitting on their hands is an ineffective way of showing their disapproval.'[4]

It should be added to Tooley's thoughts that the relative lack of Verdi voices – which very likely led to the casting of Merritt and Studer in the first place – leads to less than ideal singing in this repertoire, with audience dissatisfaction almost inevitable.

Even though Verdi singers were scarce, leggiero sopranos and bel canto voices both male and female abounded. A third generation of post-war bel canto artists had sprung up to succeed Callas, Simionato, Sciutti and Horne in the 1950s and 1960s, and Valentini-Terrani and Ricciarelli in the 1970s and 1980s. Cecilia Gasdia, one of the third-generation bel canto sopranos active in the late 1980s and the 1990s, is highly musical and a sensitive actress. Critic Stephen Hastings assessed her flexible instrument: 'Gasdia's voice is hard to pin down, perhaps because one associates it with constant motion. It is basically a soft-grained lyric soprano that delights in darting movement, rapid colour changes and lingering pianissimos. It is well projected through-out a two-and-a-half-octave range but does not expand much in the upper register, where sustained notes are rarely pushed beyond mezzo forte.'[5] Her portrayal of Beatrice di Tenda at La Scala in January 1993 was remarkable for its dramatic power. Marco Vallora found that 'There are plenty of lovely voices in the ranks of Italian female singers, but most are devoted to inexpressive purity rather than credible dra-matic qualities, and Gasdia is one of the few genuine dramatic talents in their ranks'.[6]

Verdi voices were not entirely lacking on the Scala stage. Tiziana Fabbricini scored a triumph as Violetta in the 1992 Scala *Traviata*, at long last returning the piece to the House's repertoire after the 1964 Freni–Karajan disaster. A dozen years earlier Muti had despaired of ever conducting the work in the shadow, not so much of Freni and Karajan, as of Callas and Visconti: 'I know *La Traviata* very well, and it is very difficult, perhaps impossible, today to have a good stage production of this opera. It is difficult to say never, but it is likely that in my life I will never do *La Traviata*. I should have someone like Callas again and Visconti, but they are gone.'[7] Fabbricini may not have been Callas, but she showed she has all the requisites for the part: ringing top notes, a resonant low register, flexibility, boundless colours, free and open acting, a timbre both soft and penetrating, and a lovely mi-voix which she used perhaps too infrequently. Roberto Alagna as Alfredo moved gradually from a wooden presentation in the first act, to a convincing grief in Violetta's death scene. His voice, memorable for its youthful manly richness, had a unique and extremely appealing timbre recalling no other post-war tenor. Unless moved to maximum emotional involvement, however, he was apt to sing with little subtlety or dynamic variation. In time, he was to mature as a singing actor.

Muti's view of *Traviata* stands in sharp distinction to Giulini's gently mournful reading with Callas in 1955. Not averse to thumping out a rhythm here and there, he underscores the manic, agitated element in the heroine's character, especially in Act One. He does, however, discover the mixed feelings and softer musical edges in the second act. Here and throughout the show the Scala orchestra play with a luminous tone, a singing line and a dramatic immediacy that ought to be the envy of any group of instrumentalists the world over. They create moments of musical subtlety and emotional power that contrast with the Met orchestra's precision and clarity under Levine.

Muti was reaching new and exciting conclusions about the operas he enjoyed conducting. Although he had hardly been known before as a Wagnerian, and although Wagner's works were at that time infrequently heard at La Scala, in December 1991 Muti made the unusual move of opening the season with *Parsifal*. As Vallora indicated, his approach was delicate and subtle: 'The close of the opera said it all: not a sacred apotheosis, triumphant, glorious and deeply breathed, but an interior triumph, a subdued, almost whispered glow, unwilling to drift upwards into the air. . . . I have nothing but praise for the work Muti put in with the orchestra in taking such care over details.' Vallora disapproved, however, of an excess of what he termed 'southern brightness in the dark, Nordic score'. He found Muti's optimistic reading 'forced'. Domingo in the title role was also essaying new repertoire, earning praise for his 'vocally credible, and highly musical, Parsifal'. Waltraud Meier was an almost ideal Kundry: 'Her expressive, flexible voice is utterly seductive and at the same time able to fulfil all the animalistic demands the part makes. She is at once a woman in love, a beast, a witch and Mary Magdalene.'[8]

Muti's forays into new repertoire were not limited to Wagner. In mid-March 1992 Gluck's *Iphigénie en Tauride*, conducted by him, proved one of the most esteemed successes of the Scala season. The cast demonstrated how moving certain top international singing actors could be at their best during this period. As Orestes, Thomas Allen was 'splendid', 'giving a performance full of emotion and boundless grief'. Carol Vaness played the heroine 'both as a defeated woman and a girl who has not been able to grow up'. Gösta Winbergh as Pylades, however, was not in best voice. Stage director Giancarlo Cobelli worked with imagination and clarity. Vallora wrote: 'The tyrant Thoas arrived as if in triumph, escorted by a chariot of prisoners. Orestes and Pylades hung from red cords, stretching down from above: two bloody stripes of pain which divided the stage. There was a beauti-ful, dreamlike scene where the two friends, reunited in their grief, dragged their coloured cords to the centre of the stage.'[9]

It was not only Muti who made a brilliant impact conducting at La Scala: several younger conductors were also warmly received for their work at the House. This happened at a time when Solti was complaining of a shortage of top-ranking opera conductors. It encour-aged the hope that a new generation would be available to take over when such stalwarts as Muti, Abbado, Levine and Haitink would eventually retire. Daniele Gatti was called by Vallora 'one of the most dependable of young conductors, capable of taming a mixed cast of singers'. His Scala performance of Rossini's seldom-staged *Tancredi* on 13 July 1993 was 'thoughtful and considered'.[10] Myung-Whun Chung, born in Korea in 1953, and at the time of his visit to La Scala music director at the Bastille Opera in Paris, brought to Milan a lavishly praised *Lady Macbeth of Mtsensk*; the production had first been staged at his own house. The *Opera* critic wrote, 'Chung's con-ducting was admirable, full of tension and despair, right to the last gasp, and his enthusiasm finally set the orchestra alight. It is well known that Shostakovich's orchestration . . . often drowns voices, but Chung managed to deal intelligently with this aspect, using his detailed knowledge of the score.'[11]

Fine younger conductors were active in the Italian provincial

Houses as well. Riccardo Chailly continued to stand out as a younger musician who was gradually achieving stardom. In his function as principal conductor of Bologna's Teatro Comunale he even dared to take on the *Ring*. In 1993, Fernando Battaglia was impressed by the results: 'Chailly is one of the few Italian conductors, if not the only one, to have developed his own particular reading of Wagner in recent years. This year he tackled and resolved the many problems encountered in performing *Götterdämmerung* not only with great technical expertise, but with passion and enthusiasm. If his interpretation took a while to get going, it became progressively more impassioned, especially in the first act's stupendous orchestral passages; when we arrived at Siegfried's Funeral March and Brünnhilde's Immolation, the results were really memorable.'[12]

La Scala continued its policy of deepening and expanding the operatic repertoire. On 27 March 1992 Salvatore Sciarrino, in his *Perseo e Andromeda*, gave a highly imaginative contemporary reworking of the Greek myth. The opera opened with what Vallora described as:

> a single sound, which is also the repeated, obsessive noise of the wind which imprisons the heroine. Andromeda is alone, sitting on a rock on an island. Round about there is nothing but the unchanging, monotonous loneliness of the sea. The heroine is a bored woman of the *belle époque*, a Madame Bovary who longs to escape her unchanging situation. But the one who is to arrive and rescue her is only a bored hero from an operetta. Perseus is a mindless bon viveur; it is not worth packing one's bags and trying to escape on his account.[13]

The action was also set in the *belle époque*, with furnishings and props evocative of an elegant seaside resort infected by boredom. Perseus was played by two singers in evening costume – Per Vollestand and Carsten H. Stabell – who were meant by the composer not to sing exactly together, 'thus producing manipulated sounds even without the aid of electronics'.[14]

With the Scala *cartellone* growing ever more daring, audiences had become accustomed to unfamiliar works. Performances of Rossini's *La Donna del lago*, with Muti conducting, were videotaped at the Scala in late June and early July 1992. The story of this opera, once popular but nowadays rarely performed, was derived by librettist Andrea Leone Tottola from Sir Walter Scott's poem *The Lady of the Lake*. The part of Elena, a Romantic heroine torn and grieving throughout the work, gives a talented singing actress ample opportunity for expression. Singing Elena, June Anderson was in superb form. The tone was richer and warmer than is her wont, the coloratura brilliant and smooth. Chris Merritt as Rodrigo di Dhu pushed his voice and failed to delineate a believable character. Martine Dupuy, in the trouser role of Malcolm Graeme, was a true Rossini mezzo, with solid tone, flexibility, and a huge range. Werner Herzog's direction was static, Maurizio Balò's Scottish scenes were acceptable, and Franz Blumauer dressed the noble Scots in animal pelts and decorated their heads with jungle-cat fur. Muti conducted clearly and idiomatically, imposing little of himself upon the score.

Opera houses throughout Italy were eagerly premiering new operas. In Florence, the 1992 Maggio Musicale gave one of the first stagings of *Teorema*, a new opera by the Italian composer Giorgio Battistelli based on Pier Paolo Pasolini's film of the same title. When an unknown young man enters the house of a rich Milanese family, seduces most of its members and upsets the balance of their lives, a host of themes emerges: the emptiness of bourgeois existence, the destructive and constructive power of chaos, the joy and terror of self-knowledge, the pull of mystical spirituality. All dialogue was banished from the stage: a Biblical text was read out by an announcer at the beginning of each scene, and the action was carried out by miming actors. Each character was identified with a particular instrument of the chamber orchestra, whose sounds were distributed by microphones here and there throughout the hall. Julian Budden was enthusiastic on balance:

> The English producer, Lucy Bailey, disposed her forces skilfully, though my heart went out to Bernadette McKenna (the mother), an actress of real poise, for having to lie supine with head dangling over the orchestra pit, while being symbolically ravished by three young men. Among her colleagues I would single out the nervous, athletic François Testory (the son), Tony Gillfoil (the father), condemned for long stretches to writhing, voyeuristic postures during the successive seductions; and

Philippe Giraudeau who, as the stranger, dominated the drama with a commanding presence. The inventive score was conducted with authority by Orazio Tuccelle.[15]

Muti's insistence on reviving worthy operas at La Scala bore fruit in a new staging of *La Vestale*, which opened on 8 December 1993. Spontini's work had had only five performances in the Visconti staging of 1954 in which Callas had starred. The team of Callas and Visconti proved hard to surpass. Critic Marco Vallora objected to the production's anachronisms and inappropriate allusions. Director Liliana Cavani 'mixed up the ancient and the modern, Roman arches and Restoration jackets. The women were in the ancient robes of David's paintings, while the soldiers marched past with Napoleonic guns. The confusion was indescribable: there were even comical historical blunders, like Licinius returning from having routed the Gauls wearing French clothes.' Vallora approved the self-confidence of American mezzo Denyce Graves as the Grande Vestale, writing that she 'has a powerful, clear-cut voice, but she lacks the flexibility and expressivity the role needs. . . .' Muti's contribution on the podium was praised, but his choice of singers was questioned. He had 'dedicated himself to preparing a cast which was not fully up to the demands of the work.'[16]

Financial and administrative difficulties continued to plague a number of Italian opera houses. The Donizetti Festival at Bergamo was forced to cut back and to operate biennially as from 1991. On 15 January 1993 an 'astronomical deficit' was announced for the Teatro dell'Opera in Rome,[17] a year and a half after Fernando Pinto, the Socialist sovrintendente, had been sacked and Giampaolo Cresci, a Christian Democrat, named in his place. In the face of the huge deficit, a provisional administrator was appointed for the House while Cresci remained in place. The following year the *Evening Standard* reported that Rome's opera house was subsidised in the sum of £350 per seat, per performance, with 92 per cent of its income deriving from state subsidy.[18] Even if these figures are exaggerated, they point to enormous wastage. In February 1994 the Italian public auditor described as 'insane' the financial policies pursued in Rome by Cresci, who had spent half a million pounds for floodlighting for the House and purchased Persian carpets for its floors.[19] Even in less outrageously misrun Italian opera houses, an atmosphere of permanent crisis prevailed at a time when, on average, some 70 per cent of income derived from plummeting subsidies and only some 20 per cent from ticket sales.

Muti next programmed Wagner at La Scala to open the 1994–95 season. The production of *Die Walküre*, staged by André Engel and designed by Engel and Nick Rieti, was criticised by Gualerzi for its 'bizarre' visual effects[20] but praised by Rodney Milnes for its lavish beauty. Milnes wrote in *The Times* that the field of wheat and poppies upon which the Valkyries made their Act Three appearance was alone 'worth the airfare and the price of a ticket'. Musically, he felt the show suffered from Muti's tempi, which were both overly rapid and overly slow. 'What was downright unconventional', he wrote, 'was the conducting of Riccardo Muti' whose 'general principle seemed to be that if a phrase looked lyrical on the page, then the tempo slowed right down and it was given the full Mahlerian soup treatment; if, superficially, it looked "exciting", then the tempo was doubled and off he galloped.' Milnes felt that Muti's was more than 'a restless reading: it was at times almost incoherent'.

Muti has indeed, from time to time, consciously chosen to fashion highly energetic and strongly contrasted opera interpretations, believing a full measure of the hectic may be all to the good. 'Opera', he once remarked, 'is a voyage through incessant, even feverish agitation.'[21] This philosophy, in its constructive emphasis upon energy, recalls Toscanini's readings of opera, in particular Verdi. But Toscanini avoided sentimentalising lyrical passages and rarely took presto sections faster than the singers could comfortably perform. In this *Walküre*, however, Gabriele Schnaut as Brünnhilde was hard put to keep up with Muti's tempi. Domingo's Siegmund was, Milnes felt, 'heroic' and 'smoothly sung'. Mezzo Waltraud Meier once again made a strong impact in a Wagner role at La Scala, this time in the soprano role of Sieglinde.[22]

On 4 June 1995 Muti saved the show at La Scala by playing the piano. The orchestra musicians, demanding a pay rise, had called a strike. Instead of cancelling the planned *Traviata* performance, management decided to proceed as planned, with one exception: with the striking musicians absent from the pit, Muti alone at the keyboard played the piano reduction of the orchestral score. After hurling abuse at the strikers, the audience settled down to enjoy Tiziana Fabbricini's Violetta. 'On the stage by the piano, I felt guided and dragged forward by Muti,' said Fabbricini. 'I felt the exceptional nature of the evening; it was as if I were breathing with Muti. I abandoned myself and gave everything. The public understood. They applauded with me.' Stefano Curci, the union spokesman, had reason to maintain the strike was justified. 'We are fed up. We can't take any more,' he said. 'We earn less than a plumber or a taxi driver.'[23] The take-home pay of a rank-and-file orchestra member at the time was only 2.7 million lire per month, the equivalent of some £1,100.

By the time Muti went on stage to substitute for the striking orchestra the financial condition of La Scala was so dire that radical changes were being considered. In 1992 the central government grant to all the thirteen *enti lirici* (public opera corporations) taken together, had totalled 445 billion lire, or £185 million. The following year the subsidy was reduced to 430 billion lire, or £179 million. In 1994, owing to the weak Italian economy, a further cut was announced in the amount of £21 million, a subtraction which was cancelled following protests from most of the Houses that the Rome Opera had been given an unfairly generous allocation – some 32 billion lire, or £13 million – to cover its huge debt. With salaries so low, and so many workers on the payroll in a country where overstaffed opera houses were a long-standing tradition, government funding simply did not stretch far enough. One possibility being discussed was to privatise the House, turning it into a foundation that would operate with corporate and private donations as well as the state subsidy. In 1994 private giving totalled only $1 million – a trifling sum given the huge expense of running the theatre. One reason for this penury was the unavailability of tax breaks for donors to opera.

Another strike at La Scala lasting for several weeks during the autumn of 1995 caused the cancellation of a new production of *Lucia di Lammermoor*. The season was opened instead with *Die Zauberflöte*, which was acclaimed for Muti's conducting. Gualerzi wrote, 'Muti's reading properly focused on transparency and lightness, and as he declared before the opening, he let himself "be carried away on the stream of musical purity and sweetness", without letting any of the

Above Götz Friedrich, student of Felsenstein and one of Germany's most influential directors of the 1970s and 1980s during his collaboration with Colin Davis, Covent Garden's music director from 1971 to 1986.

Above right John Tooley, general director, and Claus Moser, chairman of the Board, at the annual press conference, Covent Garden, 1981.

Norman Bailey, Heather Harper and Jon Vickers in Elijah Moshinsky's Brecht-inspired, landmark *Peter Grimes*, at Covent Garden, in July 1975.

Riccardo Muti, music director of La Scala from 1986, conducting *Macbeth* at Covent Garden, March 1981.

Jean-Pierre Ponnelle who worked at Salzburg, Covent Garden and La Scala was a favoured director at the Met during the 1980s. He is seen here rehearsing Frederica von Stade as Idamante in *Idomeneo* in October 1982 at the Met.

Right Otto Schenk, the Austrian director, who was appointed resident conductor at the Staatsoper in 1965, also worked at Covent Garden, La Scala, and the Met where he directed a romantic *Ring* from 1986 to 1989.

Left Sybil Harrington, a major Met benefactor, with her favourite director, Franco Zeffirelli, who dominated Met production in the 1980s, during rehearsals for *Tosca*, March 1985.

Below Zeffirelli's well-populated *La Bohème* in December 1981, and his even more lavish *Turandot* in March 1987, reflected Met audiences' taste for visually impressive productions.

Above Plácido Domingo, Katia Ricciarelli and Elijah Moshinsky rehearse *Otello* at Covent Garden, January 1987.

Right Carlos Kleiber, recognised by his colleagues as an extra-ordinary artist of the era, at the *Otello* rehearsals. The Domingo-Kleiber *Otello* collaboration ignited audiences in Europe and America.

Two productions of *Simon Boccanegra* in the 1990s show different approaches of the Met and Covent Garden. Giancarlo Del Monaco's first act garden, designed by Michael Scott, in 1995.

Moshinsky's and Michael Yeargan's 'shared thought on a bare stage', Covent Garden, November 1991.

Above Joseph Volpe, executive director of the Met from 1990 and general manager from 1992, at the press conference announcing the appointment of Valery Gergiev, the artistic director of the Kirov Opera, as principal guest conductor in 1997.

Below Cecilia Bartoli and Bryn Terfel in the Met *Figaro*, December 1998.

Below right Kiri Te Kanawa, Covent Garden, 1991.

Above Bernard Haitink, Covent Garden's music director from 1987 to 2002.

Below David Syrus, Covent Garden's head of music, and Georg Solti coaching Angela Gheorghiu for the role of Violetta. Theatre director, Richard Eyre, observes from behind the piano, Covent Garden, November 1994. Gheorghiu's performance was hailed as the birth of a new opera star.

Overleaf Covent Garden's restored Floral Hall after the redevelopment of 1998-2000.

work's complexity pass him by.' Muti's Mozart cast was on balance very good. Gualerzi felt Andrea Rost's Pamina was 'inspired', while British baritone Simon Keenlyside's Papageno came in for 'a special word of praise'.[24]

Even in a difficult financial climate, Italian opera found means of self-renewal. On 18 October 1991 the Carlo Felice Theatre in Genoa had been re-opened after rebuilding. The Carlo Felice was the last major opera house in Europe to be restored after damage during the Second World War. It had been inaugurated in 1828 and given the name of the then King of Sardinia, to whose realm Genoa had been annexed. The new auditorium, which seats some 2,000, is modern in design, relatively shallow and steeply raked, with open balconies on the sides rather than boxes. The total cost of rebuilding was some 150 billion lire, or £69 million, of which the Erg petroleum corporation contributed 12 billion lire. *Il Trovatore* was the work chosen for the gala evening. Raina Kabaivanska sang Leonora to muted acclaim, while Shirley Verrett's Azucena was panned by the *Opera* critic as vocally faded. Carlo Rizzi, the conductor, sometimes 'lacked the spring and feverish anxiety which the piece calls for'.[25]

Five years after the Carlo Felice was reopened, disaster struck another Italian opera house: La Fenice in Venice. On the night of 29 January 1996 the auditorium was gutted by fire. The glorious gilt interior, the decorative intaglios and mouldings and the marquetry floors of the *sale* all perished in a conflagration so strongly fanned by a west wind that embers were cast over the lagoon as far as the Giudecca. The authorities promised the Fenice would be rebuilt 'where it was, as it was'. Cinema actor and director – and jazz clarinettist – Woody Allen donated the proceeds from a concert which he played in Venice towards the rebuilding. Initial progress, however, was painfully slow, held up by legal quarrels.

Muti's *Ring* forged ahead with *Siegfried*, which opened on 1 April 1997. The conductor took a view both deep and broad, which Giorgio Gualerzi described as 'drawing the different expressive strands together in a unity of intention and result – the heroic force of the Nothung motive, the rustle of spring on its way, and the impetus of the long, impassioned love duet'. As Siegfried, Wolfgang Schmidt was 'conscientious', while Jane Eaglen, alternating with Gabriele Schnaut as Brünnhilde, was in 'robust, attractive voice'.[26] By the time *Götterdämmerung* closed the Wagner cycle on 7 December 1998, and following a concert production of *Rheingold*, Muti had matured as a Wagner conductor with the accent on the lyricism of the score, being summed up by Gualerzi as 'an excellent pilot on the stormy Wagnerian ocean'.[27]

Muti's Mozart also continued to take an honoured place at La Scala. 'Mozart', said the conductor, 'should be every musician's daily bread: performing Mozart is good for pianists, it's good for violinists, it's good for singers.'[28] Looking back in 1997, after a new production of *Le Nozze di Figaro*, Gualerzi found that nearly all Mozart's major operas had had readings by Muti:

> In sixteen years Muti has added three productions of *Don Giovanni*, two of *Così fan tutte*, and one each of *La Clemenza di Tito*, *Idomeneo*, and *Die Zauberflöte* – all the major Mozart operas, with the curious exception of *Die Entführung aus dem Serail*. This demonstrates that Muti has managed to do more than any other Italian conductor, apart from Gui, to establish Mozart's operas in Italy, and in the country's most important opera house. Muti's success has been built on two basic elements: on one hand, vigorous, alert and intelligent interpretations which never lapse into languor ... and on the other a choice of singers which, some over-dependence on non-Italians apart, has created a notable new generation of Mozart interpreters.[29]

Besides Andrea Rost and Simon Keenlyside, Muti's 'notable new generation' in Mozart roles had come to include Barbara Frittoli as the Countess, Monica Bacelli as Susanna, a role she sang with 'subtle elegance', and the incomparable Welsh bass-baritone Bryn Terfel as Figaro, performed with 'undisguised aggression'.[30]

In June 1997 the La Scala Board approved a plan worked out by the Italian minister of culture, Walter Veltroni, in which the House would fall under the control of a public-cum-private entity to be called the La Scala Foundation. When the plan went into effect on

17 November 1997 it allotted both control and funding in unequal shares: public bodies would have 60 per cent, while private companies would have 40 per cent. This meant that the State would fund the House in the amount of £33 million annually and that private companies would cover most of the remaining running costs (box office income amounted to no more than some 20 per cent of expenses). The Pirelli tyre corporation alone was scheduled to donate some £2 million each year. Insurance companies and banks were also to be involved in the funding and running of the House, and the Eni oil company agreed to participate as well. Sovrintendente Carlo Fontana pointed out the unique nature of the scheme, which was scarcely the sort of thing one would have associated with his socialist principles. 'This is more than sponsorship, which has not always been a constructive factor in the music business.' Fontana indicated that participating companies would share in the taking of decisions at La Scala. Representatives of the companies favoured innovative schemes to make money for the House, 'including the marketing of La Scala products to cash in on its reputation'.[31] Muti, none too keen on the plan, added that the foundation would have 'iron-cast written rules' to preserve 'absolute liberty and artistic autonomy'. He warned the corporate bodies not to imagine they would be allowed to dictate musical policy: 'But I say to the private investors, let us understand each other clearly: by investing money you do not acquire the right to decide whether it is better to stage Gaspare Spontini's *La Vestale* or some other lighter, romantic opera.'[32]

The shortage of dramatic sopranos continued to plague La Scala late in the decade and by then tenors had also become scarce. *La Stampa* of Turin reported on 21 June 1999 that sixty tenors were auditioned to fill ten vacancies in the Scala chorus, but only three were considered adequate. Critic Sandro Cappelletto was dumbfounded as to the cause of the problem in a land historically associated with the tenor voice. 'Is this another consequence of a male identity crisis,' he wondered, 'a mysterious hormonal mutation that reverberates in the male voice, or is it the fault of bad teachers?'[33] Muti, concerned about the tenor problem, also wondered why the weightier voices had vanished: 'Singers in the heavy repertory are becoming fewer and fewer. Certain timbres, generally the darker voices – tenore drammatico, tenore lirico spinto, soprano drammatico, mezzo-soprano drammatico, baritono verdiano, basso profondo – seem to be disappearing ... Perhaps it's a tendency to sing a greater variety of repertory: artists don't care about their voices in the same way.'[34]

Muti was nevertheless fortunate to be able to cast Maria Guleghina in heavy Verdi parts at La Scala. In early 1996 she was engaged as Abigaille (*Nabucco*), 'tackling a murderous role', as Gualerzi wrote, she 'seemed more than the others to emerge unscathed, and she gave a fine performance, both as a singer and interpreter.'[35] At the opening of the 1997–98 season Guleghina sang Lady Macbeth opposite Renato Bruson. As a French television documentary demonstrated, the pair were carefully and enthusiastically coached at the piano by Muti, who took infinite pains to correct the Russian soprano's Italian diction, help her use text, melody and rhythm to enhance her already intense dramatic expression, and even point out, as a stage director might, the atmosphere of a scene or the significance of a given utterance. The resulting performance was breathtaking. Guleghina drew on a panoply of vocal resources to portray a ferocious, obsessive, even repulsive Lady Macbeth. In the sleepwalking scene her acting was so finely detailed that one almost forgot she was singing at the time – that is, until she unleashed a pianissimo high D flat as she disappeared into the darkness.

Although Muti shared the podium with younger conductors, it was not too often that his peers were invited to La Scala. Sinopoli conducted infrequently at the House during the 1990s, with the notable exception of a *Wozzeck* in 1997. Colin Davis had a major success at La Scala with *Les Troyens* on 12 April 1996. Gualerzi wrote, 'Davis is well known for his perfect grasp of Berlioz's music, and his reputation was fully confirmed on this occasion.'[36] Riccardo Chailly, then conductor of the Amsterdam Concertgebouw Orchestra, had been established as a leading conductor of opera. In his *Butterfly* of 11 January 1996 he 'seemed in top form, more and more an operatic conductor of great sensitivity, able to maintain a good balance between pit and stage'.[37]

*   *   *

Giorgio Strehler died on 25 December 1997 at the age of seventy-six. He had been closely involved in the construction of a new small hall for chamber opera and other small-scale lyric productions, which had not had a home in Milan since the Piccola Scala had closed in 1983. The production of *Così* on which he was working went ahead after his death. In a fitting memorial, it opened La Scala's Nuovo Piccolo Teatro on 26 January 1998 and ran until late March.

In October 1998 Carlo Maria Giulini's retirement from conducting was announced by the Orchestre de Paris. Giulini, aged eighty-four, cancelled concerts scheduled for January of the following year and expressed his intention 'to spend more time teaching young musicians'.[38]

In February 1998 it was reported that the rebuilding of La Fenice had run into serious difficulties. The Italian Council of State ruled that the contract for reconstruction had been awarded in an irregular manner. The contractor was expensively recompensed and the bidding reopened. In April, David Mosford filed a story in the *Sunday Telegraph* citing speculations that the Fenice had been the target of Mafia arsonists: 'Although investigations at La Fenice will probably never resolve exactly what happened two years ago, the rumours – and rumours tend to be more authoritative than newsprint in Italy – are either that the Mafia was firing a warning shot at the Italian government for clamping down on its activities, or that Mafia-based renovators were doing themselves a little job-creation work that got out of hand, thereby reducing one of Europe's favourite Houses to rubble.'[39] Whether or not the Mafia was involved, Mosford's intimations of illegal acts were underscored the following September when the mayor of Venice was charged in court with negligence and electricians working at the Fenice the night of the fire charged with arson.[40]

Although La Scala's main building still stood, it was in urgent need of improvements. In 2001 it was decided that the auditorium would be given a refurbishing, while the backstage spaces and offices, rehearsal halls and dressing rooms would be torn down and reconstructed from the floor up. The old Piccola Scala would be transformed into much needed storage for sets. Hydraulic lifts would be installed to help make the creaky old stage machinery more efficient, but the idea of using computerised lifts on the model of Covent Garden's rebuilding was quashed on the grounds of over-complexity. The grand scheme would cost some £35 million.

While rebuilding was being carried out the company would put on regular performances in the Teatro degli Arcimboldi, a purpose-built hall funded by the Pirelli tyre company. Pirelli, involved in La Scala's management under the new scheme for the past three years, undertook to construct the Arcimboldi stage to the precise size specifications of the Scala stage, thus allowing the transfer of all the productions in the repertory. The main House shut down on 31 December 2001, after a series of Domingo's performances as *Otello*, which he intended to be his last in that role. The work chosen for its planned reopening in June 2004 was Antonio Salieri's *L'Europa riconosciuta*, the same opera which had opened the theatre in 1778. La Scala was following the lead of Covent Garden and the Met in renewing its structure. Of the houses's total annual operating budget, £1.5 million was being provided by philanthropist Alberto Vilar. With such a grand institution entering a period of uncertainty, Muti acknowledged the anxiety surrounding the move: 'This is not an *addio*, only an *arrivederci*, but one that provokes pain. There is that sense of laceration that we all feel when you are separated from places that are charged with history and extraordinary memories.'[41] The Arcimboldi underwent teething problems: during a performance at the end of January 2002 a large pane of glass fell from a wall on to seats in the auditorium which were, fortunately, empty. Many Milanese, who had dreaded the long drive out of town, came to like the daringly designed House, larger than the Scala.

The *loggionisti* were particularly apprehensive: the Teatro degli Arcimboldi had been constructed without standing room and they feared the rebuilt Scala would have no cheap places for them. Even before the closure of the old House, standing-room places in the galleries had stopped being sold. The administration suddenly discovered that allowing standees in the gods contravened fire laws. The *loggionisti* were not convinced by the excuse. Giuseppe Castagnetti, head of the organisation known as 'Gli Amici del Loggione', protested vehemently that this decision 'is very unpleasant because we will lose a traditionally passionate public that truly loves opera, lives for opera and will line up for tickets for hours, making huge sacrifices just to see a performance. A theatre is more than just its conductors and the works that are presented in it, but also its public.'[42]

As La Scala entered a new era, Muti continued to carry out his task as music director in the grand tradition of Toscanini. In the late 1980s and throughout the 1990s he had made the role of the conductor, rather than singers or stagings, the central element in the House's offerings. Muti himself often selected stage directors: 'If I've chosen the director and don't like what I see, it is my responsibility to persuade him to change things or send him away. If I got into the pit, it means I've married the ideas on stage. In the pit you take responsibility for everything.'[43] In contrast to Karajan, who used the Staatsoper as a stepping-stone to building a musical empire, Muti devoted himself largely to La Scala. He spent a good deal of time in Milan, attended to the minutest of musical details, brought well-chosen singers to a peak of excellence and took pride in his faithfulness to the tradition. At the centre of his artistic vision was a specific operatic sound, the way in which La Scala had been performing Italian repertory since 1986. 'There is a style, a Verdi style', Muti said, and he continued 'We don't pretend we are the only ones who know this style, but certainly when you hear the orchestra and chorus of La Scala in certain Italian operas, I think you hear something unique.'[44] In July 2000 Muti once again demonstrated his commitment to the House by removing himself from consideration as Kurt Masur's successor as music director of the New York Philharmonic Orchestra.

Even with the problematic refit and financial problems, Muti's leadership gave La Scala continued stability during the first years of the new millennium. His talent and tenacity, not to mention his fierce loyalty to the theatre, made him a national treasure.

TWENTY-THREE

VIENNA 1990–2002

'What Has Austria Got Besides the Staatsoper?'

THE DECADE OF THE 1990S was marked by conservative views and policies at the Staatsoper. When Eberhard Waechter and Ioan Holender took over from Claus Helmut Drese, they took a tack decidedly opposite to Drese's artistic daring and liberal spending habits, instituting a moratorium on new productions to save money during a time of belt-tightening. To Drese, the new team's policies were a capitulation to Austrian bureaucracy and a return to the problematic repertory system. Holender inherited the mantle of Staatsoper intendant when Waechter unexpectedly died on 29 March 1992 at the age of sixty-two.

Born in Romania in 1935, Holender had studied engineering and afterwards worked as a tennis coach and an assistant stage director before training as a singer in Vienna. He was down to earth about his vocal talents: 'I had a good voice – not as good as some people hoped, but not as bad as some journalists write today. Anyway, for three years I lived from it.'[1] After he took over as sole manager in Vienna Holender continued to operate under fiscal restraints. New productions were few. As he stated in an interview, 'What you find here should be of good quality.'[2] Be that as it may, if one sought excellent quality – and not mere competence – it was difficult to find in the House during the 1990s.

The first half of the decade was a somnolent time for many of the major arts in Austria. The land which early in the twentieth century had been the birthplace of the 'Second Viennese School' of composers – notably Schoenberg, Webern and Berg – was marking time with respect to new music. Nevertheless, instrumental performance remained at a high level. When the Vienna Philharmonic Orchestra was challenged by a brilliant conductor it was arguably unmatchable in the world, especially for its warm, rich, deep tone and its sensitivity of line. However, few if any star singers were emerging in the Vienna Opera, in stark contrast to the 1930s, 1940s and 1950s.

In one area of creative life Vienna was wide awake: the city's fringe opera companies prospered, nourished by the local legitimate theatre, open as it was to new styles and ideas while continuing to draw on the ever-renewed riches of the Viennese theatrical tradition, which led the German-speaking countries. The Wiener Kammeroper marked its fortieth birthday in January 1993. The Kammeroper, founded by Hans Gabor, was maintained as a private institution aided by state funding. In its lifetime it had put on an astonishing total of 162 works in 319 productions. Together with the Teatro Sperimentale in Spoleto and Ricordi, the music publishers, the Kammeroper instituted the biennial Orpheus Competition for contemporary opera composers. Among the Kammeroper's 1993 offerings was *Das Donauergeschenk* (*The Danubians' Gift*), a work commissioned by the House and composed in pure dodecaphonic style by Rainer Bischof to a 'violent libretto' by artist Friedrich Danielis.

The Kammeroper's 1993–94 season was opened with a three-sided co-production with the Staatsoper and the Volksoper: *Erendira*, with music by Violetta Dinescu to a libretto by Monika Rothmaier based upon a tale by Gabriel García Marquez. Christopher Norton-Welsh found Christina Asher 'appropriately dominating' in the role of the Grandmother. 'Alessandra Catterucia gave what life she could to the palely drawn heroine. Josef Luftensteiner sang beautifully as Ulysses, the most lyrical role, and the multitude of supporting parts were competently shared between six House regulars.'[3]

Even Carlisle Floyd's opera *Susannah*, with its American folk-music idiom and new-world setting and themes, found a place on the Kammeroper's bill, being given its first Vienna performance in October 1996. Well-known German mezzo Brigitte Fassbaender, working in her new profession as a stage director, was, as *Opera* noted, 'concentrated on the theme of a hidebound community's inhumanity to the outsider rather than the specifically American milieu. Unfortunately, the words only emerged intermittently and so much of the drama was left to the imagination. The Canadian Desmond Byrne, whose diction was crystal clear throughout, carried by a fine, rich bass-baritone, provided a dominating and more sympathetic Preacher Blitch than usual.'[4]

The offerings of the Staatsoper were pallid by contrast. A planned *Ring*, to be staged by Harry Kupfer, was dropped, while the Sanjust *Ring* had stopped short after *Die Walküre*. A new team, of Adolf Dresen as director and Herbert Kapplmüller as designer, went ahead with *Das Rheingold* which, however, was found wanting both dramatically and visually. Conductor Christoph von Dohnányi came in for praise, while following his success at La Scala in *Parsifal*, Plácido Domingo continued his exploration of Wagner tenor roles as Siegmund. He had put in a great deal of effort to improve his German and adjust his supple, Italianate vocal line to Wagner. In the end he was successful, imbuing the character with a radiant and humanising Latin passion. His singing of the tenor passaggio was a study in technical precision, and his acting was superb.

The *Opera* critic remarked of the direction, 'Dresen seems determined to deflate the gods.'[5] *Siegfried* also elicited mixed reviews: 'Herbert Kapplmüller's designs kept the general style of the previous evenings, but his solutions were more successful. . . . The loathly worm was a genuine monster with huge mouth glowing red inside, and Fafner appeared in person to sing his dying words. . . . Adolf Dresen again offered a mixture of perceptive action and gesture and rather lame stretches.' Norton-Welsh praised 'the twin glories of the evening', namely Siegfried Jerusalem in the name part and Heinz Zednik as Mime, calling them 'both well practised assumptions but both capable of finding fresh nuance and splendid in their mutual interaction'.[6]

In October 1993, to commemorate the seventy-fifth anniversary of Leonard Bernstein's birth, the Staatsoper gave a performance of the Otto Schenk production of *Fidelio*, which Bernstein had conducted when the production was unveiled in 1970. Theo Adam, singing Pizarro as he had done under Bernstein, still presented 'a frighteningly realistic picture of a small-time, horribly distorted sadist, the eyes reflecting bitterness and fear'. As Florestan Canadian tenor Ben Heppner made his debut at the Staatsoper. In the words of Alan Blyth, he 'poured out firm, solid tone into the House easily encompassing the climax of his big scena, but also managing a deal of pathos and a lean line in the aria itself and in the subsequent trio, then cutting through the ensemble in the finale. Not the most emaciated-looking of starved prisoners, he nevertheless managed to suggest Florestan's dire straits.'[7]

Returning to the Staatsoper in March 1994 after a nine-year absence, the by then legendary Carlos Kleiber conducted a cast of outstanding Strauss singers in *Rosenkavalier*. Although Michael Henderson considered Barbara Bonney's Sophie mannered and 'too knowing by half', he deemed her singing splendid. Anne Sofie von Otter's acting also found much favour. She 'conveyed Octavian's passage from joy to bewilderment to mischief to partial self-knowledge with utter radiance.' Kleiber drew from the Vienna Philharmonic generous and loving playing 'for a conductor it plainly reveres'.[8]

Austria's comfortable denial of its Nazi past was beginning to be shaken. Ioan Holender made a momentous decision for the Staatsoper as well as for the whole country when he organised an evening concert in the auditorium on 27 April 1995 in memory of the artists who had suffered and died during the Nazi era.[9] The memorial was a first step towards reawakening awareness of Austrian complicity during the war and it was fitting that it should take place within the walls of the national opera. As Holender remarked, 'This House is very important for this country.' A Jew himself, Holender deemed it crucial that the Staatsoper take the lead in facing the facts – that Austrians and the whole world see that 'at least this House has changed' in its attitude.[10] Invitations were issued to a cross-section of prominent people: politicians and intellectuals, diplomats and journalists. Outstanding singers – Domingo, Carreras, Gruberova and Baltsa among them – volunteered their services in a lengthy programme of arias and lieder emphasising the works of composers, both Jewish and non-Jewish, who had been stigmatised and banned by the Nazis as practitioners of '*entartete Kunst*' (decadent art): including Meyerbeer, Mahler, Berg, Schoenberg, Weill, Erich Korngold, Ernst Krenek and Viktor Ullmann. The printed programme included texts and photographs collected by Austrian historian Oliver Rathkolb, one of which showed the Staatsoper façade hung with swastika banners on 9 April 1938 as Hitler passed along the Opernring in an open car, receiving the Nazi salute from the assembled

Viennese. Also reproduced was a blacklist, drawn up by the Staatsoper in the same year, of its own employees branded as Jews – whether 'whole' or 'half' – and sacked from the House for no offence but their ethnic origin. The Staatsoper's lobbies were filled with an exhibition depicting anti-Semitic actions against artists during the Nazi period. Historian and journalist Hella Pick described the scene:

> In the galleries where opera-goers normally gossip idly and comment on the dress code while they wait for the performance to resume, they were shocked into looking at their past: into the way musicians had allowed themselves to be used to pervert traditions and promote the inculcation of Teutonic culture in Austria. Reaching up almost to the height of the grand staircase from the foyer, a video installation in the shape of two revolving columns had been erected with the names of more than 3000 Jewish intellectuals and artists who had either perished in the camps or been forced to leave the country.[11]

Holender, in a strong speech to the audience, recalled the memory of the sacked Staatsoper employees and the fact that none of them had been asked back to work at the House after the war. He also put paid to the myth that Austria had been the victim of Nazism by stressing the long-standing prevalence of anti-Semitism well before what Rathkolb, in the printed programme, correctly termed the 'so-called *Anschluss*'. Austrian television broadcast the event and public awareness of Austria's complicity in Nazi crimes was enhanced.

The Staatsoper, one of Austria's most prestigious institutions, thus, once again, hosted a musical event that told of the whole nation's pain and rebirth in history. In 1945 *Figaro* had symbolised continuity after wartime destruction. In 1955 *Fidelio* had announced the rebuilding of the House and the State, albeit in an atmosphere of not facing up to the past. Now, in 1995, Holender's memorial evening and the chilling pictures in the foyer pointed the way to a new future for Austria, one in which the truth might prevail and a new beginning be made.

In October 1996 another company, the Wiener Operntheater, gave the premiere performances of Reimann's opera *Das Schloss*, adapted from Kafka's novel, known in English as *The Castle*. Reimann's music, which was deemed by Norton-Welsh 'nearly as impenetrable as the castle of the title', seemed to present few difficulties to conductor Andreas Mitisek and the Györ Philharmonic Orchestra, guests from Hungary. Director-designer John Lloyd-Davies created small mazes all round the stage to suggest the absurdly impossible situation of Kafka's protagonist, who is baulked by all and sundry in his efforts to get to the castle – which in the end remains an undefined, inexplicable symbol. Norton-Welsh wrote, 'Here I must praise Martin Winkler for coping with the huge, immensely difficult part of the surveyor K with his usual intensity – on stage for the best part of three hours.'[12]

The Volksoper benefited from the services of a new music director, Israeli-born conductor Asher Fisch. Critics found that, besides enjoying a close and easy rapport with singers, Fisch raised the orchestra to a finer level. In a *Faust* which opened on 8 November 1996 Fisch 'took a lean and athletic view of the score, but while he eschewed the rich vein of latent sentimentality, he gave the music and the singers plenty of room to breathe'.[13]

In October of that year the Wiener Operntheater essayed John Adams's *Nixon in China* with considerable success. *Nixon* proved one of the few contemporary American operas which was staged widely abroad. The production's accent, refreshingly, was on humour, with Wendy Hill 'convincingly silly' as Pat Nixon and the stage dressed with oversize red armchairs and aircraft parts. Martin Winkler, wrote the *Opera* critic, 'added another intensely sung role to his many successes in such productions and looked astonishingly like "Tricky Dick" . . .'[14] Once again, Andreas Mitisek conducted the Györ Philharmonic.

The Staatsoper first presented its 'sparkling new staging' of Richard Strauss's *Die schweigsame Frau*, adapted by Stefan Zweig from Ben Jonson's *Epicoene, or The Silent Woman*, on 21 December 1996. Holender had made a vow to the rising coloratura star, Natalie Dessay, that the part of Aminta would be hers, and he fulfilled his promise. Dessay sang extraordinarily well and was judged especially effective in her interplay with Morosus, played by bass Kurt Rydl. The critics enjoyed their evening out. Norton-Welsh wrote: 'The orchestra was, as always, on its best behaviour for Horst Stein, who gave a commanding rendering of the score, both rumbustious and tender by turns, with the best soft playing I have heard in a long time.' Marco Arturo Marelli's staging was 'bright and clear . . . and fully agreeing with Dessay's conviction that Aminta does not really relish tormenting the old man: she is sorry for him but plays along to effect a reconciliation between him and his nephew Henry, her own husband.'[15]

The Viennese continued to use the Staatsoper as a focus for the preservation of their traditions. The Opernball was held, year after year, in the auditorium, with the stalls seats removed and a dancing floor laid down. The purpose of the occasion, besides seeing and being seen, was to introduce Vienna's debutantes to 'society'. The basic ticket price was £160, with a box going for £900. According to the Austrian press, the Duchess of York was paid a fee of some £35,000 for the favour of her attendance. Demonstrators renewed their annual protests outside the opera house.[16]

After six years at the helm of the Staatsoper, Ioan Holender remained the House's sole and undisputed leader. The institution continued to commemorate the murder of Austrian Jews during World War Two: on 5 May 1998, to mark the 'Austrian Day Against Violence and Racism', the Staatsoper presented *Das Tagebuch der Anne Frank*, by Grigory Frid, to both houses of the Austrian parliament as well as concentration camp survivors.

Holender had managed to secure administrative independence from the Bundestheaterverwaltung, but at the price of less than generous government support. Once again, exact facts and figures for the Staatsoper are difficult to obtain, as are yearly breakdowns. However, a broad picture emerges of financial stringency during the 1990s. Even with relatively limited funding from the Ministry, the House managed to present what it wished, and at great expense. An opera was performed on some 300 evenings each year. In the storage docks were hung an astonishing number of costumes for the Staatsoper's vast repertoire – some 200,000. All told, the House employed about 1,000 people. Even with approximately 95 per cent of available seats sold to the public, only 34 per cent of income was derived from ticket sales. 'This is not a business,' Holender remarked. 'In opera you can only lose money.' Aware that the Viennese public demanded stars, and relying on the House's cachet, Holender persuaded international singers into taking a fee cut at the Staatsoper: 'They sing here for less money,' he stated. 'The more important the House, the less must be the fee.'[17] Two-thirds of the Staatsoper's performers were not guests but contracted members of the ensemble, a fact of which Holender was proud.

As Holender had not named an artistic director, a music director or even a permanent conductor, success or failure could be laid exclusively at his door. By the mid-1990s, however, critics and audiences on balance approved his efforts, with many qualifications. Vienna was the most broadly inclusive of all the 'opera museums' worldwide, with far more productions in repertoire than any other Big Four House. As they had for years, rehearsals remained spotty, for the House was so busy putting on an opera almost every night of the week that at any given moment the main stage might well be taken up with striking and replacing sets, refocusing lights and other technical matters. Holender made full use of the ensemble singers, typically casting them in a wide variety of comprimario parts and offering them principal roles as soon as they were ready to take them on. International stars made Vienna a regular stop on their itinerary, even though the House sometimes could not match their usual fee. Quality was uneven: budgetary constraints still meant new productions were few and far between, but many of those that did get mounted were interesting on musical or theatrical grounds. Routine evenings varied from good to barely acceptable. Old stagings seemed to go threadbare very quickly. The chorus and ensemble often shone, while the orchestra veered wildly from glorious, sensitive playing to odious *Schlamperei*.

Rienzi proved one of the most talked-about Staatsoper productions of the late 1990s. David Pountney's provocative postmodern staging marked a new departure for Vienna, which was seen as bowing to contemporary trends. Nor had this early opera of Wagner's been previously staged at the House since the war. The opera, which opened on 13 December 1997, was conducted by Zubin Mehta. Pountney and Robert Israel, the set designer, gave the production 'plenty of glitz, a dash of parody and huge crowds', supplementing the House chorus with singers from the Bratislava Philharmonic Chorus and Viennese music students.

Another postmodern staging, accenting the visual element, had been unveiled earlier the same year. Boito's *Mefistofele* was staged and designed by Pier'Alli, in a co-production with La Scala, and conducted by Fabio Luisi. A performance of 14 January 1998 gave an indication of what the House might come up with on a routine night when the stars failed to smile on Vienna. Mefistofele was sung by Egils Silins, Faust by Franco Farina, Margherita/Elena by Miriam Gauci, Marta/Pantalis by Mihaela Ungureanu, and Wagner/Nerèo by Torsten Kerl. The orchestral playing was remarkably sloppy for a world-class musical organisation. The horn section produced ragged entrances, and bad intonation. Luisi seemed at first dumbfounded by the melodramatic, quasi-mystical score, allowing big holes to open up between the numerous episodes. But later he moved things along, emphasising dynamic contrasts as bearing the dramatic burden. The pianissimo choral singing was magnificent.

Pier'Alli's staging was quirky. In the Prologue he deposited six ranks of angelic choirs, male, female and child, in total immobility on a stage as dark as one of Karajan's. Their static positioning was puzzling in view of the fact that they were supposed to represent flying clouds while singing 'Siam nimbi volanti'. It is unclear how the poor children even dreamed of sailing through the air so long as they were wearing 1957 Chevrolet bonnet ornaments on their heads, perhaps in lieu of wings. When the chorus were not on view they were nonetheless sorely missed, for the stage was left nearly bare: principals, lost in the vast void, moved scarcely at all.

On many nights the Staatsoper continued to offer conventional stagings and rather better orchestral quality. The next evening a performance of *Stiffelio* showed the House in a different light. Fabio Luisi once again conducted, intelligently and competently, and this time fully at ease. His clear beat, balanced dynamics and consideration for the singers showed him well beyond the level of a routinier. The orchestral sound was clean, transparent and exquisitely balanced, the intonation very good indeed. The production was bought from Covent Garden, where it had been staged by Elijah Moshinsky with Michael Yeargan's set and Peter J. Hall's costumes. Alhough somewhat under-rehearsed, it was satisfying on the whole. Mara Zampieri as Lina took an act and a half to warm up. Although her voice was neither beautiful nor warm, she used it expressively and won the audience over. Antonio

Lotti as Stiffelio, substituting for an ailing Domingo, made intelligent use of his limited resources. Renato Bruson as Stankar was the success of the evening. Although his low tones have disappeared in the course of his long career as a Verdi baritone, what remains is a noble, authoritative and handsome sound.

David Pountney returned to the Staatsoper in October 1998 to stage Rossini's *Guillaume Tell*, with sets by Richard Hudson. The overall effect coupled symbolism with eccentricity: 'Sections of the landscape frequently split and moved on and off stage, often transporting groups of people. Gesler and his troops occupied a movable red bridge as a symbol of their oppression, and a table housing a further glassed-in section of landscape rose and sank into the stage as required . . .' *Opera* found the staging mixed: 'Pountney's direction veered from excellent theatre with flashes of human insight to unnecessarily ludicrous effects spoiling the carefully prepared dramatic tension.' As Tell, Thomas Hampson offered vocal 'flexibility and attention to textural detail', thus enriching the characterisation. Nancy Gustafson 'sang Mathilde with frigid beauty'.[18] Conductor Fabio Luisi worked wonders with the orchestra while preferring unusually rapid tempos.

The following month Richard Hudson was once again engaged, this time to provide sets and costumes for Graham Vick's staging of *Ernani*. Eccentricity was for the time being in abeyance. Hudson contented himself with 'plain grey walls relieved by high-backed Spanish chairs, a thick red rope in various forms, a huge cross that was lowered over Charlemagne's grave after Carlos had reappeared to form the podium on which he was crowned, and a stage full of flowers for the final act. His costumes veered from more or less period to late nineteenth century.' Vick's low-key direction went 'little beyond arrangement, and provided only rare dramatic moments'. Norton-Welsh found Neil Shicoff's Ernani monotonously loud, except for his moving acting in the final scene.

Partly as a result of the enlightened repertoire policy of the off-Ring Houses, and partly because of Seefehlner's and Drese's efforts in the 1980s, the Viennese had become accustomed to works other than the German, Italian and French staples. By the spring of 2001 the Staatsoper went so far as to stage – for the first time ever – Britten's *Billy Budd*, with Bo Skovhus in the title role.

Even more significant changes were coming to the Staatsoper and to Austria. In February 1999 the Vienna Philharmonic voted after a four-hour meeting to allow women to be hired for the first time as orchestra members. Austrian Chancellor Viktor Klima had pushed strongly for the move.[19] In June of that year Holender announced at a news conference that Seiji Ozawa would be leaving the Boston Symphony in August 2002 to become music director at the Staatsoper. The intendant stated that Ozawa would be coming for three years, or 'perhaps even longer'.[20] 'I didn't look for a music director,' Holender remarked afterwards. 'Ozawa created this position, just as Abbado did.' In view of Ozawa's relatively limited experience and critical success as an opera conductor, he would have his work cut out for him. And in a climate of greater political frankness in Austria, atavistic voices were also heard. In October 1999 Jörg Haider and his far-right-wing Freedom Party won 27.2 per cent of the vote in the national elections, making his grouping the second largest in parliament. In March 2000, when his party was included in government, 15,000 demonstrators used the occasion of the annual Opera Ball to gather outside the House in protest.

Following Karajan's death in 1989, the Salzburg Festival drew up a shortlist of potential successors: Gerard Mortier, the head of the Théâtre de la Monnaie, the Belgian national opera; Peter Jonas, general director of the English National Opera; August Everding, intendant at Munich. When the choice fell on Mortier it was clear the festival was in for a shake-up. Mortier had gone so far as to shut down the Monnaie for half a year at the start of his tenure in 1981 in order to decide which staff and orchestra members to sack. Within a few years he had changed the House from a somnolent, ill-attended institution to one of Europe's liveliest venues for opera. His music directors in Brussels had been Sylvain Cambreling, recognised as one of Europe's most stylish and pernickety opera conductors (Cambreling dislikes Donizetti and Puccini), and Sir John Pritchard. A mad fan of opera from childhood, Mortier was known as an effective though far from frugal opera intendant, an exceedingly hard-working administrator and a ruthless taskmaster. The tale has been told of Concorde waiting on the tarmac until Gerard Mortier arrived to take his seat. Peter Sellars termed him 'a little Napoleon, who knows exactly what he wants to do, and then does it'. Interviewed in 1990 by Rupert Christiansen in *Opera* magazine, Mortier was frank about his approach to arts administration: 'I am Machiavellian ... If you don't fight back with the same weapons as your enemy, they will surely kill you.'[21] At Salzburg he won an unusually long six-year initial contract, which in due course was extended.

Mortier did not take up his post until 1992. But as soon as his appointment was announced he went on the media warpath against Karajan, Karajan's policies, and Karajan's friends at the festival. He blasted 'the mafia that has long exploited Salzburg for its own benefit and thought about recording before thinking about programming'. He indicated dissatisfaction with the superstar system in place at the festival, maintaining it was unnecessary 'to have Domingo or Madame Te Kanawa singing in order to have a great operatic experience'. Rather, Mortier would emphasise repertoire, and repertoire of a certain kind: 'The composer must again become more important than the interpreter.' He saw 'no reason to mount *Tosca* in Salzburg. Instead I want to establish here a canon of twentieth-century classics.'[22]

Perhaps the critics were affected by Mortier's salvos. Reviewing the 1990 festival's offerings, before Mortier had taken the chair, Alan Blyth scorned 'the conservatism of the productions, the complacency and seeming ignorance of the well-heeled and ageing audience ... and the hideous architecture and questionable acoustics of both auditoriums'.[23] By the time Mortier took up his appointment in 1992, his press conferences had become one of opera's hottest tickets. His sallies against Karajan, by then three years in his grave, were so fierce that the Karajan estate was considering taking Mortier to court. His promises of revolution, having attracted worldwide attention, were amply fulfilled.

The first Mortier-run festival programme included Olivier Messiaen's six-and-a-half-hour-long *Saint François d'Assise* in its second staging ever, directed as the premiere had been in Paris, in 1983, by Peter Sellars. Rodney Milnes called it a 'Great Event':

> Messiaen's musical language is original in its highly personal utterance rather than its actual syntax; one of its most attractive

features is its acceptance in passages of daring simplicity of a peculiarly French mode of religious expression, traceable from Gounod through Massenet to Fauré. The greatest challenge Messiaen set himself was to find sound to depict the Angel's gift of music as a means of communication between man and his God, and he met it head on with heart-stopping success.[24]

Mortier had brought the Los Angeles Philharmonic under Esa-Pekka Salonen to play the score, thereby alienating some members of the Vienna Philharmonic, who considered the festival their home turf. Milnes found the orchestral playing 'a triumph of technique and stamina, and infinitely superior to that of the premiere staging'.[25] Belgian bass-baritone José van Dam, as St Francis, was superb:

> To José van Dam's account of the title role words can scarcely do justice. The extraordinary musical quality of his singing, the way he sculpted the lines, his expressive control of dynamic (a hushed pianissimo always projected easily), his uniquely communicative handling of the French language, all mark him as one of the world's greatest singers.[26]

If Mortier had chosen Peter Sellars as stage director *pour épater les Salzbourgeois*, he succeeded. Milnes felt that 'the good moments of Sellars's staging were beautiful in their simplicity and directness, and the less good ones incomprehensible in their clumsy bloody-mindedness, like placing van Dam far upstage left for the scene of the stigmata while downstage centre was occupied by 21 hyperactive TV monitors built in the shape of a cross'. He was also outraged at

> the huge neon construction suspended over the stage . . . and the 40 TV monitors variously suspended or arranged around the stage. They were showing anything up to five home movies at once, shot with hand-held cameras and thus jiggling about to irritating, not to say health-hazardous effect. . . . Anything that distracts attention from the concentration with which *St François* is composed is a mistake, if not a crime.[27]

The major scandal of that year's festival centred on Riccardo Muti's last-minute departure from the new *La Clemenza di Tito*, staged by Karl-Ernst and Ursel Herrmann (who had also produced the same opera in Brussels). Muti pulled out only a week before the opening after disagreements with the Herrmanns concerning production values and musical tempos. Milnes felt that 'the staging had its fair share of *idées*', but compared with the 'nonsense regularly dished up in front of Muti's eyes at La Scala (Ronconi's *Ernani*, last year's pretentious *Parsifal*) there wasn't much to get worked up about'. The traditionalist holdouts in the Salzburg audience, together with those whom Milnes termed 'the stars and their recording companies', applauded Muti's disappearance.

Following Karajan's death, Solti had been appointed artistic director of the Salzburg Easter Festival, which in contrast to the summer festival received no State subsidy and was organised as a company. Control of the Easter festival had been in the hands of Karajan. After his death it passed to his widow and their daughters, who did not, however, take an active part in running it. The Easter Festival was supported by subscription sales, which fell off after Karajan died. During the interregnum, arguments with Mortier erupted over the use of facilities and the sharing of co-production facilities. Before the 1993 festival had begun, Solti announced his resignation, stating, 'After over 45 years of artistic administration duties, I now wish to devote my time completely to music-making.'[28] His replacement, Claudio Abbado, also failed to find an understanding with Mortier.

In 1994, even under Mortier, Mozart remained the summer festival's stock in trade. Spoken plays were also given prominence, appealing to German-speaking audiences. More contemporary offerings were put on in smaller auditoriums. Andrew Clark in *Opera* summed it up: 'All this suggests that behind the polemics, Mortier cannot escape Salzburg's underlying conservatism. He will always need a handful of safe box-office bets as insurance.' At the same time, Clark felt Mortier had 'changed the festival's artistic culture for good', citing among other programming innovations the engagement of Nikolaus Harnoncourt to conduct the Chamber Orchestra of Europe in concerts of Beethoven symphonies and Stravinsky's opera *Oedipus Rex* 'designed by an avant-garde team of architects'.[29] The following year Mortier himself publicly confirmed Clark's suspicion:

> The problem with Salzburg is that however hard you try to realize a big idea, you know for sure you are never going to

achieve it. That is how this festival has always been. The people here don't want change. Their idea of theatre is divorced from real life – they see it as a passive, decorative activity. They don't want to be stimulated mentally or intellectually. I agree art should entertain, but it must also ask questions and stir us up.[30]

Mortier also stated that some Vienna journalists had received funding from his enemies. This accusation led to a threat of legal action by the editor of *Der Kurier*, a newspaper unfriendly to Mortier. However, the editor's wife, Frau Helga Rabl-Stadler, who was none other than the president of the Salzburg Festival, asserted her continued backing for Mortier.

An outstanding *Rosenkavalier* in the 1995 festival, staged by Herbert Wernicke, showed how stimulating Salzburg's offerings could be. Andrew Clark wrote:

Wernicke presented *Rosenkavalier* as a mirror of time – reflecting not just the imaginary eighteenth-century Vienna concocted by Strauss and Hofmannsthal, but the era of the opera's composition and our own *fin de siècle*.

The stage was lined with angled mirrors, providing *trompe l'oeil* images of the Marschallin's aristocratic boudoir, Faninal's baroque town house and the rococo intimacy of the inn. The costumes – Octavian's white tailcoat and top hat, Ochs' Lederhosen, the Marschallin's black Jugendstil outfit – suggested the pre-1914 world of the Habsburg monarchy. Every so often the mirrors would offer the audience a fractured reflection of itself. The slightest disturbance was enough to unsettle the picture – suggesting uncertainty beneath the calm exterior. Like the opera itself, the production inhabited a world of illusion which vanished as we faced our mirror-image at the final curtain.[31]

Abbado's *Otello*, the centrepiece of the 1996 Easter Festival, failed to please Andrew Clarke, who wrote: 'Film director Ermanno Olmi's staging was 'static, monochrome and, in the Act Two flower scene, soppily sentimental. Lucio Fanti's decor consisted of a stepped rock-mound, marooned like an island in the oceanic wastes of the Grosses Festspielhaus stage.' Unchecked by Abbado, the Berlin Philharmonic 'turned Verdi's music into an instrumental blockbuster, laden with dazzling brass sforzandos and deafening percussive flourishes.' Domingo's singing in the title role was judged below his usual standard, with 'the voice uncomfortably tight, with all the isolated top notes missing'.[32]

The following Easter, however, Abbado and director Peter Stein collaborated in a *Wozzeck* which Andrew Clark felt 'surpassed all expectation'. Even though many stayed away from this production of a twentieth-century work, it was memorable both dramatically and musically. Clark wrote: 'Stein's staging was incredibly precise. Played in a single ninety-minute sweep, it was simply, powerfully concentrated and, above all, realistic. The characters were subtly drawn ... There was no point-making, no Expressionist baggage, no gratuitous show of decadence.' Abbado's 'instinctive command of rhythm and structure', was in evidence. 'There was nothing cerebral about this performance – rightly so, because there is nothing cerebral about the music. Sensuality, colour, luminosity were in abundant supply ...' Replacing Bryn Terfel, who had been announced for the part of Wozzeck, was the German singer Albert Dohmen, deemed a success in every respect. And as Marie, 'Deborah Polaski has never done anything better'.[33]

Mortier had accomplished a number of feats, including the placing of Salzburg near the apex of fine opera performance worldwide, making Holender's Staatsoper offerings look threadbare by comparison. As the decade drew to a close, his position seemed secure, with a five-year extension of his contract agreed from 1996. He had made more allies among the press and secured the Vienna Philharmonic's willingness to go on playing at the summer festival, while other outstanding orchestras shared the bill. Christoph von Dohnányi had become the festival's resident Mozart conductor, while at Salzburg Natalie Dessay had grown into the leading contemporary Queen of the Night.

Mortier's plans to stage the works of leading twentieth-century composers had grown to include, among others, György Ligeti's *Le Grand macabre*, in the 1997 festival and Luciano Berios *Cronaca del luogo* in 1999. However, both Ligeti and Berio came out in public against the Salzburg productions of their operas. Interviewed in the Italian press, Berio called Claus Guth's direction of *Cronaca* 'form without content' and 'German minimalism'. Ligeti deferred his criticism of Peter Sellars's staging of his piece until the morning after the premiere, while Berio maintained he allowed Guth to continue working merely out of respect for Mortier.[34]

The festival had become a consistently fascinating institution. As Richard Law indicated, it had also begun to appeal to a wider audience, namely, 'a lot younger and less stuffy'. Law continued, 'Evening dress is nowadays by no means any longer universal (though still common), though a lot of expensive clothes and jewellery are still on show and the tourists still gather in the street after performances to gawp at the departing *Prominente*.'[35]

It came to many as a shock in summer 1999 when the President of Austria, Thomas Klestil, attacked Mortier's programming at the festival. The festival's Board named Peter Ruzicka, a German conductor and composer, as artistic leader to succeed Mortier when his contract was due to expire in September 2001.

At Bayreuth, the question of a successor to Wolfgang Wagner hung over the activities of the festival throughout the 1990s. Wagner's ageing grandson had been sole head of the festival since 1966, after the death of his brother Wieland. In an apparent effort to shore up his own position, Wolfgang had prohibited family members from working at the festival since 1980. Acrid quarrels erupted, with Wolfgang's niece Nike Wagner and his son Gottfried publishing books and making numerous public statements accusing their relative of Nazi sympathies. Wolfgang went so far as to ban Gottfried from the family home and the festival premises.

The question of Richard Wagner's own anti-Semitism was at last being tackled directly by scholars and critics. The debate centred on the question of whether the anti-Jewish sentiments Wagner expressed frequently in letters, conversation and essays ('Jewry in Music', 1850; 'Recognise Yourself', 1881) were manifested in his operas, particularly *Die Meistersinger* and the *Ring*. Although proof positive was lacking – Wagner did not clearly 'flag' Alberich, Mime and Beckmesser as Jewish types, as Mussorgsky had done with 'Shmuyle' and 'Goldenberg' in his *Pictures at an Exhibition* – the weight of evidence fell on the side of darkness. Musicologists demonstrated the likelihood that certain musical motifs, styles of singing and verbal allusions were linked in Wagner's mind to his contempt for the Jews. Festival goers at Bayreuth had to come to terms with suspicions about the defective human values implied in the composer's operas, as well as the undeniable burden of guilt borne by previous generations of the Wagner family during the Nazi era.

Wolfgang had ceased doing stagings of his own, which in any case had seldom been well received. A variety of stage directors, many of whom like Kupfer took a highly ironic view of Wagner's scores, continued to take precedence over the music in the minds of the audiences – who had by this time grown accustomed to innovative, provocative productions. Although, during the 1997 and 1998 festivals, no new productions were mounted, Bayreuth remained a powerful magnet for lovers of Wagner. In 1999 half a million people had sought tickets, with only 50,000 available. The waiting list was seven years long.[36] Daniel Barenboim, himself a Jew holding Israeli citizenship, who was named musical adviser to the festival in 1998, declared unequivocally that Wagner's music 'is not about Judaism.'[37]

Many-sided battles for the succession raged in the media. Wolfgang – who had been granted a lifetime contract by the festival Board – favoured Gudrun, his second wife. Nike belittled her qualifications: 'Everybody knows that Gudrun reached her position as a collaborator through the marriage bed and not through art and culture. My guess is that our theatre and music people will regard her candidature as the laughing stock of the nation.'[38] Nike herself proposed radical changes if she were named to run the festival, including adding another season each year, and expanding the repertoire to bring in performances of Wagner's earlier works. Wieland Lafferentz, son of Siegfried and Winifred's daughter Verena, also sought to succeed Wolfgang, as did Eva Wagner-Pasquier, Wieland's estranged daughter by his first marriage.

After several years of skirmishing, battle was fully joined on 29 March 2001, when the Richard Wagner Foundation chose Eva Wagner-Pasquier to head the festival. Wagner-Pasquier had worked in opera administration at Bayreuth, Paris and the Met. At the time of her appointment she held an administrative position at the Royal Opera House. The Foundation issued a stern statement inviting Wolfgang to take his leave. He was 'to end his leadership at the conclusion of the 2002 festival year (30 September 2002) and to respond appropriately in good time to the Foundation in writing'. The Bavarian minister of culture, Hans Zehetmair, was quoted as saying, 'In hindsight, it is not rationally explicable that Wolfgang Wagner was given a lifetime contract.' The indomitable Wolfgang (who happened to be in South Korea at the time of the Board meeting) issued his own statement, which hinted that he would not leave quietly: 'I have ascertained that the Foundation in today's meeting has not chosen a successor by naming a date of accession, but rather has decided only on a nomination. Therefore, no break in my existing contract has occurred.' Eva Wagner-Pasquier's lawyer foresaw a struggle, saying that the matter would not be resolved until Wolfgang was well out of office: 'This is not the end. It's barely the beginning.'[39] The acrimony affected Bayreuth's performers. By the summer of 2001 Plácido Domingo commented: 'Nothing is worse for all concerned when people start asking out loud or quietly, "When is this man going to go?" It is a tragic story, this farewell. Authentic Wagner.'[40]

What, then, did Austria have, at the turn of the millennium, besides the Staatsoper? In the field of opera, it also had Salzburg, even though the festival was directed by a foreigner. Salzburg possessed the character of a European rather than a national institution. Politically, Austria was beginning at last to awaken from the long sleep of denial and face the fact that xenophobia and anti-Semitism remained to trouble the national conscience. Ioan Holender had played a significant part in this awakening.

Money was still a difficult issue for the arts. In January 2001 Holender stated, 'I have the same amount of money' – from the government – 'now as I had ten years ago.' Each seat sold to the public, he said, had to be subsidised by an additional 1,200 Austrian schillings – the approximate equivalent of £50. In spite of years of effort to stage new works, many audience members preferred the standard museum pieces of the repertoire. In this respect they resembled the Met audience, who were reluctant to face new work, thus making it financially risky to stage new pieces. Said Holender,

'The public eat only what they know. Not even *Lulu* is sold here.'[41] The Staatsoper audience adored its favourite – and expensive – singers. A rich fund of talent remained in the shape of the ensemble, the orchestra and the chorus, all to be drawn on by Ozawa upon his arrival in 2002.

On 24 February 2001, Ozawa marked the beginning of his music directorship by conducting a well-received performance of Janáček's *Jenůfa*. George Loomis praised Ozawa's 'co-ordination of large musical forces' and his effective work with the orchestra: 'The orchestra's enthusiasm came across in its high-precision playing. . . . Ozawa brought out the colours handsomely.'[42] With Ozawa in charge the Staatsoper's heart was ticking over. Still uncertain, however, was whether he would prove a force for radical renewal.

TWENTY-FOUR

THE MET 1990–2002
'A Very Efficient Factory'

ONCE THE MET HAD SUCCEEDED in establishing a firm basis for its activities during the Nineties, the management would be able to take tentative steps towards educating its audience to accept a broader repertoire and more challenging interpretations by directors. The man to oversee these developments was Joseph Volpe, whom Bruce Crawford recommended to replace him as general manager. After thirty years in the company, Volpe, who was already running the entire backstage, and had been dealing with the unions since the 1975 strike, was familiar with all aspects of the administration. Both Bliss and Crawford had given Volpe increasingly heavy responsibilities, Crawford making him second in command in every area but the artistic, and he was also functioning as operational head of the House. It was Volpe who had prepared the 1989–90 budget and who convinced the orchestra that they should agree to Deutsche Grammophon's terms for a substantial recording contract of four operas in 1989–90. Phil Sipser, the orchestra's legal adviser, called Volpe 'the best negotiator in the country because he has an understanding of the problems of people who work for a living'.[1]

The Board, however, regarded Volpe as too 'coarse to lead the Met . . . too unschooled, too much the striver'. Crawford told the *New Yorker*, 'They want to stand next to someone who is very elegant and they think of the days of Rudolf Bing.'[2] Crawford later said, 'Two or three Board members were nervous; they just didn't like the style and felt he would need a very strong president to control him.' According to Crawford, there was also pressure from Sybil Harrington, who was 'not comfortable' with Volpe or 'much of anyone most of the time'.[3]

Volpe himself said, 'The Board were wondering "Who would be the spokesman" – they remembered me backstage with a hammer.' There had never been a general manager who had come up through the ranks and Volpe was an unknown quantity. 'If I had had a great college education – graduated from somewhere – they could have accepted me,' Volpe later mused, and continued, 'The reason I didn't have a college education is that I didn't have time for it. I had to get going – my last week in high school I opened up my own business.'[4] There was also opposition from James Levine and Marilyn Shapiro.

In what a member of the administration called 'an anybody but Volpe sort of attitude',[5] the Board chose an Englishman, Hugh Southern, who had been an administrator at the National Endowment for the Arts in Washington. Volpe was made assistant manager. Southern's stewardship was brief. Within a matter of weeks, Crawford later recalled, it became apparent that the task was beyond Southern's capabilities.* Levine and the Board approached Crawford to say that Southern's leadership 'wasn't working'. Southern resigned in July 1990 and it was agreed that Crawford would chair the Executive Committee and oversee the running of the House with Volpe, as executive director and with Volpe, Levine and Shapiro, as assistant manager, reporting to him. Volpe recalled, 'They came back to me – not giving me all the authority, they were still nervous.' It was, recalled Crawford, 'a trial run'. Volpe, he said, 'did not like it at all and I don't blame him'.[6] Jonathan Friend became artistic administrator.

Volpe wanted Bing's title, later recalling, 'Thick-headed me . . . it's got to be general manager.' Crawford advised him, 'It will all be yours, just be patient.' Crawford also told Volpe that the Board was afraid of him. 'You've got to calm down,' he told him. 'People are giving money here – you can't just boss them around.' At the same time Crawford told the Board, 'You'd better change his title because he's going to do what he wants anyway.' Within two years Volpe had consolidated his power and gained the title of general manager, later telling the author that he went back 'to the Bing way of operating. . . .

---

* Johanna Fiedler wrote that Southern, with his English accent and Oxford education, appealed to a powerful member of the Board, Louise Humphrey, whom he accompanied to 'quail hunts' at her Florida estate (*Molto Agitato*, p. 260).

You go to a lot of performances, you're involved closely with the singers, you know what's going on. I'm here night and day.'[7]

Volpe, a domineering and powerful general manager, was, in stark contrast to Levine, not averse to confrontation. He candidly admitted, 'I love a good fight.' Some of those who worked at the Met described him in his office as a 'lion in his den' and would refer to meetings there as 'going to the tundra'. Volpe described himself as a very controlled person who shows temperament or raises his voice only when necessary and for effect, adding, 'Unfortunately you can't say things in a nice way today – they kind of ignore you – everybody is a bully today.'[8] He confessed, 'I had a million secretaries quit . . . I'm unbearable. I do frighten people, I shout out.'[9] His relationship with the Board was defined early on. He recalled:

> Bruce Crawford, who is a tough, powerful businessman, came to complain when I was assistant manager; I did something he was unhappy with regarding one of the Board members. I sat back and I said, 'You know, Bruce, you can't bully me, I'm not afraid of you, so don't bully me' and he apologised.

'They can fire me,' Volpe added, 'but they can't interfere. I established that.'[10] Crawford later said that there was no intrusion from the Board in artistic matters during the previous fifteen years. Such a clear definition of roles would have been beneficial to Covent Garden during the next decade.

Levine, Crawford later recalled wryly, 'was not begging' for Volpe's appointment, but was anxious for Southern to be replaced.[11] To those who felt Volpe would be too strong and independent a personality to work with Levine, Bliss had explained, 'You can work with Jimmy. He doesn't want confrontations.' Volpe himself was confident: 'I'm not the insecure type'; and he said of Levine, 'I know he trusts my judgement. He is not opposed to people with different opinions if those opinions make sense.'[12] Levine put a positive gloss on the new balance of power, telling the New York Times in 1995 that it allowed him to get on with the creative artistic work with less administrative responsibilities. 'We've got another fully equipped artistic personality in the room,' he said, 'and you can increase the speed at which you can get at things.' His plans, he said, were bound up with Volpe and the Met. Volpe put it somewhat differently: 'With previous general managers, the whole responsibility of how to accomplish something Jimmy wanted to do was left with Jimmy. . . . Well, he can't do it, he doesn't have time to go to the bathroom.'[13] As a close observer wrote of Levine, 'Although he lost power he still controls the artistic side. Jimmy is a brilliant politician and a survivor.'[14] It was Levine's determination and innate optimism that enabled him to stay the course. 'I don't get up in the morning and pass a sign on the wall that says every day shall be a picnic,' he said and added, 'I get up in the morning because the exhilaration, the challenge, the difficulty is so stimulating and so involving.'*[15]

Levine, together with Friend, continued to initiate artistic ideas. With time, Friend had come to know the singers with whom Levine liked to work and a trust developed between them. Friend said that by 1999 Levine was 'less involved in the day-to-day' but that what was seen on the Met stage reflected his philosophy.[16] Casting was planned five years in advance and was based on the availability of top singers, 'starting with Plácido and Kiri and Pavarotti'. Later in the Nineties Bryn Terfel, Renée Fleming, Cecilia Bartoli and Karita Mattila were added to this select list, and Sarah (Sally) Billinghurst endeavoured to incorporate roles they were keen to sing, insofar as it was possible. Repertoire that Levine wanted to put before the audience was also part of the initial planning, as with *Lulu* in the 2000–01 and 2001–02 seasons. According to Friend the working consensus was based on the 'understanding that the dollar figure at the bottom right-hand corner is actually what means we can or cannot go on working'. Volpe was the boss, and 'nobody tries to pull the wool over his eyes more than once – and the sensible people don't even try that'. Friend added that Volpe and Levine 'disagree about priorities much less than one might think'.[17]

One of Volpe's first acts as general director was to substitute film director Werner Herzog's plans for *Die Zauberflöte* for an enlarged

---

* In the late Nineties there was concern for Levine's health because of repeated bouts of muscle tremor in his left arm.

version of David Hockney's design for the 1978 Glyndebourne production, just four months before the opening in January 1991. He saw
there would be technical difficulties. The designs, however, did not
transfer well to the Met stage and even the orchestra seemed too large,
underscoring Levine's longing for a smaller venue for eighteenth-
century opera. The sloggy tempo in the overture made the opening
ponderous rather than grand. The size of the orchestra and the
whipped-along allegros in Act One combined to give a reading of
Mozart without lightness, without daylight between the phrases. In
the same vein, Levine provided quite unstylish allargandi at the end
of several of the major arias, with Kathleen Battle's coy artifices in
'Ach, ich fühl's' too stretched out – the dramatic flow of this scene
buried in sheer musical bigness.

As Isaacs was to do at Covent Garden, Volpe intended to expand and
not cut back, believing that new productions and repertoire generated
excitement, which helped increase ticket sales throughout the year.*
Although there was to be no radical departure from the policy that
kept the core repertory in 'safe' hands, Volpe was more sensitive to
the dramatic element than some of his predecessors, having been made
aware of the demands of the stage from his years working with Dexter.
Volpe observed, 'For any conductor the score is the Bible, they would
like everything to be in concert version – forget the staging, it only
gets in the way.'[18] It was Crawford who pointed out that in the post-
Dexter period, Levine had worked with directors with whom he was
both familiar and comfortable – Ponnelle, Zeffirelli, and Schenk. It
took Volpe, 'with his knowledge of what can and can't be done, time
to open up the field and provide greater variety'.[19] Volpe also shared
Levine's hopes of infiltrating some less popular works that 'do not
involve the big blockbuster sets and scenery that we have for standard
repertory'.[20] These less popular works were to be increasingly entrusted
to directors such as Jonathan Miller and Elijah Moshinsky, who were

* Bruce Crawford, who had become Board chairman after completing a 'reorganisation
of Omnicom', reviewed plans 'because production funding is a Board matter' (Mayer,
Opera, December 1990, p. 1416). Crawford would also advise on repertory mix, marketing
and long-term strategies.

especially skilled in bringing out the dramatic potential in their singers and illuminating the essence of the works.

Jonathan Miller prepared the Met premiere of *Kát'a Kabanová*, with Charles Mackerras in the pit, in February 1991. Critics were struck by the care and intelligence that Miller and his designer Robert Israel lavished on the work. Miller's production and its spare sets, together with Mackerras's conducting, ensured that music and drama were powerfully integrated. Henahan wrote, 'The musical aspects of the performance stood out with such unusual integrity and clarity.' Czech soprano Gabriela Beňačková finally made her Met debut at the age of forty-five. According to the *New York Times*, she sang with a 'ravishing' voice and 'such fervid commitment to her role that she actually seems to glow in the dark'. Leonie Rysanek was a 'formidable' Kabanicha.[21]

It was neither Moshinsky nor Miller, however, who was to dominate the Met's Italian repertory, but a director new to the Met, Giancarlo Del Monaco. Bringing a reputation for controversial productions from Germany where he had done a *Butterfly* set in Vietnam, and a 'Saddam' *Nabucco* a year before the Gulf War, Del Monaco was happy to try what he called a 'classically progressive approach' at the Met. As he said in an *Opera News* interview in April 1992, 'I have a Eurotrash face for Europe and a classy face for Americans.' His debut production was an intensely dramatic *Fanciulla* in October 1991 with the Los Angeles-born conductor Leonard Slatkin, Domingo and Barbara Daniels. He was later to direct *Madama Butterfly*, *Stiffelio*, *Simon Boccanegra* and *Forza*.

New works were seldom seen on the Met stage, but John Corigliano's *The Ghosts of Versailles*, which had been commissioned in May 1980, originally intended for the Met centennial, was finally staged in December 1991. Corigliano described *Ghosts* as 'grand opera buffa', which was a genre that could still reach out 'in terms of tessitura, orchestration and scope into the size of the hall'.[22] The opera had as its 'central conceit' that 'the ghost of the playwright Beaumarchais, to ease the torments of the ghost of Marie Antoinette (who wishes she hadn't been killed), can rewrite history with the help of Almaviva'. Librettist William M. Hoffman, who played a central role in the project, described the opera as a love story but also a story about revolution and the nature of revolution.[23] To overcome the problem of the Figaro characters requiring a neo-classical setting in musical terms, Hoffman and Corigliano invented an opera within an opera, with the Beaumarchais characters inhabiting a ghostly world.

The New York opera audience enjoyed Corigliano's allusions to the operatic repertoire, the musical and textual quotations, the in-jokes, and the wacky, campy atmosphere, as well as John Conklin's ingenious, expensive-looking multi-purpose set. According to Mayer, the opera also had a certain 'relevance to the present condition of the arts (ravaged by a plague, suffering from the museum mentality of administrators)'.[24] The element of parody, however, was lost on many critics, and some of the musical jokes could not, in Patrick J. Smith's words, 'be apprehended easily'. The final tableau was more powerful visually than musically, with the Almaviva family escaping in a hot-air balloon and the queen going to her death, while the crowd chant the Marseillaise.[25] In general the musically slow pace added to the comprehensibility of the dense text. The pastiche quality was nicely woven into Corigliano's idiom, although melodies were less interesting than harmonies, orchestral lines and colours. At its revival in April 1995, Mayer was more impressed, describing the opera's final half-hour, with its quintet at the last ball and its sextet in the prison, 'amongst the loveliest operatic creations of recent years'. Teresa Stratas sang beautifully in a role created for her, and Gino Quilico played all Beaumarchais's Figaros 'with fiery delight'.[26]

The postmodernist and conceptual trend in stage direction was seen even more rarely at the Met than were new works. Nonetheless, as in the British provincial Houses, such work was going on in the United States, epitomised by Peter Sellars who, from 1986 to 1989, had been presenting the Mozart–da Ponte operas at the Pepsico State University of New York Summer International Festival for the performing arts. The filmed version of Sellars's *Figaro* on Decca in 1991 was replete with puzzling references, including shots of New York icons like the Rollman skating rink and Macy's shopping bags. As in Philip Glass's *Einstein*, and his *Voyage* at the Met in October 1992, the use of icons made no thematic point, but simply dressed the show in some familiarly contemporary trappings. There was little humour or piquancy in the set or the situation – the living space which Figaro and Susanna chose for their life together was a combination bedroom and laundry. Sellars was more interested in tweaking the characters into postmodernity than using the director's tools to explore motivation and class conflict. The Count, sung by James Maddalena, when divorced from the context of European class structure', became, in Milnes's words, 'little more than a stupid thug, one who threw his wife on the floor and repeatedly kicked her'. Although carefully prepared for the stage, the works were musically feeble – Figaro the flimsiest of light baritones with no low register and less than mediocre Italian diction, and conductor Craig Smith taking little trouble over the music. Diction in general was unimportant for Sellars, who prepares his own synopses for the audience, and 'cyclo-styled preface or hand-out, to explain the theory justifying what they are about to see'.[27]

Sellars's *Don Giovanni* was similarly 'relocated', the Don suffering two nervous collapses, first in the champagne aria, 'when he was restored by Leporello topping him up with a hypodermic, and then in his Serenade, which he ended slumped on the floor in tears'. Milnes wrote of Sellars, 'As a director of nervous breakdowns he is without rival today.' Sellars also trivialised *Così*, as the recognition of the men early on reduced the action 'to little more than group therapy'. *Così* also had its share of breakdowns and sight gags, some of which Milnes found of dubious value such as 'Despina-as-doctor attaching electrodes to the men's genitalia'.[28]

Tom Sutcliffe sought to explain that Sellars's 'interpretative principle has been to repatriate European classical art-works to his native homeland, recasting them in the street clothes and tone of California or the east coast'. Sellars's Mozart, he believed, has 'commanded attention not as art history detritus – exercises in re-creating a vanished society – but as vital modern theatre'.[29]

The Met, though not given to such radical production style, gave another new work on 12 October 1992, Philip Glass's *The Voyage*, in a spectacular production to commemorate the Centennial. The audience, according to Edward Rothstein, was 'a piquant mixture of uptown and downtown'. The work had been commissioned in 1988 for the reported sum of $325,000 at Glass's suggestion. Playwright David Henry Hwang wrote the libretto, Robert Israel designed the sets, and David Pountney directed.

The production itself cost $2 million. Paul Griffiths in the *New*

Yorker wrote that the work's sole purpose was 'to fill the Met'. The authors' own explicit lack of empathy for their subject led Griffiths to note, 'Unfortunately in order to qualify as the Met's quincentennia piece it had to make some reference to Columbus, but this was an obstacle briskly circumvented.' Columbus appeared in just two scenes in both of which he was portrayed as 'abandoned to doubt'. Otherwise Griffiths wrote, he was 'shoved aside to make way for heroes better suited to contemporary taste'. These included a wheelchair-bound Stephen Hawking and the female commander of a spaceship. Other icons included alien spaceships, a rocket blasting out of the Statue of Liberty, and New Ageish invocation of magic crystals. But for all its pretensions to engage in the general concept of exploration, Griffiths found no effort to engage with any of its subject matter – a weakness not aided by the repetitive music combined with 'ritual stage action' The work contained no theme, no dramatic centre, no characterisation and no narrative, merely adding up, in Rothstein's words, to 'an operatic variety show'.[30]

Milnes thought the libretto's 'ironic edge' a relief for those who found Glass's previous work 'unrelievedly portentous'. According to him the music was also developing. 'Chromatic elements have crept in, even the odd dissonance; in their wake comes counterpoint.' Glass enthusiasts might 'consider that it sullies the pure spring of minimalism', he wrote, but Glass detractors might say that 'the closer his idiom strays in the direction of non-minimalism, the more threadbare its sounds'.[31] Griffiths referred to the vocal writing's 'uniformly declamatory' style and the music's lack of movement, and its dependence on 'getting louder or quieter'.[32]

Rodney Milnes was struck by the conspicuous expenditure on *Voyage*, writing, 'To poverty-stricken UK eyes it was a spectacle beyond their wildest dreams. Robert Israel's sets whizzed up and down on lifts and singers flew in and out – it was a good twenty minutes before anyone's feet touched the ground ... The court of Ferdinand and Isabella dissolved before our very eyes and turned into the deck of the *Santa Maria*.' David Pountney, who 'after years of achieving near spectacle on tiny budgets in London ... suddenly found himself in the biggest toy shop in the world and was having a whale of a time'. He ensured that the audience did too, by providing 'humour and zaniness'.[33] Like Zeffirelli's *Bohème* and *Turandot*, the production was a spectacle that could 'keep the eyes occupied when the mind is not'.

Glass continued to be popular, with *Voyage*'s six performances nearly sold out. John Rockwell wrote in *Opera* in November 1988, 'However erratic his record of critical respect may be, he wins commissions and first performances and repeat performances.' Rockwell defended Glass and 'the basic tenets of minimalism', especially against British critics, whether of either 'conservative-romantic or modernist-gnomic persuasion', for whom, Rockwell wrote, Glass sounds 'like a stuck record'. For Rockwell and other Glass admirers 'the repetition can attain a compelling, meditative, hypnotic intensity'.

There were many new American operas premiered throughout the late Eighties and Nineties testifying to the health of the medium, but like *Ghosts* showing little potential for establishing themselves in the repertoire, in spite of serious and substantial initial productions with fine casts. One exception was John Adams's *Nixon in China*, which was conceived by director Peter Sellars and was premiered on 22 October 1987 at the Houston Grand Opera. It later played to full houses in the year 2000 at English National Opera. Sellars and Adams, together with poet Alice Goodman as librettist and choreographer Mark Morris, created, according to Milnes, a 'genuine American artefact'.

Nixon shows an obnoxious figure involved in an act of historical importance with a grand-opera approach appropriate to the event. Goodman's libretto is set with effective and poetic characterisation, although Sellars, as is his wont, resorts to caricature rather than characterisation, especially of the role of Kissinger. Excitement is generated musically rather than from any intrinsic character or dramatic conflict. Adams's music is eclectic, with echoes of Gershwin and Wagner as well as minimalist figuration akin to that of Glass. It has a mesmeric and exhilarating effect, with its endlessly repeated motifs punctuated by electronic and orchestral (brass and wind) spikes of sound worked up to frequent frenzied climaxes, while inducing an uneasy awareness of hypnotic manipulation. The recitative is more typically twentieth-century, reminiscent of Britten or Stravinsky rather than Glass. The work is also more singable than Glass, remindful of Musgrave's work.

Pat Nixon's aria at the beginning of Act Two has Richard Rodgers melodies and orchestration reduced like a sauce to minimalism – headachingly repetitious. *Nixon* was, in Milnes's words, such a 'dazzlingly theatrical experience for most of the time that you fail to notice a certain lack of musical – and indeed dramaturgical – specific gravity until after curtain-fall'.[34]

Other new work testified to the vigour of operatic life in the United States. There were thirteen world premieres of new and old, American and foreign works in 1991–92 alone, and although *Madama Butterfly* remained the most performed work, companies in general were broadening their repertoires.[35] Premieres of new operas in the United States, which received as lavish new productions as had *Voyage* at the Met, included Conrad Susa's *Dangerous Liaisons* in September 1994, produced by Colin Graham for San Francisco Opera, with Thomas Hampson, Renée Fleming and Frederica von Stade. Donald Runnicles conducted. Milnes described it as 'well-made' with a 'hugely competent' score. It did not, however, tell much about the characters but tended 'to chunter on . . . in a blameless neo-romantic idiom, illustrating rather than amplifying'.[36]

In late 1998 San Francisco premiered the conductor André Previn's *A Streetcar Named Desire*, which had been commissioned as part of San Francisco Opera's Pacific Visions programme for the creation of new American operas. The production starred Renée Fleming and Rodney Gilfry. A year later, on 9 October 1999, Lyric Opera of Chicago premiered William Bolcom's opera based on Arthur Miller's *A View from the Bridge*, after a four-year gestation period. Anthony Tommasini contrasted the work with Previn's *Streetcar*, suggesting that Miller's contribution to Arnold Weinstein's libretto, and the operatic nature of the play, helped to create an 'admirable and often affecting work'. Previn's adaptation, on the other hand, added little to Tennessee Williams's 'richly poetic and allusive' text.[37]

Levine remained, according to Billinghurst, devoted to the commissioning process, and in December the Met premiered John Harbison's *The Great Gatsby*, for which the composer wrote the libretto using much of Fitzgerald's text. Just as Miller's play had an operatic element, so *Gatsby* abounds with references to popular music of the jazz age. Harbison composed his song music to Murray Horowitz's

920s-style lyrics. Anthony Tommasini wrote, 'The songs are spiked with contemporary harmonic touches and blended into the continuous musical flow of the score, which has a consistent compositional voice.'[38] The transition from novel to opera was not, however, without its problems. Although David Stevens found that the combination of 1920s dance music and the composer's own style worked well, the pacing of the dramatic scenes was less assured. Stevens felt they went on too long, and that the 'inventive orchestral conversation was often more interesting than the vocal lines going on above'. The unobtrusive production had a fine cast, with Dawn Upshaw as Daisy Buchanan, Jerry Hadley as Jay Gatsby and Susan Graham as Jordan Baker. Levine, in honour of whose twenty-fifth anniversary the work had been commissioned, 'was in firm control of an event that needed a strong hand in the pit'.[39] A tightened-up version of the opera was presented at Chicago, and returned to the Met in the 2001–02 season. More commissions were scheduled for the 2002–03 season.

As well as providing this premiere, the Met produced Carlisle Lloyd's *Susannah*, composed in 1955. It was, in Bernard Holland's words, a 'rare example of a successful American opera'. Nevertheless the strong cast, led by Fleming, Hadley and Ramey, did little, in Holland's view, to cover the innate weakness of the score. Furthermore, the size of the House made its provinciality yet more striking.[40]

New works were a sign of a healthy operatic environment. Indeed, Opera America's survey for 1991–92 showed that in general opera was flourishing in spite of economic turmoil. Opera was, in fact, the only art form to have grown in attendance during the previous five years, by 30 per cent since 1988, with audiences holding steady at just over 4 million. This was in spite of dwindling public funding and a sharp rises in the companies' aggregate deficits. (The National Endowment for the Arts funding was down 5.2 per cent to $5.3 million.) The regional companies were faced by the same financial challenges in the Eighties and Nineties as the Met and Covent Garden. Many companies showed box office gains of 11 per cent, with earned income from all sources making up 53.4 per cent of all the companies' income.

Some companies fared better than others in the worsening economic situation. In Dallas, Nicola Rescigno resigned in January

1990, after thirty-three years, during which time the Board manage‹
to double their budget while reducing artistic standards and losin;
the Dallas Symphony Orchestra. Sarah Caldwell's Boston compan·
fared even worse, closing down completely in 1991. The Board the›
joined the Boston Lyric Opera, which worked on a suburban artisti‹
level.

Ardis Krainik was more successful in adapting Chicago to th·
unfavourable economic climate. Its 1990 season went from Septembe·
to February, with 60 per cent of its expenses recouped at a full bo›
office. Three or four performances a week and its smaller stage gave th·
company great advantages over the Met with its seven performances ›
week. Artistic director Bruno Bartoletti continued to be highly success·
ful into the late Nineties, with full houses, using good casts and conduc·
tors. Impresario and opera manager Matthew Epstein, as artisti·
adviser from 1980, brought Sellars's *Tannhäuser*. New work presentec
at Chicago included Argento's *Voyage of Edgar Allan Poe* and, in Sep·
tember 1991, Barber's *Antony and Cleopatra* which, in Moshinsky'·
hands, and with Michael Yeargan's clever minimalist sets, redeemec
itself after its unhappy Met premiere.

New York City Opera after 1988, under Christopher Keene, recov·
ered standards that had slipped at the end of the Sills era. But corporat·
funding was becoming harder to get and in 1992 Janáček's *The Excur·
sions of Mr Brouček* had to be abandoned in order to keep the defici›
under $3 million. In October 1997 Paul Kellogg, who was also directo·
of the Glimmerglass Festival company, took over City Opera, witl
John Conklin as director of productions. By bringing in production·
like Santa Fe's *Xerxes*, New York City Opera hoped to raise standard·
and experiment without 'being locked into mistakes for years to come'·
Christopher Alden's wildly updated *L'Italiana in Algeri*, with Mustaf‹
as a Middle Eastern dictator, was the second production from Glim·
merglass.[41] The presence of Mayor Giuliani and high society at specia·
performances helped boost the company's fund-raising activities i›
the late Nineties.

San Francisco faced a difficult period after the death of Kurt Her·
bert Adler, its director of almost three decades, in 1988. That same yea·
Terence McEwen resigned. In June 1990 Scottish conductor Donalc
Runnicles became music director, making a fine impression con·

ducting the *Ring*. Lotfi Mansouri, Alden and Francesca Zambello remained active directors with the company, and in the mid-Nineties its fortunes revived. In September 1997 San Francisco returned to the War Memorial Opera House – after the earthquake and after an eighteen-month closure for a $88.5 million backstage and seismic reinforcement refit. The city had allocated $49.5 million from its bond issue for the repair of earthquake damage. All the stars were there for the reopening on 14 September 1997, including locally trained Ruth Ann Swenson.

In November 1993 Virginia Opera opened its $10 million renovated home in Norfolk, named after Edythe Harrison who had founded Virginia Opera in 1975. The Board managed to raise $5 million before any public money was committed. Peter Mark continued the successful formula of combining non-standard works like *I Capuleti e i Montecchi* with popular works such as *Man of La Mancha*. He also managed to reduce the accumulated deficit. More capital expenditure was also spent at Houston Grand Opera, for which the Wortham Center for the Performing Arts was built at a cost of $72 million, on a three-acre plot donated by the city. Its central arch was modelled on Tewkesbury Abbey in Britain. Its 2,176 seats were much scaled down from the Met's 3,800; this allowed it, according to its general director David Gockley, to keep a repertory system and up to eighty more performances a season.

Adaptability and a careful balancing of the more daring with the traditional was generally the formula for success in the unsubsidised American art world of the Nineties. In November 1992 the Met engaged in a rare experiment with a conceptual production. It was Francesca Zambello's *Lucia di Lammermoor*, with June Anderson. Zambello, an American director working mainly in Europe, placed *Lucia* 'in a landscape apparently based on televised representations of Bosnia, grey mountainous terrain, with a lot of grey buildings tipped on their side and lots of suffering people'. Zambello saw Lucia's madness as 'her way of expressing a kind of freedom'. In the nineteenth century, she went on to explain, 'people weren't afraid of madness in the way we are now, because we live in a clinical, over-analysed, post-Freudian world'.[42] The production proved too controversial for the Met audience and administration, and was removed from the repertoire within a season. Zambello was not invited back to the Met for many years.*

Although Zambello's *Lucia* was not appreciated at the Met, there was a slowly but steadily increasing boldness in planning as Volpe's team mastered the balancing of repertoire to maintain the necessary box office. Zambello herself later agreed that Volpe soon brought in other directors with approaches new to the Met and that she had been unfortunate to have been the first.† Directors hitherto not in favour at the Met included Jonathan Miller, who produced *Kát'a* in April 1993, and Elijah Moshinsky who was brought back to the Met on Jessye Norman's suggestion to direct her in *Ariadne* in March 1993. Norman had enjoyed working with Moshinsky at Covent Garden on a revival of *Tannhäuser* and had insisted on his taking over when a director fell through at the Met. Moshinsky recalled, 'She didn't know that I had a bad history at the Met and she was a star. . . . it was a Jessye show.' Moshinsky remembered on opening night Volpe saying to him, '"I think it's one of the best things I've ever seen" and adding, "I've forgotten your *Ballo*." '[43]

Rothstein found in the production 'the thrill of beauty encased in irony, of sincerity at the edge of self-consciousness'. It showed, he wrote, 'the best of the Met's musical and dramatic imagination'. Rothstein praised Michael Yeargan's set, especially during the grand backstage scene 'in which the Composer strains to maintain the integrity of his *opera seria* in the face of incipient farce'.[44] Leighton Kerner applauded the 'jolting contrast between the prologue's realistic preparatory desperation and the opera-within-an-opera's giddy fantasy'. He also admired the singers' 'belief in their characters', Norman's 'sumptuous singing', the 'emotional directness' of Susanne Mentzer's

---

* Zambello began working in the straight theatre in Frankfurt and then worked at San Francisco from 1981 to 1986, and for five years as assistant to Ponnelle in Europe from 1983 to 1989, taking charge of revivals of his productions. Her work ranges from the spare, almost naturalistic Donizetti *L'Assedio di Calais* at Wexford in 1991 to the popular Earls Court *Tosca* in 1991 and to the postmodern *Les Troyens* in Los Angeles the same year. She was considered for the role of artistic director at Covent Garden in 1999. She had been dismissed from the Met, she later said, 'like being expelled from school' and only in 2001 'got invited back by the headmaster'. She was to prepare *The Trojans* in 2002–03 and a new opera by Tobias Picker based on Theodore Dreiser's *An American Tragedy*.

† When the Met produced its bland *Lucia* in December 1998 there were even nostalgic references in the House to Zambello's production.

Composer and Swenson's sparkling Zerbinetta – who 'seduced the Composer with a heady burst of erotic philosophy'.[45]

It was as the *Ariadne* rehearsals were finishing that John Schlesinger submitted his plans for *Otello*. Joseph Clark's technical department decided the set would be too large and Moshinsky was hired to direct the show in 1994. *Ballo* was indeed forgotten. Volpe later said that he appreciated Moshinsky's willingness to 'think carefully and to use different designers and bring something fresh'.[46] It was not Moshinsky, however, but Del Monaco who was given the task of introducing Verdi's unfamiliar *Stiffelio* to the Met in October 1993. Edward Rothstein was won over by the work itself, which he described as 'ripe with melodic invention, vigorous dramatic sequences and inventive ensemble pieces'. In contrast to Moshinsky's riveting realisation at Covent Garden, Del Monaco gave the drama an impersonal setting in an outsized and static production, set in a charmless and gloomy mock Gothic-style church hall and prototype German Schloss. For much of the time the protagonists were separated by a forty-foot-long table, which meant that they were not within eye contact, let alone touching distance. The production was not enhanced by the Met's new Verdi soprano Sharon Sweet, who gave an unconvincing portrayal of the tortured adulteress. Sweet has 'a gorgeous octave in the middle', Mayer wrote in *Opera* but 'no support in the lower register and an exposed top'.[47] She began roughly, 'stitching her melodic line with seams, lunging at high notes and singing sharp', but according to Rothstein, later displayed 'size, intensity and beauty of sound'.[48] Domingo, celebrating his twenty-fifth anniversary season with the Met, created a more than believable Stiffelio. His understanding of Verdi's musical line and Verdi's hero – passionate, divided, obsessive – gave dramatic weight to an otherwise bland production, and in spite of Sweet's uninvolved stage presence and uneven vocal talent.

In the same season as *Stiffelio* the Met introduced two more works new to its repertory, *I Lombardi* and *Rusalka*. *I Lombardi* received a bad press, although Levine, according to Mayer, conducted with 'energy and more gusto than has been his wont of late'. *I Lombardi* starred Ramey, Pavarotti and Millo, who sang badly on opening night and withdrew. Pavarotti, wrote Mayer, was now 'almost disconnected from the body which appeared to be in considerable pain'.[49] In the late Nineties Pavarotti had health and vocal problems, and in 1998 underwent hip and knee surgery. In spite of withdrawing from *Forza* in 1996 and from a recording of *I Lombardi*, and in spite of mixed reviews for his 1997 Calafs, Pavarotti remained a favourite of the Met audiences.

Millo's and Pavarotti's weakness, and the casting of Sweet in so many dramatic roles at this time, underlined that while Mozart, Rossini and Handel were increasingly easy to cast – given the improvement in teaching standards and a plethora of relatively small and flexible voices – it was still hard to fill the main Verdi roles. In the mid- and late-Nineties the no longer youthful Domingo and Pavarotti were still the first port of call for Verdi tenor casting, with José Cura attempting heavier Verdi roles after his debut in *Cavalleria* in 1999, and Roberto Alagna the more lyric roles.

By the mid-Nineties the opening up of Eastern Europe and Russia produced singers like soprano Maria Guleghina, whose debut at the Met was in January 1991 as Maddalena in *Andrea Chénier*, as well as mezzo Olga Borodina and baritones Chernov and Leiferkus, who on leaving Russia had originally made his home in England. Guleghina had the technique and sturdiness to cope with the heaviest of Verdi's demands, but she was almost alone in the repertoire. The Met's regular Verdi baritone was Vladimir Chernov. Levine told *Gramophone* that Chernov had fallen into his lap 'in the most amazing way' and that he now needed him 'for all the big Verdi parts'.[50] In the Met *Boccanegra* in 1995 Chernov's tone was unvaried and slightly dry but with appealing bright glints atop the dark Verdi baritone. His musicality and good upper-middle register were essential for Verdi baritone roles in which over-singing can make for vocal dryness.

In the non-Verdi repertoire the story was different. Levine was sanguine about the changing patterns of singing. It was possible by 2002, he said, to cast Mozart *opera seria*, twentieth-century pieces, French works, Handel, Strauss and Wagner with many different singers, which 'was absolutely not the case in the Forties and Fifties when in any week you could hear a middle-Verdi or Puccini performance that was first-rate'.[51] Particularly in Mozart, one of the most intelligent American stars of the Nineties was baritone Thomas Hampson, who was also a dedicated lieder singer. He sang in Düsseldorf from 1981 to

1984 and in Zurich from 1985 to 1989, when he steadily built up his roles. His Met debut was in October 1986 as Count Almaviva. He sang Don Giovanni in October 1990 and Billy Budd in April 1993. Hampson described his voice to Milnes as 'a mixture of spirit and air ... tenor mentality and a baritone metabolism'.[52] This 'mixture' brought him to sing the baritone version of Massenet's *Werther* in January 1999 opposite mezzo Susan Graham's Charlotte. Anthony Tommasini described Hampson's 'customary intelligence, plaintive lyricism and plush sound', whose 'darker colourings enhance the melancholia of Goethe's sorrowful character'.[53]

There were also the American tenors Frank Lopardo and Richard Leech. Milnes described Leech in June 1997 as having a 'disposition as sunny as his voice and very sensible', with a voice production 'easy ... unstrained ... effortless'. His Raoul in *Les Huguenots* in Hamburg in 1987 'had the audience yelling its approval'.[54] Lopardo, a favourite of Solti, specialised in Mozart and Rossini with his elegance of phrasing, sure legato, clean forthright tone throughout the range, and warmth and sweetness on the high notes. Canadian heldentenor Ben Heppner had been trained in Canada, as were tenor Richard Margison and lyric baritone Gerald Finley. Heppner won the Met's 1988 National Council Auditions and, after building up his roles mainly in the German repertoire, in 1999 sang Tristan at the Met with both lyricism and strength.

Levine's support for the young artists programme, which had begun in 1979, started to bear fruit in the Nineties. Lyric soprano Dawn Upshaw had been working her way up from a lady-in-waiting in *Francesca da Rimini* to Zerlina in 1990, and continued to gain experience at the Met. In 1992 Dwayne Croft was well received when he stood in for Hampson in *Onegin*. Croft, a nervous man who felt that he would never have survived the Met's National Council Auditions, gave total credit to Levine for his career. 'James Levine took so much time to plan ahead, to think "What do I hear his voice doing?"' he explained and added, 'Every role they gave me was a little bigger, so I felt prepared for everything I did.'[55]

Other young North American talents to emerge in the Nineties included Ruth Ann Swenson, who revealed breathtaking technical ability at her debut on 27 February 1993 as Gilda. In her recording of *Romeo and Juliet* with Domingo in 1995, conducted by Leonard Slatkin, her big, sweet, lyric tone flowers out from an almost mezzo-ish lower middle to an open bright top with a fine sense of line. Another young talent was Renée Fleming, who sang Desdemona opposite Domingo in 1995. Fleming has appealing silvery tones and an impressive lower register, but at that time seemed to lack the necessary warmth for Desdemona, emotionally and vocally. In an interview in *Opera News* she said that the role of Desdemona suited her perfectly: 'She is a very nervous lady who had a self-esteem problem.'[56] Rupert Christiansen, who wrote a profile of Fleming in the March 2000 *Opera*, felt that her artistry had grown gradually to match her technical and vocal prowess. Solti's two years of 'ardent patronage' before his death in 1997 helped her to such an extent that her Alcina in Paris and her Susanna at the Met, as well as her recording of *Rusalka*, 'ravished' Christiansen 'into submission'.[57]

Other rising stars were Dolora Zajick, whom Horne described as 'a force of nature', and the Wagnerians Jane Eaglen, Deborah Polaski, and Deborah Voigt. The *New York Times* wrote of Voigt's 'sumptuous sound, gleaming high notes, a consistency of delivery of tone . . . and astonishing breath control'.[58] The agile mezzos were Susanne Mentzer, Jennifer Larmore and Susan Graham. Graham, at home in Handel, Strauss, Mozart, Massenet and Berlioz, was described by Donald Runnicles as an intuitive singer with a 'magnetic personality on stage'.[59] In March 2000 Rupert Christiansen wrote, 'One of the more significant trends of the last decade has been the increasing dominance of the American soprano. . . . This versatile and industrious breed, with its well-schooled power-dressed efficiency, has proved a godsend to managements the world over.'[60]

Volpe's determination to bring in fine guest conductors resulted in some excellent performances. Both Mackerras's *Kát'a* and Slatkin's *Fanciulla* were idiomatic and dramatic. In December 1993 Seiji Ozawa made his debut conducting *Onegin*. In March 1994 Kent Nagano conducted Dexter's production of Poulenc's *Carmelites*, with Dawn Upshaw. Jonathan Friend later attributed an overall improvement in the roster to an increase in talented conductors like Conlon, Gatti, Pappano, Runnicles, Rizzi and Thielemann.[61]

One of the most significant guest conductors to appear in the Nineties was Valery Gergiev, who was to widen the Met's Slavic repertoire. He brought his Kirov Opera Company to the Met in July 1992, conducting fourteen performances. Co-productions with Covent Garden and the BBC had made large-scale productions possible for the company, including a Prokofiev festival in 1991 and the Covent Garden Maryinsky co-production of Prokofiev's *Fiery Angel* in April 1992. In the video recording of *The Fiery Angel* Gergiev showed musical and dramatic leadership, choosing his tempi in sympathetic understanding for the needs of the moment on stage and for the singers' breathing.[62] Mayer wrote of Gergiev, 'He can sustain rhythmic vitality at *any* tempo. . . . He closes his eyes a lot but when he opens them he is looking at someone for "emphatic *attacca subito*".' He had a small baton and sometimes uses no baton at all but is capable of grandiose, almost-Bernstein gestures that would seem self-aggrandising, except that they are so obviously effective.'[63] Gergiev made his debut with the Met forces in March 1994, conducting Moshinsky's new production of *Otello*, with Domingo, and in the 1995–96 and 1999–2000 seasons he conducted Moshinsky's production of *The Queen of Spades*.

As general manager, Volpe's directness was in stark contrast to Levine's predilection for avoiding confrontation. Joseph Clark said of his boss and friend, 'Joe Volpe rules by terror. . . . He's good at invisible assassinations when he needs to be. He is also good at visible discipline.'[64] In 1994, when Volpe dismissed Kathleen Battle, he announced his decision without any attempt at diplomatic language, explaining that her 'unprofessional actions were profoundly detrimental to artistic collaboration'. Levine was quoted as saying he would have 'let her do her performances and never hire her again', but that it was for Volpe to make the decision.[65] Volpe later said that he had had no choice: 'She was havoc in the rehearsal room, other singers could not rehearse' and 'people were in tears every night.' He added 'She has a real problem. Everybody hated it.'[66] One story circulated which told of Battle phoning her agent from the back of a limousine to phone the driver to ask him to turn down the air conditioning. Beverly Sills said of Battle, 'I think she's frightened to death.'[67]

Volpe was instrumental in bringing in more adventurous directors as well as repertoire and with greater frequency. Along with Miller and Moshinsky, another British director to be entrusted with non-core works was Graham Vick. He directed *Lady Macbeth of Mtsensk* in November 1994 when it had its Met premiere. It was heartily booed and was described by John Freeman in *Opera News* as 'Eurotrash', with its updating from the 1850s to modern times, and its on-stage collection of fridge, car and garbage bags. Freeman said that the unit set made it difficult to conceive what it would be like 'to trudge across a Siberian wasteland'. Rothstein too was unimpressed, believing that Vick had treated the work in the spirit of *Pravda*'s notorious denunciation of the piece, published two days after Stalin had attended a performance on 26 January 1936, as a 'sort of vulgar farce in which the satiric overshadows the tragic'. He felt that the production lacked Shostakovich's concern for 'understanding the tragic meeting of nature and culture'.[68]

There were others who were thrilled by the production. Met archivist Bob Tuggle thought it was one of the great evenings in the theatre and later said that he came to judge his friends and critics by their response to it. Paul Griffiths wrote that Vick's production 'combines amazement with parodic self-deflation' and he believed that Vick, together with designer Paul Brown, the choreographer Ron Howell and the lighting designer Nick Chelton with their 'effrontery', had brought 'more life to this stage than it's seen in years'.[69] Conductor James Conlon was impressive, obtaining 'startling clarity of sound from the pit'. Maria Ewing had returned after her row, and gave, in spite of vocal problems, a 'terrific impression of a provincial wife who begins to find fulfilment in lust'.[70]

Jonathan Miller was employed again with designer John Conklin to direct his small-scale *Pelléas* on 23 March 1995. The collaboration between Miller and Levine was a fruitful one, Levine later explaining that his previous experience and Miller's previous inexperience with the work ensured 'that it was set up without a weak link anywhere'. Levine worked with the designer and the cast, and Miller was 'stimulated to come up with his end of it – which he did'.[71] The production, inspired by Proust, was set at the turn of the century in a large chateau ruled by an ancient 'bourgeois seigneur'. The set, with its 'draped statues and crates, a leafless tree and creaky scaffolding', evoked 'a disintegrating world on the verge of abandonment'. Claire Mitchell's costumes consisted of Debussy-era suits and dresses. Rothstein referred to Miller's 'strange and marvellous universe' with its rejection of 'the accoutrements of ersatz medievalism'.[72]

The production marked von Stade's twenty-fifth anniversary, for which she received an ovation, and a tribute from the management. Mayer wrote, 'She has maintained the bloom in her voice . . . smooth as silk vocally and intelligent dramatically.'[73] Miller's ability to create a powerful ensemble, however, meant that this was no mere star vehicle. Dwayne Croft, the Pelléas, considered the rehearsal period 'among the highlights' of his singing career. Miller had made him 'feel so comfortable' and freed him 'to focus on the character he was playing rather than on his surroundings'. He had, he felt, been given 'permission to be creative'. Rothstein wrote of the 'lyrical auburn sheen' of Croft's Pelléas. He also admired the 'almost breathless sense of erotic mystery' of the couple's scene in Miller's staging, 'in which yearning and reaching were as crucial as the actual touching'.*[74]

Volpe's formula of a smooth working organisation combined with a repertoire carefully balanced between artistic and financial needs was enhanced in April 1995, when he negotiated a five-year labour agreement with the musicians, fifteen months early. There was to be no wage increase in the first year but a total of nearly 15 per cent in stages up to $81,000 a year by 2001. There was also to be a pension package, which Phil Sipser called 'probably the best in the world'.[75] Volpe's own contract was renewed for five years in 1995.

The year before, in August 1994, Volpe had brought in Sarah Billinghurst as his assistant manager, in charge of the administration of the artistic department. She was responsible for casting and artistic planning, videos and telecasts, her work overlapping with that of Friend, who continued to work closely with Levine and maintained his preparation of the schedules. Billinghurst had worked for twenty-two

---

* Thomas Allen also enjoyed working with Miller, later recalling his working method, 'Jonathan Miller works from anecdote to anecdote – you laugh incessantly – at the end you wonder what you've got. A producer tries not to annoy his artists and get in their way.'

years at San Francisco Opera where she had been artistic administrator since 1982, and it was she who had undertaken co-productions with the Kirov Opera.

In September 1997 Stewart Pearce also officially became a member of the artistic planning team, as assistant manager, to work closely with the artistic department on long-term planning as well as on marketing. He had been working at the Met since 1976, and had been recruited by Volpe when he had been assistant manager to work for him in the budgeting department in finance and planning. After the artistic department prepared programmes, Pearce did box office projections and adjusted the balance in great detail, including rehearsal schedules.[76] 'Joe wanted to see on a piece of paper that the season would do 90 per cent,' Pearce explained. 'If it would not, he would say "No".'[77] After so many years of planning experience, Friend was confident that he, Billinghurst and Pearce knew what would make 90 per cent and 'Volpe rarely had to say no'.*[78]

An essential element of the management team and one who worked closely with his old colleague Volpe was technical director Joseph Clark. Jonathan Miller described him as a genius: 'If he approves of what you are doing,' Miller told *Opera News*, 'and you know what you are doing, he throws everything behind you.' He continued, 'It's like working for a very efficient nuclear submarine.'[79] John Copley agreed: 'The Met is just the best place to work in. It's the most efficient and professional – a bit like a factory but a fantastic artistic factory. I love being there more than anywhere in the world.'[80] Those who did not gain Clark's approval were less enthusiastic, claiming that he could reduce a designer's vision to the dull and conventional or even be responsible for designs being totally rejected.† Nonetheless the machine worked smoothly. According to Friend, the Met was 'a very efficient factory doing seven performances a week for thirty-two weeks a year'. He was proud that 'the level of product we produce is very

---

* Pearce had worked first at the Metropolitan Opera Guild, then in development and then as budget director in the finance department in charge of a smaller budgeting group fund-raising. He went over to Met merchandising and stayed at the Guild before the centennial in 1983 in order to keep all fund-raising under one roof.

† Johanna Fiedler refers to the opinions of several resident designers who claimed that Clark had 'a certain prim and proper taste and loved to push people around'. According to her unnamed source he often did Volpe's 'dirty work' for him (*Molto Agitato*, p. 264).

ꞱIigh . . . higher than anywhere I know'. He believed that singers who ꝡorked at the Met would call it a 'family' rather than a factory – it ꝡas, he said, 'Plácido's home House'.[81]

With the confidence that the planning team could ensure an aver-Ꞧge box office of 90 per cent, Volpe continued to introduce yet more ꝛaried fare to the Met audience. He defended the Met from charges Ꝺf conservatism, arguing that he was slowly educating the audience to Ꞧccept works such as *Lady Macbeth of Mtsensk*.[82] The education process ꝡas, however, slow and painful, the box office often disappointing. ꝛady Macbeth did 72.2 per cent and was not revived until 2000. *Kát'a* Ꞧade 82.5 per cent in its first season but only 64.1 per cent on its revival Ꞧn the 1998–99 season. Dvořák's *Rusalka* was staged for Beňačková in ꞨNovember 1993, conducted by John Fiore in a very Germanic perform-Ꞧnce which, in Mayer's words, 'exaggerated the influence of Wagner'. ꞨSchenk–Schneider-Siemssen provided another of their 'nineteenth-Ꞧentury originals'. The unfamiliar work had a disappointing box office Ꝺf 82.3 per cent. Levine, however, remained convinced that if the Met Ꞧould 'put the pieces in front of the audiences enough so that they Ꝺlo not have to start generationally from scratch' the situation would Ꝺbe very different, and referred to *Pelléas et Mélisande* as being success-fully sold out for the first time.[83]

Stars were, as always, an important ingredient for success. *I Lom-*Ꝛbardi did 98.4 per cent box office with Pavarotti but was not repeated. *Stiffelio* did well at 95.6 per cent in 1993–94 with Domingo. *Ariadne* Ꞧin 1993–94 with Norman did 94.3 per cent. An all-star cast was assembled for the old Ponnelle *Idomeneo* on 15 March 1995, with Dawn ꝰUpshaw, Anne Sofie von Otter, Carol Vaness and Plácido Domingo.

Although the Met endeavoured to provide a consistently fine roster of singers, Billinghurst pointed out that in the late Nineties there were few singers who could be guaranteed to sell tickets. Even though singers Ꝺlike Terfel and Bartoli had joined the ranks of Domingo and Pavarotti as those who could, the old star system had somewhat changed by the Ꝺlate Nineties, when punters bought tickets for many reasons, including the production or the opera itself, and not only as they had in the past to hear a Tebaldi or a Vickers.[84]

* * *

The *New York Times* praised the Met for its slightly more adventurou
policy, which brought *Queen of Spades* and *The Makropoulos Case* in
the 1995–96 season. 'The ratio of standard to offbeat is pretty good
for a major grind house like the Met,' said Robert W. Wilson, chairman
emeritus of New York City Opera.[85] On 26 October 1995 Moshinsky'
Queen of Spades successfully managed to find 'faces, not windmills
by creating, with his designer Mark Thompson, a false proscenium
It framed an arcade-like corridor through which the audience view.
Hermann's descent into despair. Gergiev conducted and was respon
sible for the casting: Dmitri Hvorostovsky as Prince Yeletsky, Karita
Mattila as Lisa and Ben Heppner as Hermann. Leonie Rysanek, in he
farewell to the Met, was the Countess. Its revival in 1999 was one of
the great successes of the 1999–2000 season, when Domingo sang his
first Hermann. The show made 98.4 per cent when Domingo sang.

With all these innovations, however, the core repertoire, and Verdi
in particular, remained subject to the concept that 'grand' means big
and that big means safe. Bernard Holland wrote at the end of the
1998–99 season, 'There is part of our operatic hearts that will always
long for shallow spectacle . . . opera's loyal majority worldwide clam-
ours for opera to be grand: it wants operas that it knows and it wants
them to be big.'[86] Furthermore, too often the pit continued to take
precedence over the demands of the stage. One close observer commented, 'Jimmy doesn't like people to move on the Met stage' and
recalled hearing Levine say, '"If I see anyone singing in profile, I'll
stop."' Thomas Allen reflected, 'They don't believe in drama – it's
about noise . . . Jimmy likes a big sound – lots of it would seem to
be the primary interest at the Met. Drama takes second place to the
music.'[87] Someone else who worked at the Met spoke of how Levine's
lack of feeling for character led to his inhibiting the development of
ensemble work. Unexpected changes of tempo during rehearsals could
result in singers having to look at him and left them no freedom to
interpret their roles or hold a consistent view of their characters.

Levine's primary concerns and interests remained musical and
visual, with a preference in the visual arts for the contemporary and
avante-garde. He thus saw the choice in production as limited to
either representational and abstract imagery or deconstruction, with
no reference to the subtleties and nuances of dramatic interaction. In

defending Zeffirelli's *Bohème* from criticism he said, 'I haven't seen anybody come up with a deconstructionist *Bohème* that was as good as that . . . I'm a person who does not expect the Anselm Kiefer show to look like a Rembrandt show.'[88] In an interview with Levine in *Opera* in August 1995, Rodney Milnes nervously asked Levine if his love of music took 'precedence over dramatic requirements' and reported that Levine 'chose to misunderstand the point and turned instead to production style' and in particular to the question of updating. Levine expressed his belief that there is a conflict between the conductor who is 'trying to get closer to the composer's vision' and some directors for whom that is 'not even a starting point'. He described Vick's *Lady Macbeth of Mtsensk* as a 'chainsaw-'n'-kitchen chair' production. He had personally found it 'fascinating' but, he added, 'there were many critics who disagreed as to the type of chainsaws and kitchen chairs they would have preferred'.[89] Levine preferred to work with directors who did not, as he saw it, come between him and his singers. 'I need a director', he said, 'who understands his function and mine rather than a director who may have a completely different philosophy.'[90]

It was Verdi who fared the worst from the supposed conflict between conductor and director, and the misconception that fidelity to the music must entail production devoid of personality. For it was to Giancarlo Del Monaco, who responded to Levine's needs, and with whom he enjoyed working, that he turned to direct *Simon Boccanegra* in 1995. Met and Covent Garden productions of this work starkly reveal the difference in approach to drama in nineteenth-century grand opera between the two companies in the 1990s, as well as the strengths and weaknesses of their musical-cum-dramatic orientations.

Del Monaco's *Boccanegra* at the Met was a bland, standard, easily revivable costume drama. In contrast, Moshinsky's *Boccanegra* at Covent Garden in November 1991 was, in Milnes's words, 'one of the most profoundly stirring stagings of recent years'. It laid bare the verity of Fiesco's words, 'All earthly happiness is a lying illusion, and the human heart the source of unending tears.' Milnes pointed out that *Boccanegra*, like *Idomeneo* for Mozart, 'was an opera into which the composer put his whole soul' and to this Moshinsky, together with his designer Michael Yeargan, responded with intense conviction. Yeargan's ingenious and beautiful set, inspired by Piero della Francesca, together with Peter J. Hall's costumes, 'added up to a series of Renaissance pictures that ravished the eye, pictures that breathed the colours of the Mediterranean world under John Harrison's careful and informed lighting'.[91]

Moshinsky's delicate and sensitive delineation of the work contrasted with the broad sweep and superficial grandeur of Del Monaco's Met production, which was typically big, cumbersome and literal, cluttered with crenellated walls and a variety of flora in full bloom. The external props focused attention away from the music and the emotional developments on stage, and the over-ornate costumes rendered the protagonists almost disembodied, restricting movement, and diminishing physicality and sensuality. In Del Monaco's Council Chamber scene Domingo literally staggered under the weight of his armour, and the principals were all but obscured by the massed and massive chorus and the irrelevant brandishing of arms.* This was in sharp contrast to the clarity, intensity and lightness of Moshinsky's production, where unencumbered bodies moved and interacted freely. Unlike Del Monaco, Moshinsky worked from the inside of the opera outwards, not shifting his people about on stage unless there was a dramatic reason to do so.

The musical approach, as well as that of the design and direction, also revealed a contrasting philosophy. Levine's impressive control over the strings in the few measures of prelude provided deep, sad, elegant tone, together with lovely nuances of timbre and timing. The winds, particularly the brass, were similarly responsive. The mark of Solti's players, on the other hand, was warmth and depth of feeling. Moreover, the blend was better, as opposed to the Met's perhaps too cleanly delineated choirs and sections. Solti also took pains to maintain a dialogue between the orchestra and the on-stage happenings, conductor and stage director together creating grand opera–chamber music, in an intimate stage setting which was emotionally authentic and involving. Each voice and character, each solo instrumental line, was articulated and individualised, the orchestral lines brought out to underscore on-stage events and moods. By contrast, Levine approached

---

* A member of staff later commented that the Met's Council Chamber had been wrongly located in Venice rather than Genoa in a style which he described as 'literal but absurd'.

he orchestra as an autonomous entity, using its power and precision
adiciously, toning it down when necessary to accompany singers
ather than 'dialogue' with them as Solti does. Solti's musical pacing
vas dramatic in the full sense of the word, with big moments, little
nd middle-sized moments each given appropriate weight, and all
nked together in organic sequence. Levine's pacing tended rather to
nove from climax to climax, with swathes of recitative in between
enerally sounding very well, but somewhat all of a piece.

Volpe later said that he had tried to dissuade Del Monaco from
lways using Michael Scott as his designer, and that Del Monaco had
lone 'too much in a row', taking over Bonn and becoming 'too
usy'.*[92] The director's *Forza* on 4 March 1996 was even more bland
han his *Boccanegra*, with what Hoelterhoff described as a cast of
milling hordes of 'pedlars, pilgrims and peasants'. Of Sharon Sweet,
Holland wrote, 'The part's emotional life is miles beyond her.'[93] Dom-
ngo struggled valiantly in difficult circumstances.

Peter Davis felt that since his *Fanciulla* Del Monaco had gone
teadily downhill, with *Forza* 'showing a production aesthetic now
obbled by creative exhaustion or, worse, sheer cynicism . . .' with its
incessant flag waving, aimless milling and operetta posturing'. Davis
oncluded, 'As so often happens when nearly everything is wrong on
tage, James Levine seems to lose interest as well, and his musical
lirection is lacklustre.'[94]

Perhaps Levine himself was not fully aware of his own need for
lrama on the stage. He told Milnes, in his interview in *Opera*, that
inging counted for 80 per cent of operatic performances and
xplained:

> The human voice expressing feeling through text, sound and
> inflection, the tragedy and comedy of human existence ex-
> pressed in these terms must be the most daunting, challenging

Someone who worked at the Met believed that because Del Monaco had 'split himself
nto two different styles' for Europe and the Met, he had become 'cynical' and consequently badly behaved. The same observer believed that the technical department, and
not Del Monaco, who had wanted to set *Boccanegra* in Fascist Italy, was responsible for
he picture postcard appearance of the production. Fiedler wrote that Del Monaco's
personal style during rehearsals . . . involved more yelling than the company expected,
ven from an Italian opera director, no less one who walked out and sulked' (*Molto
Agitato*, p. 307).

and ultimately satisfying large art form. Living your life inside the imagination of a composer and librettist is about as thrilling as any man-made activity can get.[95]

Levine gave the impression of someone suffering from deconstruc tionist director abuse, going so far as to state the view that singer should not interpret the words, 'because it has already been done b the music'. But by this he was referring to the antics sometimes associ ated with postmodern productions: 'If one starts to illustrate an exaggerate words, pretty soon the fact that they are set to music doesn' work its magic. . . . No amount of running around the stage an pounding the floor and taking off your clothes or singing standing o your head is going to take the place of making the audience feel th expression in the singing direct from the singer to the listener.'[96]

Levine brought production staff to the Met who were 'consisten with his aesthetic principles'. One of the in-house directors wa Levine's protégé, California-born Lesley Koenig, who joined the Me staff in 1995–96 and, having been Zeffirelli's assistant, was often i charge of revivals of La Bohème. Koenig told Opera News, 'Director like us are endangered. Everyone wants to have a concept and plac it in Iraq. One European intendant said to me, "Make a huge scanda somewhere and then we will hire you." . . . I like to travel back i time – maybe it's all that art history.'

Leslie Koenig, as production director, prepared the new Met Cos in 1996, in which one of the great new stars, Cecilia Bartoli, appeared On 22 February 1996 Terry Teachout wrote that 'opera goers wh favor a no-nonsense Così will find this one satisfactory'.[97] Manuel Hoelterhoff observed rehearsals during which Thomas Allen, Susann Mentzer, Jerry Hadley and Dwayne Croft seemed bored while bus 'executing Koenig's tightly choreographed movements'.[98] Thoma Allen later said that Koenig had 'thought of every moment . . . ever little detail was there – the sand in my shoe was there from the firs day, it wasn't something that grew and developed as time wore on' In the event, however, he recalled, 'some sparks flew, in the sense tha the drama wasn't killed stone dead'.[99] Hoelterhoff reported Levine' joint production meetings in which the maestro was said to have tol Koenig: 'It's in C major . . . it's optimistic. The ending has to be up.'[10]

Koenig's production was the right framework for Levine's musical interpretation, and the Met orchestra was displayed to full advantage, with Mozart's fine line delineated and stylishly stroked. The transparency of sound was magical, with little gurgles here and there from the second clarinet.

In this production of Così Cecilia Bartoli's Despina revealed her extraordinary talent less well than did her Cenerentola on 27 October 1997. After her Cenerentola, Martin Mayer wrote that she 'not only has the great artist's power to concentrate our attention on her from the moment of her appearance but also has the genius to make that power create authenticity for the character she plays'. Her wonderful instrument is capable of moving quickly from lightest lyric tone to rich spinto with a range encompassing both mezzo-soprano and soprano. Her articulation is as rapid as a Gatling gun's and her sense of wit, merriment and grace is particularly appealing. Although Levine rarely conducted Rossini, he enjoyed working with Bartoli who, in Mayer's words, managed to bring out a 'true Rossinian spirit in him'.[101]

Levine, with his great love of the human voice and enjoyment of coaching, retained his ability to lure the world's greatest singers to the Met for less money than they would get in some Houses, as well as nurturing the home-bred singers. He never allowed extraordinary European talent like that of Bartoli to rest for long in Europe. One of the most exciting visitors was Bryn Terfel, with whom Levine made a solo recording of opera arias in 1996 for Deutsche Grammophon. Terfel made his Met debut on 19 October 1994 in Figaro with his 'big creamy, beautiful voice and teddy-bear manner'. Levine found inspiration in the line-up of Hampson, Terfel, Vaness and Yvonne Gonzales on 10 October 1995, when a performance of Don Giovanni came alive 'within the shell of the old scorned Zeffirelli production'.[102]

Other foreign stars at the Met included London-based Finnish soprano Karita Mattila, whose debut in May 1990 was in Don Giovanni, and British baritone Simon Keenlyside, who had his debut as Belcore in L'Elisir in 1996. Another exciting young artist was Natalie Dessay from France, who has described herself as a 'soprano légère', but whose voice has a most thrilling thrust. On 4 February 1998, when Dessay sang Olympia in Hoffmann, Mayer noted that all the old voice connoisseurs were left 'without exception sputtering speechless'. There was no one in the previous fifty years to compare with her 'interpolated top notes, to the precision of the coloratura and the richness of the melodic phrasing ... firm authority ... and to the hilarious quasi-mechanical gestures of the doll that has, somewhat to its own surprise, achieved humanity'.[103]

Home-bred talent was also flourishing. Dawn Upshaw's Ann Trulove, in November 1997 in a performance of *The Rake's Progress* was fresh, pert and youthful. She spun the sound forward, slipped up and down the middle and upper-middle registers with acrobatic ease and a vibrato out of another era, almost as clean and fast as that of Conchita Supervia. Her superb command of diction and nuance makes her a fine artist, if not a vocal comet along the lines of Dessay. Dolora Zajick's high mezzo is powerful, smooth and appealing in tone. Her vocal weight and penetration make her a splendid Azucena, while her free top enables her to sing Dalila with aplomb. She can shift effortlessly from piano to fortissimo, from lowest register to highest, and her range is one of the biggest among mezzos currently singing.

On 27 April 1996 Levine's twenty-fifth anniversary gala ran from six in the evening to two the following morning. It was a monument to his relationship with the international and American singing community. Dawn Upshaw, Dwayne Croft, and Heidi Grant Murphy were products of the young artists programme. Other American stars were Renée Fleming, Deborah Voigt, and Dolora Zajick, and Met stalwarts Morris, Ramey, Hampson and von Stade. The international group included Domingo, Pavarotti, Kraus, von Otter, Te Kanawa, Terfel, Meier, Gheorghiu and Alagna. Nilsson offered a spoken tribute. Levine conducted everything, as he had 1,646 performances in twenty-five years. In *Opera News*, Patrick J. Smith described the event as a celebration of someone who, with 'his commitment to the long term' had 'devoted his adult life to the Metropolitan Opera'.[104] At the Metropolitan Opera Guild lunch ten days before, Volpe had said, 'No music or artistic director anywhere gives as much time or energy as Jim does season after season.'[105]

Much as Levine was admired and appreciated, Volpe was sensitive to the continued criticism that world-class conductors did not appear regularly at the Met. Billinghurst admitted that it was still 'practically impossible' to get the obvious conductors like Colin Davis, Riccardo Chailly and Simon Rattle. The Met had given up trying to get Muti and Abbado, even though Volpe stressed that he was 'putting more and more pressure on them to come here'.[106] Billinghurst pointed out that it was only Gergiev's boundless energy that enabled him to rehearse at the Met while maintaining his other commitments. Most top conductors were not prepared to adopt such a frenetic lifestyle, and this reality was reinforced after the tragic and sudden death of Giuseppe Sinopoli in April 2001, from a heart attack during a performance of *Aida* in Berlin.

On 15 September 1997 Gergiev's appointment as principal guest conductor enabled Volpe to claim that he was 'really beginning to get the world's premier conductors into the House'.[107] Gergiev would conduct two productions a season, mainly in the Russian repertoire, but also *Don Carlos* in the 2001–02 season, in order to ensure, as the Met's announcement put it, 'that he will become an integral part of the artistic life of the company' and that the Russian repertoire would be better represented.* Gergiev was keen, he told the *New York Times*, to be involved with a company of world-class stature and was impressed by the organisation of the place.[108] Bernard Holland thought it a good thing to have 'some musical brutishness to counterbalance the amazing beauty of Mr Levine's conducting'.[109]

Gergiev maintained a gruelling schedule. By 1999 he was director and principal conductor of the Kirov company in St Petersburg, principal guest conductor at the Met, principal conductor of the Rotterdam Philharmonic, a sought-after guest of American and European orchestras, a director of festivals including the White Nights Festival in St Petersburg, and was involved in an annual project with the London Philharmonia. In February 1999 he agreed to conduct an electrifying revival of *The Queen of Spades* at the Met, with Domingo.

---

* This was shortly before Gergiev conducted *Boris Godunov*, with Ramey and a cast mainly of his own Russian colleagues, including Olga Borodina as Marina. Gergiev's position meant that the Russian repertoire would be given its due weight. Levine had only conducted *Onegin* and Stravinsky's *Le Rossignol*, preferring not to conduct pieces whose language he did not understand, but making an exception of *Onegin*, which he loved (Friend Interview, 23.3.00).

Gergiev has a great flair for approaching a given opera on its own terms. Warming to the fire and pagan glory of Mussorgsky's *Khovanshchina* in March 1999, he laid down great semi-opaque swathes of sound. His Dionysian approach, as well as the deep, sometimes snarling string tone, gave the Met orchestra an unaccustomed hint of fierceness. In contrast to Levine, at some points Gergiev seemed to abandon control in favour of an insistent, driving pulse, while still managing, like Levine, not to pressure the singers. Although choral entrances were sometimes ragged, the timing in the ensembles was exquisite. Eschewing a blasting or bombastic approach, pensive passages were sensitively brought out, as were the many delicate dynamic contrasts. Gergiev gave every impression of a rich, authentic emotional reaction to the uniqueness of the score.*[110]

By 1999 Volpe's team had managed to build up subscription sales to 53 per cent, which allowed the Met freedom of planning and, unlike at Covent Garden, still allowed enough single-sale tickets to be sold to keep the House accessible to non-subscribers.[111] Volpe and Pearce had succeeded in maintaining the policy of not raising the lower prices as much as the higher prices. The lowest price was still $25 per ticket in 2002, for family circle seats Monday to Thursday, by which time top prices in the centre of the parterre were $265.†[112] It was hoped that this would maintain the Met's audience base but, with 800,000 seats to sell each season, the Met continued to be concerned to bring in new audiences. The education department of the Guild organised workshops with teachers in schools. By 2002 the 'Creating an Opera' teacher workshops, begun in 1993, involved twelve full-time teachers and three part-time. The Guild also arranged a choral music initiative

---

* Johanna Fiedler quotes the reactions of some of the Met's musicians to Gergiev's conducting. One complained of Gergiev's inability to explain what he wanted of them, saying, 'I can understand "you're sharp. You're flat, you're too loud, you're too fast", but I can't understand "I want a silvery tone".' On the other hand, another said, 'We never know what he's going to do next. There's no mystery left for us with Jimmy. Gergiev gets a visceral response from us' (*Molto Agitato*, p. 318).

† Sales were 40 per cent in the New York area, 30 per cent all over the United States and 30 per cent in Europe and Asia. Tickets were available from 1999 via the Met's website.

to teach singing in schools in 2002, as well as lectures by experts and interviews with Met artists. Other ways of reaching potential new audiences included the Met's website, which had information about fifty-five operas by 2002, and which the education department believed received between 65,000 and 60,000 hits a month. The Met broadcasts also continued.*

Unlike at Covent Garden, education did not become a political issue at the Met, even though its foundation stone, the students' performances, had to be abandoned in 1996 when the cost for the Guild's education department to hire the auditorium for mid-week performances became too great at $176,000. Instead, the House arranged a discounted ticket system for students for popular or less familiar shows in the early part of their runs. These might include the opening night of *Luisa Miller* or *War and Peace* in 2002. Met School membership also included forty-four passes for students to attend dress rehearsals and receive preparatory materials. But, as Robert Tuggle wrote in 1970, the 'information without the performance is meaningless', and Covent Garden, with all its financial headaches, remained committed to the schools matinées, reintroducing them after the closure with Vivien Duffield's sponsorship.

While the strong subscription base did not bring in new audiences, it did give the financial security, which meant there could be more adventurous planning. There were some pleasant surprises, as in 1997 when *Clemenza di Tito* did 89 per cent at the box office. Jonathan Miller's *Rake's Progress* in November 1997, however, did not fare so well at 75 per cent. Together with his designer, Jennifer Tipton, Miller turned to Auden and Stravinsky rather than Hogarth for his inspiration, positioning the work, according to Holland, in a 'non-specific twentieth-century city' evocative of Berlin. Miller managed successfully to humanise 'an opera that may be more about style than people. His care and concern for the people on stage never wavers.' The raked stage reached to the audience over the pit. Its 'unassailable all-American cast'[113] included Ramey, Upshaw, Hadley and Denyce Graves as Baba the Turk. Levine was less convinced than Holland, believing

---

* Robert Bucker was head of education from 1995 to 1997, organising chamber performances of *Gianni Schicchi*, and lecture series. David Dik took over in 1997.

that Miller had left behind a 'great deal of nonsense' which they 'would have to fix in revival'.[114]

Peter Grimes in December was sensitively conducted by David Atherton. Tommasini welcomed Philip Langridge's penetrating yet lyric delivery, but found him too elegant in moments of abuse and anger.[115] *Grimes* did even worse than *Rake* at 61.4 per cent, a close observer noting that it was still too gloomy a subject after a long, hard day at the office.

It was Volpe who backed Robert Wilson's controversial production of *Lohengrin*, later recalling, 'I supported Robert Wilson. I would stand behind him. I would be there at the rehearsal.' In March 1998 *Lohengrin* was greeted with 'banshee shrieks of apparently homicidal intent' against Robert Wilson.[116] A new development was the stirring up of hostility by opera chat postings on the Internet.* Musically and visually stunning, it was dramatically perverse. The Texan, Robert Wilson, whose previous visit to the Met had been the independent production of Glass's *Einstein on the Beach* in 1986, was in John von Rhein's words, an 'unconventional theatre artist' from Waco. He was a cult celebrity in Europe and well known for his 'tai chi manoeuvres and slow motion processionals'.[117] Like Zeffirelli, Wilson's great strength lay in the visual, and it provided *Lohengrin* with a brilliantly lit backdrop of richly and beautifully changing hues. Mel Gussow, in the *New York Times* on 16 March 1998 described how his 'shimmering Rothko-like rectangle changed colour according to mood and, in Mr Wilson's signature style, bars of light, both horizontal and vertical, were substituted for traditional woods and palaces'. Movements, however, were so ritualised that the protagonists became ensnared in an inexplicable oriental masque. Even such a passionately physical and involved actress as Mattila, in the revival in November 1998, moved like a clockwork doll in a straitjacket. *Lohengrin*, though abstract in appearance, was ultimately closely akin to *Turandot*, substituting visual appeal and the grand gesture for dramatic content and nuanced interaction between the protagonists.

However radical some of the Met's new departures were, traditional

---

* There had been months of opera chat postings on the Internet with hate-mongering threats about the production, which called upon the public to destroy it with boos, as Zambello's *Lucia* had been.

productions remained what Met sponsors and Met audiences demanded for what Volpe called the 'bread and butter operas'. He explained, 'When we do the *Bohèmes, Toscas*, the *Traviatas*, we have to find something that will serve us for twenty or twenty-five years in the style that works for our public.' New productions cost up to $7 million a year and were fully funded, either by individuals or a consortium. Although the Samuels Foundation supported the 1999 production of *Moses und Aron*, it was still easier to find donations for popular works and producers.

In the late Nineties new money was finding its way on to Boards all over the United States. Lisa Gubernick reported in the *Wall Street Journal* on 7 May 1999, 'Eight years into a stock market boom, the entrance fee for those invited to join some boards has become as blatant as a price tag on a toaster.' New York's Carnegie Hall, she wrote, 'examines prospective Board members' real estate records, trusts and stock holdings and securities'. At the Met there were still Board members who were not major donors, like Risë Stevens and Beverly Sills. Volpe explained, 'Risë turns up at dinners and patrons love the opportunity to rub shoulders with her.' On the whole, however, Met Board members were generally expected to give $150,000, paid over three years. Volpe said, 'The people on the Boards are changing – the people with money are changing. . . . The people who are involved today are people who have worked their way up.'[118]

Leading patrons were Mr and Mrs George Lindemann, whose support for the young artists programme was such that the programme was renamed in their honour. In June 1999 the Lindemanns gave their daughter's wedding reception on the stage of the Met, resplendent with *Die Fledermaus* scenery, three small monkeys, five red caged birds, shocking-pink feather hanging pieces, bands, black and red drapery, audio-mix equipment, mirrored table decorations, 'Screaming Queens', red velvet cushions, two bands, two pianos, piped music for cocktails, lighting rehearsed to fit in with events – not to mention masses of garish pink flowers, caviar and 'blackamoors' who were employed to lead the guests to the stage, and then to open the backstage scenery for the 'after' party, where breakfast was served at 2 a.m.

After Sybil Harrington's demise in September 1998 another major new sponsor in the late Nineties was Alberto Vilar, a Cuban-born

American who had made a fortune in high-tech investment. Vilar gave $25 million to the Met's Endowment Fund as well as backing many new productions. In 1999 he expressed his ambition to outdo Sybil Harrington's donations of $26 million. The Met grand tier was renamed the Vilar grand tier. He pledged $20 million to the Met's new endowment as well as sponsoring new productions and contributing to the young artists programme.* He contributed to many other opera houses, including St Petersburg,[119] and in return for his £10 million donation to Covent Garden insisted on the redeveloped Royal Opera House's Floral Hall being named after him in 1999. By August 2001 Vilar claimed to have given more than $200 million to the classical performing arts throughout the world, with opera the main beneficiary.[120] He told writer Johanna Fiedler in May 2000 that the Met was 'a marriage between two forces – the artist and the donor', and that he did not understand why the donors are treated 'like second-class citizens'. 'What makes me less important than Plácido Domingo?' he asked and added, 'Why shouldn't I take curtain calls?'[121]

Although management stressed that Vilar did not interfere in artistic decisions, and indeed that no donors did, and that he did not look at designs and models, he did have his preferences. Like Harrington, he was a fan of Zeffirelli, explaining, 'The Met does lavish things and the best person for lavish is Franco Zeffirelli.' If a set he had sponsored were to be sparse like that of *Onegin* or *Lohengrin*, Vilar would wonder where his money had gone. He would be satisfied, however, with the response evoked by the second act of *Turandot* when the 'audience applauds like mad'.[122] Volpe was content to turn to Zeffirelli for traditional productions, explaining that it was difficult to find directors who were willing to do such work.[123] In the mid- and late Nineties Volpe chose Zeffirelli for new productions of *Carmen*, *Traviata* and *Pagliacci*. Zeffirelli's *Carmen* in November 1996 was described by Manuela Hoelterhoff as a 'clueless chaotic disaster' with so many 'overdressed Spaniards, lurching cripples, cavorting urchins, and raggedly beggars milling around the plaza that Maria Callas herself could have gone unnoticed'.[124]

---

* Productions that Vilar sponsored included Zeffirelli's *Traviata*, Miller's *Figaro*, Cesare Levi's *Cenerentola* and Jürgen Flimm's *Fidelio* between 1998 and 2000.

Zeffirelli's *Traviata* in 1998 cost $2.5 million. Volpe had rejected Erich Wonder's designs, because he said they 'made Paris look like Vienna'. Friend later said of Wonder's set, 'It was not going to work here – it was conceptual ... too close to Zambello's *Lucia*.' Volpe telephoned Zeffirelli and said, 'Franco, I really need you to do it.' He felt that giving *Traviata* to Albery, Vick, Moshinsky or Zambello would have been 'too big a gamble', and he asked Zeffirelli for a smaller and technically lighter *Traviata*, which he believed was then provided. Volpe called Act One the perfect set: 'Easy to get the chorus in, easy to get them out.' He had some reservations, however, telling Zeffirelli that his belief that the Met audience 'likes to see things move' was mistaken, and that the Flora scene was over the top. But, he concluded, 'Zeffirelli's productions last a long time and our audience loves it'.

The new production had been fraught with mishaps. Roberto Alagna and Angela Gheorghiu were chastened when Volpe withdrew their contract after they had delayed signing it and had urged Volpe to dismiss Zeffirelli's designs, presenting him with Alagna's brother's designs instead. Volpe told them that although artists' suggestions were taken into account, approval always rested with the production team. He asked them to sign their contracts 'like grown-ups'. He stressed that they had not been banned and were indeed singing *Roméo et Juliette* to full houses during that season. There had been another incident on tour in Japan, when Volpe had insisted that Gheorghiu wear an unattractive blond wig that Zeffirelli had designed for Micaëla in *Carmen* and had actually put on her understudy during the first performance. 'The problem', Volpe later explained, 'was not just the refusals, but the way it was handled, storming on stage and shouting that she would not wear this wig and didn't care who knows it and that's that.' Volpe was not to be crossed. He said that he hoped this experience would make them realise that he was 'a serious person'. Later, with agent Herbert Breslin as their new adviser, Alagna and Gheorghiu were, Volpe said, 'doing better'.*[125]

Volpe had got *Traviata* on the stage and Vilar was happy. The critics were less so. Peter Davis accused Zeffirelli of 'abandoning the

---

* According to the *New York Times* on 8 April 1998 Alagna and Gheorghiu signed an exclusive joint contract with EMI. The company's massive promotion campaign at Alagna's Met debut misfired when expectations were disappointed.

cast – and Verdi's opera for that matter – to revel in his obsession with interior design'. He continued, 'Violetta's overstuffed salon is just a teaser for the country villa we behold in act two, as huge as a Mussolini train station and cluttered with bric-à-brac and a jungle of plants. . . . Flora's party takes place in a garish hotel lobby choking in lace and spangled red drapery, an appropriately tacky setting for a bullfight ballet that has to be seen to be believed.' Neither Patricia Racette, who took on Violetta, nor the talented young lyric tenor Marcelo Alvarez as Alfredo, was given help to fathom the depths of their respective characters.[126] When Allan Kozinn saw the second cast, he thought it was possible that the first cast had got lost in the scenery. The first party scene was so busy that he suspected a 'where's Waldo–Wally' popular cultural reference. Volpe put it differently, 'Zeffirelli found a way to pinpoint her even though there was a lot going on. . . . You never lose the characters in a Zeffirelli set – he has an eye for that – making sure that the costumes were distinguishable.'[127] Alberto Vilar was content: 'If the guy at the *Times* didn't like *Traviata*, then he ought to try fishing, because he missed his sport. The audience was happy.'[128]

The 1998–99 season was full of interesting ventures. In December 1998 Jonathan Miller was even entrusted with one of the most central pieces of the Met repertoire, *Figaro*. According to Holland it had 'more good theatre than is normal at the Met with all the characters responding with looks and gestures'.[129] The cast alone would have insured the 98.7 per cent it did at the box office, bringing together, as it did, Bryn Terfel and Cecilia Bartoli, as well as Fleming, Mentzer and Croft. It was full of vigour and life, although Bartoli's comic high jinks bordered on farce. 'She tore around like a Disney character let loose in a Vermeer,' wrote Alex Ross in the *New Yorker*. Holland was struck by her 'bouncy charm and high-energy comedy', but warned of adulation, suggesting that Bartoli was confusing Rosina and Susanna – pure comedy versus a complete human figure.[130] Ross praised Terfel's 'boldly phrased, rhythmically vital singing'.

The orchestra were crisp and precise, with every accent, every semiquaver in the violins executed as one player, with no feeling of chill or mechanical accuracy. The performance was far more stylish than the 1991 *Zauberflöte* and the string sound warmer than before. As a member of the orchestra said at this time, Levine was generally seeking a 'rounder deeper velvety sound'.[131] The orchestra was also astonishingly together on the trills, and controlled in the dynamics. Terfel provided heat and anger, while Levine provided a brilliantly played orchestral accompaniment. The orchestra's degree of accuracy and responsiveness remained, while Levine was achieving a deeper understanding of Mozart.

Not only was Miller entrusted with *Figaro*, but Moshinsky was given *Samson et Dalila* – with Domingo – in February 1998. It was Volpe who, after hesitation, finally approved Robert Hudson's abstract designs with their oranges, clashing reds, corals and yellows. 'I'm happy about it – that's all that counts,' Volpe said. Moshinsky recalled, 'We had to do three sets for *Samson*. We sat in a meeting. They just didn't know what to do with it . . . and then Mercedes Bass who put up the money said, "Red's my favourite colour." '[132] Moshinsky explained to Ralph Blumenthal of the *New York Times*, 'We play it as desire, for sexual possession, we thought primitive emotion, we thought Matisse . . . not a palm tree in sight.' The palm trees were missed by some members of the audience, and Blumenthal felt that the phallic towers of Act Two suggested the cooling towers of Three Mile Island, the site of the nuclear reactor disaster.[133] Domingo, however, filled the House.

Moses und Aron in February 1999 was the greatest challenge to be faced by the Met, not least because it could not be cast with Met stars. Stewart Pearce mused, 'If we had done *Moses und Aron* with Plácido Domingo and Bryn Terfel it would have been budgeted a lot higher.' With Langridge and Tomlinson, *Moses und Aron* was budgeted to do 75 per cent while actually achieving 78 per cent on its first showing.

The performances of *Moses und Aron* in February 1999 were brilliantly conceived, precisely executed, and lovingly led by Levine, after ample rehearsal time during which the thorny problems of the score had been overcome by careful, dedicated work. Dense orchestral textures were injected with light and balance achieved again and again with apparent ease. Levine's orchestra was as usual crisp and clear, and even the choral diction was comprehensible. This labour of love, so faithfully presented, shows how far Levine had brought his players, and how full of vigour and professional imagination he remains after so many years in the Met harness. The casting of the brothers also demonstrated an excellent and, for the Met, daring solution: Tomlinson and Langridge were decidedly not Terfel and Domingo but nonetheless, sympathetically accompanied by Levine, they were ideal for their roles, even though Langridge in the fiendishly difficult role of Aron occasionally pushed his voice.

The critics were excited. Paul Griffiths found *Moses und Aron* 'glorious' in February and 'overwhelming' at its revival.[134] Tomlinson, he wrote, used 'Schoenberg's speech-song to find fiercely expressive regions of growl and lament'. Langridge was 'persuasive, capricious, unrepentant, clever ... with his voice and eyes and his nimble movements he provides everything the role requires'. Griffiths described Vick's interpretation of the tragedy as lying in Aron's 'penchant for drama more even than his power over the crowd'. When Aron, according to Griffiths, tells the children of Israel that Moses might have been killed by his God, he was falling victim to his 'weakness for drama at the expense of truth'. Griffiths's analysis reflected a weakness in the production which blurred the deeper meaning of the work. The discussion between the two brothers of how you present God and about inventing a religion, and the question as to whether it was a true source of inspiration or an intellectual invention were not given due weight. Peter Davis was concerned about the lack of depth, describing the production as 'hopelessly inappropriate and trivial' at its revival in October 1999. He found the 'ridiculously staged golden calf orgy' to be particularly silly: '*West Side Story* meets *Samson and Delilah*.'[135] Visually the production, although relatively sparse, was very striking with its simple deep orange sand dunes in Act One and 'arching black monolith' in Act Two.[136]

With all these – for the Met – great adventures, which also included *Khovanshchina* and *Kát'a Kabanová* for six performances, and *Wozzeck* for three performances during the 1998–99 season, management was delighted and surprised to succeed in sustaining a box office average of 92 per cent. But in spite of this, the educational process at the unsubsidised Met was a slow one and not relevant to much of its audience. Crawford was content that the education process was slowly working and that a reasonable box office could be secured for such challenging productions as *Billy Budd* and Miller's *Pelléas*.[137]

Billinghurst also believed that the Met had succeeded in persuading the public that opera is not an elitist art form, with new and younger 'Brooklyn Academy of Music' type audiences approaching such productions as the Robert Wilson *Lohengrin* or the 2000 *Dr Faust* and able to afford the tickets.[138] Nonetheless, the season's box office success was in fact sustained by twenty-one *Aidas*, which consistently played to 99 per cent houses, together with nineteen *Bohèmes*, fourteen *Toscas* and thirteen *Traviatas*. How disappointed Levine must have been when the revival of *Moses* in September 1999 was down to 49.4 per cent while *Tosca* did 96.6 per cent and *Aida* 96.6 per cent.

Levine reflected that *Moses* had been introduced to the Met, 'about twenty years later than I wanted'.[139] In an unsubsidised world, which both Volpe and Levine appeared to be facing harmoniously together by 2000, it was a tough artistic struggle. Bernard Holland wrote on 2 May 1999, 'Through all the missteps and victories of this last season, one feels a new conscience in place. Works that must be done are being done, and pragmatic businessmen who care about art are finding ways to make it possible.'*[140] The path was not without its hazards, nor were the new directors' futures at the Met assured. Graham Vick's starkly modern *Trovatore*, updated to the nineteenth century, provoked derision in December 2000. At the premiere the audience laughed so much at Neil Shicoff's entrance, balancing on a huge cross lowered from the wings in his Countess Maritza costume, that the performance stopped for the only time in Met history other than for a death on stage. The resulting anxiety caused an instant refit, and a shaken Vick asked that his name be removed from the credits, reportedly saying that he would never work at the Met again.

In October 2001 it was announced that in 2004–05 Levine would succeed Seiji Ozawa as music director of the Boston Symphony Orchestra, a position he had long desired. His contract at the Met was extended to 2007 and he would maintain his twenty-three-week-a-year commitment to the Met, but after the 2004 season his title would once again be music director, as it had been before 1986.

* * *

---

* By 2001 the $100 million endowment was worth $160 million, and fund-raising efforts were geared towards raising it to $200 million.

The dispute continued between the Met and its neighbours in the Lincoln Center, which had, by 2001, organised its $1.5 billion renovation project with a $240 million commitment from Mayor Giuliani's New York City. The redevelopment included a glass dome over the campus and the reconstruction of Avery Fisher Hall. Volpe and Paul Monterone decided to withdraw from the project, declaring that the Met would renovate independently, dissatisfied with planning decisions and having conducted its own renovation projects in previous years. Volpe was concerned that major redevelopment of the Lincoln Center would affect the Met's fund-raising operations. The problems were exacerbated when the new mayor, Michael Blomberg, announced that the recession-stricken city could not honour its commitment, and when the City Opera declared it wanted to build a new theatre adjacent to the Lincoln Center in Damrosch Park. City Opera's director, Paul Kellogg, argued that City Opera felt like a stepchild with the poor acoustics of the New York State Theater and could not 'achieve the status' it aspired to if it remained there. Volpe was, however, adamant that the Met did not want to add to the House's annual budget by becoming responsible for subsidising a new home for City Opera. The rows continued for many months with two Lincoln Center presidents resigning amid much speculation in the press as to chairman Beverly Sills's role in their resignations and in hampering agreement among the constituent bodies.[141]

With annual expenses of nearly $200 million by 2001, and an enlarged endowment of $250 million, the Met was determined not to endanger its hard-won economic security. The House was not, however, spared from the fall-out from the disaster of 11 September, and faced a sharp decline in box office receipts even for *La Bohème*. Sponsors were also affected by the stock market downturn, even Alberto Vilar giving cause for concern in the new year with reports of unfulfilled sponsorships as well as ill health. Such were the rumours that the new editor of *Opera* magazine, John Allison, wrote in the editorial of March 2002, 'These events show just how vulnerable the operatic world has become and raise the question of whether companies should be banking so heavily on one volatile source.'[142] Bruce Crawford said he believed that the Met was in solid shape but he also warned, 'Every opera house is fragile' and added, 'There is fragility still.'

TWENTY-FIVE

COVENT GARDEN 1988–94
'Bricks without Straw'

NONE OF THE MAJOR OPERA HOUSES was more 'fragile' and vulnerable than Covent Garden, as its new general director, Jeremy Isaacs, was to discover in the Nineties. But Isaacs was an intrepid new force at Covent Garden and, under his leadership, the House took a strikingly different path from the other major opera houses by deciding to present a varied, lively and daring artistic vision, rather than retrenching in the face of financial problems and a declining subsidy. Isaacs was fully aware of the potential hazards of taking such a course when he took up his position as general director in September 1988: he had been on the Board and opera committee for three years and had witnessed at first hand the constant financial problems. He later said, 'I plunge into things.'[1] But having worked in independent television, where resources were plentiful and he had been his own master, and with no experience of running an opera house, his new position was to prove a culture shock.

This was also a dangerous period for the House as there was an insidious but increasingly damaging attack on the concept of subsidy for the arts in general and for opera in particular. At the time Isaacs took on the directorship, the novelist Iris Murdoch offered a potential defence of the Royal Opera House: 'First, any attack on opera would be the first step in an attack on all the arts. And then the real reason opera matters is that it keeps the myths alive in the world.'[2] The myths were in dire danger in England in the Nineties, and Covent Garden found itself at the forefront of the battle to maintain them.

Isaacs had a clear idea of what he wanted to achieve. In his memoirs he mentions a telegram he received from the French opera producer

Jean-Louis Martinoty, welcoming him as '*un moderne*'. Isaacs later recalled that when Haitink had told the Board that nothing like the 1986 Ashman–Fielding *Flying Dutchman* 'should ever be seen again', Isaacs had felt differently, writing in his memoirs that 'creative activity has a licence to fail'. Isaacs admired Peter Jonas for having created 'an enviable creative energy' at English National Opera even though many of the productions of his era had not withstood a second airing and the company had had a 'substantial deficit when he left'.[3] He wanted to use producers, preferably British, who were 'making waves' in the profession, including Hytner, Vick, Tim Albery, David Freeman, Pountney, Richard Jones, Ian Judge and Steven Pimlott. Isaacs also intended to employ a dramaturg, Patrick Carnegy, editor of Faber music, who, together with himself and Findlay, would have 'critical discussions about the approach to new productions'.*

Isaacs was also determined to improve the standard of revivals and in general liven up the House. Even before Tooley left, in November 1987, Isaacs wrote papers for the Board setting out 'policy and future plans for the ROH'. During discussions in the opera Board on 17 November 1987, while acknowledging Tooley's achievements, he argued that there should be fewer productions performed each year, better rehearsed and in longer runs. The object was, he wrote, that 'every customer for opera arrives to find the House humming with excitement and leaves rapt in delight'. This could not be achieved, he wrote, by having to 'churn out too many performances on inadequate resources to meet box office targets'. Nor could it be by churning out 'reliable old war horses' and ancient revivals that were 'musty and uninspiring'. There needed to be, he argued, 'a portfolio of new productions'. In design he preferred 'light and illusion' to 'massive building work and supposed reality ... more of a contemporary feel'.[4] 'What I offered', Isaacs later wrote, 'was a mix of innovation and the secure popularity of the golden oldies.'[5]

To achieve his ends and consolidate his authority, Isaacs wanted to bring in his own team. He tried to get Brian McMaster of Welsh National Opera and Nicholas Payne of Opera North, who had previously worked with McMaster at Welsh National Opera. He was not

---

* Carnegy left Covent Garden in September 1992 and was not replaced.

so keen to keep on Paul Findlay, who was left over from the Tooley regime. Haitink, however, stood up for Findlay, who later recalled that the music director was 'desperate for someone with whom he could work' and in the end 'made it clear he wanted someone with experience, in the House'.[6] Tooley advised Isaacs that he had to keep Findlay or lose both him and Haitink, who threatened to resign.[7] Isaacs kept Findlay.

Findlay was to have more responsibility than he had anticipated, soon discovering that Haitink was not a music director in the Solti or Davis mould. Findlay recalled that he soon came to realise that 'Bernard's time-span in a meeting was forty minutes, and that I didn't have a colleague. I was suddenly on my own.' He went on to explain, 'It became very clear that Bernard didn't have the time because he was a musician through and through. Haitink would say, "I can't just open a score, like Gergiev and Zubin, and conduct. I have to work and prepare."' Haitink was, however, always willing to give his forty minutes and was, in Findlay's words, 'a tremendous support' throughout his time as opera director.

Haitink's relationship with Isaacs was to prove more problematic, as Isaacs recalled, 'Bernard took a habitually gloomy view of every prospect . . . Eeyore, someone said, rather than Tigger', and he continued:

> Bernard used to complain to anyone who would listen that he did not see enough of me and, sometimes, that he did not like what he saw . . . The press wrote that we did not get on. I never allowed myself to feel that, and always relished the four flights of stairs up to the Music Director's room.[8]

A member of the company described Haitink as a 'much respected, mild and patient man . . . more likely to accept that he was not going to get what he wanted and be terribly sad . . . that's why he's rather morose'.[9] Tooley later said that Haitink needed time for reflection and explanation, and that without due consideration he tended to become introspective, gradually withdrawing from his role as music director.[10] Peter Conrad in the *Observer* wrote, 'Haitink, as prone to depression as the North Sea, broods about the human value of his work. "I have sad thoughts of people marching to the gas chambers: their last thoughts were not of music. But Goethe said something which consoles me – although we doubt ourselves, so long as we give happiness to others, our lives are worthwhile." '[11]

Isaacs recognised the stature Haitink would give the House. He was, according to Isaacs, 'the cornerstone on which our hopes are built ... he demonstrates by his musicianship and dedication an ambition to excellence'. The more performances he conducted, Isaacs concluded, 'the better our performances will be'.*[12]

The two leaders of the organisation, Haitink and Isaacs, did not provide Solti's highly experienced and domineering style of opera house direction, but Isaacs was good at delegating, and the combined talents of those involved were to insure a fine period artistically. Findlay recalled, 'Jeremy would be the first to say he was not an arts administrator,' but, he reflected, 'Jeremy would argue, "I had an opera and ballet director who would do that for me."'

The instructions Isaacs gave Findlay were succinct: 'Bring in the public and make the place exciting.' Revival standards must improve, Isaacs told Findlay, Faggioni and Pavarotti must be brought back, and the repertory made more interesting. However, he told Findlay, 'We've got to have things better prepared. We're not going to have any of that under-rehearsed stuff.'†[13] In order to achieve the objective, Findlay put a greater emphasis on freshening up the repertoire than on adding rehearsals, believing that Covent Garden 'achieved more in terms of rehearsals and preparation than most international Houses'. Tooley

---

* According to Isaacs, 'Bernard remained modest in his demeanour and moderate in his demands.' With his commitments to the Boston Symphony and Berlin Philharmonic, Haitink gave about a third of his time to Covent Garden, conducting three or four productions a season – and up to thirty performances (Isaacs, op. cit., pp. 57, 159). He would conduct two new productions a year and one revival. In order to attract musicians to the orchestra there had to be 'adequate financial rewards'. Haitink also asked for the removal of the carpet to improve the acoustics, an increase in the size of the pit and more strings, as well as opportunities for the orchestra to give concerts which would help them develop their tone. Haitink offered to waive his fee for conducting concerts at the House (Royal Opera House Archives, Opera Board, 19/4/3, 17.5.88). Increasing the size of the pit was deemed too costly as losing eighteen stalls seats meant the loss of £150,000 a year. Haitink was pleased by the removal of the carpets, which had revealed fine American hardwood flooring, perhaps laid at the time of the 1941 dance hall (ibid., 13.9.88).
† Findlay explained that Isaacs had observed Welsh National Opera's exceptional rehearsal conditions which, with its short seasons and few productions, were quite unlike those of an international House.

was later infuriated by the suggestion that work had been under-rehearsed during his later years, and pointed to eight new productions in his 1983–84 year.[14] Nevertheless, as Forman put it, although the peaks (*Turandot* and *Otello*) were high, the low threshold was too low and the middle ground was filled with 'moderately successful new productions' and 'boring revivals'. Failure, he argued was 'accepted too readily'.[15]

To improve revivals Findlay asked John Cox, who had worked with Haitink at Glyndebourne, to become director of productions. Isaacs's paper of January 1988 had suggested that Cox could be responsible for starting from scratch with productions that had gone wrong, like Noelte's *Manon*, that he should keep a close interest in other revivals, and prepare a limited number of new productions himself.*[16]

Cox and Findlay met each week to talk over plans. Findlay and Peter Katona,† responsible for casting, met most days. They prepared a brief for Isaacs, whom Findlay met weekly, to endorse. Their recommendations went to the opera Board for discussion prior to referral to the main Board, upon which Isaacs insisted he should remain – a dual position that no former director had held. Isaacs had for the time being to accept Findlay and Cox, describing them as a 'strong team, if more than a shade conservative'.[17]

Isaacs was a powerful force for change, telling the Board on 9 February that financial limitations 'had to be overcome'.[18] In order to expand rather than retrench, and with the subsidy fast declining in real terms, sponsorship was to assume an even more crucial role in the House's financing. 'The moment John had gone,' Findlay recalled, 'Isaacs was given his head. Alex Alexander came in with three million of sponsorship' and 'the flood gates' were opened. Alexander raised sponsorship for new productions from the chairmen of corporations, never giving up, in Isaacs's words, 'till he had extracted a promise or pocketed a cheque'.‡[19] He succeeded in raising private subvention

---

* John Cox's early work had been with Ebert at Glyndebourne, where he had had many successful productions in the 1970s and 1980s.

† Appointed artistic administrator in November 1982 to work full time from September 1983.

‡ Isaacs recalled one prized cheque which was not brought to the boardroom but was banked forthwith. It was £500,000 from Polly Peck chairman Asil Nadir, who 'hopped off to Cyprus' shortly afterwards (Isaacs, *Never Mind the Moon*, p. 102).

from £3.4 million in 1986–87 to £5.9 million in 1989–90, through sponsorship, membership or donations. When the schools matinées were threatened in early 1990, Alexander came up with sponsorship worth £750,000 over three years.[20]

Membership of the Opera House Trust gave corporations and wealthy individuals the opportunity to buy booking privileges for sums ranging from £2,500 to £10,000. The guaranteed purchase of premium seats brought in a further £1 million. By June 1990 £1 million was already earning interest in the bank and £5 million had been committed for the current year.[21] Premium and Trust members took up 15 per cent of the seats and nearly half of the most expensive seats. In October 1988 Margaret Thatcher hosted a dinner at 10 Downing Street to launch the First Night Club, membership of which entitled individuals to certain privileges for £10,000 a year. It was expected to bring in an extra £325,000 a year. As Isaacs succinctly put it, 'The Prime Minister was showing her support for "centres of excellence" by encouraging private citizens to pay for them.'[22]

The Friends continued to have priority booking and their resources were used for new works like Luciano Berio's *Un Re in ascolto* and Birtwistle's *Gawain*. The Drogheda Circle was introduced for those who could give about £1,000 over three years, which was a higher donation than that of the regular Friends.* In March 1990 a gala performance of *L'Elisir d'amore* with Pavarotti, sponsored by Mountleigh plc, was a glittering evening which raised £500,000.† 'Such a gala', Isaacs wrote, 'furnished a key portion of our income.'[23] It did little, however, to reduce perceptions of snobbery.

Encouraged by Isaacs, Findlay immediately set about his task, recalling, 'After two terms we got it back artistically . . . We did forty-seven productions new to Covent Garden in five years.' These included operas brought by visiting companies whose work Findlay believed would help to vary the repertoire. More than half the productions

---

* Premium seats in the stalls were sold at 120 per cent of their face value and corporate members could buy top-price seats for an annual subscription or a £2,500 donation to the Trust. These schemes were handled by the Trust, the subscription schemes by the Friends and the mailing list.

† As Isaacs had wished, Pavarotti also sang Cavaradossi in 1992–93 and Renato in *Un Ballo in maschera* in April 1995 during which he was in far from his best form.

were borrowed or rented at a fraction of the cost. He wanted to put on shows that 'the public had never seen at Covent Garden' – just as Bliss and Joe Volpe, general manager of the Met, believed, 'you don't balance your books by retrenching'. It took two years to reach a consistently high standard of new production and borrowed productions often proved to be disappointing. The box office, however, responded in spite of vastly increased seat prices.

Technical improvements were needed if productivity was to be increased. At the beginning of 1989 Findlay installed a night gang. It was impossible in the antiquated building to get the stage ready for rehearsals in the morning unless the crew who had worked the previous day were requested to work through the night as well. The night gang, Isaacs told the opera Board on 10 January, would allow eleven extra performances a year.[24] 'The unions have been criticised,' Findlay later recalled but explained that it was 'not socially fair to ask men who have done a fifteen-hour day for two days to then stay all night – two shifts'.

During Isaacs's first season there were five new productions: *Rheingold* in September, *Butterfly* in October, *Rigoletto* in December, *Un Re in ascolto* in February 1989 and *Così* in March. Lyubimov's *Rheingold* had been commissioned by Tooley with a very simple set designed by Paul Hernon and Claire Mitchell, and had been intended to be suitable for the closure period. Lyubimov was trying to find a theatrical means to realise the *Ring* using light and shade, but at its premiere on 29 September 1988 Milnes felt that the set looked as though it had been 'dictated by financial stringencies'. The opera, he wrote, was reduced to 'a Victorian magic lantern show' with little character, motivation or meaning. Michael Kennedy was less harsh in the Saturday *Telegraph*, praising Lyubimov's 'lucid, narrative approach' and Robert Bryan's 'inspired lighting effects' on the back-projected screen over the tilted central disc. But as was to become a feature of the 1990s, it was the high musical standards that were most appreciated. Haitink's real love, Milnes pointed out, was the German repertoire and Wagner in particular, and the music director's 'pacing, structure, balance (every word audible) were faultless'.[25]

Lyubimov was not long for Covent Garden. Although his intention was to produce 'visual symbols of what he accepted as marvellous music', when it came to the rehearsals it became clear that he was unfamiliar with the work. Findlay reported to the Board on 11 October that Lyubimov had been 'feeling his way', which had led to great strain with members of the cast. There were major disagreements between Lyubimov and Haitink, who soon 'expressed a preference for another route forward'.[26] The 'final straw', Findlay recalled, 'was at the end of *Rheingold* at the pre-dress rehearsal when Loge appeared from the prompt box and chucked the *Walküre, Siegfried* and *Götterdämmerung* scores into the pit. That Bernard never got over! That was it!'* When in February 1989 it was announced that Lyubimov had been released from his contract, Findlay hoped to revive Tooley's idea of a Moshinsky *Ring*, but 'Bernard would not come round'.

In order to save money while freshening up the repertoire, many productions were to be borrowed – a method of working that was often to prove less successful than tailor-made work. One that did work well was Scottish Opera's *Madama Butterfly*, updated to Ezio Frigerio's three-storey Nagasaki tenement, in October 1988. Directed by the talented Spanish theatre director Nuria Espert, its impact was heightened by Catherine Malfitano's dramatic talents. It was as a result of this production that Espert was engaged to direct what turned out to be a disappointing *Rigoletto* in November 1988. Frigerio's setting for *Rigoletto* was monumental, dark and enclosed, the faces of the

---

* David Syrus recalled Lyubimov during rehearsals for *Rheingold* 'sitting with his Russian translation, he hadn't even got as far as the vocal score'. He also recalled a stormy meeting the day after *Rheingold* to discuss *Walküre* when he lost his temper with Lyubimov. He told Lyubimov, who was planning to start rehearsals by working on the roles with students: ' "The only reason artists like Gwyneth [Jones] who, at this stage has done endless *Ring* cycles, wants to come and sign on for a new *Ring* cycle, is because she wants the excitement, which any artist wants, of a new director and rediscovering it with you. The notion that she should come and be told that two weeks ago a totally inexperienced student from the Royal Academy moved left here, so would you please move left here is insulting. It is absolutely no way to deal with people." I was furious, I was absolutely steaming at this meeting.' Isaacs asked Syrus to move down the far end of the table away from Lyubimov. Syrus continued: The next day Bernard asked "how did the meeting go" and Jeremy said, "David Syrus has got some good ideas but he's a bit abrasive, isn't he?" Coming from Jeremy, of all people, this was a real compliment!' (Syrus, Interview, 6.12.00). Tooley later pointed out that directors like Lyubimov need constant dialogue and control such as he, Tooley, had in fact maintained during the *Jenůfa* rehearsals (Tooley, Interview, 11.4.02).

singers obscured by poor lighting and a front gauze. Isaacs later said, 'You could have played a history of the Roman empire in it.'[27] Findlay felt Espert would have been more successful 'if she had had better designers but she wanted architectural designers'. Espert updated *Rigoletto* to the nineteenth century. Unlike *Butterfly*, whose pre-World War Two setting was apt and stimulating, *Rigoletto*'s updating merely created problems. According to Robert Henderson the 'spangled Jester's ruff, and buffoon's traditional staff of office' looked quite out of place in an obviously bourgeois society. The characters remained emotionally disengaged and June Anderson was 'very much the knowing girl of the 1980s'.[28]

An exciting new production was Berio's *Un Re in ascolto*, which had its premiere on 9 February 1989, conducted by Berio himself, and directed by Graham Vick, in a production that was later rented by Chicago. Donald McIntyre was Prospero, Kathryn Harries Protagonista the singer, and Robert Tear the Director. Andrew Clements in the *Financial Times* called it one of the Royal Opera's 'most significant achievements of recent years'.[29] Peter Hall sent Isaacs a postcard saying he did not know that Covent Garden could put on such a show.*[30] Berio himself had been 'astonished' by Vick's production, Isaacs told the opera Board.[31]

As intended, revivals during the 1988–89 season were of a consistently high standard. Cox breathed new life and vibrancy into the restaging of Massenet's *Manon* with Leontina Vaduva, a Romanian soprano who conveyed Manon's high spirits and eroticism with looks, voice and acting ability. Soon after, Milnes found himself in an 'operatic paradise' during a revival of Copley's *Semele* in December 1988, when Ruth Ann Swenson provided a 'feast of brilliant singing'.

---

* Director Graham Vick began his substantial operatic career, which was to include the production directorship of Glyndebourne, as a staff producer at Scottish Opera where he later became director of productions. Born in 1953 in Merseyside, he trained at the Royal Northern College of Music but left before completing his course. Vick was a man of complex attitudes and a varied CV from his provocative *Don Giovanni* at Scottish Opera to the virtually classical *Figaro's Wedding* at ENO in 1992. Vick supported Opera Go Round, a small-scale, piano-accompanied group that toured remote parts of Scotland. He was artistic director of City of Birmingham Touring Opera, which introduced *Ring Saga*, Jonathan Dove's adaptation of the *Ring* in two nights, which has delighted audiences around Birmingham. Vick was also involved, in an unpaid capacity, in Adam Pollock's Do-It-Yourself Music Festival at Batignano in southern Tuscany.

According to Milnes, Swenson 'surpassed wildest expectations . . . her tone in the flesh is sweeter than on record, her technique fail safe, with dazzling pointillist staccatos and triplet runs delivered with an accuracy and both a musical and dramatic point . . . sensuality and pathos too – pure perfection'. One of Cox's greatest contributions was a fine last revival of Visconti's thirty-year-old *Don Carlos* on 26 March 1989. So successful was the revival policy that Milnes commented, 'It is on the quality of revivals that the health of an opera company depends.' In that respect, he concluded, 'it had been an auspicious season'.[32] The box office was also responding and, as finance director Philip Jones told the opera Board on 10 January 1989, the encouraging audience trends revealed for *Semele, Manon* and *Butterfly* might succeed in recouping the 1988 deficit.[33]

Plans for the House's redevelopment had continued to meet with strenuous opposition from the local Covent Garden Community Association at every planning application. Westminster Council, sensitive to electoral issues, took the opposition seriously and Isaacs was slow to focus on the need to 'appease' the opponents by setting up a Community Liaison Group. In June 1987 Westminster City Council had granted the Royal Opera House full planning permission but the Covent Garden Community Association applied to the High Court for a judicial review of Westminster's decision, 'citing guidelines against offices in the area as their principal ground'.

In February 1988 the High Court vindicated Westminster but the Royal Opera House decided nevertheless to go 'back to the drawing board'. The new technical director, John Harrison, who joined the company in 1988, insisted that the company needed more space for storage and for service facilities, and that the most modern scenery-moving equipment be installed. Isaacs wote that he was 'easily persuaded'. Westminster stopped insisting on a deep basement car park, which freed space for the House's workshops. The changes in plans were the cause for adverse press comment, with fifteen years of planning and 'little to show for it'.[34] The Treasury favoured a step-by-step approach – with the office buildings finished first to pay for the development. It was just such a system, Isaacs pointed out, that had caused the British Library's 'vast overspend'. Vivien Duffield, Board director and deputy chairman of the Royal Opera House Trust who, together with Sainsbury, was to be in charge of fund-raising for the development, immediately said she could not raise funds over such a protracted period. Both Duffield and Sainsbury later involved themselves closely in matters of design and policy.

The urgent need for modernisation was highlighted by the tragic death of a stagehand, Greg Bellamy, during a rehearsal of *Clemenza di Tito* on 31 March 1989. Bellamy, a popular member of staff who had been working at the House for ten years, was killed when an A frame trolley, loaded with flats, fell and crushed him. Colin Davis conducted the Verdi *Requiem* in Bellamy's memory and to benefit his wife and two young children. Isaacs paid a condolence visit to the family but later reflected, 'This terrible accident exacerbated tensions between stage and management.' Technical director Harrison tightened up safety procedures. Nevertheless, Isaacs realised that the House 'desperately needed stage mechanisms that would end the need for manual labour twice a day, every day. . . . Greg Bellamy's death called attention, as nothing else could, to the urgent need for the redeveloped opera house.'[35]

In spite of the success of the revivals, towards the end of Isaacs's first season he was telling Findlay, 'You can't spend that sort of money. We've got to cut back.' He continued, as Findlay recalled: 'I have never done a job where I didn't have the money to do my job. I've never done a job where I couldn't push a button and stop something I did not like.' Findlay concluded, 'The reality of being intendant had sunk in.'[36]

On 10 January 1989 Isaacs again recommended another increase in seat prices. Findlay recalled, 'Jeremy was always the first to cure problems by more sponsorship and more box office – that's how he balanced his budgets.' The House's average price was now the highest in the world and the top prices were second only to Vienna. Some members of the Board were concerned that the House would be seen as a 'place for corporate entertainment rather than for opera lovers'. They also were afraid that estimates of fund-raising up to £9.6 million were based on 'heroic assumptions'. Alexander said that even the following year's target of £7.6 million was 'daunting', especially in the light of a less favourable economic climate. Philip Jones told the Board on 7 February that although they had caught up on the previous year's deficit, it meant that for the first time in the company's history the box office would take more than was being received in subsidy. Isaacs's conclusion was that 'the House has been underpriced for a decade'.[*37] It was, however, the increase in seat prices that did the most harm to Covent Garden's image during the Nineties. The combination of what were perceived as snobbish social events and corporate entertainment, together with the very high seat prices and the lack of availability of tickets, gradually destroyed Covent Garden's public image.

The challenge to Covent Garden's management was far greater than that of the Met. Findlay recalled that during 1989 he asked Jonathan Friend at the Met how he worked out how much he could spend on singers. Friend told him, 'We don't have all these complicated models . . . we know that the best casting brings in the best box office.' That, Friend added, 'is the objective of the Met'. With the financial cushion of the subscription and endowment, Friend had none of Findlay's variables, which included the ballet company's demands on the orchestra.[38]

'The best casting' at Covent Garden was often with young singers yet to find stardom at the Met. One such was Anne Sofie von Otter who sang Sesto to Carol Vaness's Vitellia in *La Clemenza di Tito* in April 1989, with Colin Davis's conducting. This was the role in which she had made her debut at Covent Garden in December 1985, again under Davis's direction. 'Looking every inch the part,' Alan Blyth

* Finance director Philip Jones created financial models of planning whereby Findlay could see through 'a whole series of lines, the cost consequence of his plans'. According to well-established practice, there was a constant reassessment according to box office indications. If something was not doing well at the box office, Jones would ask Findlay how he could 'bring these results back on course'. Jones pointed out, 'If we budgeted for a small surplus of £50,000 in the year – we would get there not necessarily for the reasons we made in the plan but by the constant readjustments.' Isaacs later acknowledged Jones's contribution, writing that he provided management with 'prompt and accurate information on income and expenditure on request' (Isaacs, op. cit., p. 131).

wrote in 1989, 'von Otter vividly conveyed the youth's obsession with Vitellia and his terrible sense of guilt in betraying the merciful monarch.'[39] In von Otter's live recording of this role with John Eliot Gardiner in 1991 at the Queen Elizabeth Hall, her singing is both passionate and technically flawless, her Sesto glowing with sadness and regret.[40] She laid down supple, long-breathed phrases, her tone pure, focused and almost tangibly soft, with a rich alto register and a shining soprano-like top.* Her female tragic women, especially Alceste, grieve with a unique human warmth.

Findlay fulfilled Isaacs's second commandment, that of bringing in director Piero Faggioni after his successful *Fanciulla* and *Manon Lescaut*. Faggioni was duly contracted to do four productions as the main guest director. His *Trovatore* in June 1989, however, proved problematic. According to Findlay, Faggioni, in the mould of Visconti and Zeffirelli, had insisted on 'doing everything himself', lighting, design and production. The results were, in Isaacs's words, 'baleful, dark . . . half-designed and half-lit'.[41] Faggioni solved the eight different locations problem with a permanent set which was supposed to look like a volcano but which Nicholas Kenyon in the *Observer* on 11 June 1989 thought looked more like a giant 'papier-mâché chocolate whirl' and which dangerously restricted movement for the singers. Domingo managed to negotiate the set, however, and John Higgins in *The Times* marvelled at his 'richly burnished glow with no hint of strain'. Higgins added, 'Whenever Domingo steps on stage the temperature of the House rises.'[42]

Faggioni's contract stated that he would have complete control of the television production, but Channel 4 wanted their director to do it, so it was lost to television. Findlay recalled that the production alienated Faggioni from the company: 'Because he could never get things quite right and he always thought it was somebody else's fault.' Covent Garden finally parted company with Faggioni over the rehearsal

---

* The daughter of a Swedish diplomat, von Otter grew up in Bonn, London and Stockholm. She went to the Stockholm Academy of Music and thence to the Guildhall in 1981–82. Her London teacher was Vera Rosza. Von Otter spent two happy years at Basle after Guildhall, carefully building up a select repertoire including Alcina, Cherubino, Sesto, Hänsel, Clairon and Hermia. Von Otter's repertoire is surprisingly broad: in trouser roles such as Cherubino, and Romeo in Bellini's *I Capuleti e i Montecchi*, she can be impish or impetuous as the part demands.

schedule of *Don Quichotte* in August 1990, when Findlay was instructed to give him three uninterrupted weeks on stage and Faggioni insisted that Friedrich had been given more.* The substitution of ten *Turandots* for the seven *Don Quichottes* would contribute £444,000 to the budget.

Haitink had also not been at his happiest with *Trovatore*. Milnes could not understand why the music director would want to be involved in a 'mucky rough and tumble' like *Trovatore* and found his reading 'careful, deliberate and responsible', which is 'not what you need with middle-period Verdi. *Trovatore* was not part of the usual repertoire for Haitink, who was aware that he lacked 'a certain Italianate lightness of touch' for the bel canto works and Puccini.[43] *Butterfly* and *Bohème*, like *Otello*, had been spoilt for him by Kleiber. Haitink told the *Financial Times* on 1 June 1991 that he would like to get his teeth into *Don Carlos*, *Falstaff* and *Simon Boccanegra*, which were pieces he described as 'the dark Verdi', the first two of which he had indeed tackled before his time as music director was completed. When he later conducted *Don Carlos* and *Falstaff*, Haitink bridged the 'Italianate' gap, bringing intensity, human warmth and dramatic flexibility to the works as well as his emphatic self-immersion in the score.

Wagner, on the other hand, was very much the music director's domain. A new director had to be found for the *Ring* after Lyubimov's departure in November. Haitink wanted to work with Friedrich, for whom he had enormous respect,[44] and Findlay and Katona therefore decided that the easiest solution was to borrow Friedrich's 'Time Tunnel' production, designed by Peter Sykora for the Deutsche Oper, Berlin, and already seen in Tokyo and Washington, as a 'stopgap'. Management was later criticised for not using the old Friedrich production, which Findlay preferred, and for which he had found a technical solution to avoid dark nights and lost income during the Wagner cycle. Friedrich, however, had insisted that Covent Garden 'had to have his latest view'.

Isaacs pointed out that the production of *Walküre* in September 1989 had been visually stunning in its original Berlin setting where it 'not only took the eye away, past the singers towards infinity, but

---

* The *Sunday Telegraph* also quoted Mike Bolland, Channel 4's Controller of Arts, as saying, 'If you wrote Mr Faggioni into a sitcom, my feeling is you would be asked to tone him down.'

when closed off, brought the action to the front of the stage'. The touring version, however, 'confined the eye to a box', and the walls of the set with their graffiti and signs distracted from the singers.[45] Cairns agreed that the reduced tunnel had little of its Berlin impact and even felt that it was less 'audacious' than Friedrich's own platform production with Davis.[46]

Michael Kennedy in the *Sunday Telegraph* questioned Friedrich's 'Ride of the Valkyries', which he described as 'a lesbian gang-bang in a mortuary'.[47] The production's main merit was its practicality for singers 'to come and go with little rehearsal', which was ideal for the standard international cast that included James Morris, Gwyneth Jones, Helga Dernesch, and René Kollo.[48] Once again it was the musical qualities that received greater appreciation, Max Loppert describing Haitink's *Walküre* as 'lean in texture, rich in emotional impact'.[49]

Although Denis Forman and the opera Board fully supported Isaacs's drive to put on 'fresh, adventurous and dramatic productions', they were troubled by Johannes Schaaf's productions of *Così* in March 1989 and *Idomeneo* in November of that year. They were concerned that the House's adopted policy was not being well served by what was described as a 'certain strain of intense intellectual and sometimes brutal Germanic productions associated with the names of Friedrich, Schaaf and Kupfer'. Isaacs stood by his vision. 'The world and the stage', he argued, 'look different' and the work itself was no longer regarded as an 'immutable text, it is seen as a happening in theatrical performance'.[50] He did agree, however, that Schaff had marred his 'coherent' approach with 'silly' business, citing the drunk in *Così* and the teacup in *Idomeneo*.

Haitink loved working with Schaaf and was sad when the management decided not to employ him after his irredeemably dark *Don Giovanni* in 1992. 'I love Johannes,' Haitink said, 'but he is completely mad and an extremely difficult man to work with – he changes his mind so often.'[51] Furthermore, as Isaacs told the opera Board, he 'cruelly overworked his singers' and exhausted them.[52]

It was Haitink's musical leadership that was to be a firm fixture throughout the turbulent Nineties. In November 1989 the orchestra manager, Bram Gay, said the orchestra had 'warmed to his deeply musical approach' and that he 'handled the players as a whole brilliantly'.[53] His *Don Giovanni* was marked by accuracy, clarity and self-assured authority, his upbeats indicated with particular care, and accents, crescendi and diminuendi attended to with concern for the smallest nuance. Totally immersed in the music, eschewing any hint of exhibitionism, Haitink's beat was firm and strong, with minimal left-hand gestures used to cue, encourage and subdue.

In 1991 the orchestra hired its youngest leader and first concert master, Sofia-born Vasko Vassilev, a brilliant solo player as well as a fine team captain. David Syrus later said that Vassilev was an 'immensely mature and big human being' whose close relationship with Haitink was the cornerstone of the orchestra's achievements at this time. 'Bernard would talk to him about how sections of the orchestra were doing,' Syrus recalled, 'and Vasko would talk quietly to the people involved – he was a very clever and very supportive leader.'[54]

Findlay maintained Tooleys belief that 'the strength of the opera house depended on the conductor'. The policy of bringing in top conductors in no way created a conflict with Haitink, as had also been the case with Davis, and remained one of the strengths of the House. Isaacs wrote of Haitink, 'His lack of jealousy of others' talents, this opportunity he offered them to perform on his patch, made a singular contribution to the quality and ambition of our work.'[55]

Findlay's connections with Solti brought the octogenarian maestro back to the House for outstanding Strauss and Verdi performances in the Nineties. Solti had not performed much at Covent Garden during the Tooley–Davis era and was hurt by what he felt was an exclusion.* Findlay recalled, 'When I became opera director I went to see Solti. We had become very good friends. He said, "I'm not really welcome."' Findlay told Solti, 'Georg, you've got an open plate, please come, we want you back.' The two men discussed *Pelléas* and Solti told Findlay, 'I've got to have a *Traviata*.' Solti's first – and last – *Traviata* was to be one of the triumphs of the 1994–95 season.

In the 1989–90 Annual, Report Findlay wrote that Haitink's orchestra could 'now claim to be one of the finest opera house orchestras

---

* Tooley later ascribed Solti's absence to his own outburst to Tooley after the 1983 Bayreuth *Ring* – that he did not wish to conduct opera again. Solti in his memoirs referred to a 'four-year silence' after his 1979 *Parsifal*.

in the world'. When Solti came to conduct *Elektra* in March 1990 he announced that he was 'delighted with the orchestral playing'.[56] During the season Kleiber conducted Domingo's *Otello*, Christoph von Dohnányi *Meistersinger* and Simon Rattle *The Cunning Little Vixen*. Tate remained principal conductor, and Davis, Downes and Rizzi were also on the roster.

Simon Rattle's debut, planned by Tooley,[57] was similarly impressive, when he conducted *The Cunning Little Vixen* in June 1990 with, in Milnes's words, 'extraordinary tenderness and compassion'. Milnes described the show as a 'big, heart-warming success'.[58] Rattle, for whom Janáček's work is second only to Mozart as 'completely compelling music drama', was involved in every stage of the preparation including the translation, the choice of the team and all rehearsals. Bill Bryden, Rattle's choice of director, and William Dudley, the designer, contributed to a splendid visual-musical connection. 'Dudley', wrote Paul Griffiths, 'cleverly extrapolates from all the ostinato patterning of the score to create a stage abundant in rotating devices.'[59] Rattle made every detail of the score audible and his humanity and compassion for the 'hopeless human beings' shone through his reading, wrote Milnes.[60] During the season the other strikingly successful new production was a 'noble' Borodin *Prince Igor*, in February 1990.

The policy of reducing costs by borrowing productions was, however, proving less rewarding. Michael Hampe's 1988 Salzburg *Cenerentola* did not work for technical reasons in April 1990. Its set was too large and heavy for Covent Garden's stage which, Isaacs recalled, was 'discovered a little late'. The lighting designer did not turn up on the day he was supposed to, which entailed cancelling a ballet performance in order to fit in a rehearsal. Isaacs later wrote in his memoirs, 'I found it hard to forgive Paul Findlay for helping to put us in this fix.'[61] Findlay, whose successes, by contrast, were not always so readily recognised, remembered other problems with the set: 'We knew we had to do some work on it but we did not know how badly it had been made. This was a failure of the Royal Opera House's technical department to identify at the outset the viability of a borrowed production. We had to fit it to the Covent Garden stage and Hampe would not let me open it up so that it would have better sight lines.' Milnes found the production to have no more merit than a very pretty and charming fairy tale set in the nineteenth century rather than a recognisable social milieu. The one redeeming feature was Carlo Rizzi, making his House debut, whom Findlay had engaged after hearing him at the Buxton festival. Milnes found him to be a 'Rossinian to be reckoned with', with 'a sense of appreciative enjoyment in the phrasing, ideal rhythmic buoyancy, steely control of the crescendos'.[62]

The Board continued to be deeply concerned with the deteriorating financial situation, and Sainsbury was beginning to realise that his implicit deal with the government – that if the company increased its revenue the government would help – was not going to work. He was enraged when the Arts Council did not give the Royal Opera House an 'incentive award', when it had more than fulfilled the requirements of finding additional income. Having been led to believe that it would receive it, the House had budgeted accordingly. Sainsbury told the Board on 4 April 1989, 'The House had been thoroughly misled. Faith had been broken.'[63]

As a result of this Arts Council decision there was no way the House would be able to break even the following year, and on 9 March 1989 Sainsbury wrote to Arts Minister Richard Luce to say that there was a likelihood of a deficit of £2 million for 1990–91 and of £3 million for 1991–92. If the grant had kept pace with inflation since the Priestley report it would have been £2 million higher.[*64] In July, Sainsbury met Peter Palumbo, chairman of the Arts Council, and told him that 'even though we had raised box office and sponsorship', this was 'not enough to compensate for the very real reduction in the Arts Council grant over the past four years'.[†65]

In the autumn, with sponsorship in Jones's words, 'drying up', due to the downturn in the economy, Sainsbury had meetings with the Minister, Richard Luce, and Palumbo to explain the 'cause and

---

* A visit of the Komische Oper had been an artistic success but had lost £200,000 and there was a £730,000 shortfall in sponsorship (Royal Opera House Archives, Board, 18/2/6, 26.9.89).
† Palumbo, a property developer who contributed to Conservative Party funds, was described by Jeremy Isaacs as a 'polished, generous host, with a taste for fine wine'. Isaacs added that he had not 'chaired a public body in his life' (*Never Mind the Moon*, p. 108). He chaired the Arts Council from 1989 to 1994.

scale of the deficit'. Sainsbury even warned of insolvency.[66] Luce was sympathetic but non-committal. In November Palumbo agreed that it was 'sensible' to plan for a £2 million deficit and that he was trying to get the grant on to 'a sensible basis'.[67] In December Sainsbury wrote to the Minister specifically to confirm that the House was budgeting for a £2 million deficit. He also warned that if the unacceptable reduction in the grant continued, he could not see himself 'remaining as chairman of the Royal Opera House'. Palumbo agreed that the Board should work to the budget which included the deficit, while preparing to put their case to the government in the autumn.

When the Board met on 10 January 1990 Isaacs described how he was endeavouring to reduce the expected £2 million deficit for the following year by yet again increasing seat prices and also by curtailing the programme. Opera Board discussions were once again concerned with the reduction of plans. It was the Faggioni *Don Quichotte* that finally went in August 1990, although it was to have celebrated Colin Davis's twenty-fifth anniversary with the House. Lost too was a production of *Iphigénie en Tauride*.[68]

Covent Garden was not alone in its financial dilemmas. Government funding policy was creating a conundrum that was to be repeated in many arts institutions during the Nineties. Subsidy was reduced, and the resulting declining standards, or failure to live within the reduced means, was used to call into question the survival of the particular institution as well as the whole concept of public subsidy. The threat was made abundantly clear when Kent Opera was finally and cruelly axed in January 1990. The company had faced a reduction of 15 per cent in its grant in four years and this had resulted in declining artistic standards along with declining audiences.

The decision about Kent had been made in an offhand way and with no reference to the advice of the Arts Council music panel. The ensuing uproar in the press forced the Arts Council to announce a review, which reported on 18 December 1989, by which time the initial protest had died down. The review supported the decision, although reasons for the axing were not given. Kent Opera's director Norman Platt was enraged that only two of the thirteen responsible members of the Arts Council committee had actually been to a performance. The cut was considered particularly cruel as it was made just after Ivan Fischer had become artistic director in June 1989 and he and his managing director, David Pickard, had submitted a thorough business plan to eliminate their deficit within three years.*

Norman Platt had, in Milnes's words, 'an uncanny ability, genius even, for spotting and enabling talent'.[69] Kent had played a pioneering role for many years – giving commissions to Peter Maxwell Davies and Michael Berkeley.† Its first music director was Roger Norrington who stayed for sixteen years. It was one of the first companies to produce Monteverdi, with its 1969 production of *Poppea*. Jonathan Miller felt he had done some of his best early work for Kent Opera. The careers of Nicholas Hytner, Richard Jones, Elijah Moshinsky and Adrian Noble also started in Kent. It was frugal in its housekeeping and was one of the first companies to have an education department. To its bitter end Kent Opera was innovative, putting on Scottish composer Judith Weir's *A Night at the Chinese Opera* at the Cheltenham Festival in July 1987.

Platt had modelled his Kent company on Lilian Baylis's theory that 'if you give people the best they will like it – not immediately perhaps but eventually'.[70] The growth and enthusiasm of his audience proved the value of the theory and the axing made a mockery of the Arts Council's declared aim of accessibility. Baylis's aspirations to educate or expand the audience had no more secure a place in the populist mentality of the Nineties than they had had in the Thatcherite economics of the Eighties. Platt warned that if the companies did not fight together they would be in more serious trouble later.

The serious trouble was imminent. Sainsbury had continued his series of meetings with the Arts Council and the Minister for the Arts, and on 30 January Sainsbury told the Board that he had met Richard Luce,

---

* David Pickard was appointed director general of Glyndebourne in 2001.
† Michael Berkeley became a member of the opera Board in June 1994 and of the main Board in March 1996. The son of composer Lennox Berkeley, he was artistic director of the Cheltenham Festival from 1995. His chamber opera, *Jane Eyre* was performed in the Linbury Theatre at the Royal Opera House in November 2000.

the Minister, and confirmed that the House faced a deficit of £2 million during this year and £3 million the year after. He urged the need for an immediate injection of £1 million and an increase of £2 million in the annual grant. The Board, Sainsbury told Luce, 'could not continue indefinitely trying to run a great international House with a subsidy less than half of that of any other international House in Europe'. Palumbo had given, in Sainsbury's words, 'his whole-hearted support for this approach' and said that he would increase the grant to the flagship companies and, in particular, the Royal Opera House.[71]

In spite of Luce's and Palumbo's involvement and informal agreement, there was an uproar when, on 29 April 1990, Isaacs talked about the built-in £1.9 million deficit, in announcing the 1990–91 season. He defended the House's policy of maintaining artistic standards by going into deficit, saying that he had to compete with the world's leading opera houses, declaring: 'Rather than make slashing cuts, we have decided to carry on regardless.' Hugh Canning in the *Sunday Times* said Isaacs was 'throwing down the gauntlet to the Arts Council' and described his handling of the press as 'bullish' and 'brinkmanship'. He added that the cancellation of the press's extra free ticket added to an atmosphere 'already heavy with ill feeling'.*[72] After the press conference Isaacs told two journalists, when questioned, that if he were forced to cut back the next season's plans the company would face 'Armageddon'. He later explained that he had not envisaged a 'bloody battle' but rather that the programme would have to be 'savagely cut'.[73] His remark, however, made headlines, enraged Palumbo and the Arts Council, and added to the public relations damage.†[74]

Although both the Minister and the Arts Council had been fully aware of the decision to budget for a deficit, both immediately feigned

---

* There had been pressure on the administration to reduce the number of complimentary tickets for some time. In July 1988 *Salome* did 92 per cent capacity but only 85 per cent budget due to complimentary tickets (Royal Opera House Archives, Opera Board, 19/4/3, 14.7.88). Isaacs reported that complimentary tickets were costing £700,000 a year (ibid., 10.4.90). He had already warned the critics and had explained that the policy would be flexible so that if the House was not full they might still get the extra ticket (ibid., 19/4/5, 13.3.90).

† As a result of this incident Isaacs dismissed Ewen Balfour, the head of public affairs, causing yet more bad publicity, as Balfour's dismissal resulted in a much publicised 500-name petition, which included Haitink, Tate, Moshinsky and Findlay ,unsuccessfully calling for his reinstatement.

horror. The Arts Council wrote to Sainsbury to express its anger and leaked its letter to the press. The Minister for the Arts, Richard Luce made a statement saying that Isaacs's plans were 'unacceptable and totally irresponsible'. Sainsbury defended Isaacs in *The Times* and wrote to Palumbo to say that it was a 'disgrace' that the letter had been leaked, and that he and the Board were 'as one' with their general director. He reminded Palumbo that he would not have proceeded without both his and the Minister's agreement. The Arts Council, Isaacs later explained to the Board, were embarrassed at having had to admit that they had acquiesced in the deficit plan.[75]

Palumbo later withdrew his suggestion that Isaacs's statement had come as a surprise and Luce apologised for the leak, but the damage was done. As Sainsbury said, 'All in all the House had been badly treated and the surrounding publicity had been most unfortunate.' The Arts Council announced another team of assessors and told the House that it had to be in the black in three years' time. Nonetheless, Sainsbury told Palumbo in July that he was still hoping to obtain more funding for Covent Garden the next year and that neither he nor Richard Luce felt that the House 'had to take drastic steps to eliminate the deficit'.*[76]

Sainsbury saw a sinister development in the deficit incident, telling the Board that he had 'doubts about the survival of the arm's-length policy'. There was, he said, evidence of the Arts Council taking a more active role in the management of all four major companies.[77] The Arts Council's effectiveness as a buffer between clients and government was indeed being weakened at the same time as were its clients. Luke Rittner, the secretary general of the Arts Council, resigned in May 1990 because he believed that the arm's-length principle had been severely undermined by the choice of a political appointee, property developer Peter Palumbo, as chairman.

The events surrounding the deficit statement controversy had also undermined the working relationship of Sainsbury and Isaacs. Findlay recalled, 'Sainsbury had had a good relationship with Isaacs till he

---

* The House decided to commission a report from Peat Marwick to help them make their case to the government for extra funding. There had been, Isaacs said, 'too many reports and too little action'. Peat Marwick, he believed, would point to 'drastic underfunding' (Royal Opera House Archives, Board, 18/1/1, 5.6.90).

blew his top and compromised Sainsbury with his conversations with the Prime Minister ... suddenly Jeremy had gone public. It's why the media loved Jeremy because he came up with those statements, unpredictable, a showman. He believed totally in adequate funding for Covent Garden – that's why he has no remorse now.'[78] Isaacs did, however, at the 5 June Board meeting, express regret at having 'expressed a determination to implement the plans in all circumstances'. He rather should have said, he told the Board, that he did not know what the House would do if there was no increase in the grant.[79] Isaacs later confessed that he was not 'a dab hand at PR ... I don't enjoy buttering people up.' He had found not having adequate funds 'so taxing and demanding'.[80]

Discussions as to how the closure was to be handled were particularly sensitive in the light of the need to reduce the deficit. Estimates of the redevelopment costs had continued to be overwhelming. In January 1990 Westminster City Council had approved the revised planning application, but the construction costs of the theatre were now estimated at £130 million and the commercial sections at £35 million. Isaacs continued to press for the company's operations and educational considerations to be given precedence over the commercial buildings but with no funding from the recently abolished London County Council or the Treasury forthcoming, there seemed to be no alternative than to incorporate offices into the plan.

The question of what the company should do during the closure also needed to be resolved. On 30 January Isaacs had advised that the ballet company and the orchestra be maintained and the chorus reduced. There had been talk of separating the opera and ballet after the closure, as the Paris Opera had decided, but it was agreed that, in spite of tension and rivalries, neither company 'could sustain a nightly programme of its own'. For the closure, the opera company was considering short seasons in different venues, including *Ring* cycles at the Albert Hall. When Friedrich saw the Albert Hall he pronounced, 'The organ is Valhalla.'[81]

At the 5 June Board, Sainsbury expressed his scepticism at Isaacs's hopes that *Miss Saigon* was going to close in time for the House to take up Drury Lane, which was by far the preferred venue. He suggested the idea of a temporary home. Isaacs said that the Lyceum might be available – its owner wanting a partner with whom to develop the theatre. On 10 July 1990 Sir Martin Jacomb, chairman of the development Board, together with Isaacs, successfully urged the Board to delay closure to Easter 1994.[82]

During Isaacs's early years, public and critics responded enthusiastically to the opportunity to see unfamiliar works, although not all the productions were of a uniformly high standard. John Cox, who was so good at keeping up the standards of revivals, did less well with an unimaginative and dull Rossini *Guillaume Tell*. Findlay was confident that things were moving in the right direction, later recalling, 'At the beginning we didn't quite get it right, misfired a little but the ideas were right and successes came.' Loppert recognised the ingenuity of the planning and praised the company for tackling works with 'specific performance styles' like *Idomeneo*, *Prince Igor* and *Guillaume Tell*.[83]

One of the next season's most striking successes was a production of a rarely seen early Verdi work, *Attila*. One of Findlay's shrewdest moves was to continue Elijah Moshinsky's Verdi productions, so happily inaugurated with the 1987 *Otello*, and to link them to Edward Downes. Downes conducted the new *Attila* in October 1990. Loppert praised Moshinsky's contribution and his natural feeling for early Verdi, writing, 'His production is neither radical nor conservative. It seems simply right.' Moshinsky, he argued, did not 'patronise, in modish deconstructionist clichés', instead he sought and found the 'muscle and sinew of both music and words, and his handling of the chorus was faultless'.[84] Even Tom Sutcliffe, who preferred modernist productions, was impressed, writing that the 'sub-Balkan costumes suggest barbarians without seeming like Hollywood parody'.[85]

Peter Heyworth gave Downes credit for resurrecting the work with his 'unerring grasp of tempo'.[86] Milnes wrote that Downes enabled the four principals to sing at their best: Ruggero Raimondi, with great accuracy and 'elemental power', Giorgio Zancanaro with uncommon warmth and firmness, Josephine Barstow with total security and meaning, and Dennis O'Neill whose 'deployment of mezza voce' put Milnes in mind of Bergonzi. Loppert called the production 'an absolute winner' that had been greeted with cheering and stamping, and had 'put heart' into the foot soldiers of the beleaguered House.[*87]

While Downes was giving new life to early Verdi, the music director continued to give stature to the controversial *Ring* cycle. In December 1990 Alan Blyth praised Haitink's reading of *Siegfried*: 'I can't recall hearing in the theatre in recent times a reading that so ably and thrillingly fulfilled every aspect of the score . . . Above all he seems to have uncovered the secret of maintaining an overview of each act through a seamless line and ideally related tempos while at the same time catching what Goodall called the *Klang* of each section.' In Act Three the 'sense of erotic passion breaking out all over, sublime and dangerous, was conveyed by Haitink's ecstatic conducting'. The production, however, he found 'mean and drab'.[88] Edward Greenfield agreed, contrasting Erda emerging from under a grey bedspread with Friedrich's previous stage picture of a flying platform with the Wanderer peering over 'the edge of a chasm'.[89] Canning described the London *Siegfried* as a 'pale replica' of the Berlin production and wrote that *Siegfried* seemed to be a 'parable for Jeremy Isaacs's woes as operatic King of the Gods' in desperate need of a Siegfried to 'kill the dragons of government underfunding'.[90]

Efforts to complete the *Ring* cycle had indeed become embroiled in the hopes of Isaacs and Sainsbury to force the government's hand. On 27 November it was decided Sainsbury would tell Palumbo that the House could not continue indefinitely to make the contribution it was then making to the artistic life of the country and London with 'half the subsidy per performance of any comparable European House'. *Barbiere* had been so underprepared it was a 'disgrace'. If the rest of the *Ring* had to be cut, in order to make savings of £30,000, it would be a 'bitter blow to Haitink'. In January 1991 Haitink had gone so far

---

[*] The production had also improved on budget by £139,000 (Royal Opera House Archives, OB, 19/4/5,11.12.90). *The Times Saturday Review* published an in-depth study of Covent Garden's financial plight based on the costs of *Attila* on 24 November 1990. In the article it was pointed out that the sets and costumes came in at a reasonable £205,000 but that the work required chorus, actors as well as unpaid but fed and taxied children – in all a cast of 428. The complete cost of putting on the opera was £1,272,000. The question the Treasury and Arts Council therefore should have been asking themselves was whether grand opera is just 'too grand' for English cultural life.

as to say that if the *Ring* were to be cancelled he would not remain as music director.[91] In a message to the government and Arts Council, the Board noted that 'scaling down the scale of activity to a point where *Ring* cycles could not be accommodated would not be compatible with maintaining an international opera company'.[92]

Findlay, however, unaware that the loss of *Götterdämmerung* was intended to be a symbol of government neglect and intransigence, managed to work out an ingenious solution whereby it could be saved. He got Friedrich's agreement to do fewer stage rehearsals, while not reducing the orchestral rehearsals, 'so we didn't compromise Bernard's preparation', and managed to squeeze in thirteen performances of *Rigoletto* between performances of the *Ring*. Findlay recalled that Isaacs's reaction to his solution was, 'You bloody fool . . . you don't realise what you've done. You have just destroyed the chairman's opportunity to go to Thatcher and say, "This House can't get on with the money it's got."' Findlay asked Isaacs, 'Are you telling me that that was the game plan and you didn't have the nerve to tell the opera director? That the real objective was to lose the *Ring*?'[93] It had indeed been his intention. Cancellation, Isaacs later told the Board, 'would have demonstrated our need to government and public'.[94] When the *Ring* was staged in the autumn of 1991 the extra *Rigolettos* brought in a net gain of £350,000 and the opera Board complimented the management for the 'great skill' in putting on a non-*Ring* production at the same time as the *Ring* – something that had never been done before.[95]

Neither Thatcher nor Sainsbury was soon to be a player. On 30 November 1990 the Prime Minister was replaced by John Major, giving some hope to arts institutions. Major was known to be better disposed to a national lottery that would support cultural institutions than Thatcher had been.* On 31 December the new Prime Minister and his wife attended Sutherland's farewell *Fledermaus*. During the interval Isaacs encouraged Major in his deliberations concerning the introduction of a national lottery, and after the performance, appearing on stage, he offered a tribute to Joan Sutherland and welcomed the Prime

---

* Major's wife, Norma, was an opera enthusiast who had written a biography of Joan Sutherland, published by Queen Anne Press in London in 1987.

Minister. The BBC broadcast was seen all over the world by 3 million people.*

Covent Garden's hopes for a more sympathetic government response were not immediately realised. Sainsbury hoped that the new and outspoken Minister for the Arts, David Mellor, would press the case for Covent Garden more strongly, but he was to be sadly disappointed. When Isaacs met Mellor, he recalled, the Minister 'barked at me across his office as I entered that there would be no more money'. In September 1990, Mellor told Sainsbury and Isaacs that 'the circumstances of this year's expenditure round could hardly be less favourable' and strongly criticised the House for the pay increases awarded to staff.† In October Mellor warned Isaacs that the deficit incident had not 'furthered the House's cause'.[96]

In December the distribution of Mellor's £7.5 million enhancement fund 'for rewarding high standards and sound financial management' was announced. The fund was designed to earmark funds of £6 million a year for three years to enable the Arts Council to upgrade the subsidies of selected clients. It was for 'high quality of work' and not to help alleviate the accumulated deficits. Mellor did not put Covent Garden on the enhancement grant, but his successor Timothy Renton (1990–92) later reversed the decision and Covent Garden received £200,000.

The seemingly arbitrary decisions as to who was to receive the extra funding did nothing to lessen the growing crises among the companies. Although Welsh National Opera had been expecting £500,000 and faced a £325,000 shortfall in its 1991–92 budget, it was not to receive enhancement funding. Opera North, on the other hand, was to receive £685,000. Mellor had been reported as saying that Welsh National Opera should cease operating if the Arts Council could not give it increased funds. The company was reprieved at the last moment with an extra £300,000. This was a major about-turn by the Arts Council after a team of officers had rushed down to Cardiff and

---

* Also seen on television that year were *Vixen* and the ballet *Hobson's Choice*. An open-air *Bohème* was seen by 10,000 at Kenwood lakeside.
† Of the 22.4 per cent extra earnings, 18.7 per cent had been for staff, 3.7 per cent for producers, 4.2 per cent for the night gang and 1.7 per cent for overtime due to the number of new productions (Board, 18/3/1).

declared themselves 'extremely impressed' by what they saw 'based on a very thorough investigation'. This, they argued, is what influenced them and not the public outcry following their initial decision. The Welsh Office agreed to write off the remaining £842,000 debt. Brian McMaster, Welsh National Opera's managing director, was delighted that the company had been spared Kent Opera's fate, but he left the company in the autumn of 1991. In July 1992 Mackerras also retired and Carlo Rizzi's appointment as music director was announced.*[97]

The enhancement fund was too little and too late for Sainsbury, who told the Board in January 1991 that he had decided to relinquish his chairmanship a year before he was due to do so. 'With all the lobbying and financial problems,' he explained to the Board on 29 January, he felt he could not do justice both to Covent Garden and to Sainsburys. His retirement was announced on 8 April 1991. The government had not played their part in what he had believed to be an implicit understanding, and had instead allowed the grant to fall in real terms, while the House had successfully increased its income from sponsorship and box office. Isaacs was 'shattered' by Sainsbury's decision, especially as Denis Forman was also due to retire from the chairmanship of the opera board.[98]

Board member Angus Stirling took over from Sainsbury. He had been a Deputy Secretary General of the Arts Council from 1979 to 1983 and Director General of the National Trust since 1983 – a position he decided not to relinquish on becoming Covent Garden chairman, rather opting to appoint Sir James Spooner as deputy director.[99] Jeffrey Tate departed at this time and Alex Alexander also left in December 1991.

With Sainsbury's departure there was a slackening in the rigid financial controls. Jones contrasted Sainsbury's and Stirling's working methods: 'I was called into a Board meeting, where I was on parade for three hours and if I did not produce an answer I would be pinned against a wall, and going in to Stirling one was totally relaxed – it

---

* *Time Out* pointed out that the Royal Shakespeare Company was in debt to the tune of £3 million and the South Bank Centre after careful pruning by £350,000, with its accumulated shortfall reaching £9 million over the previous five years. It referred to a 'big funding mess' (9. 91). In 1990 the Royal Shakespeare Company had closed the Barbican theatre from the autumn to the spring of 1991.

was like going to a tea party.' Under Sainsbury there had been a 'well-organised drill – as soon as one Board meeting finished I would fax him the draft agenda for the next meeting and he'd come back to me within twenty-four hours either yea or nay and challenges ... It was the way he ran Sainsburys – it was all controlled through the Board and the agenda.' The growing dependence on sponsorship was also, as predicted, proving a destabilising element. Jones explained that costs and box office were forecast with accuracy close to 100 per cent but as private funding increased, the confidence in the forecasting went down by 3 or 5 per cent.[100]

Government indifference reflected a growing hostility to the arts in general and Covent Garden in particular in the early Nineties. There were ominous press attacks on the House and on Isaacs, whose contract was due to run out in 1993. Isaacs had felt compelled to challenge a particularly vicious article in the *Daily Mail* in March 1991.[101] The *Sunday Telegraph* on 14 April 1991 questioned the resignations and also some of Isaacs's appointments, asking what role Patrick Carnegy, whom Isaacs had appointed as dramaturg, was really playing. They also quoted critical comments about Isaacs from Board members, and accusations that the Board itself was a 'complacent, inward-looking, snobbish, self-perpetuating oligarchy'. The *Mail on Sunday* as usual was even more vehement in its attack, with the headline on 23 March 1991 WHY IS THE OPERA HOUSE SUCH A SHAMBLES? and asking why the Arts Council continued to pour money down the 'bottomless pit' of Covent Garden when productions had gone from 'admittedly bad to unimaginably worse'. Isaacs fought back, saying that he was not going to leave until he had made his 'full contribution'. Milnes defended the 'Glaswegian outsider' from what he called a 'nasty whispering campaign'.[102]

The press had, however, decided that the Royal Opera was a villain, and with its inclination to herd instinct its voice became increasingly uniform and hostile as the House's problems intensified.* *The Times*

---

* Maggie Sedwards, who had been English National Opera's head of public relations, had found a very supportive press during her years at ENO but she pointed out that press criticism tended to be cyclical and fuelled by cuttings that perpetrated factual

was already making the suggestion that the English National Opera and Royal Opera House should be amalgamated. There was also major criticism of the company in *Opera Now* in its March 1991 edition. The magazine cast doubt on the Arts Council's argument that the House deserved its 'enhancement fund' grant on the grounds that its work was 'of a particularly high quality'. It accused management of being a team with no leader, and attacked John Cox for employing Gianni Versace to design the costumes for *Capriccio* in January 1991, and for evading 'the moral duties of a director'. The more serious critics were also unimpressed by *Capriccio*. Milnes described the production as 'a gloomy evening', with Te Kanawa sporting a 'sort of puzzled "what am I doing?" look on her face' when she was not 'gazing fixedly at the prompt box'.[103]

Even more ominous than the criticisms of productions and the number of new productions was the reference in *Opera Now* to complaints that Covent Garden was not sufficiently sensitive to the needs of the corporate donors. Among the complaints was that of one sponsor, Frank Pearce of the Midland Bank, who said that there were too 'few rooms to entertain at Covent Garden'. The Minister for the Arts, Timothy Renton, picked up on the complaints, arguing that the House would have to make certain that there were 'much better entertainment facilities' for corporate clients and that they should be better looked after.[104] Without actually articulating it, the message was clear. Covent Garden should become what Tooley had described as 'a place for corporate entertainment rather than a theatre for opera and ballet lovers'.[105]

By dint of devoted and energetic effort, and despite some mishaps, the so-called 'leaderless' artistic team continued to compete successfully as a top international House. It was also at last getting on to an even keel financially as the box office picked up (94 per cent capacity) and with fewer new and fewer borrowed productions planned. There were to be more Italian works and to this end Edward Downes was to be put back on

---

errors and which it was virtually impossible for institutions to overcome. Like Covent Garden, the National Theatre, after its move to its new home, had also suffered from a bad press in spite of excellent work.

the payroll, as associate music director and principal guest conductor.[106] This was announced on 25 April 1991. The Italian repertoire was also to be enhanced with guests like Daniele Gatti, Carlo Rizzi, and Evelino Pido.[107] Downes would 'attend auditions, planning meetings and work with the chorus'. That, said Findlay, made 'a huge difference'.

Edward Downes has made a major contribution to the Royal Opera House over fifty years. Denis Forman, then the chairman of the opera Board, described Downes as the 'most unlucky and underestimated conductor'.[108] When he conducted *Macbeth* on 7 June 1988 Milnes had been moved to write of him, 'Born at a different time by a year or two, in a different place or with a different name, Edward Downes would be basking in public acclaim and probably be the happy recipient of an exclusive recording contract on a yellow label instead of being just – just! – an outstanding and serious musician greatly admired by his peers in the profession and by all those who work with him.' He believed that Downes's Verdi was on a par with the great.

Downes's appointment was all the more timely as Haitink was, according to Tooley, feeling 'increasingly isolated' from Isaacs, and leaving things not of his own concern to others. 'He did not choose the producer or designer; dolefully he left that to us,' wrote Isaacs; and often he did not like the choices made.[109] According to Findlay there was 'no gratuitous ill will' on Isaacs's part. It was, in his view, more due to Isaacs's lack of experience and his not understanding the make-up of musicians. Isaacs would say, 'Well, he's not here. I can't talk to him. He does not want to talk.'[110]

In April 1991 it was also announced that a new chorus-master was being appointed from the end of the season, and that the chorus would be reduced from seventy-two to sixty; a retirement age of sixty-five was also imposed and some members took early retirement.[111] Choral standards in the late Eighties had been severely criticised and the chorus had been, according to Findlay, 'woefully underpaid'.* The chorus, according to one of its members, had, by 1989–90, become

---

* The previous year Denis Forman had suggested to Findlay and Isaacs that as 75 per cent of the standard repertoire does not require a chorus bigger than sixty-two, their numbers should be accordingly reduced. Unlike English National Opera and Houses like Vienna, which perform every night, the Royal Opera does not have to divide the chorus in two. In September 1989 there had been an increase in pay for the choristers from £205 to £245 a week.

'tired'. Many of its members had been there a long time and had become 'very disillusioned and bitter – their voices were not what they had been and many were not musicians'. The chorister recalled, 'They could not sight-read, did not know when they were singing flat, did not know choral discipline – placing a consonant in the right place at the end of a phrase. They had been taught to sing instinctively.' Findlay explained, 'So we went into the question of reducing the chorus not only with the objective of money but to improve the artistic standard.'

David Syrus, in his paper for the opera Board in July 1987, had suggested that a new chorus-master whom 'they can respect' would be the best way to improve standards and discipline. The new chorus-master was Terry Edwards, who ran his own London Voices, engaged at a high salary. In employing Edwards, Findlay asked Isaacs, 'Do you want the best chorus or not?' and added, 'You can't get quality without the leaders.' The concept of a reduced chorus, augmented when necessary, fitted in with Edwards's methods and his experience as a freelance chorus director.

In spite of the press criticism of Covent Garden, the new arrangements worked well. Haitink, although not involved in the daily running of the House, gave great stature to Covent Garden. If indeed there were 'too many chiefs' at Covent Garden, the House only benefited – from 1991 until the closure – from the combination of Downes and Haitink, together with chorus-master Edwards. Their joint work insured some of the highest levels of musical attainment in the House's history. During performances of *Boccanegra*, in November 1997, Solti said that the orchestra had never been better prepared.

Isaacs's perseverance meant that the company succeeded in premiering Harrison Birtwistle's *Gawain* on 30 May 1991, even though, in Tooley's words, 'toughest of all to schedule is the completely new work'.[112] Isaacs recollected, 'If we had rescheduled Harry's opera with *Tosca*, the year's figures would certainly have improved by over £600,000. But Paul Findlay and I never doubted we must stay with it.' Isaacs displayed admirable dedication in presenting *Gawain* to the highest possible standards and later insisting on its revival.

It had been Peter Hall who had first tried to commission a work from Birtwistle, who had worked with him at the National Theatre, and with whom he planned to prepare a libretto, in the late Sixties. Tooley had later commissioned Birtwistle to write an opera about the Orpheus myth but this had been taken over by Glyndebourne without Tooley's knowledge and had then lapsed. It was finally performed in 1986 by English National Opera. It was Birtwistle who had approached Tooley for another commission: this had emerged as *Sir Gawain and the Green Knight.*[113]

Andrew Clements believed that *Gawain* placed Birtwistle at the heart of 'the operatic establishment'. The work succeeded, he wrote, in sustaining 'a single narrative thread from beginning to end in a magnificent, sweeping arc which nevertheless manages to contain the repetitions, the verse-and-refrain structures that have always been central to Birtwistle's music'. David Harsent's libretto pares down the Middle English text – making Morgan le Fay and Lady de Hautdesert control the action. 'Each act contrasts slabs of linear narration with big set-pieces.'[114] Birtwistle's dramatic material integrates a fairly simple storyline with complex ritual elements and recurrent, sometimes cyclical, themes and motifs. Finally Gawain realises he has only survived his trial by dishonesty and lying, not by heroic deeds, and thus is set apart from the noble figure of Arthur.

In the opera stylised emotions are expressed in difficult, jagged vocal lines and powerful orchestration. While Birtwistle's compositional approach is descended from Berg's expressionism, he declines to make use of the twelve-tone system in favour of an idiosyncratic atonality. The work displays nobility and grandeur without pomposity, and develops a wide variety of musical material in fascinating structures. However, unlike Aribert Reimann's *Lear* – which it superficially resembles in its musical lines and textures – *Gawain* keeps feelings somewhat at a distance. This ritualised music theatre, brilliantly worked out, appeals strongly to thought and aesthetic appreciation. It stands in contrast to John Corigliano's campy, allusive *The Ghosts of Versailles* and Stockhausen's symbolic, occasionally thrilling *Licht* operas.

Clements found John Tomlinson, who had worked closely with Birtwistle when he was writing the opera, a terrifying and 'magnificent vocal presence' with 'exemplary diction'. Tomlinson himself later said that for him the 'wonderful thing about this music' was its 'primeval power'.[115] With Alison Chitty's spare yet evocative designs, a fine cast and production, dramatic tension was maintained despite occasional evidence of the composer's idiom being at odds with the emotional content of the libretto. Dramatic tension was improved in the 1994 and 2000 revivals when cuts were made to the 'Turning of the seasons' ritual in Act One and the purification of Gawain.* Birtwistle told management that 'no composer of opera had been better served that he had by the Royal Opera'. Michael Tippett said, 'It was a most important event for all those who cared for opera.'[116]

On 25 June 1991 Isaacs told Findlay that he would not renew his contract when it expired at the end of the 1992–93 season. Peter Jonas was leaving the English National Opera and Isaacs wanted to catch Nicholas Payne before he was chosen to succeed Jonas. Haitink and Downes had not opposed, 'while expressing warm feelings towards' Findlay.[117] Payne would immediately be involved in planning.

In his memoirs Isaacs sought to explain the decision not to renew Findlay's contract. He cited some of the unsatisfactory hired productions – in particular the Friedrich *Ring* and the undermining of the chairman's plan to prove to the Thatcher government that Covent Garden needed more subsidy because it could not afford a complete *Ring* cycle. He also cited Findlay's failure to get a co-production of *War and Peace* with the Kirov on to the Covent Garden stage. *War and Peace*, a co-production with the Kirov, Paris Opéra and the BBC, was supposed to have been conducted by Downes in 1994, designed by Timothy O'Brien and directed by Graham Vick, but it became technically too big and caused great problems at its premiere in St Petersburg.† Findlay had committed £200,000 to the joint venture and later admitted that Covent Garden's technical people, who had built the set in England, let it get too big and could not get it on the

---

* According to Philip Jones, it was the uncut version that had caused David Hockney to mutter, 'Thank God there are only four seasons.'
† *War and Peace* had been Downes's choice to open the Sydney Opera House with, when he was music director there in the early 1970s.

Covent Garden stage within the normal repertory even in its planned modified version.* Findlay believed that his unwitting undermining of Sainsbury's and Isaacs's *Ring* cancellation strategy had also weakened his position.

Isaacs argued, however, that 'the real point' about Findlay's removal was that he thought that Covent Garden 'could do even better'. Somewhat disingenuously, he stated that 'the opera Board found Findlay's restless activity disquieting'.[118] But it had been Isaacs who had instructed Findlay to widen the repertoire and make the place exciting. To this Findlay had responded, and it was soon after Isaacs decided not to renew his contract that his planning achieved the artistic coherence and consistency that he had been seeking. Jones felt that Findlay did not get the credit he deserved for his many achievements, among them surtitles, the big screen in the piazza, and computerising the box office in 1986–87, which transformed the way bookings were controlled. But, Jones added, Findlay 'did tend to fly by the seat of his pants and this didn't go down well with Jeremy and certainly not John Sainsbury'.

The start of the 1991–92 season witnessed the last of the unsuccessful borrowings, with a universally disliked *Huguenots* and conclusion of Friedrich's disappointing recycled *Ring* with *Das Rheingold*. The November 1991 *Les Huguenots* was the 1987 Deutsche Oper, Berlin production directed by John Drew, which by 1991 seemed outdated and inappropriate. The setting was a modern strife-torn city, possibly Berlin or Belfast, with Marguérite de Valois and her ladies, in Gottfried Pilz's designs, 'reclining on deckchairs and popping into an on-stage swimming pool, with cheerleaders with twirling batons, camp waiters, strippers and leather-jacketed paras'.[119] It was a waste of a fine cast that included Richard Leech and Jennifer Larmore as Urbain.

The unanimity of critical disapproval for *Les Huguenots* was rare and Loppert reflected that the policy of 'buying in' productions had

---

* Findlay later argued that had his contract been renewed he would have put on *War and Peace* at the beginning of the season, for nine performances night after night, with a triple cast and using the Kirov chorus, as his *Prince Igor* experience had shown him that it was hard to get an English chorus to sing Russian idiomatically.

too often led to 'artistic compromise'. He cited, among others, the 1987 *L'Italiana* from Vienna, the 1990 *Cenerentola* from Salzburg, and the 1991 *Capriccio* from San Francisco as well as the *Ring*, which was ruined in the process of making it fit the Covent Garden stage.[120]

At the time of *Les Huguenots* the orchestra went on strike, demanding a 20 per cent pay increase, after years of minimal pay rises and a freeze on earnings in order to balance the books in 1990–91. In 1991 the basic pay of rank-and-file members of the orchestra was £17,000, which could be augmented with overtime up to £24,000. The Covent Garden musicians did not enjoy the opportunities that other London orchestral players had of picking up session work, as management did not permit deputies, and all players had to play for each opera and ballet. It was, wrote Isaacs, 'hard to keep a family and meet a mortgage'. But he argued that with the margin so tight there was no hope of 'meeting a claim that was not in low single figures'. Management offered 5.5 per cent. Negotiations became tense. Shop steward Robert Trory suggested the musicians insist on an interval between each of *Les Huguenots*' five acts instead of one as planned.

Management responded to the orchestra by insisting on one interval and the orchestra stayed at home. Three performances of *Huguenots* had to be cancelled and the House was dark for a week. A gala opening of *Simon Boccanegra*, directed by Moshinsky and conducted by Solti, was threatened. The dispute went to arbitration, at which Isaacs explained that the demand could not be met. Agreement was reached at 11 p.m. the night before the last possible day to begin orchestral rehearsals for *Boccanegra*. There was to be a 5 per cent increase in salary and for payments of £9 a week the orchestra agreed to twelve radio relays a year. This Isaacs described as 'a major breakthrough'.[121] As a result of the strike, there was a loss of £450,000.

In spite of the less than encouraging start with *Les Huguenots*, it was during the 1991–92 season that Covent Garden succeeded in establishing a firm grasp on artistic standards, with interesting and innovative repertoire and productions, a high level of casting and at the centre high musical standards. A little golden age ensued beginning on 12 November 1991 with the triumphant *Boccanegra*, directed by Moshinsky on Solti's insistence, and movingly conducted by the maestro. The contrast between Moshinsky's production and that of Del Monaco's for the Met is described on p. 747.

Isaacs's wish to see Vick employed was fulfilled in December 1991, when he directed the fourteen-year-old Mozart's *Mitridate re di Ponto*.* He brought the drama of sibling rivalry and culture clashes to life by using elements of Indian and Japanese drama. It was designed by Paul Brown with Vick's favoured vibrant colours and exotic costumes, which, according to Canning, evoked 'a breathtakingly imaginative illusion of baroque strangeness'.[122] An outstanding cast included Bruce Ford and Yvonne Kenny, who gave a commanding assumption of the fiendishly difficult role of Aspasia, as well as Ann Murray splendid as Sifare.

By 1991–92 the possibility of insolvency was beginning to cause grave concern to management. The Arts Council grant had fallen from 53 per cent of the House's receipts in 1985–86 to 38 per cent in 1991–92, and sponsorship was proving an unreliable source of income as it began to be adversely affected by the changing economic climate. Jones later explained that Alexander had 'called in all his favours' in 1987–89. Although the 1990–91 season had in fact broken even despite the high seat prices and recession at the time of the Gulf War, this was achieved, Isaacs explained, as the result of 'a quite exceptional box office boom' of 94 per cent and was misleading.[123]

Isaacs's concern was not misplaced. By September 1991 the recession was affecting the advance booking, upon which the House depended for its cash flow. Far from being able to reduce the deficit by March 1994, there was the prospect of a further deficit of £850,000 for the year. It was at this moment that Philip Jones warned that the question of advance bookings and cash flow would be particularly acute during the forthcoming closure. Sir Martin Jacomb pointed out that the fundamental point was that 'no commercial organisation could continue to work with an endemic deficit'.[124]

A radical attempt to widen the Covent Garden audience also caused serious problems at the turn of the year 1991–92, when *Turandot* was

---

* First performed in 1770 and not again until the 1971 Salzburg Festival.

presented with amplification to audiences of 7,000 at the Wembley arena in conjunction with impresario Raymond Gubbay, and with sponsorship from the *Daily Telegraph* and *Emap*.[125] The estimated 60,000 audience turned out to be nearer 40,000. Although that figure was the equivalent of twenty full houses, the sponsors and Gubbay lost between them £1 million. Instead of the estimated profit of £100,000 for the House there was a £100,000 overspend and a loss of £27,000.[126] It was, according to Sainsbury, 'a grievous new blow to the opera's finances' and revealed a 'defect in the administration's budgetary control arrangements'.[127]

In November, Stirling said 'it was difficult to exaggerate how serious the House's financial situation was', the auditors having sent a severe warning letter. Philip Jones warned of the possibility of insolvency. The Arts Council had extended the March 1994 deadline to March 1995 for eliminating the deficit but Isaacs said an 11 per cent increase in the subsidy would be required to break even.[128]

In December 1991 government support for the Arts Council increased by 13.9 per cent at the express wish of the Prime Minister, John Major, but in January 1992 Covent Garden was told it was to receive just 6.5 per cent for 1992–93. This was a very disappointing settlement in the light of another looming deficit of £1.5 million, and management were once again looking for cuts. On 29 January Isaacs proposed ten redundancies. At a special meeting over 11–12 January 1992 the Board thrashed around for solutions and decided to commission a study from Price Waterhouse. One Board member, according to Isaacs, suggested wall-to-wall *Carmens* and *Bohèmes*, *Sleeping Beauties* and *Swan Lakes*. Another suggested opera without scenery. Stirling warned that the deficit imbroglio the previous year had 'profoundly upset' the Arts Council, and that in future they must not be made to feel that the House was being 'aggressive'. They should make the desperate financial situation clear without 'confrontation'.[129]

The season continued with another thoughtfully worked out and rewarding production, the Colin Graham – Steuart Bedford *Death in Venice*, which had its premiere on 10 March 1992. Most striking were its original John Piper backdrops of Venice, and a series of wonderful

Mario Fortuny photographs from between 1900 and 1910. Director, designer, singers, and each member of the orchestra as soloists, according to Michael Kennedy, revealed Britten's 'crowning masterpiece of an amazing operatic career'. Philip Langridge, an 'English tenor' with a welcome measure of tonal depth and colour, was described by Michael Kennedy as an ideal Aschenbach, in strong middle age, looking uncannily like Thomas Mann. Conductor Bedford and director Graham, who had directed the first ever *Death in Venice* in 1973 for Britten, showed great subtlety in the handling of Aschenbach's decline as his 'dignity is stripped away scene by scene . . . walking against the revolve of the stage following Tadzio'.[*][130]

Another exciting event was the House's co-production of Prokofiev's *Fiery Angel* with the Kirov Opera, given on 14 April 1992, to mark Edward Downes's fortieth anniversary with Covent Garden as well as Prokofiev's centenary. It was Downes who not only urged the performance of the work, but had corrected the printed score from the manuscript which Nina Prokofieva had given him and from which Valery Gergiev at the Kirov worked. The production originated in St Petersburg because, Findlay recalled: 'If I put it on in St Petersburg first then I don't need so much technical time in London'.

These were dramatic times. The Kirov company had been touring at Edinburgh in August 1991 when the coup against Gorbachev took place in Moscow. Opera Factory's Australian director, David Freeman, who directed *The Fiery Angel*, pointed out that on the first day of rehearsals in December 1991 he was working in the Kirov Theatre in Leningrad and by opening night he was working in the Maryinsky Theatre in St Petersburg. The Soviet Union was itself dissolving.[131] 'Tomorrow all the republics become different countries,' Gergiev told Peter Conrad of the *Observer* the day before opening night in December 1991. 'My company is suddenly international.' Conrad felt sceptical that 'anyone would bother to put on a show when society was recreating itself or perhaps disintegrating'. But he soon realised that *The Fiery Angel* was itself a 'post-revolutionary act of restitution', as it had never been performed on stage in Prokofiev's lifetime: 'Socialist

---

* Graham, a long-standing friend and colleague of Britten, was currently artistic director of the Opera Theater of St Louis and had just directed *Ghosts* at the Met.

aesthetics could not countenance the mysticism or the neurosis' of the work. Gergiev felt a mission to stage Prokofiev's and Mussorgsky's works, comparing his own visionary feelings with that of Renata in *The Fiery Angel.*

The Kirov Opera was, in Conrad's words, 'a monument to the driven intentions of one man', Valery Gergiev, whose talents and energies restored the company to international prominence, with foreign tours at Edinburgh, Palermo and, in 1992, Covent Garden. Conrad described Gergiev as 'a Dostoevskian figure, wolfishly stubbly, wild-eyed and wilder-haired, with a pustular skin which seldom sees the daylight'.[132] Born in 1953, Gergiev had studied under Ilya Musin at the Leningrad Conservatory. Apprenticed to Yuri Temirkanov at the Kirov from 1977, Gergiev was not a Party man and did not see eye to eye with his director. Nevertheless, within ten years he had risen from assistant musical director, through permanent conductor and, in 1988, to artistic director, the first artistic director to be elected by the company members. It was Gergiev who, in a gesture that reflected the rapidly changing situation in the disintegrating Soviet Union, cancelled all the obligatory Communist Party and trade union meetings in the theatre.

At this period of extraordinary political upheaval for the new Russia, Gergiev managed to develop the company even though government funding was reduced from almost 100 per cent in the Communist era to 20 per cent by 1993. He maintained revenues with touring, recording, fund-raising and the White Nights Festival in St Petersburg. He also managed to preserve a fine ensemble of singers, moulding the company and giving them opportunities to develop artistically at home, and inviting Western directors to work with them. Realising that in post-Communist Russia there would be fierce competition, Gergiev arranged that his best artists would benefit from recording opportunities with Philips, tours and television, so that they would want to continue to work with the Kirov.

Baritone Sergei Leiferkus had been a company member at the Kirov under Temirkanov, who had invited him to sing Prince Andrei in *War and Peace* in 1977. He quickly made an international career, appearing at Wexford in 1982, then at Scottish Opera and English National Opera, before his Covent Garden debut in 1989. Born into a very poor family, Leiferkus had worked in a factory from the age of fifteen, but later joined the university chorus. He had spent seven years at the Leningrad Conservatory, from where he had joined the Kirov in 1972. Kirov stars like Chernov, Leiferkus, Olga Borodina and Galina Gorchakova kept up their links with the company after they gained major international careers, Leiferkus being invited back by Gergiev to sing Ruprecht in *The Fiery Angel*. Leiferkus shared director David Freeman's belief that the visionary Renata's persecution and Ruprecht's dangerous scientific enquiry were a parable and 'an admonition to a country which was hearing it for the first time'. David Freeman said, 'I hope that never again will a politician tell an artist or scientist what to do or think or create.'[133]

In London *The Fiery Angel* made a powerful impact on critics and public alike. Michael Tanner in the *Times Literary Supplement* expressed the general excitement of the critics when a 'neglected work' receives 'a high standard of performance'.[134] David Freeman used the company's ensemble principles to riveting effect, treating this very Russian text as a full-length chamber opera, dealing more in character than in situation or ideas. Freeman also made powerful use of a St Petersburg acrobatic troupe to portray the ghostly creatures who haunt the clairvoyant Renata. The principal singer-actors were splendid, with Galina Gorchakova untroubled by Renata's slippery vocal line, and highly dramatic both musically and in terms of stagecraft, her facial expression as interesting as her voice. Leiferkus's Ruprecht appeared particularly comfortable in his native Russian tongue, which allowed him to free his top register with an ease not always apparent in his Verdi roles. Taken as a whole, this *Fiery Angel* was a model of an integrated production: dramatically tight, musically and vocally fascinating – sparing in its use of set and spectacle. Loppert felt that it took a conductor of Downes's experience 'to squeeze theatrical juice from the less obvious features of the score, the light touches of sardonic humour, the bitter-sweet lyricism'.[135]

Ex Soviet-bloc singers began to appear increasingly widely in the West after this early visit. As well as Leiferkus, Borodina and Gorchakova, Elena Prokina, Larissa Diadkova, Maria Guleghina, Gegam Grigorian, Alexey Steblianko, and Dmitri Hvorostovsky among others, appeared in Western opera houses in the Nineties. Milnes wrote in

June 2000, 'It is virtually impossible to cast a big Verdi opera without Russian singers.'[136]

The Covent Garden season ended strongly. Daniele Gatti's debut was on 16 May 1992, conducting Bellini's *I Puritani* with a fine cast including June Anderson, Dmitri Hvorostovsky, Giuseppe Sabbatini and Robert Lloyd. The last new production of the season was *Der fliegende Holländer* directed by Ian Judge, with an exciting setting by John Gunter, which moved from scene to scene without pause and without an interval. The conductor was Christoph von Dohnányi; Julia Varady was Senta.

The House's consistently exciting artistic achievements earned the company the *Evening Standard* award for opera, and a Royal Philharmonic Society award for Birtwistle's *Gawain*. This acknowledged success in no way lessened its financial problems or the growing criticism of its administration. In his first Annual Report, the new Board chairman, Angus Stirling, showed that Isaacs's anxieties of the previous year had not been misplaced and that the 1991–92 season had indeed ended with a deficit of £1.4 million. This took the accumulated deficit to £3.6 million. The box office had held up until mid-March 1991, but then, as anticipated, the recession had begun to take its toll.* Average attendance fell to 88 per cent and sponsorship was also affected by the recession. Alex Alexander retired from the chairmanship of the Trust in December 1991, after raising £6.76 million in 1991–92.[137] The industrial action of the orchestra in the autumn of 1991 had lost more than £500,000 in revenue.

The system of constantly raising seat prices was no longer working. On 24 March Isaacs told the Board that nothing was to be gained from another increase.[138] Furthermore, prices were beginning to cause adverse comment in the press. The *Daily Telegraph* asked on 30 June 1992, 'Can we afford Covent Garden?' and went on to accuse the Royal Opera of fostering 'the most elitist and inaccessible' art form. The

---

* Tooley said that drinks sales were a good sign of public mood, and noted that champagne sales were down by 19 per cent and white wine by 16 per cent (Tooley, *In House*, p. 260).

resignations of Sainsbury and Alexander, as well as the deficit led the press to talk of a crisis.

The Arts Council did not feel strong enough to fight Covent Garden's cause and instead appointed Baroness Warnock, who had been Mistress of Girton College, Cambridge, from 1984 to 1991, to prepare another appraisal of the Royal Opera House. Other members of her team were Brian Ivory, the chairman of a Highland distilleries company, Veronica Lewis, a dance administrator, and Dennis Stevenson, chairman of SRU Ltd and a trustee of the Tate Gallery. Isaacs, who liked and respected Mary Warnock, nonetheless pointed out that she was not an expert on either opera or ballet.

The future funding of the House depended on Warnock's report and all discussion with the Arts Council and government was suspended until she completed her deliberations. In March, David Mellor, who had become Secretary of State for National Heritage, told Sainsbury that although he 'acknowledged that the House had not received its fair share of the Arts Council grant in recent years', he could do nothing to help until Warnock reported. He was still no ally and instead of making a clear statement that backed the House's development as being 'in the national interest' and having a 'legitimate claim on the lottery', expressed his concern about the elitism of the House, its expenditure and its self-appointing Board, as well as the Board's control of the executive.

The Board, in their alarm, decided on 30 March that the situation was so serious that the Prime Minister should be given advance warning of the severe cash flow crisis, 'without offending Mr Mellor in the process'. It was crucial that Warnock understood the 'immense risks in the House's financial position'.[139] By April, however, Isaacs realised that there might well be a far less satisfactory outcome to the investigation than had been true of Priestley, when he saw a draft of the report. He was disturbed, he said, that there was no sense in it 'that under-funding was the all-pervading problem'.

Amid all the anxiety there was a keen sense that the season had been a great artistic success. Isaacs wrote in his report on 24 June that the productions 'exhibited exactly the concept and design style that I believe to be appropriate to the House at this time'. The level of casting, rehearsal, music, and the improvement of the chorus under

Terry Edwards, were all sources of pride. Nonetheless, in July 1992 there was a rumour in the *Sunday Times* that Mellor was warning that any increase in Covent Garden's subsidy or any government contribution to the redevelopment would be dependent on Isaacs not having his contract renewed. There were reports of 'personal animosity' between the two men. Angus Stirling canvassed the Board as to whether Isaacs should be fired but Denis Forman pointed out that the Board had backed him and should continue to do so.

Lord Goodman would have been appalled to hear Mellor telling John Tooley that he found it hard 'just to allocate a sum to the Arts Council and not in some way be able to influence its spending'.[140] Milnes mourned the passing of the traditional 'arm's-length' policy, which had been 'one of the UK's noblest post-war assets'. He pointed out that there had been no denial from the Minister about the renewal of Isaacs's contract and commented, 'For anyone in government to criticise the ROH's seating prices is as ludicrous as it is cynical; the only way it could keep its doors open in the face of steadily reduced funding was to raise prices, and for a Minister to damn them for that is like someone starving their cat and then kicking it to death for killing birds.'*[141]

During the summer of 1992 the press raised the pitch of its attack. On 9 and 10 August there were leaks from the forthcoming Warnock report in the *Guardian* and *Sunday Times*, citing gross mismanagement and suggesting Isaacs resign. Milnes believed that the reports had been leaked by 'powerful and unscrupulous enemies' of Isaacs, who saw the articles while at Salzburg and for whom they made 'sickening reading'. Edward Downes was furious that the press was hostile after Covent Garden's golden year. 'That's what made me spit,' he later said. 'After

---

* Mellor was instrumental in getting £10 million for the English National Opera to buy the freehold of the Coliseum at this time. In his memoirs Isaacs recalled Mellor throwing a tantrum when his wife arrived late for a performance, as the guest of Sir Denis Forman, and could not get access to the royal box except by going round to Floral Street. 'Mellor blew his top; in front of others, in unrestrained language, which Mrs Isaacs (Gillian Widdicombe) inadvertently revealed at the *Observer*, where she was arts editor, and they made a story in which they said Mellor of all people should know that the opera house could ill afford "idle flunkies". Mellor was furious, demanded apologies from Forman, from me, from Gillian. We wrote grovelling apologies which were not acknowledged' (Isaacs, *Never Mind the Moon*, p. 122).

all those things that happened last season! Some of those performances! As good as you'll see anywhere in the world.'

In the autumn both Warnock's and Price Waterhouse's findings were published. As Isaacs had feared, neither Warnock nor the press addressed the central issue of how to maintain high artistic standards and reasonable seat prices with an inadequate subsidy. 'International comparisons', Warnock wrote, 'provide a more interesting insight into the differing funding cultures of the respective countries' than the 'relative cost effectiveness of the individual organisations concerned'. Nor was Warnock concerned about the maintenance of high artistic standards, explaining to the Board on 29 September that she had 'said little about the question of artistic standards and excellence' because there would have to be 'some compromising with artistic standards' in order to achieve a 'break-even strategy'. She was not even concerned about accessibility, believing that it could be better served by broadcasting than reducing ticket prices.[142] On the contrary, she saw the House's reputation, like that of the Royal Shakespeare Company, as a means of being able to charge 'premium prices'.[143]

With the crucial considerations of standards and accessibility conveniently out of the way, Warnock was able to concentrate her attentions on the weaknesses in the structure and management of the company. The 'tendency to decide what is right artistically first and to count the cost later' lay, she believed, at the heart of the House's problems.[144] She recommended longer runs of fewer productions and that plans should 'reflect known or probable resources' instead of being made and then modified if resources were not available. She also recommended that the general director's job description be redefined, as Isaacs himself had complained that too much of his time had to be devoted to managerial and financial functions. While Isaacs saw himself more as an 'overall impresario and artistic figurehead', the central task of the general director should be, according to Warnock, 'to arbitrate between competing demands for resources' from the directors of the performing companies.[145] The company was also urged to improve personnel practice – 'job descriptions and annual reports on management performance' – before there could be discussion about extra funding.

It would, however, be wrong and simplistic, the report stressed, to lay responsibility for all the problems at the door of the general director, who 'clearly had to fight many battles on many sides'. Responsibility should be borne 'by the Board, by senior management, and to a lesser degree by the Arts Council itself'. Isaacs called this a 'scattergun approach' which he believed resulted either from 'internal debate' or from a 'reluctant acknowledgement that the House was in a peculiarly difficult position'.[146]

Warnock also highlighted a problem that was to contribute to the crisis that hit the company at the time of the closure – the semi-autonomous nature of the various bodies working under the umbrella of the company structure. Warnock recommended the amalgamation of the Trust and the Friends. Findlay had ten years earlier raised the issue, and suggested to Warnock that the various marketing departments be brought under one roof as they had been at the Met. At Covent Garden each body – the Royal Opera House, the Trust and the Friends – had 'their own very powerful Boards' and was carefully guarding their own resources. Nothing was done about this problem at the time and the conflicting power bases contributed to the House's problems as the financial pressures grew and the closure got nearer.*

One of Warnock's main criticisms was that 'insufficient progress had been made in reforming backstage practices'. Both she and Price Waterhouse urged renegotiation of the stage agreements with the unions, which Isaacs had hoped to leave until the closure, originally planned for 1993 or 1995 but postponed until 1997. They recommended reducing overtime and cutting Sunday rehearsals. Restrictive work practices, Warnock said, were still rife. Findlay felt that this aspect of the House's problems was 'grossly overstated'. Although work practices at that time were archaic they were, he felt, 'also very unreasonable in the demands being made on the staff'.[147]

In the end the report, which was an uneven document, destroyed its impact and effectiveness by recommending the scrapping of the redevelopment, plans and fund-raising for which were by then twenty years in the making and despite the fact that the House had in any case to be closed down for running repairs and rewiring, which would

---

* This problem was finally addressed in 2001 when the chairman of the Board Colin Southgate amalgamated all the income-generating bodies of the House, but at the risk of losing The Friends' role of communicating with the public.

cost £25 million. The Board told her on 29 September that her recommendation to scrap the development was based on the false premise that there was no way of raising the required funds when there was in fact a distinct possibility of a national lottery. Warnock said her team had not been aware of the 'point about the lottery'.*[148]

Price Waterhouse were more even-handed than Warnock, challenging both the Arts Council and the government to declare that subsidy existed to provide accessibility and to help restore the building, as well as urging a greater sense of economy throughout the organisation and the redress of its management weaknesses. Their report 'recommended that the Royal Opera House should seek a fresh understanding with the Arts Council, based on a new and clear statement of purpose'. Both the Arts Council and the House must be clear as to its role as a House of international standing, accessible and housed in a building of national significance. The grant should reflect these 'specific agreed purposes'. They identified potential savings of £480,000 in the area of stagehands' contracts and also suggested that the general director, with a good stock of new productions already available, should concentrate on stronger management and internal discipline. 'Full costing of everything was essential' and 'a search for economy needed to pervade the organisation, including repertory planning within fixed financial envelopes'. If Covent Garden 'made a public commitment to manage well', they argued, its debt should be cleared by the end of 1992–93 by a special Arts Council grant. The worsening of the financial situation had in itself added to the weakness of the management structure, by bringing the Board into a managerial rather than trustee relationship, and leaving neither party 'properly accountable'.†

In its response, 'Putting Our House in Order', published in April 1993, management took on some of Warnock's recommendations but stressed that 'a decaying theatre in Covent Garden sooner or later derelict and empty, would be a national disgrace, a living

* Isaacs also pointed out that no one on the committee had spoken either to Sainsbury or to Sir Kit McMahon, chairman of the development Board.
† Price Waterhouse recommended £150,000 of savings during the current year, £750,000 the next, £1.25 million the next and £1.5 million the next. In general, Price Waterhouse commended Covent Garden, saying that they usually identified savings of 10–15 per cent in many organisations (Board, 18/3/3).

theatre on this site, a source of public satisfaction and national pride'.

In answer to the two reports, Isaacs produced a paper for the Board on retrenchment. 'The Board should be under no illusion', he wrote, 'what is being proposed, and what our financial plight dictates we must accept is, regrettably, a reduction in the quality of what we do.' He listed the achievements: the night gang, additional dancers, paying off 'fading' principals, livening up the repertory, engaging guest stars and great conductors, adding technical and orchestral rehearsals, hiring a new chorus-master and improving the standard of musicians in the chorus, installing surtitling equipment, increasing educational and 'In Focus' events, and offering the public a generally improved service. He did, however, admit that there might have been too many new productions.

Isaacs chose to pay £500,000 in redundancies rather than ban all new productions, losing seventy more staff, and to reduce the quantity of new productions. It was decided to cancel a production of *Die Soldaten* and a revival of *Prince Igor*. The chorus was reduced from seventy-two to sixty and all salaries and guest artist fees were frozen, and overtime kept at the 1992–93 levels. This would reduce the budget from £3.8 million to £1.95 million. There was also to be another seat price increase of 7.5 per cent.*

Isaacs responded to Warnock's 'less emphasis on quality' argument with a truth that had never been fully grasped by British politicians and civil servants from Kleiber's time on. 'Anyone who is any good in the arts', he wrote, 'wants to do the very best that can be done.' The Board had encouraged Isaacs to 'make the House the best in the world and by achieving excellence' to be able to charge high prices, attract sponsorship and claim funding. 'We have', he concluded, 'just about achieved the quality I sought and we have, in two of my four years, failed by a depressing margin to pay for it.'[149]

Lord Goodman, in the March 1991 *Opera Now* survey, had pointed out a particularly cruel aspect of the starvation funding policy: 'Some-

---

* Tooley later wrote that the redundancies meant that the numbers of employees was again similar to the numbers employed when he had been general director. In 1987–88 there had been 1,053 emloyees and in 1990–91 there were 1,152. These included twenty in the night gang, fifteen in marketing, and fourteen front of house. In the 1995–96 season the number of employees went down to 1,000 (Tooley, *In House*, p. 239).

how we seem to have arrived at a system of refined torture where the grant falls just short of the amount required. It is so often a very small amount of money that stands between the successful funding of a project and its being in jeopardy, and the government never clears the difference. It seems to take a sadistic satisfaction in not clearing it.' The *Opera Now* article concluded, 'The nation seems set to turn its cultural flagship either into a preserve of the privileged or into an insular operation increasingly unable to compete.'*[150]

Luckily for Isaacs and Covent Garden, it was Mellor who resigned on 24 September from what had become known under his stewardship as the Ministry of Fun. Peter Brook MP, who took over was, according to Isaacs, 'sympathetic but non-committal'.[151] Isaacs's contract was renewed to 1995, but he was furious when, during a meeting with the Department of National Heritage, Board member Bamber Gascoigne informed the meeting 'that all was now bound to be well, because from now on Jeremy would be kept on a short leash'.[152] Gascoigne later apologised, but the Board was increasingly unaware of the boundaries between itself and the executive. Tooley felt that Isaacs's decision to stay on the Board, of which he had been a member since 1985, while executive director, had added to the confusion of roles. For the procedure to work whereby management could question plans and policy but ultimately had to accept the director's decisions and support them or replace him, Tooley wrote, 'The independence of the management from the Board is essential.'[153]

Isaacs, however, was unperturbed by the growing involvement of the Board in relation to the director, believing it to be the inevitable result of funding problems. He later wrote of the Board, 'Once their role was to hear monthly reports from the executive and keep a watchful eye on what is going on', but 'these days, Boards are in the front line of a never-ending struggle to stay solvent'.† He continued:

---

* *Time Out* pointed out that the Royal Shakespeare Company was in debt to £3 million and the South Bank Centre's accumulated shortfall would be £9 million over the previous five years.

† In his memoirs Isaacs contrasts the Met and Covent Garden Boards. In the United States, he points out, Boards 'give money first and help raise money second'. They give generously and by belonging buy a 'ticket to New York high society'. He also points out that in the United States there are more than a million millionaires and 400 billionaires, and that charitable donations are tax deductible (op. cit., p. 226)

Serious people, without any reward except a pair of tickets, gave up hours and hours of voluntary time to help manage a private institution with public responsibilities ... As the Arts Council grant fell from over 60 per cent to under 40 per cent of revenue, we made bricks without straw. Somehow, dodging crisis after crisis, the House got by. But the constant threat of insolvency got the Board more and more closely involved in management.[154]

The need to raise massive amounts of money for the redevelopment further unbalanced the relationship. Vivien Duffield said that if people were to be expected to involve themselves in the Appeal and succeed in raising the necessary £60 million, they 'would need to feel a part of the business. Board members would need to help much more than before.'*[155]

Findlay, like Tooley, was less sanguine about this confusion of roles. He explained, 'The moment you delegate your decision-making authority ... you diminish the stature of the person at the top.... If you've got a good general director like John he would never accept that. He may be diminished in the boardroom but in the House he was the boss.' This confusion of boundaries, together with the multiplicity of power bases within the company, contributed to the ultimate breakdown of managerial control after the closure in 1997.

Even under the very difficult post-Warnock circumstances, Findlay's last season, 1992–93, was by any standards a remarkable one artistically. It included the House premiere of *Porgy and Bess*, a new production of *Die Frau ohne Schatten*, conducted by Haitink and designed by Hockney, a new *Alcina*, *Stiffelio*, Berlioz's *Damnation of Faust* and *Der fliegende Holländer*. It also included Pavarotti in *Tosca* and von Stade in *Pelléas*, conducted by Abbado, von Otter in *I Capuleti*, and Borodina and Domingo in *Samson*.

---

* Isaacs enjoyed working with Duffield, later writing in his memoirs, 'Her personality is said to be overbearing, and was hard for my successive successors to live with. I found her clear-sighted courage at all times inspiring, and her commitment to the Opera House, together with John Sainsbury's, reassuring above all things' (Isaacs, *Never Mind the Moon*, p. 103).

Extraordinary performances of Domingo's *Otello* with Solti in November 1992 showed Covent Garden, of all the companies, consistently managing to combine high musical standards with a fiercely realised dramatic thrust. Moshinsky's direction of both the London and New York *Otellos* illuminated the different styles of the two Houses. Moshinsky's London direction in the intimacy of Covent Garden, combined with the energetic contribution of Solti and the fine-tuning of the company, created a magnificent musical – dramatic experience. As in the London *Boccanegra*, Solti organised the shattering moments in order of deepening anguish, emotional clarity given precedence over the Met orchestra's precision and its impressive swathes of sound. The Met stage encouraged larger gestures while a more intimate drama was enacted on London's smaller stage. In London's Act One, Moshinsky helped encourage suggestions of erotic and domestic happiness from Domingo and the warm and innocently vulnerable Te Kanawa that were not so evident in the New York production, where Domingo was partnered by a somewhat bland Renée Fleming. Solti rarely nudged Domingo into pushing the voice whereas his New York Otello is more declamatory: a rich, baritonal sound, full of ring, which is from time to time heard straining slightly against the force of Levine's orchestra. The disintegration of Otello in Covent Garden's Act Three, culminating in Domingo's searing *'Dio! mi potevi scagliar'*, was tracked by Solti's expressive accompaniment, as was each emotional development in the opera.

Another striking success at this time, and a premiere for Covent Garden, was *Porgy and Bess* in October 1992, borrowed from Glyndebourne. It brought Trevor Nunn on an all too rare visit to Covent Garden and revealed, in Michael Billington's words, his 'ability to pierce the emotional core of a work, a nagging concern for detail and a profound seriousness about everything he undertakes'. In Nunn's hands 'Catfish Row became a genuine place; a primitive, poverty-stricken community where life was hard and work still had to be done ... a lot of ideas came from improvisations among the cast and their first-hand recollections of black community life'.[156] During the Hamlyn week, *Porgy* played to 60–70 per cent black audiences, who according to the Board minutes had expressed a desire to come back.[157]

There were other outstanding new productions, including the

Haitink–Hockney–Cox *Die Frau ohne Schatten* on 16 November 1992 – its costs shared with Los Angeles – another collaborative triumph. Michael Kennedy believed that John Cox and Hockney had 'gone a long way to vindicating those who believe that in spite of all its flaws ... it is a masterpiece of twentieth-century opera'. Hockney presented the imperial gardens in nocturnal purples and greens with other-worldly shimmerings on a lake backcloth. The mortals wore baggy Indian cotton tie-dyes and Barak's trade as dyer was represented by multicoloured patterns of overhanging cloths. Cox's clear and swiftly moving exposition of the narrative also cleverly differentiated the two worlds. Haitink's musical direction 'supplied the genuine Strauss sound' and reconciled the work's grandeur with its 'many passages of chamber-like intimacy'. Kennedy was impressed by the contributions of cello, violin, woodwind and horns, and the strings which supplied the 'soaring expression of Barak's love for his wife in their first scene together when the orchestra heartrendingly speaks what words cannot tell'. The characterisation of the individual roles was strongly prepared, especially that of Gwyneth Jones as Barak's wife and Anna Tomowa-Sintow as the Empress with her 'beautiful, secure and firmly moulded sound'. Franz Grundheber was a 'warm and dignified Barak'.[158]

Peter Katona's fine casting contributed to the general artistic success. As well as the Domingo – Te Kanawa *Otello*, Pavarotti sang Cavaradossi, von Otter sang Romeo, Thomas Hampson the Barber, Frederica von Stade Mélisande, and Carreras Stiffelio with Malfitano. Exciting new talent was also abundant. Many young singers who later became international and Met stars started and consolidated their careers at Covent Garden at this time. A young Romanian soprano, Angela Gheorghiu, sang Zerlina in 1992 and then Mimì and Liù in 1993, and Micaëla and Nina in *Chérubin* in 1994. Solti, after seeing her Mimì in May 1992, persuaded and coached her to be his first Violetta. That same month Alan Blyth greeted Roberto Alagna's debut in *Bohème* with the exclamation, 'I shall chance my arm that Roberto Alagna will be *the* Italian tenor of the new generation.' He hoped his 'extraordinary talent' would not be 'exploited too quickly', describing his tone as 'fresh, juicy, naturally produced with a truly Italian "ping" to it'.[159] On 15 June 1992 the Russian mezzo, Olga Borodina, partnered

Domingo in an electric *Samson* Promenade performance, which was relayed to the piazza in festive mood. Borodina also sang Marguérite in the Berlioz *Faust* in March 1993.

Finnish soprano Karita Mattila, who had won the 1983 Cardiff Singer of the World competition and was, like Te Kanawa and von Otter, a student of Vera Rozsa, had her Covent Garden debut in 1986 as Fiordiligi. She was a gifted and beautiful singer-actress, in what the Germans call *jugendlich-dramatisch* [youthful dramatic] fach. Mattila also sang Pamina, the Countess, Elvira and Donna Anna at Covent Garden. At her Carnegie Hall debut in February 1999 Anthony Tommasini described her voice as having a 'gleaming quality and a spareness of vibrato' while maintaining a 'meltingly warm and plaintive sound'.[160] By the time she had expanded further into the Strauss repertoire, making her debut as Arabella at the Châtelet in April 2002, John Allison described her as 'one of opera's hottest properties'. He wrote that she gave 'a characteristically committed performance; in complete control of her voice, she pours out ravishing tone and spins soft clean lines ... a fascinating creature'.[161]

One of the greatest of the new young talents was bass-baritone Bryn Terfel, who came from a farm in Pantglas near Caernarfon in Wales and for whom Welsh was his first language. Terfel later wrote, 'We have seven vowels which lend warmth to the singing.'[162] Terfel trained at the Guildhall and made his debut at Covent Garden as Masetto in 1992. One close observer called him 'a stunning actor who brings something completely new to everything he does'. He added, 'Bryn's talent affects those working around him.' In an aria collection recorded with Levine in 1996 for Deutsche Grammophon, Terfel's is the voice of a giant, perfect for Wagner as well as Mozart, with a shattering fortissimo combined with an extraordinary flexibility, including appealing glints of light in the middle and upper registers. Moreover, his head voice carries with great ease to high G, even A. In lieder as well as opera, Terfel relies on his rich tonal resources and musical understanding, emphasising the depth of the line, rather than making 'intelligent' verbal nuances in Fischer-Dieskau fashion.

As well as gifted young singers, great conductors like Solti, Abbado and Colin Davis continued to give distinction to the House. Davis conducted Berlioz's *Faust* on 8 March 1993 in Harry Kupfer's weird production set in a disused theatre with distracting apparitions. Davis was quoted as saying that Samuel Ramey's superb Méphistophélès sang his 'Voici des roses' with 'a tin of coke in his hand, walking towards Faust who is lying on a rubbish heap'. Davis reflected, 'I think I can see what he means. If you wish, you can turn a dung heap into a garden of Eden.'[163]

One of the greatest successes of this little golden age was another Moshinsky–Downes–Verdi collaboration for *Stiffelio* in January 1993. Downes was responsible for editing the score of *Stiffelio* and had been behind the project of resuscitating the piece, which Verdi had composed for Trieste but which, because of its contentious subjects of clerical marriage, adultery and Protestant forgiveness, was butchered by the censors and reworked in 1857 as *Aroldo*. In 1968 two manuscripts had been found in the Biblioteca di San Pietro a Majella and the work was given its premiere at the Brooklyn Academy of Music in 1976. Philip Gossett, dean of humanities at Chicago, gained access to the Verdi estate and recovered details such as Lina's dramatic words, which were excised by the censors: *'ministro, confessetemi'*. Gabriella Carrara-Verdi gave Covent Garden access to the archive from which Downes prepared a score 'which enabled Stiffelio to be heard as Verdi first wrote it'.[164] Covent Garden was the first major opera house to give the piece a serious production. Milnes felt that Covent Garden's first performance of the piece was 'as though, through some weird 150-year time slip, one were attending a major Verdi premiere'. *Stiffelio* was, Milnes found, 'an astonishing opera, unlike anything else in the canon – *Traviata* is the nearest – and pole-axing in its depth of feeling and dramatic impact'.[165]

Moshinsky, Michael Yeargan and Peter J. Hall relocated Stiffelio's castle to middle-America with a Nebraska rural chapel as a front drop and a Montana glacier as backdrop to the Act II graveyard scene. The opera's themes of isolation brought into focus sexual tensions and the stultifying power of rigid morality, Moshinsky effectively evoking sympathy for each character, and reflecting Verdi's own understanding of the rift between morality and instinct. The production starred Catherine Malfitano who, Andrew Porter found, commanded the stage with 'each movement of voice and of body'. José Carreras in an intense performance, sang 'with seriousness and strength, weighing and shaping each phrase, uttering it clearly'.[166] Alan Yentob, controller of BBC 2, was so 'bowled over' by the show that he cleared the schedule one evening to broadcast *Stiffelio* live. The production went to La Scala and Los Angeles, and regrettably, was finally sold to Vienna.[167]

The Royal Opera House was nominated for eight Laurence Olivier awards for 1992–93. Edward Downes won the Laurence Olivier award for *Fiery Angel* and Haitink was nominated for *Die Frau*, as were Julia Varady and Langridge for *Death in Venice*. *Stiffelio* won best opera award, and all the other nominations were for the Royal Opera. Findlay quoted the *Financial Times* in the Annual Report: 'To Royal Opera House watchers the irony in all this was that a distasteful brouhaha should have been stirred up in the year that was, by general consent, artistically the most rewarding for a very long time.' The new productions add up, it continued, 'to so richly varied and balanced a repertory . . .' The article concluded, 'A further irony of this splendid year is that it directly bears out one of the subsidiary Warnock criticisms: that the company has been favouring artistic adventurousness over economically prudent planning.'

Isaacs later recalled that for three years after Warnock there was an operating surplus, which was, in his words, unreported by press or TV. The season had in the end seen a small surplus of £349,000 as a result of the economising measures and redundancies, and a private benefaction of £2.5 million to be spread over three years from a Hong Kong businessman, Stanley Ho.[168] As Isaacs succinctly put it, 'By such acts of almost random generosity was our fate determined.'*[169]

The financial respite was indeed temporary. Findlay saw the writing on the wall, later recalling: 'All the money was beginning to be channelled into development and wasn't coming through to new productions. Jeremy was trying to have it both ways and he was cushioned by the donation from the Hong Kong gentleman.' In November 1992

---

* Covent Garden was not alone in its anxieties. In July 1993 the Arts Council announced that they were only going to fund two of London's four orchestras. Palumbo ruled that the London Symphony Orchestra and Philharmonia could live but that the London Philharmonic and Royal Philharmonic could be dispensed with. The LPO chairman threatened legal action and Palumbo gave way. Ken Baird, music director of the Arts Council, and his music panel, resigned, and Palumbo left the Arts Council in 1994.

Isaacs and the Board had decided to replace Philip Jones as finance director at the end of the season, but to keep him on for another two years as director of finances for the development. Stirling, in saying goodbye to him, told the Board, 'Without his calmness and clarity in times of crisis, the House might not have survived at all.'[170] Findlay believed that Jones had been made a scapegoat after the Warnock report. Clive Timms as finance director and Mike Morris as personnel manager were brought in – both from television.

The retirement of Board members John Sainsbury, Denis Forman and Martin Jacomb, at the same time as Philip Jones's departure, resulted in a less rigorous watch on the financial controls at an extremely sensitive time. These Board members had been, in Jones's opinion, 'the heavyweight core-centre that controlled Jeremy'. Findlay said that when Jones left, 'the expertise went ... You then had a financial team that did not have the knowledge.' Angus Stirling was 'a gentleman but not a leader ... a good committee man with a consensual approach. It was not what the House was used to.' It was the lack of a controlling central force that enabled the different power bases to pull apart, and Isaacs's lack of arbitration strengths became a handicap.

One of Findlay's last major contributions was the concept of the Verdi festival, announced in the 1993–94 Annual Report and intended to run from 1995 to 2001. Downes had presented the Verdi festival sugges-tion on 19 September 1991 to the opera Board.[171] Findlay later recalled how one night that summer, driving back from Salzburg to Bayreuth, a little weary after twelve nights of Mozart and Wagner, he had hit on an idea of how to solve a problem that had been taxing the Board: the lessening of interest and box office towards the end of the season. Findlay, who was passionate about Verdi, suddenly realised that whereas Mozart and Wagner were well represented on the festival circuit, there was no Verdi festival, which could create a focus in early summer when no one else had a festival.[172] Downes responded to Findlay's idea enthusiastically and later recalled, 'I worked out that if we started in 1995 and got a season of, say, four or six weeks each summer, we could do four Verdi operas every year in those five weeks each summer and, by the time we get to 2001, we'd have got all twenty-eight in.'

The Board hesitated because Payne was due to take over from Findlay, but the scheme was accepted in June 1993. Isaacs told the Board that Downes's employment 'greatly enhanced the House's ability to contemplate the Verdi festival'. It was, Stirling said, an 'exciting project'.[173] The Verdi festival began heroically in 1995 and livened the summer season with an exciting programme of events, lectures, discussions, interviews, and old and new Verdi productions, until it petered out and died at the closure in 1997. A revival of *Stiffelio* with Domingo was one of the high points of the June 1995 Verdi festival, during which all the great Verdi scholars – including Julian Budden, Philip Gossett, Roger Parker, Pierluigi Petrobelli and Andrew Porter – provided lectures and insights, play readings, staging editions and discussions with artists. Milnes was in awe: 'To mount performances with so visionary a sense of purpose calls for canonisation all round.'[174]

The new opera director, Nicholas Payne, described by Isaacs as 'a self-assured Etonian',[175] began his first full season at the beginning of the 1993–94 season. David Syrus, who became head of music in 1993, and whose own theatrical interests were more in line with what he described as Payne's less 'conservative ethos', felt Payne was a 'very shy person who never seemed happy' at Covent Garden.[176] But Payne was able to build on Findlay's strong foundations with his more experimental – and occasionally miscalculated – planning.

Ironically, Payne's first and perhaps greatest success was, in fact, Findlay's – it was the Graham Vick–Haitink *Meistersinger*, in October 1993. Haitink's collaboration with Vick had been a happy one from the start. Thomas Allen, singing Beckmesser for the first time, recalled how 'Graham seemed in these rehearsals to have set something in motion, and then quietly nursed it like a loving mother'. There had been, in Allen's words, a 'special chemistry' in the team during rehearsals. Allen believed that the basis of the success was Haitink's inspired conducting, describing it as 'the highest point of my career' and recalling, 'The thing that really brought home to me his greatness as an architect was the *Meistersinger* in the way he structured it, and the rehearsal period indicated something special in the offing.' Allen admired Haitink's ability 'to take everything into account in that piece – the character of David, Magdalene, Eva, Pogner (etc.) and to enrich what they have to say by what he's doing down there – to have that breadth of understanding is really extraordinary and the consistent thought that goes from the beginning of the evening right through to the end – a phenomenal piece of work'.[177]

Max Loppert called the style of the production 'a marriage of sixteenth century and late twentieth-century artistic vision'.[178] Richard Hudson's spare and witty set was like a model village with just a couple of houses, and according to Milnes, was 'reminiscent of Brueghel in technicolour – though some of the codpieces looked like the triumph of optimism over reasonable expectation'.[179] The subtle lighting shafted through open windows or cast beams from doorways, evocative of balmy, twilight-suffused midsummer northern nights giving way to sparkling midsummer mornings. Orchestral and stage colours were in total harmony in this happiest of collaborations. Vick's *Meistersinger* realised Haitink's 'dream of a sound corresponding to Vermeer's pictures, with their silent rooms in which happiness is sealed like sunlight'. It was also, according to Peter Conrad, his 'quiet revenge on Germany: this monument of what Wagner smugly entitled *"Heil'ge Deutsche Kunst"* has been made to look and sound Dutch'.*[180] At its revival in 1997 Michael Kennedy shared Allen's enthusiasm for Haitink's achievement: 'The orchestra played its collective heart out for Bernard Haitink, whose interpretation was ablaze with inspiration: all the way through, tempos were totally admirable.' Haitink 'maintained the forward impetus, held the moments of stillness, conjured up the scents of midsummer night, stopped our hearts with the sheer splendour of *"Wach auf"*, let the apprentices dance with a lightness that was truly fantastic. Great conducting.'[181]

Andrew Porter found Thomas Allen's Beckmesser to be the star of the show – 'incisive, consistent in every gesture, every stillness, every flicker of hands, eyes, or voice'.[182] John Tomlinson sang Sachs for the first time, after studying the role with Haitink for over a year. It was

---

* Haitink's grandmother was Jewish and his father spent four months in a German concentration camp. His 'revulsion of uproar and rant dates back to his boyhood in occupied Amsterdam' (*Observer*, 27.2.94).

his first Wagner role at Covent Garden, although he had been singing Wotan at Bayreuth for five years with Barenboim and was about to sing the role in the new Levine–Alfred Kirchner *Ring*.* Robert Henderson was not put off by Tomlinson's lack of a 'mellow, legato, philosophical performance', finding his rugged speech-song 'wonderfully truthful, superbly observed, profoundly moving'.[183] Later Milnes found that Tomlinson added some of the poet to his cobbler artisan, finding more legato and more variety of dynamics.[184] Tomlinson himself explained that he sought to portray Sachs as 'slightly eccentric, a bit of an odd man out. Crafty, intelligent with pain underneath, but he always jollies himself out of it. A Lancastrian streak!'[185]

Isaacs, intending to counteract the insidious and growing attack in the press on the senior arts in general and the Royal Opera House and himself in particular, decided to bring in a television company to film the company at work. Supported by Keith Cooper in charge of public relations, he believed that if it was seen what went into the running of such a complicated institution there would be greater understanding of the problems, as well as appreciation for the skills and initiative involved. Isaacs and Cooper also hoped to appeal directly to the public over the heads of the implacably hostile journalists, particularly of the *Sun*. Producer Andrew Bethell told the Board that his team 'hoped to capture the spirit of the House in all its glories and tensions'. It was not intended to be 'a PR exercise; he was confident, however, that the resulting programmes would be good for the House's image with the public'. They hoped to gain the trust of the staff and 'would promise in return not to abuse such trust'. The Board were persuaded.[186]

The House was made from September 1993 to August 1994 by Double Exposure, with executive producers Edward Mirzoeff and

---

* In an interview with Gillian Widdicombe in the *Independent* on 15 October 1993, Tomlinson expressed the belief that Wotan had brought his voice on 'in huge strides ... it puts the centre of gravity higher', and made the voice brighter and 'better placed'. He recalled singing in the chorus at Scottish Opera thirty years earlier: 'I thought I'd be a good Hagen because I had a big ugly voice. So boomy that at school, when I sang the hymn, everybody laughed. It was like giving birth to a monster even though there was no range at all, a range of only an octave.'

Andrew Bethell, and Michael Waldman for BBC 2. It was watched by up to 4 million people each week over four weeks. The decision to invite Waldman and his camera crew into the House turned out to be a serious error of judgement on Isaacs's part, particularly as he was himself an experienced television man who could have anticipated the kind of problems that were likely to arise. The programmes stressed rather than lessened the House's elitist and snobbish image, and added to it that of an uncaring and inefficient management. Isaacs later criticised the programmes, justifiably describing them not as 'documentary', but rather 'docu-soap'.[187]

The crew filmed whatever they liked, pouncing on weaknesses but never giving any indication that the season had had great artistic successes as well as a balanced budget by its end. Stories, such as the renegotiation of the stagehands' contracts, were begun for effect but not explained nor completed. Although the opening sequence of the series showed members of the Royal Ballet performing in a shopping centre in order to advertise the especially cheap performances during Hamlyn week, there was no further mention of the House's educational and outreach activities. These activities, which had been uninterrupted and growing since 1983, then included an extremely popular project called 'Chance to Dance', established in 1991 in conjunction with the Dance Theater of Harlem. By 2001 this scheme had given 14,439 children the chance to audition for a scholarship. Royal Opera artists and staff continued to volunteer their time for the educational projects. The House's educational activities remained unrecognised by the detractors and unsung by the institution itself.

There were some damaging scenes in the film showing Keith Cooper throwing tantrums and callously firing the box office manager, Andrew Follen, because he felt he would not be able to cope with the new technology.[188] Cooper was also seen on the programme dismissing Kevin McDermott of the Royal Opera House shop. Isaacs, who had hired him to 'market' the Royal Opera House, said of Cooper 'Managing staff was not his forte.'

The television series could not have come at a worse time, adding fuel to the anti-arts lobby. Hugues Gall, director of the Grand Théâtre of Geneva since 1981, was appalled by the erosion of arts subsidy in Britain in the 1980s and 1990s, and the consequent increasing dependence on private funding. His company received 75 per cent of its income from the Geneva taxpayer, and he still held the quaintly old-fashioned notion that 'the state provides not just for our physical health but our cultural well-being'. He defended the Royal Opera House, arguing that 'the ratio between quality and public subsidy is better than in any other country'. He continued, 'What British companies have achieved with limited resources is incredible. You can always make up to a certain extent with imagination, talent and management skills what you lack in money.' But he warned, 'National institutions should never be obliged to find so much private money. . . . As soon as you increase your dependence on private funding, by raising seat prices or giving blocks of tickets to sponsors, you change your public. It becomes less popular and often less discerning.'[189]

Hugues Gall's warning was constantly reflected in the television programme. One of the most damaging incidents was the much-quoted remark of a corporate donor to camera: 'We like it because it is elitist; that's why we like to come here' and he added that subsidy should 'be used to increase accessibility but not too much because part of what makes this place special is that the audience is special.' The damage to Covent Gardens public image was immediate and the programmes were repeated at home and abroad for many years to people who would never even know that it was stale and irrelevant news.

As Gall warned, the pressure for economising was beginning to damage standards as well as audience discernment. Financial discussions were patchily covered in the programme. In 1994 Isaacs was looking for £2.5 million in economies in the House as a whole – and £600,000 in the opera budget. Payne was seen on television explaining that he had already cut £1 million and asking the Board if they should cancel *Aida* next year. Isaacs suggested doing *Aida* with the Chippendales to cut costs on costumes.

The Arts Council and Warnock had asked for cut-price work, but when it was provided neither the public nor the critics liked it, and borrowing proved as risky for Payne as it had for his predecessor. When the successful Scottish Opera production of *Die Zauberflöte* was borrowed in November 1993, Rodney Milnes wrote, 'The first night of the Royal Opera's new *Die Zauberflöte* was so dispiriting that it is probably more profitable to examine the reasons behind it than to go into too much detail about the event itself.' Milnes reminded his readers that as Warnock had suggested long runs of popular works, *Die Zauberflöte* had been scheduled for fifteen performances, which was far longer than the usual length of run, with changes of cast. In Glasgow Martin Duncan's production had been zany and imbued with 'childlike fantasy'. It had been a cheap production with economical scenery relying on a youthful cast, including the young and extremely talented Simon Keenlyside, for its impact. It simply did not transfer to Covent Garden. One close observer said that on the Covent Garden stage the sets looked as though they had been made for *Blue Peter*, the children's television programme. Keenlyside was not available for Covent Garden and that 'ripped the heart out of it'. Conductor Andrew Parrot, with his 'bandmasterly beat at a steady *tempo ordinario*, achieved only an acceptable level of ensemble'. At £102 in the stalls and £37.50 in the amphitheatre, indulgence from the audience was at a premium. Milnes concluded, 'In practical terms, the Warnock principle – of cheap productions and popular works – has backfired disastrously. And after years of Dunkirk spirit somehow seeing us through, persistent underfunding is finally affecting artistic standards, and seriously.'[190] Nor did it help the box office – Cooper telling the Board on 30 November 1993 that the price schedule was 'too high for a long run'. Receipts were 'very poor'.[191]

Payne was seen in Waldman's film facing the Board and explaining in words that Findlay might have uttered, 'We went into the deals with our eyes open, but you can't always predict how these things will travel.' The last few months, he continued, had not been the House's 'finest hour' and in order to make the 1993–94 budget balance there had been an 'artistic hotchpotch', except for Findlay's October 1993 *Meistersinger.*

On 16 December Isaacs was told by Mary Allen, the deputy secretary general at the Arts Council, that there would be standstill funding for 1995–96, which meant in effect a cut of 6 per cent. The Royal Opera and Ballet companies' grant had been decreased by 18.3 per cent in four years. Isaacs was seen saying to camera: 'Although this is better than we feared (£370,000 better than we thought) it is still grim news for us.' His relations with the Arts Council chairman Peter Palumbo and secretary general Anthony Everitt had not improved. He angrily said to camera: 'They constantly deny us the funds to carry out their express wishes.'[192] Isaacs's main wish was to cut ticket prices as the box office was by then being adversely affected. Clive Timms told the Board that *Meistersinger*'s good box office had spoilt sales of *L'Italiana* and *Butterfly* because 'the House's audience did not feel rich enough to attend all three'.[193] The spare capacity in the House was now 24 per cent. On 19 April 1994 the ROH pledged to cut prices. While the Arts Council and the government evaded their responsibility for accessibility, the company members were bearing the brunt of the cutbacks. Bernard Haitink pointed out later, 'There are wonderfully dedicated people here who work really long hours for not much money. They never reach the front page because they work behind the scenes and it is sometimes amazing what Covent Garden is able to achieve with such reduced means.'[194]

In despair, opera managements, possibly inspired by Welsh National Opera's Matthew Epstein, got together to produce a document which tried to warn of the impending disaster facing the companies.* In February 1994 Epstein himself resigned from WNO after three years in the job. He cited 'the restrictions caused by central government arts funding'. Raised seat prices meant that the company 'couldn't continue to service a real public'. Cuts meant that 'the company spirit goes, morale is worn down'. He, like Gall, could not comprehend the lack of government support for what the British were best at – theatre, concerts, opera – and the failure to provide either a subsidy or tax cuts. 'To cut this enormously cultivated system down – it's a tragedy.'[195]

As Gall had warned, the audience was indeed getting less discerning. On 4 March 1994 there was an extraordinary collaboration for

---

* Milnes believed that it was Epstein who had written the document, as it expressed a certain amount of pride in British achievements under difficult circumstances – not least British singers, directors and designers being welcomed all over the world. Epstein was a New Yorker who started out twenty years earlier as an artists' manager for singers like von Stade, Ramey, Malfitano and Shicoff. He was artistic consultant to Lyric Opera of Chicago 1980.

Kát'a Kabanová, conducted by Haitink and directed by Trevor Nunn, designed by Maria Björnson, which had been planned by Paul Findlay. Good publicity pegged on Haitink's sixty-fifth birthday and radio programmes discussing Janáček's life had not succeeded in selling all the tickets for this superb collaboration: 'There was a depressing number of empty seats at the third performance of Janáček's *Kát'a Kabanová*, which only goes to show that rave reviews and true music drama don't necessarily cut much ice with the lumpen elements of public taste,' wrote Rupert Christiansen in the *Spectator*.

The *Kát'a* team, Porter wrote, powerfully conveyed the river constantly flowing throughout the piece, 'containing a timpani flood of inexorable fate, it is heard at the start, and it is heard at the close'. Porter described Maria Björnson's stage, which was set on a swirling, Munch-like river 'filling the stage with a spiral step down to the depths'. The set served to throw the action forward and allow the intense observation of Nunn's 'finely detailed, psychologically accurate account of the drama'. Once again Nunn demonstrated his gift for placing his finely drawn characters in a recognisable community – a small-town, stifling society. *Kát'a* introduced a Russian talent, Elena Prokina, who was another find from the Kirov and a formidable actress. Porter wrote that she sang softly and introspectively 'in timbres of unusual beauty and eloquence, with a purity and intensity of projection that filled the House' with 'her inestimable sadness and passionate desire to be free and find happiness'.[196]

The music director's empathy with Janáček's music and his subtle approach, brought out a finely modulated wealth of feeling: tenderness, compassion, intensity and ardently mourning passion. In an interview in March 1994 with Robert Henderson, Haitink explained the piece's appeal for him: 'I love it because it has this incredible – is it central European, or is it Slavonic? – hint of promise, this hint of a sort of liberation even in the most awful circumstances.' Janáček, he said, was 'such a human composer, with so deep an understanding of the human mind, and especially of women. He must have loved women very much, and that comes through in a very touching way.'

Sadly, it was not the passionate involvement of all those concerned in this moving and haunting production that caught the public imagination, but an incident during rehearsals shown in the television documentary. One of the horses in Act One fell through Björnson's fibreglass flooring, which had to be replaced at great expense. Equally damaging was the managerial muddle and overspend resulting from Björnson's work on *Sleeping Beauty* coinciding with *Kát'a* as a result of a change of scheduling. This created great pressures on the House's workshops and resulted in emergency funding being needed to get both completed on time. Because Trevor Nunn had rejected her first designs, the film was able to show an enraged Tessa Blackstone, chairman of the ballet Board, criticising Isaacs and the opera company for failure to co-ordinate. 'I think this is a really appalling story of incompetence,' she said to camera. Nicholas Payne pointed out that Björnson and Nunn were eminent artists and would do as they pleased. In the end both *Kát'a* and *Sleeping Beauty* were allowed to go slightly over budget – something that would have been remedied in the financial scrutinies to which the House was hitherto accustomed but was more ominous in the increasingly fraught atmosphere of the post-Philip Jones – post-Warnock era and as closure grew more imminent.

The television film had uncovered areas of discord and lack of communication within the organisation which were to overwhelm the House when the closure finally came. In the increasing bitterness one essential truth was lost, which was articulated by Trevor Nunn to Michael Waldman's camera: 'This is an expression of our culture, this is what we believe to be excellent and it should be collectively supported because it is to do with national identity and is of national significance.'[197]*

---

* Bjørnson was so distressed by the film that she considered giving up designing for the theatre. Graham Vick finally managed to persuade her to work on *Macbeth* at La Scala, and Zambello brought her back to Covent Garden for the 2002 *Don Giovanni*. She designed Zambello's Met *Trojans*, but died at the age of 53, in December 2002, before the production opened.

TWENTY-SIX

COVENT GARDEN 1994–97
'The Least-Cost Option'

THE NEW OPERA DIRECTOR, Nicolas Payne was more in harmony with Jeremy Isaac's more modernist inclinations although, in Philip Jones's words, Paul Findlay had had 'a feeling for the House and a warmth towards it that Nicholas never did'. Payne's first production, Massenet's *Chérubin*, was directed by Tim Albery, whom Isaacs had long wanted to see working at Covent Garden. Sutcliffe enjoyed its 'wickedly camp sense of absurdity'.[1] Rodney Milnes described it, 'with its near surrealist visual style' as 'a soufflé concocted from gossamer and thistledown'. It was, he said, 'so French as to make the Eiffel Tower look positively Teutonic'. Susan Graham, the American mezzo, was Chérubin. Milnes wrote, 'Her double-creamy mezzo goes up and up without either loss of quality or any hint of strain.' Angela Gheorghiu was 'just as ideal in the ingenue role of Nina'.[2] Isaacs was delighted with his new opera director: 'No one but Nicholas would have thought of giving us *Chérubin*,' he later wrote.[3]

Chérubin opened on St Valentine's Day, 14 February 1994, but it did not do well at the box office. The television programme showed the marketing department failing to make use of either the good reviews or its Valentine's Day opening to improve box office sales. Keith Cooper complained in front of the camera that Helen Anderson was too passive, having failed to place advertisements in the press. It was after the first night that Payne was caught saying to camera that he disliked hobnobbing with 'fucking raras'.

Payne's first season was no less fraught with financial pressures than that of his predecessor, and it continued to have what *Opera* dubbed a 'Warnockian' tinge, with poverty and the need for savings apparent. Although *Gawain* had been saved and, with lower seat prices, filled the House, there were sixteen *Carmens* and Anna Tomowa-Sintow sang *Tosca*, which replaced the planned revival of *Prince Igor*. In June 1994 Elijah Moshinsky's *Aida*, commissioned by Findlay, also clearly revealed at its premiere the enormous problems management faced. Shipping conglomerate P&O (Peninsular and Oriental Steam Navigation Company) who had sponsored the show with £275,000, complained that their logo was not prominent enough in the advertising. Their contribution was not sufficient, however, to prevent it looking, in Moshinsky's own words, 'a bit tacky and operatic'. There was, he reflected, 'no money at all for an opera that requires many changes of location'.[4] Although Peter Porter in the *Times Literary Supplement* wrote that there was much to be grateful for in Moshinsky's 'moderation and equanimity', he admitted that 'the problem of grandeur won't go away easily'.[5] *Aida* was Moshinsky's last new work at Covent Garden during the Payne administration.

The 1993–94 season was also the one when the Warnock and Price Waterhouse recommendations on union contracts had to be put into effect.* When closure had been planned for 1993 there had been no point in risking confrontation, but with the closure delayed to 1995 or even later, Isaacs decided to proceed with the negotiations.[6] BECTU – the Broadcasting Entertainment Cinematograph Technicians Union, representing 300 people involved in the running of the House – was the union which was to have its contracts renegotiated. The object was to secure a new cost-effective contract, whereby the twenty-eight men and one woman stage crew would end the three-day-week work practice, and would work a rostered shift system in four project teams of twelve people who would be assigned to particular productions. The crew would have to agree to be less specialised in what they were prepared to do, and undertake training courses so that different members of the crew could learn different skills. The contract would entail twenty-four redundancies, which management was prepared to meet through natural wastage and retirement.

The very tense negotiations were followed by the television team,

---

* The House's three unions were the Musicians' Union, Equity representing producers, chorus and dancers, and BECTU.

although not comprehensibly or comprehensively. In Isaacs's words, 'it was soundbites not explanation'.[7] Only after the outstanding issues were put to arbitration at ACAS on 21 July was agreement reached. The union accepted £27,000 a year rather than the £27,500 they had hoped for. The agreement made savings of £500,000 for the House. Isaacs later recalled that these negotiations did 'not take us the whole way that we needed to go to alter practice on the stage but they made a start'. Problems, he stressed, 'were blown grossly out of proportion'. He explained, 'The productivity of the ROH throughout this period was absolutely staggering, 260–270 performances a year on one stage is a remarkable state of affairs.' He contrasted Covent Garden's productivity with La Scala, La Monnaie and Vienna, which remains a repertory company 'where some things are not rehearsed at all'. Covent Garden, Isaacs stressed, continued its tradition of bringing 'collegiate groups of singers together for each individual production' and then keeping it in repertory. 'The result was that the demand on the stage was absolutely horrendous for seven days a week.'[8]

In September 1993 there was a major breakthrough in the prospects for the redevelopment, when Board member Stuart Lipton's company, Stanhope plc, was asked to look at the plans. Isaacs, who had been pressing for the elimination of the office block from the project, was delighted when Lipton declared that there was too much being squeezed on to the site. 'Offices won't pay anyway,' Lipton argued and continued, 'They were the 1980s, this is the 1990s.' Isaacs later wrote, 'This liberating view transformed the situation.' An even more crucial determining factor in a development without offices was the introduction of the National Lottery in October, three years after Mrs Thatcher, who had consistently opposed a lottery, had ceased to be Prime Minister. 'Government', wrote Isaacs of the lottery, 'had found a new way to house the arts, without spending a penny.'

In April 1994 Westminster Council recognised the 'substantial improvement' in the plans, which by then no longer included the office block and had also lowered the fly tower. Lord Gowrie took over the Arts Council from Palumbo, and Anthony Everitt, who had been deeply opposed to the redevelopment scheme, resigned as secretary general. On 30 June, in spite of opposition from the local Covent Garden community, Westminster City Council granted planning permission for the next phase of the redevelopment.

While the plans for redevelopment made progress, its funding arrangements with the Arts Council and the government remained undecided. The Waldman – Mirzoeff film covered part of the period from 1994 to 1995 when discussions were being held about the closure, including a meeting on 17 February 1994 between Sir James Spooner and Jeremy Isaacs for the Royal Opera House, and Peter Gummer and Mary Allen (deputy secretary general, Arts Council) for the Joint Action Committee of the Arts Council.* Lottery tickets were to go on sale in November 1994 and applications would be invited at the beginning of 1995. The Royal Opera House would be applying for lottery funding of no less than £45 million, Isaacs explained before the cameras. A public appeal as well as sale of property would provide the rest.

Isaacs and Spooner asked the Joint Action Committee to agree that it was sensible to apply, and also asked how the companies would be sustained during closure. Peter Gummer demanded more financial details, while an increasingly angry and frustrated Isaacs explained there were as yet no details, as there was still no decision from the Arts Council as to what the companies were expected to do during closure. Gummer did not respond to Isaacs's argument that during the closure period the companies would need an extra £4.5 million a year, suggesting instead that the Council had not agreed to subsidise the House at all during the rebuilding, and that the whole company might have to close down. Sir James Spooner, deputy chairman of the Covent Garden Board, argued that there would be no sponsorship for the bricks and mortar without the companies. Isaacs was enraged by the Arts Council's refusal to come clean. 'No other society would behave like this,' he said angrily, 'that's like saying "fuck it, we don't want you any more" – you cannot provide the arts in this country on the basis of the least-cost option – the least-cost option is no art.'

The new European Union Health and Safety regulations meant

---

* Mary Allen took over from Everitt at the Arts Council as secretary general later in 1994. That July Stephen Dorrell became the new Secretary of State for National Heritage.

the House had to be closed no later than 1997. During a performance of *Carmen* with Domingo in May 1994, rain coming in through the roof above the amphitheatre caused distress not so much because of the wetness but because of the 'noise of the drips'.[9] 'Every other great city in Europe has rebuilt its opera houses since the war,' Isaacs told Simon Tait of *The Times* on 12 January 1995, 'but we have not.' He added. 'It is a national shame.'

While Covent Garden struggled to obtain funding for its redevelopment, George Christie had successfully raised £34 million: 75 per cent from companies and 25 per cent from individuals; and supervised the development of the warm and beautiful new House at Glyndebourne. The old House had been in a very shaky condition and, in the words of John Jolliffe, there was a need 'to do something to meet the ever-increasing and excessive demand for tickets, which so often caused chagrin and disappointment among the opera-loving public'.[10] The architects were Michael and Patty Hopkins, with John Bury acting as a consultant.* The new House opened in May 1994 with Haitink conducting Gerald Finley, Renée Fleming and Alison Hagley in *Figaro*. Milnes described the acoustics in the new House as 'warm, anything but dry, all-enveloping, yet still amazingly clear'.[11]

Graham Vick, as director of productions at Glyndebourne from 1994, presided over changes and controversy. His first season included Deborah Warner's *Don Giovanni*, conducted by Simon Rattle with the Orchestra of the Age of Enlightenment. Milnes described their sound as 'warm, seductive, almost romantic' and the mood as one of 'ever-present danger' in what is 'a dangerous opera'.[12] The production, in modern dress, with Gilles Cachemaille's very nasty Don, and his indignities on a plaster statue of the Madonna, caused loud booing, and music director Andrew Davis to comment that there was less dialogue between director and conductor than there had been in the Ebert–Busch era.[13]

Anthony Whitworth-Jones's last season as chief administrator was 1995, when Nicholas Snowman took over. The 1995 season saw Graham

* Bury died on 12 November 2000, aged seventy-five.

Vick's production of *Ermione* and Birtwistle's *The Second Mrs Kong*. The 'pace of change' continued in 1998 with Nicholas de Lajatre–Pascale Cazales's production of Handel's *Rodelinda*, conducted by William Christie with the Orchestra of the Age of Enlightenment. Milnes wrote that Christie's 'faultless dramatic structure of each act', together with the fine cast, compensated for the stage business of the updated production, which was nevertheless 'utterly at odds with a hymn to marital fidelity as serious as *Fidelio* itself'.[14] Stage business included Kurt Streit as a lounge-lizard cad and Anna Caterina Antonacci's Rodelinda crawling up the walls in terror. German counter-tenor Andreas Scholl's voice was according to Milnes, 'phenomenally beautiful, pure, sweet-toned, agile, and it is allied to a musical imagination of the highest order'.

Vick's own direction was erratic. His *Pelléas* in 1999 was visually gorgeous, set as Canning wrote in an 'haut-bourgeois turn-of-the-century salon – with water cascading down the stairwell for the fountain scene and with its undulating see-through floor encasing hundreds of yellow and orange chrysanthemums'. The characterisation, however, lacked definition and eroticism – particularly in the love scene when Mélisande was required to lean backwards out of a giant light fitting. Canning felt that Vick was spreading himself too thinly.[15] John Tomlinson's Golaud dominated the evening, while Milnes felt that Andrew Davis gave a 'bland if beautiful account of the score'.[16]

The 18 July 2000 *Don Giovanni*, did little to mitigate this concern, with its pile of something brown on the floor and a disembowelled horse in the last act. Milnes thought that 'narrative values' were ignored and that it was 'negligible musically'. 'Mozart', he wrote, 'has never been Davis's bag. He beat time efficiently without ever suggesting what the music was saying.' It had been, he went on, 'a boring pointless evening'.[17] On 1 January 2000 Andrew Davis moved to Chicago, leaving Glyndebourne and the BBC. Nicholas Snowman left after his first season. In 2001 David Pickard, whose time at Kent Opera had been curtailed by the company's cruel demise, succeeded Snowman as director general. His appointment, together with Gus Christie taking over from his father as executive chairman, and Vladimir Jurowski as music director, completed a young management team.

*　　*　　*

Artistically, Isaacs's regime at Covent Garden continued to be exciting and well received, the 1994–95 season boasting 91 per cent audiences. Isaacs later wrote that 'Payne got into his stride the next season' with Jonathan Miller's belated debut at Covent Garden directing *Così*, Luc Bondy's shared *Salome* from the 1992 Salzburg Festival starring Malfitano and Terfel, and Francesca Zambello's shared *Billy Budd* from Geneva. One of the greatest successes was the Solti–Eyre *Traviata*, planned by Findlay. New to Covent Garden, but borrowed productions, included *Fedora* and Gounod's *Roméo et Juliette* from Toulouse and Paris Opéra Comique with Leontina Vaduva and Roberto Alagna. *Roméo* won the Olivier award for outstanding achievement in opera for 1994. Revivals included the Schaaf *Figaro* with Terfel and Sylvia McNair, and *Turandot* conducted by Gatti.

The season got off to a controversial start in October 1994 when the House presented its new *Ring* cycle. Payne had commissioned director Richard Jones and designer Nigel Lowery after their Scottish Opera *Ring*. By that time, according to Findlay, Haitink had 'washed his hands of it' and said 'get on with it'. One of the most damaging scenes in Mirzoeff's film showed Bernard Haitink looking at the *Ring* models without either the designer or the director present. Haitink sighs deeply and sadly while Payne tries to explain that the model symbolises the image of time passing. Haitink responds, 'What can I say ... will the audience understand this? Even at first viewing – I find it difficult to understand what he means ... the car image ... I'm not happy with it ... Maybe I'm too old-fashioned.' Payne suggests tactics to deal with Lowery, by concentrating on the car, which they are all very unhappy with, and conceding in other areas. Haitink says plaintively, 'You can't ignore everything that Wagner wanted – it will end that I don't play the music any more ... an electronic tape.' But rehearsals were well advanced by the time Haitink saw the sets and the car, along with much else, stayed in. Findlay later recalled, 'Bernard in the end can cave in because he is pragmatic: "I want to make that piece of music – I'll never do another *Ring*. I've got to do another *Ring* – I won't look at it." '[18]

That the cameras captured Haitink accepting something he was so clearly unhappy with, and to see Payne bargaining concessions with the production team, was demeaning and did little to win public confidence. When asked later if it had been a mistake to let the cameras in, Jeremy Isaacs said it had been a 'mixed blessing'. He had been disappointed it had not 'done the House more good'.[19]

Richard Jones, in an interview with Peter Conrad in the *Observer* on 2 October 1994, explained that his view of Wagner was Latin and sensuous, and one in which the colours were bright – yellow and green rather than Jungian and dark. He went on to tell Conrad, 'Wagner was a great theatrical imaginist. That is, when he wasn't being a stupid git philosophising.' Canning thought this sentiment summed up Jones himself, and described Jones as a Jekyll and Hyde character who was one of the most 'probing, fascinating, unnerving, even infuriating of imaginations among contemporary stage directors'. He also felt that it is when he is in partnership with the 'artistically challenged' Nigel Lowery 'that the monster within emerges'.*[20]

Jones's *Ring* cycle divided critics and audiences alike from its inception with *Rheingold* in October 1994 to its completion with *Götterdämmerung* in October 1995. The new *Rheingold* gave the cycle a particularly colourful and controversial launch. After Haitink and the singers had been warmly applauded, producer and designer were greeted with what David Murray in the *Financial Times* described as 'howls of fury on a truly Wagnerian scale'. *Rheingold* was, he wrote, 'unforgivably silly, facetious, inconsequent, *diminishing*'. On 14 October Dalya Alberge, *The Times*'s arts correspondent, described the production as 'near slapstick comedy', with Rhinemaidens in padded latex costumes and Alberich in frogman's flippers and a comedian's trilby. Tomlinson's Wotan was a 'lollipop man in white coat with his spear as a striped pole surmounted in a one-way sign',† Valhalla was a giant

---

* Jones had directed *Love of Three Oranges* for Opera North and ENO, *Pelléas* for Opera North, and Sondheim's *Into the Woods*. Jones explained in his interview with Conrad that the drop curtain with a French ballerina atop a crocodile with a Greek pan-pipe player balanced on the crocodile's 'tail was supposed to be reminiscent of Picasso's designs for Milhaud's Ballet *Le Train bleu* but the *Guardian* thought it more Beryl Cook than Picasso, When questioned as to its meaning, Jones grins enigmatically and refuses to decide' (15.10.94).

† Peter Hall later drew a lesson from the lollipop: 'Wotan wandering about as a lollipop man, with a lollipop – an actor wouldn't do that. He'd say, "This is daft. What does it mean?" Singers are very, very obedient. Because of their musical training, because of their integrity. It's a good thing. Singers do exactly what you tell them. The problem is that some of them don't do more than what you tell them. But I know no actor I know

orange chimney and the whole opera ended up with the Gods dancing a silly dance.

In *Walküre* Milnes, showing a greater talent for decoding than some of his colleagues, detected an ecological theme in the 'wounded tree of Hunding's house' and references to genetic engineering in Wotan's role as a spare parts surgeon. He found the evening 'positively provocative'.[21] After analysing the development of Wagner production since the war, David Murray seemed almost nostalgic for a conceptual production, concluding that the trouble with Lowery's and Jones's production was that 'it is a purely postmodernist affair, where the designer's fancies have equal weight with anything else'. This *Rheingold*, he wrote, 'founders upon inconsequence and sheer lack of purpose'.

Sutcliffe, however, was delighted by the work of the 'hyperactive theatrical wizards who believe in colour and wit and irreverent stage business'.[22] Nor was he perturbed by the obscurities, writing:

> Jones's purpose was simply the latest stage in repossessing the Wagner heritage, as reflected in the philosophical and moral consequences of his work – the German fascism to which Wagner's ambivalent genius however regrettably contributed as godfather ... Jones at last and very subtly placed the Hitler issue on the stage, also internationalising the problem ... the references in Lowery's design to a whale, like the cut-outs of bull, horse and ram suspended over the stage in *Die Walküre*, were obscure ... aimed at a new symbolism to engender a puzzled response rather than confident familiarity. Lowery's outlandish ideas finally amounted to an autonomous and coherent vocabulary of symbols and colours.[23]

Andrew Porter, a long way from his 1970s Rhine journey ideal, was also impressed, and relieved to be removed from the Met's romantic 'idea-free, Disneyesque staging' of the *Ring*. He welcomed Jones's presentation of *Rheingold* in the comic style, finding it full of 'unusual imagery, high-spirited, often playful, sometimes piercing'. At least he did not seem to be 'ramming home any tiresome concept'.[24] Seckerson

---

would have played Wotan with a lollipop.' Syrus corrected the impression that singers are too obedient, recalling, 'In fact, John Tomlinson did ask. Richard would have talked at great length about that. I think that's unfair to singers to suggest that they are not as intellectually demanding' (Interview, 28.11.00).

of the *Independent* urged audiences, 'Prepare to be a child again, prepare to shed all preconceptions.' It was, he said, 'back to the playpen, folks'.[25]

By the time the cycle was completed, the critics were largely agreed that Jones and Lowery displayed a combination of extraordinary imagination and inventiveness with downright perversity and infantile childishness, and that the completed cycle ended with a slight whimper. They were also in awe of Haitink's increasingly commanding and magisterial interpretation, which was totally at odds with the near slapstick activities on stage. Robert Henderson in the *Daily Telegraph* wondered if Lowery and Jones were 'sending up Wagner's pomposity', but if so they were working with the wrong conductor. Haitink remained deeply unhappy with the production, conducting 'the soundtrack to a different show'.[26] When he accepted the *Evening Standard* award for best opera production of 1994 he said, 'There's a lot of irony in my standing here. I am not the producer, only the conductor, who by definition must argue with the director' and added, 'Not every professional in the business liked it.'[27]

Where the *Ring* is concerned, however, the music determines success or failure, and the production did not impede Haitink from realising his musical aims. As Findlay commented, 'Bernard was loved by the orchestra; it was the one solid basis of it all. And it didn't matter what happened with the productions, how they were reviewed. If the music was right that brought a lot of prestige to the House.'[28] The 1994 *Walküre* was indeed a study in warmth, intelligence and balance. While not neglecting Wagner's occasional pagan outpourings, Haitink chose to stress the tender, compassionate moments of the score. Grief, loss and the lyric sweetness of love were clearly set forth; mania and rage downplayed. Dynamics were carefully layered, providing breadth for the climactic moments to shine forth. Since Haitink, the master of fairness, set out each dramatic moment on its own merits, the flow of the work became transparent – even though a tendency to understatement might disappoint the listener accustomed to traditionally bloated fortes. Covent Garden's dialoguing orchestra was at its finest – Haitink playing lines, colours and choirs off against each other to brilliant dramatic-musical effect.

It was also generally agreed that the casting was on an extremely high level. Deborah Polaski's Brünnhilde maintained her dignity in spite of a demeaning costume resembling a St Trinian's gymslip skirt over a black tracksuit painted with the white outlines of a skeleton. Jane Henschel was a remarkable Fricka. Tomlinson gave the 'performance of his career' as Wotan. According to Milnes he began as a 'jaunty, larky tyrant' and ended as 'an empty defeated husk'.[29] In *Götterdämmerung*, in March 1996, Anne Evans was a Brünnhilde of touching warmth and dignity, and in October, Kurt Rydl a terrifyingly dark Hagen.

Although the comic strip caricature approach tended to provoke alienation and even indifference to the plight of the protagonists on the part of the audience, Payne was content, writing of Lowery and Jones in the Annual Report that the 'denial of late nineteenth-century Romanticism has dismayed some people' but that he found their work 'rigorously truthful, responsive to music and text'.

The rest of the season was equally stimulating but less controversial. The last of Findlay's planning triumphs was Solti's first *Traviata* in November 1994. Solti had chosen to work with Richard Eyre, the director of the National Theatre. Eyre's straightforward yet tellingly detailed direction, and Bob Crowley's uncluttered and effective decor, caught the mood of each scene. Solti also chose the young Romanian, Angela Gheorghiu, to be his Violetta. Findlay recalled, 'We heard her four times. . . . Her voice wasn't big enough, she was pushing and pushing, and he kept saying give her one more chance and it worked.' They were vindicated – the critics seeing the performance as the birth of a 'new opera star'. Michael Kennedy felt that Gheorghiu sang with 'overwhelming tragic power and realism' in an 'almost unbearably poignant and vulnerable interpretation . . . ineradicable from the memory'. He saw it as an occasion when 'a singer lays claim to an inseparable association with a role'.[30] Canning described her voice as 'true, steady, ductile, with a dark attractive lustre' and was struck by her '*fil di voce* beautifully sustained . . . gradations refined and gentle'.[31] Solti's own first loving *Traviata* was also praised by Porter, who wrote that Solti's 'preludes had the detailed emotional inflection of a Mahler adagio'.[32]

On 18 January 1995 Jonathan Miller made his belated debut at

Covent Garden with a *Così* of 'bitterness and pain in reconciliation', and with inspired casting that included Ann Murray as Despina and Thomas Allen as Don Alfonso – a cynic, in Milnes's words, with 'a vein of steel, a cool indifference to the turbulences and tempests of silly youth'.*[33] The young talents were Bruce Ford, Amanda Roocroft, Susan Graham and Simon Keenlyside. Keenlyside, a naturally talented and versatile actor, had made his first impact as a brilliant Papageno in Scottish Opera's notorious *Magic Flute* in February 1993, just as Thomas Allen had twenty-four years before in Wales. Keenlyside's debut at Covent Garden had been in 1989 as Silvio, and he sang the Count as well as Guglielmo in 1995, but much of his work until then had been abroad with Muti and Abbado. Edward Seckerson, in his review of *Così* in the *Independent*, described Keenlyside as 'a natural stage animal whose easy physicality gives him such potential'.†[39]

Luc Bondy's riveting *Salome*, which was shared with the Salzburg Festival, reached London on 11 March 1995 after travelling as an ensemble since 1992 from Salzburg to Brussels and Florence. According to Canning, by the time the production reached Covent Garden it had 'matured like a good wine'.‡ Designer Erich Wonder's abstract and suggestive, set together with Susanne Raschig's costumes, placed the piece in a 'crumbling and lugubrious black and grey salon in Herod's palace'. Within this frame Bondy focused 'uncompromising attention on *Salome* as a horrific and nauseating family catastrophe'. Bondy's show was extremely well prepared, bringing out the dramatic capacities of the singers to the utmost, and ensuring fine ensemble acting with careful attention to movement and gesture.

Bryn Terfel recalled how Bondy 'worked on the chemistry' between

---

* Miller had declined to direct *Forza* in 1979, an invitation that he described as 'like being invited to defuse an IRA car bomb parked on the corner of Floral Street'. He had not been asked again until this *Così* (*Opera*, February 1994).

† Keenlyside spent six years singing in the Cambridge Choir School, but his love of animals brought him to study zoology at Cambridge. He then studied at the Royal Northern College of Music under John Cameron. He spent three years at Hamburg Opera where he did everything with little or no rehearsal, then went on to Scottish Opera. Keenlyside had been working for Muti at La Scala and sang Don Giovanni for Abbado in 1997, recording the part with Abbado in early 1997.

‡ Fifty-year-old Bondy was born in Switzerland. He studied with Jacques Lecoq in Paris before working in Germany in the 1980s, including as director of the Schaubühne 1985–87. He produced plays as well as opera all over Europe.

himself and Malfitano, whom he described as 'this beast of a Salome who jumps on John the Baptist and scratches him and pushes him and does everything to tempt him'. He ended up, he recalled 'with many scratches on my back and legs and arms' and concluded, 'Salome really put me on the road.'[35] Terfel's Jokanaan produced a furiously ecstatic roar, with his vocal openness matched by involved physical acting full of chaotic movements and gestures. His Jokanaan was deeply torn from moment to moment, caught between his prophetic destiny and his virile nature. Catherine Malfitano's lyric soprano was pushed to the limit by Strauss's dense, powerful orchestral writing, and a strident forte was occasionally the outcome. More often, however, she marshalled her vocal resources and put them carefully to work in tandem with her remarkable dramatic flair. The critics were impressed. Henderson wrote that she and Terfel 'generated an electrifying intensity and sexual danger' enacting a 'tempestuous battle of wills terrifying, grippingly powerful and menacingly erotic'.[36] There was a rapturous reception for the ensemble of stars, who also included Anja Silja's Herodias, and for Dohnányi's 'magisterial control'.[37]

The redevelopment now depended on a successful bid to the National Lottery. Isaacs had intended to leave Covent Garden in 1995, as he was involved in a twenty-four-part television series, Cold War. When the rebuilding was postponed, however, he decided to stay until the closure. He later said the ensuing two years were among the most difficult of his life. In order to obtain the lottery grant, extraordinarily detailed and extensive answers to hundreds of questions had to be prepared and, as Isaacs noted, 'each assertion backed by consultants'. Keith Cooper worked on this project throughout 1994.[38]

The single most crucial and still unresolved question remained that of running costs during the closure. It was extremely hard to predict income during closure while there was no decision on the venue and the level of activity. Although the Arts Council recognised the need for the companies to 'remain in being',[39] it still would not make a commitment as to how far it was prepared to support the House's running costs during closure. Furthermore, the lottery guidelines specifically precluded the provision of revenue.

It was also still not clear where the companies would be housed during the closure. The search for a suitable venue had been going on for many years. Technical director John Harrison knew every theatre in London in detail and Isaacs had himself often accompanied him during the 'several years of search'.[40] The Theatre Royal Drury Lane was the most suitable potential venue, with an adequate stage that had once been home to opera, a scene-dock capable of conversion, and ample seating and public spaces.* Amid rumours that the musical *Miss Saigon*'s box office was failing at Drury Lane, Isaacs had allowed himself to be 'strung along by sweet-talk propositions' from theatre impresario Cameron Mackintosh from 1993 to 1994.[41] By April 1994, however, some members of the Board were beginning to realise that 'the prospect of delivering the Drury Lane plan was remote'. Cameron Mackintosh was suggesting that Covent Garden should buy and refurbish the Lyceum Theatre instead.[42] The Lyceum Theatre option had, however, major disadvantages. The theatre would need capital investment, as not a single existing ballet or opera set would fit on its stage, and there was no indication the Arts Council would cover the extra costs entailed in using the theatre. In June Covent Garden learnt that the Apollo Leisure group were buying the Lyceum.

By September 1994 Drury Lane was looking extremely unlikely and the new owners of the Lyceum, Apollo Leisure, wanted the Royal Opera to sign up the Lyceum Theatre. Although one member of the Board suggested 'that this would give the House much needed certainty' the decision was still not taken.[43] Nor was a decision possible about the level of activity to be pursued by the companies. When costings were made for the closure in October 1994, it was estimated that no activity would cost £34.7 million gross; 'suspended animation' – which entailed a core staff with facilities for rehearsal and practice – would cost £37.3 million gross; and the Lyceum with 200 performances £49.7 million. Assuming that the Arts Council grant would be maintained, the Lyceum option left what was described as 'an extremely troublesome financing gap' of £20.5 million. The Arts Council were making no intimations that they were willing to cover

---

* Tooley had even made an unsuccessful attempt to buy the theatre in anticipation of development, but its owner, Robert Holmes à Court's Stoll Moss, had adamantly refused (Tooley, *In House*, p. 244).

it nor that it could be covered by the lottery under its guidelines.[44]

On 29 November 1994 the idea of an ad hoc construction, possibly in Hyde Park or Battersea, seemed to offer a way out of the impasse. At that time Isaacs rejected Ian Albery's offer to co-ordinate his time-table for the Royal Opera to use the newly refurbished Sadler's Wells, which it was felt would be too small, with 400 fewer seats than the Lyceum. It was not certain that it would be ready in time.[45]

The problem was still not resolved when the application to the lottery was made. According to Isaacs, there was no dispute with Peter Gummer and the Arts Council as to whether the Royal Opera should ask the government to subsidise the running costs or whether to put in a supplementary request to the lottery, for the simple reason that they had been a 'passive non-actor in the whole of this affair'. At the last moment Gummer, as chairman of the lottery advisory panel, advised that the Royal Opera House should make a request for additional funds 'not as the essence of the application but not separate from it either'.[46] As Isaacs recalled, 'They fudged the conditions that they themselves had attached to the lottery grant. They admitted to us and to themselves that funds that were supposed to be for capital could actually be devoted to revenue, provided it could be seen that the revenue arose directly from the effect of the closure.'[47]

Isaacs decided to add the figure of £20 million for running costs. As he later wrote, 'This sum was the largest I dared imagine we hoped to receive. In the event it was to prove inadequate.' If he had asked for £30 million, he later admitted, the next two years could have been a different story.[48] The revenue costs of leaving the opera house turned out to have been much greater than he anticipated. A further £17 million was needed in the end to get the company through closure even with minimum activity.*

---

* The ex-finance director, Philip Jones, believed that with his long experience he might have provided a more realistic estimate. 'With the benefit of hindsight', he later explained, that his team would have looked carefully with their knowledge and experience 'at the costs associated with the closed period and at the same time how much there would be of a drop in our working capital as a result of lower box office and then arranged finance for that'. There would have had to have been 'very modest seasons, with very modest income coming in and a decline in private funding because of the requirement for capital funding. One would have reflected this early on and said, "You have an untenable closure period. You can't do it on £20 million"' (Interview, 6.1.00).

Although there were near fatal financial repercussions resulting from the redevelopment, the Royal Opera House's case for receiving a lottery grant was very strong. As Isaacs put it:

> From a weekly spasm of gambler's optimism which would raise £4 billion a year, the public was being asked to stump up £58.5 million towards the cost of a national lyric theatre, attended by 600,000 souls a year, its music enjoyed by millions on radio and its spectacle by millions on television. The total sum being applied for, including £20 million for the closure period, was under £80 million. This represented less than a third of Lottery income to the arts in one year.[49]

Isaacs could later have added that the lottery contribution to the project was less than three months of extra funding on top of the original £700 million cost used to keep the Millennium Dome afloat during the autumn of 2000, not to mention the £40 million spent on insurance and maintenance between the Dome's closure in December and May 2002.*

On 4 January 1995 Isaacs, Thomas Allen and Simon Keenlyside, with Darcy Bussell and Bruce Sansom of the Royal Ballet, handed in the Royal Opera House's application for lottery funding. The Royal Opera would be applying for £78.5 million as a contribution to the total cost, which was £198.5 million. The rest would be raised from an appeal for private funding of £70 million and the realisation of property at £70 million. The public appeal would be led by Vivien Duffield and Lord Sainsbury.†

The pre-closure period was fraught with indecision combined with a lack of realism. In January 1995, just as the lottery application was being finalised, the Board were 'urgently examining the scope for

---

* Revenue from the lottery had been far greater than anyone had envisaged – the draw on 19 November 1994 having brought in £48.9 million. By January, when the Royal Opera House made its bid, the five good causes, the arts, sport, heritage, charities and the Millennium (which was to include the Millennium Dome at £750 million plus), stood to benefit by as much as £250 million.

† Of Duffield and Sainsbury, Isaacs later wrote, 'In the last matters of design, from options Dixon and Jones and Mlinaric put in front of them, what these two wanted they got. When they disagreed, the rest of us ducked for cover. With John Sainsbury, Vivien Duffield was the dominant personality on the Board in my time, and, in spite of her lively temper, a great force for good' (Isaacs, Never Mind the Moon, p. 225).

constructing a temporary theatre'. It could be built in fifteen months with a 2,500 capacity at a cost of £8 million. Mary Allen and Lord Gowrie at the Arts Council urged Isaacs and the Board to go to the Lyceum, as it would make a permanent addition to London's available theatres.[50] On 29 April, however, the Board agreed with Isaacs that the Lyceum would be 'expensive, unpleasant and difficult to operate'.[51] In May, Isaacs was considering delaying the closure.

Isaacs was stressed by the mounting pressure and in the spring of 1995 the Board considered asking him to leave.* Instead, they suggested that he relinquish the artistic planning for the closure period, when he would no longer be with the company. Payne took this on, together with Clive Timms, the finance director.† The Board told Isaacs that plans should be made with the looming closure challenges taken into account. At its 27 March meeting it was stressed that it was essential that the company did not return to deficit funding at such a crucial time, with the appeal about to be launched. It was also pointed out that the appeal was bound to affect funding for current operations. Isaacs's budget proposal for the 1995–96 season appeared to be 'based on a range of seemingly optimistic proposals'. He urged the Board to approve the budget with the proviso that he would review the situation month by month and raise the contingency to £400,000. By the time of the next meeting no such contingency had been raised and Pavarotti's cancellation of Ballo was costing up to £60,000 extra.[52]

Isaacs received a letter from Stirling to the effect that the 1995–96 budget was not viable, and that the finance and audit committee should review it again before the next Board meeting. Stirling urged that a 'realistic pay award' be pursued. Isaacs did not respond to the immediate problem, replying on 6 April 1995, 'In no year that I can remember, since I became general director, has it been possible to provide in our budget for a wage increase and a contingency beyond that. We do not even in what you might call an ordinary year have

---

* Isaacs in his memoirs referred to an incident the previous summer when he had failed to deal with a document concerning the terms on which some consultants were to work for the Royal Opera House. This had led to a claim that had shocked the Board and they decided that he had too much on his plate, with the development as well as the normal workload Never Mind the Moon, p. 275).

† Mike Morris was renegotiating the union agreements and overseeing the growing number of redundancies.

the resource or the reserve to fund both.' Isaacs urged the Trust to bring in more money. The situation revealed once again, he wrote, 'the serious, structural underfunding of activity from which we suffer'. He added optimistically, 'Let us hope that new sources of revenue will underpin the work of the redeveloped Royal Opera House.'[53]

By the summer there was the very real prospect of a substantial deficit after three years of surplus. Donations that would have gone to the revenue account were instead going to the appeal. The Trust's fund-raising activity had declined from £7.2 million in 1994–95 to £4.8 million in 1995–96. Box office in the summer of 1995 was also disappointing, in spite of excellent shows including *Billy Budd* and *Stiffelio*.*

The problem of a venue for closure had still not been solved, and in April, just as the reality of the double fund-raising was becoming apparent, it emerged that Southwark Council were keen to see a site near Tower Bridge developed. It was close to Shakespeare's Globe and what was to be the new Tate Modern. Covent Garden prepared a scheme for a temporary, inexpensive 2,500-seat theatre. Such a theatre could be designed to fit the existing sets and more of the present staff could be kept on, to go back to the new House.[54] Timms reported to the Board that the scheme would cost up to £17,317,000.[55]

The Lyceum needed an answer by July, which was two months before the planning decisions were to be taken for the proposed purpose-built theatre. The Arts Council were still warning of the potential pitfalls, such as possible archaeological finds or trouble with the Secretary of State for the Environment, John Gummer, but the Board were unanimously behind the project. The new theatre would cost £5 million less than to prepare the Lyceum, and would bring in new audiences and more revenue, while avoiding 300 staff redundancies. Even if Gummer called in the planning application there was still enough time, Isaacs told the Board. Gummer had told Isaacs that he would be as helpful as he could, while not making any commitment.[56] Southwark Council gave planning permission as part of a scheme to regenerate areas south of the river.

---

* After what Isaacs called Chancellor of the Exchequer Lawson's 'boomlet', many of the companies that had sponsored productions fell on hard times, like Polly Peck and Barings.

The Royal Opera's application for £78.5 million from the Arts Council lottery advisory panel was successful, and was announced by the chairman of the Arts Council, Lord Gowrie, on 21 July 1995. It was to be paid in two tranches: £55 million to enable the project to proceed and the balance of £23.5 million on receipt of satisfactory plans for the closure period. At the same time the ENO was to receive £1,384,000 to carry out a comparative study on the best way to proceed with its own redevelopment. Other grants of a similar size were being considered for the Tate, Welsh National Opera and Salford Arts Centre. Gowrie urged that there should be close supervision of the Covent Garden project by the Board.

Much of the press response to the House's successful bid was hostile. Murdoch's *Sun* was the most virulent, setting up a hotline for readers to register their opposition to the lottery grant for the 'Greedy Beggar's opera'. They inaccurately claimed that 'working-class punters' were providing £100 million (rather than the accurate figure of £70 million) for a minority pastime for the well-heeled rather than giving to genuine causes. Milnes in *Opera* criticised the poverty-stricken Royal Opera's handing out its press release on a thick red cardboard folder with gold edging while providing a table 'groaning with smoked salmon sandwiches'.[57]

The populist, right-wing, anti-culture *Daily Mail* raged that the lottery was 'robbing the poor to help the rich'. Martin Kettle in the left-wing *Guardian* concurred: 'The poor pay the money and the rich get most of the rewards.' However, Kettle wanted it both ways, warning that there was a danger of losing the capital's international House if it did not get a proper grant.[*58] As Tom Sutcliffe explained to American readers in *Opera News* in November 1995, 'Ancient British prejudice against opera resurfaced, especially in June when two reporters from Rupert Murdoch's *Sun* were sent to pay top price for tickets to the Royal Opera's *Stiffelio*, rented dinner suits (which were certainly not *de rigueur* for their visit) then left at the intermission, blaming not deadlines but deadly boredom with the tunes and absurd plot.' Isaacs wrote:

---

* The *Guardian* at least had the grace to put the attack in the context of its dislike for lotteries in general, quoting Adam Smith's dictum, 'The lottery is a tax on foolishness.'

On the next morning's television Keith Cooper was asked how he could justify an award to an opera house instead of towards providing more kidney dialysis machines; the questioner depended for her life on one. It was not easy, with a studio audience baying for blood, to point out the false dichotomy. Society can have both if it chooses.[59]

The public relations problems were not improved by the timing of the announcements of the next lottery grants by the new Minister of State at National Heritage, Virginia Bottomley. One was a massive grant of over £700 million for the Millennium Dome and the other a £13.2 million grant to purchase the Churchill papers from the wealthy grandson of the former prime minister.* Both grants were made before any charitable or sporting allocations had been announced, because other charities had failed to organise themselves in time to make early applications. The government were embarrassed by the lack of popular applicants who had not prepared in time, but it was the Royal Opera House that caught the flak. Neither the government nor the Arts Council did anything to defend the House and its grant. In Isaacs's words, Virginia Bottomley, remained 'inscrutably, unhelpfully silent'.†[60]

The hostile press reaction was not the only element in the House's nearly disastrous venture into the unknown. Two further near-fatal issues continued to dominate: one was the growing daily involvement of the Board in the running of the House during the closure, and the other was the failure to find a suitable venue for the companies for the closure period. The first became apparent when the appeal was to about to be launched. It would be, Vivien Duffield told the Board on 10 July, the 'most challenging and unpopular appeal ever launched in

---

* The Millennium Dome, to be built on a 130-acre site, was intended to portray British culture with trade-show presentations, multimedia theme-park attractions and virtual-reality displays.

† There were reports in the *Daily Mail* that Bottomley was under pressure from Cabinet ministers to veto Covent Garden's allocation. She was reported as saying that she wanted clearer guidelines about the distribution of money, which was the sole responsibility of the Arts Council, and that she wanted to 'wrest back control of arts policy from the luvvies and elitists' (21.7.95).

the donor market'. On 17 July she argued that 'there would need to be a major change in the attitude of the House. Its activities would have to be channelled towards the success of the appeal.' Stirling agreed that while the Board would not want the House to be 'donor led', there was 'general agreement that fund-raising needed to become much more closely integrated into the activities of the House'.[61]

The second near-fatal issue – that of the venue – had still not been resolved. The chairman of the Board strongly favoured the temporary theatre option, although on 24 July 1995 two Board members, Robert Gavron and Vivien Duffield, expressed grave concerns about attracting audiences to such a venue. If the Lyceum were used with minimum scenery and more performances, Gavron urged, the financial situation would 'be transformed'. On the other hand, if things went wrong at the temporary theatre, 'the disaster for the House would be much greater'. Duffield questioned whether it was feasible to take on two large projects at the same time. The Board, however, were loath to give up a plan that would be beneficial for the staff of the companies. It was decided to ask the Lyceum to keep the option open until after the Southwark planning meeting in September.[62]

In September 1995 senior management had to make the final decision about Tower Bridge before putting their recommendation to the Board. Only Nicholas Payne was firmly against Tower Bridge, preferring the Lyceum together with some other venues like the Royal Albert Hall. Mike Morris, who would be in charge of the redundancies, was in favour of Tower Bridge. Isaacs, similarly concerned about the possible 300 redundancies, also decided in favour of Tower Bridge. When the recommendation was put to the Board on 28 September only Duffield continued to express doubts, still worried that the audiences would not go south of the river.[63] Stirling said that he thought 'all the Board members wanted to believe that Tower Bridge would be the right option'. The Lyceum was still estimated to cost £7 million more than the £20 million allowed in the lottery grant. Someone ominously pointed out that the 'worst possible outcome' would be the loss of Tower Bridge and the Lyceum, and even of the Dominion Theatre.[64]

'The worst possible outcome' became more likely when, in October, the Lyceum was committed to *Jesus Christ Superstar*. On

23 October Isaacs warned the Board that GLE, a group of London boroughs, had taken over the Southwark site and were trying to raise the finances for a more 'permanent' theatre. A more permanent theatre was far more likely to be 'called in' by the Department of the Environment, even though full planning permission had been obtained from Southwark by mid-November.[65] The Board were now concerned that they risked being 'grievously exposed if the quest for planning permission failed'. If it all fell through 'some lateral thinking would be needed'.[66]

Haitink was anxious, and later angrily recalled that he had 'pleaded with the Board'. He said, 'I sent them all personal letters – begging them not to go ahead with the redevelopment until the companies had found suitable homes, but all I got back was a card from Jeremy saying, "You're wrong..."' Isaacs's plans for a temporary theatre were 'Castles in the sky'.[67] To authorise the closure of the House for redevelopment before satisfactory temporary premises had been secured was, according to Haitink, 'quite insane'. He was quoted as saying to one member of the Board, 'You are so obsessed with going down in history as the Board which brought about the new House that you ignore the fact that what you are actually doing is ruining everything we achieved in the old one.'[68]

But the Board were not listening and assumed that the government would bail them out if they got into trouble. Sir James Spooner later said in a letter to *The Times* that the Board 'assumed the State would see it through, in recognition of their generosity, and that the performing companies would continue to be supported'.[69] The Tower Bridge decision and the assumption upon which it was based proved to be costly mistakes.

With no concrete plans for a temporary home, Isaacs and the Board now had to provide a viable financial plan before the Arts Council would advance the first 'tranche' of £55 million of the development grant. But, according to Isaacs, the decision of Lord Gowrie and the Arts Council to release the money depended on the Royal Opera House replacing Board chairman Angus Stirling. Isaacs later wrote that Stirling was overburdened, as he was not only shouldering the

Royal Opera House's increasingly taxing demands but was director general of the National Trust, which was celebrating its centenary with many and 'farflung' activities.

According to Isaacs, Duffield and Sainsbury had been pressing for the appointment of Peter Gummer, chairman of Shandwick plc, brother of John Selwyn Gummer, Secretary of State for the Environment. It was Peter Gummer who had been the chairman of the Arts Council lottery advisory panel, which had awarded the Royal Opera its lottery grant and had so angered Isaacs by suggesting the company close down during the redevelopment.[70] Peter Gummer was chosen in late December to take over in September 1996 and was brought on to the Board in March 1996 so that he could serve the requisite period before becoming chairman. Board member Tessa Blackstone argued unsuccessfully for due process but, Tooley later wrote, 'two of Covent Garden's benefactors ... threatened to withdraw their committed donations if this proposal was not given a fair wind'. With the development money depending on a speedy resolution agreeable to the Arts Council, the Board decided to make a recommendation by December.[71] That same autumn the search began for a new general director.

As well as ignoring due process, Peter Gummer's appointment was the final nail in the coffin for Isaacs's Tower Bridge plan. The new chairman's brother was the Minister for the Environment and could not be seen to 'nod through' the plans, however worthy they might be. While the ministry considered, on 19 December 1995 the Board discussed the diminishing options for the company: 'suspended animation', which meant approximately eighty performances in a variety of venues within a budget of £9 million, or a complete close-down, maintaining only sufficient staff to restart the organisation like a 'pilot light', as Timms described it. Reducing the 900 staff to 60 was 'the least-cost option'. Both options were made on the assumption that the Arts Council would continue its grant.[72]

Fully aware that the Royal Opera House needed an answer to the Tower Bridge plan before the New Year, John Gummer decided to call it in for assessment on 31 January 1996. Isaacs later argued that Covent Garden had made no representations to Gummer and that he 'could have decided to let it happen'. It was in his opinion 'a failure of vision'.[73] Although in October 1996 the public inquiry 'found categorically in favour' of the Tower Bridge theatre, it was too late for it to be built in time for the closure in the autumn of 1997. The Lyceum option had only been available until October when the theatre was let. As Haitink had foreseen, the companies were now in effect about to become homeless.

Although total closure ended up being the de facto arrangement, at the time neither the Board nor the Arts Council would countenance it. The Board chose the 'suspended animation' option. According to Mary Allen, it was at this moment that the ballet and opera companies started to plan their exile independently without co-ordinated costings. In retrospect the Lyceum appeared to have been the best prospect for avoiding the more serious problems that developed from having no single base for the closure period.

The 1995–96 season had seen extra *Figaros* to bring in revenue and the end of the Wagner cycle with *Götterdämmerung*. Payne's planning did little to ease the plight of the increasingly beleaguered and anxious company. Peter Sellars's production of Hindemith's *Mathis der Maler*, which opened on 16 November 1995 in honour of the composer's centenary, achieved a box office of only 50 per cent. Sellars's characterisation and the drab business suits designed by Dunya Ramicova did not help delineate the characters, or elucidate the text. Syrus later recalled, 'Obviously just to go in to confuse is silly, to dress both sides in grey suits in the *Mathis* was crass.'[74] The whole thing took place in what Sellars described as a 'wounded skyscraper', replete with television screens to show the 'daily pressure of commercial television'.[75] Sellars's 'fetish for surtitles' meant that there were two, one of which snaked at an angle across the set. The actual titles were in what Milnes described as 'demotic Sellars-ese: "Stuff yourselves, eat, get pissed and get laid", with all references to the peasants' revolt expunged'.[76] According to John Allison, 'Nothing in this multimedia parade helped to clarify the opera, and Sellars's agenda only added layers of metaphor to what is already an allegory.' Even Sutcliffe had to concede that Sellars was 'in need of a rethink'. It was beginning to seem, he wrote, 'that not every opera could benefit from his invariable Americanising'. He added, 'Perhaps the historical German

Reformation was particularly hard to accommodate to Sellars's universal matrix of a modern United States.'*[77]

After promising that there would be no further cuts in government spending on the arts, in December 1995 the government lopped a further £5 million off the Arts Council grant and again allocated standstill funding to most of its operatic clients. Rodney Milnes pointed out that it was 'now cheaper, thanks to current arts funding policy, to go to the opera in Brussels and Paris than to Covent Garden'. In Paris prices were half those in London and all three Houses were full. 'Top price in Brussels is £50 (add a pound or two for Paris), Eurostar comes in at less than £60, and there are regular matinées. Funny old world,' Milnes commented.[78]

In order to reach a balanced budget for 1996–97, Isaacs and the Board decided to lose up to a hundred jobs during December 1995. The Arts Council on 21 December demanded 'paper requirements that would satisfy their criteria' before more lottery money was handed over. Covent Garden was instructed to bring in another firm of consultants, KPMG, to go over the figures. It was, according to Isaacs, a 'horrible' meeting. In January 1996 the Arts Council agreed to continue core funding during closure for more than minimal activity, but only if education and outreach continued. Isaacs later recalled the muddled thinking of the Arts Council during the pre-closure decision-making period. 'It was only at the end of January 1996 that the Arts Council defined the basis on which they would continue to provide any funding during the closure,' he explained, 'and what they were never willing to do at any stage was either to provide or to argue to government for provision of the money required to take the House through closure.'[79]

By January 1996 plans were progressing for the nomadic period in various venues, which would entail 200 more redundancies, but somehow ensure that the companies would continue to perform. The Royal Ballet was to appear at the Royal Festival Hall, the Barbican and the

---

* An honourable *Midsummer Marriage* for Tippett's eighty-sixth birthday, and Sandy Goehr's reinvention of Monteverdi's lost *Arianna* (see *Opera*, November 1995, p. 1271) were made possible by a grant from the Foundation for Sports and the Arts, topped up by the Arts Council.

Coliseum. The Royal Opera's plans included six months at the London Palladium, six weeks at the Barbican and touring. At this time of greatest need for careful planning, Jones's successor, Clive Timms, made David Pilcher, the chief accountant, redundant. Jones believed it was 'the single biggest mistake they ever made'. According to Jones, Pilcher, together with his management accountants, would have been able to work out what it would cost 'to go to another venue – what you could have got from the box office'.[80] As advance box office constituted a large part of the company's working capital, the single most crucial area of expertise was estimating by how much it was likely to drop, and to arrange finance to cover the loss and how to repay it. By 30 April 1996 the plans for a 'nomadic' period were beginning to cause concern to the Board as the Palladium now looked as if it too might be unavailable and none of the theatres had signed contracts.

At the end of the financial year 1995–96 Stirling's Annual Report revealed a £3.1 million deficit and pointed out that while revenue money was flooding into the arts from the lottery, revenue needs were 'as desperate as ever'. Management struggled to keep the next year's plans in the black by cutting some of the next season's productions. An opera in the Verdi festival, Il Corsaro, was cancelled and two concert performances were to be given instead.

Jones and Pilcher having been dispensed with, Timms himself was soon forced to leave. On 24 May, Isaacs wrote to the Board to say that the £20 million supplementary grant would not, in fact, cover the closure period. Timms's new estimate was that the closure would cost £34 million instead of £20 million. This he and Isaacs managed to reduce to £27 million but the Board were enraged and Timms had to resign. Isaacs was instructed to get rid of the remaining £7 million projected deficit.

Isaacs was not able to reduce the £7 million shortfall completely, and in June 1996 he presented new closure plans, which were 'projected to be £3.5 million in excess' of the provision from lottery funding, Arts Council grant, Trust and Friends, but could be charged to the development. According to Isaacs, Duffield would not let any of the money raised by the appeal be used for revenue purposes, while he continued to argue that all available funds should be pooled to get the House through closure. He recalled his arguments with Duffield who said, 'We can't do that – we're appealing for capital, we can't appeal for revenue.' Isaacs had replied, 'I don't know why not, Vivien, because what is the point of achieving a surplus on the appeal? To endow the House against difficult times ahead – why is it not reasonable to use those funds to help the House in its hour of greatest need, namely closure?' This was, he stressed, a 'wholly exceptional, appallingly difficult period' and all resources were needed to 'tide over the House and employees who are the House'.[81]

Richard Pulford, who had been appointed by the Arts Council in early 1996, worked closely with the management during the year and prepared three reports. In his first, in July 1996, he said he believed the closure plans were feasible, although tight. The closure plans were agreed by the Board, which asked for 'a close watch to be kept on financial management and control during this sensitive and demanding period pending the arrival of a new financial director'. On 22 July Isaacs said there was 'little to choose' between performing and doing nothing during the closure. The Board agreed to seek an agreement with Sadler's Wells for 1998.

As the crisis deepened, Payne and Tim Albery presented a *Nabucco* that was, in Canning's words, so wrong-headed in its 'tasteless' and 'hideously inappropriate' Holocaust analogy that Edward Downes pulled out.[82] It was part of the Verdi festival, which staggered on minus the cancelled *Il Corsaro*, but with some successes from a previous era including Domingo in a revival of Moshinsky's *Stiffelio* and Eyre's *Traviata*, which was relayed to the piazza twice in July, with Gheorghiu and Alagna.

One great achievement of this dispiriting and increasingly anxious period was Luc Bondy's joint Covent Garden–Châtelet–La Monnaie Brussels–Opéra de Nice–Opéra de Lyons production of *Don Carlos* on 11 June 1996. It was a fine ensemble work like his *Salome* and a memorable evening musically with Hampson, Mattila, Alagna and van Dam, with Haitink conducting. Bondy again showed a 'profound understanding of the opera's emotional and spiritual core' as well as an ability to create 'atmosphere by the simplest theatrical means'. He and designer Gilles Aillaud strikingly created with the minimum of props and scenery, and in what Richard Fairman called 'variations on a large grey box', the deeply mournful, snowy forest of Fontainebleau, the sun-baked monastery of San Just and the formal French garden of the king. The beautifully integrated direction left indelible visual impressions with characters simultaneously lost and looming on stage. Karita Mattila who sang Elisabetta was, according to Canning, 'in her prime – gorgeous to behold, wondrous to hear'.[83] Her subtle acting, shifts of mood and emotion were paralleled in nuances of phrase and tone colour. The voice was even in weight and lustrous from top to bottom, consistently pure, beautiful and refined, with a soft-grained production nonetheless not lacking penetration. Hampson's tone was appealingly rich, virile and tender, capable of urgency without strain. Van Dam was in most impressive vocal form after thirty-five active years on the operatic stage – his low register still smooth and rounded, the middle register penetratingly resonant, and the openness of the top reminiscent of Christoff in his prime. The five singers presented 'performances of subtlety and force rarely seen on the opera stage', Christiansen wrote, adding that 'coaxing singers to act at this level of intensity is a far more radical achievement than any posturing, postmodernist tableau, devised by the Alberys and Aldens'.[84]

Haitink was more delicate, round-toned and nuanced than Solti, whose work with the orchestra tended rather to bring out more contrasts, juxtapose piano with forte, and elicit a special sound from one instrument for a musical dramatic effect. Haitink rather tends to let one musical moment flow into the next, proceeding from a solid intellectual and emotional understanding of what Verdi is about, while never losing the expressiveness and emotional content of the moment. *Don Carlos* showed again how Haitink had built the Royal Opera House orchestra into a sensitive, responsive and resilient instrument.

At the end of the 1995–96 season Isaacs announced his intention to retire in 1997, when he would be sixty-five, to work at Turner Television. The search for the new general director, which had begun during the autumn of 1995, was proving difficult. Isaacs had recommended Payne to a reluctant Board, which hoped Gerard Mortier of Salzburg would be interested. According to Isaacs, it was Richard Eyre who had suggested that his executive director at the National Theatre Genista (Jenny) McIntosh's name be put forward. Peter Gummer was not keen on McIntosh, Isaacs believed, as she was too left-wing on 'class and ticket prices'.[85] In spite of Gummer's uncertainty it was announced on 4 July 1996 that McIntosh would succeed Isaacs as chief executive. This was a new title replacing that of general director. According to Isaacs, Gummer wanted to diminish the role of general director 'in ways which have never been explicit' and 'enhance his own role'.[86]

McIntosh had worked since 1990 at the National Theatre where she became one of the most respected and well-liked arts administrators in the country. She had been responsible for making the National Theatre more accessible and welcoming, and hoped to do the same for the Royal Opera. She had a reputation, according to Milnes, for being as 'sharp as a razor' as well as a 'person of boundless charm, warmth and humanity'.[87] She also faced another task, which Tooley described as restoring 'the former unique and inimitable spirit' backstage. Huge though the problems were, Tooley believed that McIntosh could have overcome them 'with support from the Board and a real willingness on their part to face the problems squarely'.[88] Payne, unhappy not to have got the top job, remained as opera director responsible for planning.

Isaacs left his post in mid-season, 31 December 1996, and McIntosh took over on 6 January 1997. There was no handover, as had originally been hoped. Isaacs asked to retain 'the title but in no sense the functional role of general director until the end of the season', so that he could 'for reasons of pride' be on stage for the performances associated with the closure. Although Gummer told Isaacs to leave before his contract expired and McIntosh was to start mid-season, Isaacs refuted any suggestions of 'brutality' on the part of the chairman. He recalled, 'When he put it to me that she was coming and the sooner she was allowed to get on with it, a fresh mind and all that, the better, I said immediately "of course".'*[89]

---

* Isaacs had a twenty-four-part series, Cold War, waiting for him. There were accusations that in spite of the fight to reduce the deficit, and although he was no longer working for Covent Garden, he continued to receive his salary until his contract ran out. Isaacs defended himself: 'I earned far, far less at the opera house than I would have earned if I had stayed in television and it was a perfectly reasonable settlement to say, "please go now but we will pay your contract out"' (Interview, 1.7.99).

McIntosh was walking into an impossible situation. By December 1996 Pulford of the Arts Council was concerned that the July plans had been ignored and planning had continued with no reference to them. He demanded 'decisive management action' to retrieve the situation.[90] Furthermore, McIntosh was to have serious limitations on her authority. According to Paul Findlay, 'Gummer was executive chairman – three days a week in the office. Gummer wanted to be seen to be the decision-maker.'[91] The House's image was at its lowest ebb. As Philip Jones later put it, 'The opera house, having lost its constituency in the price-hike, had the appeal of subsidised fox-hunting.'[92]

TWENTY-SEVEN

COVENT GARDEN 1997–2002

Who Owns Covent Garden?

MCINTOSH WAS DETERMINED PUBLICLY to convey a positive approach to the future, telling *The Times* about her vision for the company on 23 April 1997. 'The new building is a clear metaphor,' she said, 'because you have the old theatre, refurbished but essentially still itself, and around it new buildings implying modernity, openness and flexibility.' Behind the scenes, however, she soon came to realise what terrible difficulties the company faced. On 16 January 1997 McIntosh announced that she was doing a 'rigorous review of the programme for the next two years' to eliminate the £3.3 million deficit, of which £1.3 million savings had already been identified. McIntosh had to sort out the planning of these savings as Mary Allen at the Arts Council would not release the next tranche of lottery money without a break-even budget for the coming year.

While working on the plans for the closure period, McIntosh soon discovered the fragmented nature of the organisation. Although there were quite detailed plans for the first financial year during which closure occurred – 1997–98 – the plans had been prepared by the different departments without enough reference to each other with the result that they could not be fulfilled within the available funds. In March the Covent Garden management succeeded in presenting revised closure plans to the Arts Council. These were reviewed by a firm of professional advisers, and it was agreed that the budgets were tight but manageable as long as costs were rigidly controlled and box office targets attained. The second tranche of lottery funding was therefore released. The Arts Council decided that 'in the present political climate' this decision was not to be publicised.[1] A business plan for the first sixteen months in the new building should be completed by March 1998 and the small deficit in the closure budgets 'ironed out'.[2]

McIntosh was not only faced by the budget problems; the failure to find a suitable venue was also still causing grave concern. Payne, on instructions from Gummer, had been negotiating the contract with Sadler's Wells before McIntosh's arrival, but although the Arts Council were encouraging and brokering an agreement, Sadler's Wells was exacting onerous terms.* The negotiations further undermined the executive director, for when McIntosh met Ian Albery of Sadler's Wells in mid-February to finalise the contract, Gummer and James Butler of KPMG were both present at the meeting. At this point the gradual erosion of the director's authority in relation to the Board came home to roost. Duffield and Gummer had both installed themselves in offices in the opera house. According to Isaacs, there were reports of Gummer standing by and interrupting McIntosh at meetings and press conferences. When Gummer told Isaacs that he intended to chair McIntosh's executive management meetings, both he and the Board counselled him not to act as executive chairman.[3]

Duffield's position was increasingly powerful and unassailable as the development appeal continued. She was a formidable fund-raiser and was quoted in the *Observer* explaining the quid pro quo method of fund-raising: 'If I don't give something to the old cow for her opera house, she won't give something to my pet cause.' In November 1997 the *Guardian* reported that Duffield 'wanted to maintain exclusivity and saw more broadcasts as more access'. Gummer later told the Select Committee that he was aware that there were problems of blurred boundaries – that there was not a 'clear division between the responsibilities of the Board of Directors and the executive management'. He tried to explain to the committee that he had been working with

---

* When Allen saw the contract in September 1997 she discovered that Sadler's Wells had 'get-outs in every direction', but Covent Garden had none, even if the theatre was not ready for occupancy. Covent Garden had paid a 'substantial amount of money' into an escrow account to which the Royal Opera could only have access if Sadler's Wells failed to complete the building by the final six weeks of the third season (Allen, *A House Divided*, p. 47). Ian Albery of Sadler's Wells later told Mary Allen that the only person who had known anything about theatrical contracts had been McIntosh but that 'no sooner had she made some progress than the Board had waded in and taken over' (Allen, Ibid., p. 213).

McIntosh on the problem but his proposed solution seemed only to blur the distinctions yet further. He had suggested an executive Board under the chairmanship of the chief executive responsible for day-to-day management; 'so the Board becomes responsible for policy and the executive management becomes responsible for its implementation'. The Board would monitor whether the executive did the job. The power of the Board and the status of its members combined with the fragmented management structure of the House made McIntosh's position as chief executive untenable. Increasingly unhappy, McIntosh soon realised that she could not work there.

Payne's choice for the House's fiftieth anniversary celebrations was *Palestrina* on 24 February. Canning wondered if Pfitzner's somewhat pretentious 'long, Teutonic opera with uncomfortable "nationalistic" pretensions was the right choice to celebrate the Royal Opera House's golden jubilee'. Canning borrowed Noël Coward's immortal words to describe *Palestrina*: 'Parsifal without the jokes'. Nikolaus Lehnhoff directed an extraordinarily good-looking show with its spare sets, richly evocative of sixteenth-century Rome, designed by Tobias Hoheisal and glowingly lit by Mark Henderson. The performance on 24 February, however, became symbolic of the House's predicament in an unexpected way when rain again poured through the roof as Thomas Moser sang 'my dearest wish is to be away from here'.[4]

Jenny McIntosh was by then echoing these sentiments. In early April 1997, a week after the General Election swept the Labour party to power, McIntosh sent Gummer, now Lord Chadlington, a letter of resignation. Chadlington did not immediately accept it, as he was still entertaining hopes of trying to 'make her happier'. He later told the House of Commons Select Committee that he hoped she would 'come through it'.[5]

At the time of the announcement of her resignation, McIntosh told *The Times*, 'There is a level of ownership which people feel about the ROH; it goes right from the most senior people all the way down to people who pay the smallest amounts of money.'[6] Gerald Kaufman, the Labour chairman of the Select Committee, later asked her if she felt like an intruder and she said, 'It is not entirely unfair.' She told him that she had wanted opera to be seen by more and different people. Milnes later wrote, 'One can imagine her ideas for dragging the ROH into the twentieth century going down like a bucket of cold sick with the current power bases; since her vision could only be realised with proper funding there was no point in her staying.'

McIntosh's departure heralded a chain of events that came within a hair's breadth of totally destroying Covent Garden's companies. On 25 April Chadlington, discussed McIntosh's wish to resign with Mary Allen and on 30 April asked her if she would consider taking on the job. He did not tell the Board at its meeting on 28 April either that McIntosh wanted to leave or that he was considering signing up Mary Allen.[7] He later told the Select Committee that he was still hoping McIntosh would stay but admitted it had been 'unwise' not to tell the Board.

On 4 May Allen wrote to Chadlington to say she would consider taking on the job if other members of the Board were supportive. She did not yet contact Gowrie at the Arts Council, although she agreed with Chadlington that she should speak to him before she accepted the job. Allen later explained that she had not told Gowrie earlier because she had not believed that McIntosh would resign. 'One should not underestimate the level of stress felt by many executives working in the arts,' she explained and added that she had believed it was 'just a tough patch she was going through'.[8]

By 7 May, however, when McIntosh met Chadlington it became 'perfectly clear', as he later told the Select Committee, that 'she was not going to be able to continue in her post'. She told him that 'something had snapped and she was unable to sleep and unable to eat'. Chadlington later admitted that this was the moment he should have told the Board.[9] He also later told Kaufman's committee, 'It is difficult to imagine the depression, almost despair, that I felt when I heard that Jenny was going. . . . The degree of crisis management we were in was quite enormous.' He felt hugely relieved at the possibility of Mary Allen taking on the job.

The next day, Chadlington told Gavron that McIntosh had resigned.[10] Gavron phoned Chris Smith who had become the Secretary of State for the Department of National Heritage, which, in July 1997, was renamed the Department of Culture, Media and Sport.[11] The two Board members met Smith and told him they were in a crisis situation and wanted to appoint Mary Allen, circumventing 'the necessity to advertise and interview'. They argued that a long drawn-out search would do the Royal Opera House 'untold harm'.[12] Smith was told that McIntosh was 'suffering from stress' and wanted to 'leave the ROH as soon as possible'. Smith 'expressed concern about the propriety of the proposed process, particularly in relation to any role Ms Allen may have played in the award of the lottery grant to the ROH'. Chadlington countered that Allen had not been a decision-maker. Smith 'expressed reservations about the presentation of the situation', but 'given the very particular circumstances ... he would not raise any further objections'. Chadlington agreed to make those reservations known to the Board.[13]

Chadlington later told the Select Committee that Smith had said, 'In these very difficult and particular circumstances, I am happy.'[14] Smith's recollection was different. He said that he did not 'in any sense, betray either happiness or enthusiasm about the course which they were proposing to undertake'.[15] In fact, he went so far as to say that 'I was actually very unhappy at the situation which had developed' and that he was sorry to lose Mary Allen from the Arts Council where she was doing a good job. He also pointed out that he had no formal locus in appointments within the opera house.*

Chadlington telephoned Allen after the meeting to say that the Secretary of State was 'supportive'. Allen then made an appointment to see Gowrie the next day, 8 May, and went to discuss terms with Chadlington before she saw him. At their meeting Allen told Gowrie that she would accept the job but wanted confidentiality because the Board might not be 'supportive'. Allen later told the Select Committee that Lord Gowrie had said he 'would be personally very upset at the prospect of losing me, but he thought that it was the right thing for the Royal Opera House, the right thing for me and that it had been handled in the right way'.[16] Lord Gowrie told the Kaufman committee that he had been 'gobsmacked' to learn later that the Secretary of State

---

* It was this discrepancy which caused Michael Fabricant MP, a member of the Select Committee, to ask Smith, 'Someone is being economical with the truth. Someone is telling porky pies. Is it you?' (Select Committee, p. 96). Smith had forgotten that he had no 'formal locus' on appointments by the time he appointed Colin Southgate to the chairmanship of the Royal Opera House Board in 1998.

maintained he was a 'sympathetic listener rather than someone who gave consent'.[17]

On 12 May an emergency Board meeting 'formally ratified the fait accompli with which they were presented'.[18] Isaacs, away at a conference of cold war historians, was the last to be told. He was, he later said, 'taken aback' and reflected that had the Board not been presented with a fait accompli, he might have 'thought it right to pause and wait for a few weeks'. Payne and Morris could have held the fort for a month or so and other candidates might have come forward.[19]

Gowrie was asked hurriedly to get Arts Council agreement by midday the next day, so that an announcement could be made before the appointment was leaked to the press. At the same time Richard Hall was appointed director of finance after a nine-month hiatus. Chadlington insisted that Allen take a three-month break between working for the funding body and its client, thus becoming himself acting executive chairman. Smith in his evidence to the Select Committee expressed surprise when he discovered that Mary Allen was not going to take up her appointment for three months. 'I would', he said, 'have questioned even more strongly the circumstances of urgency which they were pressing on me.'[20]

The last moments of the season highlighted the predicament of the House, revealing both the dedication of the artists who continued to put on magnificent performances and the ineptitude of management. The 13 May revival of Friedrich's *Elektra*, with seven maids mopping blood off the walls of a sewer, inspired reviewers to comment on the similarity between on-stage and off-stage goings-on. Polaski and Mattila provided an outstanding evening vocally and dramatically, Mattila singing Chrysothemis, in John Allison's words, 'with fervour, almost whispering at times and riding the orchestral climaxes with full-throated ease', expressing her loneliness 'in the way she hugged herself nervously'.[21] Equally impressive was the 26 May *Kát'a* revival, again showing the astounding resilience of the company and the depth of Haitink's musical understanding. Milnes wrote that it was 'impossible to witness Haitink's unfolding of profound human tragedy without being stirred to the depths of your soul'.[22]

The last moments of the season revealed how lacking in realism the planning had become. Even Isaacs had to admit that Payne had 'overreached for once' by scheduling a new *Macbeth* just before closure. At the last moment it had to be given in a concert performance on 27 June. Canning wrote that the splendid orchestra and chorus were being betrayed by management and audience. Andrew Porter found a 'fully enacted, adventurous production' with the team pulling a 'triumph' out of the management failure – delivered downstage with no set.* Anthony Michaels-Moore as Macbeth showed himself to be a 'noble Verdi baritone with timbres more beautiful than Gobbi's'. Ted Downes, who was also about to say goodbye to the House after more than forty years of loyal service, 'inspired singers and players with a command of phrase and colour quick to every inflection'.

On 12 July Haitink spoke out in the *Guardian* in an interview with Andrew Clements. He defended Payne and Katona for doing their job under 'dismal circumstances', and said that the main problem was 'having a non-professional Board who think that they should be in charge; that is extremely dangerous'. These 'non-professionals', he said, 'interfere too much with the senior management, who are supposed to be the professionals and must be given the chance to do their job'. Even more serious was Haitink's suspicion that the Board wanted to close down for two years and then reopen – 'You can't throw away an opera company and then start again,' he warned, 'you have to keep the nucleus of the company going, you need to have people who have worked together.'[23] Rodney Milnes heard that Duffield was said to have demanded Haitink's resignation after his *Guardian* interview. Milnes said that 'the standards achieved by those people who actually put on the shows are little short of miraculous given the constant, cack-handed meddling by amateurs'.[24]

The Verdi festival continued in June and July with two versions of *Simon Boccanegra* – those of 1857 and 1881. The 1857 version, a rarity suited to the Verdi festival but not the general repertoire, was given a completely new production and scenery as a vehicle for Domingo.

---

* Porter explained the changes in the versions – e.g. the elimination of the old-fashioned Donizettian numbers and the exiles' chorus, and replacement of Macbeth's solo death scene by a 'triple-chorus spectacle of bards, warriors and populace in full cry' to compete with Meyerbeer's *L'Africaine* in Paris.

Solti's 1881 version was a performance of 'incredible bristling tension'. It was at this time that Solti said the orchestra had never been 'better prepared'.[25] Isaacs went on stage to thank Solti for his contribution to the House. These were Solti's last appearances at the House he had helped to build up to international status. He died in September.

Max Loppert described the 14 July closing gala as 'more a spectacle of the rich congratulating each other for being rich than a glorification of the art form, which was really the performance of *Meistersinger*'.[26] The last *Meistersinger* performances showed the company at its splendid best – the chorus, now facing mass sackings – quite radiant at '*Heil dir, Hans Sachs!*' Haitink later said that he would have left after his last *Meistersinger* 'except that so many members of the orchestra, the chorus and music staff – all the right people begged me not to abandon them', telling him, 'You are our last anchor.' Haitink agreed to do two seasons in the new House. Syrus had asked Haitink if he could absent himself on a Salzburg project for the closing performance, which was going to be 'a sad occasion'. The company would be saying goodbye to 'something that might not be reconstructed in a way that we could recognise or identify with any more'. It was also 'the final performance of a load of people who were getting the chop. . . . It was ghastly.' Haitink told him, 'If I could not be around too I would be glad.'[27]

After the closure, the circumstances of Mary Allen's appointment became further fuel for public criticism and anger, when the House of Commons Committee on Culture, Media and Sport decided to look into the running of the Royal Opera House and in particular her appointment. The committee was chaired by Gerald Kaufman and sat from 24 July to November 1997.

While the committee deliberated, Mary Allen started working at Covent Garden on 2 September 1997. On 3 September Richard Hall, the new finance director, concluded his review of the closure budgets. His aim had been to eliminate the remaining deficit of £800,000, which had been estimated and presented to the Arts Council in March. Instead, he presented Allen with his forecast of a deficit for the closure period of £9 million. The ballet season at Labatt's Apollo Theatre in Hammersmith alone, Allen wrote in her diary, 'was facing a possible deficit of £1.5 million'.[28] On 4 September Allen told Chadlington that if the Labatt's ticket sales did not pick up the company was 'in serious danger of going bust'.[29] Philip Jones later explained, 'Jenny McIntosh went and Mary Allen came in and said, "We are going to be insolvent in a week's time." All they were really saying was "we haven't got advance box office".'[30] As well as the problem of the Labatt's sales, there was an adverse forecast of £125,000 for *Otello* at the Albert Hall, and *Platée* was £175,000 over budget.*

Over the next few weeks repeated attempts were made to reduce the deficit, but it was clear that the uncoordinated planning that McIntosh had observed, together with the departure of Jones and Timms and before the appointment of the new finance director, had resulted in a breakdown of financial controls. Allen wrote in her diary on 10 September, 'The budget-making process is opaque, decision-making is incomprehensible.' By 16 September Allen was writing in her diary, 'The schism between the artistic heads and the other senior managers is becoming increasingly obvious.' She added that as far as the artistic heads were concerned they were 'running their own companies'.[31]

By 19 September it was clear to Hall and Allen that if funds could not be found from any source, the company 'could no longer trade solvently and the organisation should be closed down'. The only possible solution to such a huge deficit would be gaining 'access to the interest on the £10 million remaining in the Floral Trust'. This fund had been set up to support the development and £20 million had already been used. The interest on the remaining amount would be worth about £1.5 million in the next two years.† Panic took hold of the Board. Allen described them on 29 September as 'rabbits in headlights'. On 30 September a further £1 million went missing – Value Added Tax, which should not have been included in the figures.

---

* The finance department showed deficits of £3.7 million for 1998–99; £3.1 million for 1999–2000 in addition to the £3 million for 1997–98 (Allen, *A House Divided*, p. 29). The situation was chaotic, Moshinsky reporting that there were 'rehearsal rooms all over the place. I have a rehearsal room tomorrow for *Otello* which does not have a piano.'
† The trustees were George Magan of Hambro, Lord Carrington, Jeremy Isaacs, Angus Stirling and Chadlington.

On 3 October Chadlington told Allen he was sure he could raid the Floral Trust to prevent immediate liquidation and to carry the company through. On 8 October Richard Hall told Allen there was a cash flow crisis to the tune of £600,000, due to redundancies and two cash reviews. The cash books had not been written up since August. While Chadlington sought to arrange the £1.5 million from the Floral Trust, it became clear that some members of the Board favoured administrative receivership. Duffield repeatedly told Allen that if the government did not produce more money she would withdraw her funds for the development. If a solution could not be found by 30 October the company would have to close down.

On 20 October Duffield came out in favour of the destruction of the companies. Allen noted, 'Vivien said, over and over again, that she thought the best thing was for the company to go down. Clean sheet. Start again . . . I felt so frustrated myself that I felt like physically shaking her as I tried to explain clearly that the company could not go down without taking the development with it.' Duffield was adamant. When, on 21 October, George Magan of the Floral Trust was approached by Chadlington and Allen to get all of the £10 million for running costs, rather than the £2 million originally agreed to, Duffield was furious. Allen recorded, 'Peter said she was determined the whole organisation should go into liquidation.'[32]

Chris Smith decided to seek a radical solution to the embarrassment of the Covent Garden debacle. On 3 November he told Gowrie at the Arts Council and Paul Daniel, music director of the English National Opera since 1997, that the government was proposing that the ENO move into the Royal Opera House with all three companies under one roof to be known as Covent Garden Theatre, with a new Board. Smith further informed Daniel that Covent Garden would become an 'independent receiving House', which would offer 'cultural and financial gains for everyone'. The proposition was particularly attractive to Smith as it would also obviate the need to renovate the Coliseum. All three companies would be expected to give more performances touring outside the capital. Smith, somewhat disingenuously, said London could afford two opera companies but not two theatres for them.[33]

At the same time Smith announced that Richard Eyre would write a review by May 1998 as to how the reopened theatre would be used. The announcement of the review was somewhat unusual in that, in Allen's words, it 'set out the answers as well as the objectives'. Chadlington said weakly, 'This is a very interesting initiative which could lead to a solution.' Paul Daniel, the ENO and its audience put up an immediate and staunch fight, proclaiming, 'ENO has its own strong artistic vision and a special relationship with a large and loyal audience.'*

While Daniel defended the ENO, Duffield was 'apoplectic' about the merger proposal – donors who had already given £75 million to the development would pull out, she said. Isaacs, on 4 November, told Radio 4, 'This pig won't fly.' On 5 November a Conservative MP, Michael Fabricant, asked how Smith had set up a review and announced its conclusions in the same breath. Smith, somewhat withdrawing, said he had asked Eyre to look at other solutions too. It was, he said, 'less a plan than a proposal'. Feelings were running high. Milnes said the capital could afford two opera houses if 'the government had the political will, or any vision beyond acquiring power and maintaining it by fawning on the tabloid media and surrendering to the cultural values they promote'. Paris had four opera houses, Berlin three, Munich two. 'Make no mistake,' he warned, 'this is about the disbandment of English National Opera.' Smith, he added, could turn Covent Garden back into a dance hall, 'a feat previously achieved by one Adolf Hitler'. On 9 November Smith was reported as backtracking somewhat, saying his three-in-one scheme was designed as 'shock tactics' to shake complacency.[34] Thus the very Minister who was supposed to defend the country's cultural institutions played with them at a time when their very survival was in doubt.

On 4 November Chadlington told Kaufman's Select Committee

---

* Daniel recalled his early months as music director just after Dennis Marks left when he was faced either with 'the death blow of a merger of activity and location at the Royal Opera' or a 'stabilisation grant' to mitigate past debt and invest in what would be Daniel's artistic vision. He remembered 'sitting at home, lonely but exhilarated, with a very empty laptop screen thinking, "Here I go, I'm going to write a document which has to help this company grab its lifeline." ' Out of this grew the idea for a 'linked series with all the operas played on the same set ... an anniversary celebration of the birth of opera', the Italian season of autumn 2000 (*Coliseum*, Autumn 2000, p. 4).

that the Royal Opera House was within ten days of insolvency. He made matters worse by admitting that there had been 'no really good finance director' for twelve months. The figures were, he said, 'like catching a falling sword and they changed every month in the most alarming way'. The development, he stressed, was separate and in good shape. At the same time as announcing impending insolvency, Chadlington again said he believed 'there was a way through' and that balanced budgets could be presented to the Arts Council by the 12 November deadline.[35] He was having daily talks with benefactors to keep the House afloat. On 5 November, at the eleventh hour before the company went into receivership, the trustees of the Floral Trust – Magan, Stirling, Chadlington and Isaacs – agreed in principle to make the money available. After a lot of angry argument the Board accepted the arrangement.

On 10 November the agreement with the Floral Trust nearly came undone, with £2 million needed for pay day on 21 November. Duffield was still prepared to see the companies pulled down and there was lobbying against the Floral package. On 18 November the Floral trustees finally agreed, on condition that Allen accepted a 'professional support adviser' to review the closure budgets as well as the structure and composition of the Board. They also demanded that the Arts Council make an absolute commitment to the future funding of the House. Allen was not sure she could stay on if the 'support adviser' had decision-making powers. The Floral Trust had still not made its final decision on 19 November, the day on which the wages had to be paid and the creditors called in. The company was granted an extension to 7.30 p.m. before it was to be declared bankrupt, and at the last moment the Floral Trust gave its guarantee. Allen agreed to the appointment of Pelham Allen as adviser, which was announced on 26 November. Pelham Allen was an accountant with Coopers and Lybrand. Isaacs later expressed anger at the way in which Chadlington conducted himself at the Select Committee, 'where he did everything he could to cause alarm and shout fire but always announced, "By the way I have a bucket of water with which I am going to put out the fire."'[36]

* * *

Amid the chaos, Payne's post-closure planning had ploughed its course. He had hoped to do an interesting and varied programme of works during the exile that would not have been suitable for the Covent Garden stage. Some of the programming, as well as being without relation to other parts of the company, was more optimistic in its aspirations than in its execution and reception. On 13 September there had been a depressing, impoverished-looking *Giulio Cesare* at the Barbican. In November 1997 the controversial *Ring* designer Nigel Lowery turned his hand to production. Mary Allen recalled that when departmental heads had seen Lowery's models for *Barbiere* on 29 October 'they just stared at what they obviously felt was going to be a pretty difficult prospect'. They were, she wrote, 'at the contemporary deconstructionist end of the artistic spectrum'.[37] Andrew Porter was not amused by what he called the 'horrible *Barbiere*'. 'During "*mille grazie*",' he lamented, 'the musicians mugged and beat up the Count.' More successful was a brief season of *The Turn of the Screw* at the Barbican in October, and Moshinsky's transfer of his *Otello* to the Albert Hall in November.

Payne left for the English National Opera in February 1998. Richard Jarman, who had been general director of Scottish Opera from 1991 to 1997, took over from Payne as artistic director, responsible for artistic planning.*

The Royal Opera, although many of its wounds were self-inflicted, was equally a victim of a government indifferent to the senior arts and culture. Smith had explained in his book *Creative Britain* that the renaming of the Department of National Heritage to the Department of Culture, Media and Sport was intended to capture 'more accurately the new spirit of modern Britain'. Smith had written, 'Cultural activity is not some elitist exercise that takes place in reverential temples aimed at the predilections of the cognoscenti.'

Arts people felt increasingly betrayed by Labour and there were accusations that New Labour was more interested in populist culture

---

* Jarman had been festival administrator at the Edinburgh International Festival, 1978–84; general administrator at English National Ballet, 1984–90; and general director of Scottish Opera, 1991–97.

like pop, film and design, than theatre, concerts, art galleries and museums. Lord Gowrie, while criticising Isaacs for the closure plans, told the Select Committee on 4 November, 'The previous government was taking cash out of the arts' and continued, 'Very regrettably, the present government has decided to stick to the previous government's planning totals, and the management of these organisations at international level on a continuously diminishing revenue cash flow is a nightmare and I do not know who can do it.'*[38] Peter Jonas declared in *Opera* in January 1998 that a country that can find £750 million for a Millennium Dome can find money for opera. He added, 'This opera crisis was foreseen by all of us working in the arts during the 1980s. It could be overcome, positively in an instant, were there the political will.' Doris Lessing, the novelist, had written to *The Times* on 15 November even more bluntly about the Royal Opera House's plight: 'This can be such a nasty little country; so Philistine, so mean, and often so stupid.'†

As if to prove Lessing's point, on 2 December the report of the Culture, Media and Sport Select Committee on the Royal Opera House was published. It stated, 'We would prefer to see the House run by a philistine with the requisite financial acumen than by the succession of opera and ballet lovers who have brought a great and valuable institution to its knees.' Kaufman's report was damning, while abjectly failing to clarify the central issues of underfunding and ownership. The report also ladled out justified specific criticisms: of Isaacs and Stirling for failing to prepare viable closure plans, of Chadlington for failing to appoint a finance director and to review fully the plans for the closure period, and of the manner of Mary Allen's appointment. It also recommended that the Board should resign immediately with the exception of Duffield, Michael Berkeley and Carolyn Newbigging

---

* On 2 December Trevor Nunn, in his first letter to funders as director of the National Theatre, explained that the company had lost £1.9 million in real terms from its subsidy in the 1998–99 budget. He appealed for increased fund-raising as the only hope for avoiding a reduction in education or raising prices. The Royal Shakespeare Company announced a deficit of £1.6 million. The British Museum Trust was considering entrance fees to cover deficit and the orchestras were suffering cuts in their grants.

† Peter Hall recalled trying to get his old Royal Shakespeare Company colleague John Barton's fifteen-hour play on the Trojan war accepted by the Millennium Dome committee. He had asked them, 'Aren't you going to have any theatre?' and they said, 'No, no, it's rather elitist.' 'And I said, "Aren't we rather good at the theatre?" and they said, "Yes, but we want to be really populist"' (Hall, Interview, 29.7.99).

of the Friends. Kaufman's main target was Mary Allen, who should resign, the report stated, because 'conduct fell far below the standards to be expected of the principal officer of a public body'. If they refused to go Smith should cut off their grant and put in an administrator until the reopening.

Mary Allen defended herself in the *Daily Telegraph*: 'I absolutely reject and refute the criticisms about my appointment.' She was angry that she had been singled out for 'criticism of an intemperate kind' when she had only been working at the Royal Opera for three months.[39] Richard Morrison in *The Times* described the Select Committee's report as Gerald Kaufman's 'virtuoso masterclass in the art of scathing denunciation'. John Major wrote to *The Times* to say that the report was a 'parody': it failed to live up to the demand of being 'demonstrably fair' and 'did not serve the Commons well'.[40]

The Kaufman committee underlined how far the hapless Royal Opera had been unfairly dragged into the arenas of class consciousness and politics. At one point during the committee's proceedings Kaufman had said that the Royal Opera House was 'a private club that tolerated his presence with difficulty'. Haitink was enraged by this remark as well as Kaufman's bitter complaints in the *Spectator* on 6 December 1997 about the poor service he received at the House and the ignorant snobbish members of the audience. Haitink wrote, 'It is simply scandalous that Kaufman should be allowed to carry his personal vendetta into an official document . . . there will always be snobbery in an opera audience – it is inevitable, and universal. I don't like it, but I live with it.'[41] Starved of funding throughout the Thatcher years, the House now faced new prejudices of 'anti-elitism' as well as the more traditional brand of philistinism. While spotlighting the shortcomings of management, Kaufman's committee made no attempt to protect the professionals and artists of the company. The committee's conclusions in an indirect way served to highlight, but in no way helped to provide an answer to, the central problem of the Royal Opera House at the end of the century: 'Who owns Covent Garden?'

Chadlington resigned on 4 December. Allen agreed to stay on, when urged to do so by the Board, Haitink and Smith, for fear of instability.[42]

In February's *Opera* Haitink defended Allen: 'As the current glut of vacancies at top level in arts administration Europe-wide illustrates, they do not grow on trees, even the philistine variety.' He added, 'What is separately needed at the moment is a modicum of stability.'*

On 15 January 1998 it was announced that Sir Colin Southgate, the chairman of EMI, was to be the new chairman of the Board. Southgate, a millionaire from developing computer software, was the first chairman to be appointed by a secretary of state – Smith having forgotten his argument to the Kaufman committee that he had 'no locus in appointments'. In February 1998 the Culture Department endorsed Duffield's appointment as vice-chairman. Southgate's appointment underscored the destruction of the arm's-length principle that Arnold Goodman had so staunchly defended. Moser regretted that government had become 'more invasive'.[43] Tooley later ascribed Smith's intervention to his being 'at his wits' end about CG'. He was, wrote Tooley, 'determined to take it by the scruff of its neck and suspicious of the self-electing process of the Board decided to remove at least the right of electing the chairman from the Board'.[44] Tooley later wrote that, in Southgate, Smith had found a 'tough businessman, free of nostalgia'. He also added ruefully, 'A passion for opera and ballet might have been considered another important quality, but perhaps that had not occurred to anyone.'[45]

Rumours immediately started to circulate about the dismantling of the company and in particular the sacking of the orchestra, which was something the Arts Council had long been pondering in the context of their belief that London had too many orchestras. Someone in the Arts Council warned the Royal Philharmonic to keep itself free from 1999. On 18 January 1998 Haitink, responding to this rumour, warned in the *Independent on Sunday*, 'I do not want to resign, but my priority

---

* Perhaps stability rather than superb managerial skills. David Syrus recalled, 'I found Mary Allen incredibly arrogant. I came off the stage at the Shaftesbury having conducted the fourth performance of *Figaro* in the week. She had been working for the company by that stage for over three months. She did not know my name. I had been head of the music staff here a long time, had just conducted a performance. She should have known who I was – or the white tie and the tails should perhaps have given the game away' (Syrus, Interview, 28.11.00).

must be to fight against any cuts in the orchestra or chorus. You can only walk out once.' He added, 'My job is to lead the orchestra and chorus into the new House, and I am not a man who gives up lightly.' In February 1998 he said, 'I am walking on very thin ice ... I am a loyal man. But the gap between loyalty and mere foolishness is a very narrow one.' Syrus recalled, 'Bernard fought wonderfully for us. You only have to say the right word in his ear at the right time and he feels that he is being engaged and can do something.'[46] On 5 March Haitink conducted a brilliant *Der Freischütz* at the Barbican. The music director was by default now the main guardian of the company, but in March he had to undergo open-heart surgery. He had not recovered in time to conduct a concert performance of *Parsifal* in May with Domingo at the Festival Hall.

In February 1998 Allen sacked Keith Cooper, director of sales, and Richard Hall who had been director of finance for eight months. On 25 March, however, in spite of Haitink's appeal for stability, Allen joined those she had sacked, the Board explaining that they were looking for an artistic director with an experienced manager as number two, a solution that was not acceptable to her. At the Board meeting on 25 March Southgate just shook her hand after she had presented her vision for the future of the company and 'briefly bade her farewell'.[47] Pelham Allen became acting chief executive.*

Kaufman was jubilant at Mary Allen's departure but in an open letter to Richard Eyre in *The Times* she articulated what Kaufman's report had abjectly failed to do. She wrote, 'The Government is daft if it does not recognise that we cannot continue with the present level of artistic excellence without some additional investment,' and added, 'One of the most disgraceful aspects of Government apathy is the way in which such a highly trained human resource is being wasted.'[48]

*   *   *

---

* At the end of March there were rumours that, among others, Richard Eyre, Brian McMaster, Gerard Mortier, and Simon Rattle had been approached to take on Covent Garden.

'Apathy' was being institutionalised. In January 1998 it was announced that Gerry Robinson, chairman of Granada, the television, hotel and theme park conglomerate media group, was to become chairman of the Arts Council at the end of March 1998. A successful businessman, Robinson had presided over the expansion of Granada's interests to include London Weekend and Yorkshire Tyne-Tees TV. His appointment was perceived as yet another step in the downgrading of the senior arts. So too was Chris Smith's speech to Musicalliance '98 in March – an organisation that included representatives from all musical practitioners other than commercial pop and subsidised classical music. Smith told them, 'I think we are beginning to see a move out of the pure classical tradition. It is a good start.'[49]

The arts editor of *The Times*, Richard Morrison, pointed out the worrying implications of Labour arts policy: 'Labour is fixated on "cultural industries" that make bucks. Ideally this Government would like *all* the arts to resemble rock music; relentlessly lowbrow, vastly profitable, nakedly populist.' Milnes wrote in *Opera* in April that he felt that 'there is an anti-arts anti-funding movement afoot, and the government is encouraging it'. In June, sixty leading figures from the arts, including Peter Hall and playwright Alan Ayckbourn, complained to Tony Blair about the heavy-handed treatment they had received from Robinson.* John Tusa, the managing director of the Barbican arts centre, warned on 11 March 1998 in *The Times* that 'in backing "the arts that pay" and overlooking and undervaluing "the arts that cost", Blair shows himself a true son of Margaret Thatcher'. Indeed, grants for the new year again showed, according to Lord Gowrie the outgoing chairman of the Arts Council, a cut of £34 million in real terms, after five years of standstill. The cut to the Royal Opera House was £39,970. Opera Factory lost its £100,000 funding altogether.

Robinson's reforms enraged the arts community. Council members were no longer to advise the Council but would advise 'art form directors' who would be appointed by the Arts Council. On 20 May

---

* The impresario millionaire, Cameron Mackintosh, withdrew from a scheme to give £10 million funding to the Arts Council in a funding partnership when they tried to force him to give £150,000 to the Chard Festival of Women in Music in Somerset and £175,000 to a Bangladeshi community, when he wanted to help theatres in distress like the King's Head in Islington.

the fifteen member drama advisory panel resigned en masse.* They explained their move in a letter to *The Times* on 21 May: 'Decisions on the future of the arts in England will be made by a smaller more powerful executive drawing on the practical expertise of independent, unpaid, professional, peer group advisers.' On 22 May 1998 Morrison in *The Times* wrote of the 'burning resentment' of arts professionals, who had 'rigorously cut costs, applied every marketing trick in the book, and cajoled their staffs to work stupendous hours for tuppence a week'. They were, he wrote, being 'undermined by the blundering interventions' of amateurs. Morrison asked if the arts should be run by 'arts practitioners or by faceless bureaucrats controlled by moonlighting tycoons, such as Robinson or, at Covent Garden, EMI's Colin Southgate'.

On 29 June Blair met senior arts representatives for a 'listening exercise', in response to attacks from such Labour stalwarts as Peter Hall. The Greenwich Theatre had folded in March for want of a £330,000 grant in the same neighbourhood as the Millennium Dome was being built. The delegation was led by Dennis Stevenson of the Tate Gallery and included Simon Rattle, Richard Eyre, and John Tusa.[50] Blair acknowledged that his government had neglected the state-funded arts, but said he had been 'stung' by suggestions that he was not interested in the arts. Eyre told him that the arts needed £60 million to make up for cuts of the last few years.[51] There was a report by someone present at the meeting that the Prime Minister said he would love to increase arts funding but could not do so unless the arts community could find a way of selling it to the *Sun*.

When Southgate took over he had discovered that there were still 'no accurate figures'. It took until May, working with Pelham Allen and David Lees, one of Southgate's chosen new Board members,† to work out the figures and produce some running budgets. It became increasingly clear to Southgate, basing his figures on the estimated income from sponsors, that 'whatever scenario you came to, the subsidy to run the place fully had to be increased to £25 million'. This

---

* Including Sam Mendes, Alan Ayckbourn and Thelma Holt.
† The new Board assembled by Southgate included Sir David Lees (chairman of GKN), and Labour peer Lord Eatwell. Property developer Stuart Lipton, Vivien Duffield, Michael Berkeley and Carolyn Newbigging stayed on.

was nearly double the existing grant.[52] Even with increased sponsorship and selling out every performance – let alone thinking of reducing seat prices – the new House faced an annual deficit of between £5 and £10 million. On 19 June 1998, just before Eyre's report was published, Southgate wrote to Gerry Robinson at the Arts Council, pointing out the financial facts, which meant that an extra £10 million in subsidy was needed to bring the subsidy up to £25 million. This letter was leaked to the press. Southgate got no response to his letter. After sending a reminder eventually received a telephone call to say the Arts Council could not do anything about it. Southgate began at this point to talk to Smith.

Eyre's report 'The Future of Lyric Theatre in London' was published on 30 June. It was an impressive and timely reminder of the value of the senior arts in a decent society, and applauded the plural nature of British arts funding – a mixture of subsidy and the free market – making a striking defence of the principle of subsidy. It also made useful, if harsh, criticisms and proposals for Covent Garden's management. Where it fell down was in its failure to point to underfunding as the cause of the ownership imbroglio.

In answer to the growing hostility to the senior arts, to which Iris Murdoch had drawn attention in the early Nineties, and to counter Smith's 'some elitist exercise' in 'reverential temples' comment, Eyre explained the true meaning of 'elitism'. 'All the performing arts', he wrote, 'provoke accusations of elitism.' This was because:

> They are dedicated to creating work that can only be performed by a very few, very gifted and very skilful people to an audience limited by the number who can sit in a concert hall, a theatre, or an opera house at any one time. The use of 'elitism' as a pejorative term is only justified if the work seeks to obscure rather than illuminate, and if the performers are reluctant to communicate.

The perjorative use of the term was also justified, according to Eyre, if the institutions repelled prospective audiences through 'excessively high prices'. But he laid the main blame for growing perceptions of

exclusion where they belonged, at the door of the government, charging that the choice of going to the performing arts had not been given
to enough young people in the United Kingdom either by schools or
parents. 'The power to engender real access can only be achieved', he
stressed, 'by reducing ticket prices ... and funding education ...
making the arts truly inclusive.'* Nevertheless, Eyre also found Covent
Garden guilty of a 'selectively exclusive attitude' because of its prices
and because of the 'perceived behaviour – or the social class of its
enthusiasts', even though, he admitted, it was unreasonable 'to judge
an art by the company it keeps'.† In his view Covent Garden's exclusivity had contributed to growing doubts about subsidy in general. 'If
scepticism has increased in the past few years,' he wrote, 'it has much
to do with the fact that the Royal Opera House has come to be seen
as the barometer of the health of the performing arts.' In order to
remedy this ill, he argued, the House must also put access at the centre
of its policy-making and 'demonstrate that it has the audience at the
centre of everything it does', continuing to offer a wide range of ticket
prices, with broadcasting viewed as part of the access issue rather than
for financial reasons.‡

Although underfunding lay behind the development of exclusivity
at Covent Garden, Eyre chose not to focus on it, only at the end of
his report arguing that more money would be required and the funding
system revitalised. In this largely overlooked section he compared
Covent Garden's subsidy of £14.4 million for 1998–99 with that of La

---

* Syrus stressed that the only barrier to inclusivity was ticket prices, recalling, 'I came
to Covent Garden at sixteen and just thought "this place is for me, when I can save up
my pocket money and my paper round money I will be here". Occasionally I didn't get
the tickets I asked for but usually I did. I just loved to come here. I didn't feel it was
excluding me' (Interview, 6.12.00).

† During his introduction Eyre quoted the then Housing Minister of the 1980s, Sir
George Young, as saying that homeless people were 'the sort of people you step on
when you come out of the opera'. (The Eyre Review, p. 35).

‡ Elaine Padmore, who became opera director in 1999, later commented that there had
been much criticism of the Royal Opera for selling so many tickets to the Friends but,
she explained, 'Without the Friends' support it's a much more random business – every
opera house has Friends, has its subscribers – it's not as if we are the only company
doing that – we can't have no guaranteed income.' And she continued, 'Much as you
want to have the opportunity to offer seats to all comers on the day, what do you do
if they decide not to come? You have got to fill the House and the Friends are the loyal
supporters, the Arsenal supporters, the fans who will guarantee that we will be able to
keep going because they are giving us money' (Interview, 5.12.00).

Scala at £34 million and the Berlin Staatsoper at £30.7 million a year, or Hamburg at £28.6 million. Even the English National Opera received £11.96 million for its single company. British taxpayers, Eyre admitted, had been paying a comparatively small amount for a product of the quality being delivered by the Royal Opera House and the English National Opera.

In spite of his damning criticisms, and in contradiction to Smith's original plan, Eyre recommended that the Royal Opera and ENO maintain their separate identities and Houses. Britain deserved an international opera house and the House had a justifiably respected international reputation. But it must sort out its leadership problems and planning procedures, both of which had become 'deeply flawed'. It was 'imperative' to find 'visionary leadership in an artistic director of international repute in the opera and ballet worlds, underpinned by sound financial and managing expertise'.* There should be 'greater consultation and communication from the earliest stage and with regard for budget'. Eyre wrote, 'I cannot emphasise too strongly that the endemic lack of communication within the Royal Opera House is the cancer that will destroy the organisation unless it is treated.'

Eyre also urged that there should be 'a clear separation' between the Board and the Executive and 'in no circumstances should the main Board, or the advisory Board, attempt to act as surrogates for the artistic leaders'. He added, 'The main Board are not experts and are not qualified to make artistic policy.' Donors should be encouraged to think of 'involvement, commitment and prestige . . . rather than exclusivity which has done so much harm'.† Eyre praised the devotion of the staff, who 'are highly skilled and widely experienced . . . Many accept rates of pay well below the average because of their devotion to the work . . . they have a level of commitment and a comprehensive

---

* Eyre gave recommendations for the structure of the organisation, which he believed should have the music director at the heart of all planning. He dismissed the idea of dispensing with the orchestra: 'a permanent orchestra . . . makes for better artistic standards and the current orchestra has very high musical standards' but argued for 'more flexible working practices'. He supported Terry Edwards's 'core chorus' supplemented by freelance singers.

† At the National Theatre the Board were helpful and never interfered with artistic policy. Richard Morrison in *The Times* observed that while Eyre pleaded for clarity in the chain of command he failed 'to lift the lid on the Sainsbury and Duffield figures', and the power that their contributions gave them.

knowledge of the end product that would be the envy of many commercial organisations.'

It was the devoted staff who were now to bear the brunt of the solution to both the mismanagement and the shortage of funding. On 27 July 1998 Southgate summoned a meeting at EMI during which the various options were discussed, including that of the company being shut down, and all its members including the orchestra and chorus made redundant. The ballet company would be kept going, possibly under Sainsbury as chairman of the company's governors, but with the artistic directors fired and the company forced to accept new contracts. The building work would continue, the Friends and Trust carry on. The House would reopen in 1999. Smith agreed the next day that the 1998–99 subsidy should be spent on redundancy costs. *The Times* reported the Arts Council and Minister were determined to close the companies completely.*

In August 1998 Haitink had recovered sufficiently from his open-heart surgery to conduct another magnificent *Don Carlos* at Edinburgh. On 3 September Milnes wrote that the Royal Opera's *Don Carlos* was vastly superior to the Salzburg *Don Carlos* – which had been 'indifferently directed' by Herbert Wernicke and 'hideously conducted' by Maazel – as well as being at seat prices a quarter those at Salzburg. He also found the threatened orchestra superior to the Vienna Philharmonic at Salzburg. Haitink alone, he wrote, could hold the company together by 'his international stature and by the example of music-making like this'. When *Peter Grimes* and *Il Masnadieri* were heard in Finland, the audiences said that they had never heard such fine orchestral playing or choral singing. Milnes wrote that 'in a country less shy of its achievements' the Royal Opera 'would be regarded as a jewel in the crown, a pearl beyond price.'[53]

The fate of the orchestra and chorus was still held in the balance. Not knowing what subsidy the government would agree to, or how

---

* Michael Berkeley told the press on 29 October, 'The financial view was that we should close it all down – companies too – and start again. That works in financial terms, but in artistic and human terms it doesn't . . . it's paramount to keep the musicians playing and the dancers dancing' (*The Times*).

much could be raised from donors, the Board were negotiating contracts with the staff. It was, in Southgate's words, like 'putting virtual pieces in a three-dimensional jigsaw puzzle'.[54] Although Southgate later told the author he had always believed that the orchestra was essential to the House, he admitted that the rumour became a useful bargaining counter in the complicated negotiations between the government, unions and management which went on during 1998.[55] The perception in the House and outside, however, was that the threat was a very real one. A member of the orchestra later recalled, 'The orchestra were definitely going to go.' The sober and well-informed editor of *Opera*, writing in his editorial in September 1998, concluded from the rumours about the Royal Philharmonic, 'Message, the ROH orchestra is to be chucked away, Haitink will of course go, the Royal Opera as we know it will be no more.'[56]

On Monday, 7 September at 8.45 a.m. Southgate, accompanied by Pelham Allen, went to the Ministry and told Chris Smith that the Royal Opera House was £13 million in debt and that by March 2000 that figure could have reached £25 million. 'We have been asked to bring ticket prices down,' Southgate said. 'We want to do this, but we can't without money. It is a circle we cannot square.' If the government did not respond the House would have to close.[57]

It was becoming increasingly clear to Southgate and the Board that in order to balance the books it was going to be necessary to reduce the number of performances to match the intended funding. Southgate later recalled, 'We then came up with the proposal to cut performances in the new House to balance the books. At £20 million we could put on two hundred-plus performances in the new House.'[58] There would be radical changes to working practices. The *Daily Telegraph* reported that Southgate threatened to resign and close the opera house for good if the government did not promise extra funding.[59] When Smith was apprised of Southgate's proposals he responded that evening by letter praising Southgate for his 'visionary approach towards securing the ROH's long-term future'.

On 8 September the junior Arts Minister, Alan Howarth, met the Board to discuss the proposals and assure them that extra money would be made available through the Arts Council if the House honoured its commitment to change. Smith's demand that there should be a complete overhaul of management to ensure that proper financial controls were maintained was reiterated, and negotiations with the unions and big donors began in order to meet the new budget.

On 9 September the cancellation of the 1998–99 season was announced, including performances at Sadler's Wells from 16 January. Ian Albery of Sadler's Wells had not been informed before the announcement.* The same day staff were told about the planned reduction of performances. They were also told that they had to accept renegotiated work conditions by 26 October or redundancy notices would be issued to take effect on 18 January 1999. Phrases such as 'cost-effective use of time' and 'restructuring' and 'greater flexibility' caused anger, with one man reportedly shouting, 'Do you mean put-your-legs-behind-your-ears and-tape-them-there flexible?'[60] Southgate was reported as telling the artists' unions during the negotiations, 'You think you're tough? I'm tough. You test me. I'm tough.'[61] A member of the orchestra later recalled that Pelham Allen was quoted as saying at this meeting, 'Unfortunately you've chosen the wrong profession.' David Syrus remembered 'nearly crying'. It was, he said, 'a very bad time . . . I foresaw that the hardship was going to affect us enormously in our department. One member of the music staff had grave family problems and was most vulnerable when all this came.'[62] Tooley wrote of the House's workforce, 'They felt that they were being blamed for Covent Garden's problems and were being penalised accordingly.'[63]

According to Tooley, Bernard Haitink had not been informed or consulted about any of these decisions and was again concerned about the rumours of the threat to the orchestra. He told Canning of the *Sunday Times* that he had been 'flabbergasted' and 'furious' to receive a fax which read, 'Maybe you will be interested in this.'[64] He composed a letter of resignation and spoke three times on the telephone to Tooley, who later wrote, 'While he wanted to resign in protest, he was aware that he was the one person who could keep the orchestra in place and the orchestral musicians and chorus were looking to him for help.' Haitink also told Canning that he believed the closure decision had been 'made in a panic'.[65] Tooley also thought the closure

---

* Sadler's Wells reopened on 11 October 1998 after a £48 million lottery refit with 1,600 seats; £1.35 million compensation had to be paid to Sadler's Wells for the cancelled season.

had not been thought out, as the cancellation of the Sadler's Wells contract alone was terribly costly.*[66] There were others who felt that it was a political gesture in order to make the slightly increased funding for the reopened House more palatable.

Southgate had talked to Tooley, not Haitink, on the telephone. Tooley 'was pleased to be informed', he later wrote, 'but it demonstrated a curious sense of priorities and confirmed my opinion that Southgate is so uncomfortable with artists that he goes out of his way to avoid them'.[67] Haitink concurred. He told Canning, 'I am afraid the new chairman does not understand artists. He never comes to anything, he does not know what we are doing, he was not at the *Ring*, nor at *Don Carlos* or the other Verdi operas at Edinburgh.'[68] On 13 October the Board rallied to the defence of Southgate in the face of rising criticism from Haitink and the dancers. The ballerinas were accusing him of cruelty for trying to put 'compulsory retirement at the age of thirty-five' into their contracts, as well as a forty-week contract. Talking to the press had become a sackable offence. Michael Berkeley attempted to explain that management was trying to find enough work to keep Haitink and the orchestra 'fit' for the reopening.

The company continued to do magnificent work. In September and October 1998 there were fine semi-staged performances of the *Ring* at the Albert Hall. Before the performances musicians of the orchestra were outside the Albert Hall, appealing for support against their imminent disbandment. It was, said Canning, too 'ludicrous' to contemplate, and could only come from the Arts Council, which 'profligately commissions reviews, reports and feasibility studies while our arts institutions teeter on the brink of catastrophe'. At the end of the cycle 5,000 people rose to their feet in standing ovation.[69] Haitink later recalled, 'The existence not only of the orchestra but what was left of the company, the nucleus of the chorus, the music staff was all at stake.† At that time we all thought that we had had it ... After *Götterdämmerung*, when normally as a conductor you are totally

---

* Michael Berkeley expressed 'dismay' that the Arts Council England was insisting on £350,000 on top of the million Covent Garden in fact owed Sadler's Wells (*The Times*, 19.10.98, quoted in Lebrecht, *Covent Garden*, p. 467).
† David Syrus had been offered the position of head of music staff at San Francisco (Interview, 29.11.00).

exhausted, I found myself moving forward to say a few words to the audience: "This is a serious situation. Help us. Write to the Department of Culture because it is a matter of life and death." [70]

The Covent Garden Board had consistently misjudged the government's attitude to 'bailing out' the House in its 'hour of need'. Sir James Spooner, director of the Royal Opera House from 1986 to 1997, wrote to *The Times* on 26 November pointing out that first the state had passed the buck of rebuilding to the lottery and had then refused to commit itself to the task. 'To other nations', he wrote, 'it must seem absolutely pathetic that the administration of a country as comparatively rich as Britain has not got the will to see it through.'

Haitink had reached his limit. Syrus recalled that although he hated confrontations, 'when he does take them on he goes about them in a very stubborn way determined to win'.[71] On 11 October he offered his resignation, saying, 'There is little point in being music director when there is no music to conduct. The closing of the opera company for a season is lethal.'[72] Haitink wrote to Smith to ask him, 'Do you want an international opera company or not? If you say no, let's close the whole business down ... if you say yes then you have to make it work.' Canning wrote that Haitink's resignation would signal to the musical world that 'opera of the kind that Haitink has delivered with his *Don Carlos* and *Ring* cycles cannot be nurtured and flourish in this country and city'.[73] On 14 October Claus Moser and Denis Forman wrote to *The Times* that to lose the orchestra and Haitink would be 'a tragic act of cultural vandalism'.

The 'vandals' were co-ordinating the attack. On 14 October 1998, during his Arts Council annual lecture entitled 'An Arts Council for the future', Robinson launched a vitriolic attack on the institutions he was supposed to be supporting and defending. Although he denounced George Steiner for saying that 'a philistine, vengeful mood is being orchestrated to put in question the role of serious music', he seemed to be part of it. He accused the Royal Opera House and the national orchestras of failing to do educational work and therefore playing 'to the same middle-class audiences'. In the back of the arts institutions' minds, he sneered, 'lurks the vague hope that one day enlightenment might descend semi-miraculously upon the rest'.*

Robinson also accused the Royal Opera House of not doing out-reach to audiences, citing the Hamlyn week at the South Bank as an example of what could be done at Covent Garden. He was apparently unaware that Covent Garden had originated the scheme and that it had only moved from its twelve-year residency at the House because of the redevelopment. Isaacs in his memoirs was quietly and justifiably enraged by Robinson's 'blatant falsehood' – which was uncritically reported by the press – that the Royal Opera House did not do outreach while it had in fact done innovative and continuous work since Web-ster's time. There was never any apology for this or any of the other factual infelicities in Robinson's speech.†[74] Robinson ended with a tough warning. 'There will be no blank cheques. In the new era no one should kid themselves that the Arts Council will be a soft touch.'

As Tusa had pointed out, Robinson was focusing on what he called the cultural industries. Funding, he warned, must now be more 'flexible and not stick to traditional arts forms' – it would take into account the money-making potential of the grantee. Robinson talked excitedly about Kirklees media centre backed by £2 million of Arts Council funding, which employed 100 people in Internet, multi-media and graphic design. Iris Murdoch's 'myths' had no place on the Internet, and Richard Eyre's subsidised world, where 'the need to be good' and not profit was 'paramount', looked ever more threatened.‡

* * *

* Gillian Moore wrote an article for *The Times* on 22 October 1998 in which she exhorted Robinson to do his 'homework', explaining in detail her role as consultant to the Los Angeles Philharmonic from 1993 to 1995, on loan from the Festival Hall where she was head of education. It had been with 'astonishment', she wrote, that she had read Robin-son's speech in which he had begun with a 'paean of praise' to the Los Angeles Philhar-monic for expanding its audience through education and had castigated British performers for plying their trade 'to the same white, middle-class audiences' etc. She went on to give details of 'ground-breaking' educational work being done by the Royal Liverpool Philharmonic, the City of London Sinfonia, and the City of Birmingham Symphony Orchestra. Moore asked why the musicians were being blamed for limited audiences when the government was cutting music from the school curriculum.
† Robinson's speechwriter, Phil Murphy, was head of communications at New Labour in 1999.
‡ The 'dumbing down' fear was also underlined on 5 December. Writers including A. S. Byatt and Michael Holroyd, had been appalled to discover that Shakespeare and Chaucer would not appear in the Millennium Dome because 'leading arts organisations and figures have been excluded from the plans' and requests for meetings rejected. The

On 23 October Equity held a press conference at the new Sadler's Wells. The Equity representative reported that without agreements, management would serve redundancy notices and the companies would not survive. The general secretary of Equity criticised management for being confrontational and aggressive, arguing, 'We all know how the House has been managed ... Now the poorest people are being asked to pay for it.' In the evening the management extended its deadline by two days.

There followed two days of intense negotiations. On 24 October *The Times* reported that management had agreed better terms for the orchestra. The chorus, however, was still being asked to agree to a forty-week year instead of fifty-two and a further reduction in its size to thirty-six. The choristers were also anxious about the loss of guaranteed free time, and that they would have to be available for up to forty-eight hours a week between the hours of 9.30 a.m. and 11 p.m., Monday to Saturday, plus some Sunday performances. One chorus member explained that 'the whole skill of being a chorister is making your voice last' and 'no overtime at all means losing control of time'. History, he added, 'shows if you place yourself in that position you would be exploited'.* But there was no choice, he recalled: 'The Equity guy came and said we were at the end of the road and that we would all be sacked. I don't believe it was true.'

On 26 October, the day on which the new contracts had to be signed, the *Guardian* attempted to defend the workforce. Adam Sweeting wrote, 'The chorus has amassed a store of musical knowledge that enables it to tackle any remotely known work at a couple of days' notice.' The *Guardian* reported a member of the company as saying, 'It's a wonderful building but the heart of it is the performing com-

---

millennium organisers said literature was being excluded because it is 'more of a personal thing'. In November 1997 Jennie Page, chief executive of the New Millennium Experience Company, rejected the magnificent Peter Hall, John Barton *Tantalus* project. Michael Kustow, who was endeavouring to get funding for the project, wrote in his diary that Page had responded, ' "Really, it's not exactly the kind of thing the masses" – well she didn't actually talk about the masses, but I get the gist' (Michael Kustow, *Theatre @ Risk*, p. 20).

* The chorus member believed that with more careful working out of schedules there need not have been much overtime at all, but that the principle was the choristers' sole protection, 'where a skilled manager could schedule the year's work without incurring any overtime at all and I think the problem was they did not have a skilled manager'.

panies. By the time it opens it will need a triple bypass.'[75] That same day Davis, Barenboim, Boulez, Gergiev, Kleiber, Levine, Mehta, Rattle and Rostroprovich wrote to *The Times*, 'It takes a long time to build up so excellent an orchestra and chorus and no time at all to destroy both of them ... It is not they who have brought disrepute on the place. On the contrary many, many performances have been given by them which have been the envy of the world.' The Board and Smith were trying to persuade Haitink to stay.

On 28 October the Board met at EMI with Duffield determined not to give way. By 6 p.m. the dancers had settled and Southgate issued a statement to say that the orchestra had been saved and that Haitink might withdraw his resignation.* On 29 October Southgate announced that after an eight-hour Board meeting the threat of mass redundancies had been withdrawn. Michael Berkeley said the agreements that had been reached were to insure that the government would provide 'the money to see it through'. Management agreed to fifty weeks' employment for the dancers, instead of redundancy. The chorus agreed to a new contract and a retainer of 50 per cent of salary during the total closure from January to September 1999. A member of the chorus explained that the new contract was 'wildly undefined'. It basically permits, he explained, 'a certain number of hours in the year for which we are paid as our basic salary, and if they exceed that it would be overtime but that will be horrendously difficult to keep track of'. With no overtime at all, small parts and covers would be 'the only way of earning extra money'. Salaries were to be set at slightly less than the £25,400 secured in 1997 but for a forty-week year. Management was committed to building the season up from forty to forty-six weeks and it was agreed that those extra weeks would be bought at the same rate and the basic salary would come up to £28,000.

Some members of the chorus were bitter. One recalled, 'Bernard defended the orchestra but let us, the choristers, down – a bit embarrassed about what happened to us – everyone let us down.' Terry Edwards, he added, 'let it happen', using the opportunity to make a

---

* According to Lebrecht Sainsbury had backed the dancers in their demand for full employment and had warned that the Royal Ballet would 'go it alone' if necessary (Lebrecht, *Covent Garden*, p. 461).

fresh start. 'They should look on me as a top professional,' the chorister argued ruefully. 'I am one of the top choral singers in the country. Without the chorus there is no company.' When the House reopened staff were indeed concerned about the new conditions, although it was somewhat easier for the orchestra who were on a rota system. Syrus explained, 'We are all disappointed with the hours. The schedule is 11 to 2 and signing in for the show may well be 6.45 or something. That gives you a very short afternoon to go home and have the rest of your life.'*[76]

With the agreements in place in November, Smith told Southgate that there would be an increase in the House's grant in order to improve access through 'work to develop new audiences and education programmes'. Smith wrote to Southgate, 'Your plans for reforming and restructuring the ROH are wholly consistent with these aims, and will also address the recommendations of Eyre.' Smith was urging the Arts Council to commit to a guaranteed programme of support for the next three years.[77] On 11 November Haitink withdrew his resignation after conversations with Smith, having been told that there would be enough work the next year to maintain the orchestra.[78] Smith also tried to reassure the major donors that year-round performances would eventually be reinstated.

On 15 December, Smith and the big donors of the Board met the Arts Council, when the final decision was made to cut performances by a third in the reopened House in order to balance the books – there would be 100 performances by the Royal Opera and 120 by the Royal Ballet. There was to be a recommitment to educational work and accessibility would be assured with cheaper Friday and Saturday tickets, more matinées and at least 20 per cent of the tickets available to the general public for each performance. A department source was quoted as saying, 'Chris has never had a problem offering the ROH more money, but it could only be provided in the right context,

---

* By 2002 there were 103 members of the orchestra. Tooley said that after many calculations his administration had concluded that the optimum size for the orchestra was 140 and the minimum number of players should be 120. This allowed members of the orchestra to have a reasonable working week without bringing in extra players – a principle Tooley felt should have been adhered to even though the extra players were of a suitably high standard (Interview, 11.4.02).

otherwise the government would be accused of rewarding mismanagement and incompetence.'[79]

Southgate had believed, as Sainsbury before him, that he had secured an implicit understanding with the government. Southgate's understanding was that if the Board managed to deliver the 1998 agreement the government would provide the increased subsidy adequate for the House to reinstate a full programme within three years. But when the Board, having delivered the agreement, went back to the government for the increase, Southgate was upset to discover that the government had reneged and that the Arts Council had finally set the subsidy at £20 million plus inflation. This meant that a full season could only be reached through additional private money and would restrict the work in the other new performance spaces of the House.

On 17 December Gerry Robinson announced the increase in subsidy for the arts, from £189.6 million to £218.8 million in 1999–2000, to £228.9 million in 2000–01, and £243.7 million in 2001–02. He also addressed 'the ongoing problems of the Royal Opera House' with a three-year recovery plan to put the company back on track with an 11 per cent 'uplift', from £14.4 million to £16 million, up to £20 million in 2000–01 and at least £20 million in 2001–02.[80]

The Board had continued to search for an intendant. Southgate was keen to get Sarah Billinghurst from the Met, and it was suggested that Michael Kaiser of American Ballet Theater might be her administrator. Billinghurst recalled that Southgate had not been sure what was needed for Covent Garden until he met Kaiser in New York, when he decided that he was the right man for the job with his talent for dealing with crisis situations as well as artists. Billinghurst therefore withdrew and on 17 September 1998 Kaiser was named executive director from 12 November 1998.

Southgate, in announcing the appointment, said Kaiser's record included 'the elimination of accumulated deficits, increases in box office and fund-raising revenue and the expansion of education and outreach programmes'. The *Chicago Tribune* had called him 'the turnaround king'. His father was a violinist and he had trained as a singer before becoming a management consultant.* Kaiser told Peter Conrad of the *Observer* on 30 January 2000, 'When I walk into a troubled organisation, I put an embargo on public discussion of the past, and that whole obsession with deciding who's to blame.' Kaiser's appointment raised hopes in a grim situation but it did not fulfil Eyre's recommendation of an intendant with the experience of running a top national opera and ballet company, or answer the question of the Board's relationship to the executive.

Kaiser announced the plans for the new building in an upbeat way on 28 January 1999. After an opening festival of events in November and December, including two gala performances with Plácido Domingo, the House would be open all day for tours. Ticket prices were to be graded in a complicated way whereby top prices remained at £150 for the most popular and exciting work during the week but would be less at the weekend when the corporate members were out of town. Top prices for matinée performances of *Falstaff*, for instance, would be £65. Twenty per cent of tickets would be available for non-subscribers every day. There would be free chamber music concerts at lunchtime and the House would be open to the public during the day for the first time.†

On 16 February 1999 the renovated Royal Opera House and Floral Hall, with its glass barrel vault, was formally topped out. The public saw for the first time the Floral Hall with its 'civic dignity' taking its cue from 'E. M. Barry's grandiloquent portico'.[81] The House had new escalators up to the roof-top promenade, a much improved amphitheatre, a new cream-stuccoed 'Barry-style' fly tower, and a new studio-sized auditorium, with 400 seats, the Linbury Theatre. After years of having to work in studios in West London, the Royal Ballet had airy studios in the House, one of which contained facilities for 200 seats for the public. The press welcomed the improvements and architect Jeremy Dixon's sensitivity in maintaining the different faces of the

---

* Kaiser had succeeded in turning round the fortunes of the Kansas City Ballet Company and had then worked with the Alvin Ailey dance company and American Ballet Theater. Morrison of *The Times* wrote that he must seem to the Royal Opera a combination of 'Merlin, Midas and Mystic Meg'.
† The Royal Opera House announced several community activities including the continuation of 'A Chance to Dance', and the creation of an opera by schoolchildren of Wandsworth with the help of House staff.

theatre on its different sides. The *Sunday Times*, in a long article about the revamped House, pointed out that for the first time it was possible to approach it from the market area and concluded that in 'preserving, rebuilding and extending' rather than starting from scratch like the Met and Bastille, 'something magnificent' had been yielded.[82]

It was announced on 24 March 1999 that thirty-nine-year-old Antonio Pappano would be artistic and music director, devoting 70 per cent of his time to the House, and with substantial powers. Pappano had been born in Epping and brought up in London and the US, and had been music director in Oslo and Brussels. His father had been a singing teacher and Pappano himself had been répétiteur with Connecticut Grand Opera, New York City, Barcelona, Frankfurt and Chicago, as well as working at Bayreuth with Barenboim. Pappano insisted that the Royal Opera House orchestra come to Brussels to hear him in order 'to be included in the decision'. His appointment answered Eyre's recommendation that the music director be central to artistic planning.

The final piece of the administrative jigsaw was fitted on 9 September 1999 when it was announced that Elaine Padmore was to join management as opera director, primarily as an administrator but with artistic responsibilities. Padmore had studied music at Birmingham University and singing at the Guildhall School of Music. She had freelanced as a singer and pianist after graduation but in 1971 went to work as music programmes producer for Radio 3 at the BBC. She was head of opera there until 1982, when she became artistic director at Wexford. There Padmore enjoyed introducing little-known artists such as Sergei Leiferkus, as well as scheduling obscure repertoire. Since September 1992 she had been running the Royal Danish Opera.*

*　　*　　*

* After Haitink's retirement at the end of the House's extremely successful 2001–02 season Padmore was to have less influence and Pappano more, in planning the repertoire and its direction. There were those who, unlike Eyre, felt that the head of planning should not be a working artist. Francesca Zambello, who was not to find favour with the new music director, said, 'You can't be responsible to a full artistic vision if your own motives are inside of it'. (Interview, 25.3.02). Pappano was to bring with him many of those he had worked with in Brussels including Hans Neuenfels, Keith Warner and Robert Wilson.

Kaiser immediately set to work to restore morale and soothe the feelings of the unhappy staff. 'I love the arts and I love artists,' he explained. 'There was a lot of hurt here,' he told the *New York Times*, 'people were feeling unloved, that they were not being treated properly.' He also had to restore Haitink's confidence. He told *Classical Music* on 17 April 1999, 'Bernard's resignation was much more serious because it's not just that he is an important conductor and we need him here, but that he was truly a symbol of what was happening at the opera house, and that was something I spent a lot of time trying to address. Bernard is, I think, happy now.'

Haitink had been assuaged by the reinstatement of a much reduced season that was to include Britten's *Paul Bunyan*, *The Bartered Bride* in December and *The Golden Cockerel*, some Verdi performances and a *War Requiem*. Syrus recalled that many people including Kaiser 'spent ages of energy trying to talk to him, and keep his morale up'.[83] The orchestra was also to tour the United States, Italy and Germany. The Royal Ballet fared better with a Far Eastern tour and a season at Sadler's Wells. On 8 June, Maurizio Benini conducted *Un Giorno di regno* at the Festival Hall, and a Verdi celebration devised and conducted by Edward Downes was described by Milnes as the 'last defiant splutter of the Verdi project, the plan to perform all his works by the end of next year's centennial'. Vasko Vassilev's solo from *I Lombardi* was 'wonderfully played' in a 'rousing evening'. In the autumn of 2000 Haitink was able to say, 'I've won that battle. The orchestra is there. The chorus is now expanding in number and is in prime condition.' Haitink mentioned David Syrus, who would, he said, have gone to a full-time position in San Francisco and concluded, 'I would also have gone. But let's not look back now . . . Now we are looking forward.'[84]

Having soothed Haitink, Kaiser hoped to restore the authority of the professional management, telling the *New York Times*, 'Typically, in times of trouble, the Board gets involved in day-to-day activities, and that is what happened here.' He hoped, he explained, to make them 'realise that if this place is going to be successful, it has to be run by the staff and not by the Board'.[85] As Eyre had written, there were too many Boards acting like shadow Boards. Southgate immediately abolished the ballet and opera Boards, replacing them with a group of four or five artistic members of the Board who met four or five times a year and maintained a close relationship with the artistic team.[86] In September 2001 the Friends and Royal Opera House Trust were combined into a single charity, the Royal Opera House Foundation.

Until the £100 million redevelopment target was finally reached, however, Duffield was indispensable and omnipresent. The goal was brought nearer when, in August, Kaiser convinced his Met and Kirov friend, Alberto Vilar, to give £10 million in return for having his name tied to the Floral Hall. His was the first name to appear on any major arts institution in England. Vilar also promised money for a young artists programme and three new productions over the next five years.*

The House's final debts were written off by the sale of property. This was criticised by Philip Jones in *The Times* when he wrote that this property was 'vested in the Development Land Trust' of which the co-trustees were the Arts Council England and the House. It had been intended that any excess after the rebuilding was to be used for an endowment fund.'[87] Isaacs, however, was content. He believed that the 'realisation of property value which has enhanced beyond any forecast' as well as 'raiding the appeal' was the only sensible way to proceed in order to achieve the otherwise unrealisable objective of rebuilding the House.[88] Isaacs also recalled that the Met, after its move to the Lincoln Center had been forced to sell its last asset – the land on which the old Met had stood – to avoid bankruptcy in 1975.

The 5 December 1999 opening was a glittering black-tie event, with the prime minister Tony Blair in attendance. Fiona Maddocks in the

---

* Padmore explained that the young artists programme would be for young professionals on the threshold of international careers for whom Covent Garden would provide 'a deluxe introduction to the life of an opera house – intensive polishing, one-to-one training and coaching from stars who are in the House – a really intensive programme with a lot of performing'. Of the Linbury Theatre she said, 'We want to use it for chamber opera, the kind of repertoire that is the wrong size for the main stage – eighteenth-century work, modern operas of a chamber size, if we had a budget, which at the moment we don't at all – except for the Vilar budget for one production a year with young artists' (Padmore, Interview 5.12.00.). *Opera News* in August 2001 wrote that Vilar was urging Covent Garden, Vienna and Salzburg to introduce the titling system developed at the Met, for which he owned the technology.

Observer put the opening in proper perspective, writing, 'To call the reopening on schedule of the Royal Opera House a miracle after two years of corporate mayhem, hardly seems an overstatement.' Haitink's choice of operatic repertoire was a fair representation of the music director's mood after the traumas of the closure, described by Maddocks as 'bizarre, serious, inaccessible, protracted' and solidly German. The programme included the Weber *Oberon* overture written for Covent Garden in 1826, the Siegmund–Sieglinde duet sung by Domingo and Polaski, and the finale of Beethoven's *Fidelio* sung by such Covent Garden stalwarts as Robert Lloyd, Jeremy White, Timothy Robinson and Roderick Earle. The somewhat subdued opera opening contrasted with the rehoused ballet company's more lively fare – a history of the Royal Ballet told through two hours of ballet extracts.

On 6 December the new Vick *Falstaff* premiere revealed brighter acoustics, which Milnes described as 'brassy, immediate and slightly relentless'. Everyone was a bit nervous on opening night, Milnes reported, but by the final scene in Windsor Forest 'the music started to "sing" as it should under Bernard Haitink's care'. Paul Brown's brilliant coloured sets and Graham Vick's 'bed and broad' approach presented 'not so much an autumnal, worldly-wise human comedy in half-tones, as a romp with more than a touch of *Carry on Falstaff*. As ever fascinated by acrobatics, Vick conceived Herne's Oak as a 'human construct rising spectacularly out of the stage'.[89] Bryn Terfel's Falstaff was that of a singer in his prime, Michael Kennedy describing his 'marvellous performance, sung with majestic power and exuberance and also much subtlety'.[90] Terfel's approach to the role was that of a gleeful mischief-maker, with a deep vein of optimism running through the performance – a passionate, roguish Falstaff, dating back to Mario Stabile rather than the melancholy wise man that Bruson and others have recently portrayed.

The Millennium Dome, designed to last less than twenty-five years, was opened on 31 December at a cost to the lottery funders six times that of the Royal Opera House development. Its twenty-eight-minute show was conceived by pop impresario Mark Fisher and rock star Peter Gabriel. It was a populist spectacle of 160 acrobats, dancers, abseilers, trampoline and trapeze artists, representing earth people and sky people, performing to electronic music. Its wordless and banal non-story attempted to evoke the conflict between technology and nature. Meanwhile, Peter Hall's and John Barton's *Tantalus*, and the Royal Shakespeare Company's majestic Shakespeare history cycle, were forced to look to Denver and Michigan for their funding.

The British press were in no mood for high or low culture and soon Kaiser felt the full force of its venom in spite of the successful opening. There had been gleeful reports on 24 November that Ligeti's *Grand Macabre* had been cancelled because of small but significant delays with some of the technical equipment. It was to have been directed by Peter Sellars and conducted by Esa-Pekka Salonen. Management explained that it was taking time to master contraptions for moving heavy scenery but the rumblings continued, the *Sunday Times* reporting that 'glitches may cause a shut down'. There was also scarcely concealed delight three weeks later when the third ballet of a three-ballet evening was cancelled. Milnes put the stumblings into perspective when he pointed out that the Bastille had immediately closed down for seven months after its opening, at a loss of £31 million. He also reminded that the Bastille project had cost French taxpayers £350 million. He urged the Royal Opera to keep going rather than close down as had been suggested.

Kaiser kept his head, pointing out that 'problems are really revealed and addressed as you work a theatre for real'. He was, however, surprised by the scale of hostility, coming as he did from the United States where the arts are not news. On 30 January 2000 he told Peter Conrad that the British had 'a will to fail' and he continued, 'How grimly gratified we all are that Blair's river of fire did not ignite or that the Millennium Dome is empty – and that the computerised machinery of the Royal Opera House doesn't work.'[91] Kaiser was also assuming responsibility for planning made three years earlier, some of which looked, in retrospect, too ambitious with *Falstaff* the most standard work in the repertoire. He was concerned that press hostility might dissuade people from coming to the reopened House and stressed that it was all coming right and that the box office was strong.[92]

On 11 January the *Independent* reported a twenty-minute stop during a revival of *Gawain* because of technical hitches at the moment when the Green Knight was supposed to arrive. This made headlines more readily than did the quality of the revival itself. Michael White, however, emphasised that Covent Garden should be 'proud' of *Gawain*, which Elgar Howarth conducted with a 'clear head and calm determination', working his way through the 'terrifying complexities of the score'. Tomlinson was 'massive-voiced and generally larger than life'. The revival found *Gawain* worthy of a permanent place in the repertoire, White going so far as to call it one of the great operas of the late twentieth century.[93]

The Ursel and Karl-Ernst Herrmann *Clemenza di Tito* was a result of old planning and was a far from perfect hand-me-down, having been considered dated even at its unveiling in 1991–92 in Brussels and Salzburg. Fine music-making under conductor Nicholas McGegan with Vinson Cole as Tito, Patricia Schuman as Vitellia and Vesselina Kasarova as Sesto, and the orchestra and chorus on good form, could not redeem the show. Syrus pointed out that it was essential when bringing in borrowed productions to rehearse them in the spirit of a new production. This, he explained, had not been the case with *Clemenza di Tito*. The Herrmanns came to London, he recalled, intending to reproduce exactly what they had done before, e.g. 'Jerry Hadley did this here'. Syrus exclaimed, 'Well, excuse me, Vincent Cole is a very different singer from Jerry Hadley' and continued, 'The Herrmanns wanted to determine every appoggiatura, and quite rightly McGegan said, "That's not stylistic practice." There might be a night when a singer wants to do another appoggiatura. In rehearsals I certainly expect to have dialogue about which appoggiaturas seem appropriate.'[94]

More successful was the bought-in Pier Luigi's Rossini *Otello* from Pesaro, with a fine cast including Bruce Ford, whose range went from baritone to high Cs with ease, Mariella Devia 'an impeccable stylist with a most beautiful voice' and a 'simply sensational' Juan Diego Flórez.[95] The March 2000 *Rosenkavalier* with Renée Fleming and Susan Graham, conducted by Christian Thielemann, caused Rupert Christiansen to sigh in relief. It was, he wrote, 'a blast of something magic that the new Covent Garden has been waiting for' and 'reminded us why it is worth spending large sums of public money on the Royal Opera House'. He added that 'light shines out' of Renée Fleming's voice and to that 'radiance she adds superb technique, pellucid German and profound musicality'.[96] Susan Graham's Octavian matched Fleming's appeal and the final trio was sung with ravishing poignancy.

The May *Meistersinger* also showed that the company had lost none of its skill and fervour as a result of the closure. 'The warmth, precision and textual clarity of the orchestral playing,' wrote Milnes, 'the full-throated splendour of the choral singing: those fondly remembered qualities, the bedrock foundation of any successful opera company, were still there intact.'[97] Syrus confirmed that backstage 'to all intents and purposes it feels the same ... a company of people who do function together. When I go out and do *Traviata* next week I will feel I am surrounded by friends.' The older members of staff, he ruefully pointed out, had been saved by the length of their service to the House: 'any redundancy, however mean, was still going to involve a lot of money – that is what saved us. The amount of money for me would have been enormous because I have been here for nearly thirty years.'[98] It was Syrus's generation that had confirmed the establishment of the tradition and continuity of the Royal Opera House.

On 21 June 2000 Southgate announced that Michael Kaiser was leaving in February 2001 to go to the Kennedy Center. Kaiser told Bryan Appleyard that he had stuck to his agreement to stay for three seasons but in fact he stayed for only one and a half.* Southgate was disappointed but later recalled that Kaiser had not been happy in London.[99] There were press reports of rifts with the Board over the high corporate image of the House with its many private dining rooms. Kaiser was also, according to Milnes, 'a trouble-shooter who gets bored once the job is done'. He commended Kaiser for his achievements, for doing 'Good News which was desperately needed', for taking over at rock bottom, getting the theatre open and working in spite of attacks and difficulties, and for making the ballet company happy.[100] Syrus believed that the harshness of the press had been 'more shocking to

---

* Before he left Kaiser chose Ross Stretton as successor to Anthony Dowell as director of the Royal Ballet. Shelton resigned in 2002.

him than the stuff in the boardroom'.[101] Judith Mackerell in an interview with Kaiser wrote, 'The press didn't stop hurling mud, and although he accepts that the House requires public monitoring, his frustration over the number of misleading stories fuelled a desire to leave.'[102] Kaiser pointed to a destructive aspect of British creative life, telling Bryan Appleyard, 'This institution has become a perceived battleground over issues of class consciousness.'

In the boardroom there were changes afoot. On 23 May 2000 *The Times* reported that Duffield would be standing down from the main Board in January, officially because of the Nolan committee's recommendation that non-executive directors should remain on Boards for no more than ten years. There were also rumours that she was frustrated by Sir Colin calling to ask for money rather than to discuss strategy. Before she stood down, Duffield was on the subcommittee of the Board along with Southgate, Eatwell and Peter Hemmings to choose the new director. According to *The Times*, on 25 January 2001 she told staff at the Opera House before she left that her last year on the Board had been 'largely unpleasant' because of a 'clash of personalities' with Colin Southgate. Duffield was quoted as saying, 'I will die with the Opera House written on my heart.'

After a tame start, the 2000–01 season soon gathered momentum to produce many 'blasts of magic'. The well-revived 2 October *Hoffmann* was broadcast to the piazza, with a fine cast including Gheorghiu and Marcelo Alvarez.* The chorus, who were in splendid form, had been proved right to have been concerned at their new contract. It emerged that they were sometimes having to work from 11 a.m. to 10 p.m. with no time to go home, six days a week. As a result of these conditions the permanent members of the chorus were, according to one observer, 'totally exhausted'. By October 2000 the artistic successes of the company were compensating for the hard conditions and management were beginning to acknowledge the overwork.

Cenerentola in December was clever, contemporary and deeply human, with a fine balance between humour and seriousness. Wonder-

* BP was funding a three-year relay sponsorship for £810,000.

fully directed by Patrice Caurier and Moshe Leiser, the piece was updated to Visconti's Rome set by Christian Fenouillat in a once elegant but decaying palazzo, replete with 1950s retro plastic table and chairs. Agostino Cavalca's costumes would, according to Milnes, have suited Sophia Loren and Gina Lollobrigida. Direction was both funny and poignant and, as Milnes wrote, 'so natural that you hardly notice that there is a production at all', the directors obtaining such involved and convincing performances from their artists; Simone Alaimo's dominating Don Magnifico, Sonia Ganassi, and Juan Diego Flórez a great coloratura artist who cut a very romantic figure. Singers were finely supported by Mark Elder who was firmly in control of the Rossini idiom – rhythmically precise and disciplined, and in total harmony with the directors' balance 'between fizz and human warmth'.[103]

The season grew in strength with Padmore the moving force behind well-rehearsed and lively revivals. 'I insist that everything does come out as good as new', she said, with either the original directors or their nominated assistants preparing them. Zambello's *Budd* was revived by Swiss director Christian Räth, who had been one of her very close assistants and kept in contact with her throughout rehearsals. It was a stirring revival centred around Simon Keenlyside's 'athletic, exuberant and infinitely touching' Billy.[104] Keenlyside's effortless vocal production, soft-grained tone and magnificent diction were matched by an arching legato line and a clean shift from piano to forte and back to piano again. His understanding of Crozier's text and Britten's music, and his care for the dramatic moment, contributed to his achievement. The Covent Garden male chorus shone brightly – the piani snapping with intensity and the forti dazzling with ferocity or fun, depending on the moment. The orchestra also remained in as fine form as before the closure of the House – versatile, flexible and intelligent, with its principals perhaps on a par with those of La Scala. In January 2001 the *Falstaff* revival was also superb under Haitink's direction, bringing out every nuance in a ruminative interpretation – full of gentle humour yet underlying strong passions.

On 11 January 2001 Southgate announced the appointment of forty-nine-year-old Tony Hall to the post of executive director to start work from 2 April 2001. Southgate's press announcement said that Hall had had a long and distinguished career at the BBC as head of news, and had also been involved in management of the corporation. The announcement said that Hall's role would be a 'first-class administrator and communicator' as part of a troika that included music director designate Antonio Pappano and Ross Stretton, director of the Royal Ballet. According to one observer, the executive director as well as the music director and the ballet director would report directly to the Board – which was in contravention of good and proven managerial practice. Moser believed there should be a non-executive Board and someone who was accountable for everything.[105] Tooley also believed there should be a central figure – a *primus inter pares* with the artistic directors without whose consent they cannot act. Without a chief executive who was privy to and involved in the details of decision-making, there was no one to control the artistic directors and exert a veto 'before the die is cast' for either artistic or financial reasons. Southgate, under pressure to find a suitable candidate, felt differently, telling Tooley that the Board had decided to give the two artistic directors complete control, with a chief executive sitting in between in control of the money.[106] Southgate later explained, 'I went through everybody but I couldn't identify an intendant . . . in our circumstances where we need to control the finances very rigidly and also be brilliant artistically.'[107] If the new arrangement means that the professional team will be allowed to get on with their tasks without interference, and the artistic directors are sensitive to the traditions and needs of the House, the absence of an intendant as recommended by Richard Eyre will not undermine the fine standard of work already achieved by the company after its traumatic years in the wilderness.

The reopened House endeavoured to maintain and enhance the qualities for which it had been recognised internationally since the Kubelik–Solti years – its fine orchestra and chorus, its rigorous revivals and its imaginative integration of stage and pit. Yet still it faces uninformed criticism. During the search for a new general director there had been provocative articles suggesting that Raymond Gubbay should take over Covent Garden. Both he and Norman Lebrecht in the *Daily Telegraph* called for the disbandment of the Covent Garden orchestra. Brought to a peak under Haitink's leadership, the orchestra's fate should never again be brought into question. For both artistic and economic reasons it remains the basis of the House's standing. David Syrus explained that its accumulated experience meant it needed less rehearsal time than would other orchestras. Ultimately, however, the issue must be one of artistic concern. Of all the opera orchestras its greatest strength remains what Syrus described as its 'breathing with singers and understanding theatre' as well as its flexibility. 'It can do transparency for Bernard,' Syrus added, 'something much more grand for Colin. It can do more early music things now and with almost no rehearsals.'[108]

The season again revealed clearly the flair and devotion with which Covent Garden puts on its revivals. Elaine Padmore tried to bring back the original directors for revivals to make sure the spark is rekindled, thus avoiding the dependence of House directors on the stage notes of the original directors that can result in the blandness of some Met revivals such as *Idomeneo* in January 2002. Padmore said, 'When the press write ill of us I want to ask them if they ever go to Vienna on an average Wednesday evening? And you would realise what very high standards we are exacting of ourselves, how much we are rehearsing and paying people to be here to rehearse and so on.' It was a great challenge. Padmore continued, 'That's why we have to have enough money to do new productions. You cannot go on endlessly reviving the same old shows for financial reasons even if they have been very successful in their day. Inevitably they get further and further away from the first production and much as you try to put a charge under them the thing gets too far past its sell-by date and you have to let it go.'[109]

At the beginning of the 2001–02 season there was still insufficient funding for the Linbury Theatre to fulfil its potential role. Padmore said, showing vision, but still lacking the necessary funding, 'We'd like to turn that into our Cottesloe space – for interesting, innovative productions and a lot of top producers and designers and conductors want to do things in that sort of space.' She added, 'But we'll solve it because there is a great will to use this exciting new space.'

Education had also achieved a new status in the reopened House. Darryl Jaffray, director of education and access, believed that the closure marked a turning point for education. While there had always been those who had believed in the work of the House's education department, it had functioned semi-independently from the rest of the organisation. It was during the closure crisis that attitudes changed fundamentally throughout the House, bringing a new awareness of the original memorandum of association whereby the company had been established to promote education. Everyone recognised the need to take responsibility for education, from the directors to managers, staff and artists, as well as for the need for the work to be made known. The newly housed archive, under its archivist Francesca Franchi, now found itself with greater opportunities to make its resources available and to provide finely displayed changing exhibitions in the House's public spaces. Padmore declared, 'Anyone with an ounce of creativity can have it dragged out of them in this building – whether it's dance or opera or whatever.' The schools matinées were resumed, funded by the Clore Duffield Foundation.

Padmore also remained devoted to the cause of bringing down seat prices. But she was concerned how the books were to be balanced even with the Arts Council's increased funding of £20 million, which was not, in her words, 'a lot of money for what is expected of us – for world-class opera and ballet and lots of it, for as little state money as possible and with ticket prices as low as possible'.[110]

In the 2001–02 season, Bernard Haitink's last, the House was successful in 'squaring the circle', providing a year of stimulating new productions with outstanding casts together with finely honed, exciting revivals. Both Bryn Terfel and Simon Keenlyside gave stirring interpretations of Don Giovanni in early 2002, in Francesca Zambello's new production. The two casts and two conductors, Colin Davis and Charles Mackerras, created two powerfully different shows within the same framework. The director's central role, in Zambello's words, is that of helping the performers to 'connect and ignite'. Zambello, as a woman director, tried to create an 'unthreatening, unjudgemental, positive, family work environment' that enables the singers to reveal to the utmost 'their personal soul on stage'. The second team, under Mackerras with Keenlyside's physically and vocally alluring Don at its heart and including Ildebrando D'Arcangelo as Leporello, Christine Goerke as Donna Anna and Ana Maria Martinez as Elvira, in particular generated a youthful energy and vitality that was remarkable in its intensity. Audiences go to the theatre, Zambello reflected, to 'discover that energy' and the popularity of opera, she said, lies in 'this energy which is bigger than life and something that we are striving for'.[111]

A similar vitality and honesty were apparent in April's new production of *Il Trovatore* – one of the most difficult of Verdi's operas to stage convincingly. It brought back Elijah Moshinsky who, with his usual dedication to Verdi's aesthetic, created a framework in Risorgimento Italy that was visually traditional yet radical in its truthfulness to human emotion. Dante Ferretti's sets, Anne Tilby's costumes and the lighting of Howard Harrison provided a series of sparely beautiful tableaux for what William Weaver described as an 'inspired series of opportunities for narration and song in a broad range of mood'.[112] It also provided a context and dynamic both coherent and dramatically powerful, subtly juxtaposing savagery and violence with a tenderness rarely seen on the operatic stage. Under Moshinsky's direction, another committed ensemble of young singers – Verónica Villarroel, José Cura, Dmitri Hvorostovsky and Yvonne Naef – convincingly gave life to the complex psychological relations, obsessions and consuming jealousies of the piece.

Moshinsky's achievement derives from his conviction, as he says, that there is in Mozart and Verdi 'something that matters, and that it is in danger of being lost in a barrage of fashion'. He fears that 'if we do not hold on to the tradition no one will remember what grand opera was'. He fights to uphold that tradition, basing his work on his understanding that Verdian grand opera is rooted in the 'big idea' of the nineteenth century – 'the emergence of liberty, the balance between tyrannical and popular rule and whether you follow your individual destiny or are thrown about by it'. His successful interpretation of *Trovatore* with all its illogicalities and inconsistencies, lay in his belief that history is its 'driving force' and that it is an opera that moves forward 'by character and narrative and not visual imagery'. Moshinsky's work is occasionally misunderstood by some critics as it 'goes against the philosophical fashion' which, he explains, continues to demand 'performance art and instant pictures' from opera. It nonetheless has a universal appeal to audiences, hungry for emotional authenticity and the narrative drive. During *Trovatore* and *Boccanegra*, the last revival of the season, Moshinsky was struck by the Covent Garden chorus's ability 'to sing as characters' and by the House's resolve to maintain the Visconti tradition: the willingness of everyone involved to take part in all the rehearsals and 'try to unify it and sing from a point of view'. The result, he believed, was Covent Garden's unique achievement: 'a shared thought on a bare stage with the audience'.[113]

The Royal Opera's rebirth after its traumatic wilderness years was recognised by public and critics alike. In February 2002 Karita Mattila, for her roles in *Jenůfa* and *The Queen of Spades*, challenged Bernard Haitink for the Laurence Olivier opera award. Haitink, during his rousing last performances, as music director of *Tristan und Isolde*, won the Olivier award as director of a 'season of great distinction' by the Royal Opera and another for his contribution to the Royal Opera House from the *South Bank Show*. People who worked at Covent Garden said the House was well run, friendly and efficient.*

Although the fifty years since the war have seen the firm establishment of fine artistic companies in Britain, ambivalence towards them on the part of public and government has not diminished. Squaring circles remains the task of arts administrators on starvation and semi-starvation diets in the regional and national companies, even though they are now so established that their futures seem more assured than that of Kent Opera had been. On 7 March 2000 Milnes wrote that after years of facing a hostile Scottish Arts Council, the new Scottish parliament was meddling with Alexander Gibson's Scottish Opera. 'You can decide to fund an opera company or decide not to fund an

---

* Francesca Zambello said in March 2002 that she loved working with the 'inner fabric of the company' – the chorus and the crew and the orchestra which she knew less well. The whole technical department, she said, was 'top class' (Interview, 25.3.02). Even the choristers felt that the bitter past was receding and that the season had been an exciting and rewarding one. The one disappointment resulting from the redevelopment was the loss of the canteen as a social focal point. In contrast to the Met after the 1980 strike, when the new canteen had consciously been designed to provide a sociable environment for the whole workforce, Covent Garden had lost its canteen to the fifth floor during the rebuilding. A musician explained, 'We can't get there and back in time – you met everybody there – so we don't meet anybody any more – the family thing has gone. The whole guts have been torn out of the place.'

opera company,' Milnes wrote, quoting Sir Claus Moser, 'what you can't do without driving everyone insane is fund half an opera company.' This highly logical suggestion had fallen on different deaf ears throughout the years since the war – since Lord Waverley's similar refrain in 1955. The budget of Scottish Opera's new *Parsifal*, wrote Milnes, would have had Bavarian State Opera 'clutching its collective sides with mirth'. Yet somehow Scottish Opera manages to produce work of 'astoundingly high quality', underscored by Richard Armstrong's lyrical conducting, and fine singing from a chorus of just forty members. It was presented as a drama more than a quasi-religious rite in Silviu Purcarete's simple near permanent set 'based on three runs of mobile flats', and Christophe Forey's superb lighting. Because touring had been cut as a result of underfunding, the work only visited Edinburgh and Glasgow.[114] Scottish Opera was also attempting a *Ring* cycle, starting with *Rheingold* at the Edinburgh Festival, to be completed in 2003 and performed three times that year. Tim Albery's 'perceptive staging' preferred 'storytelling to dogma, character to symbol' in a 'timeless modern' framework.[115] Milnes wrote, 'This troubled but resolute company rises to ever greater artistic heights as its finances slip into further chaos.'

Rescued by Eyre from amalgamation with the Royal Opera and certain death, the English National Opera pursued its task under Paul Daniel's leadership. The May 1999 *Carmelites*, conducted by Daniel with 'evangelical passion and commitment', boasted a fine cast of Joan Rodgers as Blanche, Elizabeth Vaughan's prioress, Josephine Barstow's Mother Marie, Rita Cullis's Mother Lidoine in Phyllida Lloyd's 'exemplary staging'.[116] During the 1999–2000 season Mark-Anthony Turnage's powerful opera *The Silver Tassie* was premiered. Skilfully and dramatically crafted from Sean O'Casey's anti-war play, with a libretto by Amanda Holden, it was directed by Bill Bryden, conducted by Daniel, and starred Gerald Finley as Harry Heegan.

Nicholas Payne, general director since 1998, having 'banned the word closure from our vocabulary for reasons you can probably understand',[117] presented the Italian festival of the 2000–01 ENO season within a building-site permanent set – a scaffolding walkway around the dress circle. It sent out a clear message for their building appeal, while providing a flexible and exciting performing area. A disappointing

Manon Lescaut on 19 September was followed by more successful ventures, including *The Coronation of Poppea* and Leoncavallo's *Bohème* with a fine young cast. In March 2001 a £41 million restoration programme for the London Coliseum was announced with £12 million of lottery money. The aim of the programme was to restore the original Frank Matcham 1904 features as well as to provide better backstage and audience facilities, including a glass-topped terrace bar. The company would maintain its seasons and residency throughout the four-year building programme that would be carried out in bursts.

The 2000–01 and 2001–02 seasons proved highly controversial, with a particularly unsuccessful *Trovatore*, for which Daniel and Payne decided to dispense with a director, and in the following season *A Masked Ball*, which featured rape and singers on lavatories. On 11 July 2002 Nicholas Payne 'stood down' after box office sales dipped as low as 65 per cent for some performances. Payne admitted that the House had been losing some of its core supporters. The final stages of the rebuilding would see the company performing at the Barbican.

In contrast to European cities, where the opera houses retain their status, Britain's opera institutions, with all their fine artistic achievements, are still not a source of national pride. Southgate pointed out, 'Here we have this beautiful refurbished opera house but our government doesn't use it, when Chirac or other official visitors come here – there is no passion for it.'[118] The extraordinary creativity goes almost unrecognised. John Tomlinson said in 1998, 'Covent Garden is one of the three or four Eiffel Towers of the opera world with Vienna, the Met, La Scala as the others. The tradition of opera as real music theatre is second to none in Britain, if only people would realise it.'[119]

The British government, public and press on the whole, however, remain suspicious of artists and artistic achievement. Bryan Appleyard wrote in July 2000, 'Contemporary Britain does not, as a whole, admire great singers, dancers and musicians, any more than it admires poets and painters. A succession of vacant bimbos and talentless hoodlums are our heroes, and anyone who suggests they should not be will, with the collusion of a supinely populist government, be accused of elitism.

Our working class is the least aspirational in the world and our middle class the most philistine.'[120] Peter Hall put it even more starkly: 'We're a philistine, complacent, smug, stupid little nation with an enormous ability to invent and create, and then waste it.'[121]

While the British press and public opinion remain uniquely antipathetic to cultural activity, subsidy for opera on a scale sufficient to maintain standards and increase audiences is everywhere under threat. Even the Staatsoper faces belt-tightening under Holender, and La Scala, for the first time in its history, is looking increasingly towards private sources of revenue. Only the Met seems reasonably secure financially, with its unashamedly and highly successful corporate approach to funding that has enabled its endowment to reach $250 million. In Britain the Labour administration began quietly and somewhat sheepishly to provide a real increase in funding since 1998. The Arts Council's grant-in-aid increased from £184.6 million to £252.3 million in 2001–02. The drive towards 'new forms of expression' and the embracing of cultural diversity, has not been entirely at the expense of the flagship companies, even though Covent Garden was, at the beginning of 2003, still £5 million short of what the Board estimated in 1998 was needed to fulfil all its obligations and aspirations. It would require brave political leadership indeed in Britain to create a climate of pride such as still exists in Austria and Italy, and to provide the kind of subsidies Europe still enjoys. Only by positive government leadership could the idealistic post-war mood be revived, whereby the work of the national companies had the objective of being both accessible and enticing even to those not familiar with the 'senior arts'. In the political climate of the early twenty-first century, the best that the Royal Opera can hope for is a low profile and relief from press and political attack. Colin Davis in October 1972, long before the word elitism had been conjured up as a pejorative term, said, 'The reason we can't have the youngsters in here every night is that no politician will risk his reputation or his career in giving enough money to the arts to run them properly.'[122]

There is much that could be done with supportive political leadership in Britain. Isaacs pointed out to the Policy Studies Institute on 21 November 1990 that less that .05 per cent of government expenditure is on the arts. 'The sums required to sustain our success in the arts are tiny, mere minnows. It is, in the end, a political decision.'[123] Subsidy, while everywhere threatened, remains the best way of maintaining standards, innovation and access, and releasing and nurturing the extraordinary resources of talent. In Richard Eyre's words subsidy 'acts as investment, provides continuity, allows artistic risks, sustains the best of tradition, develops new talent, feeds the commercial entertainment economy, and does all this at reasonable seat prices'. In the subsidised world, he reminded, it is not profit but 'the need to be good' that is paramount.

While Austria, Italy, the United States and Britain approach the arts in general and opera in particular from very different historical perspectives, the constant factor remains that the arts are a barometer of the emotional health of nations, as well as a focus for cultural understanding in the increasingly fractured societies of the twenty-first century. As such, they should be challenging and should be made available to as many people as possible. As Eyre wrote in his report, the arts are not a luxury, they are

> ... part of our life, our language, our way of seeing; they are a measure of our civilisation. The arts tell us truths about ourselves and our feelings and our society that reach parts of us that politics and journalism don't. The arts entertain, they give pleasure, they give hope, they ravish the senses, and above all, they help us to fit the disparate pieces of the world together; to try and make form out of chaos.[124]

GLOSSARY

OF TERMS FREQUENTLY ENCOUNTERED
IN OPERA

Act drop   a curtain lowered at the end of an act

Allargando   a significant slowing of tempo

Appoggiatura   (IT.: 'leaning'); a type of ornament normally made by the singer in baroque and classical vocal music

Arpeggio   chordal notes performed successively rather than simultaneously

Aspiration   an unnecessary exhalation of breath preceding the singing of a vowel

Attack   the manner in which the singing of a note is initiated

Basso profondo   an especially low bass voice

Bel canto (1)   said of operas composed by Bellini, Rossini and Donizetti, and the fluent style of singing deemed appropriate to them

Bel canto (2)   used to denote a traditional Italianate method of voice production widely held in high esteem

Blocking   the planning of movement on stage

Cabaletta   the final, faster portion of an aria having more than one section

Cadenza   a passage, whether composed or improvised, inserted in an aria and having a free, often florid character

Cantabile   literally, singable; said of a smooth, lyrical line of vocal melody

Cantilena   a flowing vocal line generally in slow or moderate tempo

Cartellone   the playbill posted outside an Italian opera house; also used to refer to a given House's repertoire or offerings for the season

Cavatina   A song-like portion of an operatic scene; also a brief aria in one section only

Chest voice   a relatively heavy manner of vocal production in which resonance is experienced in the chest area

Coloratura   a piece of vocal writing displaying agility and rapidity; a voice, most often but not always a soprano, capable of performing such music

Comprimarii singers singing secondary roles

Diatonic in musical composition, writing which is centred in the major or minor keys; the opposite of chromatic writing, which uses tones lying outside the major and minor keys

Divisi the scoring of separate or 'divided' parts for instruments or for voices

Dramatic voice used to describe a rather heavy and powerful vocal instrument suited to the operas of Wagner and to certain Verdi roles

Dramaturg in German opera houses, the person responsible for the dramatic values of works in the repertoire; the dramaturg may translate libretti and sometimes supervises stage direction and/or production

Fach a German term (literally 'drawer') used to refer to a vocal type; e.g., the lyric tenor Fach

Fermata a pause outside strict metric time

Filato, plural *filati* a long, sustained note

Flat a portion of a stage set constructed of wood and painted muslin

Focus (of a voice) a particular centre in the body for the production of tone

Head voice a relatively light manner of vocal production in which resonance is felt in the area of the head

Heldentenor in German, 'heroic tenor'; a voice suitable for heavy dramatic roles, especially in the Teutonic repertoire

Intendant the chief administrator of a German-language opera house

Legato literally, 'tied together'; a smooth transition from note to note

Leggiero literally, 'light'; a delicately separated succession of notes in song

Lirico-spinto a voice whose weight lies between lyric and spinto (Q. V.)

Loggionisti the denizens of the upper galleries in Italian opera houses

Lyric voice a relatively light vocal instrument

Masky tone vocal production centred in the area of the cheekbones, nose and jaws; in contrast to a 'swallowed' tone centred on the soft palate

Messa di voce a gradual crescendo and decrescendo on a single held note

Mezza voce 'half voice'; a soft tone in which not all the resonance of the body is engaged

Morendo   when said of a sound: dying away

Opera buffa   comic opera

Opera seria   a sub-genre of Italian operatic composition featuring high seriousness of plot and theme, and frequently static on-stage action

Ostinato   a repeated musical phrase or figure, especially in the bass line

Parlando   a manner of singing which imitates or suggests speech

Passage work   a rapid, often florid section of vocal writing

Passaggio   the point at which vocal registers shift; often called the 'break'

Portamento, plural *portamenti*   a gently nuanced slide from one note to another; an intensification of legato

Register   one or another portion of the range of a voice that has a distinct sound and (to the singer) 'feel' of its own

Rubato   a manner of performing music in which subtle tempo changes are made liberally

Sfumato   a term borrowed from painting to describe a 'smoky', clouded sound

Sotto voce   literally, 'beneath the voice'; a very quiet, whisper-like manner of vocal production

Soubrette   a pert girl character in opera; the soprano voice suited to such a role

Spinto voice   a vocal instrument midway between lyric and dramatic

Sprezzatura   insouciance

Tenore di grazia   a flexible, smooth, 'graceful' tenor voice

Tenore robusto   a rich, powerful tenor voice

Tenuto   a musical direction to sustain a note to its full value

Tenorino   a light, high, often youthful tenor voice

Tessitura   the general range of a piece of vocal music; also, the 'lie' of a particular voice (e.g., 'What a low tessitura that baritone has')

Timbre   tone colour

Unit set   set with basic foundation that is kept the same throughout the production although props and costumes may vary

Verismo   a school of operative writing which flourished around the beginning of the twentieth century marked by realistic, sometimes sordid, narrative events and true-to-life characterisations

Vibrato   the subtle and controlled raising and lowering of vocal pitch

SOURCE NOTES

The following abbreviations are used in the notes:

Berlin papers	The Isaiah Berlin Papers, Bodleian Library, University of Oxford
DW	David Webster
MO Archives	Metropolitan Opera Archives
ROH Archives	Royal Opera House Archives
MPRC Archive	Music Performance Research Centre
OB	Opera Board
OSC	Opera Subcommittee
GDA	ROH Archives, Drogheda papers
ASA	Austrian State Archives

1 Vienna 1940–55: 'Some New Beauty Is Being Born'

1 Lanfranco Rasponi, The Last Prima Donnas, New York: Limelight, 3rd ed., 1995, p. 312.
2 P. Dusek (ed.), Kulissengespräche II: Neue Anekdoten und kostbare Aufnahmen von hundert Weltstars der Oper, Vienna: Jugend und Volk, 1995, p. 24.
3 Frederic Spotts, Bayreuth: A History of the Wagner Festival, New Haven and London: Yale University Press, 1994, p. 192.
4 Quoted in Robert Bachmann, Karajan: Notes on a Career (tr. Shaun Whiteside), London: Quartet, 1990, p. 110.
5 S. Brook, Opera: A Penguin Anthology, London: Penguin, 1996, p. 164.
6 Ibid., p. 164.
7 Penelope Turing, Hans Hotter: Man and Artist, London: John Calder, 1983, pp. 100–1.
8 Rasponi, op. cit., p. 233.
9 Opera News, July 1995, p. 8.
10 Marcel Prawy, The Vienna Opera, London: Weidenfeld & Nicolson, 1970, pp. 154–5.
11 Quoted in Charles Osborne, The Complete Operas of Richard Strauss, London: Michael O'Mara Books, 1988, p. 185.

12 Lord Harewood, *The Tongs and the Bones: The Memoirs of Lord Harewood*, London: Weidenfeld & Nicolson, 1981, pp. 93–4.
13 Ethan Mordden, *Opera Anecdotes*, New York and Oxford: Oxford University Press, 1985, p. 81.
14 C. Osborne, op. cit., p. 173.
15 Prawy, op. cit., p. 155.
16 Yehudi Menuhin, *Unfinished Journey*, London: Futura, 1978, p. 292.
17 *Opera News*, July 1995, p. 25.
18 Berta Geissmar, *The Baton and the Jackboot: Recollections of Musical Life*, London: Hamish Hamilton, 1944, p. 78.
19 Ibid., p. 80.
20 Bachmann, op. cit., p. 85.
21 ASA 784/1938, 22.6.38.
22 Rasponi, op. cit., p. 487.
23 H. Hackenberg and W. Herrmann, *Die Wiener Staatsoper im Exil, 1945–1955*, Vienna: Österreichischer Bundesverlag, 1985, p. 16.
24 Rasponi, op. cit., p. 487.
25 Ibid., p. 489.
26 Prawy, op. cit., p. 168.
27 Ibid., p. 169.
28 Dusek (ed.), op. cit., p. 169.
29 Hella Pick, *Guilty Victim: Austria from the Holocaust to Haider*, London and New York: I. B. Tauris, 2000, p. 96.
30 Quoted in Richard Osborne, *Herbert von Karajan: A Life in Music*, London: Chatto & Windus; Boston: Northeastern University Press, 1998, pp. 200, 206.
31 *New York Times*, 27.5.46.
32 Prawy, op. cit., p. 166.
33 Dusek (ed.), op. cit., p. 105.
34 *The Times*, 2.9.96.
35 Spotts, op. cit., p. 199.
36 Ibid., p. 204.
37 Ibid., p. 206.
38 Ibid., pp. 213–14.
39 *Opera*, 1951, p. 555.
40 Ibid., February 1989, p. 134.
41 Ibid., p. 230.
42 Harold Rosenthal (ed.), *The Opera Bedside Book*, London: Victor Gollancz, 1965, p. 229.
43 *Neues Österreich*, 24.5.45.
44 *New York Times*, 28.4.55.
45 *Die Presse*, 6.11.55.
46 Alexander Witeschnik, *Wiener Opernkunst von den Anfängen bis zu Karajan*, Vienna: Verlag Kremayr und Scheriau, n.d., p. 263.
47 *Wiener Zeitung*, 6.11.55.
48 *Opera*, January 1956, p. 22.
49 Prawy, op. cit., p. 22.
50 Rasponi, op. cit., pp. 539–40.
51 S. Brook, op. cit., p. 404.

2 La Scala 1945–57: Reconstruction

1 Harvey Sachs, *Toscanini*, New York: Da Capo, 1978, p. 267.
2 Ibid., p. 226.
3 Ibid., p. 286.
4 M. S. Stone, *The Patron State: Culture and Politics in Fascist Italy*, Princeton: Princeton University Press, 1998.
5 L. Arruga, *La Scala*, Milan: Electa Editrice, 1975, p. 203.
6 F. Armani (ed.), *La Scala 1946–1966*, Milan, 1966, p. ixl.
7 C. Casanova, *Renata Tebaldi: The Voice of an Angel* (tr. Connie Mandracchia DeCaro), Dallas, Texas: Baskerville, 1995, p. 28.
8 *Corriere*, 12.5.46.
9 Giorgio Gualerzi, 'La Scala's Golden Anniversary', in *Opera*, December 1995, p. 1397.
10 Quoted in Sachs, op. cit., pp. 282–3.
11 G. Mammarella, *Italy After Fascism: A Political History 1943–1965*, South Bend, Indiana: University of Notre Dame Press, 1966, pp. 119–23.
12 Claudio Sartori in H. Rosenthal (ed.), *The Opera Bedside Book*, p. 244.

13 N. Benois quoted in Sachs, op. cit., p. 292.

14 Arruga, op. cit., p. 191.

15 Sachs, op. cit., p. 292.

16 *Opera*, December 1957, p. 748.

17 Ibid., April 1968, p. 277.

18 Quoted in S. Brook, *Opera: A Penguin Anthology*, p. 184.

19 *Opera*, February 1968, p. 157.

20 Ibid., p. 156.

21 Arruga, op. cit., p. 248.

22 *Opera*, February 1961, p. 97.

23 Ibid., April 1961, p. 243.

24 Sachs, op. cit., p. 295.

25 R. Osborne, *Herbert von Karajan*, p. 295.

26 Arruga, op. cit., p. 214.

27 Ibid., p. 196.

28 Quoted in Arruga, op. cit., p. 197.

29 *L'Italia*, 31.12.47.

30 *Opera*, 1951, p. 175.

31 *Corriere della sera*, 6.6.52.

32 *Corriere lombardo*, 6–7.6.52.

33 William Weaver in *Opera*, July 1966, p. 577.

34 *Corriere della sera*, 28.12.55.

35 Franco Zeffirelli, *Zeffirelli: The Autobiography of Franco Zeffirelli*, London: Weidenfeld & Nicolson, 1986, pp. 120–1.

36 D. McGovern and D. Winer (eds), *I Remember Too Much*, New York: Morrow, 1990, p. 208.

37 Rasponi, op. cit., p. 384.

38 Ibid., p. 382.

39 Ibid., p. 385.

40 P. Dragadze in *Opera*, 1953, p. 501.

41 Ibid.

42 Michael Scott, *Maria Meneghini Callas*, London: Simon & Schuster, 1992, p. 63.

43 Ibid., p. 66.

44 *Opera*, 1952, p. 654.

45 Harewood, *The Tongs and the Bones*, p. 225.

46 Scott, op. cit., p. 82.

47 *Corriere*, 8.12.51.

48 Scott, op. cit., p. 83.

49 Ibid.

50 Plácido Domingo, *My First Forty Years*, Harmondsworth, Middlesex: Penguin, 1984, pp. 83–4.

51 Casanova, op. cit., p. 61.

3 Covent Garden 1945–55: 'Making Bricks . . .'

1 Alan Jefferson, *Sir Thomas Beecham, A Canterbury Tribute*, London: Macdonald and Jane's, 1979, p. 161.

2 *Opera*, August 1950, pp. 25–8.

3 Peter Hall, *Making an Exhibition of Myself*, London: Sinclair-Stevenson, 1993, pp. 213–14.

4 Sir Peter Hall, Interview, 19.7.99.

5 Edward Dent, *A Theatre for Everybody, The Story of the Old Vic and Sadler's Wells*, London, 1945, pp. 8–9.

6 Memorandum for informal conference at the Board of Education, quoted in Andrew Sinclair, *Arts and Cultures, The History of the 50 Years of the Arts Council of Great Britain*, London: Sinclair-Stevenson, 1995, pp. 26–7.

7 Robert Skidelsky, *John Maynard Keynes, Fighting for Britain*, London: Macmillan, 2000, p. 287.

8 Ibid., pp. 288, 289.

9 Metropolitan Opera (henceforth MO) Archives, Johnson, 1945–46.

10 Montague Haltrecht, *The Quiet Showman, Sir David Webster and the Royal Opera House*, London: William Collins, 1975, p. 55.

11 Dent, op. cit., p. 133.

12 Frances Donaldson, *The Royal Opera House in the Twentieth Century*, London: Weidenfeld & Nicolson, 1988, p. 41.

13 Sinclair, op. cit., pp. 46–7.

14 Skidelsky, op. cit., p. 294.

15　Dent to Carey, quoted in
　　Donaldson, op. cit., p. 47.
16　Royal Opera House (henceforth
　　ROH) Archives, Webster to
　　Goossens, 25.2.46.
17　Elisabeth Schwarzkopf, *On and Off
　　the Record: A Memoir of Walter
　　Legge*, London: Faber & Faber, 1982,
　　pp. 160, 93.
18　Haltrecht, op. cit., p. 58.
19　ROH Archives, Wilson, 16/074.
20　Sir John Tooley, Interview, 4.12.00.
21　*Opera*, February 1953, p. 139.
22　Cited in Michael Kennedy, *Britten*,
　　in the Master Musicians Series, ed.
　　Stanley Sadie, London: J. M. Dent
　　& Sons, 1981, p. 45.
23　Philip Reed in CD booklet, 1996.
　　Trustees of Britten-Pears
　　Foundation.
24　Kennedy, op. cit., p. 45.
25　John Lucas, *Reggie, The Life of
　　Reginald Goodall*, London: Julia
　　Macrae Books, 1993, p. 88.
26　Michael Kennedy, *Britten*, p. 41.
27　Ibid., p. 46.
28　Joan Cross, Interview with the BBC
　　in 1948.
29　Kennedy, op, cit., p. 48.
30　Ibid., p. 51.
31　Berlin to John Wheeler-Bennett,
　　The Isaiah Berlin Papers, Bodleian
　　Library, University of Oxford
　　(henceforth Berlin papers), 26.4.61.
32　ROH Archives, Statement of Policy
　　of Trust issued by Boosey, Dent,
　　Hawkes, Walton, Wilson and Sam
　　Courtauld, Covent Garden Opera
　　Trust meetings.
33　Peter Gellhorn, Interview, 27.1.00.
34　ROH Archives, Webster to
　　Goossens.
35　ROH Archives, 7.3.46, cited in
　　Donaldson, op. cit., p. 60.
36　Carole Rosen, *The Goossens, A
　　Musical Century*, London: André
　　Deutsch, 1993, p. 250.

37　Cited in Donaldson, op. cit., p. 61.
38　Ibid., 22.3.45, p. 61.
39　ROH Archives.
40　Haltrecht, op. cit., p. 68.
41　Keynes to Florence Keynes, 23.2.46,
　　cited in Skidelsky, op. cit., p. 463.
42　ROH Archives, 26.7.46, 1.8.46.
43　*Opera*, March 1958, p. 151.
44　Berlin papers, 26.4.61.
45　*Opera*, November 1968, p. 879.
46　Adolf Aber, ibid., 1950, pp. 26–7.
47　Adele Leigh, Interview, 23.4.98.
48　Ibid.
49　Gellhorn, Interview, 27.1.00.
50　John Lucas's article after Goodall's
　　death on 5 May at the age of
　　eighty-eight, *Opera*, July 1990,
　　p. 787.
51　Haltrecht, op. cit., p. 297.
52　Leigh, Interview, 23.4.98.
53　*Observer*, 10.12.46.
54　*Spectator*, 17.1.47.
55　*Time and Tide*, 29.8.47.
56　*Covent Garden, 25 Years of Opera
　　and Ballet*, p. 65.
57　*New Statesman*, 3.5.47.
58　*Manchester Guardian*, 24.4.47.
59　ROH Archives, Covent Garden
　　Opera Trust meetings 1946–51.
60　Harewood, *The Tongs and the
　　Bones*, p. 246.
61　Turing, *Hans Hotter*, p. 115.
62　*New Statesman*, 14.8.47.
63　ROH Archives, Wilson papers,
　　16/074.
64　Gellhorn, Interview, 27.1.00.
65　ROH Archives, David Webster
　　(henceforth DW) 45, Box 5, 1 of 2.
66　ROH Archives, DW 45, Box 5, 1 of
　　2, E. Hale to Mary Glasgow, 27.1.48.
67　ROH Archives, Opera Trust
　　meetings, 18.11.47, 22.12.47, 13.1.48.
68　ROH Archives, Steuart Wilson,
　　16/074.
69　ROH Archives, Opera Trust
　　meetings, 24.2.48, 20.4.48.
70　Haltrecht, op. cit., pp. 106–7.

71 ROH Archives, Opera Trust meetings, 16.11.48, 11.3.49, Steuart Wilson, 16/074.

72 Donaldson, op. cit., p. 72.

73 Gellhorn, Interview, 27.1.00.

74 ROH Archives, cited in Norman Lebrecht, *Covent Garden, The Untold Story, Dispatches from the English Culture War 1945–2000*, London: Simon & Schuster, 2000, p. 111.

75 ROH Archives, Opera Trust meetings.

76 Peter Brook, *Threads of Time, A Memoir*, London: Methuen, 1999, pp. 47, 49, 58.

77 Haltrecht, op. cit., p. 126.

78 Harewood, op. cit., p. 243.

79 Gerald Moore, *Am I Too Loud? Memoirs of a Piano Accompanist*, London: Hamish Hamilton, 1962, pp. 49, 256.

80 Adele Leigh, Interview, 23.4.98.

81 Harewood, op. cit., p. 243.

82 Peter Brook, *The Shifting Point*, London: Methuen Drama, 1987, p. 170.

83 *Opera*, February 1975, p. 143.

84 ROH Archives, Wilson, 16/074.

85 *Opera*, February 1975, p. 143.

86 Peter Gellhorn, letter to the author, 22.1.01.

87 *Sunday Times*, 27.11.49.

88 *The Times*, 12.11.49.

89 *Covent Garden, 25 Years of Opera and Ballet*, p. 102.

90 ROH Archives, Opera Trust meetings, 15.11.49.

91 Haltrecht, op. cit., p. 129.

92 ROH Archives, Opera Trust meetings, 20.12.49.

93 *Opera*, June 1950, p. 44.

94 Ibid., April 1950.

95 Donaldson, op. cit., p. 84.

96 ROH Archives, Opera Trust meetings.

97 Gellhorn, Interview, 27.1.00.

98 In MPRC Archive, now released on *Stars of English Opera*, Dutton Laboratories, CDLX 7018.

99 *Opera*, August 1950, p. 50.

100 July 1950, cited in Donaldson, op. cit., p. 84.

101 ROH Archives, 2.3.50, cited in Donaldson, op. cit.

102 Gellhorn, Interview, 27.1.00.

103 ROH Archives, Opera Trust meetings, 17.10.50.

104 Cited in Donaldson, op. cit., op. 83.

105 *New Statesman and Nation*, 16.12.50.

106 MO Archives, Bing correspondence 1950–51, A–D.

107 ROH Archives, Clark, 34/303.

108 Cited by Savage in his obituary of Kleiber in *Opera*, April 1956, p. 222.

109 Ibid. 110.

110 *Opera*, 1950, p. 91.

111 Ibid., January 1951, p. 161.

112 ROH Archives, Opera Trust meetings, 4.1.51, 16.1.51, 3.4.51.

113 ROH Archives, Wilson, 16/074.

114 Haltrecht, op. cit., p. 152.

115 *Covent Garden, 25 Years of Opera and Ballet*, p. 73.

116 ROH Archives, Opera Trust meetings, 8.5.51, 19.6.51, 15.1.52, 25.9.52, Trust Board minutes 1950–56.

117 Interview with Max Loppert, *Opera*, January 1993, p. 27.

118 Leigh, Interview, 23.4.98.

119 ROH Archives, Harewood, DW file, 4.7.51.

120 'A Personal View' by Charles Mackerras, accompanying July 1978 Decca recording, p. 25.

121 Ibid.

122 *Opera*, February 1953, p. 141.

123 Rodney Milnes, Interview, 30.4.98.

124 Lord Drogheda, *Double Harness, Memoirs of Lord Drogheda*, London: Weidenfeld & Nicolson, 1978, p. 232.

125 ROH Archives, Board minutes CGC (51).

126 Haltrecht, op. cit., p. 163.

127 Donaldson, op. cit., p. 84.
128 ROH Archives, Board minutes, 18.12.51.
129 *Opera*, January 1993, p. 27.
130 Obituary in *Opera*, July 1970, p. 601.
131 ROH Archives, Kleiber contracts, Box 34, DW files, 303 (1).
132 *Covent Garden, 25 Years of Opera and Ballet*, p. 21.
133 *Manchester Guardian*, 23.1.52.
134 ROH Archives, Kleiber contracts, Box 34, DW files, 303 (1).
135 ROH Archives, Board minutes, 7.7.53.
136 John Russell, *Erich Kleiber, A Memoir*, London: André Deutsch, 1957, p. 207.
137 ROH Archives, cited in Lebrecht, op. cit., p. 95.
138 Kennedy, op. cit., p. 60.
139 ROH Archives, Pooley to Anderson, DW 45, file 2 of 2, Board minutes, 1950–56.
140 Donaldson, op. cit., p. 86.
141 *Opera*, January 1953, pp. 37, 40.
142 ROH Archives, Board meeting, CGC 5th meeting, 16.6.53.
143 *Opera*, January 1953.
144 Joan Sutherland, *The Autobiography of Joan Sutherland*, London: Weidenfeld & Nicolson, 1997, p. 41.
145 Leigh, Interview, 23.4.98.
146 Geraint Evans with Noël Goodwin, *Sir Geraint Evans, A Knight at the Opera*, London: Michael Joseph, 1984, p. 242.
147 *Opera*, March 1953.
148 Cited in Maurice Leonard, *The Life of Kathleen Ferrier 1912–1953*, London: Hutchinson, 1988, p. 229.
149 Harewood, op. cit., p. 138.
150 15.6.53.
151 9.6.53.
152 Kennedy, op. cit., p. 62.
153 Cited in Antonia Mallo's essay 'Britten's Major Set-Back? Aspects of the First Critical Response to *Gloriana*', in Paul Banks (ed.), *Britten's Gloriana Suffolk: The Boydell Press, 1993*, p. 52.
154 David Cairns, 'Gloriana', in *Responses: Musical Essays and Reviews*, London: Secker & Warburg, 1973, p. 79, cited in Robert Hewisan's essay ' "Happy were He": Benjamin Britten and the *Gloriana* Story', Banks, op. cit., p. 16.
155 Booklet accompanying recording, Largo label 440213–2, p. 26.
156 *Opera*, February 1994, p. 143.
157 Ibid., October 1953, p. 634.
158 Harold Rosenthal, *Opera*, November 1959, p. 713.
159 Leigh, Interview, 23.4.98.
160 Donaldson, op. cit., p. 94.
161 *Manchester Guardian*, 16.5.55.
162 *Opera*, February 1955, p. 125.
163 Ibid., January 1954, p. 44.
164 ROH Archives, Board minutes, March 1954, 16.2.54.
165 *Opera*, March 1954, p. 178.
166 John Tooley, *In House, Covent Garden, 50 Years of Opera and Ballet*, London: Faber & Faber, 1999, p. 77.
167 *Daily Telegraph*, 3.12.54.
168 Harewood, op. cit., p. 156.
169 ROH Archives, Wilson to Webster, 8.3.54, Wilson, 16/074.
170 *Opera*, pp. 187–91.
171 *New Statesman*, 5.12.55.
172 *Opera*, June 1955, p. 349.

4 The Met 1941–50: *Gentleman Johnson*

1 *Opera News*, July 1995, p. 30.
2 Rasponi, *The Last Prima Donnas*, p. 220.
3 Rudolf Bing, *5000 Nights at the Opera*, Garden City, New York: Doubleday, 1972, p. 134.

4 MO Archives, Press statement, 17.7.48.
5 MO Archives, unsigned memorandum, 27.3.47.
6 Bing, op. cit., p. 138.
7 *Opera News*, 19.2.72.
8 MO Archives, Johnson to Marks Levine, 4.5.45.
9 Francis Robinson, *Celebration: The Metropolitan Opera*, Garden City, New York: Doubleday, 1979, p. 52.
10 Rasponi, op. cit., p. 127.
11 Ibid., p. 289.
12 Ibid., p. 479.
13 MO Archives, Ziegler to National Urban League, 20.4.44.
14 *Opera*, 1951, p. 51.
15 Bing, op. cit., p. 139.
16 Quoted in Irving Kolodin, *The Metropolitan Opera 1883–1996: A Candid History*, New York: Knopf, 1966, 495.
17 Ibid., p. 497.
18 *Opera News*, July 1955, pp. 32–3.
19 ASA, ms. 2312/38.
20 Quoted in Martin Mayer, *The Met: One Hundred Years of Grand Opera*, London: Thames & Hudson, 1983, p. 218.
21 *Opera News*, July 1955, p. 15.
22 'Clouds of War', *Opera News*, July 1955, pp. 10–17.
23 Quaintance Eaton, *The Miracle of the Met: An Informal History of the Metropolitan Opera 1883–1967*, New York: Meredith, 1968, p. 278.
24 D. Hamilton (ed.), *The Metropolitan Opera Encyclopedia*, New York: Simon & Schuster, 1987, p. 367.
25 Kolodin, op. cit., p. 481.
26 Ibid., p. 482.
27 Eaton, op. cit., p. 303.
28 Bing, op. cit., p. 129.

5 La Scala 1955–59: *A Golden Age*

1 Interview, *Opera News*, 13.2.71.
2 Ibid.
3 *Opera*, May 1958, p. 289.
4 BBC television programme on Luchino Visconti, April 1998.
5 Quoted in Scott, *Maria Meneghini Callas*, p. 144.
6 Quoted in R. Parker (ed.), *The Oxford History of Opera*, Oxford: Oxford University Press, 1996, p. 277.
7 Quoted in M. Stirling, *A Screen of Time: A Study of Luchino Visconti*, London: Secker & Warburg, 1979, p. 92.
8 *Corriere d'informazione*, 8–9.12.54.
9 *Il contemporaneo*, 18.12.54.
10 *Opera News*, September 1972.
11 *Corriere della sera*, 6.3.55.
12 *La patria*, 6.3.55.
13 *Corriere d'informazione*, 7–8.3.55.
14 Arruga, *La Scala*, p. 221.
15 Ethan Mordden, *Demented: The World of the Opera Diva*, New York: Simon & Schuster, 1984, p. 214.
16 Quoted in Arruga, op. cit., p. 247.
17 J. Ardoin and G. Fitzgerald, *Callas*, London: Thames & Hudson, 1974, p. 162.
18 Quoted in Scott, op. cit., p. 189.
19 Rasponi, *The Last Prima Donnas*, p. 254.
20 Casanova, *Renata Tebaldi: The Voice of an Angel*, p. 120.
21 Elvio Giudici, *L'opera in cd e video: guida all'ascolto*, Milan: Saggiatore, 1995, p. 605.
22 Arruga, op. cit., p. 214.
23 *New York Times*, 22.2.59.
24 *Opera*, December 1957, p. 560.
25 Ibid., March 1957, p. 171.
26 Massimo Mila, *Massimo Mila alla Scala: Scritti 1955–1988*, Milan: Rizzoli, 1989, 1993, p. 42.
27 *Opera*, May 1958, p. 31.

6 Vienna 1955–60: *The Advent of Karajan*

1 *Die Presse*, 8.11.55.
2 Witeschnik, *Wiener Opernkunst*, p. 265.
3 Prawy, *The Vienna Opera*, p. 182.
4 *Opera*, February 1956, p. 89.
5 John Culshaw, *Putting the Record Straight: The Autobiography of John Culshaw*, London: Secker & Warburg, 1981, p. 196.
6 G. Schmiedel in Rosenthal (ed.), *The Opera Bedside Book*, p. 292.
7 O. Fritz (ed.), *Almanach der wiener Staatsoper 1955–1956*, Vienna: Bergland Verlag, 1956, pp. 7–8.
8 *Opera*, March 1956, p. 156.
9 Ibid., April 1956, p. 239.
10 Ibid., March 1956, p. 158.
11 Prawy, op. cit., p. 183. Prawy confirmed his suspicion that Marboe had favoured Karajan's appointment all a long in an interview with one of the authors in Vienna in January 2001.
12 Franz Endler, *Karajan: Eine Biographie*, Hamburg: Hoffmann and Campe, 1992, p. 138.
13 Karajan's contract, theoretically available to researchers in the Austrian State Archives and accessed in that institution's ledgers, has in fact not been transferred from the archives of the Österreichische Bundestheaterverwaltung (Austrian State Theatres Administration). Repeated requests by the officials of the State Archives for this document and certain others to be handed over have met with no success.
14 *Opera*, August 1956, p. 488.
15 Ibid., September 1956, p. 555.
16 Norman Lebrecht, *When the Music Stops: Managers, Maestros and the Corporate Murder of Classical Music*, London: Simon & Schuster, 1996, p. 167.
17 Prawy, op. cit., pp. 189–90.
18 *Opera*, December 1956, p. 741.
19 Ibid., January 1957, p. 37.
20 Ibid., February 1957, p. 92.
21 Ibid., November 1957, p. 708.
22 Prawy, op. cit., p. 186.
23 *Opera*, June 1957, p. 365.
24 Ibid., p. 366.
25 Quoted in Endler, op. cit., pp. 139–40.
26 *Opera*, August 1960, pp. 538–9.
27 Ibid., February 1960, p. 144.
28 Ibid., Koegler surely meant the 'Florentine character' of the productions, as Botticelli did not paint in Venice.
29 *Opera*, February 1960, p. 145.

7 The Met 1951–59: *Bing Rampant*

1 MO Archives, memorandum on Mr Bing's recommendations. Rudolph Bing papers 8/12/194.
2 Bing, *5000 Nights*, pp. 138–40.
3 Ibid., p. 146.
4 Ibid., p. 147.
5 Ibid., p. 145.
6 Ibid., p. 150.
7 Kolodin, op. cit., p. 499.
8 *Opera*, 1951, p. 334.
9 Bing, op. cit., p. 148.
10 James Hinton Jr in *Opera*, April 1955, p. 237.
11 Bing, op. cit., p. 151.
12 Kolodin, op. cit., p. 500.
13 McGovern and Winer (eds), *I Remember Too Much*, p. 22.
14 Ibid.
15 *Opera*, 1951, p. 336.
16 *Opera*, 1951, p. 331.
17 Quoted in Kolodin, p. 504.
18 Ibid.
19 *Opera*, 1952, pp. 273–4.
20 Ibid., p. 274.
21 Ibid., 1953, p. 343.

22 Eaton, *The Miracle of the Met*, p. 317.
23 *Opera*, 1953, p. 343.
24 MO Archives, Bing to Diez, 25.22.50 (authors' emphasis).
25 MO Archives, Bing to Diez, 18.12.50.
26 Reiner contracted to conduct a 1963 *Götterdämmerung* at the Met but fell ill during the rehearsal period and died.
27 Eaton, op. cit., p. 321.
28 MO Archives, Board Minutes.
29 MO Archives, memo, 19.12.52.
30 MO Archives 1956–7, Special Meeting of Executive Committee.
31 Bing, op. cit., p. 154.
32 Rasponi, *The Last Prima Donnas*, p. 388.
33 Bing, op. cit., p. 154.
34 Rasponi, op. cit., p. 85.
35 Ibid., p. 81.
36 Ibid., pp. 311–12.
37 Ibid., p. 85.
38 Kolodin, op. cit., p. 603.
39 *Opera News*, 3.3.73.
40 Bing, op. cit., p. 245.
41 MO Archives, Board of Directors.
42 MO Archives, Bing to Di Stefano, 13.10.52.
43 MO Archives, Board of Directors Confidential Annex B. 16.5.57.
44 MO Archives, Bing to Engel, 20.11.50.
45 MO Archives, Engel to Bing, 12.12.50.
46 Bing, op. cit., p. 234.
47 Bing, op. cit., p. 235.
48 MO Archives, memo, 25.10.56.
49 Kolodin, op. cit., p. 577.
50 Ibid., p. 576.
51 Ibid.
52 A delightful parody of the Tebaldi cult and Callas mania is found in James McCourt's 1976 novel *Mawrdew Czgowchwz*. Tebaldi is sent up as 'Morgana Neri, a diva of yesteryear'. Neri's fans, led by Old Mary Cedrioli, assemble voodoo images of Czgowchwz, the hated rival. Critical reaction to Czgowchwz's vocal idiosyncrasies is extreme – and extremely divided. ' "Quintessential Czgowchwz!" Alice screamed. "Definitive in its own right," Paranoy insisted in the April *Opera*. Ralph, revived, lamented, "She wobbles in thirds!" Dixie, defiantly opposed to the transformation that first day, moaned, "She sounds like an Electrolux; the tops are like steel wool!" '
53 *Opera*, 1952, p. 654.
54 The bass Nicola Rossi-Lemeni in an interview recalled Callas's insecurities at the time of the first La Scala *Norma*: 'She was always afraid she had sung badly, that it wasn't as good as she wanted; her ambition was such that she was never satisfied with herself.' Michael Scott, *Maria Meneghini Callas.*
55 MO Archives, Bing to Callas, 16.2.57.
56 MO Archives, Bing to Callas, 6.1.58.
57 MO Archives, Bing to Callas, 26.9.56.
58 MO Archives, Bing to Callas, 13.1.58.
59 MO Archives, Bing to Callas, 29.10.58.
60 MO Archives, 1.11.58.
61 Bing, op. cit., p. 242.
62 MO Archives, 1.11.58.
63 MO Archives, 2.11.58.
64 *Dallas Morning News*, 1.11.58, cited in Scott, op. cit., p. 215.
65 MO Archives, Bing to Callas, 3.11.58.
66 MO Archives, Bing to Callas, 5.11.58.
67 MO Archives, Callas to Bing, 6.11.58.
68 MO Archives, Bing to Callas, 6.11.58.
69 Kolodin, op. cit., p. 606.
70 Ibid., p. 607.
71 Robinson, *Celebration*, p. 57.

8 Covent Garden 1955–60: *Kubelik and Beyond*

1   ROH Archives, Norman Fraser BBC, Kubelik papers.
2   *Opera*, June 1955, pp. 391–2.
3   Ibid., July 1955, p. 460.
4   Ibid., December 1955, p. 793.
5   *Observer*, 23.10.55.
6   Tooley, Interview, 4.12.00.
7   ROH Archives, Kubelik papers.
8   *Opera*, January 1957, p. 56.
9   Ibid., January 1956, p. 55.
10 Porter in the *Financial Times*, 20.1.56 and Mann in *The Times*, 20.1.56.
11 Harewood, *The Tongs and the Bones*, p. 158.
12 Drogheda, *Double Harness*, p. 236.
13 Ibid., p. 241.
14 Drogheda to Berlin, Berlin papers, 10.8.61.
15 Berlin, Interview, 6.12.96.
16 ROH Archives, Board minutes, 1953–64, 17.1.55, 1950–56, 22.3.55.
17 ROH Archives, Board minutes, 1950–56.
18 Haltrecht, *The Quiet Showman*, p. 204.
19 ROH Archives, Moore and Webster at Board meeting, 1950–56, 28.6.56.
20 Donaldson, *The Royal Opera House*, p. 101.
21 ROH Archives.
22 Donaldson, op. cit., p. 102.
23 ROH Archives, Board minutes, 1950–56.
24 *The Times*, 6.7.56.
25 Drogheda, op. cit., p. 247.
26 ROH Archives, Board minutes, 1950–56.
27 *Opera*, October 1956, p. 586.
28 ROH Archives, OSC minutes, 1951–59, 15.11.56.
29 ROH Archives, Board, 1950–56, 18.12.56.
30 Berlin, Interview, 6.12.96.

31 Andrew Porter, 'Opera in English', *Opera*, February 1957, p. 80.
32 *Opera*, March 1957, p. 182.
33 28.1.57.
34 *Opera*, February 1957, p. 79.
35 Evans with Goodwin, *Sir Geraint Evans*, p. 76.
36 *The Times*, 14.6.57.
37 *New Statesman*, 15.12.56.
38 *Observer*, 6.12.56.
39 *The Times*, 11.12.56.
40 William Mann in Harold Rosenthal, *Two Centuries of Opera at Covent Garden*, London: Putnam, 1958, p. 82.
41 Philip Hope-Wallace, *Manchester Guardian*, 6.6.57.
42 *Opera*, March 1958, p. 192.
43 MRPC Archive.
44 Cited in Donaldson, op. cit., p. 106.
45 ROH Archives, Drogheda papers (henceforth GDA), Webster to Drogheda on his retirement, 18.9.70., ROH Archives, Drogheda papers. Undated letter.
46 Tooley, Interview, 4.12.00.
47 *Opera*, February 1975, p. 132.
48 ROH Archives, Board meetings papers, 1953–54.
49 Berlin papers, Arts Council to Waverley, 25.7.57.
50 ROH Archives, Drogheda to William Emrys Williams, GDA, 22.5.58.
51 ROH Archives Board minutes, 21 January, 18.3.58.
52 ROH Archives, Williams to Drogheda, GDA, 30.5.58.
53 ROH Archives, Board minutes, 20.1.59, Williams to Webster, 17.3.59.
54 *Myto records* 1994 3 mcd 941.97 Myto CD 236 0060.
55 *Covent Garden, 25 Years of Opera and Ballet*, p. 74.
56 *Opera*, June 1958, p. 349.

57 *New Statesman*, 17.5.58.
58 Hall, *Making an Exhibition of Myself*, p. 222.
59 Harewood, op. cit., p. 162.
60 Jeannie Williams, *Jon Vickers, A Hero's Life*, Boston North-eastern University Press, 1999, p. 88.
61 Haltrecht, op. cit., p. 240.
62 ROH Archives, OSC minutes, 1951–59, 3.4.58.
63 Berlin papers, House receipts.
64 Berlin papers.
65 Berlin to Drogheda, Moore archive, 13.6.60.
66 Berlin, Interview, 6.12.96.
67 Berlin papers.
68 ROH Archives, Board minutes, 27.10.59.
69 Note in Berlin archives: The Post of Music Director.
70 ROH Archives, Board minutes, 21.5.57.
71 Berlin papers.
72 Harewood, op. cit., p. 162.
73 Tooley, Interview, 4.12.00.
74 ROH Archives and Berlin papers, Board minutes, 16.9.58.
75 *Opera*, December 1958, p. 806.
76 Joan Sutherland, *The Autobiography of Joan Sutherland*, p. 68.
77 ROH Archives, OSC, 1951–59.
78 Harewood, op. cit., p. 165.
79 ROH Archives, Harewood, 11.9.58.
80 Berlin papers, 11.12.57, 15.12.58.
81 ROH Archives, Drogheda to Legge, 23.9.58.
82 Berlin papers, 18.12.58.
83 ROH Archives, GDA.
84 ROH Archives, GDA, 13.9.58.
85 Berlin papers.
86 Berlin archives, Harewood to Berlin, 22.6.61, Berlin to Harewood, 26.6.61, Berlin to Donaldson.
87 Berlin papers, Berlin to James Smith, 9.1.59, Legge to Berlin, 24.2.59, Berlin to Drogheda, 4.3.59.
88 Zeffirelli, *The Autobiography of Franco Zeffirelli*, pp. 146–7.
89 Evans with Goodwin, op. cit., p. 102.
90 Zeffirelli, op. cit., p. 147.
91 Sutherland, op. cit., p. 69.
92 Donaldson, op. cit., p. 121.
93 Sutherland, op. cit., p. 72.
94 MPRC Archive.
95 Berlin papers.
96 Berlin papers, Berlin to Smith, 3.7.59, 17.7.59, 20.7.59.
97 Drogheda to Berlin, Berlin papers, 3.9.59.
98 Harewood to Berlin, Berlin papers, 30.9.59.
99 *Opera*, March 1960, p. 174.

9 Covent Garden 1960–65: *The Solti Revolution*

1 Bryan Magee, *The Solti Era, Solti's Ten Years*, BBC, *Music on Two*, July 1971.
2 Georg Solti, *Solti on Solti, A Memoir*, London: Chatto & Windus, 1997, p. 29.
3 *About the House*, Summer 1971.
4 Magee, op. cit.
5 *About the House*, vol. 3, no. 1, Summer 1971, p. 21.
6 *Omnibus* Tribute, *Solti, The Making of a Maestro*, BBC 1, 28.9.97.
7 His friend Susan Dansch in BBC Radio 3 Tribute, September 1997.
8 *Sunday Times*, 6.12.59.
9 *The Times*, 5.12.59.
10 *About the House*, vol. 5, no. 9, Summer 1971.
11 Drogheda, *Double Harness*, p. 280.
12 Solti, op. cit., p. 124.
13 *About the House*, Summer 1971, p. 18.
14 Berlin papers.
15 ROH Archives.
16 ROH Archives, GDA.

17 ROH Archives, Solti file, contracts 54/4/3.
18 ROH Archives, GDA, Hedi Solti to Drogheda, 2.4.60.
19 Haltrecht, *The Quiet Showman*, p. 258.
20 Berlin papers, Drogheda to Berlin, 10.8.61.
21 Berlin papers, 8.3.60, Berlin to Drogheda, 9.3.60.
22 ROH Archives, SC 1960.
23 *Opera*, March 1960, p. 228.
24 Berlin papers.
25 *Opera*, March 1960, p. 228.
26 Sutherland, *The Autobiography of Joan Sutherland*, p. 83.
27 Berlin papers, Berlin to Drogheda, 14.11.60.
28 Berlin papers, Legge to Berlin, 9.6.60, 13.6.60, Drogheda to Berlin 14.6.60.
29 Berlin papers.
30 Ibid.
31 Tooley, *In House*, p. 26.
32 Berlin papers, Drogheda to Berlin 16.6.60, Berlin to James Smith, 27.6.60, Berlin to Sackville-West, 27.6.60.
33 Drogheda, op. cit., p. 282.
34 ROH Archives, Board minutes, 24.5.60.
35 ROH Archives, Solti to Webster, 13.12.60, Solti contracts 54/4/3, 12.60, Solti contracts 54/4/3, GDA, Hedi Solti to Drogheda, 9.1.61, 10.1.60.
36 ROH Archives, SC, 20.4.60.
37 *Opera*, August 1961, p. 498.
38 ROH Archives, Solti contracts 54/4/3. Press conference.
39 Peter Heyworth, *Otto Klemperer, His Life and Times*, vol. 2, 1933–73, Cambridge: Cambridge University Press, 1996, p. 288.
40 Webster to Solti, 28.2.61, Solti contracts 54/4/3.
41 *Opera*, February 1960, p. 153.
42 Berlin papers, Berlin to Sackville-West, 30.5.60.
43 *Opera*, May 1960, p. 372.
44 Bella Voce BLV 107.203.
45 *The Times* 10.10.61.
46 *Opera*, August 1961, pp. 471–2.
47 Berlin papers, Drogheda to Berlin, 'Friday night'.
48 Berlin papers, Berlin to Mrs Hirshman.
49 ROH Archives, GDA, Hedi Solti to Drogheda, 9.1.61.
50 Andrew Porter quoted in Donaldson, *The Royal Opera House*, p. 124.
51 Magee, op. cit.
52 Jon Tolanski, *The Royal Opera – 50 Glorious Years*, The Royal Opera – Classic FM.
53 Magee, op. cit.
54 ROH Archives, GDA.
55 *Omnibus* Tribute.
56 Lady Solti, Interview, 6.10.98.
57 Berlin papers, Berlin to Drogheda, 1.6.61, Berlin to Keefe, 5.6.61, Berlin to Drogheda, 31.10.60.
58 ROH Archives, GDA.
59 Solti, op. cit., p. 136.
60 ROH Archives, GDA.
61 *Opera*, October 1961, p. 645.
62 ROH Archives, Board minutes, 27.9.60.
63 *About the House*, vol. 3, no. 9, Summer 1971.
64 Milnes, Interview, 30.4.98.
65 Turing, *Hans Hotter*, p. 142.
66 Berlin papers, October 1961.
67 Tooley, Interview, 4.12.00.
68 Haltrecht, op. cit., p. 290.
69 ROH Archives, GDA, Drogheda to Webster, 25.2.62.
70 Williams, *Jon Vickers*, p. 115.
71 Berlin papers, Drogheda to Berlin, 13.10.61.
72 Haltrecht, *The Quiet Showman*, p. 290.
73 Ingpen, Interview, 8.10.99.
74 Williams, op. cit., p. 123.

75 Tooley, op. cit., p. 29.
76 ROH Archives, OSC, 10.12.61.
77 Tooley, Interview, 4.12.00.
78 *Financial Times*, 10.2.62.
79 Donaldson, op. cit., 10.2.62, p. 126.
80 *Opera*, April 1962, p. 273.
81 Berlin papers, Berlin to Burdon Muller, 26.9.62, Berlin to Webster, 17.9.62.
82 *Opera*, August 1980, p. 769.
83 Ingpen, Interview, 18.10.99.
84 Solti, op. cit., p. 135.
85 Berlin papers.
86 *Omnibus* Tribute.
87 Berlin papers, Berlin to Drogheda, 1.6.61, Berlin to Bagrit, 3.6.61.
88 *Sunday Times*, 16.9.62.
89 *Opera*, September 1962, p. 693.
90 ROH Archives, Board minutes, 1960–61.
91 *Opera*, October 1991, p. 1141.
92 *About the House*, Summer 1971, p. 19.
93 *The Times*, 15.11.00.
94 *The Listener*, 11.6.70.
95 ROH Archives, Hall to Webster, 2.7.54.
96 ROH Archives, undated transcript of meeting between Tooley, Davis, Hall, O'Brien, Bury, probably December 1970.
97 *Opera*, July 1962, p. 488.
98 *Financial Times*, 29.9.62.
99 *About the House*, vol. 1, no. 1, 1962.
100 *Opera*, November 1962, p. 712.
101 *Guardian*, 2.10.62.
102 *Opera*, July 1975, p. 703.
103 Ibid., December 1962, p. 829.
104 Berlin papers.
105 ROH Archives, Board 5/1.
106 Drogheda, op. cit., p. 284.
107 Berlin papers.
108 Record of meeting between Mr Solti, Sir David Webster and Lord Drogheda, 13.12.62, Berlin papers.
109 Berlin papers, 9.1.62.
110 *Opera*, January 1993, p. 31.

111 *Observer*, 20.1.63.
112 *The Times*, 19.1.63.
113 Recording in MPRC BCT 328.
114 Evans with Goodwin, op. cit., p. 80.
115 *Opera*, July 1963, pp. 506, 492.
116 Ibid., November 1997, p. 1301.
117 Magee, op. cit.
118 Solti, op. cit., p. 149.
119 ROH Archives, undated letter, Solti contracts 54/4/3.
120 Tooley, Interview, 4.12.00.
121 ROH Archives, GDA, Drogheda to Solti, 14.3.63, GDA, undated.
122 *Sunday Times*, 14.4.63.
123 *Financial Times*, 9.4.63.
124 *Covent Garden, 25 Years of Opera and Ballet*, p. 87.
125 *About the House*, vol. 3, no. 9, Summer 1971, p. 19.
126 Hall, *Making an Exhibition of Myself*, p. 236.
127 Drogheda, op. cit., p. 290.
128 *The Times*, 12.9.63.
129 *Sunday Times*, 15.9.63.
130 ROH Archives, GDA, Drogheda to Solti, 20.10.63.
131 *The Times*, 19.5.71, interview with Edward Downes.
132 Donaldson, op. cit., p. 128.
133 ROH Archives, Solti to Drogheda, 28.10.63.
134 *Opera*, January 1992, p. 31.
135 ROH Archives, GDA, Berlin to Drogheda, 17.5.63.
136 ROH Archives, GDA, quoted in Lebrecht, *Covent Garden*, p. 257.
137 Harewood, op. cit., p. 233.
138 *The Times*, 13.4.64.
139 ROH Archives, GDA, 19.4.64.
140 ROH Archives, OSC minutes, 1963–66.
141 Solti, op. cit., p. 144.
142 *The Times*, 14.9.64.
143 *Observer*, 6.9.64.
144 *Opera*, August 1980, p. 769.
145 *Financial Times*, 4.9.64, 7.9.64.
146 *The Times*, 14.9.64.

147 Milnes, Interview, 30.4.98.
148 *About the House*, Spring 1972.
149 *Opera*, October 1964, p. 689.
150 Ingpen, Interview, 18.10.99.
151 *Opera*, July 1966, pp. 590–3.
152 Ibid., October 1978, p. 958.
153 John Jolliffe, *Glyndebourne, An Operatic Miracle*, London: John Murray, 1999, p. 93.
154 *Opera*, Festival issue, 1998, p. 39.
155 ROH Archives, Board minutes, 18/1/7.
156 *Guardian*, 29.1.65.
157 Solti, op. cit., p. 144.
158 *Times Educational Supplement*, 5.2.65.
159 ROH Archives, GDA, 7.2.65, 11.3.65, 17.3.65.
160 ROH Archives, Drogheda to Lord Cottesloe, 23.12.64.
161 Drogheda, op. cit., p. 311.
162 *Command Paper* 2601, 7.2.65.
163 Drogheda, op. cit., p. 307.
164 ROH Archives, GDA.
165 Arnold Goodman, *Tell Them I'm On My Way*, London: Chapmans, 1993, p. 275.
166 Sinclair, *Arts and Cultures*, p. 191.
167 Patricia Hollis, *Jennie Lee, A Life*, Oxford: Oxford University Press, 1997, p. 294.
168 Goodman, op. cit., p. 291.
169 Sinclair, op. cit., p. 147.
170 Tooley, op. cit., p. 209.
171 Robert Jackson, quoting Arts Council report of 1966 in *The Times*, 17.1.70.
172 Sinclair, op. cit., pp. 154–5.

10 Covent Garden 1965–70: 'The Greatest Opera Company in the World'

1 Berlin papers, Berlin to Mr White, assistant secretary ACGB, 12.10.61, 30.5.60.
2 *Omnibus* Tribute, *Solti, The Making of a Maestro*, BBC 1, 28.9.97.
3 ROH Archives.
4 *The Times*, 25.6.65.
5 Hall, *Making an Exhibition of Myself*, p. 223.
6 ROH Archives, OSC minutes, 1963–6, 16.6.65.
7 *The Times*, 7.6.65.
8 ROH Archives, Hall.
9 Hall, op. cit., pp. 224–5.
10 *The Times*, 7.6.65.
11 *Sunday Times*, 4.7.65.
12 *Omnibus* Tribute.
13 *The Times*, 7.6.65.
14 Hall, op. cit., p. 226.
15 Ingpen, Interview, 18.10.99.
16 Joan Bakewell interview, Radio 3, 1998.
17 ROH Archives, Board minutes, 1961–66, 5/1, 23.11.65.
18 *Opera*, February 1970, p. 105.
19 Ibid., April 1969, p. 357.
20 Video, *The Art of Great Conducting: great conductors of the past*, Teldec video IMG Artist/BBC in association with Teldec Classics International group (UK) inc. 1993 © International Management Group (UK) inc. 1993 (p) 1994 Teldec Classics International GMBH Hamburg A Time Warner Company.
21 Haltrecht, *The Quiet Showman*, p. 292.
22 ROH Archives, GDA, 1.7.66, undated letter.
23 Hall, Interview, 29.7.99.
24 Evans with Goodwin, *Sir Geraint Evans*, p. 223.
25 Hall, Interview, 29.7.99.
26 ROH Archives, 28.7.65.
27 *Sunday Times*, 10.7.66.
28 Drogheda, *Double Harness*, p. 313.
29 Booklet accompanying 1992 Decca CD, p. 14.
30 *Opera*, December 1984, pp. 1305–6.
31 Drogheda, op. cit., p. 325.

32 ROH Archives, GDA, Confidential annexe to Board minutes, 19.12.67.
33 Drogheda, op. cit., p. 326.
34 ROH Archives, GDA.
35 The Times, 24.3.70.
36 Alan Blyth, Opera, September 1967, p. 769.
37 Opera, November 1965, p. 787.
38 Berlin papers, Berlin to Drogheda, 23.1.67, 26.1.67.
39 ROH Archives, Inter-departmental memo, 25.3.68.
40 Hall, op. cit., p. 227.
41 ROH Archives, GDA, Davis to Drogheda, 28.1.69, 22.2.69.
42 ROH Archives, minutes of undated meeting in 1970.
43 Hall, Interview, 29.7.99.
44 Opera, October 1967, pp. 790–7.
45 Ibid., March 1967, p. 253.
46 Ibid., March 1970, p. 262.
47 Rosenthal interview with Solti in ibid., July 1968, pp. 534–7.
48 Goodman, Tell Them I'm On My Way, p. 302.
49 Tooley, In House, p. 105.
50 Goodman, op. cit., p. 303.
51 Stephen Fay, Power Play, The Life and Times of Peter Hall, London: Hodder & Stoughton, 1995, p. 264.
52 Hall, op. cit., p. 236.
53 Fay, op. cit., p. 264.
54 Ibid., p. 265.
55 Colin Davis, Interview, 24.11.99.
56 Opera, July 1969, pp. 639, 641.
57 Rosenthal in ibid., p. 644.
58 ROH Archives, OSC 1961–70, 6/1.
59 ROH Archives, GDA, 4.11.69.
60 Hollis, Jennie Lee, 5.2.70, p. 265.
61 Sutherland, The Autobiography of Joan Sutherland, p. 231.
62 Drogheda, op. cit., p. 318.
63 Solti, op. cit., p. 156.
64 Harewood, The Tongs and the Bones, p. 174.
65 ROH Archives, GDA, Drogheda to Harewood, 17.4.69, 19.4.69.
66 Drogheda, op. cit., pp. 348–9.
67 Isis, 16.2.70.
68 ROH Archives, Drogheda papers, 20.3.70, 21.3.70.
69 Hall, op. cit., p. 229.
70 Alan Blyth, The Listener, 11.6.70.
71 ROH Archives, undated minutes of meeting, December 1970.
72 Berlin papers, Joan Drogheda to Berlin, 17.1.70.
73 ROH Archives, undated minutes of meeting, December 1970.
74 Ibid.
75 ROH Archives, Hall to Davis and Tooley, 19.1.70.
76 ROH Archives, Board minutes.
77 ROH Archives, GDA, Drogheda to Hall, 16.2.70.
78 ROH Archives, Board minutes.
79 ROH Archives, GDA, Drogheda to Hall, 18.2.70.
80 Berlin papers, Pavitt to Berlin, 19.2.70.
81 ROH Archives, OSC.
82 Drogheda, op. cit., p. 331.
83 ROH Archives, OSC 1961–70 6/1, 16.9.70.
84 ROH Archives, GDA, 22.9.70, Drogheda to Tooley 31.12.70, Davis to Drogheda 29.9.70, 8.10.70, 26.11.70, 8.12.70, Drogheda to Tooley, 31.12.70.
85 ROH Archives, OSC 1961–70, 6/1, 16.12.70.
86 ROH Archives, GDA, 28.12.70.
87 Ibid.
88 ROH Archives, undated minutes of December 1970 meeting.
89 ROH Archives, GDA, 8.1.70, 16.12.70, 19.1.71.
90 Drogheda, op. cit., p. 334.
91 ROH Archives, GDA, Hall, 12.1.71, 18.1.71.
92 Tooley, op. cit., p. 37.
93 Covent Garden, 25 Years of Opera and Ballet, p. 228.
94 ROH Archives.

95 Berlin papers, Berlin to Drogheda
    15.12.69, 13.1.70, Pavitt to Berlin
    21.12.69, Drogheda to Berlin, 25.1.70.
96 ROH Archives, Hall to Tooley,
    19.1.70.
97 *Sunday Telegraph*, 21.2.71.
98 *About the House*, vol. 3, no. 9,
    Summer 1971.
99 *Opera*, August 1971, p. 693.
100 Berlin papers, Pavitt to Berlin.
101 Hall, Interview, 29.7.99.
102 Jon Tolansky on Classic FM, *The
    Royal Opera – 50 Glorious Years*,
    1.1.97.
103 *Covent Garden, 25 Years of Opera
    and Ballet*, p. 73.
104 Lady Solti, Interview, 6.10.98.
105 *About the House*, Summer 1971,
    p. 21.
106 *Omnibus* Tribute, 1997.

11 The Met 1960–72: *The Met
    Moves to Lincoln Center*

1   *Opera*, May 1963, p. 313.
2   Harold Rosenthal (ed.), *Opera
    Annual No. 7*, London: John
    Calder, 1960, p. 123.
3   Quoted in Bing, *5000 Nights*, p. 261.
4   *New York Times*, 23.7.95.
5   *Opera*, May 1962, p. 327.
6   Bing, op. cit., pp. 261–2.
7   Clive James, *Falling Towards
    England: Unreliable Memoirs II*,
    London: Pan, 1986, p. 146.
8   *New York Times*, 5.10.96.
9   Ibid., 28.1.61.
10 Quoted in Rupert Christiansen,
    Prima Donna: A History,
    Harmondsworth: Penguin, 1986,
    p. 213.
11 *Opera News*, 12.2.72.
12 *Opera*, April 1965, p. 267.
13 Giudici, *L'opera in cd e video*,
    p. 987.
14 Ibid., p. 986.
15 Rosenthal (ed.), op. cit., p. 1.

16 MO Archives, Bing to Bliss, 25.6.62.
17 *New York Times*, 20.11.60.
18 *Opera*, January 1964, p. 44.
19 Ibid.
20 MO Archives, Bing to Fisher,
    24.10.63. Fisher's firm had an
    unfortunate slogan: 'If it flows
    through pipe anywhere in the
    world ... chances are it's
    controlled by ... FISHER.'
21 *Opera*, February 1965, p. 104.
22 Kolodin, op. cit., p. 689.
23 MO Archives, Bing to Solti, 6.10.61.
24 Ibid.
25 MO Archives, Bing to Solti,
    20.10.61.
26 MO Archives, Bing to Solti, 24.9.64.
27 MO Archives, Solti to Bing, 4.12.64.
28 MO Archives, Bing to Giulini,
    23.5.62.
29 MO Archives, Zeffirelli to Bing,
    16.4.62.
30 MO Archives, Bing to Zeffirelli,
    19.5.62.
31 MO Archives, Bing to Zeffirelli,
    11.9.63.
32 Robinson, *Celebration*, p. 164.
33 *Opera*, March 1964, p. 189.
34 Robinson, op. cit., p. 167.
35 *New York Herald Tribune*, 7.3.64.
36 *Opera*, July 1964, p. 453.
37 MO Archives, Bing to Visconti,
    7.10.64.
38 MO Archives, Visconti to Bing,
    12.10.64.
39 MO Archives, Bing to Visconti,
    9.11.64.
40 MO Archives, Bing to Visconti,
    19.12.64.
41 MO Archives, Karajan to Bing,
    26.5.66.
42 MO Archives, telephone
    conversation transcript, Bing to
    Wilford, 25.2.66.
43 MO Archives, 17.5.66.
44 MO Archives, Bauer to Herman,
    10.2.67.

45 MO Archives, Bing to Abbado, 27.12.67.
46 *Opera*, May 1962, p. 308.
47 Bing, op. cit., p. 249.
48 Ibid., p. 245.
49 Ibid., p. 250.
50 Ibid., p. 251.
51 Ibid., p. 256.
52 Ibid., p. 253.
53 Eaton, *The Miracle of the Met*, p. 383.
54 Ibid., p. 390.
55 Ibid., p. 391.
56 *Opera News*, 14.11.84.
57 Ibid.
58 Robinson, op. cit., p. 19.
59 Bing, op. cit., p. 291.
60 J. Dizikes, *Opera in America: A Cultural History*, New Haven and London: Yale University Press, 1993, p. 529.
61 MO Archives, Board minutes, 18.4.63.
62 Quoted in Dizikes, op. cit., p. 530.
63 MO Archives, Board minutes, 24.2.59.
64 Bing, op. cit., p. 293.
65 Ibid., p. 300.
66 *New York Times*, 17.4.66.
67 Ibid.
68 Ibid.
69 Kolodin, op. cit., p. 745.
70 Ibid.
71 Eaton, op. cit., p. 410.
72 Robinson, op. cit., p. 26.
73 Ibid., p. 25.
74 Hamilton, *Metropolitan Opera Encyclopedia*, p. 229.
75 Robinson, op. cit., p. 26.
76 Ibid., p. 38.
77 *Opera*, November 1966, p. 841.
78 Bing, op. cit., p. 305.
79 *New York Times*, 13.10.80.
80 *Opera*, November 1966, p. 849.
81 *Opera News*, 16.1.82.
82 MO Archives, Bing to Zeffirelli, 12.12.66.
83 *New York Times*, 5.10.96.
84 MO Archives, Board minutes, 9.11.66.
85 MO Archives, 5.12.66.
86 MO Archives, Board minutes, 10.4.67.
87 Quoted in Brook, *Opera*, p. 405.
88 MO Archives, Bliss to Moore, 10.10.69.
89 MO Archives, Bing, 16.10.68.
90 *Opera News*, 13.6.70.
91 Ibid.
92 *New York Times*, 10.12.80.
93 *Opera News*, 13.6.70.
94 Ibid.
95 MO Archives, minutes, 21.5.70.
96 *New York Times*, 15.12.69.
97 *Opera*, November 1970, p. 1003.
98 Ibid., February 1971, pp. 120–1.
99 Ibid., November 1971, p. 973.
100 *New York Times*, 20.11.71.
101 Ibid., 19.2.72.
102 *Opera*, May 1972, p. 413.
103 *New York Times*, 19.2.72.
104 Ibid., 14.6.72.
105 *Opera*, July 1972, p. 614.
106 Robinson, op. cit., p. 57.
107 *Opera*, July 1972, p. 614.
108 *New York Times*, 23.4.72.
109 *Opera*, August 1964, p. 561.
110 *Opera News*, 30.1.65.
111 Mayer, *The Met*, p. 326.
112 White Paper on the Metropolitan Opera, June 1971, p. 5.
113 *New York Times*, 10.12.70.
114 *Opera*, June 1972, p. 502.
115 Robinson, op. cit., p. 57.
116 The House had not had a music director since Toscanini resigned in 1915.
117 *New York Times*, 10.6.71.
118 Ibid., 7.6.71.
119 Mayer, op. cit., p. 323.
120 S. Chapin, *Leonard Bernstein: Notes from a Friend*, New York: Walker, 1992, p. 152.

12 Vienna 1961–68: *Karajan Resigns*

1 R. Osborne, *Herbert von Karajan*, p. 36.
2 Dusek (ed.), *Kulissengespräche II*, p. 41.
3 Prawy, *The Vienna Opera*, pp. 188–9.
4 Quoted in R. Osborne, op. cit., p. 416.
5 Prawy, op. cit., p. 187.
6 *Opera*, August 1961, p. 514.
7 Ibid.
8 Ibid.
9 Ibid., March 1962, p. 172.
10 Ibid.
11 Ibid., August 1962, p. 529.
12 Ibid.
13 Ibid., April 1962, p. 243.
14 Prawy, op. cit., pp. 191–2.
15 Quoted in R. Osborne, op. cit., p. 472.
16 Ibid.
17 *Opera*, June 1963, p. 398.
18 Günther Rennert, *Opernarbeit: Inszenierung 1963–1973*, Kassel: Bärenreiter, 1974, p. 185.
19 *Opera*, June 1963, p. 398.
20 Prawy, op. cit., p. 183.
21 *Opera*, August 1963, p. 540.
22 Ibid.
23 Ibid., November 1963, p. 742.
24 Prawy, op. cit., pp. 193–4.
25 Ibid., p. 194.
26 Ibid.
27 *Opera*, February 1964, p. 101.
28 *Opera*, June 1964, p. 388.
29 Prawy, op. cit., p. 195.
30 Ibid.
31 Prawy, op. cit., p. 196.
32 Quoted in *Die Presse*, 14.5.64.
33 *Opera*, Autumn 1964, p. 43.
34 Ibid., p. 44.
35 Quoted in Bachmann, *Karajan*, pp. 182–3.
36 Schwarzkopf, *On and Off the Record*, pp. 227–8.

37 *Opera*, November 1965, pp. 820–1.
38 Ibid, p. 821.
39 Ibid., February 1966, pp. 141–2.
40 Ibid., May 1966, pp. 359–359.
41 Ibid., March 1968, p. 230.
42 Ibid., January 1968, p. 31.
43 Prawy, op. cit., p. 203.
44 Ibid., p. 202.
45 Quoted in Bachmann, op. cit., p. 186.
46 *Opera*, Autumn 1965, p. 32.
47 Even so, Wieland Wagner in 1954 had deleted the spoken text in his Stuttgart production of *Fidelio* and altered the sequence of the arias and ensembles.
48 *Opera*, Festival issue 1966, p. 54.
49 Peter Conrad, *A Song of Love and Death: The Meaning of Opera*, New York: Poseidon Press, 1987, pp. 310–11.
50 *Opera*, Autumn 1967, pp. 52–3.
51 The English version was first staged in 1956 at Santa Fe, New Mexico, in a production conducted by the composer.
52 S. Sadie (ed.), *The New Grove Dictionary of Opera*, London: Macmillan, 1997, vol. II, p. 695.
53 *Opera*, January 1965, p. 42.
54 Spotts, *Bayreuth*, p. 216.
55 Walter Felsenstein, 'The Approach to the Work: An Assemblage of Music-Theatre problems', in P. P. Fuchs (ed. and tr.), *The Music Theatre of Walter Felsenstein*, New York: Norton, 1975, pp. 56–7.
56 Ibid.
57 Felsenstein, 'Conversations During Rehearsals', in ibid., p. 112.
58 Felsenstein, 'Approach to Work', in ibid., p. 61.
59 *Opera*, January 1976, p. 26.
60 Ibid., p. 27.
61 Ibid.
62 Felsenstein in a conversation with Rolf Liebermann, 7.4.62, in *The*

Music Theatre of Walter Felsenstein, p. 119.

63 Conversation with André Boll, in ibid., p. 122.

64 Fuchs, op. cit., p. 134.

13 La Scala 1960–69: New Divas and Divos

1 Opera, August 1960, pp. 559–60.
2 Scott, Maria Meneghini Callas, p. 229.
3 Eugenio Montale, Prime alla Scala, Milan: Leonardo, 1995, pp. 319–20.
4 Ibid., p. 136.
5 Scott, op. cit., p. 230.
6 Opera, April 1968, p. 315.
7 Casanova, Renata Tebaldi, p. 159.
8 Mila, Massimo Mila alla Scala: Scritti 1955–1988, p. 174.
9 Opera, August 1962, pp. 523–4.
10 Ibid., February 1963, p. 95.
11 Corriere della sera, 13.6.64.
12 Mila, op. cit., p. 222.
13 Opera, March 1971, p. 203.
14 Ibid., March 1968, p. 236.
15 Ibid., September 1965, p. 659.
16 Giudici, L'opera in cd e video, p. 627.
17 Zeffirelli, The Autobiography of Franco Zeffirelli, p. 176.
18 Corriere della sera, 1.2.63.
19 Zeffirelli, op. cit., p. 181.
20 Ibid., pp. 179–80.
21 Ibid., p. 181.
22 Corriere della sera, 18.12.64.
23 Zeffirelli, op. cit., p. 181.
24 Ibid.
25 Montale, op. cit., p. 414.
26 Opera, July 1988, p. 770.
27 Ibid., March 1968, p. 236.
28 Corriere della sera, 8.12.67.
29 Opera, July 1998, p. 770.
30 Quoted in Mila, op. cit., p. 240.
31 Quoted in Giuseppe Pintorno, Le prime alla Scala, Gorle, Bergamo: Grafica Gutenberg, 1982, p. 256.

32 Opera, September 1962, pp. 559–60.
33 Quoted in Pintorno, op. cit., p. 259.
34 Ibid., p. 256.
35 Opera, June 1966, p. 447.
36 Ibid., May 1966, p. 393.
37 Ibid., July 1968, p. 549.
38 Ibid., April 1968, p. 317.
39 Ibid., December 1968, p. 968.
40 Rasponi, The Last Prima Donnas, p. 377.
41 Ibid.
42 Opera, February 1961, p. 97.
43 Ibid., p. 97.
44 Ibid., April 1965, p. 267.
45 Ibid., February 1981, p. 119.
46 Ibid., p. 120.
47 Quoted in Montale, op. cit., p. 432.
48 Ibid., p. 443.
49 Opera, October 1966, p. 819.
50 Domingo, My First Forty Years, p. 42.
51 Mila, op. cit., p. 248.
52 Corriere della sera, 8.12.69.
53 Domingo, op. cit., pp. 80–1.
54 Interview in Opera News, 27.3.82.
55 Opera, March 1962, p. 185.
56 Giudici, op. cit., p. 903.
57 Opera, July 1968, p. 547.
58 Ibid., November 1968, p. 931.
59 Ibid., March 1979, p. 215.
60 Opera, April 1968, p. 285.
61 Ibid., July 1968, p. 547.
62 Ibid., p. 548.
63 Ibid., August 1968, p. 654.
64 Ibid., March 1964, p. 189.
65 Ibid., November 1964, p. 704.
66 Ibid., September 1964, p. 596.
67 Ibid., February 1966, p. 148.
68 Ibid., January 1967, p. 32.

14 La Scala 1970–80: There'll Always Be an Italy

1 New York Times, 3.7.72.
2 Quoted in J. Nobécourt, L'Italie à vif, Paris, 1970, p. 208.

3 *Opera*, October 1972, pp. 900–2.
4 *New York Times*, 13.2.72, *Opera*, April 1972, p. 314, December 1996, p. 1405.
5 G. Guazzoti, quoted in D. Hirst, *Directors in Perspective: Giorgio Strehler*, Cambridge: Cambridge University Press, 1993, p. 6.
6 *Opera*, March 1973, p. 251.
7 *Opera News*, 19.4.75.
8 *Opera*, November 1978, p. 1068.
9 Ibid., March 1976, pp. 208–9.
10 Ibid., October 1972, p. 898.
11 Ibid., April 1971, pp. 278–9.
12 Ibid., March 1973, pp. 252–3.
13 Ibid., p. 254.
14 Ibid., May 1973, p. 452.
15 *Corriere della Sera*, 18.1.73.
16 *Opera*, July 1974, p. 587.
17 Ibid., pp. 587–8.
18 Ibid., pp. 588–9.
19 Ibid., June 1971, p. 485.
20 Ibid., April 1974, p. 308.
21 Mila, *Massimo Mila alla Scala*, p. 286.
22 *Corriere della sera*, 9.12.73.
23 *Opera*, February 1972, pp. 120–1.
24 *Messaggero del Lunedì*, 24.12.73.
25 Mila, op. cit., p. 265.
26 Programme booklet Deutsche Grammophon, recording 1976.
27 *Opera*, March 1976, p. 232.
28 Interview in *Opera*, November 1975, p. 1026.
29 *Corriere della sera*, 26.3.76.
30 *Opera News*, Sept. 1976.
31 *Opera*, April 1977, p. 345.
32 Domingo, *My First Forty Years*, pp. 144–5.
33 *Opera*, March 1977.
34 *Opera News*, Sept. 1979.
35 *Opera*, June 1977, p. 590.
36 Conrad, *A Song of Love and Death*, p. 302.
37 *Opera*, July 1978, pp. 713–14.
38 Ibid., July 1979, p. 799.
39 Ibid., March 1978, p. 238.
40 Quoted in H. Matheopoulos, *Bravo: The World's Great Male Singers Discuss Their Roles*, London: Victor Gollancz, 1989, p. 297.
41 *Opera*, March 1970, p. 253.
42 Quoted in Schwarzkopf, *On and Off the Record*, p. 77.
43 *Opera*, July 1974, p. 593.
44 Ibid., August 1970, p. 773.
45 Robert Pullen and Stephen Taylor, *Casta Diva: A Biography of Montserrat Caballé*, Boston: Northeastern University Press, 1995, p. 153.
46 *Opera News*, 25.9.65.
47 *Opera*, May 1971, pp. 436–47.
48 Ibid., August 1973, p. 722.
49 Ibid., June 1976, p. 533.
50 Ibid., July 1977, p. 687.
51 Ibid., April 1974, p. 806.
52 *Opera News*, June 1971, p. 29.
53 José Carreras, *Singing from the Soul: An Autobiography*, London: Souvenir Press, 1994, p. 86.
54 *Opera*, March 1974, p. 25.
55 Ibid., May 1974, p. 451.
56 Carreras, op. cit., pp. 119–20.
57 Giudici, *L'opera in cd e video*, p. 609.
58 *Opera*, October 1972, p. 981.
59 Ibid., April 1980, p. 391.
60 Ibid., December 1996, p. 1410.
61 *Opera News*, Oct. 1980, p. 20.
62 Ibid.
63 *Opera*, March 1971, pp. 211–12.
64 Ibid., May 1971, p. 439.
65 Ibid., July 1971, p. 584.
66 *Opera News*, Octo. 1980, p. 19.
67 Ibid.
68 *Opera*, February 1975, p. 190.
69 Ibid., March 1978, p. 292.
70 Ibid., July 1978, p. 669.
71 Ibid., February 1979, pp. 168–9.
72 Ibid., May 1978, p. 500.
73 Ibid., March 1992, pp. 295–6.
74 Ibid., November 1977, p. 1015.

15 Vienna 1970–80: *Manifold Pleasures of Routine, Rarer Joys of Excellence*

1 M. Prawy, *Marcel Prawy erzählt aus seinem Leben*, Vienna: Kremayr und Scheriau, 1996, p. 66.
2 *Opera*, August 1972, p. 709.
3 *Opera*, November 1970, p. 1002.
4 Ibid., July 1972, p. 599.
5 Ibid., March 1970, p. 244.
6 Ibid., July 1970, pp. 626–7.
7 *Die Presse*, 25.5.70.
8 *Opera*, August 1970.
9 Hermann Scherchen had recorded the Seventh Symphony with the Vienna Staatsoper orchestra as long ago as 1953, but Bernstein's repeated efforts, in recording and programming, helped reintroduce Mahler to the standard Viennese concert repertoire.
10 S. Chapin, *Leonard Bernstein*, p. 109.
11 *Opera*, November 1970, p. 1019.
12 Ibid., January 1971, p. 32.
13 *Die Presse*, 25.5.71.
14 *Opera*, March 1972, p. 227.
15 *Die Presse*, 27.12.71.
16 *Die Presse*, 9.9.70.
17 *Opera*, November 1970, p. 1002.
18 Ibid., January 1973, p. 60.
19 Ibid., February 1973, p. 154.
20 Ibid., April 1973, p. 324–5.
21 Ibid., p. 324.
22 *Die Presse*, 27.12.72.
23 Ibid., 24.5.73.
24 *Opera*, Festival issue 1973, pp. 45–6.
25 *Die Presse*, 22.5.73.
26 *Opera*, April 1973, p. 325.
27 Ibid.
28 Ibid.
29 Ibid.
30 R. Osborne, *Herbert von Karajan*, p. 625.
31 *Opera*, December 1973, p. 1079.
32 Ibid., February 1974, p. 151.
33 Rasponi, *The Last Prima Donnas*, pp. 105–6.
34 *Opera*, July 1974, pp. 617–18.
35 Ibid., February 1975, pp. 184–5.
36 Ibid., November 1974, p. 1000.
37 Ibid.
38 Ibid., April 1974, p. 293.
39 Ibid., Mary 1976, p. 465.
40 Prawy, op. cit., p. 229.
41 Prawy, op. cit., p. 231.
42 *Opera*, December 1976, p. 1145.
43 *Frankfurter Allgemeine*, 10.5.77.
44 Carreras, *Singing from the Soul*, p. 132.
45 *Die Presse*, 8.5.77.
46 *Opera* August 1977, p. 648.
47 Ibid.
48 Carreras, op. cit., p. 127.
49 *Opera*, June 1977, p. 558.
50 Schwarzkopf, *On and Off the Record*, p. 224.
51 *Opera*, June 1978, pp. 604–5.
52 Ibid., September 1978, p. 871.
53 Ibid., p. 872.
54 Quoted in Bachmann, *Karajan*, p. 193.
55 *Opera*, Festival issue 1973, p. 50.
56 Ibid., Festival issue 1976, p. 15.
57 Ibid., June 1974, p. 492.
58 Ibid., Festival issue 1975, p. 58.
59 Domingo, *My First Forty Years*, pp. 128–9.
60 Ibid., p. 130; *Opera*, Festival issue 1976, p. 61.
61 Spotts, *Bayreuth*, pp. 273–4.
62 *Opera*, Festival issue 1976, p. 18.
63 Quoted in Spotts, op. cit., p. 279.
64 Gottfried Wagner: *He Who Does Not Howl with the Wolf*. The Wagner Legacy Sanctuary Publishing Limited, London, 1997, p. 88.
65 Ibid., p. 282.
66 *Opera*, Festival issue 1977, p. 74.
67 Ibid., p. 78.

68 Ibid., Festival issue 1976, p. 190.
69 Andrew Porter, *Musical Events, A Chronicle, 1983–7*, London: Grafton Books, 1990, p. 18.
70 *Opera*, Festival issue 1964, p. 8.
71 Ibid., Festival issue 1979, p. 17.
72 Rosenthal, in ibid., p. 22.
73 Quoted in Spotts, op. cit., p. 285.
74 Rosenthal, in op. cit., p. 25.
75 *Opera*, Feb. 1976.
76 Ibid., August 1977, p. 779.
77 Ibid.
78 Ibid., January 1978, pp. 72–3.
79 Ibid., September 1977, pp. 880–1.
80 *Opera*, June 1970.
81 *Opera*, October 1970, pp. 957, 959.
82 Ibid., Festival issue 1977, p. 80.
83 Ibid., April 1978, p. 375.
84 *Opera*, Autumn 1978, p. 90.
85 Ibid., Festival issue 1979, p. 85.
86 Ibid., November 1971, p. 1001.
87 Ibid.
88 Ibid., January 1977, pp. 33–4.

16 Covent Garden 1971–80: 'A Drama and not a Birthday Cake'

1 *Financial Times*, 2.7.71.
2 Peter Hall, Interview, 29.7.99.
3 Sir Colin Davis, Interview, 24.11.99.
4 ROH Archives, 4.7.71, quoted in Donaldson, *The Royal Opera House*, p. 145.
5 ROH Archives, Hall.
6 Interview, 29.7.99, Hall.
7 *Evening Standard*, 11.7.71.
8 ROH Archives, GDA, Hall to Drogheda, 12.7.71.
9 ROH Archives, Tooley at OSC, 1971.
10 Tooley, *In House*, pp. 36, 93.
11 ROH Archives, Hall to Tooley, 3.8.72.
12 Tooley, Interview, 4.12.00.
13 ROH Archives, GDA.
14 *Daily Telegraph*, 19.4.72.
15 ROH Archives, GDA.
16 ROH Archives, undated minutes of meeting, 1970.
17 *Opera*, July 1990, p. 770.
18 David Syrus, Interview, 5.12.00.
19 *Opera*, July 1978, p. 671, quoting *Gramophone*, 1976.
20 Sir Thomas Allen, Interview, 21.12.99.
21 Ibid.
22 *Opera*, July 1978, p. 673.
23 Ibid., July 1971, p. 652.
24 Ibid., September 1971, p. 964.
25 Tooley, op. cit., p. 114.
26 ROH Archives, OSC, 1971, 21.7.71, Harewood to Tooley, 5.10.71, OSC, 27.9.71, Tooley to Harewood, 1.10.71.
27 Berlin papers.
28 ROH Archives, OSC, 22.12.71.
29 *The Times*, 2.12.71.
30 *Observer*, 5.12.71.
31 *Opera*, January 1972, p. 8.
32 *The Times*, 2.1.71.
33 Donaldson, op. cit., p. 156.
34 Ibid.
35 John Copley, Interview, 23.3.00.
36 ROH Archives, OSC, 22.12.71.
37 ROH Archives, undated minutes of meeting with Tooley, December 1970.
38 *Observer*, 2.4.72.
39 *Financial Times*, 28.3.72.
40 *Evening Standard*, 21.7.72.
41 ROH Archives, GDA, 6.2.73.
42 Tooley to Susie Gilbert, 29.8.01.
43 ROH Archives.
44 *Opera*, March 1973, p. 276.
45 Ibid., June 1973, pp. 553–4.
46 *Financial Times*, 2.6.72.
47 *The Times*, 9.12.71.
48 *Observer*, 8.7.73.
49 Ingpen, Interview, 18.10.99.
50 *Opera*, March 1974, p. 257.
51 Domingo, *My First Forty Years*, p. 86.
52 *The Times*, 13.7.72.
53 *Opera*, September 1972, p. 790.

54 *Daily Telegraph*, 15.7.72.
55 *Opera*, July 1970, p. 573.
56 Davis, Interview, 24.11.99.
57 *Opera*, November 1972, p. 1021.
58 ROH Archives, GDA, Drogheda to Moser, 12.12.71.
59 *Opera*, October 1991, p. 1142.
60 ROH Archives, GDA, 19.4.73, Board minutes, 1973–74, 18/1/8.
61 *Opera*, September 1973, p. 756.
62 Ibid., October 1991, p. 1142.
63 ROH Archives, Drogheda papers, 15.4.73.
64 *Opera*, June 1973, pp. 548–9.
65 *The Times*, 19.4.73.
66 *Sunday Times*, 18.4.73.
67 *Opera*, January 1974, p. 84.
68 Interview with Hope-Wallace in *Guardian*, 1.10.74.
69 Tooley, Interview, 4.12.00.
70 Tooley, op. cit., p. 93.
71 ROH Archives, GDA.
72 Lord Moser, Interview, 11.6.01.
73 Davis, Interview, 24.11.99.
74 ROH Archives, GDA, Davis to Tooley, 2.2.73.
75 Tooley, Interview, 4.12.00.
76 ROH Archives, GDA, Tooley to Drogheda, 7.3.72.
77 ROH Archives, GDA, Drogheda to Pope Hennessy, 20.4.73, Davis to Drogheda, 9.4.73, Drogheda to Davis, 26.8.73.
79 Rodney Milnes, *Opera*, January 1978, p. 13.
80 Hall, Interview, 29.7.99.
81 Hall, *Making an Exhibition of Myself*, p. 235.
82 Obituary in *The Times*, 15.11.00.
83 *Opera*, August 1978, p. 799, review by Alan Blyth of John Higgins, *The Making of an Opera: Don Giovanni at Glyndebourne*, London: Secker & Warburg, 1978.
84 Southern Television, producer

Humphrey Burton, 1973, Pickwick video, 1991.
85 Spike Hughes, *Glyndebourne, A History of the Festival Opera Funded in 1934 by Audrey and John Christie*, London: Methuen, 1965, p. 259.
86 *Observer*, 8.7.73.
87 *Opera*, March 1994, p. 270.
88 Simon Mundy, *Bernard Haitink, A Working Life*, London: Robson Books, 1987, p. 84.
89 © BBC TV, Virgin Classics, Opera.
90 ROH Archives, GDA, 23.7.73, Moser to Drogheda, undated, Board minutes 1972–74, 18/1/8, OSC, 19/3/6, 20.2.74.
91 ROH Archives, Board minutes, 18/1/8, 26.2.74, Tooley to Drogheda, 24.4.74.
92 ROH Archives, OSC, 16.10.73.
93 *The Times*, 23.4.74.
94 William Mann, *The Operas of Mozart*, London: Cassell, 1977, p. 589.
95 *Financial Times*, 23.4.74.
96 *Opera*, June 1974, p. 545.
97 Ibid., April 1974, p. 348.
98 Moser, Interview, 11.6.01.
99 ROH Archives, GDA, 20.6.73, 5.7.74, 6.7.74, 26.8.74.
100 Hall, Interview, 29.7.99.
101 Syrus, Interview, 5.12.00.
102 Davis, Interview, 28.11.00.
103 Tooley, op. cit., p. 94.
104 *Sunday Times*, 3.10.76.
105 Götz Friedrich in *About the House*, Christmas 1974.
106 *Financial Times*, 18.10.76.
107 *Opera*, November 1974, p. 950.
108 *Financial Times*, 3.10.74, 18.6.76.
109 *Observer*, 6.10.74.
110 *The Times*, 3.10.74.
111 ROH Archives, Board minutes, 18/1/7, 20.8.74, 26.11.74, 20.8.74.
112 Annual Report, 1982–83.
113 *Opera*, July 1988, p. 779.
114 Davis, Interview, 24.11.99.

115 Peter Heyworth, *Observer*, 10.7.75.
116 John Higgins, *The Times*, 3.7.75.
117 *Opera*, February 1977, p. 131.
118 *The Times*, 10.7.75.
119 Elijah Moshinsky, Interview, 10.5.99.
120 Tooley, op. cit., p. 95.
121 ROH Archives, OSC, 19/3/6, Board minutes, 18/1/7.
122 *Opera*, February 1977, p. 127.
123 *The Times*, 21.9.74.
124 ROH Archives, Board minutes, 23.3.78.
125 *Observer*, 19.9.76.
126 *Opera*, December 1976, p. 1149.
127 *The Times*, 3.10.76.
128 ROH Archives, OSC 1974–75, 19/3/6.
129 Tooley, op. cit., p. 79.
130 *Opera*, September 1976, p. 817.
131 Ibid., August 1977, p. 802.
132 *Observer*, 10.7.72.
133 *Opera*, July 1976, pp. 677–8, September 1978, p. 912, August 1978, p. 825.
134 Interview with John Higgins in *The Times*, 11.7.86.
135 Findlay, Interview, 15.12.99.
136 *Guardian*, 19.7.86.
137 Tooley, op. cit., p. 67.
138 Mundy, op. cit., p. 111.
139 Hughes, op. cit., p. 266.
140 *Opera*, Autumn 1977, pp. 24–8.
141 Allen, Interview, 21.12.99.
142 Mundy, op. cit., p. 12.
143 Joan Bakewell, Radio 3, 3.3.99.
144 Mundy, op. cit., p. 141.
145 Hall, Interview, 29.7.99.
146 Tom Sutcliffe, *Believing in Opera*, London: Faber & Faber, 1996, p. 83.
147 Hall, Interview, 29.7.99.
148 Interview with John Higgins in *The Times*, 11.7.86.
149 *Opera*, September 1993, p. 1025.
150 Davis, Interview, 24.11.99.
151 Tooley, Interview, 4.12.00.
152 Geoffrey Wheatcroft, *Opera*, April 1988, p. 156.
153 *The Times*, 10.3.78.
154 ROH Archives, Board minutes, 18/2/1, 26.2.80.
155 *Financial Times*, 19.7.86.
156 Davis, Interview, 24.11.99.
157 William Mann, *The Times*, 30.6.78.
158 *Opera*, August 1980, p. 829.
159 *Financial Times*, 6.7.78.
160 ROH Archives, OSC, 19.11.75, Board minutes, 18/1/7 5/20.
161 *Opera*, January 1979, p. 16, August 1979, p. 814.

17 The Met 1972–80: 'Faces Not Windmills'

1 MO Archives, Board of Directors, minutes.
2 George Movshom, *Opera*, March 1975, p. 234.
3 MO Archives, Board of Directors, minutes, 28.6.73, 21.9.72.
4 Schuyler Chapin, *Musical Chairs, A Life in the Arts*, New York: G. P. Putnam's Sons, 1977, p. 288.
5 *Opera*, January 1973, p. 34.
6 Conrad, *A Song of Love and Death*, p. 333.
7 Ibid., p. 34.
8 Chapin, op. cit., pp. 318–24.
9 Ibid., p. 305.
10 MO Archives, Chapin memorandum to the Executive Committee, 5.1.73.
11 Chapin, op. cit., pp. 329–32.
12 MO Archives, Executive Committee, 11.1.73.
13 Chapin, op. cit., pp. 283, 287.
14 *Opera News*, 2.7.76.
15 MO Archives, Board of Directors, minutes, 28.6.73.
16 MO Archives, Chapin's report to the Board of Directors, 28.6.73.
17 MO Archives, Board of Directors, minutes, 20.9.73.
18 Chapin, op. cit., p. 301.
19 Ibid., p. 347.

20 *Opera*, March 1974, p. 235.
21 MO Archives, Administrative Committee, 3.1.75.
22 Chapin, op. cit., p. 357.
23 *Village Voice*, 9–15.12.81.
24 Chapin, op. cit., p. 367.
25 *Opera*, June 1974, p. 501.
26 *New York Times*, 1.2.74.
27 *Opera*, June 1974, p. 502.
28 *Saturday Review*, 23.3.74.
29 *Opera*, June 1974, p. 502.
30 Ibid., December 1974, p. 1054.
31 Chapin, op. cit., p. 363.
32 *Opera*, June 1974, pp. 499, 504.
33 Chapin, op. cit., pp. 359, 367.
34 Ibid., p. 388.
35 John Dexter, *The Honourable Beast, A Posthumous Autobiography*, New York: Routledge/Theatre Arts, 1993, pp. 10, 15.
36 Richard Eyre and Nicholas Wright, *Changing Stages, A View of British Theatre in the Twentieth Century*, London: Bloomsbury, 2000, p. 213.
37 Dexter, op. cit., 11.5.74, p. 81.
38 Chapin, op. cit., p. 394.
39 Dexter, op. cit., 16.3.74.
40 MO Archives, Executive Committee, 6.6.74.
41 Chapin, op. cit., p. 387.
42 MO Archives, Board of Directors, minutes, 19.9.74.
43 MO Archives, Chapin papers, box 7, 1974–75.
44 *New York Times*, 26.10.74.
45 Ibid., 16.11.74.
46 *Opera*, March 1974, pp. 240–1.
47 MO Archives, Solti contracts.
48 MO Archives, Bliss White Paper, 1.3.76.
49 MO Archives, Board of Directors, minutes, 21.11.74.
50 Frank E. Taplin Jr, Diary, 21.11.74.
51 *New York Times*, 12.2.78.
52 Bliss obituary in *Opera*, October 1991, p. 1165.
53 James Levine, Interview, 25.1.02.
54 Taplin, Diary, 21.11.74.
55 Chapin, op. cit., pp. 397, 400.
56 Dexter, op. cit., 19.11.74, p. 86.
57 Conversation between Kerner, Levine and Dexter in *Opera*, September 1977, pp. 841–8.
58 MO Archives, Board of Directors, minutes.
59 *New York Times*, 18.12.74.
60 *Village Voice*, 30.12.74.
61 MO Archives, Chapin papers, box 15.
62 MO Archives, Administration Committee, 11.2.75.
63 MO Archives, Executive Committee, 8.1.75. Administration Committee minutes.
64 Dexter, op. cit., 19.11.74, pp. 86, 88.
65 MO Archives, Board of Directors, minutes, 26.6.75.
66 Martin Mayer, *The Met*, p. 328.
67 Chapin, op. cit., p. 396.
68 Taplin, Diary, 12.9.77.
69 *Opera*, March 1975, p. 235.
70 MO Archives, Bliss papers, 9.6.75.
71 Dexter, op. cit., p. 88.
72 MO Archives, Bliss papers, 9.6.75, Intendants, 2.7.75.
73 MO Archives, Board of Directors, minutes, 16.10.75, 18.12.75, 21.8.75.
74 MO Archives, Bliss papers.
75 MO Archives, Bliss papers, Bliss to Mrs August Belmont, 12.9.75.
76 MO Archives, White Paper.
77 MO Archives, Board of Directors, minutes, 18.3.76.
78 Ibid.
79 Taplin, Diary, 23.3.76.
80 MO Archives, Bliss papers.
81 Levine, Interview, 25.1.02.
82 *New York Times*, 2.3.76.
83 MO Archives, Board of Directors, minutes, 25.11.75.
84 Dexter, op. cit., p. 89.
85 Moshinsky, Interview, 10.11.98.
86 Dexter, op. cit., p. 91.
87 *Opera*, September 1977, pp. 841–8.

88 *New York Times/Newhouse/Chicago Daily News*, Wire, 4.2.76.
89 *Financial Times*, 1.3.78.
90 *New York Times*, 4.2.76.
91 *Opera*, August 1976, p. 714.
92 Ibid., September 1977, p. 841–8.
93 MO Archives, Letter to Bliss, 24.9.80.
94 *Washington Post*, 10.12.78.
95 Dexter, op. cit., 5.2.76, p. 100.
96 *Opera*, August 1976, p. 716.
97 Ibid., p. 717.
98 MO Archives, Bliss papers, new productions.
99 Cori Ellison's obituary in *Opera News*, November 1993, p. 58.
100 *Opera*, May 1997, p. 447.
101 *New York Times*, 27.2.77.
102 MO Archives, Bliss papers L.
103 Ibid.
104 *Saturday Review*, June 1980.
105 *Opera*, June 1981, p. 611.
106 Domingo, *My First Forty Years*, p. 73.
107 MO Archives, Board of Directors, minutes, 21.5.80.
108 *Opera News*, December 1976.
109 *Saturday Review*, June 1980.
110 Domingo, op. cit., p. 73.
111 Robert C. Marsh, *Dialogues & Discoveries, James Levine: His Life and his Music*, New York: Scribner, 1998, p. 34.
112 Interview with Robert Jackson in *Opera News*, 10.1.81.
113 *Opera News*, 13.8.82.
114 Marsh, op. cit., pp. 191, 219.
115 Thomas P. Lanier, profile of Sherrill Milnes in *Opera*, June 1980, p. 543.
116 *Opera News*, April 1990.
117 *Opera*, January 1977, p. 44.
118 Clive Barnes notebook in *New York Times*, 27.11.76.
119 Glenn Loney, *Opera News*, 11.3.78.
120 *Opera*, January 2977, p. 48.
121 John Higgins, *The Times*, 7.2.77.

122 Dexter, op. cit., 22.2.77, p. 110.
123 *Opera*, September 1977, p. 841–8.
124 *New York Times*, 6.2.77.
125 *The Times*, March 1981.
126 MO Archives, Board of Directors, minutes, 20.1.77.
127 Taplin, Diary, 15.4.77, 24.2.77.
128 MO Archives, Board of Directors, minutes, 27.4.78.
129 Taplin, Interview, 29.3.01.
130 MO Archives, Board of Directors, minutes, 20.10.77.
131 Ibid.
132 MO Archives, Bliss to Brian O'Dougherty, National Endowment for the Arts.
133 MO Archives, Bliss papers G.
134 *Opera*, February 1978, pp. 140–1.
135 Joan Ingpen, Interview 18.10.99.
136 Arlene Saunders interview in *Opera News*, 18.3.78.
137 Ingpen, Interview, 18.10.99.
138 MO Archives, Bliss contracts.
139 MO Archives, Board of Directors, minutes, 25.10.78.
140 MO Archives, Bliss papers, new productions, 25.7.78, 23.6.78.
141 Quoted in Taplin, Diary, 21.2.79.
142 Ibid.
143 *New Yorker*, 6.11.78.
144 Patrick J. Smith, *The Times*.
145 MO Archives, Board of Directors, 19.10.78.
146 *New York Times*, end of season.
147 Patrick J. Smith, *A Year at the Met*, New York: Alfred A. Knopf, 1983, p. 153.
148 *New Yorker*, December 1978.
149 *Wall Street Journal*, 28.12.78.
150 *New York Times*, 9.12.78.
151 *Newsday*, 13.12.78.
152 Dexter, op. cit., 24.9.80, p. 171.
153 Ibid., p. 110.
154 Manuela Hoelterhoff, 28.12.78.
155 Dexter, op. cit., p. 110.
156 *New York Times*, 7.2.79.
157 *Village Voice*, 10.2.80.

158 *Opera News*, September 1977, p. 15.
159 Levine, Interview, 25.1.02.
160 *Opera*, November 1988, p. 1285.
161 Levine, Interview, 25.1.02.
162 *Opera News*, May 1979.
163 *New York Times*, May 1979.
164 *Village Voice*, 28.3.79.
165 *New Yorker*, 2.4.79.
166 MO Archives, Board of Directors, minutes.
167 *New York Times*, 20.4.79.
168 MO Archives, Board of Directors, minutes, 15.11.79.
169 *Opera*, March 1980, pp. 276–8.
170 MO Archives, Board of Directors, minutes, December 1979.
171 *Time*, October 1983.
172 Taplin, Diary, 29.9.77.
173 Domingo, op. cit., p. 42.
174 Taplin, Diary, 10.1.80.
175 Dexter, op. cit., p. 164.
176 *New York Times*, 9.9.98.
177 Taplin, Diary, 28.2.80.
178 Ingpen, Interview, 18.10.99.
179 Levine, Interview, 25.1.02.
180 Moshinsky interview with Peter G. Davis, *New York Times*, 3.2.80.
181 Moshinsky, Interview, 10.2.00.
182 Davis interview in *New York Times*.
183 Moshinsky, Interview, 10.2.00.
184 Bel Canto Paramount Home video 16.2.80. © 1989, Paramount Pictures.
185 *Jersey Journal*, 6.2.80.
186 *Wall Street Journal*, 15.2.80.
187 *New Yorker*, 18.2.80.
188 *Opera*, May 1980, pp. 455–6.
189 *New York Times*, 6.2.80.
190 Smith, op. cit., p. 157.
191 Dexter, op. cit., 24.9.80, p. 175.
192 Bruce Crawford, Interview, 31.5.01.
193 Moshinsky, Interview, 10.2.00.
194 *New York Times*, 19.3.80.
195 Dexter, op. cit., memo of 24.9.80, p. 175.
196 *Women's Wear Daily*, January 1978.

197 *New York Times*, 3.2.78.
198 *Opera*, April 1980, p. 356.
199 *Saturday Review*, June 1980.
200 *Los Angeles Times*, 25.5.80.
201 Caroline Seebohm, *Saturday Review*, March 1982.
202 *Los Angeles Times*, 25.5.80.
203 *Boston Globe*, 6.4.80.
204 *Los Angeles Times*, 25.5.80.
205 MO Archives, Solti contracts, Ingpen to Ann Colbert; Davis contracts, Herbert Barret to Joan Ingpen, 28.8.80, 11.9.80; Davis contracts, Ingpen to Herbert Barret; Abbado contracts, Abbado to Rodzinski, 20.9.77; Muti contracts, R. Wilford, note, 2.11.77.
206 *New York Times*, 31.3.82.
207 *Opera*, June 1982, p. 623.
208 MO Archives, Haitink contracts, Judie Janowski, Columbia Artists Management, 29.8.79.
209 MO Archives, Bliss papers K.
210 *Boston Globe*, 6.4.80.
211 *Washington Post*, December 1978.
212 *Opera News*, September 1994.
213 Joseph Volpe, Interview, 23.6.99.
214 MO Archives, Bliss papers V.
215 Volpe, Interview, 23.6.99.
216 Ibid.
217 Bliss interview in *Opera News*, September 1980.
218 Levine, Interview, 25.1.02.
219 Dexter, op. cit., 3.3.80, p. 166.
220 Ibid., 24.11.74, p. 87.
221 *The Times*, 17.7.01.

18 La Scala 1980–90: *Italian Tossed Salad*

1 N. Abbott, *Italy in the 1970s*, London and Vancouver: David & Charles, 1975, p. 9.
2 *Opera News*, 15.3.80.
3 *Opera*, February 1980, pp. 185–6.
4 *Opera News*, March 1981, p. 34.
5 Ibid.

6 *Opera*, February 1981, pp. 138–9.
7 Ibid.
8 Hirst, *Directors in Perspective: Giorgio Strehler*, p. 121.
9 *Opera*, September 1984, p. 1029.
10 Ibid., June 1983, pp. 657–8.
11 Ibid., April 1983, p. 422.
12 Sadie (ed.), *The New Grove Dictionary of Opera*, vol. I, p. 1082.
13 *Opera*, August 1983, p. 852.
14 Ibid., May 1988, p. 539.
15 *Massimo Mila, alla Scala*, p. 425.
16 *Opera*, March 1984, pp. 260–1.
17 Ibid., Festival issue, 1984, pp. 47–8.
18 Ibid., May 1986, pp. 570–1.
19 Ibid., June 1981, p. 585.
20 Ibid., September 1985, p. 991.
21 Ibid., September 1988, p. 1064.
22 Ibid., February 2000, p. 171.
23 *Corriere della Sera*, 8.12.84.
24 *Opera*, March 1985, p. 330.
25 Ibid., December 1985, p. 1376.
26 Ibid.
27 Ibid., May 1986, p. 571.
28 Ibid., p. 1031.
29 Ibid., p. 1032.
30 *Opera News*, October 1980, p. 19.
31 *Opera*, May 1987, p. 522.
32 Ibid.
33 *Corriere della Sera*, 8.12.87.
34 Mila, op. cit., p. 299.
35 *Opera*, February 1989, p. 150.
36 Ibid., March 1990, p. 348.
37 Ibid., June 1986, pp. 687–98.
38 *Opera*, June 1988, p. 724.
39 Ibid., April 1988, p. 343.
40 Ibid., March 1986, p. 328.
41 Ibid., July 1983, p. 775.
42 Ibid., May 1983, pp. 545–6.
43 Ibid., Festival issue 1984, p. 89.
44 Conrad, *A Song of Love and Death*, p. 301.
45 Ibid., p. 90.
46 Giuseppe Barigazzi in *La Scala racconta*, quoted in Giorgio Gualerzi, 'La Scala's Golden Anniversary', *Opera*, December 1996, p. 1414.

19 Vienna 1980–90: *Efforts to Revive the Gleam*

1 Quoted in Hella Pick, *Guilty Victim*, p. 157.
2 *Opera News*, October 1979, p. 68.
3 *Opera*, May 1980, p. 476.
4 Ibid., March 1981, p. 285.
5 Ibid., May 1981, p. 501. This was unconventional opera fare. Prawy recalled in an interview that, even though *Mass* was enjoyed by the Viennese, audiences were sparse. He remembered the American Jewish impresario Sol Hurok, who had arranged for the work to be performed in Vienna, acutely disappointed at advance ticket sales. 'Terrible!' exclaimed Hurok to Prawy. 'I think we'd better leave the writing of masses to the goyim.'
6 M. Prawy, *Marcel Prawy erzählt*, p. 235.
7 Ibid., June 1981, p. 625.
8 Ibid., April 1982, p. 404.
9 Ibid., April 1982.
10 Ibid., February 1983, p. 157.
11 Ibid., May 1983, p. 527.
12 Ibid.
13 Ibid., pp. 526–7.
14 *Opera News*, October 1980, p. 19.
15 *Opera*, September 1983, p. 982.
16 Ibid.
17 Prawy, op. cit., p. 235.
18 Ibid.
19 Quoted in C. H. Drese ... *aus Vorsatz und durch Zufall: Theater – und Operngeschichte(n) aus 50 Jahren*, Cologne: Dittrich, 1999, p. 428.
20 *Opera*, July 1984, p. 775.
21 Quoted in Conrad, *A Song of Love and Death*, p. 278.
22 *Opera*, April 1985, p. 634.

23 Ibid., August 1986, p. 900.
24 Drese, op. cit., p. 435.
25 Ibid.
26 Ibid., pp. 436–7.
27 *Opera*, January 1987, p. 69.
28 Ibid., July 1987, p. 771.
29 Ibid.
30 Sadie (ed.), *The New Grove Dictionary of Opera*, vol. IV, p. 1000.
31 *Opera*, May 1987, p. 549.
32 *Opera News*, 5.1.80.
33 Ibid., December 1987, p. 1429.
34 Ibid.
35 Ibid., May 1988, p. 464.
36 Ibid., February 1988, p. 180.
37 Ibid., July 1988, p. 813.
38 Drese, op. cit., p. 428.
39 *Opera*, December 1987, p. 1429.
40 Drese, op. cit., p. 427.
41 Ibid., p. 428.
42 *Opera*, August 1988.
43 Ibid., November 1988, p. 908.
44 Ibid., May 1989, pp. 566–7.
45 Ibid., April 1985, p. 637.
46 Ibid., Festival issue 1985, p. 49.
47 Ibid., Festival issue 1987, p. 58.
48 Ibid., pp. 58–60.
49 *Opera*, Festival issue 1988, pp. 47–8.
50 *New York Times*, 7.3.82.
51 Prawy, *The Vienna Opera*, pp. 251–2.
52 Dusek (ed.), *Kulissengespräche II*, p. 43.
53 *Opera*, August 1996, p. 882.
54 Dusek (ed.), op. cit., p. 130.
55 *Opera*, June 1982, p. 631.
56 Ibid., April 1981, p. 390.
57 Ibid., December 1983, p. 1339.
58 Ibid., January 1985, pp. 79–80.
59 Ibid., p. 28.
60 A. Porter, *Musical Events*, p. 18.
61 Ibid., p. 20.
62 Ibid., p. 24.
63 *Opera*, Festival issue 1983, p. 22.
64 *Observer*, 1.10.92.
65 *Opera*, Festival issue 1983.

66 Ibid.
67 A. Porter, op. cit., p. 25.
68 *Opera*, Festival issue 1984, p. 69.
69 Ibid., pp. 70–1.
70 Ibid., p. 71.
71 Ibid., Festival issue 1985, pp. 70–1.
72 Ibid., Festival issue 1988, pp. 63–5.
73 Ibid., Festival issue 1992, p. 65.

20 Covent Garden 1980–87: *Colin Davis 2: Prima la Musica*

1 Paul Findlay, Interview, 15.12.99.
2 Claus Moser, Interview, 11.6.01.
3 *Opera*, July 1993, p. 777.
4 Tooley, Interview, 4.12.00.
5 Tooley, *In House*, p. 232.
6 Margaret Thatcher, *The Downing Street Years*, London, 1993, p. 632.
7 Quoted by Alan Blyth, *Opera*, February 1981, pp. 114–5.
8 Tooley, Interview, 4.12.00.
9 Davis, Interview, 24.11.99.
10 Berlin papers, Berlin to Moser, undated letter.
11 *The Times*, 11.7.86.
12 Findlay, Interview, 15.12.99.
13 Donaldson, *The Royal Opera House*, p. 178.
14 *Opera*, March 1994, p. 270.
15 Interview with Harold Rosenthal in *Opera*, October 1980, p. 976.
16 Tom Sutcliffe, *Believing in Opera*, p. 295.
17 Copley, Interview, 23.3.00.
18 *Opera*, February 1980, p. 193.
19 Ibid., January 1983, p. 98.
20 Ibid., April 1985, p. 371.
21 Tooley, op. cit., p. 107.
22 ROH Archives, OSC 19/4/1, 18 April, 14.6.86.
23 *Opera*, July 1991, pp. 374, 376.
24 Ibid., July 1991, p. 761.
25 Ibid., July 1993, p. 778.
26 Ibid., April 1982, p. 420.
27 Ibid., November 1982, p. 1198.
28 Ibid., March 1983, p. 332.

29 Robert Henderson, ibid., May 1983, p. 561.
30 Ibid., December 1983, pp. 1349–50.
31 Ibid., July 1991, p. 755.
32 Ibid., July 1985, p. 739.
33 Ibid., July 1993, p. 782.
34 Harewood, Interview, 6.19.98.
35 *Opera*, February 1986, p. 239.
36 Sutcliffe, op. cit., pp. 171, 173.
37 Milnes, *Opera*, June 1987, p. 608.
38 Sutcliffe, op. cit., p. 181.
39 Moshinsky, Interview, 10.2.00.
40 Sutcliffe, op. cit., p. 180.
41 Moshinsky, Interview, 10.2.00.
42 Quoted in Richard Fawkes, *Welsh National Opera*, London: Julia Macrae Books, 1986, p. 204.
43 Ibid., p. 251.
44 *Opera*, November 1988, p. 1362.
45 *The Times*, 1.8.87.
46 ROH Archives, OSC, 28.7.81.
47 Sutcliffe, op. cit., p. 49.
48 ROH Archives, Board minutes, 24.6.80.
49 Moser, Interview, 11.6.01.
50 Tooley, Interview, 4.12.00.
51 David Cairns, *Sunday Times*, 4.10.81.
52 *The Times*, 1.10.81.
53 *Financial Times*, 30.9.81.
54 *The Times*, 1.10.81.
55 ROH Archives, Carlo Maria Giulini contracts file 2.
56 *Opera*, July 1982, p. 681.
57 Tooley, op. cit., p. 58.
58 ROH Archives, OSC, 20.7.82.
59 *Financial Times*, 2.7.82.
60 *Observer*, 4.7.82.
61 *Opera*, August 1982, p. 864.
62 Peter Conrad, *Times Literary Supplement*, August 1982.
63 *Observer*, 4.7.82.
64 Tooley, Interview, 4.12.00.
65 ROH Archives, OSC, 19/4/1.
66 Goodman, *Tell Them I'm On My Way*, p. 307.
67 Moser, Interview, 11.6.01.
68 Findlay, Interview, 15.12.99.
69 Jeremy Isaacs, *Never Mind the Moon*, London: Bantam Press, 1999, p. 56.
70 ROH Archives, OSC, 19/4/1.
71 ROH Archives, Board minutes, 18/2/2, 26.2.85, B18/2/3, 11.12.85, 6.3.85.
72 *Opera*, October 1984, pp. 1101–3.
73 Milnes, *Opera*, November 1984, p. 1265.
74 ROH Archives, Board minutes, 25.6.84, B18/2/3, 29.7.86, B18/2/3, OSC, 12.9.85, 19/4/1.
75 *About the House*, vol. 7, no. 8 Spring 1987. Article written in 1986 for Glyndebourne Touring Opera.
76 Ibid.
77 *Opera News*, November 1995.
78 ROH Archives, Board minutes, OB 19.4.2, 15.12.87, OB 19/4/3.
79 *New York Times*, 31.10.95.
80 Milnes, *Opera*, August 1987, p. 951.
81 *Opera*, July 1988, p. 782.
82 Moser, Interview, 11.6.01.
83 Syrus, Interview, 28.11.00.
84 Tooley, op. cit., pp. 235, 81.
85 *Spectator*, 25.9.85.
86 *Guardian*, 30.3.87.
87 *Observer*, 5.4.87.
88 *Sunday Times*, 5.4.87.
89 Tooley, op. cit., pp. 82–3.
90 Moser, Interview, 9.6.99.
91 Davis, Interview, 24.11.99.
92 ROH Archives, Board minutes, 18/2/2.
93 Tooley, op. cit., p. 47.
94 Interview in *Records and Recording* in 1972, quoted in Mundy, *Bernard Haitink*, p. 86.
95 Hall, *Making an Exhibition of Myself*, p. 250.
96 Obituary in *The Times*, 15.1.00.
97 Jolliffe, *Glyndebourne*, p. 170.
98 *Financial Times*, 4.7.86.
99 ROH Archives, Board minutes, 19/4/2, 17.7.86.
100 *Financial Times*, 19.7.86.

101 Interview in *The Times*, 11.7.86.
102 *Sunday Times*, 26.3.86.
103 ROH Archives, OSC, 17.7.86, OSC, 19/4/2.
104 *Financial Times*, 19.11.86.
105 Isaacs, op. cit., p. 10.
106 Moser, Interview, 11.6.01.
107 Findlay, Interview, 15.12.99.
108 Moser, Interview, 11.6.01.
109 Isaacs, op. cit., p. 26.
110 Ibid., p. 26.
111 ROH Archives, Board minutes, 18/2/5.

21 The Met 1980–90: *That Plush and Crystal Whorehouse*

1 John Rockwell, *New York Times*, 20.7.80.
2 Taplin, Diary, 4.12.79.
3 Ibid., 29.9.80.
4 Robert Jackson, *Opera News*, October 1980.
5 MO Archives, Board of Directors.
6 *New York Times*, 20.9.81.
7 Taplin, Diary, 15.10.80, 25.10.80, 13.11.80.
8 Joseph Volpe, Interview, 23.6.99.
9 MO Archives, Board of Directors, minutes, 15.10.81.
10 MO Archives, Board of Directors, minutes, 20.11.81.
11 *New York*, 5.1.81.
12 *New Yorker*, 5.1.81.
13 *Opera News*, December 1980.
14 Boutwell, *New Yorker* staffer, interview in *Opera News*, September 1980.
15 John Higgins, *The Times*, March 1981.
16 MO Archives, Letter to Manuel Rosenthal, Bliss papers P.
17 *The Times*, March 1981.
18 Dexter, *The Honourable Beast*, 19.6.80, p. 161.
19 MO Archives, Dexter to Bliss, Met P, 1.5.80.
20 Basil Langton, *Opera News*, May 1980.
21 John Rockwell, *New York Times*, 13.2.81.
22 Hoelterhoff, *Wall Street Journal*, 27.2.81.
23 Patrick J. Smith, *Opera*, May 1981, p. 477.
24 *Wall Street Journal*, 27.2.81.
25 *New York Times*, 22.9.81.
26 *New Yorker*, September 1981.
27 Bernard Holland, *New York Times* magazine, 20.9.81.
28 Crawford, Interview, 31.5.01.
29 Jonathan Friend, Interview, 21.6.99.
30 Moshinsky, Interview, 10.2.00.
31 *New Yorker*, 18.12.81.
32 *New York Times*, 16.12.81.
33 Lanfranco Rasponi, *Opera News*, 16.1.82.
34 Levine, Interview, 25.1.02.
35 Ingpen, Interview, 18.10.99.
36 Moshinsky, Interview, 10.2.00.
37 *New York Times*, 10.3.82.
38 *Opera*, June 1982, p. 621.
39 MO Archives, Board of Directors, minutes, 15.4.82.
40 *New York Times*, 15.12.83.
41 *Opera News*, September 1995.
42 Levine, Interview, 25.1.01.
43 Howard Jacobson, *High Fidelity Magazine*, December 1978.
44 *Opera*, April 1982, pp. 383, 402.
45 *New York Times*, 31.1.82.
46 Ibid.
47 Ibid., 20.11.82.
48 Hall, Interview, 29.7.99.
49 Peter Hall, *Making an Exhibition of Myself*, pp. 251–2.
50 *New Yorker*, 13.12.82.
51 *Opera*, May 1984, p. 504.
52 Friend, Interview, 21.6.99.
53 MO Archives, Hall to Crawford, Hall contracts.
54 Hall, Interview, 29.7.99.
55 Dexter, op. cit., p. 181.

56 Robert C. Marsh, *Dialogues &* *Discoveries*, p. 59.
57 Levine, Interview, 25.1.01.
58 Taplin, Diary, 7.3.83.
59 Bliss's statement, *New York Times*, 16.9.83.
60 *Fortune* magazine, October 1983.
61 Holland, *New York Times* magazine, 20.9.81.
62 Levine, Interview, 25.1.01.
63 *Opera News*, September 1980.
64 Quoted in Marsh, op. cit., p. 44.
65 Interview with Robert Jacobson, *Opera News*, September 1980.
66 March, op. cit., p. 11.
67 *Opera News*, November 1983.
68 *New York Times*, 19.8.83.
69 *Opera News*, 10.2.79.
70 Donal Henahan, *New York Times*, 6.1.82.
71 Joan Bakewell interview, BBC Radio 3.
72 Ingpen, Interview, 18.10.99.
73 *Opera News*, July 1981.
74 Ibid., 17.3.84.
75 Ibid., 19.1.84.
76 *New York Times*, 21.1.84.
77 *Opera News*, 19.1.84.
78 Andrew Porter, *Musical Events, A Chronicle, 1983–6*, p. 107.
79 *Opera*, June 1984, p. 624.
80 MO Archives, Hall contracts, Hall to Ingpen, 9.10.83.
81 Dexter, op. cit., notes for a meeting, 16.5.84, pp. 183–4.
82 Volpe, Interview, 23.6.99.
83 Dexter, op. cit., notes for a meeting, 16.5.84, pp. 185, 188–9.
84 *Opera News*, September 1980.
85 Mark Schubin, Met technological consultant for radio broadcasts, *Opera News*, 8.12.90.
86 Shirley Fleming, *Opera News*, December 1991.
87 Michael Bronson, Telecast executive producer, Gary D. Lipton, ibid., September 1981.
88 ROH Archives, OSC, 19/4/1, 18.4.85.
89 Robert Jackson, *Opera News*, 14.2.81.
90 *Opera*, October 1988, p. 1172.
91 *Opera*, January 1977, p. 48.
92 Philip Glass, *Opera on the Beach: Philip Glass on his New World of Music Theatre*, London: Faber & Faber, 1988, pp. 29–32.
93 *Opera*, January 1977, p. 66.
94 Ibid., October 1988, p. 1167.
95 Ibid., January 1989, p. 14.
96 Dexter, op. cit., p. 87.
97 Taplin, Diary, 3.5.84.
98 Crawford, Interview, 31.5.01.
99 Pearce, Interview, 21.6.99.
100 *Opera News*, September 1985.
101 MO Archives, Board, 20.9.85.
102 Crawford, Interview, 31.5.01.
103 MO Archives, Board, 18.10.84.
104 Crawford, Interview, 31.5.01.
105 *New York*, March 1987.
106 *New York Times*, 25.2.87.
107 Crawford, Interview, 31.5.01.
108 Taplin, Diary, 3.5.84.
109 MO Archives, Board of Directors, minutes.
110 *Opera News*, September 1985.
111 Mayer, *Opera*, June 1985, p. 639.
112 Andrew Porter, op. cit., p. 287.
113 MO Archives, Board of Directors, minutes, 21.3.85, 21.3.85.
114 Hall, Interview, 29.7.99.
115 Levine, Interview, 25.1.02.
116 Marsh, op. cit., p. 111.
117 Allen, Interview, 21.12.99.
118 Porter, op. cit., p. 297.
119 *Opera*, February 1988, p. 150.
120 Friend, Interview, 21.6.99.
121 *Village Voice*, 7.10.86.
122 Rockwell, *New York Times*, 21.9.86.
123 Mayer, *Opera*, June 1989, p. 655.
124 Ibid., December 1987, p. 1396.
125 *Opera News*, 4.12.94, p. 222.
126 *Opera*, December 1994, p. 1372.
127 *New York Times*, 24.9.86.
128 Ibid., 21.9.86.
129 *Village Voice*, 7.10.86.

130 *Opera*, June 1989, p. 656.
131 Ibid., November 1989, p. 1372.
132 *Opera News*, May 1984, p. 42.
133 *New York Times*, October 1986.
134 Crawford, Interview, 31.5.01.
135 *New York Times*, 27.5.87.
136 Porter, *Opera*, August 1987, p. 860.
137 Henahan, *New York Times*, 29.3.87.
138 *New York Times*, 29.12.98.
139 Holland, ibid., 10.3.87.
140 *Opera*, February 1988, p. 152.
141 Deutsche Grammophon, DG VHS, 1987.
142 Porter, *Opera*, August 1987, p. 860.
143 Friend, Interview, 21.6.99.
144 Moshinsky, Interview, 10.2.00.
145 *Opera*, August 1987, p. 860.
146 *New York Times*, 12.4.87.
147 Moshinsky, Interview, 10.2.00.
148 Will Crutchfield, *New York Times*.
149 *New York*, 20.4.87.
150 Ibid.
151 *Village Voice*, 19.2.87.
152 *Opera*, May 1988, p. 565.
153 Ibid., February 1988, p. 182.
154 Ibid., p. 150.
155 Crawford, Interview, 31.5.01.
156 *New York*, 2.1.89.
157 *Opera*, April 1989, p. 426.
158 Volpe, Interview, 23.6.99.
159 Bruce Crawford to Susie Gilbert, 4.3.02.

22 La Scala 1990–2002: *The Primacy of Muti*

1 *Opera*, March 1990, p. 348.
2 Ibid., Festival issue 1992, p. 8.
3 Ibid., March 1993.
4 John Tooley to Susie Gilbert, 29.8.01.
5 *Opera News*, May 1995, p. 25.
6 *Opera*, May 1993, p. 587.
7 *Opera News*, Oct. 1980, p. 22.
8 *Opera*, April 1992, pp. 461–3.
9 Ibid., July 1992, p. 838.
10 Ibid., November 1993, p. 1230.
11 Ibid., October 1992, p. 1233.
12 Ibid., June 1993, p. 702.
13 Ibid., July 1992, p. 839.
14 Ibid., p. 840.
15 Ibid., Festival issue 1992, pp. 85–6.
16 Ibid., March 1994, pp. 342–4.
17 Ibid., July 1993, p. 383; May 1994, pp. 530–6.
18 *Evening Standard*, 28.7.94.
19 *Opera*, May 1994, p. 532.
20 Ibid., August 1997, p. 957.
21 Giudici, op. cit., p. 946.
22 *The Times*, 12.12.94.
23 Ibid., 5.6.95.
24 *Opera*, June 1996, p. 693.
25 Ibid., February 1992, p. 213.
26 Ibid., August 1997, p. 957.
27 Ibid., April 1999, p. 449.
28 *Opera Now*, January 1991, p. 30.
29 *Opera*, November 1997, pp. 1346–7.
30 Ibid., p. 1347.
31 *The Times*, 12.7.97.
32 Ibid., 18.11.97.
33 Quoted in ibid., 22.6.99.
34 *Opera*, December 1996, p. 1392.
35 Ibid., June 1996, p. 694.
36 Ibid., p. 1215.
37 Ibid., p. 693.
38 *International Herald Tribune*, 1.11.98.
39 *Sunday Telegraph*, 19.4.98.
40 *The Times*, 21.9.99.
41 Ibid., 8.12.01.
42 *International Herald Tribune*, 8.9.00.
43 *Opera*, December 1996, p. 1393.
44 Ibid., p. 1390.

23 Vienna 1990–2002: 'What Has Austria Got Besides the Staatsoper?'

1 *Jerusalem Post*, 7.3.00.
2 Holender, Interview, 19.1.01.
3 Ibid., January 1994, p. 85.
4 Ibid., January 1991, p. 179.
5 Ibid., March 1993, p. 308.
6 Ibid., June 1993, pp. 670–1.

7 Ibid., December 1993, p. 1427.
8 *The Times*, 22.3.94.
9 The date marked the fiftieth anniversary of the proclamation of the Second, or post-Nazi, Republic in Austria.
10 Holender, Interview, 19.1.01.
11 Pick, *Guilty Victim*, p. 97.
12 *Opera*, February 1997, p. 181.
13 Ibid., April 1997, p. 448.
14 Ibid., February 1998, p. 215.
15 Ibid., April 1997, p. 450.
16 *The Times*, 6.2.97.
17 Holender, Interview, 19.1.01.
18 *Opera*, January 1999, pp. 77–8.
19 *International Herald Tribune*, 28.2.99.
20 Ibid., 24.6.99.
21 Interview in *Opera*, Festival issue 1990, p. 9.
22 Ibid., pp. 11–14.
23 Ibid., p. 16.
24 Ibid., 1992, pp. 38–9.
25 This had taken place in November 1983 at the Paris Opéra.
26 *Opera*, Festival issue 1992, p. 39.
27 Ibid., pp. 38–40.
28 *Opera*, April 1993, p. 409.
29 Ibid., Festival issue 1994, p. 68.
30 Quoted in ibid., Festival issue 1995, p. 52.
31 Ibid., pp. 55–6.
32 *Opera*, August 1996, p. 937.
33 Ibid., July 1997, pp. 803–4.
34 *International Herald Tribune*, 4.8.99.
35 *Opera*, Festival issue 1998, p. 65.
36 *The Times*, 24.7.99.
37 Interview on Israeli television, 26.12.98.
38 *Observer*, 4.6.00.
39 *New York Times*, 30.3.01.
40 *The Times*, 31.7.01.
41 Holender, Interview, 19.1.01.
42 *International Herald Tribune*, 27.2.02.

24 The Met 1990–2002: 'A Very Efficient Factory'

1 *New York Post*, 16.4.89.
2 David Remnick, *New Yorker*, 22.2.99.
3 Crawford, Interview, 31.5.01.
4 Volpe, Interview, 23.6.99.
5 Pearce, Interview, 21.6.99.
6 Crawford, Interview, 31.5.01.
7 Volpe, Interview, 23.6.99.
8 Ibid.
9 Ralph Blumenthal, *New York Times*, 31.10.95.
10 Volpe, Interview, 23.6.99.
11 Crawford, Interview, 31.5.01.
12 *New York Post*, 16.4.89.
13 *Herald Tribune*, 23.4.96.
14 Johanna Fiedler, Conversation, 22.6.99.
15 Levine, Interview, 25.1.02.
16 Friend, Interview, 21.6.99.
17 Ibid.
18 *Opera News*, September 1994, p. 12.
19 Crawford, Interview, 31.5.01.
20 *Opera News*, September 1994.
21 *New York Times*, 27.2.91.
22 *Opera News*, 4.1.92.
23 *New York Times*, 15.12.91.
24 *Opera*, March 1992, p. 308.
25 *Opera News*, 21.12.91.
26 Opera, July 1995, p. 785.
27 Sutcliffe, *Believing in Opera*, p. 197.
28 *Opera*, Festival issue 1989, p. 12.
29 Sutcliffe, op. cit., pp. 197, 199.
30 *New York Times*, 14.10.92.
31 *Opera*, December 1992, p. 1414.
32 *New Yorker*, 26.10.92.
33 *Opera*, December 1992, p. 1414.
34 Ibid., October 1988, p. 1167.
35 *Opera News*, November 1993.
36 *Opera*, November 1994, p. 1295.
37 *New York Times*, 11.10.99.
38 Ibid., 26.12.99.
39 *International Herald Tribune*, 29.12.99.
40 *New York Times*, 2.4.99.

41 Heidi Waleson, *Wall Street Journal*, 17.9.97.
42 *Opera*, November 1994, p. 1267.
43 Moshinsky, Interview, 10.2.00.
44 *New York Times*, 13.3.93.
45 *Village Voice*, April 1993.
46 Volpe, Interview, 23.6.99.
47 *Opera*, January 1994, p. 47.
48 *New York Times*, 23.10.93.
49 *Opera*, March 1994, p. 300.
50 *Opera News*, 5.3.94.
51 Levine, Interview, 25.1.02.
52 *Opera*, June 1996, p. 621.
53 *New York Times*, 13.1.99.
54 *Opera*, August 1987, p. 887.
55 *Opera News*, 17.2.96.
56 Ibid., September 1994.
57 *Opera*, March 2000, p. 266.
58 *New York Times*, 26.9.97.
59 *Opera News*, January 2000, p. 47.
60 *Opera*, March 2000, p. 266.
61 Friend, Interview, 21.6.99.
62 Philips, recorded at the Maryinsky Theatre, September 1993, Brian Large TV director © 1993 BBC TV/RM Arts.
63 *Opera*, July 1993.
64 *New Yorker*, 22.2.99.
65 Ibid.
66 Volpe, Interview, 23.6.99.
67 *Time*, 21.2.94.
68 *New York Times*, 12.11.94.
69 *New Yorker*, 28.11.94.
70 Edward Rothstein, *New York Times*, 12.11.94.
71 Levine, Interview, 25.1.02.
72 *New York Times*, 17.4.95.
73 *Opera*, July 1995, p. 786.
74 *New York Times*, 17.4.95.
75 Ibid., 31.10.95.
76 Pearce, Interview, 21.6.99.
77 Ibid.
78 Friend, Interview, 21.6.99.
79 *Opera News*, 17.1.98.
80 John Copley, Interview, 23.3.00.
81 Friend, Interview, 21.6.99.
82 Volpe, Interview, 23.6.99.
83 Levine, Interview, 25.2.02.
84 Billinghurst, Interview, 1.6.01.
85 *New York Times*, 31.10.95.
86 Ibid., 2.5.99.
87 Allen, Interview, 10.11.98.
88 Levine, Interview, 25.1.02.
89 *Opera*, August 1995, pp. 890–9.
90 Levine, Interview, 25.1.02.
91 *Opera*, January 1992, p. 103.
92 Volpe, Interview, 23.6.99.
93 *New York Times*, 2.3.96.
94 *New York*, 18.3.96.
95 *Opera*, August 1995, p. 899.
96 Levine, Interview, 25.1.02.
97 *Opera News*, February 1996.
98 Manuela Hoelterhoff, *Cinderella & Company, Backstage at the Opera with Cecilia Bartoli*, New York: Alfred A. Knopf, 1999, p. 86.
99 Allen, Interview, 10.11.98.
100 Hoelterhoff, op. cit., p. 95.
101 *Opera*, February 1998, p. 168.
102 Ibid., December 1995, p. 1417.
103 Ibid., April 1998, p. 407.
104 *Opera News*, September 1995, p. 13.
105 Robert C. Marsh, *Dialogues & Discoveries*, p. 217.
106 Volpe, Interview, 23.6.99.
107 *New York Times*, 19.12.97.
108 Ibid..
109 Ibid., 2.5.99.
110 Texaco Broadcast, 13.3.99.
111 Volpe, Interview, 23.6.99.
112 Pearce, Interview, 21.6.99.
113 *New York Times*, 2.11.00.
114 Levine, Interview, 21.1.02.
115 *New York Times*, 3.12.97.
116 Albert Innaurato, ibid., 29.3.98.
117 *Opera News*, February 1991, describing the Chicago *Alceste* of September 1990.
118 Volpe, Interview, 23.6.99.
119 *New Yorker*, 22.2.99.
120 *Opera News*, August 2001.
121 Johanna Fiedler, *Molto Agitato, The Mayhem Behind the Music at the*

Metropolitan Opera, New York:
Nan Talese, an imprint of
Doubleday, 2001, p. 337.
122 *New Yorker*, 22.2.99.
123 Volpe, Interview, 23.6.99.
124 Hoelterhoff, op. cit., p. 197.
125 Volpe, Interview, 23.6.99.
126 *New York*, 14.12.98.
127 Volpe, Interview, 23.6.99.
128 *New Yorker*, 22.2.99.
129 *New York Times*, 31.10.98.
130 Sunday ibid., 2.11.98.
131 *Opera News*, September 1997.
132 Moshinsky, Interview, 10.2.00.
133 Blumenthal, *New York Times*,
12.2.98.
134 *New York Times*, 30.9.99.
135 *New York*, 18.10.99, p. 61.
136 Holland, *New York Times*, 10.2.99.
137 Crawford, Interview, 21.5.01.
138 Billinghurst, Interview, 1.6.01.
139 Marsh, op. cit., p. 108.
140 *New York Times*.
141 *New York*, 4.2.02.
142 *Opera*, March 2002, p. 269.

25 Covent Garden 1988–94: 'Bricks without Straw'

1   Isaacs, Interview, 1.7.99.
2   *Observer*, 27.9.92.
3   Isaacs, *Never Mind the Moon*,
pp. 28, 54.
4   ROH Archives, Opera Board paper,
December 1987, 19/4/4, OB, 19/4/3,
OB, 19/4/3, 17.11.87.
5   Isaacs, op. cit., p. 55.
6   Findlay, Interview, 15.12.99.
7   Tooley, *In House*, p. 234.
8   Isaacs, op. cit., p. 220.
9   Jonathan Coad, Interview, 11.6.99.
10 Tooley, Interview, 11.4.02.
11 *Observer*, 27.2.94.
12 ROH Archives, OB, 19/4/3, January
1988.
13 Findlay, Interview, 15.12.99.
14 Tooley, op. cit., p. 260.
15 ROH Archives, Forman to Isaacs,
4.1.88.
16 ROH Archives, OB, 19/4/3.
17 Isaacs, op. cit., p. 56.
18 ROH Archives, OB, 1988, 19/4/3.
19 Isaacs, op. cit., p. 102.
20 ROH Archives, OB, 19/4/5.
21 ROH Archives, Board minutes,
18/3/1, 5.6.90.
22 Isaacs, op. cit., p. 101.
23 Ibid., p. 99.
24 ROH Archives, OB, 19/4/4.
25 *Opera*, November 1988, p. 1383.
26 ROH Archives, OB, 19/4/3, 13.12.88,
OB, 19/4/3, 1.10.98, OB, 19/4/3,
13.12.88.
27 Isaacs, Interview, 1.7.99.
28 *Daily Telegraph*, 10.12.88.
29 *Financial Times*, 24.2.89.
30 Isaacs, op. cit., p. 65.
31 ROH Archives, OB, 19/4/4, 14.3.89.
32 *The Times*, 2.2.96, 29.6.89.
33 ROH Archives, OB, 19/4/4.
34 Isaacs, op. cit., p. 184.
35 Ibid., pp. 67–8.
36 Findlay, Interview, 15.12.99.
37 ROH Archives, OB, 19/4/4, 18/2/6,
31.1.89, 19/4/4, 11.4.89, OB, 19/4/4,
14.3.89.
38 Findlay, Interview, 15.12.99.
39 *Opera*, June 1989, p. 740.
40 Archiv Production, Deutsche
Grammophon.
41 Isaacs, op. cit., p. 204.
42 *The Times*, 9.6.89.
43 *Opera*, March 1994, p. 271.
44 Findlay, Interview, 15.12.99.
45 Isaacs, op. cit., p. 64.
46 *Sunday Times*, 1.10.89.
47 *Sunday Telegraph*, 1.10.89.
48 Milnes, *Opera*, November 1989,
p. 1370.
49 *Financial Times*, 29.9.89.
50 ROH Archives, OB paper, 19/4/4,
December 1989.
51 *Opera*, March 1994, p. 272.
52 ROH Archives, OB, 19/4/4.

53 ROH Archives, OB, 19/4/4. 14.11.89.
54 Syrus, Interview, 6.12.00.
55 Isaacs, op. cit., p. 58.
56 ROH Archives, OB, 19/4/5, 13.3.90.
57 Findlay, Interview, 15.12.99.
58 Opera, August 1990, p. 983.
59 The Times, 8.6.90.
60 Spectator, 16.6.90.
61 Isaacs, op. cit., p. 74.
62 Opera, June 1990, p. 736.
63 ROH Archives, Board minutes, 18/2/6.
64 ROH Archives, Board minutes, 18/2/6, 25.7.89.
65 ROH Archives, Letter of 18/3/1, 4.5.90.
66 ROH Archives, Board minutes, 18/2/6, 26.9.89.
67 ROH Archives, Board minutes 18/2/6, 28.11.89.
68 ROH Archives, OB, 19/4/5.
69 The Times, 17.7.01.
70 Opera, June 1989, p. 684.
71 ROH Archives, 18/3/1.
72 Sunday Times, 28.4.90.
73 The Times, 12.1.95.
74 Isaacs, op. cit., p. 109.
75 ROH Archives, Board minutes, 18/3/1.
76 ROH Archives, Board minutes, 18/3/1, 5.6.90, 18/3/1, 24.7.90.
77 ROH Archives, Board minutes, 18/3/1. 5.6.90.
78 Findlay, Interview, 15.12.99.
79 ROH Archives, Board minutes, 18/3/1.
80 Jeremy Isaacs interview with James Naughtie, Face to Face, BBC 2, 1998.
81 ROH Archives, Board, 18/3/1.
82 ROH Archives, Board minutes, 18/3/1, 5.6.90, OB, 19/4/5, 10.7.90.
83 Opera, August 1990, p. 898.
84 Financial Times, 15.10.90.
85 Guardian, 15.10.90.
86 Observer, 21.10.90.
87 Financial Times, 15.10.90.
88 Opera, December 1990, pp. 1489–90.
89 Guardian, 6.10.90.
90 Sunday Times, 7.10.90.
91 ROH Archives, OB, 19/4/6, 8.1.91.
92 ROH Archives, Board minutes, 18/3/1, 27.11.90.
93 Findlay, Interview, 22.10.99.
94 ROH Archives, Internal memo, OB, 19/4/6.
95 ROH Archives, OB, 19/4/6, 12.11.91.
96 ROH Archives, Board minutes, 18/3/1, 24.7.90, 18/3/1, 25.9.90, OB, 19/4/5, 9.10.90.
97 Opera, February 1991, p. 139.
98 ROH Archives, Board minutes, 18/3/2, 26.3.91.
99 Ibid.
100 Jones, Interview, 6.1.00.
101 ROH Archives, Board minutes, 18/3/2, 26.3.91.
102 Evening Standard, 6.12.90.
103 Opera, March 1991, p. 275.
104 27.2.91.
105 ROH Archives, Board minutes, 18/2/63, 1.1.89.
106 ROH Archives, OB, 19/4/6, 9.4.91.
107 Isaacs, op. cit., p. 57.
108 Forman, Interview.
109 Isaacs, op. cit., p. 159.
110 Findlay, Interview, 15.12.99.
111 ROH Archives, OB decision of 13.11.90.
112 Isaacs, op. cit., p. 112.
113 Tooley, op. cit., p. 80.
114 Opera, August 1901, p. 874.
115 Interview with Hilary Finch, The Times, 4.1.00.
116 ROH Archives, OB, 19/4/6, 11.6.91.
117 ROH Archives, 18/3/2, 24.9.91.
118 Isaacs, op. cit., p. 159.
119 Loppert, Opera, January 1992, p. 98.
120 Ibid.
121 Isaacs, op. cit., pp. 117–19.
122 Canning, Sunday Times, 8.12.91.
123 Sainsbury's final Annual Report, ROH Archives, September 1991, Board minutes, 18/3/2, 26.11.91.

124 ROH Archives, Board minutes, 18/3/2, 24.9.91.
125 ROH Archives, OB, 19/4/6, 12.11.91.
126 Tooley, op. cit., p. 255.
127 ROH Archives, OB, 19/4/6, 12.11.91.
128 ROH Archives, Board, 18/3/2, 26.11.91.
129 ROH Archives, OB, 19/4/6, 10.12.91, Board, 18/3/2, 29.1.92, Board, 18/3/3, 11–12.1.92.
130 Opera, May 1992, p. 510.
131 Nick Kimberley, Guardian, 5.3.92.
132 Observer, 5.4.92.
133 Ibid.
134 Times Literary Supplement, 1.5.92.
135 Financial Times, 16.4.92.
136 The Times, 20.6.00.
137 ROH Archives, Annual Report 1990–91.
138 ROH Archives, 18/3/3.
139 Ibid.
140 Tooley, op. cit., p. 207.
141 Opera, July 1992, p. 763.
142 'Royal Opera House Covent Garden Ltd, Appraisal', p. 35.
143 Ibid., p. 15.
144 ROH Archives, Board minutes, 18/3/3.
145 'Appraisal', p. 25.
146 Isaacs, op. cit., p. 125.
147 Findlay, Interview, 15.12.99.
148 ROH Archives, Board minutes, 18/3/3.
149 General director's report, September 1992, ROH Archives, Board, 18/3/3.
150 Antony Peattie, Opera Now, March 1991, p. 10.
151 ROH Archives, Board minutes, 18/3/3.
152 Isaacs, op. cit., p. 129.
153 Tooley, op. cit., p. 227.
154 Isaacs, op. cit., p. 230.
155 ROH Archives, Board minutes, 19/3/2, 24.9.91.
156 Opera, March 1994, p. 279.
157 ROH Archives, Board minutes, 18/3/3.
158 Opera, January 1993, pp. 10–12.
159 Ibid., July 1992, p. 851.
160 New York Times, 22.2.99.
161 Opera, June 2002, p. 658.
162 The Times, 14.6.97.
163 Ibid., 6.3.93.
164 Porter, Observer, 31.1.93.
165 The Times, 27.1.93,
166 Porter, Observer, 31.1.93.
167 Isaacs, op. cit., p. 152.
168 ROH Archives, Board minutes, 18/3/4, 26.1.93.
169 Isaacs, op. cit., p. 130.
170 ROH Archives, Board minutes, 18/3/4.
171 ROH Archives, OB/91/7.
172 Findlay, Interview, 15.12.00.
173 ROH Archives, Board minutes, 18/3/4.
174 Opera, September 1995, p. 1018.
175 Isaacs, op. cit., p. 139.
176 Syrus, Interview, 28.11.99.
177 Allen, Interview, 21.12.99.
178 Financial Times, 11.10.93.
179 The Times, 8.10.93.
180 Observer, 7.2.94.
181 Opera, June 1997, p. 721.
182 Ibid., December 1993, p. 1386.
183 Telegraph, 11.10.93.
184 The Times, 17.3.97.
185 Interview with Gillian Widdicombe, Independent, 15.10.93.
186 ROH Archives, Board minutes, 18/3/4, 28.9.93.
187 Isaacs, op. cit., p. 242.
188 Ibid., p. 247.
189 Profile by Andrew Clark, Opera, February 1993, p. 145.
190 The Times, 17.11.93.
191 ROH Archives, Board minutes, 18/3/4, Board minutes 18/3/5.
192 Kate Mosse, The House: Inside the Royal Opera House Covent Garden, London: BBC Books, 1995, p. 71.
193 ROH Archives, Board minutes, 18/3/4, 28.9.93.
194 Opera, March 1994, p. 273.

195 *Observer*, 27.9.92.
196 *Opera*, May 1994, pp. 612–13.
197 Quoted in Mosse, op. cit., p. 54.

26 Covent Garden 1994–97: '*The Least-Cost Option*'

1 *Guardian*, 16.2.94.
2 *The Times*, 16.2.94.
3 Isaacs, *Never Mind the Moon*, p. 161.
4 Moshinsky, Interview, 24.10.98.
5 *Times Literary Supplement*, 8.7.94.
6 Isaacs, Interview, 1.7.99.
7 Ibid.
8 Ibid.
9 *Evening Standard*, 18.5.94.
10 Jolliffe, *Glyndebourne*, p. 221.
11 *Opera*, Festival issue, 1994, p. 6.
12 Ibid., p. 15.
13 Jolliffe, op. cit., p. 243.
14 *The Times*, 15.6.98.
15 *Sunday Times*, 30.5.99.
16 *The Times*, 24.5.00.
17 Milnes, *The Times*, 18.7.00.
18 Findlay, Interview, 15.12.99.
19 Isaacs interview with James Naughtie, *Face to Face*, BBC 2, 1998.
20 *Sunday Times*, 23.10.94.
21 *The Times*, 17.10.94.
22 *Guardian*, 12.10.94.
23 Sutcliffe, *Believing in Opera*, p. 246.
24 *Opera*, December 1994, p. 1372.
25 *Independent*, 15.10.94.
26 Canning, *Sunday Times*, July 1995.
27 *Evening Standard*, 23.3.95.
28 Findlay, Interview, 15.12.99.
29 *The Times*, 17.10.94.
30 *Sunday Telegraph*, 4.12.94.
31 *Sunday Times*, 4.12.94.
32 *Opera*, January 1995, p. 107.
33 *The Times*, 17.12.92.
34 *Independent*, 20.1.95.
35 Interview with Joan Bakewell, *Artist of the Week*, BBC Radio 3, 15.8.99.
36 *Opera*, May 1995, p. 506.
37 Canning, *Sunday Times*, 19.3.95.
38 Isaacs, op. cit., p. 190.
39 ROH Archives, Board minutes, 18/3/5, 28.3.94.
40 Isaacs, op. cit., p. 278.
41 Ibid.
42 ROH Archives, Board minutes, 18/3/4, 25.4.94.
43 ROH Archives, Board minutes, 18/3/5, 26.9.94.
44 ROH Archives, Board minutes, 18/3/2, 24.10.94.
45 ROH Archives, Board minutes, 18/3/2, 28.11.94.
46 Isaacs, op. cit., p. 192.
47 Isaacs, Interview, 1.7.99.
48 Isaacs, op. cit., pp. 193–4.
49 Ibid., p. 193.
50 ROH Archives, Board minutes, B18/3/6, 23.1.95, 18/3/6, 27.3.95 and Culture, Media and Sport Select Committee of the House of Commons (henceforth known as Select Committee).
51 Select Committee.
52 ROH Archives, Board minutes, 18/3/6, 27.3.95, 18/3/6, 24.4.95.
53 Isaacs, op. cit., p. 294.
54 Ibid., p. 282.
55 ROH Archives, Board minutes, 18/3/6, 18.4.95.
56 ROH Archives, Board minutes, 18/3/6, 22.5.95.
57 Isaacs, op. cit., p. 196.
58 *Guardian*, 18.7.95.
59 Isaacs, op. cit., p. 197.
60 Ibid., p. 198.
61 ROH Archives, Board minutes, 18/3/6, 10.7.95, 18/3/6, 17.7.95.
62 ROH Archives, Board minutes, 18/3/6 and Select Committee.
63 Isaacs, op. cit., p. 288.
64 ROH Archives, Board minutes, 18/3/6.
65 Isaacs, op. cit., p. 288.
66 ROH Archives, 18/3/6, 23.10.95.
67 *Sunday Times*, 11.10.98.

68 *Daily Telegraph*, 28.2.98.
69 *The Times*, 26.10.98.
70 Isaacs, op. cit., p. 277.
71 Tooley, *In House*, p. 272.
72 ROH Archives, Board minutes, 18/3/6.
73 Isaacs, Interview, 1.7.99.
74 Syrus, Interview, 6.12.00.
75 *Sunday Telegraph*, 5.11.95.
76 *The Times*, 18.11.95.
77 Sutcliffe, op. cit., p. 222.
78 *The Times*, 16.2.96.
79 Isaacs, Interview, 1.7.99.
80 Jones, Interview, 6.1.00.
81 Isaacs, Interview, 1.7.99.
82 *Sunday Times*, 9.6.96.
83 Ibid., 16.6.96.
84 *Spectator*, 22.6.96.
85 Isaacs, op. cit., p. 305.
86 Isaacs, Interview, 1.7.99.
87 *Opera*, August 1996, p. 871.
88 Tooley, op. cit., p. 273.
89 Isaacs, Interview, 1.7.99.
90 Mary Allen, *A House Divided, The Diary of a Chief Executive of the Royal Opera House*, London: Simon & Schuster, 1998, p. 6.
91 Findlay, Interview, 15.12.99.
92 Jones, Interview, 6.1.00.

27 Covent Garden 1997–2002: *Who Owns Covent Garden?*

1 Select Committee.
2 Allen, *A House Divided*, p. 7.
3 Isaacs, *Never Mind the Moon*, p. 314.
4 Dalya Alberge, *The Times*, 25.2.97.
5 McIntosh before the Select Committee of House of Commons, 23.7.97, p. 41.
6 *The Times*, 14.5.97.
7 Lord Chadlington Before the Select Committee, pp. 40, 41.
8 Allen's evidence before the Select Committee, 30.10.97, p. 60.
9 Chadlington to Kaufman, Select Committee, 30.7.97, p. 42.
10 *The Times*, 8.11.97.
11 Select Committee, 30.7.97, p. 41.
12 *Sunday Times*, 18.5.97.
13 Minutes of a meeting between Secretary of State for Culture, Media and Sport, Lord Chadlington, and Mr Robert Gavron, 4.11.97, Select Committee, p. 95.
14 Chadlington's evidence before Select Committee, 30.7.97.
15 Smith's evidence, Select Committee, 4.11.97, p. 97.
16 Select Committee, 30.10.97, p. 61.
17 Gowrie's evidence before Select Committee, 25.7.97.
18 Isaacs, Interview, 1.7.99.
19 Isaacs, op. cit., p. 314.
20 Select Committee, p. 97.
21 John Allison, *Opera*, July 1997, p. 960.
22 *The Times*, 26.5.97.
23 *Guardian*, 11.7.97.
24 Milnes, Conversation, 13.10.98.
25 *New Statesman*, 21.11.97.
26 *Opera*, September 1997, p. 1036.
27 Syrus, Interview, 29.11.00.
28 Allen, op. cit., p. 18.
29 Ibid., p. 20.
30 Jones, Interview, 6.1.00.
31 Allen, op. cit., pp. 29, 36.
32 Ibid., p. 92, 29.10.97, p. 102.
33 *The Times*, 4.11.97.
34 *Sunday Times*, 9.11.97.
35 Select Committee, p. 121.
36 Isaacs, Interview, 1.7.99.
37 Allen, op. cit., p. 104.
38 Select Committee, p. 108.
39 *Daily Telegraph*, 4.12.97.
40 *The Times*, 8.12.97.
41 28.2.98.
42 *The Times*, 5.12.97.
43 Moser, Interview, 4.11.98.
44 Tooley to Gilbert, 9.1.01.
45 Tooley, op. cit., p. 283.

46 Syrus, Interview, 5.12.00.
47 Allen, Diary, p. 286.
48 *The Times*, 2.4.98.
49 Ibid., 4.3.98.
50 *Evening Standard*, 30.6.98.
51 *The Times*, 6.7.98.
52 Southgate, Interview, 12.7.01.
53 *The Times*, 3.9.98.
54 Ibid.
55 Southgate, Interview, 12.7.01.
56 *Opera*, September 1988, p. 1025.
57 *Guardian*, 10.9.98.
58 Southgate, Interview, 12.7.01.
59 *Daily Telegraph*, 10.9.98.
60 *Guardian*, 10.9.98.
61 Ibid., 17.10.98.
62 Syrus, Interview, 6.12.00.
63 Tooley, *In House*, p. 288.
64 Ibid., p. 289.
65 *Sunday Times*, 11.10.98.
66 Tooley, op. cit., p. 289.
67 Ibid.
68 *Sunday Times*, 11.10.98.
69 Canning, *Sunday Times*, 27.9.98.
70 *About the House*, vol. 1, no. 1, Autumn 2000, p. 16.
71 Syrus, Interview, 6.12.00.
72 *Observer*, 11.10.98.
73 *Sunday Times*, 11.10.98.
74 Isaacs, op. cit., p. 250.
75 *Guardian*, 26.10.98.
76 Syrus, Interview, 6.12.00.
77 Smith to Southgate, circulated by ROH with closure plans.
78 This meeting is described in Norman Lebrecht, *Covent Garden, the Untold Story*, p. 466 and has also been mentioned by members of the orchestra.
79 *Guardian*, 10.9.98.
80 Arts Council press announcement, 17.12.98.
81 *Daily Telegraph*, 16.2.99.
82 *Sunday Times*, 26.9.99.
83 Syrus, Interview, 6.12.00.
84 *About the House*, Autumn 2000.
85 *New York Times*, November 1989 and *International Herald Tribune*, 17.2.99.
86 Southgate, Interview, 12.7.01.
87 *The Times*, 1.7.99.
88 Isaacs, Interview, 1.7.99.
89 *The Times*, 7.12.99.
90 *Sunday Telegraph*, 12.12.99.
91 *Observer*, 30.1.00.
92 *Classical Music*, 11.3.00.
93 *Independent on Sunday*, 16.1.00.
94 Syrus, Interview, 29.11.00.
95 *The Times*, 2.2.00.
96 *Daily Telegraph*, 14.3.00.
97 *The Times*, 18.5.00.
98 Syrus, Interview, 6.12.00.
99 Southgate, Interview, 12.7.01.
100 *The Times*, 21.6.00.
101 Syrus, Interview, 6.12.00.
102 *Guardian*, 20.6.00.
103 *The Times*, 18.12.99.
104 Tanner, *Spectator*, 30.9.00.
105 Moser, Interview, 11.6.01.
106 Tooley, Interview, 11.4.02.
107 Southgate, Interview, 12.7.01.
108 Syrus, Interview, 6.12.00.
109 Padmore, Interview, 5.12.00.
110 Ibid.
111 Zambello, Interview, 25.3.02.
112 Covent Garden programme notes, p. 16.
113 Telephone conversation, 16.5.02 and Interview, 3.7.02.
114 *The Times*, 7.3.00.
115 Maddocks, *Observer*, 27.8.00.
116 Canning, *Sunday Times*, 30.5.99.
117 *The Times*, 30.3.01.
118 Southgate, Interview, 12.7.01.
119 *Observer*, 22.2.98.
120 *Sunday Times*, 16.7.00.
121 Hall, Interview, 29.7.99.
122 Transcript of interview with Humphrey Burton on *Aquarius*, ROH Archives, Drogheda papers, 13.10.72.
123 ROH Archives, Board minutes, 18/3/1.
124 Eyre review, p. 3.

SELECT BIBLIOGRAPHY

SECONDARY SOURCES

N. Abbott, *Italy in the 1970s*, London and Vancouver: David & Charles, 1975

Nicky Adam (ed.), *Who's Who in British Opera*, Aldershot: Scolar Press, 1993

Brian Adams, *La Stupenda: A Biography of Joan Sutherland*, Richmond, Victoria, Australia: Hutchinson, 1980

Mary Allen, *A House Divided, The Diary of a Chief Executive of the Royal Opera House*, London: Simon & Schuster, 1998

Thomas Allen, *Foreign Parts, A Singer's Journal*, London: Sinclair-Stevenson, 1993

Marian Anderson, *My Lord, What a Morning: An Autobiography*, New York: Avon, 1956

John Ardoin and Gerald Fitzgerald, *Callas*, London: Thames & Hudson, 1974

F. Armani (ed.), *La Scala 1946–1966*, Milan, 1966

Lorenzo Arruga, *La Scala*, Milan: Electa Editrice, 1975

Robert C. Bachmann, *Karajan: Notes on a Career*, tr. Shaun Whiteside, London: Quartet, 1990

Paul Banks (ed.), *Britten's Gloriana*, Suffolk: The Boydell Press, The Britten-Pears Library, 1993

Fabio Battistini, *Giorgio Strehler*, Rome: Gremese, 1980

William G. Baumol and William G. Bowen, *Performing Arts: The Economic Dilemma*, New York: The Twentieth Century Fund, 1966

Rudolf Bing, *5000 Nights at the Opera*, Garden City, New York: Doubleday, 1972

Peter Brook, *Threads of Time, A Memoir*, London: Methuen, 1999
——, *The Shifting Point, Forty Years of Theatrical Exploration 1946–1987*, London: Methuen, 1988

S. Brook, *Opera: A Penguin Anthology*, London: Penguin, 1996

Humphrey Burton, *Leonard Bernstein*, New York: Doubleday Dell, 1994

José Carreras, *Singing from the Soul: An Autobiography*, Seattle and Los Angeles: Souvenir, 1991

Carlamaria Casanova, *Renata Tebaldi: The Voice of an Angel*, Dallas, Texas: Baskerville, 1995

Schuyler Chapin, *Leonard Bernstein: Notes from a Friend*, New York: Walker, 1992

——, *Musical Chairs, A Life in the Arts*, New York: G. P. Putnam's Sons, 1977

Rupert Christiansen, *Prima Donna: A History*, Harmondsworth: Penguin, 1986

Peter Conrad, *A Song of Love and Death, The Meaning of Opera*, New York: Poseidon Press, 1987

Covent Garden 25 Years of Opera and Ballet, an exhibition organised by the Royal Opera House and the Victoria and Albert Museum in co-operation with the Friends of Covent Garden and the Arts Council of Great Britain, 19 August–10 October 1971

John Culshaw, *Putting the Record Straight: The Autobiography of John Culshaw*, London: Secker & Warburg, 1981

Edward Dent, *A Theatre for Everybody, The Story of the Old Vic and Sadler's Wells*, London, 1945

John Dexter, *The Honourable Beast, A Posthumous Autobiography*, New York: Routledge/Theatre Arts, 1993

Giuseppe Di Stefano, *L'arte del canto*, Milan: Rusconi, 1989

John Dizikes, *Opera in America: A Cultural History*, New Haven and London: Yale University Press, 1993

Plácido Domingo, *My First Forty Years*, London: Weidenfeld & Nicolson, 1983

Frances Donaldson, *The Royal Opera House in the Twentieth Century*, London: Weidenfeld & Nicolson, 1988

Claus Helmut Drese, . . . *aus Vorsatz und durch Zufall: Theater- und Operngeschichte(n) aus 50 Jahren*, Cologne: Dittrich, 1999

Lord Drogheda, *Double Harness, Memoirs of Lord Drogheda*, London: Weidenfeld & Nicolson, 1978

Peter Dusek (ed.), *Kulissengespräche II: Neue Anekdoten und kostbare Aufnahmen von 100 Weltstars der Oper*, Vienna: Jugend und Volk, 1995

Quaintance Eaton, *The Miracle of the Met: An Informal History of the Metropolitan Opera 1883–1967*, New York: Meredith Press, 1968

Mark Elder, Peter Jonas and David Pountney, *Power House, The English National Opera Experience*, London: Lime Tree, 1992

Franz Endler, *Karajan: Eine Biographie*, Hamburg: Hoffmann und Campe, 1992

Geraint Evans with Noël Goodwin, *Sir Geraint Evans, A Knight at the Opera*, London: Michael Joseph, 1984

August Everding, *Zur Sache, wenn's beliebt! Reden, Vorträge und Kolumnen*, Munich: Wilhelm Heyne, 1996

Richard Eyre and Nicholas Wright, *Changing States, A View of British Theatre in the Twentieth Century*, London: Bloomsbury, 2000

Richard Fawkes, *Welsh National Opera*, London: Julia Macrae Books, 1986

Stephen Fay, *Power Play, The Life and Times of Peter Hall*, London: Hodder & Stoughton, 1995

Johanna Fiedler, *Molto Agitato, The Mayhem Behind the Music at the Metropolitan Opera*, New York: Nan Talese an imprint of Doubleday, 2001

Gerald Fitzgerald (ed.), *Annals of the Metropolitan Opera: The Complete Chronicle of Performances and Artists*, London: Macmillan, 1990

Otto Fritz (ed.), *Almanach der Wiener Staatsoper 1995–1956*, Vienna: Bergland, 1956

Peter Paul Fuchs, *The Music Theatre of Walter Felsenstein*, New York: Norton, 1975

Berta Geissmar, *The Baton and the Jackboot: Recollections of Musical Life*, London: Hamish Hamilton, 1947

Elvio Giudici, *L'opera in cd e video: Guida all'ascolto*, Milan: Il Saggiatore, 1995

Philip Glass, *Opera on the Beach: Philip Glass on his New World of Music Theatre*, edited and with supplementary material by Robert T. Jones, London: Faber & Faber, 1988

Arnold Goodman, *Tell Them I'm On My Way*, London: Chapmans, 1993

John Goodwin (ed.), *Peter Hall's Diaries, The Story of a Dramatic Battle*, London: Hamish Hamilton, 1983

Robert Hackenberg and Walter Herrmann, *Die Wiener Staatsoper im Exil, 1945–1955*, Vienna: Österreichischer Bundesverlag, 1985

Peter Hall, *Making an Exhibition of Myself*, London: Sinclair-Stevenson, 1993

Montague Haltrecht, *The Quiet Showman, Sir David Webster and the Royal Opera House*, London: William Collins, 1975

D. Hamilton (ed.), *The Metropolitan Opera Encyclopedia*, New York: Simon & Schuster, 1987

Lord Harewood, *The Tongs and the Bones, The Memoirs of Lord Harewood*, London: Weidenfeld & Nicolson, 1981

Clemens Hellsberg, *Demokratie der Könige: Die Geschichte der Wiener Philharmoniker*, Zurich: Schweizer Verlagshaus, n.d.

Peter Heyworth, *Otto Klemperer, His Life and Times*, Vol. 2, 1933–73, Cambridge: Cambridge University Press, 1996

David L. Hirst, *Directors in Perspective: Giorgio Strehler*, Cambridge: Cambridge University Press, 1993

Manuela Hoelterhoff, *Cinderella & Company, Backstage at the Opera with Cecilia Bartoli*, New York: Alfred A. Knopf, 1999

Patricia Hollis, *Jennie Lee, A Life*, Oxford: Oxford University Press, 1997

Harald Hoyer (ed.), *Chronik der Wiener Staatsoper, 1945 bis 1995*, Vienna: Anton Schroll, 1995

——, *Chronik der Wiener Staatsoper, 1996 bis 2000*, Vienna: Anton Schroll, 2000

Spike Hughes, *Glyndebourne, A History of the Festival Opera Founded in 1934 by Audrey and John Christie*, London: Methuen, 1965

Gisela Huwe (ed.), *Die Deutsche Oper Berlin*, Berlin: Quadriga, 1984

Jeremy Isaacs, *Never Mind the Moon*, London: Bantam Press, Transworld, 1999

Alan Jefferson, *Sir Thomas Beecham, A Centenary Tribute*, London: Macdonald & Jane's, 1979

John Jolliffe, *Glyndebourne, An Operatic Miracle*, London: John Murray, 1999

Michael Kennedy, *Britten*, in the Master Musicians series edited by Stanley Sadie, London: J. M. Dent, 1981

Joseph Kerman, *Opera as Drama*, London: Faber & Faber, rev. ed. 1988

Irving Kolodin, *The Metropolitan Opera 1883–1966. A Candid History*, New York: Alfred A. Knopf, 1968

Michael Kurtz, *Stockhausen: A Biography*, tr. Richard Toop, London: Faber & Faber, 1994

Norman Lebrecht, *Covent Garden, The Untold Story, Dispatches from the English Culture War 1945–2000*, London: Simon & Schuster, 2000

——, *When the Music Stops: Managers, Maestros and the Corporate Murder of Classical Music*, London: Simon & Schuster, 1996

Maurice Leonard, *The Life of Kathleen Ferrier 1912–1953*, London: Hutchinson, 1988

Rolf Liebermann, *Opernjahre: Erlebnisse und Erfahrungen vor, auf und hinter der Bühne grosser Musiktheater*, Berne and Munich: Scherz, 1977

David Littlejohn, *The Ultimate Art: Essays Around and About Opera*, Berkeley: University of California Press, 1992

Giorgio Lotti and Raul Radice, *La Scala*, New York: Morrow, 1979

John Lucas, *Reggie, The Life of Reginald Goodall*, London: Julia Macrae Books, 1993

Giuseppe Mammarella, *Italy After Fascism: A Political History 1943–1965*, South Bend, Indiana: University of Notre Dame Press, 1966

William Mann, *The Operas of Mozart*, London: Cassell, 1977

Robert C. Marsh, *Dialogues & Discoveries, James Levine, his Life and his Music*, New York: a Lisa Drew Book, Scribner, 1998

Helena Matheopoulos, *Bravo: The World's Great Male Singers Discuss Their Roles*, London: Victor Gollancz, 1989

Martin Mayer, *The Met: One Hundred Years of Grand Opera*, London: Thames & Hudson, 1983

Dennis McGovern and Deborah Grace Winer, *I Remember Too Much*, New York: Morrow, 1990

Yehudi Menuhin, *Unfinished Journey*, London: Futura, 1978

Massimo Mila, *Massimo Mila alla Scala: Scritti 1955–1988*, Milan: Rizzoli, 1989, 1993

Eugenio Montale, *Prime alla Scala*, Milan: Leonardo, 1995

Gerald Moore, *Am I Too Loud? Memoirs of a Piano Accompanist*, London: Hamish Hamilton, 1962

Ethan Mordden, *Demented: The World of the Opera Diva*, New York: Simon & Schuster, 1984

——, *Opera Anecdotes*, New York and Oxford: Oxford University Press, 1985

Kate Mosse, *The House: Inside the Royal Opera House Covent Garden*, London: BBC Books, 1995

Simon Mundy, *Bernard Haitink, A Working Life*, London: Robson Books, 1987

Charles Osborne, *The Complete Operas of Richard Strauss*, North
　　Pomfret, Vermont: Trafalgar Square, 1988
Richard Osborne, *Conversations with Von Karajan*, New York: Harper
　　& Row, 1989
——, *Herbert von Karajan: A Life in Music*, London: Chatto & Windus,
　　1998
Roger Parker (ed.), *The Oxford History of Opera*, Oxford and New
　　York: Oxford University Press, 1996
Volkmar Parschalk (ed.), *Die Wiener Staatsoper: Jahrbuch 1996*, Vienna:
　　Barylli, 1996
Friedrich W. Pauli, *Der goldene Vorhang: Sechzehn Wegen zur Oper*,
　　Berlin: Rembrandt, 1962
Luciano Pavarotti with William Wright, *Pavarotti: My Own Story*,
　　London: Sidgwick & Jackson, 1981
Hella Pick, *Guilty Victim: Austria from the Holocaust to Haider*, London
　　and New York: I. B. Tauris, 2000
Giuseppe Pintorno, *Le Prime alla Scala*, Gorle, Bergamo: Grafica
　　Gutenberg, 1982
Andrew Porter, *Musical Events, A Chronicle, 1983–1986*, London:
　　Grafton Books, 1990
Marcel Prawy, *Marcel Prawy erzählt aus seinem Leben*, Vienna: Kremayr
　　und Scheriau, 1996
——, *The Vienna Opera*, London: Weidenfeld & Nicolson, 1970
Robert Pullen and Stephen Taylor, *Casta Diva: A Biography of
　　Montserrat Caballé*, London: Indigo, 1996
Lanfranco Rasponi, *The Last Prima Donnas*, New York: Limelight, 3rd
　　ed., 1994
Günther Rennert, *Opernarbeit: Inszenierung 1963–1973*, Kassel:
　　Bärenreiter, 1974
Francis Robinson, *Celebration: The Metropolitan Opera*, Garden City,
　　New York: Doubleday, 1979
Giandomenico Romanelli et al., *Gran Teatro La Fenice*, Cologne:
　　Evergreen/Taschen, 1999
Carole Rosen, *The Goossens, A Musical Century*, London: André
　　Deutsch, 1993
Harold Rosenthal, *My Mad World of Opera*, London: Weidenfeld &
　　Nicolson, 1982
——(ed.), *1955–6 Opera Annual*, London: John Calder, 1955
——(ed.), *1959–60 Opera Annual*, London: John Calder, 1960

———(ed.), *The Opera Bedside Book*, London: Victor Gollancz, 1965

———, *Opera at Covent Garden, A Short History*, London: Victor Gollancz, 1987

———, *Two Centuries at Opera at Covent Garden*, London: Putnam, 1958

John Russell, *Erich Kleiber, A Memoir*, London: André Deutsch, 1957

Harvey Sachs, *Toscanini*, New York: Da Capo, 1978

S. Sadie (ed.), *The New Grove Dictionary of Opera*, London: Macmillan, 1997

Elisabeth Schwarzkopf, *On and Off the Record: A Memoir of Walter Legge*, London: Faber & Faber, 1982

Michael Scott, *Maria Meneghini Callas*, London: Simon & Schuster, 1992

André Segon and Daniel Sebille, *Mario Del Monaco ou un ténor de légende*, Lyon: Laffont, 1981

Andrew Sinclair, *Arts and Cultures, The History of the 50 Years of the Arts Council of Great Britain*, London: Sinclair-Stevenson, 1995

Robert Skidelsky, *John Maynard Keynes, Fighting for Britain*, London: Macmillan, 2000

Patrick J. Smith, *A Year at the Met*, New York: Alfred A. Knopf, 1983

Georg Solti, *Solti on Solti, A Memoir*, London: Chatto & Windus, 1997

Frederic Spotts, *Bayreuth: A History of the Wagner Festival*, New Haven and London: Yale University Press, 1994

Monica Stirling, *A Screen of Time: A Study of Luchino Visconti*, London: Secker & Warburg, 1979

Marla Susan Stone, *The Patron State: Culture and Politics in Fascist Italy*, Princeton: Princeton University Press, 1998

Tom Sutcliffe, *Believing in Opera*, London: Faber & Faber, 1996

Joan Sutherland, *The Autobiography of Joan Sutherland*, London: Weidenfeld & Nicolson, 1997

John Tooley, *In House, Covent Garden, 50 Years of Opera and Ballet*, London: Faber & Faber, 1999

Penelope Turing, *Hans Hotter: Man and Artist*, London: John Calder, 1983

John Tusa, *Art Matters, Reflecting on Culture*, London: Methuen, 1999

Vienna State Opera (eds), *Festschrift zur Eröffnung des wiederaufgebauten Opernhaus*, Vienna: n.p., 1955

Christoph Wagner-Trenkwitz (ed.), *Die Wiener Staatsoper: Jahrbuch 1992*, Vienna: Locker, 1992

Joseph Wechsberg, *The Opera*, New York: Macmillan, 1972

Arnold Wesker, *As Much as I Dare, An Autobiography (1932–1959)*, London: Century, 1994

John Wheeler-Bennett, *John Anderson, Viscount Waverley*, London: Macmillan, 1962

Jeannie Williams, *Jon Vickers, A Hero's Life*, Boston: North-eastern University Press, 1999

Alexander Witeschnik, *Wiener Opernkunst von den Anfängen bis zu Karajan*, Vienna: Kremayr und Scheriau, n.d.

Franco Zeffirelli, *The Autobiography of Franco Zeffirelli*, London: Weidenfeld & Nicolson, 1986

MAGAZINES AND NEWSPAPERS

About the House, Boston Globe, Classical Music, Il Contemporaneo, Corriere della sera, Corriere d'informazione, Corriere lombardo, Daily Telegraph, Dallas Morning News, Evening Standard, Financial Times, Fortune, Frankfurter Allgemeine Zeitung, High Fidelity Magazine, Giornale della musica, Gramophone, Guardian, Independent, International Herald Tribune, Isis, L'Italia, Jersey Journal, Jerusalem Post, The Listener, Los Angeles Times, Manchester Guardian, Messaggero del lunedi, Music and Musicians, New Statesman, New York Herald Tribune, New York Post, New York Times, New Yorker, Newsday, Observer, Opera (1950–2002), Opéra International, Opera News, Opera Now, Opern Welt, Das Opernglas, La patria, Die Presse (Vienna), La Repubblica, Saturday Review, Spectator, La Stampa, Sunday Telegraph, Sunday Times, Time, Time and Tide, The Times, Village Voice, Wall Street Journal, Washington Post, Wiener Zeitung, Women's Wear Daily.

INDEX